THE OXFORD HANDBOOK OF

COMPARATIVE
LAW

THE OXFORD HANDBOOK OF

COMPARATIVE LAW

Edited by

MATHIAS REIMANN

AND

REINHARD ZIMMERMANN

OXFORD
UNIVERSITY PRESS

OXFORD
UNIVERSITY PRESS

Great Clarendon Street, Oxford OX2 6DP

Oxford University Press is a department of the University of Oxford.
It furthers the University's objective of excellence in research, scholarship,
and education by publishing worldwide in

Oxford New York

Auckland Cape Town Dar es Salaam Hong Kong Karachi
Kuala Lumpur Madrid Melbourne Mexico City Nairobi
New Delhi Shanghai Taipei Toronto

With offices in

Argentina Austria Brazil Chile Czech Republic France Greece
Guatemala Hungary Italy Japan Poland Portugal Singapore
South Korea Switzerland Thailand Turkey Ukraine Vietnam

Oxford is a registered trade mark of Oxford University Press
in the UK and in certain other countries

Published in the United States
by Oxford University Press Inc., New York

British Library Cataloguing in Publication Data

Data available

Library of Congress Cataloging in Publication Data

Data available

Typeset by RefineCatch Limited, Bungay, Suffolk
Printed in Great Britain
on acid-free paper by
Antony Rowe Ltd, Chippenham

ISBN 0–19–929606–5   978–0–19–929606–4

1 3 5 7 9 10 8 6 4 2

PREFACE

....

Over the past ten to twenty years, the discipline of comparative law has been revitalized and has made considerable progress. It has faced new tasks and challenges, arising mainly from the Europeanization of law and, more broadly, the globalizing trends in contemporary life. It has been subjected to close scrutiny from a variety of perspectives, especially in Europe and the United States. It has lost its methodological innocence as scholars began to ask hard questions about traditional approaches, such as the functional method. It has engaged in inter-disciplinary discourse with history, sociology, economics, anthropology, and other fields. As a result, comparative law has become a vibrant and intellectually stimulating field of study and research and it has advanced our knowledge in a variety of areas and contexts. At the same time, it has often been noted that there is no comprehensive account of the 'state of the art' of the discipline. This book undertakes to provide such an account.

Its three parts are preceded by an analysis of comparative law *avant la lettre*. This historical introduction shows that even before the emergence of the modern discipline of comparative law there have, of course, been comparisons of different legal systems. In fact, traces of a comparative approach can be found as far back as Ancient Greek constitutional philosophy.

In eight chapters, Part I then assesses the development of modern comparative law in a number of different countries and regions of the world. According to a widely held view, the discipline in its current form is of relatively recent origin. It evolved in the nineteenth and early twentieth centuries, that is, in an age which was characterized by the nationalization of law and legal discourse. Even though modern comparative law served to counteract legal nationalism, it was also, to some extent, affected by it: for the discipline developed differently in different legal systems, or legal families.

Part II forms, in a way, the core of the book. Its eighteen chapters look at comparative law more broadly, that is, as an intellectual enterprise. What do lawyers do when they say that they engage in comparisons? What methods and approaches do they adopt? Does comparison (have to) focus on similarity or difference? Is it plausible to distinguish different legal families, or legal traditions? Does comparative law essentially amount to the study of transplants and receptions? What can we learn from the experience of 'mixed legal systems'? What are the practical tasks of comparative law? Which challenges does the discipline face as a result of the process of globalization? What is its significance in non-Western cultures? How does comparative law relate to other disciplines? To what extent can it be described, or should it be turned into, an interdisciplinary exercise? The chapters commissioned for Part II pursue these and other questions, arriving at more or less confident answers.

Part III focuses on important individual branches of the law in which comparative studies have borne at least some fruit. The sixteen chapters assembled here are supposed to summarize the state of the art in their respective fields. What important comparative work has been done? When, where, and why has that work been performed? What have these studies been able to achieve? What does the map of the law look like in that subject-matter area? Where do we find similarity or difference? What are the specific difficulties facing scholars working comparatively in the respective area? Are there any particular contexts within that field where comparative scholarship is likely to be of greater benefit than in others? Are there important, and perhaps even urgent, tasks waiting to be tackled by comparative legal scholarship? Thus, what will the agenda for the discipline be in the foreseeable future? These were the main questions which the authors in Part III of the present book have attempted to answer.

Comparative law, today, is highly diverse. Moreover, hardly anybody possesses the linguistic skills and the background knowledge required to subject even an individual area of the law to a truly comprehensive comparative study, let alone a number of areas. Thus, a work like the present one requires the international cooperation of a great number of scholars. We have assembled a team of more than forty contributors from twelve different countries in four continents. As will be readily apparent, the individual authors have been left considerable freedom in devising their chapters within the general framework sketched above. Some of them have decided mainly to discuss substantive legal issues, others have primarily provided a survey and an assessment of the existing literature, and yet others have engaged in the discussion of specific problems which are close to their hearts or scholarly agendas and, at the same time, characteristic of a particular aspect of comparative law. In all this, the book reflects the pluralism of approaches, methods, and subject-matter areas characteristic of comparative law today.

We are very grateful indeed for the authors' willingness to cooperate in this project and to contribute their specific expertise. We appreciate their readiness to engage in, sometimes spirited, debates with the editors, to react to our suggestions or to decide to hold their ground, and, more generally, to comply with the many demands necessitated by such a large endeavour. We are also indebted to a number of people who have helped us with the preparation of this book, particularly Peter Webster and Ben Steinbrück in Hamburg, and Baiba Hicks and Nancy Paul in Michigan. And we received the support of the institutions with which we are affiliated: the Max Planck Institute for Comparative and International Private Law in Hamburg and the University of Michigan Law School in Ann Arbor. Finally, we owe a debt of gratitude to John Louth and his team at OUP for their unfailing support and encouragement.

Of course, we realize that this book has a number of shortcomings. Most importantly, perhaps, it is not truly comprehensive. Some areas of the world have received scant attention, and some of the more specialized branches of the law had to be left unexplored. But if the project was to be kept within manageable bounds, and within the confines of one volume, more could hardly be done at this stage. None the less, we hope that the book will give a vivid impression of a legal discipline which is both intellectually exciting and perhaps more practically relevant than ever before. At the same time, it is hoped that this volume will bring home to its readers how much interesting work remains to be done.

Mathias Reimann
Reinhard Zimmermann
Hamburg and Ann Arbor, February 2006

Contents

PART II APPROACHES TO COMPARATIVE LAW

PART III SUBJECT AREAS

NOTES ON THE CONTRIBUTORS

John S. Bell is Professor of Law (1973), University of Cambridge, and Fellow of Pembroke College, Cambridge

T. W. Bennett is a Professor in the Department of Public Law, University of Cape Town

Harold J. Berman is Robert W. Woodruff Professor of Law, Emory University, Atlanta, and James Barr Ames Professor of Law Emeritus, Harvard University, Cambridge, Massachusetts

John W. Cairns is Professor of Legal History, University of Edinburgh

David S. Clark is Maynard and Bertha Wilson Professor of Law, Willamette University, Salem, Oregon

Roger Cotterrell is Anniversary Professor of Legal Theory, Queen Mary and Westfield College, University of London

Vivian Grosswald Curran is Professor of Law, University of Pittsburgh, Pennsylvania

Gerhard Dannemann is Professor for British Legal, Economic, and Social Structures, Humboldt University, Berlin

Marius J. de Waal is Professor of Private Law, University of Stellenbosch

Charles Donahue is Paul A. Freund Professor of Law, Harvard University, Cambridge, Massachusetts

Jacques du Plessis is Professor of Private Law and Roman Law, University of Stellenbosch

Markus Dirk Dubber is Professor of Law, Roger and Karen Jones Faculty Scholar, and Director, Buffalo Criminal Law Center, State University of New York, Buffalo

E. Allan Farnsworth was Alfred McCormack Professor of Law, Columbia University School of Law, New York

Florian Faust is Professor of Private Law, Commercial Law, and Comparative Law, Bucerius Law School, Hamburg

Bénédicte Fauvarque-Cosson is Professor of Private Law, Private International Law, and Comparative Law, University Panthéon-Assas (Paris II)

Matthew W. Finkin is Albert J. Harno Professor of Law, University of Illinois, Champaign-Urbana

David J. Gerber is Distinguished Professor of Law, Chicago-Kent College of Law, Chicago

H. Patrick Glenn is Peter M. Laing Professor of Law, Faculty of Law and Institute of Comparative Law, McGill University, Montreal

James Gordley is Shannon Cecil Turner Professor of Jurisprudence, School of Law, University of California at Berkeley

Elisabetta Grande is Professor of Comparative Law, University of Piemonte Orientale, Alessandria, Italy

Michele Graziadei is Professor of Comparative Law, University of Piemonte Orientale, Alessandria, Italy

Klaus J. Hopt is Director of the Max Planck Institute for Comparative and International Private Law, Hamburg, and Professor of Law, University of Hamburg

Peter Huber is Professor of Private Law, Conflict of Laws and Comparative Law, Johannes Gutenberg University, Mainz

Nils Jansen is Professor of Roman Law, Legal History, German and European Private Law at the Institute for Legal History, Westfoelische Wilhelms-Universität Münster

Zentaro Kitagawa is Emeritus Professor of Private Law, Faculty of Law, University of Kyoto

Jan Kleinheisterkamp is Assistant Professor of Law, École des Hautes Études Commerciales—HEC School of Management, Paris

Harry D. Krause is Max L. Rowe Professor of Law Emeritus, University of Illinois, Champaign-Urbana

Zdeněk Kühn is Associate Professor of Law, School of Law, Charles University, Prague

Chibli Mallat is Jean Monnet Professor of Law, St Joseph's University, Beirut

Ugo Mattei, is Alfred and Hanna Fromm Professor of International and Comparative Law, University of California at Hastings, and Professor of Private Law, University of Turin

Ralf Michaels is Associate Professor of Law, Duke University, Durham, North Carolina

Horatia Muir Watt is Professor of Private Law, Private International Law, and Comparative Law, University Panthéon-Sorbonne (Paris I)

Mathias Reimann is Hessel E. Yntema Professor of Law, University of Michigan, Ann Arbor

Annelise Riles is Professor of Law, and Professor of Anthropology, Cornell University, Ithaca, New York

Ingeborg Schwenzer is Professor of Private Law, University of Basel, Switzerland

Jan M. Smits is Professor of European Private Law, University of Maastricht

Mark Tushnet is William Nelson Cromwell Professor of Law at Harvard Law School

Sjef van Erp is Professor of Private Law and European Private Law, University of Maastricht, and Marie Curie Fellow, Centre of European Law and Politics, University of Bremen

Daniel Visser is Professor of Private Law, University of Cape Town

Stefan Vogenauer is Professor of Comparative Law, University of Oxford, and Fellow of Brasenose College, Oxford

Gerhard Wagner is Professor of German and European Private Law and Civil Procedure, Private International Law and Comparative Law, University of Bonn

Joachim Zekoll is Professor of Private Law, Civil Procedure, and Comparative Law, Johann Wolfgang Goethe University, Frankfurt, and A. D. Freeman Professor of Law, Tulane University, School of Law, New Orleans, Louisiana

Reinhard Zimmermann is Director of the Max Planck Institute for Comparative and International Private Law, Hamburg, and Professor of Private Law, Roman Law, and Comparative Legal History, University of Regensburg

ABBREVIATIONS

....

AALS	Association of American Law Schools
ABA	American Bar Association
AC	Law Reports, Appeal Cases; Appeal Court
AGBG	Gesetz zur Regelung des Rechts der Allgemeinen Geschäftsbedingungen (Standard Terms of Business Act, Germany)
AH	anno Hegirae (the year according the Muslim calendar)
AJCL	*American Journal of Comparative Law*
ALADI	*Asociación Latinoamericana de Integración* (Latin American Association of Integration)
ALI	American Law Institute
All ER	All England Law Reports
ALR	Australian Law Reports
Ann Bull	Annual Bulletin
Anon	Anonymous
ASIL	American Society of International Law
Ass plén	*Assemblée plénière* of the *Cour de cassation*
B & Ald	Barnewall & Alderson's King's Bench Reports
BGE	*Entscheidungen des Schweizerischen Bundesgerichts* (Decisions of the Swiss Supreme Court)
BGB	*Bürgerliches Gesetzbuch* (German Civil Code)
BGH	*Bundesgerichtshof* (German Federal Supreme Court)
BGHZ	*Sammlung der Entscheidungen des Bundesgerichtshofs in Zivilsachen* (Collection of the Decisions of the German Federal Supreme Court in Private Law Matters)
B & S	Best & Smith's Queen's Bench Reports
Bull civ	*Bulletin des arrêts des chambres civiles de la Cour de cassation*
BVerfG	*Bundesverfassungsgericht* (German Federal Constitutional Court)
BVerfGE	*Sammlung der Entscheidungen des Bundesverfassungsgericht* (Collection of the Decisions of the German Federal Constitutional Court)
BW	*Burgerlijk Wetboek* (Dutch Civil Code)
C.	Justinian's Codex
CA	Court of Appeal

CAFA	Class Action Fairness Act
Cal	California; California Reports
Cal App	Court of Appeal, California
CALE	Centre for Asian Legal Exchange
CAN	*Comunidad Andina de Naciones* (Andean Community)
Cass civ	*Arrêt des chambres civiles de la Cour de cassation*
Cass com	*Arrêt des chambres commerciales de la Cour de cassation*
CC	Constitutional Court, South Africa
CE	common era
CE Sect	*Conseil d'État, Section*
CFR	Common Frame of Reference
Ch	chapter
Ch App	Law Reports, Chancery Appeal Cases
CIDIP	*Conferencia Interamericana de Derecho Internacional Privado* (Inter-American Specialized Conference on Private International Law)
CISG	United Nations Convention on Contracts for the International Sale of Goods
CLR	Commonwealth Law Reports
Cmnd	Command Papers
COM	European Commission documents
Cong	Congress (USA)
d.	deceased
D	*Recueil Dalloz*
D.	Justinian's Digest
DLR	Dominion Law Reports
Drew	Drewry's Vice Chancellor's Reports tempore Kindersley
EC	European Community
ECHR	European Convention of Human Rights and Fundamental Freedoms; European Court of Human Rights
ECJ	European Court of Justice
ECR	European Court Reports
EEC	European Economic Community
EGBGB	*Einführungsgesetz zum Bürgerlichen Gesetzbuch* (Introductory Act to the German Civil Code)
EHRR	European Human Rights Reports
El & Bl	Ellis & Blackburn's Queen's Bench Reports
ER	English Reports
ERA	*Europäische Rechtsakademie* (Academy of European Law)
ERPL	European Review of Private Law
ETS	European Treaty Series
EU	European Union

Ex	Exchequer Reports
F Supp	Federal Supplement
F 2d/3d	Federal Reporter, Second/Third Series
fol.	folio
FTAA	Free Trade Area of the Americas
FRCP	Federal Rules of Civil Procedure (USA)
IMF	International Monetary Fund
Gai.	The Institutes of Gaius
GATT	General Agreement on Tariffs and Trade
Gaz Pal	*Gazette du Palais*
Gen.	Book of Genesis
GG	Grundgesetz (Basic Law, Germany)
H Res	House of Representatives Resolution (USA)
HCA	High Court of Australia
HCJ	High Court of Justice (Israel)
HL	House of Lords
HLC	Clark & Finnelly's House of Lords Reports, New Series
HR	*Hoge Raad* (Supreme Court of the Netherlands)
ICLQ	*International and Comparative Law Quarterly*
Inst.	The Institutes of Justinian
KB	Law Reports, King's Bench
LJ	Law Journal
LJR (NS)	Law Journal Reports (New Series)
LQR	*Law Quarterly Review*
LR	Law Reports; Law Review
Lloyd's Rep	Lloyd's Law Reports
M & W	Meeson & Welsby's Exchequer Reports
MERCOSUR	*Mercado Común del Sur* (Common Market of the South)
Misc	Miscellaneous Reports (New York)
MPI	Max Planck Institute
NAFTA	North American Free Trade Agreement
NCCUSL	National Conference of Commissioners on Uniform State Laws
NE 2d	North Eastern Reporter, Second Series
NGO	Non-governmental Organization
NS	New Series
NW	North Western Reporter
NYS	New York State; New York Reporter
NYU	New York University
OAS	Organization of American States
OASTS	Organization of American States Treaty Series
OECD	Organisation for Economic Cooperation and Development
OHADA	*Organisation pour l'Harmonisation en Afrique du Droit des*

	Affaires (Organization for the Harmonization of Business Law in Africa)
OJ	Official Journal of the European Communities
OR	*Obligationenrecht* (Swiss Code of Obligations)
orig	originally
P	Pacific Reporter
Pa D & C	Pennsylvania District & County Reports
PC	Privy Council
PECL	Principles of European Contract Law
PETL	Principles of European Tort Law
PICC	UNIDROIT Principles of International Commercial Contracts
Ps.	Book of Psalms
QB	Law Reports, Queen's Bench
RabelsZ	*Rabels Zeitschrift*
repr	reprinted
RIDC	*Revue internationale de droit comparé*
RGZ	*Sammlung der Entscheidungen des Reichsgerichts in Zivilsachen* (Collection of Decisions of the German Imperial Court in Private Law Matters)
S Ct	Supreme Court; Supreme Court Reporter (USA)
SA	South African Law Reports
SC	Session Cases, Scotland
SCA	Supreme Court of Appeal, South Africa
SCR	Supreme Court Reports, Canada
SEC	Security and Exchange Commission
Sess	Session
SJD	Scientiae Juridicae Coctor (Doctor of Legal Science)
SPTL	Society of Public Teachers of Law
StGB	*Strafgesetzbuch* (German Criminal Code)
Tenn	Tennessee; Tennessee Supreme Court Reports
TGI	*Tribunal de Grande Instance*
trans	translator(s)
UCC	Uniform Commercial Code
UK	United Kingdom
UKHL	United Kingdom, House of Lords
UKNCCL	United Kingdom National Committee of Comparative Law
ULF	Convention relating to a Uniform Law on the Formation of Contracts for the International Sale of Goods
ULIS	Convention relating to a Uniform Law on the International Sale of Goods
UN	United Nations
UNCITRAL	United Nations Commission on International Trade Law

UNESCO	United Nations Educational, Scientific and Cultural Organization
UNIDROIT	International Institute for the Unification of Private Law
UNTS	United Nations Treaty Series
US	United States Supreme Court Reports; United States
USC	United States Code
UST	United States Treaties and other International Agreements
USCS	United States Code Service
Wisc	Wisconsin; Wisconsin Reports
WLR	Weekly Law Reports
WLSA	Women and Law in Southern Africa
X	Liber Extra (Decretales Gregorii IX.)
ZGB	*Zivilgesetzbuch* (Swiss Civil Code)

INTRODUCTION

COMPARATIVE LAW BEFORE THE *CODE NAPOLÉON*

CHARLES DONAHUE

Cambridge, Massachusetts

MODERN comparative lawyers, the editors of this *Handbook* assure me, tend to date the foundation of their discipline to the nineteenth century and to the promulgation of the great European codes. As a legal historian, I found that notion a bit strange and puzzled as to where I would put the origins. I decided that one could make an argument that comparative law is to be found in the ancient world, that despite the multiplicity of legal sources it is not often found in the early or high middle ages, that there are hints of it in the commentators of the later middle ages, that in a very real sense it can be found in French legal thinkers of the sixteenth century, and that one can trace a relatively clean line from the sixteenth century to whatever nineteenth-century authors one chooses to focus on as the founders of the discipline that produced the First International Congress of Comparative Law in 1900.[1]

I. The Ancient World

There are more than hints of the comparative method in Aristotle's *Politics*.[2] Aristotle, or more likely members of Aristotle's school, compiled the 'constitutions' of 158 Greek city-states, and the same school is probably responsible for a lost work in four books on the customs of the Greeks, Romans, and barbarians.[3] Only one of the constitutions, 'the Athenian constitution', survives, and that by the chance discovery at the end of the nineteenth century of a papyrus in an Egyptian rubbish pit.[4] Its authorship is hotly debated, but the most recent commentator concludes that it is the work of a student of Aristotle.[5] The uncertainty of the dates of the lost works (and of the one surviving one) makes it equally uncertain whether the influential generalities of the *Politics* were based on intensive empirical study or whether they were the admittedly brilliant products of a first-rate speculative mind informed by a more casual empirical knowledge. There can be little doubt, however, both that Aristotle espoused the comparative method in the *Politics* and that he, or his school, or both, engaged in a massive empirical investigation of the governmental systems of a large number of Greek city-states and a somewhat more casual investigation of the world beyond that which spoke Greek.

When we put the *Politics* together with the information-gathering efforts, there can also be little doubt that what Aristotle and his school were doing should be classified as comparative law. The fact is, however, that all that survives is a treatise written at a rather high level of generality and an exploration of the constitution of

---

[1] A sketch of the argument that is elaborated here is to be found in Charles Donahue, 'Comparative Legal History in North America: A Report', (1997) 65 *Tijdschrift voor Rechtsgeschiedenis* 1–17. That article, however, was devoted to comparative legal history, a somewhat different enterprise from comparative law itself.

[2] The standard edition is Alois Dreizehnter (ed), *Aristoteles' Politik*, Studia et testimonia antiqua, 7 (1970). I have used the translation of Sir Ernest Baker as revised by R. F. Stalley (1995). For the comparative nature of the work, see, conveniently, R. G. Mulgan, *Aristotle's Political Theory: An Introduction for Students of Political Theory* (1977), 60–77, 116–38.

[3] On the lost works, including the probability, but not certainty, of the number 158 for the constitutions, see P. J. Rhodes, *A Commentary on the Aristotelian Athenaion politeia* (rev edn, 1993), 1–2, and Paul Moraux, *Les Listes anciennes des ouvrages d'Aristote*, Aristote, traductions et études (1951), 115–16, 130–3, 199, 200, 265, 303–4, 319.

[4] F. G. Kenyon (ed), *Aristotelis Atheniensium Respublica* (1920).

[5] Rhodes (n 3), 61–3.

one Greek city-state. The former can be regarded as political theory (or, at best, comparative government), and the latter is not comparative and was lost until quite recently. Hence, there is no continuity between the Aristotelian effort and later efforts at comparative law. The method had to be rediscovered.

There is another reason for not making Aristotle the founder of Western comparative law. He shared with all the ancient Greek thinkers a seeming uninterest in private law. We look in vain in the Greeks for the manipulation of middle-level generalities in private law that characterizes the developed legal systems that comparative lawyers are so fond of classifying. Hence, while Aristotle and his school can certainly be said to have been engaged in comparative law, they confined their comparative legal work to what we would call comparative public law.

The Romans certainly were interested in the manipulation of middle-level generalities in private law. Indeed, the Roman jurists devoted the bulk of their efforts, at least the bulk of those efforts that survive, to private law. The one work of a Roman jurist that survives almost complete, Gaius' *Institutes* (written roughly AD 160), does contain a few comparative remarks. We learn, for example, that the Galatians had an institution that they regarded as similar to Roman *patria potestas*, though Gaius, seemingly basing himself on a rescript of the emperor Hadrian, argues that the institution of *patria potestas* is unique to the Romans.[6] Such remarks are, however, relatively few, and there is certainly no systematic exploration of the similarities and differences between the Roman and non-Roman institutions to which he refers.

As is well known, Gaius does recognize that Roman law is based in part on what he calls *ius gentium*, which he describes as 'the law that natural reason establishes among all mankind [and] is followed by all peoples alike'.[7] 'Thus', he tells us, 'the Roman people observes partly its own peculiar law [*ius proprium*] and partly the common law [*ius commune*] of mankind'.[8] He promises to tell us throughout the work, which institution is which. He does not completely keep his promise, but he gives us enough markers so that we can get a reasonably good idea of what he regarded as the *ius proprium* of Rome and what the *ius commune* or *ius gentium*. Thus, acquiring title by delivery from the owner is an institution of the latter (here he calls it *ius naturale*), while acquiring title by mancipation, cession in court, or usucapion is an institution of the former (here he calls it *ius civile*).[9] The partnership that is contracted by plain consent is an institution of the *ius gentium*, but the partnership among heirs that once prevailed among the Romans is proper to Roman citizens.[10]

Clearly, there lies behind these remarks a comparative effort. Over a quite long

---

[6] Gaius, *Institutes* [Gai.], 1.55. Of many editions and translations, I have used that of Francis de Zulueta, *The Institutes of Gaius* (2 vols, 1946–53).

[7] Gai.1.1 (the translation is Zulueta's (n 6)).

[8] Ibid.   [9] Gai.2.65.   [10] Gai.3.154–154a.

period of time, the Romans had engaged in a relatively comprehensive comparison of specifically Roman institutions with those of other peoples, principally those who spoke Greek, in the Mediterranean basin. What Roman law had in common with those other peoples they called *ius gentium*, or *ius commune*, or, sometimes, *ius naturale*, and they conceived of this law as being the product of human reason. It has been suggested that this understanding of the division between what is specifically Roman and what is shared with other peoples in the Mediterranean basin is the product of a specific Roman institution, the *praetor peregrinus*, whose function was to hear legal cases at Rome between non-citizens or between a citizen and a non-citizen.[11]

Unfortunately, the process by which the comparison was made was not committed to writing, or, if it was, it has not survived.[12] The process had happened by the time of Gaius, and he merely reports some of the conclusions. By Gaius' time, the institutions of the *ius gentium* had been thoroughly integrated into the Roman legal system.[13]

Although Gaius' work as a whole was lost to the West until early in the nineteenth century, fragments and epitomes of it were known or knowable throughout Western legal history. Perhaps more important, Gaius' *Institutes* was the basis of Justinian's *Institutes*, an elementary textbook of Roman law written in the name of the Byzantine emperor Justinian and published in 533. Gaius' division of the sources of Roman law into *ius civile* and *ius gentium* was carried over into Justinian's *Institutes*, as were most of his identifications of what pieces of Roman law belonged in each category. Justinian also reports a tripartite classification of law, derived from the Roman jurist Ulpian (d. 228), in which *ius gentium* is sharply separated from *ius naturale*. The latter is what 'nature has taught all animals', whereas the former, following Gaius' definition, is 'those rules prescribed by natural reason for all men [and] observed by all peoples alike'.[14] The confusion between the Gaian and Ulpianic conceptions of natural law in Justinian's *Institutes* is profound and was to prove provocative of thought wherever the work was studied as virtually a sacred text. Even within the Gaian conception there is a tension, which would become particularly noticeable when it became apparent that there are practically no rules that are 'observed by all peoples alike'. What 'natural reason' prescribes may or may not be evidenced by what all, or even most, peoples observe.

---

[11] See H. G. Jolowicz and Barry Nicholas, *An Historical Introduction to Roman Law* (3rd edn, 1972), 103–4.

[12] The edict of the peregrine praetor has not survived, and not enough of the provincial edict has survived to allow a reconstruction.

[13] In addition to the bibliography cited in Jolowicz and Nicholas (n 11), see most recently Max Kaser, *Ius gentium* (1993).

[14] Justinian, *Institutes* [Inst.] 1, 2pr, 1. Of many editions and translations, I have used that of J. B. Moyle, *The Institutes of Justinian* (2 vols, 1913).

Late antiquity produced a curious comparative work, the *Lex Dei quam praecepit Dominus ad Moysen* ('The Law of God which the Lord Commanded unto Moses'), also known as the *Collatio legum mosaicarum et romanarum* ('A Comparison of the Mosaic and Roman Laws').[15] The date of the work is controverted, but the basic text seems to have been compiled in the early fourth century with some later additions.[16] What survives of the work (it is generally thought that we have only the beginning, but how much is missing cannot be determined) is divided into sixteen titles, each of which begins with a quotation from the Pentateuch attributed to Moses, followed by extracts on the same topic from works of the classical Roman jurists. Title 9 is typical of, if somewhat shorter than, most of the others:[17]

Concerning [the fact that] the testimony of members of a family is not to be admitted.

[I.] Again Moses [says]: 'Thou shalt not bear false witness against thy neighbour'.

[II.] Ulpian in the 8th book 'Concerning the office of the proconsul' [under the title] 'On the *lex Julia* concerning public and private force': [1.] By the same law, in chapters 87 and 88, certain people are entirely interdicted from testimony and certain from testimony if they are unwilling. [2.] [In chapter 88] in these words for these men: 'By this law let there not be permitted to speak testimony against the defendant anyone who was freed [*se liberaverit ab*] by him, his parent, the freedman of either of them or of his freedman, or by a freedwoman [sc. of them], or who is under the age of puberty, or who [has been condemned in a public judgment and who] has not been reinstated [*qui eorum in integrum restitutus non est*], or who is in chains and public custody, or who has pledged himself for fighting, or who has hired or hires himself out for fighting with beasts, except someone who has been or is sent to the city to fight with javelins, or who has publicly made or makes gain with his body, or who has been adjudged to have taken money to give testimony'. And none of these gives testimony against the defendant according to this law, even willingly. [3.] In chapter 87 in these [words]: 'Unwilling let them not speak testimony against the defendant who is cousin to the defendant or joined by closer relation, or who is his father-in-law, son-in-law, stepfather, or stepson'. And the rest.

[III.] Paul in the fifth book of 'Opinions' under the title 'Concerning witnesses and torture [*quaestionibus*]': It has been decided that witnesses who are suspected [of partiality], and especially such as the accuser produces from his own household, or whose low station in life renders them of bad repute, should not be interrogated; for in the case of witnesses, their style of life, as well as their dignity, should be considered. Witnesses cannot be examined with reference to anyone if they are related to them by either marriage or blood. Neither parents, children, [patrons,] nor freedmen should be admitted to testify

---

[15] The standard modern edition is by Theodor Mommsen in *Collectio librorum iuris anteiustiniani* (1890), iii. I have used the edition by Giovanni Baviera, in Salvatore Riccobono, Giovanni Baviera, Contardo Ferrini, Giuseppe Furlani, and Vicenzo Arrangio-Ruiz (eds), *Fontes iuris romani anteiustiniani* (1968), ii, 543–89. There is an English translation by Moses Hyamson (1913). For commentary, see Edoardo Volterra, *Collatio legum mosaicarum et romanarum*, Memorie della R. Accademia nazionale dei Lincei: Classe di scienze morali, storiche e filologiche, 6.3.1 (1930); Giorgio Barone-Adesi, *L'età della Lex Dei*, Pubblicazioni dell'Istituto di diritto romano e dei diritti dell'Oriente mediterraneo, 71 (1992), and the bibliographical references in the latter.

[16] Barone-Adesi (n 15), 175–96.

[17] Baviera ed (n 15), 565–6 (my translation).

against one another, if they are unwilling to do so; for the near relationship of persons generally destroys the truth of evidence.

From the time of its rediscovery by the humanists, the principal interest of this text has been in the fact that it provides evidence of the writings of the classical jurists and of classical Roman law independent of the texts in the *Corpus Iuris Civilis*. Our concern here, however, is with the comparison between the Mosaic law and the Roman. It is an understatement to say that it is not very exact. The focus of the Mosaic law (Exod 20: 16, Deut 5: 20) is on perjury, particularly on perjury that harms another Jew. The principal concern of the Roman texts is to prevent certain people from testifying, admittedly and in all probability, with an underlying concern that such people will perjure themselves. Hence, our example supports what seems to be the current trend in scholarship on the work as a whole: that the underlying purpose of the compiler was to demonstrate that Roman law was consistent in principle with the Mosaic and that it in some sense implemented the Mosaic.[18]

II. The Early and High Middle Ages

The entry of the Germanic peoples into the Roman empire produced an awareness of quite radical differences in legal systems and the opportunity for comparison. In at least one instance, we have some evidence that the opportunity was taken. During the brief period in which there was a separate kingdom of the Burgundians, in the late fifth or early sixth centuries, two 'codes' were produced, one of which seems to be a law for the Burgundian inhabitants of the area, and the other for the Roman.[19] The Roman code is a pastiche of late classical sources, mostly rules, not always accurately stated, from such works as the *Opinions of Paul* and the Theodosian Code. The Burgundian code is an original work, although some scholars have found echoes in it of the code of the Visigothic king Euric. Both works are arranged into titles, usually with several provisions under each heading. The titles themselves are, however, in no discernible order. What is discernible is that the order of the titles in each work is remarkably similar. Either the com-

---

[18] Barone-Adesi (n 15), 175–96.

[19] The standard edition of both is by L. R. de Salis, *Leges Burgundionum*, Monumenta Germaniae Historica, Legum 1.2.1 (1892). The English translation of *Lex Burgundionum* by Katherine Fischer [Drew] (*The Burgundian Code*, 1949) is unreliable. That into German by Franz Beyerle (*Gesetze der Burgunden*, 1936) is more reliable. So far as I am aware the *Lex romana Burgundionum* has never been translated into English.

piler of the *Roman Law of the Burgundians* had the basic text of the *Law of the Burgundians* before him or vice versa, because there is no other reason for the correspondence of the subject-matter of the titles.[20] That the author or authors of these codes were making comparisons is clear enough, but we cannot tell what they made of their comparisons.

Awareness of different sources of law and occasional attempts to lay different sources side by side continued throughout the early middle ages,[21] but pressure of space dictates that we skip to northern Italy in the first half of the twelfth century and to the revival of legal study at Bologna. While the origins are obscure, and becoming more obscure as the result of recent scholarship, it seems clear that by the year 1150, there were *studia* at Bologna in which Roman law was taught on the basis of quite good editions of virtually all of the Justinianic *corpus* and in which canon law was taught on the basis of Gratian's *Concordance of Discordant Canons*, a work that may still have been growing at this date but which was shortly to receive, if it had not already received, its vulgate edition.[22] That a systematic arrangement of Lombard laws, known as the *Lombarda*, was made, probably in the late eleventh century, suggests that this body of law was also being studied, probably at Pavia.[23] A source book of feudal law, known as the *Libri feudorum*, was being compiled at this time, and was almost certainly being used for study in northern Italy, though it is unclear where.[24] There was also study of Roman and canon law going on in the south of France, though, again, it is difficult to determine precisely where.[25] The method of teaching, at least of Roman and canon law in Italy, was that the master read the basic text (slowly, many students did not own the book and were trying to memorize it); he then commented on individual passages. These comments were recorded in the manuscripts as glosses.[26]

The glossatorial effort could have given rise to a considerable amount of comparative work. It certainly did within each tradition. Texts within the four

[20] See de Salis (n 19), 164–7.

[21] Notable in this regard is the so-called 'code' of the Anglo-Saxon king Alfred (r. 871–99). See Patrick Wormald, *The Making of English Law; King Alfred to the Twelfth Century* (1999), 265–85.

[22] On the study of Roman law, see most recently, Hermann Lange, *Römisches Recht im Mittelalter. 1: Die Glossatoren* (1997), with copious references. (He wrote, however, before Winroth.) On canon law, see most recently Anders Winroth, *The Making of Gratian's Decretum* (2000).

[23] The radical suggestions on this topic by Charles Radding, *The Origins of Medieval Jurisprudence: Pavia and Bologna 850–1150* (1988), have not been generally accepted. For the standard account, see Peter Weimar, in Helmut Coing (ed), *Handbuch der Quellen und Literatur der neueren europäischen Privatrechtsgeschichete. 1: Mittelalter* (1973), 165–6, with references.

[24] Ibid. 166–8.

[25] This topic is best pursued in the widely scattered studies of André Gouron: *La science juridique française aux XIe et XIIe siècles. Diffusion du droit de Justinien et influences canoniques jusqu'à Gratien*, Ius romanum medii aevi, 1.4.d–e, (1978); *La science du droit dans le Midi de la France au moyen age* (1984); *Études sur la diffusion des doctrines juridiques médiévales* (1987); *Droit et coutume en France aux XIIe et XIIIe siècles* (1993); *Juristes et droits savants, Bologne et la France médiévale* (2000).

[26] A number of other forms of literature were also produced, including treatise-like works called *summae*.

corners of the basic texts were sought, and their differences expounded. But the fundamental thrust of the glossatorial effort was to harmonize the texts, not to outline different systems of law. That the *Corpus Iuris Civilis* provides insights into Roman law in many different periods seems obvious enough to us, and today we sharply distinguish the classical law from the post-classical and from that of Justinian. The glossators were aware that Justinian had made changes (they could hardly be unaware of it, because he says so in many places), but their vision seems to have been one that sought, if at all possible, to reconcile the texts within the *Corpus* and form them into a coherent whole. The same may be said of canon law. It seems obvious to us that the canons of the church councils and the writings of the fathers of late antiquity envisage a rather different system of law from that of the penitentials and councils of the early middle ages, different again from that of the writings and papal decretals of the reform movement of the eleventh and twelfth centuries. But comparing these systems is not what the canonists were trying to do. They had a system for preferring one authority over another in the case of irreconcilable conflict, but they rarely saw irreconcilable conflicts. Most of the material proved to be malleable into a single system by means of clever distinctions and creating a hierarchy of general rules and exceptions.

When it came to comparisons between Roman law and canon law, the effort at harmonization continued. This is particularly noticeable in the case of the canonists of the glossatorial period, because the basic canonical sources were deficient, particularly in what we would call private law. Since the church was said to live by Roman law, it was relatively easy to borrow whole areas of Roman law and incorporate them into the canonical system. A particularly remarkable achievement of this period was the creation of a system of Romano-canonical procedure, an effort in which both canonists and civilians participated, and which resulted in the procedural system which is the direct ancestor of that in Continental Europe today.[27]

The system of land-holding described in the *Corpus Iuris Civilis* was quite different from that of twelfth-century Italy. The glossators reacted to this fact in two ways. They manipulated the Roman-law texts to create a *dominium directum* for the lord and a *dominium utile* for the tenant.[28] They also elaborated the *Libri feudorum*, but confined its reach to land that could be clearly identified as a fief. The *Libri feudorum* was thus brought into the overall system in such a way that in the sixteenth century it could be printed without embarrassment as part of the *Corpus Iuris Civilis*. The Lombard law proved to be more intractable. While some

---

[27] R. C. van Caenegem, *History of European Civil Procedure*, International Encyclopedia of Comparative Law, 16.2 (1973).

[28] See Robert Feenstra, 'Dominium utile est chimaera: nouvelles réflexions sur le concept de propriété dans le droit savant', (1998) 66 *Tijdschrift voor Rechtsgeschiedenis* 381–97, with ample references to earlier literature.

effort was made to interpret it in the light of Roman law, it was never brought into the Romano-canonical system as fully as were the *Libri feudorum*.

Differences between Roman law and canon law and between the developing Romano-canonical system and customary law remained. Two examples may suffice to show how the glossators, or at least some of the glossators, dealt with them. In Roman law there was apparently some debate, pitting, as we are told, the Republican jurist Trebatius against the Antonine jurist Gaius, as to whether mortally wounding an animal was sufficient to give title to it, or whether one must actually seize the animal.[29] Justinian resolved the debate in favour of the latter (Gaian) view, on the ground that 'it may happen in many ways that you will not catch it'.[30] That does not seem to have been the customary law of northern Italy in the twelfth and thirteenth centuries, where priority was almost certainly given to the huntsman who had wounded the animal and perhaps even to one who was simply in hot pursuit.[31] Accursius interprets Justinian's quite clear ruling to mean that the judge must inquire into the likelihood that the huntsman will catch the animal.[32] If it is clear that he will, then priority goes to the first huntsman. It is hard not to see customary law as exerting a pressure, to put it mildly, on Accursius' interpretation.

The canon law, which had jurisdiction over the formation of marriage, differed from what seems to have been the Roman law on the issue. The glossators of the Roman law bent their interpretations of the Roman law of marriage to accommodate the canon. For example, the Bolognese civilian Azo early in the thirteenth century suggested that when it came to the question whether a sacramental marriage had been formed, canon law prevailed, but a leading of the bride into the house of the groom was required for the marital property consequences of marriage to ensue.[33] Hence, as in the case of the *Libri feudorum*, the two laws are accommodated under one roof by creating a category to which each will apply. In one area, however, the civilians did not bend the Roman law. In Roman law the father of a child in power (who could be of any age) had to consent to that child's marriage. Canon law did not require parental consent. Although a number of ways to do so were available to them, the civilians did not attempt a reconciliation in this instance, perhaps because they sided with fathers in the generational battle that has a long history in the West.[34]

---

[29] *Digest* [D.] 41.1.5. The standard edition is by Theodor Mommsen. It is conveniently reprinted in Alan Watson (ed), *The Digest of Justinian* (4 vols, 1985), with an English translation that should be used with caution.

[30] Inst.2.1.13.

[31] See below, text at notes 35–6, 77–8.

[32] *Glossa ordinaria ad* Inst.2.1.13 s.v. *difficile, ceperis, capias* (Lyon, 1604), col 126.

[33] See Charles Donahue, 'The Case of the Man Who Fell into the Tiber', (1978) 22 *American Journal of Legal History* 30–2.

[34] Ibid, at 9–10, 34–53.

III. The Later Middle Ages

Except in the case of Roman and canon law, the glossators rarely mention the existence of bodies of law different from the ones that they are expounding. This characteristic of legal writing changed in the period of the commentators (fourteenth through sixteenth centuries) perhaps as a result of university-trained jurists' attempting to come to grips with strong customary legal systems in the north of France. Mainstream Italian jurists of the fourteenth century frequently cite differing customs and statutes of the Italian city-states, and when they cannot reconcile them with their learning (which they normally attempted to do), they simply recognize that they are different. Thus, when Bartolus is discussing the same issue about wounding a wild animal that Accursius had attempted to reconcile with the customary law in a way not true to the Roman-law text, Bartolus holds to the obvious meaning of Justinian's (and Gaius') ruling: 'The Lombard Law, "On hunters," next-to-last law,[35] is opposed [i.e., suggested as an authority for reaching a contrary result]. Solution: that law is one thing this law is another, but by custom the opinion of Trebatius is approved'.[36]

Not only did the commentators acknowledge the existence of differing bodies of law, they also began, at first quite tentatively, to explore why there might be such differences. For example, the fifteenth-century canonist Panormitanus considers the difference between Roman law and canon law on the topic of parental consent: 'Canon law', he says, 'considered the freedom of marriage. The civil law, however, considered the crime of the ravisher[37] and deception of women'.[38] The past tense will be noted; having considered these things, the law became fixed.[39]

Open acknowledgement of the differences between laws necessitated the creation of a system to deal with conflicts of laws. Bartolus's justly famous *repetitio* on the

---

[35] The reference is to the 'vulgate' edition of the Lombard laws with the gloss. Lombarda 1.22.6 (Venice, 1537), fol. 56ra–56rb. The standard edition of the original text is Friedrich Bluhme (ed), *Leges Langobardorum*, Monumenta Germaniae Historica, Legum, 3 (1868). There is an English translation by Katherine Fisher Drew: *The Lombard Laws* (1973). The law being referred to is Rothair 314 (trans Drew, p 114).

[36] Bartolus, *Commentarius ad* D.41.1.5 (Basel, 1562), 183.

[37] The man who married a woman, at least a young woman, without obtaining her father's consent was considered to have committed rape (*raptus in parentes*), the consent of the woman being irrelevant.

[38] Nicholaus de Tudeschis (*abbas Panormitanus*), *Commentarius ad* X 5.17.6 (Venice, 1569), iv, fol. 140r.

[39] Some literature developed outlining the differences between Roman law and canon law, eg Galvanus de Bononia, 'Differentie legum et canonum', in *Modus legendi abbreviaturas* ([Strassburg, before 1478]), sig. z4ra–z7vb, and many times reprinted. The heyday, however, of 'difference' literature lies in the early modern period and is to be associated with the comparative effort of the humanists, discussed below. Eg Christoph Zobel (1499–1560), *Differentiae iuris ciuilis et Saxonici* (Leipzig, 1598).

imperial constitution *Cunctos populos* (*Code* 1.1.1) is not only the first extended treatment of the topic, it also makes considerable use of what we would call policy analysis in an effort to determine the legitimate scope of conflicting laws.[40]

It has recently been argued, correctly in my view, that in at least one place the Bartolan *repetitio* shows considerable sophistication in comparative analysis.[41] Most of the conflicts with which the *repetitio* deals are relatively standard ones involving the statutes of Italian city-states. In one example, however, Bartolus poses a conflict between the *ius commune*, with its provision for equal inheritance in intestacy among children of the deceased, and English law with its system of primogeniture. The relevant variables for determining which law will apply, as Bartolus sees them, are the citizenship of the deceased (English or Italian) and the location of the property (in England or Italy). He then adds one more: 'The words of the statute or custom are to be carefully examined, for they either make a determination about a thing (*circa rem*) "The goods of the deceased shall go to the eldest son" . . . or [they] make a determination about a person (*circa personam*): "The eldest son shall succeed" '.[42] This distinction has long been criticized on two grounds: first, that the English law was customary and not redacted, and second, that a difference as important as this one should not be made to depend on wording. A statute-making body (or a redactor of a custom), aware of this distinction, would always use the personal wording in order to increase the scope of the statute or custom. If, however, we assume that Bartolus was reasonably well-informed about the differences between the English legal system and the Italian ones in his period, and that he phrased the problem in terms of the language of statutes or redacted customs because that is the way his listeners thought about local law, then the distinction may be quite sophisticated. The Italian city-states in Bartolus's period used the Roman system of universal succession. 'Let the first-born succeed' to an Italian of Bartolus' period would mean that the first-born was the universal heir, inheriting all the property and the active and passive of the obligations. He was charged with the responsibility of paying the legacies and frequently also charged with *fideicommissa*, roughly the equivalent of the modern Anglo-American trust. 'The property shall go to the eldest son', by contrast, means just that. Nothing is implied about obligations, administration, or trusts. In fact, it is the second alternative that corresponds to the English legal system of

---

[40] Bartolus, *Commentarius ad* C.1.1.1 (Venice, 1602), fol. 4r–7r, nos. 13–51. The printed text has a number of misprints. The English translation by Joseph Henry Beale (*Bartolus on Conflict of Laws*, 1914) cannot be recommended. That by J. A. Clarence Smith ('Bartolo on the Conflict of Laws', [1970] 14 *American Journal of Legal History* 174–83, 247–75), is better, but it is harder to use because Smith does not repeat the portions of the text that correspond to Bartolus's commentary on D.1.3.32 (which he translates in ibid 163–74).

[41] Nikitas Hatzimihail, *Pre-Classical Conflict of Laws* (SJD Dissertation, Harvard Law School, 2003), 169–70, 221–7. (Dr Hatzimihail has not yet submitted his dissertation to the Harvard Law Library, and when he does, the page references will probably change somewhat.)

[42] Bartolus (n 40), fol. 6ra–b, no. 42 (my translation).

Bartolus' day. Primogeniture applied only to land and not even to all land.[43] In short, if we focus not on the wording of the 'statute', but on the underlying substantive differences between the English and the Italian systems of succession in Bartolus' day, his distinction may be based on an important comparative insight.

Considerable work that can be regarded as comparative is found in the *consilia* of the fifteenth- and sixteenth-century Italian commentators that deal with conflicts between the statutes of the Italian city-states and between those statutes and the *ius commune*. Systematic exploration of these *consilia* is in its infancy. We will have something to say about them when we consider the better-known work of the sixteenth-century French legal thinkers.[44]

Contemporary with the commentators, but operating in a decidedly different legal tradition is Sir John Fortescue, a mid-fifteenth-century English judge of the Lancastrian party. Fortescue made numerous comparisons between the legal systems of England and France, both in his *De laudibus legum Anglie* and in his *Governance of England*.[45] The purpose of both works, however, was to show how English law and governance were in all respects superior to those of France. Whether one regards Fortescue as a practitioner of the comparative method depends on whether just making comparisons—which Fortescue surely did—is sufficient. One may, however, argue that the comparative method requires more. In particular, it may require an openness to the comparative process, a willingness to admit that what is on the other side of the comparison is better than what is on one's own side, or—if one does not want to be normative—an openness to seeing that some differences may be more apparent than real and that the remaining differences may have quite intelligible explanations. If that is required, then Fortescue was not a true practitioner of the comparative method. He made comparisons, but the result of his comparisons was a foregone conclusion: English law was better than French.

---

[43] Most land in boroughs and most land held by servile tenure descended according to different systems; much of the land of Kent descended according to a different system.

[44] Below text at nn 53–8.

[45] Christopher Plummer (ed), *The Governance of England: Otherwise Called, the Difference between an Absolute and a Limited Monarchy by Sir John Fortescue* (1885; repr 1979); S. B. Chrimes (ed), *De laudibus legum Anglie: Sir John Fortescue*, Cambridge Studies in English Legal History (1942; repr 1979).

IV. SIXTEENTH-CENTURY FRENCH LEGAL THINKERS

> And so having compared the arguments of Aristotle, Polybius,
> Dionysius [of Halicarnassus], and the jurists—with each other and
> with the universal history of commonwealths—I find the
> supremacy in a commonwealth consists of five parts. The first and
> most important is appointing magistrates and assigning each one's
> duties; another is ordaining and repealing laws; a third is declaring
> and terminating war; a fourth is the right of hearing appeals from
> all magistrates in last resort; and the last is the power of life and
> death where the law itself has made no provision for flexibility or
> clemency.[46]

The author of this quotation is Jean Bodin, although the quotation is not from the *Six livres de la République* but from the earlier *Methodus ad facilem historiarum cognitionem*. My concern here is not with Bodin's definition of supremacy in a commonwealth, what he elsewhere calls 'sovereignty'; my concern is with his method, that is to say, with the way by which he arrived at his definition. He did it, he tells us, by comparing 'the arguments of Aristotle, Polybius, Dionysius [of Halicarnassus], and the jurists—with each other and with the universal history of commonwealths'.

We are becoming increasingly aware that Bodin was not as original in his political and legal thought as he claimed to be.[47] The same is true of his method. A number of Bodin's contemporaries engaged in more or less systematic comparison of top-level philosophical and political abstractions like those of Aristotle (Polybius and Dionysius are in exalted company) and of the middle-level generalizations found in the writings of the Roman jurists and of the 'universal history of commonwealths', a topic that turns out to include large amounts of more or less accurate history of the ancient Mediterranean world with considerably less accurate histories of the Celtic and Germanic worlds. One has only to mention the names of Éguinaire Baron, François Baudouin, and François Hotman to indicate how common the method of comparative legal history was among the French

---

[46] *I. Bodini Methodus ad facilem historiarum cognitionem* (Amsterdam, 1650, repr 1967), 175–6. The translation is derived from J. H. Franklin, 'Sovereignty and the Mixed Constitution: Bodin and His Critics', in J. H. Burns (ed), *The Cambridge History of Political Thought: 1450–1700* (1991), 302 (based on the edition of P. Mesnard, in *Oeuvres philosophiques de Jean Bodin*, 1951). Cf *Method for the Easy Comprehension of History* (trans B. Reynolds, 1945), 172–3.

[47] See, most notably, the first three volumes of Aramand Fell's massive *Origins of Legislative Sovereignty and the Legislative State: 1. Corasius and the Renaissance Systematization of Roman Law; 2. Classical, Medieval, and Renaissance Foundations of Corasius' Systematic Methodology; 3. Bodin's Humanistic Legal System and Rejection of 'Medieval Political Theology'* (1983–7).

humanists of the sixteenth century. Indeed, it has been argued that the French legal humanists invented modern historical method.[48]

Be that as it may be, the use of the comparative method in law and history is certainly a characteristic of the French sixteenth century. The homologation of French customary law in this period produced material that cried out for comparative treatment, and comparisons began even before the effort was finished. Most notably, the comparative method can be found in writers who can be classified as 'humanists' in only the most extended of senses. Guy Coquille's (1523–1603) *Institution au droict des François* is illustrative.[49]

Coquille was a practising lawyer in the customary courts of Nivernais, but he had been trained in Italy. He mentions Mariano Socini, junior, who taught at Bologna and died in 1556, as one of his teachers. Coquille's *Institution* begins with the titles of the homologated custom of Nivernais. He first states the rules of that custom relevant to the title, but he immediately broadens out comparatively. Let us examine some of Coquille's comparative arguments, for they show considerable sophistication.

In his title on marital property, Coquille states that the rule in Nivernais is that a married woman must obtain the consent of her husband in order to make a testament.[50] The same rule applies in Burgundy. In Poitou, Auxerre, Berry, and Rheims the rule is to the contrary. This is the kind of conflict that comparative analysis uncovered quite quickly in dealing with 285 diverse customs.[51] Once the customs had been redacted, it is a relatively mechanical task to lay them side by side to see how the rules are similar and how they differ. But once the conflict has been discovered what are we to do about it? One way to resolve such a conflict would be simply to say that a married woman in Nivernais or Burgundy should get her husband's permission to make a testament but one in Poitou, Auxerre, Berry, and Rheims need not. But in general that is not the way Coquille and most of his contemporaries thought. The question they seem to be asking is what is the 'true rule'. This would suggest that we are still in a world in which there is a true rule; law is not simply a matter of the will of the legislator or even of the will of the community expressed in the homologated custom. The true rule is that a testament cannot depend on the will of another. That is in the nature of a testament. How does Coquille know that? Because Roman law says so, and he cites relevant passages from the *Digest* to show it.[52] But he will not simply override the custom of

---

[48] Donald Kelley, *Foundations of Modern Historical Scholarship: Language, Law, and History in the French Renaissance* (1970). cf *idem, History, Law, and the Human Sciences: Medieval and Renaissance Perspectives* (1984).

[49] 1st edn, Paris, 1607. I have used the edition of Paris, 1608.

[50] *Idem*, at 184–5.

[51] They were ultimately published in four massive folio volumes, Charles A. Bourdot de Richebourg (ed), *Nouveau coutumier général* (Paris, 1724).

[52] Citing D.28.5.32 (on point).

Nivernais or Burgundy. The rule still has some force in those areas. But what he will do is limit the scope of the rule. If the custom is abolished, then the rule has no force because the *ius commune* is to the contrary. But even more important, he will limit the number of people who can raise the objection. If the husband in Nivernais or Burgundy does not raise an objection to his wife's testament, then no one can. A rule contrary to the *ius commune* will be held to be a kind of privilege, exercisable only by those to whom it has been granted it.

On the basis of this example, it looks as if the *ius commune* and juristic inter-pretation always win the day. But the *ius commune* was malleable stuff. Let us take a look at how Coquille handles the problem of when a marriage is deemed to be complete for marital property purposes.[53] Coquille begins with a basic proposition: Almost all the customary jurisdictions have community property. Indeed, almost all of them have the version that is the basic version in France today, community property of movables and acquests. The community does not arise, Coquille tells us, until there are words of the present tense (a requirement of canon law as old as the twelfth century) and solemnization of the marriage in the face of the church (which was not a requirement of the classical canon law for either validity or legitimacy).

Some customs require a nuptial blessing. But this, Coquille tells us, makes no sense because in canon law a blessing can be done privately or clandestinely with-out assembly.[54] Coquille does not derive his requirement that marriages must be public for community property to arise from the decree *Tametsi* of the council of Trent (1563) or the *ordonnance* of Blois (1579), both of which might have been used to support such a publicity requirement.[55] Rather, he relies on a *consilium* of his teacher, Mariano Socini, junior, and Socini had, in turn, relied on a *consilium* on the same topic of Panormitanus.[56] Panormitanus was dealing with a different issue: He had interpreted statutes of Italian city-states to require that for purposes of giving the husband a share in the dowry of his predeceased childless wife there must be a leading of the bride into the house of the groom in addition to the canonical requirement of present consent. Panormitanus considered, but apparently rejected, interpreting the statutes to require that the marriage be consummated. But for Panormitanus the policy that the statutes supported was that the husband be compensated for bearing the expenses of the wedding and

---

[53] Coquille (n 49), 185–6.   [54] Ibid.

[55] Council of Trent, sess 24 (1563), Canones super reformatione circa matrimonium, c 1 (*Tametsi*), in Giuseppe Alberigo (ed), *Conciliorum oecumenicorum decreta* (1972), 755–7; Ordonnance of Blois (May, 1579), arts 40–4, in *Recueil des grandes ordonnances, édits et déclarations des rois de France* (Toulouse, 1786), 173–4.

[56] The numbers that Coquille gives for Socini's *consilia* (1.31, 1.86) do not correspond to those in Mariano Socini, *Consilia* (Venice, 1571). The *consilium* of Panormitanus that he cites is *Facti contin-gentia*, Nicholaus de Tudeschis, *Consilia* 1.1 (Lyon, 1562), fol. 2ra–vb. Cf *Sante stututo*, ibid, 2.79 (Venice, 1569), fol. 162v–163v.

maintaining his wife in his household. Coquille was concerned about publicity *tout court*. He simply rejects the customs that call for consummation. He sharply distinguishes the canonic requirements from the civil requirements. He does not say so, but he almost certainly comes to his conclusion because it is critically important in a community property system that creditors know with whom they are dealing. Publicity is essential for community property not only for the relatively rare instances of disputes about the division of the property but for the day-to-day dealings of the couple with others.

What Coquille has done is to take *consilia* in the tradition of the *ius commune* that raised the question of what is to be done about local law that seemed inconsistent with the *ius commune* and interpreted that law in the light of an imagined purpose relevant to the local system of marital property. In the case of Panormitanus that purpose had to do with a dotal system; in Coquille's case the system of marital property was community property. The imagined purpose of the local law is quite different in the two cases: compensating the husband in one case, giving publicity to the formation of the community in the other. What links the two is that in both cases the local law adds something to the present-consent requirement of the canon law (and of the *ius commune*), and in both cases the teleological interpretation of the local law is connected to the local system of marital property.

My last example shows Coquille at his most radical.[57] All the customs that Coquille cites make the contract of a married woman absolutely void. This means that the contract has no effect even after the death of the husband or upon the divorce of the couple. Coquille does not like this rule, although it is not completely clear why. He apparently does not think that there is anything about being a woman that makes her incompetent to contract, and he cites the proposition that an unmarried woman who has reached the age of majority can contract. He also notes that women may be sued for their delicts, that they can trade, and that they have capacity to sue when there has been a separation of goods. We may speculate that Coquille feels that absolute incapacity does not correspond to social reality. In any event the problem is how is he going to get around the unanimous testimony of his customary authorities. He does it by saying that the rule was derived from Roman law. Not only was it derived from Roman law, it was derived by an analogy, from the contractual incapacity in Roman law of the *filiusfamilias*. Therefore the authorities do not require an absolute rule of (female) incapacity. The true rule, he says, is that a woman is incapacitated from contracting only in respect of the power of her husband. Take away the power, and the rule ceases. In other words, the incapacity is not personal but relational. Hence, presumably, as in the case of the testament, only the husband can object. I am not sure that this is a good argument, but it is interesting that Coquille makes it.

What is also interesting is Coquille's method. Perhaps the easiest of his moves to

---

[57] Coquille (n 49), 181.

see is where he makes a comparison and the comparison reveals that there is a difference among the customs. Here he has a tendency to look to the rule of the *ius commune*, and to privilege that rule. He will not deny that the contrary custom exists, but he will require that it be clearly stated, and he will apply it only in those situations to which it clearly applies. Basically the same techniques were being used by the Italian jurists in the fifteenth century when they were dealing with statutes that were contrary to the *ius commune*: Statutes in derogation of the common law (*ius commune*) are strictly construed. But Coquille's search for principle goes further. Sometimes he will ask what the purpose of the custom is and will refuse to apply it in situations where he does not believe that its purpose applies. Again, the same technique was used in the interpretation of the statutes of the Italian city-states. Occasionally we will find an argument that the custom is just flat-out wrong, either that it contradicts other higher principles or that it—this argument is usually only hinted at—does not correspond with social reality. The former argument is found in the fifteenth-century Italian jurists, though it is not often used; the latter is so rare as to be virtually non-existent. Coquille and others writing in the French tradition go beyond what the Italian jurists did in another respect. They attempt to find principles that unite the divergent French customs among themselves when no reference to the *ius commune* can be made, and they use methods and principles of the *ius commune* in analysing a customary system of law that, unlike the statutes of the Italian city-states, did not assume the *ius commune* as its basis.

The comparative method was not universally followed in sixteenth century France, at least not as broadly as Coquille used it. Christophe de Thou, *premier président* of the *parlement* of Paris and the man who more than any other was responsible for the homologation of the French customs, seems to have been hostile to comparisons involving Roman law.[58] We must be cautious, however, in making this statement. De Thou's thought is quite difficult to reconstruct. He did not write any general works about his method, and what we know of his thought is largely derived from what he did and what his contemporaries said about him. He was probably not hostile to comparisons among the various French customs, and he was willing to allow Roman law to be called *ratio scripta* in some of the homologations. On the other hand, he never spoke of Roman law as being the *droit commun* in France, a phrase that he seems to have reserved for the common elements among the customs, and he seems to have been less open to argument from Roman law than was his predecessor Pierre Lizet. De Thou's *discours* pronounced on 11 May 1565 in the presence of the prince de Condé is replete with citations to classical authors, but it contains relatively little Roman law.[59] Citation

---

[58] See generally René Filhol, *Le premier président Christofle de Thou et la réformation des coutumes* (1937).

[59] ed Sylvie Daubresse, 'Un discours de Christophe de Thou premier président du Parlement de Paris', (1995) 153 *Bibliothèque de l'École des chartes* 380–7.

of classical authorities increased markedly in the *plaidoyers* during de Thou's tenure as *président* of the *parlement* (1554–82).[60] But citation of classical authorities for rhetorical purposes is not quite the same thing as citing Roman law as authoritative or making comparisons between French customary law and Roman law.[61]

Pierre Pithou, in what may have been a daring move in 1572, dedicated his edition of the newly discovered *Lex Dei* to de Thou, arguing in the preface that de Thou had nothing to fear from the authority and sanction of Roman law and much to gain from its reason and equity. De Thou's reaction, so far as I know, is not recorded. Perhaps he did not even notice; Pithou's dedication is dated five weeks after the St Bartholomew's day massacre.[62] De Thou may well have had other things on his mind.

De Thou did, in fact, have something to fear from Roman law and from the comparative method, but the source of the danger was not the authority of a Byzantine emperor dead for a thousand years, nor that of Rudolf II, the nominal successor of the Roman emperor in the west. What de Thou had to fear was that compared to Roman law, French customary law was an intellectual mess, and in an intellectual age, intellectual messiness was not a desirable characteristic. Ultimately, of course, French customary law acquired intellectual respectability, but it did so by using the very tools of analysis and comparison that de Thou seems to have feared, tools that by and large had been developed by men like Pithou working on Roman law. In the process French customary law changed; it became less local and less particular. While it retained characteristics that were peculiarly French, there were fewer such characteristics when the process was over than there had been before it began. De Thou may have saved French customary law as a category and its practitioners as a profession, but what emerged was not the same as what he had saved, and, perhaps, what he hoped to save.

I think there can be no doubt that French legal thinkers of the sixteenth century employed the comparative method widely. Unlike Fortescue, they were open to

---

[60] The evidence given for this proposition in Professor Elizabeth A. R. Brown's forthcoming study of the subject is powerful. I am grateful to her for allowing me to see the study in draft. She is also the source of the qualifications of de Thou's views given in the previous sentences.

[61] The traditional view, espoused, for example, by Filhol (n 58, at 125–40), that de Thou was opposed to the latter, is shaken but not quite upset. For opposition to Roman law among customary lawyers in the early modern period generally, see Gerald Strauss, *Law, Resistance, and the State: The Opposition to Roman Law in Reformation Germany* (1986); Daniel Coquillette, *The Civilian Writers of Doctors' Commons, London: Three Centuries of Juristic Innovation in Comparative, Commercial and International Law*, Comparative Studies in Continental and Anglo-American Legal History, 3 (1988), esp 84–94.

[62] The first printing is *Fragmenta quaedam Papiniani Pauli Vlpiani Gaii Modestini . . . cum Moysis legibus collata* (Paris, 1573), 116 ff, separately published as *Mosaycarum et romanarum legum collatio* (Basel, 1574). I have used the edition in *Petri Pithoei opera, sacra, ivridica, historica, miscellanea* (Paris, 1609). The dedication is dated 1 October 1572. Pithou, in *Opera*, 76. The massacre, of course, took place on 24 August.

what their comparative sources were telling them. We certainly cannot accuse most of them of jingoism, an accusation that it is not unfair to apply to Fortescue. They also dealt with their sources from the ancient Mediterranean world with considerable sophistication.

Let us return to what Jean Bodin confidently asserted that he had done in order to arrive at his definition of sovereignty. He had, he tells us, compared the arguments of Aristotle, Polybius, Dionysius of Halicarnassus, and the jurists with each other and with the universal history of commonwealths. He had, in short, comparatively examined abstractions of the highest order, comparatively examined the middle-level abstractions found in juristic writing, and had laid both comparisons against the history of the societies in which they emerged. Only then was he able to arrive at his generalizations about the nature of sovereignty. In his day it was just barely possible for a genius and polymath like Bodin actually to execute this programme.

Even Bodin took shortcuts. It is probably just as well that Bodin spent little time examining the Germanic and Gallic background of the French constitution, because the work that his contemporaries, such as Hotman, did on the topic seems today embarrassingly tendentious and amateurish.[63] What the sixteenth-century humanists have to say about the Greek and Roman worlds is more solidly based. One can still gain insights into Greek and Roman law and legal thought from reading the work of the humanists. The work of Jacques Godefroy (1587–1652) on the Theodosian Code has, in some sense, not been replaced.[64] None the less, the humanists' vision of the development of law and legal thought in Greece and Rome is not ours. While they were aware of the problems that interpolation and omission in the juristic texts caused, they did not systematically explore the effects of these phenomena. They knew some of the epigraphic evidence, but not enough. The study, for example, of Roman public law cannot be done today as it was done in the sixteenth century because of the work of Mommsen and his followers.[65] I am still old-fashioned enough to believe in progress in knowledge, but progress means that the number of areas that one can cover in a lifetime gets smaller.

---

[63] See eg Donald Kelley, *François Hotman; A Revolutionary's Ordeal* (1973), 238–52; *idem*, 'The Rise of Legal History in the Renaissance', (1970) 9 *History and Theory* 187–90, repr, in *History, Law, and the Human Sciences* (n 48), V:179–80; Ralph Giesey, 'When and Why Hotman Wrote the *Francogallia*', (1967) 29 *Bibliothèque d'humanism et renaissance* 581–611.

[64] Published posthumously, Jacques Godefroy (ed), *Codex Theodosianus cum perpetuis commentariis Jacobi Gothofredi* (Lyon, 1665). For a recent assessment, see Bruno Schmidlin and Alfred Dufour (eds), *Jacques Godefroy (1587–1652) et l'Humanisme juridique a Genève* (1991), 44–5, 259. For a recent work dependent on Godefroy's, see Renate Frohne, *Codex Theodosianus. 16, 8, 1–29: über Juden, Himmelsverehrer und Samaritaner*, Europäische Hochschulschriften, 3.453 (1991).

[65] In this regard the Mommsen of the *Corpus inscriptionum latinarum* (1862–) (currently 18 vols in 54 parts) may be more important than the Mommsen of the *Römisches Staatsrecht*, Handbuch der römischen Alterthümer, 1–3 (3 vols, 3rd edn, 1887), which has recently been challenged as anachronistic. See Jochen Bleicken, *Lex Publica: Gesetz und Recht in der römischen Republik* (1975).

What we have just said raises some doubt about whether the French legal thinkers of the sixteenth century can truly be said to be the founders of modern comparative method. As was the case with Fortescue, so too with the case of the French legal thinkers of the sixteenth century, it is a question of definition. If we require that the comparative method be value-neutral, that its practitioners not seek to act on the results of their studies, that they seek only to explain similarities and differences, that they be 'scientific' in one of the modern senses of that term, then the French legal thinkers of the sixteenth century, for the most part, were not practitioners of the modern comparative method. Bodin sought not only to understand sovereignty but also to influence French constitutional development in his own time. On a less exalted level, Coquille sought to shape the customs with which he was dealing so that they moved in the direction of what he regarded as right. Both believed in a supranational body of law. For Coquille it was the *ius commune*; for Bodin and Pithou it was the principles derived from the experience and writings of the ancients. Neither would have agreed that law is solely a matter of the will of the legislator.

If, however, we insist that comparative law be 'scientific' in the sense that I have just defined it, then a great deal that passes for comparative law today is not comparative law. Many comparatists look to other legal systems for possible solutions to the problems that are plaguing some legal systems, perhaps even their own, or for explanations of why one legal system, perhaps even their own, has succeeded in an area in which another has not. Many comparatists look to legal systems other than their own to see if it is possible to develop a dialogue across systems, for example, by finding common principles, if not specific rules. Most would agree that the task of the comparatist must involve careful examination of top-level ideas, middle-level legal discourse, and actual practice and development. In all of these endeavours modern comparatists are the descendants of the French legal thinkers of the sixteenth century.

V. The Seventeenth and Eighteenth Centuries

With the decline of French humanist legal thought, the comparative method passed to the natural law school.[66] To put the matter too simplistically, the French humanists had shown how classical Roman law was very different from what

---

[66] Limitations of space prevent me from tracing the line that runs from writers like Coquille to the more practically inclined Dutch legal thinkers of the seventeenth century and German practitioners of

passed under the name of Roman law in the Italy of their day and suggested that the real lessons to be learned from Roman law were on a level of generality higher than the specific rules of the system.[67] It was to this higher level of generality that the natural law school turned its attention. Whether their principles were derived from comparative study or whether they were illustrated and confirmed by comparative examples, many members of the natural law school, among whom Hugo Grotius (1583–1645), John Selden (1584–1654), and Samuel von Pufendorf (1632–1694) provide notable examples, set their natural law principles in a broadly comparative framework.[68] The comparative method is also found among writers of the Enlightenment who were not members of the natural law school, for example, Charles de Secondat, baron de Montesquieu (1689–1755),[69] and to a lesser, but still substantial, extent, among Enlightenment authors who were only partially members of the natural law school, for example, Robert-Joseph Pothier (1699–1772).[70]

The previous paragraph avoided the question whether the method of the natural law school was genuinely inductive, so that comparative material was used to derive larger and larger principles until the ultimate principles emerged, or whether these principles were found deductively, so that the comparative material was there simply by way of illustration, example, or confirmation of what had been determined by other means. I am not sure that such a question can be answered when one is dealing with men as complex and learned as Grotius, Selden, and Pufendorf. The distinction, however, is an important one if one defines comparative law as being necessarily empirical. If an author has already made up his mind that the true principle of law is, for example, that man has a natural right to private property as that term is normally understood in the West, then the empiricist is likely to regard that author's comparative material as not truly comparative but as propaganda for the predetermined conclusion.

Certainly some members of the natural law school—Christian von Wolff (1679–

---

the *usus modernus pandectarum* in the seventeenth and eighteenth centuries. These complex lines can be explored in Franz Wieacker, *A History of the Private Law of Europe*, Tony Weir (trans, of 2nd edn of *Privatrechtsgeschichte der Neuzeit* (1967)) (1995), particularly at 159–95.

[67] The division of Europe along confessional lines probably also played a role in this search for a higher level of generality. See, somewhat controversially, Harold Berman, *Law and Revolution, II: The Impact of the Protestant Reformations on the Western Legal Tradition* (2003).

[68] A good general account of the natural law school is needed, the relevant volume of the *Handbuch der Quellen und Literatur der neueren europäischen Privatrechtsgeschichte* (n 23) having, apparently, been abandoned. In the meantime see Richard Tuck, 'Grotius and Selden' and Alfred Dufour, 'Pufendorf', in *Political Thought: 1450–1700* (n 46), at 499–529, 561–88; Wieacker (n 66), 199–256.

[69] Charles de Secondat, baron de Montesquieu, *De l'esprit des lois*, most recently Gonzague Truc (ed) (2 vols 1962); see eg Robert Shackleton, *Essays on Montesquieu and on the Enlightenment* (1988); Judith Shklar, *Montesquieu* (1987).

[70] Jean-Joseph Bugnet (ed), *Œuvres de Pothier: annotées et mises en corrélation avec le Code civil et la législation actuelle* (10 vols, 1890). See eg Jean-Louis Sourioux and Aline Terrasson de Fougères (eds), *Robert-Joseph Pothier: d'hier à aujourd'hui* (2001).

1754) comes immediately to mind—wanted to make law a rigorously deductive science.[71] In this Wolff was probably following the jurisprudential ideas of Gottfried von Leibniz (1646–1716), but he was also being true to his own formation: He began his career as a professor of mathematics. Some of his work can be regarded as comparative in the sense that he occasionally uses examples drawn from a variety of legal systems, but it is certainly not empirical in the normal sense of that term. He may be a comparatist in the broad sense but his approach does not lead to the method employed by most, if not all, modern comparatists.

As previously suggested, Grotius, Selden, and Pufendorf are more complicated. Their methodological premises are less apparent than Wolff's. All may have realized that at least in the human sciences the distinction between inductive and deductive tends to break down. They certainly ranged very widely indeed with regard to the materials they considered, perhaps no one more so than Selden.

We have space for only one example, but it is one that, I believe, illustrates the mainstream of the natural law school, at least in its seventeenth-century manifestations, quite well. It is also one that will allow the reader to decide for him- or herself whether these thinkers should be classified as comparatists.

Our example is taken from Pufendorf's treatment of the occupation of wild animals, a topic discussed earlier.[72] Although Pufendorf struggled against Thomas Hobbes, his thought on property has a decidedly Hobbesian cast.[73] For Pufendorf, as for Hobbes, there is no natural right to property in the state of nature. All property is dependent upon the compact among men. According to this compact things seized by one man out of the common stock are protected from seizure by another. But since the core of the compact is that men surrender their autonomy to the sovereign, the sovereign may change the rule about first occupancy, as in most places he had with regard to hunting wild animals. None the less, the law cannot change the rule that what is in no one's dominion cannot be owned.[74]

This proposition leads Pufendorf to spell out the negative implications of Justinian's text: A wild animal is not reduced to possession except by bodily seizure, either directly or by instruments. That, in turn, brings Pufendorf to the problem of the wounded animal:[75]

The question is also raised whether, by wounding a wild animal, we seem to make it at once our own. Trebatius once said that we did, supposing that we pursue it, while if we do not do

[71] I am thinking here more of the Wolff of *Jus naturae methodo scientifica pertractatum* (8 vols, Frankfurt, 1741–8) than I am of the Wolff of *Jus gentium methodo scientifica pertractatum* (Magdeburg, 1749). On Wolff's thought in general, see Wieacker (n 66), 253–5.

[72] I have used the edition of *De jure naturae et gentium* in *The Classics of International Law* series (1934), a reprint of the Latin text (Amsterdam, 1688), with a translation by C. H. and W. A. Oldfather.

[73] He may have succeeded more in freeing himself from Hobbes in his views about contract than he did in his views about property. See Wieacker (n 66), 243–8.

[74] Ibid 4.4.1–14, 4.6.1–9, trans i, 532–56, 569–78.

[75] Ibid 4.6.10, trans i, 579 (altered on basis of original).

so, it ceases to be ours, and goes to him who first secures it. Others take the opposite position, namely, that it is not ours unless we have caught it, since many things can happen that may keep us from catching it.[76] On this Godefroy[77] observes that Frederick [Barbarossa] drew some distinctions in cases like this, to wit: 'If a man has discovered an animal with large deer hounds, or Molossian dogs, and was pursuing it, the animal goes to him rather than to the one who seizes it; and likewise if he wounds or kills it with a spear or sword. If he pursued it with beagles or Spartan dogs, it falls to the seizer. If he slew it with dart, stone, or arrow, it belongs to him and not to the seizer, provided that he is pursuing it'. According to a law of the Lombards,[78] he who killed or found an animal wounded by another, may carry off the fore-quarter with seven ribs, the rest belonging to him who had wounded it, though his right endured only twenty-four hours. In my opinion the general statement should be that, if an animal has received a mortal wound or been seriously crippled, it cannot be taken by another so long as we keep up the pursuit of it, and provided we have the right to be in that place; while this is not true, in case the wound be not mortal, nor such as seriously to hinder its flight. Therefore, it was more from affection than right that Meleager allowed Atalanta to share in the glory of the slaying of the Caledonian boar, as the story is given by Ovid.[79] But the game which my dogs have killed without any urging is not mine until I seize it.[80]

Pufendorf is not known to have had a sense of humour, but it is hard to imagine that he did not at least smile when he brought to bear on the problem both the chronicler's account of the elaborate ruling of Frederick Barbarossa and the story of Meleager and Atalanta.[81] The Roman legal texts and the Lombard, as we have seen, were already very much in the tradition. Pufendorf's own opinion on the topic is within the mainstream of the Roman legal tradition (though more on the Trebatian than on the Gaian side) but it is also derived from, or is at least consistent with, his Hobbesian view of property. Law has no place where the sovereign does not have power over the subject, and property has no place where the subject does not control the object of property. Now if we ask where this idea comes from, we would say that for Hobbes it is derived from a story about how human beings banded together and surrendered themselves to the sovereign in order to escape from their nasty, mean, brutish, and short existence. Pufendorf replaces that account with one much more based on the account of the original situation of humans found in the book of Genesis, but he retains Hobbes's insistence on sovereign power. There is no natural right to property in the sense that such a right existed in natural law before the compact that created the state, and hence, the sovereign may institute whatever rules he chooses about who is entitled to hunt and where. For Pufendorf, there is a master narrative that trumps all other

---

[76] Citing D. 41, 1, 5.

[77] Citing Radevicus [Frisingensis], *De gestis Friderici* 1.26.

[78] Citing Lombarda 1.22.4, 6 ((n 35), fol. 55vb–56ra, 56ra–56rb).

[79] Citing Ovid, *Metamorphoses* 8.427.

[80] Citing Alberico Gentili, *Pleas of a Spanish Advocate* 1.4.

[81] The former certainly gave rise to considerable drollery in the dissenting opinion of Livingston J, in *Pierson v Post*, 3 Caines 175, 181–2 (New York Supreme Court, 1805).

narratives. From this master narrative, principles are derived, which are then used to control the wide variety of examples that comparative inquiry produces. The principles are, however, derived from a narrative, not from ever more abstract propositions about the nature of man or the nature of human societies.

If we change the master narrative, we get different results. Jean Barbeyrac (1674–1744) accepted John Locke's master narrative about the origins of property (the Indian and his acorns), from which he, like Locke, derived the notion of a natural right to property that antedated the social compact.[82] If we say that the purpose of property is to protect human labour in reducing resources to human use, then we will not find any particularly powerful dividing line at the point where the resource is actually seized. We are much more likely to say that the huntsman who has announced his intention to others to pursue a particular animal will be protected in that endeavour so long as he continues the pursuit. And this is precisely what Barbeyrac says in his trenchant and highly critical commentary on the passages of Pufendorf just summarized.[83] Methodologically, however, the Hobbes–Pufendorf and Locke–Barbeyrac approaches are the same: Principles derived from the master narrative control the examples produced by comparative inquiry.

When we move from writers in the natural law school of the seventeenth century to Montesquieu, one of the things that is most noticeable is the great increase in the geographical and cultural range of his examples, a product, among other things, of the greater knowledge that was reaching Europe of places like Japan, China, and India. There is correspondingly less emphasis on examples from antiquity, although these are certainly not wanting. Notable too is the absence of a master narrative from which principles are derived and then used to control the examples. Rather than condemning practices that the master narrative has shown to be contrary to reason, Montesquieu seeks to explain the variety of laws and practices that he reports as the product of geographical (or ecological), institutional, and social forces. His method, then, is more like that of modern empirical social science. As such, it is no better than the data on which it is based, and some of what Montesquieu took from travellers' accounts was clearly just wrong.[84] Of course, the fact that Montesquieu has no master narrative does not mean that his account is value-free. Perhaps what we see from the vantage point of more than two centuries indicates the impossibility of a totally value-free account in the social sciences.

The following example is atypical only in that it does not range so widely

---

[82] Jean Barbeyrac (ed and trans), *Le droit de la nature et des gens par le baron Pufendorf* (London, 1740). The English translation by Basil Kennet (London, 1749) is quite adequate.

[83] Ibid 4.4.1–14, 4.6.1–9 (notes). The critical note with the reference to Locke that sets up the rest of the argument is at 4.4.4.

[84] See, for example, his remarks on the different proportions of male and female births in different countries. Montesquieu, *The Spirit of Laws* (trans Thomas Nugent, 2nd edn, London, 1752), 443.

geographically as do many of Montesquieu's. It deals with a topic previously con-sidered, the consent of fathers to the marriage of their children:[85]

The consent of fathers is founded on their authority, that is, on the right of property. It is also founded on their love, on their reason, and on the uncertainty of that of their children, whom youth confines in a state of ignorance and passion in a state of ebriety.

In the small republics, or singular institutions already mentioned, they might have laws which gave to magistrates that right of inspection over the marriages of the children of citizens which nature had already given to fathers. The love of the public might there equal or surpass all other love. Thus Plato would have marriages regulated by the magistrates: this the Lacedaemonian magistrates performed.

But in common institutions, fathers have the disposal of their children in marriage: their prudence in this respect is always supposed to be superior to that of a stranger. Nature gives to fathers a desire of procuring successors to their children, when they have almost lost the desire of enjoyment themselves. In the several degrees of progeniture, they see themselves insensibly advancing to a kind of immortality. But what must be done, if oppression and avarice arise to such a height as to usurp all the authority of fathers? Let us hear what Thomas Gage says in regard to the conduct of the Spaniards in the West Indies.[86] . . . [Gage's account describes the Spanish as forcing the Indians to marry at a young age in order to increase the amount of tribute that the Spanish receive.] Thus in an action which ought to be the most free, the Indians are the greatest slaves.

In England the law is frequently abused by the daughters marrying according to their own fancy without consulting their parents. This custom is, I am apt to imagine, more tolerated there than anywhere else from a consideration that as the laws have not established a monastic celibacy, the daughters have no other state to choose but that of marriage, and this they cannot refuse. In France, on the contrary, young women have always the resource of celibacy; and therefore the law which ordains that they shall wait for the consent of their fathers may be more agreeable. In this light the custom of Italy and Spain must be less rational; convents are there established, and yet they may marry without the consent of their fathers.

Montesquieu begins with some general assumptions about the way that paternal power is organized the world over and about how fathers and children behave and are disposed. From this he derives the proposition that the laws will require that fathers consent to the marriage of their children. He then notes that there are exceptions in 'small republics' and 'singular institutions', a phrase that he uses for institutions that are rarely found. In Sparta and in the Platonic Republic, magis-trates chose the marriage-partners of the citizenry. Perhaps that might be justified in a tightly knit community where 'the love of the public might there equal or surpass all other love'. But the 'common institution' is that fathers control the marriage of their children, a provision that Montesquieu attributes both to the greater prudence of fathers and also to a natural desire of fathers to see themselves continue in their offspring. Montesquieu regards it as an abuse that a colonizing

---

[85] Ibid 440–2.
[86] Citing Thomas Gage, *A New Survey of the West Indies* (3rd edn, London, 1677), 345.

power has taken over the marriage choices of a subservient population in order to increase its revenue: 'in an action which ought to be the most free, the Indians are the greatest slaves'. He does not consider the possibility that a parental consent requirement might also be inconsistent with liberty of marriage. He then notices that in England children frequently marry without parental consent. His observation is acute and in comparison with France in his period, he may well be right. He then suggests that the reason for the difference is that English women do not have the alternative of going to the convent, as French women do. His explanation then causes him puzzlement because he also thinks that Spanish and Italian women frequently marry without parental consent, and they, like French women, have the option of going to the convent.

This is not Montesquieu at his best. He has jumped too quickly to an assumption about a common institution without the empirical survey of institutions that we sometimes find in his work. His analysis of the motivations of fathers smacks of natural-law analysis without the rigour of the best of the natural-law thinkers. (He seems to suggest that the desire of fathers to see the prosperity of their offspring is somehow biological rather than rational.) His comparison of England and France is made without careful consideration of the difference in laws between the two countries. (France in his period, at least arguably, did require parental consent for the civil validity of a marriage; England did not.) His proposed explanation for the difference between England and France fails in its own terms when he considers Spain and Italy, and he does not pause to consider whether his generalization about practice in Spain and Italy may be mistaken (as it may well be).

All of this should not, however, obscure the fact that Montesquieu employs something very close to, if it is not the same thing as, modern comparative method. He posits a virtually universal requirement for parental consent. If that is right, then the explanation for it must be virtually universal, perhaps something biological, the lack of prudence of the young, their passion, the desire of fathers to see their line succeed. There are exceptions. They must be explained. Small, tightly knit communities may share a commonality of values and purposes that will lead them to entrust such decisions to the magistracy. Colonial powers may repress subject peoples. Montesquieu then moves from the law to its evasion or violation. He sees a difference among countries and seeks, though he fails, to explain that difference on the basis of religious differences.

We close with a glimpse at a somewhat younger contemporary of Montesquieu's, Pothier. His approach can be seen well in his treatment of the topic of property in wild animals.[87] Like Locke and Pufendorf, but with more religious emphasis than either of them, Pothier begins with God's dominion over and creation of the universe and God's grant to humankind of a dominion over

---

[87] Robert-Joseph Pothier, *Traité du droit de domaine de propriéte* 1.2.1.1, in *Œuvres* (n 70), ix, no. 21, ⁱ0. The translation is mine.

creation subordinate to his own.[88] He then outlines, as had Pufendorf and others before him, the negative community that existed from the beginning:

... which consisted in that these things which were common to all belonged no more to one of them than to the others and in that no one could prevent another from taking from among these common things that which he judged fitting to take in order to satisfy his needs. While he was satisfying his needs with it, the others were obliged to leave it to him, but after he ceased to satisfy his needs with it, if the thing were not one of those which were consumed in the use that one made of them, that thing returned to the negative community and another could satisfy his needs with it in the same manner.

Humankind having multiplied, men divided the land and the majority of things that were on the surface among themselves. That which fell to each of them began to belong to him to the exclusion of others. That was the origin of the right of property. . . .

So far as wild animals are concerned, *ferae naturae*, they remained in the ancient state of the negative community. . . . [N]o one has property in them so long as they remain in that state, and they cannot be acquired except by seizing them.

Pothier next takes up the Roman law of hunting. He notes the basic proposition that conforming to the natural law, Roman law made the chase available to every-one. He correctly interprets *Digest* 41.1.3.1 as making it irrelevant whether the capture took place on the hunter's property or on another's land. He notes, as does the same *Digest* passage, that the landowner may, however, prohibit the hunter from entering on his land (which he takes as a consequence of land-ownership), and seems to support the opinion that if one takes an animal contrary to the prohibition of the landowner, he none the less acquires title to the animal but the landowner has an *actio iniuriarum* against him. Pothier goes on to point out, as had Pufendorf, that the Romans did not require actual manucaption. An animal caught in a trap, he seems to hold, belongs to the trapper if it cannot get out.

Pothier then proceeds to consider the question of wounding and of interference with the hunt. He notes the conflict between Trebatius and Gaius on the topic. He makes no mention of how Justinian resolved the question, but he reports Pufendorf's resolution, which he describes as allowing the huntsman an action if the wound was *considérable* and the animal could not escape. He then reports Barbeyrac's opinion that pursuit alone is enough and concludes:[89]

Barbeyrac . . . thinks that it suffices that I be in pursuit of the animal, even though I have not already wounded it, in order that I be regarded as the first occupant, with the result that another will not be permitted to seize it from me during this time. This idea is more civil; it is followed in usage; it conforms to an article of the ancient laws of the Salians [5.35]: where it is said: 'If anyone kills and steals a tired wild boar whom another's dogs have stirred, let him be adjudged liable for 600 *denarii*'.

So far Pothier has been quite consistent. He has grounded the privilege of the

---

[88] Citing and quoting Ps. 24(23): 1–2; Ps. 8: 4, 6; Gen. 1: 28.

[89] Pothier, *Domaine* (n 87), 1.2.1.2.1, in *Œuvres* (n 70), ix, no. 26, pp 112–13.

huntsman in a divine grant as a matter of natural law, and he has supported the huntsman at every turn. He prevails over the landowner even when he is expressly forbidden from entering onto the land. He prevails over the later huntsman in the case of wounding, and perhaps simply in that of hot pursuit, following a much more Lockian than Hobbesian version of the story. When Pothier gets to the law of France, however, he is surprising. This broad right of the huntsman does not apply in France. Hunting rights are restricted to the nobility. Proprietary rights prevail everywhere over poachers. How can this be?[90]

Some of the old doctors have doubted whether the sovereigns had the right to reserve hunting for themselves and to forbid it to their subjects. They argue that God having given men power (*l'empire*) over beasts, as we have seen above, the prince had no right to deprive his subjects of the right that God had given them. The natural law, one says, permits everyone to hunt; the civil law that forbids it is contrary to the natural law and exceeds, by consequence, the power of the legislator, who is himself subject to the natural law and cannot ordain the contrary to that law.

It is easy to respond to these objections. From the fact that God gave power over the beasts to humankind it does not follow that it ought to be permitted to every individual member of humankind to exercise that power. The civil law ought not to be contrary to the natural law. That is true with regard to what the natural law commands or that which it forbids. But the civil law can restrain the natural law in that which it only permits. The majority of civil laws do nothing but make restrictions on what the natural law permits. That is why, although in terms of pure natural law, the hunt is permitted to every individual, the prince was within his rights to reserve it to himself and [grant] it to a certain kind of person and forbid it to others. Hunting is an exercise likely to turn peasants and artisans from their work and merchants from their commerce. It would be useful and for their proper interest and for the public interest to forbid them from it. The law which forbids hunting is therefore a just law which it is not permitted to those who are forbidden from it to contravene either in the forum of conscience or in the external forum.

The distinction between a requirement and a permission of the natural law goes back to the first glossators of canon law, when they were seeking to justify private property.[91] Though I cannot recall having seen this argument in medieval authors with regard to wild animals, a medieval jurist would certainly have understood it. Indeed, there is much about Pothier's method that reminds us of the middle ages. Although he cites, and accurately reports, the results in many different legal systems, divine law, natural law, Roman law, the Salic law, the customary law of France, his effort is not one to explore and explain the differences and similarities of these systems, as Montesquieu's had been. His effort is basically integrative. He wants to reconcile all of these systems into one coherent whole. This causes him considerable difficulty when he comes to the customary French law of hunting, for it seems very far from his coherent account integrating all of the other systems.

---

[90] Pothier, *Domaine* (n 87), 1.2.1.2.2, in *Œuvres* (n 70), ix, no. 28, p 113.
[91] See Brian Tierney, *The Idea of Natural Rights* (1997), 131–69.

He succeeds in integrating the French customary law by appealing to a general principle of the natural-law tradition concerning property. Remove the supporting superstructure of divine, natural, and Roman law, and one can see how Pothier's statement of the rules could be used—as it frequently was, though emphatically not in this area—as a basis for the *Code Napoléon*. It is much harder to see a line from Pothier to the comparatists of the nineteenth century and today.

The discovery of the sixteenth-century French humanists was that the comparative method, when applied to law, involves laying two legal systems side by side in all of their aspects. One must understand the top-level generalizations that lie behind the statements of rules and doctrines; one must understand the rules and doctrines themselves; one must understand the history in which they are embedded; one must understand how the society and institutions affect the way in which the rules and doctrines operate. Only when one understands all of these things can one safely make comparisons. The French humanists and the natural lawyers who followed them differed from modern comparatists in that most of them believed that the results of their study would be the discovery of a supranational body of principles, if not rules, that ought to be applied in their own day. Montesquieu may not have been alone among the thinkers of the eighteenth century to emphasize the importance of the geographical, institutional, and social contexts in which different rules were embedded and which in some sense explained the differences in the rules, but he certainly illustrates an approach quite different from that of the natural law school and from that of Pothier. He is at once the most positivistic and the least normative of the writers we have examined. In the former aspect he is the ancestor of virtually every comparative lawyer today; in the latter he is the ancestor of many.

If Montesquieu emphasized the geographical, institutional, and social forces that shaped the laws that he was studying, he tended to underemphasize the intellectual. By contrast, the French humanists, and even more the natural law school, tended to overemphasize the intellectual. Also, because they did not range very far outside the Western context, they failed to see how different the underlying intellectual contexts of different legal systems might be. The methodological vision of Jean Bodin remains ours, but we know a great deal more about different legal systems, and what we know makes us aware that the first comparatists made a lot of mistakes, particularly when they ventured to look at systems outside the Latin tradition. It is a tall order today to examine even one legal system in all the aspects that Bodin regarded as relevant for comparative inquiry. It is a very tall order to do it with more than one system. Thus, one cannot study 'the universal history of commonwealths' and adhere to contemporary scholarly standards.

BIBLIOGRAPHY

The history of the discipline of comparative law before the *Code Napoléon* is not, so far as I am aware, the subject of any monographic treatment. In my focus on France in the sixteenth century, I am indebted to the works of Donald Kelley:

Foundations of Modern Historical Scholarship: Language, Law, and History in the French Renaissance (1970)

History, Law, and the Human Sciences: Medieval and Renaissance Perspectives (1984) (collected essays)

For the rest, the essay is based on primary sources, principal among which are (in chronological order):

Aristotle, *Politics*: Alois Dreizehnter (ed), *Aristoteles' Politik*, Studia et testimonia antiqua, 7 (1970), trans Sir Ernest Baker, rev R. F. Stalley as Aristotle, *The Politics* (1995)

Lex Dei quam praecepit Dominus ad Moysen, sive Collatio legum mosaicarum et romanarum: Theodor Mommsen (ed), in *Collectio librorum iuris anteiustiniani* (1890), iii; trans Moses Hyamson as *Mosaicarum et romanarum legum collatio* (1913, repr 1997)

Bartolo of Sassoferrato, *Repetitio ad Cunctos populos* (*Code* 1.1.1), in Bartolus, *Commentarius ad C.1.1.1* (Venice, 1602), fol. 4r–7r, nos. 13–51; trans Joseph Henry Beale as *Bartolus on Conflict of Laws* (1914), trans J. A. Clarence Smith, as 'Bartolo on the Conflict of Laws', (1970) 14 *American Journal of Legal History* 174–83, 247–75

Sir John Fortescue, *De laudibus legum Anglie*: S. B. Chrimes (ed) (Cambridge, 1942; repr 1979)

Jean Bodin, *Methodus ad facilem historiarum cognitionem* (Amsterdam, 1650, repr 1967), trans B. Reynolds as *Method for the Easy Comprehension of History* (1945)

Guy Coquille, *Institution au droict des François* (Paris, 1607), and many times reprinted

Samuel von Pufendorf, *De jure naturae et gentium* (Amsterdam, 1688), trans C. H. and W. A. Oldfather (1934); Jean Barbeyrac (trans and annotated) as *Le droit de la nature et des gens par le baron Pufendorf* (London, 1740), trans Basil Kennet (London, 1749)

Charles de Secondat, baron de Montesquieu, *De l'esprit des lois*, Gonzague Truc (ed) (2 vols 1962), trans Thomas Nugent as *The Spirit of Laws* (2nd edn, London, 1752)

Robert-Joseph Pothier, *Traité du droit de domaine de propriété*, in Jean-Joseph Bugnet (ed), *Œuvres de Pothier: annotées et mises en corrélation avec le Code civil et la législation actuelle* (1890), ix

PART I

THE DEVELOPMENT OF COMPARATIVE LAW IN THE WORLD

CHAPTER 1

DEVELOPMENT OF COMPARATIVE LAW IN FRANCE

BÉNÉDICTE FAUVARQUE-COSSON

Paris

FRANCE has a long and solid tradition of comparative law. This chapter traces the discipline's development in France, describing its strengths and weaknesses. As universal a science as it is, comparative law has distinctive features in each country. While there is currently no such thing as French or Italian comparative law in the sense that there is French or Italian contracts law, there is an identifiable French style in comparative law that is closely related to the development of French legal thought in general.

The twentieth century witnessed the rise, the decline, and the renaissance of comparative law in France. In 1900, simultaneously with the *Exposition universelle*, its capital hosted a Congress on comparative law, known throughout the world as the Congress of Paris,[1] under the auspices of the *Société de législation comparée*. It was the first major world congress on the discipline. It has become famous because it symbolizes if not the birth of comparative law then at least the emergence of the discipline as a new branch of legal science in its own right. The Congress of Paris rang in an era often referred to as the *Belle Époque* of comparative law, and it gave rise to the dream of a common worldwide legal system.[2]

Great scholars in that discipline notwithstanding, comparative law gradually lost much of its importance in France during most of the twentieth century. This decline can be attributed to various factors, including a very positivistic, legicentric, and parochial method of teaching law in universities.

When a French lawyer, especially an academic, thinks about the past, he cannot help but feel a twinge of nostalgia. All over the world, the influence of the French language, French law, and, consequently, the influence of France herself have diminished. In thinking about the past, the French tend to say, 'Let us commemorate'.[3] Of course, one must accept that when one's Code has influenced foreign legal systems, one way or another, it will be eventually superseded by local

---

[1] *Congrès international de droit comparé, Procès-verbaux des séances et documents* (vol 1, 1905). See in particular: Edouard Lambert, 'General Report', 3 ff; Raymond Saleilles, 'Rapport sur l'utilité, le but et le programme du Congrès', 9 ff; 'Conception et objet de la science du droit comparé', 167 ff.

[2] The centennial of this Congress was celebrated in Louisiana by the Tulane University School of Law. To commemorate the event, the contributions of scholars throughout the world have been reproduced in 'Centennial World Congress on Comparative Law', (2001) 75 *Tulane LR*.

[3] On this past glory of the French Civil Code, see Konrad Zweigert and Hein Kötz, *An Introduction to Comparative Law* (trans Tony Weir, 3rd edn, 1998), 98 ff.

laws. However, it is more difficult to admit that, even in France, the influence of the Civil Code, and more generally speaking of French internal law, is declining: many sources of inspiration now come from abroad or from supranational orders. In France, this has led to a sort of 'reverse comparative law', based upon importing, rather than exporting, norms.

Yet, there is a time for commemoration of past achievements,[4] and a time for the development of new enterprises. While French law has lost part of its past importance, it still has a role to play, especially in the development of a new European private law. Recently, European private law has injected new energy into legal studies, and this has created a renewed interest in comparative law. At the dawn of this new century, the renaissance of comparative law in France is just beginning. The discipline is leaving the dusty shelves of old law libraries to play an active role in the day-to-day activities of modern legal practice: legislators seek inspiration from foreign or international models; judges use comparative law as a device to reach a decision, or to justify the one they have already chosen; academics enrich their work with comparisons of various sorts; and students more frequently engage in comparative studies, often eventually ending up working abroad.

The never-ending question of the purpose of comparative law emerges as one of the fundamental jurisprudential debates of the twentieth century. In France, comparative law has long been viewed as a discipline with a highly scientific profile—a means of becoming more knowledgeable, albeit not necessarily more efficient. In particular, French jurists have considered comparative law a static, not dynamic, field. This may explain why, by the end of the twentieth century, comparative law had been relegated to the modest status of an ancillary discipline. Indeed, why study comparative law when it is not directly applicable to legal practice and when there are so many areas of law that seem so much more practical and useful?

Yet, mentalities are currently changing. The internationalization and Europeanization of life and law have shown that legal insularity is no longer an option. The rise of immigration and international trade has dramatically increased the number of cases in which French judges must apply foreign law. Though proving and applying foreign law is not 'comparative law' *per se*, it does require the use of a form of the comparative method. For these and other reasons, comparative law is

---

[4] In 2004, commemorations of the bicentenary of the Civil Code took place worldwide. Across continents, leading academics from all nations outlined the decline of the influence of the French Civil Code. In the richly decorated *Grand Amphithéatre* of the Sorbonne, while the French were commemorating the birth of a 200-year-old code, they were also announcing the possible rise of a new, modern, and extraneous instrument: the European Civil Code. Far from completed, the European Civil Code is already well on its way in certain fields of the law such as contract law. In 1904, during the centenary of the Civil Code, scholars extensively debated whether or not to reform the French Civil Code. By 2004, the debates had evolved to consider the possible replacement of the French Civil Code. See Michel Grimaldi, 'A propos du bicentenaire du Code civil', in *De tous horizons, Mélanges Xavier Blanc-Jouvan* (2005), 739 ff. See Bénédicte Fauvarque-Cosson and Sara Godechet-Patris, *Le Code civil face à son destin*, Documentation française, 2006.

increasingly considered a useful tool rather than a mere hobby, and is praised as an effective way to lead France out of national isolation.

In some ways, however, comparative law is still marginal, because it is based on outdated concepts. There is a lingering fundamental assumption that comparative law is merely the study of foreign law as classified into René David's legal families or '*Grands systèmes de droit*'. This assumption is no longer appropriate for a variety of reasons. First, the ongoing process of regionalization and internationalization blurs the notion of 'frontiers', a notion that is challenged, *inter alia*, by the concept of cultural centres or '*foyers culturels*'.[5] Second, some legal systems are much more foreign than others, especially where they have been either unified or harmonized under the guidance of European law and fundamental rights.[6] In areas of law that have been so unified, or at least harmonized, the EU member states' internal legal systems are no longer really 'foreign' one to another, even if some differences do subsist. Third, the scope of comparative law must reach beyond the mere study of foreign law. Since comparative law consists primarily of the application of the comparative method, it should include comparisons among internal, international, European, as well as foreign sources of law. Unfortunately, in France the 'comparatist' is still considered the specialist who studies foreign law and who thus forms part of a small and rather marginal community. Perhaps oddly, French 'internists' refuse to consider themselves comparatists, even when they engage in various forms of comparison.[7] And French internationalists, themselves divided into public international and private international lawyers, also view comparative studies as a branch of law clearly distinct from their own. But there are signs of change here as well: the creation, in 2002, of a new chair at the prestigious Collège de France, appropriately named '*Etudes juridiques comparatives et internationalisation du droit*', may prove significant in that it may point to a gradual convergence between international law and comparative law.[8]

In sum, there is still a stark contrast between the rather modest position of

---

[5] Paul Ricoeur, 'Conférence in Entretiens du XXI siècle', reproduced in *Le Monde*, 28 April 2004.

[6] Although these rights are often considered 'universal', they remain purely occidental in origin.

[7] For instance, all recent contract law textbooks now compare the French internal rules with international conventions, European directives or regulations, European case law, and even private codifications such as the UNIDROIT Principles or the Principles on European Contract Law.

[8] This chair was awarded to Professor Mireille Delmas-Marty who advocates the use of comparative law to identify general common principles on an international level and whose major recent publications deal with pluralism and harmonization of the law: Delmas-Marty, 'The Contribution of Comparative Law to a Pluralist Conception of International Criminal Law', (2003) 1 *Journal of International Criminal Justice*, 13 ff, Delmas-Marty, *Les forces imaginantes du droit. Le relatif et l'universel* (2004); Delmas-Marty, 'Préface', in Delmas-Marty (ed), *Critique de l'intégration normative. L'apport du droit comparé à l'harmonisation des droits* (2004), 18 ff; Delmas-Marty, 'Avant-propos : Droit commun et droit comparé', in *Variations autour d'un droit commun* (2001).

On the relationship between comparative law and international law, see George Bermann, 'Le droit comparé et le droit international: alliés ou ennemis?', (2003) *RIDC* 519 ff, followed by Bénédicte Fauvarque-Cosson, 'La réponse', 530 ff.

comparative law as an academic discipline and the ever-increasing need for comparative work in both theory and practice. If comparative law has recently become a primary source of inspiration in drafting national, regional, and international[9] norms in many national legal systems, this is also true, albeit to a limited extent, in France where today, there is a broad consensus that comparisons provide a useful tool, *inter alia*, for lawmakers when contemplating new legislation.

Section I of this chapter details the historical rise of comparative law in France, Section II then chronicles its decline. Section III finally predicts its renaissance, provided the French give the study of comparative law the regard it is due.

I. THE RISE OF COMPARATIVE LAW IN FRANCE

French comparative law rose to prominence in the first part of the twentieth century. The first steps of comparative law—*premiers pas*—led to the above-mentioned Paris Congress of 1900 which opened a new phase sometimes referred to as *la Belle Époque du droit comparé*.

1. The *premiers pas* of Comparative Law in France

Charles de Montesquieu (1689–1755) is often considered to be the first major comparatist in modern times. In his principal work, *L'esprit des lois*, Montesquieu first ponders the idea that laws are by nature universal, but then rejects this approach, insisting instead that diverse societies bring about legal diversity.[10] Some French

---

[9] Patrick Glenn, 'Comparative Legal Reasoning and the Courts: A View from the Americas', (2001) 75 *Tulane LR* 219 ff.

[10] 'Laws, in their most general signification, are the necessary relations arising from the nature of things. In this sense all beings have their laws'. Charles Louis de Secondat and Baron Montesquieu, *De l'Esprit des lois* (1748), I,1.
Though Montesquieu's climate theory may appear simplistic today, his famous words against unification of the law remain strikingly modern in the current debate about the European unification of law. 'There are certain ideas of uniformity, which sometimes strike great geniuses (for they even affected Charlemagne), but infallibly make an impression on little souls. They discover therein a kind of perfection, which they recognize because it is impossible for them not to see it; the same authorized weights, the same measures in trade, the same laws in the state, the same religion in all its parts. But is this always right and without exception? Is the evil of changing constantly less than that of suffering? And does not a greatness of genius consist rather in distinguishing between those cases in which uniformity is requisite, and those in which there is a necessity for differences' (XXIX, 18).

scholars today view Montesquieu as the father of sociology, political science, and comparative law.[11] Others emphasize the crucial part he played in comparative constitutionalism.[12] All scholars agree, however, that in recognizing the need to understand other legal systems before being able truly to understand your own, Montesquieu provided a new perspective that fundamentally changed legal thinking.[13]

Before the French Civil Code of 1804, French universities did not teach French national law. French national law was not unified and the universities, as elsewhere in Europe, focused on the law common throughout Europe, that is, on the Roman-canon *ius commune*, written not in the vernacular but in Latin. Although some legal historians have expressed doubts as to the practical effectiveness of the *ius commune* in Europe, the fact remains that, in the eighteenth century, there existed a common European legal culture on the basis of Roman civil and canon law in legal academia as well as in practice.[14] The diversity of French law and the predominance of the *ius commune* were overcome only with the enactment of the *Code civil* in 1804.

Montesquieu had considerable influence on the drafters of the French Civil Code. Thus, Portalis expressed Montesquieu's famous view that laws should be drafted simply and concisely: 'the task of legislation is to establish general principles, rich in implications, rather than to descend into the details of every question which might possibly arise'.[15] The drafters of the French Civil Code used comparative law in a variety of ways to unify and harmonize conflicting legal regimes in France. First, the drafters conducted internal comparisons between the *Ancien droit*[16] and the intermediary law of the revolutionary period. This was all the more difficult since the *Ancien droit* itself was divided between the *pays de droit écrit* of the South, influenced by Roman law, and the *pays de coutumes* or *droit coutumier* in the North, based on Germanic customs.[17] Second, the drafters

---

[11] Raymond Legeais, *Grands systèmes de droit contemporains, Une approche comparative* (2004), 401 ff.

[12] David-Louis Seiler, *La méthode comparative en science politique* (2004), 17 ff.

[13] Yet, comparatism was at that time practised without a well-defined comparative method. According to Marc Ancel, it was pursued with a sort of non-systematic 'curious cosmopolitism'. 'Cent ans de droit comparé en France', *Livre du centenaire de la Société de législation comparée* (1969), 3 ff.

[14] Jean-Louis Halperin, 'L'approche historique et la problématique du jus commune', (2000) 4 *RIDC* 717 ff; Reinhard Zimmermann, *The Law of Obligations, Roman Foundations of the Civilian Tradition* (1996), IX ff; René-Marie Rampelberg, *Repères romains pour le droit européen des contrats* (2005).

[15] Quoted by Zweigert and Kötz (n 3), 87 ff: '*le style doit en être concis . . . Le style des lois doit être simple . . . Quand le style des lois est enflé, on ne les regarde que comme un ouvrage d'ostentation . . . Les lois ne doivent point être subtiles; elles sont faites pour des gens de médiocre entendement . . .*'.

[16] The law before the French Revolution.

[17] By the end of the eighteenth century, all the important customs had been recorded, and this division was no longer entirely clear-cut. Zweigert and Kötz (n 3), 75 ff.

explored foreign law, particularly the Prussian code.[18] In order to draw on foreign models, Napoléon Bonaparte created a specific office called the *Bureau de legislation*, whose function was to translate major foreign statutes into French.

It is often said that once a country enacts its own national code, it tends toward national isolation. The pride of possessing a new and modern national code discourages lawyers from looking abroad for alternative sources of law. Indeed, when the French law faculties were reorganized in 1805 after being suppressed during the Revolution, their teaching no longer concentrated on the all-European *ius commune* but on the French Napoleonic Codes as the embodiment of the national legal system. Throughout the eighteenth century, major philosophers had emphasized the *droit naturel*, the idea that universal law exists and precedes all existing laws, both in time and epistemological foundation. Scholars now proclaimed that the new Codes described and established this rational and universal law. This is the philosophical context in which the *Ecole de l'Exegèse* developed. This school encouraged scholars to teach and comment only on the French Civil Code which, of course, left little if any room for comparative law. Its spirit is captured in Professor Bugnet's famous quote: '*Je ne connais pas le droit civil, j'enseigne le Code Napoléon*' ('I do not know civil law, I teach the Code Napoléon').

Somewhat surprisingly, and in spite of this positivistic and legalistic attitude so characteristic of the nineteenth century,[19] major steps were undertaken to promote comparative legal scholarship in France. As early as 1831, the highly prestigious *Collège de France* created a special chair for *Histoire générale et philosophique des législations comparées*. In 1834, Jean-Gaspard Foelix, a Parisian lawyer and *avocat*, founded the *Revue étrangère et française de législation et d'économie politique*. He did so not only in order to help French lawyers improve their knowledge of foreign law, but also to improve French law through comparison. Unfortunately, the time was not ripe for such an ambitious effort—the French still regarded their Civil Code as the only relevant source of law—and the *Revue* was discontinued in 1850. None the less, in 1838, the *Faculté de droit de Paris* instituted a new course on comparative criminal law, and in 1846, it created a chair for *Droit criminel et législation pénale comparée*. This comparative approach to criminal law focused on the *Code Pénal*, first enacted in 1810 (revised, first in 1832 and then again in 1863). Thus, criminal law was one of the fields in which comparative studies were developed in France at the time. By the end of the nineteenth century, comparatism had spread to other areas of French law as well, in particular to the discipline of civil law. The *Faculté de droit de Paris* offered lectures on the '*droit*

---

[18] Jean-Louis Sourioux, 'Notule sur le droit comparé, dans les travaux préparatoires du code civil des français', in *Mélanges Xavier Blanc-Jouvan* (n 4), 159 ff.

[19] Case law was only recognized as a real source of law by the end of that century.

civil approfondi et comparé.[20] It is worth noting that during this period, the term 'comparative law' was never used alone, that is, in the sense of an independent field of study. Instead, it was always paired with, and integrated into, a specific subject such as comparative criminal law or comparative civil law.[21]

One of the most important events in the *premiers pas* of comparative law in France was the creation in 1869 of the *Société de législation comparée*, a society that is still very active today. Its purpose is to promote the study and comparison of various legal systems as well as the search for practical means of improving the law.[22] To this end, the *Société* published the *Annuaire de législation étrangère*, an internationally noted and successful work. In France, this prompted the Ministry of Justice to establish the *Comité de législation étrangère* in 1876. Its primary task was to translate all existing national codes into French under the direction of the *Société de législation comparée*. In 1889, the *Société* held an extraordinary session to celebrate its twentieth birthday. On this occasion, its president, Professor Bufnoir, expressed the view that legislation should no longer be a local enterprise; instead, it should draw on the experience of the whole world. He also insisted that comparative law should not only play an informative role but that it should also be an important tool for the legislator.

2. The *belle époque* of Comparative Law

As in other European countries from 1900 to the second half of the twentieth century, a major shift occurred leading from an academic and idealistic approach to a more concrete and functional view in comparative law.

(a) The Paris Congress of 1900

In 1900, the Congress of Paris gathered a large group of non-common law jurists who expressed their optimism regarding the future unification of law. In spite of the achievements already made during the nineteenth century, both in France and abroad, this Congress is often considered the birthplace of comparative law as we know it. The Congress of Paris developed the modern conception of comparative

---

[20] Edouard Lambert (n 1), 58 ff; Adhémar Esmein, 'Le droit comparé et l'enseignement du droit', in *Congrès international de droit comparé* (n 1), 445 ff. Not only was comparative law taught in French universities, but, at that time, French academics exerted great influence abroad. For example, on Boissonade's influence in Japan, see Olivier Moréteau, 'Boissonade revisité: de la codification doctrinale à une langue juridique commune', in *Mélanges Blanc-Jouvan* (n 4), 103 ff.

[21] Xavier Blanc-Jouvan, 'Prologue', in *L'avenir du droit comparé* (2000), 10 ff; Patrick Glenn, 'Vers un droit comparé intégré?' in ibid 105 ff; James Gordley, 'Is Comparative Law a Distinct Discipline?' (1998) 46 *AJCL* 607 ff.

[22] According to the Statute, it promotes '*l'étude et la comparaison des lois et du droit des différents pays ainsi que la recherche des moyens pratiques d'améliorer les diverses branches de la législation*'.

law as a legal science, closely linked to philosophy, legal history, ethnology, and sociology.

The contributions of Saleilles and Lambert, in particular, have remained famous because they signalled a new direction in comparative law.[23] While Raymond Saleilles was already a well-known professor and an important author,[24] Edouard Lambert, who was eleven years his junior, had not yet published a major book when Saleilles asked him to write a General Report at the Paris Congress.[25] Both scholars played very important roles in the recognition of comparative law as a new science in its own right. They insisted that comparative law should not be merely part of the study of foreign law and thus restricted to information about foreign systems.[26] Saleilles and Lambert observed that comparative law, as a legal science, extends beyond observation and discovery of foreign legal systems to influence domestic law and prompt a convergence among different legal regimes. Their conception of comparative law was ambitiously orientated towards the discovery of universal law.

Both scholars criticized the classical exegetic method, and tried to replace it with a new approach going beyond mere legislative interpretation. While Saleilles advocated an historical role for comparative law, Lambert had greater ambitions. He was a firm proponent of comparative law as a new science and viewed it as a genuine surrogate for the method then famously advocated by François Gény, the '*libre recherche scientifique*'. Since Gény's approach focused primarily on the interpretation and application of existing legislation,[27] Lambert considered it too narrow. According to Lambert, comparative law should be oriented toward action rather than limited to observation and discovery.[28] Saleilles shared this position, though he remained faithful to the historical method rather than following Lambert's new approach to legal reasoning.

(b) From the Paris Congress of 1900 to World War I

For many years after the Paris Congress, its agenda regarding the aims and uses of comparative law, the place of comparative law in legal science, and the harmonization and unification of positive law, fascinated legal academics.

---

[23] n 1.

[24] Saleilles first taught the History of Law in Grenoble and Dijon. In 1895 he moved to Paris where he held the chair of comparative criminal law, and, as of 1898, the chair of comparative civil law.

[25] For more details, see Christophe Jamin, 'Le vieux rêve de Saleilles et Lambert revisité. A propos du centenaire du Congrès international de droit comparé de Paris', (2000) *RIDC* 733 ff.

[26] See in particular, Lambert (n 1), 58 ff. This idea was also defended, at the same Congress, by Esmein, in his contribution entitled 'Le droit comparé et l'enseignement du droi' (n 1), 445 ff. Today, scholars often make the distinction between the mere study of foreign law and comparative law. With the development of internationalization and exchange programmes, law students who want to study foreign legal systems can now go abroad.

[27] See Jamin (n 25), showing how the invention of modern comparative law at the beginning of the twentieth century 'served as an instrument in laying the foundation of the authors' hegemony'.

[28] Lambert (n 1), 35 ff.

Following Saleilles's and Lambert's highly regarded ideas, comparison was held to be a necessary approach in the search for a '*droit commun législatif*'.

While the prevailing view found comparative law useful as a tool for unification, this applied only to legal systems with similar systematic structures. Comparing civil law systems to common law regimes was thus excluded. Additionally, the German and Swiss national codifications of 1900 and 1907, respectively, led the French to consider their Code outdated, especially on the occasion of the centenary anniversary of the French Civil Code in 1904. As a result, comparative law became more orientated towards the improvement of national legislation.

At the same time, French legal thinkers gradually turned away from a glorification of the French Civil Code and embraced a more pluralistic conception of law. They emancipated themselves from the *Ecole de l'exégèse*, and began teaching civil law more generally rather than just the Code Civil. This shift opened new doors for the development of comparative law, which was now being firmly established at the university level with the creation of new chairs, one in Paris[29] and others in other cities.

(c) From World War I to World War II

After World War I, comparative law entered a new phase. Germany was defeated, and the Treaty of Versailles consecrated the triumph of French nationalism. The Allied victory was also considered the victory of democracy over authoritarianism. The new states formed by this Treaty, including Poland, Czechoslovakia, and Yugoslavia, looked to the French model, copied some of its institutions, and imitated its constitution. Meanwhile, French lawyers began to pay more attention to the English and American legal systems, that is, to the common law.

World War I also led Europe to discover its fragility,[30] and the cruelty of the war led to the dream of a unified international political system that would guarantee peace. The League of Nations, fostering the international development of democratic principles such as public discussions and majority vote, also symbolized the triumph of law in that it implemented a legal order designed to overcome violence. One of the League's major accomplishments was the foundation of the *Institut pour l'unification du droit privé* (UNIDROIT) in 1926. In the view of many, the time had finally come for the international unification of the law. In French legal academia, Lambert, Lévy-Ullmann, and Julliot de la Morandière were the main advocates of this new agenda. All this tied into the belief, widespread during the 1920s, that the pre-eminence of law and democracy would lead to a better, that is, more human, free, and just, society.

---

[29] Chair created by Saleilles in 1902.

[30] The famous French writer, Paul Valéry, published his article 'Nous autres civilisations savons maintenant que nous sommes mortelles'. In 1920, a geographer, Albert Demangeon, wrote a book entitled, *Le Déclin de l'Europe*, where he foresaw a shift of the 'centre of gravity' of the world from Europe to the populations of America and Asia.

After World War I, various institutions renewed their dedication to the study of comparative law. The foundation of several comparative research institutes led to the emergence of expert teams and specialized libraries. In 1920, Edouard Lambert created an Institute of Comparative Law in Lyon, the first of its type. In 1932, Lévy-Ullmann founded the Institute of Comparative law at the *Faculté de droit* of Paris. The *Revue internationale de droit comparé* was created in 1949. The same year saw the foundation of an international faculty of comparative law in Strasbourg.[31] French comparatists were deeply involved in many of these international associations and academic projects. Notably, the International Academy of Comparative Law was founded in 1924 with André Weiss, a French Law Professor at the Faculty of Law of Paris, as its first President. Since its creation, the Academy has held quadrennial International Congresses of Comparative Law with strong French participation.

(d) After World War II

In the post-war period, French jurists changed the way they approached comparative law. Edouard Lambert, like Ernst Rabel in Germany, advocated intensive comparison especially with the common law systems. By showing the benefit of comparing rather different systems, they overcame the then prevailing assumption that only similar regimes can be fruitfully compared. Thus moving beyond the assumptions at the heart of the Paris Congress of 1900, comparative research expanded to new legal systems and embraced the functional approach as its new methodological foundation. The new trend postulated that in order to be profitable, comparison must take as its baseline the 'similarity of function and of social need'[32] which particular legal rules or institutions were designed to fulfil. Also, instead of searching for unity in law, comparative law began to take differences more seriously and sought to discover ways to overcome them and the difficulties they created. This shift from a universalistic mentality to a pluralistic perspective[33] also entailed a move from a theoretical to a more practical approach according to which comparative law was to be purposefully aimed at reforming and improving the law.[34]

(e) René David's Book, Les grands systèmes de droit contemporain

In post-World War II France, as elsewhere in Europe, a great deal of academic energy was spent on the theory of legal families. Many scholars attempted to divide the legal world into various great systems. In 1964, René David published his

---

[31] At the same time, the *Max-Planck-Institut für ausländisches und internationales Privatrecht* in Hamburg became a very active centre of comparative legal studies in Germany.

[32] Zweigert and Kötz (n 3), 62 ff.

[33] Rodolfo Sacco, 'Epilogue', in *L'avenir du droit comparé* (n 21), 339 ff.

[34] In Germany, Ernst Rabel, a great supporter of comparative law, advocated a more concrete and diverse approach to the discipline, Zweigert and Kötz (n 3), 60 ff.

soon-to-be famous model in his book *Les grands systèmes de droit contemporains*. It was a completely revised version of a once influential book he had written in 1950, the *Traité élémentaire de droit civil comparé*. The work was soon translated into several major languages and became perhaps the most widely known comparative law book of its time. David divided legal systems into five families: Western systems, socialist systems, Islamic law, Hindu law, and Chinese law. These categories were based on two main factors: ideology, and legal techniques.[35] Subsequently, David slightly modified his categories by first distinguishing three legal families: the Romano-Germanic family, the common law, and the (now-dismantled) socialist family. Next, David identified another group of systems, consisting of Jewish law, Hindu law, the law of the Far East, African regimes, and Malagasy law.[36] Of course, David's classifications have met with criticism. In particular, some scholars disliked the defining factors he used to group the world's legal systems. None the less, David's categories have by and large retained their prominence in French law faculties where, often enough, comparative law courses continue to be entitled *Grands systèmes de droit contemporains*.[37] Thus, outdated as it may seem in today's world, René David's book is still the leading comparative law text in France. His classifications will remain one of the landmarks of twentieth-century comparative law in France, if not worldwide.

David was not without famous colleagues in France. They have trained minds, created or directed research centres, strengthened links with other legal systems and lawyers, played an active role in the *Société de legislation comparée*, and often served as presidents of the law faculty of Paris.[38] Several French academics have concentrated their efforts on the harmonization of contract law through private codifications. Most notably, Denis Tallon, Georges Rouhette, and Claude Witz actively participated in the Lando Commission's work on the drafting of the European Principles on Contract Law. Ultimately, and more recently, this academic enterprise became a matter of animated debate among French jurists because it came to be seen as a step towards a European Civil Code—a project which is enormously controversial in France.

---

[35] Bertrand Ancel, *Dictionnaire de la culture juridique* (2003). For a different perspective, in terms of tradition rather than families, see Patrick Glenn (2004). It is interesting to read René David's autobiography *Les avatars d'un comparatiste* (1982), especially chapter 18 where he presents his work in comparative law to which he dedicated his entire life.

[36] In the latest edition of the influential *Les grands systèmes de droit contemporain* (2002), his coauthor, Camille Jauffret-Spinosi, distinguishes three legal families: the Romanistic-German family, the common law family and the Russian family (which can no longer be classified as the socialist family) and adds a fourth part entitled 'other conceptions of the social order and of the law', which includes Muslim, Indian, Chinese, Japanese, and African law.

[37] See Legeais (n 11).

[38] Former Société de législation comparée presidents include Henri Lévy-Ullmann, René Demogue, Louis Josserand, Jean-Paulin Niboyet, Jules Basdevant, René Cassin, Henri Solus, Marc Ancel, Roland Drago, Xavier Blanc-Jouvan and Guy Canivet.

Last, but not least, André Tunc (1917–99) deserves special mention as one of the most brilliant members of French legal academia in the field of comparative law. Firmly convinced that it was necessary to teach common law, including American law, in French law schools, Tunc created the first *Diplôme d'études approfondies* in American and English business law. He was also instrumental in the establishment of the first joint degree in French and English law, which was soon followed by joint degrees involving American and German law. Tunc also paved the way for the expansion of exchange programmes in French law schools. These joint-degree options and exchange programmes led to the emergence of a new generation of comparatists.[39] Tunc was also a great law reformer, both directly and indirectly. His publications on the United States Securities and Exchange Commission contributed to the creation of the French *Commission des opérations de bourse* in 1967. He was one of the first scholars in France to draw attention to theories of corporate governance and he was among the pioneers in studying, in depth, English corporate law which led to the publication of his *Droit anglais des sociétés anonymes*. As a tort law specialist, Tunc was an editor and co-author of the *International Encyclopedia of Comparative Law*. In 1985, he drafted a project that gave birth to one of France's most famous and practically relevant statutes: the Law on Road Traffic Accidents. Tunc was known and influential throughout the world, including the United States, Great Britain, Japan, Brazil, and Tunisia, and many eminent scholars throughout the world have paid tribute to him.[40]

Yet, in spite of the highly significant comparative law scholarship generated in France,[41] in spite of the creation of the *Revue internationale de droit comparé* in 1948, and in spite of René David's and André Tunc's efforts to bring comparative law to the forefront of the curriculum, comparative law has not yet succeeded in becoming a major academic subject in France. Instead, comparative law has long been regarded as a mere ancillary subject.[42] We will thus have to take a look at the reasons behind the decline of comparative law in the latter decades of the twentieth century.

---

[39] For a moving homage and a detailed biography, see Blanc-Jouvan, 'In memoriam André Tunc (1917–1999)', (2000) *RIDC* 5 ff. The Institut André Tunc at the Panthéon-Sorbonne (Paris I) keeps his memory alive.

[40] See the homages of von Mehren, Jolowicz, Hoshino, Wald, and Charfi (2000) *RIDC* 12 ff.

[41] In France, comparison was first orientated towards criminal and constitutional law. A solid tradition of comparison in public law still exists today, especially in constitutional law (constitutional law is often taught on a comparative basis and French treatises on constitutional law contain a lot of information on foreign models). The same could be said of criminal law, albeit to a lesser extent, for it mainly concerns academic writings rather than teaching.

[42] Blanc-Jouvan, 'Prologue' (n 21), 15 ff.

II. The Decline of Comparative Law

The decline of comparative law was largely a result of its low status in French law schools. Although there has been a rich comparative law tradition, the discipline has not been treated as a major subject in French universities. Many leading academics still consider it simply an exoticism.[43] As a result, comparative law has found itself limited to an ancillary function, not only in legal academia but also among judges and other practitioners.

This marginal status has also been linked to a double identity crisis. After the two world wars, comparatists lost their belief in universalism and found themselves vexed by the question 'Who are we really?' Internists, that is, scholars focusing on domestic law who taught French law as a national science and who felt no need for comparison, in turn asked the question from the other end: 'Who are they?' Since the teaching of French law remained overwhelmingly positivistic and legicentric[44] throughout the twentieth century, it should not come as a surprise that comparative law was considered a marginal field in French law faculties.

1. Comparative Law: A Collateral Science

The works of Jean Carbonnier provide a striking illustration of the modest status of comparative law as a legal discipline in France. Carbonnier was one of the greatest private lawyers[45] of the twentieth century, a leading academic, and a great legislator. He was particularly open-minded and intimately familiar with many foreign languages, cultures, and legal systems. As a jurist, Carbonnier advocated new, non-positivistic approaches. As the father of French legal sociology, he stressed the importance of comparative law to legal sociology.[46] Since Carbonnier's scholarship is replete with comparisons to foreign legal systems, he can appropriately be considered a comparatist. Yet, in spite of his extensive knowledge of foreign cultures and legal systems, and despite his interest in comparison, Carbonnier never tried to put comparative law as a discipline at the forefront of French academia. In his Introduction to Law, a compulsory subject for first-year

---

[43] Philippe Malaurie and Patrick Morvan, *Droit civil, Introduction générale* (2005), 296 ff.

[44] This positivistic attitude has been criticized by major French academics and, by the end of the twentieth century, case law has taken on a major role, as have other sources of the law, such as general principles, customs or usages, lex mercatoria, academic works and academic codifications. However, positivistic attitudes have prevailed during the second half of the twentieth century, and in many respects, still do.

[45] A civilist is a specialist in non-commercial private law.

[46] Jean Carbonnier, 'L'apport du droit comparé à la sociologie juridique', *Livre du centenaire* (1969), 75 ff.

students, Carbonnier classified comparative law as a 'collateral' science as opposed to the truly legal sciences, or *sciences proprement juridiques*. More precisely, Carbonnier considered comparative law (together with legal history) a 'classical collateral science', as opposed to one of the 'new' collateral sciences, which included sociology, ethnology, psychology, linguistics, and law and economics. Since Carbonnier profoundly influenced French scholarship throughout the second half of the twentieth century, his views on comparative law were widely shared by most leading French academics of that period.

Interestingly, Carbonnier also defined comparative law as 'the application of the comparative method to the various systems of law as they exist at our time'.[47] Whether comparative law is a method or not is a question that has been endlessly debated, and it is not the purpose of this chapter to revisit that discussion. Suffice it to say that Carbonnier believed comparative perspectives should be integrated into all legal disciplines using proper comparative methods. The problem, however, is that nobody seems to agree on which method to use, and the extensive debate over that question has left many participants and observers with the feeling that further discussion would be rather useless. While many academics throughout the world have attempted to define the comparative method, all have both succeeded in one sense and failed in another because there is no such thing as one universal method. Instead, there are as many comparative methods as there are practising comparatists. Furthermore, it is futile to impose a universal method, because the perfect method does not, and cannot, exist. There are various functions of comparative law, and the proper method depends entirely on the goals the comparative scholar pursues. Due to the lack of consensus, and because of the widespread conviction of the futility of this theoretical endeavour, most French scholars practise comparative law without giving thought to methodology.[48]

While Carbonnier believed that the primary function of comparative law was to be an instrument for legislative reform, his scepticism made him reluctant to adopt foreign institutions that might interfere with, or disrupt, the internal coherence of the French legal system. Although he had a clear sense of pluralism in law, of reciprocal influences, and the necessity of comparison,[49] Carbonnier was concerned with the possible *déviances* of comparative law. While acknowledging that comparative law was primarily a 'tool for legislative reform', Carbonnier expressed two major concerns with that application of comparative law. The first stemmed

---

[47] Carbonnier, *Droit civil, Introduction* (2002), 26 ff.

[48] For a criticism of this philosophy, see Etienne Picard, 'L'état du droit comparé en France en 1999', in *Blanc-Jouvan* (n 21), 153 ff. An exception is Léontin Jean Constantinesco who attempted to reconcile various methodological differences: after presenting the current methods, Constantinesco proposed adopting a device he called '*outils opératoires*', rather than just one method, see Constantinesco, *Traité de droit comparé, vol. I, Introduction au droit comparé, vol. II, La méthode comparative, vol. III, La science des droits comparés* (1972, 1974, 1983).

[49] Carbonnier (n 47), 152 ff, (paragraph entitled 'Le droit civil français en face des systèmes juridiques étrangers', see especially paragraph 85 on the main legal systems, including canon law).

from the powerful effects of comparative law. In some of his famous articles, Carbonnier denounced the myth of the foreign legislator and criticized the practice that consists of distorting foreign examples in order to make them more persuasive for the French legislator.[50] As the father of 'law and sociology' in France, Carbonnier's concern was both sociological and cultural. He believed comparative law could contribute to legal sociology and vice versa, but he also observed that recourse to foreign institutions often entailed difficult attempts to transplant foreign laws. In his essays, Carbonnier criticized the phenomenon of inter-nationalization and Europeanization of French law and denounced its impact on French international law: he thus stigmatized reception of a *droit cosmopolite*[51] which gives rise to a form of *acculturation juridique*.[52] Still, while Carbonnier praised comparison as a tool for understanding technical concepts, he expressed some reluctance as to the use of comparative law in the legislative process. In particular, Carbonnier rejected Edouard Lambert's idea of using comparative law to identify common law or '*droit commun législatif*' capable of filling the lacunae of French internal law.[53] According to Carbonnier, there are no general common law principles as such; nor is comparative law a transnational legal order. No norm, institution, or rule commonly adopted elsewhere, should, for that reason, become a source of French law. Along the same line of thinking, Ernst Rabel's programme using comparative law for the resolution of conflict of law issues was considered improper by many French academics. More generally, the leading view is that the existence of international terminology detached from internal rules is only justified if it developed in conjunction with international or European texts,[54] such as the common set of concepts and definitions of European contract law.[55]

Carbonnier's criticism of the use of comparative law as a tool for the French legislator appears rather representative of many French legal academics in general. For many years, most French internists did not feel the need to engage in the process of comparison before reforming internal laws at all. Many internists believed they had little to learn from foreign cultures and were convinced that comparison was not a necessary component of their search for excellence in law

---

[50] Jean Carbonnier, 'A beau mentir qui vient de loin', *Essais sur les lois* (1995), 227 ff; Jean Carbonnier, *Sociologie juridique* (1994), 23 ff. For an example of such distortions, see Mathias Reimann, 'Liability for Defective Products at the Beginning of the Twenty-First Century: Emergence of a Worldwide Standard?', (2003) 51 *AJCL* 751 ff.

[51] Jean Carbonnier, *Droit et passion du droit sous la Ve République* (2000), 37 ff.

[52] Carbonnier (n 47), 79 ff.

[53] Carbonnier (n 47), 79 ff. This concern is based on Lambert's famous ideas. See Jamin (n 25), 741 ff; Constantinesco (n 48), vol II, 108, 296 ff.

[54] For a fierce critic of such an '*esperanto juridique*', see Constantinesco (n 48), vol 2, 314 ff.

[55] Klans Peter Berger, 'Harmonisation of European Contract Law. The Influence of Comparative Law', (2001) 50 *ICLQ* 877.

reform. This parochial attitude is not a matter of French character[56] but more likely the result of history: France has historically exported its legal system and is simply not accustomed to importing legal ideas from other countries. French internists also believed that while comparison may be helpful, it was certainly not necessary in order to understand one's own legal system because each legal system exists independently of others. In fact, a few extreme internists blame comparative law scholars for attempting to weaken and trivialize the French legal tradition by pointing to solutions adopted abroad. Understandably, such attitudes have contributed to the decline of comparative law in France.

Fortunately, such negative views were somewhat counterbalanced by more positive approaches. In their leading book, R. David and C. Jauffret-Spinosi advocated practical applications of comparative law and praised its legislative function.[57] While this function may be strongest in the international context, comparative analysis should not, according to these authors, be confined to that context—the French legislator drafting French law should also use comparative analysis. When used with appropriate care, the French legislator is likely to borrow only from legal systems that are already similar to the French. And in doing so, a legislator is likely to find commonalities, or at least a consensus by way of compromise.[58] Thus, as long as one admits that comparison may serve a multitude of purposes and that its distinctive features will vary according to the purpose it serves, comparative law is not distorted by such a legislative use. Comparison is simply practised with different techniques and methods than when used in a more scientific fashion to obtain pure knowledge.

During the twentieth century, the French legislator did not always view comparative law kindly. At the conclusion of the work of the 1945 Commission for the revision of the Code Civil, one of its members reported that comparative law had certainly exerted some influence, but when a foreign solution was brought before the Commission, it was regularly viewed with suspicion because of its non-French origin.[59] French judges were similarly sceptical of foreign law for a variety of historical and personal reasons. Historical factors include the rise of specific national codifications with their own principles and rules, the decline of the French empire, and the absence of a common legal space and language in civil law countries comparable to that found in common law countries. Among the more personal reasons for many judges' reluctance to consider foreign law were the lack

[56] See, for a more universal point of view, Thomas Hobbes, *Leviathan* (1651) (chapter III): 'For such is the nature of men that howsoever they may acknowledge many others to be more witty, or more eloquent or more learned, yet they will hardly believe there be many so wise as themselves; for they see their own wit at hand, and other men's at a distance'.

[57] David and Jauffret-Spinosi (n 36), 8 ff.

[58] Mathias Reimann, 'Stepping out of the European Shadow: Why Comparative Law in the United States Must Develop its Own Agenda', (1998) 46 *AJCL* 637 ff.

[59] Juliot de la Morandière, quoted by Marc Ancel (n 13), 17 ff. The work of this Commission was never enacted.

of knowledge and a pronounced reluctance to apply the traditional maxim '*jura novit curia*' (the court knows the law) to foreign materials.[60]

2. The Marginal Position of Comparative Law in French Law Faculties

Comparative law occupies a marginal position in French law schools because it is not taught enough and because students are discouraged from studying abroad as well as from specializing in comparative law. Fortunately, these matters are quickly changing.

(a) Insufficient Teaching of Comparative Law

In 2000, Professor Antoine Lyon-Caen submitted a report to the French Minister of Education and Research, and a member of parliament subsequently presented it to the French National Assembly.[61] In that report, Lyon-Caen denounced the poor status of comparative law in France, its brilliant tradition notwithstanding. He insisted that French scholarship had not moved beyond the most fundamental research and that this was detrimental not only to the elite strata of the profession but to all practitioners. The purpose of the report was to convince Members of the French Parliament to vote for a law creating a Foundation for Comparative Law Studies.[62] While the law was indeed passed, the Foundation was never established because soon after the vote the government changed and the Foundation was not one of the new leadership's priorities.[63]

---

[60] For a comparative survey, see Trevor C Hartley, 'Pleading and Proof of Foreign Law: The Major European Systems Compared', (1996) 45 *ICLQ* 271. For different French perspectives, see Bénédicte Fauvarque-Cosson, 'Foreign Law before the French Courts: The Conflicts of Law Perspective', chapter 1, 3 ff, and see Richard Fentiman, 'Foreign Law in National Courts', chapter 2, 13 ff; both contributions are published in Guy Canivet, Mads Andenas, and Duncan Fairgrieve (eds), *Comparative Law before The Courts* (2004). Olivier Remien, 'European Private International Law, the European Community and its Emerging Area of Freedom, Security and Justice', (2001) 38 *Common Market LR* 78 ff, notes the 'enormous diversity' on this subject in Europe and advocates a European regulation of conflict law with regard to the status, judicial notice, and proof of foreign law. The modern choice-of-law approach chooses the applicable law to apply, in whole or in part, based on the *content* of the conflicting laws. Therefore, practical knowledge of foreign laws and comparison between various laws is inevitable: Symeon Symeonides, 'Private International Law at the End of the Twentieth Century: Progress or Regress?' in Symeon Symeonides, *Private International Law at the End of the Twentieth Century: Progress or Regress?* (1999), 36–42, 62–73 ff.

[61] See <http://www.assemblee-nationale.fr/rapports/r3072.asp>.

[62] Loi no. 2002–282 du 28 février 2002, *Journal officiel* no. 51, 1 March, 3903 ff.

[63] Another project is currently under way which consists in creating a Foundation which would serve the 'promotion of continental law' (this project was launched after the French civil law tradition had been attacked by a World Bank's Report mentioned and criticized below, nn 99–101 and text).

Still, since the end of the twentieth century, there has been an increasing aware-ness that comparative law should play a much more important role in legal education. In April 1988, the French Centre for Comparative Law, *Centre français de droit comparé*, held an international conference on this topic,[64] and in 2002, the same subject was chosen by the International Academy of Comparative Law for the Sixteenth Congress in Brisbane. The General Rapporteur, Professor Gabriel Moens from Australia, concentrated on a number of current questions: alternative teaching methods such as moot court, development of foreign exchange pro-grammes, the creation of a new educational model of the 'global lawyer', the establishment of a 'global law faculty', and the impact of multinational law firms on comparative law. By comparison, the French law faculties appeared to be very backward. Such backwardness could be overcome if comparative law was taught at all French law faculties, instead of only the largest ones that could offer many electives, and if comparative law was taught as an early and mandatory course instead of an optional subject available only in the third or fourth year and focusing only on '*Les grands systèmes de droit*'.[65] It is critical to develop student interest in comparative law through an introduction to the discipline at a much earlier stage, preferably in the first year.[66]

Regarding foreign exchange programmes, virtually all French law schools have made some important improvements. These programmes allow students to study abroad for either a term or a full year and, since their creation, the '*double maîtrises*' programmes in particular have met with continual success. Instead of taking trad-itional first-year courses at a French law school, the French exchange students spend their first two years as law students in a foreign university and return to France to complete their third and fourth years. After four years of study, these students have earned a double degree in French law and either English, American, or German law. But the respective students are not only dual-degree holders, they are also, and perhaps more importantly, conversant in two legal cultures.[67]

(b) Insufficient Incentives for Students to Engage in Comparative Legal Studies

The students who have obtained a *double maîtrise* are privileged since the respec-tive programmes are highly selective and recognized as such by French academics

---

[64] The contributions have been published in 'Journée d'étude organisée par le Centre Français de droit comparé', (1988) *RIDC*, no. 4, 703–63.

[65] Bénédicte Fauvarque-Cosson, 'L'enseignement du droit comparé', (2002) *RIDC* 293 ff, esp 307 ff.

[66] This was also suggested, as a 'dream', by Blanc-Jouvan (n 21) 8 ff.

[67] The exchange programme between Paris I and King's College (London), created by Professor André Tunc, run for many years by Professor Xavier Blanc-Jouvan, were the first of this type. It has been recognized by the European Commission as the best exchange programme. It has since been successfully imitated by law faculties from the UK (see for instance the double *maîtrise* between Paris II and Cambridge) and all over Europe and the United States.

and professionals. Other students, however, often hesitate to go abroad during their four years of law school because they fear the risk of rejection by selective post-graduate programmes. A detour into a foreign legal system costs them time, money, and, most importantly, the opportunity to take all the standard French law courses needed to compete for the best masters programmes. It is true that it may well be more important for law school students to understand a variety of legal systems than to memorize the myriad ever-changing cases and laws of their country. But as long as studying abroad decreases their chance of postgraduate admission, such know-ledge of foreign laws and the practice of comparison has little immediate payoff.

The situation does not improve upon graduation. Young French researchers aspiring to academia have long been discouraged from engaging in comparative studies. Indeed, legal academics have tended to view comparative theses with sus-picion. Fortunately, the current situation is rapidly changing due to an increasing number of professors who know foreign languages, have experience abroad, and are therefore truly open to foreign legal systems and comparative law.[68] Recently, several scholars have published excellent theses in comparative law and have succeeded at the academically all-important *'Agrégation de droit'*[69] despite the nature of their topic. Soon, these scholars will have their own doctoral students whom they will most likely encourage to pursue comparative research. As a result, a new school of comparative law may well be in the making.

Some law schools are now establishing research centres dedicated to com-parative law.[70] Outside the universities, the *Société de législation comparée*, which encompasses academics, judges, and practitioners from all over the world, acts as an important forum for discussions on comparative law. It publishes comparative studies[71] in collaboration with the *Revue internationale de droit comparé* and the *Centre national de la recherche scientifique* (CNRS).[72]

Although these signs are encouraging, there is still a long way to go. Compara-

---

[68] In the field of contract and tort law, see, in particular, the great comparative insight in Muriel Fabre-Magnan, *Les obligations* (2004) or in Geneviève Viney, *Traité de droit civil. Introduction à la responsabilité* (1997), Viney and Patrice Jourdain, *Les conditions de la responsabilité, Les effets de la responsabilité* (1998). See also, in the recently launched new *Review on Contract Law* (*Revue des contrats*), the specific section dedicated to comparative law of contracts (by Pascal Ancel and Fauvarque-Cosson). See also, for an overall view of English commercial law, Olivier Moréteau, *Droit anglais des affaires* (2000).

[69] The '*Agrégation de droit*' enables a French doctor to become a professor.

[70] There is also a sort of superstructure, called the *Groupement de droit comparé* (GDR), which tries to reassemble some of these centres but this is a difficult and complex task. The well-known *Association Henri Capitant* is also doing comparative research, focusing on the various laws of French-speaking countries all over the world. Its aim is to promote Romanistic legal culture.

[71] For example, see the *Mélanges Denis Tallon* (1999) and *Melanges Xavier Blanc-Jouvan* (2005), two books dedicated to comparative law.

[72] In 1999, a special volume, entitled *L'avenir du droit comparé* (n 21), was published to celebrate the fiftieth anniversary of the *Revue internationale de droit comparé*. It contains twenty contributions from comparatists from all over the world (nine of them come from Europe, none from Africa).

tive law must be pursued with a less nationalistic spirit and aimed at providing 'a comparative basis on which to develop a European common law'.[73] After a long decline, we can now confidently predict the renaissance of comparative law in France.

III. The Renaissance of Comparative Law in France

In France, comparative law is currently undergoing an important change as both new initiatives and new directions are transforming the discipline.

1. New Initiatives

The construction of a European private law has recently boosted comparative law in France and provided the discipline with a new form of legitimacy.[74] Moreover, criticisms of comparative law and of the civil law tradition coming from the United States also seem to be waking the sleeping beauty.

(a) The Development of European Law and its Impact on Comparative Law in France

The development of European law has played an important part in the renaissance of French comparative law. The change was first felt in academic circles, then by French judges, and finally among the practising bar.

In academic circles, there is a growing awareness that comparative law has become a basis of lawmaking at the European level. This is particularly true regarding 'hard law' such as EC directives or regulations. It is also true, however, for the elaboration of soft law such as common European principles of, for example, contract law. The role of comparative law is particularly important because of the fragmented nature of most European (private) law.

Since much of the existing '*acquis communautaire*' has developed in a piecemeal fashion, it is seen as having no overall coherence, rationality, predictability, or even

---

[73] Hein Kötz, 'Comparative Law in Germany Today', in *L'avenir du droit comparé* (n 21), 28 ff. Kötz's book, *European Contract Law* (trans. T. Weir, 1997) constitutes one of the first examples of such a European approach, because it follows the functional approach and uses comparative research to find functional equivalents rather than to identify conceptual dogmatic differences.

[74] Mathias Reimann, 'The Progress and Failure of Comparative Law in the Second Half of the Twentieth Century', (2002) 50 AJCL 691 ff; see also chapter 16 in the present *Handbook*.

legitimacy. At the initiative of Professor Ole Lando, a group of recognized European scholars regularly met from the 1970s to the 1990s and formed what has come to be known as the Lando Commission. The Commission drafted the well-known 'Principles of European Contract Law' which, among other things, now constitute the basis for teaching contract law in a European context, a course already established in some European universities, including several French postgraduate programmes.

The Study Group on the European Civil Code, led by Professor Christian von Bar, included some French academics in spite of great reluctance and criticism expressed by several leading French scholars. In January 2005, the group formed a large network of European researchers whose function is to create a Common Frame of Reference (CFR) in the field of contract law. Their goal is to improve lawmaking in Europe and, it is hoped, unify European contract law. This CFR will be based on comparative studies and may well constitute the first necessary step for a European contract code. One can only hope that the work on the CFR will unite European comparatists and strengthen their sense of belonging to a larger community of European scholars.[75] French scholars have also created new European organizations, such as the Social Justice Group, which published a manifesto arguing for more social values in European law.[76] In the coming years, most European comparatists will either be committed to cooperation or join various critical circles. Thus, jurists are now taking on a new identity, that of 'European comparatists' engaged in the discipline at the European level, though not necessarily for the purpose of drafting legislation. For instance, a large group of scholars meets every year in Trento to pursue The Common Core of European Private Law. The project seeks to identify similarities as well as differences among European legal systems through the analysis of case studies. A variety of results have already been published in a series of books.

Many recent publications reflect the emergence of a genuine European private law. Some books are compilations of the main texts on European Private Law, and in this respect closely resemble a 'codification-compilation',[77] while others, such as the *Common Law of Europe Casebooks* edited at the initiative of Walter van Gerven, also include case law and some doctrinal excerpts. A third revised and expanded edition of *Towards a European Civil Code*, published in 2004, assembles forty-four contributions from European scholars on various topics. The success of several European law reviews is also noteworthy, notably the *Zeitschrift für Europäisches Privatrecht* (*ZEuP*), the *European Review of Private Law*, and the *European Review on Contract Law*. The *European Review on Contract Law*'s lead article in its first volume was written by Ole Lando. Encouraged by the success of the 'Troika', the

---

[75] See also the recently created *European Legal Forum* which reports on the development of the European *ius commune* (<www.european-legal-forum.com>).

[76] 'Social Justice in European Contract Law: A Manifesto', (2004) 10 *European Law Journal* 653 ff.

[77] See Oliver Radley-Gardner, Hugh Beale, Reinhard Zimmerman, and Reiner Schulze (eds), *Fundamental Texts on European Private Law* (2003).

CISG, PECL, and Unidroit Principles, Lando called for a World Code on international non-consumer contracts based on the Principles of European Contract Law and the Unidroit Principles of International Commercial Contracts, both of which were inspired by the United Convention on Contracts for the International Sale of Goods (CISG).[78]

Each of these enterprises has contributed to a gradual convergence of legal reasoning towards a European model. Clearly, comparatists no longer live in national isolation, and the distinction between common law and civil law no longer appears as clear-cut as it originally seemed. The emergence of European private law is being accompanied by European legal scholarship focused on soft law rather than controversial legislative reform. The 'European success story' is therefore the 'success of soft law'.[79]

French jurists should not miss the opportunity to think and work on a European level. Many French scholars have already joined European projects and have thus begun to move away from the traditional French view of legal research as an individual process. The creation of a common European legal science is indispensable to the future development of the European Union because it will enable European private law to develop within an established framework.

Yet, as mentioned, the prospect of a European contract code, not to mention a European civil code, has sparked heated debate and a great deal of criticism in France. The objections are many and include the project's lack of legitimacy, the absence of economic necessity, the relatively poor quality of European legislation compared to the French Civil Code, and the fear that European legislation will inevitably lead to the decline of both French civil law and the French language.[80] Still, non-participation in European academic projects is both useless and irresponsible because it will not stop the process of Europeanization. A related, and important issue, is whether to use French in all the working groups; at least in theory, unified texts could be written in more than one language, and indeed, most international documents, including those aimed at the harmonization or unification of law, come in more than one official language. But the larger the groups become, the more difficult it is to use several languages in plenary sessions. This suggests the use of a basic working language, and English is, for better or worse, the inevitable choice. French scholars need to accept that fact, as have their German, Italian, and other colleagues.

---

[78] Ole Lando, 'The European Principles in an Integrated World', (2005) 1 *European Review of Contract Law* 3 ff.

[79] Martijn Hesselink, *The New European Legal Culture* (2001), 58 ff.

[80] For a collection of leading French articles on that topic, see Bénédicte Fauvarque-Cosson and Denis Mazeaud (eds), *Pensée juridique française et harmonisation européenne du droit* (2003); See also, Bénédicte Fauvarque-Cosson, 'Faut-il un Code civil européen?' (2002) *Revue trimestrielle de droit civil* 463 ff; Denis Mazeaud, 'Faut-il avoir peur d'un droit européen des contrats?' *Mélanges X. Blanc-Jouvan* (n 4), 309 ff; Rampelberg (n 14).

On the bench, the development of European law has prompted much more liberal use of comparative law in French cases. Since French judges are bound to apply EC law, they have increasingly developed a comparative methodology to incorporate European rules and principles into the French legal system. The growing influence of fundamental rights, through the application of the European Convention on Human Rights (ECHR), has also affected the discipline of comparative law by expanding the scope of comparison beyond national norms to encompass transnational, international, and supranational sources of law.[81]

The use of comparative law is especially important in French administrative law courts because French administrative law is not based on a codification comparable to the Code Civil. Since the European perspective has become paramount, the need for comparison with other regimes is increasing.[82] This is rarely obvious from the decisions themselves since French administrative courts rarely cite other cases. The best way to detect the existence of comparative reasoning is to read the conclusions of the *Commissaire du gouvernement*.

The new importance of comparative perspectives was signalled by the visit, in June 2005, of United States Supreme Court Justice Breyer to the Collège de France at the invitation of Professor Delmas-Marty. Justice Breyer discussed the use of comparative law by the American Supreme Court and by French judges. Bruno Genevois, former President of a *Conseil d'Etat* Section, mentioned the role of comparative law in difficult cases involving new economic, political, or social questions, such as the financing of political parties or issues of abortion. However, Genevois believed it was proper to use comparative law only in exceptional cases where the issue is either novel or difficult, or where views on an issue have undergone significant change. It is possible, however, that a few years down the road, even French judges will use comparative law much more liberally. The judge as comparatist is a new conception of the judges' role, much favoured by the Premier President of the *Cour de cassation*, Mr Guy Canivet.[83]

The *Cour de cassation*, the French Supreme Court in the field of private law, also frequently draws on comparative studies. Since this Court is bound by its traditional and elliptic style of opinion writing that prohibits judges from openly relying on, or

---

[81] Mathias Reimann, 'Beyond National Systems. A Comparative Law for the International Age', (2001) 75 *Tulane LR* 1103 ff; Richard Buxbaum, 'Die Rechtsvergleichung zwischen nationalem Staat und internationaler Wirtschaft', (1996) 60 *RabelsZ*, 203; Bénédicte Fauvarque-Cosson, 'Le droit comparé: art d'agrément ou entreprise stratégique?', *Mélanges Blanc Jouvan* (n 4), 69 ff; *idem* (n 65), 2, 293 ff. In fact, the ECHR also affects most internal disciplines. For instance, in private international law matters, the ECHR leads to a more frequent use of the ordre public exception as a means of displacing foreign laws that do not conform to Western conceptions of fundamental rights.

[82] Roger Errera, 'The French Administrative Law Courts', in *Comparative Law before the Courts* (n 60), 153 ff.

[83] Guy Canivet, 'La pratique du droit comparé par les cours suprêmes. Brèves réflexions sur le dialogue des juges dans les expériences françaises et européennes: en commentaire de l'article de Sir Basil Markesinis et Jörg Fedtke Le juge en tant que comparatiste', (2005) 80 *Tulane LR* 221 ff.

even mentioning, foreign rules, it is difficult to know the extent to which comparative law influences the decisions. One way to measure this influence is to consult the main French law reviews, the reports of the *Avocat Général* or *Conseiller rapporteur*, and the annual report of the *Cour de cassation*. According to Guy Canivet, the Premier Président of the *Cour de cassation* and former President of the *Société de Législation Comparée*, 'the use of comparative law is essential to the fulfillment of a supreme court's role in a modern democracy',[84] along with economic and scientific data.[85] President Canivet further advocated 'the role of the judge as a guardian of social values through the use of comparative law'[86] and encouraged the 'expression of the general interest', for example as '*amicus curiae*'.[87] When confronted with new and important social issues, such as homosexual marriages or questions of bioethics, the *Cour de cassation* engages in comparative research to discover the best available solution. To conduct effective comparative research, the *Cour de cassation* may order a comparative report from a new Comparative Law Centre at the University Panthéon-Sorbonne (Paris I). The report is then shared with the parties and the *Court de cassation's* public prosecutor, the *Ministère public*.[88]

In the meantime, networks of European judges, particularly among the various supreme courts, facilitate a new type of dialogue between civil law and common law jurisdictions. As a result, the decisions of national judges are contributing to the convergence of the European legal systems.[89] In this and other ways, the development of European law is thus forcing French judges to overcome the parochialism that dominated the twentieth century.

International commercial arbitration has become a particularly important context for the use of comparative law in recent years. A comparative approach not only brings a sense of legitimacy to the process, it is also useful as a source of law.[90] Arbitrators often like to refer to a variety of legal sources in order to justify the application of one national rule instead of another, or in order to fill a gap when

[84] Guy Canivet, 'The Use of Comparative Law before the French Private Law Courts' in *Comparative Law before the Courts* (n 60), 81 ff; Thomas Koopmans, 'Comparative Law and the Courts', (1996) *RIDC* 545 ff, with this optimistic conclusion : 'The future belongs to comparative law'.

[85] Guy Canivet, 'Le juge entre progrès scientifique et mondialisation', (2005) *Revue trimestrielle de droit civil* 44 ff.

[86] Guy Canivet's conference, 21 February 2003, at the British Institute of International and Comparative Law in London.

[87] Guy Canivet, 'L'amicus curiae en France et aux Etats-Unis', (2005) *Revue de jurisprudence commerciale* 99 ff.

[88] Guy Canivet, 'The Use of Comparative Law before the French Private Law Courts' in *Comparative Law before the Courts* (n 60), 191 ff. The first two expert reports were based on a case of wrongful birth, and a possible manslaughter conviction of a driver responsible for a traffic road accident that resulted in a pregnant woman requiring an abortion.

[89] Guy Canivet, 'La convergence des systèmes juridiques par l'action du juge', *Mélanges X. Blanc-Jouvan* (n 4), 11 ff.

[90] Emmanuel Gaillard, 'Du bon usage du droit comparé dans l'arbitrage international', (2005) 2 Revue de l'Arbitrage 375 ff.

there is no satisfactory solution in domestic law. The Unidroit Principles are often invoked, not only because they attempt to reconcile and merge the civil law and common law traditions, but also because they are presented as a modern *lex mercatoria*, and because they are easily accessible. By contrast, practitioners seem not to regard the Principles of European Contract Law as highly, partly because they are European instead of international, and partly because they are still fairly new. The development of European law can also foster the use of comparative law among practitioners more generally. Though the EC Commission stressed the need for standard contract terms at the European level in its recent Action Plan,[91] the Commission correctly found that it was not the appropriate body to lead this process and limited its involvement to the creation of a website for the purpose of exchanging information. As a result, practitioners are now in a position to compare their own contractual clauses not only with those of other countries or institutions, but also with the quasi-codifications such as the UNIDROIT Principles and Principles of European Contract Law. In particular, the development of an optional European law of contracts, initiated by the Principles of European Contract Law, and the current development of the CFR may encourage practitioners to rely on these European texts. The more practising French lawyers are involved in the elaboration of the future European contract law, the more they will refer to this corpus, at least in the context of European disputes. This in turn will strengthen the new sense of convergence in European law.

(b) American Critique and its Perception in France

Towards the end of the twentieth century, comparative law was subjected to a great deal of criticism from American scholars.[92] The critical allegations were many: comparative law is too 'heavily oriented toward private law'; it envisages an 'old civil v. common law scenario;' it rests on an idealistic notion of law as science; it lacks professional orientation,[93] methodological reflection, and theoretical foundation; and it remains primarily nationalistic while the importance of the nation-state is diminishing. Moreover, American scholars have stressed that the harmonization of mere blackletter law puts the discipline of comparative law on an 'extremely traditional and narrow path', and transforms it into 'a soundly positivistic, methodologically simplistic, and an amazingly biased enterprise'.[94] It is

---

[91] 'Action Plan on a More Coherent European Contract Law', COM (2003) 68, *Journal officiel* 2003 C63/01.

[92] See in particular the symposium 'New directions in Comparative Law', (1998) 46 *AJCL* 597.

[93] See in particular Mathias Reimann, 'Stepping out of the European Shadow: Why Comparative Law in the United States Must Develop Its Own Agenda,' (1998) 46 *AJCL* 637, 642 ff; see in the same volume, Ugo Mattei and Mathias Reimann, 'Introduction', 597 ff; for a different view which seeks to explain the current state of affairs, see George Bermann, 'The Discipline of Comparative Law in the United States', in *L'Avenir du droit comparé* (n 21), 305 ff and the references.

[94] Reimann, (2002) 50 *AJCL* 691 ff.

indeed this last concern that has kept some French academics from participating in projects attempting to harmonize or unify the law. These French scholars have argued in favour of diversity and multiculturalism, and they emphasize comparative law's potential benefit as applied to one's own legal system, instead of its unifying potential on an international level.

In response to American criticism of comparative law as stagnant,[95] and a hindrance to legal diversity and multicultularism,[96] comparative law took a new turn.[97] In her leading article, Horatia Muir Watt demonstrated how powerful a weapon comparative law could be against positivism and dogmatic approaches: it demonstrates the relative nature of national systems, exposes the parochialism of positivism, and contributes to a less formal approach to law more generally. At the same time, Pierre Legrand strongly opposed the process of Europeanization and internationalization of the law and questioned the idea of a convergence among legal systems, especially between the civil and the common law.[98] One may wonder, however, whether such protests are not lagging behind the times. The Europeanization of law is already taking place and European legal systems are already converging, for better or for worse. And when Legrand advocates complex cultural and interdisciplinary comparison, his approach renders the discipline so complicated that it may well discourage and deter scholars from becoming involved in the first place. It should also be noted that this highly exclusive approach to comparative law is in complete opposition to the present needs of French society. Due to the relative low number of French comparatists and to their traditionally limited influence, comparative law has suffered from its marginal position for too long already. Especially in light of the lingering bias that it is impossible to be both a comparatist and a good French lawyer, it seems not only unrealistic but also counterproductive to insist that French comparatists become interdisciplinary specialists or social scientists.

In practice, the impact of these critiques has been fairly limited outside a relatively small academic circle as such matters are of rather little concern to the French legal community as a whole. In contrast, the publication of a recent World Bank report entitled *Doing Business in 2004. Understanding Regulation*,[99] has provoked a real '*electrochoc*' affecting a much broader spectrum of French jurists. The report, written by American economists, criticizes the 'French civilist tradition' and endeavours to demonstrate that it is counterproductive in the business

---

[95] See the symposium (1998) 46 *AJCL* and in particular: Ugo Mattei and Mathias Reimann, 'Introduction', 597 ff; George Fletcher, 'Comparative Law as a Subversive Discipline', 683 ff; ibid, Ugo Mattei, 'An Opportunity Not to be Missed: The Future of Comparative Law in the United States', 709 ff.

[96] For articles on post-modernism in comparative law, see Reimann, (2002) 50 *AJCL* 681 ff; David S. Clark, 'Nothing New in 2000? Comparative Law in 1900 and Today', (2001), 75 *Tulane LR* 895 ff; Sacco, 'Epilogue' (n 33), 347 ff.

[97] See for instance Horatia Muir Watt, 'La fonction subversive du droit comparé' (2000) *RIDC*, 503ff. Marie-Claire Ponthoreau, 'Le droit comparé en question(s)', (2005) *RIDC* 7 ff.

[98] Pierre Legrand, *Le droit comparé* (1999).

[99] This report is available on the World Bank's website.

world.[100] Several conferences were held criticizing the report as a misguided comparison, based upon a fundamental opposition between the common law and the civil law world, when, in reality, the legal world map was truly much more complex. In addition, the report was attacked for using comparison merely as a means of asserting the superiority of the common law system.[101] While the issues are far from closed, the whole incident has already shown the potential political explosiveness of comparative studies. At the same time, it has demonstrated that a change in attitude might be necessary in order to preserve the civil law tradition against such charges of inefficiency. In particular, it may be necessary to translate more French civil law scholarship into English to make the civilian tradition more accessible to common law professionals, educators, and students and thus to counteract misunderstandings, distortions, and biases.

2. New Challenges

In France, a profound change of attitude towards comparative studies is necessary on a broad basis. Unless the French want to succumb to isolationism, they must make a determined effort to forge an alliance between the French legal tradition and the construction of a European and international legal order, and to build bridges between legal science and practice. Comparative law as a revitalized discipline is likely to face several new challenges. It must construct an international approach of comparative law; allow for a wider recognition of the practical uses of comparison; and embrace a pluralistic and pragmatic conception of the goals and methods of the discipline.

(a) An International Approach to Comparative Law

The first challenge for French comparative law is a greater integration of comparative law and international law. At a time when supranational legal systems and

---

[100] There would be a lot to say about this biased report which puts forward the idea that 'one size fits all' and expressly states or implicitly admits that, of course, the common law is the ideal model as it is the most efficient, but this is not the proper place to do so. Suffice it to mention here that in France and in other countries where the civil law tradition is still very much alive (particularly in Canada), the report has been much criticized (it should also be noted that it was criticized by the World Bank itself). The views of the proponents of French civil law have been heard by the World Bank whose 2005 Report (*Doing Business in 2005. Removing Obstacles to Growth*) is much more respectful of the civil law tradition.

[101] See Frédéric Rouvillois (ed), *Le modèle juridique français: un obstacle au développement économique* (2005), with a postface by the former Ministry of Justice (Dominique Perben) announcing the forthcoming creation of the '*Foundation pour la promotion du droit*', 143 ff; see the Research programme '*Attractivité économique du droit*', created in December 2004 (<http://www.gip-recherche-justice.fr/aed.htm>); les droits de tradition civiliste en question, 'À propos de Reports *Doing Business* de la Banque Mondiale', Association H. Capitant, vol. 1, 2006.

norms impact nearly every national legal system, comparative law can no longer be viewed as merely the study of foreign law as classified into legal families. Such a view is thoroughly outdated. In today's world, comparative law must incorporate the progress made by international law.[102] In a pluralistic context, the task of the comparatist is not only to compare, but also to identify the norms, to categorize them[103] by level (national, regional, or supranational), and to ascertain their role and impact. For more than two centuries, comparative law was essentially horizontal in so far as it dealt with comparisons of national legal systems. From now on, it must integrate transnational material and, to be effective, comparatists must become international lawyers capable of drafting a legal map illustrating the way in which each legal system connects with other legal systems within the multidimensional forest of legal regimes. They can then leave it to (private) international law specialists (who are often also comparatists) to identify the appropriate conflict rules.

(b) A Wider Recognition of the Practical Uses of Comparison

French practitioners still largely consider comparative law a purely academic endeavour far removed from the case at hand. This tends to be true despite the fact that today, more than ever before, the need for comparative perspectives has increased as practitioners frequently encounter difficult foreign legal questions. It is also both important and possible to use comparative law in the lawmaking process. The French parliament has its own resources to research foreign law, as do most of the *Ministères*. Most notably, the Ministry of Justice has at its disposal the *Service des affaires européennes et internationales* (SAEI). Members of parliament, as well as academics advocating reform, should also engage in deeper comparative research, though some areas of the law are obviously more suited for that than others. For instance, the recent use of comparative law by European Community judges in conjunction with the European Human Rights Convention has led to the development of a European administrative law.[104] In the field of international commercial law, the elaboration of international commercial rules, such as the CISG, necessarily rests on comparative analysis, as do the so-called *lex mercatoria* and the general principles of international commercial law as enshrined in the UNIDROIT project. Of course, it is considerably easier to model, unify, and harmonize business law, commercial law, and, more generally, contract law, than it is in the areas of family law or individual rights.

---

[102] Buxbaum, (1996) 60 *RabelsZ* 211–12, 229 ff; See also Leslye Amede Obiora 'Toward an Auspicious Reconciliation of International and Comparative Analyses', (1998) 46 *AJCL* 669 ff (advising resort to 'internal comparison').

[103] Reimann, (2001) 75 *Tulane LR* 1103 ff; Delmas-Marty, (2003) 1 *Journal of International Criminal Justice* 13 ff; Fauvarque-Cosson (n 81).

[104] David and Spinosi (n 36).

Most French academics focus on comparative law's epistemological function rather than its legislative role. The discipline is considered socially useful in so far as it fosters better understanding, interpretation, and critical analysis of French law. Yet, French academics are critical of the 'normative' use of comparative law for three reasons. The first reason, which is fortunately a minority view, is political. In this view, comparative studies are grounded in a nationalistic conception of law that stands in opposition to the processes of internationalization or Europeanization. Advocates of this position also question the value of looking for inspiration in foreign legal systems. The second criticism is ontological—it is one thing to compare, but quite another to enact rules. Thus, comparison must remain non-normative. This criticism is legitimate in so far as it opposes the creation of new rules from mere comparison,[105] but it misses the mark when it becomes a critique of rule-oriented comparison as such.[106] The third objection is methodological. A rule-oriented comparison is not a proper approach because it is too positivistic, too nationalistic, and it fails to respect (and perhaps even foster) diversity. Such critiques, even when they are valid, may have some merit with regard to pure legal scholarship. Yet, comparative law is much more than just that—it is also, if not primarily, a tool for legislators and judges who are not charged with multicultural and multidisciplinary agendas but simply with reaching practical results.[107]

In addition, comparative law has a variety of goals that can easily coexist. While considerable attention has recently been paid to the unification of European private law, there is a great deal of non-private and non-blackletter comparative law in Europe. In fact, most of the discipline as it is actually practised in Europe is non-positivistic: judges refer to experiences in other European jurisdictions, practitioners rely on general principles, and academics such as the Trento group try to identify legal convergences and divergences by resorting to the case method, publish 'jus commune casebooks', or add comparative sections to existing books or study materials.

(c) A Pluralistic and Pragmatic Conception of the Goals and Methods of Comparison

The third challenge consists of recognizing and promoting the diverse functions of comparative law. Traditionally, common law systems are empirical and therefore tend towards a functional approach; the civil law tradition, by contrast, favours a scientific approach so that comparison is based on concepts and general

---

[105] On this point, see Carbonnier's idea on comparative law (n 47).

[106] See also Otto Pfersmann, 'Le droit comparé comme interprétation et comme théorie du droit', (2001) RIDC 275 ff.

[107] Bermann, in L'avenir (n 21), 305 ff.

principles.[108] Yet, rather than conflicting, these two approaches are actually com-plementary. Obviously, the methodology changes according to the goals pursued and the subject-matter studied. For example, in family law, religious, cultural, and historical considerations are much more important than they are in commercial law. Further, in family law comparability is much more an issue so the scope is quite narrow while in commercial law, contract law, intellectual property law, and corporate law, the geographical scope can be quite broad, as demonstrated by important international conventions.

Thus, comparatists use different methods depending on their goals, the subject-matter, and the geographical areas under scrutiny. When scholars engage in comparison as a basis for legal unification, they concentrate on countries that share a common heritage. But if they are looking for differences, they may include, or focus on, very different legal systems and their work will soon resemble that of an ethnologist.

Up to now, French academics have paid too little attention to the method-ological aspects of comparative law.[109] While Europeanization and globalization have increased interest in comparative law, its methodological foundation has not been solidified and, in practice, each researcher actually follows more or less his or her own method depending largely on the individual's background and knowledge. Of course, this touristic approach to comparative law irritates scholars who view comparative law as a truly scientific discipline[110] but one cannot be too demanding and should guard against calling for a perfect method and further dividing the French comparatists who work as scholars and those who search for practical results. In addition, excessive obsession with methodological questions entails the risk that internists will write off comparative study as a mere discourse in legal philosophy and fail to recognize it as true legal analysis. French comparatists should thus follow a middle path and formulate basic maxims of comparison, similar to the current principles of textual interpretation that can serve as guidelines and help to prevent fundamental errors.

---

[108] However, in some civil law countries, this practical approach to the common law has been attractive to jurists and practitioners, especially in Italy where the 'casebook method' was adopted by some comparatists opposing the dogmatic Germanic approach; see Pier Giuseppe Monateri, 'Critique et différence: le droit comparé en Italie', (1999) *RIDC* 990 ff.

[109] Etienne Picard, 'L'état du droit comparé en France en 1999', in *L'avenir* (n 21), 165 ff; Béatrice Jaluzot, 'Méthodologie du droit comparé. Bilan et prospective', (2005) *RIDC* 29 ff.

[110] Legrand (n 98).

IV. Concluding Remarks

The renaissance of comparative law in France is a recent phenomenon and far from fully developed. As a result, there are many encouraging aspects to its development as well as many opportunities for continuing criticism.

To begin with, French comparatists have a highly scientific vision of what comparative law is or should be. This is both good and bad. It is good because it discourages a touristic approach; it is bad because it tends to restrict comparative law to the academic context. Also, it is not helpful that comparatists sometimes adopt an exclusivist attitude—comparison is a universal process and comparative law should be used and practised by all lawyers.

Furthermore, the standing of comparative law in French universities is still rather modest and French students interested in pursuing comparative studies are often discouraged, especially if they wish to become academics. Nineteenth-century French law professors enjoyed saying that they did not teach French law but the Civil Code. During the twentieth century, they broadened their teaching and taught French law with equal emphasis on statutory rules and case law. Today, few French scholars describe themselves as full-fledged comparatists; instead they identify themselves with other fields of interest in which they then think more and more comparatively. Most of them are fully aware that they can no longer teach just French internal law but must also include European and international dimensions and view legal issues from a comparative perspective. While the study of national legislation remains the core of French legal education, most academics genuinely believe that comparison can be included in lectures or books on French law and do not really see the need for comparative law as a distinct science when it can be integrated into the curriculum as a whole. They are right, of course, but there is rarely enough time and space for this to happen in practice.

Also, French comparatists often have a chip on their shoulder: they either bemoan the lack of real interest in comparative law (a mere '*art d'agrément*') or doubt whether it has a solid intellectual and methodological basis.[111] None the less, French comparatists are fully aware that a major change of attitude must occur in order to integrate the international dimension of law into their discipline and that this integration requires some serious thought about comparative law as a whole. French comparative law also needs to revitalize its methodological reflection and work towards a set of basic principles that take into account the various goals of comparison.

The recent changes that have occurred in French law faculties could eventually

---

[111] Picard (n 21), 153 ff.

lead to a revival of the brilliant French tradition in comparative law, provided French comparatists understand today's challenges and come to grips with them. New paradigms (e.g. a reorientation from merely foreign laws to transnational sources) and new goals (e.g. turning from a purely scientific conception to a more practical orientation) are currently shaping new approaches to the discipline in France. In addition, the ongoing unification of European private law has opened up new prospects.

Finally, the development of comparative law in France and elsewhere must overcome nationalistic attitudes. It must embrace the prospect for peace among states and operate in the context of a convergence of civilizations. Thus, comparative law requires a certain degree of international harmony and here, as elsewhere, comparative law is inextricably intertwined with the internationalization of law.

BIBLIOGRAPHY

Congrès international de droit comparé, Procès-verbaux des séances et documents (2 vols, 1905)

Marc Ancel, 'Cent ans de droit comparé en France', *Livre du centenaire de la Société de législation comparée* (1969), 3 ff

Jean Carbonnier, 'L'apport du droit comparé à la sociologie juridique', *Livre du centenaire de la Société de législation comparée* (1969), 75 ff

Léontin Jean Constantinesco, *Traité de droit comparé, vol. I, Introduction au droit comparé, vol. II, La méthode comparative, vol. III, La science des droits comparés* (1972, 1974, 1983)

Rodolfo Sacco, *La comparaison juridique au service de la connaissance du droit* (1991)

Pierre Legrand, *Le droit comparé* (1999)

L'avenir du droit comparé, Un défi pour les juristes du nouveau millénaire (2000)

Horatia Muir Watt, 'La fonction subversive du droit comparé', (2000) *RIDC* 503 ff

Etienne Picard, 'L'état du droit comparé en France en 1999', in *L'avenir du droit comparé* (2000), 165 ff

René David and Camille Jauffret-Spinosi, *Les grands systèmes de droit contemporains* (11th edn, 2002)

Bénédicte Fauvarque-Cosson, 'L'enseignement du droit comparé', (2002) *RIDC* 293 ff

Christophe Jamin, 'Saleilles' and Lambert's Old Dream Revisited', (2002) 50 *AJCL* 701 ff

Guy Canivet, 'The Use of Comparative Law before the French Private Law Courts', in Guy Canivet, Mads Andenas, and Duncan Fairgrieve (eds), *Comparative Law before the Courts* (2004), 153 ff

Mireille Delmas-Marty, *Les forces imaginantes du droit. Le relatif et l'universel* (2004)

Bénédicte Fauvarque-Cosson, 'Le droit comparé: art d'agrément ou entreprise stratégique?' *Mélanges Blanc Jouvan* (2005), 69 ff

De tous horizons, Mélanges Xavier Blanc-Jouvan, Société de législation comparée (2005)

Le devenir du droit comparé en France (2005)

CHAPTER 2

....

DEVELOPMENT OF COMPARATIVE LAW IN GERMANY, SWITZERLAND, AND AUSTRIA

....

INGEBORG SCHWENZER

Basel*

* This article could not have been written without the collaboration of the historian lic. phil.
Simone Peter. It is only for editorial reasons that she is not mentioned as a co-author. All translations
from German texts, unless otherwise indicated, are by the author.

I. Introduction

THIS chapter attempts to give an overview both of the development of comparative law as a field of research, and of its impact on legal changes in Germany, Switzerland, and Austria. General aspects of the methodology, institutionalization, and the use of comparative approaches by courts and legislators in each of those three countries are therefore considered, with a primary focus on the development of comparative law in the field of the law of obligations.

Any attempt at periodization is to some extent arbitrary, for it suggests a division of historical time, which is, as such, continuous. Historians generally mistrust dividing history into periods following the so-called 'political' or 'diplomatic' framework narrative. In fact, it is questionable whether political events have importance for any fields other than politics. Furthermore, cultural and social developments do not follow a precise decimal chronology. Nevertheless, the use of historical periods of time can be helpful. Also, in this particular case, there appear to be convincing reasons for relying upon the political framework to produce a history of comparative law. Moreover, this history, especially in Germany, is linked very closely to the large-scale events of European history.

Section II of this chapter deals with the long nineteenth century. It is followed by a section on the golden age of comparative law, which covers the period of the Weimar Republic (III). The 'dark age' of the 1930s and the first half of the 1940s will be referred to as the period of rupture and remorse (IV). The section on recovery encompasses post-war developments until the end of the cold war (V). The final section of this chapter focuses on the attempts to unify the law and on the new approaches to comparative law which have gained in importance in the course of the Europeanization of private law (VI).

II. THE LONG NINETEENTH CENTURY

The 'long nineteenth century' covers the period between 1789 and World War I (1914–18). Historians first coined this large-scale narrative to stress the importance of the French Revolution and to characterize the whole nineteenth century as a response to the revolutionary ideas which launched Europe into modern times. Obviously, the century is also crucial for the development of modern legal systems as well as modern legal science. The growth of comparative law—seen both as a method and as a field of research—also falls into this long century.

1. Philosophical and Political Traditions

The great codifications around 1800, that is, the *Allgemeines Landrecht* (Prussia, 1794), the *Code civil* (France, 1804), and the *Allgemeines Bürgerliches Gesetzbuch* (Austria, 1811) can be regarded both as the end of the Age of Enlightenment and as the beginning of the 'Age of Comparison', which was Nietzsche's suggested label for the nineteenth century. The 'lost unity of natural law'[1] made legal comparison between different laws not only possible, but also necessary. Thus, thanks to its

---

[1] Anne Peters and Heiner Schwenke, 'Comparative Law beyond Post-Modernism', (2000) 49 *ICLQ* 800, 803.

philosophical premises and its deductive method, Natural Law had been focusing on common and general principles. The legal diversity of the recently adopted codes enabled comparison which, however, did not merely follow a purely scientific motivation. In the eyes of contemporaries, those codifications not only represented the glory and triumph of modern and rational law making, but could also be viewed as the spectre of the liberal agenda of a bourgeoisie, which demonstrated its explosive potential in the French Revolution.

Neither Germany nor Switzerland represented unified units in the first half of the nineteenth century, nor did they have a unified law at that time. The territorial entities such as, for example, Prussia, Bavaria, Württemberg, or the Swiss cantons used to have laws of their own. In some French-occupied territories, French revolutionary laws became effective automatically; in others, they were introduced by choice, either *tel quel* or in a modified version, such as the *Badisches Landrecht* (1810), which was an adaptation in German of the *Code civil*. In the aftermath of the Vienna Congress in 1815, any interest in the French *Code pénal* and the *Code civil* corresponded not only to the actual territorial scope of those codifications, but also to the political preferences of liberal scholarship prevailing at that time. Consequently, the *Code civil* was retained in some Swiss cantons, for example, Geneva and Vaud, as well as in Baden. By way of contrast, conservative scholars and politicians were happy to overthrow the revolutionary heritage, with its dangerous ideas of freedom, equality, and fraternity, as soon as the French occupation had come to an end and the return to a pre-revolutionary society seemed possible. The rather aristocratic and restorative cantons of Bern, Solothurn, and Lucerne in Switzerland favoured the Austrian *Allgemeines Bürgerliches Gesetzbuch*, against the background of Metternich's conservative political regime.

Last, but not least, the famous dispute between Friedrich Carl von Savigny and Anton Friedrich Justus Thibaut on the necessity of a codification for Germany can be mentioned as the most outstanding example of the impact of political preferences. Thibaut, holding the chair of Roman law at the liberal University of Heidelberg, argued in favour of a uniform code, with a Natural law basis, as an instrument of German unification. He stressed the importance of a better knowledge of foreign laws, and he was soon supported by the so-called Heidelberg School and the first journal of comparative law, which was founded in 1829: the *Kritische Zeitschrift für Gesetzgebung und Rechtssetzung des Auslandes*, edited by Karl Josef Anton Mittermaier and Karl Salomo Zachariae von Lingenthal.

Conversely, Savigny and the Historical School corroborated their aversion to a German Civil Code by reference to the 'shallow philosophy' of Natural Law with its 'infinite arrogance'—an aristocratic hostility to the presumed dangers of egalitarian ideas. Many scholars of comparative law are astonished that the Historical School was unwilling to take foreign law into consideration. In fact, the Romantic idea of a *Volksgeist* as the source of every nation's law was not, as such, opposed to empirical observation, which could have verified (or falsified) any theoretical assumptions. Therefore, ignoring contemporary foreign law was not only a scientific choice; it also demonstrated a disapproval of liberal thought patterns and liberal scholarship in idealizing the Ancient Roman World in an ahistoric way.

Political preferences had an impact on philosophical orientation as well. Whereas the Historical School was influenced by romantic philosophers such as Herder, early comparatists instead referred to Hegel and a universalistic conception of law and history. Thus, Eduard Gans published his work on the law of succession in 1824 as a contribution to a universal history of law.[2] Anselm von Feuerbach elaborated drafts of a Bavarian Civil Code (1808) and a Bavarian Penal Code (1813), both based on the French codes, but with a strong claim to legal universalism and strongly influenced by Hegel's philosophy.

However, all these promising attempts at comparative law completely disappeared by the middle of the nineteenth century under the all-dominant Historical School.[3]

2. The Evolutionary Paradigm

In the second half of the nineteenth century, an ethnological branch of legal science appeared under the name *Vergleichende Rechtswissenschaft*. It was based on a belief in legal progress, which was shared by a cross-section of the legal community. However, differences existed about its means. Names such as Georg Cohn, Franz Bernhöft, Albert Hermann Post, and Josef Kohler stood for the ambivalent attempt of defining the 'idea of law'[4] by the description of different systems of law, present and past. This evolutionary paradigm assumed a hidden 'law' to be the actual originator of historical change, which could be gauged by observing 'primitive' tribal law as a mirror, at least partly, of one's own past. The *Zeitschrift für vergleichende Rechtswissenschaft* (Journal of Comparative Legal Science) was founded by members of that circle, and appeared for the first time in 1878. The programmatic foreword to the first issue contemplated the 'enlargement of the boundaries of legal science'[5] and the overcoming of the national restriction which the Historical School had imposed on German legal science.

Although some authors are inclined to see one source for the development of modern comparative law in those ethnological studies,[6] most scholars today deny

---

[2] Eduard Gans, *Das Erbrecht in weltgeschichtlicher Entwicklung: Eine Abhandlung der Universalrechtsgeschichte* (4 vols, 1824–34).

[3] See Konrad Zweigert and Hein Kötz, *Einführung in die Rechtsvergleichung* (3rd edn, 1996), 56. English translation under the title *An Introduction to Comparative Law* by Tony Weir (3rd edn, 1998), 58.

[4] Franz Bernhöft, 'Über Zweck und Mittel der vergleichenden Rechtswissenschaft', (1878) 1 *Zeitschrift für vergleichende Rechtswissenschaft* 1, 37.

[5] Ibid 2.

[6] Otto Sandrock, *Über Sinn und Methode zivilistischer Rechtsvergleichung* (1966), 14.

the importance of that school of thought or even ignore it completely. In fact, the careless accumulation of heterogeneous sources, the imprudent use of different methods, and the combination of observations and purely speculative thoughts, make it difficult to appreciate the work of those authors. This becomes all the more apparent when we consider an article by Josef Kohler, in which he admitted, self-critically, the mistakes committed by him and others and the lack of both scientific precision and reflection.[7] But instead of abandoning what he referred to as 'wild products of speculation', Kohler himself, in the same article, continued to engage in further such speculations.

3. Legislative Comparative Law

Despite the dominance of the Historical School, another branch of modern comparative law emerged during the second half of the nineteenth century which may be referrred to as legislative comparative law. In Germany, intensive comparative studies preceded the elaboration of several specific commercial statutes, which became necessary as a result of the development of trade and industry, for example, the *Allgemeine Deutsche Wechselordnung* (General German Bills of Exchange Act 1848), the *Allgemeines Deutsches Handelsgesetzbuch* (General German Commercial Code 1861), and the *Geschmacksmusterrecht* (Registered Designs Act 1878), as well as statutes on company law such as the *Aktiengesetz* (1870 and 1884). The preparatory work not only focused on the various laws prevailing in Germany at the time, but for the first time also encompassed other European Commercial Codes, such as those of France and the Netherlands, as well as sometimes even English law. Comparative law also played a prominent role in preparing the *Konkursordnung* (Insolvency Act 1881) and the *Zivilprozessordnung* (Civil Procedure Act 1880).

The two great Civil Codes at the dawn of the twentieth century, the German *Bürgerliches Gesetzbuch* (1900) and the Swiss *Zivilgesetzbuch* (1912), which unified private law in the German *Reich* and in Switzerland respectively, were firmly based on comparative research. In accordance with the aim of unification, the starting-points were the particular laws of the *Länder* (in Germany) and the Cantons (in Switzerland). Thus for Eugen Huber, who may be called the father of the Swiss codification, comparative legal science had the task of 'stating the differences, comparing what is lying apart, emphasizing commonalities, investigating the reasons for the differences, and revealing the usual lines of development'.[8] Likewise, the preparatory works for the German Civil Code show that comparative efforts were primarily focused on the *ius commune* of the nineteenth century as

---

[7] Josef Kohler, 'Zur Urgeschichte der Ehe', (1897) 12 *Zeitschrift für vergleichende Rechtswissenschaft* 187, 203.

[8] Eugen Huber, *System und Geschichte des schweizerischen Privatrechtes* (vol I, 1886), 3.

well as the specific laws of the various German *Länder*. However, foreign laws did not go unnoticed by the creators of the two codes, the main sources of comparison being the existing Natural law codifications of Austria, France, and Prussia. Last but not least, the new codes influenced each other to a certain degree in various fields. The German Civil Code, furthermore, had a considerable impact on the amendments to the Austrian Civil Code; from 1914 to 1916, three *Teilnovellen* were enacted, relying heavily on German solutions.

Although this seems to be a success story for comparative law, we must not forget that the German *Bürgerliches Gesetzbuch* is a product of the nineteenth-century Historical School and the conceptual jurisprudence (*Begriffsjurisprudenz*) generated by it. Doctrinal considerations often prevailed over pragmatism. One notable example was the conception of a 'general part' of the Civil Code, which purported to create general rules that could be applied to all parts of private law, from the law of obligations to property law, family law, and the law of succession. Gustav Radbruch therefore famously characterized the *Bürgerliches Gesetzbuch* as being more the cadence of the nineteenth century than the upbeat to the twentieth century. This was despite the promising and symbolically chosen date of 1 January 1900, upon which the new code was to enter into force.

In the context of a history of comparative law in Germany, however, the year of 1900 is not generally associated with the entry into force of the *Bürgerliches Gesetzbuch*, but rather with the first World Conference of Comparative Law in Paris, often identified as the cradle of modern comparative law. The organizer of that conference, Raimond Saleilles, and the principal speaker, Edouard Lambert, expressed their hope that the use of the comparative method would finally lead to a *droit commun de l'humanité civilisé*, a unified law for the entire civilized world. This ambitious aim stood in stark contrast to the limited scope of comparison. Only statutory law was deemed to be comparable, thus confining the whole undertaking to continental law.

4. Early Stages of Institutionalization

Even before the Paris Congress, German comparative lawyers had formed associations and founded comparative law journals in what may be called a process of institutionalization of comparative law.[9] In 1893–94, first the *Gesellschaft für vergleichende Rechts- und Staatswissenschaft* (Association for Comparative Legal and Politcal Science) and then—initiated by Felix Meyer—the *Internationale Vereinigung für vergleichende Rechtswissenschaft und Volkswirtschaftslehre* (International Association for Comparative Legal Science and Political Economics) were

---

[9] See Léontin-Jean Constantinesco, *Rechtsvergleichung* (vol I: *Einführung in die Rechtsvergleichung*, 1971), 132 ff.

founded. The latter focused on 'our European-American World Culture'.[10] The application of the comparative method on a historical and ethnological basis, mainly represented by Josef Kohler, was not to be neglected, although it was soon to lose popularity. From 1895 onwards, the association published a yearbook[11] that was supplemented in 1902 by a monthly journal.[12] The association had a genuinely international orientation, having not only close contacts to corresponding societies abroad, but also members from numerous countries. Highlights in the history of the association were conferences in Heidelberg in 1911 and Berlin in 1914, where the twentieth anniversary was celebrated by a gathering of 200 members, friends, and sponsors.[13] Comparing the state of comparative law with that twenty years previously, Meyer, as president of the association, drew an overly optimistic picture on the very eve of World War I:[14] 'How different the situation is today, at a time when the internationalization of law has made enormous progress, no statute is prepared without the assistance of comparative law. . . . Indeed, spring has come, also in Germany'.

Apart from the activities of the International Association, further endeavours enhancing the importance of comparative law can be encountered, such as the establishment of the journal *Rheinische Zeitschrift für Zivil- und Prozessrecht* (1909) that replaced the former *Zeitschrift für Deutsches Bürgerliches Recht und französisches Civilrecht* (1869). It counted Josef Kohler and Ernst Rabel among its editors.

World War I ended the early optimism and some ambitious projects, such as that of a German commentary on English law. Although comparative law was not held in high esteem during the war through being associated with an interest in the laws of the enemies, the process of institutionalization nevertheless continued at university level. As early as 1914, an *Institut für Internationales Recht* was founded in Kiel, to be followed by the famous *Institut für Rechtsvergleichung* in Munich in 1916, which, in turn, became the model for all later foundations, such as the *Seminar für wirtschaftliche und rechtsvergleichende Studien* at the University of Heidelberg in 1917, the *Seminar für englisches Recht* in Würzburg, the *Seminar für deutsches und nordisches Recht* in Hamburg, both in 1919, and finally the *Universitäres Institut für Auslands- und Wirtschaftsrecht* in Berlin in 1920.

The Versailles Treaty ended the 'long nineteenth century'. At the same time, the political consequences of the war laid the ground for a new era of comparative law, closely linked to the name of Ernst Rabel, who was to influence comparative law more than any other person throughout the twentieth century.

---

[10] Elmar Wadle, *Einhundert Jahre rechtsvergleichende Gesellschaften in Deutschland* (1994), 32.

[11] Franz Bernhöft and Felix Meyer (eds), *Jahrbuch der Internationalen Vereinigung für vergleichende Rechtswissenschaft und Volkswirtschaftslehre* (vol I, 1895).

[12] *Mitteilungen der Internationalen Vereinigung für Rechtswissenschaft und Volkswirtschaftslehre* (vol I, 1902).

[13] Wadle (n 10), 40.   [14] See Wadle (n 10), 41.

III. A Golden Age (1919–1933)

1. The Weimar Republic and the Pre-eminent Influence of Ernst Rabel

The real flourishing of comparative law in Germany only began with the work of Ernst Rabel.[15] He was born on 28 January 1874 in Vienna. All of his grandparents had been of the Jewish faith; his parents belonged to the Catholic church. Ernst Rabel was raised as part of the contemporary Viennese society with its conservative values, enjoying piano lessons with the old Anton Bruckner. After having completed his studies in his home town, Rabel worked as an attorney for a short while, but soon returned to the university, completing his second doctorate (*Habilitationsschrift*) in Leipzig in 1902 under the supervision of Ludwig Mitteis. Even this early work on the seller's liability for defects in title[16] took account of the comparative dimension, but its focus was historical. In 1906, Rabel became a full professor and judge in Basel. In 1910 he went to Kiel, but left again in 1911 to go to the University of Göttingen. During those early years, Rabel's publications were mainly in the fields of Roman law and juristic papyrology. But he also argued, for instance, that the newly adopted rules of the German Civil Code on breach of contract, centred on the notion of 'impossibility', were based upon misunderstandings reflecting '*Windscheid*'s pseudo-romantistic doctrine'.[17]

In the middle of World War I, in 1916, Rabel moved to the University of Munich. By granting him more money to found an Institute of Comparative Law, Bavaria prevailed over the University of Frankfurt. This fact sheds light both on the early reputation of Ernst Rabel and on the importance which, at the time, was attributed to the emerging discipline of comparative law.

The practical use of comparative law and the need for comparative research soon became visible with the Versailles Treaty of 1919, which had a deep impact not only on public, but also on private, law. As Rabel emphasized, the treaty had been worked out by lawyers of the coalition that had won World War I, using terminology based upon Anglo-American or French law, without any attempt to pay attention to different conceptions of German law and legal practice.[18] To Rabel,

---

[15] See Gerhard Kegel, 'Ernst Rabel—Werk und Person', (1990) 54 *RabelsZ* 1; Rolf Ulrich Kunze, *Ernst Rabel und das Kaiser-Wilhelm-Institut für ausländisches und internationales Privatrecht 1926–1945* (2004); Timo Utermark, *Rechtsgeschichte und Rechtsvergleichung bei Ernst Rabel* (2005).

[16] Ernst Rabel, *Die Haftung des Verkäufers wegen Mangels im Rechte* (1902).

[17] See Ernst Rabel, 'Die Unmöglichkeit der Leistung. Eine kritische Studie zum Bürgerlichen Gesetzbuch' (1907), in Hans G. Leser (ed), Ernst Rabel, *Gesammelte Aufsätze*, vol I: *Arbeiten zum Privatrecht* (1965), 1, 26.

[18] Ernst Rabel, 'Rechtsvergleichung vor den Gemischten Schiedsgerichtshöfen' (1923), in Hans G. Leser (ed), Ernst Rabel, *Gesammelte Aufsätze*, vol II: *Arbeiten zur internationalen Rechtsprechung und zum internationalen Privatrecht* (1965), 50, 53.

a man used to comparative legal thinking, it was obvious that a real understanding of the Treaty was only possible by a truly comparative method. Furthermore, the need for basic research became obvious. Again, Rabel's vision was far ahead of its time, compared to the majority opinion of German legal scholarship.

Rabel's famous speech on the aims and purposes of comparative law in 1924[19] has been called the 'foundational text of modern comparative law'.[20] In fact, the speech is often cited and used as an example of Rabel's functional approach. He disapproved of the naïvity displayed in the comparison of isolated statutory rules, which were not considered in their context. He argued that the preoccupation with statutory law was not conducive to a full understanding of a legal system.

Instead of using a foreign legal system as a quarry, comparative law research should analyse not only the individual rules, but also the problems to which they refer and the solutions which they propose.[21] It should take into account 'the law of the whole world, past and present, and everything that affects the law, such as geography, climate and race, developments and events shaping the course of a country's history . . .'.[22] The functionalist method was to take real life problems as its starting point; and the new science of comparative law, according to Rabel, was to have the same aim as all other sciences: to promote knowledge and understanding.[23] This set the course for the further development of comparative law. One result of that programmatic foundation was the 'discovery' of the common law as a necessary object of comparison.

Still, however, Rabel's speech addressed an audience of practising lawyers and not of legal scholars. The focus was therefore on the practical importance of comparative law. Rabel stressed the political difficulties of the post-war period, he deplored the lost influence of German legal science, and he stressed the danger of its isolation as a result of the Versailles Treaty.[24] Twenty years later, in 1954, Rabel looked back somewhat ambivalently:

A comparative lawyer is exposed to be distrusted alternatively as a nationalist or as an antinationalist. 'A sound national law develops like a sound human being only in a social common life with the fellow others.' I must confess I underestimated for a long time the full bearing of this truth. Today I repeat that if all lawyers of the world knew it and would take it to heart, new hopes would arise—immense hopes for our often challenged and just now seriously shaken faith in justice.[25]

---

[19] Ernst Rabel, 'Aufgabe und Notwendigkeit der Rechtsvergleichung' (1924), in Hans G. Leser (ed), Ernst Rabel, *Gesammelte Aufsätze*, vol III: *Arbeiten zur Rechtsvergleichung und zur Rechtsvereinheitlichung* (1967), 1.

[20] Kunze (n 15), 20.   [21] Rabel (n 19), 1, 3.

[22] Ibid 5.   [23] Ibid 6.   [24] Ibid 18.

[25] Ernst Rabel, 'Vorträge. Unprinted lectures 1954', (1986) 50 *RabelsZ* 282, 283.

2. The Kaiser-Wilhelm Institutes

The political situation in Germany after World War I and its legal implications played an important role in the establishment of the first independent institutes of comparative law not affiliated with an existing university. The Union of German Industry founded the *Institut für ausländisches Recht beim Reichsverband der deutschen Industrie*. The aim of re-establishing the international trading relationships which Germany had enjoyed before the war had to be supported by the necessary knowledge of international instruments and foreign law. The first director of the Institute was Felix Meyer, who strongly stressed its practical function. When he died in 1925, he was followed by Josef Partsch, who attempted to shift the focus to academic research.[26] Both Meyer and Partsch were close friends of Ernst Rabel, and Partsch was involved in the first plans to found a major institute of comparative law in Berlin,[27] where all the ministries and the important associations of German industry were situated.

In December 1924, the *Kaiser-Wilhelm-Gesellschaft* agreed to establish an *Institute of Public International Law* in Berlin, with Victor Bruns as its first director. The Institute was to be financed by the *Kaiser-Wilhelm-Gesellschaft*, the *Reich*, and members' contributions. Considering that the importance of the Versailles Treaty extended to private law matters, the new Institute was first intended also to conduct research on international private law and the trade law.[28] That idea was soon abandoned in favour of an independent institute. In the meantime, Rabel had been offered a chair at the University of Berlin, succeeding Josef Partsch who had died in 1925 at the age of 42.[29] The *Kaiser-Wilhelm-Gesellschaft* made the autonomy of the new institute a condition of Rabel's nomination, and when Rabel accepted the post, the *Kaiser-Wilhelm-Institut für ausländisches und internationales Privatrecht* was established in Berlin in 1926 and housed in the old castle in the centre of Berlin, next door to the Institute for Public International Law. It built up an extensive library as a necessary basis of its work. By 1932 it contained more than 200,000 volumes, including the largest collection of American legal materials and legal literature outside the United States.[30]

Also as a judge, Rabel faced the difficulties arising not only from the Versailles Treaty, but also from the war and its economic consequences in general. He was a member of the German-Italian Arbitral Tribunal in 1921 and served as a member of the Permanent International Court of Justice in The Hague from 1925 to 1928.

---

[26] On Partsch, see Rudolf Meyer-Pritzel, 'Der Rechtshistoriker und Pionier der modernen Rechtsvergleichung Josef Partsch (1882–1925)', (1999) 7 *Zeitschrift für Europäisches Privatrecht* 47 ff.

[27] Wadle (n 10), 56.   [28] Kunze (n 15), 48.   [29] Wadle (n 10), 55.

[30] See Max Rheinstein, 'In Memory of Ernst Rabel', (1956) 5 *AJCL* 185.

The Union of German Industry expected to be able to make practical use of the new Institute, which was entirely to replace its own *Institut für Auslandsrecht*. In exchange for financial contributions, German firms had access to the legal opinions produced by the Institute. Max Rheinstein, one of Rabel's early collaborators, directly linked the high quality of the work done by Rabel and his staff to the German successes before international courts of law.[31] Nevertheless, Rabel tried to place the Institute's main focus on basic research. It was predominantly the German and international community of legal scholars who were to benefit from this type of research. To further this aim, Rabel established a comparative law journal, edited within the Institute, which was not only to provide the necessary information about different countries and legal subjects, but also to be a main source of reference for international comparative legal science.

The *Zeitschrift für Ausländisches und Internationales Privatrecht* first appeared in 1927. It replaced not only the former journals of *Blätter für vergleichende Rechtswissenschaft und Volkswirtschaftslehre and Auslandsrecht*, but also the *Rheinische Zeitschrift für Zivil- und Prozessrecht*. Rabel featured as its main editor. He later described the aims of the review and the difficulties encountered as follows:[32]

It had more than a thousand pages of big size every year and was entirely either worked on or supervised by the institute. I had laid much stress, from the beginning, on an ample and reliable publication of materials, that is, an annual survey of the enactments, decisions, literature and business forms of the important countries. I wanted them reported as quickly, as precisely and as comprehensively as possible, having complained myself often that all endeavours of such kind either came too late or were too vague. And I thought indeed that the first task of such an institute, with its skilled and paid staff, was to collect the facts, a task too hard and annoying for the single student but indispensable for theory and practice.

From 1928 onwards, the Institute figured as the editor of the series *Beiträge zum ausländischen und internationalen Privatrecht*, which published monographs focusing mainly on Anglo-American law. Nevertheless, the review continued to publish long studies on selected problems, among them the first volume of Rabel's monumental study on the law concerning the sale of goods[33] in 1936.

3. Sale of Goods

From 1927, Ernst Rabel served as a member of the Board of the Institute for the Unification of Private Law in Rome. This Institute had been set up in 1926 as an

---

[31] Max Rheinstein, 'Ernst Rabel', in *Rechtsvergleichung und internationales Privatrecht, Festschrift für Ernst Rabel* (vol I, 1954), 1, 2.

[32] Rabel (n 25), 298.

[33] Ernst Rabel, 'Das Recht des Warenkaufs, eine rechtsvergleichende Darstellung', *Sonderheft der Zeitschrift für ausländisches und internationales Privatrecht* (1936).

auxiliary organ of the League of Nations. It had been initiated by the Italian Government under Benito Mussolini, who was endeavouring to found an institution which was to have members of international standing and so a worldwide reputation.

In 1929, Rabel initiated the project of unification of the law concerning the sale of goods, arguing that this subject, with its far-reaching international implications, would be most suitable for that purpose. In several articles, all published in the Institute's review, Rabel tried to promote the idea and the contours of the project. Rabel and the staff of the Berlin Institute were to furnish the necessary basic research. Rabel's study on the sale of goods is the first attempt to give a comprehensive assessment of the law of sales, based on a truly comparative functional method. After a general discussion of the scope and the aims of the unification of sales law, he laid down the principles concerning the formation of sales contracts, the general duties arising out of this type of contract, as well as the duties of the seller. Further topics such as the duties of the buyer, the seller's liability for non-conformity of the goods, the passing of risk, as well as secured transactions, were to be left to another special issue of the Institute's journal. As a result of Rabel's expulsion from the Institute and from Germany, however, this did not appear during his lifetime, but was published only in 1958.

Rabel's work provided the intellectual foundations for the unification of international sales law. In 1929, Rabel delivered the famous 'Blue Report' to the Institute's Council in Rome.[34] Soon thereafter, a committee was established with members from the English, French, Scandinavian, and German legal systems; it published the first draft of a Uniform Sales Law in 1935. Due to the political situation of the time, the idea was not pursued any further, but was only resumed by the Hague Conference. It was on the basis of Rabel's work that the (Hague) Uniform Law on the Sale of Goods and the Uniform Law on the Formation of Contracts for the International Sale of Goods were passed in 1964. These uniform laws, in turn, were to become the predecessor of the United Nations Convention on Contracts for the International Sale of Goods (CISG), adopted at the Vienna Conference in 1980.

The list of persons whose contribution was acknowledged in the foreword of *Das Recht des Warenkaufs* of 1936 reads like a 'Who's Who' of leading scholars in post-war Germany and the United States, especially in comparative law. To name but a few: Friedrich Kessler, Ludwig Raiser, Max Rheinstein, Eduard Wahl, Ernst von Caemmerer, Arwed Blomeyer, Fritz Korkisch, and Konrad Duden. They had all been assistants at the Institute, which in its heyday had been the intellectual home of more than forty young scholars.

---

[34] Ernst Rabel, 'Rapport sur le droit comparé en matière de vente', in *idem, Gesammelte Aufsätze,* vol III (n 19), 381.

IV. Rupture and Remorse (1933–1950)

In general presentations on legal history, the story of the 'dark age' of the Nazi period in Germany is generally told very quickly or even left out altogether. The section on the history of comparative law in the standard *Introduction to Comparative Law*[35] ends with the optimistic claim that Rabel's functional method had ultimately come to be accepted for comparative law worldwide—without even mentioning that Rabel was forced to leave the Institute, his chair at the University of Berlin, and the editorial board of the Institute's review. In recent years, however, an extensive amount of research about the Nazi period has been undertaken,[36] which permits the following assessment.

1. The Policy of Gleichschaltung

The German notion of *Gleichschaltung* describes the process by which the Nazi regime successively established control over public life in Germany. This was not only enforced from the top down; it was also a bottom-up process, which the British historian Ian Kershaw refers to as 'working towards the *Führer*'. With this notion he attempts to characterize Hitler's personalized form of rule, which 'invited radical initiatives from below and offered such initiatives backing, so long as they were in line with his broadly-defined goals. This promoted ferocious competition at all levels of the regime.'[37] Kershaw's account can also be helpful to describe the attitude of German legal science.

The ever-increasing incidence of civil unrest and riots was evidence of the difficulties of the late Weimar Republic. The universities too were affected. When Hitler was appointed as Chancellor of the Reich on 30 January 1933, the majority of the organized student body had already become members of the National Socialist student organization, but only a small minority of law professors openly sympathized with Hitler's party.[38] However, the National Socialist *Rechtswahrerbund*—literally: union of professors of the law—already comprised 30,000 members by October 1933, compared with only 1,400 members in January.[39] Rabel was the Dean of the law faculty in Berlin in the winter term of 1932–33, but he resigned from this

---

[35] Zweigert and Kötz (n 3), 47 ff (48 ff of the English translation).

[36] See, most recently, Reinhard Zimmermann, ' "Was Heimat hieß, nun heißt es Hölle" ', in Jack Beatson and Reinhard Zimmermann (eds), *Jurists Uprooted: German-Speaking Émigré Lawyers in Twentieth-Century Britain* (2004), 1 ff (with comprehensive references).

[37] Ian Kershaw, *Hitler 1889–1936: hubris* (1998), 530.

[38] Bernd Rüthers, *Geschönte Geschichten—Geschonte Biographien, Sozialisationskohorten in Wendeliteraturen* (2001), 35.

[39] Ibid 45.

position prematurely; his successor was Ernst Heymann, the director of the *Institut für Auslands- und Wirtschaftsrecht*.[40] There were fifteen chaired professors in the Berlin faculty, five of whom were to be dismissed because they were 'non-Aryans', to use the Nazi terminology. Heymann was not willing to support his Jewish colleagues; on the contrary, along with colleagues such as Carl Schmitt, Carl August Emge, and Graf von Gleispach, he supported the establishment of a National Socialist school of thought. Gleispach became Dean of the faculty in 1935. Heymann had tried to persuade Martin Wolff and Rabel to leave the faculty, but both of them refused, so Gleispach reported their names to the Ministry of Education with an appeal to expel them for being a 'heavy burden for the German student body' and an 'obstacle for the implementation of the National Socialist spirit'.[41] Then, in October 1935, Rabel, like so many of his 'non-Aryan' colleagues before him, was forced to leave the University.

The *Kaiser-Wilhelm-Institut für ausländisches und internationales Privatrecht* was also forced to face the consequences of the National Socialist regime. Many of its scholars left Germany because they were Jewish. Max Rheinstein had won the prestigious Rockefeller scholarship and went to New York in 1933. This was both the chance to leave and the reason for his expulsion from the Institute and the University, which he was unable to prevent. Friedrich Glum, the president of the *Kaiser-Wilhelm-Gesellschaft*, and a member of the Berlin faculty, argued that 'non-Aryan Rockefeller scholars' were no longer to be hired.[42] Of all the emigrants, Rheinstein seems to have been one of the most fortunate. He was young; moreover, he was a specialist in comparative law and well acquainted with the common law. In 1935, he secured a position on the faculty of the University of Chicago Law School.[43] Friedrich Kessler left Germany in 1934 at the age of 33. As a specialist in American law he, too, had relatively favourable conditions for a new start abroad: he went to Yale and Chicago, returned to Yale and—after his retirement from Yale—finally moved to Berkeley.[44]

After his forced retirement from the university, Rabel was still allowed to act as the Director of the Institute until 1937, when Heymann succeeded him. The protocol of the meeting of the chairman of the Institute's governing body and a representative of the Ministry of Science and Education stated:[45]

---

[40] For details on the change in the Berlin law faculty, see Anna-Maria Gräfin von Lösch, *Der nackte Geist: die Juristische Fakultät der Berliner Universität im Umbruch von 1933* (1999), 156 ff.

[41] See Kunze (n 15), 64.

[42] Gräfin von Lösch (n 40), 214.

[43] Mary Ann Glendon, 'The Influence of Max Rheinstein on American Law', in Marcus Lutter, Ernst C. Stiefel, and Michael H. Hoeflich (eds), *Der Einfluss deutscher Emigranten auf die Rechtsentwicklung in den USA und in Deutschland* (1991), 171, 172.

[44] Herbert Bernstein, 'Friedrich Kessler's American Contract Scholarship and its Political Subtext', in Lutter *et al* (n 43), 87.

[45] Kunze (n 15), 166.

We arrive at the following conclusion: Professor Rabel, whose merits concerning the Institute are recognized by the Ministry, has to resign from his position as head of the Institute. It is intolerable for the State that a person presides over the Institute who must be superannuated as a result of the Nuremberg Laws.

The name of Ernst Rabel was to disappear from the journal as well: 'Henceforth, only the Director of the Institute shall be named on the Journal, which will make it easier for Prof. Rabel to accept the embarrassment of the disappearance of his name'.[46] Consequently, the *Zeitschrift für Ausländisches und Internationales Privatrecht* began to appear under the name of Ernst Heymann.

Not until the very eve of World War II, in March 1939, did Rabel leave Germany for the United States. He first went to Philadelphia and subsequently became a visiting lecturer at Ann Arbor, Michigan, where he devoted himself to work on his second monumental work, *The Conflict of Laws*. However, Rabel, by then in his late sixties, did not really flourish in the United States. His study on the law of sales was unknown there. Although he tried to adapt his own draft to the proposals of the Uniform Commercial Code, Karl N. Llewellyn did not intend to collaborate with the famous German professor whom he had met in Europe some years before.[47] The Dean of the Michigan Law School was to state many years later: 'We did not know who he actually was'.[48] In Germany, his name disappeared not only from the journal of the Institute, but also from footnotes and bibliographies in legal scholarship. Walter Erbe did not even refer to Rabel when he published his article on the purpose of comparative law in the journal of the Institute in 1942.

Rabel's co-founder of the Munich Institute in 1916, Karl Neumeyer, had been forced to retire in 1934. In 1940, he had to sell off his entire library by auction. To escape imminent deportation, Neumeyer and his wife committed suicide in 1941.

2. National Socialist Comparative Law?

The *Zeitschrift für Ausländisches und Internationales Privatrecht* continued to appear until 1942. A recent study on the Institute and its role during the Third Reich[49] has shown that Ernst Heymann tried to give the Institute a new National Socialist profile. Although the journal maintained its basic structure, more and more book reviews began to focus on the new trend in German legal scholarship. Not only the journal, but also the second International Conference of Comparative Law, which took place in The Hague in 1937, seemed to offer the German delegation a chance to promote National Socialist legal theories. The majority of assembled scholars welcomed the new regime and contributed to the attempts to

---

[46] Ibid 167.
[47] Bernhard Grossfeld and Peter Winship, 'Der Rechtsgelehrte in der Fremde', in Lutter *et al* (n 43), 197.
[48] Ibid 190.   [49] Kunze (n 15).

nazify German law. Wolfgang Siebert gave a lecture on the general change of the notion of contract, and came out in favour of the new view that regarded contract as an instrument of the 'people's' (*völkisch*) order.[50]

In 1968, Bernd Rüthers analysed the details of the legal change during the Third Reich. He demonstrated how German scholars were eager to 'work towards the Führer' by turning the existing German private law into an instrument of racist and anti-Semitic oppression.[51] Although there was never a comprehensive system of National Socialist legal theory, but rather a vast diversity of different approaches,[52] the new ideas were all centred on vague notions such as race, *Volk*, *Führer*, honour, or blood and soil. Authors such as Karl Larenz, Wolfgang Siebert, and Hans Dölle (who was to become Director of the Institute in the post-war era) advocated the transformation of the existing private law into an instrument of National Socialist ideology.[53]

Only a few scholars stuck to the ideal of classical comparative legal scholarship. Ernst von Caemmerer, who was among the German members of the delegation at the above-mentioned Hague Congress in 1937, was an example. His lecture on the role of the media still reveals the differences in quality when compared to the Nazi ideas in the same field of law as they were advocated by another member of the delegation, Alexander Elster, in his lecture on copyright law.[54] When Georg Dahm finally argued that the legal principle of *nullum crimen sine lege* in reality signified a renunciation of substantive justice, the German delegation revealed its complete isolation. Heymann reported that the Congress had been a success and that further participation of German scholars in international conferences would be useful— without being aware of the reality that Germany had lost her leading position in comparative law. Not being willing to collaborate, von Caemmerer was among the few who decided to leave the Institute. He refused to accept a chair at the University of Rostock during the Nazi period and only resumed his plans for an academic career with a *Habilitation* after World War II.[55]

During the late 1930s and the early 1940s the journal of the Institute and the Institute itself became more and more involved with the Nazi regime and its

---

[50] Wolfgang Siebert, 'Die allgemeine Entwicklung des Vertragsbegriffs', in Ernst Heymann (ed), *Deutsche Landsreferate zum II. Internationalen Kongress für Rechtsvergleichung im Haag 1937* (1937), 199–215.

[51] Bernd Rüthers, *Die unbegrenzte Auslegung: zum Wandel der Privatrechtsordnung im National-sozialismus* (1968).

[52] See Michael Stolleis, *Recht im Unrecht* (1994), 32.

[53] For Hans Dölle see eg 'Das deutsche bürgerliche Recht im nationalsozialistischen Staat', 1933 *Schmollers Jahrbuch* 649; *idem*, 'Vom alten zum neuen Schuldrecht', 1934 *Deutsche Juristen-Zeitung* 1017; *idem*, 'Die Neugestaltung des Deutschen Bürgerlichen Rechts', (1937) 4 *Zeitschrift der Akademie für Deutsches Recht* 359.

[54] See Kunze (n 15), 175.

[55] Albin Eser, 'Begrüssung zur Akademischen Gedenkfeier für Ernst von Caemmerer am 18. Februar 1987', (1987) 98 *Freiburger Universitätsblätter* 47, 48.

ideology. Legal opinions were furnished not only to the government, but also to the National Socialist Party, and more and more articles which welcomed the attempts to change German private law into a *völkische Ordnung* were published. The new approach was not comparative in method; it was largely an exercise in self-promotion, which aimed to show the rest of the world the superiority of the new ideology and its impact on the law. To this end, the German Rechtswahrerbund founded a new international association, the *Internationale Rechtskammer* in 1941; it was composed of members of the allied or occupied countries. Hans Frank, Imperial Minister without Portfolio, became chairman of the association. Frank had once attended Rabel's lectures in Munich; now he discredited traditional legal scholarship by speaking out against a formalistic and over-zealous approach to law.[56] Despite the preponderance of shallow literature which served only to glorify Nazi ideology, there were still a number of publications emanating from the Institute which can be regarded, even today, as good examples of comparative research. Among them is *Die Einwirkung des Krieges auf Verträge* by Gerhard Kegel, Hans Rupp, and Konrad Zweigert, published in 1941,[57] which, in addition to German law, encompassed also French, English, and US law in particular.

One of the consequences of Heymann's collaboration with the Nazi regime was that the Institute was classified as *kriegswichtig*, or important for the purposes of the war. This is why the Institute, with its precious library, was evacuated from Berlin to Tübingen at the initiative of Konrad Zweigert and Hans Rupp in 1944 and was thus saved from destruction when the old castle in Berlin was bombed later in the same year.

The Institute for Foreign Private Law and Private International Law's twin sister, the Institute of Public International Law, managed to preserve much more of its independence, even though it was supposed to furnish the legal basis for German expansionist foreign policy.[58] Although its director, Bruns, had become a member of the Nazi legal association, he opposed the new Nazi tendencies in the field of international law. Despite having initially welcomed the policy of conquest, in the course of time the Institute developed a climate of resistance towards a regime which showed disdain for international law in general, and international humanitarian law in particular. A group of scholars later supported the armed resistance of 1944, among them Berthold Graf Schenk von Stauffenberg and Helmuth James Graf Moltke.

[56] Hans Frank, 'Ansprache aus Anlass der Gründung der Internationalen Rechtskammer in Berlin vom 3. bis 5. April 1941', in Helmut Pfeiffer (ed), *Tagungsbericht der Internationalen Juristen-besprechung aus Anlass der Gründung der Internationalen Reichskammer* (1941), 103, 104.

[57] Gerhard Kegel, Hans Rupp, and Konrad Zweigert, *Die Einwirkung des Krieges auf Verträge* (1941).

[58] See Ingo Hueck, 'Die deutsche Völkerrechtswissenschaft im Nationalsozialismus', in Doris Kaufmann (ed), *Geschichte der Kaiser-Wilhelm-Gesellschaft im Nationalsozialismus* (vol II, 2000), 490.

3. Continuity

German legal scholarship and, with it, comparative law, remained devastated during the years immediately after World War II. The interruption was, however, brief, for very soon many academics who had been proponents of the new German legal culture were allowed to return to their chairs at German law faculties. This continuity is also to be seen in the history of the Kaiser-Wilhelm Institute. Heymann remained the director of the Institute until his death in 1946, when he was succeeded by Hans Dölle.

In 1949, the Institute was formally dissolved and re-established under the auspices of the *Max-Planck-Gesellschaft* (the successor of the *Kaiser-Wilhelm-Gesellschaft*) as the *Max-Planck-Instiut für ausländisches und internationales Privatrecht.* While the Institute was to flourish, the personal fate of its founder, Ernst Rabel, was much less fortunate.[59] In 1946 Dölle invited Rabel to join the Tübingen Institute. Rabel was indeed eager to come back to Germany, since he felt out of place in the United States. However, his return proved to be very difficult, not only for organizational reasons, but also because of a considerable reluctance on the part of the German scholarly community to welcome him among them. This in turn was largely due to the contemporary tendency to repress the shameful past and one's own personal and scholarly contribution to it. Still, Rabel was able to continue his work in the Tübingen Institute. In 1951 he finished the second volume of the law concerning the sale of goods, which he was able to present as a manuscript at the Hague Conference that had gathered to discuss the uniform law of international sales. The work was not published, however, until 1956, one year after his death.

The difficulties encountered by non-Nazi comparatists in post-war German law faculties can also be illustrated by Ernst von Caemmerer, whose comparative contributions were to have considerable influence on the development of German law. Von Caemmerer did not pass his *Habilitation* until after the war at the University of Frankfurt-on-Main under the supervision of Walter Hallstein. When the law faculty of Freiburg im Breisgau had to appoint a person for the chair for private law, commercial law, and conflicts of law, it first attempted to nominate scholars who were considered to be more senior, even if they had been been involved with Nazi ideology. It was only the military government which reversed the nomination lists and appointed Ernst von Caemmerer—against the will of the faculty.[60]

For a long time in post-war Germany the Nazi period tended to be hidden behind the phrase the 'dark years'; the cultural and academic elites attempted to live as though those twelve years had never happened.[61] Compensation often

---

[59] Kunze (n 15), 230 ff.   [60] Eser (1987) 98 *Freiburger Universitätsblatter* 49.

[61] Michael Stolleis, *Reluctance to Glance in the Mirror: The Changing Face of German Jurisprudence after 1933 and post-1945* (The Maurice and Muriel Fulton Lecture Series of the Law School, University of Chicago, 2001).

remained at a symbolic level. Thus, in 1950, Rabel was made an honorary member of the newly founded Society of Comparative Law, and the *Zeitschrift für Internationales und ausländisches Privatrecht* was renamed *Rabels Zeitschrift* with effect from 1960.

V. RECOVERY (1950–1989)

1. General Aspects and Institutionalization

The revitalization of comparative law on an international level began in the late 1940s. In 1949, UNESCO gathered an organizing committee in Paris that was to establish an international association for comparative law; the committee consisted of eighteen leading scholars, among them Ernst Rabel. It set itself the task of 'organizing research, legal literature, and teaching in the field of comparative law as a means towards international understanding and peace':[62] a universalistic aim just as ambitious as the one announced at the Paris World Conference almost fifty years before. One of the suggestions was to establish national committees as the basis for the international association. In Germany Hans Dölle, Walter Hallstein, and Eduard Wahl were charged with the preparations. Finally, in 1950, the *Gesellschaft für Rechtsvergleichung* was established. It held its first conference in Tübingen and was presided over by Dölle. The association regarded itself as the direct successor of the *Vereinigung für vergleichende Rechtswissenschaft und Volkswirtschaftslehre*, which had ceased to exist in 1933.[63] In 1950, a German delegation was sent to the IIIrd International Congress of Comparative Law in London, and an impressive volume brought together the German contributions delivered at this conference.[64] However, the association did not intend to become an independent research institution; its aim was limited to supporting and initiating projects.[65] From its very beginnings, the association was divided into a number of sections according to the main branches of the law; thus, there were sections on comparative private law, comparative public law, comparative criminal law, comparative commercial law, foundational research, and even for comparative legal history and ethnological research. From time to time, new sections were added, such as those on intellectual property law and labour and social security law.

---

[62] See Wadle (n 10), 77.   [63] Ibid 73.

[64] Ernst Wolff (ed), *Deutsche Landesreferate zum III. Internationalen Kongress für Rechtsvergleichung in London 1950* (1950).

[65] Wadle (n 10), 79.

The importance of research in comparative law at the universities began to increase in the aftermath of World War II. Institutes that had their origins in the time before Hitler's seizure of power, such as those in Munich, Heidelberg, and Frankfurt, were eager to re-establish the tradition. New institutes were also created, among them the *Institut für ausländisches und internationales Privatrecht* at the University of Freiburg. However, the most important projects of comparative law remained linked to the *Max-Planck-Institut für ausländisches und internationales Privatrecht*, which moved to Hamburg in 1956. The Institute for Comparative Public Law and Public International Law had been re-established under the auspices of the *Max-Planck-Gesellschaft* in Heidelberg.

Later, other Max Planck Institutes (MPI) were founded, partly as successors of earlier university institutes: the MPI for European Legal History in Frankfurt-on-Main (1964), the MPI for Foreign and International Criminal Law in Freiburg (1966), and the MPI for Foreign and International Social Law in Munich (1980). Another important institution was the *Deutscher Rat für Internationales Privatrecht* (German Council for Private International Law), which was established in 1954 on Dölle's initiative. It is composed of two commissions and serves as an advisory body to the German government in the preparation of important statutes or conventions with an international element. It played a crucial role in the elaboration of the UN Convention on Contracts for the International Sale of Goods (CISG) in the 1970s.

In the German Democratic Republic, the *Institut für ausländisches Recht und Rechtsvergleichung* was established in 1967 at the *Akademie für Staats- und Rechtswissenschaft der DDR* (Academy for Political and Legal Science of the German Democratic Republic) in Potsdam-Babelsberg.[66] It was to furnish legal opinions to the Ministry of Justice concerning the unification of law between the socialist countries. Studies focusing on the comparison between socialist and capitalist legal systems were done either to stress the superiority of the socialist law, or to prepare or interpret internationally uniform law such as the CISG.

The institutionalization of comparative law in Austria and Switzerland did not begin until the late 1950s. Hans Köhler was the editor of the *Österreichische Hefte für die Praxis des internationalen und ausländischen Rechts*, which was published from 1956 to 1960. In 1960, an Association for Comparative Law was founded, followed by an Institute for Comparative Law at the University of Vienna. From 1960 onwards, the Institute and the Association edited the journal *Zeitschrift für Rechtsvergleichung*, which became the *Zeitschrift für Rechtsvergleichung, internationales Privatrecht und Europarecht* in 1991. Even today, no university institute of comparative law exists in Switzerland. However, there is the Swiss Institute of

---

[66] On the role of comparative law in that academy, see Akademie für Staats- und Rechtswissenschaft der DDR (ed), *Die Rolle der Rechtsvergleichung in der Rechtswissenschaft, Rechtsausbildung und Rechtspraxis der DDR sowie in der ideologischen Auseinandersetzung* (1982).

Comparative Law in Lausanne, which was founded in 1982 as an independent entity of the Swiss administration. It prepares legal opinions on behalf of individuals and governmental agencies and has an impressive library on foreign and comparative law. The only journal that addresses comparative issues at all, although not as its main focus, is the *Schweizerische Zeitschrift für internationales und europäisches Recht*, which commenced publication in 1991.

2. Methods and Fields of Interest

(a) Methodological Foundations

In the 1950s, there was a general consensus that the functional method should be the basis of comparative research. Konrad Zweigert's famous inaugural lecture in 1949 on the subject of comparative law as a universal method of interpretation[67] laid down the principles that were to rule comparative law for the years to come. Zweigert's call to use comparative law for the purposes of interpreting existing law was firmly based on the functional method. However, he deviated slightly from Rabel's approach by focusing on the need for a critical evaluation which searched for the best, rather than the prevailing, solution. Moreover, and somewhat over-optimistically, he suggested that not only law makers, but also courts, should bring comparative reflections to bear in their everyday work.

During the 1950s and the 1960s, the functional method was enriched by embracing sociological considerations. This can be traced mainly to Josef Esser who, in his great work *Grundsatz und Norm in der richterlichen Fortbildung des Privatrechts* (1956), familiarized not only comparative lawyers in Germany but also German legal scholarship at large with the intricacies of American legal realism and sociological jurisprudence concerning judicial law making and law finding. On Zweigert's initiative, a group for socio-legal research was established at the Hamburg Max-Planck Institute in the 1970s, but its success was limited and the group was soon to be dissolved. Although some texts did include consideration of the sociological aspects of their topics, this was usually only at a superficial level and was more a result of pandering to modern trends than of a desire for truly interdisciplinary research.[68]

Although the theory of families of legal systems never attained as much importance in Germany as it did in France,[69] German comparatists did attempt to identify

---

[67] Konrad Zweigert, 'Rechtsvergleichung als universale Interpretationsmethode', (1949/50) 15 *Zeitschrift für ausländisches und internationales Privatrecht* 5.

[68] Michael Martinek, 'Wissenschaftsgeschichte der Rechtsvergleichung und des internationalen Privatrechts in der BRD', in Dieter Simon (ed), *Rechtswissenschaft in der Bonner Republik: Studien zur Wissenschaftsgeschichte der Jurisprudenz* (1994), 529, 552.

[69] René David, *Les grands systèmes de droits contemporains* (1964).

characteristic features of legal systems, or groups of legal systems, in order to distinguish them from each other. In 1961, Zweigert transferred the notion of 'style', as it was used in literature and in the fine arts, to the description of legal systems and he identified historical background and development, predominant modes of legal thought, especially distinctive institutions, the kind of legal sources and the ways of handling them, and the prevailing ideology as important factors for determining the 'style' of a legal system.[70] Looking back, this endeavour seems rather arbitrary and unfruitful. Thus, in the first edition of Zweigert and Kötz's *Introduction to Comparative Law*, published in 1971,[71] the style of the French legal family was characterized by the position of illegitimate children and by the famous provision of Art 340 *Code civil* (which was at that date still in force): '*La recherche de la paternité est interdite*'.[72] Shortly thereafter, however, the French legislature abandoned this rule. This incident probably contributed to Zweigert and Kötz's abandoning the attempt to define typical stylistic factors for legal systems in the second edition of their work in 1984, although the concept, as such, was retained.[73]

It was generally understood that comparison presupposed comparability. Thus, even in 1949, Zweigert stressed the boundaries of comparative law, both concerning the areas of the law which could be subjected to the comparative method and the countries whose laws might be considered. Comparative studies were taken to be fruitful only for those areas that were not of a specifically national character. Family law or the law of succession thus remained largely excluded. Moreover comparison was limited to those legal systems 'that were more or less on the same cultural level as one's own'.[74] This excluded the so-called primitive laws, religious laws, and also the laws of the socialist legal systems.

(b) Fields of Interest

During the 1950s, the main focus was on the law of obligations, with an ongoing special interest in the law of sales. Whereas the fields of interest were soon expanded, the reluctance to consider socialist legal systems was to persist. The reason for this was said to be the different function attributed to law in socialist systems. This approach received institutional support. Whereas the German Association of Comparative Law did not have any problem establishing a section on European Law in 1962, a proposal to set up another section dealing with socialist legal systems was rejected.[75] However, institutes with a special focus on 'eastern

---

[70] Konrad Zweigert, 'Zur Lehre von den Rechtskreisen', in *20th Century Comparative and Conflicts Law: Legal Essays in Honor of Hessel E. Yntema* (1961), 42.

[71] Konrad Zweigert and Hein Kötz, *Einführung in die Rechtsvergleichung auf dem Gebiete des Privatrechts* (vol I: *Grundlagen*, 1st edn, 1971, vol II: *Institutionen*, 1st edn, 1969).

[72] Ibid, § 10.

[73] Konrad Zweigert and Hein Kötz, *Einführung in die Rechtsvergleichung* (2nd edn, 2 vols, 1984).

[74] Zweigert, (1949/50) 15 *Zeitschrift für ausländisches und internationales Privatrecht* 13.

[75] Wadle (n 10), 84.

law' (*Ostrecht*) were established at universities; the subject-matter thus became a specialized field of study which remained outside the general comparative discourse.[76] From 1968, the Institute for Eastern Law of the *Freie Universität Berlin* furnished a basis for research by editing the legal sources of socialist countries.[77]

A certain shift of focus concerning the legal systems studied by comparative lawyers can be observed during the 1950s. Much work after World War I had been centred on Anglo-American law.[78] This interest continued after World War II; it was even fuelled by the influence of eminent German comparatist scholars who had predominantly emigrated to the United States and to England.[79] Nevertheless, for a number of reasons, a special interest in French law became apparent by the middle of the 1950s. One reason for this was that the Saar area did not become a *Land* of the Federal Republic of Germany until 1957, after a period of formal autonomy, during which it had maintained strong economic and administrative links with France. Thus, it was only natural that at the new University of Saarbrücken, founded in 1948 in cooperation with France, comparison with French law was nurtured from the very beginning, the main advocate being Léontin-Jean Constantinesco. Consideration of French law was also forcefully promoted by Murad Ferid, who was the director of the Institute for Comparative Law at the University of Munich. A further, and probably the most important, reason was that the European countries began to come closer to each other, particularly after the formation of the European Economic Community (EEC) in 1957 with Belgium, the Netherlands, Luxembourg, France, Italy, and the German Federal Republic as its founding members. The influence of France, and of the countries influenced by French law and culture, was very significant in the EEC.

Until the 1990s, comparative law in Austria and Switzerland focused primarily on German law. This is due partly to the similarity of language and partly to the fact that a number of German scholars occupied chairs at law faculties in Austria and Switzerland. The reception of German ideas was not always a happy experience, since it occurred without much consideration of their background.[80] Two examples will demonstrate this. In its Code of Obligations, the Swiss law of delict is based on a so-called general provision, much inspired by Art 1382 of the French *Code civil*. However, when interpreting the provision of Art 41 OR, legal scholars and courts did not consider the legal developments in France since 1804, but heavily relied on the German *Bürgerliches Gesetzbuch* with its § 823 I, where delictual liability is

---

[76] Martinek (n 68), 563.

[77] Osteuropa-Institut an der Freien Universität Berlin (ed), *Quellen zur Rechtsvergleichung* (1968 ff).

[78] See, as one outstanding example, Fritz Kessler, *Die Fahrlässigkeit im nordamerikanischen Deliktsrecht: unter vergleichender Berücksichtigung des deutschen und des englischen Rechts* (1932).

[79] See Lutter *et al* (n 43); Beatson and Zimmermann (n 36).

[80] Ingeborg Schwenzer, 'Rezeption deutschen Rechtsdenkens im schweizerischen Obligationenrecht', in *eadem* (ed), *Schuldrecht, Rechtsvergleichung und Rechtsvereinheitlichung an der Schwelle zum 21. Jahrhundert* (1998), 59.

based on the infringement of one of the specific rights and interests listed in this provision. This rather narrow list was adopted by Swiss legal scholars and courts in defining the requirement of unlawfulness in Art 41 I OR, thus effectively abandoning the very notion of a general provision and its Natural law heritage. Another, more recent, example is the Swiss reception of the notion of *faktisches Vertrags-verhältnis*, that is, the idea that contracts are not always based on the intention of the contracting parties, but can also come into existence as a result of mere facts and behaviour. Very much in line with the anti-liberal thought patterns prevailing during the Nazi regime, this concept had been developed by Günter Haupt in his Leipzig inaugural lecture in 1941[81] and was later, for some time, also espoused by Karl Larenz (though by few other German authors).[82] Swiss literature, however, welcomed this principle, and in 1984 it even found its way into decisions of the Swiss Federal Tribunal.[83] This was at a time when the principle had been abandoned in Germany, even by Larenz.[84]

3. Comparative Law Scholarship in the Post-War Era: Some Highlights

In the post-war years, comparative law seemed to flourish. Even in many doctoral dissertations reference to other legal systems could be found. More often than not, however, a truly comparative approach was lacking; instead, we merely find reports on foreign laws. Nevertheless, throughout this period, prominent comparative work was published, considerably influencing legal developments in Germany.

(a) Comparative Law in General

It must be mentioned at the outset that the late Konrad Zweigert and Ulrich Drobnig, who was to become one of his successors as Director of the Max Planck Institute in Hamburg, set up the International Encyclopedia of Comparative Law, a truly universal endeavour covering all areas of private law in seventeen volumes. The first fascicles were published in 1972; to date, the work is still in progress.

The most prominent contribution to comparative law, which is unequalled anywhere else in the world, is the introduction to comparative law by Konrad Zweigert and Hein Kötz, first published in 1969.[85] In 1977, Tony Weir's English translation

---

[81] Günter Haupt, 'Über faktische Vertragsverhältnisse', in *Festschrift der Leipziger Juristenfakultät für Heinrich Siber* (vol II, 1943), 1.

[82] Karl Larenz, 'Die Begründung von Schuldverhältnissen durch Sozialtypisches Verhalten', [1956] *Neue Juristische Wochenschrift* 1897.

[83] BGE 110 II 244.

[84] Karl Larenz, *Allgemeiner Teil des deutschen Bürgerlichen Rechts: Ein Lehrbuch* (7th edn, 1989), § 28 II.

[85] See n 71.

appeared, as a result of which the book also became a classic of comparative legal literature in the Anglo-American legal world. Another major scholarly contribution is the three-volume study by Léontin-Jean Constantinesco.[86]

Great services to the understanding of French law in Germany were rendered by Murad Ferid and later Hans Jürgen Sonnenberger, with their comprehensive work on French Private Law,[87] the characteristic feature of which is its presentation of the French law according to the system of the German Civil Code.

(b) Law of Sales

The law of sales continued to be a matter of primary interest to German scholars in the aftermath of World War II, when the idea of the unification of international sales law was resumed. The discussions at the Hague Conference concerning the Uniform Law on the International Sale of Goods and the Uniform Law on the Formation of Contracts for the International Sale of Goods were closely followed by German comparatists, among whom Ernst von Caemmerer occupied a leading position.[88] Hans Dölle was the first to edit a commentary on the Uniform Law on the International Sale of Goods in 1976.[89] Although the Hague Conventions were not a success—they were implemented by only nine states—they served as a model for the work of the United Nations Commission on International Trade Law (UNCITRAL) concerning the United Nations Convention on Contracts for the International Sale of Goods (CISG), which was eventually adopted in Vienna in 1980.

The preparatory work of UNCITRAL in Germany was followed, and commented upon, by the Commission on the Law of Obligations of the German Council for Private International Law, chaired by Ernst von Caemmerer. His successor to the chair of the Institute of Foreign and Comparative Law at the University of Freiburg, Peter Schlechtriem, was a member of the German delegation to the Vienna Conference in 1980. He published a monograph on the CISG as early as 1981,[90] which was soon to be translated into English and later editions of which have now been translated into many other languages. In the 1990s, Schlechtriem started editing a commentary on the CISG that was to become one of the main authorities in this field.

---

[86] Léontin-Jean Constantinesco, *Rechtsvergleichung* (3 vols, 1971–83).

[87] Murad Ferid, *Das französische Zivilrecht* (2 vols, 1971); Murad Ferid and Hans Jürgen Sonnenberger, *Das französische Zivilrecht* (2nd edn, 1986).

[88] See Ernst von Caemmerer, 'Internationales Kaufrecht', in *idem*, *Gesammelte Schriften* (vol I, 1968), 79; Ernst von Caemmerer, 'Die Haager Konferenz über die internationale Vereinheitlichung des Kaufrechts vom 2–25. April 1964', in ibid 97.

[89] Hans Dölle (ed), *Kommentar zum einheitlichen Kaufrecht: die Haager Kaufrechtsübereinkommen vom 1. Juli 1964* (1976).

[90] Peter Schlechtriem, *Einheitliches UN-Kaufrecht* (1981).

(c) Tort Law

The intricacies of German tort law, which is strongly rooted in the nineteenth century, were at least partly brought to light by von Caemmerer's comparative studies in tort law, especially his masterpiece, *Wandlungen des Deliktsrechts*,[91] where an intellectual link was established to negligence liability in the common law. Furthermore, von Caemmerer conducted fundamental research in the field of causation. Building upon Rabel's ideas, he introduced the central notion of *Schutzzweck* (protective ambit) into German law, using it as a means to limit liability in the same way as Anglo-American law specifies the scope of a duty of care.

The development of products liability was firmly based upon comparative research. After quite a number of studies on products liability had already been published, some of which supported the French regime of contractual liability, it was Werner Lorenz who provided the decisive impulse for the German development. His general report on the liability of producers of goods[92] at the 1965 Conference for Comparative Law in Kiel relied heavily on the American solution, which was based on (strict) extra-contractual liability. Three years later, in 1968, the German Supreme Court followed this approach by making available a delictual claim and approximating it to strict liability by shifting the burden of proof for negligent misconduct to the producer. The concept of *Verkehrspflichten*, which comes close to the duty of care, was also strongly influenced by Anglo-American legal thinking.[93]

(d) Law of Restitution

Again, it was von Caemmerer who revolutionized the law of restitution. He declared all attempts to find a comprehensive formula to cover unjust enrichment claims to be unfruitful. Instead, he stressed the fundamental difference between the *Leistungskondiktion*, or claim for the restitution of a benefit conferred by the plaintiff's own act, and the *Eingriffskondiktion*, a claim based on an interference with the rights of another person.[94] Von Caemmerer's former assistant, Detlef König, subsequently elaborated the comparative foundations for a new system of restitutionary claims[95] that was to culminate in the monumental two volume study

---

[91] Ernst von Caemmerer, 'Wandlungen des Deliktsrechts', in *idem, Gesammelte Schriften* (n 88), 452.

[92] Werner Lorenz, *Die Haftung des Warenherstellers* (1966).

[93] See the impressive monograph by Christian von Bar, *Verkehrspflichten: Richterliche Gefahrs-teuerungsgebote im deutschen Deliktsrecht* (1980). Another important comparative work is Hans Stoll, *Das Handeln auf eigene Gefahr* (1961).

[94] Ernst von Caemmerer, 'Bereicherung und unerlaubte Handlung' in *idem, Gesammelte Schriften* (n 88), 209.

[95] Published only posthumously; Detlef König, *Ungerechtfertigte Bereicherung: Tatbestände und Ordnungsprobleme in rechtsvergleichender Sicht* (1985).

on restitution by Peter Schlechtriem (another of von Caemmerer's pupils) in 2000–01.[96] These ideas were adopted by several Swiss authors in the 1980s.[97]

(e) Family Law and the Law of Succession

Comparative studies in family law first dealt with the problems concerning equal rights for women, which had to be addressed as a result of the equality clause in the Basic Law (*Grundgesetz*) of 1949. Soon thereafter, comprehensive studies on family law emanated from the Hamburg Max Planck Institute, such as Dölle's two volumes on family law in 1964 or Paul Heinrich Neuhaus's study on marriage and the law of children.[98] One of the great, early comparatists in family law was Wolfram Müller-Freienfels, who not only incorporated Anglo-American law into his research, but also Japanese law. He even took account of revolutionary family law legislation, such as Chinese or Russian law.[99]

Comparative research depends upon the availability of foreign legal sources. Two comprehensive projects have to be mentioned here, one by Ferid and Firsching on the international law of succession, the other by Bergmann and Ferid on the international law of marriage and children. Both are compilations of the translated and annotated statutory provisions in the respective fields from all over the world.[100]

(f) Conflict of Laws

One would expect the field of conflict of laws to be especially open to comparative legal research, in view of its international character.[101] However, in post-war Germany the approach to conflict of laws was still firmly based on Savigny's conceptual ideas. Substantive policy considerations, except for the *ordre public* reservation, were not taken into account. This restrictive approach was only rarely challenged among German legal scholars. It was not until 1971 that the German Constitutional Supreme Court, in what was to become one of its most important leading cases, decided that the provisions of German private international law, as well as the applicable foreign law, have to be measured in conformity with the value

---

[96] Peter Schlechtriem, *Restitution und Bereicherungsausgleich in Europa* (2 vols, 2000–01).

[97] See the references provided in Schwenzer (n 80), 74.

[98] Hans Dölle, *Familienrecht* (2 vols, 1964–65); Paul Heinrich Neuhaus, *Ehe und Kindschaft in rechtsvergleichender Sicht* (1979).

[99] Wolfram Müller-Freienfels, *Ehe und Recht* (1962); idem, 'Zur revolutionären Familiengesetzgebung, insbesondere zum Ehegesetz der Volksrepublik China', in *Ius privatum gentium: Festschrift für Max Rheinstein zum 70. Geburtstag* (1969), 843; idem, *Familienrecht im In- und Ausland, Aufsätze* (3 vols, 1978–94).

[100] Murad Ferid and Karl Firsching (eds), *Internationales Erbrecht: Quellensammlung mit systematischen Darstellungen des materiellen Erbrechts sowie des Kollisionsrechts der wichtigsten Staaten* (1955 ff); Murad Ferid and Alexander Bergmann, *Internationales Ehe- und Kindschaftsrecht: mit Staatsangehörigkeitsrecht* (1952 ff).

[101] For what follows see Martinek (n 68), 581.

system laid down in the *Grundgesetz*.[102] Although the creative US-American 'conflicts revolution', with its governmental interest analysis (Currie), lex-fori-approach (Ehrenzweig), or better-law approach (Cavers, Leflar, Juenger), did not go totally unnoticed, the conservative approach in Germany prevailed. The so-called political school of conflicts analysis, which mostly relied on modern thinking from the United States and is linked to the names of Rudolf Wiethölter and Christian Joerges, has been isolated by the prevailing traditionalists and their representatives, such as Eric Jayme, Gerhard Kegel, Paul Heinrich Neuhaus, Egon Lorenz, or Klaus Schurig.

4. Comparative Law in Legislation and Courts

'Legislative comparative law' has been described as one of the oldest, as well as most fundamental, purposes of comparative legal scholarship.[103] However, Rabel's uneasiness with legislative comparative law, which he tended to regard as methodologically suspicious, has not lost its relevance today. Consequently, although foreign laws are usually considered in the preparation of major law reform projects, more often than not a truly comparative approach is lacking, and only a very restricted selection of legal systems is taken into account. Political reasons, such as the systematic ignorance of the law of the socialist countries, were part of the cause, but there were also more practical problems, such as those arising from a failure to understand foreign languages. Thus, in 1981, Ferid accused the German legislature of not having taken account of French law in the family law reform projects of 1969 and 1976, and of ignoring French and Italian solutions when drafting the Act on Standard Terms of Business in 1976.[104]

But even in Switzerland, with its linguistic diversity, the comparative consideration of foreign legal systems outside the 'Germanic legal family' cannot be taken for granted. Very often, German solutions are simply adopted into Swiss law. Thus, although the preparatory works for the Swiss family law reform in 1995 demonstrated considerable interest in the broader European legal development,[105] some of the articles eventually adopted are a mere reproduction of German law. Thus, for example, Art 125 III ZGB on the exclusion of maintenance claims between divorced spouses has its direct counterpart in § 1579 BGB. Even more significantly, the elaboration of a Swiss Federal Code of Civil Procedure, which is under way at the moment, is based upon a comparison of the statutory provisions

---

[102] BVerfGE 31, 58 = [1971] *Neue Juristische Wochenschrift* 1509.
[103] See Helmut Coing, *Europäische Privatrecht*, vol II: *19. Jahrhundert* (1989), 56 et seq.
[104] Murad Ferid, 'Die derzeitige Lage von Rechtsvergleichung und IPR in der Bundesrepublik Deutschland', (1981) 22 *Zeitschrift für Rechtsvergleichung* 86, 87 ff.
[105] Bundesblatt der Schweizerischen Eidgenossenschaft 1996 I 1.

of the twenty-six Swiss cantons, whereas foreign laws are almost completely disregarded.

The use of comparative law by courts was one of the subjects of the XIVth International Congress of Comparative Law in Athens. Using as a starting-point Zweigert's famous assertion in 1949, that comparative law was to be regarded as a universal method of interpretation, most contributors to the Congress had to acknowledge that comparative law is usually no more than an additional argument for supporting a decision that has already been arrived at on other grounds. It has been suggested that one should classify court decisions which rely upon comparative law according to the motivation behind the courts' use of foreign law (which can be necessary or voluntary), and that one should additionally distinguish its use in cases involving rules with an international element from those which are of purely domestic character.[106] Rules with an international element seem particularly suitable for a comparative approach to interpretation. This proposition has, on a general level, even received support from the German Federal Supreme Court. It has held that rules of internationally uniform law cannot be interpreted as one would any other rule of national law, but rather must be approached with the aim of guaranteeing a uniform interpretation in all contracting states.[107] However, the practical consequences of this assertion are less visible. Very often, provisions of international origin are implemented into German law as if they were genuinely indigenous German law, passed by the German legislature. The result is that those who have to apply the law, especially the courts, tend to forget that a provision is part of an international convention, and so do not pay attention to its comparative origins. As a result, these 'international' provisions are interpreted from a merely national point of view which, in turn, leads to a 'renationalization' of international law. This is especially true for the implementation of many Hague Conventions in the field of conflict of laws.

It has already been noted above that German law dominates in Swiss legal scholarship. The consequences can be observed by analysing not only Swiss legislation but also the decisions of the Swiss Federal Supreme Court. A comprehensive study has revealed that—even if, compared to other Supreme Courts in Europe, the Federal Supreme Court displays a relatively friendly attitude towards foreign legal systems—90 per cent of all references to foreign law were to German law.[108] Furthermore, in most cases comparative arguments do not play a decisive role in the process of decision-making.

---

[106] Ulrich Drobnig, 'General Report', in Ulrich Drobnig and Sief van Erp (eds), *The Use of Comparative Law by Courts* (1999), 3, 6.

[107] See Ulrich Drobnig, 'National Report Germany', in Drobnig and van Erp (n 106), 127, 132.

[108] Alexandra Gerber, 'Der Einfluss des ausländischen Rechts in der Rechtsprechung des Bundesgerichts', in *Perméabilité des ordres juridiques: Rapports présentés à l'occasion du colloque-anniversaire de l'Institut suisse de droit comparé* (1992), 141, 143.

VI. LEGAL HARMONIZATION AND NEW APPROACHES TO COMPARATIVE LAW

The end of the cold war in 1989 may be seen as the beginning of a new chapter in the development of comparative law.

1. Development of the German Bürgerliches Gesetzbuch

There were a number of legal scholars who hoped that the reunification of the two German states in 1990 might trigger an increased interest in comparison. Especially in the field of family law, it was expected that the solutions adopted in the German Democratic Republic's Family Code of 1965 would be taken into account. Though partly influenced by socialist legal thinking, many of its provisions reflected a modern approach that had also manifested itself in a number of other Western legal systems, for example in the law concerning children in France or the Scandinavian countries. However, these hopes were dashed by the Unification Treaty of 1990, which introduced the provisions of the BGB as it was still in force in the German Federal Republic, with only a few reservations.[109] Thus, the distinction between marital and non-marital children, which had been abolished in 1965 in the German Democratic Republic, was reintroduced into the so-called new German *Länder*. It was not until 1998 that the entire law relating to children was comprehensively revised, based mainly upon the deliberations of the *Deutscher Juristentag* in 1992, with its thorough comparative report.[110]

In the late 1970s, the German government had started the process of a fundamental revision of the German law of obligations. As a first step, leading German scholars were asked to prepare comparative reports which were to serve as a basis for the reform.[111] In 1984, a Reform Commission was established to prepare a draft. As a result of the influence of two eminent comparatists who were members of the commission, Hein Kötz and Peter Schlechtriem, the final report of 1992[112] represented modern comparative legal thinking. In the fields of breach of contract and

---

[109] Art 230 I EGBGB and Art 235 § 1 II EGBGB. See Dieter Schwab (ed), *Familienrecht und deutsche Einigung: Dokumente und Erläuterungen* (1991).

[110] Ingeborg Schwenzer, *Empfiehlt es sich, das Kindschaftsrecht neu zu regeln? Gutachten A zum 59. Deutschen Juristentag* (1992).

[111] Bundesministerium der Justiz (ed), *Gutachten und Vorschläge zur Überarbeitung des Schuldrechts* (3 vols, 1981–83). Later, a further comparative report concerning the development of the law of sales was given on behalf of the Hamburg Max Planck Institute: Jürgen Basedow, *Die Reform des deutschen Kaufrechts* (1988).

[112] Bundesministerium der Justiz (ed), *Abschlussbericht der Kommission zur Überarbeitung des Schuldrechts* (1992).

the law of sales, the draft mostly reflected the solutions found in the CISG. The draft was favourably received by the sixtieth *Deutscher Juristentag* in 1994. However, apart from that, there was no broadly based discussion of the draft, which appeared to be consigned, increasingly, to oblivion. It was only the enactment of the EC Consumer Sales Directive and the need for its implementation by 1 January 2002 that revitalized the idea of a fundamental revision of the law of obligations. However, the so-called Discussion Draft published by the German government in September 2000 was heavily criticized by German traditionalists, who were still inspired by nineteenth-century pandectist legal thinking. The Ministry of Justice, therefore, charged another commission, whose members were not comparatists, with the task of revising the Discussion Draft. This led to modifications diluting the international and comparative approach, and reintroducing peculiarly pandectist thinking into the final draft which came into force in 2002.

2. The Interpretation of Uniform Law

The tendency to interpret internationally uniform legal instruments against a national legal background has already been mentioned. This was also true, initially, for one of the most successful uniform laws so far: the international sales convention (CISG). Thus, for example, German courts at first interpreted the CISG provisions requiring the buyer to give notice in case of a delivery of non-conforming goods in precisely the same way as the corresponding provisions in the German Commercial Code. The courts thus simply ignored the fact that other national sales laws do not recognize a notice requirement at all, and that courts from these countries would never adopt an approach as rigorous as that favoured by the German courts, who apply time limits of less than one week. Modern commentaries on the CISG, on the contrary, follow a truly comparative approach. They not only consider the differences in national sales laws that influenced the drafting of the convention, but also closely observe and register the application and interpretation of the convention by foreign courts and scholars all over the world.[113] Slowly, this approach is also influencing the judiciary.

3. Europeanization

Over the past fifteen years, EC Directives have had an ever-growing impact on core areas of private law. These Directives have to be implemented by the various

[113] See the leading commentary by Peter Schlechtriem and Ingeborg Schwenzer, *Commentary on the UN Convention of the International Sale of Goods (CISG)* (2nd edn, 2005). This approach is supported by the operation of a database that gathers all relevant court decisions; see <www.cisg-online.ch>.

national legislatures in the EU member states. However, it is commonly under-stood that national judges should take account of the judicial and academic interpretation of the harmonized provisions in the other member states, although this ideal is hard to realize in the real world of national courts. Still, uniform interpretation is facilitated by the existence of the European Court of Justice and the European Court of First Instance.

Switzerland, despite not being a member of the EU, has enacted several statutes which automatically follow the relevant EC Directives, and thus also pursue the aim of European legal harmonization. In many cases, however, the European origin of these statutes is not obvious. This is one of the reasons why no consideration is usually given to the judicial development of these matters in the EU member states or by the European Court of Justice.

In spite of the growing number of Community Directives, they are nothing more than 'islands' in 'the great ocean of international private law', as the Euro-pean Parliament has described the situation.[114] Outside those 'safe harbours', economic players 'risk running aground on shallows consisting of either unresolved conflicts of individual private law regulations or the absence of coordination between European law and international private law'. What is still lacking to this very day is a general contract law, or general rules for the law of obligations. The call for unification, or at least harmonization, in this field is constantly growing. International unification has always been one of the aims of comparative law, and so it is not surprising that the 1990s saw scholars in this field eagerly taking up the challenge of Europeanization of private law. Two different movements may be distinguished, both of them emanating from Germany:[115] the one may be called the classical comparative approach, the other the *ius commune* approach.

(a) The Classical Comparative Approach

During the last decade, comprehensive research has revealed a 'common European core' of national solutions in many areas within the law of obligations. It is charac-teristic of these studies that they no longer consist of country reports; instead, they focus on the functional treatment of practical issues. In 1996, Hein Kötz published the first volume of *Europäisches Vertragsrecht*,[116] which deals with the formation, validity, and content of contracts, as well as the participation of third parties in contractual relationships (agency, contracts for the benefit of third

---

[114] European Parliament, *Report on the Approximation of the Civil and Commercial Law of the Member States* of 6 Nov 2001 (A5–0384/2001).

[115] For details, see Chapter 16 in this *Handbook*.

[116] Hein Kötz, *Europäisches Vertragsrecht* (1996) (English translation under the title *European Contract Law* by Tony Weir, 1997).

parties, and assignment). In his two-volume work, *Gemeineuropäisches Delikt-srecht*,[117] Christian von Bar, in 1996 and 1999, set out the common core of European tort law. Similarly, in his work entitled *Restitution und Bereicherungsausgleich in Europa*,[118] Peter Schlechtriem elaborated the comparative basis for projects of harmonization and unification in the field of restitution and unjustified enrichment.

(b) *The* Ius Commune *Approach*

In 1947, in the aftermath of World War II, Heinrich Mitteis called for legal history to focus not on the specificities of national legal development, but on the *ius commune* in order to devise a 'pan-European legal history on a comparative basis'.[119] The idea of a European *ius commune* has gained new ground as a result of important research which stresses the similarities between the common law and civil law, closely linked to the name of Reinhard Zimmermann, who is one of the current directors of the Max Planck Institute in Hamburg. In 1990, he initiated the discussion with his work on the Law of Obligations, which adopts both a historical and a comparative approach.[120] The proximity of legal history and comparative law has long been accepted by comparative scholars. It may be recalled in this context that Ernst Rabel himself was originally a legal historian who never neglected to trace the historical origins of legal rules. Leading comparatists have often referred to legal history as 'vertical comparative law'. Among legal historians, however, this approach is strongly challenged by scholars who argue that legal history constitutes an integral part of historical scholarship. For them, it cannot be the aim of legal history to scrutinize the development of legal systems in order to gain a better understanding of the modern law. Legal history, in other words, should not serve as an instrument of contemporary law making.

Whereas Zimmermann and others take the view that a common tradition can be the starting-point for harmonizing and unifying European law today, others doubt that an unbroken continuity exists between the *ius commune* and modern law.[121] They suspect that the ideas of nineteenth-century pandectist scholarship are being re-animated without, however, being able to contribute to the solution of modern problems. All too often, the reference to Roman roots only serves to reinforce national legal preoccupations. Thus, for example, the study group on a European Civil Code discussed at length the unfruitful question whether the transfer of

---

[117] Christian von Bar, *Gemeineuropäisches Deliktsrecht* (2 vols, 1996 and 1999) (English translation under the title *The Common European Law of Torts*, 1999 and 2001).

[118] Peter Schlechtriem, *Restitution und Bereicherungsausgleich in Europa* (2 vols, 2000 and 2001).

[119] Heinrich Mitteis, *Vom Lebenswert der Rechtsgeschichte* (1947), 54.

[120] Reinhard Zimmermann, *The Law of Obligations: Roman Foundations of the Civilian Tradition* (1990; paperback edn, 1996).

[121] Regina Ogorek, 'Rechtsgeschichte in der Bundesrepublik (1945–1990)', in Simon (n 68), 12, 57.

property should be causally linked to the underlying contract, or whether the principle of abstraction should be adopted.[122]

(c) Practical Endeavours

Since the 1980s, several projects have been launched, with strong participation of German scholars, to elaborate European principles that might conceivably serve, one day, as a basis for a European Code. The working method has been influenced by the American Restatements. A Commission on European Contract Law has drafted Principles of European Contract Law (PECL) and presented them to the public in three stages.[123] Whereas the Commission on European Contract Law concentrated on general contract law, the Study Group on a European Civil Code, founded in 1998, expanded their agenda to special contracts, property law, and non-contractual obligations. In the field of family law, a Commission on European Family Law was established in 2001 and published the first part of its Principles of European Family Law in 2004.[124] But there are also other groups which have set themselves the task of formulating uniform rules. Thus, the so-called Pavia Group published a preliminary draft of a European Contract Code in 2001,[125] which, however, is heavily based on continental and pandectist legal thinking and may not, therefore, really be attributed to modern comparative legal research. Finally, a European Group on Tort Law, based in Vienna and coordinated by the Austrian scholar Helmut Koziol, published a set of Principles of European Tort Law in 2005.[126]

4. Criticism

The postmodern criticism of traditional comparative law that has been formulated, especially by American legal scholars, has gone virtually unnoticed among German comparatists.[127] One of the major points of criticism is that comparative law scholarship still focuses on a limited number of national legal orders. This is

---

[122] Peter Schlechtriem, 'Europäisierung des Privatrechts—vom Beruf unserer Zeit für ein europäisches Privatrecht', 2004 *Juridica international* 24, 31.

[123] Ole Lando and Hugh Beale (eds), *Principles of European Contract Law*, Part I (1995); Ole Lando and Hugh Beale (eds), *Principles of European Contract Law*, Parts I and II (2000); Ole Lando, Eric Clive, André Prum, and Reinhard Zimmermann (eds), *Principles of European Contract Law*, Part III (2003).

[124] Katharina Boele-Woelki, Frédérique Ferrand, Cristina González Beilfuss, Maarit Jänterä-Jareborg, Nigel Lowe, Dieter Martiny, and Walter Pintens, *Principles of European Family Law Regarding Divorce and Maintenance between Former Spouses* (2004).

[125] Giuseppe Gandolfi (ed), *Code européen des contrats* (2001).

[126] European Group on Tort Law (ed), *Principles of European Tort Law: Text and Commentary* (2005).

[127] See Peters and Schwenke (n 1).

particularly valid in view of the fact that German comparative lawyers are strongly involved in the above-mentioned projects concerning the harmonization of private law on a European level. Prominent authors have even claimed that questions of European harmonization should be clearly distinguished from comparative law in general.[128] Whether or not one subscribes to this view, it is obvious that a restriction of the comparative law agenda to European private law carries with it the inherent danger of isolation. Further legal development in Europe, from a global point of view, should not lead merely to the implementation of specifically European solutions, that is, of a kind of nationalism on a larger scale. Future comparison and harmonization projects should take account, apart, of course, from the United States, of Australia and New Zealand, two vigorous common law jurisdictions which have many interesting and innovative solutions to offer. Traditional laws may also harbour unknown treasures which provide answers to current problems.

VII. Conclusion

Professional historians deeply distrust lawyers who write about the history of legal scholarship, for they often regard them as over-optimistic and prone to telling uncritical stories of success. Professional historians prefer to see gaps and ruptures.

The history of comparative law during the last century can indeed be seen as a success story: institutes have been founded which are flourishing and which have produced much impressive work. Most law makers today no longer adopt new rules without referring to comprehensive comparative research. In addition, courts of law increasingly take comparative aspects into consideration. Although the Nazi period can be regarded as a deep rupture, post-war comparative legal scholarship built upon the successes of the glorious past of the Weimar Republic. The age of globalization shows its impacts on legal scholarship too: all attempts at harmonization are based on comprehensive research, and scholars in comparative law are highly esteemed experts, not only in their respective areas of research, but also in the field of law in general. English has effectively become the new *lingua franca* and also has a considerable impact on legal research, which is becoming more and more international. Students and young scholars often go for postgraduate studies to Anglo-American law schools,[129] which also contributes to a gradual convergence

---

[128] Christian von Bar, 'Comparative Law of Obligations: Methodology and Epistemology', in Mark van Hoecke (ed), *Epistemology and Methodology of Comparative Law* (2004), 123, 131.

[129] See Wolfgang Wiegand, 'The Reception of American Law in Europe', (1991) 39 *AJCL* 229.

of legal systems. This type of narrative is very common in articles which focus on the history of comparative law, and it also underlies the present chapter, at least to some extent.

In contrast, contributions which refer to the contemporary state of comparative law have often referred to, and still refer to, the relative insignificance of this branch of legal scholarship. The authors of such contributions deplore the ignorance of the rest of the legal community of other legal systems, the bad institutionalization of comparative law, and its shadowy existence in the general curriculum at universities. They criticize bad decisions of national courts of law which ignore foreign solutions or, on the contrary, adopt them blindly without taking into consideration their functional context. Traces of those complaints can also be found in the present chapter. We need only recall the recent revision of the law of obligations in the *Bürgerliches Gesetzbuch* in Germany in 2002.

Thus, the question arises as to how these divergent views should be evaluated and how comparative law is going to develop in the future. Comparative law undoubtedly has achieved much, and it has enhanced legal knowledge in an impressive way. But it cannot be denied that it has always been confined to a minority of scholars, who may be regarded as an elite. It has never gained broad recognition, either as a special branch of legal scholarship, or as an integrated part of legal scholarship in general. It has been said that there has never been a meaningful communication between comparative law and the traditional core of German legal doctrine. It has been argued that Ernst Rabel himself contributed to this estrangement by insisting on high professional standards, thus raising fears among those who might otherwise have been willing to venture beyond the purely national sources of law that they might be accused of dilettantism.[130]

On the other hand, one would love to speculate about what would have happened if the 'dark age' of German legal history had not taken place and if, instead, Rabel and his staff could have continued their work without disruption and thus possibly have achieved their ambitious goal, which was to remodel German law on a comparative basis.[131]

In the future, the importance of comparative law will largely depend on whether students are trained in this field from the very beginning of their studies. Up until now, this has not been the case in Germany, Switzerland, or Austria. Comparative law (if it exists at all) is still only one optional course among many others, and it even runs the danger of being further reduced in view of the rapid rise of European Community law. The tendency mentioned above of more and more young people studying abroad does not, *per se*, replace the need for a basic comparative

---

[130] Jürgen Basedow, 'Der Standort des Max Planck-Instituts—Zwischen Praxis, Rechtspolitik und Privatrechtswissenschaft', in Jürgen Basedow and Ulrich Drobnig (eds), *Aufbruch nach Europa: 75 Jahre Max-Planck-Institut für Privatrecht* (2001), 3, 12.

[131] Rabel (n 19), 19.

education. Much too often, those exchanges only add knowledge of a foreign legal system to that of the respective person's own legal system, without really furthering a comparative understanding. This can result in an uncritical reception of foreign legal notions and practices, as has indeed happened in many fields of the legal profession where American customs and rules have simply been blindly adopted.

To summarize, then, the history of comparative law bears testimony to remarkable successes as well as constant obstacles which, to this very day, still prove hard to overcome.

BIBLIOGRAPHY

Hans Dölle, 'Der Beitrag der Rechtsvergleichung zum deutschen Recht', in Ernst von Caemmerer, Ernst Friesenhahn, and Richard Lange, *Hundert Jahre deutschen Rechtslebens: Festschrift zum hundertjährigen Bestehen des Deutschen Juristentages 1860–1960* (vol II, 1960), 19 ff

Léontin-Jean Constantinesco, *Rechtsvergleichung* (3 vols, 1971–83)

Marcus Lutter, Ernst C. Stiefel, and Michael H. Hoeflich (eds), *Der Einfluss deutscher Emigranten auf die Rechtsentwicklung in den USA und in Deutschland* (1991)

Michael Martinek, 'Wissenschaftsgeschichte der Rechtsvergleichung und des internationalen Privatrechts in der BRD', in Dieter Simon (ed), *Rechtswissenschaft in der Bonner Republik, Studien zur Wissenschaftsgeschichte der Jurisprudenz* (1994), 529, 552

Elmar Wadle, *Einhundert Jahre rechtsvergleichende Gesellschaften in Deutschland* (1994)

Reinhard Zimmermann, *The Law of Obligations: Roman Foundations of the Civilian Tradition* (1990; paperback edn, 1996)

Ingeborg Schwenzer, 'Rezeption deutschen Rechtsdenkens im schweizerischen Obligationenrecht', in *eadem* (ed), *Schuldrecht, Rechtsvergleichung und Rechtsvereinheitlichung an der Schwelle zum 21. Jahrhundert* (1998), 59 ff

Konrad Zweigert and Hein Kötz, *Einführung in die Rechtsvergleichung* (3rd edn, 1996); English translation under the title *An Introduction to Comparative Law* by Tony Weir (3rd edn, 1998)

Rolf Ulrich Kunze, *Ernst Rabel und das Kaiser-Wilhelm-Institut für ausländisches und internationales Privatrecht 1926–1945* (2004)

CHAPTER 3

DEVELOPMENT OF COMPARATIVE LAW IN ITALY

ELISABETTA GRANDE

Alessandria

I. Introduction: Layers of Reception

SINCE its unification in 1861, Italian law has mainly been a 'context of reception'.[1] In contrast to contexts of production, where legal scholarship tends to unfold in a self-centred mode, contexts of reception tend to search for legal innovation abroad. Thus, the Italian legal culture has often copied (albeit with some adaptations) legal ideas, norms, and institutions from foreign countries but only rarely produced original work of its own. Jurists in the united Italy have looked first to France, later to Germany, and most recently to the United States for legal innovation. This culture of borrowing also provides the framework for the discipline of comparative law in Italy.

In the nineteenth century, France provided the leading model. In 1804, France produced one of the most successful export items in legal history, the *Code civil*. The French codification was first introduced into Italy in the early nineteenth century as a consequence of the Napoleonic conquest. After the restoration and the birth of a unified Italy, however, the continuing adherence to the model of the French *Code civil* was not the result of imposition but the choice of admiring jurists. It is no wonder then, that the Italian *Codice civile* of 1865, while presented as partially original, was heavily indebted to the French model. That model was widely admired as a symbol of liberalism and modernity and its imitation gave the Italian legal system an aura of progressiveness and civility. At the time, Italian legal scholars were scarcely creative and initially interpreted their code according to French scholarship, filling their bookshelves with French legal literature. It was only after quite some time that Italian jurists began to emancipate themselves from the intellectual domination of French legal thought and to offer their own, original, contribution to the interpretation of their code.

Beginning in the late nineteenth and early twentieth centuries, German learning gradually succeeded French law as the leading paradigm. In fact, the early twentieth century was marked by a wave of reception of German legal formalism. The leading group within the academic legal profession, the private law scholars, were fascinated, in Italy as elsewhere, by the elegance and logical consistency of German pandectism. Despite Savigny's nationalistic notions of law as the expression of a people's spirit (*Volksgeist*), later nineteenth-century German legal science was characterized by a remarkably universalistic spirit, culminating in the German Civil Code (BGB) of 1900. It was this universal and quasi-geometric nature of legal concepts that captured the legal imagination worldwide and attracted, in particular, the Italian Romanists who played the leading role in the reception of German

---

[1] For an in-depth discussion of this notion, see Diego Lopez Medina, *Teoria impura del derecho* (2000).

ideas.[2] French-style commentary on black-letter rules went out of fashion and was superseded by conceptual jurisprudence and admiration of system-building. Moreover, after World War I, the intellectual admiration for the German professorial tradition was in tune with the political sympathies of the Fascist regime which emphasized all sorts of connections with Germany. In this climate, Italian jurists not only abandoned earlier projects of cooperation with their French colleagues (such as the Italo-French project of a law of obligations of 1927), they also paid little or no attention to critical currents emerging in Germany (such as the *Freirechtschule* or the *Kathedersozialismus*). Tainted by a leftist reputation, such movements remained either unknown or uninfluential in mainstream Italian legal academia.

It is thus somewhat surprising that the making of a new Italian civil code resulted in a codification that betrayed only limited influence of German private law and was by no means an imitation of the BGB. To be sure, the German formalist heritage remained visible in a variety of concepts, used by Italian scholars in interpreting the code, such as the *Rechtsgeschäft*. But looking at the fundamental structure of the *Codice civile* of 1942, one finds a rejection of the (very German) idea of a General Part, a rather innovative combination of civil and commercial law, and the inclusion of subjects entirely foreign to the German codification. The wind was changing and gradually began to blow from a less formalist direction. The more advanced Italian jurists began to import—albeit somewhat randomly— the social and functionalist approach not only of von Jhering but also of Duguit and Josserand. And the new 1948 Constitution helped to create a climate of a more anti-formalist style of legal interpretation.

After World War II, the Anglo-American model began to capture the attention of jurists in Italy. As in much of the (Western) world, US-American law in particular became the primary supplier of legal innovation in Italy. This trend continues today, although Italian law has also come increasingly under the influence of European law, originating in Brussels, Strasbourg, and Luxembourg.

In Italy, comparative law as a discipline played at best a minimal role in all these changes. The academic leadership consisted of the private law scholars who understood themselves as Romanists, and Roman law was considered the foundation of all true legal learning. As we will see, Italian comparative law came into its own only in the second half of the twentieth century. Still, Italian comparatists, eager for respectable pedigree, have sought to trace the origins of their discipline to much earlier times. Thus, philosophers like Muratori, Romagnosi, and Beccaria, that is, the best part of the Italian enlightenment, have been enlisted as founding fathers of the discipline. In 1985, at a conference of the *Associazione Italiana di Diritto Comparato* in Palermo, the early nineteenth-century Sicilian jurist Emerico Amari,

---

[2] On the German reception in Italy, see, among many others, Antonio Gambaro and Rodolfo Sacco, *Sistemi giuridici comparati* (2002), 383 ff.

author of an encyclopaedic survey of foreign legislation, was officially declared the ancestor of the discipline. This allowed Italy to claim a place in the pre-modern (encyclopaedic) phase of comparative law.[3]

This search for a tradition should not be taken too seriously. The present chapter will therefore begin the story of comparative law in Italy in the early part of the twentieth century. It will distinguish three fundamental layers: a commercial law branch, a reformist tradition, and a mainstream, 'scientific', approach. It will discuss the current state of Italian comparative law resulting from the academic and cultural influence of these three layers. And it will attempt to assess the impact of the more significant and original contributions of Italian comparative law at the European and global levels.

II. Development: The Emergence
of the Modern Discipline

1. Civil and Commercial Law Scholars in the Early Twentieth Century: To Cross or Not to Cross (the Channel)

During the Fascist era (1922–43), England was at the top of the list of official (political) contempt, and English law was simply not on the radar screen of Italian jurists at all. The same was true for the United States and American law. The common law tradition was treated with contempt, and Italian jurists tended to doubt whether Anglo-American 'law' really even deserved that name. This attitude resulted in a deep and self-inflicted ignorance virtually about the entire common law tradition.

Yet, there was a major exception. A small group of commercial law scholars, among them masters such as Tullio Ascarelli, Mario Rotondi, and Angelo Sraffa, worked in the less parochial and more cosmopolitan spirit traditionally associated with commercial law and thus began to look across the Channel and even across the Atlantic. They were the first to take an interest in topics later to become classics of comparative law—questions of the nature and sources of law or institutions like the trust. This group, consisting in part of Jewish scholars who were forced into emigration by racist laws, was instrumental in working towards 'integrative' comparison. Its members rejected the idea that the diversity of positive law created by national codifications (even in the domain of commercial law) essentially

---

[3] Emerico Amari, *Critica di una scienza delle legislazioni comparate* (1857).

precluded effective communication among different legal systems—an idea that left international legal practice without a useful legal regime altogether. Their early efforts at comparative studies were motivated by practical and professional concerns but, at the time, they nevertheless constituted the cutting edge of comparative legal scholarship in Italy. Their methodology was remarkably open-minded, and they were fully capable of looking through legal forms to the substance underneath. Tullio Ascarelli in particular has justly been considered a founding father not only of comparative law in his country but also of economic and social approaches to legal reasoning.[4] Angelo Sraffa inspired an early comparative law institute in Milan.[5] And Mario Rotondi began to publish the internationally recognized series *Inchieste di diritto comparato* in 1970.[6]

Yet, while highly influential in the domain of commercial law, these scholars had little influence in the general domain of Italian jurisprudence. The institutionalized separation among the various branches of legal scholarship, so typical of the Italian academic system, prevented a major spillover of their comparative law efforts into the realm of general private law. This realm has long been the centre-piece of Italian legal academia, and it continues to be dominated by the guild of private law scholars as the elite of the teaching profession. Thus, despite the intellectual profile of Filippo Vassalli as the father of the 1942 *Codice civile*, and despite the codification's merger of private and commercial law, the code was prepared without any systematic comparative studies and in complete ignorance of what the common law tradition had to offer. This tradition therefore remained completely uninfluential until after World War II.

2. The Reformists in the Post-World War II Period: Broadening the View

In the aftermath of World War II, the United States exerted pressure on Italy, as well as on Germany and Japan, to (re-)establish at least a local version of the rule of law. In this political climate, the German influence on Italian law began to decline and the common law tradition, associated with the victorious Anglo-Americans, rapidly gained prestige, at least with the avant-garde of the legal profession. After all, the civil law tradition with its emphasis on legislation and codification had proved impotent to prevent the rise of totalitarianism and dictatorship. The new institutional order of the free world thus had to recognize a significantly increased

---

[4] Tullio Ascarelli, *Interpretazione del diritto e studio del diritto comparato* (1952).

[5] The *Istituto di diritto comparato A. Sraffa* at the Bocconi University was founded in 1934 on the initiative of the then Chancellor, Gustavo del Vecchio, and of Mario Rotondi, who was its first Director.

[6] Published by Giuffrè, Cedam, and Kluwer.

role of judicial power in order effectively to protect individual rights. And Italy was firmly committed to becoming part of the new free world. As a result of the agreements made between Churchill and Stalin as early as 1944, there was little doubt that Italy would end up on the Western side of what was to become the iron curtain, although formally speaking, that decision was made only with the socialist and communist defeat in the 1948 elections.

One of the lead players in the anti-Fascist resistance in Florence, Piero Calamandrei, had an early fascination with the common law tradition. When Calamandrei became a member of the Italian constitutional convention, the first chief justice of the Italian Constitutional Court, and a famous attorney and leading civil procedurist, his predilections became widely influential. Calamandrei admired in particular the important role of practising lawyers in the making of the common law tradition. He was convinced that the influence of the practitioners could also cure the civilian tradition of its abstractness and frequent lack of realistic perspective. Calamandrei was also an early advocate of adversary procedure, a critic of the ambiguous role of the Italian prosecutor-judge, and a supporter of reorganizing the legal profession along less bureaucratic and more policy-oriented lines.

While fighting in the mountains around Trento in the Italian north, Calamandrei met a 13-year-old boy who was assisting the resistance as a messenger. The teenager's name was Mauro Cappelletti. In due course, he was to carry Calamandrei's torch, to share his passion for the common law tradition, and to become the founder of the Italian reformist tradition of comparative law. For many years, Cappelletti served as the director of the European University Institute in Florence, was a full professor of Civil Procedure at the University of Florence, and a Distinguished Professor of International and Comparative Law at Stanford University. For a long time, Cappelletti was the only Italian legal scholar with a worldwide reputation. His name is linked to two major collective projects, *Access to Justice* (1978–9) and *Integration through Law* (1985). In particular, his scholarly and policy contributions to our understanding of the implications and potential of judge-made law have remained unmatched.[7] In 2003, the seventeenth meeting of the *Associazione Italiana di Diritto Comparato* was dedicated to him.[8] When Cappelletti died in 2004, he left behind a firmly established Florentine school of comparatists.

---

[7] Mauro Cappelletti (gen ed), *Access to Justice: 1. A World Survey 2. Promising Institutions 3. Emerging Issues and Perspectives 4. The Anthropological Perspective* (1978–9); Mauro Cappelletti, Monica Seccombe, and Joseph Weiler (eds), *Integration through Law, Europe and American Federal Experience.* (1985); Mauro Cappelletti, *Giudici Legislatori?* (1984); idem, *The Judicial Process in Comparative Perspective* (1991).

[8] For a recent contribution in his honour, see Nicolò Trocker and Vincenzo Varano (eds), *The Reforms of Civil Procedure in Comparative Perspective. An International Conference dedicated to Mauro Cappelletti, Florence, 12–13 December, 2003* (2005).

3. The Emergence of the Mainstream in the 1950s and 1960s: From Gorla's *Contracts* to Sacco's *Formants*

Oddly enough, the mainstream tradition of Italian comparative law has its birth-place, at least in a sense, in a small college town in the Eastern United States, that is, in Ithaca, New York. Ithaca was the place where, since the 1950s, Rudolf B. Schlesinger, the German emigrant, was conducting the preparation of his most ambitious project, his study of the Common Core of the rules governing contract formation. This project involved several key figures in the development of Italian comparative law: the young Mauro Cappelletti; Giovanni Pugliese, a distinguished Roman law scholar; and, perhaps most importantly, Gino Gorla, later recognized as the true founding father of modern comparative law in Italy.[9]

In 1955, Gorla, a somewhat heretical civil law professor at the University of Rome, published his highly original comparative book on contract law, *Il Contratto*. In this work, he pioneered the use of the case method and of a factual approach, introducing both into an area of law hitherto largely dominated by formalistic dogmatism.[10] Thus, the publication of this masterpiece shook the pro-fession. Tullio Ascarelli called it 'the first Italian wide-ranging comparative work'. Gorla's *Il Contratto* was the result of years of searching for alternatives to the 'dogmatic-conceptual' approach (as he defined it) prevailing in the Italian legal culture. Gorla had looked for such alternatives mainly in the United States. Between 1948 and 1949, he visited many American law schools and established particularly close ties with the Cornell Law School where he met Rudolf Schlesinger with whom Gorla began a seminal scholarly dialogue. He found that American casuistic and inductive approach freed from the intellectual strait-jacket of the broad and abstract concepts that Italian jurisprudence had borrowed from the German *Allgemeine Rechtslehre*. To Gorla, the American approach was like a breath of fresh air. *Il Contratto* was the product of this encounter with the American legal culture. Here, for the first time, not only in Italy but in all of continental Europe, key questions of contract law were addressed from an historical and comparative per-spective, discussed in a case method fashion and with reference to four major legal systems—the Italian, French, English, and American.

The impact of Gino Gorla's work on comparative law was simply enormous. It opened completely new vistas for legal research. It also attracted the particular interest of Rodolfo Sacco, a young private law scholar then teaching at the University of Trieste. Sacco was not directly involved in the Common Core project at Cornell and had never studied the common law in a systematic fashion, but he was greatly

---

[9] On the Cornell Common Core Project, results of which have been published in two monumental volumes (Rudolf B. Schlesinger (ed), *Formation of Contracts. A Study in the Common Core of Legal Systems* (1968)), see Ugo Mattei, 'The Comparative Jurisprudence of Schlesinger and Sacco: A Study in Legal Influence', in Annelise Riles (ed), *Rethinking the Masters of Comparative Law* (2001), 240 ff.

[10] Gino Gorla, *Il Contratto. Problemi fondamentali trattati con il metodo comparativo e casistico* (1955).

inspired by Schlesinger's approach as well as by Gorla's foundational work. Once interviewed about his own contribution to comparative law, Sacco declared with excessive modesty: 'I have been a notary who put into writing, using some neologism when necessary, the new things discovered by R. David, R. Schlesinger and G. Gorla'.[11]

Sacco's remark is certainly a serious understatement but it remains true that the most influential version of Italian comparative law today—Sacco's theory of 'legal formants'—has its roots in the post-World War II tradition founded by René David in France, Konrad Zweigert in Germany, and Gino Gorla in Italy. The hallmark of this tradition is the idea of functionalism-structuralism which is now part of the mainstream of professional Western comparative law.[12]

After having tested it in his teaching at Trieste as early as 1958–59, Sacco first formulated his theory of 'legal formants' under the label of 'legal components' in an article exploring some aspects of the law of the Romanist tradition.[13] He fully developed his theory in a report for the International Academy of Comparative Law meeting in Teheran in 1974.[14] It became widely known through Sacco's treatise *Introduzione al diritto comparato*[15] and finally became available in English through a translation by James Gordley in 1991.[16]

As described in the leading American comparative law casebook, the methodology of legal formants looks deceptively simple:

Professor Sacco has shown that there often is not, in a given legal system, a single unvarying rule on a particular point, but rather a series of different (sometimes conflicting) formulations of the applicable rule, depending on the kind of source consulted. The code may say one thing, the courts another; scholars may state the rule differently; the tacit rule actually followed may again be different from what anyone says it is. These different possible formulations are 'formants' (the term being borrowed from phonetics, the science that studies sounds) of the rule as it obtains in that particular jurisdiction. Understanding a legal system requires attention to the different incidences of its rules at various levels of practice and layers of discourse. An important reason for such differences may be that the 'formants' of a rule derive from different sources: for instance, the legislature's rules may derive from a particular foreign system, while scholars have systematized them using concepts and principles borrowed from another. This phenomenon is particularly noticeable in

---

[11] Rodolfo Sacco, *Che cos'è il diritto comparato?* (1992), 284 f.

[12] On the notion of functionalism-structuralism in comparative law, see Mattei (n 9), 252 f; see also Michele Graziadei, 'The Functionalist Heritage', in Pierre Legrand and Roderick Munday (eds), *Comparative Legal Studies: Traditions and Transitions* (2003), 100 ff.

[13] Rodolfo Sacco, 'Définitions savantes et droit appliqué dans les pays romanistes', (1965) *Revue Internationale de Droit Comparé* 827 ff.

[14] Rodolfo Sacco, 'Les buts et les méthodes de la comparaison du droit', in *Rapports Nationaux Italiens au IX Congrès International de droit comparé, Téhéran 1974*, (1974), 113 ff.

[15] 1980, 1st and 2nd eds.

[16] Rodolfo Sacco, 'Legal Formants. A Dynamic Approach to Comparative Law', (1991) 39 AJCL 1 ff, 343 ff. See also in English, Rodolfo Sacco and Pier Giuseppe Monateri, 'Legal Formants', in Peter Newman (ed), 2 *The New Palgrave Dictionary of Economics and the Law* (1998), 531 ff.

the many civil law systems which, like Italy, initially adopted codes based on the French prototype but later fell under the spell of German legal scholarship.[17]

Sacco's idea of 'legal formants', that is, of a legal landscape consisting of components not necessarily coherent with each other, provided a theory for the demise of the paradigmatic Kelsenian idea of law as a pyramid of orders from the sovereign at the top to the subject at the bottom. From now on, the comparatist could no longer be content with such a rigid order. Instead he or she needed to discover, analyse, and contrast with each other, a variety of 'formants' in order to capture the complexity of a legal system and of its 'rules'. This represented a significant step forward in our understanding of the nature and life of the law. Yet, it has recently been observed that the theory of 'legal formants' does not accomplish complete liberation from positivistic notions of law. As a tool of inquiry, the theory is still remarkably narrow, for example, in its complete lack of interdisciplinarity, an aspect to which we will return.

So far, the theory of 'legal formants' is probably the most important and lasting contribution of Italian scholarship to the discipline of comparative law. Its impact is particularly noticeable in the ongoing search for a common private law of Europe. In recent years, comparative law has been boosted in Europe by the practical needs of legal integration, and Italian comparatists have actively participated in this search in a variety of contexts and capacities. This is particularly true with regard to one of the most visible undertakings in this area, that is, the search for a *Common Core of European Private Law* organized at the University of Trento (see Section V). This undertaking builds on Schlesinger's Cornell project but then takes a step forward by using Sacco's 'legal formants' approach to distinguish the various elements of law in a given system. In one of the earlier books emerging from the Trento project, its editors, Mauro Bussani and Vernon Palmer, aptly described the resulting methodological credo:

A full understanding of what the legal formants are and how they relate to each other allows us to ascertain the factors that affect solutions, making it clear what weight interpretative practices (grounded on scholarly writings, on legal debate aroused by previous judicial decision, etc.) have in molding the actual outcomes. Hence the notion of legal formant is more than an esoteric neologism for the traditional distinction between 'Loi', 'Jurisprudence' and 'Doctrine', i.e., between enacted law, case law and scholarly writings. Within a given legal system, the legal rule is not uniform, not only because one rule may be given by case law, one by scholars and one by statutes. Within each of these sources there are also formants competing with each other. For example, the rule described in the headnotes of a case can be inconsistent with the actual rationale of the decision, or the definition in a code can be inconsistent with the detailed rules contained in the code itself. This complex dynamic may change considerably from one legal system to another as well as from one area of the law to another. In particular, in each legal system certain legal formants are

---

[17] Rudolf B. Schlesinger, Hans W. Baade, Peter E. Herzog, and Edward M. Wise, *Comparative Law. Cases, Text, Materials* (6th edn, 1998), 288.

clearly leading in a different way—differences in formants' leadership are particularly clear in the (traditional) distinction between common law and civil law.[18]

In Italy, the mainstream approach to comparative law put private law in the Western tradition at its centre. Enriched by various methodological innovations, this has become the core around which comparative law in Italy has grown as a professional project. While Gino Gorla's later work focused on historical inquiries into the sources of law in the traditions of the common law and of the *ius commune*,[19] and while Rodolfo Sacco broadened the field, particularly through his many disciples, the Italian mainstream continued to focus on the study of private law, which was kept rather strictly separate from comparison in other areas. This has also shaped the institutionalization of the field which occurred in two major ways: through the creation of a 'disciplinary group' (for purposes of academic recruitment) called 'private comparative law', and through the foundation of the *Associazione Italiana di Diritto Comparato*, the corresponding institution to the International Academy of Comparative Law, in 1971.

4. Institutionalizating the Field in the 1970s and 1980s: The Dominance of Private Law Comparison

When the *Associazione Italiana di Diritto Comparato* was created in 1971, there was only one full chair of comparative law in Italy. Today, largely thanks also to the increasing number of new Italian Law Schools, there are 51 full professors of private comparative law and 56 full professors of public comparative law. All this growth occurred in just one generation, and it has been particularly impressive over the last seven years when the number of comparative law chairs doubled.

The continuing distinction between private and public law is becoming obsolete on the domestic level and even more so in the comparative law context. Its persistence is largely the result of the peculiar structure of Italian academic organization and power. Academic appointments in Italy are decided by a committee that is elected by all professors whose chairs belong to the same 'academic group'. There is one group for private comparative law (IUS/02) which is the result of the gradual merger of the various branches described above; this group has a well-defined history and tradition. There is another group for public comparative law which is an offshoot of the powerful academic group of constitutional law professors; understanding its genesis is still work in progress.[20] Finally, there are a few other

[18] Mauro Bussani and Vernon Palmer, 'Pure Economic Loss in Europe', in Mauro Bussani and Ugo Mattei (gen eds), *The Common Core of European Private Law* (2003), 168.

[19] Gino Gorla, *Diritto comparato e diritto comune europeo* (1981).

[20] Compare Giorgio Lombardi, *Premesse al corso di diritto pubblico comparato: problemi di metodo* (1986).

comparative law chairs in various areas, such as criminal law and procedure or labour law; they do not have autonomous academic groups so that scholars in these fields cannot produce the critical mass necessary to wield serious academic power. At the end of the day, private comparative law still dominates the definition and direction of comparative law in Italy, thus reinforcing the centrality of the private law approach more generally.

When the *Associazione Italiana di Diritto Comparato* was created, it became clear that the comparative law guild consisted of three discrete groups of scholars: the uniform commercial law experts, the reformists, and what I call the mainstream. These three groups have been centred in Rome (where Gorla failed to have one of his disciples appointed as his successor), Florence (where Cappelletti left a fairly cohesive group of reformist scholars), and Turin (the capital of the School of Sacco), respectively. This tripartite division continues to define the fundamental structure of Italian comparative law today.

III. THE CONTEMPORARY SCENE: FROM PURITY TO PLURALISM

1. The Theses of Trento

In 1979, the biannual meeting of the *Associazione Italiana di Diritto Comparato* was dedicated to Gino Gorla. It became the venue of the last truly intense methodological discussion in comparative law in Italy. This discussion occurred mainly between two camps. One group of scholars, lead by Mauro Cappelletti and Vittorio Denti, insisted that comparative law had a mission to improve the law and to participate in policy-making. The other group, headed by Rodolfo Sacco, advocated a 'purely scientific' approach and saw the purpose of comparative legal studies as the pursuit of pure knowledge. The latter group ultimately won the day. Ever since, it is paid homage, more or less routinely, in most comparative law books and law review articles and it has never seriously been challenged in its leadership role. Ultimately, it became closely associated with a newly founded university in the North of Italy and formulated its programme in the so-called 'Theses of Trento'.

In 1982, Rodolfo Sacco was elected chairman of the special committee that established the law school at the University of Trento. At the time of its opening, the teaching staff was very young—most law faculty members were full-time scholars in their mid-twenties. When the law faculty began operations in 1984, observers noted that the curriculum looked very peculiar: all courses taught by full professors were labelled 'comparative'. In contrast, courses on purely domestic law were taught by junior faculty members. This pattern was the exact opposite of the traditional set-up where senior professors had given the domestic (compulsory) lectures while comparative law, if taught at all, was offered by junior or adjunct faculty. While the traditional pattern was quickly restored, the experiment still linked the name of Trento with the rise of comparative law in general, and with Sacco's programme in particular. In 1987, this programme was formalized in five theses. They are worth reproducing here in translation because they have had a significant influence on the direction of, and the debate about, comparative law in Italy.

First thesis. 'Comparative law, understood as a science, necessarily aims at the better understanding of legal data. Ulterior tasks, such as the improvement of law or its interpretation, are worthy of the greatest consideration but nevertheless are only secondary goals of comparative research.'

Second thesis. 'There is no comparative science without measuring the differences and similarities among different legal systems. Mere cultural excursion into, or parallel exposition of, certain fields is not comparative science.'

Third thesis. 'Comparison turns its attention to various phenomena of legal life operating in the past or the present; it considers legal propositions as historical facts including those formulated by legislators, judges, and scholars, and so verifies what genuinely occurred. In this sense, comparison is an historical science'.

Fourth thesis. 'Comparative knowledge of legal systems has the specific merit of testing the coherence of the various elements present in each system after identifying and understanding these elements. In particular, it checks whether the unrationalized rules present in each system are compatible with the theoretical propositions proffered to make the operational rules intelligible'.

Fifth thesis. 'Understanding a legal system is not a monopoly of the jurists who belong to that system. On the contrary, the jurist belonging to a given system, while enjoying the advantage of an abundance of information on the one hand, is, on the other hand, suffering from the disadvantage that he, more than any other jurist, is under the assumption that the theoretical formulations present in his system are completely coherent with its operational rules.'[21]

Over the next decade and a half, it became apparent, though, that a canon thus formalized and presented as a form of scientific truth had to meet with resistance in a period of emerging post-modernist scholarship, in Italy and elsewhere. A later

---

[21] The Theses of Trento can be found in the entry by Antonio Gambaro, Pier Giuseppe Monateri and Rodolfo Sacco, 'Comparazione giuridica', (1988) 3 *Digesto 4 ed. Discipline privatistiche* 52. For an English translation, see Sacco (1991) 39 *AJCL* nn 6, 27–9.

meeting in Trento was again devoted to a discussion of the continuous validity of the pure comparative method advocated by Sacco. Unfortunately, however, the conference ended with much self-congratulation but little substantive discussion.[22]

Interestingly, the pattern established in the founding phase of Trento's new law faculty, that is, ranking the comparative aspects of a field as equal to, or even higher than, its purely domestic side, characterized another major project launched in the mid-1980s: the new edition of the *Digesto*, that is, the leading Italian legal encyclopaedia. The whole work is organized so that legal subjects are analysed not only from a domestic perspective, as in previous editions, but also in their comparative dimension. In fact, entries on domestic law are put side by side with entries on comparative, foreign, and international law. This structure expressed the fundamental idea that (Italian) law must be studied, and can perhaps only be understood, in a broader comparative context.

Both moves, the path-breaking initial organization of the Trento law curriculum and the innovative structure of the *Digesto* in its fourth edition, were revolutionary. They can be interpreted as frontal attacks by Sacco and his school on the traditional patterns of prestige in Italian Academia. Yet, while Italian comparatists have by and large shared the goal of fighting the dominant parochial approach in Italian legal education and scholarship, they did not necessarily subscribe to the methodological purism codified in the theses of Trento. As Vittorio Denti, one of Italy's most prominent civil procedure scholars, has pointed out, it is important to understand that different methodologies and concerns are equally legitimate, and it is a form of dogmatism to consider one method legitimate and scientific while denying alternative approaches academic standing on dignity.[23]

Despite the general open-mindedness of Sacco as their author, the theses of Trento could be understood as such a form of dogmatism. Thus, they have encountered considerable resistance from scholars who regard such a canon as an intellectual strait-jacket. It is true, indeed, that the theses contain an element of scientific positivism that is troublesome in an age of methodological anxiety. For example, they express great faith in the distinction between 'is' and 'ought'. Today, however, such a distinction is widely regarded as epistemologically obsolete. Perhaps more importantly, it may well be in outright conflict with the 'legal formants' approach which postulates, after all, that the interpretation of a rule is part of the rule itself.[24]

Thus, one should not overrate the influence of the Trento canon on comparative law in Italy. This influence is overshadowed by the impact of the much more open-minded 'legal formants' approach. This approach is the most influential

[22] The new version of the Theses of Trento is discussed by Antonio Gambaro, 'The Trento Theses', (2004) *Global Jurist Frontiers*, available at <http://www.bepress.com/gi/frontiers/vol4/iss1/art2>.

[23] Vittorio Denti, 'Diritto Comparato e scienza del processo', in Rodolfo Sacco (ed), *L'apporto della comparazione alla scienza giuridica* (1980), 204.

[24] For this critique, see more extensively, Mattei (n 9), 253.

formulation of the current structuralist methodology and the most characteristic feature of the Italian comparative mainstream.

2. Letting Many Flowers Bloom: The 1990s and Beyond

In the introduction to this chapter, I divided the Italian comparative law community into a commercial law school, a policy-making group, and a structuralist mainstream. Yet this division suggests clear boundaries that no longer exist. Thus, it should be not considered ontological but merely as a device to help us understand the major trends in today's highly diverse community of comparative law scholars.

In current Italian comparative law scholarship, these three sub-traditions (to which we could add a fourth if we included the historical approach of the late Gino Gorla as a separate variant of the structuralist mainstream) often mix and blend in the work of individual scholars. For example, while the school of Florence is primarily pursuing policy-oriented work, many of its members also explore structural regularities determining the solutions to particular problems.[25] Also, members of the earlier commercial law group (whose most important contributions are the UNIDROIT Principles on International Commercial Contracts) often appreciate the structural differences and economic variables in conflict with legal uniformity.[26]

Yet, the current comparative law landscape in Italy is also populated by a great variety of other, non-traditional, schools and approaches. Some scholars, mostly affiliated with the law faculties of Napoli and Salerno, have enriched comparative law by introducing normative elements and value judgements imported from mainstream private law scholarship, which in turn has taken the respective values from post-war constitutional law and theory.[27] The historical tradition, still deeply connected with mainstream structuralism, is also alive and well and, within it, normative critique has become an openly pursued element of the discourse (mainly in Genoa).[28] A current emerging from links between the law faculties at

[25] In this vein, for a recent contribution from the school of thought whose best-known leaders are Vincenzo Varano and Nicolò Trocker, see Vittoria Barsotti, *L'arte di tacere* (1999).

[26] See eg Guido Alpa, Michael J. Bonell, Diego Corapi, Luigi Moccia, and Vincenzo Zeno-Zenchovich, *Diritto privato comparato, Istituti e problemi* (1999).

[27] For a recent contribution from a school of thought that finds its mentor in the Italian private law scholar Pietro Perlingeri, see Felice Casucci, *Il diritto 'plurale'. Pluralismo delle fonti e libera circolazione delle norme giuridiche* (2004).

[28] See Maurizio Lupoi, *Alle radici del mondo giuridico europeo. Saggio storico comparativo* (1994), but also Antonio Gambaro and Carlo Augusto Cannata, *Lineamenti di storia della giurisprudenza europea. Dal medioevo all'età moderna* (1984).

Turin and Harvard is characterized by a penchant for irony and story-telling.[29] In Sicily, there is a school mostly devoted to 'thick descriptions' of the common law tradition.[30] A number of Italian comparatists, influenced by US-American ideas, have developed an openly functionalist methodology, often evaluating different solutions from an efficiency perspective.[31] In response, a more critical current has exposed the sham neutrality of the efficiency principle and has discussed various hegemonic patterns in which dominating legal systems 'dress up' in order to persuade the periphery of their superiority.[32] In addition, the development of a dialogue between comparative law and other social sciences—including not only economics but also anthropology and sociology—has blurred the boundaries of the discipline. As a result, the current generation of Italian comparatists is less and less willing to comply with the Trento canon by leaving the evaluation of legal structures to the 'other sciences' and more and more confident in its normative stance.[33]

Yet, a closer look at this pluralism of approaches also reveals several common denominators. To begin with, the study of 'legal transplants' continues to enjoy widespread attention; here, a quasi-historical tradition, seeking to understand whence law comes and where it goes, is characteristic of large parts of the Italian comparative law community. The terminology, if not the methodology, of legal formants is constantly used and has become almost a password for academic membership. Much attention is devoted to issues of legal translation and legal language;[34] in part, the reason is that, on the global level, Italian is not a dominant language so that scholars have to be particularly careful when it comes to

---

[29] Anna di Robilant and Fernanda Nicola, 'Il liberalismo alle prese con identità e redistribuzione: le critiche al "Right Discourse" da parte della sinistra americana', (2004) *Rivista Critica del Diritto Privato* 673.

[30] See Giovanni Criscuoli, *Il contratto nel diritto inglese* (1990); Antonello Miranda, *Il testamento nel diritto inglese: fondamento e sistema* (1995).

[31] See Giuseppe Bellantuono, *I contratti incompleti nel diritto e nell'economia* (2000); Carlo Marchetti, *La 'Nexus of Contract Theory'* (2000); Alberto Monti, *Buona fede e assicurazione* (2002).

[32] See Ugo Mattei, 'A Theory of Imperial Law. A Study on U.S. Hegemony and the Latin Resistance', (2002) 10 *Indiana Journal of Global Legal Studies*, 383 ff; Gianmaria Ajani, 'Navigatori e giuristi. A proposito del trapianto di nozioni vaghe', in Valentina Bertorello (ed), *Io comparo, tu compari, egli compara: che cosa, come, perché?* (2003), 3 ff; Elisabetta Grande, *Imitazione e diritto. Ipotesi sulla circolazione dei modelli* (2000).

[33] See the proceedings of the biannual meeting of the *Associazione Italiana di Diritto Comparato* of 2003, held in Pisa and dedicated to the start of cooperation of Italian comparative law with other sciences and disciplines, in Giovanni Comandé and Giulio Ponzanelli (eds), *Scienza e diritto nel prisma del diritto comparato* (2004).

[34] See the works of Rodolfo Sacco, 'Les problèmes de traduction juridique', in *Rapport Nationaux Italiens au XII Congrès International de Droit Comparé, Sidney* (1986); Ajani (n 32); Antonio Gambaro, 'A proposito del plurilinguismo legislativo europeo', (2004) *Rivista trimestrale di diritto e procedura civile* 287 ff, or the recent series of books edited by Barbara Pozzo, entitled, *Le lingue del diritto*, the first volume of which is *Ordinary Language and Legal Language* (2005). These are just few examples of the Italian comparatists' interest in legal language and in problems arising from legal translation.

terminological issues. Italian comparatists—especially, though not exclusively, in private law—are also very actively involved in the unification of European law, with some of them exploring the dynamics of the new European legal order as a matter of competition among various formants.[35]

There is some persistent ethnocentrism, still based on the idea that comparative assessments are really possible only among Western systems because such assessments require sufficient social and economic commonalities and because looking for variations of professional 'style' (in John Merryman's sense) is useful only among sufficiently related regimes. Yet, such ethnocentrism is more and more openly resisted. A school of Islamic studies, strongly rooted in the structuralist canon, is thriving and there are actually a (small) number of academic chairs devoted to Islamic law.[36] African law, post-Soviet law, Chinese and Japanese law, and even gypsy law are also studied, both by mainstream scholars and specialists, although one cannot yet speak of full-fledged schools in these areas.[37] Other contexts have traditionally been explored by various professional groups. For example, Latin American studies are mostly the domain of Roman law specialists; the relationship between Hebrew, Islamic, and Canon law is analysed by an emerging group of comparative religion scholars coming from a canonistic tradition;[38] and the globalization of the economy has mostly attracted experts on administrative and international law, legal history, and sociology who explore issues revolving around the—real or imagined—demise of the nation-state.[39]

When it comes to the role and status of comparative law in legal education, Italy is ahead of most other countries in the world: comparative law is a central element in the curriculum. Practically all law schools teach a general introduction to the subject, as do a number of economics and political science departments. This situation is also reflected in the great variety of introductory textbooks for first- and second-year law teaching. In this regard as well, Italy is, as proudly pointed out by Sacco, truly '*en tête*'.[40] This literature also reflects the continuing

---

[35] Luisa Antoniolli Deflorian, *La struttura istituzionale del nuovo diritto comune europeo* (1996).

[36] Among others, Italian Islamists Francesco Castro, Roberta Aluffi, Gianmaria Piccinelli, and Massimo Papa deserve mention.

[37] See, among others, Rodolfo Sacco, *Il diritto africano* (1995); Marco Guadagni, *Il diritto in Mozambico. Introduzione al sistema giuridico di un paese africano* (1989); Elisabetta Grande, Marco Guadagni, and Lyda Favali (eds), *New Law for New States: Politica del diritto in Eritrea* (1998); Gianmaria Ajani, *Diritto dell'Europa Orientale* (1996); Gabriele Crespi Reghizzi, *L'impresa nel diritto sovietico* (1969); Marina Timoteo, *Il contratto in Cina e Giappone nello specchio dei diritti occidentali* (2004); Alessandro Simoni (ed), *Stato di diritto e identità Rom* (2005).

[38] See eg Silvio Ferrari, *Lo spirito dei diritti religiosi: ebraismo, cristianesimo e islam a confronto* (2002); Roberto Mazzola, *La pena latae sententiae nel diritto canonico: profili comparati di teoria generale* (2002).

[39] See eg Sabino Cassese, *La crisi dello Stato* (200); Maria Rosaria Ferrarese, *le diritto al presente: globalizzazione e tempo delle istituzioni* (2002); Paolo Grossi, *Mitologie gioridiche della modernità* (2001).

[40] Rodolfo Sacco, 'L'Italie en tête: à propos de l'enseignement du droit comparé', (1995) *Revue Internationale de Droit Comparé* 131.

strength of the so-called 'systemological approach' (associated mainly with René David), that is, the continuing interest among Italian comparatists in looking for deep constants, located at the level of legal sources or of legal style.

IV. Current Challenges and Future Directions: The Discipline Struggles with its Past

1. Beyond the Private Law Bias?

The private law bias referred to above continues to be an issue in Italian comparative law. There are signs that it is about to be overcome but, on the whole, the evidence is contradictory.

On the one hand, there are now, in each part of the Italian academic landscape, a few fairly well-established comparatists who function as chains of transmission for knowledge produced by core, private law-oriented, scholars to a variety of more peripheral subjects. The emergence of comparative work in areas outside private law, however, is not exactly a recent phenomenon. Even at the Gorla conference in 1979, one could identify experts not only in comparative civil procedure (itself the core business of Italian comparative law because of the Cappelletti school) and constitutional law (now an organized sub-field in its own right) but also in criminal procedure, labour law, and other fields. For a long time, though, these fields were largely ignored by the private law-oriented mainstream. While this is changing today, change comes slowly, and private law remains at centre stage.

On the other hand, recent developments have forced scholars in many legal areas beyond the traditional private law subjects to become comparatists of sorts. One of these developments is the significant 'Americanization' of Italian law in the post-cold war era. The influx of American ideas and institutions has stimulated (if not forced) a number of domestic law scholars across a variety of fields to come to grips with the transplants they are suddenly facing. The most obvious example is the attempted Americanization of Italian criminal procedure. It has, by necessity, attracted the interest of the respective specialists, who find it increasingly difficult to stick to their traditional positivistic and parochial attitude and who can no longer avoid looking at, and thinking about, models prevailing in a foreign legal culture. Another significant development is the ongoing legal integration of Europe and, beyond it, the globalization of law. This integration forces foreign, international, and comparative perspectives into many areas of domestic law, especially in the realm of economic regulation. As a result of these developments, areas outside private law are now experiencing what private law experienced in earlier decades: a 'comparativization' from the top down, so to speak, driven by the emerging shape of the international legal order. In other words, comparative perspectives are injected into many, if not most, areas of erstwhile purely domestic law.

Yet, despite these processes, and despite a general spread of comparative law to other areas, private law continues to remain at the centre of the discipline, at least for the time being.[41] Whether such a situation is defensible or not, at least at the academic level, comparative law in Italy is still primarily the business of an initiated circle whose members share professional interests and affiliations and are reluctant to share their traditional territory with newcomers from the outside.

2. The Lack of Political Influence

Unfortunately, in recent years, the influence of comparative knowledge on law reform in Italy has dramatically decreased. The reasons for this are mainly the often esoteric and academic nature of the comparative law discourse and the increasingly parochial attitude of the domestic law mainstream. It must be admitted that most of the recent law reforms in Italy were mainly the results of the above-mentioned 'Americanization' and the much trumpeted globalization of law, and that this has taken most core comparatists by surprise and thus with little to contribute.

Hard as it is to believe, the reception of the US-American model of criminal procedure, for example, occurred without any general comparatist pointing out the deep structural differences between Anglo-American and continental procedure. Had these differences been discussed (and understood), one could easily have predicted a general failure of the experiment.[42] Nor have comparatists been involved in the recent reform of crucial elements of substantive criminal law, such as the introduction of a new provision on self-defence which, again, was based on the US-American model; nor have they participated in the latest changes of sentencing rules which are based on an incapacitation rationale new to modern Italian legal culture. In a similar vein, the recent neo-liberal transformation of labour law occurred without any deep comparative understanding and without much attention to its impact on the Italian culture of rights. Almost incredibly, the same is true in the domain of corporate governance—a topic traditionally of great interest to a core group in the Italian comparative law tradition. Many other examples of

---

[41] For more on this subject, see Elisabetta Grande, 'Uno sguardo oltre il confine. La comparazione giuridica al di là del diritto privato', in Bertorello (n 32), 133 ff.

[42] For further discussion, see Elisabetta Grande, 'Italian Criminal Justice: Borrowing and Resistance', (2000) 48 AJCL 227 and *eadem* (n 41).

such failures to draw on the academic expertise of comparative law scholars could be cited. As a result, the practical impact of Italian academic comparatists in policy-making has been rather trivial, to say the least.

This does not mean that Italian law makers do not consider foreign models. Quite to the contrary, as we have seen, Italy has a long tradition of importing foreign legal ideas and, even today, numerous foreign rules and solutions find their way into the Italian legal system. The respective services in the Italian parliament provide legislators with short descriptions of foreign law but the knowledge derived from these briefings remains technical, a-contextual, and superficial. It is a far cry from the thick and thorough knowledge of foreign law that is necessary in order to make sound and circumspect decisions about what law to import from abroad.

It is tempting to explain this lack of academic influence on law reform as a result of the mainstream's commitment to a descriptive approach (as in the Theses of Trento) and thus, in a sense, to a 'conservative bias'. Yet, even assuming that such a bias really exists, the structuralist mainstream is not nearly the only player in Italian comparative law. As we have seen, there are other branches and traditions, such as the school of Florence. Its members have long openly rejected a strictly descriptive approach in favour of a policy-making and normative agenda. Perhaps the primary explanation for the negligible impact of Italian comparatists on law reform, and for the lack of critique of legal transformation in their own country, lies in the rapid growth of the discipline. The expansion from a very small number of academic chairs to a veritable industry in a matter of a few years has kept comparatists busy constructing their own professional project and thus focused overwhelmingly on academic concerns.[43] Paying so much attention to recruitment and appointments, methodological debates and academic conferences, they have had few resources left to participate in the realm of actual law making.

3. Interdisciplinary Trends

It is somewhat of a paradox that, while there is still very little dialogue between different areas of *legal* scholarship, Italian comparative law has made considerable progress towards an interdisciplinary approach involving *other* social sciences.

Beginning in the 1980s, Italian comparatists developed an interest in the 'Law and Economics' movement in the United States and soon began to import its paradigms.[44] The original hope that economics could offer a way to evaluate

---

[43] For a harsh critique from this perspective of Italian comparative law academia (and of comparative law academia in general), see Basil Markesinis, *Comparative Law in the Courtroom and Classroom: The Story of the Last Thirty-Five Years* (2003).

[44] See above n 31.

alternative institutional solutions in an objectively measurable way was eventually abandoned, albeit without much empirical experimentation. But economic analysis of law has also been combined with comparative analysis more generally and is now widely used for purposes of legal interpretation. More recently, it has also been discussed in a critical mode, especially for the purpose of exposing the economic fallacies underlying hegemonic patterns of dominance through law.[45]

Italian comparatists have also played a fairly significant role in the area of 'comparative law and critical legal studies' which is discussed in a separate chapter in this *Handbook*; in particular, scholars have noted certain analogies between the work of Rodolfo Sacco in Turin and Duncan Kennedy at Harvard.[46]

Last, but not least, Italian comparative law scholars have explored the possibilities of cooperation with legal anthropology. In fact, Italy is one of the few places in the world where both the French and English traditions of legal anthropology have been known and discussed for quite some time.[47] Italian translations of the leading books of both traditions have long been available. The study of legal anthropology (as well as of legal ethnology) has sought to understand unwritten and even completely non-verbalized legal phenomena in various contexts.[48] One should add that notions of legal pluralism were developed by Italian scholars as early as the 1920s (Santi Romano[49] and Venezian,[50] among others) and that an archaeological method of inquiry into African law has been used by several Italians, including Rodolfo Sacco in his early work on Somalia.[51]

On the other hand, the role of Italian scholars in the law and society movement has been minimal. As a result, an Italian version of 'comparative law and society'

---

[45] Mattei (2002) 10 *Indiana Journal of Global Legal Studies*, 383 ff.

[46] Elisabetta Grande, 'Ai confini delle responsabilità (prime riflessioni per un programma di ricerca in diritto comparato)', *Rassegna di Diritto Civile* 857, 897. The strong interest of Italian comparatists in the CLS (critical legal studies) movement can be detected in the following works: Giovanni Marini, 'I Critical Legal Studies', (1986) *Rivista critica di diritto privato* 187 ff; Ugo Mattei and Anna di Robilant, 'The Art and Science of Critical Scholarship: Postmodernism and International Style in the Legal Architecture of Europe', (2001) 75 *Tulane LR* 1053.

[47] Compare Gioseppe Mazzarella, *Studi di etnologia giuridica* (16 vols, 1903–37); Francesco Remotti, *Temi di antropologia giuridica* (1982); Riccardo Motta, *Teorie del diritto primitivo: un'introduzione all'antrolopologia giuridica* (1986).

[48] See Sacco, 'Mute law', (1995) 43 *AJCL* 455 ff, *idem*, 'Crittotipo', in Rodolfo Sacco (ed), 5 *Digesto 4 ed, Discipline privatistiche* (1989), 39; Alberto Gianola, 'L'analisi etologica del diritto', (1995) *Rivista di Diritto Civile* I, 805; Raffaele Caterina, 'Dominanza e possesso (e proprietà?) in alcune società non umane', (2000) *Rivista di Diritto Civile* II, 449 ff; Alba Negri, *Il giurista romanista di fronte all'etnologia giuridica* (1983); Elisabetta Grande, 'L'apporto dell'antropologia alla conoscenza del diritto (Piccola guida alla ricerca di nuovi itinerari)', (1996) *Rivista critica di diritto privato* 467 ff.

[49] Santi Romano, *L'ordinamento giuridico* (1951).

[50] Giacomo Venezian, *Opere giuridiche. 3. Scritti vari giuridici, sociali, politici* (1925).

[51] Rodolfo Sacco, *Le grandi linee del sistema giuridico somalo* (1985). See, also, above (n 38).

has yet to be invented, a translation of Lawrence Friedman's *History of American Law* notwithstanding.[52]

These interdisciplinary efforts aim to go to the very heart of legal phenomena and avoid the assumption that all law must be written or even spoken, let alone cast in official form. Overcoming this assumption, in turn, has improved and enriched the theory of legal formants. For example, collaboration between a comparatist and an economist has brought into sharper relief the observation that there is a competitive relationship among legal formants. Notably, the idea that there is competition among legal orders was discussed among Italian comparatists as early as the late 1980s, that is, years before this idea became much acclaimed in US-American legal scholarship in the field of corporate governance.[53]

Moreover, interdisciplinary work has broadened the focus of the legal formants approach. In its original version, this approach challenged the traditional hierarchical view of legal sources, showing, for instance, that an article in the civil code competes with a court decision in producing the governing rule. But this challenge had remained within the confines of legal positivism, so to speak. Recent work in legal anthropology has elucidated other, non-positive, factors that are at work as well. Thus, 'users' of law also influence legal change, for example, by making (non-professional) decisions that have an impact on how the law works, as when a victim's feeling of injustice drives him or her to bring a lawsuit or to pursue an appeal, or when a company seeks to maximize its profit by cutting (legal) corners. Today, Italian comparatists thus also consider 'meta-legal formants' among the components that constitute a legal rule, such as political backgrounds, economic environments, ideas currently in vogue, and the need for social cohesion. This has enabled them fully to appreciate the context in which a legal rule arises, operates, and has effects. Such an enriched, broader, version of the legal formants approach goes beyond officialdom and professionalism. It shows that legal formants are not independent of social, economic, and cultural factors and that dimensions of power, and especially of power disparity, play an important role in shaping the law.[54]

[52] Lawrence M. Friedman, *Storia del diritto americano*, (1995), translated for the series *Giuristi stranieri di oggi*, on which see n 55, by Guido Alpa Michele Marchesiello and Giorgio Rebuffa.

[53] Ugo Mattei and Francesco Pulitini, 'A Competitive Model of Legal Rules', in Albert Breton, Gianluigi Galeotti, Pierre Salmon, and Ronald Wintrobe (eds), *The Competitive State. Villa Colombella Papers on Competitive Politics* (1991), 207 ff.

[54] Laura Nader and Elisabetta Grande, 'Current Illusions and Delusions about Conflict Management, in Africa and Elsewhere', (2002) *Law and Social Inquiry* 579 ff.

V. FROM IMPORT TO EXPORT?
ITALIAN CONTRIBUTIONS TO COMPARATIVE LAW IN EUROPE AND BEYOND

'Contexts of reception' that import from abroad usually do not themselves contribute to the global legal landscape. For most of its modern history, Italian legal culture, expressing itself in a recessive language, has been no exception. Italian legal scholars, particularly specialists in purely domestic law, have, by and large, exercised little, if any, influence on the global level, with the possible exception of Spain and some regions in Latin America.

Yet, in recent years, several Italian jurists have become quite well-known and influential abroad. They have written in, or been translated into, English or French and have thus reached a wider audience. Thus, Italian legal scholarship has begun to play a more important role on the world stage.

To begin with, it is worth mentioning that the size of the group of Italian comparatists participating in the quadrennial congresses of the International Academy of Comparative Law has recently been second only to the US-American delegation. At every such congress, a significant number of Italian scholars have served as reporters. Italian comparatists regularly visit (as teachers or scholars) prestigious foreign institutions and a few are regular or semi-regular faculty members at universities in Europe, the United States, Asia, and Africa. In 2004, the prestigious Clarendon Lectures at Oxford University were delivered by an Italian.[55] Through these and other contacts, Italian comparatists are in permanent touch with scholarly developments on the global level, and foreign cutting-edge scholarship is often promptly translated into Italian.[56]

Several Italian comparatists have led major cooperative projects on an international scale. I have already mentioned Mauro Cappelletti, probably the most famous Italian comparative law scholar of recent times. Cappelletti's work on access to justice involved jurists from many countries and made a lasting contribution to the world of comparative legal scholarship.[57] More recently, the Trento Project on the 'Common Core of European Private Law', also described above, was launched, and has since been directed, by two Italian comparatists. Here, Sacco's

---

[55] Michele Graziadei, 'Against Self-Interest? Making Sense of Fiduciary Obligations in Comparative Perspective', (2005) Clarendon Lectures at Oxford University.

[56] Three series of translations promoted by Italian comparatists deserve mention here. Cosimo Mazzoni and Vicenzo Varano (eds), *Giuristi stranieri di oggi* (1986); Pietro Perlingeri (ed), *Traduzioni della Scuola di perfezionamento in diritto civile dell'Università di Camerino* (1980), and Ugo Mattei and Luisa Antoniolli (eds), *Diritto contro frontiere* (vol 1, 2003, vol 2, 2005).

[57] Cappelletti (n 7).

legal formants analysis, perhaps the most influential theoretical contribution of an Italian comparatist worldwide, is being combined with the factual approach developed by Schlesinger at Cornell a generation ago. Involving more than 200 scholars from all EU countries and beyond, the Trento project puts Italian comparative law methods to work on the European level.[58] Another notable project prominently involving an Italian comparatist is the 'Principles and Rules of Transnational Civil Procedure'. The project, a joint enterprise of UNIDROIT and the American Law Institute (ALI), was led by Michele Taruffo, a well-known Italian comparative law scholar, and Geoffrey Hazard, a prominent US-American proceduralist. In short, Italian comparatists are heavily involved in numerous projects, both in the context of European legal integration[59] and on a global scale.

Beyond all this, there are various other international projects involving Italian jurists who are specialists in commercial, private, criminal, or international law, rather than full fledged comparatists. In particular, one of the most significant international codifications of so-called 'soft law' is largely the work of an Italian scholar: the 'UNIDROIT Principles of International Commercial Contracts' are the product of an international working group under the leadership of Joachim Bonell, Gino Gorla's successor in Rome. The 'Principles' are a hugely important contribution not only to comparative legal scholarship but also, and perhaps more importantly, to international commercial law practice. Furthermore, there is the Gandolfi group, centred in the University of Pavia, which is producing a draft civil code for Europe. Italian experts are also contributing to the drafting of a European criminal code (the *Corpus Juris* project). And Italian jurists are participating in various international criminal tribunals, such as the International Criminal Court (ICC) and the tribunals for Yugoslavia (ICTY) and Rwanda (ICTR), thus helping to shape the new landscape of international criminal law.[60]

Finally, a few articles written by Italians (mostly in English) are widely discussed and cited abroad. Ugo Mattei's innovative taxonomy of the world's legal systems, proposing a dynamic classification, has been the object of international debate.[61] The same scholar was the first to present a combination of comparative law and economics to a wider international audience, creating a logo that is now in general use.[62]

It would perhaps go too far to say that we Italians are currently experiencing

---

[58] So far, seven volumes have been published under the general editorship of Mauro Bussani and Ugo Mattei; this number will increase in the near future.

[59] See Mauro Bussani, 'Integrative Comparative Law Enterprises and the Inner Stratification of Legal Systems', (2000) *ERPL* 83 ff.

[60] See eg Antonio Cassese and the journal that he recently launched: the *Journal of International Criminal Justice*, published by Oxford University Press.

[61] Ugo Mattei, 'Three Patterns of Law: Taxonomy and Change in the World's Legal Systems', (1997) 45 *AJCL* 5 ff.

[62] Ugo Mattei, *Comparative Law and Economics* (1997).

something of an inversion of the traditional situation, that is, a development from a 'context of reception' to a 'context of production'. Yet, in the last few decades, we have made fairly significant contributions to the progress of the discipline on a worldwide scale. Thus, for the first time in our modern history, we are not only importing foreign ideas but also exporting our own.

BIBLIOGRAPHY

Giorgio Lombardi, *Premesse al corso di diritto pubblico comparato: problemi di metodo* (1986)

Giuseppe De Vergottini, *Diritto costituzionale comparato* (1987)

Marco D'Alberti, *Diritto amministrativo comparato. Trasformazioni dei sistemi amministrativi in Francia, Gran Bretagna, Stati Uniti, Italia* (1992)

Ugo Mattei, *Common Law. Il diritto anglo-americano* (1992)

Rodolfo Sacco, *Introduzione al diritto comparato* (5th edn, 1992)

Aldo Mazzacane and Reiner Schulze, *Die deutsche und italienische Rechtskultur im Zeitalter der Vergleichung* (1995)

Gianmaria Ajani, *Il modello post-socialista* (1996)

Marco Guadagni, *Il modello pluralista* (1996)

Paolo Gallo, *Grandi sistemi giuridici* (1997)

Ugo Mattei and Pier Giuseppe Monateri, *Introduzione breve al diritto comparato* (1997)

Pier Giuseppe Monateri, *Il modello di civil law* (2nd edn, 1997)

Guido Alpa, Michael J. Bonell, Diego Corapi, Luigi Moccia, and Vincenzo Zeno-Zenchovich, *Diritto privato comparato, Istituti e problemi* (1999)

Rolando Tarchi (ed), *Corso di diritto comparato, vol I: Forme di Stato, Diritti di libertà, Forme di governo* (1999)

Christof Dipper, *Rechtskultur, Rechtswissenschaft, Rechtsberufe im 19. Jahrhundert: Professionalisierung und Verrechtlichung in Deutschland und Italien* (2000)

Mario Losano, *I grandi sistemi giuridici. Introduzione ai diritti europei ed extraeuropei,* (2000)

Francesco Palazzo and Michele Papa, *Lezioni di diritto penale comparato* (2000)

Maurizio Lupoi, *Sistemi giuridici comparati. Traccia di un corso* (2001)

Christian Resch, *Das italienische Privatrecht im Spannungsfeld von Code civil und BGB* (2001)

Antonio Gambaro and Rodolfo Sacco, *Sistemi giuridici comparati* (2nd edn, 2002)

Vittoria Barsotti and Vincenzo Varano, *La tradizione giuridica occidentale, vol I: Testo e materiali per un confronto common-law civil law* (3rd edn, 2006), *vol II: Argomenti per un confronto civil law-common law* (2003)

Gianmaria Ajani, *Sistemi giuridici comparati. Lezioni e materiali* (2005)

Ugo Mattei, *Il modello di common law* (2nd edn, 2005)

Alessandro Pizzorusso, *Comparazione giuridica e sistema delle fonti del diritto* (2005)

CHAPTER 4

DEVELOPMENT OF COMPARATIVE LAW IN GREAT BRITAIN

JOHN W. CAIRNS

Edinburgh

I. Introduction

In 1934, F. P. Walton (1858–1948) claimed that interest in foreign law had increased greatly in the last fifty years. He also pointed out that, despite the importance of the work of Sir Henry Maine (1822–88) on early customs, 'comparative law' now meant something different from evolutionary jurisprudence.[1] The view that it was towards the end of the nineteenth century that comparative law emerged in Britain as a scholarly domain still garners general agreement. Walton was here influenced by Sir Frederick Pollock (1845–1937), who had expressed the view that the 'complete recognition of the new branch of legal science' could be dated from 1869. This has been repeated and accepted. This was the year in which the French Society of Comparative Legislation was founded and Maine appointed as the first Corpus Professor of Historical and Comparative Jurisprudence in Oxford.[2]

Other symbolic events supporting Walton's claim include the foundation of the Society of Comparative Legislation in December 1894, which had the practical

---

[1] F. P. Walton, 'The Study of Foreign Laws', (1934) 46 *Juridical Review* 1.

[2] See H. C. Gutteridge, *Comparative Law: An Introduction to the Comparative Method of Legal Study and Research* (2nd edn, 1949), 17; J. A. Jolowicz, 'Comparative Law in Twentieth-Century England', in Jack Beatson and Reinhard Zimmermann (eds), *Jurists Uprooted: German-Speaking Émigré Lawyers in Twentieth-Century Britain* (2004), 345 f; Frederick Pollock, 'The History of Comparative Jurisprudence', (1903) 5 (NS) *Journal of the Society of Comparative Legislation* 74 ff, 86; Walton (1934) 46 *Juridical Review* 1; L. Neville Brown, 'A Century of Comparative Law in England: 1869–1969', (1971) 19 *AJCL* 232.

primary aim of 'promoting knowledge of the course of legislation', particularly in the Empire and the United States, and the First Congress of Comparative Law at Paris in 1900, where there was a small British delegation including Pollock. The Congress had no immediate impact of consequence in Britain, probably because Raymond Saleilles (1855–1912), the main organizer, saw comparative law as revealing the universal, but not immutable, principles common to all civilized legal systems—a view not especially sympathetic to British scholars.[3]

The late-Victorian crystallization of comparative law reflected the period's increased focus on law as a national rather than universal discipline. The term, 'comparative law', started to become fixed in the years around 1900; by 1914, it was normal.[4] As a discipline, however, it was full of tensions, and the significance ascribed to different dates arose from different emphases among comparatists. Despite such variation, most strands in the early development of British comparative law were closely linked to the experiences and needs of the British Empire.

II. Empire: Evolution and Legislation

Development of comparative philology, comparative anatomy, and comparative geology had popularized the idea that there was a scientific 'comparative method'.[5] Legal scholars adopted the idea that comparative investigation of law could lead to advances in understanding law, as the analytical jurisprudence associated with Bentham and Austin became increasingly unfashionable. James Bryce (1838–1922), Regius Professor of Civil Law in Oxford from 1870–93, provided a powerful account of this view. In *Studies in History and Jurisprudence*, he stated that four methods were 'employed in legal science'. He largely dismissed the first two—the metaphysical and the analytic—arguing that the third—the historical method— had superior explanatory force. The 'youngest of the four' was the comparative, which allowed construction of a system that was 'Natural', 'Philosophical', and 'Serviceable'. The 'comparative science of jurisprudence' had two forms. The first was historical. The second, though it could not 'dispense with the aid of history',

---

[3] 'Statement of the Objects of the Society', (1896–7) 1 *Journal of the Society of Comparative Legislation*, vi; Courtney Ilbert, 'The Society of Comparative Legislation', (1895) 38 *Nineteenth Century* 142 ff; 'Notes', (1900) 2 (NS) *Journal of the Society of Comparative Legislation* 190, 404 ff; Gutteridge (n 2), 5–6.

[4] Edward Jenks, 'On the Study of Comparative Jurisprudence', (1900) 2 (NS) *Journal of the Society of Comparative Legislation* 446 ff, 446 f.

[5] See Stefan Collini, Donald Winch, and John Burrow, *That Noble Science of Politics: A Study in Nineteenth-Century Intellectual History* (1983), 207 ff; J. W. Burrow, *Evolution and Society* (1966), 42 ff, 149 ff.

had 'a palpably practical aim' and was 'directed to contemporary phenomena'. Bryce considered the 'historical form' of the comparative method useful for 'legal training and legal theory'. Practical use of the comparative method helped courts explore 'questions of liability and responsibility and negligence', but primarily belonged to 'the province of legislation than to that of law'.[6] These two under-standings of comparative law dominated the period from the later nineteenth century to World War I and beyond. The growth of the Empire from the eighteenth century onwards provided the context in which both approaches developed.

1. Problems of Empire

English law was exported to the colonies, which were largely self-governing. But when colonial territories of other states were acquired, Britain generally preserved the existing civil laws. This meant that the Empire included colonies governed by Roman-Dutch law, French customary law, Spanish law, and the *Code civil*. Indigen-ous legal traditions, particularly Hindu and Muslim law, were also recognized. Contact with such laws and traditions stimulated reflection on evolution and legal theory.[7]

By 1895, it could be written that '[n]o monarch has ever formed a constituent part of so many Legislatures as the Queen of England. . . . Some sixty Legislatures are at work in the British Empire'.[8] Thus, even those colonies that had received English common law developed their own statutes and precedents. It was possible to appeal from the courts of most colonies and overseas territories and dominions to the monarch in his or her Privy Council, which was presumed to know the differing laws of all. This echoed the problem that had arisen in the eighteenth century with Scottish appeals to the House of Lords, only resolved in this era with regular appointment of Scots lawyers to the Lords.

In 1838, William Burge, drawing on extensive experience in dealing with appeals to the Privy Council from a variety of colonies, published *Commentaries on Colonial and Foreign Laws*. His aim was to provide useful information about 'those systems of foreign jurisprudence which are most frequently presented to the consideration of an English tribunal'. A massive, four-volume work, this encompassed the law of Scotland and of other European states, as well as of the colonies.[9] Though a brave attempt, it was inevitably soon out of date.

---

[6] James Bryce, 'The Method of Legal Science', in James Bryce, *Studies in History and Jurisprudence* (2 vols, 1901), vol 2, 172 ff, 174, 184 ff.

[7] See generally M. S. Amos, 'The Common Law and the Civil Law in the British Commonwealth of Nations', (1937) 50 *Harvard LR* 1249 ff.

[8] Ilbert, (1895) 38 *Nineteenth Century* 142.

[9] William Burge, *Commentaries on Colonial and Foreign Laws Generally, And in their Conflict with Each Other, and with the Law of England* (vol I, 1838), Dedication (dated 1837), ii–v.

2. Comparative Evolutionary and Historical Jurisprudence

As early as 1810, Anselm von Feuerbach (1775–1833) had argued that empirical comparative legal studies would lead to a universal jurisprudence.[10] Maine crucially took up this idea. Briefly Regius Professor of Civil Law at Cambridge, where his classes were 'concerned with general jurisprudence, illustrated by Roman and English law', he was appointed Corpus Professor of Historical and Comparative Jurisprudence in Oxford in 1869.[11] In *Ancient Law* (1861), he had divided societies into progressive and stationary: Hindu society was stationary, while Roman and English were progressive. Mirroring contemporary comparative philology, Maine investigated the legal history of what he considered to be the Aryan or Indo-European races. Understanding of the early legal history of Europe could thus be deepened—in his view—by comparative consideration of the institutions of other Aryan peoples. By such comparative study he hoped to develop a historical jurisprudence that demonstrated rules of legal progress.[12]

This approach led to an emphasis on the comparison of English with Roman law, especially since Maine thought that the former, as it matured, became more like the latter.[13] This was taken up by Pollock, who claimed that 'vindication of the historical and comparative method in law . . . may be thought superfluous'. In his valedictory lecture as Corpus Professor, he still echoed the views of Maine, remarking that comparison of the Roman law of property with the current English law of real property would not throw light 'on anything in the past history of English law, but on what English law may tend to become in the days of our children or grandchildren'.[14]

Similar emphasis on comparison of English with Roman law is found in the work of Bryce. In his inaugural lecture at Oxford, he stated that the comparative method had taught 'us much respecting the structure of primitive society, and has [become] the means of illustrating many curious phenomena in the politics and philosophy of more recent times'. Of modern systems of law, there were 'besides those of Teutonic origin' (such as English) only three really worth mentioning: Hindu law; 'Muhamadan' law; and Roman law. The first was 'fully developed only

---

[10] Konrad Zweigert and Hein Kötz, *Introduction to Comparative Law* (trans Tony Weir, 3rd edn, 1998), 52 f.

[11] Peter Stein, 'Maine and Legal Education', in Alan Diamond (ed), *The Victorian Achievement of Sir Henry Maine: A Centennial Reappraisal* (1991), 195 ff, 197.

[12] Henry Maine, 'The Effects of the Observation of India on Modern European Thought', in *idem, Village-Communities in the East and West. Six Lectures Delivered at Oxford. Fourth Edition to which are added other Lectures, Addresses and Essays* (1881), 205 ff, 223 f; see also *idem, Village-Communities*, 6 f; *idem, Ancient Law: Its Connection with the Early History of Society and its Relation to Modern Ideas* (8th edn, 1880), 7; Peter Stein, *Legal Evolution: The Story of an Idea* (1980), 93 ff.

[13] Henry Maine, 'Roman Law and Legal Education' (1856), in *idem, Village-Communities* (n 12), 330 ff, 332 f.

[14] Pollock, (1903) 5 (NS) *Journal of the Society of Comparative Legislation* 74, 76, 79; Neil Duxbury, *Frederick Pollock and the English Juristic Tradition* (2004), 7 f, 85 ff.

in two or three directions'; the second was 'deficient on some of the sides we should deem the most important'. This meant that, '[s]o far . . . as the doctrines of law in its civilized and developed forms, suited to a progressive modern nation, are concerned, the comparative method is virtually restricted to a comparison of English and Roman conceptions and rules'.[15] W. Jethro Brown (1868–1930), Professor of Constitutional and Comparative Law at Aberystwyth, though holding different views on legal philosophy, agreed, and his first-year Roman-law course involved a comparison of the historical development of Roman law with English law and of their respective laws of obligations.[16]

Supporting such comparisons of Roman and English law was a belief that both had an imperial mission. In the 1890s, Sir Courtenay Ilbert (1841–1924), a parliamentary draftsman with experience of India, regretted that a jurist was still wanted who would 'expound the Spirit of English Law', and who would 'show how it seems destined to play in India and in the new continents the part that has been played in the continent of Europe by the law of Rome'.[17] Bryce produced a number of comparative studies of English and Roman law in an imperial context, while J. E. G. de Montmorency (1866–1934), in the 1920s Quain Professor of Comparative and Historical Law in University College London, also argued for parallels between the British and Roman Empires.[18]

Maine's thought long continued influential. The admiration of Maine by Sir John Macdonell led him to value Rudolf von Jhering's posthumously published works as a study of the 'Aryan' peoples and their laws as the background to Roman law. A founder of the Society of Comparative Legislation and for long editor of its *Journal*, and (from 1901) de Montmorency's predecessor in the Quain chair, Macdonell's enthusiasm led to lectures on 'Comparative Law since Maine', emphasizing the need to pursue his legacy.[19] De Montmorency characterized the chief task of the

---

[15] Bryce, 'The Academical Study of the Civil Law', in *idem, Studies in History and Jurisprudence* (2 vols, 1901), vol 2, 475 ff, 484 f; *idem* (n 6), 188 f.

[16] W. Jethro Brown, 'The Purpose and Method of a Law School', (1902) 18 *LQR* 78 ff (Part I), 192 ff (Part II), 193 ff. See John Andrews, 'A Century of Legal Education', (2003) 34 *Cambrian LR* 3 ff, 8 ff. On Brown's theories, see R. W. Ireland, 'John Austin, H. L. A. Hart . . . Oh, and W. Jethro Brown', (2003) 34 *Cambrian Law Review* 57 ff.

[17] Ilbert, (1895) 38 *Nineteenth Century* 142, 154.

[18] James Bryce, 'The History of Legal Development at Rome and in England' and 'Marriage and Divorce in Roman and in English Law', both in *idem, Studies in History and Jurisprudence* (2 vols, 1901), vol 2, 338 ff and 381 ff; J. E. G. de Montmorency, Letter, (5 September 1929) *The Times* 8A; *idem*, 'India and the Roman Empire', (14 November 1931) *The Times* 7F (report of lecture).

[19] John Macdonell, 'Rudolph von Ihering', in John Macdonell and Edward Manson (eds), *Great Jurists of the World* (1913), 590 ff, 593, 597. On Macdonell, see Michael Lobban, 'Macdonell, Sir John (1845–1921)', in H. C. G. Matthew and Brian Harrison (eds), *Oxford Dictionary of National Biography* (2004); Jolowicz (n 2) 350 ff; H. J. Randall, 'Sir John Macdonell and the Study of Comparative Law' (1930) 12 (3rd Series) *Journal of Comparative Legislation and International Law* 188 ff; Anon, 'The Value of Comparative Law' (1919) 148 *Law Times* 189; John Macdonell, 'Introduction', in John Macdonell and Edward Manson (eds), *Great Jurists of the World* (1913), ix ff, xv.

jurists as 'to show how the spirit and history of each nation is revealed in its laws' while the 'comparative method' would demonstrate 'how much there is in common between the various systems of law, and the historic reasons why there are these common elements'.[20] The brilliant medievalist Paul Vinogradoff (1854–1925), Pollock's successor as Corpus Professor, maintained the importance of the comparative method and the thought of Maine. In his final major, unfinished work, *Outlines of Historical Jurisprudence*, he developed a scheme of 'ideological' evolutionary stages of jurisprudence.[21] C. K. Allen (1887–1966), once Vinogradoff's assistant, wrote in 1927 that the 'science of "comparative" jurisprudence', which had steadily grown 'for the last sixty years at least', was the 'study of racial origins and early social institutions'—a sentence essentially preserved until 1964.[22]

Legal evolutionists, however, started to develop a more ethnological approach, mindful of the needs of the Empire. Edward Jenks (1861–1939) saw 'comparative jurisprudence' as providing practical assistance in humane dealing with the 'subject races' of the Empire. Macdonell argued for a survey of the 'primitive laws' of the Empire. 'Few things', he wrote, were 'more needed in the interest of comparative jurisprudence'.[23] The work of S. G. Vesey-Fitzgerald (1884–1954), who considered himself a pupil of Vinogradoff, underlined the practical significance of such studies. After a career in the Indian Civil Service, he taught probationers for the Indian and Tropical Administrative Services in Oxford, also becoming Lecturer in Hindu and Mohammedan Law for the Council of Legal Education in 1927. In 1937, he became Reader in Indian Law and then, in 1946, Professor of Oriental Laws in the University of London, demitting office in 1951. He guided the establishment of the Law School at the School of Oriental and African Studies. He argued that comparative law was important 'in the present-day problems of the British Empire, whose administrators we had to train'. The comparative method was necessary for 'the right understanding of any one of the immense variety of

---

[20] J. E. G. de Montmorency, 'Danish Influence on English Law and Character', (1924) 40 *LQR* 324 ff, 325. His inaugural lecture was entitled 'The Natural History of Law': Obituary, (10 March 1934) *The Times* 14D. In 1931 he lectured on 'Sir Henry Maine and the Historical Jurists', (30 October 1931) *The Times* 9D.

[21] Paul Vinogradoff, 'The Teaching of Sir Henry Maine', (1904) 20 *LQR* 119 ff; *idem*, 'Presidential Address', in *idem* (ed), *Essays in Legal History Read before the International Congress of Historical Studies Held in London in 1913* (1913), 3 ff; H. A. L. Fisher, 'Paul Vinogradoff: A Memoir', in Louise Vinogradoff (ed), *Collected Papers of Paul Vinogradoff* (2 vols, 1928), vol 1, 3 ff, 62; Paul Vinogradoff, *Outlines of Historical Jurisprudence* (2 vols, 1920–22), vol 1, 155. See Peter Stein, 'Vinogradoff, Sir Paul Gavrilovitch [Pavel Gavrilovich Vinogradov] (1854–1925)', in H. C. G. Matthew and Brian Harrison (eds), *Oxford Dictionary of National Biography* (2004).

[22] C. K. Allen, *Law in the Making* (1927), 21 f.

[23] Jenks, (1900) 2 (NS) *Journal of Comparative Legislation* 446, 448 ff; John Macdonell, 'Primitive Laws and their Investigation: A Suggestion', (1907) 8 (NS) *Journal of the Society of Comparative Legislation*, 104 ff. Jenks saw Josef Kohler as having supplied the necessary methodology: see Leonard Adam, 'Josef Kohler und die vergleichende Rechtswissenschaft', (1920) 37 *Zeitschrift für vergleichende Rechtswissenschaft* 1 ff.

systems by which the King's subjects lived'. The 'study of primitive law' was 'vitally important for tropical Africa', but 'required constant comparison with more civilized systems to prevent its degenerating into anthropology'.[24] In 1946, he wrote that 'comparative jurisprudence in the sense in which those words are usually associated with the name of Sir Henry Maine is suffering from a neglect'—this was 'largely undeserved'.[25] He regretted that scholars had not followed Maine's insights about the significance of the Sanskrit law books to develop 'a new science of Comparative Jurisprudence'.[26]

3. The Society of Comparative Legislation

Maine himself wrote in 1871 that, 'the chief function of Comparative Jurisprudence is to facilitate legislation and the practical improvement of the law'.[27] A state that lived by trade also needed to develop understanding of the commercial laws of other countries. Study of foreign legislation of other parts of the Empire and the world not only assisted litigation, but also helped develop better statutes on particular topics. In November 1894, Ilbert accordingly pointed out to the Imperial Institute that it would be expedient to take 'steps towards arranging, organising, and completing our stock of knowledge about the course of legislation in different parts of the British Empire and in the United States of America'.[28]

A meeting followed on 19 December 1894, chaired by Lord Chancellor Herschell (1837–99), with the aim of considering 'the best means of furthering the study of Comparative Legislation'. This led to the foundation of a 'Society for Comparative Legislation', which had 'the object of promoting knowledge of the course of legislation in different countries, more particularly in the several parts of her Majesty's Dominions, and in the United States'. The Privy Council's needs also justified the initiative, the main movers behind which were Macdonell and Ilbert.[29]

Ilbert explained that it was most important to acquire knowledge of the legislation not only of the sixty or so colonial legislatures, but also of the fifty more found in the United States, which he considered part of 'Greater Britain'.

---

[24] See his remarks quoted in the discussion in H. C. Gutteridge, 'The Value of Comparative Law', (1931) *Journal of the Society of Public Teachers of Law* 26 ff, 31 f. See S. G. Vesey-Fitzgerald, *Muhammadan Law: An Abridgement According to its Various Schools* (1931), vi; *idem, The Future of Oriental Legal Studies: An Inaugural Lecture Delivered at University College London* (1948), 1; *Who Was Who, 1951–1960* (4th edn, 1984), s.v. 'Vesey-Fitzgerald'; Obituary, (30 September 1954) *The Times* 8E; letter by J. N. D. Anderson, (6 October 1954) *The Times* 8E.

[25] S. G. Vesey-Fitzgerald, 'Sir William Jones, The Jurist', (1946) 11 *Bulletin of the School of Oriental and African Studies* 807 ff, 816.

[26] Vesey-Fitzgerald, *Future of Oriental Legal Studies* (n 24), 9 f.

[27] Maine, *Village-Communities* (n 12), 4.   [28] Ilbert, (1895) 38 *Nineteenth Century* 142 ff.

[29] 'Statement of the Objects of the Society' (n 3), vi f.; Randall, (1930) 12 (3rd Series) *Journal of Comparative Legislation and International Law* 188, 189.

Different solutions were being everywhere attempted for similar problems: '[o]ur colonies present specimens of almost every type of legislation on subjects such as education, the regulation of labour, the relief of the poor, the control of the liquor traffic'. While similar problems might arise in France or Germany, 'the laws and institutions of the English speaking-world are differentiated by a characteristic mode of approaching the problems with which they have to deal'. Spread around the world, 'the English-speaking race' approached similar problems 'in substantially the same spirit'—a spirit rather different from those of the Germans or French. It was accordingly 'not surprising that different legislatures, dealing with similar problems, and animated by a common spirit should copy each other's laws'. One of the 'chief aims of [the Society] will be the collection of information as to the statute law and forms and methods of legislation in the British Empire and the United States'. In 1902, the Society expressed the aim to the colonial premiers present in London, that it should become 'a legal consultative Council of the Empire', indicating areas in which it could help in gathering and disseminating information about legislation and assist in codifying the commercial law of the Empire. It even considered itself representative of 'the scientific spirit, the movement towards unity, in law, never so much needed as in these days'.[30]

To fulfil the Society's aspirations various standing committees would be appointed, the first of which would be a Statute Law Committee. The Society would also pay attention to those issues of interest more to the jurist and student than practitioner, by which Ilbert meant comparative jurisprudence in the tradition of Maine. The practical advantages to be derived from the work of the Society were better legislation, awareness of what might work from knowledge of what had happened elsewhere, and further stimulation and promotion of 'that tendency towards uniformity of law which is so marked among the English-speaking races'.[31] Further underscoring the importance of such work was the complex nature of the Privy Council's jurisdiction over many different legal systems.[32] Four standing committees were established to fulfil scientific and practical ambitions: on Statute Law; on Mercantile Law; on Procedure; and on Comparative and Historical Jurisprudence. It is easy to trace the activity of all of them other than the last, though it contained such luminaries as Professors A. V. Dicey (1835–1922), F. W. Maitland (1850–1906), and Pollock.[33]

[30] Ilbert, (1895) 38 *Nineteenth Century* 142, 144 f.; 'Notes', (1902) 4 (NS) *Journal of the Society of Comparative Legislation* 85 ff, 96 ff. The idea of 'Greater Britain' was drawn from the thinking of Charles Wentworth Dilke.

[31] Ilbert, (1895) 38 *Nineteenth Century* 142, 153.

[32] 'Statement of the Objects of the Society' (n 3), vi ff. The similarity to Ilbert, (1895) 38 *Nineteenth Century* 142 ff suggests this 'Statement' was drafted by him. He evidently had Burge (n 9) in front of him.

[33] 'Departmental Committees', (1896–7) 1 *Journal of the Society of Comparative Legislation*, v; see 'Annual Meeting', (1897) 2 *Journal of the Society of Comparative Legislation*, iii f.

The content of the first two series of the Society's *Journal* indicates the interests of the members as understood by the editors. Most obvious is the concern with the laws of the Empire combined with the practical aim of improving legislation. Until merger with the *International Law Quarterly* in 1952, a substantial proportion of the *Journal* consisted of a review and index of imperial and other legislation. Related issues were assimilation and codification of imperial law: in general, if codification was not considered feasible, assimilation of mercantile law was thought both possible and desirable. Proposals to erect a suitable final appeal court for the entire Empire, ending the distinction between the Judicial Committees of the Privy Council and the House of Lords, so that there be one court for the colonies, Scotland, England, and Ireland, also interested the Society. Grounds for appeal to the Privy Council from 'the Queen's dominions beyond seas' also were considered. The *Journal* noted the first time a Colonial judge sat on a British appeal in the House of Lords in 1914, when Lord de Villiers, the Chief Justice of South Africa, sat on a Scottish appeal; the similarity of Scottish and South African laws made this appropriate. Indeed, the development of extensive gold and diamond mining in South Africa had made Roman-Dutch law the common law of a rich and important part of the Empire, and the attention devoted to it far outweighed occasional discussions of the use of Spanish and French law in the Empire.[34]

The *Journal* paid great attention to mercantile and commercial law, particularly international conventions on topics such as bills of exchange, including provision of information about other countries. Practical information, such as the problems arising for English companies with assets in France issuing debentures and the difficulties for British companies carrying on business in Germany were noted and analysed. There were some genuinely comparative studies, such as a brief consideration of the penal consequences of bankruptcy in England and the United States and descriptions of partnership and patent law in the Empire.

In 1900, Jenks, a member of the Society's original committee on 'Comparative and Historical Jurisprudence', challenged the Society's aims, pleading for a remedy of the neglect of the study of 'comparative jurisprudence'. He did note, however, that the contents of the Society's *Journal* were wider in scope than the title of the Society might suggest.[35] Ilbert replied to Jenks in a paper taking stock of the Society's achievements. He argued that the aim of the Society had been very specific: to acquire 'better, fuller, more accurate information about the course of legislation in different parts of the world', on the model of the French Society. Further, the title of the Society had not limited its operations. He added that study of comparative legislation was in some ways wider than that of comparative law

---

[34] 'Notes', (1914) 14 (NS) *Journal of the Society of Comparative Legislation* 283 ff, 285; Alexander Wood Renton, 'Indian and Colonial Appeals to the Privy Council', (1899) 1 (NS) *Journal of the Society of Comparative Legislation* 345 ff.

[35] Jenks, (1900) 2 (NS) *Journal of Comparative Legislation* 446 f.

or jurisprudence, transcending the disciplinary boundary of law and crossing into political science, economics, and sociology.[36]

In 1917, the Society's Executive Committee appointed an Editorial Committee, under the chairmanship of Macdonell, to produce its *Journal*, now renamed *Journal of Comparative Legislation and International Law*. This included de Montmorency and two other distinguished international lawyers, given 'the present importance of the subject of International Law'. The Executive Committee stressed, however, that 'this development should not affect in any way the primary objects of the Society, which are to publish an annual review of legislation and to record the development and working of the laws passed in the different parts of the Empire'.[37]

Into the 1920s, the focus of the Society thus remained the Empire. World War I made imperial connections seem more important, even starting debates over its future government and potentially closer union. This made 'the appeal for such a record of legislation . . . even stronger'.[38] Given the financial and other support given the Society by the Dominions, Crown Colonies, Foreign Office, Board of Trade, and Colonial Office, this attitude was not surprising. It is important to remember, however, that during its first twenty-five years, the *Journal* established a tradition of a broad approach to comparative law, practical, legislative, and academic. The attitude was ultimately catholic and pragmatic, encompassing studies of foreign law and legislation, evolutionary historical legal theorizing, and, if much of the periodical was simply informative about foreign legal systems, this was a growing body of useful information.

III. Modern Foundations

In 1936, B. A. Wortley (1907–89) described H. C. Gutteridge and Sir Maurice Amos (1872–1940) with 'other enthusiasts' as having carried out 'admirable pioneer work'. Ten years later, Wortley described Gutteridge as 'the *doyen* of English comparative lawyers', and 'mainly responsible' for the development of comparative law in England since the end of World War I.[39] Without denigrating Gutteridge's

---

[36] Courtney Ilbert, 'The Work and Prospects of the Society', (1908) 9 (NS) *Journal of the Society of Comparative Legislation* 14 ff.

[37] 'Notes', (1918) 18 (NS) *Journal of Comparative Legislation and International Law* 302 ff, 306 f.

[38] See the discussion of 'The Coming of Age of the Society' in 'Notes', (1916) 16 (NS) *Journal of the Society of Comparative Legislation* 67 ff, 78 f.

[39] B. A. Wortley, 'Some Reflections on Legal Research', (1935) *Journal of the Society of Public Teachers of Law* 52 ff, 54; *idem*, 'Review', (1947) 23 *International Affairs* 396.

importance as an advocate for comparative law, it is important to stress that he was not alone in pursuing an agenda to establish the subject in Britain; also important were Walton, Frederic M. Goadby (1875–1956), R. W. Lee (1868–1958), and Vesey-Fitzgerald.

If building on the tradition of pragmatism already established, these men institutionalized a modernizing vision of comparative law, somewhat different from that associated with Macdonell and Ilbert, that lasted beyond World War II. They achieved this through involvement with the Societies of Comparative Legislation and Public Teachers of Law, development of international links, engagement with international bodies, and persuasive scholarship. Aiding this were strong bonds of friendship and cooperation. Other than Gutteridge, all had shared experiences in the British Empire.

1. The Pioneers

(a) Gutteridge

Called to the bar in 1900, Gutteridge developed a practice in commercial law, to which he devoted much of his scholarship, having been a pupil of his life-long friend, the future Lord Atkin. An establishment man, with good links to the judiciary and the world of politics and power, he was appointed as British delegate to The Hague Conference on Private International Law, to the Geneva Conferences on unification of the law of bills of exchange, and served on government commissions and committees. In 1919 he was elected Sir Ernest Cassel Professor of Industrial and Commercial Law in the London School of Economics, though continuing some practice at the bar. The holder of this chair had 'the duty of promoting the study of Comparative Commercial Law'. Private means allowed him to leave his London chair in 1930, accepting a Fellowship at Trinity Hall, Cambridge combined with a University Lectureship. Promoted Reader by 1933 and to a personal chair in Comparative Law in 1934, he retired in 1941. His involvement in the world of affairs and the authority of his Cambridge chair helped establish his credentials and promote his discipline.[40]

Between 1904 and 1909, he provided the 'Review of the Legislation of Newfoundland' for the *Journal of the Society of Comparative Legislation*. He was an Honorary Secretary of the Executive Committee of the Society from 1921–45, when he became

---

[40] Lord McNair, rev, 'Gutteridge, Harold Cooke (1876–1953)', in H. C. G. Matthew and Brian Harrison (eds), *Oxford Dictionary of National Biography* (2004); Obituary, (31 December 1953) *The Times* 8D; C. J. H[amson], 'H. C. Gutteridge at Cambridge', (1954) 3 *ICLQ* 377 ff; C. J. H[amson], 'Harold Cooke Gutteridge', (1954) *Cambridge LJ* 197 ff, 198; Kurt Lipstein, 'H. C. Gutteridge at Cambridge', (1954) 3 *ICLQ* 381 ff, 382; H. C. Gutteridge, 'The Study of Comparative Law in France and England', (1922) 4 (3rd Series) *Journal of Comparative Legislation and International Law* 84 ff, 86.

assistant to the Honorary Editors of the *Journal*, until it amalgamated into the *International and Comparative Law Quarterly*.

Gutteridge's first publication as Cassel Professor was on commercial documents and partly comparative. By 1925, three further articles touching on international commerce demonstrated the two main themes that run through all of his work in comparative law: unification and private international law.[41] These were prominent in the first (published 1922) of a number of essays he produced arguing for the importance of comparative law and sketching out a methodology, comparing achievement abroad with inactivity in Britain. This essay contrasted the position in England with that in France, with the Institutes in Paris under Henri Lévy-Ullmann (1870–1947) and Lyons under Edouart Lambert (1886–1947). If unification of law 'throughout the civilized world' was a dream, he argued that it was important to know the laws of other countries. The 'function of the comparative lawyer' was to ascertain definitely the 'conflicting rules of law' and to consider whether they resulted from 'differences in fundamental conceptions of rights and duties' or were 'merely excrescences on the general body of the law': the latter could easily be abolished. Gutteridge stressed that comparative research involved collaboration with scholars in other countries. He argued that a central, international body might usefully be created to bring together 'comparative lawyers of all nations' to promote collaboration. The importance of such bodies featured in his next essay on comparative law (a report of the address Lambert made to the Society of Public Teachers of Law (SPTL) in 1925) in which the recent foundation of the International Academy of Comparative Law and of an Institute for the Unification of Law in Rome by the Italian government were prominent.[42]

In 1931, Gutteridge addressed the annual meeting of the SPTL on 'The Value of Comparative Law'. Again stressing how vital comparative study was for private international law, he regretted modern authors' neglect of the 'exhaustive comparative study of the rules of conflict [that] would in many instances have yielded very valuable results'. He also argued that knowledge of comparative law was vital to trade. It was necessary 'to understand the structure of foreign law, the meaning of foreign legal terminology, and the mentality of foreign lawyers'. Furthermore, knowledge of foreign law would help in national legal reform. This need not wait

---

[41] H. C. Gutteridge, 'The Law of England and America relating to Warehouse Receipts', (1921) 3 (3rd Series) *Journal of Comparative Legislation and International Law* 5 ff; *idem*, 'The Limitation of the Liability of Shipowners', (1921) 2 *Economica* 180 ff; *idem*, 'The Law Relating to "Received for Shipment" Bills of Lading', (1922) 4 *Economica* 17 ff; *idem*, 'The Law of Bankers' Commercial Credits', (1923) 7 *Economica* 35 ff. For a listing of his publications, see C. J. Hamson, 'Publications of Professor H. C. Gutteridge', (1954) 3 *ICLQ* 386 ff which is incomplete and in parts inaccurate.

[42] Gutteridge, (1922) 4 (3rd Series) *Journal of Comparative Legislation and International Law* 84, 86 ff; *idem*, 'The Institutes of Comparative Law in France and Italy', (1925) 7 (3rd Series) *Journal of Comparative Legislation and International Law* 212 ff.

for legislation, but jurists could use their knowledge of foreign law to help shape their own laws. He instanced the problem of abuse of rights.[43]

On retirement, Gutteridge published an essay on 'Comparative Law as a Factor in English Legal Education'. The picture was gloomy: '[v]ery little is left of the effort made in England over a period of rather more than seventy years to find a place for the comparative method in the teaching of the law'. For Scotland he cited the statement of J. C. Gardner (1902–57) that there was 'no course of Comparative Law at any of the Scottish Universities, and no facilities for studying it'. During the war years, he followed this with essays on comparative law and the conflict of laws and comparative law and the law of nations, as he explored further the nature of the discipline, leading in 1946 to his *Comparative Law: An Introduction to the Study of the Comparative Method of Legal Study and Research*, in which he summed up his views. As the first British book to address the subject of comparative law it proved very influential. A broad-ranging, even diffuse, work, its message was: comparative law was simply a method; unification was an important issue (though some scepticism was obvious); and that comparative law was important in private international law and the law of nations.[44] It was well received.[45]

(b) Walton

Walton was the most important pioneer after Gutteridge. After classics at Oxford, he studied law in Edinburgh and Marburg, being admitted an advocate in 1886. In 1894, he was appointed Lecturer in Civil (i.e., Roman) Law in the University of Glasgow, before appointment as Professor of Roman Law and Dean of the Faculty of Law at McGill University in Montreal in 1897. In 1915 he succeeded Amos as Director of the Khedivial School of Law in Cairo. He returned to Britain in the early to mid–1920s, settling in Oxford. In 1932, he retired to Edinburgh.[46]

Walton's training in Scots law, interest in Roman law, and imperial career determined his approach to comparative law. A 'profound canonist', Walton's earliest publications were on the Scots law of marriage, while he edited a collection

---

[43] Gutteridge, (1931) *Journal of the Society of Public Teachers of Law* 26, 28 ff, 30.

[44] H. C. Gutteridge, 'Comparative Law as a Factor in English Legal Education', (1941) 23 (3rd Series) *Journal of Comparative Legislation and International Law* 130 ff; J. C. Gardner, 'The Study of Comparative Law in Great Britain', (1932) 14 (3rd Series) *Journal of Comparative Legislation and International Law* 201 ff, 201.

[45] See the reviews in (1946) 58 *Juridical Review* 253 ff; E. J. Cohn, (1947) 10 *Modern LR* 224 ff; Lord Macmillan, (1947) 63 *LQR* 227 ff; Wortley, (1947) 23 *International Affairs* 396. The second edition of 1949 was only very slightly changed.

[46] H. G. Hanbury, rev Eric Metcalfe, 'Walton, Frederic Parker (1858–1948)', in H. C. G. Matthew and Brian Harrison (eds), *Oxford Dictionary of National Biography* (2004); 'F. P. Walton, Esq., Advocate, Professor of Roman Law in the McGill University, Montreal', (1914) SLT (News) 21; Appointments, (1894) 10 *Scottish LR* 230, 298; F. H. L[awson], 'Dr F. P. Walton', in 'Notes' (1949) 31 (3rd Series) *Journal of Comparative Legislation and International Law* 98 ff, 98.

of eighteenth-century Scottish consistorial decisions.[47] In 1903 he published *Historical Introduction to Roman Law*, a straightforward account, well adapted for law students. He emphasized that in 'a country of the Civil Law, like the Province of Quebec', it was important 'to show the way in which the Roman Law has grown into the modern Civil Law'.[48] This made him sceptical of the value of some modern trends that he thought were contributing to the decline in the study of Roman law.[49]

By 1900, Scots lawyers had come to see their legal system as having a 'mixed and varied character', because of its 'large debt to the jurisprudence of other countries, especially to the Roman and English law'.[50] In Quebec, Walton found another jurisdiction in which 'the law occupies a position midway between the Common law and the Civil law'. In 1913, he wrote that 'the two countries whose legal systems present the closest analogy to that of Quebec are Louisiana and Egypt'. An advocate of codification who thought the form of law of profound importance, Walton considered this was because of their shared background in French law and the influence of the French civil code.[51]

The legal position in Egypt was of particular interest to a comparative lawyer. As well as special religious jurisdictions, 'Mixed Courts' had been introduced to deal with matters involving the foreign community and 'Native Courts' to deal with matters exclusively involving Egyptians. Mixed Courts had a bench consisting of Egyptian judges and jurists from sixteen Western countries. Similar codes, based on those of France, but which also gave scope for equitable development, were employed in both sets of courts.[52]

In Quebec, Walton developed a profound interest in the French law of obligations, especially delictual liability or torts, and state liability. He analysed the French approach to abuse of right in comparison with the relevant English law. He became an expert on workmen's compensation. He also wrote on the responsibility of the state for the faults of its officials in France and England, state immunity, cause and consideration, libelling the dead, the right to privacy, delictual responsibility, and damage by inanimate objects. In 1920 he produced his two-volume

[47] Hanbury (n 46). See David Fraser and Suzanne Drapeau, 'Walton's Bibliography', in F. P. Walton, *The Scope and Interpretation of the Civil Code of Lower Canada* (ed Maurice Tancelin, 1980), 133 f. This is incomplete.

[48] F. P. Walton, *Historical Introduction to Roman Law* (1903), v.

[49] F. P. W[alton], 'Professors of Roman Law, Old Style and New Style', in 'Notes', (1929) 11 (3rd Series) *Journal of Comparative Legislation and International Law* 268 ff, 273 ff.; *idem*, 'The Teaching of Roman Law in the United States', in 'Notes', (1931) 13 (3rd Series) *Journal of Comparative Legislation and International Law* 128 ff, 133.

[50] J. Dove Wilson, 'The Sources of the Law of Scotland', (1892) 4 *Juridical Review* 1 ff, 4; The Editors [in fact Henry Goudy], 'Prefatory Note', (1889) 1 *Juridical Review* 1 ff, 1.

[51] F. P. Walton, 'The Civil Law and the Common Law in Canada', (1899) 11 *Juridical Review* 282 ff, 291; *idem*, 'The Legal Systems of Canada', (1912–13) 5 *Law Library Journal* 55 ff, 57.

[52] J. Y. Brinton, *The Mixed Courts of Egypt* (rev edn, 1968).

Egyptian Law of Obligations: A Comparative Study with Special Reference to the French and English Law (second edition, 1923). In 1935 he published with Amos their well-known *Introduction to French Law* for English readers.[53]

Experience of Scotland, Quebec, and, in particular, Egypt led Walton to scepticism about intimate links between nations and laws: Savigny's theories could not be accommodated even with the facts of German history. Egypt, Japan, and Turkey were examples of nations with 'an ancient customary law' which had 'deliberately thrown overboard this heritage of race' and introduced 'at one blow a legal system entirely foreign'. If these were countries trying to modernize, and it was unlikely that anything similar could be done in countries such as France and England, because of the conservatism of an established legal profession, the adoption of French law in Romania by wholesale transplant in the 1860s further negated 'the doctrine of the historical school of jurisprudence'.[54] Walton's study of civil codes had demonstrated that legal borrowing was common: 'Codifiers are arrant thieves, and every new civil code ought to contain some articles which the legislators of other countries will make up their minds to steal so soon as a favourable opportunity occurs'.[55]

In 1926, Walton became joint editor of the *Journal of Comparative Legislation and International Law* with Amos (the latter served only for one year). Walton served until 1933, exercising considerable influence on the development of comparative law in Britain. F. H. Lawson (1897–1983) described Walton as one 'of the great pioneers in Comparative Law', holding a 'central position . . . in comparative studies'. A 'master of French law in its practical as well as in its academic aspects . . . [who] was perfectly able to draw into comparison not only English, but also German law', Walton 'was exceptionally modern in his outlook and *au fait* with all contemporary developments in foreign law', but he remained 'a firm believer in the importance of Roman Law'.[56]

(c) *Amos*

Born in London, Amos studied moral sciences at Cambridge before being called to the bar in 1897. To qualify as an inspector for the Egyptian Ministry of Justice, he learned Arabic and graduated *licence en droit* in Paris. He also taught at the Khedivial School of Law. First appointed a judge in the Native Court in 1903, he was promoted to the Native Court of Appeal in 1906, becoming Director of

[53] See Fraser and Drapeau (n 47).

[54] F. P. Walton, 'The Historical School of Jurisprudence and Transplantations of Law', (1927) 7 *Journal of Comparative Legislation and International Law* 183 ff, 184 ff, and 189 ff; *idem*, (1934) 46 *Juridical Review* 1, 11 ff, 13.

[55] F. P. Walton, 'Civil Codes and their Revision: Some Suggestions for Revision of the Title "Of Ownership" ', (1916) 1 *Southern Law Quarterly* 95 ff, 116.

[56] F. H. L[awson], 'Dr. F. P. Walton', (1949) 31 *Journal of Comparative Legislation and International Law* 98.

the Khedivial School of Law in 1912 before leaving to work in the ministry of munitions in London. In 1917, he returned as Legal Adviser to the Egyptian Government, staying on after the Protectorate ended in 1922. Returning to England in 1925, he practised at the bar, succeeding de Montmorency in the Quain Chair in 1932, which he held until 1937.[57]

Though familiar with Ottoman and Islamic law, Amos's scholarly interests were largely confined to French law, particularly obligations, and constitutional and administrative problems. His earliest publications were thus on abuse of right and specific performance in French law. Returning from Egypt, he wrote on the government of Egypt, comparative civil procedure, comparative statutory interpretation, and the constitutional law of Britain, the Empire and the United States. He also regularly reviewed books in these fields. While working with Walton on their *Introduction*, he published a study of perpetuities in French law.[58]

Despite Amos's undergraduate studies, his writings show little interest in legal philosophy. In 'Some Reflections on the Philosophy of Law', he argued that the future for legal philosophy lay with development of the Austinian systematic tradition. He thought Bentham's utilitarianism was dead. The third school of law he identified—the historical—he associated with Maine. It had enjoyed excessive prestige 'during the last two generations', but its emphasis on evolution had potentially restricted the legislator's freedom to act. What he saw worthwhile in it, however, was its offshoot, anthropology of law, and its enlargement of 'our understanding of backward races subject to our government or influence'.[59]

Amos's rejection of Maine reflected the similarity of his experience to Walton's. The *Code Napoléon* could be received round the world, even in Egypt 'by a people totally alien to Europe in language, religion, and social and political traditions'. The Japanese had adopted a version of the new German code. In his inaugural lecture in London, he asserted that 'the truth is that in the world of to-day most civilized countries are governed not by home-grown law, but by law received from abroad'. This was because, when legal institutions went 'beyond a comparatively primitive stage of culture', they were influenced by 'the type of thought which we recognize as that of the professional jurist'. Receptions were normal; laws were not the products of national and natural evolution. There was little necessary, intimate

---

[57] Marie-Louise Legg and T. S. Legg, 'Amos, Sir (Percy) Maurice McLardie Sheldon (1872–1940)', in H. C. G. Matthew and Brian Harrison (eds), *Oxford Dictionary of National Biography* (2004); Norman Bentwich, 'Sir Maurice Amos', in 'Notes', (1940) 22 *Journal of Comparative Legislation and International Law* 226 ff; H. A. H[anbury], 'Sir Maurice Sheldon Amos, K.B.E., K.C.', (1939–41) 7 *Cambridge LJ* 403 f.

[58] See eg M. S. Amos, 'Abusive Exercise of Right According to French Law', (1900) 2 (NS) *Journal of the Society of Comparative Legislation* 453 ff; *idem*, 'Specific Performance in French Law', (1901) 17 *LQR* 372 ff; *idem, England and Egypt, Cust Foundation Lecture* (1929); *idem*, 'The Interpretation of Statutes', (1933–5) 5 *Cambridge LJ* 163 ff; *idem, The English Constitution* (1930); *idem, Lectures on the American Constitution* (1938).

[59] M. S. Amos, 'Some Reflections on the Philosophy of Law', (1927–9) 3 *Cambridge LJ* 31 ff, 32 f, 37 ff.

connection between laws and nations. Codification facilitated such borrowing. English law was not easily borrowed, so it was found only in the United States and parts of the British Empire. This was the reason why he favoured codification.[60]

(d) Goadby

A solicitor and Oxford graduate, Goadby moved to the Khedivial School of Law in the early 1900s, later serving in Jerusalem as Director of Legal Studies to the Government of Palestine under the British Mandate, training magistrates and clerks in the Trilingual Law School.[61] Knowing Amos and Walton through the Khedivial Law School, the latter secured Goadby, on his return to Britain, as his successor as editor of the *Journal of Comparative Legislation and International Law* in 1933, which he edited until 1944.

In 1910, Goadby published an introductory textbook for Egyptian law students, which reached a third edition in 1923. He also published what was ultimately a three-volume *Commentary on Egyptian Criminal Law and the Related Criminal Law of Palestine, Cyprus, and Iraq* (1924), based on an earlier work on Egyptian law. With no particular interest in the French private law in force in Egypt, Goadby developed a particular concern with Islamic and Ottoman law, and the separate religious jurisdictions dealing with personal law and status found in Egypt and Palestine. In Palestine, the growing influence of English law and procedures created a fascinating mixture. This resulted in a book based on his Jerusalem lectures on *International and Inter-Religious Private Law in Palestine* (1926). He also wrote on the personal law of British subjects in Palestine, a particular problem when British Jewish subjects were settling there under the influence of the Zionist movement, but did not take up Palestinian citizenship. There being no modern code in Palestine, Goadby also studied the *Mejelle*, the Ottoman codification of Islamic law and produced (with M. J. Doukhan) an account of Palestinian land law.[62]

(e) Vesey-Fitzgerald

Though Vesey-Fitzgerald published a discussion of family property in Beaumanoir, his real interests were Hindu and Mohammedan law.[63] More typical were his studies of the place of Hindu law in comparative law, usury in Hindu and Roman law, the legal personality of a 'Hindu idol', a projected codification of Hindu law, and

---

[60] See M. S. Amos, 'The *Code Napoléon* and the Modern World', (1928) 10 (3rd Series) *Journal of Comparative Legislation and International Law* 222 ff, 233 ff; *idem*, 'The Legal Mind', (1933) 49 *LQR*, 27 ff; *idem*, 'Should we Codify the Law?', (1933) 4 *Political Quarterly* 357 ff.

[61] See Norman Bentwich, 'Dr Frederic Maurice Goadby', (18 August 1956) *The Times* 11B.

[62] F. M. Goadby, 'Personal Law of British Subjects in Palestine', (1929) 45 *LQR* 498 ff; *idem*, 'Notes on the Law of Delicts in the Mejelle', (1924) 15 *L'Égypte contemporaine* 493 ff; F. M. Goadby and M. J. Doukhan, *The Land Law of Palestine* (1935).

[63] S. G. Vesey-Fitzgerald, 'Family Property in Beaumanoir', (1926) 8 (3rd Series) *Journal of Comparative Legislation and International Law* 71 ff, 79.

succession of collaterals in Hindu law.[64] In 1931, he published a book on Islamic law for students who were 'probationers entering the Civil Service of the tropical African dependencies', and he produced an analysis of his lectures. He explored the influence of Roman on Islamic law.[65] Practical concerns led him to discuss the conflict arising from application of Islamic law in common-law courts, and between 1935 and 1940 he discussed in the *Journal* of the Society of Comparative Legislation cases arising in India, Burma, and the Far East on conflict of laws, dealing with issues arising from Buddhist, Muslim, Hindu, and customary Chinese law, with some more specialized notes on such cases.[66] His experience in India also led him to write on the curious status of the Province of Berar, Bentham and the Indian Codes, and polygamous marriages.[67]

(f) Lee

After studying classics at Oxford, Lee entered the Ceylonese Civil Service in 1891, acting as a magistrate and commissioner of requests. Health problems led to his return to England and he was called to the bar in 1896. He taught law at a number of Oxford colleges and the University of London, and practised before the Privy Council in Ceylonese appeals. In 1905 he added the office of Professor of Roman-Dutch Law in the University of London. The part-time chair did not attract students every year. According to his pupil at Oxford, Lucas, Lee had not yet 'begun his close study of Roman-Dutch law' and only subsequently started to learn Dutch and begin serious work on the discipline. In 1914, he married one of the daughters of Macdonell, still Quain Professor, before succeeding Walton in his posts in McGill in 1915. In 1921 he returned to the new Rhodes Chair of Roman-Dutch Law in Oxford, concurrently holding office as Reader in Roman Law and Roman-Dutch Law to the Council of Legal Education. He retired from the Rhodes Chair in 1956.[68]

---

[64] S. G. Vesey-Fitzgerald, 'The Place of Hindu Law in Comparative Jurisprudence', (1923) 39 *LQR* 357 ff; *idem*, 'Dum Dapat—Alterum Tantum', (1925) 7 (3rd Series) *Journal of Comparative Legislation and International Law* 171 ff; *idem*, 'Idolon Fori', (1925) 41 *LQR* 419 ff; *idem*, 'The Projected Codification of Hindu Law', (1947) 29 (3rd Series) *Journal of Comparative Legislation and International Law* 19 ff; *idem*, 'The Succession of Cognate Collaterals in Hindu Law', (1948) 12 *Bulletin of the School of Oriental and African Studies* 677 ff.

[65] Vesey-Fitzgerald, *Muhammadan Law* (n 24) v; *idem*, *Analysis of Lectures on Muhammadan Law: To Probationers at Oxford for the Tropical Administrative Services of the Colonial Office* (nd); *idem*, 'The Alleged Debt of Islamic to Roman Law', (1951) 67 *LQR* 81 ff.

[66] S. G. Vesey-Fitzgerald, 'Le droit anglo-musulman', (1954) 6 *Revue internationale de droit comparé* 250 ff.

[67] S. G. Vesey-Fitzgerald, 'The International Status of Berar', (1926) 42 *LQR* 33 ff; *idem*, 'Bentham and the Indian Codes', in G. W. Keeton and Georg Schwarzenberger (eds), *Jeremy Bentham and the Law: A Symposium* (1948), 222 ff.

[68] 'Professor Robert Warden Lee', (1922) 39 *South African LJ* 1 ff; R. W. Lee, 'The Teaching of Roman-Dutch Law', (1929) *Journal of the Society of Public Teachers of Law* 31 ff; Tony Honoré, rev, 'Lee, Robert Warden (1868–1958)', in H. C. G. Matthew and Brian Harrison (eds), *Oxford Dictionary of National Biography* (2004); F. A. W. Lucas, 'Robert Warden Lee: A Tribute', (1958) 75 *South African LJ* 235 f. A list of his publications may be found in 'Robert Warden Lee: Publications', (1958) *Acta Juridica* 3 ff.

Appointment to the London chair led to a number of articles on Roman-Dutch law, culminating in the brilliant *Introduction to Roman-Dutch Law* (1915), which made his career, reaching a fifth edition in 1953. Experience of Quebec led to publications on cause and consideration, and comparative views of civil law and common law on torts, though these were not profound analyses.[69] After appointment to Oxford, Lee tirelessly propagandized for Roman-Dutch Law both in Britain and in international organizations as 'a body of laws transplanted from its native land to distant dependencies overseas', South Africa in particular.[70] He also studied Grotius, hoping to overcome the popular vision of him simply as the 'father of international law'. In 1926 he published the text with translation (as *The Jurisprudence of Holland*) of Grotius' *Inleidinge tot de Hollandsche rechts-geleerdheid*, a commentary following in 1936.

In 1907, Lee contributed substantial entries on obligations to Jenks's famous multi-volume *Digest of English Law* (1905–17). This later inspired him to publish, structured as a code, *The South African Law of Obligations* (1950) and *The South African Law of Property, Family Relations and Succession* (1954) with Tony Honoré (born 1921) and other contributors. These volumes reflected Lee's belief in the virtues of codification. Experience had shown that the codified civil law in Quebec was tougher, more resilient, and more resistant to infiltration of common law than was Roman-Dutch law in South Africa. In a world in which he thought law would and should come together, the uncodified common law was under threat; codification would allow it to exercise influence in emerging countries comparable to that exercised by the codes of France and Germany.[71]

Lawson described Lee as likely considering himself a 'cosmopolitan rather than a comparative lawyer'—yet he was important in developing the subject.[72] It was impossible for him not to think comparatively in dealing with the mixed systems of South Africa, Ceylon, and Quebec. From the start of his career he was involved with the Society of Comparative Legislation, later publishing accounts of conflicts in dominion and colonial cases in the *Journal* from 1934–9. He was also much involved with the International Academy of Comparative Law after its foundation, for which, with Vesey-Fitzgerald, between 1928 and 1932, he reported on conflicts of law in colonial and dominion cases.[73] In 1930, Lee noted that there was no chair in comparative law in Britain, asking: 'How long shall we remain indifferent to a movement which is revolutionizing legal studies upon the continent and which

---

[69] See 'Robert Warden Lee: Publications', (1958) *Acta Juridica* 3 ff.

[70] See eg R. W. Lee 'What has become of Roman-Dutch Law?', (1930) 12 (3rd Series) *Journal of Comparative Legislation and International Law* 33 ff.

[71] R. W. Lee and A. M. Honoré, *The South African Law of Obligations* (1950), v.

[72] F. H. Lawson, 'In Memoriam Robert Warden Lee', (1958) 7 *AJCL* 659 ff, 660.

[73] S. G. Vesey-Fitzgerald, 'Indian and Far Eastern Cases on the Conflict of Laws, 1928–1933', (1934) 16 (3rd Series) *Journal of Comparative Legislation and International Law* 116 ff, 116 n 1.

includes our law within its scope?'[74] In 1936, as President of the SPTL, Lee's address, 'Comparative Law and Comparative Lawyers', urged progress in teaching and research in the British Isles.[75]

2. Foreign Links: Institutes and Academies

Interest in international and foreign links grew after World War I. In the 1920s British comparatists paid most attention to Lambert's Institute in Lyons and Lévy-Ullmann's at Paris, partly, undoubtedly, because both were interested in English law. Lévy-Ullmann also gave an important address on 'The Law of Scotland' at the Assembly of the French Society of Comparative Legislation in February 1924 that his friend Walton translated into English.[76] Both addressed the SPTL.[77] It was presumably Lambert who secured honorary doctorates for W. W. Buckland (1859–1946), Lee, and Gutteridge at the fiftieth anniversary celebrations of his Faculty in 1926. His brief period as Dean of the Khedivial Law School from 1906–7 also brought him into contact with Goadby and Amos.[78]

British scholars followed the activities of the French institutes with interest and, one suspects, some envy, their progress being regularly reported in the 'Notes' section of the *Journal* of the Society of Comparative Legislation. It is no surprise that Goadby revised and edited the translation into English of Lévy-Ullmann's work on English law and that both Frenchmen were invited to become honorary members of the SPTL in 1930.[79] The universalist views of French scholars, of Lévy-Ullmann in particular, were not, however, sympathetic to most British comparatists.

The International Academy of Comparative Law was founded in Geneva on 13 September 1924, while, on 3 October 1924, the Council of the League of Nations in Geneva approved the International Institute for the Unification of Private Law

---

[74] R. W. Lee, 'Istituto di Studi Legislativi', in 'Notes', (1930) 12 (3rd Series) *Journal of Comparative Legislation and International Law* 109 ff, 115 ff, 117.

[75] R. W. Lee, 'Comparative Law and Comparative Lawyers', (1936) *Journal of the Society of Public Teachers of Law* 1 ff.

[76] Henri Lévy-Ullmann, 'The Law of Scotland', (1925) 37 *Juridical Review* 370 ff.

[77] Henri Lévy-Ullmann, 'The Teaching of Comparative Law: Its Various Objects and Present Tendencies at the University of Paris', (1925) *Journal of the Society of Public Teachers of Law* 16 ff; Gutteridge, (1925) 7 (3rd Series) *Journal of Comparative Legislation and International Law* 212.

[78] 'Report of the General Committee for 1925–26', (1926) *Journal of the Society of Public Teachers of Law* 58 ff; Amr Shalakany, 'Sanhuri and the Historical Origins of Comparative Law in the Arab World (or How Sometimes Losing your *Asalah* can be Good for You)', in Annelise Riles (ed), *Rethinking the Masters of Comparative Law* (2001), 152, 163 ff.

[79] Henri Lévy-Ullmann, *The English Legal Tradition: Its Sources and History* (trans M. Mitchell and rev and ed by F. M. Goadby, 1935); 'Report of the General Committee for 1930–31', (1931) *Journal of the Society of Public Teachers of Law* 57 ff.

to be located in Rome, established and funded by the Italian Government.[80] Except for Gutteridge and Wortley, who participated in its work on mercantile law, British comparative lawyers in general do not seem to have taken particularly great interest in the Rome institute. This may have had to do with Italian politics, but was mainly because of British scepticism of large-scale projects of unification, despite interest in unification within the Empire.[81]

British comparatists were, however, much more involved with the International Academy, the 'principal object' of which was 'study of comparative law on an historical basis and the improvement of legislation in the various countries, particularly in connection with private law, by systematically comparing and reconciling laws'.[82] These broad objectives were sympathetic to most British comparative lawyers, and Jenks, Lee, Walton, and Goadby were present at the first ever session of the Academy at The Hague, written up by Goadby for the Society of Comparative Legislation. Total membership of the Academy was initially restricted to thirty. British members from 1924 were Goadby, Walton, and Lee, who by 1930 was a General Secretary of the Academy (later becoming Vice-President and President) (all of them being in the Oriental and Colonial section), and Pollock, Vinogradoff (replaced by Sir William Holdsworth (1871–44)), and Jenks (who were in the Anglo-American subject section). Lee and Walton contributed to the first volume of the Academy's *Acta*, while Walton and Goadby provided studies, respectively on Egyptian law and Palestinian law, for the first fascicle of the Academy's *Opera*, on *Les sources du droit positif*. Walton addressed its meeting of August 1927 on 'The Historical School of Jurisprudence and Transplantations of Law'. Lee and Vesey-Fitzgerald produced joint reports on conflicts of law in the British colonies and dominions for the Academy.[83]

The sizable British delegation at the first International Congress of the Academy, held at The Hague in 1932, included, as President of the General Section of the Congress, Lord Macmillan (1873–1952), who in 1932 became Chairman of the Council of the Society of Comparative Legislation. Macmillan gave an address on 'Scots Law as a Subject of Comparative Study'. General Reports provided by British

[80] For details, see J. H. Wigmore, 'The Movement for International Assimilation of Law: Recent Phases', (1925–6) 20 *Illinois LR* 42 ff, 45 ff; also René David, 'The International Institute of Rome for the Unification of Private Law', (1933–4) 8 *Tulane LR* 406 ff; Lee, (1936) *Journal of the Society of Public Teachers of Law* 1, 5.

[81] See M. D. Chalmers, 'The Movement for International Assimilation of Private Law' in 'Notes', (1925) 7 (3rd Series) *Journal of Comparative Legislation and International Law* 248 ff.

[82] Wigmore, (1925–6) 20 *Illinois LR* 42, 46.

[83] F. M. G[oadby], 'International Academy of Comparative Law', in 'Notes', (1925) 7 (3rd Series) *Journal of Comparative Legislation and International Law* 248 ff, 258; F. P. W[alton], 'International Academy of Comparative Law', in 'Notes', (1930) 12 (3rd Series) *Journal of Comparative Legislation and International Law* 299 ff, 305; 'International Academy of Comparative Law', in 'Notes', (1926) 8 (3rd Series) *Journal of Comparative Legislation and International Law* 292 ff, 299; Walton, (1927) 7 (3rd Series) *Journal of Comparative Legislation and International Law* 183; Vesey-Fitzgerald, (1934) 16 (3rd Series) *Journal of Comparative Legislation and International Law* 116.

scholars included those of Walton on Delictual Responsibility, of Holdsworth on Formation and Breach of Contract, of Gutteridge on Opening of Bank Credits, and A. D. McNair on Modes of Concluding International Treaties. Goadby gave a Special Report on 'Religious Communities and Courts in Palestine'. Amos, Lee, and Wortley also attended.[84] Though Robert Candlish Henderson, Professor of Scots Law in Edinburgh, established a Scottish Committee in connection with the Congress, the only Scots lawyer, other than Macmillan and Walton, who attended was Gardner, a member of the Society of Comparative Legislation.[85]

By 1936, a Second International Congress of Comparative Law was planned, and in that year the SPTL appointed a small delegation of five, including its current President, H. F. Jolowicz (1890–1954), Lee (now a Vice-President of the Academy), and Wortley, to attend. Gutteridge was later included.[86] British attendance was good. The judges again included Lord Macmillan, who gave an opening address. As a General Reporter in delict, Walton provided an account of 'Liability for Damage done by Inanimate Things, Moveable and Immoveable'. Other British reports included those of Gutteridge on 'The Comparative Aspects of Legal Terminology', Lee on 'The Interaction of Roman and Anglo-Saxon Law', and Goadby on civil liability in Muslim law. Amos and Wortley attended. International tensions affected aspects of this Congress, the last before the war.[87]

3. The Society of Comparative Legislation

On 18 December 1919, the Society of Comparative Legislation celebrated its twenty-fifth anniversary. Sir Albert Gray, in reference to the digest of legislation, stated that, by this work of 'keeping a record of those experiments and of the success or

[84] Lord Macmillan, 'Scots Law as a Subject of Comparative Study', in *idem, Law and Other Things* (1938), 102 ff; F. M. Goadby, 'The International Congress of Comparative Law at The Hague', (1932) 14 (3rd Series) *Journal of Comparative and International Law* 244 ff; H. Milton Colvin, 'The International Congress of Comparative Law', (1932–3) 7 *Tulane LR* 53 ff; 'Report of the General Committee for 1932–33', (1933) *Journal of the Society of Public Teachers of Law* 50 ff; F. P. Walton, 'Delictual Responsibility in the Modern Civil Law (More Particularly in the French Law) as Compared with the English Law of Torts', (1933) 49 *LQR* 70 ff; F. M. Goadby, 'Religious Communities and Courts in Palestine', (1933–4) 8 *Tulane LR* 215 ff; 'Report of the General Committee for 1930–31', (1931) *Journal of the Society of Public Teachers of Law* 57; 'Report of the General Committee for 1931–32', (1932) *Journal of the Society of Public Teachers of Law* 62 ff, 62.

[85] Gardner, (1932) 14 (3rd Series) *Journal of Comparative Legislation and International Law* 201, 206.

[86] 'The Second Congress of Comparative Law', in 'Notes', (1936) 18 (3rd Series) *Journal of Comparative Legislation and International Law* 127 ff; 'Report of the General Committee for 1935–36', (1936) *Journal of the Society of Public Teachers of Law* 58 ff, 61; 'Report of the General Committee for 1936–37', (1937) *Journal of the Society of Public Teachers of Law* 80 ff; 'Report of the General Committee for 1937–38', (1938) *Journal of the Society of Public Teachers of Law* 66 ff, 67. There was one other adjustment.

[87] Murray Seasongood, 'The Second International Congress of Comparative Law', (1938) 31 *Law Library Journal* 47 ff, 54 ff.

ill success of the endeavours', the Society made reform easier. This was because 'in most cases we find nowadays that the subject has been dealt with in some way or another in some country'.[88] The suffering of World War I initially created a desire for closer imperial unity, which led, for example, C. E. A. Bedwell (1878–1950), Keeper of the Library of the Middle Temple, and an active member of the Society, to propose the establishment of a committee for legal research for the Empire. Facilitating such thinking was the view that the joint heritage of English common law unified the Empire. The 'notable exceptions' were India and South Africa, but even they were 'considerably influenced' by the common law.[89]

The focus of the Society of Comparative Legislation now started to change, however, leading to increasing scepticism about unification within the Empire. Careful reading of the 'Notes' section of the *Journal* suggests that, after the mid-1920s, the topic of imperial unification of law became of much less interest. In 1923, Berriedale Keith (1879–1944), Regius Professor of Sanskrit and Comparative Philology in the University of Edinburgh, recognized that the 'circumstances of the Empire and the diversity of its legislative organs are fatal to that uniformity of legislation in favour of which Imperial Conferences periodically declare themselves'.[90]

Crucial in this re-orientation was the increasing influence of men such as Gutteridge, Amos, Walton, and Goadby, Walton's editorship of the *Journal* being especially important. Drawing on his varied experience, he commented that 'the importance of [uniformity] is frequently exaggerated', adding that it was 'in fact, only within a somewhat narrow field of legislation that uniformity presents obvious advantages'. Thus, while it was important for 'bills of exchange, bills of lading, bankruptcy, copyright, the reciprocal enforcement of judgments and extradition', pressing for uniformity in other areas was likely 'to do more harm than good'. Canada gave a good example of this: uniformity was not only unnecessary, but detrimental, as the diversity of systems was creative as they influenced each other, with differing advantages and solutions that could be copied if necessary by the other.[91] Though judged not to have 'forgotten the interests of the Dominions and other parts of the Empire', Walton widened the scope of the *Journal* by 'enlisting the help of a number of foreign writers of reputation'. Reflecting the importance he placed on this, he personally translated several such articles by foreign authors on French and German law.[92]

---

[88] 'Twenty-Fifth Anniversary of the Society', (1920) 2 (3rd Series) *Journal of Comparative Legislation and International Law* xv ff.

[89] C. E. A. Bedwell, 'Imperial Unity and Legal Research', (1920) 2 (3rd Series) *Journal of Comparative Legislation and International Law* 144 ff.

[90] A. Berriedale Keith, 'Introduction', (1925) 7 (3rd Series) *Journal of Comparative Legislation and International Law* xxviii ff, xxviii.

[91] 'Introduction', (1926) 8 (3rd Series) *Journal of Comparative Legislation and International Law* xxviii ff, xxix.

[92] Lord Atkin, 'The Editorship', in 'Notes', (1933) 15 (3rd Series) *Journal of Comparative Legislation and International Law* 124 ff. I have counted fourteen items translated by Walton.

Developments in the nature of the Empire reinforced this trend, as different structures of government had developed while the self-governing dominions had already acquired effective independence.[93] Imperial unity was challenged by Dominions being represented at new international bodies such as the League of Nations and having their own diplomatic dealings with each other. These changes interested the Society of Comparative Legislation, and Berriedale Keith, the most important theorist in this field, regularly contributed to the *Journal* on these issues, including annual 'Notes on Imperial Constitutional Law'.[94]

Further imperial administrative problems arose from the mandates created by the League of Nations in the Middle East out of the collapse of the Ottoman Empire. The Privy Council decided it could deal with appeals from the Mandated Territories, the inhabitants being under the protection of the British Crown. The Mandated Territories offered new opportunities and projects for comparatists. Palestine started to feature in the *Journal*, with frequent discussion of its legal position and legislation, notably by Goadby and Norman Bentwich (1883–1971), because of the system of personality of law inherited from the Ottomans by the British. Thus, the application of late-Roman or Byzantine law by the Courts of the Orthodox Church in Jerusalem, using their Codes on the law of family and succession, attracted interest. This was a topic Goadby pursued in the 'Notes' section of the *Journal*, notably after succeeding Walton as editor. The new Mandates also reinforced the practical and scholarly interest in Islamic law already fostered by the Empire. Both Goadby and Vesey-Fitzgerald enjoyed teasing out the complex problems of conflicting jurisdictions, particularly with reference to Islamic law.[95]

By the outbreak of World War II, the Society's *Journal* also rejected any attempt to discover any essential or universal nature of comparative law. Influential comparatists stressed that government of the Empire did not depend on a unified legal system. Pragmatism was enshrined as orthodoxy in the Society.[96]

4. Comparative Law in the Universities

In 1918, only the Quain Chair and the Corpus Chair were in any way designated for comparative law or jurisprudence. After the war, Macdonell and de Montmorency pursued an essentially legal evolutionary agenda in their teaching in London,

---

[93] See eg A. P. Poley, 'The Privy Council and the Problems of Closer Union of the Empire', (1917) 17 (NS) *Journal of the Society of Comparative Legislation* 30 ff.

[94] See R. F. Shinn, *Arthur Berriedale Keith, 1879–1944: The Chief Ornament of Scottish Learning* (1990), which contains details of Keith's voluminous publications at 353 ff.

[95] See eg S. [G.] V[esey-]F[itzgerald], 'Conflict of Jurisdiction in Palestine', in 'Notes' (1937) 19 (3rd Series) *Journal of Comparative Legislation and International Law* 280 ff, 287 ff.

[96] 'The Functions of Comparative Law', in 'Notes', (1940) 22 *Journal of Comparative Legislation and International Law* 93 ff, 100.

including courses of lectures on famous trials. De Montmorency taught customary law as the basis of law.[97] Vinogradoff taught comparative historical jurisprudence, but his successors were legal theorists. At the London School of Economics, Gutteridge taught Comparative Commercial Law to candidates 'for the Bachelor of Commerce Degree (Trade Group)'.[98]

It is none the less important to note that much 'foreign' law was taught, such as Islamic, Hindu, and Roman-Dutch. Both the Inns of Court and Oxford accepted Roman-Dutch law as an alternative to land law in the curriculum.[99] At London, reforms in 1925 permitted students to offer the Indian Penal Code and Procedure as one paper in the intermediate examination, while they could also offer as an alternative to Property Law, one of: 'either Roman-Dutch, Muhammadan, Hindu, Ottoman, or French law (*Code civil français*)'. Further papers offered at London included the Indian Evidence Act and Civil Procedure of the Indian Courts and Constitutional Laws of the British Empire.[100]

The 1930s saw significant development. Gutteridge's move to Cambridge allowed him to hold a postgraduate seminar in comparative law, the success of which depended on 'the presence in Cambridge of foreign advanced students', though he was not always able to attract sufficient for a class. The refugee Kurt Lipstein (born 1909) contributed as his assistant (Gutteridge finding his salary). No option in comparative law was available to undergraduates. In the postgraduate LLB degree, there was a compulsory paper on a comparative aspect of Roman law and English law, the topic varying from year to year: it is no surprise that Buckland and McNair published *Roman Law and Common Law: A Comparison in Outline* in 1936. Gutteridge reported that he taught conflicts of law as comparatively as possible in the time available. Further, a Diploma in Comparative Legal Studies was eventually developed.[101]

Amos as Quain professor reported that his students averaged around a dozen in number, and contained several refugee Germans. Only foreign students, however, had approached him about pursuing research in comparative law. He gave lectures

[97] See the reports of Macdonell's lectures under the headings 'The Value of Comparative Law', 'The Uses of Comparative Law' and 'The Evolution of Comparative Law', in (1919) 148 *Law Times* 189, 208 f, 226; John Macdonell, *Historical Trials* (ed R. W. Lee, 1927); Jolowicz (n 2), 350. On de Montmorency, see 'Province of Case Law', (14 November 1930) *The Times* 5C; Gutteridge, (1931) *Journal of the Society of Public Teachers of Law* 26, 31 f.

[98] Gutteridge, (1922) 4 (3rd Series) *Journal of Comparative Legislation and International Law* 84, 86.

[99] Lee, 'Roman-Dutch Law', (1929) *Journal of the Society of Public Teachers of Law* 31 ff; F. H. Lawson, *The Oxford Law School, 1850–1965* (1968), 103 f, 132 f, 151 f.

[100] H. C. Gutteridge 'The Faculty of Laws of London University', in 'Notes', (1925) *Journal of the Society of Public Teachers of Law* 34 ff.

[101] Lee, (1936) *Journal of the Society of Public Teachers of Law* 1, 6; 'Society of Public Teachers of the Law: Report on Comparative Law', (1940) 22 (3rd Series) *Journal of Comparative Legislation and International Law* 74 ff; Christian von Bar, 'Kurt Lipstein—The Scholar and the Man', in Jack Beatson and Reinhard Zimmermann (eds), *Jurists Uprooted: German-Speaking Émigré Lawyers in Twentieth-Century Britain* (2004), 749 ff, 753.

on the comparative law of marriage and comparative constitutions. Comparative Industrial Law was added to the existing courses in London. Otto Kahn-Freund (1900–1979) became an assistant lecturer at the London School of Economics in 1936, enriching the teaching of comparative law. Vesey-Fitzgerald, in a discussion in 1936, further emphasized that 'the comparative *method* was used in his own seminars at London'.[102]

In Oxford, students were required to study Digest 18, 1 and 19, 1, and 'show a knowledge of the relevant topics of the English Law of Sale' for Roman law in the honours school. Lawson, currently All Souls Reader in Roman Law at Oxford, tried to incorporate comparative methods of study in all his classes where possible. Thus, he 'gave informal instruction in the Law of Obligations', treating the subject 'comparatively, with special reference to French Law, Scots Law and Roman-Dutch Law', considering topics such as 'Cause and Consideration, *stipulatio alteri*, and unjust enrichment'. Once Martin Wolff (1872–1953), sometime Professor at Berlin, had settled in Oxford, he assisted with this seminar.[103]

At Birmingham, Professor C. E. Smalley-Baker (1891–1972) discussed 'comparative history of sources of the law' in 'Introduction to English Law'. By 1936, Wortley, Reader in Jurisprudence and Comparative Law at Manchester, stated that a 'department of Comparative Law existed in embryo'. By the outbreak of the war, however, it was only said of Manchester that the introduction of 'five or six lectures on the topic of Comparative Law into the course on Jurisprudence has been continued'.[104] The nature of the curriculum at the Scottish law faculties gave no scope for comparative law as such.[105]

On retirement in 1941, Gutteridge stated accurately that the 'Quain Chair of Comparative and Historical Law ... has, in effect, been suppressed', while the Oxford Chair 'is ... devoted primarily to the general theory of the law'. He concluded that there was 'no Chair of Comparative Law in the British Universities'.

[102] Lee, (1936) *Journal of the Society of Public Teachers of Law* 1, 6, 8; Bentwich, (1940) 22 *Journal of Comparative Legislation and International Law* 226, 227; Mark Freedland, 'Otto Kahn-Freund (1900–1979)', in Jack Beatson and Reinhard Zimmermann (eds), *Jurists Uprooted: German-Speaking Émigré Lawyers in Twentieth-Century Britain* (2004), 299 ff, 307; Gardner, (1932) 14 (3rd Series) *Journal of Comparative Legislation and International Law* 201.

[103] Lee, (1936) *Journal of the Society of Public Teachers of Law* 1, 7; J. K. B. M. Nicholas, 'Lawson, Fredrick Henry [Harry] (1897–1983)', in H. C. G. Matthew and Brian Harrison (eds), *Oxford Dictionary of National Biography* (2004); 'Report on Comparative Law', (1940) 22 (3rd Series) *Journal of Comparative Legislation and International Law* 74, 75.

[104] Lee, (1936) *Journal of the Society of Public Teachers of Law* 1, 6 f, 8, 9; 'Report of General Committee for 1935–36', (1936) *Journal of the Society of Public Teachers of Law* 58 ff, 61; 'Report on Comparative Law', (1940) 22 (3rd Series) *Journal of Comparative Legislation and International Law* 74, 76.

[105] During the war Polish and French refugees encouraged some interest in comparative law in Scotland: see H. L. MacQueen, ' "A Picture of What Will some day be the Law of the Civilised Nations": Comparative Law and the Destiny of Scots Law', in K. Michalowska (ed), *Festschrift Rajski* (forthcoming).

Lee had stated in 1936 that the position of Comparative law in Britain was 'shocking'; Gutteridge said this was 'not without justification'. He thought comparative law was not taught at all in Scotland, and survived in England only as a few lectures in courses on jurisprudence. The problem was that the curricula of the law faculties and professional schools were 'so tightly packed with subjects for examination that a latecomer such as Comparative Law must almost inevitably be excluded'. This is slightly exaggerated. Lee (whom Gutteridge described as a 'comparative lawyer of great distinction') still held the chair of Roman-Dutch Law at Oxford. Jolowicz, though primarily a Romanist, had been a delegate at the International Congress of Comparative Law in 1937, and occupied the Chair of Roman Law in London. Lawson was well embarked on his career, though his significant comparative work was still ahead of him. Much the same could be said of C. J. Hamson (1905–87) and Wortley, though the latter was ultimately to become better known in international law.[106] Seeds had been sown that germinated after the war.

5. An Imperial Law School and Advanced Legal Studies

In 1919, Henry Goudy (1848–1921) addressed the members of the SPTL on founding an Imperial Law School. Mooted since the 1890s, the proposal had already been discussed in *The Times*. Some, such as de Montmorency, thought such a School would serve as an 'Imperial War Memorial' to those who had fought 'for the maintenance of law and good faith amongst men'. During the Imperial Conference of 1923, de Montmorency argued that an Imperial Law School 'would not only promote the comparative study of the existing systems of law within the Empire, but would also involve scientific study and comparison of the customary law of native races through a greater part of the world'. This was important for proper imperial government of the Empire and, while much was already done, the 'fullest application of the comparative method to the vast masses of material [was] essential, and the work of comparison need[ed] organizing'.[107]

The proposal in 1926 that the Triennial Congress of the Empire's Universities

---

[106] Gutteridge, (1941) 23 (3rd Series) *Journal of Comparative Legislation and International Law* 130 f; Lee, (1936) *Journal of the Society of Public Teachers of Law* 1, 5; H. F. Lawson (rev J. K. B. M. Nicholas), 'Jolowicz, Herbert Felix (1890–1954)', in H. C. G. Matthew and Brian Harrison (eds), *Oxford Dictionary of National Biography* (2004); Nicholas (n 103); J. A. Jolowicz, rev, 'Hamson, Charles John Joseph [Jack]' (1905–1987)', in H. C. G. Matthew and Brian Harrison (eds), *Oxford Dictionary of National Biography* (2004); 'Professor B. A. Wortley', (13 June 1989) *The Times* 20F. In 1930 Lee, (1930) 12 (3rd Series) *Journal of Comparative Legislation and International Law* 109, 117 had already claimed that in Britain 'no university has yet established a chair of Comparative Law'.

[107] 'Public Teachers of Law', (4 July 1919) *The Times* 11A; 'Legal Education for the Empire', in 'Notes', (1900) 2 (NS) *Journal of the Society of Comparative Legislation* 173 ff, 180; J. E. G. de Montmorency, Letter, (3 February 1919) *The Times* 8E; Walter Trower, Letter, (6 February 1919) *The Times* 2D; J. E. G. de Montmorency, Letter (9 July 1926) *The Times* 10F; *idem*, Letter, (4 October 1923) *The Times* 8A.

should consider the topic of 'The Establishment in London of an Advanced School of Legal Study' led to another debate developed in the columns of *The Times*. Professor H. A. Smith (1885–?) of McGill stressed that any such School should be postgraduate in nature and neither propagate English common law nor affect admission to the legal profession in any part of the Empire. He argued that on 'its scientific side the main work of the school should be the advanced study of comparative law and legislation'. Finally, the 'school should be equipped with a real library of Imperial law'. Gutteridge agreed that the School should be postgraduate, and should not be 'a centre of propaganda on behalf of the common law', while 'the study of comparative law and legislation should be in the forefront of [its] curriculum'. He thought, however, that what was needed was coordination of existing institutions, not a new institution. Smith's and Gutteridge's near-exclusive focus on comparative law did not please everyone. De Montmorency once more stressed that, as well as modern law, 'scientific study and comparison of the customary law of the native races . . . for whom the Empire stands as trustee' should be pursued. A broadly approving, if measured, leader was published.[108]

On 9 July 1926, Smith addressed the SPTL on the topic at its annual conference. He pointed out that the chief need was for advanced comparative legal study. Acknowledging that the sole chair of comparative law in the Empire was the Quain Chair in London, he stressed that the Imperial Law School should be primarily devoted to 'the scientific study of the laws and legislation of this and other countries, particularly comprised within the British Empire'. He emphasized that no impression should be given that the School was intended 'to hold up the lamp of the common law as a light to enlighten those who sit in the outer darkness of the civil law'. Following de Montmorency, he also argued that the School should 'promote an intimate understanding, not only of the civil law but also of Hindu and Mohammedan law and the other systems which obtain in the Empire'.[109] Gutteridge reported that the participants (including Atkin) at the Triennial Congress on 14 July 1926 unanimously favoured 'an Imperial postgraduate school of advanced legal studies in London', many stressing that it would aid comparative law.[110]

These discussions produced no immediate result. Comparative law collections were, however, developing in London. Ernest Schuster (1850–1924) had bequeathed his library to the Society of Comparative Legislation, which, in 1925, deposited its

---

108 H. A. Smith, Letter, (7 April 1926) *The Times* 13F; H. C. Gutteridge, Letter, (12 April 1926) *The Times* 10C; H. A. Smith, Letter, (15 April 1926) *The Times* 10C; J. D. Falconbridge, Letter, (30 June 1926) *The Times* 12C; J. E. G. de Montmorency, Letter, (9 July 1926) *The Times* 10F; H. Goitein, Letter, (17 July 1926) *The Times* 13D; Leader, 'An Imperial School of Law', (10 July 1926) *The Times* 15C; H. F. J[olowicz], ' "The Times" Correspondence on the Subject of an Imperial School of Law in London', in 'Notes', (1926) *Journal of the Society of Public Teachers of Law* 26 ff, 31.

109 H. A. Smith, 'An Imperial School of Law', (1927) *Journal of the Society of Public Teachers of Law* 11 ff, 15 f. See also 'An Imperial Law School', (12 July 1926) *The Times* 11F.

110 H. C. Gutteridge, 'Note', (1926) 42 *LQR* 436 ff, 437.

entire library, including this bequest, in the London School of Economics. On the initiative of Gutteridge, gaps were filled. The Society donated the library to the London School of Economics in 1936.[111]

In 1932 the Lord Chancellor established a Committee under the chairmanship of Lord Atkin 'to consider the organisation of legal education in England' with a view to '[c]loser co-ordination between the work done by the Universities and the professional bodies and . . . [f]urther provision for advanced research in legal studies'. Gutteridge and Atkin were friends and Atkin was currently Chairman of the Executive Committee of the Society of Comparative Legislation (he resigned in 1933), of which Gutteridge was one of the two honorary secretaries. Gutteridge was appointed to the new committee.[112]

The *Report* of the Atkin Committee analysed legal research into 'Historical Legal Research, Comparative Legal Research, and Clinical Legal Research'. Saying nothing specific of the first and basically dismissing the third as covered by the Lord Chancellor's appointment in 1934 of a Standing Committee on Law Revision, it emphasized that 'much remains to be done in the domain of Legal Research in its wider sense'. It noted that comparative legal research had been neglected in England, so that 'we lag[ged] behind many of the Continental countries'. Arguing that a specialized institution for academic research was needed, it proposed the foundation of an 'Institute of Advanced Legal Studies' in London. The report stressed that the Institute 'would . . . serve as a centre of study for many of the students who come to this country from our overseas Dominions and Colonies' and collect information on foreign and commonwealth laws. To some extent 'it would operate . . . to embody the ideals of those who have envisaged the establishment in England of an Imperial School of Law'. The *Report* largely embodied Gutteridge's vision for an Institute of Advanced Studies primarily devoted to comparative law.[113]

At the Annual Meeting of the SPTL in 1934, Gutteridge 'regretted that failure had hitherto met the attempt to establish an Imperial School of Law in London'. At the next Annual Meeting in July 1935, Wortley endorsed the Atkin Committee's proposals. The Meeting requested its General Committee to consider and report on the proposed Institute of Advanced Legal Studies. A Sub-Committee was appointed to meet with Lord Macmillan, as member of the Court of the University of London. Following this, the President, Lee, wrote to Lord Hailsham, the current

---

[111] H. C. Gutteridge, 'The Schuster Library of Comparative Law', in 'Notes', (1927) 9 (3rd Series) *Journal of Comparative Legislation and International Law* 260 ff, 265 f; 'The Schuster Library of Comparative Law', in 'Notes', (1928) 10 (3rd Series) *Journal of Comparative Legislation and International Law* 311 ff, 320 f; W. C. Dickinson, 'The Schuster Library of Comparative Legislation', in 'Notes', (1938) 20 (3rd Series) *Journal of Comparative Legislation and International Law* 119 ff, 122 f.

[112] *Report of the Legal Education Committee*, Cmnd 4663 (1934) 2 f.

[113] Ibid, 12 ff; E. C. S. Wade, 'The Legal Education Committee', (1934) *Journal of the Society of Public Teachers of Law* 30 f.

Lord Chancellor, in May 1936. Attempts to take the matter forward were stymied by the war.[114]

6. The Society of Public Teachers of Law

A small, relatively informal body that met annually, the SPTL provided a campaigning platform for the development of education in comparative law of which Lee, and, above all, Gutteridge made use. Gutteridge was very active in the Society, becoming Vice-President in 1926 and President in 1928. Lee was President in 1936. Vesey-Fitzgerald became a member in 1929. Goadby and Walton joined as corresponding members in 1931. Wortley was elected by 1932. Amos joined after appointment to the Quain Chair in 1932.[115]

Gutteridge's 1931 paper, 'The Value of Comparative Law', and Lee's Presidential Address of 1936 on 'Comparative Law and Comparative Lawyers' exemplify the comparatists' campaign to raise the subject's profile. Perhaps prompted by the outcome of the Atkin Committee, Lee's Address proposed that the SPTL should send a delegation to the International Congress scheduled for 1937 (which was done) and form a Comparative Law Committee. The next year, the General Committee reported that it had invited Gutteridge, Lee, and Wortley (as convenor), along with the President *ex officio*, to form a Standing Committee on Comparative Law. The first report of this Committee was adopted at the Society's meeting in Edinburgh in 1939, when international events overtook further progress. The Report highlighted the issue of libraries. By the 1940s, comparative law collections had improved.[116]

7. The Achievements of the Pioneers

Returning to Britain as Gutteridge started to campaign for the recognition of comparative law, Amos, Walton, Lee, and Vesey-Fitzgerald, and later Goadby,

---

114 'Public Teachers of Law' (16 July 1934) *The Times* 7E; B. A. Wortley, 'Some Reflections on Legal Research', (1935) *Journal of the Society of Public Teachers of Law* 52 ff, 54 ff; 'Public Teachers of Law', (22 July 1935) *The Times* 9B; 'Annual Meeting of the Society', (1935) *Journal of the Society of Public Teachers of Law* 92; 'Report of the General Committee for 1935–36', (1936) *Journal of the Society of Public Teachers of Law* 58 ff; Willi Steiner, 'The Establishment of the Institute of Advanced Legal Studies of the University of London', (1994) 17 *Bulletin of the Institute of Advanced Legal Studies* 6 ff, 15; Lord Macmillan, *A Man of Law's Tale* (1952), 217–18, 228.

115 See the various Reports of the General Committee in the *Journal of the Society of Public Teachers of Law*.

116 Lee, (1936) *Journal of the Society of Public Teachers of Law* 1, 8; Gutteridge, (1931) *Journal of the Society of Public Teachers of Law* 26; 'Report of General Committee for 1936–37', (1937) *Journal of the Society of Public Teachers of Law* 80; Gutteridge, (1941) 23 (3rd Series) *Journal of Comparative Legislation and International Law* 130, 134; 'Report on Comparative Law', (1940) 22 (3rd Series) *Journal of Comparative Legislation and International Law* 74 f.

raised the profile of the subject. In doing so, they took advantage of bodies such as the Societies of Comparative Legislation and Public Teachers of Law, and the International Academy at The Hague that stimulated and inspired them. They thus set the agenda for comparative law for the post-war period.

Despite different interests, they had some views in common. Rejecting the views of the historical school, they did not accept that 'the law of a country . . . is one form in which the national consciousness expresses itself'.[117] This had three consequences. It made study of other modern systems central to comparative law. It prompted realization of the importance of borrowing in legal development. Finally, it liberated the study of non-Western systems of law from the burden of being understood as embryonic Western systems, allowing development of the type of anthropological comparative law associated with the School of Oriental and African Studies.

They generally rejected international unification of law other than in matters of international commerce. Lee emphasized in the pages of the *Journal of Comparative Legislation* that the 'idea of a *droit civil mondial* which hovers before the eyes of so many Continental jurists is not one to make an appeal to English lawyers'. Likewise, any idea that there was some kind of 'essence' to comparative law was rejected as a 'will-o'-the-wisp'. There was no essential ' "common law" of humanity'.[118]

Despite this, Walton translated for publication in the *Juridical Review* the address on 'The Law of Scotland' given by his friend Lévy-Ullmann in 1924. The Frenchman argued that Scots law showed how laws of Roman and 'Anglo-Saxon' origin combined 'by this work of fusion preparing the way for the legal unification of Western Europe'. He added that 'the Scots law as it stands today gives us a picture of what will be, some day . . . the law of the civilised nations, namely, a combination between the Anglo-Saxon system and the continental system'.[119] Amos, lecturing at Harvard, expressed a similar view.[120] This relied on Walton's analysis of Scots law as a 'mixed system', which was becoming widespread by the 1930s.[121]

Finally, it is important to note that these men looked almost exclusively to French law as 'continental' law. The interest that Walton, Gutteridge, and Amos all had in German law was completely overwhelmed by their focus on French law. If affected by politics, much of the concentration on French law was due to the

---

[117] Walton, (1934) 46 *Juridical Review* 1, 13.

[118] Lee, (1930) 12 (3rd Series) *Journal of Comparative Legislation and International Law* 109, 117; R. W. L[ee], 'Istituto di studi legislativi', in 'Notes', (1931) 13 (3rd Series) *Journal of Comparative Legislation and International Law* 266 ff, 274 ff, 275; 'The Functions of Comparative Law', in 'Notes', (1940) 22 (3rd Series) *Journal of Comparative Legislation and International Law* 93 ff, 100.

[119] Lévy-Ullmann, (1925) 37 *Juridical Review* 370, 390.

[120] Amos, (1937) 50 *Harvard LR* 1249, 1274.

[121] J. C. Gardner, 'Judicial Precedent in the Making of International Public Law', (1935) 17 (3rd Series) *Journal of Comparative Legislation and International Law* 251 ff, 259.

profound knowledge of it acquired by influential individuals such as Walton and Amos. French law came to seem the obvious law to study comparatively, as the modern civil law to compare with common law. Reinforcing this was the fact that, after Latin, French was the language most likely to be encountered in law students—an important consideration when building up comparative law in the universities. Certainly Gutteridge said of his students that 'German Law is beyond them'.[122]

IV. Beyond Empire: New Directions

Britain has never produced a dominant theorist of comparative law; after World War II, however, teaching boomed, leading L. Neville Brown (born 1923) to describe the years from 1946 to 1969 as those of the 'efflorescence of comparative law'. It is easy to see why. Between 1953 and 1965 the number of law students increased by more than 50 per cent both north and south of the border; the increase between 1965 and 1975 was yet again over 50 per cent, while dropping Roman law as a requirement for admission to the English bar in 1966 left more scope for courses in comparative law.[123]

   The end of Empire had two obvious effects. It progressively removed the necessity to train administrators in Hindu, Muslim, and indigenous laws. Centred on the School of Oriental and African Studies in London, under the leadership of individuals such as Sir Norman Anderson (1908–94), Anthony Allott (1924–2002), and Simon Roberts (born 1941), such studies specialized, diverging from 'mainstream' comparative law. It was as recently as 2000 that a conference first again brought together those working on the comparison of civil and common law with those working on African and Asian laws.[124] Second, it eventually brought to an end the teaching and study of Roman-Dutch law in the universities, especially after the political isolation of South Africa under apartheid. Into the 1970s, however, candidates for the English bar could substitute for land law in Part I of the exams Roman or Roman-Dutch law, or two of Hindu law, Mohammedan law as applied in India or Pakistan, Mohammedan law as applied elsewhere, general African law, or African customary law.[125] Development of debates on unification in the EU have led

---

[122] Quoted in Lee, (1936) *Journal of the Society of Public Teachers of Law* 1, 6.
[123] Brown, (1971) 19 *AJCL* 232, 241, 250; J. F. Wilson and S. B. Marsh, 'A Second Survey of Legal Education in the United Kingdom', (1974–5) 13 *Journal of the Society of Public Teachers of Law* 239, 249.
[124] See Andrew Harding and Esin Örücü (eds), *Comparative Law in the 21st Century* (2002), vii.
[125] Wilson and Marsh, (1974–5) 13 *Journal of the Society of Public Teachers of Law* 239, 291.

scholars again to assess the view that mixed systems bridge the gap between civil and common laws, leading once again to increased interest in Roman-Dutch law.

1. Scholarly Legacy of the Pioneers

(a) The Fundamental Role of Roman Law

Barry Nicholas (1919–2002) commented that, for Lawson, 'Roman law provided the common lawyer with the key to the conceptual structure of continental civil law'. In his inaugural lecture as first Professor of Comparative Law in Oxford (appointed 1948), Lawson stated 'the most fruitful field to till' was comparison of civil and common law, particularly where they contacted and conflicted in the mixed systems.[126] He followed this agenda from his early (1936) paper, 'Error in Substantia'. Like Walton and Amos, his most important work was on obligations, with *Negligence in the Civil Law* (1950) being profoundly influential. His aim was to make the student, through close examination of the Roman law on a special subject, generally aware of the fundamental thinking of the continental legal systems. His new (1952) edition of Buckland and McNair's *Roman Law and Common Law: A Comparison in Outline* and his brilliant study, *A Common Lawyer Looks at the Civil Law* (1955), exemplify his approach. It is worth noting that, between 1956 and 1965, he travelled to New York to teach a triennial class on Roman and comparative law.[127]

Lawson's work was crucial in post-war development, and most other British comparatists also continued to see Roman law as central, given the continuing focus on comparison of civil with common law and interest in mixed systems. Though best known for work in international and European law, Lipstein, who became Professor of Comparative Law in Cambridge in 1973, held the firm view that a thorough knowledge of Roman law 'enables the student of comparative law to see the motives and changes of legal institutions that provide him with the opportunity of picking out the most useful features'.[128] Nicholas himself pursued the comparison of civil law and common law in Lawson's manner, focusing on obligations, with a related interest in mixed systems, publishing, for example, important studies of unjustified enrichment in the civil and Louisiana law. He also

---

[126] Barry Nicholas, 'Professor FH Lawson 1897–1983', in Peter Wallington and R. M. Merkin (eds), *Essays in Memory of Professor FH Lawson* (1986), 3 ff, 5; F. H. Lawson, 'The Field of Comparative Law', (1949) 61 *Juridical Review* 16 ff, 35. For a list of his publications, see F. H. Lawson with Bernard Rudden, 'F. H. Lawson—A Bibliography', in Peter Wallington and R. M. Merkin (eds), *Essays in Memory of Professor F. H. Lawson* (1986), 11 ff, 13–15. The details are not always accurate. His earliest publications were on Byzantine law and constitutional law.

[127] F. H. Lawson, *The Roman Law Reader* (1969), vi.

[128] Christopher Forsyth, 'Kurt Lipstein (1909–)', in Jack Beatson and Reinhard Zimmermann (eds), *Jurists Uprooted: German-Speaking Émigré Lawyers in Twentieth-Century Britain* (2004), 463 ff, 465.

had a particular interest in problems in contract, such as frustration and mistake, and how they were differently handled by the civil and common law systems. Succeeding Lawson as All Souls Reader in Roman Law, and holding the Oxford Chair of Comparative Law from 1971, Nicholas became best known for his *Introduction to Roman Law* (1962) and a new edition of Jolowicz's *Historical Introduction to the Study of Roman Law* (1972).[129]

One curiosity of this dominant framework was that when distinguished comparatists, such as Albert Kiralfy (1915–2001) and Bernard Rudden (born 1933), started to study Soviet law after the war, they found it to some extent possible to accommodate it within the opposition between civil law and common law, viewing it as a form of 'civil' law, despite its different ideology.

(b) The Importance of French Law

While Lawson's *Negligence in the Civil Law* included very varied extracts from modern sources, such as those from the Mexican and Soviet codes, the main focus was on French law, with extensive resort to French case-law and 'notes'. Lawson also assumed that students would understand French and be able to supplement his textbook with modern French literature. This emphasis on French law led him in 1963, with Neville Brown and A. E. Anton (born 1922), to produce a new edition of Amos and Walton's work (reaching a third edition in 1967). Lawson considered comparative study of French law as of primary significance for the English lawyer.[130] His successor in the chair, Otto Kahn-Freund, in the words of André Tunc, 'brilliantly developed' the practice of studying French law at Oxford established by Lawson.[131] He published (with Claudine Lévy and Bernard Rudden), *A Source-Book on French Law* (1973), in which, after sources and methods, the focus was on contract. Nicholas, on succeeding Kahn-Freund, maintained this emphasis, publishing the *French Law of Contract* (1982).

Hamson, appointed to a personal chair in Comparative Law in Cambridge in 1953, also focused on French law. His scholarship largely explained French law to the British and English law to the French. He developed an influential course in Cambridge on 'French and English Legal Methods' and became expert on French administrative law, his study, *Executive Discretion and Judicial Control: An Aspect of the French Conseil d'État* (1954), being particularly notable.[132] Mentored by Hamson, Neville Brown completed a doctorate at Lyons on the French notary. His

---

[129] See eg Barry Nicholas, 'Unjustified Enrichment in the Civil Law and Louisiana Law', (1962) 36 *Tulane LR* 605 ff (Part I), (1962) 37 *Tulane LR* 49 ff (Part II); Barry Nicholas, '*Force Majeure* and Frustration', (1979) 27 *AJCL* 231 ff.

[130] F. H. Lawson, 'A New Book on French Law', (1961) 6 (NS) *Journal of the Society of Public Teachers of Law* 132 ff; *idem*, 'Comparative Judicial Style', (1977) 25 *AJCL* 364 ff.

[131] See André Tunc, 'Preface', in Otto Kahn-Freund, Claudine Lévy, and Bernard Rudden, *A Source-Book on French Law: System, Methods, Outline of Contract* (1973), xii.

[132] Jolowicz (n 106); Brown, (1971) 19 *AJCL* 232, 250.

most important individual publication was probably *French Administrative Law* (1967), written with the distinguished administrative lawyer, J. F. Garner (1914–97). Brown differed from other contemporaries in his scholarly emphasis on family law, in particular that of husband and wife, rather than obligations.[133]

Focus on French law has continued strong in teaching comparative law. No longer quite so powerfully emphasized in research, there is still distinguished work, such as that of John Bell (born 1953), now professor in Cambridge.

(c) Unification

Along with Wortley, R. H. Graveson (1911–91), educated at Sheffield, London, and Harvard, was the British comparatist most associated after the war with unification, particularly of private international law (on which he was a leading author). He represented Britain at The Hague Conference on private international law and on legal committees of the Council of Europe. He wrote regularly on unification, reflecting his belief in its importance in bringing differing peoples together.[134]

Britain was often seen as ambivalent and obstructing 'the realisation of unified law from selfish motives'. Gutteridge argued that the movement for unification in fact owed much to British 'initiative and collaboration'. The 'English-speaking countries' had already arrived at 'a very degree of uniformity of law as between themselves', which would be jeopardized if Britain acted independently with other nations.[135] But when UNIDROIT resumed activity at Rome after the war, the only British scholars listed as members of Expert Committees were Andrew Dewar Gibb of Glasgow (1888–1974), Gutteridge, and Wortley. Only four British lawyers attended UNIDROIT's 1950 congress. For around twenty years, only Wortley and Graveson had much association with the institution.[136]

---

[133] L. Neville Brown, *Law without Frontiers: Memoirs of a Comparatist* (2004), 57–63.

[134] Obituary, (9 January 1991) *The Times*. See reports by Graveson through the 1960s in the *International and Comparative Law Quarterly*. See also eg R. H. Graveson, 'L'influence du droit comparé sur le rapprochement des peuples', (1958) 10 *Revue internationale de droit comparé* 501 ff; *idem*, 'L'unification des différents systèmes juridiques en vigueur dans les îles britanniques', (1966) 18 *Revue internationale de droit comparé* 395 ff.

[135] H. C. Gutteridge, 'Great Britain and the Movement for Unification', (1948) 1 *Unification of Law* 285 ff.

[136] 'Members of Expert Committees', (1948) 1 *Unification of Law* 10, 11. See Massimo Pilotti, *Activity of the International Institute for the Unification of Private Law (1926–1946)* (1947), 5 f; H. C. G[utteridge], 'The Institute for the Unification of Private Law', in 'Notes', (1946) 28 (3rd Series) *Journal of Comparative Legislation and International Law* 122 ff, 123 f; 'Bureaux du congrès et liste des participants', (1951) 2 *Unification of Law* [*Actes du Congrès International du Droit Privé*] 13 ff, 24.

(d) Mixed Systems

Sir Thomas (T. B.) Smith (1915–88) particularly cultivated the study on mixed systems in which Lawson, Nicholas, and Neville Brown also maintained an interest. Educated in law at Oxford before being called to the English bar in 1938, Smith was admitted an advocate in Scotland in 1947, before appointment to a chair in the University of Aberdeen in 1949. In 1958, he moved to the Chair of Civil Law in Edinburgh, transferring to that of Scots Law in 1968. In 1972 he became a full-time member of the Scottish Law Commission, of which he had been a part-time member since 1965.[137]

Smith's interest in mixed legal systems developed in the 1950s as a means of understanding Scots law and its place in the legal world, at a time when René David (1906–90) was popularizing his powerful idea of 'legal families'. Smith saw the concept of 'mixed system' as providing a means of protecting Scots law from further English influence, which he was inclined to view as generally detrimental. This led him to oppose views in favour of unification of law in Britain expressed by Lord Denning (1899–1999) and Graveson. While occupying the Chair of Civil Law in Edinburgh, he transformed the course of civil law into one in which the comparative study of obligations in mixed systems played a significant part.[138] Partly influencing this was Smith's view in the early 1960s that, if Britain joined the European Economic Community, Scots law would 'help promote . . . a rapprochement between the somewhat insular South Britons and their fellow Europeans'.[139] The failure of Britain's early attempts to join the EEC deprived of immediate practical interest this development of Lévy-Ullmann's ideas.

2. Institutional Legacies

(a) Institute of Advanced Legal Studies

The Institute of Advanced Legal Studies was formally established within the University of London on 1 October 1946. While 'as an aid to the study of comparative law' the Institute did aim 'to build up' a 'good library of foreign law', comparative law featured less than the Atkin Report might have led one to expect.

---

[137] For an account of his life and career, see Lord Hunter, 'Thomas Broun Smith, 1915–1988', (1993) 82 *Proceedings of the British Academy* 455 ff.

[138] T. B. Smith, 'Unification of Law in Britain: Problems of Co-Ordination', (1965–6) *Acta Juridica* 93 ff, 95 ff; K. G. C. Reid, 'While One Hundred Remain: T B Smith and the Progress of Scots Law', in Elspeth Reid and D. L. Carey Miller (eds), *A Mixed Legal System in Transition: T B Smith and the Progress of Scots Law* (2005), 1 ff; *Edinburgh University Calendar 1959–1960* (1959), 94.

[139] See, T. B. Smith, 'The Influence of the "Auld Alliance" with France on the Law of Scotland', in *Studies Critical and Comparative* (1962), 28, 44.

It was none the less recognized that the Institute provided a useful focus for comparative work. Bedwell of the Society of Comparative Legislation advised on collection of commonwealth material.[140]

(b) British Institute of International and Comparative Law

The Society of Comparative Legislation sustained publication of its *Journal* through the war, despite financial problems and twice losing its premises to enemy action. Graveson, Hamson, Lawson, and Wortley (along with E. J. Cohn (1904–76) and E. G. M. Fletcher MP) represented it at the celebration of the eightieth anniversary of the French *Société* in 1949. The Annual Report for 1950 expressed anxiety about the 'financial future of the Society', noting that '[s]teps [were] being taken by the Executive Committee' to remedy this.[141] In 1952, the *Journal* amalgamated with the *International Law Quarterly* (first published in 1947) to create *The International and Comparative Law Quarterly*. In 1958, the Society of Comparative Legislation and International Law (as it was now known) merged with the Grotius Society to create the British Institute of International and Comparative Law. The new Institute took over publication of the journal, quickly merging it with the *Transactions of the Grotius Society*.

This consolidation created a strong institution, which has provided an important forum for colloquia and seminars, while pursuing a publication programme, including monographs, the *Quarterly*, and, between 1965 and 1977, the *Annual Survey of Commonwealth Law*.[142]

(c) International Academy of Comparative Law

The first Congress of the International Academy of Comparative Law after the war took place at London in 1950, under Lee's presidency. Thereafter, the programme of a congress every fourth year has been maintained with consistent and extensive British participation.[143]

(d) International Committee of Comparative Law and the UKNCCL

In 1950, under the auspices of UNESCO, the International Committee of Comparative Law was established. The British delegation included Hamson, Graveson,

[140] Steiner, (1994) 17 *Bulletin of the Institute of Advanced Legal Studies* 6, 16 ff; D. Hughes Parry, 'The Institute of Advanced Legal Studies', (1947–51) 1 (NS) *Journal of the Society of Public Teachers of Law* 183 ff, 184 and 187; Willi Steiner, *The Institute of Advanced Legal Studies in London 1947–1976* (2000), 7.

[141] 'Annual Report', (1950) 32 (3rd Series) *Journal of Comparative Legislation and International Law* xxvi; 'Annual Report', (1951) 33 (3rd Series) *Journal of Comparative Legislation and International Law* xxvi.

[142] 'The British Institute of International and Comparative Law', (1959) 8 *ICLQ* 245 ff.

[143] R. W. L[ee], 'International Congress of Comparative Law', in 'Notes', (1950) 32 (3rd Series) *Journal of Comparative Legislation and International Law* 91 ff, 101.

Lawson, Lipstein, and Wortley (Gutteridge was unable to attend). The membership of this body consists of national committees, the United Kingdom National Committee of Comparative Law (UKNCCL) being a founder member. Bodies represented on the UKNCCL originally included representatives from the SPTL, law faculties teaching comparative law, the Institute of Advanced Legal Studies, the Society of Comparative Legislation, and the School of Oriental and African Studies.[144]

Later styled the International Association of Legal Science, the International Committee provided a new forum for British comparative lawyers through its organization of international colloquia. Meeting annually—in 1952 in Cambridge, in 1953 in Copenhagen—it held its first international congress at Barcelona in 1956, Lipstein and Lawson being general reporters for two of the four colloquia. British comparatists were much involved, Hamson being a member of the Committee and Lipstein Director of Research. Later Graveson represented the common law systems.[145]

Under the chairmanship of Graveson (Neville Brown being Secretary) the UKNCCL started to hold colloquia linked to the meetings of the SPTL. The first, prior to the Society's Edinburgh meeting in July 1955, was on 'The Influence of English Law within the Commonwealth', the success of which led to the decision to hold another colloquium at Aberystwyth in 1956.[146] Thereafter the practice of holding a two-day colloquium prior to the meeting of the SPTL became firmly established through the 1960s and 1970s. The UKNCCL was important in stimulating work in comparative law, in recent years sustaining a successful series of publications, arising out of themed conference proceedings, in collaboration with the British Institute of International and Comparative Law.

(e) The Law Commissions

In 1965, two Law Commissions, one for England and Wales, the other for Scotland, were established. Both were instructed to consider foreign law in deliberations over reform. There can be little doubt that their manner of working has sometimes involved quite considerable comparative work.[147]

---

[144] 'International Committee of Comparative Law', in 'Notes', (1950) 32 (3rd Series) *Journal of Comparative Legislation and International Law* 91 ff, 99 f; 'Report of the General Committee for 1950–51', in (1947–51) 1 (NS) *Journal of the Society of Public Teachers of Law* 465 f.

[145] Alexis Coudert, 'International Committee of Comparative Law', (1953) 2 *AJCL* 128; J. N. H[azard], 'University of Cambridge Conference of Teachers of Law', (1953) 2 *AJCL* 131 f; H. E. Y[ntema], 'International Committee of Comparative Law', (1956) 5 *AJCL* 704.

[146] 'Conferences in 1955', (1952–4) 2 *Journal of the Society of Public Teachers of Law* 190; 'Annual Meeting of the Society, 1954', (1952–4) 2 *Journal of the Society of Public Teachers of Law* 228; 'U.K. National Committee of Comparative Law', (1955–6) 3 *Journal of the Society of Public Teachers of Law* 179 f; 'United Kingdom National Committee of Comparative Law', (57) 6 *ICLQ* 160 ff.

[147] Law Commissions Act 1965, s 3. See generally, J. H. Farrar, *Law Reform and the Law Commission* (1974).

3. New Developments

(a) German Law and Comparative Legal Science

From Walton onwards, there had been minor interest in German law, but even the presence of the émigrés had failed particularly to develop it. Thus, Cohn's two-volume *Manual of German Law* (1950–2) was prepared for Allied use in Germany after the war: it reached a second edition in 1968 and 1971. Kahn-Freund's occupation of the Oxford Chair (1965–71) might have raised the profile of German scholarship, but other than two theoretical essays, he produced virtually nothing on comparative law. In these, given his strong interest in sociology of law, he argued for a functional approach to comparative law, rather different from that of most British scholars in the field.[148]

Publication in 1977 of the translation by Tony Weir, himself a distinguished comparatist, of *Einführung in die Rechtsvergleichung auf dem Gebiete des Privatrechts* of Konrad Zweigert (1911–96) and Hein Kötz (born 1935) helped develop interest in German law and the German approach to comparative law. The translation, as an *Introduction to Comparative Law*, reached a third edition in 1998. Thus, when Basil S. Markesinis (born 1944) produced a new edition of Lawson's *Negligence in the Civil Law* in 1982, as *Tortious Liability for Unintentional Harm in the Common Law and the Civil Law*, one of the obvious changes was the inclusion of much more German material. Since then, publication of works such as Markesinis's *Comparative Introduction to the German Law of Tort* (1986) has led comparisons of English or Scots law with German law to become more common, as interest in French law has declined. Further, the increasingly international nature of academic life has brought a number of German scholars to work in British universities, encouraging the development of courses on German law. It is worth noting that the present holder of the Oxford Chair of Comparative Law is German.

(b) Legal Transplants

Walton's (and Lee's) terminology of legal transplant or transplantation and emphasis on borrowing still exerted influence in the 1950s. Thus, Wortley reported that the 1950 Rome conference of UNIDROIT concluded 'that the time was [not] ripe for the transplanting of the Trust into other countries'. In 1955 a colloquium of the International Committee of Comparative Law in Istanbul was described by

---

[148] Otto Kahn-Freund, 'Comparative Law as an Academic Subject', ((1966) 82 *LQR* 40 f his inaugural lecture, also published separately as a pamphlet in 1965); *idem*, 'On Uses and Misuses of Comparative Law', (1974) 37 *Modern LR* 1 ff (both were reprinted in Otto Kahn-Freund, *Selected Writings* (1978), 275 ff and 294 ff).

Hamson as considering the 'effect of the transplantation of a system of law into a significantly different culture'.[149]

The development of medical techniques of organ transplant revivified the metaphor for British comparatists in the 1970s. A short, sharp controversy over legal borrowing was generated by the work of Kahn-Freund and Alan Watson (born 1933), then Professor of Civil Law in Edinburgh, a leading scholar of Roman law educated in Glasgow and Oxford. In a lecture on 26 June 1973, Kahn-Freund focused on 'transplantation' as a tool of law reform. He argued that it was necessary to examine, not rules, but social and economic factors in differing societies that made laws successful to determine whether a transplant of law from one jurisdiction to another was possible.[150]

In 1970, Watson had delivered a series of lectures at Virginia that were published in 1974 as *Legal Transplants: An Approach to Comparative Law*. He argued that, as an academic discipline, comparative law should focus on relationships, particularly historical, between legal systems. He drew a comparison with comparative philology. Developing the thesis that there is only a very limited, necessary relationship between law and society, Watson stressed that most legal development takes place by borrowing and that societies need not be similar to societies from which they borrow. The economic and social similarities that Kahn-Freund emphasized were unnecessary.[151] Though found challenging by sociologists as well as comparatists, Watson's attack on functionalism did not initially generate much, other than hostile, response. The seductive metaphor of 'transplant' was used from time to time by authors who would not necessarily have accepted Watson's wider thesis.

In the course of the 1990s, however, Watson's theory of transplants became widely discussed, since it seemed to present possibilities for proposals to harmonize or even unify law in Europe. His views could be understood as implying that unification, particularly through codification, would be easy. This led to vigorous criticism by Pierre Legrand (born 1959), a French-Canadian who briefly held a minor academic post in Lancaster and who has repeatedly opposed the idea of codification of private law in Europe.[152] This has engendered a lively debate that has rendered the idea of legal transplants part of normal discussion in comparative law in Britain.

---

[149] B. A. Wortley, 'Report on the Rome Conference, 1950', in 'Notes', (1950) 32 (3rd Series) *Journal of Comparative Legislation and International Law* 91; C. J. Hamson, 'The Istanbul Conference of 1955', (1956) 5 *ICLQ* 26 ff.

[150] Kahn-Freund, (1974) 37 *Modern LR* 1, 5 ff.

[151] Alan Watson, 'Legal Transplants and Law Reform', (1976) 92 *LQR* 79 ff. The preface of *idem*, *Legal Transplants: An Approach to Comparative Law* (1974) is dated June 1973. I mention this as Freedland (n 102), 311 states that Kahn-Freund invented the concept of 'legal transplantation' or 'legal transplant'.

[152] Pierre Legrand, 'The Impossibility of "Legal Transplants"', (1997) 4 *Maastricht Journal of European and Comparative Law* 111 ff.

(c) The Revival of Interest in Mixed Systems

In 1990, Reinhard Zimmermann (born 1952) published *The Law of Obligations: Roman Foundations of the Civilian Tradition*, in the preface of which he commented that South African law offered 'valuable experiences for anyone interested in the prospect of a future European common law'. With moves towards harmonization in Europe, the importance of the idea of mixed systems has been reassessed. Revival of interest dates strongly from the mid-1990s, leading to works such as Jan Smits, *The Making of European Private Law: Towards a Ius Commune Europaeum as a Mixed Legal System* (2002) and Reinhard Zimmermann, Daniel Visser, and Kenneth Reid (eds), *Mixed Legal Systems in Comparative Perspective: Property and Obligation in Scotland and South Africa* (2004). Concern has been stronger in Scotland than England, with a special issue of the *Juridical Review*, in 2002, while in 2003 the University of Aberdeen hosted a conference devoted to the legacy of T. B. Smith. Scots were also present in numbers at the first World Congress on Mixed Jurisdictions held in New Orleans in 2002.[153]

V. DISCIPLINARY UNCERTAINTY

Many British comparatists still work within the parameters established by the pioneers in the 1920s and 1930s, so that comparisons of civil with common law remain a staple. Some, such as Markesinis, regret this, arguing for the importance of methodology, often favouring the functionalist model associated with Ernst Rabel (1874–1955) in Germany. In *Comparative Law in the Courtroom and Classroom: The Story of the Last Thirty-Five Years* (2003), Markesinis has forcefully and controversially expressed the view that what comparatists ought to do is produce research that judges can use to develop the law. Comparative law none the less remains a domain of study and research that is, at best, fuzzy round the edges, potentially linked to legal history and legal philosophy, and pursued for a whole variety of very different purposes in differing ways in all areas of law; at worst, it is simply indeterminate. It is notable that no British comparatist has yet produced a textbook for students to rival the third edition of Zweigert and Kötz. Were a book more suited to British approaches produced, it might well start to give greater definition to the topic, at least in the universities.

In the recent past, comparative studies in Britain have been most energized by

---

153 See Elspeth Reid and D. L. Carey Miller (eds), *A Mixed Legal System in Transition: T B Smith and the Progress of Scots Law* (2005), vii; Vernon V. Palmer, 'International Update: Report on the first World Congress on Mixed Jurisdictions', (2003) 18 *Tulane European and Civil Law Forum* 123 ff.

developments in the European Union, and British scholars have been involved with initiatives such as the Trento 'common core' project and the Lando Commission on the Principles of European Contract Law. Perhaps most important is the way legal scholarship is transcending the national focus of the last 150 years. It is a rare, advanced-level, course in a university that would not adopt a comparative approach, while courts draw on comparative studies in cases such as *McFarlane v Tayside Health Board* 2000 SC (HL) 1.

BIBLIOGRAPHY

Frederick Pollock 'The History of Comparative Jurisprudence', (1903) 5 (NS) *Journal of the Society of Comparative Legislation* 74 ff

H. C. Gutteridge, *Comparative Law: An Introduction to the Comparative Method of Legal Study and Research* (2nd edn, 1949)

L. Neville Brown, 'A Century of Comparative Law in England: 1869–1969', (1971) 19 *AJCL* 232 ff.

J. A. Jolowicz, 'Comparative Law in Twentieth-Century England', in Jack Beatson and Reinhard Zimmermann (eds), *Jurists Uprooted: German-Speaking Émigré Lawyers in Twentieth-Century Britain* (2004), 345 ff

CHAPTER 5

···

DEVELOPMENT OF COMPARATIVE LAW IN THE UNITED STATES

···

DAVID S. CLARK

Salem, Oregon *

  * I thank Mathias Reimann for thoughtful insights and suggestions that improved this chapter and Willamette University College of Law for a summer research grant that facilitated completion of my research.

I. INTRODUCTION

COMPARATIVE law is as old as the American republic. That was the view of Roscoe Pound (1870–1964),[1] one of America's great comparatists in the first half of the twentieth century. Pound, the founder of sociological jurisprudence in the United States, spoke from a position of influence as a professor (1910–47) and dean (1916–36) at Harvard Law School. He supported a cyclical view of comparative law's importance, arguing that it went into decline after 1850. Michael Hoeflich, the leading US scholar today on the significance of Roman and civil law in nineteenth-century America, confirms Pound's view on the civil law's early role, but argues that it continued in importance, although in different ways, later in that century.[2]

After a brief review of a highly visible discussion of the role for comparative law in America's highest oracle of the law—the United States Supreme Court—we will

---

[1] Roscoe Pound, 'The Revival of Comparative Law', (1930–1) 5 *Tulane LR* 1–2. 'It was an element of the first order in the building of American law'. Ibid.

[2] Michael H. Hoeflich, *Roman and Civil Law and the Development of Anglo-American Jurisprudence in the Nineteenth Century* (1997), 2, 6–8, 51, 74–5.

visit the origins of comparative law activities during the formative era of the United States. Natural law thinking predominated during this intense period of debate after 1776 about the ideal in law and legal institutions. Comparison acted as a filter for the importation of rules and structures meant to serve an emerging nation in the new world. This process continued during the post-Civil War period after 1865, but under the influence of historical and analytical jurisprudence. Instead of looking at the utility of codifying areas of the law or adopting specific foreign rules, comparatists favoured the prestige of modifying civilian university legal education and its legal science for American circumstances or using ideas from European legal philosophy to develop a comparative jurisprudence.

In the twentieth century, sustained scholarly comparative law activity, together with organized networks of communication, began along with the successful effort to establish scientific teaching and research mostly at university law schools. Interested law teachers and practitioners founded the Comparative Law Bureau, part of the American Bar Association, in 1907. The Bureau published an *Annual Bulletin* for many years and supported a series of books reflecting and supporting comparative law activities. In the 1920s, comparative law figures were closely involved with the establishment of the American Law Institute in 1923 and Bureau members decided in 1925 also to organize a new entity in New York City, the American Foreign Law Association, to further their comparative law interests through publications and meetings. United States jurists through the 1930s, furthermore, were active in the Bureau's successor entity, the Section of International and Comparative Law, and in international comparative law organizations and conferences.

After World War II, leading comparatists incorporated the American Association for the Comparative Study of Law (today the American Society of Comparative Law), which in 1952 began publishing the *American Journal of Comparative Law*. Several of these founders were immigrants who had fled Nazi Europe in the 1930s, which helped initially to set the scholarly agenda. These professors created the organizational framework that would permit comparative law securely to establish itself in American legal education. The *Journal* today has the largest worldwide circulation of any comparative law publication and American comparatist representation in international conferences is strong if not dominant. Exportation of legal rules and structures is a major activity that occupies scholars, lawyers, and government officials.

One should not forget that comparative law has been especially strong in the two jurisdictions within the United States that are mixed civil law and common law systems: Louisiana and Puerto Rico. Chapter 14 in the *Handbook* treats their interesting history.[3]

---

[3] See Chapter 14 of the present book; Vernon Valentine Palmer, *Mixed Jurisdictions Worldwide: The Third Legal Family* (2001); (2003–4) 78 *Tulane LR* 1–501 (special issue on First Worldwide Congress on Mixed Jurisdictions).

II. COMPARATIVE LAW IN THE
US SUPREME COURT

At the beginning of the twenty-first century, the nine justices on the United States Supreme Court are engaged in a controversial debate, both on and off the Court, about the role of comparative law in their judicial decision-making. The two sides reflect grander philosophical perspectives that have supported the ebb and flow of interest in foreign law (and public international law) in American legal history.

For example, in *Roper v Simmons*,[4] Justice Anthony Kennedy delivered the Court's majority five–four opinion that the Eighth and Fourteenth Amendments of the US Constitution prohibit execution of individuals who were under 18 years of age at the time of their capital crimes. Kennedy wrote:

Our determination that the death penalty is disproportionate punishment for offenders under 18 finds confirmation in the stark reality that the United States is the only country in the world that continues to give official sanction to the juvenile death penalty. This reality does not become controlling, for the task of interpreting the Eighth Amendment remains our responsibility. Yet at least from the time of the Court's decision in *Trop* [1957], the Court has referred to the laws of other countries and to international authorities as instructive for its interpretation of the Eighth Amendment's prohibition of 'cruel and unusual punishments.'[5]

Justice Antonin Scalia, with two others joining, dissented. He wrote:

The Court reaches this implausible result by purporting to advert, not to the original meaning of the Eighth Amendment, but to 'the evolving standards of decency' [citation omitted] of our national society. . . . The Court thus proclaims itself sole arbiter of our Nation's moral standards—and in the course of discharging that awesome responsibility purports to take guidance from the views of foreign courts and legislatures. Because I do not believe that the meaning of our Eighth Amendment, any more than the meaning of other provisions of our Constitution, should be determined by the subjective views of five Members of this Court and like-minded foreigners, I dissent.[6]

Justice Sandra O'Connor, dissenting since she did not find a sufficient American state consensus on the issue, nevertheless had this to say on the comparative law issue:

I disagree with Justice Scalia's contention [citation omitted] that foreign and international law have no place in our Eighth Amendment jurisprudence. Over the course of nearly half a century, the Court has consistently referred to foreign and international law as relevant to its assessment of evolving standards of decency. . . . [T]his Nation's evolving understanding of human dignity certainly is neither wholly isolated from, nor inherently at odds with, the

---

[4] 125 SCt 1183 (2005).   [5] Ibid at 1198.   [6] Ibid at 1217.

values prevailing in other countries. On the contrary, we should not be surprised to find congruence between domestic and international values, especially where the international community has reached clear agreement—expressed in international law or in the domestic laws of individual countries—that a particular form of punishment is inconsistent with fundamental human rights.[7]

Whatever view one takes on the place for foreign law in providing support for particular meaning to the US Constitution's language, it is clear that for over 200 years the Court has influenced foreign legal systems and in turn has been influenced by legal opinion abroad. There are many different perspectives on comparative law, admirably described in later chapters of this *Handbook*. Leaving aside the concern, expressed by some comparatists, that the study or use of foreign law is not comparative law, we can point to the Supreme Court's 1803 decision in *Marbury v Madison*.[8] It implied a model of judicial review of legislative and executive acts that was transplanted in the 1820s and 1830s to newly independent nations in Latin America and later influenced constitutional review and constitutional courts in Europe and East Asia. The transplant metaphor also helps to explain the spread of the Court's doctrine on freedom of expression and association, and some concepts from criminal procedure, to many parts of the world during the twentieth century.

This transmission of legal ideas in the United States has been a two-way street, where importation is facilitated by lawyers who are familiar with more than one legal system. In general, when transmission is voluntary, and not coerced through colonization or war, the superior prestige of the exporting system, such as Roman law, or the obvious usefulness of the legal rule, such as comparative negligence, or of the institution, such as the ombudsman, motivates jurists. The more lawyers knowledgeable in multiple legal systems, that is, comparatists, the more sophisticated this transmission may be.

In nineteenth-century US Supreme Court reports, there are many instances of Roman law and civil law citations, in addition to the expected references to English common law doctrine and institutions. The two most famous Supreme Court justices of that century to favour Roman and civil law references were Joseph Story (1779–1845) and Oliver Wendell Holmes (1841–1935). The flow of foreign legal citation for constitutional interpretation was variable in the twentieth century, but has returned to some attention in the twenty-first century in *Lawrence v Texas*.[9] Here Justice Kennedy cited foreign examples, including several decisions from the European Court of Human Rights, in holding that a Texas criminal sodomy law violated the constitutional right to privacy for same-sex consenting adults. Rather than an example of transplantation, one may better understand this as an example of legal convergence resulting from similar social and cultural developments in Europe and America.

---

[7] Ibid at 1215–16.   [8] 5 US 137 (1803).   [9] 539 US 558 (2003).

Even those justices who believe that foreign law has no place in interpreting the United States Constitution admit that it may well be relevant in interpreting a treaty that the United States has ratified—such as the Warsaw Convention regulating international air carrier liability (with French as its authentic language)—or multilingual treaties in which interpretive uniformity is expressed as a goal. Foreign law might also influence domestic law reform. Furthermore, foreign law has today become a common issue in transnational litigation before both federal and state courts throughout the American judicial system.

III. Comparative Law in the Formative Era (1776–1865)

1. The American Revolution and Natural Law

American interest in foreign and comparative law has waxed and waned over the more than 200 years that the United States has been a republic. To some extent, this paralleled the nation's cultural and intellectual fashion, economic wealth and institutional development, increased racial, ethnic, and religious diversity as a land of immigrants, and self-perceived place in the world. Initial optimism and utopian natural law views defined the early years of the nation. The Declaration of Independence (1776), the United States Constitution (1787), and its first ten amendments, the Bill of Rights (1791), early stated the ideal in law and government. Many of the Founding Fathers were not only trained in English common law, but read European political philosophy and considered Roman law an important element in the Roman republic's success.

Prior to the American Revolution (1776) colonists' arguments against English political domination insisted nevertheless on an Englishman's common law rights as also the colonists' rights. As Roscoe Pound explained, the same events that separated colonists from England politically prepared them to receive the common law. The publication of William Blackstone's four volume *Commentaries on the Laws of England* (1765–9) provided an authoritative statement, although not up to date, that facilitated this reception. The substantial minority of Americans of German descent also supported natural law principles of liberty. Their 1794 petition to Congress to publish federal laws in German, which failed in the House of Representatives by one vote, would have opened the door to more continental sources.

At the same time, law comparison found a place through the importance put on natural law as a legal theory. John Adams (1735–1826), for instance, a student of both the common law and the civil law, argued against parliamentary authority in his *Dissertation on the Canon and Feudal Law* (1765) as well as against the common law in *Novanglus* (political essays published in 1775). Instead, he asserted that New Englanders derived their laws from natural law. His 1779 draft of the Massachusetts Constitution prescribed a government of laws, not men. In 1801, as United States president, he appointed John Marshall (1755–1835) chief justice of the US Supreme Court. Marshall in 1803 wrote the opinion in *Marbury v Madison* that asserted the power of judicial review.

Another natural lawyer was Thomas Jefferson (1743–1826), trained in law by George Wythe (1726–1806), who knew civil law and in 1779 became the first law professor in the United States at the College of William and Mary. Jefferson drafted the Declaration of Independence, which defined legitimate government as one that supports the inherent individual natural rights of life, liberty, and the pursuit of happiness. He served as minister to France from 1785 to October 1789, where he witnessed the early French Revolution and advised the Marquis de Lafayette on the French Constitution. As United States president, Jefferson was careful to try to limit presidential power, ironically concluding the Louisiana Purchase in 1803 that more than doubled the size of the United States.

2. Resistance to English Law

Pound pointed to five factors that impeded an easy American reception of English law after the war of independence.[10] First, English law seemed to embrace medieval scholasticism. Its presentation was often alphabetical, abridged, and disorganized. This contrasted to the order and system of continental treatises, which influenced Story and others. Second, American social and economic conditions, emphasizing individualism in a pioneer society, were very different from those in England, which was in the process of industrialization and urbanization. American lawyers felt they had to work out their own rules favouring the exploitation of abundant natural resources. Third, Puritans, reacting against their hostile treatment in England, tended to distrust lawyers and disfavour lawyers' law. Fourth, many Americans were bitter at the English after the war. Since some states had lay judges even in their high courts, they expressed this sentiment by preferring French or natural law. Fifth, an economic depression followed the war. Lawyers, active in collecting debts, enforcing the British subjects' treaty rights, and invoking English criminal law against persons involved in disturbances, provoked some politicians to resist using English law.

In the formative era of the United States legal system, comparative law was not an organized force, certainly not a discipline, simply because lawyers learned law itself through reading and apprenticeship rather than formal schooling. Few law

---

[10] See Roscoe Pound, *The Formative Era of American Law* (1936).

books were available. Law schools that developed in the nineteenth century were nothing more than law training offices, and this was true even at Harvard until Story provided a more scholarly flavour. Comparative law in this social and economic context could only be a method; as such, it was a method for borrowing Roman or civil law (as natural law), comparing it with positive common law, or providing prestige to a decision that local sources could otherwise reach.

Under the influence of natural law, a person's reason could discover a universal, immutable set of principles that positive law might reflect. For public law, the theories of Hugo Grotius (1583–1645), Samuel Pufendorf (1632–94), and Emer de Vattel (1714–67) could philosophically support an Englishman's immemorial common law rights, with Edward Coke's (1552–1634) idea of 'due process of law' in *The Second Part of the Institutes of the Lawes of England* and Blackstone's *Commentaries* supplying the content. However, for private law and especially commercial law, English materials were insufficient and less generally available.

3. Use of Roman and Civil Law

After the French Revolution, some liberal sentiment favoured French law. There were early English translations of Robert Pothier's (1699–1772) *Traité des Obligations* (1777), but other English translations of French treatises by Pothier and Jean Domat (1625–96) came much later. Hoeflich's research reveals that more translated foreign law books were available in English in ante-bellum United States than previously believed. Many of these, published in England or in American periodicals, served a practical comparative law with liberal translations to convey the sense of the original language.[11]

In addition, R. H. Helmholz has shown that American lawyers and judges made much more use of Roman and civilian sources than previously believed. He surveyed the cases reported in fourteen states and the federal system between 1790 and 1825. In each jurisdiction, there were multiple references of considerable variety in source material and subject-matter. Usually American judges and lawyers commented favourably on Roman law as *ratio scripta* or civil law with its extensive development, but others regarded it as overly elaborate in its distinctions or associated with tyrannical governments. The subject areas of greatest use were maritime disputes and commercial law. Jurists generally used Roman and civil law to cure deficiencies in English common law, support public natural law principles, or reinforce the common law rule.[12]

[11] Michael H. Hoeflich, 'Translation and the Reception of Foreign Law in the Antebellum United States', (2002) 50 *AJCL* 753–75.

[12] R. H. Helmholz, 'Use of the Civil Law in Post-Revolutionary American Jurisprudence', (1992) 66 *Tulane LR* 1649–84.

4. Livermore, Lieber, Story, and Kent

An early comparatist who facilitated the work of later jurists was Samuel Livermore (1786–1833). He spent half his career as a lawyer in Boston and Baltimore and the other half in New Orleans, where he moved in 1819. He wrote the first comparative law study on agency published anywhere in the world and the first American treatise on conflict of laws using a comparative methodology. He devised his huge 400 volume collection of European law books, printed from the invention of the press until 1800, to Harvard University. Joseph Story relied on this collection in writing his *Commentaries*.

Pound identified two judges from the formative era (out of the six he considered most important) who had the background to understand Roman and civil law and use it as practising comparatists. These were, first, Joseph Story, who served for thirty-two years on the US Supreme Court, taught as the Dane Professor at Harvard Law School, and wrote nine *Commentaries* and two other treatises on various subjects of American law between 1832 and 1845. The second was James Kent (1763–1847), the first law professor at Columbia College, who worked for twenty-five years on the New York bench, including nine years as chancellor of the New York Court of Chancery. He published his four volume *Commentaries on American Law* between 1826 and 1830.

Hoeflich documents Story's knowledge of Roman and civil law through his book collection (part of which he gave to Harvard Law School in the 1830s), his citation of foreign sources in the *Commentaries*, and his friendships with Romanists such as John Pickering (1777–1846) and Charles Follen (1796–1840) and other civilians such as Francis Lieber (1800–72). Lieber, a German émigré like Follen, corresponded extensively with Story, kept him current with German scholarship, and introduced him by mail to Carl Mittermaier (1787–1867), who made Story an editor and contributor to his *Kritische Zeitschrift für Rechtswissenschaft und Gesetzgebung des Auslandes*. Hoeflich argues that Story adopted the treatise form, unusual in the common law, for his *Commentaries* based on the civilian example of systematically explaining a specialized field. He could use it for his teaching at Harvard and it certainly filled an important need among practitioners. Besides borrowing a civilian form, Story made use of Roman and civil law rules to fill gaps in the common law and, where a rule already existed, as an argument for the universality of the common law doctrine.

Story was an ally of Chief Justice Marshall, both of whom supported federal (over state) rule-making power implied from clauses in the Constitution and strong federal judicial power. In *Swift v Tyson*,[13] Story wrote for a unanimous Court to create a general federal common law for civil obligations (contracts and torts) and commercial law for business litigants. They could either sue in federal court, or as defendants remove their cases from state court, if their domicile was different from

---

[13]   41 US 1 (1842).

that of their opponent. This restricted local, less favourable, state precedent from interfering with what federal judges, who could rely on Story's treatises, considered the reasonable expectations of the parties in interstate commercial affairs.

Kent's *Commentaries*, modelled on those by Blackstone, Americanized the common law, leavening it with his insights from civilian sources. He favoured strong property rights against the state, which he considered essential for liberty and economic development. The *Commentaries*, extremely popular among judges and lawyers who might not have access to the limited case reports, were reprinted in numerous editions during the 19th century.

Story's volumes came into general use along with those by Kent. Together, they helped to ensure the reception of English common law in the United States during the first half of the nineteenth century. Considering Story's treatises on commercial law, the irony of *English* 'reception' is that the Scotsman William Murray (Lord Mansfield, chief of the English King's Bench from 1756 to 1788) had liberally used Roman and civilian sources in developing English commercial law. Much of the usefulness of the earlier European *lex mercatoria* thus infused American commercial law either through Mansfield or through Story, since the latter cited French commentators in his treatise. Kent, as chancellor in New York, did the same, which served overall to liberalize American commercial law. Pound found that this tendency to rely on Roman and civilian sources spread to private law generally. He concluded:

A skilful use of comparative law, seeming to show the identity of an ideal form of the English common-law rule with an ideal form of the Roman-law or civil-law rule, and thus demonstrating the identity of each with a universally acknowledged law of nature, was the most efficient of the instruments by which Kent and Story, and many who followed them, were able to insure that the English common law should be the basis of the law in all but one of the United States.[14]

English equity rules were absorbed into American law in much the same way, although there was particular resentment in some states against equity jurisdiction with its technicalities and many formalistic rules. For instance, Pennsylvania did not have equity jurisdiction until 1836 and Massachusetts maintained only partial acceptance until after the Civil War. Story's treatise on equity again made a difference and brought many Roman law ideas into play as universal statements of natural law.

5. Lieber, Legaré, Walker, Hoffman, and Cushing

In addition to the great jurists that Pound recognized, there were groups of others familiar with Roman and civil law, whose published work was influential, who

---

[14] Pound (n 1), 12.

should qualify as comparatists. Hoeflich identifies Story's friend, Francis Lieber, Hugh Legaré (1797–1843), and James Walker (1813–54), all in South Carolina. Lieber's principal Romanist book was *Legal and Political Hermeneutics* (1839), which synthesized numerous sources and perspectives, including ethics, on the proper interpretive principles to use in reading legal materials including constitutions, treaties, statutes, precedents, and documents.[15] After 1857, Lieber left South Carolina and taught at Columbia College in New York City and at Columbia's law school until 1872. Helmholz adds Thomas Cooper (1759–1839). His *Institutes of Justinian with Notes* (1812, 2nd edn, 1841) was the first book to specifically relate American case law to the civil law.

David Hoffman (1784–1854) was interested in legal education. In 1814, he was appointed a law professor at the University of Maryland, where he published *A Course of Legal Studies* (1817, 2nd edn, 1836). Hoffman had studied at the University of Göttingen and believed that a thorough knowledge of Roman and civil law should be a significant part of the training of any American lawyer. He taught regularly at Maryland from 1822 until 1833 and teachers used his *Course* at Harvard and Columbia.

Another important comparatist was Luther Cushing (1803–56). He taught Roman law at Harvard, which led to *An Introduction to the Study of the Roman Law* (1854), and translated or edited civilian law books by Jean Domat, Robert Pothier, Carl Mittermaier, and Friedrich Carl von Savigny (1779–1861). Like Story, he served on the editorial board of Mittermaier's *Kritische Zeitschrift*. His *Introduction* dealt with the philosophy and sources of Roman law rather than substantive rules, emphasizing the practical utility of its study. Cushing argued that many American legal rules and institutions were derived from Roman law and, in addition, several American jurisdictions such as Louisiana, Florida, Texas, and California had civilian systems.

6. David Field and his Codes

To this list of influential comparatists, I add David Dudley Field (1805–94). Most jurists know Field, a successful New York lawyer, as a law reformer who advocated codification of both procedural and substantive law to replace the chaotic common law. Field's greatest success came as the pivotal member of the New York commission that submitted its draft Code of Civil Procedure to the legislature in 1848. Enacted in 1849, more than half the other American states and territories adopted the Code in one of its versions by 1873. It was revolutionary since it abolished the English feudal writ and bill system of pleading and replaced it with a single civil

---

[15] Lieber, *Legal and Political Hermeneutics, or Principles of Interpretation and Construction in Law and Politics* (Boston: Charles Little & James Brown, 1839).

action guided by 'code' pleading. It also merged law and equity, a distinction that had caused great confusion and delay.

The major source of Field's ideas about codification and the content of his civil procedure rules came from the 1825 Louisiana Code of Procedure. Edward Livingston (1764–1836), a New Yorker who moved to Louisiana in 1804, was trained in the civil law of France and Spain, which influenced his successful Louisiana Practice Act of 1805. He, Louis Lislet (1762–1832), and Pierre Derbigny (1767–1829) drafted the Louisiana Code's *projet*, drawing from French, Spanish, and Roman law sources, common law tradition, and Livingston's 1805 Act. The cumulative impact of the civilian idea of codification, the numerous similarities in form and substance between the New York Code and the Louisiana Code or the French Code of Civil Procedure (1806), make it likely that Field directly or indirectly borrowed significant elements from civil law sources. Much of the French influence probably made its way to New York via Louisiana, making Louisiana the cultural intermediary between civil law Europe and common law America.

IV. Comparative Law and Historical Jurisprudence (1865–1904)

1. Historical Jurisprudence

After the Civil War (1861–65), natural law ceased to be a creative theory that could work hand in hand with comparative law by borrowing from civil law jurisdictions. In both Europe and the United States, jurists looked inward and revelled in the particular over the universal. Italy in 1861 and Germany in 1871 became modern nation states. Jurists, along with others, emphasized the uniqueness and virtue of their national culture, language, and law. The primary jurisprudential theories that replaced natural law were historical, searching for law in a people's spirit, or analytical, organizing legal rules and discovering principles in a scientific manner. Neither of these approaches seemingly left much room for valuing how other societies solved legal problems. Pound saw this period as a nadir in American comparative law activities.

More recently, Hoeflich and others have demonstrated that comparative law did not so much go into decline, rather its focus shifted. Instead of looking at the utility of adopting specific foreign rules or the codification form, post-bellum comparatists considered the prestige of modifying civilian university legal education and its legal science for American circumstances or using ideas from European and especially

German legal philosophy to develop a comparative jurisprudence. Hoeflich considers Savigny the most influential civilian during this period, especially his ideas on historical jurisprudence.

Savigny wrote that one would not find the sources of law in logic or nature, but in the common life of a people. Good law arises from a nation's history and reflects its unique qualities. Sir Henry Maine (1822–88) in England supported this basis for an historical approach to Roman and civil law. He became the first reader in Roman law at the London Inns of Court in 1852 and, after some time in India, returned to teach at Oxford in 1869. His most influential book was *Ancient Law* (1861), a polemic for comparative law study and law reform.

Pound identified four judges from the latter nineteenth century that he considered most important in developing American law. Only one of these—Oliver Wendell Holmes, Jr (1841–1935)—had the background to understand Roman and civil law, but given the philosophical tenor of the period, he more subtly incorporated civilian insights into his influential court decisions and writings. Holmes's famous book, *The Common Law* (1881), provided a systematic historical and philosophical critique of its subject, which served as the basis for much of American private law development in the twentieth century. For twenty years as justice and then chief justice of the Massachusetts Supreme Judicial Court, Holmes applied his pragmatic jurisprudence to private law. He then served for thirty more years on the US Supreme Court, where his influence on public law was equally important.

2. Making Legal Education Scientific

This period saw the complete transformation of American legal education from a modified English apprenticeship approach, even at Harvard Law School, where instruction relied primarily on lectures, memorization, and recitation. The new system embraced university law schools that adopted major elements related to the goals, method, structure, and ceremony of German legal education, the leading European model. Harvard was the centre of this transformation under the presidency of Charles Eliot (1834–1926) and the Law School's first dean, Christopher Langdell (1826–1906), who served from 1870 until 1895. Eliot, who had travelled for two years in Europe in the 1860s studying educational systems, was the more important. He actively initiated and supported reform throughout the university and presided over most Law School faculty meetings. He hired law professors who lacked a background of professional practice but could be full-time teachers and scholars.

Langdell, with the help of Eliot's leadership, from 1870 to 1885 institutionalized five important changes: (1) an entrance examination; (2) a progressive three-year curriculum, leading to an undergraduate bachelor of laws degree (LLB); (3) requisite annual examinations before students could proceed to the next year's subjects;

(4) support for a research function similar to that existing at German universities; and (5) an instructional method utilizing Socratic dialogue to discuss appellate court cases, justified as a scientific process to elaborate general, organic principles of the common law. Langdell contended that he was trying to put American law faculties on a level with universities in continental Europe. Professors and students should together work through questions and answers to discover common law principles, aided by classroom research manuals called casebooks. Langdell's theory of legal science and organic development was similar to that of Savigny.

As dean, Langdell recruited James Barr Ames (1846–1910) as an assistant professor in 1873. Ames was the new breed of academic lawyer, with limited practical experience, that met Eliot's goal for teaching and scholarship. Ames had studied for over a year at German universities. He became a popular instructor, using Langdell's Socratic method, and produced many casebooks that were widely used in American law schools. Legal science promised a complete and orderly system of norms; it brought prestige to law as a science. The American Bar Association Committee on Legal Education and Admissions to the Bar accepted this model in 1879. Harvard Law School's influence on the rest of American legal education up through the twentieth century is unequivocal. Jurists could build the discipline of comparative law upon this foundation.

3. The First Academic Comparatists

An important American jurist to embrace comparative law full time as a scholar and teacher was William Hammond (1829–94). After reading to become a New York lawyer, Hammond studied law at Heidelberg University and elsewhere in Europe. Savigny's historical approach heavily influenced him in his Roman and civil law work. From 1869 to 1881, he served as chancellor at the University of Iowa Law Department, where he taught civil law and comparative law. During this time, he pushed for a broad, philosophical, and scientific education, including knowledge of Roman law, of the type he had witnessed in Heidelberg, appropriate for a university law school. He published an edition of Justinian's *Institutes*, which included a comparative survey of civil and common law classification systems, and his own edition of Lieber's *Legal and Political Hermeneutics*. In 1881, he became dean of Washington University (at St Louis) Law Department, where he continued until his death to advocate a more scientific legal education and write on civil law, comparative law, and legal history. In 1890, he published his own edition of Blackstone's *Commentaries*. During the last quarter of the nineteenth century, Roman and civil law gained support for study at the university, but were at the same time of less practical import to modern lawyers. Hammond saw the historical approach as intimately connected to comparative law. Together they clarified one's understanding of the common law while serving as a basis for reform. John Pomeroy

(1828–85), a prolific treatise writer and law professor from 1878 to 1885 at Hastings Law College (in San Francisco), took a similar view.

Perhaps the institution that best supported comparative law at the end of the nineteenth century and beginning of the twentieth century was Yale College and Law School. James Hadley (1821–72) taught Roman law at Yale College for many years. His lectures, first published after his death in 1873, were so popular that there were several reprints well into the twentieth century. The crucial figure, however, was Simeon Baldwin (1840–1927). John Langbein describes this Yale Law School professor, appointed in 1869, sometime treasurer and major benefactor, as the person who carried the law school into the twentieth century.[16] Although Baldwin wrote about public international law and taught private international law using civilian sources, he was not a comparatist in the scholarly sense. His principal contribution was to lend his prestige as one of America's leading jurists to the development of comparative law and its institutionalization as director of the Comparative Law Bureau from 1907 to 1919.

Professors taught Roman, canon, and civil law at Yale Law School from the 1870s. Albert Wheeler's Roman law class from 1876 until his death in 1905 was required for all doctor of civil law (DCL) candidates. One of those doctoral students, Charles Sherman (1874–1960), who also studied in Rome and Paris, replaced Wheeler at Yale from 1905 until 1917. He taught three courses on Roman law and one on canon law. He used a comparative and historical approach that emphasized the relevance of Roman law not only for civil law countries, but also for Anglo-American law. Other professors lectured on the French codes and Savigny's views on obligations.

By the end of the nineteenth century, scholars taught Roman law in several law schools over a wide area of the United States. Munroe Smith (1854–1926), a comparatist at Columbia University, expressed a common view at that time about the role of Roman law in instructing future lawyers. Roman law was no longer of practical use, since courts had stopped citing it (with the exception of cases involving private international law). Furthermore, it was not necessary in teaching the process of legal reform, since a course on English or American legal history could do just as well. However, Roman law was central to teaching law as a science, which required a method, and that method should be the one used by comparative law.

To judge the type of articles written about Roman and civil law during this period, Hoeflich surveyed the leading law journal, the *Harvard Law Review*, which began publication in 1887. Most of the articles up to 1904 were historical in treating their subjects, and their authors were academics interested in gaining a comparative perspective on modern common law issues. Prominent young comparatists who

---

[16] John H. Langbein, 'Law School in a University: Yale's Distinctive Path in the Later Nineteenth Century', in Anthony T. Kronman (ed), *History of the Yale Law School: The Tercentennial Lectures* (2004), 53, 59–63.

wrote during this seventeen-year period included Samuel Williston (1861–1963), who authored three articles on contracts, Ernst Freund (1864–1932), who described the new German civil code, and John Wigmore (1863–1943), who published a comprehensive comparative survey on the pledge in three articles. In 1894, William Howe (1833–1909), a Louisiana Supreme Court justice, delivered the Storrs Lectures at Yale and wrote about the development of civil law in America.

In summing up the role served by Roman and civil law in American legal thought during the nineteenth century, Hoeflich found that they gave common lawyers a comparative benchmark by which to analyse their own solutions to problems affecting law and legal institutions. Teachers like Hammond saw the comparative method as a tool for teaching jurisprudence and training law students to be problem solvers. More particularly, they provided models of systematic legal structure, such as codification or those found in treatises, by which jurists could organize common law rules. Scientific university legal education was another example. Furthermore, Roman and civil law, in contrast to the medieval flavour of the common law, appeared to have conceptual and linguistic precision. Scholars such as Lieber attempted to redefine civilian terms and introduce them into the common law. In Latin, they seemed appropriate for university law study and superior to the casuistic nature of law office training. Finally, Roman and civil law, requiring some knowledge of a foreign language, bestowed intellectual prestige on common lawyers.

V. Organized Comparative Law: The First Effort (1904–1950)

1. A Timeline

Sustained scholarly comparative law activity in the United States, together with organized networks of communication, commenced early in the twentieth century, which one can conveniently date from 1904. Largely associated with the successful effort to establish scientific teaching and research at mostly university law schools, twenty-five of which in 1900 created the Association of American Law Schools (AALS), this new field of juristic inquiry emerged from both idealistic as well as practical concerns. Moreover, it was as successful in the United States as the much better-known contemporary national developments in Belgium, France, Germany, and Great Britain.

Organized American comparative law began with the 1904 St Louis Universal

Congress of Lawyers and Jurists, the first international congress of comparative law in the United States, held only four years after the justly celebrated 1900 Paris *Congrès international de droit comparé*. The timeline that follows shows how the discipline of comparative law first developed. I emphasize five stages in this evolution that take us to 1950, when academic comparative law achieves a firmer footing.

First, organizational efforts to establish the Comparative Law Bureau began in 1905, which led the American Bar Association (ABA), the leading national organization of lawyers and judges, to create that entity as a section in 1907. Bureau members met annually at the ABA's summer meeting and published a 200 or so page *Annual Bulletin* from 1908 until 1914, when World War I disrupted cross-Atlantic connections. This was the first comparative law journal in the United States.

Second, the ABA, although organized in 1878, only started publishing a *Journal* in 1915. Established as a quarterly, the Bureau's editorial staff controlled the second issue each year, which was devoted primarily to the subjects previously handled in the Bureau's *Annual Bulletin*. Bureau members continued to meet annually, while the publishing arrangement with the ABA continued through 1929. After that date there were no more special Bureau issues of the *ABA Journal*, but comparative and foreign law articles still appeared with regularity, about five to ten per volume. In 1931, the Bureau made the *Tulane Law Review* its official journal, where it published meeting reports and some papers in a special section.

Third, since interest in foreign and comparative law was especially strong in New York City during the 1920s, Bureau members decided to organize a new entity in lieu of simply creating a New York branch of the Bureau in the manner that the International Law Association (London) created branches. Therefore, they established the American Foreign Law Association (AFLA) in 1925, which until 2000 was a sponsor member of the American Society of Comparative Law with a special subscription relationship to the *American Journal of Comparative Law*.

Fourth, due to the Great Depression, the Bureau fell into financial difficulty in the 1930s. It published one more *Annual Bulletin* in 1933, 215 pages long, but neither it nor the Bureau could survive. John Wigmore, on the Bureau's council, urged the ABA executive committee to sponsor an amendment to the ABA's constitution, which successfully merged the Comparative Law Bureau with the International Law Section. From 1933, Wigmore served as the first chair of the Section of International and Comparative Law. The Section provided useful publications in its official journal, the *Tulane Law Review*, and its annual meetings had sessions for academic comparatists, especially the Comparative Jurisprudence Committee and the Teaching of International and Comparative Law Committee. It levied Section dues beginning in 1942 and by the end of World War II the Section had over 1,000 members.

Finally, in 1950, members of the American Foreign Law Association and the ABA Section decided to make a sustained effort to support a more scientific comparative law and its teaching and research in American law schools. The American

Foreign Law Association had issued proceedings from its periodic meetings since 1926 (some of its articles also appearing in law journals) and it published biblio-graphies. Also in 1950, the American Foreign Law Association began publishing a *Bulletin*, edited by Harvard professor Kurt Nadelmann (1900–84), which according to the American Foreign Law Association president, Phanor Eder (1880–1971), served as an example for the new *American Journal of Comparative Law* in 1952. In May 1951, the American Foreign Law Association voted to establish the American Association for the Comparative Study of Law, which its directors incorporated in New York in June. In 1992, the Association was renamed the American Society of Comparative Law.

2. The 1904 Universal Congress of Lawyers and Jurists

The St Louis Universal Congress of Lawyers and Jurists was the first international congress of comparative law in the United States. It resulted from a proposal that the 'Louisiana Purchase Exposition Company' made to the ABA. After reciting the fact that President Thomas Jefferson purchased the Louisiana Territory for $15 million from France in 1803, the Company proposed to hold a centennial in St Louis in 1903. The proposal noted: 'The wilderness of 1803 has developed into fourteen States and Territories' and stated that the city of St Louis, with the help of $5 million from the US Congress and $1 million from the state of Missouri, was willing to devote more than the purchase price (ie $16 million) to a celebration of its centennial. The Centennial Exposition contemplated a 'World's Fair greater and more wonderful than any ever held', and 'to gather together the learned men of the world in the several departments of arts and sciences, including the science of jurisprudence'.

The ABA accepted the proposal, which it postponed until 1904 to further coordinate preparations, and which would now celebrate the centennial of the official transfer of sovereignty from Spain to France to the United States. The World's Fair was a great success, attracting 20 million visitors. St Louis also hosted the third modern Olympics that same year. In 1903, the ABA president had appointed Simeon Baldwin of Yale to the ABA's Executive Committee to implement the Congress, which occurred from 28–30 September 1904, immediately after the ABA's annual meeting.[17] Baldwin was one of the ABA's founders (drafting its consti-tution), a former ABA president (1890–1), and AALS president (1902), Yale law

---

[17] The Congress's aims 'were the consideration of the history and efficacy of the various systems of jurisprudence and the discussion of those questions of international, municipal and maritime law which concern the welfare of all civilized nations; the hope of contributing to greater harmony in the principles and the forms of procedure upon which the law of civilized nations should be based; the bringing into contact of lawyers and jurists from all parts of the world for the purpose of exchanging views on the principles and methods of the correct administration of justice'.

professor until his death, and member of the *Institut de droit comparé* in Brussels. He would later be chief justice of the Connecticut Supreme Court, Governor of Connecticut, and director of the Comparative Law Bureau from 1907 to 1919.

Unlike the 1900 international comparative law congress in Paris, lawyers and judges organized and ran this one, with a smaller representation from academia. The Congress president was Associate Justice David Brewer (1837–1910) of the US Supreme Court, who was also an international law professor at George Washington University. Brewer was born in Smyrna, Asia Minor (now Turkey), where his father worked as a missionary. His mother was Emilia Field, sister of Supreme Court Justice Stephen Field and the New York codifier, David Field. His experience in Asia came through in strong dissents in cases limiting the rights of Chinese and Japanese immigrants. His 1893 dissent in *Fong Yue Ting v United States*[18] illustrates the view that made him a natural favourite later to preside at a congress of comparative lawyers. In *Fong*, the Court determined that Congress's power to deport aliens was plenary and inherent in federal sovereignty. Brewer responded: 'In view of this enactment of the highest legislative body of the foremost Christian nation, may not the thoughtful Chinese disciple of Confucius ask, Why do they send missionaries here?' Brewer was an anti-imperialist who believed that the United States should give the Philippines its independence and then guarantee its neutrality.

Of the fourteen Congress vice presidents, one from each of the Congress nations, most were judges or lawyers, but four were professors. These persons formed a Committee of Nations and voted on Congress propositions. The majority of the voting members were European: from Austria, Belgium, the British Empire, France, Germany, Italy, the Netherlands, Sweden, and Switzerland. The remaining Congress countries were Argentina, Brazil, China, Mexico, and the United States.

Delegates could present reports and discuss in any language, but Congress staff provided translations into English. Comparative law panels included: (1) the preferable method of regulating the trial of civil actions with respect to pleading and evidence; (2) a review of the four Hague Conferences on private international law; and (3) the extent to which local courts should recognize the judicial action of foreign country courts.

There were 481 registered delegates at the Congress, which was a huge number for such an event, even though most were from the United States. Forty American law professors attended from almost 30 law schools, including deans from leading law schools such as Chicago (Joseph Beale, 1861–1943), Harvard (James Barr Ames), Northwestern (John Wigmore), Pennsylvania (William Draper Lewis, 1867–1949), and Stanford (Nathan Abbott, 1854–1941). Some, in addition to Beale, Lewis, and Wigmore, would publish comparative law research or contribute to comparative law activities, such as Eugene Gilmore (1871–1953, Wisconsin), Charles Huberich (1877–1945, Texas), William Mikell (1868–1945, Pennsylvania), James Brown Scott

---

[18] 149 US 698 (1893).

(1866–1943, Columbia), Munroe Smith (Columbia), and William Walz (b. 1860, Maine). The most famous foreign law professors in attendance were Georges Blondel (1856–1948, Paris), Josephus Jitta (1854–1925, Amsterdam), and Friedrich Meili (1848–1914, Zurich).

3. The Comparative Law Bureau

Soon after the 1904 Congress, the question of creating a comparative law society received its first organized recognition by the Pennsylvania State Bar Association in 1905. At the Association's annual meeting, the president appointed a committee to discuss such a project. The committee's report considered the initiative too large for any one state and recommended bringing the matter before the ABA. The ABA created a committee to investigate and recommend the best method to accomplish the goals of comparative law. At its 1907 annual meeting, the ABA authorized the organization of the Comparative Law Bureau, which published its first *Annual Bulletin* surveying foreign legislation and legal literature in July 1908.

It is likely that the French *Société de législation comparée*, founded in 1869, which organized the 1900 Paris Congress, served as the model for the American Bureau. In 1896, Professor Henri Lévy-Ullmann (1870–1947, Montpellier, also *avocat* at the Paris Cour d'appel), wrote a report describing the French Society in the *Harvard Law Review*. Lévy-Ullmann served as the general reporter to section 4 (civil law) at the Paris Congress, which had five United States delegates, including Professor John Burgess (1844–1931) of Columbia University, a specialist on comparative constitutional law.

Lévy-Ullmann described several elements of the French Society that later came to parallel aspects of the American Bureau. First, the Society's members were lawyers and judges as well as scholars. Second, its principal tasks were to translate and publish interesting foreign laws and to stimulate comparative law studies that could aid legislatures in law reform or simply provide useful information (such as a series of essays on bar organizations in diverse countries). Third, it published a periodic *Bulletin*, which included translated legislation and comparative law studies. Fourth, it published translations of foreign codes, constitutions, and statutes (by 1896, from England, Germany, Hungary, Italy, Montenegro, Netherlands, Portugal, Russia, Scandinavia, United States, and Zurich) and a few comparative studies, for instance, on the treatment of aliens or notarial law. He concluded: 'Its main object is, by putting the knowledge of the laws of all countries within the reach of everybody, gradually to bring about uniformity in legislation through the development of the science of law; this is pre-eminently a work of civilization and of progress.'[19]

---

[19] Henri Lévy-Ullmann, 'Account of the French Society of Comparative Legislation', (1897) 10 *Harvard LR* 161, 166–7.

The Bureau's officers included Simeon Baldwin (Yale and Connecticut Supreme Court) as director and William Smithers (1864–1947) as secretary. Smithers was from Philadelphia, where the International Printing Company published the *Bulletin*, and he also served as the chairman of the *Bulletin*'s editorial staff. The Bureau's managers included James Barr Ames, dean at Harvard, George Kirchwey (1855–1942), dean at Columbia, William Draper Lewis, dean at Pennsylvania and later the first director of the American Law Institute, and John Wigmore, dean at Northwestern. In 1911, Roscoe Pound, then Story professor at Harvard, became a manager. In the *Bulletin*'s first issue, the Bureau presented its aims.[20]

The *Bulletin* was circulated to all ABA members, numbering over 2,000, and to other subscribers. The editorial staff in 1908 included: Baldwin for general jurisprudence; Robert Shick (b. 1869) for Austria-Hungary; Arthur Kuhn (1876–1954) for Belgium; Smithers for Egypt, France, and Turkey; Ernest Lorenzen (1876–1951, George Washington) and Roscoe Pound (then at Northwestern) for Germany; Charles Wetherill for China and Great Britain; Masuji Miyakawa (d. 1916, first Japanese admitted to a state bar) for Japan; Leo Rowe (1871–1946, Pennsylvania) for Latin America; William Hastings (1853–1937, dean at Nebraska from 1909) for Russia; Samuel Scott (1846–1929) for Spain; and Gordon Sherman (1854–1925) for Switzerland.[21] In 1910, Smithers added Charles Huberich (Stanford) to the *Bulletin*'s editorial staff for the British Colonies and Edwin Borchard (1884–1951) and Samuel Williston (Harvard) for Germany. In 1911, he added Charles Lobingier (1866–1956) as editor for the Philippine Islands, where he was a judge (1904–14) and law professor at the University of the Philippines (1911–21). Borchard became law librarian at the Library of Congress in 1911 and then librarian and professor at Yale Law School in 1917. In 1910, the Bureau had five law libraries and seventeen law schools as institutional members. By 1914, that number had grown to fourteen law libraries and twenty law school institutional members.

4. The Bureau's Support for Publications

The Bureau entered into a publishing arrangement with the Boston Book Company in 1910 for a foreign law series. This included Samuel Scott's translation of *The Visigothic Code* (1910) and Robert Shick's translation of *The Swiss Civil Code*

---

[20] The Bureau's aims were to: (1) publish an annual *Bulletin* with foreign legislation and reviews of foreign legal literature; (2) translate and publish foreign legislation and relevant expert opinions; (3) hold an annual conference to discuss comparative law generally; (4) provide a more thorough means by which foreign laws could become available to American lawyers; (5) promote research in foreign law; (6) establish a list of foreign correspondents; and (7) gather information on foreign law, including bibliographies, for the benefit of practising lawyers, law teachers, and students.

[21] There were foreign correspondents from fourteen countries, including Gaston de Leval (1874–1944, avocat, Brussels court of appeal) and Eugen Huber (1849–1923, Bern).

(1915). The latter was a team effort by Bureau members, since Wetherill annotated and Huber and Sherman made corrections. Boston Book also published *The Civil Code of the German Empire* (1909), N. M. Korkunov's *General Theory of Law* (1909, Dean Hastings's translation), and twenty-four volumes, out of thirty-five projected, of the *Commercial Laws of the World* (1911–14, Huberich's general introduction). The German Civil Code was a collaborative effort between the University of Pennsylvania and the Pennsylvania Bar Association. Walter Loewy (1881–1932) translated, Smithers wrote an historical introduction, and Wetherill wrote reference notes referring to analogous provisions in other foreign codes.

In addition, Boston Book (and its successor, Macmillan Company) published twelve volumes in the Modern Legal Philosophy Series between 1911 and 1925, which an Association of American Law Schools (AALS) committee, chaired by John Wigmore and dominated by comparatists, edited.[22] The volumes primarily consisted of civilian legal science books, articles, and excerpts translated into English. Besides making continental legal theory accessible in English, the editors (who sometimes also translated) and others wrote useful introductions and editorial prefaces.

In 1911, the United States Government began to support financially the comparative law movement by devoting resources to the Library of Congress 'to collect the essential materials necessary for an accurate knowledge of the legal institutions of every civilized country'.[23] Edwin Borchard, Bureau editor and law librarian, was supervising the work. The Library also started to publish critical surveys of foreign country legal literature, beginning with Germany, printing portions also in the *Bulletin*. This series, known as *Guide to the Law and Legal Literature of . . .*, was very useful for academic comparatists. Borchard published two in this series, one on Germany (1912) and the other on Argentina, Brazil, and Chile (1917), as well as the *Bibliography of International Law and Continental Law* (1913). The Library of Congress finished this run by publishing volumes on Spain (1915) and France (1931). In 1943, the Library picked up the series again with twelve new volumes, this time concentrating on Latin America. Helen Clagett (1905–89), chief of the Hispanic Law Section, authored ten of these books from 1945 to 1948.

5. The 1920s and 1930s: American Comparatists Look Abroad

The 1920s and 1930s were decades during which American comparatists became actively involved in European legal research and European legal conferences,

---

[22] The AALS president selected the committee members in 1910: Albert Kocourek (1875–1952, Northwestern), Lorenzen (then at Wisconsin), Floyd Mechem (1858–1928, Chicago), Pound (Harvard), and Wigmore (Northwestern). Ernst Freund (Chicago) and Huberich (Stanford) joined the committee in 1912, Joseph Drake (1860–1947, Michigan) in 1913, and Morris Cohen (1880–1947, College of the City of New York Philosophy Department) in 1922.

[23] William W. Smithers, 'Editorial Miscellany', (1911) 4 *Ann Bull* 11.

although also with substantial interest in Asia and Latin America. *ABA Journal* special sections devoted to comparative law reflected this as did American submissions to foreign legal publications. The 1925 *Journal* reported that foreign law had become increasingly important in the United States, both for the goals of comparative law as well as private international law. The *Journal* went to all ABA members, numbering around 4,000 in 1920, but increasing to 30,000 in 1936. In 1930, fourteen law schools reported offering a comparative law course, usually to graduate students.

In 1924, Munroe Smith, a professor at Columbia University, together with Élemér Balogh (1881–1955), Antonio de Bustamante (1865–1951), Henri Lévy-Ullmann, Vittorio Scialoja (1856–1933), and André Weiss (1858–1928) formed the International Academy of Comparative Law in Geneva, which moved its seat in 1925 to The Hague. The number of full members was set at a maximum of thirty, although they could elect additional correspondents. Members must be professors or published scholars. The other American members were: John Bassett Moore (1860–1947), a member of the Columbia faculty since 1891 and a judge on the Permanent Court of International Justice since 1921; Roscoe Pound; James Brown Scott, a professor at Georgetown and editor-in-chief of the *American Journal of International Law* since 1907; and Harlan Stone (1872–1946), dean of Columbia Law School from 1910 to 1923 and US Supreme Court justice since 1925.

6. The American Foreign Law Association and the American Law Institute

In 1924, the Comparative Law Bureau adopted a resolution to create a New York section of the Bureau. That same year, during a visit of hundreds of American lawyers to the ABA annual meeting held in London, the *Société de législation comparée* entertained a group of the lawyers who had travelled to Paris. At that meeting, some suggested that the Americans form a *Société* branch in the United States. There followed a meeting between the president of the New York City Bar Association, the chair of its special committee on private international law and conflicts of law, and the Bureau's chairman and vice chairman. They decided to form an organizational committee that led to the 1925 founding of the American Foreign Law Association (AFLA).[24]

---

[24] Art II of the American Foreign Law Association's Constitution reads: 'The objects of the Association shall be the advancement of the study, understanding, and practice of foreign, comparative and private international law, the promotion of solidarity among members of the legal profession who devote themselves, wholly or in part, to those branches, the maintenance of adequate professional standards relative to members and active cooperation with learned societies, devoted to such subjects, like the Comparative Law Bureau of the ABA, the *Société de Legislation Comparée*, etc.', 'American Foreign Law Association', (1925–26) 20 *Illinois LR* 110, 111.

American Foreign Law Association dues were set at $10 annually. The first elected president was William Smithers. The General Council included Manley Hudson (1886–1960, Harvard), Judge Otto Schoenrich (b. 1876, New York City), Judge Charles Lobingier (United States Court for China and professor, Comparative Law School of China, 1914–24), Phanor Eder (New York City), and Arthur Kuhn (New York City). In 1925, the American Foreign Law Association had forty-two American members and nine foreign members.

It is also worth noting the significant relationship between comparative law and the founding of the American Law Institute (ALI) in 1923. William Draper Lewis, one of the Comparative Law Bureau's managers since 1907, became the first director of the ALI. Among the forty person committee organizing the ALI were four individuals with experience in foreign law: Ernst Freund, Roscoe Pound, John Wigmore, and Samuel Williston. Williston was the reporter for the ALI's first restatement, on contracts, which appeared in 1932. Mitchell Franklin (1902–86), a Romanist at Tulane, chided the ALI for its unwillingness to admit (what Williston had recognized) that its restatement represented the first step toward codification.[25]

7. Tulane College of Law

After 1929, when the ABA discontinued publishing the Bureau's reports, three young Harvard law professors, Walther Hug (1898–1980), Gordon Ireland (1880–1950), and James Thayer (1899–1976), together with Mitchell Franklin, a recent Harvard JSD graduate, convinced the *Tulane Law Review* to provide the Bureau with a section in the *Review* devoted to comparative law. Franklin had begun teaching at Tulane University College of Law in 1930, and the Bureau selected the *Review* to be its official periodical in 1931. The College had developed a special relationship with the Bureau dating from 1916, when the College began publishing the *Southern Law Quarterly*. John Wigmore wrote its lead article, 'Louisiana: The Story of its Legal System', and Charles Lobingier wrote two articles.

In 1931, Ernst Feilchenfeld (1898–1956), assistant professor at Harvard (1926–32), joined the original Harvard group and they all were listed on the *Review* masthead as 'Comparative Law Editors'. Hug and Feilchenfeld earned their doctorate of law degrees in Zurich and Berlin, respectively. After the Bureau merged with the

---

[25] Franklin went on: 'Restatements cannot be very creative. Restatement, therefore, is summation; it is an inventory, taken in the twentieth century, of nineteenth century resources. Moreover, due to the unwillingness of the Institute to describe its work as codification, the Restatements are not expected to have political sanctions put behind them. As they are to lack legislative approval, apparently the Restatements must become efficacious through an eighteenth century view as to the compulsiveness of reason'. Mitchell Franklin, 'Restatement of the Law of Contracts', (1933–4) 8 *Tulane LR* 149, 150 (book review).

ABA International Law Section in 1933, the new Section of International and Comparative Law, with Wigmore its first chair, chose the *Tulane Law Review* to be its 'official organ'. Section reports included articles by American and foreign comparatists, which continued until World War II no longer made it feasible. Besides Section reports, the *Review* organized a group of comparatists to contribute to a new part of the journal that digested interesting articles appearing in foreign legal periodicals.

In 1932, the *Tulane Law Review* further expanded its comparative law mission. The faculty editor announced that if the *Review* was to 'fulfil its place as a comparative law journal its organization must be on a broader and more comprehensive basis; it must not only reflect the developments and achievements of comparative law in the United States, but in the rest of the civilized world as well'.[26] To reflect this new role, the *Review* announced that it was the official 'American medium of expression of the International Congress of Comparative Law', held at The Hague in 1932, and that it would publish the official American report of the proceedings and several general reports from that Congress. The *Review* continued this role for reports from the Second International Congress of Comparative Law, held in 1937 in The Hague.

In 1949, the dean at Tulane announced the establishment of the Tulane Institute of Comparative Law, led by Ferdinand Stone (1908–89), based on the school's early support for comparative law and Louisiana's French and Spanish legal heritage and relationship with Latin American jurists. Stone, who earned a civil law degree at Oxford as a Rhodes Scholar and a JSD at Yale, reported on the 1950 London International Congress of Comparative Law in the *Tulane Law Review*, where he also published the national report he presented in London. In 1956, the Ford Foundation provided the Institute with $275,000 to strengthen the Tulane civil and comparative law programme and in 1957, the Rockefeller Foundation added $114,000 to establish a programme in Latin American legal studies.

8. Roscoe Pound

America's leading comparatist during the first half of the twentieth century was Roscoe Pound. After attending Harvard Law School, Pound began his academic career at the University of Nebraska in 1895, where he taught Roman law in the Latin department. In 1899, he continued that course even after his appointment as professor in the law department, where he became dean in 1903. In 1907, he joined the law faculty at Northwestern University and later the University of Chicago, after which he accepted the Story professorship at Harvard Law School in 1910.

---

[26] James J. Morrison, 'Editorials', (1932–3) 7 *Tulane LR* 96.

There he served as dean from 1916 until 1936. Pound continued to lecture and publish at Harvard until 1947 and elsewhere nearly until his death in 1964.

Pound learned German in his youth, earned a PhD in botany that involved reading the work of German scientists, and minored in Roman law. Michael Hoeflich divides Pound's scholarship into three areas: first, legal philosophy, where he was especially interested in Rudolf von Jhering's (1818–92) jurisprudence of interests (*Interessenjurisprudenz*) and other civilian jurists' writing about sociological jurisprudence; second, the development of Roman law into modern civil law and its use for comparison; finally, the influence of Roman and civil law on United States law. Pound's teaching materials reveal his interest in comparative law. Part one was published as *Readings in Roman Law and the Civil Law and Modern Codes as Developments Thereof: An Introduction to Comparative Law* (1914).

9. John Wigmore

Another major American comparatist with a worldwide reputation during this period was John Wigmore. He began his comparative law career when Harvard's president, Charles Eliot, selected him in 1889 to be the first professor of Anglo-American law at Keio University in Tokyo. Japan at the time was intensely interested in transplanting the best features of Western law. Wigmore became an expert in Tokugawa law and corresponded with scholars such as Josef Kohler (1849–1919, Berlin), who was a German delegate at the 1900 Paris Congress.

In 1893, Wigmore joined the Northwestern University Law School faculty, serving as dean from 1901 to 1929. He attended the 1904 St Louis Congress and was on the founding board of managers of the Comparative Law Bureau in 1907, remaining until its merger in 1933. Wigmore chaired the AALS editorial committee (all typically Bureau members), created in 1909, that oversaw the publication of the extremely useful ten-volume Continental Legal History Series. The other committee members were usually the same persons who organized and edited the Modern Legal Philosophy Series. The history volumes provided translated excerpts from books and articles and some original material on important aspects of European legal history and jurists. There were separate volumes on French, German, and Italian law as well as on civil procedure and criminal law and procedure. Wigmore was actively involved—editing, translating, and writing prefatory and introductory material.

Between 1915 and 1918, Wigmore and Albert Kocourek compiled and edited the three-volume *Evolution of Law*, bringing into one place English language excerpts and translated foreign writing about ancient and primitive legal systems, the rules themselves, and the physical, biological, and social factors influencing legal development. The authors intended the first volume, carrying the specific title *Sources of Ancient and Primitive Law* to be used as a book of materials to accompany the case method of teaching originally developed at Harvard. Consequently, *Sources*, published in 1915, is the world's first published comparative law 'casebook'. Although it is commonplace to think of comparative law as the study of similarities and differences in the laws of distinct systems, Wigmore and Kocourek were concerned primarily with similarities. Like other comparatists of their era, they saw unification of law as an important task (or at least insight) for the discipline. As with other comparatists in America and Europe, they also viewed the discipline broadly to include history, jurisprudence, and ethnology.

In 1928, Wigmore published the three-volume *A Panorama of the World's Legal Systems*, an attempt to open comparative law to a broader understanding beyond that provided by merely textual exegesis. Wigmore decried the narrowness of most foreign law studies and defined comparative law to mean: 'tracing of an identical or similar idea or institution through all or many systems, with a view to discovering its differences and likenesses in various systems, . . . in short, the evolution of the idea or institution, universally considered'. He then added: 'Modern scientific thought has made it generally understood that a legal institution can be fully [comprehended] only in the light of the social, economic, religious, political, racial, and climatic circumstances which surround it'.[27]

Wigmore wanted comparatists to have as much contact with the living law of a foreign system as possible, preferably learning the foreign language and residing in the country. Since he knew that this was often not possible, and if so, only for one or two countries, he advised scholars, in preparing their comparative studies, to adopt three perspectives. First, learn about the ethical, economic, and social background of their subject legal system. Second, review legal materials used in everyday social life, such as deeds and contracts as well as travellers' accounts of legal places and events such as courthouses and trials. Finally, use pictures so that a reader could visualize the legal reality.

Wigmore argued for this methodology, which he applied in his *Panorama*. There he surveyed sixteen principal legal systems, past and present: Egyptian, Mesopotamian, Hebrew, Chinese, Hindu, Greek, Roman, Japanese, Mohammedan, 'Keltic', Slavic, Germanic, maritime, papal, Romanesque, and Anglican. To bring his subject to life he incorporated 500 illustrations. He followed this in 1941 with *A Kaleidoscope of Justice: Containing Authentic Accounts of Trial Scenes from All Times and Climes*. The book's subtitle suggests the author's intent, which is to 'tell us of Justice as it is done, not of Justice as by the books'. Predating television broadcasting, Wigmore relied on the 'records of travel and adventure by eye-witnesses of the scenes described' to provide 'informational entertainment' and a 'collection of pen-pictures'. Nevertheless, Wigmore the scholar, could not restrain the temptation to 'draw inferences from these scattered instances to some general truths,

[27] John H. Wigmore, 'Comparative Law: Jottings on Comparative Legal Ideas and Institutions', (1931–2) 6 *Tulane LR* 48, 51.

truths of evolution and principles of policy', which he did in his twenty-four-page epilogue.

10. The 1930s: Achievement during a Difficult Period

In 1932, Wigmore wrote an article in the *ABA Journal* entitled 'An American Lawyer's Pilgrimage on the Continent'. His purpose was to interest lawyers in attending the upcoming international congress of comparative law at The Hague. In the notice following this article, he explained: 'This is the first Congress of this kind to be held since the International Congress of Lawyers at the Louisiana Purchase Exposition in 1904 in St Louis. It is organized by the International Academy of Comparative Law, of which the American members are Edwin Borchard, John Bassett Moore, Roscoe Pound, James Brown Scott, and Justice Harlan F. Stone.'[28] In 1930, Wigmore had translated and published Edouard Lambert's report calling for such a congress. Wigmore mentioned that forty countries had formed national committees. Those would designate national reporters for the topics in which they cared to participate. Although the United States attorney general headed the American committee, and forty state, county, and city bar associations appointed delegates, Wigmore was the driving force in soliciting attendance.

At the end of 1932, Wigmore dutifully reported in the *ABA Journal* about the Hague Congress and its major American presence. Delegates represented thirty-one countries. Of the 305 delegates registered in attendance, seventy-two came from the United States. Of these, at least twenty-eight were professors who represented sixteen law schools or university faculties. The second largest contingent of fifty-two participants came from France. Shortly thereafter, the ABA merged the Comparative Law Bureau in 1933 with the International Law Section, whose first chair was Wigmore.

Near the end of his deanship, Pound gave the address at the 1935 annual meeting of the newly constituted ABA Section of International and Comparative Law. In magisterial form, he surveyed the history of comparative law since the twelfth century, described its importance for development of law in the nineteenth-century United States, and argued that current comparative law was one of five universalizing elements helping to break the cult of local law. He also supported comparison beyond mere legal rules to embrace legal systems, and described the utility of the functional method of comparison.

Although the Great Depression, and later World War II, made serious comparative law research difficult, there was a surprising amount of important activity in the United States, partly supported by the wave of émigré legal scholars from

---

[28] John H. Wigmore, 'International Congress of Comparative Law', (1932) 18 *ABA Journal* 92.

Germany and Austria. Scholars examined this fascinating process of legal trans-plantation through the stories of individual scholars, which fully blossomed in the post-war period, at a conference held in Bonn in 1991. Refugee jurists had a very difficult time finding positions in American law schools, often only after a period of 're-education' in American law. Even then, since fewer than ten law schools offered a course in comparative or Roman law, most refugees had to settle for a research position, at least during the 1930s and early 1940s.

In 1934, Francis Deák (1898–1972) prepared and used at Columbia School of Law one of the earliest American-style casebooks for his comparative law class. Although focusing only on torts, it examined selected statute or code articles, legislative debates, *projets*, and *motifs*, American restatements, and judicial decisions of England, France, Germany, and the United States. Its innovative synthesis of the civilian emphasis on legislation (but without the scholarly overlay) and common law reliance on cases was only part of its distinctiveness. It also included briefs, references to other materials, hypothetical cases, and questions for the students.

The International Academy of Comparative Law called for a second inter-national congress at The Hague in 1937. Wigmore was the chair of the United States committee and again actively encouraged attendance. The United States had the largest national contingent of delegates among the thirty-five nations represented, forty-seven out of 240 jurists in attendance. It also had the largest number of universities represented, eleven compared to the next highest national group, which was Germany with professors from seven universities. Americans wrote general reports for twelve of the topics. Among those who attended were Harriet Daggett (1891–1966, Louisiana State), America's first female comparatist.[29]

Most of the work for organized comparative law in the late 1930s and 1940s fell to the American Foreign Law Association and the ABA Section on International and Comparative Law. The ABA Section, reorganized in 1937, elected Eder as vice chair and Vance as secretary. Wigmore was on the Council and its Advisory Com-mittee included Frederic Coudert (1898–1972), a partner in the eponymous Coudert Brothers law firm in New York (then America's leading firm for foreign law issues), Edwin Dickinson (1887–1961, University of California, Berkeley, who attended the 1932 Hague congress while at Michigan), and Pound.

Some other organizations, however, also helped. In 1939, William Draper Lewis, director at the ALI, created a research position in Philadelphia for perhaps

[29] Others were Phanor Eder, Mitchell Franklin, Jerome Hall (1901–92, Louisiana State), Albert Kocourek, Charles Lobingier (National University), Paul Sayre (1894–1959, University of Iowa), and Hessel Yntema (1891–1966, University of Michigan). American professors present who wrote national reports were Edwin Borchard, Harriet Daggett, and Karl Loewenstein (1891–1973, political science and jurisprudence professor at Amherst College, who was a German refugee Privatdozent, 1929–33, at the University of Munich and then an associate professor of government at Yale, 1934–36). Other attending American professors, besides Wigmore, came from law schools at George Washington, Valparaiso, William and Mary, and the Universities of Cincinnati and Wisconsin. John Vance (1884–1943), Library of Congress law librarian, also participated.

Europe's most famous comparatist, Ernst Rabel (1874–1955), director until 1937 of the *Kaiser Wilhelm Institut für ausländisches und internationals Privatrecht* in Berlin. Hessel Yntema helped to arrange a two-year stipend to pay Rabel while he prepared a companion volume to the *Restatement of Conflict of Laws* (1934). Although this project to present the conflicts rules of major countries according to the Restatement's arrangement was a promising opportunity for the ALI explicitly to embrace the comparative method, Rabel simply could not complete the book in such a short time. He returned to his four-volume magnum opus, *The Conflict of Laws: A Comparative Study* (1945–58), which the University of Michigan financed.

In 1941, the ABA Section of International and Comparative Law authorized John Vance, for the duration of the war, to offer to publish the English *Journal of the Society of Comparative Legislation*, but that Society decided to continue publishing from London. Vance, Congress's law librarian since 1924, thought that American comparatists should do more to support Latin American comparative law. He died the same month in 1943 as Wigmore. The sun was setting on the first sustained period of organized comparative law in the United States. A new dawn waited at the creation of the American Association for the Comparative Study of Law.

VI. Firmly Establishing Comparative Law (1950–2005)

1. The Post-War Period

At the beginning of the twentieth century, the United States was already a powerful nation with an overseas empire and an even greater reach for economic hegemony. After finishing on the winning side of two world wars, America emerged as the world's leading economic power, which after the collapse of Soviet communism in 1989 confirmed that it was *the* superpower. During the last fifty years of the twentieth century, consistent with this new status, American comparatists—both scholars and practising lawyers—engaged more actively in the exportation of American law and legal institutions in contrast to the net importation that occurred in the nineteenth century.

Some of this influence stemmed from American military occupation, such as that in the late 1940s and 1950s in Germany, Japan, and South Korea. One can see the impact in public law, especially constitutional law, and in institutions such as judicial review. During the cold war contest with communism in the 1960s and 1970s, the US Government and some American foundations with law and development programmes supported the battle in developing nations, many newly independent as part of the United Nations' effort toward decolonization. These programmes sought to implant certain American legal features such as active teaching in law schools, or social engineering for lawyers and judges, as a spur to economic and political development. In the 1990s, the American Bar Association's Central European and Eurasian Law Institute programme, 'promoting the rule of law', provided thousands of advisers to help write constitutions and laws in Russia, its former republics, and a few other developing nations.

2. UNESCO, American Foreign Law Association, and the AALS

From 1949 to 1951, American and European comparatists made concerted efforts to place comparative law studies on a firmer institutional basis. In 1949, UNESCO sponsored a conference of experts in Paris, which recommended the creation of the International Committee for Comparative Law. This was part of a UNESCO programme to develop international institutes of social science. Among comparatists resident in the United States, the 1949 conference included John Hazard (1909–95), Arthur von Mehren (1922–2006), and Ernst Rabel. UNESCO in 1950 created and funded the Committee, whose members were limited to national comparative law committees, while international organizations such as the Rome Institute for the Unification of Private Law were eligible as associate members. The Committee (which became the executive committee of the new International Association of Legal Science in 1956) would admit a national committee if it was satisfied that the national committee was representative of those entities or persons engaged in comparative law in that state.

By 1952, the Committee had accepted twenty members, including the United States. A Council and Bureau conducted the Committee's business. Each national committee had one delegate to the Council, which elected the rotating members of the seven-member Bureau. The Bureau took on an organizational element from the United Nations' Security Council: it had three permanent members—France, the United States, and the United Kingdom. The American delegate was Alexis Coudert (1914–80); the Bureau's first secretary-general was René David (1906–90).

The American Foreign Law Association undertook the task in 1950 of becoming the United States 'national' committee to the International Committee, whose agenda was primarily scholarly and involved sponsoring conferences and book publication. Since the American Foreign Law Association was largely a body of practising lawyers from the northeast, it needed to broaden its membership (about 170 in 1950) to include both more law professors and more residents from beyond the eastern seaboard. In 1951, it organized chapters in Chicago and Miami, and by

1952, it listed 38 law professors out of a total membership of 253. Both Germany and the United Kingdom in 1950 also created national committees for comparative law.

Comparative law also moved forward on other fronts. In 1950, probably due to the effort of John Hazard, the Association of American Law Schools created the Committee on Comparative Law, which was now independent of its International Law Committee. Arthur von Mehren chaired the Comparative Law Committee's annual programme from 1952 to 1953 and Hazard chaired in 1954. In addition, the Comparative Law Division within the ABA Section of International and Comparative Law remained active with seven committees, some of which took a scholarly perspective or interest in comparative law teaching.

3. The American Association for the Comparative Study of Law

Many of the law school affiliated members of the American Foreign Law Association believed that comparative law needed an organization, principally of law school sponsors, that could support a quality journal dedicated to the subject, similar to those existing in France, Germany, Great Britain, and Italy. Since the United States did not have a funded institute or centre of comparative law like that in Berlin or Paris, Americans would need to invent the functional equivalent. That entity would be the American Association for the Comparative Study of Law (AACSL), whose directors filed its certificate of incorporation with the New York Department of State in June 1951.[30] The founders believed that comparative law was too vast a field for a single institution to pre-empt it, and, even if possible, it would be undesirable in a nation as diverse as the United States. This attitude precluded tying the Association or its journal financially with the Parker School of Foreign and Comparative Law[31] at Columbia University or the new Tulane Institute of Comparative Law and the *Tulane Law Review*. Although the Parker School was a founding member of the American Association for the Comparative Study of Law, Tulane only joined in 1956.

The American Association for the Comparative Study of Law held its first meeting in July 1951 during the ABA annual meeting. Representatives of twenty law

---

[30] The Association's incorporation certificate stated its purpose: 'to promote the comparative study of law and the understanding of foreign legal systems; to establish, maintain, and publish without profit a comparative law journal; and to provide for research and the publication without profit of writings, books, papers, and pamphlets relating to comparative, foreign, or private international law'.

[31] Judge Edwin Parker left most of his estate in trust to support a school that would train students in foreign affairs. The trustees, including Justice Harlan Stone, Henry Stimson (secretary of state), and William Mitchell (attorney general and head of the American delegation to the 1932 Hague congress), exercised their power in 1931 to select Columbia University as the site for what would be the Parker School of Foreign and Comparative Law. In the 1950s, the Parker School had an ambitious publication programme that resulted in twelve books on foreign and comparative law.

schools met at New York University (NYU) Law School to discuss joining the Association, which changed its name in 1992 to the American Society of Comparative Law. That first year, ten schools plus the American Foreign Law Association joined as sponsor members, each with one director.[32] These directors elected Phanor Eder president, Hessel Yntema vice president, Alexis Coudert secretary, and David Cavers treasurer. This election continued the pattern of mixing scholarly and practice-oriented interests that had characterized American comparative law since its beginning. Both Eder and Coudert were prestigious New York City attorneys involved in foreign practice, although all the remaining directors were full-time law professors. Coudert was a law professor at Columbia and acting director of its Parker School from 1949 to 1955, when he succeeded Eder as president of the American Association for the Comparative Study of Law.

4. The *American Journal of Comparative Law*

Plans for the *American Journal of Comparative Law* began even before the Association's creation. The first meeting occurred at the Parker School in April 1950, followed a year later by a similar meeting at Harvard. The initial meeting of the *Journal's* board of editors took place at the University of Michigan in November 1951. By the first issue in 1952, two more sponsor members (Cornell and the University of California, Berkeley) had joined—that is, paid their $500 annual dues to—the Association, each of which had the right to select one editor for the board (who could also be its Association director).[33] Although all were full-time law professors, Hessel Yntema, the editor-in-chief, emphasized both the practical and scientific objectives of the *Journal.*[34]

Roscoe Pound wrote the lead article in the *Journal.* Reminiscent of the earlier Comparative Law Bureau's *Bulletin* and its continuation in the *Tulane Law Review* during the 1930s, the *Journal* had sections on documents, foreign law case digests,

[32] American Foreign Law Association (Phanor Eder), Chicago (Max Rheinstein, 1879–1977), Parker School at Columbia (Alexis Coudert), Georgetown (Heinrich Kronstein, 1897–1972), Harvard (David Cavers, 1902–88), Indiana (Jerome Hall), Louisiana State (Joseph Dainow, 1906–78), Miami (Russell Rasco, 1897–1970, dean), Michigan (Hessel Yntema), NYU (Miguel de Capriles, 1906–81), and Yale (Myres McDougal, 1906–98).

[33] In addition to Hessel Yntema, the editor-in-chief, these editors (along with their sponsor members) were Kurt Nadelmann (American Foreign Law Association), Albert Ehrenzweig (1906–74, California), Rheinstein, John Hazard (Parker School), Rudolf Schlesinger (1909–96, Cornell), Kronstein, Arthur von Mehren (Harvard), Hall, Dainow, David Stern (1919–2000, Miami), Walter Derenberg (1903–75, NYU), and McDougal.

[34] '[O]n the one hand, to encourage *general* investigation of legal problems, whether theoretical or empirical, as essential to the advancement of legal science and, on the other, to provide information respecting foreign legal developments, as increasingly requisite in legal practice and for legal reform'. Hessel E. Yntema, 'The American Journal of Comparative Law', (1952) 1 *AJCL* 11.

book reviews, book notices, and foreign law periodicals. The American Foreign Law Association printed its 'Bulletin', which it began in 1950, in the *Journal*. Most of the *Journal*, however, had a distinctly scholarly tone dedicated to articles, notes, and comments.

5. Growth and Maturity: The American Society of Comparative Law

The Association grew slowly through the 1950s and 1960s. In 1963, the International Association of Legal Science named the American Association for the Comparative Study of Law its American member and national committee. The American Association for the Comparative Study of Law had only thirty sponsor members by 1970. However, the *Journal* found its place as the centre for the discussion in the United States of important issues related to comparative law and private international law. Many foreign comparatists also published their work in the *Journal*. When the ABA Section of International and Comparative Law, with Edward Re as chair, established *The International Lawyer* as a quarterly in 1966, it relieved any remaining pressure to achieve a balance between practical and scholarly concerns either in the Association or with the *Journal*. Both more clearly reflected, from the 1970s on, an academic flavour.

The Association rotated its annual meeting among sponsor schools. In the 1980s, the Association began to hold a one-day scholarly programme in addition to its dinner and half day business meeting for the Association and the *Journal*. In 1990, the Association broke from the tradition of maintaining a president who did not hold a full-time position at one of the sponsor member law schools. Edward Re, chief judge of what later became the United States Court of International Trade, was the last such president (1971–90). Phanor Eder (1951–5) and Alexis Coudert (1955–60 and 1965–71) were his predecessors. The only exception was the presidency (1960–5) of Miguel de Capriles, director of the NYU Inter-American Law Institute (1947–57) and dean of its School of Law (1964–7). Also in 1990, the members modified the Association by-laws so that they elected all officers for two-year terms, with four years of maximum service as president or vice president. In 1992, the Society changed its name to the American Society of Comparative Law.

After the collapse of the Soviet Union, there was an accelerated globalization in economic, social, and cultural life in the 1990s. These forces affected law primarily through improvements in information dissemination and via the spread of American-style law firms worldwide. American lawyers are at the front of this expansion in transnational legal services, earning billions of dollars. American law schools, even after the 2001 terrorist attack on the World Trade Centre in New York City, train about 2,000 foreign lawyers annually, most of whom earn the one-year LL M degree. More than a thousand of these foreign graduates then go on to pass the New York state bar examination each year. This globalization of law, or what some call Americanization, occurs in English and cannot help but provide a much larger base on which to build a multifaceted comparative law.

Comparative law in the United States today is more vibrant than ever before. The willingness of American comparatists to subject their discipline to serious critique illustrates its health.[35] Virtually all of the 184 fully accredited law schools offer one or more comparative law courses. A majority of these schools offer summer or semester programmes abroad for their students. In addition, over thirty of these schools offer international and comparative LL M graduate programmes for specialized study in this area and more than forty offer an LL M programme for foreign-trained lawyers to study for a year in the United States. The ABA Section of International Law and Practice, which includes comparative law as well as business transactions and disputes as two of its five divisions, has 13,000 members worldwide.

Finally, the American Society of Comparative Law now has over 100 law school and institute sponsor members (most with multiple representatives). These even include members from Canada, France, Italy, Germany, Singapore, and Switzerland and there are, in addition, over twenty foreign corresponding institutional members. Besides its annual scholarly meeting, the Society is co-sponsoring more academic conferences than ever before, both in the United States and abroad. Its *Journal* has the largest worldwide circulation of any comparative law publication. Moreover, Society members have been active in establishing student-run comparative and international law journals at their home institutions. These journals number more than seventy-five, which provide a written outlet for Americans and others to express their every thought related to foreign and comparative law.

6. Scepticism and Assessment

At the same time as there seem to be many indicators of success, there are sceptics of American comparative law's position in legal education or more generally its influence in American legal life. Measured from the 1930s, there appears little doubt that there has been important progress in the acceptance of foreign and comparative law teachers and journals in United States law schools. American lawyers and judges deal with foreign law issues every day. The globalized law firm is a fact of modern legal practice.

What is the case for scepticism? No law school makes comparative law a core discipline or puts comparatists at the centre of scholarly debate. This is true even of New York University School of Law, which claims to be the country's pre-eminent global law school. In the United States, the centre of most attention at most schools

---

[35] eg Mathias Reimann, 'The Progress and Failure of Comparative Law in the Second Half of the Twentieth Century', (2002) 50 *AJCL* 671.

is constitutional law, its various subdisciplines, and the United States Supreme Court. Faculty hiring decisions and budget allocations reflect this situation, which is simply a reality of American legal history and culture. Another complaint is that domestic American law students are generally ill prepared to take on serious comparative law study, since they lack a rigorous background in history, philosophy, or languages. This has some merit, but may be changing as law faculties are hiring more professors with doctoral degrees outside law and creating more post-JD degree programmes, and as students come to appreciate the demands of global legal practice. US law schools are also willing to hire a few foreign-trained professors, which add to the school's global perspective.

A more pessimistic critique appeared in 1997 and 1998 in two symposium law journal issues on comparative law.[36] Several essays from the Michigan-Hastings conferences decried a stagnating discipline's lack of methodological reflection and theoretical foundation and comparatists' failure to re-examine goals and methods in light of new realities. Since most comparatists believe that the history of American comparative law began with the émigré group in the late 1930s and 1940s, it is easy to conclude that the discipline is really a mostly German import that never really fitted American circumstances and is thus today badly out of date.

Part of this critique, nevertheless, contains the seeds for improving the importance of comparative law in legal academia. As a 'subversive' discipline, it can promote cultural criticism, which allows us better to understand our basic assumptions about law and perhaps to stimulate us to consider change. Critics call for comparative jurisprudence, or efforts to conduct research with scholars from outside law in interdisciplinary projects, or movement away from norm-centred research toward system dynamics.[37] Some of this critique seems to ignore the best work accomplished, particularly in the latter half of the twentieth century, toward these very ends. Of course, more would be desirable, but it is hardly easy, and some of the proposals might simply be impossible to achieve.

The Utah conference drew a mixed group of participants. Some older comparatists pointed out that many of the papers used approaches that were hardly new, but rather solid examples that drew from the toolbox already available for comparative research. Others borrowed heavily from the jargon of critical legal studies, identity politics, literary theory, or feminism to criticize what most comparatists do. From much of that, it would be hard to map a path forward.

Another approach to assess the importance of American comparative law would not line it up against other American legal or allied disciplines, or contrast it with some mythical scholarly universe, but rather use its own methodology to measure its activity relative to the strength of comparative law in foreign countries. Here,

---

[36] Symposium: 'New Approaches to Comparative Law', (1996) *Utah LR* 255–663; Symposium: 'New Directions in Comparative Law', (1998) 46 *AJCL* 597–756 (Michigan, 1996 and Hastings, 1997).

[37] Ugo Mattei and Mathias Reimann, 'Introduction', (1998) 46 *AJCL* 597–606.

I present two examples. First, in this *Handbook* itself, one of the two co-editors holds his academic position in the United States and sixteen authors for forty-three chapters affiliate with American universities. Germany, the next most represented country, has eight authors. Second, consider the most ambitious comparative law project of all time, the *International Encyclopedia of Comparative Law*. As described by its executive secretary and current responsible editor, Ulrich Drobnig, the existing comparative law treatises in 1965 did 'not satisfy the current demand for a compendium containing a comparison of all legal systems on an international scale and covering broad segments of the law'.[38] To call this project ambitious would be an understatement, although it was limited to private civil and commercial law. Originally conceived to cover 17,000 pages and to cost $3 million, the publisher released the first instalment of chapters in 1971. The first (and only) full 'volume', in two books, appeared in 1983. As of 2004, for the anticipated seventeen volumes, United States comparatists were chief editors of five volumes; Germany provided the next greatest number of chief editors, four.

Perhaps surprisingly, with historical perspective, there is a sense in which American comparative law today is less significant in legal academia than it was in the first quarter of the twentieth century. This approach would consider the national leadership of United States law schools, persons with whom all law teachers would be familiar, and ask whether those leaders were active in organized comparative law. In recent decades, the answer in general would be no. Looking at the first quarter of the twentieth century, however, seven of the first twenty-five presidents of the AALS were active in comparative law activities. These were Simeon Baldwin (Yale, 1902, the Comparative Law Bureau's director), George Kirchwey (Columbia, 1907, Bureau manager), Roscoe Pound (1911, Harvard, Bureau manager and original member of the International Academy of Comparative Law), Joseph Beale (1913, Harvard), Harlan Stone (1916–19, Columbia, original member of the International Academy), Eugene Gilmore (1920, Wisconsin), and William Draper Lewis (1924, Pennsylvania, Bureau manager).

VII. CONCLUSION

The first 125 years of United States history saw some exportation of American laws and legal institutions, primarily to the newly independent Latin American nations in the 1820s. These included concepts from the Constitution of 1789, the 1791 Bill of

---

[38] Ulrich Drobnig, 'The International Encyclopedia of Comparative Law: Efforts toward a Worldwide Comparison of Law', (1972) 5 *Cornell International LJ* 113, 113.

Rights, and public law structures such as federalism, a presidential executive, and judicial review of legislative and executive action. American comparatists did not pay much attention to this process of outbound law, but concerned themselves with comparison as a filter for the importation of rules and structures meant to serve an emerging nation in the new world.

By the twentieth century, American comparative law began to form as an organized activity, with its own journal and annual meetings. This process was uneven, but steady. When the Comparative Law Bureau folded into a more comprehensive ABA section, the American Foreign Law Association kept the flame alive. Comparatists dealt with more complex methods and issues, some debated in international meetings. They developed the first American comparative law 'casebooks' to educate students in the discipline.

However, the full flowering of American comparative law bloomed only after World War II, with a healthy push by émigré scholars from Europe. This process accelerated with the economic and cultural dimensions of globalization after 1990, which involve most aspects of law from business to the family as well as the larger issues of legal institution building. Just as the justices of the United States Supreme Court debate the utility and meaning of these forces for the American legal system, other *Handbook* chapters that treat comparative law approaches and subject areas illustrate the rich American contribution to the field during the contemporary era.

BIBLIOGRAPHY

There is no tradition of treatises about comparative law or surveys of the world's legal systems of the type developed in France and Germany (although the most important of these are available in English translation). A partial exception to this is John Henry Merryman, *The Civil Law Tradition: An Introduction to the Legal Systems of Western Europe and Latin America* (2nd edn, 1985).

Instead of treatises, American comparatists have developed comprehensive 'casebooks' to instruct students and some practitioners about the field. As noted in the text, Pound, Wigmore, Kocourek, and Deák developed early exemplars. Rudolf Schlesinger, an original *Journal* editor, ushered in the modern era in 1950 with the path-breaking *Comparative Law: Cases, Text, Materials* (6th edn, 1998), now with several co-authors. Other important casebooks of the post-war period include Mary Ann Glendon, Michael Wallace Gordon, and Christopher Osakwe, *Comparative Legal Traditions: Text, Materials, and Cases on the Civil and Common Law Traditions* (2nd edn, 1994); John Henry Merryman, David S. Clark, and John O. Haley, *The Civil Law Tradition: Europe, Latin America, and East Asia* (successor edn, 1994); and Arthur Taylor von Mehren and James Russell Gordley, *The Civil Law System: An Introduction to the Comparative Study of Law* (2nd edn, 1977).

The number of excellent American monographs treating comparative law, foreign law, and their many dimensions is too large to list.

Roscoe Pound, *The Formative Era of American Law* (1936)

Peter Stein, 'The Attraction of the Civil Law in Post-Revolutionary America', (1966) 52 *Virginia LR* 403–34

James E. Herget, *American Jurisprudence, 1870–1970* (1990)

Marcus Lutter, Ernst C. Stiefel, and Michael H. Hoeflich (eds), *Der Einfluß deutscher Emigranten auf die Rechtsentwicklung in der USA und in Deutschland: Vortäge und Referate des Bonner Symposions im September 1991* (1993) (1991 Bonn Conference)

Mathias Reimann (ed), *The Reception of Continental Ideas in the Common Law World: 1820–1920* (1993)

David Clark, 'The Civil Law Influence on David Dudley Field's Code of Civil Procedure', in Mathias Reimann (ed), *The Reception of Continental Ideas in the Common Law World: 1820–1920* (1993), 63–87

David Clark, 'The Use of Comparative Law by American Courts (I)', (Supp 1994) 42 *AJCL* 23–40; reprinted in Ulrich Drobnig and Sjef van Erp (eds), *The Use of Comparative Law by Courts* (1999), 297–314

David Clark, 'Tracing the Roots of American Legal Education—A Nineteenth Century German Connection', (1987) 51 *RabelsZ* 313–33; reprinted in Steve Sheppard (ed), 1 *The History of Legal Education in the United States: Commentaries and Primary Sources* (1999), 495–508

David S. Clark, 'Nothing New in 2000?: Comparative Law in 1900 and Today', (2001) 75 *Tulane LR* 871–912

Kyle Graham, 'The Refugee Jurist and American Law Schools, 1933–1941', (2002) 50 *AJCL* 777–818

CHAPTER 6

....

DEVELOPMENT OF COMPARATIVE LAW IN CENTRAL AND EASTERN EUROPE

....

ZDENĚK KÜHN

*Prague**

  * I am grateful to Mathias Reimann for his comments and invaluable advice, the Summer Stipend
for Issues of European Integration provided by the Milton and Miriam Handler Foundation, and the
Horace H. Rackham School of Graduate Studies at the University of Michigan for their financial
support. All translations are mine unless otherwise indicated. The responsibility for errors rests solely
with the author.

THE region of Central and Eastern Europe covers a variety of the European nations east of Germany. The dominant nation of the region is Russia. Between Russia and Germany there are, first, a number of small nations composing the region known as Central Europe (Poland, Hungary, the Czech Republic, and Slovakia); second, the nations which formed the western part of the Soviet Union; and, third, the states on the Balkan peninsula.[1] This chapter briefly shows the rich history of comparative law before the instalment of communist regimes, and then discusses in detail comparative law under communism and the role and status of comparative law after the fall of communist rule.

The first part of the chapter demonstrates that we cannot fully understand the role of comparative law in the region without a brief outline of its legal history, tracing back to the time when the region was dominated by empires. When new nations arose in Central and Eastern Europe after World War I, most of them had complex legal systems originating in a plethora of often very different legal cultures. This made comparative law issues the agenda not only within academic research (as was the case in most Western European nations before World War II), but for daily legal business as well.

The instalment of communism unified national legal systems, while often destroying or at least undermining national legal cultures. Research on comparative law was likewise influenced. During the era of Stalin, any form of comparative research was discredited and ultimately prohibited. I will show, however, that in the later decades of communist regimes, some scholars of comparative law did appear and some works even achieved high levels of academic quality.

Section III, which constitutes the core of this chapter, describes the current issues in comparative law in the region of Central and Eastern Europe. I will describe the return of comparative law as a practical discipline, but also the ongoing problems continuing to plague comparative law research. I will argue that the influence of comparative law was considerable not only in the making of new laws, but also in the transplanting of Western constitutional doctrines into the legal environment of new constitutional courts.

---

[1] cf especially Jenö Szücs, 'The Three Historical Regions of Europe', (1983) 29 *Acta Historica Academiae Scientiarum Hungaricae* 131–84; a substantial part was reprinted in Volkmar Gessner, Armin Hoeland, and Csaba Varga, *European Legal Cultures* (1996), 14–48.

I. Comparative Law in Central and Eastern Europe before Communism

The role of comparative law in the region of Central and Eastern Europe has traditionally been defined by practical needs rather than by theoretical interests. Two primary reasons explain this.

Western European nations achieved their national legal unity through codes in the nineteenth century. That is why their 'lawyers concentrated exclusively on their own legislation, and stopped looking over the border'.[2] In contrast, most of the modern nations of Central and Eastern Europe emerged out of the collapse of four empires: the Ottoman, Austro-Hungarian, German, and Russian (or in the 1990s, the Soviet Union). The laws of many of these new states were composed of differing legal systems and cultures. Working in the diverse legal systems of Central and Eastern Europe meant facing challenging comparative issues every day. Proficiency in a number of languages was the rule for scholars in Central Europe between the wars. Central Europe itself had been a blend of many nationalities and languages until the outbreak of World War II. After all, even the Russian Empire prior to 1917 was a vast muddle of different legal systems, ranging from Scandinavian laws in Finland to French codifications in parts of Russian Poland, to Russian customary laws as collected in *Svod zakonov*, to Islamic law in Central Asia.[3]

For instance, Czechoslovakia inherited Austrian law in the western part of its territory and Hungarian law in what is now Slovakia and (since 1945 Ukrainian) Ruthenia. Even German law applied for a few years in the parts of Czech territory acquired from Germany in 1918. Before World War II changed this permanently, the Czechoslovak legal system had been formed by collaborations of Czechs, Czech Germans, Slovaks, Slovak Hungarians, and, after 1917, even a large community of Russian émigrés. Major early decisions of the Czechoslovak Constitutional Court, the second oldest tribunal of its kind in the world, received extensive comment from a comparative standpoint by both domestic scholars and foreign observers.[4]

Similarly, Poland, reborn in 1918, was a rather curious mélange of five distinct legal systems. In the southern part of Poland, formerly the Austrian province of

---

[2] See Konrad Zweigert and Hein Kötz, *An Introduction to Comparative Law* (3rd edn, 1998), at 15.

[3] Anatolii A. Tille, *Sotsialisticheskoye sravnitelnoye pravovedenie* (Socialist Science of Comparative Law), (1975), 50–1. On the history of comparative law in pre-Soviet Russia in English, cf Vladimir G. Grafsky, 'From the History of Comparative Jurisprudence in Russia', in *Problems of the Contemporary World* (*No. 168*). *The Development of Soviet Law and Jurisprudence* (1978), 173–81; Akmal Kholmatovich Saidov, *Comparative Law* (trans W. E. Butler, 2003), 60 ff, 338 ff (describing the history of Russian law).

[4] See the decision of the Czechoslovak Constitutional Court of 7 November 1922 (concerning the power of the legislature to delegate issues to the executive power), (1923) 62 *Právník* 390.

Galicia, Austrian law applied. As Polish political and legal life had been most developed in the Austrian province of Galicia, the most outstanding scholars and lawyers came from this region. They were, however, familiar with German legal systems as well; as a rule, these professionals had also studied in Germany. German law was in force in the formerly Prussian (German) western province of Posen. Russian law could be found in the ex-Russian provinces in the east. Furthermore, in some parts of Polish territory previously belonging to Russia, the Napoleonic Civil Code, taken from early nineteenth-century revolutionary France, applied. This was a hangover from the legal system of the Grand Duchy of Warsaw, which existed briefly during the Napoleonic wars when French legislation was introduced there. To make the legal system of the newly emerged state even more complex, the Hungarian legal system applied in small parts of the country.[5] In subsequent developments, German legal influence prevailed in the area of public law, as did French legal culture in private law.[6] Despite numerous attempts at national legal unification, much of this legal hotch-potch survived until the installation of communist regimes in Central Europe, which unified the legal systems over the course of the 1950s.

The second and more enduring reason for the practical use of comparative law was a self-perception of backwardness and an inferiority complex in many Eastern European domestic legal cultures. To help resolve the fact that it lagged behind its Western counterpart economically, Eastern Europe was supposed to receive Western European legal systems by imitating those systems.[7] By the early eighteenth century, Czar Peter the Great had already invited foreign legal experts, primarily German, to give lectures on law in the Russian Empire. Moreover, until the 1917 October Revolution, Russian legal education was generally based on comparative approaches, as foreign law was considered superior to the backward Russian legal systems.[8]

The legal system most famous for utilizing a comparative approach in making its own laws was that of Hungary, the country that used to proudly call itself a 'nation of lawyers'.[9] In replacing their ancient laws, Hungarian drafters based their work on careful comparisons of German, Austrian and other models. The Hungarian

---

[5] For details, see W. W. Soroka, 'The Law in the Polish Lands during the Partition Period', in Wenceslas J. Wagner (ed), *Polish Law throughout the Ages* (1970), 123 ff.

[6] Polish criminal law was largely modelled after German law, while the new Polish civil law was largely based on French examples. See Zbigniew Gostynski and Alan Garfield, 'Taking the Other Road: Polish Legal Education during the Past Thirty Years', (1993) 7 *Temple International and Comparative LJ* 243 ff, at 250.

[7] cf Kalmán Kulcsár, *Modernization and Law (Theses and Thoughts)* (1987), 81 ff.

[8] Tille (n 3), 45 ff.

[9] Laszló Boroa, Ágnes Gyulavári, and Zoltán Fleck, 'Juristenausbildung und Rechtserziehung in Ungarn von 1945 bis 1990', in Gerd Bender and Ulrich Falk (eds), *Recht im Sozialismus, Analysen zur Normdurchsetzung in Osteuropäischen Nachkriegsgesellschaften (1944/5–1989). Band 2. Justizpolitik* (1999), 337 ff, at 345.

procedural codes so developed in the early twentieth century enjoyed very high regard. Some even considered them the best procedural codes in Europe.[10]

II. Comparative Law during Communism

1. Comparative Law before Stalinism

The 1917 October Revolution declared that it had broken radically with all pre-revolutionary Russian law. In the first phase of 'war communism' during the Russian civil war, the old law was completely abolished and replaced by revolutionary law based on 'class revolutionary consciousness'. The old czarist judicial structure was entirely eradicated and replaced by new informal revolutionary tribunals (people's courts). In fact, it was legal anarchy caused by the lack of a proper judicial structure, civil war, and the absence of established rules.[11] A few years after the civil war ended, new laws and codes were drafted, considerably influenced by the German law of that era.[12]

The first wave of legal scholarship in Soviet Russia after the 1917 October Revolution rested on idealist theses concerning the withering away of law that would soon occur in a new revolutionary state, a transitional society heading in the direction of a stateless and classless communism. Throughout the 1920s, the scholars of the first Soviet decade developed a number of Marxist theories on the interaction between state and law and the inevitable demise of law in the Soviet state. Soviet law was supposed to be 'bourgeois law without bourgeoisie', destined for an early disappearance. Pashukanis, the most prestigious Soviet scholar of the 1920s, professed, 'We have no need for any sort of juridical system of proletarian law'.[13]

---

[10] cf Arpad Erdei, 'Law of Criminal Procedure', in Attila Harmathy (ed), *Introduction to Hungarian Law* (1998), at 202.

[11] Janet Campbell, *An Analysis of Law in the Marxist Tradition. Studies in Political Science* (vol 12, 2003), 77 ff. A classic work on this period is John Hazard's book, *Settling Disputes in Soviet Society. The Formative Years of Legal Institutions* (1960).

[12] Konrad Zweigert and Hein Kötz, *An Introduction to Comparative Law I* (trans T. Weir, 1977), at 309 (noting that the structure and some of the content of the Civil Code of the Russian Soviet Republic of 1922 derived from the pre-revolutionary drafts based on the German Civil Code of 1900, although the Russian Code was much simpler and shorter); Inga S. Markovits, 'Civil Law in East Germany—Its Development and Relation to Soviet Legal History and Ideology', (1968–9) 78 *Yale LJ* 1, 23 ff.

[13] Evgenii B. Pashukanis, 'The Soviet State and the Revolution in Law' (in Russian, 1930), in John N. Hazard (ed), *Soviet Legal Philosophy* (trans Hugh W. Babb, 1951), at 279. For more details in English, see Piers Beirne and Robert Sharlet, *Pashukanis: Selected Writings on Marxism and Law* (1980).

The comparative method was employed rather frequently as the new scholars compared their images of the new socialist legal system with legal systems in Western societies. The function of this early Soviet approach was in principle critical; comparisons served above all to criticize Western European laws, to find peculiar features of new 'proletarian' law, as well as to enhance radically new legal concepts in the Soviet society. For instance, a Soviet textbook of criminal law based fully on the comparative method was published in 1930. Its conclusions were that the Russian Criminal Code of 1922 was very close in its form and substance to Western criminal codes and as such it should have been replaced, as the new proletarian states should not perpetuate flawed concepts of bourgeois criminal law.[14]

2. Comparative Law during Stalinism

With the end of the short-lived Soviet anti-formalist school of the 1920s, serious comparative research disappeared for a long time. When the Soviet Union stabilized and its totalitarian and oppressive features strengthened, the idealist claims about the early end of the state and law became dangerous for the new rulers. Since even doctrinal differences were viewed as high treason by Stalin, he accused the old scholars of sharing the deviations of Trotsky. Consequently, most 1920s scholars soon met their ends on Stalin's gallows.[15]

The new intellectual leader of Soviet legal doctrine, A. Y. Vyshinsky, rejected the thesis that law was supposed to disappear under socialism. It would do so only when the stage of communism was attained, when law would wither away, when the people would have become accustomed to following the basic rules without any need for compulsion. During that transitional phase, law fulfilled the important mission of preserving order and the communist hold on power in the socialist state.[16]

Although it might have seemed acceptable to acknowledge the use of bourgeois law for that purpose, the atmosphere of Stalinism was extremely unreceptive to any sort of comparative legal research. The Stalinist school, which generally prevailed in Central and Eastern Europe after World War II, espoused the view that socialist

[14] See A. I. Estrin, *Nachala sovetskogo ugolovnogo prava (sravnitielno s burzhuaznym)* (Foundations of Soviet Criminal Law (A Comparison with Bourgeois Law)) (1930).

[15] As Hans Kelsen noted, 'If science is considered to be an instrument of politics, then it is a punishable crime to advocate a wrong theory; and, then, a theory is wrong if it is a deviation from the orthodox doctrine, the orthodox doctrine being the one established by the political party in power.' Hans Kelsen, *The Communist Theory of Law* (1955), at 127. For an English summary of the development of Soviet legal thought up to the beginning of the 1950s, see Hazard's introduction in: Hazard (n 13).

[16] See Andrey Y. Vyshinsky, 'The Fundamental Tasks of the Science of Soviet Socialist Law' (an address in 1938), in Hazard (n 13), 303 ff, 330–41 *passim*.

law was substantially different from bourgeois law. Although the form of law might be similar, this similarity, for instance in the textual provision of the code, did not extend to the substance. 'The dictatorship of the proletariat is a state of a new type, and the law created by that state is law of a new type; Soviet democratic law which protects the interests of each and every one of the majority of the people: toilers.'[17] 'Of necessity, Soviet legislation still reflects certain survivals of the old bourgeois legislation without ceasing thereby to be socialist legislation.'[18]

Significantly, the leading Stalinist textbook on the 'theory of state and law' (as legal theory was called in the Soviet bloc) characterized comparative law as one of the methods of 'bourgeois legal theory',[19] or in other words, a method improper for new socialist legal scholars. Although Stalinist law books frequently referred to Western law, these references were nothing other than empty ideological slogans without any real content. Quotations from, and the serious study of, foreign law vanished in the 1940s when the 'struggle against cosmopolitanism' was declared by the Soviet authorities.[20]

After 1945, this xenophobic trend continued in the Central and Eastern European countries that imported Soviet-style communism. Radical discontinuity of the domestic legal heritage and abandonment of the links to Western legal cultures were applauded by many Central European Stalinist lawyers. This hostile attitude of socialist scholars towards comparative legal science did not change until the end of the Stalinist era in the 1950s. The sole exception was Yugoslavia, the one communist country that remained independent from Moscow.[21]

3. Comparative Law from the 1960s through the 1980s

The first new scholarly papers on comparative law in the Soviet bloc appeared in the 1960s. In the Soviet Union, the first indication of a new approach was the article appearing in 1964 in the leading Soviet legal journal, *Soviet State and Law*.[22] Major

---

[17] P. Yudin, 'Socialism and Law' (in Russian in 1937), in Hazard (n 13), 281 ff, at 290–1. See also ibid. 293–6.

[18] Ibid at 295.

[19] Sergei A. Golunskii and Mikhail S. Strogovich, *Teoria gosudarstva i prava* (Theory of State and Law) (1940), at 11.

[20] cf Olimpiad S. Ioffe, *Development of Civil Law Thinking in the USSR. Studies in Comparative Law* (1989), 20 ff.

[21] In 1955 the Institute of Comparative Law was established, with Professor B. Blagojević as its head. Cf also Borislav T. Blagojević (ed), *Introduction aux droits socialistes* (1971).

[22] Samuil L. Zivs, 'O metode sravnitelnogo pravovedenia v nauke o gosudarstve i prave' (On the method of comparative law in the science of state and law), (1964) 3 *Sovietskoie gosudarstvo i pravo* 23–35. This article is described as a breakthrough by Tille (n 3), at 60. Cf also Samuil L. Zivs, *Razvitie formy prava v sovremennykh imperialisticheskikh gosudarstvakh* (Developments of Form of Law in Contemporary Imperialist States) (1960).

Western treatises on comparative law were translated into Russian. René David's *Major Legal Systems in the World Today* had an especially substantial impact on re-emerging Soviet comparative legal scholarship.[23] At the same time, the situation also changed in the Soviet satellites of Central and Eastern Europe. Harsh Stalinist attitudes towards the Continental legal heritage were re-evaluated, at least rhetorically, in most communist countries.

Comparative science flourished to different degrees throughout the communist region. Much depended both on how liberal the regime in a particular state was and on the extent to which its legal academia had been purged. Although the early 1950s were disastrous for intellectual development throughout the Central and Eastern European region, we can point to important differences. Unlike the Czechoslovak legal academia's massive purges in the early 1950s, which was repeated after the Prague Spring in 1968, Polish universities never resorted to such radical measures. In fact, unlike Czechoslovakia, most Polish pre-war professors survived in their chairs throughout the Stalinist era and managed, albeit to a limited degree, to assure some continuity in domestic legal developments.[24]

At the top of socialist comparative scholarship were obviously the countries with the most liberal regimes in the Soviet bloc, Poland and Hungary. In Poland, for example, by the early 1960s the Minister of Justice had already expressed regret for the excesses of Stalinism in Poland:

The mechanical opposition of the law, legislation and judicial practice of the socialist state to the corresponding institutions of the capitalist state has been one of the negative factors exerting an influence on our legal development. The fact that these institutions were the product of a centuries long heritage has been underestimated; in the interests of socialism it would be better to perfect rather than to suppress them.[25]

Polish legal scholarship rested on its strong legal theory, exemplified by a renowned scholar, Jerzy Wróblewski. His works covered a vast area of law and were always based on a strong comparative perspective.[26] Later in the 1970s and

---

[23] The first Russian translation of R. David's *Les grands systèmes de droit contemporain* was published in 1967. See the introduction of Tille (n 3); similarly Saidov (n 3), 3, 6. For the development of Soviet comparative law after the end of Stalinism in English see Saidov (n 3), 84–6.

[24] See John Connelly, 'The Sovietization of Higher Education in the Czech Lands, East Germany, and Poland during the Stalinist Period, 1948–1954', in Michael David-Fox and György Péteri (eds), *Academia in Upheaval, Origins, Transfers, and Transformations of the Communist Academic Regime in Russia and East Central Europe* (2000), 144.

[25] Quoted by René David and John E. C. Brierley, *Major Legal Systems in the World Today. An Introduction to the Comparative Study of Law* (3rd edn, 1985), 200.

[26] See Jerzy Wróblewski, 'Statutory Interpretation in Poland', in Neil MacCormick and Robert S. Summers (eds), *Interpreting Statutes—A Comparative Study* (1991), 258 ff, Jerzy Wróblewski, *The Judicial Application of Law* (1992). The first edition of the latter piece appeared as early as 1959: *Zagadnienia teorii wykladni prawa ludowego* (Problems of the Theory of the Interpretation of the People's Law) (1959). With its knowledge of foreign legal concepts, the book was an outstanding piece of comparative legal scholarship, and contrasted strikingly with most of the socialist writings on law of that era.

1980s, Polish academia developed an influential field of comparative constitutionalism. This was influenced by the fact that Poland was, after Yugoslavia, the second communist state to experiment with constitutional review. The fact that Poland enjoyed one of the oldest constitutional traditions in the world, with a written constitution enacted as early as 1791, might have also played a role in this development.[27]

The Hungarian scholarship of comparative private law re-emerged in the 1960s. Several books on comparative law by Hungarian scholars were published in English, including Gyula Eörsi's influential book on comparative private law,[28] which is generally considered a masterpiece of socialist comparative legal literature.[29] In this book, Eörsi attempts to develop a sophisticated Marxist approach to comparative law. He starts from a traditional perspective of comparative law and limits his approach to the field of civil (or private) law. Though from today's perspective some parts of the book seem to be outdated, especially in light of the fall of the socialist regimes in Central and Eastern Europe, a number of important issues discussed are still relevant. A Western reader may find the critical perspective on legal development in Western Europe and the United States very interesting. With few exceptions, his critical description of the convergences of Western legal cultures avoids empty ideological clichés.

Both Poland and Hungary kept their civilian heritage, which allowed for openness to comparative law. The Polish Civil Code, adopted in 1964, attempted to preserve continuity with the Continental tradition. The only major structural deviation was the exclusion of family law from the field of civil law;[30] however, that was a typical and unavoidable feature of the socialist ideology of that period. Similarly, the Hungarian Civil Code, enacted in 1959, was based on earlier pre-war proposals, and the substantive content of the civilian heritage was preserved. The Hungarian tradition of comparative law remained to a substantial extent undisturbed, with the exception of an extreme, albeit temporary, interruption in the first decade of the communist era. The practical use of comparative law re-emerged in Hungary long before the collapse of communism; a comparative agenda with Western legal systems already played an important role in the 1977 amendment to the Civil Code.[31]

---

[27] Among representatives of the Polish constitutional comparative scholarship that emerged during the 1980s one should name especially Lech Garlicki. See eg Lech Garlicki, *Sądownictwo konstytucyjne w Europie Zachodniej* (Constitutional judiciary in Western Europe) (1987).

[28] Gyula Eörsi, *Comparative Civil (Private) Law. Law Types, Law Groups, the Roads of Legal Development* (1979).

[29] cf also another important book of Hungarian comparative scholarship: Csaba Varga, *Codification as a Socio-historical Phenomenon* (1991), which is the translation of an older work published in Hungarian in the late 1970s.

[30] Aleksander W. Rudziński, 'New Communist Civil Codes of Czechoslovakia and Poland: A General Appraisal', (1965) 41 *Indiana LJ* 33, 47 ff.

[31] Attila Harmathy, 'A Survey of the History of Civil and Commercial Law', in Harmathy (n 10), 19 ff.

In contrast, developments in Czechoslovakia went in a different direction. The end of Stalinism in Czechoslovakia encouraged the local communist movement to annihilate the remnants of bourgeois legal science and to create truly socialist codes.[32] This made it much more difficult to develop comparative legal research. Despite several promising attempts at comparative law writings during the period of political liberalization preceding the 1968 Prague Spring, Czechoslovak purges in the early 1970s deprived legal academia of most of the people capable of pursuing valuable comparative research. The most important Czechoslovak figure of that era, Viktor Knapp, an editor of the *International Encyclopedia of Comparative Law* in the 1970s, did not publish his comparative treatises at home; his major work in the field was published in Czech only after the fall of communism.[33]

Romania presents a special case of the success of comparative law despite an oppressive dictatorship. Romanian comparative legal scholarship was traditionally influential in the Central and Eastern European region. Professor Tudor Popescu of Bucharest, for instance, was one of three principal figures behind the UNIDROIT Principles of International Commercial Contracts.[34] The strength of comparative legal scholarship in Romania might be explained by a traditional self-perception of Romanian elites as part of the Romance family, which also encompasses knowledge of Romance languages, naturally important for comparative studies. Unlike most other socialist countries, Romania did not abolish its pre-communist civil code throughout the four decades of the socialist era. Characteristically, its Civil Code of 1864 closely tracked the French Napoleonic Civil Code.[35]

In their treatises on comparative law, socialist scholars by and large spent much of their energy defending the thesis that socialist legal culture was a legal culture separate from and superior to that of both common law and Continental law.[36] However, the answer to the question of whether or not socialist legal systems formed a genuinely independent legal culture depended on one's point of view. If we had tried to find the answer in the rules and the codes of the socialist nations,

---

[32] So thinks John Hazard, *Communists and their Law. A Search for the Common Core of the Legal Systems of the Marxian Socialist States* (1969), at 313, at 329 ff (examples cited). In more detail see Rudziński, (1965) 41 *Indiana LJ* 47 ff.

[33] Viktor Knapp, *Velké právní systémy (Úvod do srovnávací právní vědy)* (Great Legal Systems. (An Introduction to Comparative Legal Science)) (1996). This work characteristically reflects upon comparative law, including literature and major opinions, two decades before its Czech publication.

[34] Arthur Hartkamp, 'Principles of Contract Law', in Arthur Hartkamp, Martijn Hesselink, Ewoud Hondius, Carla Joustra, and Edgar du Perron (eds), *Towards a European Civil Code* (2nd edn, 1998), 105–20, 107–8.

[35] On Romanian law, see eg Flavius Baias, 'Romanian Civil and Commercial Law', in Stanislaw Frankowski and Paul B. Stephan III (eds), *Legal Reform in Post-Communist Europe. The View from Within* (1995), 211–31; Victor Dan Zlătescu, *Panorama marilor sisteme contemporane de drept* (The Panorama of Contemporary Great Legal Systems) (1994), 67–77. One of the products of the prolific relationship between Romanian and French legal science is eg Yolanda Eminescu and Tudor Popescu, *Les Codes Civils des Pays Socialistes. Étude comparative* (1980).

[36] Most prominently in Central Europe see Eörsi (n 28), 38 ff.

we would have found that the law was still more or less close to its Continental roots. Of course, socialist codes and laws were substantially simplified; some rules were not used, some traditional institutions and principles disappeared, and many strange new principles were added. Many legal paradigms of classical European legal thought were destroyed or disappeared, and some traditional categories and concepts were abolished. Putting aside law's ideological deadwood, the core of the Soviet concept of law and legal process which spread into Central Europe was a set of formalistic doctrines, rules, and institutions resembling classical Continental positivism.[37]

The pedigree of Continental legal thinking might have been discovered, *inter alia*, in the doctrine of sources of law, in many legal institutions, and in the fundamentals of legal reasoning. Characteristically, Hazard noted the frustration experienced by many scholars of comparative law who searched in vain for a method of socialist law distinctive from the Continental legal tradition.[38] Some socialist legal scholars even proudly acknowledged that their theory of legal sources went back to the early nineteenth century. For instance, a Hungarian scholar discussed the allegation that socialist devotion to statutory law was inherited from Continental culture and that socialist methodology was similar to the Continental style:

If we can speak of any similarity in this field, we might say rather that Socialist legal systems have returned—although in different social conditions—to the views on the sources of law professed in Continental states at the outset of Bourgeois legal development.[39]

In contrast, if we go beyond the 'sources of law' and 'law in books' comparisons, we might encounter even more complicated issues. The ideological difference between socialist and Western legal culture might be seen as essential. Socialist law was considered to have fully served the interests of the Communist Party, which was the only recognized authority capable of leading its nation towards the alleged objective of the very existence of socialist society—a classless community of communism.[40] Socialist law in this sense was perhaps closer to the family of religious

---

[37] Hazard (n 11), 478–9 ('What the Soviet draftsmen retained after seven years of evolution [since 1917] to differentiate their revolution born-system from those of other lands lacked novelty, except for those tending to see difference in kind in a difference of degree').

[38] Hazard (n 32), at 521.

[39] Imre Szabó, 'The Socialist Conception of Law', in *International Encyclopedia of Comparative Law, Volume II, The Legal Systems of the World. Their Comparison and Unification. Chapter 1, The Different Conceptions of the Law* (1975), 49, at 73 (in addition emphasizing that 'even in appearance there is only outer similarity, because the social reasons for Socialist solutions are not identical with those reasons which once set legislative activity in opposition to the arbitrary practices of feudalism making it not merely the main, but the exclusive source of law').

[40] According to a standard Western treatise on comparative law—quoting the edition when it still covered the socialist legal family: Zweigert and Kötz (n 12), 294 ('The legal systems which form the socialist legal family have a special character owing to their common foundation on the world view of Marxism-Leninism').

legal systems, as the element of the holy book (the role of classical writings of Marxism-Leninism in legal reasoning), typical of religious legal cultures, might be uncovered in socialist legal culture.[41]

One of the ways to keep in contact with the legal issues that go beyond national legal borders and at the same time to study elements common to a European legal culture is research into and education on Roman law. This is especially true if this education is realized not as education in a dead legal system but in introducing students in an intelligent way to the common principles of European law.[42] It might fairly be said that Roman law persisted as a separate legal discipline during the communist period, which also reflects the fact that many communist rules and institutions had their unquestionable basis in Roman law.[43]

Last but not least, one should not overlook the many lawyers and scholars from the region who emigrated to the West, where they achieved success in comparative legal research. In the twentieth century, there were two main waves of emigration from the region, the first during World War II and the period immediately preceding the war, and the second coinciding with the instalment of communist regimes and during the era of communism. Eric Stein of Czechoslovakia, one of the founders of European legal studies, is a leading representative of the former wave;[44] Vera Bolgar of Hungary, Jaro Mayda of Czechoslovakia, Mirjam Damaška of Croatia, Olympiad S. Ioffe of Russia, and Wojciech Sadurski of Poland represent the latter wave.[45] Both waves deprived the region of many brilliant lawyers and lowered the intellectual power of these nations.

[41] Hazard (n 32), 521 (quoting the opinion of a distinguished scholar of Islamic law). As René David put it, in socialist states 'everything does take place as though the Marxist-Leninist doctrine were a revealed dogma; it does not occur to Soviet jurists to question its merits; for them it is beyond any possible discussion'. David and Brierley (n 25), 179.

[42] Reinhard Zimmerman, 'Roman Law and European Legal Unity', in A. S. Hartkamp et al (eds), Towards a European Civil Code (1994), 65.

[43] On the role of Roman law in the Soviet Union, see Olympiad S. Ioffe, 'Soviet Law and Roman Law', (1982) 62 Boston University LR 701 ff; in Poland, Gostynski and Garfield, (1993) 7 Temple International and Comparative LJ 259. In Czechoslovakia, the widespread notion that a completely new civil law had been established (see the text accompanying n 32) also downgraded the role of Roman law in legal education.

[44] See eg Eric Stein, Thoughts from a Bridge: A Retrospective of Writings on New Europe and American Federalism (2000).

[45] Vera Bolgar assisted Hessel Yntema in founding the American Journal of Comparative Law and was an associate editor of that journal in the 1950s and 1960s: cf 'Vera Bolgar 1913–2003', (2004) 52 AJCL 5. Jaro Mayda was a law professor at the University of Puerto Rico. See Jaro Mayda, 'Quelques Reflexions Critiques sur le Droit Comparé Contemporain', (1970) 22 Revue Internationale de Droit Comparé 7–82; Jaro Mayda, François Gény and Modern Jurisprudence (1978). Mirjam Damaška is a renowned professor of comparative law at Yale University. See eg Mirjam Damaška, The Faces of Justice and State Authority. A Comparative Approach to the Legal Process (1986). Olympiad S. Ioffe, a former dean of Leningrad State University Law Faculty, was expelled from the Soviet Union in the 1970s and helped to start the comparative programme at the University of Connecticut School of Law. Olympiad S. Ioffe and Peter Maggs, Soviet Law in Theory and Practice (1983); Ioffe and Maggs, The Soviet Economic System: A Legal Analysis (1987). Wojciech Sadurski left Poland in the early 1980s for

In conclusion, though socialist comparative scholarship achieved some success, its real impact was limited by the all-pervading official state ideology of communist dictatorships and the extreme difficulty in many Central and Eastern European states of obtaining access to Western literature. This situation forced most legal scholars to choose between two options: to resort to tedious textual and positivistic analysis of the legal texts in order to evade omnipresent ideology, or to join the political mainstream and produce works of socialist comparative law that were scarcely readable and of little value (they had precious little content buried under a mass of political propaganda demonstrating the superiority of socialist law over its capitalist counterpart).[46]

III. COMPARATIVE LAW AFTER THE FALL OF COMMUNISM: FROM COMPARATIVE CIVIL LAW TO COMPARATIVE CONSTITUTIONALISM?

1. The Transformation of Communist Law and the Role of Comparative Law

After the collapse of communism, the countries were challenged by the most unique transformation which probably has ever happened there. While the transformation of political systems occurred in many European countries, the post-communist countries faced 'the radical reorganization of both politics and the economy'.[47]

Australia; he is now head of the legal studies department at the European University Institute, Florence, Italy. Wojciech Sadurski (ed), *Constitutional Justice, East and West: Democratic Legitimacy and Constitutional Courts in Post-communist Europe in a Comparative Perspective* (2002); Sadurski, *Rights before Courts: A Study of Constitutional Courts in Postcommunist States of Central and Eastern Europe* (2005).

[46] cf discussion by Tille whether or not it is possible and desirable to compare socialist and bourgeois legal systems because of the radical material difference between socialist and bourgeois societies. Tille (n 3), 177–85.

[47] András Bozóki, 'Post-communist Transition: Political Tendencies in Hungary', in András Bozóki, András Körösényi, and George Schöpflin (eds), *Post-communist Transition, Emerging Pluralism in Hungary* (1992), 13, at 15. As Bozóki explains, '[a]uthoritarian right-wing dictatorships are *political* dictatorships. They are often more cruel than those of the left, but when they fail, society can more quickly resume its normal functioning'. Ibid at 15.

The collapse of communism in the late 1980s also entailed the collapse of legal wisdom accumulated under that regime, to the extent that it belonged to a different sort of society than that to which post-communist states have aspired since the end of the 1980s. To different degrees in different states, based on their respective levels of independence and the capabilities of domestic legal academia during the communist era, piles of socialist-era law books were discarded and the search for new sources began quite suddenly, virtually overnight. While some works of Polish or Hungarian scholarship were suitable even for the era of the 1990s, this was not the case for most other post-communist states. The process of legal transplantation and the very practical use of comparative law, which I have already discussed as the typical aim of most comparative legal studies in the region of Central and Eastern Europe, emerged again.[48]

In redrafting their civil or criminal legal systems, some post-communist nations were able to utilize their own pre-communist legal heritage.[49] Foreign models were also considered; however, they were often translated word for word, without proper comparative analysis. Comparative research, if done at all, was often done mechanically, without any consideration of the differences between the circumstances prevailing in the national legal system and those of the donor systems.

After the major deficiencies of the communist legal systems were eliminated, especially in those areas in which the systems had most lost contact with their Continental roots, a second wave of changes was ushered in. In anticipation of joining the EU, the Central European nations were required to Europeanize their legal systems, that is, to make their laws consistent with the accumulated body of European law, the *acquis communautaire*.

In this regard, European directives have had a clearly disruptive effect on national legal orders, resulting in the questioning of old values of legal science and the call for novel answers to old problems.[50] The following comment on the problems encountered in Poland, as described by the prominent Polish internationalist, W. Czapliński, is relevant more or less to all post-communist law-makers:

[F]rom the substantive point of view the process of adaptation of Polish law to Community law suffers from certain shortcomings. The sponsors of the relevant legislation, followed by the Council of Ministers and the Sejm [the Polish lower house of the Parliament], seem sometimes to have settled for the simplest way out, limiting their activities to (often

---

[48] Few doubted the necessity of substantial borrowing from Western European, or perhaps to some extent, American, law. For a critical discussion of this issue, see the article by the Slovenian author, A. Perenič, 'Must the Transition Necessarily be an Uncritical Imitation?', in Werner Krawietz, Enrico Pattaro, and Alice Erh-Soon Tay (eds), *Rule of Law. Political and Legal Systems in Transition* (1997) 17 *Rechtstheorie* 123–9.

[49] Gianmaria Ajani, 'By Chance and Prestige: Legal Transplants in Russia and Eastern Europe', (1995) 43 *AJCL* 93, at 95.

[50] In Central and Eastern Europe, this is happening to an even more striking extent than in the old EU Member States. For this process in Western Europe see Martijn Hesselink, *The New European Legal Culture* (2001).

incorrect and careless) translation of directives. Their nomenclature is often translated word for word, thereby introducing concepts which are not known to the Polish legal system. Alternative options are omitted—even when a Directive requires a choice between them.[51]

The mixture of often incompetently drafted post-communist law, immaturity of post-communist legal systems, and judges adhering to textual positivism has deepened the post-communist legal crisis. A more thorough study of comparative law is often seen as a sort of cure for these problems. The fact is, however, that the practical use of foreign models in legislating has rarely been accompanied by the development of solid scholarship in comparative law. Thus far, only a few law schools in the region have modified their curricula to satisfy these new needs.

2. Post-Communist Legal Academia and Comparative Law

One of the most conservative elements of Central and Eastern European legal systems remains legal academia. Despite the fact that foreign law is used in legislating, education in comparative or transnational law at universities is still rare and haphazard, and the processes of globalization and internationalization of law are rarely reflected in law school curricula.[52]

In general, it is possible to say that much of Central and Eastern European legal education still has resilient parochial features, with topics concentrating on national laws without their comparative context, usually disregarding entirely the fact that much of national law consists of foreign transplants implemented in the course of post-communist transition and the EU accession process. The situation is made even worse by insufficient funding of higher education throughout the region as well as by the fact that many academics able to pursue comparative legal studies left for the EU institutions.[53]

The lack of funding also results in low salaries, which forces most academics to divide their energy between academia and legal practice. This further hinders any valuable comparative law scholarship and makes their academic posts merely supplementary. The sole purpose of being in academia is to increase the prestige of practising academics in public and thus attract more clients. The paradox that the

[51] Władysław Czapliński, 'Harmonisation of Laws in the European Community and Approximation of Polish Legislation to Community Law', (2001) 25 *Polish Yearbook of International Law* 45, at 54.

[52] My information on this is taken from the Internet sites of respective law schools, and based on my personal experience as a lecturer in the Czech Republic. In addition, I have received information based on my interviews with academics from Croatia, Poland, Slovakia, Romania, and Russia.

[53] An example among Czech professors is Irena Pelikánová, an expert in comparative business law and an author of *Úvod do srovnávacího práva obchodního* (An Introduction into Comparative Commercial Law) (2000), (appointed to the Court of First Instance of the European Communities in May 2004), and in Poland Jerzy Makarczyk, an expert in international law and comparative human rights (appointed to the Court of Justice in May 2004).

quality of legal research declined in many countries after the collapse of communism can be explained in this way. While before the 1990s there were not many possibilities for skilful lawyers able to do research in foreign languages, the open market for lawyers in the 1990s drastically changed this situation.

My description is general and there are important exceptions to the rule. For instance, the situation at the Warsaw Law School seems to be very different: it was the first law school in the Central and East European region to introduce training in foreign law as part of the regular curriculum. Moreover, in May 2005, the Warsaw Law School offered studies in Polish, American, German, French, Italian, and English law.[54]

The general rule seems to be different, however. For instance, at the two most important Czech law schools, Prague and Brno, a general course in comparative law has not even been offered in the first fifteen years after communism. The Charles University Law School in Prague redressed this problem to a certain extent by special electives in German, French, and English Law taught by foreign lecturers in their respective tongues. The impact of these courses is rather small though, as the language barrier still plays a role and only a tiny number of students attend these lectures.[55] At less prestigious law schools in the region, even this is very problematic due to insufficient resources and lack of interest by foreign academics.

The Central European University (CEU) in Budapest presents a picture very different from mainstream legal academia in the region. An internationally renowned institution of postgraduate education in the social sciences and humanities was built by its Founding Fathers (including the billionaire George Soros) to be a supranational institution that would attract a number of postgraduate students from throughout the region. The department of legal studies includes a number of important scholars of comparative law;[56] its comparative constitutional law programme headed by András Sajó has become a leader of comparative constitutionalism in the region and an important global player in the field of comparative constitutional law.[57]

[54] See <http://www.wpia.uw.edu.pl/en/> (visited 24 April 2005). The Warsaw Law School included chairs of comparative civil law, chair of comparative criminal law, and chair of comparative administrative and economy law in May 2005. It is also true that funding of Polish law schools seems to be better than of those in most other Central and Eastern European nations because funds come from both public and private sources. The introduction of tuition fees also meant higher competition among Polish law schools themselves.

[55] See <http://www.prf.cuni.cz> (visited 30 June 2005). A class on comparative business law was taught at the Charles University Law School by Professor Irena Pelikánová before her appointment to the Court of First Instance in 2004.

[56] For instance Tibor Varady, a chair of the international business law programme and a co-author (with John J. Barceló III and Arthur T. von Mehren) of *International Commercial Arbitration: A Transnational Perspective* (2003).

[57] András Sajó is a prominent Hungarian legal philosopher and a chairman of Comparative Constitutional Law programmes. See eg András Sajó, *Limiting Government. An Introduction to Constitutionalism* (1999), or Michel Rosenfeld, András Sajó, Susanne Baer, and Norman Dorsen (eds),

3. Comparative Constitutional Law

It was in the process of establishing a new constitutional law that indigenous legal roots were most challenged, as many scholars considered them largely obsolete in the field. In contrast with other branches of law, where it appeared feasible to utilize national legal traditions, in constitutional law it was evident that something other than the translation of the constitutional text from elsewhere was needed for the successful emergence of a new culture of constitutionalism. That is why comparative scholarship in the region increasingly directed its attention from comparative civil (private) law to comparative constitutional law.

It is true that many post-communist constitutions have been influenced by their pre-communist legal predecessors. An extreme example is Latvia, which in 1993 reinstated its 1922 constitution to emphasize the illegality of the Soviet occupation in 1940.[58] However, a contemporary Western influence is clearly evident in almost all post-communist constitutions, particularly in their human rights provisions. Most of all, the influence of Western doctrines on constitutional adjudication in some post-communist nations seems to be overwhelming.

It was in the staffing of the new constitutional courts that domestic comparative scholarship was most extensively utilized. The leading figures of the constitutional courts were generally scholars experienced in Western doctrines and not compromised by close relations with the former communist regimes. Poland was able to make use of its own domestic scholarship; many of its scholars (most notably Lech Garlicki) had elaborated on doctrines and written on comparative constitutional law before the collapse of communism.[59] Hungary used scholars of comparative civil (private) law for this purpose; the 'Founding Father' of Hungarian constitutional jurisprudence, László Sólyom (the Court's Chief Justice between 1990 and 1998, elected in 2005 as a president of the Republic of Hungary) was himself a civil lawyer and an expert in comparative civil studies.[60] The leading figure in the Slovenian Constitutional Court in the 1990s was Boštjan M. Zupančič, an expert in comparative criminal law.[61] Lawyers who had emigrated during

---

Comparative Constitutionalism, Cases and Materials. American Casebook Series (2003). Sajó is also an organizer of annual conferences such as 'The Individual vs. the State', which took place in Budapest and attracted prominent scholars of comparative constitutional law (2005 was the twelfth year this conference was held).

[58] See Caroline Taube, *Constitutionalism in Estonia, Latvia and Lithuania: A Study in Comparative Constitutional Law* (2001), 46–55.

[59] The composition of the Polish Constitutional Tribunal and the professional background of its justices, many of them visiting professors at prestigious Western European and American universities, make this court one of the academically strongest constitutional tribunals in Europe and certainly the strongest one in Central and Eastern Europe.

[60] Among the justices appointed in the late 1990s Attila Harmathy, a scholar of comparative civil law, must be mentioned.

[61] Boštjan M. Zupančič (ed), *Ustavno kazensko procesno pravo* (Constitutional Law of Criminal Procedure) (1st edn, 1996, 2nd edn, 1999).

the communist era played an important role in some courts.[62] Considering the true nature and mission of these new courts—to introduce a new vision of constitutionalism, thereby challenging the status quo of legal systems which are extremely resistant to change[63]—there was little choice but to call upon the services of such exceptional figures.

The process by which constitutional courts westernized post-communist constitutional orders presents a chief example of the practical use of comparative law and constitutional philosophy.[64] Faced with numerous gaps and empty fields in their domestic constitutional systems,[65] and in order to avoid the pitfall of 'reinventing the wheel',[66] they made extensive use of comparative constitutional law in the gradual formation of new post-communist constitutional systems. Another reason for the resort to comparative law, however, was that it afforded these new constitutional courts a legitimate explanation for decisions that were not clearly required by the text of their constitutions. In other words, the courts could demonstrate that they 'discovered' rather than 'invented' the law. This was openly acknowledged by the Hungarian Constitutional Court, which remarked per its President L. Sólyom:

For interpreting individual fundamental rights, there is a comprehensive, comparative international case law and theoretical opinions at hand so that there is no need to turn directly to ideological or political arguments. Constitutional interpretation of such methodology is protected from the direct enforcement of ideologies by emphasizing formal

---

[62] In the Czech Republic the most significant example was Vladimír Klokočka, a Czech constitutional scholar who left Czechoslovakia for West Germany after the 1968 Soviet-led invasion; among his most important works is *Ústavní systémy evropských států* (Constitutional Systems of European States) (1996), which challenges the parochial approaches of mainstream Czech constitutional scholarship.

[63] According to Kahn-Freund, the concept of legal transplantation is difficult and depends on the nature of the transplanted rules. The law forms a continuum of legal rules of which 'some can be readily transferred by mechanical insertion (not unlike a carburettor or a wheel transferred from one car to another)' and, on the other end, a rule comparable to a living organism which can be 'transplanted' only like a transplant of kidney, 'with the attendant risk of rejection by the home environment'. Kahn-Freund concludes that '[a]ny given rule or institution may be placed at an appropriate point of this continuum'. Otto Kahn-Freund, 'On Use and Misuse of Comparative Law', (1974) 37 *Modern LR* 1, 2 ff.

[64] Some authors prefer to call this process 'law importation'. Cf Catherine Dupré, *Importing the Law in Post-communist Transitions. The Hungarian Constitutional Court and the Right to Human Dignity* (2003).

[65] 'In want of constitutional precedents, conventions, and customs, in short, of established practice, the field where the political and legal game is played is rather empty. The transition period now is the dramatic high time for Central and Eastern Europe nations to set the style for their future.' Csaba Varga, *Transition to Rule of Law. On the Democratic Transformation in Hungary* (1995), at 75.

[66] As Anne-Marie Slaughter pointed out, foreign legal standards and reasoning were borrowed because post-communist courts needed to fill the gaps in their constitutional systems. See Anne-Marie Slaughter, 'A Global Community of Courts', (2003) 44 *Harvard International LJ* 191, at 197.

guarantees, and the elaboration on the value content of individual rights provides protection against the abuse of positivism.[67]

The German model, a paradigm of constitutional adjudication in Central and Eastern Europe, has dominated post-communist constitutional adjudication, though its pre-eminence is not unchallenged. In several cases the published judicial opinions made explicit the criteria they used for selecting models for inspiration: it was noted that the courts take their examples from 'our civilization circle',[68] from the states with whom the judges share 'the common values and principles' of constitutionalism,[69] or, most concretely, 'the member states of the EU and other developed states of Western Europe'.[70] The former Chief Justice of the Hungarian Constitutional Court, L. Sólyom, once remarked that during his term the Constitutional Court (1990–8) was inspired mainly by Germany, although this 'nearly overwhelming' influence was balanced by the American, Italian, Portuguese, and Spanish constitutional experiences.[71]

To give one clear example of the intentional reception of foreign doctrines into post-communist legal discourse, I might cite the decision of the Czech Constitutional Court to borrow the German concept of indirect horizontal effect of basic rights, thus constitutionalizing civil law. Throughout the 1990s, the Czech Constitutional Court made a systematic effort to transplant major Western European constitutional doctrines into the national legal order, including the doctrine of the 'radiation' of constitutional law throughout the legal order. This doctrine is known and was developed originally in German constitutional law ('Ausstrahlungs-wirkung') and characterizes mainstream German tendencies towards the horizontal effect of basic rights.[72] The Czech Constitutional Court directed ordinary courts that:

---

[67] The case concerning the minimum age for membership in homosexual organizations, decision no. 21/1996 of 17 May 1996, translated in László Sólyom and Georg Brunner, *Constitutional Judiciary in a New Democracy: The Hungarian Constitutional Court* (2000), at 341–2 (emphasis added). Cf Juliane Kokott, 'From Reception and Transplantation to Convergence of Constitutional Models in the Age of Globalization—with Special Reference to the German Basic Law', in Christian Starck (ed), *Constitutionalism, Universalism and Democracy—A Comparative Analysis* (1999), at 78: 'The reception of a concept common in another jurisdiction may lend this concept the appearance of a general principle discovered, and not invented, by the judges'.

[68] Dissenting opinion of Justice Lech Garlicki in the Polish Abortion case, explaining a general approach of the Polish Constitutional Tribunal, see the case K 26/96 of 28 May 1997, *Orzecznictwo Trybunalu Konstytucyjnego* (The collection of decisions of the Constitutional Tribunal), no. 12/1997, 173 ff, at 230 ff. (my translation).

[69] The Czech Constitutional Court's decision III ÚS 31/97, *Sbírka nálezů a usnesení* (The collection of decisions), vol 8, p 149, justifying the use of European law and case law in Czech law.

[70] The Czech Constitutional Court's decision Pl ÚS 5/01 (Milk Quota Case), published as no. 410/2001 Sb (Official gazette), translated on the Court's Internet site <http://www.concourt.cz/>.

[71] László Sólyom, 'Introduction to the Decisions of the Constitutional Court of the Republic of Hungary' in Sólyom and Brunner (n 67), at 5.

[72] In English see Robert Alexy, *A Theory of Constitutional Rights* (trans J. Rivers, 2002), 350 ff.

One of the functions of the Constitution, and especially of the constitutional system of basic rights and freedoms, is its 'radiation' throughout the legal order. The sense of the Constitution rests not only in the ordering of basic rights and freedoms, as well as institutional mechanism and process of making legitimate state decisions, not only in the direct applicability of the Constitution and its status as the immediate source of law, but also in a duty of public authorities to interpret and apply law while considering the protection of basic rights and freedoms.[73]

The use of constitutional comparative law was brought about by the need to create a new constitutional culture in the shortest time possible. Conceived in this way, the reception of foreign models by post-communist parliaments was only the tip of the iceberg; it was not the end of transformative process but rather an activation of much more important processes of deliberate creation of new constitutionalism via adjudication. There are two basic conditions for this development, and they are both present in the region. First, the post-communist political system, similar to the post-World War II situation (though in the opposite direction), 'rejects the past, the essence of which is that the society was subjected to the colonial or exploiting regime, or to both, and accepts the new society to be created as a superior one solving all problems'.[74]

The second condition correlates with the first. In post-communist nations one may find an almost complete rejection of the legal values developed during the existence of the communist legal system. Therefore, the previous legal system and its values lost their significance (at least on the surface) to the present application of law.[75]

In conclusion, at least some post-communist nations developed a working constitutional review, which in the more than fifteen years of its existence has enjoyed considerable public acceptance and prestige.[76] However, it is still too early to judge the extent to which transplants of new constitutionalism into post-communist legal systems might be considered successful. While post-communist courts have quite often used foreign legal sources and ideologies in their attempts to include them within the national legal systems, the new constitutional culture is still far from being internalized by domestic lawyers and most ordinary courts.[77]

[73] The decision of the Czech Constitutional Court published in the Collection of Decisions vol 12, p 97 (III ÚS 139/98). Cf with the German Federal Constitutional Court's decision BVerfGE 7, 198 (206), *Lüth*.

[74] Kulcsár (n 7), at 81.   [75] Ibid 81 ff.

[76] See, generally, Radoslav Procházka, *Mission Accomplished. On Founding Constitutional Adjudication in Central Europe* (2002), analysing the constitutional courts of Hungary, Poland, the Czech Republic, and Slovakia during the first post-communist decade. The book is a doctoral dissertation submitted at Yale Law School, written by a young Slovak scholar of comparative constitutional law. For a critical study of post-communist constitutional courts, cf Wojciech Sadurski, *Rights before Courts: A Study of Constitutional Courts in Postcommunist States of Central and Eastern Europe* (2005).

[77] See Zdeněk Kühn, 'Worlds Apart: Western and Central European Judicial Culture at the Onset of the European Enlargement', (2004) 52 *AJCL* 531.

IV. THE PROSPECTIVE OF COMPARATIVE LAW IN THE REGION OF CENTRAL AND EASTERN EUROPE

The current situation of comparative law in the region of Central and Eastern Europe is characterized by both the extensive use of foreign models in legislating and underdeveloped comparative legal studies in academia. The ongoing European integration increases the importance of comparative legal research and comparative legal studies.[78] That is one reason a significant increase in the role of comparative law can be expected in the eight post-communist nations which joined the EU in May 2004 (Poland, the Czech Republic, Slovakia, Estonia, Latvia, Lithuania, Slovenia, and Hungary). The same can be said for other EU applicants, such as Romania, Bulgaria, and Croatia,[79] which intend to join the EU in the foreseeable future.

Increasing criticism of parochial approaches towards legal education, as well as the necessity to make legal studies more attractive for exchange students in the EU programme Socrates-Erasmus, are likely to put further pressure on the universities in the region to add more foreign language courses as well as to increase the overall comparative and transnational orientation of legal education. If this occurs, the once strong tradition of comparative legal scholarship in the region of Central and Eastern Europe may be revived.

BIBLIOGRAPHY

John N. Hazard (ed), *Soviet Legal Philosophy* (1951)

John N. Hazard, *Communists and their Law. A Search for the Common Core of the Legal Systems of the Marxian Socialist States* (1969)

Imre Szabó, 'The Socialist Conception of Law', in *International Encyclopedia of Comparative Law, Volume II, The Legal Systems of the World. Their Comparison and Unification. Chapter 1, The Different Conceptions of the Law* (1975), 49 ff

[78] cf eg A5–0384/2001 European Parliament Resolution of 15 November 2001 on the approximation of the civil and commercial law of the Member States (COM (2001) 398, C5–0471/2001, 2001/2187(COS)), para 14 (f) (accessible through <http://europa.eu.int/eur-lex/>), urging the Commission to submit an action plan comprising, *inter alia*, 'measures to promote the dissemination of comparative analysis and common legal concepts and solutions in academic training and in the syllabuses of the legal profession, as well as promote dissemination of Community law to the same academic and legal circles'.

[79] In Croatia, the department of European public law of the Zagreb Law School headed by Professor Siniša Rodin seems to be another rising centre of comparative constitutional studies in the region, connected with the research on European constitutional law. See the *Croatian Yearbook of European Law and Policy* (vol 1, 2005), initiated by S. Rodin.

Gyula Eörsi, *Comparative Civil (Private) Law. Law Types, Law Groups, the Roads of Legal Development* (1979)

Kalmán Kulcsár, *Modernization and Law (Theses and Thoughts)* (1987)

Csaba Varga, *Codification as a Socio-historical Phenomenon* (1991)

Csaba Varga, *Transition to Rule of Law. On the Democratic Transformation in Hungary* (1995)

Gianmaria Ajani, 'By Chance and Prestige: Legal Transplants in Russia and Eastern Europe', (1995) 43 *AJCL* 93

Laszló Sólyom and Georg Brunner (eds), *Constitutional Judiciary in a New Democracy: The Hungarian Constitutional Court* (2000)

Radoslav Procházka, *Mission Accomplished. On Founding Constitutional Adjudication in Central Europe* (2002)

Akmal Kholmatovich Saidov, *Comparative Law* (1st Russian edn, 2000, W. E. Butler trans, 2003)

Wojciech Sadurski, *Rights before Courts: A Study of Constitutional Courts in Postcommunist States of Central and Eastern Europe* (2005)

CHAPTER 7

DEVELOPMENT OF COMPARATIVE LAW IN EAST ASIA

ZENTARO KITAGAWA

Kyoto

I. INTRODUCTION

In discussing the development of comparative law in East Asia, this chapter focuses on the area of private law. It also focuses primarily on Japan, since this is my major area of expertise, although it does consider developments in Korea and China as well. The essay also looks beyond the development of the discipline and outlines more generally some challenges and perspectives for comparative law in the near future.

II. The Modern History of Comparative Law in East Asia

1. The Influence of the German Pandectist System

(a) The Formative Era of Modern Civil Law in Japan and East Asia

About half a century ago, Paul Koschaker described Japanese legal theory as 'a pressure gauge which registers changes within the German legal boiler before the Germans themselves are aware of them'.[1] This curious statement indicates the intimate relationship between German legal theory and its Japanese counterpart. Given the geographic distance between these two countries, one might well wonder what the reasons for this close relationship might be. Is it just a peculiarity in the legal history of Japan? As we shall see, pursuing this question will ultimately lead us to new perspectives on comparative law today and tomorrow.

The basic idea of comparative legal studies is to investigate the similarities and differences between legal systems. The situation is somewhat different, however, where we deal with the reception of legal elements from one country into another. Still, the study of such legal transplants, which is discussed in greater detail in Chapter 13 of this *Handbook*, has long been recognized as a special subcategory of comparative law. This is so not only because of the theoretical interest in such reception processes but also for at least two rather practical reasons. First, deciding which elements of foreign law to import requires their comparison with the domestic system in order to determine which foreign law elements could fit in and which would not. Second, even after a reception has taken place, comparison may be necessary between the 'mother law' and the 'child law' in order to comprehend the meaning of the import and to make it work in its new environment.

It is no wonder, then, that the study of comparative law in Japan started with the reception of Western laws in the nineteenth century. The Japanese civil code was enacted in 1896 and entered into force in 1898, that is, two years earlier than the German Civil Code. The subsequent development of Japanese private law can be roughly divided into the three stages: the era of commentaries (Section II.1.b), the era of imported doctrine (Section II.1.c), and the era of comparative law proper (Section II.1.d).[2]

---

[1] Paul Koschaker, *Europa und das Römische Recht* (3rd edn, 1958), 132.

[2] Yoshiyuki Noda, *Introduction to Japanese Law* (trans and ed by A. H. Angelo 1976), 41; Zentaro Kitagawa, 'Minpoten to *Hikakuho* (Two Civil Codes and Comparative Law)', in '100 Years German Civil Code' (1996), 58 *Hikakuho Kenkyu*, 68. See also Zentaro Kitagawa, 'Drei Entwicklungsphasen im japanischen Zivilrecht', in H. Coing, R. Hirano, Z. Kitagawa, J. Murakami, K. Nörr, T. Oppermann, and H. Shiono (eds.), *Japanisierung des Westlichen Rechts* (1990), 125.

(b) The Era of Commentaries

In the second half of the nineteenth century, Japan ended its policy of isolation, which dated from the Edo era, and opened its market to the world. It was in this context that Japan decided to import Western laws. Their reception in Japan was considered one element in a much more comprehensive programme of modernization in accordance with Western models of government, industry, higher education, and military power.

The major step in the area of private law was the making of the civil code of 1898. It was the fruit of approximately thirty years of preparatory work. The drafters of the code considered the laws of over forty foreign countries so that Professor Nobushige Hozumi, a member of the drafting committee, could proudly characterize the new code as 'a product of the comparative law method'.[3]

A civil code was enacted in 1890, primarily based on the French civil law system, but because of ideological and political controversy was abolished without coming into force. The 1898 civil code, however, imported the German Pandectist system into Japan. This system was the result of nineteenth-century German legal science (mainly in private law) which had organized the classical Roman law (mainly contained in the *Digest*, or *Pandects*) into a conceptual and logical system, finally culminating in the German civil code (*BGB*) of 1900. In approach, spirit, and structure, the Japanese civil code was likewise a manifestation of the Pandectist version of private law. Its substantive content, however, was a mixture of various foreign laws, particularly the German and French. In that regard, the Japanese codification was quite eclectic.

The first stage of development of Japanese private law, immediately following the enactment of the civil code, may be called the era of commentaries. The interpretation of the civil code was mainly a matter of commenting on the meaning of its provisions by looking at the various foreign laws which had been used as models. This method of interpretation amounted to a rather literal explanation of each provision, illustrating its various principles and concepts. Since the civil code was still very new, this method was an obvious, and perhaps even inevitable, choice—in the absence of any kind of proper pedigree, modern Japanese private law had to start, so to speak, from scratch. Another reason for the prevalence of this approach was the fact that most commentaries and textbooks on the civil code were written by the scholars who had been involved in its drafting in one way or other.

(c) The Era of Imported Doctrine

While the Japanese civil code drew upon a variety of legal systems, the Japanese private law system as we know it today was built overwhelmingly by looking to German theories, concepts, and rules. As a result, a gap developed between the text

---

[3] Nobushige Hozumi, *Lectures on the New Japanese Civil Code* (1912), 22.

of the code and prevailing legal doctrines. In other words, there arose what is sometimes called the 'dual structure' of Japanese private law.

Let us look at a couple of illustrative examples. With regard to the law of damages available for breach of contract, the code distinguishes between damages arising normally and damages arising through special circumstances (art 416). This distinction is in accord with the rule set forth in the common law case of *Hadley v Baxendale* (9 Exch 341, 1854). Later, however, Japanese scholars came to accept the German doctrine that the scope of liability for damages is determined merely by adequate causation, not by foreseeability. Since then, and until today, the Japanese law of damages has followed the German pattern, not the letter of the code (and not the rule of *Hadley v Baxendale*). Another example is the approach to non-performance of obligations. The civil code envisages a uniform concept of non-performance in a quasi-general clause which applies '[i]f an obligator fails to effect performance in accordance with the tenor and purport of the obligation' (art 415). Private law doctrine, however, follows the German model of distinguishing essentially three categories: delayed performance (*riko chitai*), impossibility of performance (*riko funo*), and improper performance (*fukanzen riko*) or positive violation of obligations (*sekkyokuteki saiken shingai*). A final illustration of the duality between code and doctrine is the seller's liability for latent defects (*kashi tampo sekinin*). The code (art 570) treats both defects in rights (*kenri no kashi*) and defects in substance (*mono no kashi*) identically and does not provide special remedies for such defects. Doctrine developed during the era of imported doctrine, however, adopted the German distinction between these two types of defects; it saw the delivery of things defective in substance not as outright non-performance but as a breach of warranty resulting in special forms of liability. Here again, we see a faithful adoption of German theory in deviation from the code's actual provisions. There are many other examples.

The importation of German doctrine and theory began right after the enactment of the civil code and lasted mainly until the end of World War I. Thus, in this second stage of its development, Japanese private law was shaped along the lines of the German system. I have coined this process 'the reception of German civil law theory'.[4] And, indeed, it was in this period that the framework of present Japanese private law was formed and the now familiar style of textbook analysis and explanation of the system and its basic concepts was developed. This was the era foremost in Paul Koschaker's mind.

---

[4] Zentaro Kitagawa, *Nihon Hogaku no Rekishi to Riron—Minpogaku o Chushin to shite* (The History and Theory behind Japanese Legal Studies: A Focus on the Study of Civil Law) (1968); *idem*, 'Rezeption und Fortbildung des europäischen schen Zivilrechts in Japan', (1970), 45 *Arbeiten zur Rechtsvergleichung* 67. See also *idem*, 'Theory Reception: One Aspect of the Development of Japanese Civil Law Science, (1970) 4 *Law in Japan* 10; see also Claus-Wilhelm Canaris, 'Theorienrezeption und Theorienstruktur', in *Wege zum Japanischen Recht, Festschrift für Z. Kitagawa* (1992), 59.

The adoption of German private law doctrine was motivated by a variety of factors. Japan had essentially chosen the German Empire, then the emerging power in Europe, as its primary model for building a modern Japan. The comprehensive set of reforms initiated during the Meiji coup was pursued under the slogan *ukoku kyohei* (enrich the country and strengthen the military) and affected all areas of public life[5] from the system of administration to the economy, and from public education to the military. Legal modernization was but one, albeit very important, part of the whole and, as in other contexts, Germany was considered to provide the ultimate guidance.

(d) The Comparative Law Era

The third stage of the development of Japanese private law, the comparative law era, began after the end of World War I. The 1920s, in particular, witnessed two trends that ran counter to the reception of German legal theory. First, as a result of contacts with the United States legal system, the case method began to make inroads into Japanese legal reasoning. Japanese court decisions were increasingly analysed with regard to how legal rules applied to a concrete set of facts. This tradition has continued all the way to the present. Second, there was a growing interest in the sociology of law. Here, the contribution of Eugen Ehrlich was essential.[6] Thus, Japanese jurists were no longer content to consider merely the law on the books but were beginning to pay attention to law in action. In the wake of these trends, Japanese scholars increasingly looked at their own legal practice. Thus, while the influence of German theory remained strong at least until the end of World War II, Japanese private law gradually emancipated itself from the German model and began to develop a system of its own.

Yet, it was really only after World War II that Japan entered what I call the comparative law era. At that time, Japanese scholars began to react against the reception of almost exclusively German theory and to pay increasing attention to French private law—an entirely appropriate corrective move in light of the eclectic (mainly German-French) origins of the civil code. Moreover, US-American influence was gradually beginning to make itself felt and to create an additional layer of reception on top of the German and French ingredients. United States influence was boosted, of course, when post-war legal reforms took place under the guidance of the American occupation regime, up to and beyond the American-influenced new Constitution of Japan of 3 May 1947. All these developments significantly weakened, and in some instances actually neutralized, the German influence. Still,

[5] For the modernization of Japan in general, see George Bailey Sansom, *The Western World and Japan* (1951); William Gerald Beasley, *The Modern History of Japan* (1963); William Gerald Beasley, *The Meiji Restoration* (1972); Edwin Oldfather Reischauer, *Japan. The Story of a Nation* (3rd edn, 1981).

[6] Eugen Ehrlich, *Grundlegung der Soziologie des Rechts* (1912). At that time, leading professors on Japanese civil law were eager to study the new field of sociology of law. See Kitagawa, 'Rezeption und Fortbildung' (n 4), 143 and n 8 (with further references).

the structure of the civil code and the grand outlines of the private law system have largely remained intact.[7]

While German theories had been received more or less uncritically in the first two or three decades of the twentieth century, the foreign doctrines and ideas imported after World War II were not necessarily incorporated in their pure and original form. Instead, they were adopted in Japan only after they had been examined from a comparative point of view and after they had been adapted as necessary to make them fit into the domestic system.

2. Lessons for Comparative Law

(a) The German Pandectist System in East Asia and its Significance for Comparative Law

In the history of comparative law, and more specifically in the history of legal transplants, Japan played a pivotal role important for the reception of the German Pandectist system into East Asia more generally. In particular, Japan's rise and role as a new power in twentieth-century East Asia led to the further transmission of German legal theory to China and Korea.

Like Japan more than a century ago, developing countries have often emulated Western models in modernizing their legal systems. It is generally agreed that in the case of Japan, the reception of Western law was a success—foreign law was usually assimilated to, and integrated into, the Japanese legal system. Moreover, in Japan, the reception of German legal theory, especially of the German tendency to systematize and integrate new elements into the private law system, greatly facilitated the assimilation of a complex variety of foreign legal elements, first into the civil code, then into the private law system more generally: it catalysed a process of organic integration of heterogeneous foreign legal elements. This assimilation, based on the reception of the German systematic approach, was accomplished so superbly that we can speak of an 'assimilation through systematization'.[8]

It is no wonder, then, that the Japanese experience itself quickly became influential in other areas of East Asia. After the first Sino-Japanese War (1894–5) and the Russian-Japanese War (1904–5), Japan became the dominant military and economic force in the region. Later, the war with China established Japan's strong interest in Formosa (now Taiwan), which eventually came under Japanese

---

[7] For a general survey, see Kenzo Takayanagi, 'The Development of Japanese Law 1868–1961', in Arthur von Mehren (ed), *Law in Japan* (1963), 5.

[8] Franz Wieacker, *Privatrechtsgeschichte der Neuzeit* (1952), 73, 128.

jurisdiction, and in Korea, which was occupied and formally annexed by Japan from 1910 to 1945.

In China, the civil code enacted in 1929 was influenced by the Japanese private law theory of the time which was itself the product of the reception of German ideas and doctrines. This code continued to apply in Taiwan after the end of World War II. After Korea became independent from Japan again, it enacted a civil code in 1958. Recent research has shown that this code was deeply indebted to the codification in the Manchurian Empire (1937), which in turn was nothing but a product of Japanese legal doctrine and thus, ultimately, of German private law theory. As a result, the civil code of Korea is closer to the German Pandectist system than the civil code of Japan.[9]

In this manner, the Japanese influence on the modernization of private law in East Asia in the first half of the twentieth century transmitted German law and legal theory to the leading countries in the region. Thus, Japanese law created a broad and unique base for the German Pandectist style, as well as much substantive German private law thousands of miles away from Germany itself.

(b) The Search for Japanese Legal Identity

As we have seen, the modern Japanese system of private law is the product of numerous foreign ingredients: the 1898 civil code built on French and German law; the system of private law that drew heavily on German doctrine; after World War II, more French influence combined with US-American transplants, and so on. All this leads us to the question of the ultimate identity of Japanese law. What is the heart and soul of Japanese private law? How should it be classified for comparative law purposes? Is it part of Western law, perhaps even of the civil law tradition, part of Asian law, or yet something else?

Leading comparatists have answered these questions in different ways. René David saw Japanese law as a legal system of the Far East and in the same group as Chinese law. In contrast, Léontin Jean Constantinesco treated Japanese law as part of the Western legal system, and John Merryman, David Clark, and John Haley consider it part of the 'Civil Law Tradition'. Konrad Zweigert and Hein Kötz take an intermediate position and see Japanese law transforming from an Asian to a Western legal system.[10] According to all these views, however, the identity of Japanese law is

---

[9] For China, see Karl Bünger, 'Die Rezeption des europäischen Rechts in China', *Deutsche Landesreferate zum III. Internationalen Kongress für Rechtsvergleichung* (1950), 178; for Korea, see Jeong Jong Hyu, *Kankoku Minpoten no Hikakuho teki Kenkyu* (A Comparative Study of the Korean Civil Code) (1989).

[10] René David and Günther Grasmann, *Einführung in die großen Rechtssysteme der Gegenwart* (1966), 559; Léontin-Jean Constantinesco, 'Über den Stil der Stiltheorie in der Rechtsvergleichung', (1979) 78 *Zeitschrift für vergleichende Rechtswissenschaft* 170 f (mainly on the continental European legal family); John H. Merryman, David Clark, and John Haley, *The Civil Law Tradition: Europe, Latin America, and East Asia* (1994); Konrad Zweigert and Hein Kötz, *Einführung in die Rechtsvergleichung auf dem Gebiete des Privatrechts*, vol I (1971), 71 (finding Japan's membership of the Far Eastern legal family increasingly doubtful).

apparently to be judged by Western standards. Japanese comparatists recognize, of course, that their system successfully received and assimilated Western law. Yet, they are reluctant to consider Japanese law as a part of the Western tradition and thus have considerable reservations *vis-à-vis* the views summarized above.[11]

While this chapter does not directly deal with the problem of classifying Japan among the world's legal systems, it does address the issue of the identity of Japanese law. To be sure, this identity problem is not unique to Japanese law; it is a universal question for all non-Western legal systems. Finding an answer requires comparing two kinds of Western law—that in the country of origin and that in the receiving country. Thus, we need to look at the question from a broader perspective, employing a new kind of comparative law.

III. COMPARATIVE LAW THEORY IN AND FROM EAST ASIA

1. Introduction

It is generally accepted today that we must not compare legal rules, concepts, or institutions in the abstract but rather on the basis of the function they fulfil. This puts the emphasis on comparison of law in practice and, when we look at how courts apply a norm, we want to understand primarily the purpose for which they employ it.

This 'functional method', which is discussed in greater detail in Chapter 10 of the present *Handbook*, raises the question of how to deal with traditional, especially non-Western and semi- or unofficial, norms. On the one hand, an approach to comparative law based on the Western legal tradition would tend to regard such norms as extra-legal or even simple matters of fact. On the other hand, a functional approach, looking at what problem a rule helps to solve, must not disregard traditional norms lest it completely misunderstand non-Western legal traditions. After all, even where traditional legal systems received Western laws, perhaps even codifying them in Western form, indigenous, non-Western norms usually continue to function in practice. Thus, comparison according to the functional method must extend to these traditional norms which vary from country to country.

---

[11] This reservation can be limited to the cultural infrastructure of law in Japan, which is different from the Western tradition. See eg K. Igarashi, *Gendai Hikaku Hogaku no Shoso* (Various Aspects of Modern Comparative Law Theory) (2002), 245. This view can be traced back to Nobushige Hozumi (n 3). See eg Hitoshi Aoki, 'Nobushige Hozumi: A Skillful Transplanter of Western Legal Thought into Japanese Soil', in Annelise Riles (ed), *Rethinking the Masters of Comparative Law* (2001), 129.

Thus, when comparative law looks at systems like Japan, it must take their pluralism into account and look at them as combining Western and traditional elements. It must recognize that the two elements supplement each other and that traditional norms can, indeed, sometimes even override the more official, Western, side of the law. Herein lies, at least in my view, a major challenge for comparative law today and tomorrow.

2. Functionalism

(a) The Functionalist Approach in Comparative Law

At the Paris Congress of 1900, the French comparatist Raymond Salleiles described the subject of comparative law as the discovery of concepts and principles common to all civilized legal systems. This original, formalist and universalist conception of the discipline was eventually replaced by the functionalist approach first introduced by Ernst Rabel in the 1920s. According to this approach, the starting-point of comparative analysis is not the rules themselves, but the concrete social problems which the rules then help to resolve. After World War II, this functionalist approach migrated from Europe to the United States, and has become the prevailing theory of comparative studies in the second half of the twentieth century.[12]

Comparative law in Japan developed its own version of the functional approach by emphasizing that the comparison should be extended to social, economic, and cultural factors. In other words, functional analysis should consider the entire legal milieu. Of course, it is well-nigh impossible in practice to study every issue in such an all-encompassing fashion, and it was widely recognized that the *legal* function of a rule is the least useful subject of comparison.

Generally speaking, comparison should focus on three objects: factual elements, logical elements, and normative elements. Let us look at them in turn.

As to the first, a functional comparison of law is meaningless if the factual situations in question are not identical, at least in their relevant respects. As to the logical elements, one must take into account that legal concepts, institutions, and constructions are shaped by the history of each country so that they acquire distinctive characteristics; thus, identical constructions may have different legal significance so that their functions are not necessarily identical. Therefore, seeking

---

[12] Raymond Salleilles, 'Conception et objet de la science juridique du droit comparé', in *Procés verbaux et documents du Congrés internationale du droit comparé 1900*, vol I (1905), 167; Ernst Rabel, *Aufgabe und Notwendigkeit der Rechtsvergleichung* (1925), 4; Konrad Zweigert and Hein Kötz, *Introduction to Comparative Law* (trans Tony Weir, 3rd edn, 1998), 32–47; Max Rheinstein, *Einführung in die Rechtsvergleichung* (2nd edn, 1987), 33. See also Anne Peters and Heiner Schwenke, 'Comparative Law beyond Post-Modernism', (2000) 49 *ICLQ* 806 (with further references).

similarities or differences between legal constructions is merely preparatory work for functional comparison and it does not itself lead to functional analysis. Finally, as far as normative elements are concerned, there are certain legal principles which constitute the basis for evaluation; we may call them 'law formation principles'. When we have identical facts and the law formation principles applicable to them are identical as well, then similar legal constructions can also be considered functionally equivalent. Thus, the equivalence of these law formation principles is the fundamental subject of comparison.[13]

(b) Functionalism and the German Pandectist System in East Asia

As a result of the reception of German theory, Japanese private law shares many legal constructions with its German equivalent. Thus, Japanese and German private law employ common legal constructions to handle identical legal facts. On the other hand, since the basic structure of Japanese private law is so different from that of US-American law, a comparison between these two regimes makes it much harder to coordinate legal facts and legal constructions. Thus, we can expect to find more exact functional equivalence between Japanese and German private law than between Japanese and US-American law. We can see here how the unique connection between the German and the Japanese legal systems (which were originally very different from each other) is valuable material for exploring the problem of functional equivalence in comparative law.

The influence of the German Pandectist system in East Asia as the result of the Japanese reception of German theory is, thus, of special importance for comparative law. But a functional approach to this unique context may also find situations in which virtually identical private law doctrines play different roles in the German and in the East Asian contexts.

3. Law in Practice

(a) Traditional Laws

As we have seen, developing countries in East Asia, as in many other parts of the world, have transplanted Western models in order to modernize their legal systems. This phenomenon raises the issue of what is the law in practice in such countries. In particular, it suggests that the indigenous, traditional laws must be included in a functional analysis.

This makes it particularly important that legal studies, including those of a comparative nature, focus increasingly on traditional, community-based norms,

---

[13] Kitagawa, 'Rezeption und Fortbildung' (n 4), 105; *idem*, 'Theory Reception' (n 4), 10.

such as village law. For example, village law in Vietnam consists of written rules formulated in each traditional village and based on the customary law of the country. In Indonesia, however, it has been pointed out, fundamental village law principles, concerning the family, cooperative economic and social equality, and community responsibility, are raised to the constitutional level, while the country's natural resources are placed at the disposal of the state apparatus without reference to indigenous ownership rules or the access of society to commonly held goods. Another interesting example is Uzbekistan where traditional Islamic law was discussed in the process of reforming the 1997 civil code; while Uzbekistan is not an East Asian country, we can recognize the same problem here, that is, what law really governs in practice. Traditional village law is basically a form of social control which is more or less systematically enforced by authority structures at the village or community level. This control is exercised in part through customary status and systems of meaning, in part through power hierarchies. It has two major dimensions. First, it is based on customary law. Second, it represents a world consisting of rules and regulations in quasi-legal form, governing groups which operate largely outside the official systems of courts and law but are still embedded in various ways in the state and its legal system.[14]

A functional approach to comparative law must extend to these systems if it truly wants to understand which rules solve which problems in practice.

(b) Pluralistic Legal Models

In the post-war world of the United Nations, Western models of governance and law are no longer the universal standard. Today, we increasingly emphasize a deeper understanding of the non-Western perspective on politics, economics, culture, and so on. As a result, the emerging Asian, Central and South American, Arabic, and African legal systems are receiving more attention. Their non-Western models are based on legal pluralism. Recognizing such pluralism means recognizing

---

[14] See generally, Antony Allott and Gordon R.Woodman (eds), *People's Law and State Law* (1985); Trend Vedeld, 'State Law versus Village Law: Law as Exclusion Principle under Customary Tenure Regimes', in Erling Berge and Nils Stenseth (eds), *Law and the Management of Renewable Resources* (1998). For Indonesia, see Mason C. Hoadley, *Why You Can't Go Home. The Legacy of Law and Indonesian Public Administration* (2002); The World Bank, *Village Justice in Indonesia. Case Studies on Access to Justice, Village Democracy and Governance* (2004), Working Paper Report No. 31616. For Vietnam, see Takehiro Oya, 'Village Law and its Reorganization in Vietnam' (in Japanese), in *Ajia hoseibi shien kenkyukai Houkokushu* (2003), 13–20; Symposium on 'Village Law and Law Reforms' (Hanoi, 27–8 December 2002), CALE News (Centre for Asian Legal Exchange, Nagoya University), no. 9 (25 March 2003), 1–9 (in Japanese); 'International Symposium on the Village Law (*go-yaku*)', in *Ajia hoseibi shien kenkyukai Houkokushu* (2003) (in Japanese), 139 (briefly introducing village law in China, Korea, and Vietnam). For Uzbekistan, see T. Ito, 'Traditional Law and Legal Aid in Uzbekistan (in Japanese)', in *Ajia hoseibi shien kenkyukai Houkokushu* (2003), 21–31, and the Symposium on 'Traditional Law in Uzbekistan and Japan' (Tashkent, 11–13 September 2002), CALE News no. 8 (12 December 2002), 1–8 (in Japanese); see also CALE Update, vol 1, no. 4 (2002), 1–2 (in English).

that non-Western legal systems do not become Western simply by having contact with Western law, even if that contact is profound and lasting. Continuing traditional fundamentals will often preclude classifying a legal system as Western.

These fundamentals are inseparably interrelated with traditional norms and, as mentioned before, they must not be treated as phenomena outside the law. Where traditional norms, village laws, or community customs operate as law in practice, they constitute an important element in a pluralistic legal system.[15] We will revisit this subject in the context of discussing current trends in international legal assistance (below Section IV.2).

(c) A Case Study in Pluralism: Contracts in Japan

Soon after the end of World War II, Japanese legal academics began to emphasize the uniqueness of Japanese legal thinking. In particular, they claimed to find a pre-modern attitude toward contracts among the Japanese. They critically compared the careful and detailed drafting of contracts as well as the strict insistence on contract rights prevailing in the United States with the Japanese preference for informality and simplicity in contract drafting and the tendency to resolve disputes through compromise. These scholars contended that the unique Japanese attitude toward contracts demonstrated the continuing importance of traditional norms. Theories of this nature have exercised considerable influence not only on Japan's own post-war ideology but also on the way in which Japanese law was perceived abroad.

These views eventually met with criticism from both insiders and outsiders. Perhaps the main thrust of this critique was that the differences between Japan and the United States in regard to contract drafting and enforcement were not the result of divergences in general legal consciousness. Japanese and American businessmen both observe contracts, and there are no signs that lawyers in the two countries have fundamentally different views of the law. This critique also pointed out (correctly) that the traditional view was distorted because it looked at different groups on the respective sides: it really compared the attitudes of Japanese businesspeople with those of American lawyers. Empirical research indicates that American businesspeople also hesitated to resort to legal rules that contradicted their common sense, so that the differences between American and Japanese expectations regarding contracts are not nearly as great as was once believed.

---

[15] See Zentaro Kitagawa, 'A Reflection on Three Law Models', in *Festschrift für Manfred Rehbinder* (2002), 559; *idem*, '*Kinmirai no Ho Modern* (Law Models of the Near Future)' (1999) (its Chinese translation by H. Xia and W. Xiaoyan in Journal of Comparative Law, CUPL, 2006, n 61, p 130); *idem*, 'Law Models of the Near Future for a New Dimension of Law', in *Festschrift für Knut Wolfgang Nörr* (2003), 445. The idea of pluralistic legal models in this paper is related to the theory of legal pluralism, which has been developed in sociological, cultural, and anthropological studies. Considering these contexts is useful for understanding the interface between law in practice and traditional norms; see Masatoshi Chiba, *Legal Pluralism: Toward a General Theory through Japanese Legal Culture* (1989).

Today, the traditional view is no longer prevalent in Japan but similar opinions are still often found abroad. When Japan, with the growth of its economy and the development of its technology, came to occupy an established position in international society in the last quarter of the twentieth century, it also became a target of revisionist critiques from both Europe and the United States. Many foreign pundits pointed to an alleged uniqueness of Japanese society. And even though Japan had successfully incorporated Western legal models, many Western observers continued to focus mainly on the differences between the Japanese legal system and their own.[16]

It is indeed an essential question for comparative law how important the non-Western elements in the Japanese legal system are in practice. To the extent that real problems are actually being solved according to traditional norms, comparative studies must include these norms as well. Japanese law consists of both Western transplants and non-Western elements. The same is more or less true in many non-Western countries in the world.

4. Functionalism Modified

(a) Post-modernist Critiques

Where non-Western countries have imported Western law, indigenous and received elements interrelated in many and complex ways, creating a pluralist legal order. This pluralism presents a challenge to the orthodox functional approach because, as mentioned, it cannot limit its focus to the more familiar, that is, the imported Western elements.

Here, the post-modernist critique of the functionalist approach deserves attention. This critique is primarily directed against functionalism's express or implied universalism. Functionalism is based on the assumption that basic legal problems and their solutions are more or less the same everywhere and that there are a limited number of (standardized) solutions. According to its critics, functionalism imposes a Western view of problems and solutions on the whole world. It thus amounts to a justification of the Western model of law. There is much truth in this critique. The functional approach can easily lead to universalist assumptions and biases in favour of Western perspectives and evaluations, although its post-modernist critics pay less attention to non-Western, pluralistic models than is desirable.

Some post-modernist critics also contend that a true understanding of a foreign legal culture (ie other than the observer's own) is essentially impossible. Since the

---

[16] See Whitmore Gray, 'The Use and Non-use of Contract Law in Japan: A Preliminary Study', 17 *Law in Japan* (1984) 103, and Zentaro Kitagawa, 'Use and Non-Use of Contracts in Japanese Business Relations: A Comparative Analysis', in Harald Baum (ed), *Japan: Economic Success and Legal System* (1995), 145.

intellectual processes of comparison and evaluation are inescapably subjective, personal, and contestable, the functionalist claim to objectivity and neutrality is deemed untenable.[17] The validity of this criticism is questionable, however. Comparatists supporting a functional approach do not necessarily have to seek scientific objectivity or complete neutrality. They may well content themselves with an understanding of what norms—be they Western or traditional—do in terms of solving problems actually observed in a society.

(b) The Interface between Western and Pluralistic Models

We thus need to reconsider the functionalist approach in light of the relationship between purely Western and pluralistic legal systems. This relationship is of fundamental importance in the modern world because it results in a tension between competing trends. On the one hand, with the ongoing globalization of the economy, Western legal models, in particular the US-American version,[18] increasingly claim a leadership role *vis-à-vis* more traditional and pluralistic legal systems. On the other hand, these traditional and pluralistic systems are frequently consolidating themselves and take on greater global significance. Comparative law must therefore explore the relationship between the two sides, both on the theoretical level and in its practical ramifications.

This exploration of the interface between Western and pluralistic legal systems is an enormously promising field for comparative law today. It is important, however, not to generalize too broadly in this regard. The extent to which Western imports prevail, how they coexist with traditional elements, and where they may actually be obliterated by indigenous structures, varies greatly. It is also important not to conceive of traditional norms as a negation of, or as a substitute for, Western legal elements but rather to understand the interplay between both sides.

5. Functionalism in Law in Practice

(a) Japanese Contracts as an Example

Modern Japanese law provides an example of a pluralistic legal model since it operates within an imported Western framework while also resorting to more traditional norms and methods. Looking at this combination of the received and

---

[17] For a summary and critique of post-modernist theories, see Peters and Schwenke (n 12), at 811, and J. H. M. (Sjef) van Erp, 'European Private Law: Postmodern Dilemmas and Choices. Towards a Method of Adequate Comparative Legal Analysis', (1999) 3.1 *Electronic Journal of Comparative Law* <http://www.ejcl.org/31/art31–1.html>, item 4 (comparative law from the perspective of a post-modern ideal).

[18] cf Martin Shapiro, 'The Globalization of Law', (1993) 1 *Indiana Journal of Global Legal Studies* 37–64 (United States models as universal).

the indigenous, we can acquire a better understanding of the identity of modern Japanese law, previously discussed in the context of its historical development (above Section II). Japanese contracts provide an illustration of the interplay between the various elements involved in conflict resolution.

It has often been pointed out that Japanese contracts tend to be much shorter and simpler than their US-American counterparts. But that in and of itself tells us little about how well one version or another works. Even a long, detailed, and perfectly drafted agreement may not guarantee smooth solutions to all problems, and even a short and simple document may function well for the parties involved. Thus, in order to understand the impact of drafting styles, we have to know how contracts actually function in their respective environments. For example, we need to ask, perhaps right at the outset, whether particular problems are solved by reference to the terms of the contract or rather by resorting to customs of trade, good faith principles, or *ex post* additional agreements between the parties. If these avenues lead to acceptable solutions, we can say that the contract is actually functioning. On the other hand, if issues between the parties are being resolved by extra-legal standards—such as political considerations, administrative inter-ference, or economic necessities—one could conclude that the contract is not functioning properly.[19]

Yet matters are hardly that simple. Instances in which contract problems are resolved in the business world according to extra-legal considerations present complex problems. To be sure, strictly from the perspective of contract law in a narrow sense, resort to such standards may be said to indicate a failure of the agreement. There is, however, another way of looking at the matter. If the parties actually agree (albeit silently and implicitly) or simply presuppose that certain problems will be resolved, at least *inter alia*, by reference to extra-legal consider-ations, it would be wrong to say that the contract is not functioning as intended. This is often the situation in pluralistic legal orders where hard, Western-style, rules coexist and interact with traditional norms and cultural habits in the back-ground. In a similar vein, even if a contract were to contain unconscionable (though not outright illegal) terms, it could still function if the parties perform their obligations without disputing them in court, as is frequently the case in practice.

As long as the respective extra-legal standards do not violate mandatory legal rules, resolving contract disputes by means of such standards is not against public policy and good morals. Again, in a sense, this way of looking at the functioning of agreements goes beyond the legal nature of the contract itself, but there are deals that do function like that quite well in practice. A functional comparison of contracts in action must take this into account.

---

[19] See for further examples Kitagawa (n 16).

(b) Standards in Law in Practice

In Japan, administrative standards have long influenced private contractual relationships, often in a profound manner because even when business transactions
are purely private in nature, Japanese administrative agencies often intervene. A
famous illustration of this practice is the administrative guidance (*gyosei shido*)
provided by various Japanese ministries. To be sure, such government interference
is highly problematic from the perspective of party autonomy but it should not
be rejected too quickly because it may, under certain circumstances, have a very
salutary effect. For example, administrative guidance can be used to prevent the
stronger party from imposing unfair terms on the weaker party. In case of a
dispute, administrative intervention can also contribute to a solution, though in an
informal and not altogether uniform fashion. Of course, such informal justice
has its limits, and my intention here is not to justify it. It is rather to point to an
element which a functional comparative analysis must take into account. In other
words, Japanese administrative standards are examples of extra-contractual norms,
and where they help to define the contractual relationship and to resolve potential
issues, they become part of contract law as it functions in practice.[20]

The phenomenon is not limited to administrative standards. There are also, for
example, technological norms, quality, environmental, educational, health, and
safety standards. 'Standards' thus come in all shapes and sizes and amount to a
complex set of guidelines under which legal problems are, or at least can be, solved.
Such guidelines are more than mere facts—they have a heuristic function. They
can help to resolve problems arising out of the tension between a Western and a
pluralistic approach and are thus part of law in practice.[21]

IV. NEXT-GENERATION ISSUES AS A TASK OF COMPARATIVE LAW IN EAST ASIA

1. Next-Generation Issues and Comparative Law

We now live in a global society and face new legal problems arising out of
the progress of computer and information technology, the increasing impact

---

[20] Ibid. For this theory of comparative law in action, see Stewart Macaulay, 'The Real and the
Paper Deal: Empirical Pictures of Relationships, Complexity and the Urge for Transparent Simple
Rules', (2003) 66 *Modern LR* 44; Steward Macaulay, 'Freedom from Contract: Solution in Search of a
Problem?', (2004) *Wisconsin LR* 777.

[21] Regarding legal aspects of such standards, see Zentaro Kitagawa, 'Standard als Weg zur "besseren
Privatautonomie" ', in *Festschrift für Karl Larenz zum 80. Geburtstag* (1983), 329.

of the Internet, research in biotechnology, the need for environmental protection, and so on. Some of these problems have very broad implications, such as the emergence of a virtual society on the Internet; some are serious enough to potentially endanger human existence itself, such as environmental pollution or biohazards. Neither Western nor pluralistic legal models can handle them all, and neither has yet developed appropriate solutions. In many respects, there is a legal gap because neither Western law nor traditional norms are designed to handle the questions involved. We thus need to come up with new legal ideas, theories, and rules.

In order to do so, we must understand the precise nature of the issues we are facing. Once a problem is clearly identified and defined, we have to undertake research necessary to find out how to resolve it. Here, again, comparative law can be highly useful. In particular, it can explore the interrelationship between Western and pluralistic or even traditional legal orders and thus help us to discover solutions to the urgent problems we face today.

2. The Competition for Legal Assistance

(a) Competing 'Code Donors'

The collapse of the Union of Soviet Socialist Republics (USSR) in 1991 lead to the creation of several newly independent states. They share an ambition to reform their legal systems in order to make them compatible with a market-oriented economy. In many cases, this entails the introduction of new civil and commercial codes as the basic laws governing market activity. This has rung in a new era of codification. These efforts are often supported by international cooperation programmes which constitute a veritable network of legal assistance projects. These projects have been developed under the umbrella concept of Official Development ment Assistance (ODA) and often with the financial support of the World Bank, the European Bank of Restoration and Development, and the Asian Development Bank (ADB). Their main purpose is to help developing countries transplant Western legal models by enacting new legislation or by amending existing laws. But contemporary legal assistance projects do not stop here. Legal and judicial reform (as envisaged by the World Bank) and law and policy reform (as envisaged by the Asian Development Bank) have not simply been concerned with offering a menu of Western legal models to recipient countries. They also seek to force each country to make a choice about the direction of its legal system and to prioritize its reform needs.[22] The recipient countries often face some tough choices. For example,

---

[22] These are lessons the World Bank as well as the Asian Development Bank have learned. See World Bank Legal Department, 'The World Bank and Legal Technical Assistance. Initial Lessons' Policy Research Working Paper (1995). In my view, Official Development Assistance is a highly

when importing Western law, there can be a conflict between codification in the continental European fashion and the enactment of piecemeal statutes in the US-American style, not to mention competition between different policies and substantive provisions. This, in turn, leads to competition among the Western donor systems.

For these reasons, it is unclear at the moment how helpful Western donor systems really are to developing nations. Fortunately, the Western aid projects have recently become more generous and more flexible in their attempt to export their ideas of law to other parts of the world.

(b) Japanese Legal Assistance

In the case of Japan, legal assistance is provided by the Japan International Cooperation Agency (JICA) and the International Cooperation Department of Research and Training Institute of the Ministry of Justice. Japan is also contributing to the drafting of new codes in accordance with Western legal models. In 2003, Japan helped to prepare drafts of a Civil Code and a Code of Civil Procedure for Cambodia.[23] The drafts are the work of a preparatory committee which consisted of experts from the two countries. Another joint committee prepared amendments to the Civil Code of Vietnam; they will be part of the new Vietnamese civil code which came into effect on 1 January 2006 and replaced the older code of 1995.[24]

Although Western legal models continue to be important, they are no longer the only designs available to recipient countries. In addition to the official assistance from the governmental sector, large research projects at various universities supported by the Japanese government are now playing an important role in this regard. The Centre for Asian Legal Exchange (CALE), Nagoya University, for example, has been quite active in expanding its academic and educational activities, including academic exchange agreements with universities in Vietnam, Laos, Mongolia, Uzbekistan, and so on.[25]

(c) A Legal Interface for the Next Generation of Law

It is becoming clear that international legal assistance programmes have helped the respective recipient countries to transplant Western legal models into their legal systems. At the same time, these countries are now facing the problem of the interrelationship between the Western imports and their own traditional norms.

important framework for pluralist legal models. For the history of Official Development Assistance, see Helmut Führer, 'The History of Official Development Assistance. A History of the Development Assistance Committee and the Development Co-operation Directorate in Dates, Names and Figures' (OECD, 1996) at <http://www.oecd.org/dataoecd/3/39/1896816.pdf>.

[23] See <http://www.jica.go.jp/english/evaluation/project/term/as/archives/13–1–02.html>.

[24] See <http://vietnamnews.vnagency.com.vn/showarticle.php?num=07POL200505>.

[25] See <http://cale.nomolog.nagoya-u.ac.jp>.

They are often perplexed by the complexities and sometimes outright contradictions they face—both with regard to the competing Western systems themselves and with regard to the relationship between the Western approach as a whole and indigenous norms.

Japanese contributions are well on their way to finding a workable solution to the problem of handling the interface between the imported and the indigenous. The Japanese approach reflects the country's own historical experience as a place of reception and the valuable lessons it has learned in this regard. Japanese jurists understand that there is a need for a new approach. The interface between Western transplants and pluralistic legal orders in the context of international legal assistance is a new horizon for comparative law.[26] The discipline must help us understand how Western models can be supplemented and enriched by exploring how the traditional law in the respective countries functions.

3. The German Pandectist System in East Asia in the Near Future

Let us conclude this chapter by paying short visits to the three East Asian countries in which the German Pandectist system has had considerable influence. As discussed before (Section II), this system was introduced in East Asia at the end of the nineteenth century. What role does it play a century later, and what are its prospects for the future?

(a) Three Countries

Let us first look at Korea. Here, the German Pandectist approach continues to prevail. Since its entry into force, the Korean civil code had been amended only insubstantially until October 2004, when a draft for a major overhaul was introduced into parliament. The project entails the amendment of about 130 code provisions concerning topics as diverse as the definition of a minor, legal persons, juristic acts, the substantive effect of provisional registration, security rights in real estate, implied warranties, sureties as well as new types of transactions such as travel contracts and brokerage. The goals of the reform are to modernize the respective institutions, to adjust the law to changed market situations, and to cope with issues caused by the internationalization of law. A quick look at the various items gives the impression that the reform was influenced by recent developments in Japanese private law on the one hand, and by the 2001 reform of the German law

---

[26] A report of the World Bank illustrates this point when it 'recommends that village-level development programs can be good vehicles for access-to-justice interventions. The kinds of broad-based local justice interventions can complement a national reform program in a way that avoids ineffective legalisms and focuses assistance on where it is most wanted', The World Bank (n 14), 70.

of obligations on the other hand. On the whole, Korea appears to remain faithful to the German Pandectist tradition.

China has been active in codifying its private law in order to make it compatible with a socialistic market economy. The project began with General Provisions of the Civil Code of the People's Republic of China (PRC) in 1986 and continued with the Contract Law of 1999. Initially, the codification proceded along the lines of the German Pandectist approach. The General Provisions contain the basic legal concepts and institutions that correspond, at least roughly, to the Pandectist system: fundamental principles, natural persons, juristic persons, juristic acts, agency, private rights, real rights and obligatory rights, intellectual property rights, rights of personality, civil liability (breach of contracts and tort), and conflict of laws provisions. The 1999 Contract Law consists both of general rules governing the formation, validity, performance, amendment and assignment, and breach of contracts, and of specific provisions covering twenty-three types of civil and commercial contracts.

Some time ago, however, the focus began to shift away from the Pandectist system to a more pragmatic approach. This trend was obvious in the Draft for the Civil Code of China of 17 December 2002. The Draft was discussed at a Japanese-Chinese symposium held in March 2003 at Yunnan University. To the surprise of the Japanese participants, it did not contain the general provisions on the law of obligations; this became a major point of controversy between Chinese and Japanese jurists. Yet this omission is not as radical as it first appears because most of the general provisions on obligations really address contract issues, both in theory and practice. Thus the law of contracts can cover most of the pertinent issues—just as in common law jurisdictions. How eventually to codify them will be a matter of legislative policy. The 2002 Draft shows, however, that the legislative trend in China is not faithful to the German Pandectist approach but prefers a solution of issues in their respective practical contexts.

If, finally, we look at the Japanese civil code, we find that it has been frequently amended over the last couple of years. In part, these amendments have simply modified traditional concepts and institutions. For example, they have introduced new types of limited legal capacity, regulated secured transactions. and addressed the transfer of obligatory rights. These reforms were not solely fashioned after German models but rather the product of comparative studies of European laws, US-American law, and other sources.

In part, however, Japanese law reforms have also created a variety of new legal rules and ethical norms that respond to cutting-edge issues. Two areas are particularly noteworthy in this context: the digitalization of information and the progress of biotechnology. In both regards, the civil law system of the classic age of codification is woefully out of date. A century ago, there were no computer-based contracts, no human intentions reduced to digital codes, no virtual personalities, and information *per se* was not considered a marketable good. Today, we live in the digital age which presents huge challenges to law.[27] Contracts, for example, are frequently created by, and operated through, computer systems.[28] A century ago, there were also no issues of stem cell research, DNA manipulation, or ovum or sperm donation, and jurists did not have to worry about who owns DNA or ES cells physically separated from the human body. Today, we must face these and other issues, some of which are vital for the future of mankind.[29] The question then is how civil law systems can handle them. Certainly, new legislation is called for and, certainly, comparative legal studies can help in the process of making it. But once made, there is also the question of how the respective norms can be integrated into the existing legal system. We are now beginning to understand that this cannot always be done in the form of hard legal rules nor in the comprehensive and systematic fashion characterizing the codifications in the German Pandectist tradition a century ago.

Recent Japanese reforms have made some progress towards a more open-textured approach. With regard to the digitilization of information, for example, there are new norms governing electronic signatures and contracts, online registration of immovables and of security interests. In the area of biotechnology, there are softer standards, such as guidelines for the treatment of the human embryo. In this fashion, innovative concepts and norms have been steadily incorporated into the civil law of Japan. This has not changed the basic structure of the civil code but it has made the Japanese civil law system more flexible and diverse. Thus, Japanese law is gradually changing its identity and finding its own path toward the future. Moreover, these developments in Japan indicate that in order to deal with cutting-edge issues, the civil codes of the near future may have to contain a greater variety of legal material than their precursors. Much of this material will take on the shape of so-called 'soft law'—ethical standards, technological, administrative, or business norms, and so on.[30]

---

[27] See generally, M. Ethan Katsh, *Law in a Digital World* (1995); David R. Johnson and David G. Post, 'Law and Borders—The Rise of Law in Cyberspace', (1996) 48 *Stanford LR* 1367; Aron Mefford, 'Lex Informatica: Foundations of Law on the Internet' (1997) 5 *Indiana Journal of Global Legal Studies* 21; Henry H. Perritt, 'The Internet as a Threat to Sovereignty? Thoughts on the Internet's Role in Strengthening National and Global Governance', (1998) 5 *Indiana Journal of Global Legal Studies* 423. The Uniform Computer Information Transaction Act (UCITA) Section 2(35) defines information. See also Lawrence Lessig, *Code and Other Laws of Cyberspace* (1999).

[28] Regarding system contracts, see Zentaro Kitagawa, 'Der Systemvertag. Ein neuer Vertragstyp in der Informationsgesellschaft', in *Festschrift für Murad Ferid* (1988), 219.

[29] See eg Graeme Laurie, *Genetic Privacy—A Challenge to Medico-Legal Norms* (2002), Zentaro Kitagawa, 'Gedanken über DNA und Recht—Prolog zum Recht des "Lebenselements" ', in *Festschrift für Hyung-Bae Kim* (1995), 229.

[30] Zentaro Kitagawa, '*Minpo no Kinmirai Moderu* (Civil Law Models of the Near Future)', (2004) 54 *Kobe LR* 161; *idem*, 'A Comparative Study of the Civil Code Legislation of the PRC', (2003) *Renmin University LR* 43 (in Chinese). See also *idem*, 'Law Models for the Near Future' (n 15). The characterization of the civil code of the near future in this paper is also inspired by recent progress towards a European private law, particularly towards a European civil code; see eg Arthur Hartkamp, Martin Hesselink, Ewoud Hondius, Carla Joustra, Edgar du Perron, and Muriel Veldman (eds), *Towards a European Civil Code* (3rd edn, 2004).

(b) Three Ways Ahead

The German Pandectist heritage will experience a different fate in each of the three countries examined. Korea will continue to adhere to the Pandectist approach. China is deviating from that approach and pursuing a more pragmatic course, even though its most ambitious reforms have yet to be enacted. And Japan is on its way to building its own civil law model but is still experimenting and deciding exactly which course to pursue. Comparative law focusing on this area of the globe now faces the task of coming to grips with these developments and with the way law functions in these countries.

Especially from a comparative law perspective, the present developments in East Asia are both fascinating and challenging. In some of the current trends, we are beginning to see the emergence of new civil law models which incorporate new issues and introduce new kinds of norms. Their comparative study is particularly important in light of the fact that international legal assistance programmes are presently transplanting elements of the German Pandectist tradition into various recipient countries in the world. With the help of comparative law, these countries may learn valuable lessons from the East Asian experience.

V. CONCLUSION

The modern legal systems of Japan, Korea, and China were once all shaped by the reception of Western legal models, albeit to varying degrees and in a variety of ways. A century has passed since their formative stage. This makes it timely for comparative law to analyse their development and to assess the status quo.

In that context, it is particularly important for comparative law to explore the interface between imported Western elements and indigenous culture which, in their combination, have produced complex pluralist systems. But comparative law can also do its share in helping us understand how to incorporate new rules in response to new challenges, especially those presented by the information age and the progress of biotechnological research, into the established structures of civil law. Here, especially, Japan is beginning to set a noteworthy example.

As a result, the comparative study of East Asian legal systems is worthwhile not only in its own right but also more generally because it can add new material to comparative law and because it may provide some guidance for the solution of current and future legal problems.

Bibliography

Zentaro Kitagawa, 'Rezeption und Fortbildung des europäischen Zivilrechts in Japan' (1970) 45 *Arbeiten zur Rechtsvergleichung* 1–221.

Yoshiyuki Noda, *Introduction to Japanese Law* (1976)

Zentaro Kitagawa (ed), *Doing Business in Japan*, 7 vols (looseleaf, 1980–)

Masatoshi Chiba, *Legal Pluralism: Toward a General Theory through Japanese Legal Culture* (1989)

Harald Baum (ed), *Japan: Economic Success and Legal System* (1995)

Kochiro Fujikura, *Japanese Law and Legal Theory* (1996)

Sang Hyan Song, *Korean Law in the Global Economy* (1996)

John O. Haley, *The Spirit of Japanese Law* (1998)

Hiroshi Oda, *Japanese Law* (2nd edn, 2001)

Kenneth Port and Gerald McAlinn, *Comparative Law. Law and the Legal Process in Japan* (2nd edn, 2002)

Stephen C. Hsu (ed), *Understanding China's Legal System: Essays in Honor of Jerome A. Cohen* (2003)

Stewart Macaulay, 'Freedom from Contract: A Solution in Search of a Problem?' (2004) *Wisconsin LR* 777–820.

Neil Jeffrey Diamant, Stanley B. Lubman, and Kevin O'Brien (eds), *Engaging the Law in China: State, Society, and Possibilities for Justice* (2005)

CHAPTER 8

DEVELOPMENT OF COMPARATIVE LAW IN LATIN AMERICA

JAN KLEINHEISTERKAMP

Paris

I. Introduction

Latin American law has largely been neglected by mainstream comparative law.[1] Common wisdom has been that Latin American law is largely an offspring of and, at best, a variation of French law due to its reception of the *Code Napoléon*.[2] Accordingly, Latin-American law has typically been put in the box of the 'French' or 'Romanistic' legal family—and left there without much more attention.[3] A striking example is Merryman's *The Civil Law Tradition—An Introduction to the Legal Systems of Western Europe and Latin America*, where one will, on the whole,

---

[1] This has already been observed in 1878 by Léonel Oudin, 'Étude sur le *Code civil* du Chili', (1878) VII *Bulletin de la Société de Législation Comparée* 506 ff: 'Notre Société, dans ces études sur les législations de divers pays, n'a pas eu souvent l'occasion de s'occuper des États de l'Amérique du Sud . . .'.

[2] For the repercussions of such simplistic classification see eg the astonishing conclusions drawn by economists trying to show that legal origins predetermine legal efficiency and even economic performance: 'Latin America suffers from relatively uninformative financial statements and relatively weak protection of shareholders, partly due to its Napoleonic legal heritage': Ross Levine, 'Napoleon, Bourses, and Growth in Latin America', (1998) *Inter-American Development Bank—Office of the Chief Economist Working paper no. 365*, available at <http://www.iadb.org/oce> (accessed 13 January 2006).

[3] See eg Imre Zajtay, 'Les destinées du *Code civil*', (1954) 6 *Revue internationale de droit comparé* 792, 804. For an overview of the works of the first half of the twentieth century, following this scheme, see René David, 'L'originalité des droits de l'Amérique latine', in *idem, Le droit comparé: Droits d'hier, droits de demain* (1982), 161, 164 (a reprint of an unpublished *polycopie* of 1953), citing, *inter alia*, the works of Wigmore, Schnitzer, Gutteridge, Sarfatti, and Ionesco. The same attitude can still be found today in Konrad Zweigert and Hein Kötz, *An Introduction to Comparative Law* (trans Tony Weir, 3rd edn, 1998), 113–15.

search in vain for any reference to Latin American law.[4] The presumed 'familiarity' and the consequent perception of Latin American law as lacking sufficient originality,[5] or rather exoticism, may explain why comparative works have often dedicated considerably more attention to Islamic, Hindu, and East-Asian law (not to speak of 'giants' such as Switzerland, Austria, Louisiana, etc.).[6] The topics of both Latin American law as the object of comparative law, and comparative law as a subject in Latin American jurisprudence, have remained in the shade with the result that they have, as we shall see later on, become battlegrounds for influence and domination. The present contribution tries to provide a rough sketch of the development of comparative law in Latin America and its significance for, and impact on, the legal systems of the Latin American countries today.

II. THE COLONIAL PERIOD

1. First Legal Structures

Latin American law existed even before it had been discovered by Europeans. Some of its indigenous populations, especially the Aztecs, but probably also the Incas, developed highly complex legal systems that well reflected their social and political structures.[7] Moreover, the Spanish Catholic monarchs had already established the legal bases that were to govern the new world, which was yet to be discovered, with the *Capitulaciones de Santa Fe* of 17 April 1492, that is, even before Columbus's departure into the unknown.[8] Spanish law poured into the newly discovered territory, which was formally taken into possession on behalf of the Spanish Crown.

---

[4] John H. Merryman, *The Civil Law Tradition: An Introduction to the Legal Systems of Western Europe and Latin America* (2nd edn, 1985), referring at 89, 96, 137, 139, and 140 only very briefly to Latin American constitutional law.

[5] See the provocative introduction by René David, 'Structure et idéologie du Droit brésilien', (1954) 17–18 *Cahiers de Législation de Bibliographie juridique de l'Amérique latine* 7, 8: 'The first impression of both Brazilian law as well as all other aspects of the Brazilian spirit is without doubt the absence of originality'. See also *idem* (n 3), 161 for all of Latin American law.

[6] See eg in quantitative terms Zweigert and Kötz (n 3), who dedicate as much space (one and a half pages) to all of Latin American law as to the law of Louisiana or Quebec (at 115–18), which is still only a small fraction of the attention given to the civil codes of Austria or Switzerland.

[7] John Merryman, David S. Clark, and John O. Haley, *The Civil Law Tradition: Europe, Latin America, and East Asia* (1994), 352–62 (on the legal system of the Incas and Aztecs); Jerome A. Offner, *Law and Politics in Aztec Texcoco* (1983); Miguel Bonifaz, *Derecho Indiano* (1955), 72–121 (sketching the legal systems of the Aztecs, the Maya-Quitches, the Chibchas, the Kollas, and the Incas).

[8] See José María Castán Vázquez, 'El sistema de derecho privado iberoamericano', (1969) 28 *Estúdios de Derecho* 5, 12.

However, Spanish law did not wipe out the pre-existing indigenous laws and customs: these continued—at least in theory—to be valid and enforceable as long as they were not in conflict with the religion and the laws of Spain.[9] To some extent, this created the first challenge to comparative law in Latin America. Indigenous law was frequently found to be largely compatible with Spanish legal institutions, such as the payment of tributes, slavery, forced labour, jointly held land, or special courts for particular classes of litigants.[10] Accordingly, indigenous laws and customs continued to govern many aspects of intra-indigenous relations and were apparently applied by royal courts.[11]

2. The Existing Spanish Legal Order

The strict control of access to the Americas and the prohibition of trade with non-Spaniards meant that there was no need to worry about foreign laws or conflict of laws.[12] However, Spanish law in itself was everything but consolidated and very much marked by the need to analyse and compare legal provisions of different provenance. The key role in the contemporary legal jumble was held by Roman law, the foreign law *par excellence*, whose popularity among legal scholars and practitioners constantly undermined the Spanish Crown's authority in legislative matters. As early as AD 654, the Visigoth King Recceswinth had provided in his *Liber Iudicum*:[13] 'We instruct, allow, and wish that everybody studies the laws of the foreign people for his own benefit; but as regards the decisions in courts we prohibit them and reject their use'.

This prohibition was reiterated many times during the following thousand years, as lawyers continued virtually to ignore the chaotic royal law of Castile and resorted to the writings of scholars in the Roman-Canon *ius commune* when arguing their cases. The result was a considerable degree of legal uncertainty.[14] Disgusted by the court practices in Castile, and apparently worried about maintaining the legal order on the new continent, the Crown in 1509 prohibited lawyers from travelling to the

---

[9] *Ordenanzas* of 6 August 1555 and of 13 July 1530, restated by the 'Recopilación de las Leyes de las Indias' (1681) Book 2, Title 1, Law 4 and Book 5, Title 2, Law 22, in Juan Manzano Manzano, *Recopilación de leyes de los reynos de las Indias* (1943, reprint 1973); see also <http://www.congreso.gob.pe/ntley/LeyIndiaP.htm> (accessed 13 January 2006).

[10] cf Ricardo Levene, *Manual de historia del derecho argentino* (5th edn, 1985), 199–200; Matthew C. Mirow, *Latin American Law: A History of Private Law and Institutions in Spanish America* (2004), 6–7.

[11] See Clarence Henry Haring, *The Spanish Empire in America* (1975), 101; Mirow (n 10), 51.

[12] See Alfonso García Gallo, *Los origenes españoles de las instituciones americanas* (1987), 269.

[13] *Liber Iudicum* (AD 654) Book 2, Title 1, Law 8, in *Los códigos españoles concordados y anotados* (vol I, 2nd edn, 1872), 5; this rule can also be found in the Castilian version of the *Liber Iudiciorum*, the *Fuero Juzgo* (AD 681), ibid at 111.

[14] For many others, see Mirow (n 10), 16–17.

West Indies.[15] This prohibition was only abolished after legal practice in the Indies had been heavily regulated in 1563.[16] Nevertheless, the *conquistadores* brought with them to the new continent the legislative confusion of their homeland, and it was soon increased by specific legislation *de las Indias*.[17] Eventually this led to the same troublesome court practices that had existed in Castile: litigation was slow, costly, highly unpredictable, and often prone to corruption.[18] It is also this context of legislative confusion and remoteness from the centralist power of the Crown, combined with vacillating policies, corrupt administrative personnel, and contradictory messages from the motherland, that gave rise to the practice of *la ley se acata pero no se cumple* (the law is acknowledged but not enforced),[19] a proverb that is still frequently used today to describe the role of the law in Latin America.[20] In view of this, lawyers and judges in both the motherland and overseas remained strongly attached to the Roman-Canon *ius commune* for arguing their cases and founding their decisions,[21] thus dashing any hope that Castilian and colonial legislation would be learned in practice.[22] This was only natural: contemporary lawyers had been trained exclusively in Roman law and Canon law, and their libraries were predominantly stocked with Romanist literature.[23] As a result, the law of the Spanish Empire remained desperately chaotic and barely able to provide a satisfactory basis for legal practice.

[15] Alfonso García-Gallo, *Antología de las fuentes del antiguo Derecho* (1982), 145.

[16] See the *Ordenanzas de Audiencia* of 1563, restated in the *Recopilación de la Leyes de las Indias* (n 9), Book 2, Title 24, Laws 1–28.

[17] See the *Ordenanzas de Audiencia* of 1530, restated in the *Recopilación de las Indias* (n 9), Book 2, Title 1, Law 2.

[18] Keith S. Rosenn, 'Brazil's Legal Culture: The *Jeito* Revisited', (1984) 1 *Florida International LJ* 1, 9–12; *idem*, 'The Success of Constitutionalism in the United States and its Failure in Latin America: An Explanation', (1990) 22 *University of Miami Inter-American LR* 1, 25–6; Woodrow Borah, 'Assistance in Conflict Resolution for the Poor and Indians in Colonial Mexico', (1996) 63 *Recueils de la société Jean Bodin pour l'histoire comparative des institutions* 217, 222.

[19] Guillermo F. Margadant S., *An Introduction to the History of Mexican Law* (1983), 72–3. For an analysis based on the conflicting standards hypothesis, see John L. Phelan, 'Authority and Flexibility in the Spanish Imperial Bureaucracy', (1960) 5 *Administrative Science Quarterly* 47–65.

[20] For the Latin American concepts of 'flexibility', see Howard J. Wiarda, 'Law and Political Development in Latin America: Towards a Framework for Analysis', (1971) 19 *AJCL* 434, 460–3; Keith S. Rosenn, 'The *Jeito*: Brazil's Institutional Bypass of the Formal Legal System and its Developmental Implications', (1971) 19 *AJCL* 514–49.

[21] Javier Barrientos Grandón, *La cultura jurídica en la Nueva España* (1993), 116–22; Guzmán Brito (below n 23), 87–9.

[22] Margadant (n 19), 44–5.

[23] See eg Alejandro Guzmán Brito, 'La vigencia del derecho romano en Indias según el jurista Juan del Corral Calvo de la Torre', in *Justicia, Sociedad y Economía en la América Española (Siglos XVI, XVII y XVIII)* (1983), 71, 88–9 (with further references in n 70); see also Castán Vázquez (n 8), 14, referring to Irving A. Leonard, *Los libros del Conquistador* (1953), 269–358.

3. The Cradle of Comparative Law in Portugal and Brazil

The development of the legal order of the Portuguese empire, which had legalized its claim to Brazil in the Treaty of Tordesillas (1493), was equally marked by considerable legislative confusion despite various attempts at consolidation in *Ordenações*,[24] related to the exclusive teaching of Roman and common law,[25] the rules on the application *in subsidio* of these two 'learned laws',[26] and their resulting use and abuse in legal practice.[27] The Crown's struggle against this phenomenon culminated in 1769 when the Empire's governor, the Marquis de Pombal, a man who was fiercely anti-clerical and imbued by the spirit of Natural law, decreed the so-called *Lei da Boa Razão*: Roman law could still be consulted, but was not to be applied unless it passed the test of the *boa razão* (ie good reason), either as found in the most fundamental principles of Natural law, in the rules of the *ius gentium* of the civilized nations, or in political, economic, commercial, and maritime matters, 'as reflected by the modern laws of the civilized nations'.[28] This radical shift from the *ratio scripta* to the *rectius ratio* revolutionized Portuguese and Brazilian jurisprudence, legal education, and practice. Not only did the *usus modernus pandectarum*, as reflected by contemporary German and Dutch doctrines, become the benchmark for the application of Roman law,[29] the shift also brought about the massive and systematic, but sometimes also excessive, use of comparative law in general,[30] especially the comparison with German and Italian law, and later also with French law.[31] A good example of the new impact of comparative law has been given by the Portuguese professor Moncada,[32] who shows how the Portuguese law of succession changed substantially under the influence of the statutes of the German cities of Hamburg and Lübeck, as cited in Heineccius' *Elementa Iuris Germanici*. A Brazilian writer has concluded as follows:[33]

[24] For the development of the *Ordenações Afonsinas* (1447), *Manuelinas* (1521), and *Filipinas* (1595), see in detail Mário Júlio Almeida Costa, *Historia do Direito Português* (3rd edn, 1996), 273–93.

[25] See Almeida Costa (n 24), 229–32.   [26] Ibid 308–16.

[27] Ibid 316–17 (printing out that even Spanish law was sometimes applied despite not being admitted as a source of law).

[28] § 9 *Lei da Boa Razão*. See also the *Estatutos da Univ. de Coimbra do ano de 1772* (vol II, 1773), 269 (Book 2, Title 5, Law 3), cited by L. Cabral de Moncada, *Estudos de História do Direito* (1948), 103 (n 1).

[29] Moncada (n 28), 104: '. . . thereby placing the entire Portuguese [and thus Brazilian] legal life under the influence of the German and Dutch doctrine, humanism and legal rationalism'.

[30] Clovis Bevilaqua, *Resumo das Licções de Legislação Comparada sobre o Direito Privado* (2nd edn, 1897), 27 (still using the *Lei da Boa Razão* to justify the necessity of comparative law in 1897); Francisco C. Pontes de Miranda, *Fontes e Evolução do Direito Civil Brasileiro* (1928), 87–98 (noting that this did not bring about the relief for judicial practice that had been hoped for, but rather contributed to the chaos by citing contradictory sources); see also below n 185.

[31] Almeida Costa (n 24), 377; Moncada (n 28), 124; Clóvis V. Couto e Silva, 'O direito civil brasileiro em perspectiva histórica e visão de futuro', (1988) 97 *Revista de Informação Legislativa* 163–180, at 167 and 171 (referring to the influence of the Prussian *Allgemeines Landrecht* of 1794 and then of the French *Code civil* of 1904).

[32] See in detail Moncada (n 28), 105–24.   [33] Couto e Silva (n 31), 171–2.

The result was a passion—. . . still undiminished in our days—for arguing with the opinions of foreign authors and writings in order to contrast and to supplement national law. This exchange of ideas can be considered as a permanent reception of foreign law by which the fatal immobility of the Codes is compensated.

III. INDEPENDENCE AND CODIFICATION

Following Napoleon's occupation of the Iberian Peninsula in 1807, the independence movements in Spanish America benefited from Spain's weakness. This finally culminated—after bloody wars against the Spanish forces—in the constitution of the new republics of Latin America between 1810 and 1825.[34] At the same time, the constitution of these new republics frustrated the dream of the main leader of the movement, Simón Bolívar, which was to maintain the political unity of former Spanish America, and thereby also marked the end of legal uniformity.

Brazil also experienced some fighting; none the less, its independence came about quite differently. Portugal's King Dom João VI, who had fled from Napoleon's troops to Brazil, returned to Lisbon in 1821. His son Pedro, Regent-Prince of Brazil, refused to obey when called back to Lisbon and declared Brazil's independence on 22 September 1822. He ejected his father's troops and eventually suppressed the republican independence movements himself. Brazil remained a centralist empire until 1889, when it became a federal republic.[35]

1. The Latin American Constitutions

The Spanish-American independence movement was very familiar with the French enlightenment philosophy and the French Declaration of Human and Civil Rights of 1789,[36] as well as the United States Constitution of 1787 and Hamilton and Madison's Federalist Papers, which had been translated into Spanish and

---

[34] The countries resulting from the break-up of the former Spanish American empire were Argentina, Bolivia, Chile, Colombia (including Panama), Costa Rica, Cuba, Ecuador, El Salvador, Guatemala, Honduras, Mexico, Nicaragua, Panama, Paraguay, Peru, and, eventually, Uruguay and Venezuela.

[35] For the general history from 1808 to 1889, see Mary del Priore and Renato Pinto Venâncio, *História do Brasil* (2001), 198–268.

[36] See Ovidio García Regueiro, '1789 y la América española: eco ultramarino de los acontecimientos franceses', in *Revolución, contrarrevolución e independencia: La Revolución Francesa, España y América* (1989), 108.

circulated widely in Latin America during the wars of independence.[37] Bolívar himself, who had been a pupil of Andrés Bello (who was to become Chile's great codifier), had studied the writings of Locke, Montesquieu, and Rousseau, and kept in his library various treatises on Roman, Canon, and Spanish royal law. Like most Latin American independence leaders, he was also in contact with Jeremy Bentham.[38] It is therefore not surprising that all these sources influenced—in varying degrees—the drafting of the first constitutions of the newly created Latin American states.[39]

Bolivia's first Constitution of 1826, for example, based on a draft written by Bolívar himself, contained elements of Roman antecedents (such as the three-chamber legislature consisting of the senate, the tribunate, and the censor).[40] Traces of the Roman model could also be found in Argentina's and Chile's first republican period, which recognized temporary dictatorship (*director supremo*) in times of crisis.[41] More interesting is the clear influence of Spain's short-lived liberal Constitution of 1812 (repealed with the restoration of Ferdinand VII in 1814 but reinstated on several occasions thereafter), as evidenced, for example, by the cumbersome procedure for electing members of the Parliament (by provincial electors who were, in turn, elected by parish electors), which was inserted in various early constitutions with only slight modifications.[42]

Much more influential was the US American model, especially where the federal system was adopted, as in Mexico and Brazil (1891).[43] The most typical example of United States influence, however, is Argentina, which had seen many years of war between the provinces before they united (1810–29, followed by a dictatorship lasting until 1852). Although its direct affiliation with the United States Constitu-

---

[37] Gerald E. Fitzgerald, *The Constitutions of Latin America* (1968), x–xi; David S. Clark, 'Judicial Protection of the Constitution in Latin America', (1975) 2 *Hastings Constitutional Law Quarterly* 405, 413. For the Brazilian independence movement, which was destined to fail, see Haroldo Valladão, 'L'étude et l'enseignement du Droit comparé au Brésil: XIXᵉ et XXᵉ siècle', in Marc Ancel (ed), *Livre du centenaire de la Société de législation comparé: Évolution internationale et problèmes du droit comparé* (1971), 311–12.

[38] Later on, however, Bolívar prohibited the writings of Bentham for being too liberal; Jürgen Samtleben, 'Menschheitsglück und Gesetzgebungsexport: Zu Jeremy Benthams Wirkung in Latein-amerika', (1986) 50 *RabelsZ* 451, 454–5.

[39] For an analysis of the influence of the different sources, see Otto Carlos Stoetzer, *El pensamiento político en la América española durante el período de la emancipación (1789–1825)* (1966).

[40] Fitzgerald (n 37), x–xi.

[41] For Argentina see section 3 of the *Estatuto Provisional* of 5 May 1815; for Chile see Art 80 of the Constitution of 30 October 1822 and Art 14 of the Constitution of 29 December 1823; available at <http://www.cervantesvirtual.com/portal/constituciones/> (accessed 13 January 2006).

[42] See Ignacio Fernández Sarasola, 'La constitución española de 1812 y su proyección europea e iberoamericana', (2000) 2 *Fundamentos* (Spain) 359–466.

[43] For the troubled Mexican constitutional history, see Helen L. Clagett and David M. Valderrama, *A Revised Guide to Law & Legal Literature of Mexico* (1973), 1–13; for Brazil, see Jacob Dolinger, 'The Influence of American Constitutional Law on the Brazilian Legal System', (1990) 38 *AJCL* 803, 823.

tion has been disputed,[44] it remains a fact that the wording of the Argentinean Constitution (1853, amended in 1860) is in many respects similar to the United States model and that almost all treatises on constitutional law published in Argentina during the nineteenth century turned particularly to the United States for their comparative analysis.[45] Moreover, from the outset Argentina's *Corte Suprema* has systematically referred to United States Supreme Court case law and United States legal doctrine when interpreting the Argentinian Constitution:[46] a tradition that continues today.[47]

It is in respect of the writ of *amparo* that the influence of the Constitution of the United States has attracted the greatest attention of comparative lawyers. This is a special and extraordinary legal remedy against abusive acts of public authorities which embraces elements of *habeas corpus* and writs of injunction, error, *mandamus*, and *certiorari*.[48] The origin of the most prominent Mexican *amparo* is much less clear than claimed by many (especially North American) authors.[49] There have been fierce debates as to whether the *amparo*'s origin lies in French, the United States, or more recent Spanish constitutional law,[50] but there is also much evidence that the writ of protection against abuses of public discretion was already practised under Spanish rule as early as the seventeenth century.[51] Nevertheless, and despite the fact that the Mexican *amparo* developed into a genuinely local institution, the comparison with United States constitutional law remained an important element in Mexican legal scholarship.[52] *Habeas corpus* and writs of protection also developed, under the influence of Anglo-American doctrine,

[44] For details, see Jonathan M. Miller, 'The Authority of a Foreign Talisman: A Study of U.S. Constitutional Practice as Authority in Nineteenth Century Argentina and the Argentine Elite's Leap of Faith', (1997) 46 *American University LR* 1483, 1514–22.

[45] See Edwin M. Borchard, *Guide to the Law and Legal Literature of Argentina, Brazil and Chile* (1917), 123–8; also Miller (n 44), 1508–32 and 1545–61.

[46] The very first decisions are Corte Suprema de Justicia de la Nación, 12 April 1864, *Fiscal General de la Nación c/ M.G. Argerich*, (1865) 1 *Fallos* 130–48 (on the question of whether the Federation has jurisdiction to prosecute insults made in the press, with a thorough discussion of the writings of Story and Kent and of case law from the US Supreme Court) and 3 May 1865, *Domingo Mendoza y Hermano c/ Provincia de San Luis s/ derechos de exportación*, (1865) 1 *Fallos* 485–98 (discussion of United States doctrine on the question of federal jurisdiction in cases of a claim against a province by a 'foreigner').

[47] See below, n 198.

[48] For the development of the *amparo*, see Clagett and Valderrama (n 43), 38–61 (who characterize it as a legal remedy that is unique to Mexico).

[49] See eg Phanor J. Eder, 'The Impact of the Common Law on Latin America', (1949–50) 4 *Miami Law Quarterly* 435, 436–7: 'It is one of the best fruits of comparative law in action'.

[50] See the references by Clagett and Valderrama (n 43), 39–40.

[51] Alfonso Noriega Cantú, 'El origen nacional y los antecedents hispánicos del juicio del amparo', (1942) 9 *Jus* (Mexico) 151–7; see also Merryman *et al* (n 7), 396.

[52] See eg the comparative work of Ignacio Vallarta (President of the Supreme Court from 1879–83): *El juicio de amparo y el writ of habeas corpus* (1881).

though always with distinct peculiarities,[53] in the Latin American countries, such as in Argentina,[54] Chile,[55] Peru,[56] and much of Central America.[57] The first specific *habeas corpus* provisions in Latin America were found in Brazil as early as 1830 and have since developed into much broader writs of protection, especially the *mandado de segurança*.[58] It is interesting to note that these were based on the English *Habeas Corpus* Acts of 1640, 1689, and 1816, and the practice as expounded by Blackstone and other English authorities.[59] This heritage can still be seen today in the fact that the word 'writ' has become part of the Brazilian legal vocabulary.

2. Codification Efforts

As regards the law below the level of the constitution, the young Latin American states inherited the legislative jumble described above: the Spanish *Siete Partidas, Leyes de Toro, Leyes de las Indias, Recopilaciones*, and so on (and, in Brazil, the equally confusing Portuguese law) remained in force provisionally, but only as far as they did not conflict with the *orden público* of the new constitutions. This only increased the uncertainties inherent in the application of these legal sources.[60] Partly because of Bentham's writings, the independence leaders were already considering the idea of bringing some order into the prevailing legal chaos by means of comprehensive codifications.[61] A contemporary source said that '[Bentham's]

---

[53] See eg Pedro P. Camargo, 'The Right to Judicial Protection: "Amparo" and Other Latin American Remedies for the Protection of Human Rights', (1971) 3 *Lawyer of the Americas* 191, 211–16; Fix Zamudio, 'Diversos Significados Jurídicos del Amparo en el Derecho Iberoamericano', (1965) 18 *Boletín del Instituto de Derecho Comparado de México* 119.

[54] Art 18 of the first Argentine Constitution (1853/60) (*habeas corpus*); Corte Suprema de Justicia de la Nación, 5 September 1958, *Samuel Kot S.R.L. s/habeas corpus*, (1958) 241 *Fallos* 291, 292. See today Art 43 of the Constitution (1994), *Ley del Amparo* No. 16986 (18 October 1966), *Ley del Habeas Corpus* No. 23098 (28 September 1984), *Ley de Habeas Data* Law No. 25326 (4 October 2000); Kenneth L. Karst and Keith S. Rosenn, *Law and Development in Latin America: A Case Book* (1975), 160; J. P. Mandler, 'Habeas Corpus and the Protection of Human Rights in Argentina', (1991) 16 *Yale Journal of International Law* 5–12.

[55] Richard Cappalli, 'Comparative South American Civil Procedure: A Chilean Perspective', (1989–90) 21 *University of Miami Inter-American LR* 239, 296–301.

[56] Art 200 of the Constitution of 1993.

[57] Karst and Rosenn (n 54), 182–3; see also Phanor J. Eder, 'Habeas Corpus Disembodied, The Latin-American Experience', in Kurt H. Nadelmann, Arthur T. von Mehren, and John N. Hazard (eds), *XXᵗʰ Century Essays in Honor of Hessel E. Yntema* (1961), 463; Clark, (1975) 2 *Hastings Constitutional Law Quarterly* 405.

[58] For the *habeas corpus, habeas data*, and the *mandado de segurança* see now Art 5 § 63, 69–73 of the Brazilian Constitution of 1988. For details, see Keith S. Rosenn, 'Brazil's new Constitution: An Exercise in Transient Constitutionalism for a Transitional Society', (1990) 38 *AJCL* 773, 794–8.

[59] Eder (n 57), 465–9.

[60] For a list of the different national provisions see Alejandro Guzmán Brito, *La Codificación Civil en Iberoamérica—Siglos XI–XX* (2000), 186–9.

[61] Samtleben, (1986) 50 *RabelsZ* 468.

name is little known in England, better in Europe, best of all in the plains of Chile and the mines of Mexico'.[62] However, his massive lobbying in 1822 to be appointed as the draftsman of a general code for all of Latin America[63] failed and his influence remained quite limited. Most of the young constitutions contained a mandate for codifying the criminal, civil, and commercial law, following the model of the Spanish Constitution of 1812, whose respective provision had, in turn, been taken from the French Constitution of 1791.[64] Codification evolved in a peculiar way in each country and, as shown by Guzmán Brito, differently from the general understanding that codification meant the mere adoption of French law.

(a) Early Copying of Foreign, especially French, Law

The military—and later political—leaders of the independence movement, such as Bolívar himself, Chile's *Director Supremo* O'Higgins, or Bolivia's (and later also Peru's) *Protector* Santa Cruz,[65] did, indeed, push for the adoption of the French Codes. This preference, however, can probably best be explained by the leaders' personal admiration for Napoleon. Most evidence points in this direction rather than supporting the alternative thesis that they were seeking legislation which represented the revolutionary ideals of liberalism as opposed to those of the hated Spanish regime. After all, the liberal Spanish Constitution of 1812 had been quite influential in most of the new republics;[66] also, all provisions of the Spanish *ancien régime* contrary to the liberal spirit of the new constitutions had already been abolished right after the attainment of independence.[67] Furthermore, no liberal legislation was wanted for family law and the law of succession, which continued to be governed by the restrictive principles of Canon law and the Spanish and Portuguese royal law based on them.[68] As a consequence, for example, marriage and divorce were governed in Brazil by the canons of the Council of Trent (1563) until 1890, that is, the advent of the Republic.[69]

In fact, only Santa Cruz was able successfully to imitate Napoleon with the promulgation of Bolivia's *Código Santa Cruz* of 1830, which was imposed with few

---

[62] William Hazlitt, 'The Spirit of the Age', (1825), in A. R. Waller and A. Glover (eds), *The Collected Works* (vol IV, 1902), 185, 189.

[63] Kurt Lipstein, 'Bentham, Foreign Law and Foreign Lawyers', in George Keeton and Georg Schwarzenberger (eds), *Jeremy Bentham and the Law: A Symposium* (1948), 216.

[64] Guzmán Brito (n 60), 231–7.   [65] Ibid 238–40.   [66] See text accompanying n 42.

[67] See Guzmán Brito (n 60), 184–5 (pointing to the partial abolition of slavery, the abolition of privileges of the nobility and of the primogeniture inheritance pattern for land (the *mayorazgo*), the introduction of legal capacity of the Indians, marriage between non-Catholics, intellectual property rights, the abolition of the discretionary remission of debt by the royal administration, and the right of privileged withdrawal from contracts).

[68] Ibid 263.

[69] Law of 3 November 1827 (maintaining *Alvará* of 11 September 1564 and Law of 8 April 1569) was only abolished by Decree No. 181 of 24 January 1890; see Pontes de Miranda (n 30), 95–6.

modifications on North and South Peru in 1836. In 1841 it became part of Costa Rica's first *Código General*.[70] The French *Code civil* also continued to be in force in the former French Haiti (1825). When the Spanish-speaking Dominican Republic was first annexed by Haiti, the *Code civil* was imposed upon it; the French language version was retained even after the Dominican Republic regained independence in 1844, and it was only forty years later that a Spanish translation came to be enacted.[71] As early as 1827, the Mexican State of Oaxaca had also adopted a literal translation of the *Code civil* in order to assert its autonomy within a future Mexican federation.[72]

Other examples of the more or less direct influence of French law can be found in the field of commercial law. Santa Cruz's Bolivian Commercial Code (1830) was, of course, also copied directly from the French Code of 1807.[73] In 1831, shortly after splitting from Bolívar's Federation of *Gran Colombia*, Ecuador directly enacted the Spanish Commercial Code of 1829,[74] which—despite some innovations—was largely a copy of the French Code of 1807. The Commercial Codes of Colombia and Peru (both of 1853) were also, like some others, literal copies of the Spanish Code, that is, essentially based on French law.[75] The same holds true—although to a lesser degree—for the Brazilian Commercial Code, which was enacted in 1850 on the basis of a draft elaborated in 1834 by a commission of two jurists, two merchants, and the Swedish Consul in Rio.[76] This draft was based on the French *Code commercial*, the Spanish Code of 1829, and the Portuguese Code of 1833 (which itself had been based on the first two codes mentioned).[77] Despite being considered by contemporaries as the 'most advanced legislation' of its time,[78] it is not surprising that these rather unsophisticated transplants subsequently came to be qualified as being out of date and badly adapted to the new nations' usages and requirements.[79]

---

[70] Ibid 307–24.   [71] Ibid 289–302.   [72] Ibid 304–5.

[73] Julio Olavarría Ávila, *Los Códigos de Comercio Latinoamericanos* (1961), 245–7.

[74] In fact, by a mere reference to the Spanish code in Law No. 4 of 1831; Luis Monsalve Pozo, *Derecho Mercantil Ecuatoriano* (1968), 60–1.

[75] José Gabino Pinzón, *Introducción al Derecho Comercial* (2nd edn, 1966), 33; Miguel Antonio de la Lama, *Código de Comercio* (1902), xxxvii. For one of the few, but significant, deviations of the Spanish Code of 1829 from French law, see the text accompanying n 121.

[76] Sílvio Meira, *Teixeira de Freitas: O jurisconsulto do Império* (1983), 272. See also generally W. R. Swartz, 'Codification in Latin America: The Brazilian Commercial Code of 1850', (1975) 10 *Texas International LJ* 347 ff.

[77] Dylson Doria, *Curso de Direito Comercial* (vol I, 4th edn, 1986), 24–9; Olavarría (n 73), 245–7.

[78] Candido Luiz Maria de Oliveira, *Curso de Legislação Comparada* (1903), 198.

[79] For Brazil, see Waldemar Martins Ferreira, *Tratado de Direito Comercial* (vol XIV, 1965), 3 and Olavarría (n 73), 214 (referring especially to the provisions on bankruptcy); for Colombia, see Robert C. Means, *Underdevelopment and the Development of Law: Corporations and Corporation Law in Nineteenth-Century Colombia* (1989), 151.

(b) Indigenous Attempts to Codify Civil Law and the Role of Foreign Law

It is striking that in virtually all Latin American countries the idea—propagated mostly by their politicians—of replacing the old legal institutions by modern foreign law faced stern opposition by lawyers in the field of civil law. Nevertheless the conviction prevailed that there was a need to bring order to the existing legislative mess and, once it had been consolidated, to modernize it in line with the latest international standards. In this context, the supplementary recourse to foreign law built on an inverse logic to that underlying the Portuguese *Lei da Boa Razão*: foreign law was used where it best reflected the existing law, especially where that existing law was based on Roman law. This was particularly clearly stated by Uruguay's Eduardo Acevedo (1852) and Venezuela's Julián Viso (1853):[80]

[O]ur work, with some rare exceptions, is no more than the editing in the form of a modern code of the same laws and doctrines which our tribunals use each day. If it were to come into operation tomorrow . . . nobody, except for the lawyers, would notice that our legislation had changed. It would seem to the general public as if we had never left the *Fuero Juzgo*, the *Siete Partidas*, and Roman law. [Acevedo]

In the plan of the Code there is absolutely no intention to vary the substance of the existing law, but only to bring it up to the level of the intellectual movement of the most advanced nations and to overcome the numerous divergences of some Spanish scholars on various questions of law. [Viso]

Guzmán Brito offers two clear examples for the recourse to foreign law: he shows that the formulations of Art 1135 of the Chilean *Código civil* and Art 3383 of the Argentine Code (both addressing the problem where a testator bequeaths a piece of property, but then sells or pledges it) are based upon Art 1038 of the French *Code civil*, though only because the French rule constituted the best generalized formulation (taken, in fact, from Pothier) of the respective Roman law rules (D. 32, 10, 12; 34, 4, 18 and 34, 4, 15), which were, in turn, the sources of the then still applicable Laws 6, 9, 17 and 6, 9, 40 of the *Siete Partidas*. In the same fashion, Art 1645 of the Chilean and Arts 877 and 886 of the Argentine Code (on the return of a document of indebtedness which is taken to be part of discharge), which seem to be taken from Arts 1282, 1283, and 1286 of the *Code civil*, are based on the French provisions because they best reformulated the Roman origin of Laws 5, 14, 9 and 5, 13, 40 of the *Siete Partidas*.[81]

Determining which points require codification and searching for the best solutions by systematizing the national law and analysing it in the light of foreign law require much time and effort as well as considerable legal talent. These resources

---

[80] Eduardo Acevedo, *Proyecto de un Código Civil para el Estado Oriental del Uruaguay* (1852), 12; Julián Viso as cited by Gonzalo Parra-Aranguren, 'Nuevos Antecedentes sobre la codificación civil venezolana (1810–1862)', in *La codificación de Paez: Código Civil de 1862* (vol I, 1974), xiii, liii; cf also the overview by Guzmán Brito (n 60), 258.

[81] Guzmán Brito (n 60), 264–71.

were not readily available in the new Latin American states, most of which experienced difficult periods of civil strife after gaining independence. The scarcer these resources were, the more codifiers simply tended to copy from foreign sources.

The first successful attempt at enacting an indigenous civil code was undertaken by Peru. After having been freed from Bolivian occupation by a Chilean intervention in 1839, the despised 'Bolivian codes', that is, the copies of French law imposed by Santa Cruz in 1836, were immediately abolished and a commission was formed to elaborate new codes on the basis of the existing law. The resulting draft of 1847 was enacted with some minor changes as the Peruvian *Código Civil* in 1852, which remained in force until 1936. Despite some borrowing from the French *Code civil* (as eg in the chapter on the essential requirements for the formation of a contract), the Peruvian Code of 1852 was essentially based on Spanish law and the Roman *Corpus Iuris Civilis*.[82]

This pattern of indigenous codification using comparative law as a catalyst was to characterize the Latin American civil codes much more than Napoléon's code. Three men, in particular, were to perfect this method of codification and become the most influential codifiers—and *de facto* comparative scholars—of the nineteenth century in Latin America: Chile's Andrés Bello, Brazil's Augusto Teixeira de Freitas, and—laying the foundations of a tradition of eclecticism—Argentina's Dalmacio Vélez Sarsfield.

(c) Bello and Ocampo in Chile

Andrés Bello (1781–1865) was born in Caracas as the son of a lawyer. He started to learn Latin at the age of 7 and, aged 15, began his studies at the University of Caracas, where he read philosophy and experimental physics, followed by the study of laws. Initially, under the old regime, this entailed Canon law and Roman law (which were abolished after independence and was replaced by the teaching of Natural law, national law, and civil law based on the Spanish *Instituciones* by Asso and Manuel of 1775). During his studies he was the private tutor of Simón Bolívar, who was almost of the same age. After participating in Humboldt's famous expedition and serving in public administration, he was sent to London in 1810 as part of a delegation headed by the young Bolívar. He stayed there until 1829 as an envoy of his newly created country. During this period Bello studied English law and the law of the United States, and apparently also deepened his knowledge of Roman and medieval Spanish law. He also worked as a secretary for Jeremy Bentham, despite his rejection of Bentham's utilitarianism due to his Catholic faith. In 1829 he moved to Chile, becoming a Chilean citizen a few years later. In 1830 he started teaching a general introductory course to law based on Bentham's writings, followed in 1831 by a course on Natural and international law, and in 1834 by a course on modern Roman law (reintroduced at his insistence). For the latter, in 1843 he

---

[82] Ibid 317, 338–42.

eventually published his *Instituciones de Derecho Romano*, which were based primarily on Heineccius' *Elementa juris civilis secundum ordinem Institutionum*. In that year, in which he also inaugurated the University of Chile in Santiago as its first rector, Bello (who had also become a senator) was heavily involved in the works of the parliamentary commission (1840–5) that reviewed his proposal for a Chilean Code, which the Minister of Justice had asked him to prepare in 1833.[83]

Bello's *Código Civil*, which was finally enacted in 1855 and—with some reforms—is still in force today in Chile, is the product of his broad legal, but also linguistic and literary, genius. (Bello is still highly admired for his fundamental work on Spanish grammar and his other writings and poems.) The structure of his codification is based—with few modifications—on Justinian's *Institutes*. Bello's rich annotations show the sources which he used, as far as the substance is concerned. As for the consolidation of 'national' law, his primary source was the *Siete Partidas* as glossed by Gregorio López, but he also directly relied upon the *Corpus Iuris Civilis* and, to a lesser degree, on the other sources of Spanish law, as well as the writings of Spanish scholars. For his comparative research with a view to modernizing the national law, like all other codifiers, he mainly used the *Concordance entre les Codes Civils Étrangers et le Code Napoléon* by Anthoine de Saint-Joseph, the leading French comparative work that elaborated the parallels between the provisions of the *Code civil* and the codes of Bavaria, Prussia, Austria, Sardinia, Louisiana, the Netherlands, and the Swiss Canton of Vaud, many of which were apparently also at his disposal. For doctrinal help, Bello turned primarily to the writings of many French scholars available at that time, especially the *Traités* of Pothier and the later works of Delvincourt and Rogron, but also, although to a lesser degree, to Savigny's Treatise on modern Roman law.[84] As explained above, the role of comparative law, especially French law, was rather that of a source of inspiration. Comparative law was one of Bello's tools to find the best reformulation of Roman law rules contained in the ancient Spanish law. Among the foreign influences, the French was certainly predominant;[85] however, as Guzmán Brito put it:[86]

[T]he code of Bello turned out to be a body that is substantially based on the ancient law, reformulated in the style of the modern codifications by means of a number of technical operations, and reformed, according to the precepts of legal liberalism, in the spirit of his time; for the rest, he stuck with devotion to the old Roman-Castilian institutions.

A similar, but more eclectic, approach could be found in the codification of

---

[83] See, with further references, Máximo Pacheco G., 'Don Andrés Bello y la formación del jurista', in *Andrés Bello y el Derecho Latinoamericano: Congreso Internacional Roma 10/12 diciembre 1981* (1987), 185–7; Sandro Schipani, 'Andrés Bello Romanista-Institucionalista', in ibid, 205, 232–43; M. C. Mirow, 'Borrowing Private Law in Latin America: Andrés Bello's Use of the Code Napoléon in Drafting the Chilean Civil Code', (2001) 61 *Louisiana LR* 291, 297–99.

[84] See eg Guzmán Brito (n 60), 368–73 (with further references).

[85] For more detail on the use of the *Code civil* see also Mirow, (2001) 61 *Louisiana LR* 291–329.

[86] Guzmán Brito (n 60), 373.

Chilean commercial law, prepared by José Gabriel Ocampo Dávila (1799–1882). Ocampo Dávila was an experienced and highly successful Argentinian lawyer who arrived in Chile in 1841, after fleeing Buenos Aires when the persecutions under the regime of the first Argentine *caudillo* Ortiz de Rosas (1829–52) became too threatening for him.[87] Ocampo, who also became a member of the Commission revising Bello's Civil Code (1853–5), was commissioned to codify Chile's commercial law in 1852 after previous attempts had failed. Despite following the structure of the Spanish Code of 1829, his work has been hailed as highly sophisticated and original.[88] Parting from the still governing old Spanish law and especially the *Ordenanzas de Bilbao*, Ocampo applied the same method as the draftsman of the United States Uniform Commercial Code, Karl Llewellyn, that is, he investigated contemporary commercial practices through interviews, discussions, and scholarly writings.[89] Although he created many new provisions himself where ancient Spanish law appeared to be incomplete (as, for example, with respect to the rules regarding corporations) or deficient (as in the case of the rules concerning bankruptcy),[90] Ocampo turned primarily to French law; apart from that, guided by Saint-Joseph's *Concordance entre les codes de commerce étrangers et le code de commerce français*, he also used solutions from the Codes of Portugal, the Netherlands, Hungary, Prussia, and Buenos Aires, as well as from the writings of French, Spanish, and Italian authors.[91]

(d) Teixeira de Freitas in Brazil

The biography of Augusto Teixeira de Freitas (1816–83) is strikingly different from Bello's. Born into a noble family in the province (today state) of Bahia, Freitas at the age of sixteen started to study law at the Academy of Olinda, which was one of the two universities founded in 1827 and modelled on Coimbra. In his second year he switched to the University of São Paulo, but after quarrelling with his professors and almost failing in his fourth year, he returned to the poorly equipped Olinda. Legal training focused on the interpretation of the Imperial Constitution of 1823 and the constitutional theories of the Swiss Benjamin Constant, on the *Ordenações*, the rules and definitions of Roman law, and, as part of 'the study of the law comparable to that of the civilized nations', the *Code civil*, for which the knowledge of French was mandatory (English became mandatory in 1853, German becoming

---

[87] For the background of Ocampo, see Armando Braun Méndez, *José Gabriel Ocampo y el Código de Comercio de Chile* (1951), 13–21.

[88] Means (n 79), 194.   [89] Braun Méndez (n 88), 26–9; Mirow (n 10), 159.

[90] Ángel Fernández Villamayor, *El régimen legal de la sociedad anónima en Chile* (1977), 20–1; Villar Laheras, 'Comentario al Mensaje del Código de Comercio', in Universidad de Chile (ed), *XVI Memorias de Licenciados: Derecho Comercial* (1951), 13, 83.

[91] Olavarría (n 73), 272. The city and province of Buenos Aires had left the Argentine Federation one year after its formation in 1852 and only rejoined, after protracted negotiations in 1861. During this time, Buenos Aires enacted a Commercial Code; see below text after n 107.

an alternative option in 1891).[92] After political quarrels in his home province of Bahia, Freitas moved to Rio de Janeiro in 1843, where he soon built a reputation as a brilliant lawyer and became the co-founder of the influential *Instituto dos Advogados Brasileiros*, the forerunner of the National Bar Association.[93]

In 1855 the Empire's Minister of Justice approached Freitas to draft a civil code. Freitas rejected the Portuguese draft Code prepared by the Viscount of Seabra (1857–9, finally enacted in 1867) as too heavily influenced by French law (one of the most controversial points being the automatic transfer of property upon the conclusion of a contract of sale[94]). Instead he proposed an approach which was similar to Bello's, although more cautious. Before attempting a new codification, Freitas prepared a consolidation of the existing Portuguese law: the *Consolidação*, which he finished in 1858 and which consisted of 1,332 articles. While strictly keeping to the content of national law (which he described as incomplete and poor), he restructured it, faithful to the tradition of the Portuguese *Lei da Boa Razão*:[95]

[H]e went to search for the foundations of his systematization of the law in the profound analysis of the nature of legal relations contained in the works of recent German Romanists, and presented them with the help of Hugo, Heineccius, Savigny, Mackeldey, Ortolan. In presenting the character of this work he does not pretend to absolute originality to which he could not aspire; but without ceasing to be traditional, he gave his thoughts a serious sense of modernity; he gathered from the Roman jurisprudence, restored in Germany, not what could be found in its primitive form but in its modern substance; and, without any revolutionary spirit, he managed to bring about a transformation which gave a modern meaning to the legislation.

A result of this quest for a new structure was the extraction of rules that govern all specific provisions in a general part, a structure that was kept by the later Brazilian Civil Codes of 1916 and 2002, and which Brazilian law shares with the German Civil Code of 1900.[96]

[92] Meira (n 76), 44; Valladão (n 37), 312–13.

[93] See eg Meira (n 76), 39–87; Rodrigo Octávio, 'La codification du droit civil au Brésil : Teixeira de Freitas et l'unité du droit privé', (1930) 29 *Revue trimestrielle de droit civil* 727–50.

[94] See Art 1549 of the Portuguese Civil Code of 1867 (based on Art 1583 of the *Code civil*), retained in Arts 408 and 874 of the new Code of 1966 (which is otherwise primarily influenced by the German *BGB*); see António dos Santos Justo, 'O direito brasileiro: Raízes históricas', (2002) 20 *Revista Brasileira de Direito Comparado* 131, 142, 151–2.

[95] Enrique Martínez Paz, *Freitas y su influencia sobre el Código Civil argentino* (1927), 35, cited by Octávio, (1930) 29 *Revue trimestrielle de droit civil* 738–9.

[96] It has been suggested, *inter alia*, by Meira (n 76), 455 ff that the draftsmen of the German Civil Code may have been inspired by Freitas' structure—a not very convincing theory, in view of the fact that the use of a general part for civil law codifications was already widely discussed in German pandectist scholarship which, in turn, had inspired Freitas; the idea had already been implemented by the draft Saxonian Civil Code of 1852; see Mathias Schmoeckel, 'Vor § 1—Der Allgemeine Teil in der Ordnung des BGB', in Mathias Schmoeckel, Joachim Rückert, and Reinhard Zimmermann (eds), *Historisch-kritischer Kommentar zum BGB* (vol I, 2003), 123, 146 ff.

The imperial government officially approved the *Consolidação* in 1858; and even though it lacked any legal force, it was enthusiastically embraced by courts and lawyers as a clear and structured body of rules with complete references to its sources.[97] Freitas was immediately commissioned to elaborate a draft civil code, but he opted for yet another intermediary step: the elaboration of a 'sketch', the *Esboço*, which was to be published in parts as soon as these were finished in order to allow a public discussion before submitting a draft to Parliament. In 1860 Freitas published the general part (on persons, objects and (legal) facts), in 1861 the beginning of the social part: the second book (on rights in general) and sections 1 and 2 of the third book (on personal rights in general and in family relations), and only in 1865 its massive section 3 (on personal rights in civil relations, ie the law of obligations). The fourth book (on real rights) was finished in 1866, but the fifth book (on provisions common to real and personal rights, ie succession and prescription) remained incomplete. There are numerous reasons for this; in particular, he was annoyed by the French influenced Commercial Code of 1850 (which already contained many provisions on general civil matters) and decided in 1867 that a codification of civil law without the integration of commercial law would not make sense. (He was apparently unaware of a similar proposal of the Italian Montanelli from 1847.)[98] The government refused to change its approach and assured him that it was very pleased with the parts of the *Esboço* that had already been published. Freitas replied in great detail that he was not pleased at all, and—possibly already affected by his subsequent serious mental illness—abandoned his work after having already drafted almost 5,000 articles.

For the elaboration of the *Esboço*, Freitas also consulted the foreign codes available through Saint-Joseph's *Concordances*. For doctrinal guidance, for his structure and for the reformulation of many concepts, Freitas relied fundamentally on the works of Savigny. Furthermore he considered 'all the literature that was *en vogue* in the mid nineteenth century', ie the leading German, French, and Belgian works on civil law.[99] Nevertheless, his work remained genuinely indigenous, a perfection of the law inherited from Portugal, to such a degree that the Brazilian Civil Code of 1916, which relied largely on Freitas' *Esboço*, is held to have preserved the legal tradition of Portugal, based on Roman law, much more than the Portuguese codes.[100]

[97] See eg Octávio, (1930) 29 *Revue trimestrielle de droit civil* 739–40.

[98] Ibid 746, referring to the position of Giovanni Montanelli, *Introduzione filosofica allo studio del diritto commerciale positive* (1847) in chapters XIII and XIV. Teixeira de Freitas had already insisted on the necessity of abolishing the existing codes of commercial law and civil procedure in his initial acceptance to draft the *Consolidação* of 10 July 1854; letter reproduced by Meira (n 76), 92.

[99] Meira (n 76), 351.

[100] Guilherme Braga da Cruz, 'A formação histórica do moderno direito privado português e brasileiro (1)', (1955) 50 *Revista da Faculdade de* 32, 69; Justo, (2002) 20 *Revista Brasileira de Direito Comparado* 150–3.

(e) Vélez Sarsfield, Acevedo, and Narvaja in Argentina and Uruguay

The interplay between commercial law and civil law was more fortunate in Argentina and Uruguay, where the difficulties under Rosas's dictatorship had paralysed all efforts at codification. After Rosas's fall in 1852, the cooperation between the Uruguayan Eduardo Acevedo and the Argentinian Dalmacio Vélez Sarsfield pushed comparative law even closer to the centre of codification efforts due to their high degree of eclecticism.

Dalmacio Vélez Sarsfield (1800–75) was born in Córdoba (Argentina), where he studied at the *Colegio de Montserrat* and the University of Córdoba, from which he graduated in 1820. Both institutions had also been attended, first two years earlier, by José Gabriel Ocampo, the later codifier of Chilean commercial law, which suggests that the two knew each other. Vélez's studies probably included works on Roman law by Cujas, Vinnius, and Heineccius, as well as the French *Code civil* and the *Cours de droit civil français* by Aubry and Rau (based on the German work of Zachariae).[101] Once admitted to the bar in Buenos Aires in 1823, he had his first experiences of drafting legislation as a young deputy to the Constituent Congress of 1824 and also taught political economy at the University of Buenos Aires. Having being persecuted during Rosas's dictatorship and after a period of exile in Montevideo, Vélez engaged in national politics in Buenos Aires after Rosas was overthrown in 1852. In 1853 he was named as a member of a commission for the elaboration of a civil code, which, however, never started work due to Buenos Aires' splitting from the Confederation.[102] His misfortune ended in 1856 when he joined the efforts of the Uruguayan Eduardo Acevedo in drafting a commercial code.

Acevedo (1815–65) had worked as a young lawyer in Ocampo's law firm in Buenos Aires between 1836 and 1839.[103] Back in Uruguay, Acevedo had pursued his private project of producing a draft civil code for his country, which he finished sometime between 1848 and 1851. He had abandoned his original idea of merely translating and adapting the French *Code civil* for fear of being reproached with wanting to transplant 'exotic' foreign legislation which was out of tune with the local realities. Instead, he followed the approach of the Peruvian and Chilean projects, that is, he based his draft primarily on the governing law inherited from Spain.[104] It is interesting to note that Acevedo nevertheless relied significantly on the works of the French writers Domat, Pothier, Toullier, Merlin, and Troplong, but confessed that he avoided citing them in order 'to give everything a national character, taking away the foreign appearance which would be criticized. This

---

[101] Ricardo Levene, *Manual de historia del derecho argentino* (5th edn, 1985), 427–33; Mirow (n 10), 138.

[102] Guzmán Brito (n 60), 444–5.

[103] Guzmán Brito (n 60), 460 n 1130; Levene (n 102), 447–8; Mirow (n 10), 158.

[104] See the text cited at n 81.

reached such a level that whenever an article had been suggested to us by Toullier, we would justify it with an opinion of [the Spanish] Sala or Acevedo'.[105] Despite becoming a bill in the Uruguayan Parliament in 1853, Acevedo's draft was never adopted, apparently due to lack of political support. An initiative to enact his draft for the Argentine province of Buenos Aires in 1856 was also unsuccessful for the same reason.[106]

The alliance between the ambitious Vélez and Acevedo proved more successful. Their privately drafted commercial code was adopted by the Province of Buenos Aires in 1859 and in 1862, after the reintegration of Buenos Aires into the Confederation, also for all of Argentina. This was many years before a civil code was adopted. This commercial code was primarily based on Acevedo's draft civil code for Uruguay, the *Ordenanzas de Bilbao*, the Brazilian Commercial Code (itself based on the French, Spanish, and Portuguese codes) and the Dutch Code, but also the Code of Württemberg (for the bills of exchange provisions), combined with the drafters' knowledge of local experience and commercial practice.[107] Nevertheless, this Code, which was also enacted in Uruguay in 1865, followed the fate of most other commercial codes of the time: it soon became outdated due to the rapid development of trade. Thus, it was amended in 1889; the general civil law provisions were removed and other rules were introduced which had been partly copied not only from Italian and Portuguese law, but also from German and English legislation.[108] The Code, and its clumsy amendment, have been blamed for the serious commercial crisis which occurred at the end of the century, when a wave of poorly handled bankruptcies shook the country.[109]

Vélez's next project was to prove a greater success. In 1864 he was finally officially commissioned to draft a civil code for Argentina. Following the tradition of Florencio García Goyena's Spanish draft Civil Code of 1851 (which was based heavily on the French *Code civil* and annotated according to Saint-Joseph's *Concordances*),[110] and also Freitas's method (with whom Vélez was in close contact),[111] Vélez was requested by the government to justify each draft provision with annotations concerning their conformity with, or divergence from, the existing law and 'the civil codes of the leading nations of the world'.[112]

---

[105] Guzmán Brito (n 60), 462.   [106] Ibid.

[107] Guillermo Sánchez Sorondo, 'Introduction', in George Wilson-Rae and Bernardo de Speluzzi (eds and trans), *Argentine Republic: Code of Commerce* (1904), vii–viii; Salvador Perrota, 'Introducción al Estudio de las Fuentes del Código de Comercio de 1862', in *Libro del Centenario del Código de Comercio* (1966), 95, 132, and 143 (qualifying the provisions for corporations as original legislation 'fortified by foreign concepts').

[108] Report of the Commission, cited by Carlos R. S. Alconada Arambrurú, *Código de Comercio Anotado* (vol I, 1954), xlvi, lxxi, lxxvi, lxxiii.

[109] Sánchez Sorondo (n 108), ix–x; Borchard (n 45), 77–8.

[110] See Florencio García Goyena, *Concordancias, Motivos y Comentarios del Código Civil Español* (1852, reprinted 1974).

[111] Meira (n 76), 267–345.   [112] Guzmán Brito (n 60), 453 n 1110.

The final count of the different sources was as follows: roughly 1,200 provisions from Freitas's *Esboço*, 800 directly from the Roman *Corpus Iuris Civilis*, 700 provisions from the French textbook of Aubry and Rau (based on Zachariae), 300 from the Spanish draft of García Goyena, 170 (or maybe 300) from the Chilean Code, 145 directly from the French *Code civil* (although almost half of the content of Vélez's code is indirectly reflected in the Argentinian Code as they are based on the same Roman law foundations), 70 from Zachariae's (German) work on French law, 52 from Demolombe's commentary to the French *Code civil*, 52 from the Code of Louisiana, 50 from Troplong's (French) treatises on contracts and succession, 27 from the Uruguayan draft Civil Code of Acevedo, 13 from the Russian Code, 11 from the writings of the Belgian author Molitor on possession and servitudes, and 4 from the statutes of the State of New York. The number of provisions inspired by the French Pothier, Mercadé, and Duranton, by the French translations of Savigny's treatises on modern Roman law and the law of obligations, and by the Italian Code of 1865 has not been ascertained.[113] Rejecting the structure of Justinian's *Institutiones* and of the French *Code civil*, Vélez followed the structure of Freitas's *Consolidação*, yet dissolved its general part. Thus the structure of his code was as follows: I. Persons (legal and natural persons, family); II. Personal rights in civil relations (creation and extinction of obligations, general theory of legal facts and legal acts, general theory of contracts, specific contracts); III. Real rights (property and possession); IV. Provisions common to personal and real rights (succession, rights of creditors, prescription). The final code, a massive work of 4,051 articles, was approved *en bloc* by Congress in 1869 and entered into force in 1871.[114]

Despite the works of Acevedo, Uruguay finally received its civil code from an Argentinian, Tristán Narvaja Dávila, who was a relative of Ocampo. Supported by Ocampo, through whom he probably got to know Bello, Narvaja spent eight years in Chile between 1845 and 1853, that is during which time Bello finalized his draft Civil Code. After moving to Montevideo, and apparently inspired by the Chilean efforts, he started a private attempt at drafting a civil code based on Acevedo's draft. This was finally enacted by the Uruguayan dictator Flores in 1868. It has been calculated that about one-third of that code is based on the Chilean model, one-fifth on the Spanish draft of García Goyena (which was itself based on the French Code), and one-sixth on Acevedo's draft, while the drafts of Freitas and Vélez had only little influence as they were considered to be too lengthy and complicated.[115]

---

[113] cf Guzmán Brito (n 60), 451–2, relying on Lisandro Segovia, 'Introduction', in *idem* (ed), *El Código Civil de la República Argentina* (1881), xix–xxiv; also Karst and Rosenn (n 54), 46; Mirow (n 10), 130–40; Ignacio Winizky, 'Le droit comparé en Argentine durant les cent dernières années', in Ancel (n 37), 301, 305.

[114] Guzmán Brito (n 60), 448–50.   [115] Ibid 463–6 (with further references).

(f) Further Developments between Mimicry and Wild Eclecticism

The Chilean codes were to prove to be the most influential models of codification in Latin America. Bello's and Ocampo's codes were adopted by Ecuador, Colombia, and Venezuela (where Julián Viso had dropped his own project in favour of Bello's code in 1861), as well as by the Central American states of El Salvador, Nicaragua, and Honduras.[116] Guatemala also adopted Chile's Commercial Code, but preferred in 1877 to copy Peru's Civil Code of 1852, apparently for political reasons.[117] Argentina's Civil Code was enacted in Paraguay in 1876 after the country had lost its war against the Triple Alliance of Argentina, Brazil, and Uruguay, and with it much of its territory and four-fifths of its male population.[118]

A striking example of the adoption of foreign codes is Venezuela. It had adopted the Chilean Civil Code under the regime of General Páez in 1862. Along with most legislation of that regime, the Code was revoked in 1863 after the dictator's fall, leading to the return to ancient Spanish law. After fruitless efforts at drafting a new code, a commission of experts was given forty days in 1867 to present a new proposal. This eventually resulted in the plain copying of the Spanish draft of García Goyena (1851). In 1873 this second Civil Code was itself dropped in favour of a modestly amended copy of the Italian *Codice Civile* of 1865, which was itself largely an imitation of the French *Code civil*.[119]

Colombia provides another example of an unsophisticated transplant.[120] In 1853 it had copied the Spanish Commercial Code of 1829, and with it—unconsciously—its ground-breaking innovation: the freedom of incorporation subject only to registration, which, at that stage, was recognized only by Spain and England. The Colombian draftsmen, however, were not aware that in 1848, after a severe crash that had followed the early founders' boom, Spain had revoked the freedom of incorporation and had returned to the previous system that required government authorization for incorporation. Colombian entrepreneurs, on the other hand, were not very aware of the possibilities that incorporation offered and continued to operate as unlimited partnerships rather than seeking the protection of limited liability that the law now offered, with the result that neither a founders' boom nor a crash occurred. Nevertheless, Colombia abandoned free incorporation—again unconsciously—in 1887: the Commercial Code of Panama (at that time a state of the Colombian Federation) of 1867, which was essentially based on Ocampo's code of 1852 for Chile, was enacted for all of Colombia as it was considered to constitute the state of the art. Once again, the Colombian draftsmen had ignored the fact that, a few months after the enactment of Panama's code, in

---

[116] For the civil codes, see Guzmán Brito (n 60), 374 ff; for the commercial codes, see Olavarría (n 73), 299 ff.

[117] Guzmán Brito (n 60), 348.   [118] Ibid 455–7.   [119] Ibid 414–18, 428–9.

[120] See Katharina Pistor, Yoram Keinan, Jan Kleinheisterkamp, and Marc D. West, 'Evolution of Corporate Law', (2002) 23 *University of Pennsylvania Journal of International Economic Law* 791, 806–8, 842–7.

1867, France had followed England in accepting free incorporation, as had Spain in 1869, Germany in 1870, and Delaware in the United States in 1883. A year later the Colombian draftsmen became aware of their ignorance and abolished the requirement of two presidential decrees of incorporation,[121] but left untouched the remaining provisions, which were structured around a principle of strict government surveillance.

Other countries, such as Costa Rica (1886), eventually opted to try to develop their own code.[122] These generally followed the highly eclectic method adopted by Vélez Sarsfield, yet rarely with as much sophistication. An unfortunate example of unsophisticated eclectic copying is the Civil Code of Nicaragua of 1907, which is said to have taken 878 articles from the Argentine Code, 811 from the Mexican, 609 from the Chilean, 373 from the Costa Rican, 329 from the Spanish, 254 from the Portuguese, 181 from the Italian, 116 from the Guatemalan, and 51 from the Uruguayan Code. It is hardly surprising that this code suffered from a serious lack of coherence and from irremediable contradictions.[123]

(g) Bevilaqua and Comparative Law in Brazil

However, there has been at least one other highlight of successful codification: the Brazilian Civil Code of 1916, which entered into force on 1 January 1917. After numerous attempts to produce a draft civil code on the basis of Freitas's *Esboço*, the task was finally entrusted in 1899 to Clovis Bevilaqua (1859–1944).[124] He was an academic and the first professor of comparative law at the University of Recife (an offspring of the Academy of Olinda).[125] Coinciding with the tradition of the *Lei da Boa Razão* and Teixeira de Freitas, Bevilaqua had a strong affinity for German pandectist jurisprudence, as he was part of the *Escola de Recife*, a modernist and republican movement that opposed the traditional orientation towards French culture and that emphasized the study of German literature, philosophy, and legal doctrine (especially the works of Rudolf von Jhering). It was the chapter on the method of comparative law in Bevilaqua's book summarizing his lectures on comparative legislation of 1893 (2nd edition, 1897) that first introduced to Brazil (at least in theory) the modern concept of comparative law, which—inspired by psychology, ethnology, anthropology, and sociology—went beyond the mere

---

[121] Art 17 of Law 27 of 1888; Means (n 79), 267.

[122] On the Costa Rican Code of 1886 see Thilo Scholl, *Die Rezeption des kontinental-europäischen Privatrechts in Lateinamerika am Beispiel der allgemeinen Vertragslehren in Costa Rica* (1999); Guzmán Brito (n 60), 467–9.

[123] Guzmán Brito (n 60), 469–71, relying on Carlos Morales, Joaquín Cuadra Zavala, and Mariano Argüello, 'Cómputo general de los orígenes de los artículos de este Código Civil y del Reglamento del Registro Público', in *idem, Código Civil de la República de Nicaragua* (vol II, 3rd edn, 1931).

[124] For the history of the different drafts see Borchard (n 45), 240–4.

[125] On Clovis Bevilaqua, see Rodrigo Octávio, 'La codification du Droit civil au Brésil: Clovis Bevilaqua et la codification du Droit civil', (1930) 29 *Revue trimestrielle de droit civil* 1011, 1024 ff.

comparison of statutes and sought to identify the underlying reasons for commonalities and differences.[126]

Bevilaqua produced his draft civil code in eight months; it was based both on the existing drafts, especially Freitas's *Esboço*, and also on his own comparative experience. What followed were four years of intensive parliamentary and academic discussions, which were equally dominated by comparative arguments.[127] After having been massively reformulated in terms of drafting and linguistic style (but not as regards substance) by Senator Ruy Barbosa, the eminent mastermind of the Brazilian Constitution of 1891 and another pupil of the *Escola de Recife*, the first Brazilian Civil Code was finally approved in 1916 and remained in force between 1917 and 2002. Strangely enough, the German *BGB*, which was promulgated in 1896, did not have much impact on the content of the Brazilian Code.[128] (Bevilaqua apparently only possessed a French translation by Raoul de la Grasserie.)[129] Nevertheless, the structure of both codes is very similar due to extent to which Freitas was influenced by German pandectist doctrine. The Brazilian Code of 1916 had 1807 articles, and it was divided into a general part containing three books on persons, goods, and legal facts, and a specific part containing four books on family law, real rights, obligations, and succession. An introductory law regulated the Code's applicability. Following Freitas's tradition, the Brazilian Code was predominantly an indigenous product: more than a third of its provisions are based on the pre-existing law, and another third are new provisions of original Brazilian pedigree, taken mainly from Freitas's *Esboço*. Accordingly, only about one-quarter of its provisions are based on exogenous sources, the most influential of which was the French *Code civil*. Again, as shown by Pontes de Miranda, French law was resorted to 'less for its own sake than for the modern formulation which it gave to Roman law'.[130]

---

[126] Bevilaqua (n 30), 19–29.

[127] For details of many of the comparative arguments, see the Report of the Baron of Loreto on secured transactions in *Projeto do Código Civil Brasileiro: Trabalhos da Commissão Especial da Câmara de Deputados* (vol I, 1902), 13 ff, where every provision of the draft is placed in the comparative context of a host of foreign codes (including the Japanese Code of 1896) and commented upon, mainly on the basis of French writings.

[128] Pontes de Miranda (n 30), 108; the Report of the Baron of Loreto (n 127), 14 also complains about the failure to consider the German *BGB*.

[129] Bevilaqua (n 30), ii–iii and *idem, Código Civil dos Estados Unidos do Brasil* (vol I, 1926) (where he refers to the *Code civil allemand, publié par le Comité de législation comparé*); the Report of the Baron of Loreto (n 127), merely mentions the French translation of de la Grasserie.

[130] Ibid 119–20.

3. Summary of the Development in the First Century of Independence

The creation of the new Latin American states and the development of their young legal systems was marked from the beginning by the influence of comparative law. In constitutional matters the quest for new models led to the law of the United States exerting considerable influence. In commercial and civil matters, initially the most important model was French law; however subsequently new models were developed, based mainly on the pre-existing law, which was corrected and complemented by references to modern foreign law. Roman law and its *usus modernus* was originally the most important source for the indigenous codifications. However, the trend towards an increasing eclecticism for justifying the solutions proposed the basis for a new approach to comparative law in Latin America: the focus slowly shifted from the search for the best available modern reformulation of Roman law towards a direct interest in the foreign legislative solutions on their own merits. Apart from being a source for legislative reform, comparative law was a highly practical discipline, as underlined by Clovis Bevilaqua in 1897 (who was still alluding to the *Lei da Boa Razão*):[131]

Ultimately, the judge cannot limit himself to the knowledge of his own law, because in many cases he will have to study conscientiously the foreign sources which have inspired the legislator, in order to understand the provisions of his own law . . .; because in many other cases the gaps and deficiencies of the law of his country can be remedied by recourse to suitable provisions of the laws of the civilized nations; and in yet other cases because he will find himself obliged to apply the foreign law as a result of the commands of the principles of conflict of laws.

IV. FROM THE TWENTIETH CENTURY TO THE PRESENT DAY

1. The Growing Influence of the Common Law

While the codifications created more or less stable frameworks for civil law, by the end of the nineteenth century commerce and commercial law were evolving at a much faster pace. As already mentioned, the commercial codes quickly became outdated and required urgent amendment. At that point the Anglo-Saxon impact

---

[131] Bevilaqua (n 30), 26–7; also Oliveira (n 78), 30.

became significant as a result of England's, and later the United States', domination of international trade in Latin America.

In commercial law the great role has been played by international commercial usages, as the real living law—what civilians call international corporative law—not by the bare text of a statute. Insurance policies, sales contracts, charter parties, bills of lading, warehouse receipts, corporation by-laws, letter of credit and other bank documents and usages of all kinds have tended to follow British or [United States] American models. This practical incorporation has been facilitated by the historical fact that our law itself had its roots in the general law merchant of the European continent. But our law has found its way also into express legislation. Argentina even adopted the English word 'warrant' in its law on warehouse receipts, as it did 'debentures.' Maritime mortgages arose in England, spread to the Continent and thence to South America. Stoppage in transit of common law origin has been recognized in Brazil, Chile and elsewhere. The Argentine law of cheques was intended to be based on the English law, and the Costa Rican Bills of Exchange Act was modelled on Chalmers' codification.[132]

It is not surprising that the United States' growing economic interest in Latin America (evidenced, for example, by Theodore Roosevelt's capture of the Panama Canal in 1903, or the sharp rise of United States investments in Latin America in the first third of the twentieth century) started to have an impact on Latin American legislation. The leading example is the reform of the banking sector in Guatemala, Colombia, Chile, Ecuador, Bolivia, and Peru between 1919 and 1934, which was promoted by a United States mission headed by Edwin W. Kemmerer, Professor at Princeton. As well as establishing central banks and banking surveillance along the lines of the United States model, these reforms led to the adoption of provisions on negotiable titles that were modelled on the United States Uniform Negotiable Instruments Law. The literal (although deficiently translated) copy of United States law in Colombia proved to be 'a striking example of how not to legislate' and was apparently completely ignored by Colombia's banking sector.[133] The Chilean experience was more positive, as Kemmerer's proposals only served as a source of inspiration for indigenous reforms of the Commercial Code.[134] Upon Kemmerer's recommendations, banks in Colombia, Peru, Chile, and Bolivia were authorized to open trust departments (*comisiones de confianza*). This sign of the recognition of the express trust of the common law caused much excitement among lawyers in the United States.[135] Before the trust was adopted in Argentina, Colombia, Ecuador, Mexico, Peru, Uruguay, and Venezuela,[136] its introduction into a civil law jurisdiction had been spearheaded by Panama in 1924, which modelled

---

[132] Eder, (1949–50) 4 *Miami Law Quarterly* 438–9.
[133] Eder, (1949–50) 4 *Miami Law Quarterly* 439; Olavarría (n 73), 304, 309–11 n 40.
[134] Olavarría (n 73), 279–80, 295 n 54.   [135] Eder, (1949–50) 4 *Miami Law Quarterly* 438.
[136] For an overview see Maurizio Lupoi, *Trusts: A Comparative Study* (2000). For the new Uruguayan Law 17703 of 27 October 2003 (Fideicomiso. Certificados de Depósito y Warrants. Régimen) see its justification of 20 November 2002 at <http://www.parlamento.gub.uy/repartidos/camara/D2003091413–00.htm> (accessed 13 January 2006).

its corporate law on that of Arizona and Florida.[137] The result is that 'Panama . . . has become a haven for corporations—thousands have been organized there, owned by foreigners, especially Americans, to the profit of the country and its bar'.[138] That conclusion might today, with hindsight, have been formulated less enthusiastically.

The liberalization of Chile's economy under Pinochet's regime and the influence of the 'Chicago boys' introduced more important changes originating in the United States; these affected, *inter alia*, the legislation on corporations and securities. The experiences of many other Latin American countries are similar.[139] In 1981 Chile—at least indirectly inspired by United States' legislation—abandoned its traditional concept of governmental supervision of corporations in favour of a system relying on individual court actions being brought by shareholders in case of mismanagement. It further introduced concepts such as the distinction between open and closed corporations, or shares without par value.[140]

Another interesting example of legislation inspired by common law ideas is the Brazilian adoption of legislation allowing various types of class actions.[141] Based on studies of the class action, as recognized in the United States, and its compatibility with the civil law system by Italian scholars in the 1970s (among them Professor Mauro Cappelletti, who is highly esteemed especially among Latin American jurists), a group of prestigious Brazilian jurists elaborated a proposal to adopt the possibility of group actions for pursuing public interests. The law was passed by the Brazilian parliament in 1985 and has subsequently been extended and applied to a variety of situations in which collective interests are affected.[142] Brazilian courts and lawyers have quickly accepted the new instrument, which has, however, developed independently of the North American model, and thus quite differently.[143] About 95 per cent of all group actions are initiated by the *Ministério Público*, official prosecutors who act in the public interest;[144] and in most cases, such as those related to local taxes and increases in bus fares, defendants are public bodies. But there have also been some actions against private enterprises relating to misleading advertisements, environmental damage, defective products, and

[137] Phanor J. Eder, 'Common and Civil Law Concepts in the Western Hemisphere', in *A Symposium on the Law of Latin America* (1959), 1, 4.

[138] Ibid.

[139] For Mexico's securities regulations law of 1953, see Mirow (n 10), 169; for Brazil's Capital Market Law of 1965 and its effects, see Rosenn, 'Teaching Latin-American Law', (1971) 19 *AJCL* 692, 693–4.

[140] Law 18045 (*Ley de Mercado de Valores*) and Law 18046 (*Ley de Sociedades Anónimas*), both of 21 October 1981; see Álvaro Puelma Accorsi, *Sociedades: Sociedad Anónima* (vol II, 1996), 397–8.

[141] Law 7347 of 24 July 1985 (*Lei da Acão Civil Publica*).

[142] António Gidi, 'Class Actions in Brazil: A Model for Civil Law Countries', (2003) 51 *AJCL* 311, 323–30.

[143] See Gidi, (2003) 51 *AJCL* 311, 404 n 296: 'American law, and particularly American civil procedure, is virtually unknown in Brazil. Even though the class action debate began in Brazil as early as 1977, the first studies of class action that used American sources were published only in the 1990s.'

[144] Author unknown, 'Ação Civil Pública completa 20 anos', (2005) (May/June) *RT Informa* 4–5.

consumer matters; and there have been a few, albeit rather rudimentary, mass tort claims.[145] One of its advocates views the Brazilian *ação civil pública* as a 'responsible transplant' and promotes it as a model for all civil law countries, especially the other Ibero-American countries:[146]

Adapted to the civil-law tradition and the peculiarities of local culture and needs, the Brazilian class action legislation is a unique regulation addressing standing to sue, types of group rights, *res judicata, lis pendens*, and several other important aspects. The Brazilian experience demonstrates that civil law systems can employ a class suit procedure but cannot transplant the American class action model into their systems without substantial adaptation.[147]

It is interesting to note that in Argentina an attempt by a representative of the public interest (*Defensoría del Pueblo*) to bundle mass claims of a large number of aggrieved parties who had suffered damages due to the interruption of electricity by the privatized provider has been rejected by the court. After a detailed analysis of the system of class actions in the United States, the court concluded that, in the absence of a specific legal basis, the existing provisions on *Defensoría*'s powers could not interpreted as allowing a collective action.[148]

2. A Battlefield for Influence: The Unification of Law

The general shift 'from Europe to America'[149] has accelerated since the end of World War II. Many young Latin American jurists now prefer LL M courses in the United States over French or German doctorates.[150] The change was also supported by the efforts of the short-lived 'law and development' movement in the 1960s, which sought to implement the rule of law in Latin America by means of legal education.[151] This change of emphasis must be seen in the larger context of 'Pan-Americanism', the United States' answer to the French concept of *l'Amérique latine*, by means of which France had tried to invoke a common linguistic and cultural

---

[145] Gidi, (2003) 51 *AJCL* 332–3.

[146] See Ada Pellegrini Grinover, Kazou Watanabe, and Antonio Gidi, 'Anteproyecto de Código Modelo de Procesos Colectivos para Iberoamérica', (2004) 5 *Revista Iberoamericana de Derecho Procesal* 13.

[147] Gidi, (2003) 51 *AJCL* 314.

[148] Cámara Nacional de Apelaciones en lo Civil y Comercial Federal, 14 March 2000, Case No. 539/99, *Defensoría del Pueblo de la Ciudad de Buenos Aires c/ EDESUR SA s/ responsabilidad por daños*, available at <http://www.csjn.gov.ar/jurisp/principal.htm> (accessed 13 January 2006).

[149] Mirow (n 10), 167–70.

[150] See generally Yves Dezalay and Bryant Garth, *The Internationalization of Palace Wars: Lawyers, Economists, and the Contest to Transform Latin American States* (2002).

[151] For a critical evaluation, see James Gardner, *Legal Imperialism: American Lawyers and Foreign Aid in Latin America* (1980); for a denial of the alleged legal imperialist intentions, see John H. Merryman, 'Law and Development Memoirs I: The Chile Law Program', (2000) 48 *AJCL* 481 ff.

heritage during its military intervention in Mexico in 1864–6. Pan-Americanism is a child of the Monroe Doctrine, which was first formulated in 1823, that is, the claim by the United States to be entitled to exclude European interference in the Americas. French hegemony and legal influence eventually gave way to US American predominance, contrary to what a Francophile author still hoped in 1954:[152]

It would be erroneous, however, to draw pessimistic conclusions as to the destiny of French law in Latin America. The existence of French law on this part of the American continent is not jeopardized by an invasion of common law concepts. . . . It even seems probable to me that if one day a real Latin American law should be born out of the diversity found currently in these countries, it would have to be a system based on French law.

(a) Pan-Americanism versus Ibero-Americanism

At the First Pan-American Conference in Washington in 1889–90, the United States proposed, *inter alia*, the adoption of uniform systems of weights and measures, protection of intellectual and industrial property rights, common rules on imports and exports, and an American customs union similar to the German *Zollverein* of 1834, which helped to pave the way towards the unification of Germany in 1871.[153] This resulted in the creation of the Commercial Bureau of the American Republics, which became the Pan-American Union in 1910 and had the task of promoting the commercial and cultural links between the countries of the Americas, *inter alia*, through the elaboration of conventions, that is, the unification of laws.[154] Despite considerable activities and a large budget, this institution, which became the Organization of American States (OAS) in 1948, has always been confronted with Latin-American suspicions concerning the interests of the *Yanquis*, as they were bitterly formulated by the Peruvian writer and diplomat García Calderón in 1917:[155] 'Pan-Americanism, by the end of the last century, is a delusive synonym for arrogance, for the association of nations brought about by force, [as a result of which] the peoples of the tropics obey the orders of Washington and work for the benefit of a distant dictator . . .'.

The rejection of the growing influence of the United States gave rise to a competing model of legal unification, grounded in the Ibero-Americanism movement. It invoked the old dream of a reunification of law, especially private law, in Latin America on the basis of the historical legal unity which had existed under the Spanish and Portuguese reign and under the auspices of Roman law. It is in this context that the vision of using comparative law as a tool for the unification of law,

---

[152] Imre Zajtay, 'Les destinées du *Code civil*', (1954) 6 *Revue Internationale de Droit Comparé* 792, 802.

[153] Emílio Miñana y Villagrasa, *La unificación del derecho mercantile Hispano-Americano: Bases para una legislación común* (1925), 111–12.

[154] For these efforts, see the collection of texts by the Carnegie Endowment for International Peace (ed), *Conferencias Internacionales Americanas 1889–1936* (1938).

[155] Francisco García Calderón, cited by Miñana (n 153), 110.

as formulated by Raymond Saleilles at the International Congress on Comparative Law of Paris in 1900,[156] was extended to Latin America, as in the highly polemical proposal of the Spanish professor Emílio Miñana y Villagrasa for *The Unification of the Hispano-American Commercial Law* in 1925.[157] The Ibero-American spirit of legal unification can still be found today in a small number of specifically Ibero-American congresses and institutes, such as the influential *Instituto Iberoamericano de Derecho Procesal*, which currently promotes the Brazilian version of class actions in the form of an 'Ibero-American Model Code'.[158]

(b) Unification of Home-Grown and Transplanted Law: CIDIP

The adherents of the Pan-American ideal have also recognized comparative law as a central tool for the unification of law.[159] However, their perspective is often quite different. Rather than searching for a common core as the basis for unification, the focus has been on the quest for new solutions adapted to the new social reality. This has entailed the the rejection of traditional sources, such as, in particular, Roman law.[160] Comparative studies, therefore, also became relevant for finding the means of transplanting new, and often foreign, concepts into the existing, often outdated legal structures. The degree of sensitivity to the compatibility of the old native and the new foreign concepts with each other has varied significantly, and has often depended on the economic interest lying behind the proposed innovations. Examples of this kind of influence can be found in the activities of the OAS's Inter-American Specialized Conferences on Private International Law which have taken place since 1975 and are mostly known under the Spanish abbreviation CIDIP. The CIDIP was originally intended to merge the efforts of the Lima Conference of 1877 (the first international conference in this field), the Treaties of Montevideo 1889 and 1939–40, and the Bustamante Code, which was signed in Havana in 1929, in the light of the American Law Institute's Restatement of the Law of Conflict of Laws (1934/71).[161] Beginning in 1975, the CIDIP focused for some time on the enforceability of foreign titles, judgments, and awards, as well as on the

[156] Raymond Saleilles, 'Conception et objet de la science du droit comparé', (1900) XXIX *Bulletin de la Société de législation comparé* 383, 397.

[157] Emílio Miñana y Villagrasa, *La Unificación del Derecho Mercantil Hispano-Americano* (1925), 322–6.

[158] See n 146.

[159] See International Commission of Jurists (of the Pan-American Union), 'Projects Concerning Permanent Technical Organs—Resolution Concerning the Unification of Legislation', (1928) 22 *American Journal of International Law* (Supplement: Codification of International Law) 328–9.

[160] See especially the preface written by Antonio Sánchez de Bustamante (the Cuban draftsman of the *Código Bustamante* of 1928, an important treaty establishing uniform rules in the field of private international law) to Francesco Consentini, *Código Civil Pan-Americano* (1929), v–vii.

[161] See generally Alejandro Garro, 'Unification and Harmonization of Private Law in Latin America', (1992) 40 *AJCL* 584, 593–604; Jürgen Samtleben, 'Neue interamerikanische Konventionen zum Internationalen Privatrecht', (1992) 56 *RabelsZ* 1–115; Diego P. Fernández Arroyo, *La codificación del Derecho Internacional Privado en América Latina* (1994).

conflict of laws. While most initiatives regarding classical questions of family law or status have Latin American origins (frequently duplicating the efforts of the Hague Conference on Private International Law), initiatives in commercial matters were typically proposed by the United States. One example is the Panama Convention of 1975 on the recognition of foreign arbitral awards, which was proposed as a regional solution in order to overcome the rejection of the New York Convention of 1958 by most Latin American countries.[162]

The latest CIDIP VI, held in Washington in 2002, brought about a new dimension:[163] the harmonization of substantive law through model laws, making the CIDIP the vehicle for the preparation of a uniform legal framework for the functioning of the Free Trade Area of the Americas (FTAA), the negotiations for which had been formally launched in 1998.[164] The first Inter-American model law has been yet another effort of 'selling' a common law-based concept to the Latin American partners. Based on the conviction that a transplanted version of Art 9 Uniform Commercial Code (UCC) may be able to reproduce its success story of stimulating economic growth by providing more flexible and cheaper credit, the United States had proposed an Inter-American Model Law on Secured Transactions that would allow the creation of a security interest without the actual possession of the collateral. This proposal faced much resistance from the Latin American countries as it was conceived as being incompatible with the Roman law basis of their legal systems. Furthermore, the proposal's significant strengthening of creditors' rights gave rise to much suspicion about the interests at work. Nevertheless, because Mexico had already partly accepted a similar reform under the influence of its partners in NAFTA,[165] and in view of a complete re-writing and 'latinization' of the draft by the Uruguayan *rapporteur* Ronald Herbert the night before the final session, the Model Law was finally adopted—yet with the general implicit understanding that, in any case, 'no Latin American parliament would enact such a solution'.[166] However, it remains to be seen whether the Latin American countries

---

[162] For details, see Jan Kleinheisterkamp, *International Commercial Arbitration in Latin America: Regulation and Practice in the MERCOSUR and the Associated Countries* (2005), 18–28.

[163] For details, see Diego P. Fernández Arroyo and Jan Kleinheisterkamp, 'The VIth Inter-American Specialized Conference on Private International Law (CIDIP VI): A New Step Towards Inter-American Legal Integration', (2002) IV *Yearbook of Private International Law* 237–55.

[164] The plan for the FTAA has its origin in the US Government's 'Enterprise for the Americas' of 1990, (1990) *International Legal Materials* 1567. For the FTAA see <http://www.ftaa-alca.org>.

[165] See John Wilson Molina, 'Secured Financing in Latin America: Current Law and the Model Inter-American Law on Secured Transactions', (2000) 33 *Uniform Commercial Code Journal* 46, 63–5; Mario de la Madrid Andrade, 'La prenda sin transmisión de posesión: Estudio comparativo con la Ley modelo interamericana de garantías mobiliarias', (2001) 9 *Revista Mexicana de Derecho Internacional Privado* 11 ff; Lionél Pereznieto Castro, 'Comentarios al 'Proyecto México-Estadounidense para una Ley Modelo en Materias de Garantías Mobiliarias', (2001) 10 *Revista Mexicana de Derecho Internacional Privado* 66 ff.

[166] Remark made to the author, who was the observer for the Federal Republic of Germany at the CIDIP VI, by a number of Latin American delegates.

will be able to ignore this model, which they have officially endorsed, in any future negotiations with the IMF, the World Bank, or the Inter-American Bank of Development for the raising of finance. These institutions, too, have already played a role in bringing about important legislative changes as is evidenced, for example, by the adoption of new laws on arbitration in Bolivia and Paraguay on the basis of the UNCITRAL-Model Law on International Commercial Arbitration.[167] It can only be hoped that Latin American countries will listen to the warnings formulated in this respect:[168]

The practical field for uniformity is very limited. It is restricted to private international law and to a few phases of commercial law, such as bills of exchange, overseas sales and the like. In many branches of the law, attempted unification would do more harm than good. The law should be adapted to the specific conditions and customs of each people. It is these countries that are creating their own law that are making the greatest progress in the field of law. Copying foreign legislation may well be highly disastrous.

(c) The Role of 'Sub'-Regional Integration: MERCOSUR and the Andean Community

A certain counterbalance to the United States dominated Pan-Americanism can be found in 'sub'-regional projects of integration: the Common Market of the South (MERCOSUR) between Argentina, Brazil, Paraguay, Uruguay, and now also Venezuela[169] and the Andean Community (CAN) which includes Bolivia, Colombia, Ecuador, Peru, and Venezuela[170] (which are—together with Chile—also associated with the MERCOSUR). Both of these alliances were founded under the institutional umbrella of the (otherwise insignificant) Latin American Association of Integration (ALADI).[171] Both projects aim at the formation of a true common market, such as the one established by the European Union, that is, economic and social integration flanked by legal integration. To date, however, the degree of legal integration is still far from being comparable to that of the European model.

Some significant efforts have been undertaken by the MERCOSUR states in the field of international civil procedure (recognition of foreign decisions, cooperation and jurisdictional assistance, international arbitration).[172] But because the

---

[167] Kleinheisterkamp (n 162), 7, 10, 190.

[168] Phanor J. Eder, 'Common and Civil Law Concepts in the Western Hemisphere', in The Washington Foreign Law Society (ed), *A Symposium on the Law of Latin America* (1959), 1 (referring to the Colombian example cited at n 133).

[169] See <http://www.mercosur.org.uy>.

[170] See <http://www.comunidadandina.org>. The term 'sub'-regional integration is widely used with regard to CAN and MERCOSUR in contrast to ALADI which comprises the entire region (of Latin America).

[171] See <http://www.aladi.org>.

[172] See Jürgen Samtleben, 'Das Internationale Prozeß- und Privatrecht des MERCOSUR—Ein Überblick', (1999) *RabelsZ* 1–63; *idem*, 'Die Entwicklung des Internationalen Privat- und Prozessrechts im MERCOSUR', (2005) *Praxis des Internationalen Privat- und Verfahrensrechts* 376–83.

legislative process is still dominated by political rather than legal issues, preparatory comparative studies have apparently rarely played a significant role. Attempts
at a harmonization of the laws on consumer protection, based on the Santa Maria
Protocol of 1996 on jurisdiction in consumer matters (which was never ratified by
any of the four signatory states), failed due to fundamentally different national
conceptions in this area; Brazil, in particular, refused any harmonization, for fear
that it would lower its existing standard of protection.[173] Interestingly, however,
Brazilian judges turned, *inter alia*, to the definition given by the failed Protocol
when interpreting the term 'consumer' in the Brazilian *Código de Defesa do
Consumidor*.[174]

In the absence of an institution comparable to the European Court of Justice,
another key role that comparative law may be expected to play in the context of
South American unification and harmonization of laws is that of guaranteeing the
uniform interpretation and application of the 'community law' in all member
states of the MERCOSUR.[175] The recent publication by the Secretariat of the
MERCOSUR on the application of the law of the MERCOSUR by national courts
shows that this necessity is finally being recognized.[176]

3. Developments Determining, and Determined by, Comparative Law

The significant growth in the influence of US American law since the beginning of
the twentieth century is just one of the facets of the development of comparative
law in Latin America. Today the picture is far from being as homogeneous or linear
as it may have appeared in the mid-nineteenth century. A number of highly particular aspects have to be taken into consideration in order to understand the
crucial role of comparative law for Latin American law.

(a) The High Degree of Eclecticism

The high degree of eclecticism, already mentioned above, is certainly the most
striking feature of the recourse to foreign law, both by draftsmen of legislation and

---

[173] See Claudia Lima Marques, 'Direitos do consumidor no MERCOSUL: Algumas sugestões frente
ao impasse', (1999-III) *Jurisprudencia Argentina* 912 ff = (1999) 32 *Revista de Direito do Consumidor*
16 ff.

[174] *Tribunal de Justiça de Santa Catarina* (3ª *Câmara de Direito Comercial*), 26 June 2003, AC
2002.022015–4/So; and 11 September 2003, AC 2003.001897–2/Bl; cited by Secretaría del MERCOSUR
et al (eds), *Primer informe sobre la aplicación del derecho del MERCOSUR por los tribunales nacionales*
(*2003*) (2005), 82–3.

[175] For details, see Jan Kleinheisterkamp, 'Legal Certainty in the MERCOSUR: The Uniform Interpretation of Community Law', (2000) 6 *NAFTA: Law and Business Review of the Americas* 5, 29–34.

[176] See Secretaría del MERCOSUR (n 174).

scholars. Its extent often depends on the intellectual and educational background of those who resort to comparative law. One example of this is the Peruvian Civil Code of 1984. Like the Bolivian Code of 1976 and the Paraguayan Code of 1985, its general source of inspiration was the Italian *Codice civile* of 1942 (a model that was generally popular in Latin America, particularly as a result of its language being easily accessible).[177] The chapter on agency (*mandato*) was drafted on the basis of a careful study of the concept's historical origins, the confusion between *mandat* and *représentation légale* in French law and its transplants, as well as the subsequent clarification by Windscheid and Laband; essentially it follows the models of Italian and Portuguese law.[178] The chapter on the general provisions on contracts, on the other hand, is primarily based on Italian law, but also adopted provisions from various European codes (Germany, the Netherlands, Portugal, and Switzerland), and Latin American codes (Bolivia, Cuba, Mexico, and Portugal), as well as those of the Philippines, Lebanon, and Ethiopia.[179] The chapter on unjustified enrichment (*enriquecimiento sin causa*), which switched from a system of restitution to a system of compensation of damages (*indemnización*),[180] is commented upon laconically in the *Exposición de Motivos*:[181]

In comparative law, unjustified enrichment is regulated by Articles 812 to 822 of the German Civil Code, Articles 703 ff. of the Japanese Civil Code, Articles 2041 and 2042 of the Italian Civil Code, Articles 62 to 67 of the Swiss Federal Code of Obligations, Articles 399 ff. of the Soviet Civil Code, Articles 179 to 183 of the Chinese Civil Code, Articles 123 to 127 of the Polish Code of Obligations, Articles 66 to 73 of the Franco-Italian Draft Code of Obligations and Contracts, Articles 1882 to 1895 of the Mexican Civil Code.

Just a few years earlier, the renowned Peruvian professor and Supreme Court judge Roberto G. MacLean had already lamented:[182]

Legislation often is drafted without the necessary studies and information. The national reality has just begun to be explored and, faced with a lack of facts and figures and ignorant of precise situations to be regulated in many cases, legislation is done 'by ear,' frequently working from the legislative models available from other countries. Recourse to comparative

---

[177]   For the development of these three codes, see Guzmán (n 60), 522–8.

[178]   Carlos Cárdenas Quirós, 'Exposición de Motivos y Comentarios: Mandato', in Delia Revoredo de Debakey (ed), *Código Civil: Exposición de Motivos y Comentarios* (vol VI, 1984), 481–520, relying on the study by Luis Díez Picazo, *La representación en derecho privado* (1979).

[179]   Max Arias Schreiber Pezet, 'Exposición de Motivos y Comentarios: Contratos en General', in Delia Reveredo Debakey (ed), *Exposición de Motivos y Comentarios* (vol VI, 1984), 10 ff.

[180]   Delia Revoredo de Debakey, 'Comentarios: Enriquecimiento sin causa', in *idem* (ed), *Código Civil: Exposición de Motivos y Comentarios* (vol VI, 1984), 775, 778; see Arts 1954 and 1955: 'Aquel que se enriquece indebidamente a expensas de otro está obligado a indemnizarlo'. 'La acción a que se refiere el artículo 1954 no es procedente cuando la persona que ha sufrido el perjuicio puede ejercitar otra acción para obtener la respectiva indemnización.'

[181]   Debakey (n 180), 775–8.

[182]   Roberto G. MacLean, 'Judicial Reasoning and Social Reality in Peru', (1980) 28 *AJCL* 489, 490.

law as an aid to the legislator, if made injudiciously, carries with it the danger of causing a serious distortion of the juridical function. Laws are a reflection of the conflicting interests existing in a society and its duty is to neutralize them and put them in equilibrium. For this reason, when a law is transplanted from one country to another, it may be then in the new country the law does not satisfactorily resolve the conflicts between interests, simply because the conflicts are distinct. In such cases, they remain at least partially up in the air and without resolution.

Some—but certainly not all—academic studies also seriously suffer from a wild eclecticism which lacks reflection. An extreme example for this is a recent Colombian publication on unjustified enrichment, which—besides citing a host of Roman, Spanish, French, Italian, English, and German authors—develops the analysis of forty-eight national laws, but spends only five pages on the law of Colombia.[183] This phenomenon has also been observed by Kenneth L. Karst and Keith S. Rosenn:[184]

Student theses tend to be in the scissors and paste tradition—back-to-back quotations from German, French, Italian, and Spanish authors. The law of the author's own jurisdiction may receive little attention, and rarely is there an attempt to appraise a particular legal rule against the background of the Latin-American socio-economic scene.

(b) The Authority and Challenges of Comparative Law

The degree of authority of foreign law is certainly a striking feature of Latin American law in general, and of Brazilian law in particular. An example of the heritage of the *Lei da Boa Razão*, that is, the overriding authority of foreign law where positive national law does not provide satisfactory solutions, can be found in the Brazilian law of delict. The Brazilian Civil Code of 1916 had not adopted the solution of Teixeira de Freitas's *Esboço* of 1865 that accepted a special responsibility of the owner for his belongings.[185] Rather, the spirit of individualism led Bevilaqua to tie extra-contractual liability to the strict necessity of fault, with only limited exceptions for owners of animals or houses, and the *actio de effusis vel deiectis*, thus adopting a much more restrictive regime than the original French *Code civil*.[186] Between 1896 and 1930 the French courts further developed the system of liability on the basis of the general wording of Art 1384 al 1 *Code civil* by accepting the *responsabilité du fait de chose*, that is, liability for things 'which one has under one's

---

[183] Jorge Fabrega Ponce, *El enriquecimiento sin causa* (vol I, 1996) (apparently after having visited the Max Planck Institute's library in Hamburg).

[184] Karst and Rosenn (n 54), 67. See also already Augusto Teixeira de Freitas, *Consolidação das Leis Civis* (1st edn, 1858, 3rd edn, 1896), xxxii: 'All of this resulted in our jurists loading their works with foreign materials, going far beyond the mere filling of gaps. Matters have gone so far that our own law is hardly known and studied on the basis of our own statutes . . .'.

[185] Silvio de Salvo Venosa, *Direito Civil* (vol IV, 4th edn, 2004), 92.

[186] Compare Arts 159, 1518, 1521, 1523, 1527–29 of the Brazilian Civil Code of 1916 to Arts 1382–6 (esp 1384) of the French Civil Code.

control', irrespective of fault.[187] This very extensive concept of liability, in sharp contrast to the concept of the Brazilian Civil Code of 1916, soon caught the attention of a Brazilian scholar, who held in 1944:[188] 'If the French Civil Code has accepted this solution, there can be no doubt that it is also adequate for our law, since it was inspired by the former as regards the general framework and the details of delictual liability'. After having been originally rejected by the courts, the *teoria do risco* was ultimately accepted about ten years later, in cases of car accidents and defective machines, on the model of the French solution.[189] Based on that case law, the *teoria do risco* also came to be incorporated into the new Civil Code of 2002.[190]

The phenomenon of citing foreign legal doctrine when interpreting legal provisions that are fundamentally different from those to which the foreign doctrine refers is not rare. Another example of this is the monumental and highly influential *Tratado de Direito Privado*, a treatise in sixty volumes by Francisco Pontes de Miranda,[191] who, as a pupil of the *Escola de Recife*, had developed close ties to Germany. In this work Miranda cites almost every available German publication on any topic treated in his work, often regardless of whether the Brazilian solution coincides with the German one or not. It is in this light that one has to understand the somewhat exaggerated assertion by René David (who had lived for some time in Brazil) that every law has to be studied according to its own methods:[192]

In Brazil, scholarly writings, both foreign and national, seem to play a prominent role: French, Italian, Portuguese, Spanish and Argentine authors are constantly cited and commented upon by the judges in their decisions. Whoever studies a question of Brazilian law has to take this into account and should not pretend to resolve that question by considering only the Brazilian laws, court decisions and scholarly opinions.

The *grand connaisseur* of Latin American law, Phanor J. Eder, identifies two particular difficulties with this approach. For one, there is a constant danger of distortion with the resulting possibility of creating obstacles to the development of the national law; furthermore, there is a gulf between the sophisticated approach of the elite and the much poorer local practice:[193]

---

[187] The landmark decision was *Cour de Cassation*, Ch réunies, 13 February 1930, D. 1930, I, 57; for an overview of the case law, see Philippe Malaurie, Laurent Aynès, and Philippe Stoffel-Munck, *Les obligations* (2003), 88–90.

[188] José de Aguiar Dias, *Da Responsabilidade Civil* (vol II, 1944).

[189] *Tribunal de Justiça Rio Grande*, 9 December 1955, Ap 10872, (1957) 170 *Revista Forense* 300; *Supremo Tribunal Federal*, 4 August 1955, RE 27857, (1957) 2 *Revista Trimestral de Jurisprudência* 264, 266 (in a case of concurring contractual and extra-contractual liability); and especially *Tribunal de Justiça da Guanabara*, 19 May 1964, Ap civ 34314, (1966) 365 *Revista dos Tribunais* 285, 286.

[190] *Código Civil* (2002), Art 927 *Parágrafo único*.

[191] Francisco C. Pontes de Miranda, *Tratado de Direito Privado* (vols I–LX, 1954–69).

[192] René David, *Traité élémentaire de Droit civil comparé* (1st edn, 1950), 243. David, incidentally, forgot to mention the German legal writing.

[193] Phanor J. Eder, 'Law and Justice in Latin America', in *Law: A Century of Progress 1835–1935* (1937), 39, 63–4.

In the dearth of published reports of the courts, and in view of the fact that the codes are in such large part of foreign origin, the Latin American lawyer is compelled to resort to comparative law. Nowhere else does comparative law become of such practical value. Nearly every treatise of note is a comparative study, and the contribution of Latin American law to the field of jurisprudence is of high merit. The shelves of prosperous lawyers are filled with foreign books. In the bookstores one is apt to find a more extensive stock of French books and of translations into Spanish from all Continental languages than of national law books. The lower and intermediate courts, on the other hand, are rarely, if ever, supplied with adequate libraries, and the judges are too poorly paid to buy books. Except for a few enlightened and well-educated judges, court decisions are not directly influenced by foreign law to the extent one may expect. They turn, rather, on a refined, generally casuistic, and narrow interpretation of articles of the codes and statutes, which does not help the evolution or the growth of the law. It is to the universities, not the courts, that one looks for progress. Practical conditions and business requirements are rarely taken into account.

The difficulties associated with the comparative approach also led the abolition of the principle of nationality by Brazil, a traditional country of immigration, in its rules on conflict of laws in favour of the principle of residence (which has always been the standard of its neighbours Argentina and Uruguay):[194] 'What is incomprehensible is the massive application, especially by judges in rural areas, who are poorly paid and incapable of having perfect knowledge, of the laws of Syria, Japan, Germany, etc.'.

The other aspect mentioned by Eder may be a key to understanding the large role of comparative law in Latin America: the exclusivity of knowledge of, and access to, foreign and presumably better developed law has been a crucial factor for building and securing the positions of the local elites. Yves Dezalay and Bryant G. Garth have demonstrated how the new generations of young Latin American lawyers (and economists) that invested in their legal training in the United States since World War II have managed to enjoy important careers back home, whereas the older elites with their traditional orientation towards Continental Europe could not always keep up with the changes of the internationalized and US dominated economy, not to mention those who had no means of internationalizing their professional portfolio.[195] Individual legal and linguistic capacities have been important determinants for the development of comparative law and of Latin American law as such. The struggle for influence in Argentine administrative law between the traditional French and the more recent US American approach provides a good example. The former school of thought is represented by Juan Carlos Cassagne, professor at the *Universidad de Buenos Aires*, who speaks French as a foreign language and has close contacts with France and Spain; the latter is headed by Hector Mairal, the holder of the other chair of administrative law at the same university,

---

[194] Press conference of the Brazilian Minister of Justice Campos in July 1939, (1939) 79 *Revista Forense* 355, 360–1.

[195] Dezalay and Garth (n 150).

who speaks both French and English, holds a masters in Comparative Law from the United States, and has been a visiting professor at Harvard and Cambridge.[196] This aspect of individual capacities, but also that of the diversification of foreign sources and the role of the authority of comparative arguments is illustrated by a snapshot of the role of comparative law in two Latin American Supreme Courts whose constitutional traditions have their roots in US American constitutional law.

(c) Comparative Law in Action: The Supreme Courts of Argentina and Brazil

As noted above in the discussion of nineteenth-century constitutional law, the Argentine *Corte Suprema* readily turned to constitutional doctrine and case law from the United States to interpret its own Constitution, and still regularly does so today wherever it seems appropriate.[197] US law, however, is no longer the only persuasive authority from abroad. One example is a sensitive case in 1998 in which the brother of a victim of the military regime, who had disappeared in 1976, sued for access to government sources of information. The opinions delivered by most of the judges contained numerous references to, and sometimes even detailed analyses of, not only international treaties and soft law on the matter, but also foreign developments on the question of *habeas data*, such as in Colombian, Brazilian, and German constitutional law, in addition to that of the United States.[198] On the question of whether somebody condemned *in absentia* could be extradited, the judges also, apart from US law, referred in some detail to English, Italian, French, and German law, as well as to the case law of the European Court of Human Rights.[199] In general, it is interesting to note that comparative arguments are also often found in dissenting opinions,[200] and that they are regularly invoked by the same judges.

---

[196] Jonathan M. Miller, 'A Typology of Legal Transplants: Using Sociology, Legal History and Argentine Examples to Explain the Transplant Process', (2003) 51 *AJCL* 839, 878–9.

[197] For the most recent examples, see Corte Suprema de Justicia de la Nación, 5 April 2005, A.126.XXXVI, *Angel Estrada y Cía. S.A. c/ resol. 71/96—Sec. Ener. y Puertos* para 13 (on the admissibility of attribution jurisdiction to adjudicate to government agencies in administrative matters); 5 April 2005, G.2181.XXXIX, *Galli, Hugo Gabriel y otro c/ PEN s/ amparo sobre ley 25.561*, opinion of Judges Zaffaroni and Lorenzetti para 10 (on the support of the Constitutional Court for the monetary sovereignty of the Congress).

[198] Corte Suprema de Justicia de la Nación, 15 October 1998, U.14.XXXIII, *Urteaga, Facundo Raúl c/ Estado Nacional—Estado Mayor Conjunto de las FF.AA.—s/ amparo ley 16.986* para 13, but especially the opinion of Judge Petracchi paras 10–11.

[199] Corte Suprema de Justicia de la Nación, 5 November 1996, N.1.XXXI, *Nardelli, Pietro Antonio s/ extradición*, opinion of the Judges Fayt, Petracchi, and Bossert paras 21–9.

[200] For some recent examples, see Corte Suprema de Justicia de la Nación, 8, March 2005, A.869.XXXVII, *Arancibia Clavel, Enrique Lautaro s/homicidio y asociación ilícita*, dissenting opinions of Judge Petracchi, paras 7, 17, Judge Belluscio paras 15–16, Judge Fayt paras 15, 18 (relying on case law of the European Court of Human Rights and on German case law and legal authors for the principle of due process in criminal proceedings); 30 March 2004, R.663.XXXVII, *Roviralta, Huberto c/ Editorial Tres Puntos S.A. s/ daños y perjuicios*, dissenting opinion of Judge Fayt paras 7–9 (referring to US law and to the case law of the Constitutional Court of Spain concerning the right to privacy).

A look at some recent cases of the Brazilian *Supremo Tribunal Federal* shows a very similar but even more complex picture. While references to foreign sources sometimes serve as mere 'decoration' of the judge's opinion,[201] serious comparative arguments are quite frequent.[202] Recourse to US constitutional case law can be found in some sensitive decisions by Judge Celso de Mello (who went to high school in the United States) and the recently appointed Judge Joaquim Barbosa (who wrote his doctorate in France and has been a visiting professor at the University of California, Los Angeles and Columbia Law School);[203] these decisions, *inter alia*, concern the limitations of a foreign state's immunity,[204] the limitations of the jurisdiction of martial courts,[205] or abortion in case of anencephaly.[206] It is, however, another recently appointed judge who has been particularly conspicuous for bringing insights from comparative law to bear upon the decisions of the Court: Judge Gilmar Mendes (who had studied for an LL M and written his doctorate on comparative constitutional law in Germany).[207] A number of his opinions in fundamental cases contain elaborate comparative arguments. On the question whether the declaration of unconstitutionality of a law operates only *ex tunc*, he relied not only on constitutional doctrine and case law from the United States, but also Austrian, German, Spanish, and Portuguese law, as well as the case law of the European Court of Human Rights.[208] In a case on whether pensions of public servants may be privileged in terms of taxation he referred mainly to German, but also to French and Italian, constitutional law. In other cases, his

---

[201] See eg the opinion of Judge Grau in STF, 18 August 2004, ADI 3105, on the question whether pensions of public servants may be privileged as regards taxation, citing Ulpianus, Alexy (a German professor of legal theory), Kelsen, Aristotle and Plato; available at <http://www.stf.gov.br/jurisprudencia/jurisp.asp> (accessed 13 January 2006).

[202] For the fiercest battle, so far, of comparative arguments see STF, 17 September 2003, HC 82424 (the entire judgment is 488 pages long), where the judges had to decide whether the publication of a book denying the Holocaust and describing the German people as the real victims of World War II has to be qualified as an 'act of racism' which, according to Art 5 No. XLII of the Brazilian Constitution, is a crime that is not subject to any statutory time-limitation; French, Spanish, Portuguese, German, English, and US law were used to defend both the extensive and the restrictive interpretation of the Constitution.

[203] For the judges' backgrounds, see <http://www.stf.gov.br/institucional/galeria/> (accessed 13 January 2006).

[204] Supremo Tribunal Federal, 20 June 1995, AgRg 139671, opinion of Judge de Mello, 12–13 (invoking the Foreign Sovereign Immunities Act of 1976 against the defence of immunity of the US Embassy against a claim by a former employee).

[205] Supremo Tribunal Federal, 18 June 2002, HC 81963, opinion of Judge de Mello, 9–13 (reproducing large parts of the 'valuable historic precedent' *ex parte Milligan* of 1866 to argue that the mere injury to a serviceman cannot give rise to martial jurisdiction in times of peace).

[206] Supremo Tribunal Federal, 4 March 2004, HC 84025, opinion of Judge Barbosa, 17–19 (relying, *inter alia*, on citations from the leading US case *Roe v Wade* of 1973); for the parallel case in Argentina see Corte Suprema de Justicia de la Nación, 11 January 2001 (n 197).

[207] Furthermore, he is fluent in English, French, and German, and received a decoration from the German President in 1982, ie before he took his doctorate in Germany, see n 204.

[208] Supremo Tribunal Federal, 9 June 2004, AC 189, opinion of Judge Mendes, 3–8.

comparative arguments have been limited to German constitutional doctrine.[209] But also in the field of private law, Mendes's recourse to comparative law has had some impact. An example is a decision according to which the invalidity of labour contracts has no retroactive effect. This was based on the German doctrine of *faktisches Arbeitsverhältnis*, with additional support being derived from French, Mexican, and Italian law.[210]

V. FINAL REMARK

The almost paradoxical and Janus-faced character of comparative law is probably inevitable as it is part of the highly complex legal tradition and culture of Latin America.[211] In respect of Latin America, one may certainly not end a summary of the past one hundred years of modern comparative law with the conclusion that 'its influence on legal practice, at least outside the legislation of Western states [of the "First World"], has been rather marginal'.[212] Although often not directly visible, the influence of comparative law in Latin America has been—and still is— pervasive, sometimes almost excessively so.

The result of this mixture is a mosaic of highly diverse legal systems which, even if located in the circle of the 'civil law' family, show a special coloration with its own and particular characteristics. It is thus not surprising that Latin America has been qualified as 'a comparatist's dream'. The fact that much Latin-American legislation has foreign origins explains why comparative law is of paramount practical importance. The Latin-American lawyer is obliged to turn to comparative law. Accordingly, comparative studies are so familiar to Latin-American lawyers that they are often not even noticed.[213]

---

[209] Supremo Tribunal Federal, 23 October 2003, Rcl 2363, opinion of Judge Mendes, 4–10 (citing from his own book).

[210] Supremo Tribunal Federal, 30 November 2004, AI 476950, opinion of Judge Mendes, 3–12.

[211] Eder (n 193), 42–3: 'How can we reconcile and understand the curious combination of an outward respect for legal formalities and rituals, evidencing a real reverence for law, and a complete disregard of the substance and essence of parts of the written law?'; cited by Karst and Rosenn (n 54), 58.

[212] Ralf Michaels in his otherwise brilliant essay 'Im Westen nichts Neues: 100 Jahre Pariser Kongreß für Rechtsvergleichung—Gedanken anläßlich einer Jubiläumskonferenz in New Orleans', (2002) 66 *RabelsZ* 97, 112.

[213] Eugenio Hernández-Bretón, 'Sueño o pesadilla de un comparatista: el derecho en Suramérica', (1998) 109 *Revista de la Facultad de Ciencias Jurídicas y Políticas* 33, 35 (the expression 'South-America' has been replaced by 'Latin-America'); the quotation 'a comparatist's dream' refers to Rosenn, (1971) 19 *AJCL* 692.

BIBLIOGRAPHY

Phanor J. Eder, 'Law and Justice in Latin America', in *Law—A Century of Progress 1835–1935* (1937), 39 ff

Phanor J. Eder, *A Comparative Survey of Anglo-American and Latin-American Law* (1950)

Julio Olavarría Ávila, *Los Códigos de Comercio Latinoamericanos* (1961)

Kenneth L. Karst and Keith S. Rosenn, *Law and Development in Latin America: A Case Book* (1975)

Alejandro Garro, 'Unification and Harmonization of Private Law in Latin America', (1992) 40 *AJCL* 584 ff

John H. Merryman, David S. Clark, and John O. Haley, *The Civil Law Tradition: Europe, Latin America, and East Asia* (1994)

Alejandro Guzmán Brito, *La Codificación Civil en Iberoamérica—Siglos XIX y XX* (2000)

Yves Dezalay and Bryant G. Garth, *The Internationalization of Palace Wars* (2002)

Matthew C. Mirow, *Latin American Law—A History of Private Law and Institutions in Spanish America* (2004)

PART II

APPROACHES TO COMPARATIVE LAW

CHAPTER 9

COMPARATIVE LAW AND COMPARATIVE KNOWLEDGE

NILS JANSEN

Münster *

* For very helpful stylistic advice I wish to express my thanks to Tony Weir, Trinity College, Cambridge.

I. INTRODUCTION

COMPARATIVE law may be seen as a special legal subject within the broader field of the comparative disciplines which explore the similarities and dissimilarities of different cultural or social phenomena. Such research always consists of two 'steps', which should be clearly distinguished in analysis. The comparatist must first understand and describe the foreign phenomenon before proceeding to formulate a system of similarities and differences which can serve as a basis for further analysis. Only at this second stage does comparison come into play: it is— alongside the analysis of transfers or 'transplants'—one of the two main methods of international and intercultural research.[1]

For a long time, comparative lawyers have regarded it as their methodological problem to be gaining knowledge of another system and understand its way of reasoning: in applying concepts, rules or precedents, and, more basically, in knowing the relevant sources of knowledge. Here, the well-known epistemological problems of comparative law arise: it may be difficult to understand a foreign legal system, because legal rules and legal texts are typically deeply rooted within a specific economic, political, moral, and cultural background, which can often only be explained from a historical perspective.[2] Thus, the comparative lawyer, as some have put it, must be 'culturally fluent' in another legal language.[3] This is necessary not only for understanding foreign norms and legal texts, but also for identifying

---

[1] cf Hartmut Kaelble, 'Die interdisziplinären Debatten über Vergleich und Transfer', in Jürgen Schriewer and Hartmut Kaelble (eds), *Vergleich und Transfer: Komparatistik in den Sozial-, Geschichts- und Kulturwissenschaften* (2003), 469, 471 ff.

[2] William Ewald, 'Comparative Jurisprudence (I): What Was it Like to Try a Rat', (1995) 143 *University of Pennsylvania LR* 1889 ff, 1945 ff; Vivian Grosswald Curran, 'Cultural Immersion, Difference and Categories in U.S. Comparative Law', (1998) 46 *AJCL* 43, 49, 90 ff; for an illuminating historical overview and critique, see James Q. Whitman, 'The neo-Romantic turn', in Pierre Legrand and Roderick Munday (eds), *Comparative Legal Studies: Traditions and Transitions* (2003), 312, 315 ff, 329 ff.

[3] Mitchel de S.-O.-l'E. Lasser, 'The Question of Understanding', in Legrand and Munday (n 2), 154 ff; Pierre Legrand, *Fragments on Law-as-Culture* (1999), 4 ff and *passim*.

parallel rules or parts of the law.[4] What is more, even if a foreign proposition is perfectly understood, it may prove difficult to translate it into one's own language.[5] This is especially the case with law, which constitutes a partly autonomous reality created by the norms, doctrine, and concepts of a legal system[6] that do not necessarily find exact counterparts in another.

The second step in comparing different systems is commonly regarded as a minor problem in comparison with the first step, which requires the comparatist to understand and describe the foreign law. While it is true that comparative lawyers insist that their subject cannot be reduced to a mere description of other legal systems (*Auslandsrechtskunde*), and while it is also true that comparative law is sometimes seen more as a method than a special field of knowledge,[7] and that it is even occasionally emphasized that comparative law shares its method with other comparative disciplines, such as comparative linguistics, comparative religion, or comparative social studies,[8] none the less, comparatists are commonly engaged in contrasting different systems rather than genuinely comparing them. The question of what comparison really means has until recently[9] never been seriously asked, let alone answered.[10] Thus, both 'traditional' mainstream comparative lawyers and 'modern' interpretative approaches to comparative legal studies normally treat comparison pragmatically, without any solid theoretical basis. On the one hand, interpretative approaches are typically more interested in the foreign law as such than in comparison.[11] Even where it is argued that comparison should look at 'differences' instead of 'similarities', it is apparently assumed that the meaning of such concepts is obvious and causes no methodological problem. Is it not the case that all knowledge is based on comparison and that for lawyers, used to drawing analogies, comparison is a familiar way of thinking? On the other hand, traditional comparative lawyers, mainly interested in discovering which legal system fulfils certain legal demands most smoothly, take it for granted that these demands are instrumental in nature. The law, as we have been told by Jhering, the

---

[4] cf Konrad Zweigert and Hein Kötz, *An Introduction to Comparative Law* (trans Tony Weir, 3rd edn, 1996), 35 ff.

[5] Pierre Legrand, 'How to compare now', (1996) 16 *Legal Studies* 232, 234 f.

[6] Herbert L. A. Hart, *Definition and Theory in Jurisprudence* (1953), 5 ff; Nils Jansen, ' "Tief ist der Brunnen der Vergangenheit". Funktion, Methode und Ausgangspunkt historischer Fragestellungen in der Privatrechtsdogmatik', (2005) 27 *Zeitschrift für Neuere Rechtsgeschichte* 202, 213 ff.

[7] Léontin-Jean Constantinesco, *Rechtsvergleichung*, vol II: *Die rechtsvergleichende Methode* (1972).

[8] Erich Rothacker, 'Die vergleichende Methode in den Geisteswissenschaften', (1957) 60 *Zeitschrift für vergleichende Rechtswissenschaft* 13 ff; Max Rheinstein, *Einführung in die Rechtsvergleichung* (2nd edn, 1987), 16 f; Constantinesco (n 7), 30 f, 70 ff, 111 f.

[9] Hiriam Chodosh, 'Comparing Comparisons: in Search of Methodology', (1999) 84 *Iowa LR* 1025 ff.

[10] cf Legrand, (1996) 16 *Legal Studies* 234; Mathias Reimann, 'The Progress and Failure of Comparative Law in the Second Half of the Twentieth Century', (2002) 50 *AJCL* 671, 689 f. For similar observations in other disciplines, cf the contributions to Schriewer and Kaelble (n 1).

[11] cf Geoffrey Samuel, *Epistemology and Method in Law* (2003), 112 ff.

Interessenjurisprudenz, and early American realists, is a means for organizing or controlling society and social change, and for pursuing social goals. Here, as long as different legal systems face identical problems,[12] the functional approach to comparative law[13] apparently offers easy answers as to which rule is superior. All in all, comparative lawyers may assume that common sense normally suffices for satisfactory comparisons. Comparative law has even been praised for not being infected with the 'disease' of methodological reflection or even debate.[14]

It is debatable whether it is more dangerous to be knowingly ill or to be entirely ignorant of one's ailment. Today signs of comparative law's being infected by the methodological disease have become apparent, and this part of the *Handbook* is one of them.[15] In fact, the following chapters do discuss method. Whereas some authors propose alternatives to the pragmatic 'functional method', others seek to clarify or specify the ideas underlying this approach: they make the idea of what constitutes a 'better solution' to a given problem more explicit, and they discuss the presuppositions and limits of functionalism.[16] In fact, comparative law has long gone beyond simply comparing rules and outcomes as functional solutions to universal problems. Thus, comparative lawyers have always analysed legal rules and systems in their historical context,[17] reconstructing the individual functions of rules from within the individual legal system.[18] What is more, comparatists have been aware that, although it is helpful to see the law as a means of achieving social goals, it may at the same time be the outcome of a distinctive legal tradition and an expression of a specific culture or collective identity.[19] But this dimension of the law cannot be compared from a merely pragmatic point of view. Alan Watson has even argued

---

[12] Max Salomon, *Grundlegung zur Rechtsphilosophie* (2nd edn, 1925), 32 f. For a critique of such an assumption, see Nils Jansen, *Binnenmarkt, Privatrecht und europäische Identität* (2004), 67 ff; Alan Watson, *Legal Transplants* (2nd edn, 1993), 4 f; Günter Frankenberg, 'Critical Comparisons: Re-thinking Comparative Law', (1985) 26 *Harvard International LJ* 411, 435 ff.

[13] Zweigert and Kötz (n 4), 34 ff; Rheinstein (n 8), 25 ff; Otto Sandrock, *Über Sinn und Methode zivilistischer Rechtsvergleichung* (1966), 66 ff.

[14] Zweigert and Kötz (n 4), 33 f.

[15] Others are symposia on 'New Approches to Comparative Law', (1997) *Utah LR* 255, or on 'New Directions in Comparative Law', (1998) 46 *AJCL* 597 ff; further, see Merk Van Hoecke (ed), *Epistemology and Methodology of Comparative Law* (2004); Legrand and Munday (n 2).

[16] See, for very clear expositions along these lines, Michele Graziadei, 'The functionalist heritage', in Legrand and Munday (n 2), 100 ff and the contribution by Ralf Michaels to the present volume.

[17] cf Paul Koschaker, *Europa und das Römische Recht* (4th edn, 1966); John P. Dawson, *The Oracles of the Law* (1968); Reinhard Zimmermann, *The Law of Obligations: Roman Foundations of the Civilian Traditions* (paperback edn, 1996); James Gordley, *The Philosophical Origins of Modern Contract Doctrine* (1991).

[18] For the functional method in the historical work of Ludwig Mitteis and Ernst Rabel, see Reinhard Zimmermann, ' "In der Schule von Ludwig Mitteis": Ernst Rabels rechtshistorische Ursprünge', (2001) 65 *RabelsZ* 1, 35 f.

[19] For a comprehensive picture, see H. Patrick Glenn, *Legal Traditions of the World* (2nd edn, 2004).

that the law can only be understood and explained from a genuinely legal, internal perspective, which makes meaningful comparison altogether impossible.[20]

Here, the 'methodological infection' will serve not as a justification for another discussion of the different approaches to comparative legal studies, but rather for an examination of the ideas of 'comparison' and 'comparative knowledge' themselves. The focus is thus on the second step of comparison. Unfortunately, the lack of legal literature on this question will disappoint readers who expect a critical evaluation of the discipline's state of the art. Instead, comparative law will be compared to other comparative disciplines in the humanities and social sciences[21] that have addressed methodological questions of comparative research more thoroughly. Most comparative disciplines face problems similar to those of comparative law. Of course, their approaches cannot simply be transferred to legal analysis, but some of these disciplines have developed specific methods and conceptual instruments for describing similarities and dissimilarities that, it will be shown, can be useful for the comparative study of law as well. Thus, even if the lawyer is an amateur in other disciplines, a comparative analysis will also prove helpful on a methodological level. This will be explored more fully as far as historical linguistics, comparative religious studies, and comparative history are concerned.

Before drawing comparative conclusions or even inferring lessons, however, it will be necessary to present the other comparative approaches in some detail: only after an individual discipline has been analysed, can its specific relevance for comparative law become apparent. Thus, we will ask why other disciplines engage in comparative research. What is their specific epistemological interest? Which methods do they apply in order to draw comparisons, and how do these methods relate to the epistemological interest? Does comparison presuppose a scholarly neutral point of view? And how does comparison relate to theory, typology, and classification: are there special conceptual instruments for describing comparative judgments? To address such questions, however, it is probably helpful first to clarify the basic concept of 'comparison': what does it mean 'to compare' and how is this concept related to the ideas of 'similarity' and 'difference'?

---

[20] Watson (n 12), 4 ff.
[21] Chodosh, (1999) 84 *Iowa LR* 1025 ff, focuses more narrowly on political and anthropological studies of law.

II. Analysing Comparison

Comparison is the construction of relations of similarity or dissimilarity between different matters of fact. However, a statement that two persons *a* and *b* 'are similar' is hardly a meaningful proposition; such statements normally mean only that they *look* similar, that they share a certain property, or that they behave similarly. Thus, properly comparative propositions in their simplest form draw a triadic relation between two objects and a certain quality, the *tertium comparationis*. 'S *ab*T' signifies that *a* and *b* are similar with regard to T, which is a common property of *a* and *b*. The similarity of *a* and *b* is due to their sharing the property T. Likewise 'D *ab*T' states that *a* and *b* are dissimilar with regard to T: whereas *a* or *b* is T, the other is not.

1. Comparison and Classification

Comparison has often been understood as the search for either common or distinguishing properties. For a long time, the focus was on the intuition of similarity that shed light on common properties theretofore concealed. This helped not only to detect previously unknown laws of nature, but also to understand and explain metaphors or parables,[22] because, in this sense, every analogy draws on comparison. Likewise, however, the search for distinguishing properties ('distinguishing comparison') may be equally fruitful, where the focus is on the individual. Difference is essential for constructing identity, especially where the uncertain feeling of 'otherness' becomes a first step in developing a more mature personality. Thus, as we are told, a major motive for Joseph's chaste resistance to Pothipar's wife was his deep desire to define himself as different from the Egyptians,[23] and likewise historiography has often been used to construct a nation's identity by portraying its history as being different from others.[24]

Now, all this depends on having a classifying concept of comparison that is based on a common-property model of similarity and difference. Analogies are plausible in so far as they point to common features; constructions of difference emphasize distinctive characteristics. Within such a model of comparison, the

---

[22] cf Erhard Weigel, *Philosophia Mathematica, Theologia naturalis solida . . .* (Jena, 1693), 62: Isaak and Jaakob (or Israel) connected by the *tertium comparationis* 'vis (activa viz. passiva)'. Weigel (1625–99), professor in Jena, was an academic teacher of Leibniz.

[23] 'Denn nur durch Vergleichung unterscheidet man sich und erfährt, was man ist . . .': Thomas Mann, *Joseph und seine Brüder*, vol II: *Joseph in Ägypten, Sechstes Hauptstück: Die Berührte. Von Josephs Keuschheit.*

[24] Martha Howell and Walter Prevenier, *From Reliable Sources. An Introduction to Historical Methods* (2001), 9 ff; Hartmut Kaelble, *Der historische Vergleich* (1999), 70 ff.

similarity of a and b with regard to T apparently just means 'aT $\wedge$ bT': both a and b are T. Thus comparison, understood in this way, becomes a mere conceptual abstraction leading to a scheme of generic terms (the *tertia comparationis*) and species.[25] Whereas common-property similarity is the identity of certain properties, dissimilarity is based on a defining *differentia specifica*. Normally, however, comparison is supposed to entail more than simply applying pre-existing categories; it is an intellectual process and not a single mental act. Thus, comparison is meant to encompass the search for new categories for understanding relevant similarities or dissimilarities, or rethinking existing ones: classifying comparison is the process of reflecting upon and categorically applying a *tertium comparationis* in order to construct relations of similarity and dissimilarity.

2. Comparison and Qualification

Yet this classifying concept of comparison does not fully capture what is meant by judgments of similarity or dissimilarity. Assessing similarity involves more than simply allocating various things to one category. To say that two brothers are alike in being beautiful does not imply that they possess the same degree of beauty: one of them may be even more beautiful than the other. And to argue that judge-made law is of similar importance in civilian systems and in the common law is not a (wrong) statement of sameness. Thus, judgments of similarity are especially useful where the property in question can be a matter of degree. It appears strange, for example, to say that what two cars have in common is that they are both cars and therefore similar, when the similarity might be in their speed or in their colour. Similarity, rightly understood, entails the possibility of difference. It follows that the similarity of a and b with regard to a *tertium comparationis* T may be defined as a and b's sharing a common property T, although the intensity of a's being T ($I_T(a)$) may differ from that of b.[26]

This is the conceptual nucleus of the concept of 'similarity' and, thus, of every genuine qualifying comparative proposition. None the less, it does not fully capture the meaning of similarity. This becomes apparent when we consider the meaning of the corresponding concept of 'difference'. It has been explained above that a and b are different with regard to T, if T is a property only of a or of b. But a and b can likewise differ with regard to T if, while sharing that property, they do so to a different degree. This is presupposed, for example, by the use of comparative adjectives: one thing which is larger than another is different in size, although both

[25] cf Christian Wolff, 'Von den fruchtbaren Begriffen', in *idem, Gesammelte kleine philosophische Schriften*, Zweyter Theil: *Vernunftlehre* (Halle, 1737), 80 ff, § 2.

[26] **S** abT $=_{df}$ aT $\wedge$ bT $\wedge$ {**P** $I_T(a) \neq I_T(b)$}. **P** $I_T(a) \neq I_T(b)$ indicates the possibility (**P**) of $I_T(a)$ differing from $I_T(b)$.

share the property of extension. And if one of two brothers is very intelligent whereas the other is extraordinarily intelligent, it may be misleading to judge them as similar in being both very intelligent. Their different degrees of intelligence may be more important than their intelligence being above average. It follows that the first definition of similarity[26] may also be true, if a and b are justly judged to be different. Thus, similarity apparently presupposes that the intensity of T is similar for a and b; this can be formulated in an improved definition of similarity: a and b are similar with regard to T if both share that property and if a's and b's degrees of T, although different, are similar.[27]

3. Judging Similarity and Difference

Of course, this result is perplexing, and many will regard the definition as unsatisfactory. It defines 'similarity' as similarity, and in both instances the term is used in the same sense. Propositions of similarity must therefore be narrowly circular or lead to an infinite regress when trying to explain the similarity of I_T. It may be objected either that the analysis is wrong or the concept of similarity useless. For is it not obvious that the *definiens* must not be part of the *definiendum*?

Certainly the definition does not explain the meaning of 'similarity' to a person with no prior idea of this concept. But that is not its aim. Instead, clarifying the meaning of similarity and dissimilarity will improve the understanding of genuine comparative research. Here, the analysis casts new light on the often useless debates of difference and similarity, because it makes clear that propositions of similarity or difference can be objective in a strict sense only where they rely on the common-property model explained above. Outside this narrowly confined area similarity must be accompanied by corresponding dissimilarity, that is, the conceptual distance to identical properties. In these cases, it may therefore prove difficult to have a meaningful debate on whether things 'are' similar or different, for similar things are also dissimilar. Where two violinists are said to possess a similar sound, it may be difficult to perceive any differences, but it is presupposed that it is possible.

It follows that propositions of similarity express irreducibly subjective *judgments*. Whereas the layman might find our violinists similar, the professional critic will perhaps listen only for the differences. Of course, this does not mean that comparison is an intrinsically 'political' or normative process. Similarity is not conceptually related to evaluative terms: two observers may agree on two cars being similarly fast without agreeing upon whether the quality of cars depends on their speed. But there is no empirical criterion that defines the meaning of 'similar speed' or 'similar sound'. Comparative judgments mostly depend on the comparatist's standpoint, on his epistemological interest, and on his prior expectations: two

---

[27] $S\ abT =_{df} aT \wedge bT \wedge \{P\ I_T(a) \neq I_T(b) \wedge I_T(a)\ S\ I_T(b)\}$.

sisters who look similar may justly be thought to look different when they turn out to be twins, and members of a family may be expected to exhibit a greater degree of similarity than strangers.

Thus, similarity and dissimilarity are matters of degree that are difficult to describe objectively in ordinary language. For example, whereas 'a difference in temperature of 5° Celsius' is an objective concept, 'slightly' or 'much warmer' are seemingly not: such statements may have a different meaning for different speakers. One might therefore wonder whether it is a precondition for meaningful comparisons that there be objective, metric scales. Since such scales are normally available only in the empirical sciences, it might be feared that comparative judgments in social or cultural studies lack any substantial propositional content: they may not be arbitrary, and they may have a 'meaning', but perhaps this meaning is purely subjective, a mere expression of opinion.

At its extreme, such a thesis is misleading or even wrong. The statement that a 5° Celsius difference in human body temperature was 'little' or that the same difference in a star's temperature was 'large' would be perplexing. It is true that there is no agreement as to where a difference in human body temperature ceases to be 'little' and where a 'significant' or 'large' difference begins, but the same could be said of the question when day ends and night begins. In fact, because we know the relation between body temperature and human health, in many—if not most—cases there would be agreement as to where the boundary between an insignificant and a significant difference in temperature lies. A shared perspective and common opinion make comparison intersubjectively meaningful. This depends on a common understanding of 'what matters' and on basic scales that differentiate 'little', 'medium' and 'large' differences.[28] Often it is even possible to formulate thresholds for qualifying comparative judgments. Thus, it may plausibly be said that whereas 1.8 m distinguishes between tall and short men, the threshold for women is 1.75 m.

From all this it finally follows that, although comparison is to a certain degree subjective, it is not arbitrary, because indirectly it refers to objective facts, and if we share or even recognize the author's perspective and his epistemological interests, we can perfectly understand his judgment of similarity and dissimilarity. This explains why comparisons comparing comparisons ('comparative comparisons') are often especially meaningful: if we are told that the European law of contract exhibits a greater degree of similarity and homogeneity than the law of torts, we may question the homogeneity of the national contract laws, but we can perfectly understand the state of tort law as compared to contracts. If we doubt the possibility of reconstructing a common understanding of European contract law, we will realize that this is certainly not possible for tort law. Agreement will remain a question of plausibility, not of truth, but in cultural sciences and humanities

---

[28] cf Robert Alexy, *A Theory of Constitutional Rights* (2002), 402.

plausibility is often all we can hope for. What is more, judgments of similarity become more comprehensible the more completely the relevant facts are reported. If we are told that two wines are of similar quality, we can understand this judgment much better, if we know not only their varietal, but also their origins, producers, and vintages, and our understanding will be even deeper, if we are told the *terroir* and the methods of vinification: meaningful comparison depends on full factual description.

4. Choosing *Tertia Comparationis*: What Matters?

It has been explained above that comparative judgments are not necessarily normative or 'political', but, of course, this does not mean that comparative studies are a neutral, purely 'objective' business. On the contrary, comparisons are always related to a *tertium comparationis* that is often implicit in the conceptual structure chosen for the comparative description of foreign law. Such *tertia comparationis* are not objectively 'in the air'; rather they result from a choice about 'what matters', that is, which aspects of the law are relevant for the comparative lawyer, and which aspects of the law might benefit from the additional knowledge which comparison provides. Of course, such 'choices' may be subconscious; they are often influenced by an inherited conceptual and cultural understanding of the law. Nevertheless, they bear a normative character, because they are guided by normative assumptions about the law and by specific epistemic interests, which may even be dependent on a 'political' programme.[29]

Thus, although comparisons can be described as normatively neutral, it is misleading to suggest that evaluations come into play only after the process of comparison is finished.[30] However, such an a priori 'biased' perspective is neither problematic nor avoidable: comparative lawyers should not and cannot stop participating in legal discourse, and it is neither possible nor useful to compare all legal systems in all respects at the same time. Thus, a wholly neutral perspective is neither possible nor desirable for comparative law. This is true of both qualifying and quantifying comparison: the search for differentiating or common properties, and judgments about the importance of differences in degree of a common property, are both based on normative evaluations of what is interesting and what is important in the law, namely the researcher's assessment of 'what matters'.

This should be borne in mind when arguing for a common comparative method or when trying even to 'prescribe specific comparative procedures to be followed'.[31]

---

[29] cf Chodosh, (1999) 84 *Iowa LR* 1065 ff.

[30] But see Ernst Rabel, 'Aufgabe und Notwendigkeit der Rechtsvergleichung', in *idem, Gesammelte Aufsätze* (vol III, 1967), 1, 3, 8; Zweigert and Kötz (n 4), 46 f.

[31] Mark Van Hoecke and Mark Warrington, 'Legal Cultures, Legal Paradigms and Legal Doctrine: Towards a New Model for Comparative Law', (1998) 47 *ICLQ* 495, 510.

It is not easy to justify the imposition of one's normatively defined interests on others. Compelling arguments for looking only for doctrinal parallels, or only for commonalities in function and results, or only for differences in legal culture are difficult to see. Comparative legal studies may be helpful both for the normative endeavour of constructing a common European law of obligations and for socio-logically discovering the commonalities and differences in how 'the law' is under-stood and used in different societies. Surely, it is improbable that the same point of view and comparative interest will help to answer such divergent questions. Thus, if we think that others ask boring questions, we should answer the right ones instead of blaming them for not investigating what happens to interest us. Of course, the question 'what matters' will often require normative answers that may be heavily disputed. But this is not a methodological but a substantive question of what is important in the law. Comparative lawyers should therefore reflect their epistemological interests[32] and openly inform others of the reasons or motives for their choice of *tertia comparationis*. This is a postulate of clarity and sincerity. But on a methodological level, clarity is all that can be demanded. In the end, it must be the common interest and fruitfulness of the results which justify the approach and the *tertia comparationis* chosen.

5. Complex Comparisons: Family Similarity and the Idea of an *Idealtypus*

In both everyday discourse and comparative cultural or legal studies, meaningful comparisons rarely relate only to one *tertium comparationis*; instead there will usually be a range of *tertia comparationis* $T_{1, \ldots, n}$. For example, if we are trying to understand democracy it is probably not very useful to compare political systems solely with regard to whether elections take place; and if the traditional concept of a 'legal family' is to make any sense, it must be characterized by more than one or two defining features. As a consequence, however, the concepts of similarity and dissimilarity become significantly more complex: a and b are similar with regard to a list of *tertia comparationis* $T_{1, \ldots, n}$, if a and b share the common properties $T_{1, \ldots, n}$, and if the intensities of a's being $T_{1, \ldots, n}$ are partly identical or similar to those of b.[33] What is more, the complexity of 'similarity' increases further if complex similarity (plausibly) allows for dissimilarity with regard to certain properties, as long as the most important *tertia comparationis* are similar.

Correspondingly, most social concepts are also highly complex: their meaning cannot usually be defined by simply pointing to a *genus proximum* and respective

---

[32] cf Frankenberg, (1985) 26 *Harvard International LJ* 443 ff.

[33] $S_{complex} \, abT_{1, \ldots, n} =_{df} aT_{1, \ldots, n} \wedge bT_{1, \ldots, n} \wedge \{P \, I_{T1}(a) \ldots I_{T\,n}(a) \neq I_{T1}(b) \ldots I_{T\,n}(b) \wedge I_{T1}(a) \ldots I_{T\,n}(a)$ S $I_{T1}(b) \ldots I_{T\,n}(b)\}$.

differentia specifica. Thus, Wittgenstein argued that many concepts—including that of 'games' and thus law—can only be explained by giving examples. What is more, although this does not entail abolishing the traditional 'metaphysical' assumption of a concept's meaning,[34] these examples need not share a list of specific common features. Instead, they should be characterized as 'a complicated network of similarities overlapping and criss-crossing: sometimes overall similarities, sometimes similarities of detail'.[35] Comparison is the mode of application of such concepts[36] which do not normally allow for exclusive classification: a (mixed) legal system may belong to more than one legal tradition or family; middle and modern English, although deriving from an early form of German, both exhibit strong Romance influence;[37] and a thing used as a chair is capable of use as a little table. In such instances exclusive taxonomies may be misleading.

However, examples alone do not help us to structure and understand reality. Scholars need precisely defined concepts. Here, in order to avoid misleading or impossible classifications and taxonomies, Max Weber introduced the concept of an ideal type (*Idealtypus*) as a means of describing social facts, like 'law', 'rule', 'feudalism', or 'capitalism'. Of course, Weber was fully aware that the price of giving such concepts a precise meaning was to deprive them of empirical significance: they are abstract reconstructions on the basis of complex comparisons. Reality does not fit neatly into such clinically idealized standards. Again, the application of an *Idealtypus* is a comparative process—reality is understood as an 'approximation' to the *Idealtypus*.[38]

Thus, the use of ideal types, 'prototypes',[39] or constructed types both allows for a rational, structured description of social reality and replaces misleading taxonomic classifications with complex typologies. Such concepts offer a means of comparing complex matters of fact: similarities and differences may be formulated as deviations from the idealized concept.[40] For example, classifying the German *Verkehrspflichtenhaftung* (liability for the breach of rather strict civil

[34] Wilhelm Lütterfelds, 'Familienähnlichkeit als sprachanalytische Kritik und Neukonzeption des metaphysischen Essentialismus?', in Karen Gloy (ed), *Unser Zeitalter—ein postmetaphyisches?* (2004), 138 ff.

[35] Ludwig Wittgenstein, *Philosophische Untersuchungen/Philosophical Investigations*, (trans Gertrude E. M. Anscombe, 1953), §§ 66 ff, 164; see also *idem, Philosophische Grammatik* (vol IV of the *Werkausgabe* [Collected Works], 1984), 75 f.

[36] Wittgenstein, *Philosophische Untersuchungen* (n 35), § 69: 'das, *und Ähnliches*, nennt man "Spiele" '.

[37] Radoslav Katičić, *A Contribution to the General Theory of Comparative Linguistics* (1970), 121 ff, 126; Hans Henrich Hock, *Principles of Historical Linguistics* (1986), 421 ff, 479 ff; Terry Crowley, *An Introduction to Historical Linguistics* (3rd edn, 1997), 275 f.

[38] Max Weber, *Wirtschaft und Gesellschaft* (5th edn, 1972), 1 ff, 9 f; *idem*, 'Die "Objektivität" sozialwissenschaftlicher und sozialpolitischer Erkenntnis', in *idem, Gesammelte Aufsätze zur Wissenschaftslehre* (3rd edn, 1968), 146, 190 ff.

[39] cf Martin Shapiro, *Courts: A Comparative and Political Analysis* (1981), 1 ff, 63 f, and *passim*.

[40] John C. McKinney, *Constructive Typology and Social Theory* (1966), 11 ff, 21 ff, 41 f, 49 ff, 100 ff.

duties) either as 'liability for fault' (because of its conceptual relation to negligence) or as 'strict liability' (because of its functional equivalence to the French
liability for *faits des choses*) would be equally unsatisfactory. Instead, as a complex
concept based on the related ideas of wrongful behaviour, individual accountability, and moral blameworthiness, it may prove more illuminating to put it
somewhere in the middle of a continuum ranging from the ideal type of strict
liability to the conceptually opposed type of liability for fault.[41] Such approaches
to defining concepts need not be discussed in more detail here. It is enough to
note that clearly classifying definitions are often not possible, and that a plausible
alternative approach is characterized by complex comparisons. This should be
borne in mind when comparatively defining and using concepts like contract/
contrat/Vertrag or fault/*faute/Verschulden*. Of course, these concepts are used
slightly differently in the specific contexts of different legal systems, but it would
also be wrong to suppose that these words express different concepts. The concept of a game/*Spiel*, too, changes its meaning when applied to different contexts,
like chess or soccer or *Anspielung*[42] (the English word 'allusion' similarly plays on
the Latin *ludere*), but this is not because the words themselves are equivocal.
Thus, whereas it may be misleading to use the concept of a 'contract' without
further explanation when comparing the English gift to the German *Schenkung*
(which is understood as a *Vertrag*), this concept creates no problems in the
context of sales.

From all this, it follows that complex comparisons and the comparative use of
complex social concepts must be even more a question of judgment than simple
comparisons. They are necessarily based on the selection of a limited range of
criteria or variables that are regarded as relevant or important, and, when applying
such variables, comparison includes evaluations as to which properties and simple
similarities or differences are more important in the given context. Again, all these
evaluations depend on epistemic interests and on the point of view adopted. It can
be illuminating to characterize French law as a member of the Western tradition
and yet to emphasize the many differences between French law and German,
Spanish, or the common law. After all, members of a family are *individuals* that are
characterized by *common features*. Thus, where comparison leads to the formulation of complex concepts or is based on their use, it is helpful to clarify their
meaning by making explicit the relevant criteria, because typologies must be
relative to the criteria chosen. This is obvious for the taxonomy of 'legal families':
depending on one's perspective, one may or may not accept that the Japanese
law of obligations belongs to the civilian tradition.[43] But the question whether

---

[41] Nils Jansen, *Die Struktur des Haftungsrechts* (2003), 554, 607 ff, 614 ff, 620 ff.

[42] 'Die liebste und lieblichste Form des Spielens aber war ihm [i.e. Joseph] die Anspielung . . .':
Thomas Mann, *Joseph und seine Brüder*, vol IV: *Joseph der Ernährer, Erstes Hauptstück: Die andere
Grube. Joseph kennt seine Tränen.*

[43] cf Glenn (n 19), 304 f.

classification 'must' look to the doctrinal structure or rather to the cultural attitude towards the law as a means for conflict resolution probably admits of no cogent answer. It depends on the epistemic interest. Again, translating questions of interest into debates of method would be mistaken.

III. Comparing Comparisons: Interests and Methods

As a scientific method, comparison has a long history and has been used in most academic disciplines. Bishop Cusanus argued in the fifteenth century that all research is done through comparison and by setting comparative relations;[44] and in subsequent centuries comparison was also seen as a universal method. By the end of the nineteenth century the French anatomist Baron Couvier (1769–1832) had established a comparative organismal biology that successfully set about reconstructing the skeletons and phenotypes of extinguished species; and in the nineteenth century comparative linguistics tried optimistically to reconstruct an original Indo-European language. Thus, comparison reached the social sciences and the humanities: John Stuart Mill formulated logical principles of inductive comparative research;[45] and the German architect Gottfried Semper (1803–79), working on Couvier's ideas, even tried to lay the foundations of comparative stylistics.[46] Comparative religion and comparative law were introduced as new disciplines, and comparison became an important instrument for social sciences such as ethnology. Thus, it was used to reconstruct the unwritten origins of religion and law by observing undeveloped present-day societies.[47]

Here, however, problems arose, because in order to use comparison to reconstruct the origins of law and religion it must be presumed that such elements of human culture follow identical or similar patterns of development. Yet this was challenged by scholars of the Historical School, who argued that historical developments must be understood individually. In fact, in many cases where comparative scholars had proudly pointed to collective property as a universal feature

---

[44] Nikolaus de Kues (1401–64), *De docta ignorantia, liber* I, *capitulum* I, II (§§ 2 f, 31 f); cf also above p 310.

[45] *A System of Logic Ratiocinative and Inductive, Collected Works* (vol VII, 1973), 389 ff.

[46] 'Entwurf eines Systems der vergleichenden Stillehre', in *idem, Kleine Schriften* (1884), 259 ff.

[47] Wilhelm Dilthey, 'Der Aufbau der geschichtlichen Welt in den Geisteswissenschaften', part II. 3, in *Gesammelte Schriften* (vol VII, 1927), 77, 98 f; Erich Rothacker, *Logik und Systematik der Geisteswissenschaften* (1948), 92 ff.

of early culture, it could be shown that this form of land-use was introduced only in later times for specific historical reasons. If the evolution of different societies appeared to follow distinctive paths, there could be no presumption that separate legal systems had a shared pattern of development. Instead, similarities were often shown to be due to mutual influence, not to parallel evolution. Conversely, monotheistic elements in Australian aboriginal culture showed that the evolutionist theory of religious development from 'primitive' forms of animism to high-cultural monotheism was untenable.[48] Thus, the comparative approach seemed methodologically misleading, because it could not account for the individual history of any social system.[49]

Today it is generally accepted that there may be inherent limits to the comparative approach, which make it inadequate for certain types of research. Nevertheless, with regard to the study of the earliest law the winds have changed again. On the one hand, the act of applying the same concepts to different societies unavoidably relies on comparative judgments. On the other hand, ethnologists have realized that the very concepts of 'one's own' and 'another society' are conceptual constructions that depend heavily on a specific European understanding of 'culture' and may influence the perception of human societies.[50] In fact, there are distinctive common features in the development of early societies, and their religions and laws, which cannot be attributed to mutual influence. Even if different societies do not follow identical patterns of development, their history can be better understood if compared to others: the relation between individual and universal factors in the development of societies can only be perceived from a comparative perspective.[51] In some cases comparison can even help to reconstruct legal and pre-legal history.[52] In fact, this is what early historical comparatists in the tradition of the Historical School, such as Paul Koschaker or Ernst Rabel, had done without assuming parallel historical developments.[53] In such instances, as in the case of comparative palaeontology, comparison is used as a basis for drawing conclusions relating to (historical) matters of fact. It offers answers to 'how it probably was'. Obviously, comparison is a method that can be used for a vast range of sciences with totally divergent epistemic interests.

Often, comparison is seen as the social sciences' equivalent of experiments, as a

---

[48] Johann Figl, 'Gott—monotheistisch', in *idem* (ed), *Handbuch Religionswissenschaft* (2003), 545, 547 f.

[49] Rothaker (n 47), 97 ff; Uwe Wesel, *Frühformen des Rechts in vorstaatlichen Gesellschaften* (1985), 36 ff.

[50] Laura Nader, 'Comparative Consciousness', in Robert Borofsky (ed), *Assessing Cultural Anthropology* (1994), 84 ff; Wolfgang Kaschuba, 'Anmerkungen zum Gesellschaftsvergleich aus ethnologischer Perspektive', in Schriewer and Kaelble (n 1), 341, 346 ff; Martin Fuchs and Eberhard Berg, 'Phänomenologie der Differenz: Reflexionsstufen ethnographischer Repräsentation', in *idem* (eds), *Kultur, soziale Praxis, Text* (2nd edn, 1995), 11 ff.

[51] Below, pp 332 ff.   [52] Wesel (n 49), 46 ff.

[53] Zimmermann, (2001) 65 *RabelsZ* 31 ff.

test for general theories of human behaviour. Thus, in comparative economics[54] or cross-cultural psychology[55] general hypotheses are applied to different nations or cultures: the culturally relativistic idea of an individual *Völkerpsychologie* (Wilhelm Wundt), assuming a 'unity of culture and mind', has never been accepted.[56] Legal systems, however, are normally understood as individual entities defining their boundaries from within.[57] Thus, they must be genuine objects of comparative research, with the comparative method contributing to the knowledge of individual legal systems. What is more, lawyers normally explain the law not in causal but in normative terms: they ask for reasons rather than empirical correlations. Economics and psychology are therefore of little interest for our methodological comparison. Nevertheless, the comparative analysis of social change will be examined in some detail, because comparative lawyers have often argued for an empirical, sociological understanding of their discipline.[58] From such a perspective the combination of generalizing explanations with the description of individual peculiarities may prove rewarding. This will be preceded by an examination of comparative religious studies, not only because the oldest law, as we are told, was stolen from the priests,[59] but more importantly because comparison here concerns individual traditions of autonomous normative thought and revelation. The first place, however, must be given to comparative linguistics, both for its extraordinary success and because grammar has often been understood as an intellectual model for the status of law's doctrines.[60]

1. Historical Linguistics: Searching Genetic Relations

It is in the field of comparative linguistics that the 'comparative method' may be said to have produced the most spectacular results. Until 1780 the comparative

---

[54] cf Ulrich Ritter, *Vergleichende Volkswirtschaftslehre* (2nd edn, 1997), 38 f, 50 ff.

[55] cf John W. Berry, Ype H. Poortinga, Marshall H. Segall, and Pierre R. Dasen, *Cross-Cultural Psychology: Research and Applications* (1992), 1 ff; for culture-independent developments, see Lutz H. Eckensberger and Roderick F. Zimba, 'The Development of Moral Judgment', in John W. Berry, Pierre R. Dasen, and T. S. Saraswathi (eds), *Handbook of Cross-Cultural Psychology* (vol II, 2nd edn, 1998), 299 ff.

[56] John D. Greenwood, 'From *Völkerpsychologie* to Cultural Psychology: The Once and Future Discipline', (1999) 12 *Philosophical Psychology* 503 ff, with further references.

[57] cf Herbert H. L. Hart, *The Concept of Law* (2nd edn, 1994), 100 (the 'rule of recognition' providing 'authoritative criteria for identifying primary rules'); similarly Hans Kelsen, *Reine Rechtslehre* (2nd edn, 1960), 196.

[58] Arthur T. von Mehren, 'An Academic Tradition for Comparative Law?', (1971) 19 *AJCL* 624, 626 ff; Ulrich Drobnig, 'Methods of Sociological Research in Comparative Law', (1971) 35 *RabelsZ* 496 ff; cf Roger Cotterell, 'Comparatists and sociology', in Legrand and Munday (n 2), 131 ff.

[59] Livius, *Ab urbe condita*, 9, 46, 4 f.; Pomponius, D. 1, 2, 2, 6 f.

[60] Maximilian Herberger, *Dogmatik. Zur Geschichte von Begriff und Methode in Medizin und Jurisprudenz* (1981), 37 f, 74 ff, 119, 257 f; Zenon Bankowski, D. Neil MacCormick, Robert S. Summers, and Jerzy Wróblewski, 'On Method and Methodology', in D. Neil MacCormick and Robert S. Summers (eds), *Interpreting Statutes* (1991), 9, 20.

knowledge of language had largely been guesswork based on etymologies which often proved to be erroneous. This changed only when European linguists became aware of Sanskrit and when the rise of the comparative method resulted in more thorough grammatical studies.[61] Scholars recognized the similarities between this old Indian language and Latin, Greek, and old German, which could be explained neither by chance nor by mutual influence; they therefore guessed that they had 'sprung from some common source, which, perhaps, no longer exists', as Sir William Jones, an English judge in Bengal and a founding father of comparative law,[62] put it in 1786.[63] The idea of a reconstructive *Vergleichende Grammatik* (comparative grammar) was coined by the Schlegel brothers by analogy with comparative biology,[64] but it remained a mere aspiration until 1816 when the German linguist Franz Bopp was the first to present a more specific comparative study of the conjugation systems of Sanskrit, Greek, Latin, Persian, and German.[65] At that stage it became feasible to draw family trees representing the genetic relationships between different languages,[66] perhaps in analogy to the *Stammbaum* of manuscript variants of historic texts.[67] However, while comparative linguistics remained intellectually in the tradition of Romanticist cultural studies, the idea of a 'kinship' between different languages remained vague. Scholars still relied on the somewhat unclear notion of similarities in the 'inner structure' of grammar, which limited the extent to which the presumed ancestor of European and Indian languages could be traced.

---

[61] cf Lyle Campbell, 'The History of Linguistics', in Mark Aronoff and Janie Rees-Miller, *The Handbook of Linguistics* (2001), 81, 85 ff; Hans Arens, *Sprachwissenschaft: Der Gang ihrer Entwicklung von der Antike bis zur Gegenwart* (2nd edn, 1969), 155 ff; Paolo Ramat, 'Da Humboldt ai neogrammatici. Continuità e fratture', in Tullio de Mauro and Lia Formigari, *Leibniz, Humboldt, and the Origins of Comparativism* (1990), 199 ff.

[62] David Ibbetson, 'Sir William Jones as Comparative Lawyer', in Alexander Murray (ed), *Sir William Jones 1746–1794* (1998), 17 ff; see also the other essays in that volume. Jones, today mainly known as a Sanskritist, was a polymath who also contributed substantially to classics, to Arabian philology, and to ancient Indian history. His primary profession, however, was the law, and in that regard he is still known not only for his influential *Essay on the Law of Bailments* (1781), but also, perhaps even more importantly, for his achievements as a comparative lawyer.

[63] 'The Third Anniversary Discourse', in *Discourses Delivered at the Asiatick Society* (1993), 24, 34; likewise Friedrich Schlegel, *Über die Sprache und Weisheit der Indier* (Heidelberg, 1808), 1 ff. On possible earlier intellectual sources for Jones's statement, see Rosane Rocher, 'Nathaniel Brassey Halhed, Sir William Jones, and Comparative Indo-European Linguistics', in *Recherches de Linguistique. Hommages à Maurice Leroy* (1980), 173 ff.

[64] August Wilhelm Schlegel, 'Ankündigung. Sprachlehre von A.F. Bernhardi', (1803/5) 2 *Europa: Eine Zeitschrift*, part 1, 193, 203; Schlegel (n 63), 28.

[65] *Conjugationssystem der Sanskritsprache . . .* (Frankfurt am Main, 1816).

[66] August Schleicher, *Die Darwinsche Theorie und die Sprachwissenschaft* (3rd edn, 1873), 12 ff and the attached print.

[67] cf Henry M. Hoenigswald, 'On the History of the Comparative Method', (1963) 5 *Anthropological Linguistics* 1, 7 ff; more generally on the intellectual origins of the discipline's conceptual instruments, see *idem*, 'Descent, Perfection and the Comparative Method since Leibniz', in Mauro and Formigari (n 61), 119 ff.

(a) A 'Science of Language'

The precise analysis of sound changes marked the discipline's breakthrough to a more exact form of scholarship. Here, among others, Jakob Grimm (subsequently of fairy-tale fame) was able to observe highly significant correspondences of consonants in different Indo-European languages (today known as 'Grimm's law') and identified these as the major evidence of linguistic kinship (eg Greek P $\cong$ Gothik F $\cong$ Old High German B).[68] Thus, the cultural comparison of different languages was supplemented by attempts to reconstruct the exact genetic relations between languages, and whereas Grimm still believed that his observations allowed for certain irregularities, these were later satisfactorily explained in the form of more complex regularities.[69] The 'Neogrammarian Manifesto', according to which 'every sound change, in as much as it occurs mechanically, takes place according to laws that admit of no exceptions',[70] soon became a general standard of research; and as a hypothesis it has stood the test of time until today.

Within a short time, the discipline had wholly changed its face. On the one hand, it was no longer concerned with mere comparisons, but with the historical reconstruction of languages and their development; thus, today the discipline is called 'historical linguistics'. On the other hand, on the basis of its firmly established method, the discipline could claim to have become an exact 'science of language'.[71] It is true that it has been challenged in the twentieth century by structuralist and other new approaches to language, but, rather than really questioning the results of historical research, these have only refined and complemented the methodological reservoir for linguistic reconstruction.[72] Despite critique, the method continues to define the starting-point for any comparative analysis in the discipline.[73] Today, large parts of Proto-Indo-European and other languages have been reconstructed. Even if taking such reconstructions for a realistic and complete picture of ancient languages is to misunderstand the method,[74] they may still tell us something about the culture and origins of former peoples, especially when complemented with archaeological evidence.[75]

---

[68] Jacob Grimm, *Deutsche Grammatik* (vol I, 1819), 581 ff, 588 ff.

[69] Karl Verner, 'Eine ausnahme der ersten lautverschiebung', (1877) 23 *Zeitschrift für vergleichende Sprachforschung* 97, 113 ff.

[70] Hermann Osthoff and Karl Brugmann, *Morphologische Untersuchungen auf dem Gebiete der indogermanischen Sprachen* (vol I, 1878), XIII.

[71] F. Max Müller, *Lectures on the Science of Language* (vol I, 1861), 1: 'The science of language one of the physical siences'; cf Schleicher (n 66), 5 f: 'naturwissenschaftliche Methode'.

[72] Anthony Fox, *Linguistic Reconstruction* (1995), 37 ff, 145 ff, 210 ff.

[73] Fox (n 72), 122 ff, 137 ff, and *passim*; Hock (n 37), 556 ff, 562 ff, 581 ff; Crowley (n 37), 87 ff; Brian D. Joseph, 'Historical Linguistics', in Aronoff and Rees-Miller (n 61), 105, 122 ff; see also Mark Durie and Malcolm Ross (eds), *The Comparative Method Reviewed: Regularity and Irregularity in Language Change* (1996).

[74] Fox (n 72), 7 ff, 140 f; but see Hock (n 37), 568 ff: 'approximation'.

[75] Winfried P. Lehmann, *Historical Linguistics* (1992), 294 ff; Lyle Campbell, *Historical Linguistics* (1998), 339 ff.

(b) The Comparative Method

As a result of these nineteenth-century developments, comparative evidence of similarities between languages is today no more than a starting-point for an analysis of genetic relations.[76] The 'comparative method' is no longer an evaluation of similarities; such judgments have become only the first step of a 'set of mechanical procedures' in the process of reconstructing proto-languages.[77] The linguist does not settle for apparent similarities of words or grammatical structure, but continues to search for regular 'correspondence sets' that identify items as genetically equivalent. Accordingly, as a result of comparative research, judgments of similarity have been replaced by laws of language change: whereas there exists no such correspondence between the Latin and Greek words for 'god' (*deus/theós*), their striking similarity being mere chance, the Greek and Armenian words for 'two' (*dúo/erku*) do correspond to each other despite the apparent difference, because it is possible to trace these words by *general* rules of sound change to a common ancestor.[78] Conversely, two words, like the German *selig* (blessed) and the English 'silly', may be closely related despite bearing different meanings. Accordingly, the degree of similarity between two languages is not necessarily parallel to their genetic relation:[79] members of a family, as one knows, may appear rather different, and sometimes a friend is said to fit better into a family than an actual relative.

(c) Some Observations

Now, such a 'comparative method' might prima facie be judged irrelevant for the comparative lawyer. The method is not uniformly applicable even to all aspects of language—it is apparently of little help with syntactical structures, and when applied to the lexicon the results are less certain and based to a larger degree on intuition.[80] How, then, can it be relevant for complex legal systems? Furthermore, is it not true that comparative law is concerned with the synchronic similarities and differences between legal systems, whereas genetic relations may be the historians' business?

However, this is exactly the point that needs clarification. Not everybody feels comfortable with superficial similarities such as between *deus* and *theós*, or between different legal systems which reach similar results on the basis of fundamentally divergent doctrinal bases. For example, European legal systems are all reluctant to grant a claim in negligence in cases of negligent misstatements unless there is a special relation of responsibility. But whereas this is decided in Germany

---

[76] For a detailed analysis, see Fox (n 72), *passim*; Malcolm Ross and Mark Durie, 'Introduction', in *idem* (n 73), 3 ff; Johanna Nichols, 'The Comparative Method as Heuristics', in Durie and Ross (n 73), 39, 48 ff.

[77] Fox (n 72), 57.   [78] Fox (n 72), 65; Hock (n 37), 557 f, 583.

[79] Hock (n 37), 219 f, 247 f.

[80] cf Stephen Ullmann, *Semantics. An Introduction to the Science of Meaning* (1970), 30 f, 193 ff; Fox (n 72), 109 ff. But see David P. Wilkins, 'Natural Tendencies of Semantic Change and the Search for Cognates', in Durie and Ross (n 73), 264 ff.

and England on the basis of a theory of specifically protected interests ('rights') and 'pure economic loss', French lawyers rely on considerations of 'fault' or 'causation'. Both approaches are the result of a specific traditional understanding of the law of delict that may be traced back to Natural law thinking, the split having taken place as early as in the theory of Grotius.[81] Thus, it is difficult to reconcile such divergent views on the law. Here, similarities of result explain little; they do not deepen our comparative understanding and they are not helpful when searching for a common basis for a restatement of the law. This is confirmed by the familiar fact that lawyers faced with the same set of facts may often reach opposite results: the empirical similarity or dissimilarity of results may be a mere chance. Two legal systems deciding a hard case differently despite a traditionally common intellectual approach may be 'closer' to each other than systems coming to the same result on a divergent legal basis: discourse will be easier in the former case. Thus, comparative studies may become much more exact and useful when complementing the idea of 'similarity' with a conception of 'genetic relatedness': the two aspects of comparative knowledge may add to each other. Whereas linguistics has complemented the reconstruction of individual genetic relations with abstract typological analyses of universal linguistic structures,[82] comparative legal studies may profit from genetic analyses. Such knowledge is indispensable for a deeper understanding of intellectual legal unity and diversity.

Of course this cannot be done by a purely mechanical analysis of micro-elements of the law. What is more, lawyers cannot proceed from the assumption that every system has only one ancestor and that creoles (pidgins developed into native languages) are a modern irregularity. We know that legal systems develop in close contact to others: new ideas may evolve within one line of tradition and then spread quickly, with great effect on other legal systems. This happened with Natural law ideas during the eighteenth and nineteenth centuries and it seems today to be the case with the American instrumental view of private law, which is becoming increasingly influential in discussions on European consumer protection. However, the investigation of genetic relations is not dependent on the linguistic method of reconstruction. There are other methods of examining historical material from a genuinely comparative perspective: whereas the historian describes former developments of individual legal systems (perhaps also investigating genuine transplants of parts of a legal system), comparatists will analyse the relations between different legal systems more comprehensively. They will identify a set of specific intellectual legal units, like normative ideas, legal values, conceptions of basic legal concepts (such as 'right', 'duty', 'contract', or 'tort') and perhaps even

---

[81] Nils Jansen, 'Duties and Rights in Negligence. A Comparative and Historical Perspective on the European Law of Extracontractual Liability', (2004) 24 *Oxford Journal of Legal Studies* 443, 444 ff, 454 ff.

[82] Fox (n 72), 617 ff; Lehmann (n 75), 96 ff; William Croft, 'Typology', in Aronoff and Rees-Miller (n 61), 337, 341 ff.

doctrinal elements, in order to trace these units to common or divergent sources, and reconstruct points of departure, merger, or transfer.[83] Here, even if difficult to draw, the linguistic distinction between a system 'borrowing' foreign elements and systems being 'genetically related',[84] may also be illuminating for addressing questions about the common law's place within the Western legal tradition: otherwise most contemporary legal systems would turn out to be related to each other.[85] But again, lawyers will have to develop special methodological instruments. Thus, it will probably become necessary to allow for different ancestors for different parts of a legal system. Whereas German constitutional rights are closely related to the Constitution of the United States, large parts of German private law have never experienced any influence from America.

Of course, all this cannot be developed in more detail. Here it suffices to recall that identifying genetic relations may be a highly illuminating complement to the traditional description of similarities and differences. This is especially the case, where comparative analysis aims at reconstructing a common system: such systems presuppose a common inheritance of basic intellectual elements. Comparatists with such aims would clearly distinguish similarity from genetic relatedness. Instead of being content with prima-facie judgments of similarity or dissimilarity, they would seek to ascertain whether basic intellectual elements of the law have 'sprung from some common source' or result from different lines of thinking.

2. Comparative Religion: Complex Typologies for a Complex Reality

Comparative religion has always been the English equivalent of the German *Religionswissenschaft*: by definition, there can apparently be no scientific treatment of religion but a comparative one.[86] Interestingly, however, the comparative method has never been a central issue for sociological studies of belief systems, although, beginning with the writings of Max Weber and Émile Durkheim, such research had quite naturally proceeded in a comparative manner.[87] Even today

---

[83] cf, by way of example, Jansen, (2004) 24 *Oxford Journal of Legal Studies* 443 ff, 456 ff for hidden genetic relations; James Q. Whitman, 'Enforcing Civility and Respect: Three Societies', (2000) 109 *Yale LJ* 1279, 1313 ff, 1344 ff, 1372 ff for divergent intellectual traditions with respect to human dignity.

[84] cf the references above, n 37.

[85] cf Esin Örücü, 'Family Trees for Legal Systems: Towards a Contemporary Approach', in Van Hoecke (n 15), 359, 363 ff, 371 ff.

[86] See eg Eric J. Sharpe, *Comparative Religion: A History* (2nd edn, 1986); Christoph Bochinger, 'Religionsvergleiche in religionswissenschaftlicher und theologischer Perspektive', in Schriewer and Kaelble (n 1), 251 ff.

[87] Max Weber, 'Die Wissenschaftsethik der Weltreligionen', in *idem*, *Gesammelte Aufsätze zur Religionssoziologie* (1920), vol I, 237 ff, vol II and vol III; Émile Durkheim, *Les formes élémentaires de la vie religieuse* (1968); today Stephen Sharot, *A Comparative Sociology of World Religions* (2001).

methodological discussion within comparative religion does not pay much attention to these classical works. What is it, then, that comparative religion seeks to
explore, and why is it that comparison occupies such a central place?

(a) The Idea of a Comparative Religionswissenschaft

Although the intellectual roots of all scientific treatment of religion must be traced
back to the Enlightenment's critiques of religions, it would be a mistake to see
comparative religion as being necessarily critical of religious belief: '. . . the study
of ancient religions of mankind, if carried on in a bold, but scholar-like, careful
and reverent spirit, will remove many doubts and difficulties which are due entirely
to the narrowness of our religion's horizon'.[88] This was the motivating conviction
of the discipline's founding father, Friedrich Max Müller, for establishing comparative religion as an academic subject. Müller, who taught in Oxford from 1850, was
of German origin (his father's poems were set to music by Franz Schubert as *Die
Winterreise* and *Die schöne Müllerin*), and, as he had studied under Schelling and
the linguist Bopp, his intellectual background included Romantic idealism and
the modern school of comparative linguistics. To this day Müller's definition of
linguistics as a 'science'[89] has remained authoritative, and he was equally convinced
that a scientific treatment of religion could reveal theological truth. Thus, although
he was not interested in the theological views of other religions from a genuinely
Christian perspective (be it for apologetic or missionary motives), his project
was neither to analyse sociologically the impact of religion on society, nor to
understand religion from the perspective of human society. Rather, each religion
was to be taken seriously as religion. Drawing on the methods of philology and
anthropology, different religions of early times and within different cultures were
to be compared in order to recognize general features of religion, to understand the
peculiarities of individual religions, and to group religions (according to their
linguistic background) into fundamental 'families' or traditions. Such knowledge
promised answers to questions about the essence of religion, the stages of the
development of religions, and the origin of belief (*Urreligion*). It was a matter of
course that such research had to be done comparatively. Only such a perspective
could account for the obvious plurality of religious traditions and thus offer a full
picture of human belief and religious thinking.

From early on, this approach has raised intriguing problems, for belief, being a
deeply 'normative' subject, cannot easily be treated in a scientific way. 'Holiness'
is more than, and different to, 'completely good';[90] it cannot be translated into
or explained by recourse to empirical, more objective terms. In this respect it
corresponds to legal categories, like 'obligation', 'right', and the 'lawful-unlawful'

---

[88] F. Max Müller, *Introduction to the Science of Religion* (1873), ix.
[89] Above n 71; cf 'Preface', in Aronoff and Rees-Miller (n 61), xiv.
[90] Rudolf Otto, *Das Heilige* (29/30th edn, 1936), 5 ff.

dichotomy, but whereas the existence of the law and of rights may be taken for granted, this is less evident in the case of the Lord and other holy matters. On the one hand, it seems impossible objectively to distinguish 'real' awe from the imagination of awe or thrill; and thus, scholarly objectivity requires the comparatist to avoid having recourse to such ideas. On the other hand, religious comparatists have often argued that religion can only be understood from a religious standpoint that presupposes an intuitive knowledge of deity and thus the feeling of holiness. Of course, they wanted to analyse the fundamental categories of religion in a rational way. But they insisted that these categories, and thus the object of comparative research, are meaningful only for those who possess a *sensus numinis*. Today, proponents of pluralistic approaches[91] argue that there are different ways to salvation; some even search for the 'common core' of the different religions of the world, with the possible aim of revealing an ultimate truth. In these approaches, the comparative study of religions has been transformed into comparative theology.[92]

For comparatists who want to base their work on a more objective understanding of scientific research such a deeply religious point of view is unacceptable. For them, the question whether there actually is some sort of deity, or whether belief is an illusion based on a fundamental mistake of human consciousness, must be left open. They therefore argue for a more descriptive approach, avoiding the question of religious truth. Their aim consists, less pretentiously, in understanding and systematizing different religions and common structures of belief. The individual motive for pursuing such studies may well be to deepen the scholar's *sensus numinis*, but the perspective must be a purely scholarly one.[93] Thus, the comparative description of different religions and the contrasting analysis of their historical development, the formulation of categories suitable for such work, and the theoretical typological description and analysis of the religious world, become the genuine business of a positive *Religionswissenschaft*.[94] Questions as to the essence of religion are left unanswered.

As in present legal debates, it has often been argued that such a positivistic comparison of religions unavoidably causes misunderstanding, because it neglects the religions' claim to incomparability, which can be seen not only in the Abrahamic religions but also, for example, in Buddhism.[95] However, such a view is highly questionable, since even the command 'Thou shalt have no other gods

---

[91] cf John Hick, *God Has Many Names* (1982), 41 ff; Thomas Dean (ed), *Religious Pluralism and Truth* (1995); Perry Schmidt-Leukel, *Theologie der Religionen* (1997), 237 ff.

[92] Sharpe (n 86), 262 f; Bochinger (n 86), 276 ff.

[93] Joachim Wach, *Religionswissenschaft. Prolegomena zu ihrer wissenschaftstheoretischen Grundlegung* (1924), 21 ff; *idem, The Comparative Study of Religions* (1958), 9 ff; Annemarie Schimmel, 'Summary of the Discussion', (1960) VII *Numen* 237; Johann Figl, 'Einleitung', in *idem* (n 48), 17, 27, 35 ff, 51 ff.

[94] Hubert Seibert, 'Systematische Religionswissenschaft: Theoriebildung und Empiriebezug', (1977) 61 *Zeitschrift für Missionswissenschaft und Religionswissenschaft* 1 ff; Gustav Mensching, *Die Religion* (1959).

[95] On the discussion, see Bochinger (n 86), 268 ff.

before me' (Exod. 20: 3; Deut. 5: 7) appears to be based on comparison: 'Gods' is not just Yahweh's name, but a noun for different supreme beings all belonging to one class. Likewise, early Christians characterized their new belief with the term that Romans applied to their heathen beliefs (*religio*): for them, Christian belief was not conceptually incomparable; they only *qualified* it as superior (*religio vera*). Thus, discourse between different religions presupposing a shared basic understanding of belief has always been possible and in fact happens even today.[96] The story of Joseph and Pharaoh discussing the truth of one highest God may be fictional, but it might have happened just as both the Bible and, in a much more elaborate fashion, Thomas Mann, tell it.[97] It is true that religions are normally exclusive: a person believing in Mohammed the prophet cannot be a Christian. But this is because all are different species of one genus 'religion'. In this respect, understanding a religion's claim to exclusiveness presupposes comparison.

(b) The Comparative Method

All in all, comparative religion has to proceed descriptively and cannot base its research on the conceptual structure of a scholar's personal belief. Functionalism is no alternative either, because such a sociological view of belief is inadequate for a genuine internal understanding of religion: whereas lawyers may often plausibly interpret the law from a functional perspective, such an understanding of religion is impossible for the devoted believer. Seeing the Lord's commands and Christ's resurrection as functional solutions to our mundane problems would be a ridiculous misunderstanding. Thus, it may be asked how comparison can be possible at all under such circumstances. What are the *tertia comparationis*, and how is it possible to develop criteria for assessing different religions?

As to the last question, the simple answer is that there can be no such evaluations within a positive science. Answers to the first question, however, are more difficult to find. It is apparently regarded as a technicality, depending on the scholar's skill: normally, after identifying a prima-facie common phenomenon in two or more religions, it is exemplarily described and both the smaller and larger differences and similarities with regard to this phenomenon are analysed.[98] This has been done for a number of different areas: for abstract ideas of supreme beings, be they theistic or non-theistic, monotheistic or polytheistic, as well as for the traditional foundations of religion, that is, myths or holy scriptures, and their understanding in present religious life. More specific are the practical dimensions of religion, both

---

[96] Günter Lanczkowski, *Begegnung und Wandel der Religionen* (1971); cf also the references in n 91 f, and n 110.

[97] Gen. 41: 25 ff; Mann (n 42), *Drittes Hauptstück: Die kretische Laube*. On the disputed mutual influence between the Egyptian and other religions, cf Leonard H. Lesko, 'Egyptian Religion', in Mircea Eliade (ed), *The Encyclopedia of Religion* (vol V, 1987), 37, 53.

[98] William E. Paden, *Religious Worlds: The Comparative Study of Religion* (1988), 3 ff, 161 ff.

cultic elements, like rituals and sacred rooms or times, and spiritual features, such as prayer, meditation, and ecstasy. Here comparison is less difficult than in the case of abstract concepts like 'holiness', because here it is easier to point to prima-facie common structures.[99]

The more intensively such comparisons rely on thick, precise descriptions of the different religions, and the more they are aware of the specific use and meaning of the concepts compared, the more illuminating they are. They are, then, anything but trivial: they offer both a picture of human belief that is conceptually clear, and a rich analysis of the complexities of religions. What is more, such comparison reveals highly interesting insights, such as that it is not a common constitutive element of all religions to have a God or gods, or even perhaps holiness.[100] We learn that monotheism and polytheism are not mutually exclusive concepts, but different elements which may be present in one religion; famous examples are the people of Israel worshipping only Yahweh although there were other gods[101] or the Egyptian belief that one highest god *(Atôn)* manifests himself in a plurality of other, local gods.[102] We even see three different ideal types of the prima vista simple idea of monotheism and we realize that other religions do not see Christian belief as being purely monotheistic.[103] The supreme beings in different religions are classified in complex, 'Weberian' typologies according to a variety of criteria, such as cultural history, natural phenomenology, or social function.[104] We realize that, although there are holy scriptures in Christianity, Islam, and Buddhism, these texts are read, interpreted, and translated in very different ways. What is more, they have assumed different theological functions and status: whereas Islamic belief centres on the *Koran,* for Christians the centre is the person of *Christ,* and in Buddhism it is the holy doctrine *Dharma,* which transformed *Siddhartha* into *Buddha.* Interestingly, all these central elements are said to have come into being in a holy night that is today remembered in ritual feasts.[105] This is a complex comparison combining the aspects of 'theological centre' and 'holy scripture', and unearthing a structure of both 'overall similarities and similarities of detail'[106] and significant differences.

---

[99] cf Carsten Colpe, 'Wie universal ist das Heilige?', in Hans-Joachim Klimkeit (ed), *Vergleichen und Verstehen in der Religionswissenschaft* (1997), 1 ff.

[100] cf Nathan Söderblom, 'Holiness (General and Primitive)', in James Hastings and John A. Selbie (eds), *Encyclopaedia of Religion and Ethics* (vol VI, 1928), 731 ff; Mensching (n 94), 126 ff; Colpe (n 99).

[101] Figl (n 48), 550, 554 f.

[102] Birgit Heller, 'Götter/Göttinnen', in Figl (n 48), 530, 531 f.

[103] Figl (n 48), 546, 548 ff.

[104] Theodore M. Ludwig, 'Gods and Goddesses', in Eliade (vol VI, n 97), 59, 61 ff; Heller (n 102), 535 ff; Gerard van der Leeuw, *Religion in Essence and Manifestation* (paperback edn, 1986), 52 ff.

[105] Udo Tworuschka 'Heilige Schriften', in Figl (n 48), 588, 589 f.

[106] For Wittgenstein's idea of family similarity, see above p 316.

(c) Some Observations

Comparative religion could not simply opt for a normative *tertium comparationis*, such as 'function' or a theological concept of 'holiness', because in religious studies the scholarly acceptability of research depends on avoiding such a normatively biased perspective. As a result of this, religious comparatists have become more and more aware of the problems of formulating 'neutral' *tertia comparationis*. Today, it is a matter of course that the formulation of adequate conceptions of concepts, such as 'creation', 'prayer', or 'meditation', is part of the comparative process,[107] which is described as an inductive practice in contrast with the deductive application of concepts of a prior idea of religion.[108] Thus, *tertia comparationis* cannot be defined as part of the method; comparison must remain open for new insights. Nevertheless, as a result of successful comparisons, the discipline has—perhaps unconsciously—developed a comparative second-order language describing the concepts that constitute the different religions' beliefs. It has become highly useful for analysing the complex commonalities and differences of religion; all in all it represents a large body of comparative knowledge.

All this shows that even with normative objects a largely intersubjective, descriptive comparison is possible without necessarily adopting a sociological perspective. The question of 'what matters' is partly answered from the point of view of the religions compared. Although still normative, answers can be evaluated as more or less adequate depending on the insights they produce. Correspondingly, the comparative lawyer becomes aware of his 'functional' approach as being just one—simplifying and normative—*tertium comparationis* that precludes a more subtle, complex analysis. At the same time it becomes apparent that the search for differences is not the only alternative to a unifying functional approach: it is possible to develop complex conceptual structures that allow for simultaneously formulating commonalities and distinguishing peculiarities; such concepts become the basis of a comparative second-order language. What is more, such forms of comparatively contrasting analysis deepen the understanding of the objects compared, as was shown in the case of monotheism: the aim of comparative religious studies is not merely seen in reducing complexity but in structuring and systematically representing a highly complex religious world.[109]

None the less, comparing religions objectively is difficult, and this has quite naturally led the attention of scholars to the way religions perceive each other's belief. On a practical level, this was a motivation for theological discourse between different religions;[110] on the theoretical level, it has stimulated second-order comparisons of the representations religions may make of each other. Understanding the other's view of oneself may not only enhance one's own understanding of

---

[107] cf Jürgen Mohn, 'Schöpfungsvorstellungen', in Figl (n 48), 612 ff; Bettina Bäumer, 'Gebet/ Meditation/Mystik—Ekstase', in Figl (n 48), 702 ff.

[108] Paden (n 98), 3.   [109] Paden (n 98), 162 f.   [110] Sharpe (n 86), 251 ff.

oneself and of the other; it also reveals the common strategies of argumentation which most religions use aggressively to identify themselves as different from others. When such strategies include 'typical forms of *epistemological* or *genetic dissociation* attributing the (wrong) belief of the "Other" to mental confusion or to a basic dependence on base instincts',[111] the comparative lawyer is reminded of striking parallels in recent methodological debate.

3. Understanding Social Change: General Explanations for Historic Developments?

Comparative politics and international social sciences aim at formulating general theories that explain the structure and change of political and social systems as results of their economic, cultural, and historical conditions. Thus, the 'comparative' view on the similarities and dissimilarities of different systems is the obvious method for such investigations. Relying on inductive strategies already developed by John Stuart Mill,[112] social scientists isolate explanatory factors that may have caused social structure or change. Here, explicability presupposes empirical regularity. Accordingly, comparative statements are usually based on a simple classifying concept of similarity: societies and political systems are taken as applications of abstractly formulated concepts or general hypotheses about human action.[113] Such a method is no more comparative than Newton's treatment of apples when exploring the laws of gravity: it does not use qualifying or even complex comparisons and does not treat comparison as an intellectual process for discovering unknown similarities and dissimilarities.

During the twentieth century, this approach faced enormous difficulties. To begin with, classification proved difficult. Thus, it is not easy to find a neutral description for entities such as 'political systems' (ranging from the United States of America to pre-modern systems),[114] 'classes', or 'parties'. Even more serious problems, however, arose in the second place, when it came to testing political theories empirically. First, it remains unclear whether social structures can be

---

[111] Andreas Grünschloß, *Der eigene und der fremde Glaube. Studien zur interreligiösen Fremd-wahrnehmung in Islam, Hinduismus, Buddhismus und Christentum* (1999), 231 ff, 232.

[112] Above n 45.

[113] cf Jan Berting, 'Why Compare in International Research? Theoretical and Practical Limitations of International Research', in Manfred Niessen and Jules Peschar (eds), *International Comparative Research* (1982), 5, 14 f; Wil Arts and Loek Halman, 'New Directions in Quantitative Comparative Sociology: An Introduction', (1999) 40 *International Journal of Comparative Sociology* 1, 3 ff; Klaus von Beyme, *Der Vergleich in der Politikwissenschaft* (1988), 50–68.

[114] For the prevailing system-theoretical standard model (inspired by a Weberian definition of government), see Gabriel A. Almond and G. Bingham Powell, Jr, *Comparative Politics* (2nd edn, 1978), 3 ff, 52 ff, 79 ff.

described in the form of genuine scientific 'laws'. The idea of causal explanations of social action is disputed, and strict empirical correlations are rare. Second, social reality is complex, and complexity cannot artificially be reduced in a laboratory. Thus, empirical studies have mostly reduced the complexity of reality by using dichotomizing variables, which unavoidably leads to a loss of important information and so to unduly simplistic theories without explanatory value.[115] Third, all political comparisons face the dilemma that the number of cases (political systems) is low and the number of relevant variables (possible explanatory factors) high. What is more, variables are usually highly interdependent and cannot easily be isolated. Of course there are ways of addressing such problems, but none of them works smoothly. Thus, although the discipline has collected a large amount of social data,[116] comparative analysis is only rarely reliable, often superficial, and nearly always disputed.[117]

(a) Towards a 'Histoire Comparée'

It is hardly surprising in the light of such problems that there is a fundamental methodological debate in the comparative social sciences. Highly influential voices plead for a more historical approach, which would limit the analysis to specific structures and processes. Generalizations, they argue, are only plausible if they leave room for individual factors and circumstances, and they must often be limited to specific historical conditions. On the other hand, these scholars insist that historical processes often cannot be understood from a narrow historical focus on the society of a particular nation. Such societies are neither homogeneous nor easily distinguished from other societies, and thus the social change within one political system is normally embedded in larger processes of social change.[118]

Similarly, historians have long debated the alternatives of individual historiography without explanatory value and implausibly 'great theories', based on abstract generalizations, both of which are unsatisfactory. Historical explanation must steer clear of the Scylla of mere description and the Charybdis of generalizations abstracted from reality. What is more, historians found themselves caught—not unlike scholars of religious studies or law—within the boundaries of national scholarly languages which had developed in isolation, and it had proved difficult even to identify and describe comparable events in different societies.

---

[115] Jack A. Goldstone, *Revolution and Rebellion in the Early Modern World* (1991), 39 ff.

[116] Charles Lewis Taylor and David A. Jodice, *World Handbook of Political and Social Indicators* (2 vols, 3rd edn, 1983).

[117] Dirk Berg-Schlosser, 'Comparative Studies: Method and Design', in *International Encyclopedia of the Social & Behavioral Sciences* (vol 4, 2001), 2427 ff; Gisèle de Meur and Dirk Berg-Schlosser, 'Comparing Political Systems: Establishing Similarities and Dissimilarities', (1994) 26 *European Journal of Political Research* 193 ff.

[118] Charles Tilly, *Big Structures, Large Processes, Huge Comparisons* (1984), 74 f, 80 ff, and *passim*; Kaelble (n 24), 8, 93 ff, and *passim*.

In consequence, Marc Bloch argued in 1928 for an *histoire comparée* which could develop a common academic language and help to understand history adequately.[119] This did not mean that comparative historians would suppress differences. On the contrary, according to Bloch, only such a common language could create a sensitivity to the different meanings of prima-facie similar or related concepts; only by comparison was it possible to observe the peculiarities of one's own history. A theory of a German *Sonderweg* is meaningful only from a comparative perspective.

All in all, historical comparison is today seen as an 'intellectual . . . process . . . determining the relation between the general and the specific' which is necessary because universal features of social action and social change are typically embedded within specific cultural and historical circumstances.[120] Individual developments are thus understood as 'historical variations' of 'robust processes'.[121] Accordingly, comparative history is a field of research common to historians and social scientists. It has, however, never become a homogeneous discipline, mainly because contrasting comparison, which explains the individual as distinct from other developments, and universalizing approaches, which search for uniform patterns of development, have—perhaps wrongly—been widely regarded as different approaches to history.[122] Nevertheless historical comparative studies have yielded highly innovative explanations, for example for great revolutions, for the different ways and the speed of processes of industrialization, and for patterns of professionalization.[123] Today it is even possible to identify a set of common methodological assumptions.

(b) Comparison and Theory

Similar developments can be explained either as the results of mutual influence or of similar conditions and historical regularity. Thus, relying on the distinction in linguistics between similar structure and genetic relatedness, historians offer

[119] 'Pour une histoire comparée des sociétés européennes', (1928) 48 *Revue de synthèse historique* 15 ff; cf Otto Hintze, 'Über individualistische und kollektivistische Geschichtsauffassung' (1897), in *idem, Soziologie und Geschichte* (2nd edn, 1964), 315 ff; *idem,* 'Der Beamtenstand' (1911), in the same volume, 66, 78 ff, 86 ff.

[120] Hannes Siegrist, 'Perspektiven der vergleichenden Geschichtswissenschaft: Gesellschaft, Kultur und Raum', in Schriewer and Kaelble (n 1), 305 ff, 321, 330.

[121] Goldstone (n 115), 51 ff; cf also Tilly (n 118); Heinz-Gerhard Haupt, 'Comparative History', in *International Encyclopedia of the Social & Behavioral Sciences* (vol IV, 2001), 2397 ff.

[122] cf Theda Skocpol and Margaret Somers, 'The Uses of Comparative History in Macrosocial Inquiry', (1980) 22 *Comparative Studies in Society and History* 174 ff; Tilly (n 118); Jürgen Osterhammel, *Geschichtswissenschaft jenseits des Nationalstaats* (2001), 17 ff, 25 ff.

[123] Theda Skocpol, *States and Social Revolution: A Comparative Analysis of France, Russia and China* (1979); Goldstone (n 115); Alexander Gerschenkron, *Economic Backwardness in Historical Perspective* (1962); Hannes Siegrist, *Advokat, Bürger und Staat: Sozialgeschichte der Rechtsanwälte in Deutschland, Italien und der Schweiz* (1996).

different kinds of explanations for different forms of social change.[124] From a methodological point of view, historical parallels that are independent of mutual influence are most interesting. Here an explanation is usually based on generalizing, causal theories. Of course, these may be, and are even expected to be, limited in space, but the generalization is always in the form of a specific question or theoretical hypothesis that forms the guideline for and the result of comparative historical research and thus becomes the *tertium comparationis*. Conversely, comparative historical studies may be understood as a process of developing, testing, and reformulating general theories of social change.[125] Dissimilarities in historical development must be explained as deviations from the general theory for particular reasons or circumstances. It follows that—as in the case of comparative religion—the *tertium comparationis* must be seen as a substantial element of comparative research, not as part of the method. However, it is normally not a concept, but a historical theory that forms such a point of reference: comparative history typically either develops or examines distinctive theories of social change.[126] Comparative legal studies, too, might profit from structuring analyses by different theoretical hypotheses (functionalism being only one of them) instead of merely accounting comprehensively for the commonalities and differences of legal systems. Comparative lawyers would then become aware of the fact that there may be normative 'political' implications not only in the choice of a *tertium comparationis* but also in the prior choice of the systems to be compared:[127] a *Sonderweg* presupposes a 'normal' path followed by the nations chosen for comparison.

Excluding the formulation of a *tertium comparationis* from the domain of methodology has not prevented the discipline from formulating methodological guidelines for such theories. Thus, hypotheses have to be specific and relate to observable matters of fact. For example, an unspecific comparison of marriage in different countries would not be accepted, unless a hypothesis—perhaps about the relation between religious belief and legal order—is clearly stated. It is also emphasized that comparative hypotheses must be designed so that it remains possible to account for both commonalities and differences in historical development.[128] Now, because of the complexity of social change, historical explanations are normally not plausible if they do not embrace a range of factors. It follows that comparisons are normally complex: they try to lay open different explanatory factors and they must be embedded in thick, detailed descriptions of the relevant historical processes. Again, ideal types have long been taken to be

---

[124] Bloch, (1928) 48 *Revue de synthèse historique* 19 ff, 41 ff; Osterhammel (n 122), 56 f.

[125] Skocpol (n 123), 36; Goldstone (n 115), 51 ff.

[126] See eg Tilly (n 118), 82; Siegrist (n 120), 319 f, 333 f; Kaelble (n 24), 120 ff, 124 f, 130 f; Haupt (n 121), 2401 f.

[127] cf Chris Lorenz, 'Comparative Historiography: Problems and Perspectives', (1999) 38 *History and Theory* 25, 39.

[128] Tilly (n 118), 118 f; Kaelbe (n 24), 122 ff.

suitable instruments for formulating comparative historical theories, especially for contrasting forms of analysis. It would otherwise be difficult to apply concepts like 'feudalism', 'industrialization', or 'profession' to different, partly dissimilar processes in different countries and different times. Only such an approach permits a rational description of similarities and differences in terms of the *degree of deviation* from an idealized theory of historical process.[129]

IV. Concluding Remarks

Methodological investigations should—as far as possible—abstain from normatively imposing one's own epistemological interests on others. The foregoing survey accordingly analysed different forms of comparison and comparative knowledge in order to clarify these ideas, without prescribing specific procedures for others to follow in their comparative research. Nevertheless, the analysis was guided by the hope that the experience of other disciplines might enrich the comparative lawyer's methodological reservoir; it was therefore restricted to obvious achievements of other disciplines—a comprehensive critique being neither possible nor intended. After all, two lessons may be particularly important for the comparative lawyer. First, historical linguistics reminds other comparative disciplines not to be content with judgments of similarity. Unearthing genetic relations between different systems may add considerably to our comparative knowledge. It may lay the foundations for, and show the limitations of, any project to reconstruct a common understanding of the law.

The second lesson concerns the conceptual and theoretical structure of *tertia comparationis*. Of course, lawyers have always been aware of the fact that comparison may entail the necessity of developing suitable instruments for neutrally describing the legal systems compared.[130] But compared to practitioners of comparative religion or comparative history, lawyers have made relatively little progress in this regard. Perhaps because they (mistakenly) took common comparative

---

[129] Otto Hintze, 'Max Webers Soziologie' (1926), in *idem, Soziologie und Geschichte* (n 119), 134, 143 ff; *idem*, 'Soziologische und geschichtliche Staatsauffassung' (1929), in the same volume, 239, 250 ff, 269, 277 f, 294 ff; *idem*, 'Wesen und Verbreitung des Feudalismus' (1929), in *idem, Staat und Verfassung* (2nd edn, 1962), 84 ff, 99 ff; McKinney (n 40), 57 ff, 140 ff, 150 ff; Siegrist (n 123), 12 ff, 67 ff, 925 ff; further references in *idem* (n 120), 309 ff, 320, 333 f.

[130] Ulrich Drobnig, 'Methodenfragen der Rechtsvergleichung im Lichte der "International Encyclopedia of Comparative Law" ', in *Ius Privatum Gentium: Festschrift für Max Rheinstein* (vol I, 1969), 221, 228 ff.

concepts to be a kind of ideal, 'natural' law,[131] or perhaps because of the dominance of the functional approach, lawyers have developed neither neutral comparative concepts nor comparative theories. Instead, most standard works of comparative law still rely on the national terminology inherited from the respective author's system and refrain from theoretically analysing causes or reasons for commonalities and differences. Only very recently have scholars begun to research the determining factors of legal change. What is more, comparative lawyers have only exceptionally realized that the virtues of comparative and doctrinal concepts are not identical: whereas doctrine needs clearly limited, classificatory concepts, genuine comparative knowledge presupposes precise, but complex, typologies that can both unearth commonalities and help to perceive and rationally describe the peculiarities of the world's different legal systems. Weberian *Idealtypen* may be more useful than Aristotelian definitions.

V. Summary

(1) Comparison is the process of constructing relations of similarity and dissimilarity. Whereas *classifying* comparison reflects and *categorically* applies a *tertium comparationis, qualifying* comparison relates to a *shared tertium comparationis* T; here judgments of similarity are based on the compared objects' degree of T. *Complex comparisons* are judgments of family-similarity based on a bundle of classifying and qualifying comparisons.

(2) The core of comparative knowledge consists in a structured system of similarities and differences of the objects compared.

(3) Although qualifying and complex judgments of similarity and difference are irreducibly subjective, they are not meaningless if they relate to a clearly defined epistemological perspective or to a common understanding of the relevant circumstances. Differences can be expressed by elementary scales like 'little—medium—large'. Comparisons gain empirical content the more they are based on a full factual description of the objects compared: meaningful comparison presupposes full factual description.

(4) Complex comparisons may be rationalized by formulating *tertia comparationis* in the form of ideal-type typologies. Such typologies structure the description of similarities and dissimilarities and thus allow both individual peculiarities

---

[131] cf Constantinesco (n 7), 43 f (against Radbruch); for such a Natural-law approach to comparative law today, see James Gordley, 'Comparative Legal Research: Its Function in the Development of Harmonized Law', (1995) 43 *AJCL* 555 ff.

and general commonalities to be accounted for as degrees of deviation from or correspondence with a common standard.

(5) Comparative judgments are not evaluative. However, comparative investigations are determined on the one hand by the choice of objects compared, and on the other by the choice of the comparative question (*tertium comparationis*). These choices are influenced by epistemic interests and evaluations about what matters or what counts as normal. They should be openly stated and may be measured by both non-academic (eg legal) values and academic standards relating to the quality of the result of comparative research.

(6) The choice of *tertia comparationis* should be understood as part of the comparative process, not as a defining element of the comparative method. *Tertia comparationis*, for example structuring typologies or general explanatory theories, should be formulated in a specific way relating to observable similarities and dissimilarities. They can thus become a central element of comparative knowledge.

(7) Comparisons of partly autonomous normative systems, such as religion or law, should be formulated in a neutral second-order language. Such a language bears a descriptive character and must not be confused with an ideal (Natural law) system.

(8) The analysis of genetic relations traces prima-facie similarities to a common ancestor. Comprehensive comparative knowledge requires an analysis both of similarities and dissimilarities, and of genetic relations, for they complement each other.

(9) Evaluation of the objects compared is not a part of the comparative process. Comparative knowledge may be used to justify normative statements, but comparison itself neither proves the truth of a belief nor reveals one legal rule or doctrine to be superior to others.

BIBLIOGRAPHY

Marc Bloch, 'Pour une histoire comparée des sociétés européennes', (1928) 48 *Revue de synthèse historique* 15 ff

Ludwig Wittgenstein, *Philosophische Untersuchungen/Philosophical Investigations* (trans Gertrude E. M. Anscombe, 1953)

Erich Rothacker, 'Die vergleichende Methode in den Geisteswissenschaften', (1957) 60 *Zeitschrift für vergleichende Rechtswissenschaft* 13 ff

Max Weber, 'Die "Objektivität" sozialwissenschaftlicher und sozialpolitischer Erkenntnis', in *idem, Gesammelte Aufsätze zur Wissenschaftslehre* (3rd edn, 1968), 146 ff

Léontin-Jean Constantinesco, *Rechtsvergleichung*, vol II: *Die rechtsvergleichende Methode* (1972)

Charles Tilly, *Big Structures, Large Processes, Huge Comparisons* (1984)

Eric J. Sharpe, *Comparative Religion: A History* (2nd edn, 1986)

William E. Paden, *Religious Worlds. The Comparative Study of Religion* (1988)

Anthony Fox, *Linguistic Reconstruction* (1995)

Hiriam Chodosh, 'Comparing Comparisons: in Search of Methodology', (1999) 84 *Iowa LR* 1025 ff

Mark Aronoff and Janie Rees-Miller, *The Handbook of Linguistics* (2001)

Johann Figl (ed), *Handbuch Religionswissenschaft* (2003)

Jürgen Schriewer and Hartmut Kaelble (eds), *Vergleich und Transfer: Komparatistik in den Sozial-, Geschichts- und Kulturwissenschaften* (2003)

CHAPTER 10

THE FUNCTIONAL METHOD OF COMPARATIVE LAW

RALF MICHAELS

Durham, North Carolina*

* This essay was finalized while I was a Lloyd Cutler Fellow at the American Academy in Berlin. Special thanks for comments to Donald Horowitz, Joan Magat, and the editors.

I. 'The Functional Method'

THE functional method has become both the mantra and the *bête noire* of comparative law. For its proponents it is the most, perhaps the only, fruitful method;[1] to its opponents it represents everything bad about mainstream comparative law. The debate over the functional method is indeed much more than a methodological dispute. It is the focal point of almost all discussions about the field of comparative law as a whole—centres versus peripheries of scholarly projects and interests, mainstream versus avant-garde, convergence versus pluralism, instrumentalism versus hermeneutics, technocracy versus culture, and so on.

This functional method is a chimera, in both theory and practice of comparative law. As theory it hardly exists, at least in an elaborated version. The standard reference text for supporters and opponents alike is a brief chapter in an introductory textbook, a text that in its original conception is almost half a century of age[2] and whose author, Zweigert, expressed both disdain for methodological debate[3]

---

[1] See, eg, for the United States, John Reitz, 'How to do Comparative Law', (1998) 46 *AJCL* 617, 620–3; Mathias Reimann, 'The Progress and Failure of Comparative Law in the Second Half of the Twentieth Century', (2003) 50 *AJCL* 671, 679 f; for France, Marc Ancel, *Utilité et méthodes de droit comparé* (1971), 97 f, 101–3; *idem*, 'Le problème de la comparabilité et la méthode fonctionnelle en droit comparé', in *Festschrift für Imre Zajtay* (1982), 1–6; for England, Hugh Collins, 'Methods and Aims of Comparative Contract Law', (1989) 11 *Oxford Journal of Legal Studies* 396–406; Peter de Cruz, *Comparative Law in a Changing World* (2nd edn, 1999), 230 ff; for Germany, Hein Kötz, 'Comparative Law in Germany Today', (1999) 51 *RIDC* 753, 755 f; for Scandinavia, Michael Bogdan, *Comparative Law* (1994), 59–60; for a socialist perspective, Imre Szabó, 'Theoretical Questions of Comparative Law', in Imre Szabó and Zoltán Péteri (eds), *A Socialist Approach to Comparative Law* (1977), 9, 36–8; for rise and fall in Italy, Pier Giuseppe Monateri, 'Critique et différence: Le droit comparé en Italie', (1999) 51 *RIDC* 989, 991 f.

[2] Konrad Zweigert and Hein Kötz, *An Introduction to Comparative Law* (trans Tony Weir, 3rd edn, 1998), 32–47, first published in *Einführung in die Rechtsvergleichung* (vol I, 1971), 27–48; Konrad Zweigert, 'Methodological Problems in Comparative Law', (1972) 7 *Israel LR* 465–74. Earlier versions are Konrad Zweigert, 'Méthodologie du droit comparé', in *Mélanges offerts à Jacques Maury* (vol I, 1960), 579–96 = 'Zur Methode der Rechtsvergleichung', (1960) 13 *Studium Generale—Zeitschrift für die Einheit der Wissenschaften im Zusammenhang ihrer Begriffsbildung und Forschungsmethoden* 193–200; Ernst von Caemmerer and Konrad Zweigert, 'Évolution et état actuel de la méthode du droit comparé en allemagne', in *Livre du Centenaire de la société de législation comparée* (1969), 267, 282–97. The functional approach to comparative law had been practised in Germany and elsewhere earlier; see Max Rheinstein, 'Comparative Law and Conflict of Laws in Germany', (1934–5) 2 *University of Chicago*

and a preference for inspiration over methodological rigour as the comparatist's ultimate guide.[4] Even a seminal text like Zweigert's cannot possibly provide all elements of a theory, nor suffice to refute all criticism directed against it. Moreover, even a spurious overview of comparative law theory reveals that functionalism is, and has always been, only one of several approaches towards micro-comparison. At least three main current approaches other than functionalism remain:[5] comparative legal history, the study of legal transplants, and the comparative study of legal cultures.

Concerning practice, the functional approach underlies some famous successful and methodologically explicit studies, but they are famous in no small part because they are so rare.[6] More often, for supporters and opponents alike, 'functional method' merely serves as shorthand for traditional comparative law. Two recent works on similar topics illustrate this. Stefan Vogenauer explicitly places his comprehensive comparative study of statutory interpretation within the functional tradition,[7] although his analysis focuses on forms of legal argument rather than functions. In contrast, Mitchel Lasser describes the method behind his comparison of judicial styles as a (cultural) analysis of *mentalités*,[8] but then he explains different

LR 232, 250; Hans G. Ficker, 'L'état du droit comparé en Allemagne', (1958) 10 *RIDC* 701, 716–18; M. Schmitthoff, 'The Science of Comparative Law', (1939–41) 7 *Cambridge LJ* 94, 96 ff; Tullio Ascarelli, *Studi di diritto comparato e in tema di interpretazione* (1952), 1 ff.

[3] Below, n 109.

[4] See Zweigert and Kötz (n 2), 33, expressing approval of a statement by Gustav Radbruch, *Einführung in die Rechtswissenschaft* (9th edn, 1958), 242 ('Wissenschaften, die sich mit ihrer eigenen Methodenlehre zu beschäftigen Anlaß haben, sind kranke Wissenschaften'; '. . . sciences which have to busy themselves with their own methodology are sick sciences'); but cf the more distanced attitude in Zweigert, 'Zur Methode' (n 2), 193 ('mag auf sich beruhen'). See already Franz von Liszt, 'Das "richtige Recht" in der Strafgesetzgebung', in Konrad Zweigert and Hans-Jürgen Puttfarken (eds), *Rechtsvergleichung* (1978), 57, 58; originally in (1906) 26 *Zeitschrift für die gesamte Strafrechtswissenschaft* 553–7: 'Es pflegen nicht eben die schaffenskräftigsten unter den Gelehrten zu sein, die sich der Erörterung methodologischer Fragen zuwenden' (Usually, the scholars who deal with issues of methodology are not the most productive ones).

[5] cf the lists in Béatrice Jaluzot, 'Méthodologie du droit comparé: Bilan et prospective', (2005) 57 *RIDC* 29, 38 ff; Alessandro Somma, 'Al capezzale del malato? Riflessioni sul metodo comparatistico', (2005) 23 *Rivista critica del diritto privato* 401–47; also in *idem, Tecniche e valori nella ricerca comparatistica* (2005), 3–71.

[6] Michele Graziadei, 'The Functional Heritage', in Pierre Legrand and Roderick Munday (eds), *Comparative Legal Studies: Traditions and Transitions* (2003), 100, 100 f.; Vernon Valentine Palmer, 'From Lerotholi to Lando: Some Examples of Comparative Law Methodology', (2005) 53 *AJCL* 261, 285. Annelise Riles, 'Wigmore's Treasure Box: Comparative Law in the Era of Information', (1999) 40 *Harvard International LJ* 221, 236 f calls functionalism a 'compromised methodology'.

[7] Stefan Vogenauer, *Die Auslegung von Gesetzen in England und auf dem Kontinent* (vol I, 2001), 18 n 105; see now also *idem*, 'Eine gemeineuropäische Methodenlehre des Rechts: Plädoyer und Programm', (2005) 13 *Zeitschrift für Europäisches Privatrecht* 234, 246–9.

[8] Mitchel de S.-O.-l'E. Lasser, *Judicial Deliberations* (2004), 362; cf *idem*, 'The Question of Understanding', in Legrand and Munday (n 6), 197–239.

styles of legal systems as equivalent regarding the functions they serve: transparency, judicial accountability, and control.[9]

In short, 'the functional method' is a triple misnomer. First, there is not one ('the') functional method, but many. Second, not all allegedly functional methods are 'functional' at all. Third, some projects claiming adherence to it do not even follow any recognizable 'method'. Does functionalist comparative law actually have any meaning? Functionalist comparatists agree on some important elements. First, functionalist comparative law is factual, it focuses not on rules but on their effects, not on doctrinal structures and arguments, but on events. As a consequence, its objects are often judicial decisions as responses to real life situations, and legal systems are compared by considering their various judicial responses to similar situations. Second, functionalist comparative law combines its factual approach with the theory that its objects must be understood in the light of their functional relation to society. Law and society are thus thought to be separable but related. Consequently, and third, function itself serves as *tertium comparationis*. Institutions, both legal and non-legal, even doctrinally different ones, are comparable if they are functionally equivalent, if they fulfil similar functions in different legal systems. A fourth element, not shared by all variants of functional method, is that functionality can serve as an evaluative criterion. Functionalist comparative law then becomes a 'better-law comparison'—the better of several laws is that which fulfils its function better than the others.

This chapter tries to reconstruct and evaluate functionalist comparative law by placing it within the larger framework of other disciplines, especially the social sciences. It is of course a risk for a comparative lawyer to use disciplines foreign to his own—sociology, anthropology, philosophy—as lenses on his own discipline. But comparatists know that looking through the eyes of foreign law enables us better to understand our own, so looking through the eyes of foreign disciplines should similarly help us better to understand our own discipline. Such an interdisciplinary analysis yields three promises. First, the interdisciplinary look should enable a (re-)construction of a more theoretically grounded functional method of comparative law than is usually presented (Section II). This should reveal its connections with and its peculiarities within both the development of comparative law and the development of functionalism in other disciplines. Second, the interdisciplinary approach should help formulate and evaluate the concept in order to determine how functional the method really is (Section III). Just as comparative law can borrow from the development of functional methods in the social sciences, so it can borrow from the development of critique. However, comparative law is not a social science, and herein lies the third promise of an interdisciplinary

---

[9] Lasser, *Judicial Deliberations* (n 8), 299 ff; see also *idem*, 'Is there a Transatlantic Common Core of Judicial Discourse?', in Mauro Bassani and Ugo Mattei (eds), *The Common Core of European Private Law* (2003) 213–9.

approach: The comparison with functionalism in other disciplines may reveal what is special about functionalism in comparative law, and why what in other disciplines would rightly be regarded as methodological shortcomings may in fact be fruitful for comparative law.

II. Concepts of Functionalism

In 1971, Konrad Zweigert postulated a methodological monopoly: 'The basic methodological principle of all comparative law is that of functionality.'[10] Twelve years before him, Kingsley David had done something similar for sociology and social anthropology when he had called structural-functional analysis, 'in effect, synonymous with sociological analysis'.[11] Similarly again, Laura Kalman remarked that the statement that we are all (legal) realists now 'has been made so frequently that it has become a truism to refer to it as a truism'.[12]

Such claims of monopoly suggest a lack of conceptual clarity, or a lack of theoretical sophistication, or both. If functionalism is the only method in a discipline, chances are that either the discipline does not recognize all of its potential, or the notion of functional method is itself inflated into a meaninglessly broad concept. Indeed, neither Davis nor Kalman thought a specified version of functionalism had won the day in their respective disciplines. Davis proposed to drop the notion of functionalism because it blurred the underlying methodological differences.[13] Similarly, the 'we are all realists now' quote has been used as a strategy to conceal the special contributions of legal realism[14] rather than to adopt their general ones, a way of beating realism by embracing it to death. If we are all functionalists of comparative law, as Zweigert proclaims, then functionalism cannot mean very much. (Nor, as one tends to overlook, can its rejection by its critics.)

The reconstruction of a more precise concept of functionalism in each discipline

---

[10] Zweigert and Kötz (n 2), 34.

[11] Kingsley Davis, 'The Myth of Functional Analysis as a Special Method in Sociology and Anthropology', (1959) 24 *American Sociological Review* 757, 757.

[12] Laura Kalman, *Legal Realism at Yale, 1927–1960* (1986), 229. See also Lawrence Rosen, 'Beyond Compare', in Legrand and Munday (n 6), 493, 504, ending his critique of functionalism by proclaiming: 'In some sense, of course, we are all functionalists and that is all to the good inasmuch as it leads us to see connections we might not otherwise have thought obtained'.

[13] For example Radcliffe-Brown called himself an anti-functionalist just in order to distinguish himself from the other great functionalist, Malinowski: Alfred R. Radcliffe-Brown, 'Functionalism: A Protest', (1949) 51 *American Anthropologist* 320, 321.

[14] See, most recently, Hanoch Dagan, 'The Realist Conception of Law', (2005) *Tel Aviv University Law Faculty Papers* 21.

reveals another, less obvious but more important, problem—functionalism means different things in different disciplines. Superficially, one would expect to find similarities. After all, the turn in the nineteenth and twentieth centuries away from essentialist to functionalist methods, from observation of objects themselves to observation of their relations amongst each other and to the whole, was so widespread that one could speak of a general 'functionalist turn' away from essentialism in all academic disciplines and beyond, for example, in architecture and design ('form follows function'). There may indeed have been no more fashionable concept in the twentieth century than that of function.[15] This simultaneous rise and fall of functionalism in different disciplines suggests a parallel, perhaps even a common development, or evolution, of ideas.[16] Similarity becomes even more plausible in view of cross-fertilizations between disciplines:[17] Ernst Cassirer transposed the notion from mathematics and science to philosophy;[18] sociologists from Comte and Spencer via Durkheim to Parsons and Luhmann borrowed biological concepts; lawyers like Jhering and Pound were inspired by sociological ideas of function.

But such cross-fertilization, as comparatists know well from the legal transplants debate, is not immune to misunderstandings and alterations, known or unknown. The story of a common development, alluring as it may be, tends to overlook the differences between concepts and disciplines and, as a consequence, the differences between different kinds of functionalism. This is especially problematic for a discipline like comparative law that sees its place somewhere between the social sciences on the one hand and legal studies on the other, and that draws methodological inspiration from both. If the concepts and methods in these disciplines are different, the result can only be methodological mishmash.

In fact, one can distinguish at least seven different concepts of functionalism across disciplines:[19] (1) finalism, a neo-Aristotelian functionalism based on inherent teleology, (2) adaptionism, an evolutionary functionalism in a Darwinian tradition, (3) classical (Durkheimian) functionalism, explaining institutions through their usefulness for society, (4) instrumentalism, a normative theory of using law for social engineering, (5) refined functionalism, a functionalist method that replaces certain postulates of classical functionalism with empirically testable hypotheses,

---

[15] Reiner Wiehl, *Subjektivität und System* (2000), 375.

[16] Connections are drawn eg by Rudolf B. Schlesinger, Hans W. Baade, Peter E. Herzog, and Edward M. Wise, *Comparative Law* (6th edn, 1998), 49; Rosen (n 12), 504.

[17] For examples from writers in two different disciplines, see the references in Robert K. Merton, 'Manifest and Latent Functions', in *idem, Social Theory and Social Structure* (1968), 73, 101 n 50; reprinted eg in N. J. Demerath III and Richard A. Peterson (eds), *System, Change, and Conflict: A Reader on Contemporary Sociological Theory and the Debate over Functionalism* (1967), 10; Felix S. Cohen, 'Transcendental Nonsense and the Functional Method', (1935) 35 *Columbia LR* 809, 824–9; *idem*, 'The Problems of a Functional Jurisprudence', (1937), *Modern LR* 5, 9.

[18] Ernst Cassirer, *Substanzbegriff und Funktionsbegriff* (1910).

[19] For another classification of different concepts of functionalism, see Martin Mahner and Mario Bunge, 'Function and Functionalism: A Synthetic Perspective', (2001) 68 *Philosophy of Science* 75–94.

(6) epistemological functionalism, an epistemology that focuses on functional relations rather than on the ontology of things, and (7) equivalence functionalism, building on these concepts but emphasizing the non-teleological, non-causal aspect of functional relations. Largely oblivious of incompatibilities, functionalist comparative law (8) uses all of these.

1. Finalism

Functionalist comparative law shares its emphasis on generalities that transcend national boundaries with the Natural law tradition, and indeed finds one of its origins there. Kant, while positing a strict separation between 'is' and 'ought,' had conceived the possibility of universal law based on reason. Neo-Kantians hoped to use comparative law as a response to Kirchmann's famous verdict on law as non-scientific and as a way towards a rational law. In 1905, Gustav Radbruch proposed a Kantian version of ideal law as *tertium comparationis* for solutions to similar problems. This ideal law could not be deduced from the insights of comparative law (that would have been an is/ought crossover), but its formulation could help psychologically in the quest for better law.[20] Twenty years later, Max Salomon expanded on these thoughts and formulated the credo of modern functionalist comparative law: Legal science, like every science, deals with universals, but these universals are not legal norms but rather legal problems. As a consequence, a comparison of legal norms is possible only of norms responding to the same legal problems.[21] Legal science is possible only as comparative law.

Another source lies in Aristotle's philosophy, where the idea that law performs some function for society in an unspecific sense can already be found. For Aristotle, the purpose of things, their *telos* or *causa finalis*, belonged to their nature.

---

[20] Gustav Radbruch, 'Über die Methode der Rechtsvergleichung', (1905–6) 2 *Monatsschrift für Kriminalpsychologie und Strafrechtsreform* 422–5; reprinted in Zweigert and Puttfarken (n 4), 52–6 and in Heinrich Scholler (ed), *Gustav Radbruch—Rechtsvergleichende Schriften* (Gustav Radbruch Gesamtausgabe, vol 15, 1999), 152–6. See also *idem, Rechtsphilosophie* (1932), 120 (*Wertbeziehung* [value relation] as scientific criterion for legal science). For a stricter application of the is/ought argument and critical response to both Radbruch and Salomon, see Julius Binder, *Philosophie des Rechts* (1925), 951 ff; for the possibility of a Natural law derived from the comparison of positive laws, see von Liszt (n 4), 61 f; Konrad Zweigert, 'Rechtsvergleichung als universale Interpretationsmethode', (1949) 15 *RabelsZ* 5, 19–20.

[21] Max Salomon, *Grundlegung zur Rechtsphilosophie* (1925), 34 ('Rechtswissenschaft ist nicht eine Wissenschaft von den Rechtsnormen, sondern von den Rechtsproblemen'; legal science is a science not of legal norms but of legal problems), 33 ('Rechtsvergleichung ist Vergleichung von Lösungen eines einheitlichen Problems'; comparative law is the comparison of solutions to a uniform problem); for approval, see Radbruch, *Rechtsphilosophie* (n 20), 120 n 19; Schmitthoff (n 2), 96; Willis Santiago Guerra Filho, 'A dimensão processual dos direitos fundamentais e da Constituição', (1998) 137 *Revista de Informação Legislativa* 13, 20–1; cf Otto Sandrock, *Über Sinn und Methode zivilistischer Rechtsvergleichung* (1966), 16 f.

Underlying this was a teleological image of the world, in which everything strove towards perfection. 'Is' and 'ought' were connected: the correct laws could be deduced from the nature of things. Such thoughts were later rejected both in philosophy and in legal theory, before the crisis of legal positivism spurred a simultaneous return to Natural law and comparative law, and to Aristotelian ideals, in the twentieth century. Once it could be shown that not only problems but also their solutions were similar, a return to a minimal version of Natural law or at least *ius gentium*, based on an Aristotelian notion of function, seemed possible. To this end, the revived rhetorical tradition of topics could be made fruitful.[22] Topics, taking the role of problems, did not spur universal solutions by themselves, but inspired similar analyses that might lead to similar results. Comparative law became phenomenological:[23] Comparatists viewed the solutions in different legal systems as responses to common problems, contingent in their form but none the less required by the nature of the problem.

The most important theoretical treatise in this tradition and, at the same time, one of the most important works for functionalist comparative law is Josef Esser's book on principles and rules in judicial lawmaking.[24] Esser's functionalism is richer and more sophisticated than the one developed later by Zweigert, but its central elements are strikingly similar: Institutions are contingent while problems are universal, the function can serve as *tertium comparationis*, different legal systems find similar solutions by different means, so universal principles of law can be found and formulated as a system with its own terminology.[25] The reason for the similarity is that solutions are deemed inherent in problems and arguments can be made from the *Natur der Sache* (the thing's nature); a commonality of values is both the basis for and the consequence of this. Another comparatist, more openly in the tradition of Aristotle and Thomas Aquinas, is James Gordley.[26] His general approach is more philosophical than Esser's, but in effect quite similar: Gordley

---

[22] Fritz von Hippel, *Zur Gesetzmäßigkeit juristischer Systembildung* (1931); Theodor Viehweg, *Topik und Jurisprudenz* (1954, 5th edn, 1974; English translation under the title *Topics and Law* by W. Cole Durham, 1993); Ernst A. Kramer, 'Topik und Rechtsvergleichung', (1969) 33 *RabelsZ* 1–16; for the history of legal topics, see also Jan Schröder, *Recht als Wissenschaft* (2001), 23–48 with references at 23 n 97.

[23] Alois Troller, *Überall gültige Prinzipien der Rechtswissenschaft* (1965), especially at 4–5; *idem*, 'Rechtsvergleichung und Phänomenologie', in Mario Rotondi (ed), *Inchieste di diritto comparato*, vol II: *Buts et méthodes du droit comparé* (1973), 685–705, especially at 694; both with references to functionalist comparatists.

[24] Josef Esser, *Grundsatz und Norm in der richterlichen Rechtsfortbildung* (1956), especially at 31 ff, 346 ff. Unfortunately no English translation exists; for reviews in English, see Max Rheinstein (to whom Esser dedicated his book), (1959) 24 *University of Chicago LR* 597–605; Wolfgang G. Friedmann, (1957) 57 *Columbia LR* 449–51; Arthur T. von Mehren, (1957) 22 *RabelsZ* 548–9. For an application of Esser's method by one of his students, see Dieter Rothoeft, *System der Irrtumslehre als Methodenfrage der Rechtsvergleichung* (1968).

[25] Esser (n 24), ch 10.

[26] James Gordley, 'The Universalist Heritage', in Legrand and Munday (n 6), 31–45; *idem*, *The Foundations of Private Law: Property, Tort, Contract, Unjust Enrichment* (2006), 1 ff.

also sees different laws as different responses to the same, universal problems.[27] Neo-Aristotelians postulate that comparative law can lead us to universal, common legal principles. Different laws provide answers to similar problems that are doctrinally (formally) different but substantively similar, and their relative similarity suggests inherently correct solutions to these problems—a Natural law, a *ius commune* (Gordley), a *ius gentium* (Esser), or 'universal legal principles' (Troller).

Both Esser and Gordley call their approaches functional, and both have been influential in functionalist comparative law. But they use function in a very specific sense: For them it is synonymous with purpose and *causa finalis*. This is quite different from the modern notion of function as developed by Durkheim. Durkheim explicitly distinguished an institution's functions from its cause and from its nature, rejected the Aristotelian fourfold concept of *causa* by confining 'cause' to *causa efficiens*, and replacing end or goal (*causa finalis*) with function.[28] Since then, the function of a thing (or a law) is normally separated not only from the reasons for its origin and evolution,[29] but also from its essence; functional relations are separate from the things themselves. Esser's and Gordley's functionalisms are different; they must be understood against the background of Aristotelian ontology and metaphysics and answer the criticisms brought forward against these.

2. Adaptionism

Darwinism discarded the Aristotelian worldview, but it did not simultaneously discard the teleological view of the world.[30] The *telos* was now transferred into the world at large; the struggle of everyone against everyone was thought to contribute to the progress of the whole. Darwinian ideas influenced all disciplines in the nineteenth century, including the new discipline of sociology and the concept of function within it. Auguste Comte, who gave sociology its name, introduced a vision of society as a complex organism which evolved as a whole, while its elements all performed certain functions in this evolution. Herbert Spencer, closer to Darwinism, conceptualized society more as a struggle of all against all, but he also emphasized the important interplay between structures and their functions

---

[27] See eg, James Gordley, 'Is Comparative Law a Distinct Discipline?', (1998) 46 *AJCL* 607–15.

[28] Émile Durkheim, *Les règles de la méthode sociologique* (5th edn, 1988, originally published in 1894–5), 188: 'Nous nous servons du mot de fonction de préférence à celui de fin ou de but, précisément parce que les phénomènes sociaux n'existent généralement pas en vue des résultats utiles qu'ils produisent' (we use the word function rather than that of end or goal precisely because social phenomena do not generally exist in view of the useful results they produce).

[29] Durkheim (n 28), 183: 'Faire voir à quoi un fait est utile n'est pas expliquer comment il est né ni comment il est ce qu'il est' (showing for what a fact is useful is not the same as explaining how it comes about nor why it is the way it is).

[30] This is in dispute; for Darwin's own views of Aristotle (whom he discovered late in life), see Allan Gotthelf, 'Darwin on Aristotle', (1999) 32 *Journal of the History of Biology* 3–30.

for society.[31] Not surprisingly, evolutionist thought also influenced lawyers of the time, none more perhaps than Jhering, who argued that law developed in response to the needs not of individuals but of society.[32] For all these scholars, institutions like the law respond, adapt to social needs; those institutions that adapt best will survive.

This version of functionalism, which one may call adaptionism, seemed especially apt for comparative law.[33] That field had hitherto consisted largely of comparative legal history, understood as the history and diffusion of ideas and doctrines. The new sociological interest in interrelations between law and society changed this focus. Now ideas about law were drawn neither from texts nor from the spirit of a particular people, but from general ideas about societies and their development. Consequently, generalization across borders became possible; comparative law could become a science of the way in which societies dealt with similar problems on their paths toward progress. Central to this new approach was the focus on the functions that both law at large and its individual institutions fulfilled for society. An early example comes from Franz von Liszt, a supporter of a functional criminal law in the tradition of Beccaria (and a cousin to the famous composer). Liszt suggested that because punishment was necessary for maintenance of the legal order and because the legal order in turn was necessary for the maintenance and development of the state, criminal law norms had to be judged against their ability to maintain the legal order.[34] This function was useful for comparative law; it served as the *tertium comparationis* for the (functional) comparison of criminal law in different legal orders.[35] Philipp Heck, the most important proponent of a jurisprudence of interests, also argued for functionalist comparative law: Similarities of values among societies created laws different in doctrine but similar in results.[36] Also, Roscoe Pound, while not a strict functionalist himself, shared

---

[31] cf Jonathan H. Turner and Alexandra Maryanski, *Functionalism* (1979), 2–14; Richard Münch, 'Funktionalismus—Geschichte und Zukunftsperspektiven einer Theorietradition', in Jens Jetzkowitz and Carsten Stark (eds), *Soziologischer Funktionalismus* (2003), 17, 23–6.

[32] Rudolf von Jhering, *Der Zweck im Recht* (1877–83; English translation under the title *Law as a Means to an End* by Isaac Husik, 1913); idem, *Der Kampf ums Recht* (1872; English translation under the title *The Struggle for Law* by John J. Lalor, 1979); on Jhering's concept of evolution see Okko Behrends (ed), *Privatrecht heute und Jherings evolutionäres Rechtsdenken* (1993); Marc Amstutz, *Evolutorisches Wirtschaftsrecht* (2002) 148–67.

[33] Konrad Zweigert and Kurt Siehr, 'Jhering's Influence on the Development of Comparative Legal Method', (1971) 19 *AJCL* 215–31.

[34] cf Franz von Liszt, *Der Zweckgedanke im Strafrecht* (1882–3).   [35] von Liszt (n 34), 60.

[36] Philipp Heck, *Begriffsbildung und Interessenjurisprudenz* (1929), 133 f; idem, *Grundriss des Schuldrechts* (1929), 11: 'Die nationalen Rechte unterscheiden sich weniger in der Entscheidung der Interessenkonflikte als in den angewendeten Gebotsbegriffen und Gebotssystemen. Auch in dieser Hinsicht findet sich eine Aequivalenz der Konstruktionen und der Gebotssysteme. Die Verlegung des Schwergewichts auf die Interessenwirkung verringert den Gegensatz.' (National legal systems differ from each other less in how they decide between conflicting interests but rather in the norms and normative systems they apply. In this way, too, we find equivalence of constructions and systems. Moving the emphasis on interests reduces the difference.) Heck was inspired by a review of his

some of functionalism's convictions. Pound was interested in 'law in action, not law in the books'[37] and in 'how the same things may be brought about, the same problem may be met by one legal institution or doctrine or precept in one body of law and by another, quite different institution or doctrine or precept in another'[38]—both central elements of functionalist comparative law.

Today, after the catastrophe of two world wars has rattled the faith both in teleological evolutionism and in progress through law, adaptionism survives in only a very reduced form. In political science it is used in some integration studies as an explanation of convergence, especially of the European Union.[39] But the loss of teleology and awareness of the complexity of the world have made the simple functionalism of means and ends harder to justify both as an explanatory theory and as a guiding principle. Adaptionism seemed to suggest a false determinism.[40] Evolutionary functionalism in political science has therefore been called ideological and ethnocentric, a criticism replicated in reference to comparative law.[41]

3. Classical Functionalism

Sociologists interested in a value-free sociological science perceived this as an illegitimate faith in progress and tried to develop a non-teleological functionalism instead. These efforts can be traced back to Émile Durkheim, who introduced two important ideas. First, he separated functions from origins and established functions as relations between, not qualities of, elements. Second, he emphasized that the goals of individuals were contingent and therefore not the valid material of scientific endeavours; sociology as a science had to focus on objective functions.[42] Both steps had crucial implications. As long as the ends or goals of an institution

property book by Max Rheinstein, (1931) 60 *Juristische Wochenschrift* 2897, 2899: 'Die Rechtsvergleichung ist eine notwendige Ergänzung und Weiterführung der Interessenjurisprudenz' (comparative law is a necessary supplement and continuation of jurisprudence of interests). See also Heinrich Schoppmeyer, *Juristische Methode als Lebensaufgabe* (2001), 69 f with n 154.

[37] Roscoe Pound, 'Law in the Books and Law in Action', (1910) 44 *American LR* 12–36; cf Karl H. Neumayer, 'Fremdes Recht aus Büchern, fremde Rechtswirklichkeit und die funktionelle Dimension in den Methoden der Rechtsvergleichung', (1970) 34 *RabelsZ* 411–25.

[38] Roscoe Pound, 'What May We Expect from Comparative Law?', (1936) 22 *ABAJ* 56, 59.

[39] David Mitrany, *A Working Peace System: An Argument for the Functional Development of International Organization* (1943); Ernst B. Haas, *Beyond the Nation-State: Functionalism and International Organization* (1964); David Long and Lucian M. Ashworth, 'Working for Peace: the Functional Approach, Functionalism and Beyond', in *idem* (eds), *New Perspectives on International Functionalism* (1999), 1–26; Jürg Martin Gabriel, 'Die Renaissance des Funktionalismus', (2000) 55 *Aussenwirtschaft* 121–68.

[40] Robert W. Gordon, 'Critical Legal Histories', (1984) 36 *Stanford LR* 57–125; Günter Frankenberg, 'Critical Comparisons: Re-thinking Comparative Law', (1985) 26 *Harvard International LJ* 412, 438.

[41] Léontin-Jean Constantinesco, *Traité de droit comparé*, vol III: *La science des droits comparés* (1983), 74.

[42] Durkheim (n 28), 194 ff.

had been its inherent elements, any explanation had to be teleological, and an analysis would have to focus either on the will of a transcendent creator or on the inherent nature of things. If institutions were defined by the purposes defined by their creators, a systematic analysis had to be impossible, for individual goals were hard to observe as well as arbitrary and contingent. The emphasis on objective functions on the other hand, distinct from both origin and purpose, allowed the search for general laws, the goal of all sciences. Still, Durkheim did think an institution's existence and its function interrelated. On the one hand, causes often determine functions: An institution is established in order to maintain a certain status quo, and it then fulfils that function. On the other hand, functions often determine if not the origin then at least the persistence of institutions:[43] Dysfunctional institutions cannot compete with more efficient institutions, societies with wasteful, dysfunctional institutions cannot survive.[44]

Several elements of Durkheim's functionalism reappear in functionalist comparative law: the scientific character and objectivity of research, a perception of society as a whole that transcends the sum of its parts because its elements are interrelated, the idea that societies have needs, the idea that law can be understood in terms of the needs it meets, a focus on observable facts rather than individual ideas (law in action versus law in the books), the discovered similarity of institutions of different societies, and the competitive advantage of more functional institutions within one society's law and of societies with better laws *vis-á-vis* other societies. None the less, although Durkheim himself was a trained lawyer, his functionalism had less immediate impact on comparative law than his concept of social facts. Saleilles followed Durkheim (and Weber) in maintaining that comparative law 'cherche à définir le type d'idéal tout relatif qui se dégage de la comparaison des législations, de leur *fonctionnement* et de leurs résultats' and in emphasizing 'l'unité des résultats dans la diversité des formes juridiques d'application'.[45] But most comparatists in the Durkheimian tradition focused rather on a non-teleological comparative legal history than on functional analysis[46] and opposed more functionalist versions of comparative law.[47]

---

[43] See also Wsevolod W. Isajiw, *Causation and Functionalism in Sociology* (1968), eg 127 f.

[44] Durkheim (n 28), 189 f.

[45] Raymond Saleilles, 'Conception et objet de la science du droit comparé', in *Congrès international de droit comparé: Procès verbaux* (vol I, 1905), 167, 173, 178.

[46] Roger Cotterell, 'Comparatists and Sociology', in Legrand and Munday (n 6), 131, 136 ff.

[47] Pierre Lepaulle, 'The Function of Comparative Law: With a Critique of Sociological Jurisprudence', (1921–2) 35 *Harvard LR* 838–58; also in Zweigert and Puttfarken (n 4), 63–84.

4. Instrumentalism

One reason why comparatists lacked interest in Durkheimian sociology may have been that they did not share the social scientists' fear of normativity. Instead, comparatists embraced an offspring of adaptionism that was popular in law: instrumentalism. If law fulfils functions and meets societal needs, then the lawyer's job is to develop laws that perform these tasks ('social engineering'), and comparative law can help compare the ability of different solutions to solve similar problems, and spur similar degrees of progress.

These ideas, which can be found already in Jhering's work, became prevalent in legal realism. Realism made functionalism fashionable not only in academic writing but also for curriculum reform proposals.[48] One strand of realism starts from the sociological concept of function, but then translates objective functions into purposes to be set by legislatures. These realists substitute teleological analysis for Durkheim's objective science, and they assume that the effect of laws on society can be both measured and controlled. While American legal realists remained surprisingly uninterested in comparative law, European comparative law was influenced. Zweigert and Kötz put it bluntly: 'Law is "social engineering" and legal science is a social science. Comparative lawyers recognize this: it is, indeed, the intellectual and methodological starting point of their discipline.'[49] Such ideas became especially attractive to the law and development movement, which hoped to use law in order to aid the economic progress of developing countries—a combination of the Darwinian faith in progress and teleology with the instrumentalist's hope placed in law. Such ideas, out of fashion for some time,[50] have recently been revitalized, specifically for former communist economies, generally in the World Bank's 'Doing Business' project.[51] Yet they face problems.[52] First, researchers frequently place naïve faith in both the mono-functionality and effectiveness of legal institutions. Second, they are often insufficiently aware of the non-legal elements of success or failure of societies, including cultural differences.[53] Experience in domestic contexts has shown that social engineering through law is far more complex than one thought; the insight still has to make its way into comparative law.[54]

---

[48] Brainerd Currie, 'The Materials of Law Study, (1955) 3 *Journal of Legal Education* 1–78.

[49] Zweigert and Kötz (n 2), 45.

[50] David M. Trubek, 'Towards a Social Theory of Law: An Essay on the Study of Law and Development', (1982) 82 *Yale LJ* 1–50.

[51] www.doingbusiness.org (last accessed 21 July 2006).

[52] See, most recently, Kerry Rittich, 'Functionalism and Formalism: Their Latest Incarnations in Contemporary Development and Governance Debates', (2005) 55 *University of Toronto LJ* 853–68.

[53] Jan Torpman and Fredrik Jörgensen, 'Legal Effectiveness', (2005) 91 *Archiv für Rechts- und Sozialphilosophie* 515–34; Association Henri Capitant, *Les droits de tradition civiliste en question—A propos des Rapports Doing Business de la Banque Mondiale vol 1* (2006).

[54] A more nuanced analysis is Daniel Berkowitz, Katharina Pistor, and Jean-François Richard, 'The Transplant Effect', (2003) 51 *AJCL* 163–203.

5. Refined Functionalism

Developments in the social sciences also contributed to their disjunction from comparative law: sociological functionalism became more complex and thereby less useful for functionalist comparative law. The work of Radcliffe-Browne, Malinowski, and Parsons has had little direct response in comparative law, mostly because their interest in a *theory* of societal systems was not congruent with the search in comparative law for a *method*. But comparative lawyers have also ignored sociologists interested in functionalism as a method. In particular, Robert Merton's seminal text on latent functions should have shown the problems of translating functionalism into comparative law.[55]

First, Merton introduces the important distinction between manifest functions (functions intended and recognized by participants) and latent (unknown and unintended) functions.[56] Separating objective functions from subjective intentions has a pedagogical effect: it points researchers to the importance of latent functions, which yield more important insights precisely because they previously went unrecognized.[57] Comparative lawyers are sometimes in accord when they focus on what the courts do in fact, as opposed to what they say they are doing. Yet when lawyers wish to use comparative law for social engineering, they forget that legislatures cannot know latent functions precisely because these functions are only latent. Social engineering presumes unrealistically simple relations between society and laws.

A second contribution is Merton's challenge to the postulate of functional unity of society—the axiom, shared by Rabel and Zweigert,[58] that societies are so integrated and interdependent that changing one element affects all others. In response, Merton suggests that different societies are integrated to different degrees and empirical tests are necessary to determine this degree.[59]

Merton's third challenge attacks the assumption that every element in society fulfils some vital function, ignoring non-functional or even dysfunctional institutions. Such institutions, so-called survivals, were known in both sociology and

---

[55] Merton (n 17). An early version of the argument was published as 'Sociological Theory', (1945) 50 *American Journal of Sociology* 462–73.

[56] Merton (n 17), 105, 114–36; see already *idem*, 'The Unintended Consequences of Purposive Social Action', (1936) 1 *American Sociological Review* 894–904.

[57] Merton (n 17), 122.

[58] See eg Ernst Rabel, 'Aufgabe und Notwendigkeit der Rechtsvergleichung', (1924) 13 *Rheinische Zeitschrift für Zivil- und Prozeßrecht* 279, 283; reprinted in Hans G. Leser (ed), Ernst Rabel, *Gesammelte Aufsätze* (vol III, 1967), 1, 5 and in Zweigert and Puttfarken (n 4), 85, 89: 'Alles das bedingt sich gegenseitig in sozialer, wirtschaftlicher, rechtlicher Gestaltung ... Alle diese vibrierenden Körper zusammen bilden ein noch von niemandem mit Anschauung erfaßtes Ganzes' (Everything in the social, economic, and legal fields interacts ... All these vibrating bodies in their ensemble form a whole that no one has yet fully realized); quoted approvingly by Zweigert and Kötz (n 2), 36.

[59] Merton (n 17), 79–84.

functionalist comparative law.[60] But traditional sociologists and anthropologists, and likewise comparative lawyers, consider survivals to be unstable and only temporary. Merton in turn emphasizes that whether institutions are functional or not is a matter of empirical research,[61] a point made forcefully in comparative law from an anti-functionalist perspective by Alan Watson.[62]

Merton's critique was powerful, while his constructive 'paradigm for functional analysis in sociology',[63] was less successful. (This is similar to Felix Cohen's article on legal functionalism,[64] which contains, in its first part, a brilliant critique of conceptualism, while its second part, developing a constructive theory of values, is much weaker.) Criticism of sociological functionalism grew.[65] Functionalism is criticized as intrinsically teleological and therefore unable to fulfil Durkheim's own postulate of a value-free social science.[66] Related to this is a criticism of implicit tautology and circularity,[67] mirrored in comparative law:[68] The survival of societies is explained by the existence of institutions, while the existence of these institutions is explained in turn by the needs of society. For critics this means either that functional relations are no different from causal relations (and therefore dispensable as a separate category) or that teleology is reintroduced into sociology.[69] Other critics go against the programme of functionalism. For them, emphasis on the stability of systems makes its proponents both politically conservative and methodologically incapable of explaining social change[70]—again, a criticism raised also

[60] See eg Durkheim (n 28), 184; also Zweigert and Kötz (n 2), 35 on the non-functional German provision on 'joke transactions', § 118 BGB; ibid 634 on the dysfunctional role of § 831 BGB (delictual liability for others) and functional equivalents in German law.

[61] Merton (n 17), 84–6.

[62] See eg Alan Watson, *Legal Transplants* (1974), 12–15; cf Folke Schmidt, 'The Need for a Multi-axial Method in Comparative Law', in *Festschrift für Konrad Zweigert* (1981), 525, 528; Frankenberg, 26 *Harvard International LJ* 437 f; Graziadei (n 6), 123.

[63] Merton (n 17), 104–8.

[64] Cohen, 35 *Columbia LR* 809 ff. On Cohen's own concept of functionalism, akin to sociological positivism rather than to sociological functionalism, see Martin Golding, 'Realism and Functionalism in the Legal Thought of Felix S. Cohen', (1981) 66 *Cornell LR* 1032, 1051 ff.

[65] Two influential collections of essays are Demerath and Peterson (n 17) and Don Martindale (ed), *Functionalism in the Social Sciences: The Strength and Limits of Functionalism in Anthropology, Economics, Political Science, and Sociology* (1965).

[66] Ernest Nagel, 'A Formalization of Functionalism', in *idem, Logic without Metaphysics* (1965), 247 ff; reprinted in Demerath and Peterson (n 17), 77–94; Carl G. Hempel, 'The Logic of Functionalism', in Llewellyn Gross (ed), *Symposium on Sociological Theory* (1959), 271–307; Frankenberg, 40 *Harvard International LJ* 439.

[67] See Turner and Maryanski (n 31), 128 ff; Mark Abrahamson, *Functionalism* (1978), 37 ff.

[68] Vivian Curran, 'Cultural Immersion, Difference and Categories in U.S. Comparative Law', (1998) 46 *AJCL* 43, 67.

[69] Ernest Nagel, 'A Formalization of Functionalism with Special Reference to its Application in the Social Sciences', in *idem, Logic without Metaphysics* (1956), 247–83, reprinted in abbreviated form in Demerath and Peterson (n 17), 77–94; for a defence, see Isajiw (n 43).

[70] Ralf Dahrendorf, 'Struktur und Funktion', (1955) 7 *Kölner Zeitschrift für Soziologie und Sozialpsychologie* 491–519; idem, 'Out of Utopia: Toward a Reorientation of Sociological Analysis', (1958) 64 *American Journal of Sociology* 115–27; reprinted in Demerath and Peterson (n 17), 465–80.

against functionalist comparative law.[71] And finally, and perhaps most importantly, sociological functionalism is considered unable to account for culture, in particular to explain practices that serve no function—another critique also of comparative law.[72] In general, Parsons's 'grand theory' was considered too abstract and therefore often unable to predict all empirical findings,[73] again a concern shared in comparative law.[74]

After these critiques, functionalism lost ground; a proclaimed 'neofunctionalism' has not been successful.[75] Within sociology and especially social anthropology, functionalism made way for cultural and hermeneutic methods[76]—a 'cultural turn' reflected in legal studies generally[77] and comparative law specifically.[78] At the same time, sociology as a discipline, not least due to the perceived lack of methodological sophistication, had to yield its once leading position within the social sciences to economics, again, a development replicated in comparative law.[79]

Legal functionalism has faced similar challenges. Already before 1900, criticism of the German Civil Code's structure as non-functional remained unheard;[80] later

[71] Jonathan Hill, 'Comparative Law, Law Reform and Legal Theory', (1989) 9 *Oxford Journal of Legal Studies* 101, 106 f; David Kennedy, 'The Methods and the Politics', in Legrand and Munday (n 6), 345, 391.

[72] One author representing the trend in both anthropology and comparative law is Clifford Geertz; for anthropological anti-functionalism, see his 'Ritual and Social Change: A Javanese Example', (1957) 59 *American Anthropologist* 32–54; reprinted in Demerath and Peterson (n 17), 231–49; Clifford Geertz, *Interpreting Cultures* (1973); for anti-functionalist comparative law, see *idem*, 'Local Knowledge: Fact and Law in Comparative Perspective' in *idem, Local Knowledge—Further Essays in Interpretive Anthropology* (1983), 215–34, especially at 232. See also Pierre Legrand, 'The Same and the Different', in Legrand and Munday (n 6), 240, 292 f.

[73] Wright Mills, 'Grand Theory', in *idem, The Sociological Imagination* (1959); reprinted in Demerath and Peterson (n 17), 171–83.

[74] See the references in n 6; William Alford, 'On the Limits of "Grand Theory" in Comparative Law', (1985) 61 *Washington LR* 945–56.

[75] Jeffrey C. Alexander, *Neofunctionalism and After* (1998); cf Michael Schmid, 'Der Neofunktionalismus: Nachruf auf ein Forschungsprogramm', in Jetzkowitz and Stark (n 31), 279–303.

[76] Victoria E. Bonnell and Lynn Avery Hunt (eds), *Beyond the Cultural Turn: New Directions in the Study of Society and Culture* (1999).

[77] See eg Austin Sarat and Jonathan Simons (eds), *Cultural Analysis, Cultural Studies and the Law: Moving beyond Legal Realism* (2003).

[78] The general theme for the 2007 Conference of the American Society of Comparative Law will be 'Comparative Law and Culture'.

[79] For connections, see Anne Sophia-Marie van Aaken, 'Vom Nutzen der ökonomischen Theorie des Rechts für die Rechtsvergleichung', in *Prinzipien des Privatrechts und Rechtsvereinheitlichung: Jahrbuch junger Zivilrechtswissenschaftler 2000* (2001), 127–49; Reinier Kraakman, Paul Davies, Henry Hansmann, Gerard Hertig, Klaus J. Hopt, Hideki Kanda, and Edward Rock, *The Anatomy of Corporate Law: A Comparative and Functional Approach to Corporate Law* (2004); Peter Behrens, 'Ökonomische Wirkungsanalyse im Kontext funktionaler Rechtsvergleichung' (unpublished paper delivered at the 2005 Conference of the German Society for Comparative Law in Würzburg; summary in [2006] *Juristenzeitung* 454).

[80] Ralf Michaels, 'Strukturfragen des Schuldrechts', in Reinhard Zimmermann, Joachim Rückert, and Mathias Schmoeckel (eds), *Historisch-kritischer Kommentar zum BGB* (vol II, forthcoming), vor § 241, no. 50.

abuses of functionalism by the Nazis[81] made the concept unattractive in the post-war period. Instead, the paradigm for statutory interpretation and legal argumentation moved from a functionalist jurisprudence of interests to a jurisprudence of values, thereby substituting the legislator's individual goals or a specific society's values for objective functions and abolishing the universalist aims of functionalism which had made it attractive for comparative law.

6. Epistemological Functionalism

All proponents of functionalism discussed so far stand before a dilemma. Either they must explain function as mere causality, or they have to insert some kind of teleology into their worldview, some '*Natur der Sache*'. A way out can be found in Ernst Cassirer's functionalist epistemology. Cassirer posits that, since Kant suggested laws of nature as human constructs, there has been a seismic shift from a focus on substance to a focus on function, from attempts to understand how things 'really' are (their substance, ontology) to understanding them only in their (functional) relation to particular viewpoints (their function, epistemology).[82] No longer could classes of elements be defined simply by common traits, because such an abstraction would ignore the necessary relation between the element and the whole. Rather, individual elements had to be understood in relation to particular aspects, as different results to the same function. A series of elements $a\,a_1\,\beta_1, a\,a_2\,\beta_2, a\,a_3\,\beta_3 \ldots$ cannot be understood merely by the common criterion a, but rather by the regularity in which its elements are brought about through the function $a\,x\,y$, in which the variable x defines all a, the variable y defines all β, and all these elements stand in a functional regularity so that it is possible to create new elements in the series.

This move has two decisive advantages. First, it is not necessary to recognize some essence of a particular element; it is sufficient to understand the element as variable result of a functional connection with another variable element. Individual numbers do not have an essence, but the totality of all numbers does.[83] Functionalism need not declare the existence of any a or any β but only that if there is a certain a there will be a certain β. Second, it is possible to conceive of groups of elements and to describe them without the loss of specificity that comes with traditional classifications requiring abstraction.[84] The function $a\,x\,y$ describes all elements of the

---

[81] Vivian Grosswald Curran, 'Fear of Formalism: Indications from the Fascist Period in France and Germany of Judicial Methodology's Impact on Substantive Law', (2002) 35 *Cornell International LJ* 101, 151 ff.

[82] Cassirer (n 18); for a less influential approach, see Laurence J. Lafleur, 'Epistemological Functionalism', (1941) 50 *The Philosophical Review* 471, 476 ff. Heinrich Rombach, *Substanz, System, Struktur: Die Ontologie des Funktionalismus und der philosophische Hintergrund der modernen Wissenschaft* (vol 1, 1965), 140 ff, sees the roots of functionalism in the work of Cusanus and Descartes.

[83] Cassirer (n 18), 420 f.   [84] cf Cassirer (n 18), 18 ff, 313 ff.

series completely, whereas a focus on the common element *a* as classificatory criterion would ignore both the differences between two elements $a\,a_1\,\beta_1$ and $a\,a_2\,\beta_2$ as well as the specific functional relation between *a* and *y* that creates the respective elements.

Although Cassirer had no direct influence on functionalist comparative law,[85] several parallels exist. First, functionalist comparative law is also interested not in some essence of legal institutions, but rather in their functional relation to particular problems. Second, functionalist comparative law also aims at avoiding the abstraction inherent in both conceptual comparisons and the macro-comparison of legal families, and instead focuses on a legal institution's relation to the whole. Third, Cassirer's emphasis on the totality of elements as opposed to individual elements is akin to Max Salomon's attempt to define universal jurisprudence beyond individual national institutions. Cassirer's concept of function, which he borrowed from mathematics, can work as a formalization of functional equivalents in comparative law: If we define *a* as a particular problem, '*x*' as the variable for legal systems $a_{1,\,2,\,3}\,\ldots$, and '*y*' as the variable for legal institutions $\beta_{1,\,2,\,3}\,\ldots$, we can formalize the functional comparison of different legal institutions as a series, where, for example, $a\,a_1\,\beta_1$ is French law's (a_1) response (β_1) to problem *a*, $a\,a_2\,\beta_2$ is German law's (a_2) response (β_2) to the same problem *a*, and so on. This approach enables the comparatist to focus not only on the similarity between institutions (the common problem *a* and the institutions' similar ability to respond to it) but also on the differences (between a_1 and a_2, and between β_1 and β_2, respectively), and furthermore allows her to explain these differences between institutions as a function (!) of the differences between legal systems. Such formalization, while raising many problems (eg whether the social sciences reveal the same degree of regularity as do mathematics and the natural sciences), is a promising step towards more rational comparative law.

7. Equivalence Functionalism

The insight that different elements can respond to the same problem is crucial. Finalism, adaptionism, and classical functionalism all contain traces of determinism and teleology: if similar problems cause similar solutions, then the solutions must somehow be inherent in the problems, and similar functions must be fulfilled by the same kinds of institutions. Durkheim expressly rejected functional equivalence as finalist and proclaimed a remarkable similarity between institutions of different

---

[85] However, Max Hartmann's somewhat comparable philosophy of science did influence Georges Langrod, 'Quelques réflexions méthodologiques sur la comparaison en science juridique', (1957) 9 *RIDC* 353, 364 ff; reprinted in Zweigert and Puttfarken (n 4), 225, 234 ff.

societies as responses to functional requirements.[86] Goldschmidt's otherwise original study of comparative functionalism in anthropology claimed that 'certain social needs repeatedly call forth similar social institutions, that correlations between institutional forms can be found because, broadly speaking, they are the "natural" or "preferred" means by which certain necessary social tasks may best be performed in given circumstances'.[87] Even Rabel marvelled at the finding of 'essentially related institutions and developments'.[88]

Given how different institutions are in detail, such a view is hard to maintain except in very abstract analysis; the similar institutions must be ideal types. Comparative lawyers, with their focus on details and specificities, have long known this. They knew on the one hand that similar institutions can fulfil different functions in different societies or at different times,[89] and they found, on the other hand, that similar functional needs can be fulfilled by different institutions, the idea of the functional equivalent. This idea, central to functionalist comparative law, appears in all kinds of functionalism: Max Salomon's focus on problems as the unifying element of general jurisprudence enabled scholars to see different solutions as functionally equivalent;[90] Josef Esser developed the concept for comparative law;[91] and Konrad Zweigert made it the central point of his approach to comparative law and an important tool in seeing universalities in what may look like differences.[92]

Indeed, the recognition of functional equivalents gave a boost to the possibilities for comparative law. In particular, the comparison between common law and civil law has traditionally tempted functionalists, for two reasons: First, functionalist comparison overcomes the epistemic/doctrinal difference between civil and common law by declaring it functionally irrelevant. Second, the common law with its

---

[86] Durkheim (n 28), 187: 'En fait, quand on est entré quelque peu en contact avec les phénomènes sociaux, on est . . . surpris de l'étonnante régularité avec laquelle ils se reproduisent dans les mêmes circonstances. Même les pratiques les plus minutieuses et, en apparence, les plus puériles, se répètent avec la plus étonnante uniformité.' (In fact, once on gets into some contact with social phenomena, one is surprised at the astonishing regularity with which they are reproduced under the same circumstances. Even the most minute practices and the seemingly most puerile ones are repeated with the most astonishing uniformity.)

[87] Walter Goldschmidt, *Comparative Functionalism: An Essay in Anthropological Theory* (1966), 30; see also 122: 'similar problems evoke similar solutions'.

[88] Rabel, 13 *Rheinische Zeitschrift für Zivil- und Prozeßrecht* 284 ('wesensverwandte Einrichtungen und Entwicklungen').

[89] Karl Renner, *Die Rechtsinstitute des Privatrechts und ihre soziale Funktion: ein Beitrag zur Kritik des Bürgerlichen Rechts* (1929; English translation under the title *The Institutions of Private Law and their Social Functions* by Agnes Schwarzschild, edited by Otto Kahn-Freund, 1949).

[90] Salomon (n 21).   [91] Esser (n 24), especially at 354 ff.

[92] Konrad Zweigert, 'Des solutions identiques par des voies différentes', (1966) 18 *RIDC* 5–18; for a German version, see 'Die "praesumptio similitudinis" als Grundsatzvermutung rechtsvergleichender Methode', in Rotondi (n 23), 735–58; a partial English translation can be found in Volkmar Gessner, Armin Hoeland, and Csaba Varga (eds), *European Legal Cultures* (1996), 160–4.

organic development should be particularly apt for functional understanding. Not surprisingly then, some of the most influential works applying the functional method have focused on institutions from the common law and their functional equivalents in the civil law, for example trusts[93] and consideration.[94] Some even found functionalism helpful for intersystemic comparison between socialist and capitalist legal systems.[95] Yet equivalence functionalism in comparative law has always been explicated by examples rather than developed theoretically.[96] Thus, it is not clear whether functional equivalence suggests some uniformity of values beyond the universality of problems. Likewise, the concept of a function suggests a comparatively naïve relation between the problem and the institution, either between cause and effect (so that the problem causes an institution to exist), or between purpose and implementation (so that a legal solution serves the purpose of solving a recognized problem).

Here, comparative law could profit from sociological equivalence functionalism as developed especially by Niklas Luhmann (who in turn was influenced not only by Merton but also by Cassirer). Merton questioned the postulate of indispensability, according to which every element in a society is indispensable for the working of the system, and pointed out that even indispensable necessities can be met by different institutions that act as functional substitutes or functional equivalents.[97] Cassirer's epistemology provided a formalized version of the argument. Functional equivalence means that similar problems may lead to different solutions; the solutions are similar only in their relation to the specific function under which they are regarded. Luhmann brings the two together to overcome a main problem of classical functionalism—the problem that functions either are nothing more than causal relations, or contain an element of teleology. Equivalence functionalism by contrast explains an institution as a possible but not necessary response to a problem, as one contingent solution amongst several possibilities. As a consequence, the specificity of a system in the presence of (certain) universal problems lies in its decision for one against all other (functionally equivalent)

---

[93] eg Hein Kötz, *Trust und Treuhand* (1963); Henry Hansmann and Ugo Mattei, 'The Functions of Trust Law: A Comparative Legal and Economic Analysis', (1998) 73 *New York University LR* 434–79.

[94] Arthur T. von Mehren, 'Civil-Law Analogues to Consideration: An Exercise in Comparative Analysis', (1959) 72 *Harvard LR* 1009–78; Zweigert and Kötz (n 2), ch 29—'Indicia of Seriousness'; Basil S. Markesinis, 'Cause and Consideration: A Study in Parallel', (1978) 37 *Cambridge LJ* 53–75; Ferdinand Fromholzer, *Consideration* (1997).

[95] See Zweigert, 7 *Israel LR* 470 f; Konrad Zweigert and Hans-Jürgen Puttfarken, 'Possibilities of Comparing Analogous Institutions of Law in Different Social Systems', (1973) 15 *Acta Juridica Academiae Scientiarium Hungaricae* 107–30, German translation in *idem* (n 4), 395–429; Szabó (n 1).

[96] But see now Kirsten Scheiwe, 'Was ist ein funktionales Äquivalent in der Rechtsvergleichung? Eine Diskussion an Hand von Beispielen aus dem Familien- und Sozialrecht', (2000) 83 *Kritische Vierteljahresschrift für Gesetzgebung und Rechtswissenschaft* 30–51.

[97] Merton (n 17), 86–90.

solutions.[98] Legal developments are thus no longer necessary but only possible, not predetermined but contingent.[99] This method in turn requires an understanding of society (and its subsystems, including law) as a system constituted by the relation of its elements, rather than set up by elements that are independent of each other.[100] It does not avoid the criticism of tautology—institutions are still understood with regard to problems, and problems are understood as such by their relation to institutions. But because Luhmann's functionalism is constructivist, he can use these tautologies as the means by which societies constitute themselves, by which they make sense of institutions.

Although Luhmann emphasizes that 'the functional method is ultimately a comparative one'[101] and occasionally suggests the comparison of systems as a valuable project of verification,[102] he does not, apart from a passing reference to Josef Esser,[103] use this for comparative law. Functionalist comparative law in turn has rarely reacted to Luhmann's method,[104] despite the similar focus on functional equivalence.[105] This is unfortunate. Of course, Luhmann's systems theory has been criticized severely—as being indifferent to individuals, inherently conservative (again), and as ignorant of the permeability of systems. Yet all these criticisms can also be launched against functionalist comparative law as it stands; they are not reasons against enriching current functionalism with Luhmann's constructivism.

[98] Niklas Luhmann, 'Funktion und Kausalität', (1962) 14 *Kölner Zeitschrift für Soziologie und Sozialpsychologie* 617–44; reprinted in *Soziologische Aufklärung* (vol I, 7th edn, 2005), 1–38. For the parallel concept of equifinality, see Ludwig von Bertalanffy, 'Der Organismus als physikalisches System betrachtet', (1940) 28 *Naturwissenschaften* 521; idem, 'General Systems Theory', in idem, *Main Currents of Modern Thought* (1955), 71, 75; reprinted in Demerath and Peterson (n 17), 115, 121 ff.

[99] cf Gunther Teubner, *Recht als autopoietisches System* (1989), 64 f against Gordon's criticism of functionalism (n 40).

[100] 'Niklas Luhmann, 'Funktionale Methode und Systemtheorie'; (1964) 15 *Soziale Welt* 1–25; reprinted in idem (n 98), 39–67; idem, *Soziale Systeme* (1984), especially at 83 ff, English translation under the title of *Social Systems* by John Bednarz and Dirk Baecker (1995), 52 ff; cf Stefan Jensen, 'Funktionalismus und Systemtheorie—von Parsons zu Luhmann', in Jetzkowitz and Stark (n 31), 177–203.

[101] See eg Luhmann, *Soziale Systeme*, 85 = *Social Systems*, 54 (both n 100); cf idem, 'Funktionale Methode und Systemtheorie' (n 100), 43 ff; idem, *Die Gesellschaft der Gesellschaft* (vol II, 1997), 1125 f.

[102] See eg Luhmann (n 98), 31 f.

[103] Luhmann, 'Funktionale Methode und systemtheorie' (n 100), 63 n 17; see also idem, *Das Recht der Gesellschaft* (1993), 13 f, 573 f; English translation under the title of *Law as a Social System* by Klaus A. Ziegert (2004), 56 f, 481.

[104] A notable exception is Volkmar Gessner, 'Soziologische Überlegungen zu einer Theorie der angewandten Rechtsvergleichung', (1972) 36 *RabelsZ* 229–60, especially at 240 ff; reprinted in Ulrich Drobnig and Manfred Rehbinder (eds), *Rechtssoziologie und Rechtsvergleichung* (1977), 123–50.

[105] On systems theory and autopoiesis in comparative law, see eg Lynn M. LoPucki and George G. Triantis, 'A Systems Approach to Comparing U.S. and Canadian Reorganization of Financially Distressed Companies', (1994) *Harvard International LJ* 267, 270 ff; Gunther Teubner, 'Legal Irritants: Good Faith in British Law or How Unifying the Law Ends Up in New Divergences', (1998) 61 *Modern LR* 11 ff; Mark van Hoecke, 'Legal Orders between Autonomy and Intertwinement', in Karl-Heinz Ladeur (ed), *Public Governance in the Age of Globalization* (2004), 177–94; Catherine Valcke, 'Comparative Law as Comparative Jurisprudence: The Comparability of Legal Systems', (2004) 52 *AJCL* 713–40.

8. Functionalist Comparative Law: Synthesis or Eclecticism?

Which of these concepts underlies the functional method of comparative law? The answer is: all of the above. Comparative lawyers pick and choose different concepts, regardless of their incompatibility.[106] There is still a strong faith that the similarities between different legal orders revealed by the functional method are neither the result of circular reasoning, nor mere evidence of similar needs between societies, but proof of deeper universal values. While this suggests an Aristotelian background, elsewhere functionalists place themselves outside of legal philosophy and within legal sociology and emphasize objective needs over contingent values. In the concept of function itself, comparative lawyers borrow, if inadvertently, the anti-metaphysical focus of epistemological functionalism as opposed to an essential concept of legal institutions; they understand institutions through their relation to problems. But it is not clear whether this concept of function is teleological or not. Sometimes comparatists use functions in an openly teleological fashion, as a way towards progress reminiscent of adaptionism—when only legal systems at similar stages of evolution are deemed comparable,[107] or when the development of the law is deemed important for the discovery of its function,[108] a combination of cause and function that is anathema to Durkheim's postulates. Sometimes comparatists focus on legal institutions as tools for the preservation of stability, something more akin to classical functionalism. But then it is often unclear whether they include latent functions in their focus on what laws do in effect, or whether they confine themselves to manifest functions, as in instrumentalism and social engineering. And finally, the claim that 'there will always remain . . . an area where only sound judgment, common sense, or even intuition can be of any help'[109] has an irrational ring to it that would, it seems, altogether distance functional comparative law from the scientific aspirations of functionalism in all other disciplines.[110]

In particular, the functionalism of sociology and that of law are different. First, sociologists and lawyers use different concepts of function.[111] While sociological

---

[106] See also Dimitra Kokkini-Iatridou, 'Some Methodological Aspects of Comparative Law. The Third Part of a (Pre-)paradigm', (1986) 33 *Netherlands International LR* 143, 168 ff.

[107] Zweigert and Kötz (n 2), 3 (referring to Lambert).

[108] Zweigert and Kötz (n 2), 8: '. . . if the comparatist is to make sense of the rules and the problems they are intended to solve he must often investigate their history'.

[109] Zweigert and Kötz (n 2), 33; see also 34 ('feeling'), 35 ('imagination').

[110] But see, for the possible need of irrationality for comparison, Luhmann, *Soziale Systeme*, 90 f = *Social Systems*, 57 f (both n 100) and his cite to Alfred Baeumler, *Das Irrationalitätsproblem in der Ästhetik und Logik des 18. Jahrhunderts bis zur Kritik der Urteilskraft* (1923, reprinted 1967), 141 ff.

[111] Niklas Luhmann, 'Funktionale Methode und juristische Entscheidung', (1969) 94 *Archiv für öffentliches Recht* 1–31; reprinted in *idem, Ausdifferenzierung des Rechts* (paperback edn, 1999), 273–308; Hans – Joachim Bartels, *Methode und Gegenstand intersystemarer Rechtsvergleichung* (1982), 77–9; cf also Jean Carbonnier, 'L'apport du droit comparé à la sociologie juridique', in *Livre du Centenaire* (n 2), 75, 77–9; Jerome Hall, *Comparative Law and Social Theory* (1963), 107; Zweigert and Kötz (n 2), 11 f N. A. Florijn, Leidraad Voor Zinvolle rechtsvergelijking (1995), 45.

functionalism is interested in latent functions (and largely ignores the intention of lawmakers), lawyers focus precisely on manifest or even imagined as opposed to latent functions: The judge must interpret a statute according to the function intended by the legislator even if the statute is dysfunctional; the legislator can consider only manifest functions because by definition he does not know about latent functions.[112] Sociologists could be said to take an external, and lawyers an internal point of view.[113] Second, the goals of functionalism in sociology and law are different. This is only partly due to the difference between normative and descriptive analytical goals—after all, a large part of the judge's task is descriptive, too.[114] Rather, sociologists use functionalism in order to raise complexity, so their picture of observed societal systems becomes more accurate than a mere listing of its elements. Lawyers, on the other hand, use functionalism to reduce complexity—they hope for functionality to tell them which of several alternative decisions they should take.[115] The effects of judicial decisions are only partly the responsibility of judges;[116] even legislators must take decisions in necessary partial ignorance of effects. Finally, sociologists and legal philosophers often focus on the differentiated functions of relatively broadly defined institutions, while comparative lawyers take the existence and functionality of law for granted and focus on very specific legal issues.

The clash between sociological and legal concepts of comparative law is some-times observable—when Roscoe Pound's sociological comparative law is criticized from the Durkheimian tradition as unsociological,[117] when a lawyer rejects a ques-tionnaire proposal by a sociologist as too unspecific and too oblivious of legal categories,[118] or when Zweigert's concept of functional comparative law is criti-cized by lawyers as not sufficiently legal and by sociologists as not sufficiently sociological.[119] Whereas sociological functionalism has been criticized as inher-ently conservative, legal functionalism and social engineering have been rejected as overly progressive and activist. Whereas sociological functionalism is rejected as tautological, legal functionalism is criticized for its open introduction of new values into legal arguments. A big interdisciplinary project at the Hamburg

---

[112] Of course, lawmakers may learn about latent functions over time. Sunset clauses for legislation are a response to the problem: lawmakers make laws, then observe their latent functions and dysfunc-tions, and then react to this learning experience.

[113] William M. Evan, Angelo Grisoli, and Renato Treves, 'Socialogia del diritto e diritto compa-rato—Considerazione conclusive', (1965) *Quaderni di sociologia* 376, 389 (quote by Treves); German translation in Drobnig and Rehbinder (n 104), 34, 51.

[114] See Ralf Michaels and Nils Jansen, 'Die Auslegung und Fortbildung ausländischen Rechts', (2003) 116 *Zeitschrift für Zivilprozeß* 3, 8–12.

[115] Luhmann (n 98), 10, 6; cf Gessner, (1972) 36 *RabelsZ* 247 f.

[116] See Gunther Teubner (ed), *Entscheidungsfolgen als Rechtsgründe: Folgenorientiertes Argumentieren in rechtsvergleichender Sicht* (1995).

[117] Lepaulle, 35 *Harvard LR* 838–58.   [118] Evan *et al* (n 113).

[119] Keebet von Benda-Beckmann, 'Einige Bemerkungen über die Beziehung zwischen Rechtssozio-logie und Rechtsvergleichung', (1979) 78 *Zeitschrift für vergleichende Rechtswissenschaft* 51–67; Gessner, 36 *RabelsZ* 229, 240 ff.

Max Planck Institute involving both sociologists and lawyers largely failed due to these incompabilities; the interaction between sociology and comparative law has focused more on empirical sociology than on theory.[120]

One reason for the methodological mishmash in comparative law is that the founders of the functional method were more pragmatically than methodologically interested. In suggesting, almost in passing, that the function of institutions has to stand at the centre of the comparative endeavour,[121] Ernst Rabel did not develop an elaborate method from this insight. His approach was deliberately pragmatic rather than theoretical; he was not interested in expansive methodological debate,[122] but in solving practical problems. Ascribing a 'functional method' to him was rather the work of his student Max Rheinstein, who introduced his thoughts to the United States.[123] Josef Esser came closer to developing an elaborate functional method, but his influence did not extend to the details of the method, and few would have shared his philosophical foundations. Konrad Zweigert,[124] despite the disdain for methodological debates uttered in his textbook, published quite extensively on methodological questions. Yet he was driven primarily by an interest in universalist humanism and in legal unification; the functional method was simply the best tool to reach these goals.

Methodological eclecticism could be justified as pragmatism. But it has invited criticism, and functionalist comparatists react surprisingly defensively. One defensive strategy is to acknowledge the relevance of culture as an add-on for functionalist comparative law. Yet with no clear view of the relationship between culture and function, this must lead to an eclectic, internally inconsistent method. Another strategy is to postulate a 'methodological pluralism' in which functionalism is only one of several methods, and the comparatist picks (*ad hoc?*) whichever method seems most appropriate for a given purpose.[125] Neither strategy seems promising unless the strengths and weaknesses of a more clearly functional method are recognized. If the functional method is deficient, it is not clear why a moderated version

---

[120] Michael Martinek, 'Wissenschaftsgeschichte der Rechtsvergleichung und des Internationalen Privatrechts in der Bundesrepublik Deutschland', in Dieter Simon (ed), *Rechtswissenschaft in der Bonner Republik* (1994), 529, 552 f.

[121] Rabel, 13 *Rheinische Zeitschrift für Zivil- und Prozeßrecht* 282; also in Zweigert and Puttfarken (n 3), 88.

[122] Max Rheinstein, 'In Memory of Ernst Rabel', (1956) 5 *AJCL* 185, 187; cf Hans G. Leser, 'Ein Beitrag Ernst Rabels zur Privatrechtsmethode: "Die wohltätige Gewohnheit, den Rechtsfall vor der Regel zu bedenken" ', in *Festschrift für Ernst von Caemmerer* (1978), 891–906; David J. Gerber, 'Sculpting the Agenda of Comparative Law: Ernst Rabel and the Façade of Language', in Annelise Riles (ed), *Rethinking the Masters of Comparative Law* (2001), 190, 196 ff.

[123] Rheinstein, 2 *University of Chicago LR* 246–50, especially at 248 f.

[124] Rabel's importance for Zweigert becomes clear in von Caemmerer, Zweigert (n 2). Zweigert wrote a short foreword for Esser's book; see Esser (n 24), VII.

[125] See eg Jaakko Husa, 'Farewell to Functionalism or Methodological Tolerance?', (2003) 67 *RabelsZ* 419, 446 f; Palmer, 53 *AJCL* 290; see also A. E. Onderkerk, *De preliminaire fase van het rechtsvergelijkend onderzoek* (1999) 79 ff.

should be maintained; if it is not deficient, it is unclear why it should be moderated. Yet we cannot evaluate this as long as we lack a coherently formulated functional method, with a consistent concept of function.

III. FUNCTIONS OF FUNCTION

One could thus be excused for thinking functionalist comparative law indefensible. The functional method has turned out to be an undertheorized approach with an undefined disciplinary position, assembling bits and pieces from various different traditions, which, while mutually incompatible, are similar in their decline. But to think so would be hasty. If the substance of a functional method in comparative law is unclear, our analysis should move from a substantive to a functional one and focus on what it does, instead of what it is. In the spirit of Durkheim and Merton, we should measure the method neither by its origins nor by the intentions of its proponents, but by its functionality. We should look at the functions and dysfunctions of the concept of function, including its latent functions, in the production of comparative law knowledge. We should look at whether it is functional or dysfunctional, and we should see whether alternative proposals could serve as functional equivalents. This should enable us at the same time to start reconstructing the functional method as a constructive, interpretative,[126] rather than positive enterprise, as a way of making sense of legal systems—constructing them as meaningful, instead of merely measuring them. Of course, such a method must use the same concept of functionalism throughout. I propose to use equivalence functionalism, both because it is the most robust concept in sociology and because it represents the central element of functionalist comparative law as developed by Rabel and Zweigert: functional equivalence.

This section focuses on seven functions: (1) the epistemological function of understanding legal rules and institutions, (2) the comparative function of achieving comparability, (3) the presumptive function of emphasizing similarity, (4) the formalizing function of system building, (5) the evaluative function of determining the better law, (6) the universalizing function of preparing legal unification, and (7) the critical function of providing tools for the critique of law.

---

[126] Otto Pfersmann, 'Le droit comparé comme interprétation et comme théorie du droit', (2001) 53 *RIDC* 275–88; see also Anne Peters and Heiner Schwenke, 'Comparative Law beyond Post-Modernism', (2000) 49 *ICLQ* 800, 833 f.

1. The Epistemological Function: Understanding Law

The first function of function is epistemological. Functionalism provides a tool to make sense of the data we find. We understand this function of function if we distinguish functionalist comparative law from an approach that shares some of its methodology and is often referred to as functionalist: the factual method,[127] especially as applied in common core research.[128] There are two important differences that strip the factual method of much of the explanatory power that functionalism claims for itself and that suggest that the factual method and common core research should not be called functionalist.[129] First, the factual method shows us similarities across legal systems, but it does not tell us whether these are accidental or necessary, or how they relate to society. Second, the factual method, in focusing on cases, is limited in two ways: its problems are only disputes, and its solutions are only court decisions. Functionalism promises more. It aims at explaining the effects of legal institutions as functions (a specific kind of relation), and it promises to look at non-legal responses to societal requisites, too. The functional method asks us to understand legal institutions not as doctrinal constructs but as societal responses to problems—not as isolated instances but in their relation to the whole legal system, and beyond, to the whole of society.

This suggests why a frequent criticism of functionalism as being too rule-centred[130] may apply to much mainstream comparative law, but not to the functional method. Functionalists explicitly ask that comparatists look not only at legal rules ('law in books'), nor only at the results of their application ('law in action'), but even beyond at non-legal answers to societal needs.[131] Few comparatists may practise this, but this is a flaw in practice, not in the method. Similarly, the frequent criticism that functionalism is reductive[132] is unwarranted. The great advantage of functionalism over substantivism, emphasized first by Cassirer, is precisely that it makes generalizations possible without loss of specificity.[133] Functionalism emphasizes relations in addition to institutions, and it focuses on latent in addition to manifest functions. In this sense, a functionalist view of legal institutions, focusing on the complex interrelatedness of societal elements, creates a picture not less but more complex than that created by the participants in a legal system.[134]

---

[127] eg Stefan Rozmaryn, 'Etude comparative de cas administratifs concrets', (1967) 19 *RIDC* 421–4.

[128] Rudolf Schlesinger (ed), *Formation of Contracts: A Study of the Common Core of Legal Systems* (vol I, 1968), 30–41.

[129] cf Ralf Michaels, 'Common Core?', *ERPL* (forthcoming).

[130] Frankenberg, 26 *Harvard International LJ* 438; Graziadei (n 6), 110; Rosen (n 12), 504; Constantinesco (n 41), 69–70: 'Begriffsjurisprudenz' (conceptual jurisprudence).

[131] See eg Ascarelli (n 2), 30, 40; Zweigert and Kötz (n 2), 38 f.

[132] See eg Mark Tushnet, 'The Possibilities of Comparative Constitutional Law', (1999) 108 *Yale LJ* 1225, 1265 ff.

[133] Above pp 355 f.   [134] Luhmann, *Soziale Systeme*, 88 = *Social Systems* 56 (both n 100).

The same is true for the criticism that functionalism makes no room for culture.[135] Rightly understood, functionalist comparative law assumes that legal rules are culturally embedded, especially once latent functions are accounted for. In fact, functionalists can sound like their critics: 'Le fait que tout droit est un phénomène culturel et que les règles de droit ne peuvent jamais être considérées indépendamment du contexte historique, social, économique, psychologique et politique est confirmé avec une force particulière par les enquêtes de droit comparé';[136] 'cette méthode fonctionnelle ... permet d'atteindre ... le système dans son homogénéité, dans son esprit, dans ce qu 'on a justement appelé sa "mentalité" ...'.[137] What distinguishes functionalists from culturalists is not the degree of attention to culture, but the kind of attention. What critics call acultural is the functionalists' resistance to adopting an insider's view, their unwillingness to limit themselves to culture as such, and of course their reconstruction of culture as functional (or dysfunctional) relations. This can of course account for only one aspect of culture. But once the futile hope to grasp any holistic 'essence' of culture is given up, a functionalist outsider's account need not be inferior to a culturalist insider's account; it just highlights a different perspective. To do so, functionalism must assume that 'law' can somehow be separated from 'society' because otherwise law could not fulfil a function for society. This assumption of separability has been criticized,[138] but it can be defended at least as a heuristic device. The separation is more in tune with both the use of the term 'law' and the functional differentiation of modern societies; it carries more analytical force than collapsing all law into society and culture would.

Obviously, functionalism is not the only available epistemological scheme for understanding a legal system.[139] Functionalists take an observer's perspective as an alternative to, not a substitute for, the participant's perspective inherent in cultural approaches, and emphasize the view of law in a specific (namely functional) relation, while ignoring other relations. Functionalism can thus not claim to capture some essence or 'ultimate truth' of legal institutions;[140] but such a claim would run counter to its own programme, anyway. Functionalism in sociology as in philosophy is the fruit of a move away from metaphysical concepts like 'substance' and 'essence'; function is not an ontological category. Such a functionalist comparative law, driven by a particular interest of the comparatist, cannot be fully objective and

[135] Above, n 72.
[136] Zweigert, 18 *RIDC* (n 92), 13 f.   [137] Ancel, 'Problème' (n 1), 4.
[138] cf Frankenberg, 26 *Harvard International LJ* 424; Gordon, 36 *Stanford LR* 102 ff; Geoffrey Samuel, 'Epistemology and Comparative Law: Contributions from the Sciences and Social Sciences', in Mark van Hoecke (ed), *Epistemology and Methodology of Comparative Law* (2004), 35, 39 ff.
[139] Geoffrey Samuel, *Epistemology and Method in Law* (2003), 301 ff.
[140] Graziadei (n 6), 112.

neutral in the way traditional sciences aim at objectivity and neutrality,[141] but this is not a shortcoming.

If functions are relations between institutions and problems, then the first task is to find the problem to be solved by legal institutions. And this is itself a problem.[142] For evolutionists, a problem is a situation in society that spurs legal and ultimately social change; the solution is only a temporary step forward that will lead to new problems. For neo-Kantians, a problem is a legal problem ('Rechtsproblem') and thus a problem defined by the law and not by social reality, an aprioristic philosophical concept.[143] A solution cannot be found in an analogy to the sciences because it requires a value judgment.[144] For functionalists, finally, a problem is only one side of a bipolar functional relation, the other side taken by the institution that meets the need, so society can stay in equilibrium: problems and institutions mutually constitute each other.

There are real issues with functionalism as a social science or as philosophy, but less so for constructivist functionalism in comparative law. Explaining legal institutions functionally drives hypotheses that consider the problems and the structure of a society not as realities (either empirical or philosophical), but rather make proposals about how societies can and should be understood, not just how they work. That a problem exists and that an institution is a response to it need not be proven; but the connection between events and institutions must be made plausible as a way of understanding. We may well say that problems are constructed[145] and still maintain explanatory power; we may analyse from a particular non-universal viewpoint and offer this analysis as one of several possible interpretations. Functionalism thereby turns from a scientific to a constructive approach to law, a way of 'making sense' that is distinct from the participants' way of making sense of their legal systems. This would be problematic for a positive science. It is not so for an argumentative and normative, purpose-oriented discipline like comparative law.

---

[141] Frankenberg, 26 *Harvard International LJ* 439; Mark van Hoecke and Mark Warrington, 'Legal Cultures, Legal Paradigms and Legal Doctrine: Towards a New Model for Comparative Law', (1998) 47 *ICLQ* 495, 535; Husa, 67 *RabelsZ* 443.

[142] Gessner, 36 *RabelsZ* 232 ff; Hans F. Zacher, 'Vorfragen zu den Methoden der Sozialrechtsvergleichung', in *idem* (ed), *Methodische Probleme des Sozialrechtsvergleichs* (1977), 21, 41 ff; Hill, 9 *Oxford Journal of Legal Studies* 108; Onderkerk (n 125) 70 ff; Teemu Ruskola, 'Legal Orientalism', (2002) 101 *Michigan LR* 179, 189 f. See already Ernst von Hippel, Book Review of Salomon (n 21), (1926) 49 *Archiv des öffentlichen Rechts* 274, 279 f.

[143] See Arwed Blomeyer, 'Zur Frage der Abgrenzung von vergleichender Rechtswissenschaft und Rechtsphilosophie', (1934) 8 *RabelsZ* 1, especially at 12 f.

[144] Salomon (n 21), 51 ff.

[145] Luhmann, *Soziale Systeme* 86 = *Social Systems* 54 (both n 100); Florijn (n 111) 45; Nils Jansen, 'Dogmatik, Erkenntnis und Theorie im europäischen Privatrecht', (2005) 13 *Zeitschrift für Europäisches Privatrecht* 750, 772.

2. The Comparative Function: *Tertium Comparationis*

Of course, this interpretative reconstruction of functionalism immediately raises the question why one functional explanation should be more plausible than another. How can functions be tested empirically? How can we prove values? Comparison can help here, and this leads to the second function of function—that of *tertium comparationis*.

Comparison traditionally requires an invariant element. In theory, a functional method could set either problems or institutions as invariant;[146] in reality, as long as institutions are non-universal, only problems can play the role of a constant. Functionalists often claim that comparative law can serve as the closest substitute for an experiment to test a hypothesis on functional relations.[147] Yet this still begs the question whether needs and problems are universal.[148] It is not even clear what universality of problems means: Philosophers like Max Salomon understand these problems as philosophically universal problems of general jurisprudence, while the sociological strand understands them as empirically universal problems of societies. As a consequence, it is not clear whether function as *tertium comparationis* refers to (manifest) value judgments by legislatures or to (latent) sociological needs or, as Rabel said somewhat opaquely, to both.[149] In addition, sociologists and anthropologists who define substantive problems often fall into one of two traps.[150] Either their lists of societal needs[151] are too abstract for meaningful comparative law—the stability of society is relevant on a different level than the enforcement of

---

[146] Luhmann (n 98), 21; Scheiwe, 83 *Kritische Vierteljahresschrift für Gesetzgebung und Rechtswissenschaft* 30 n 2.

[147] Lepaulle, 35 *Harvard LR* 853 f; reprinted in Zweigert and Puttfarken (n 3), 77 f ('recoupement'); Roscoe Pound, 'Some Thoughts about Comparative Law', in *Festschrift für Ernst Rabel* (1954) 7, 12 f; similarly Merton (n 17), 108.

[148] Watson (n 62), 4 f; Jerome Hall (n 111), 108–10; Constantinesco 63 ff; Wolfgang Mincke, 'Eine vergleichende Rechtswissenschaft', (1984) 83 *Zeitschrift für vergleichende Rechtswissenschaft* 315, 324; Richard Hyland, 'Comparative Law', in Dennis Patterson (ed), *A Companion to Philosophy of Law and Legal Theory* (1996), 184, 189; de Cruz (n 1), 228–30; James Q. Whitman, 'The Neo-Romantic turn', in Legrand and Munday (n 6), 312, 313.

[149] Ernst Rabel, 'El fomento internacional del derecho privado', (1931) 18 *Revista de derecho privado* 321, 331; reprinted in *Gesammelte Aufsätze* (n 58, vol III) 35, 50: 'el *tertium comparationis*, constituido de un lado por las intenciones sociales económicas y éticas de las leyes, y de otro por las exigencias practicas de la vida que se presentan como parecidas entre sí' (the *tertium comparationis*, constituted on the one hand by the law's social, economic, and ethical purposes, on the other hand by the practical exigencies of life as they similarly present themselves). See also idem, 'In der Schule von Ludwig Mitteis', (1954) 7–8 *Journal of Juristic Papyrology* 157, 159; reprinted in *Gesammelte Aufsätze* (n 58, vol III) 376, 378: 'die funktionelle Betrachtung—die man auch die soziale, aber am wichtigsten die juristische nennen konnte . . .' (the functional analysis—which could also be called social, but most importantly juristic..).

[150] Tushnet, 108 *Yale LJ* 1238.

[151] eg D. F. Aberle, A. K. Cohen, A. K. Davis, M. J. Levy, Jr, and F. X. Sutton, 'The Functional Prerequisites of a Society', (1950) 60 *Ethics* 100–11; reprinted in Demerath and Peterson (n 17), 317–31; cf Marion Levy, *The Structure of Society* (1950), 34–55.

consumer rights. Or problems are contingent on specific societal structures and thus no longer universal[152]—the problem of protecting shareholder rights will not exist in societies without capital markets. For example, we may think that societies require deterrence of wrongdoing and that tort law is there to fulfil this need. But how do we know that this is the problem that tort law solves? Why is its function not compensation, instead, or the effectuation of certain societal values? Or is tort law perhaps even dysfunctional?[153]

Some comparatists try to avoid these challenges by restricting the analysis to societies at similar stages of development and in certain relatively value-neutral areas of the law.[154] Yet not only have such more complex comparisons been made frequently.[155] Also, the restriction to societies at the same stage of development smacks of the now-discarded functional adaptionism; and the restriction to value-neutral areas of the law assumes the similarity of problems precisely by designating areas of the law as value-free and therefore non-contingent.

It seems more fruitful to differentiate between levels of analysis. We can assume relatively safely that certain abstract problems—for example, the need to survive—are universal, at least in the sense that all societies face them qua being societies.[156] Such general problems cannot simply be broken down into the specific problems that interest comparative lawyers by mere deduction, just as discussions about the function of law in general do not yield answers addressing the functions of specific legal institutions. Many problems are contingent on the solutions to other problems.[157] But they enable the comparatist who does not find universality of a certain problem at a high degree of specificity to step down one level because derived needs arise, if in a contingent way, from original needs. The more specific a problem is, the less likely its universality, but a focus on the more general level enables us to see not only the contingency of certain problems but also what the analogous problems in other legal systems are. This leads to a much more complex, but also a richer, functional analysis.

Furthermore, functionalist epistemology makes it unnecessary to assume universal problems. Once the formulation of a problem is understood as a constructive move rather than an empirical one, the universality of problems is likewise a constructive move rather than a mere representation of reality. Comparability is

---

[152] Goldschmidt (n 87), 106 ff.

[153] Nils Jansen, *Binnenmarkt, Privatrecht und europäische Identität* (2004), 67 ff. For another example, see Iain D. C. Ramsay, 'Functionalism and Political Economy in the Comparative Study of Consumer Insolvency: An Unfinished Story from England and Wales' (2006) 7 *Theoretical Inquiries in Law* 625, 632 ff.

[154] See eg Zweigert (n 92), 756.

[155] See the examples given by Graziadei (n 6), 109 f; cf also the criticism by Frankenberg, 26 *Harvard International LJ* 437 f; Constantinesco (n 41), n 40.

[156] Wilbert E. Moore and Joyce Sterling, 'The Comparison of Legal Systems: A Critique', (1985) 14 *Quaderni fiorentini per la storia del pensiero giuridico* 77, 98; cf Goldschmidt (n 87), 118 ff.

[157] Goldschmidt (n 87), 106 ff.

attained through the construction of universal problems as *tertia comparationis*. This is where the notion of functional equivalent has its bite. Even if legal institutions are understood as responses to societal needs, they are not caused by these needs in the sense of logical necessity. Rather, they are contingent responses to these needs that can be identified with reference to the other possible responses, the functional equivalents, that were not chosen.[158] These functional equivalents may not be known until they appear in other legal systems, but their appearance enables the comparatist to construct the underlying problem and thereby to recognize the functions of a legal institution. The similarity of results to certain fact situations, regardless of differences in doctrine, strongly suggests that the respective legal institutions can be seen as different (but functionally equivalent) responses to a similar problem. This reasoning is of course circular—it goes from problems to functions and from functions to problems. But this circularity resembles the way in which mathematicians recognize functions, and it appears justified for constructivist comparative law as interpretation because it mirrors the hermeneutic circle between the comparatist and the legal systems observed that is characteristic of comparative law.[159]

3. The Presumptive Function: *Praesumptio Similitudinis*

The universality of problems leads to the question of difference and similarity. Zweigert suggested the (in)famous *praesumptio similitudinis*, a presumption of similarity: The comparatist should assume that different societies face similar needs and that, to survive, any one society must have (functionally equivalent) institutions that meet these needs. As a consequence, if the comparatist finds no functional equivalent in a foreign legal order, he should 'check again whether the terms in which he posed his original question were indeed purely functional, and whether he has spread the net of his researches quite wide enough'.[160]

Perhaps no statement in the history of comparative law has been criticized more than this short passage. Three types of this criticism deserve attention here. First, the postulate violates requirements of scientific method: Following Popper's critical rationalism, the comparatist should try not to prove but to falsify hypotheses.[161] Second, the postulate violates requirements of ideological neutrality, or requirements of the correct ideology: The comparatist should not favour similarity over difference, but should either be objective and neutral as between similarity and difference or should even openly advocate difference over

---

[158] See above, pp 358 f.   [159] cf Zacher (n 142), 39 f; Ruskola, 101 *Michigan LR* 232 f.

[160] Zweigert and Kötz (n 2), 40; for an earlier version see already Zweigert, 'Praesumptio Similitudinis' (n 92) 755 f. Zweigert first mentioned the *praesumptio* in 'Méthodologie' (n 2), 297 = 'Zur Methode' (n 2), 198.

[161] von Benda-Beckmann, (1979) 78 *Zeitschrift für vergleichende Rechtswissenschaft* 57.

similarity.[162] Third, the postulate is reductionist: Similarity will only appear once legal orders or institutions are stripped of culturally relevant and contingent details.[163] Some defendants of functionalism yield to the critique; they are ready to give the presumption up.[164] But things are not that easy.

First, the presumption of similarity must be placed in its historical context. It was formulated after a war had been fought on the allegation of insurmountable differences; this is one reason why comparatists tried to counter the presumption of difference prevailing among ordinary lawyers of that time.[165] In this sense, the presumption of similarity was as critical of the state of affairs of its time as is the current emphasis on difference, which may likewise be just a rhetorical strategy.[166] Calls for 'falsification' of the presumption are, then, as misplaced as calls for a switch to a *praesumptio dissimilitudinis* because they only shift the relation between rule and exception.[167]

More to the point, the presumption is closely linked to the methodological assumptions. If only functionally equivalent institutions are comparable, then by definition these institutions must be similar in the sense that they respond to the same problem. To this extent, the presumption is not just Zweigert's naïve idea, but a necessary element of functionalist comparative law. Here the caveat that only societies at similar stages and institutions in value-neutral areas of the law can be compared becomes important. Of course, this caveat turns the assumption into a tautology: problems are universal in so far as we exclude all problems that are not universal.[168] But this tautology is not fatal once we understand functionalism as a constructive method: it describes the thought process between the general and the specific, between presumed problems and institutions as presumed responses, that creates legal knowledge. The claim of universality of a problem is a first interpretative step that can be challenged, but this is a fruitful way of making sense of one legal system in relation to another.

If therefore the presumption of similarity is central to the functional method, it

---

[162] Curran, 46 *AJCL* 67; Pierre Legrand, *Le droit comparé* (1999), 110: '*principium individuationis*'; Hyland (n 148), 194: '*coniectura dissimilitudinis*'.

[163] Geertz, 'Local Knowledge' (n 72); Volkmar Gessner, 'Praesumptio similitudinis?—A Critique of Comparative Law', in *1995 Annual Meeting of the ISA Research Committee on Sociology of Law 'Legal Culture: Encounters and Transformations', Section Meetings, August 1–4, 1995* (1995), 41, 50: 'the praesumptio similitudinis is nothing but a consequence of poor data collection in comparative legal studies'; see already *idem*, 36 *RabelsZ* 235.

[164] See eg Ancel, *Utilité* (n 1), 55 ff; de Cruz (n 1), 230; Husa, 67 *RabelsZ* 440 f, 442 f; cf Hein Kötz, 'The Common Core of European Private Law: Presented at the Third General Meeting of the Trento Project', (1998) 21 *Hastings International and Comparative LR* 803, 807, slightly revised from (1997) 5 *ERPL* 549, 552: 'must be rebutted when there is evidence for doing so'; see also Ruskola, 101 Michigan LR 191.

[165] Curran, 46 *AJCL* 67 ff.   [166] Thus Legrand (n 72), 302; see also Husa, 67 *RabelsZ* 442 f.

[167] cf Nathaniel Berman, 'Aftershocks: Exoticization, Normalization and the Hermeneutic Compulsion', (1997) *Utah LR* 281–6.

[168] Hiram Chodosh, 'Comparing Comparisons: In Search of Methodology', (1999) 84 *Iowa LR* 1025, 1122 f.

becomes vital to understand clearly what the presumption does and does not say. What is presumed to be similar are neither the legal institutions, nor the problems to be solved by them and the need for societies to respond to them, but the functional relation between problems and solutions: if a society has a certain problem *a*, it must have a legal institution *y*, and different solutions to *a* are functionally equivalent. This does not mean that different solutions to similar problems, the core element of the functional method, are really 'similar'; Zweigert's own formulation of 'similarity' is misleading. Tort law and insurance law are not similar just because they fulfil the same function of providing accident victims with compensation for their accidents. They are obviously different—not only in their doctrinal structures but also (a point often neglected by comparatists) in their effects and functions (or dysfunctions) regarding problems other than that of compensation, such as deterrence, the creation of certain kinds of jobs (judges or insurers), litigiousness, or a welfare mentality. They are similar regarding only one element—namely, the solution of one specific problem. This is not similarity. This is functional equivalence.[169]

Some critics consider the *praesumptio similitudinis* to be internally inconsistent, because comparatists claim that different legal systems find similar results although at the same time they advocate differences between the legal institutions they compare.[170] They are partly right. Comparatists do indeed look at difference and similarity at the same time, but that is not inconsistency. Rather, functional equivalence is similarity in difference; it is finding that institutions are similar in one regard (namely in one of the functions they fulfil) while they are (or at least may be) different in all other regards—not only in their doctrinal formulations, but also in the other functions or dysfunctions they may have besides the one on which the comparatist focuses. The decision to look at a certain problem, and thus at a certain function, therefore becomes crucial for finding similarity. But this is always similarity regarding only that one function. The finding of similarity is contingent on the comparatist's focus.

It follows that this degree of similarity cannot explain a whole institution. First, by choosing one institution β_1 a society decides against other possible functionally equivalent institutions β_2 and β_3. The choice of tort law for compensation purposes is, at least in part, a choice against insurance law for the same purposes. It would therefore be wrong to say that 'really' tort law and insurance are the same, because this would strip the decision for one and against the other institution of its relevance. Second, when the comparatist uses one function as his *tertium comparationis*, he deliberately leaves other functions out of his view for which

---

[169] cf Scheiwe, 83 *Kritische Vierteljahresschrift für Gesetzgebung und Rechtswissenschaft* 35; Hein Kötz, 'Abschied von der Rechtskreislehre?', (1998) 6 *Zeitschrift für Europäisches Privatrecht* 493, 504 f.
[170] Hill, 9 *Oxford Journal of Legal Studies* 103, 109; cf Frankenberg, 26 *Harvard International LJ* 440.

institutions may well be different.[171] In so far as functional equivalence means similarity regarding one function, the presumption is tautological:[172] because only institutions fulfilling the same function are comparable, by definition they must be similar regarding their quality of fulfilling this function. Nothing is said about any further similarity or difference. Because critics have spilled much ink on a misunderstanding, this insight deserves repeating: Functionalism leads to comparability of institutions that can thereby maintain their difference even in the comparison. It neither presumes, nor does it lead to, similarity.

4. The Systematizing Function: Building a System

As a last step in the comparative method, Zweigert proposes the 'building of a system' with its own 'special syntax and vocabulary'.[173] How is it possible to do so, given that 'comparative law is by its nature a functional and antidoctrinal method'?[174] Must such a system not necessarily be as formalist and as doctrinal as the national systems that the functional methods try to overcome?[175]

In one way the answer is yes: scientific approaches aim at building systems, and systems are by their nature formalist. We see this development in social anthropologists who hoped that function would lead to a general heuristics of societies and societal systems; in sociologists like Parsons who developed his elaborate AGIL system;[176] and in legal philosophers who linked comparative law to the system-building project of general jurisprudence. All these system-building projects have been criticized as being insensitive to details and as technocratic.

---

[171] Luhmann (n 98), 25: 'Einzelne funktionale Leistungen sind nur in einer bestimmten analytischen Perspektive äquivalent' (individual functional achievements are equivalent only from a specific analytical perspective); Scheiwe, 83 *Kritische Vierteljahresschrift für Gesetzgebung und Rechtswissenschaft* 36 f.

[172] For this criticism, see Scheiwe, 83 *Kritische Vierteljahresschrift für Gesetzgebung und Rechtswissenschaft* 34, 35.

[173] Zweigert and Kötz (n 2), 44–6; Max Rheinstein, 'Teaching Comparative Law', (1937–8) 5 *University of Chicago LR* 615, 620 f. For problems of systematization and terminology in a practical example of functionalist comparative law, see Ulrich Drobnig, 'Methodenfragen der Rechtsvergleichung im Lichte der "International Encyclopedia of Comparative Law" ', in *Ius Privatum Gentium—Festschrift für Max Rheinstein* (1969), 221, 228–33. The prominent position of the system in Zweigert and Kötz's treatise may be due to Zweigert's interest in a system of comparative law before he advocated functionalism. See eg Konrad Zweigert, Book Review, (1949) 15 *RabelsZ* 354–8; Bernhard C. H. Aubin and Konrad Zweigert, *Rechtsvergleichung im deutschen Hochschulunterricht* (1952), eg at 39 ('Einheit eines überpositiven Systems', unity of a suprapositive system).

[174] Konrad Zweigert, 'Rechtsvergleichung, System und Dogmatik', in *Festschrift für Eduard Bötticher* (1969), 443, 448.

[175] For criticism, see Ernst Kramer, 33 *RabelsZ* 10–12, against Esser and Rothoeft. Riles, 40 *Harvard International LJ* 244 f, posits that the postmodern attack against modernist comparative law parallels the modernist attack against earlier comparative law.

[176] Adaptation, Goal attainment, Integration, Latency.

Comparative lawyers may first respond that they do what functionalist lawyers like Philipp Heck did: if rules and systems cannot be discarded altogether, they should at least be improved. For example, comparison reveals that ownership is transferred by mere consent in some legal systems, while others require the passing of possession, but the answers to specific fact situations are remarkably similar. These results can be formalized in three easy rules: Between transferor and transferee ownership passes through mere consent; with regard to third parties ownership passes through transfer of possession; third parties with notice must accept the transfer of ownership between transferor and transferee under the first rule.[177] The ensuing system is still doctrinal and thus open to external criticism, but at least it describes the state of the different legal systems better than their own rules.

Of course this leaves the more fundamental criticism against any kind of system-building at large. This criticism cannot be avoided, because system-building is inherently linked with equivalence functionalism.[178] Three kinds of relations are indispensable for functional comparison: the similarity relation between the problems in different societies, the functional relation between each individual problem and the legal institution with which a given legal system responds to it, and the equivalence relation between the institutions in different legal systems. The question phrased by functionalist comparison therefore already entails a system; Zweigert's system-building only formalizes it. It would be a mistake to consider this functional system as somehow more real than the doctrinal legal systems from which it is derived, if only because its formulation is necessarily formal, too. The system created by equivalence functionalism is a construction, and as such it is open to criticism like any other system. But it may be a better, more appropriate system than others, it may provide new angles on the legal systems we compare, and it may thereby help us both understand and critique those systems.

5. The Evaluative Function: Determining the Better Law

While the construction of a system is thus an implicitly normative-critical project, functionalist comparative law sometimes asserts an explicitly normative function: Functionality should serve as a yardstick to determine the 'better law'. This step from facts to norms is always problematic in comparative law. Saleilles proposed to look to the majority solution of legal orders to find a 'droit idéal relatif',[179] but

---

[177] Ralf Michaels, *Sachzuordnung durch Kaufvertrag* (2002), especially 188 ff; cf already Fr. Vinding Kruse, 'What Does "Transfer of Property" Mean with Regard to Chattels? A Study in Comparative Law', (1958) 7 *AJCL* 500–15; Rodolfo Sacco, 'Diversity and Uniformity in the Law', (2001) 49 *AJCL* 171, 183 f.

[178] Luhmann, 'Funktionale Methode und Systemtheorie' (n 100).

[179] Saleilles (n 45); *idem*, 'École historique et droit naturel', (1902) 1 *Revue trimestrielle de droit civil* 80, 101, 106, 109 ff; Zweigert, 15 *RabelsZ* 19–21.

why should majority suggest superiority? The Common Core projects look to commonalities among *all* legal orders, but even the fact of commonality (to the extent it exists) does not have intrinsic normative force.[180] Indeed, functional comparatists often hesitate to move to such normative conclusions. Rabel, for example, argued that evaluation was not strictly an element of comparative law.[181] The neo-Kantians' concept of ideal law is independent of existing legal orders.[182] Both approaches thus face the same problem from different sides. The sociologist cannot deduce an 'ought' from an 'is'; comparative material gives no guidelines; even commonality has no independent normative force. The idealist philosopher can develop his ideal law in the abstract; but it is not clear how the knowledge of the different legal orders can help him or why that knowledge is even relevant.

Zweigert himself was aware that the empirical material collected by the comparatist did not have legal authority[183] and that the comparative lawyer, in order to determine the better law, 'must operate with assumptions which . . . would rightly be derided by the sociologist of law as simple working hypotheses'.[184] But he thought that, whenever functionalist comparative law studies find similarity in result among different legal orders, all that needs to be evaluated is the better doctrinal formulation, and this is a task that the jurist is both able and entitled to do.[185] Others seem more ambitious.[186]

The unease is justified: equivalence functionalism provides surprisingly limited tools for evaluation.[187] The specific function itself cannot serve as a yardstick, for functionally equivalent institutions are by definition of equal value with respect to that function—equivalence means, literally, of equal value. Once a specific function has been used to determine relative similarity, the same function cannot determine superiority, for this would require a relative difference. It is impossible first to isolate the function of a legal institution from its doctrinal formulation and to measure this remaining functional element against some ideal function, for no such ideal function exists beyond the mundane reality of the legal order. In this strict sense, better-law theory is not compatible with functionalist comparative law.

---

[180] Hill, 9 *Oxford Journal of Legal Studies* 103; J. P. Verheul, 'Così fan tutte', in *Comparability and Evaluation: Essays on Comparative Law, Private International Law and International Commercial Arbitration in Honour of Kokkini-Iatridou* (1994), 143–9.

[181] Rabel, 13 *Rheinische Zeitschrift für Zivil- und Prozeßrecht* 280 (but see 286 ff).

[182] Radbruch, 'Über die Methode' (n 20); Salomon (n 21), 30 ff; Blomeyer (n 143), 2.

[183] Zweigert, 15 *RabelsZ* 14 f; idem, 'Die kritische Wertung in der Rechtsvergleichung', in *Law and Trade: Recht und Internationaler Handel. Festschrift für Clive Schmitthoff* (1973), 403, 405.

[184] Zweigert and Kötz (n 2), 11 f; cf 47.

[185] Zweigert, 'Kritische Wertung' (n 183), 408 f; for a more explicit is/ought cross-over, see idem, 15 *RabelsZ* 20.

[186] Rheinstein, 5 *University of Chicago LR*, 617 f: '[E]very rule and institution has to justify its existence under two inquiries: First: What function does it serve in present society? Second: Does it serve this function well or would another rule serve it better? It is obvious that the second question cannot be answered except upon the basis of a comparison with other legal systems' (internal footnote omitted).

[187] cf Niklas Luhmann, *Zweckbegriff und Systemrationalität* (1968), 120.

This may explain why so many comparative studies list similarities and differences and then run out of criteria to determine which of the laws is better.

If the yardstick must therefore lie outside the specific function under scrutiny, it can be found either in the costs of an institution, or in its functionality or dysfunctionality regarding other problems. This, however, makes a comprehensive evaluation almost impossibly complex. Take, for example, the different responses to car accidents of the New Zealand insurance system and the English tort law system. Arguably, New Zealand's law is functionally superior to English law regarding the function of compensation, because its transaction costs are lower. English law in turn is arguably superior with regard to the function of deterrence, because it creates better incentives for careful driving. Now, equivalence functionalism suggests that New Zealand meets the latter function of deterrence with other institutions— criminal liability, for example—so we have to account for this in our evaluation, too. But criminal law is costly and perhaps dysfunctional in so far as it clutters court-houses, so we must also take the costs of court procedures into account, and so forth. Micro-comparison regarding individual functions turns into macro-comparison between whole legal systems.

This example illustrates the crux of equivalence functionalism: its advantages in achieving comparability turn into disadvantages for evaluation. The focus on func-tional equivalence instead of similarity or difference is a deliberate way of mastering complexity without reducing specificity: institutions are made comparable precisely by reducing them to one function. To evaluate these institutions, however, it is not enough to focus only on this one function, because institutions are multifunctional; yet the focus on all other functions and dysfunctions reintroduces complexity.

This does not make an evaluation of the results of functionalist comparison impossible, but it shows its limits.[188] First, the criteria of evaluation must be different from the criteria of comparability. Ultimately, evaluation remains a policy decision, a practical judgment, under conditions of partial uncertainty. The func-tional method can show alternatives and provide some information and thereby greatly improve this policy decision, but it cannot substitute for it. Second, any evaluation of functionally equivalent solutions is valid only with regard to the function scrutinized in the comparative inquiry—one law, one institution is not better than the other *tout court*. At best it may be better regarding a certain function. Thus, equivalence functionalism makes comparability possible, but simultaneously suggests restraint in evaluating results.

A good example for the strengths and limits of functionalism for evaluation is the House of Lords decision in *White v Jones*.[189] The question was whether a solicitor who had negligently failed to finalize a will was responsible to the intended bene-ficiaries. The Court starts by assessing several functions of liability: Tort-feasors

---

[188] Prudent functionalists admit this much, eg Rheinstein, 5 *University of Chicago LR* 618.
[189] [1995] 2 AC 207.

should not go 'scot-free', solicitors should maintain a high standard, legacies play an important role in society, etc. Then the Court compares various functionally equivalent foreign doctrinal constructions that would support the solicitor's liability as to their adequacy within English law. However, while these foreign solutions are comparable because they are responses to the same problem (functionalism), the second step, assessing whether these solutions could be adopted in English law, is a matter of doctrinal fit within English law. Functionalism could play no role in this.

6. The Universalizing Function: Unifying Law

Evaluation is closely linked to another function connected with the functional method since its early days: to be a tool for the unification of law. Functionalist comparatists advocate their method as ideal for this purpose, whether regionally (eg in Europe), or worldwide. Their argument rests on functionalism's ability to identify similarities among seemingly different laws; it should enable lawmakers to write an optimal uniform law that overcomes and transcends the doctrinal peculiarities of local legal systems. Once the functional similarities of different laws are realized, the argument goes, it becomes easier to unify them on the basis of these similarities.

Two problems with this argument have been treated above: the functional method alone cannot reveal the best legal system (Section III.5), and as an antidoctrinal method it is not well equipped for the formulation of legal rules that must be doctrinal (Section III.4). Lawmakers cannot ignore lawyers' actual experiences with legal doctrine and the creation of systems if they want to create a new doctrine and a new system.[190] Functionalist comparative law works well for critiquing doctrine, far less well for its establishment.

Yet there is an additional, slightly less obvious reason why functionalist comparative law is a particularly bad tool for the unification of law. A teleological version of functionalism may well contain a preference for convergence, some elements of which appear in the work of both Rabel and Zweigert. Equivalence functionalism, on the other hand, provides arguments against unification. If different legal systems are already similar regarding individual functions, as the functional method shows, then the benefits from unification lie only in formal improvements[191] and may well be outweighed by the costs.[192] First, it is often

---

[190] Christian Baldus, 'Historische Rechtsvergleichung im zusammenwachsenden Europa: Funktionelle Grenzen der funktionellen Methode?', (2003/2004) 1 *Zeitschrift für Gemeinschaftsprivatrecht* 225; cf Jansen (n 153), 72 ff.

[191] See eg Ugo Mattei, 'A Transaction Cost Approach to the European Code', (1997) *ERPL* 537, 540.

[192] See eg Hein Kötz, 'Rechtsvereinheitlichung: Nutzen, Kosten, Methoden, Ziele', (1986) 50 *RabelsZ* 1–17; Christian Kirchner, 'A "European Civil Code": Potential, Conceptual, and Methodological Implications', (1998) 31 *University of California Davis LR* 671, 686 ff.

inefficient for lawyers to learn new formal rules if these fulfil the same functions as the old ones; this is one important reason for practitioners' continuing lack of interest in the UN Sales Convention and for the reserved reactions of European business to proposals for a unified European contract law.[192a] Second, the functional method assumes that each legal institution performs a variety of functions within its legal system and that there is a sensitive interaction among the various institutions in each system that accounts for intersystemic differences. Unification of individual areas of the law is then likely to unsettle this balance. This can be observed in the difficult coordination between the United Nations Sales Convention (CISG) and national legal systems.[193] The functional method with its emphasis on functional equivalence shows why unification may be easier than one might think, but also why it is less important.

Of course, the last argument of interactions within a system can also provide an argument in favour of unification. That different legal systems respond to similar problems with different needs leads to problems in choice of law if actors, willingly or unwillingly, pick and choose solutions from different legal orders that do not combine into a whole. For example, one legal system may protect surviving spouses through the law of succession, the other through family law; one legal system protects poor parties through the law of damages, the other through the law of procedure. This can lead to inconsistencies if, under a choice of law analysis, different laws are applicable for different areas. Most of these problems, however, can be countered through a functionalist approach to choice of law.[194]

It becomes evident, somewhat surprisingly, that the functional method is not only a bad tool for legal unification, but even provides powerful arguments for maintaining differences. Indeed, modern law makers often prefer functional equivalence to unification. For example, in European Union law, directives must be implemented not in their doctrinal structure but only with regard to their results; the implementing laws in the member states are not similar but functionally equivalent. Similarly, the principle of mutual recognition in European Union law requires not similarity, but equivalence—presumably functional equivalence.[195] The OECD Convention on Corruption requires its member states to use not

[192a] But see now Stefan Vogenauer and Stephen Weatherill, 'The European Community's Competence to Pursue the Harmonisation of Contract Law—an Empirical Contribution to the Debate', in Vogenaur and Weatherill (eds), *The Harmonisation of European Contract Law* (2006), 105, 119 ff.

[193] For use of functionalist comparative law here see Franco Ferrari, 'The Interaction between the United Nations Convention on Contracts for the International Sale of Goods and Domestic Remedies (Rescission for Mistake and Remedies in Torts)' (forthcoming 2007) 71 *RabelsZ* Issue 1.

[194] Below, pp 378 f.

[195] cf the examples of education degrees and data protection in Scheiwe, 83 *Kritische Vierteljahresschrift für Gesetzgebung und Rechtswissenschaft* 31 f.

similar, but functionally equivalent measures against corruption.[196] So does international trade law: In the famous semi-conductors case, Europeans complained that through monitoring Japanese corporations, the Japanese government was effectively preventing those companies from exporting below certain company-specific costs. Japan countered that monitoring measures were not restrictions. However, a GATT panel made clear that the formal character of a governmental measure was irrelevant as long as it operated in a manner equivalent to mandatory restrictions.[197] In the Japanese legal culture, even formally non-binding measures imposed by the government were considered and treated as binding. They were, in other words, functionally equivalent.

7. The Critical Function: Critique of Legal Orders

This leaves the last proclaimed function of functional analysis, its critical function in various ways: tolerance of foreign law, critique of foreign law, critique of our own law, and critique of law in general. Functionalism does not fare equally well for all of these.

Functionalist comparative law can overcome a home bias against foreign law.[198] This shows particularly well in the conflict of laws, in which the question of accepting foreign law gains practical relevance, and functionalist comparison is often applied.[199] The most famous example for functionalism in the conflict of laws is Rabel's proposal to use functional comparison for the purpose of characterization.[200] Similarly, substitution and adaptation, the (somewhat idiosyncratic) methods of aligning different legal orders, require functional comparison. But the most important use of functionalist comparisons and functional equivalence concerns the question whether application of foreign law violates the forum's public policy. The German *Bundesgerichtshof*, holding that a foreign judgment on punitive

---

[196] Gemma Aiolfi and Mark Pieth, 'How to Make a Convention Work: the Organisation for Economic Co-operation and Development Recommendation and Convention on Bribery as an Example of a New Horizon in International Law', in Cyrille Fijnaut and Leo Huberts (eds), *Corruption, Integrity and Law Enforcement* (2002), 349, 351–3; Mireille Delmas-Marty, *Le relatif et l'universel* (2004), 253–7.

[197] *Japan: Trade in Semi-conductors*, Report of the Panel adopted on 4 May 1988, L/6309, Basic Instruments and Selected Documents 35S/116, especially nn 109, 117.

[198] Martijn W. Hesselink, *The New European Legal Culture* (2001) 51, 55.

[199] For the usefulness of functionalist comparison for conflict of laws, see Arthur T. von Mehren, 'An Academic Tradition for Comparative Law?', (1971) 19 *AJCL* 624, 625.

[200] Ernst Rabel, 'Das Problem der Qualifikation', (1931) 5 *RabelsZ* 241–88. Graziadei (n 6), 103 ff, even posits that the roots of functional comparative law are in problems of characterization. Yet while early texts on functionalism draw the connection frequently, Rabel himself pointed to his education in legal history as the source for his functional approach: Rabel, 'In der Schule' (n 149) 158 f; and see Reinhard Zimmermann, ' "In der Schule von Ludwig Mitteis": Ernst Rabels rechtshistorische Ursprünge', (2001) 65 *RabelsZ* 1, 35 f.

damages did not automatically violate German public policy, relied on an extensive analysis of the various functions of punitive damages and its German functional equivalents.[201] A Californian Court of Appeal relieved a French company of the requirement that it attain workers' compensation insurance from a Californian insurer, holding that the manifest function of the requirement—that employers should be adequately insured by a solvent company—could be attained by different means, in this case insurance with a French company.[202] Western courts are now more willing than before to recognize Islamic divorce based on unilateral repudiation because it is functionally equivalent to divorce in Western democracies, which, though nominally consensual, can effectively be brought about against or without the will of one of the spouses.[203] Between EU member states, community law restricts the application of mandatory norms of the forum law if the foreign law contains functionally equivalent norms.[204] In all these cases, the tolerance for foreign law is brought about by the recognition of functional equivalence.

At the same time, functionalist comparison can aid in critiquing foreign law, especially when a legal system insists on its cultural autonomy. For the sake of plurality and autonomy, critical strands in comparative law often invoke culture against functionalism. But culture is sometimes invented and sometimes undesirable. Distinguishing 'good' from 'bad' culture is difficult for an insider lacking a critical perspective, as well as for an outsider lacking sufficient insight. Functionalist comparative law can be helpful here in preparing the ground for critique, because it combines two important perspectives: awareness of culture on the one hand, and a perspective from outside on the other. By reconstructing legal culture in functional terms, functional comparative law helps preserve the culture's otherness while making it commensurable with our own law—we see the foreign law's functions and dysfunctions, both manifest and latent, and we know from comparison how else these effects can be brought about. The method does not provide us with the tools to evaluate the foreign law. But without the groundwork laid by functionalist comparisons, such evaluation is hard to formulate.

On the other hand, functionalist comparative law helps less in critiquing one's own law. The reason is again functional equivalence: Because we cannot say easily whether a foreign law is better than our own, recognizing different solutions abroad does not show us deficiencies at home. Functionalist comparison can open

---

[201] BGH (4 June 1992), BGHZ 118, 312; English translation in (1993) 32 *International Legal Materials* 1327.

[202] *Tucci v Club Mediterranee, SA*, 89 Cal App. 4th 180, 192 f.

[203] See eg Mathias Rohe, 'The Application of Islamic Family Law in German Courts and its Compatibility with German Public Policy', in Jürgen Basedow and Nadjma Yassari (eds), *Iranian Family and Succession Laws and their Application in German Courts* (2004), 19, 28 ff. But see Cass Civ (17 February 2004), D 2004, 825.

[204] Hélène Gaudemet-Tallon, 'De nouvelles fonctions pour l'équivalence en droit international privé?', in *Le droit international privé: esprit et méthodes. Mélanges en l'honneur de Paul Lagarde* (2005), 303, 315 ff.

our eyes to alternative solutions, but it cannot tell us whether those alternative solutions are better or not. Functionalism can provide us with a view of our own law from the outside, but whether what we thus see is deficient must be determined by other criteria. Functionalism can be critical of doctrinalism by revealing the contingency of any one doctrine, but it cannot show a way towards law without any doctrine, and it cannot itself provide such law.

Finally, functionalism is unhelpful in various respects in which critique may be desirable. First, functionalism does not help in evaluating functionality and purposes.[205] Quite to the contrary, in showing that other societies pursue the same goals by different means, it may reinforce our conviction that certain purposes are somehow necessary. Second, functionalism does not help us much in a fundamental critique of law. Functionalism may show how other societies fulfil certain needs with other institutions than law, but it cannot provide alternatives to the functionalist thinking inherent to our thinking about law. Third, with its emphasis on understanding the status quo and on apolitical analysis, functionalist comparative law is of little use for political governance projects.[206] Fourth, because functionalist comparative law presumes separate societies and separate legal systems as objects of comparison, it is unable to conceptualize the way in which these systems and societies are interdependent and overlap, a growing problem under conditions of globalization. Fifth, functionalist comparison is unable to account for tensions within legal systems, at least so long as it focuses on the relations between whole legal systems rather than on legal subsystems. All of these are real shortcomings, not only of the functional method in comparative law, but of traditional comparative law at large, and to this extent critiques of the functional method that are really aimed at mainstream comparative law are justified. But it remains doubtful whether any method of comparative law can fare better here.

IV. CONCLUSION

Section III has rendered some surprising results. Generally, one assumes that the strength of the functional method lies in its emphasis on similarities, its aspirations towards the evaluation and unification of law. This is the main reason why its

---

[205] Hill, 9 *Oxford Journal of Legal Studies* 106 f.

[206] David Kennedy, 'New Approaches to Comparative Law: Comparativism and International Governance', 1997 *Utah LR* 545, 588 ff; but see, for a promising proposal, Richard Buxbaum, 'Die Rechtsvergleichung zwischer nationalem Staat und internationaler Wirtschaft', (1996) 60 *RabelsZ* 201, 211 ff.

supporters since Rabel have considered it such a powerful tool, and why opponents have felt the need to combat it so fiercely. Yet the discussion has revealed that the functional method emphasizes differences within similarity; it does not provide criteria for evaluation; and it supplies powerful arguments against unification. Further, one generally assumes that the functional method does not account sufficiently for culture and is reductionist. But as the analysis demonstrates, the functional method not only requires us to look at culture, but it enables us to formulate general laws without having to abstract the specificities.

These misunderstandings about the utility of the functional method arise because comparatists unknowingly use different concepts of function, as demonstrated in Section II. Because the relation between these different concepts within the method was unclear, some of the hopes placed in the functional method were unrealistic. Comparatists' shift from a sociologically inspired to a legally inspired concept of function within the functional method occurs quite precisely when they move from description to systematizing and evaluation. A method reconstructed plainly on the basis of functional equivalence as the most robust of the concepts and following a constructive epistemology can make fewer claims in these last four areas; in fact, it can suggest reasons for caution and restraint. At the same time, such a method is less open to some of the criticism levelled against the functional method as an explanatory tool.

Other disciplines have discarded functionalism only after utilizing its insights. Functionalist comparative law has not yet made sufficient use of the benefits of functionalism. This study can only hint at the possibilities, but its findings suggest that a more methodologically aware functionalism will provide us with better insights into the functioning of law. In addition, functionalism in comparative law may well be immune to some of the criticism voiced against functionalism in the social sciences. After all, law is a normative discipline for which teleology may be useful or even necessary. Of course, this requires the construction of a more robust functional method. This chapter proposes to base such a method on equivalence functionalism and on an epistemology of constructive functionalism. Whether such a method can hold its own—against the uncritical version of functionalism on the one hand, and against the alternatives to functionalism on the other—remains to be seen. But the attempt seems well worth the effort.

BIBLIOGRAPHY

Émile Durkheim, *Les règles de la méthode sociologique* (1895, 5th edn 1988)

Ernst Cassirer, *Substanzbegriff und Funktionsbegriff* (1910)

Ernst Rabel, 'Aufgabe und Notwendigkeit der Rechtsvergleichung', (1924) 13 *Rheinische Zeitschrift für Zivil- und Prozeßrecht* 279–301; reprinted in Hans G. Leser (ed), Ernst Rabel, *Gesammelte Aufsätze* (vol III, 1967), 1–21

Max Rheinstein, 'Teaching Comparative Law', (1937–8) 5 *University of Chicago LR* 615–24

Josef Esser, 'Universale Prinzipien als Basis der Funktionsvergleichung von Privatrechtsinstituten', chapter 10 of *Grundsatz und Norm in der richterlichen Fortbildung des Privatrechts* (1956), 346–81

Niklas Luhmann, 'Funktion und Kausalität', (1962) 14 *Kölner Zeitschrift für Soziologie und Sozialpsychologie* 617–44; reprinted in *idem, Soziologische Aufklärung* (vol I, 7th edn, 2005), 1–38

Robert K. Merton, 'Manifest and Latent Functions', in *idem, Social Theory and Social Culture* (enlarged edn, 1968), 73–138

Niklas Luhmann, 'Funktionale Methode und juristische Entscheidung', (1969) 94 *Archiv für öffentliches Recht* 1–31; reprinted in *idem, Ausdifferenzierung des Rechts* (paperback edn, 1999), 273–307

Konrad Zweigert and Hein Kötz, *Einführung in die Rechtsvergleichung* (1st edn, 1969–71, 3rd edn, 1996; English translation under the title *An Introduction to Comparative Law* by Tony Weir, 3rd edn, 1998)

Volkmar Gessner, 'Soziologische Überlegungen zu einer Theorie der angewandten Rechtsvergleichung', (1972) 36 *RabelsZ* 229–60

Robert W. Gordon, 'Critical Legal Histories', (1984) 36 *Stanford LR* 57–126

Günter Frankenberg, 'Critical Comparisons: Re-thinking Comparative Law', (1985) 26 *Harvard International LJ* 412–55

Kirsten Scheiwe, 'Was ist ein funktionales Äquivalent in der Rechtsvergleichung? Eine Diskussion an Hand von Beispielen aus dem Familien- und Sozialrecht', (2000) 83 *Kritische Vierteljahresschrift für Gesetzgebung und Rechtswissenschaft* 30–51

Jaakko Husa, 'Farewell to Functionalism or Methodological Tolerance?', (2003) 67 *RabelsZ* 419–47

Michele Graziadei, 'The Functionalist Heritage', in Pierre Legrand and Roderick Munday (eds), *Comparative Legal Studies: Traditions and Transitions* (2003), 100–27

CHAPTER 11

COMPARATIVE LAW: STUDY OF SIMILARITIES OR DIFFERENCES?

GERHARD DANNEMANN

Berlin

I. Introduction

THERE is no point in comparing what is identical, and little point in comparing what has nothing in common. It is therefore inevitable that comparing legal systems involves, at least to some degree, exploring both similarities and differences. For some writers, this forms part of the definition of comparative law.[1] Yet there appears to be a somewhat limited debate which has not led to any consensus on why and where a comparison between different legal systems should focus on differences, and why and where on similarities. We can note that, both in the past and the present, some comparative lawyers have generally emphasized differences, while others see similarities, particularly in problems and their results, and a third group has sought to strike a balance between observing and analysing similarities and differences (Section II). Drawing on a debate in comparative history, the present chapter argues that the proper balance between looking for similarities and

---

[1] See eg Richard Hyland, 'Comparative Law', in Dennis Patterson (ed), *A Companion to Philosophy of Law and Legal Theory* (1996), 184 ff; David Kennedy, 'The Methods and the Politics', in Pierre Legrand and Roderick Munday, *Comparative Legal Studies: Traditions and Transitions* (2003), 345 ff, 355.

for differences depends on the purpose of the comparative enquiry (Section III). Furthermore, the issue of difference or similarity will be linked to the various steps which are involved in a comparative legal enquiry and it will be suggested that some steps require more focus on similarity, others on difference, and many call for a balance of both (Section IV).

II. History and the State of the Debate

In Europe, before the emergence of modern nation states, the uniting legal culture of the *ius commune* provided a perspective for legal writing which took similarity for granted and saw differences between regional or local laws as variations on a common theme.[2]

The situation changed during the eighteenth century. It may well be that Montesquieu was the first European scholar to discuss the issue of similarity or difference in a comparative legal enquiry, although by his time it was against the backdrop of existing nation states which were keen to show their particular identities. Montesquieu places the emphasis on difference. Which laws are appropriate for a country depends on climatic, geographical, cultural, religious, economic, moral, and political factors, so that 'it is very unlikely that the laws of one nation can suit another'.[3] He therefore urges us in the preface to his work 'not to consider as similar cases with real differences or to overlook differences in those which appear similar'.[4] Throughout *The Spirit of the Laws*, Montesquieu employs a difference-oriented comparison in order to show unique features of various historic and contemporary legal systems.

---

[2] See also Charles Donahue's introduction to this book.

[3] Montesquieu, *The Spirit of the Laws* (1748, trans and ed by Anne M. Cohler, Basia Carolyn Miller, Harold Samuel Stone, 1989), part I, ch 3, 8–9. For the comparative aspect of this work, see Iain Stewart (ed and trans), 'Montesquieu in England: his "Notes on England", with Commentary and Translation', 2002 *Oxford University Comparative Law Forum* 6 at <http://ouclf.iuscomp.org>.

[4] Montesquieu (n 3), preface, p xliii. The omitted first words of the sentence are: 'When I turned to antiquity, I sought to capture its spirit in order . . .'. It can be said, though, that Montesquieu did not limit this approach to antiquity.

1. Unification, Functionalism, and the Presumption of Similarity

(a) Unification

At some time during the late nineteenth century, just when the last of the great national codifications were being undertaken, the attention of a growing number of comparative lawyers focused on a new goal, namely the harmonization of national laws through a process of unification, as notably discussed at the 1900 *Congrès international de droit comparé*, but also evidenced in legislative efforts to harmonize some areas of commercial law and private international law. It has been stated that this limited the scope of comparative enquiries, as 'its assumption that only similar things could be compared led to rather a narrow concentration on statutory law and on the legal systems of Continental Europe'.[5] It generally brought a strong shift towards observing similarities rather than differences.[6] However, it must equally be remembered that unification can only occur where there are substantial differences to begin with,[7] and that any serious enquiry aimed at unification must take note of these differences.

(b) Functional Approach

When efforts at unification were revived some time after World War I, they helped to shape a new methodological approach towards comparative law, and towards perceiving similarities and differences. In particular, Ernst Rabel advocated the system of using case studies for comparative law enquiries, whereby emphasis would be given to the practical solutions achieved by the legal systems under consideration, thus unearthing substantive legal ideas which had hitherto been hidden under 'technical-juridical constructions. . . . When viewed in this manner, the similarities will prove to be extraordinarily strong and thoroughly profound.'[8] This developed into the functional approach towards comparative law which dominated much of the twentieth century.[9] Before we can evaluate its impact on perceiving similarities and differences, a few words are appropriate about legal families, and about macro- and microcomparison.

---

[5] Konrad Zweigert and Hein Kötz, *An Introduction to Comparative Law* (trans Tony Weir, 3rd edn, 1998), 59.

[6] Hyland (n 1), 187.

[7] Similarly, John H. Merryman, 'On the Convergence (and Divergence) of the Civil Law and the Common Law', in Mauro Cappelletti (ed), *New Perspectives for a Common Law of Europe* (1978), 195 ff, 223 (writing about convergence).

[8] Ernst Rabel, *Das Recht des Warenkaufs* (vol I, 1938), 67; English translation of this quote by Hyland (n 1), 187. The German original speaks of 'Verwandtschaften', literally: kinships, rather than 'Ähnlichkeiten' (similarities).

[9] See Ch 10 of this book. The functional approach has been developed and advocated, *inter alia*, by the leading treatise of Zweigert and Kötz (n 5), 34 ff.

(c) Legal Families

The notion of different legal families, which was aired at the 1900 *Congrès*[10] and was subsequently developed and refined,[11] exerted an important influence on how similarities and differences have been perceived in the comparative law debate. Entire legal systems, or at least large parts of them (notably: private law), are placed into different groups which are called 'families'. Members of each family show similarities which distinguish them from other families. The fact that this allows 'a concurrent investigation of difference and similarity' has been viewed as a benefit.[12] This investigation is, however, channelled in a certain way. Once agreement has been reached on those families and their constituent legal systems, the notion of legal families may lead to the similarities within each family being stressed (eg between French and Mexican law as members of the French legal family). It may also lead to the emphasizing of the differences between members of different legal families (eg French and Swiss law, the latter belonging to the German legal family).

The notion of legal families has also exerted considerable influence on the question of which legal systems should be chosen for a comparison by giving preference in particular to three European legal systems which are considered 'parent systems' within their family, that is, English, French, and German law.[13] This concentration on English, French, and German law may have produced similarities which are less related to the law in those countries and more to what else they have in common. Generally speaking, the choice of legal systems to be compared is a factor which exerts great influence on whether the researcher will find more differences or more similarities (see below, Section IV.1(b)).

(d) Macro- and Microcomparison

The above can be related to a distinction which Zweigert and Kötz have drawn between macrocomparison (with a focus on general questions) and microcomparison (with a focus on specific legal problems).[14] If individual legal families are categorized according to differences between families and similarities amongst their members, macrocomparison of members of different legal families is likely to reveal differences, and macrocomparison of members of the same family is likely

---

[10] Adhémar Esmein, 'Le Droit comparé et l'enseignment du Droit', in *Congrès international de droit comparé, Procès-verbaux des séances et documents* (vol I, 1905), 445 ff, 451.

[11] See Zweigert and Kötz (n 5), 63 ff, who follow the classification by Pierre Arminjon, Boris Nolde, and Martin Wolff, *Traité de droit comparé* (vol 1, 1950), 49. Patrick Glenn, *Legal Traditions of the World* (2nd edn, 2004), has recently proposed a similar type of classification which gives more prominence to cultural factors.

[12] Hyland (n 1), 191.

[13] Zweigert and Kötz (n 5), 41 advise this choice for more general comparative enquiries, and, 'as a rule of thumb', the inclusion of one additional member for each family, namely US, Italian, and Swiss law, for research into particular institutions or questions.

[14] Zweigert and Kötz (n 5), 4–5; Hyland (n 1), 184.

to reveal similarities. If we additionally follow the advice to compare primarily parent systems of different legal families, macrocomparison will predominantly focus on differences. For macrocomparison, this built-in affinity towards noting difference is not mitigated through a functional approach, because that approach has rarely been applied to macrocomparisons. It is indeed difficult to find answers to the general questions which macrocomparisions raise by comparing results in similar cases.

(e) Similarity of Problems and Results

On the other hand, if one follows the functional approach towards microcomparison, one should generally expect different legal systems to produce similar results for similar cases. Zweigert and Kötz have elevated Rabel's notion as follows:[15]

one can almost speak of a basic rule of comparative law: different legal systems give the same or very similar solutions, even as to detail, to the same problems of life, despite the great differences in their historical development, conceptual structure, and style of operation.

This similarity 'almost amounts to a *"praesumptio similitudinis"*, a presumption that the practical results are similar'. This presumption works as a heuristic principle, showing us 'where to look in the law and legal life of the foreign system in order to discover similarities and substitutes'. It also provides a checklist, for if the researcher[16]

finds that there are great differences or indeed diametrically opposite results, he should be warned and go back to check again whether the terms in which he posed his original question were indeed purely functional, and whether he has spread the net of his researches quite wide enough.

A second aspect of perceived similarity, which has not been elevated to a presumption, relates to legal problems:[17]

If law is seen functionally as a regulator of social facts, the legal problems of all countries are similar. Every legal system in the world is open to the same questions and subject to the same standards, even countries of different social structures or different stages of development.

However, it would be going too far to state that a functional approach, or the presumption of similarity, turn the entire comparison into an exercise of comparing similarities. It must not be overlooked that the 'basic rule' of Zweigert and Kötz mentions great differences not only in historical development, but also in conceptual structure and style of operation. The presumption of similarity relates only to the practical results, the outcome in the case studies which form the basis of a microcomparison.

This combination of the functional approach with the expectation that different

---

[15] Zweigert and Kötz (n 5), 39.   [16] Ibid 40 (this and the preceding two quotes).
[17] Ibid 46.

legal systems, institutions and rules produce similar results in solving similar problems has remained highly influential and has in recent times received a further boost through various projects which aim, to a different degree and in different ways, at the harmonization or unification of European Private Law.[18]

2. Critique of Functionalism and the Emphasis on Difference

(a) Gutteridge and Ancel

Nevertheless, the same combined approach has been challenged throughout the second half of the twentieth century. In an important textbook published directly after World War II, Harold Gutteridge focuses on differences between legal systems when describing the method of comparative law.[19] Perhaps motivated by existing significant differences in the laws, Gutteridge urges us to look for similarity in 'the stage of legal, political and economic development' when selecting the legal systems under comparison, in order to avoid what he calls 'illusory comparison'.[20] Twenty-five years later, with the Cold War showing no signs of abating, Marc Ancel developed the notion of a *comparaison contrastée* in which more prominence is given to the opposition between legal systems than to their possible convergence.[21] In Ancel's view, all comparative study poses itself in terms of contrast. On a subjective level, differences will be the first thing which a comparative lawyer, trained in one legal system, will notice when encountering the rules of another. He further suggests that comparing radically different legal systems might yield more significant results than comparing similar legal systems.[22] At the same time, this difference is not limited to capitalist and socialist legal systems. Ancel remains critical of the notion of an 'occidental law' group which combines the Roman-German and Anglo-American legal systems. While some similarities exist within that group, there are other aspects which Roman law and socialist law may have in common and which distinguish them from the common law.[23]

(b) Difference Theory

The perspective of the researcher, which had already provided Ancel's subjective argument for difference, became a central plank in an attack on functionalism which Günter Frankenberg launched in 1985. He urged comparative lawyers 'to

---

[18] See Ch 16 of this book.
[19] Harold C. Gutteridge, *Comparative Law* (1946), 8–9.   [20] Ibid 73.
[21] Marc Ancel, *Utilité et méthodes du droit comparé: Eléments d'introduction générale à l'étude comparative des droits* (1971), 65.
[22] Ibid 67.   [23] Ibid 67–9.

recognize that they are participant observers'[24] who understand other legal systems primarily from the perspective of their own and are thus unable to be as neutral as functionalists would like to see them. In consequence, the presumption of similarity is 'to be abandoned for a rigorous experience of distance and difference'.[25] A group of difference theorists emerged.[26] They reject functionalism and its focus on result-based comparison. They urge, in Hyland's words, that 'all levels of difference among legal systems—whether in terms of concepts or results—should be acknowledged rather than suppressed', and establish a presumption of dissimilarity.[27] From a *tour d'horizon* which encompasses, *inter alia*, discourse theory, sociology, philosophy, and psychology, Pierre Legrand, perhaps the most outspoken and radical proponent of a 'priority of difference',[28] perceives law as part and product of individual cultures and argues on this basis, *inter alia*, that common law and civil law are 'irrevocably irreconcilable'.[29]

(c) Diversity in Legal Process and Dynamics

The presumption of similarity is also challenged by several works which shift the comparative perspective away from finding similar results to explaining difference and diversity through studying legal processes (Mirjan Damaška) or dynamics (Rodolfo Sacco). Transcending legal families, and giving greater prominence to political factors, Damaška classifies legal processes into hierarchical or coordinate types of authority, and into policy-implementing or conflict-solving types of procedure, thus producing a framework of four models of justice which serve to examine the legal process, whereby all four can co-exist within one and the same legal system.[30] While Damaška is equally interested in similarities and differences,[31] one of his main points is nevertheless to show how different models of justice produce different procedural and substantive outcomes. And where Zweigert and Kötz warn of superficial differences, Damaška warns us not to fall for superficial similarities when, for example, 'all states subscribe to the view that judges should be independent'.[32]

---

[24] Günter Frankenberg, 'Critical Comparisons: Re-thinking Comparative Law', (1985) 26 *Harvard International LJ* 411 ff, 441.

[25] Ibid 453.

[26] See, in particular, Hyland (n 1), 193–7; Pierre Legrand, 'The Same and the Different', in Pierre Legrand and Roderick Munday, *Comparative Legal Studies: Traditions and Transitions* (2003), 240 ff (further developing his previous work in this area).

[27] Hyland (n 1), 194.   [28] Legrand (n 26), 286.

[29] Ibid 245, against James Gordley, 'Common law und civil law: eine überholte Unterscheidung', (1993) 1 *Zeitschrift für Europäisches Privatrecht* 498 ff. Gordley argues that US common law today is closer to civil law than to its own historic roots on account of it having taken over the civil law classification into contract, tort, and property.

[30] Mirjan R. Damaška, *The Faces of Justice and State Authority* (1986), 181 ff.

[31] Ibid 240: '. . . the sense of similarities and differences can be sharpened, and new relationships can be detected where none were perceived before'.

[32] Ibid 1.

Sacco has developed the notion of 'legal formants' in order to demonstrate and explain the diversity of law within as well as between legal systems.[33] Different sources account for different formants, and legal solutions presented by statute, judgments, and academic opinion may diverge. Comparative law serves to bring out, and find explanations for, this divergence within one system, as well as divergence between different legal systems. Even where different legal systems appear to agree on a rule, a different combination of legal formants may lead to a different application of that rule.[34] Comparative law also allows us to find what Sacco calls cryptotypes, that is, hidden formants, rules which lawyers apply without being aware of their presence. Any difference between a rule and a decision purporting to be based on this rule indicates the presence of a cryptotype. The cryptotype can be revealed through comparison with another legal system, in particular if the same rule is explicit in that system.[35] By showing how the outcome of a case depends on the interplay of different legal formants, Sacco appears to strengthen the case of those who argue for a perspective of difference.[36] On the other hand, some of Sacco's writing reads like enthusiastic support for a functional comparison which employs the presumption of similarity and which aims at improving the law through convergence or unification.[37]

3. Reconciliation?

Over the last decade, we have seen some reconciliation of proponents and critics of the functionalist approach, and an agreement might be in sight that propositions of either similarity or difference should be abandoned in favour of an approach which allows for both similarity and difference and has no presumption in favour of either.

From the side of the critics, Bernhard Großfeld and Vivian Curran take up many

[33] Rodolfo Sacco, *Introduzione al diritto comparato* (5th edn, 1990), ch 2. An English version of the first four chapters was published as 'Legal Formants: A Dynamic Approach to Comparative Law', (1991) 39 *AJCL* 1 ff and 343 ff, and of the fifth chapter as 'Diversity and Uniformity in the Law', (2001) 49 *AJCL* 171 ff. A German translation of the entire book appeared as *Einführung in die Rechtsvergleichung* (trans Jacob Joussen, 2001).

[34] Sacco, (1991) 39 *AJCL* 21 ff.   [35] Sacco, (1991) 39 *AJCL* 384 ff.

[36] Sacco's legal formants have been hailed by a supporter of a presumption of difference, Hyland (n 1) 195, in that they 'may well represent the most significant contribution to the understanding of difference in recent comparative law'. I agree with Michele Graziadei, 'The functionalist heritage', in Pierre Legrand and Roderick Munday, *Comparative Legal Studies: Traditions and Transitions* (2003), 100 ff, 125, that Sacco's formants provide 'both an alternative and a supplement to the functional approach'.

[37] Sacco, (2001) 49 *AJCL* 188: '[Conceptual] categories are different in various countries and lawyers in these countries do nothing to free themselves from these differences. The contrasts we have before us exist in taxonomy qualifications, languages, descriptions, explanation and concepts. They do not exist however in the operating rules. The task of scholars is then that of comparing, and then banishing and exorcising these absurd conceptual contrasts'.

of the issues raised by the difference theorists.[38] Großfeld uses primarily the relationship between language and law to demonstrate the difficulties of a participant observer approach, urging us not to mistake apparent similarity in the language used in legal sources for similarity in law.[39] Curran relates the participant observer approach to the generation of *émigré* lawyers who fled the national socialist regime and who are seen as the driving force behind the presumption of similarity.[40] For Curran, comparative law is a process of 'cultural immersion', whereby 'a valid examination of another legal culture requires an immersion into the political, historical, economic and linguistic contexts that molded the legal system'.[41] In this, 'the original legal culture should be viewed in untranslated form, but comparatists need to retain their stance as outsiders even as they acquire insight into the insiders' view'.[42] Großfeld and Curran agree that understanding is possible, although difficult; Curran adds that 'the comparatist will fail to grasp a foreign legal culture completely from within'.[43] However, unlike the difference theorists, she expressly rejects a reversal of the presumption of similarity into a presumption of difference.[44] The comparative lawyer must be ready to look for and accept both, including 'the possibility of irreconcilable differences at a fundamental level'.[45] For this, it is important not to associate sameness with inclusion, and difference with exclusion, because otherwise our perception might be blurred by political issues relating to inclusion and exclusion.[46] It is interesting to note in this context that David Kennedy places the preference for observing either similarity or difference in other legal systems on a rough political matrix of left and right, whereby, from a Western viewpoint, left stands for exoticizing the neighbour, familiarizing the Orient, and generally emphasizing diversity, whilst the right will tend to exoticize the Orient, familiarize the neighbour, and emphasize uniformity in comparative law.[47]

James Whitman, who complains that 'tone-deafness to difference in our comparative law literature has grown worse',[48] at the same time warns us not to repeat the mistakes of nineteenth-century Romanticism in overemphasizing otherness to

---

[38] Bernhard Großfeld, *Kernfragen der Rechtsvergleichung* (1996); Vivian G. Curran, 'Cultural Immersion, Difference and Categories in U.S. Comparative Law', (1998) 46 *AJCL* 43 ff.

[39] Großfeld (n 38), 106–7.   [40] Curran (n 38), 66 ff.   [41] Ibid 51.   [42] Ibid 57.

[43] Ibid 58. One could wonder whether this is also Curran's verdict on the generation of *émigré lawyers*, or lawyers operating in mixed legal systems, or the fast-growing number of young lawyers who have received their legal training in two or more countries. It is noteworthy that Großfeld (n 38), 292–3, calls for 'patient optimism'.

[44] Curran (n 38), 85.   [45] Ibid 86.   [46] Ibid 87.

[47] Kennedy (n 1), 417. Graziadei (n 36), 124 offers a similar observation. Alan Watson, *Legal Transplants* (2nd edn, 1993), 95, 108 has suggested that it is extremely common for different legal systems to borrow from each other. According to Graziadei, Watson has predominantly been criticized for this suggestion from scholars on the left side of the political spectrum.

[48] James Q. Whitman, 'The Neo-Romantic turn', in Pierre Legrand and Roderick Munday, *Comparative Legal Studies: Traditions and Transitions* (2003), 100 ff, 312.

the point of 'colossal silliness and of distasteful moral relativism'.[49] And Michele Graziadei finds no difficulty in combining a call for comparative law to be 'strongly attuned to diversity'[50] with sympathy for the achievements of functionalism and the prospect of its reform through ongoing comparative research in the form of the bargaining processes which take place when defining the parameters of multilateral comparative projects.[51]

From the other end, Jaakko Husa defends a moderate functional approach which discards three elements associated with what he calls hardcore functionalism, namely the presumption of similarity, 'causal explanations' for similarity (see below, Section III.1), and the notion of a neutral framework in comparative law. On the other hand, Husa supports 'the desire for strict comparability and an effort to give explanations to revealed similarities and differences'.[52] More particularly, Husa believes that the presumption of similarity 'is pointless as a basic methodological rule of thumb' for comparisons between culturally remote systems, and explains (rather than defends) the presumption by stating that it is 'quite natural to think like Zweigert and Kötz . . . if one compares systems within the same cultural sphere as for example common law and Romano-Germanic law'. He also criticizes the fact that the presumption of similarity calls for suspicion only if the results do not appear similar, and urges us 'to treat any "results" of comparative study with natural in-built suspicion'.[53]

Moreover, the surviving co-author of the textbook which did so much to advance both functional approach and presumption of similarity, has recently taken what looks like a moderated stance. After defending a functional approach in terms of helping to avoid mistakes and misunderstandings, and as being indispensable for practical comparative work, Kötz concedes:[54]

. . . but it also has the disadvantage that it sometimes distracts from the truly interesting and important questions. For it can be compared with a 'black box', into which the 'problem' is inserted on the one end, and which spits out the 'solution' at the other. What really happens within the 'black box' receives little attention, and is not particularly important for the principle of functionality. However, sometimes the solutions are not as interesting as the procedure by which they are generated. Therefore, much can be said for the assertion that 'comparative legal studies are most fruitful when they focus on styles and techniques rather than on the substantive law'. This is particularly true when one seeks to unify 'substantive law,' and if such unification can occur only by way of a codification which will necessarily have to operate with overt and covert general clauses. That gives particular

---

[49] Ibid 313.   [50] Graziadei (n 36), 114.   [51] Ibid 127.

[52] Jaakko Husa, 'Farewell to Functionalism or Methodological Tolerance?', (2003) 67 *RabelsZ* 417 ff, 443.

[53] Ibid 424.

[54] Hein Kötz, 'Abschied von der Rechtskreislehre?', (1998) 6 *Zeitschrift für Europäisches Privatrecht* 493 ff, 505 (my translation). The quote within this quote is from Donald Harris and Denis Tallon (eds), *Contract Law Today: Anglo-French Comparisons* (1989), conclusions, 394.

relevance to what cannot be unified by order of the legislator: styles, procedures, techniques, mentalities, and value judgments.

While this statement does not repeal the presumption of similarity of 'solutions', it nevertheless shifts the attention of the comparative lawyer into those areas where more differences are to be observed. For Kötz, it is generally interesting to understand these differences, and particularly important to do so in order to ensure that law is unified not only by name, but also in terms of practical application.

4. Evaluation of the Contemporary Debate

In his recent evaluation of present comparative law methodology, Mathias Reimann is highly critical of the state of debate on similarity or difference between legal systems. 'If there is no articulated set of criteria which define and measure likeness, agreements or disagreements about the similarity of, say, the common law and the civil law at best reflect mere differences in perspective; at worst they are empty word games'. If some proponents of similarity discuss the similarity of black-letter law, and some proponents of difference discuss the differences between mental habits, 'the two arguments cannot be connected in a sensible way'.[55]

The above supplies some further evidence for his analysis. It appears on closer inspection that much of the opposition between a presumption of similarity and a presumption of difference does not relate to whether laws are generally similar or different. What is more controversial is which aspects of law and its context are most relevant for comparative research, and which steps within a comparative enquiry deserve most attention.

The presumption that laws are the same all over the world does exist, but not in comparative law textbooks. It is practised as a rule of law. According to the English rules of conflict of laws, in the absence of evidence to the contrary, all foreign law is presumed to be the same as English law.[56] It is true, on closer inspection, that this rule has much to do with the burden of proof and little to do with any genuine

---

[55] Mathias Reimann, 'The Progress and Failure of Comparative Law in the Second Half of the Twentieth Century', (2002) 50 *AJCL* 671 ff, 690, referring to the dispute between Gordley and Legrand (n 29). Similarly, Lawrence Rosen, 'Beyond Compare', in Pierre Legrand and Roderick Munday, *Comparative Legal Studies: Traditions and Transitions* (2003), 493 ff, 505, arguing that the issue of similarity versus difference 'is false because there are no natural lines of differentiation that, in some science-like quest, we can discover'.

[56] *Dynamit AG v Rio Tinto Co* [1918] AC 260, 295 (HL). Taken at face value, this could be seen as 'the most daring and least accurate of all legal presumptions': Gerhard Dannemann, 'Establishing foreign law in a German Court', *German Law Archive* at <http://www.iuscomp.org/gla/literature/foreignlaw.htm> near note 22 (last accessed on 27 January 2006).

belief that laws are the same throughout the world.[57] Nevertheless, it is easily overlooked that the presumption of similarity as proposed by Zweigert and Kötz has a much more limited field of application.[58] It applies only to those areas of (a) substantive (b) private law which (c) are not culturally or politically sensitive, thus excluding all of public law, criminal law, procedural law, and even family and inheritance law. So the vast majority of the law taught at universities, applied by courts, and—this is a more recent and welcome development—examined by comparative lawyers is not caught by the presumption. Furthermore, the presumption applies to only one aspect in the process of comparison, namely the results, that is, practical outcomes, which legal systems deliver in response to specific situations.

It is for this reason that some of the critics of the presumption of similarity may have been preaching to the converted when they emphasized existing differences in terms of legal culture. It has been explained above why the combination of functionalism with the notion of legal families is likely to produce studies in macro-comparison which also emphasize difference between legal systems. And indeed, some of the most active supporters of the presumption of similarity of practical results have been preaching the difference between legal systems on a more general level. For example, one such supporter, who goes as far as stating that 'skilful (and well-meaning) manipulation' needs to be applied to bring out this similarity of results,[59] argues in the same article against codifying European civil law *inter alia* on the ground that differences between English and Continental drafting techniques are too great.[60] The same author has produced a comparison between the English and the German style of judgments which is so contrastive that it could have been formulated by a difference theorist.[61] Moreover, few of those who criticize functionalism for overemphasizing similarity appear to have noticed that Zweigert and Kötz, in the general part of their treatise, make much use of the contrastive method to bring out particular features of the different legal families they describe.[62]

Both supporters and opponents of the presumption of similarity have argued that it has value as a heuristic principle, that is, for leading our search into direc-

---

[57] Following Richard Fentiman, 'Foreign Law in English Courts', (1992) 108 *LQR* 142 ff, 147–8, the true and much less problematic content of the rule is that English law applies unless foreign law is proven.

[58] Zweigert and Kötz (n 5), 40.

[59] Basil S. Markesinis, 'Why a Code is Not the Best way to Advance the Cause of European Legal Unity', (1997) 5 *European Review of Private Law* 519 ff, 520, leaving Legrand (n 26), 247 to wonder whether 'comparativists who make an ideological investment in sameness . . . are being tenaciously *delusional* or stubbornly *disingenuous*'.

[60] Markesinis (n 59), 521–2, an aspect which is overlooked by the vociferous critique of Legrand (n 26).

[61] Basil S. Markesinis, 'A Matter of Style', (1994) 110 *LQR* 607 ff.

[62] Zweigert and Kötz (n 5), an aspect which is overlooked eg by Frankenberg, (1985) 26 *Harvard International LJ* 436. For a view which emphasizes similarity between common law and civil law, see Gordley, (1993) 1 *Zeitschrift für Europäisches Privatrecht* 498 ff.

tions we might otherwise have missed.[63] This almost presupposes that the existing differences between legal systems would *per se* suggest the opposite, that is, different results. Also, what merit would a work have which finds similarity, if everything is the same to begin with? The functional comparatist will find greatest satisfaction in unearthing similarities in results which are hidden deep inside a jungle of different styles, methods, procedures, and sources of law—just as critics of functionalism may derive the greatest pleasure from uncovering hidden differences even where the law appears similar.[64] Both need similarity and difference as a matter of job satisfaction.

The discussion between those who see similarity and those who see difference might be more fruitful if this debate were more structured. Such a structure could be provided by two distinctions. The first is between the different aims of a comparative enquiry (below, Section III.3.). The second distinction relates to the individual steps which such an enquiry is likely to take (below, Section IV). It is therefore within the context of comparing results that an evaluation of the presumption of similarity will be located (Section IV.2.(d)). Similarly, the functionalist rule which proclaims similarity of problems faced by legal systems worldwide (and which, despite being formulated much more widely, may have attracted less attention),[65] will be treated in the context of identifying the basis of comparison (IV.1.(a)).

The present debate also seems to focus much more on stating that we should expect similarities, or that we should expect differences, than on explaining why we should look for similarities or for differences in the first place. The following section will look beyond law for assistance in identifying such reasons.

III. Reasons to Look for Similarities or Differences

1. Linking Rules to Effects

Comparative law has long been used to show the effects which certain legal institutions or rules produce. Perhaps the oldest example can be taken from Plato's *Laws*.[66]

---

[63] Zweigert and Kötz (n 5), 40; Hyland (n 1), 190.

[64] Whitman (n 48), 336: 'Indeed, uncovering differences in unarticulated assumptions will frequently be the most revealing and gratifying work a comparatist can do'.

[65] Zweigert and Kötz (n 5), 46. For a discussion, see Peter de Cruz, *Comparative Law in a Changing World* (2nd edn, 1999), 230 ff.

[66] Plato, *Laws*, book 3, 12–16.

An Athenian, Spartan, and Cretan test the theory that there are two basic forms of statehood, monarchy and democracy, and that a combination of the authoritarian aspects of monarchy and the libertarian aspects of democracy is ideal, by comparing the constitutional arrangements in Persia, Athens, and Sparta throughout the ages. The conclusion is that all three states were better off whenever there was a proper balance between monarchy and democracy, and worse off if either monarchy or democracy gained the upper hand (despotism during some of Persia's history, libertarianism during some of Athens' history). Plato compares similarities to show what the better periods of Persian, Athenian, and Spartan history had in common, and differences to distinguish these better periods from worse periods, for which he again finds a common denominator, that is, the undue dominance of one model of statehood.

The methodological basis of establishing causal links through a process of elimination based on comparing differences and similarities appears to have received little attention from comparative lawyers. This process was described in the nineteenth century by John Stuart Mill, who distinguished the 'method of agreement' and the 'method of difference' as the first two out of four methods of experimental inquiries 'into the cause of a given effect or into the effects or properties of a given cause'.[67] Mill shows that the 'method of agreement' and the 'method of difference' do not work in isolation, but in combination. Using examples from natural sciences, Mill demonstrates how comparing differences and similarities can be used to find the cause of a certain effect through a process of elimination in which a common denominator is found for situations where this effect occurs and which is absent in situations in which the same effect does not occur. Mill thus describes the very process which Plato employed to find out what good states have in common, and what distinguishes them from bad states. And indeed, this is how differences and similarities between different legal systems continue to be used in order to test a hypothesis that a certain legal rule or institution will lead to a certain desired or undesired effect.

All legal norms strive to attain certain effects. The study of links between rules and effects is not limited to comparative enquiries. However, comparative law can add a new dimension to such causal enquiries, which are most frequently related to law reform.

For example, if it is debated whether a lower speed limit should be introduced for road traffic, it will be helpful to know which other countries have introduced such a speed limit, and whether or not road traffic accidents have declined since the law was changed. Thus, the comparative lawyer compares differences in speed limits and links them to the development of the number of road traffic accidents; a different development (reduction of accidents) might indicate a causal link to

---

[67] John Stuart Mill, *Philosophy of Scientific Method* (ed Ernest Nagel, 1950), 211 ff, 211.

the different rule, and a similar development (no reduction of accidents) could indicate that a lower speed limit would not help to reduce accidents.

Similarly, comparative law can help to alleviate or strengthen fears about possible negative side-effects of changes in the law. For example, whenever the principle of equal treatment of the sexes forced the German legislature to derogate from the traditional German notion that a husband and wife, and their common children, must have the same surname (traditionally the husband's), fears were raised that such a change would gravely damage family ties. The comparative lawyer can point to Latin America as an almost entire continent where no such common family name exists (difference), and where family ties appear no less strong than in Germany (similarity). The similarity in result and the difference in rule can serve to indicate that the rule does not affect the result. Thus, for the comparative lawyer, the legal systems of the world combine to form a large laboratory in which different legal solutions are constantly being tested.

This method appears to work reasonably well for rules which operate in low context situations and cultures,[68] and independent of their particular legal context, such as the above-mentioned speed limit. But even then it may be difficult to establish causal links with sufficient certainty. Even if one common denominator can be found for a group with similar results which is absent in a group with different results, it will often be difficult to find and eliminate all other common denominators or individual factors which could explain the difference. In the speed limit example one would have to establish through such a process of elimination that (a) a drop in motor traffic casualties not only coincided with the introduction of a particular speed limit in country X but was caused by the speed limit, and (b) that the introduction of the same speed limit in country Y would have a similar effect on motor traffic casualties in country Y.

The laboratory of different legal systems has one main disadvantage, namely that the differences between legal systems and their historical, economic, social, geographical, political, and cultural contexts are often too great to allow safe conclusions about the effect which certain legal rules will produce outside their native environment. Some have therefore argued that comparative lawyers should give up altogether the idea of establishing such causal links.[69]

On the other hand, with these limitations in mind, comparative legal studies may at least provide arguments even where causal links cannot be established with certainty, for example by suggesting (without proving) that a different speed limit can reduce traffic accidents, and that no damage will occur to family ties if husband, wife, and their children are no longer legally required to share the same surname. In this way, comparative law can help to establish links which would be more difficult to prove within one legal system. To stay within our example, if it can be shown that the number of road traffic accidents has dropped in all legal

---

[68] Edward T. Hall, *Beyond Culture* (1976), ch 7.   [69] Husa, (2003) 67 *RabelsZ* 417, 433.

systems after they introduced a certain lower speed limit, and that no similar drop could be observed in those legal systems which did not, this will provide much stronger evidence for such a link than an enquiry into only one of those systems could have provided.

Therefore, even if comparative law cannot deliver full proof of a causal link between rule and effect, it can still produce more evidence for such a link than an enquiry which limits itself to one legal system. This is sufficient justification for comparative lawyers to direct their enquiries to causal links between rules and effects.

Obviously, the more deeply legal rules are embedded in their context, the more difficult it becomes to suggest, let alone prove, causal links. An interesting and perhaps hitherto somewhat neglected branch of comparative law could shed more light on this phenomenon by comparing situations in which identical or similar rules have produced different results in different contexts.[70] Quite generally, one should not take for granted that similarities and differences in the laws under consideration are more important than similarities in terms of economy, social structures, geographical factors, politics, or culture. While it is true that some rules will only make sense within a given legal environment, it is not particularly important whether a speed limit is imposed in a common law or a civil law system; much more important is the degree to which traffic rules are obeyed or ignored, whether they are enforced or not, and how similar or different the road systems are in the countries under consideration.

Finally, there is one lesson we can take from Mill and the issue of causal enquiries, namely that similarities and differences are equally important to a comparison, and that the interplay of both will advance our knowledge substantially more than focusing on either similarities or differences.

2. Complex Enquiries

In his criticism of what he regards as the undue preoccupation of traditional functionalist lawyers with establishing causal links, Husa states that law 'is simply too complex a phenomenon for this', that is, that it has too little in common with natural sciences or even empirical social sciences which engage in causal enquiries. He advises comparative lawyers to look at legal history for the type of explanations which the law can provide for such highly complex phenomena.[71] The present author would go one step further and look towards history as a discipline which

---

[70] For an unusual example in which a new rule worked better 'abroad' than 'at home', see Alan Berman, 'The Law on Gender Parity in Politics in France and New Caledonia: A Window into the Future or More of the Same?', 2005 *Oxford University Comparative Law Forum* 2 at <http://ouclf.iuscomp.org>.

[71] Husa, (2003) 67 *RabelsZ* 417, 433.

has for quite some time debated one important question which appears to have been less on the minds of comparative lawyers, namely, why (and not just where) should we look for differences or for similarities when comparing two different complex systems?

Writing in 1928, Marc Bloch stated that a comparison had to take note of both similarities and differences, and had to explain both, to the degree that this was possible. For this purpose, there had to be a 'certain similarity between the facts observed . . ., and a certain dissimilarity between the environments in which these facts occur'.[72]

One year later, Otto Hintze gave us the following clue to the reasons why comparative studies should search for similarities or for differences: 'Comparison may look for something general on which the compared objects are based; comparison may seek to gain a sharper image of the individuality of one of the objects compared'.[73]

While Hintze believed that sociologists look more for common ground (ie similarity), and historians more for a sharper image (ie difference), contemporary writers such as Heinz-Gerhard Haupt and Jürgen Kocka show that both approaches can be found in comparative history scholarship. They argue, however, that the search for both differences *and* similarities is the most distinctive feature of comparative work.[74] Similarly, Jürgen Osterhammel distinguishes between convergent and divergent comparison; whereas the former is searching for similarities, the latter searches for differences.[75] Osterhammel writes:[76]

Whereas the divergent approach works on the assumption of a universal history which is not fragmented in postmodern fashion, but can be structured by distinguishing between

---

[72] Marc Bloch, 'Pour une histoire comparée des sociétés européennes', (1928) *Revue de Synthèse historique*, reprinted in: *Mélanges historiques* (vol I, 1963), 16 ff, 17 (my translation). The original reads: '. . . une certaine similitude entre les faits observés . . . et une certaine dissemblance entre les milieux où ils se sont produits'.

[73] Otto Hintze, 'Soziologische und geschichtliche Staatsauffassung' (1929), in Otto Hintze, *Gesammelte Werke* (ed G. Oestreich, vol II, 1964), 239 ff, 251 (my translation). The German original reads: '[M]an kann vergleichen, um ein Allgemeines zu finden, das dem Verglichenen zugrunde liegt; man kann vergleichen, um den einen der möglichen Gegenstände in seiner Individualität schärfer zu erfassen'.

[74] Heinz-Gerhard Haupt and Jürgen Kocka, 'Historischer Vergleich: Methoden, Aufgaben, Probleme', in Heinz-Gerhard Haupt and Jürgen Kocka (eds), *Geschichte und Vergleich* (1996), 9 ff.

[75] Jürgen Osterhammel, 'Sozialgeschichte im Zivilisationsvergleich', [1996] *Geschichte und Gesellschaft* 143 ff, 158. This seminal article draws together eight important distinctions in approaches to comparative studies.

[76] Ibid 159, my translation. The German original reads: 'Geht der divergente Ansatz von der Annahme einer nicht postmodern fragmentierten, sondern durch die Unterscheidung von Entwicklungspfaden strukturierbaren Universalgeschichte aus, legt eine konvergente Perspektive (sofern sie nicht teleologisch auf ein einheitliches Modernitätsziel hin entworfen wird) Wert auf die Beobachtung, daß Völker auf verschiedenen Kontinenten und in unterschiedlichen Zivilisationsbereichen ähnliche Grundformen der Vergesellschaftung und ähnliche Problemlösungsstrategien ausgebildet haben'.

different paths of development, a convergent perspective (unless specifically designed to fit a unitarian aim of modernity) will emphasize the observation that people on different continents and in different areas of civilization have created similar basic forms of societalization (*Vergesellschaftung*) and similar strategies for solving problems.

Osterhammel stresses that the two approaches are not contradictory. Ideally, they should be combined.[77] Their proper balance depends on the purpose of the enquiry (*Erkenntnisziel*).

What can comparative lawyers learn from this debate?

First, it offers some insights into what comparative lawyers have done in the past, and why. We learn that unitarian modernizers will use a convergent approach, as indeed those who have advocated legal unification from the 1900 *Congrès international de droit comparé* until today have done. We learn that, even beyond an agenda of unification, a convergent approach will discover similar strategies for solving similar problems, and we note that problems and solutions are precisely the two areas in which Zweigert and Kötz see most similarity between different legal systems. We learn that a divergent approach need not be associated with postmodern fragmentation but can be used to show the different paths of development which different societies have taken, and this is how comparative lawyers who seek to explain law in the context of the history and culture of the legal system in question operate: they use a divergent approach in order to gain a sharper image by emphasizing differences to other legal systems and their history and culture. To this one could add that lawyers using a convergent approach tend to emphasize similarity by linking primarily legal rules of one system to legal rules of another, whereas lawyers using a divergent approach tend to emphasize difference by primarily linking legal rules to the society in which they operate.

Second, the debate on comparative history confirms what Mill advocates: a comparison will normally yield the best results when the researcher keeps an eye open for both similarities and differences. We also learn that the proper balance between discovering common features and detecting contrasting features depends on the purpose of the enquiry, or the *Erkenntnisinteresse*. It therefore appears appropriate to discuss how such a balance might be achieved for the main purposes of comparative legal enquiries.

3. Purposes of Comparative Legal Enquiries

There can be as many purposes of comparative legal enquiries as there are comparative lawyers, or objects of enquiry. All the present chapter can do is to use a simple typology of purposes which provides basic models for when and where

---

[77] Ibid 163.

comparative lawyers tend to look for differences or similarities.[78] We will begin with applied comparative law, from the perspectives of those who shape legal rules, who apply them, and who are regulated by them. Then we will take a look at comparative legal studies which are directed more at understanding than at changing, applying, or using law.

(a) Unifying Law

As has been stated above, unification or at least harmonization of legal rules within various legal systems has been a major concern of comparative legal scholarship and has found expression, in particular, in the areas of the law of obligations, intellectual property law, and conflict of laws. We have also witnessed a substantial amount of uniform legislation being enacted. This has greatly influenced the way comparative law is seen in general, but also more particularly the views on whether and where comparative lawyers look for differences, and whether and where for similarities.

It should therefore not come as a surprise that the unification or harmonization of private law rules is the type of applied comparative scholarship where the traditional functionalist approach towards similarities and differences appears to work with the greatest ease. Unifying legal rules makes sense only if the problems experienced by the legal systems involved are at least roughly similar, and unification is more easily justified if the rules in the different systems involved produce identical or at least similar results. If results are similar, this helps when looking for a common denominator—perhaps in the form of unformulated policy—behind the way in which different rules are applied to produce those results. Similar results also make it easier to phrase a unified rule which accurately reflects the situation in the legal systems under consideration. Ideally, such a unified rule reflects this situation even more accurately than the slightly ill-fitting domestic rule which has been bent and pushed in order to produce the desired outcome. And if the comparative researcher or legislator can indeed formulate one rule which encapsulates those similar results, this will help to justify unification. In other words, comparative enquiries which aim at unification or harmonization have two distinct reasons to look for similarity of results: first because the search for similarity provides a heuristic principle, and second because similarity of results makes unification easier. The two should not be confused, because the second reason is more dangerous and more questionable from a methodological viewpoint than the first.

It would be wrong to think that comparative enquiries which aim at unification or harmonization cannot accept difference. It has been explained above why the functionalist approach recognizes and sometimes perhaps even exaggerates

[78] For example, the following typology does not include comparative enquiries in the context of codification of entire areas of law without unification.

differences when it comes to macrocomparative issues, and this also applies in the present context. Below we will see that there are several steps within unification enquiries where one will look primarily for difference. Problems may arise, though, when these differences are subsequently ignored for the purpose of the enquiry. It has been mentioned above that Kötz has warned that a 'black box' approach towards comparative law can cause damage to unification projects, because uniform law tends to show a greater need for general clauses than domestic laws. The application of such general clauses depends on factors such as 'styles, procedures, techniques, mentalities, and value judgments' which cannot be unified.[79] In other words: comparative enquiries aimed at unification must keep a watchful eye on those differences.

(b) Solving Particular Problems

Comparative legal enquiries are frequently made as part of an effort to improve a legal rule or institution which has been suspected or recognized as a source of problems. Thus, the legislature, or courts within their powers of shaping legal rules, or those who advise or seek to influence drafters or courts, will often take an interest in how other legal systems solve the same problem for which a solution is sought. We can use as an example the doctrine of privity of contract in English law. The Law Commission discussed the experience of countries which allow for contracts in favour of third parties, and so did the House of Lords in one related case.[80]

Similarity of problems is essential for such an enquiry when deciding which other legal systems should be chosen for a comparison. However, for many other aspects of the enquiry, the desire for reform (ie unhappiness with the existing situation) places a strong emphasis on difference. The enquiry seeks to establish whether different rules or institutions would reduce or eliminate the problem in question because of the different effects which these rules or institutions are likely to produce. In exceptional cases, the problem may not be the results but the unsatisfactory way in which they are reached; such an enquiry would look for similar rather than different results, but would still look for different rules. We can observe that only one of the two areas where the traditional functionalist approach expects or presumes similarity can be of assistance to this type of comparative enquiry, namely the expectation that legal systems throughout the world face similar problems. On the other hand, a presumption of similarity of results would normally be fatal to such an enquiry precisely because it usually aims at achieving a different result.

In spite of this tendency towards observing differences, it would be wrong to lose

---

[79] Kötz (n 54), 505; see above Section II.3.

[80] The Law Commission, *Privity of Contract: Contracts for the Benefit of Third Parties* (1996), Appendix B: Legislation from some Other Jurisdictions; *White v Jones* [1995] 2 AC 207 (HL). The doctrine of privity was largely abolished by the Contracts (Rights of Third Parties) Act 1999.

sight of similarities. Comparative enquiries aimed at solving existing problems will always take an interest in establishing causal links, so that what has been said above (Section III.1) of the need to discover similarity for this purpose needs to be taken into consideration.

(c) Applying Foreign Law

Comparative legal enquiries may become necessary when foreign law is applied by domestic courts or public authorities. This has been particularly discussed in the context of classification in private international law. For example, on marrying, a Muslim couple has agreed on a *mahr* (dower) to be paid to the bride under certain conditions.[81] The conflict rules of the forum say nothing about *mahr*. So which conflict rules should point to the applicable law—those on marriage, on matrimonial property, on maintenance, on divorce, or those of contract law? The same question can turn into an issue of substantive law once the first question has been resolved, and a substantive law has been invoked which does not provide for *mahr*. Should this agreement be fitted into the categories of a marriage contract, an agreement on matrimonial property, on pre- or post-divorce maintenance, or general contract law? Different formal requirements may apply, or the extent of the parties' freedom of contract may vary, depending on the category into which one chooses to slot a *mahr*. In this situation, the judge—perhaps assisted by an expert witness—must engage in a comparative legal enquiry. What is the function of *mahr* as agreed between the parties? Under the given circumstances, which institution of the forum or of the applicable law does it resemble most closely? Or does it have to be understood as an agreement *sui generis*? Judges and those who advise them will apply the same legal skills, and the same approach to similarity and difference, which they use in their daily work: finding similarity through comparison with other rules in order to establish common ground, leading to the application of a particular rule which is thus generalized or extended, or finding difference through comparison with other rules in order to establish distinction, leading to non-application of a particular rule which is thus isolated or restricted. This process of rule finding can function properly only if the judge is ready to look for both similarity and difference without giving priority to either. The same applies to academic enquiries which discuss on a more general level such problems of squeezing foreign law into ill-fitting categories provided by the *lex fori* or another applicable law.

(d) Facilitating Choice between Legal Systems

A different type of comparative enquiry aims to facilitate the choice between different legal systems from the perspective of those who are subjected to legal

---

[81] BGH 28.1.1987, [1988] *Praxis des Internationalen Privat- und Verfahrensrechts* 109.

rules. Perhaps the most obvious examples arise in the commercial context. Which corporate law, tax law, labour law, intellectual property law, etc. would best suit the interests of a particular business? In which country should a ship be registered? Which contract law regime provides the best solution for a particular contract, or best serves the particular interests of one party to the contract? If a dispute has arisen, which forum offers the most attractive combination of procedural and applicable substantive law for a particular party? This type of enquiry is not limited to commercial contexts but can arise wherever there is an element of choice between legal systems, regardless of whether this choice is facilitated by legal rules (eg choice of applicable contract law) or frowned upon, as in the case of a criminal who looks for the best country from which to operate an Internet fraud, or to resist an extradition request. With the possible exception of the last two examples, rich literature exists which compares particular features of different legal systems in order to facilitate this choice, and a substantial number of international practitioners make their living out of providing this sort of advice. Nevertheless, this area of applied comparative law has been somewhat neglected by the methodological discussion, perhaps because of its highly practical purpose.

This type of comparative enquiry has in common with the others the fact that it will look for a certain amount of similarity as far as the basis of comparison is concerned. In the case of the business which looks for the best legal system in which to operate, this means that the various corporate vehicles which are being compared should offer similar functionality. However, for almost all other aspects of this enquiry, the emphasis is on difference. The purpose is to establish which legal system is the most favourable for a particular purpose, so the choice will be made on the basis of these differences. Similarities are interesting only to the extent that they reduce the complexity of choice: if the tax laws of countries X and Y result in a similar overall tax burden, issues of, for example, corporate governance may be given more prominence when choosing the best legal system. A presumption of similarity of results would be almost fatal to this type of enquiry. Moreover, the niceties of macrocomparative issues—with the possible exception of anything which has a bearing on litigation likelihood and costs—are almost completely irrelevant. If there is any type of comparative legal enquiry for which a 'black box' approach is appropriate, it must be this one; at the same time, it is the type which shows the greatest interest in difference.

(e) Understanding Law

Lastly, we will take a look at comparative enquiries which do not or do not primarily aim at practical application but which chiefly serve to gain understanding and enhance knowledge. One could call these simply academic enquiries were it not for the fact that so many enquiries which are undertaken by academic comparative lawyers aim at practical application.

What Zweigert and Kötz have called macrocomparisons will generally fall into this category, but there are also comparative enquiries on particular issues which do not principally aim at any practical application of their results. Works on comparative legal history tend to fall into this category, regardless of whether they deal with rather general or more particular features of certain legal systems. It is those comparative legal studies which show the greatest similarities with studies in comparative (general) history, so that the methodological debate in comparative history which has been briefly outlined above (Section III.2) is particularly relevant to this type of enquiry.

Therefore, it is generally advisable for the researcher to look for both similarities and differences; the particular research interest will be decisive for the right balance and also for the places where one should look more for similarity or for difference. It appears to add spice and offer greater potential for understanding if one aspect of the enquiry concentrates more on similarity, and another on difference. Enquiries which establish similarities in development, arguments, structures, and, indeed, results in spite of substantial general differences between the systems under consideration have proven to be particularly attractive not just for comparative lawyers who follow the functional approach, but also for various historians.[82] Conversely, differences in development, arguments, structures or results in spite of substantial similarities between the systems under consideration are also intellectually attractive, because they also unearth what was hidden from view. Studies which see similarity everywhere can appear as pointless or boring as studies which only note differences. While this technique of contrasting similarities with differences produces more attractive results, the researcher would nevertheless be well advised to keep an eye open for differences in an area of perceived similarities, and for similarities in an area of perceived difference.

IV. Steps of Comparative Enquiries

We will now carry the issue of similarity or difference through the stages and steps which comparative enquiries will typically go through. There can obviously be no uniform structure which fits all types, but most comparative enquiries will involve three major stages: selection (of what will be compared), description (of the law and its context in the legal systems under consideration), and analysis. Further distinctions can be drawn within each of those stages, which will be called steps. Not all of those steps apply to each enquiry. It should be kept in mind that the

---

[82] See Osterhammel, [1996] *Geschichte und Gesellschaft* 143 ff, 159.

following should not serve as an outline for comparative enquiries, but rather as a structure for a discussion of where comparative lawyers look for similarities, where for differences, and where for a balance of both.

1. Selection

When comparative lawyers select what they want to compare, they choose their topic, define the basis of their comparison, and choose the legal systems which they want to include. The choice of topic is not particularly relevant for the present chapter beyond what has been stated above about purposes of comparative enquiries.

(a) Basis of Comparison

The basis of comparison is formed by the objects of research which, within the chosen topic, are selected for comparison, and also includes the sources which are consulted. The selection of the basis of comparison appears to be the only stage of the comparative enquiry for which there seems to be full agreement that we must strive for similarity.[83] As we have seen above (Section III.3), similarity of the basis of comparison is also essential for achieving each of the main aims of comparative enquiry. There is, however, disagreement on what should ideally be selected as the basis of comparison. This decision can have a bearing on which differences within the basis of comparison we are most likely to overlook.

In the functionalist approach, microcomparisons should proceed on the basis of case studies, that is, sets of factual situations which arise in connection with the topic under comparison. A traditional functionalist would therefore not just compare strict liability under §§ 7, 18 of the German Road Traffic Act with fault-based liability for road traffic accidents under the English law of negligence, but would look at the treatment of various cases of accidents for which the driver bears little or no subjective blame. He would not be impressed by the fact that one system is based on strict and the other on fault-based liability, because that difference does not affect the sets of facts. One could, of course, opt instead for a rule-oriented approach. For example, one could write about comparative strict liability in tort and omit English road traffic law on the ground that it is based on negligence.

The reader will notice that both approaches can miss out on something: the functionalist approach because the choice between strict and fault-based liability might yield significant information about the legal systems involved, and the

---

[83] See eg Zweigert and Kötz (n 5), 34–5. Even the most outspoken advocate of a priority for difference accepts that a minimum of similarity must be achieved for the basis of comparison: Legrand (n 26), 283.

rule-oriented approach because it is likely to end up comparing rules which relate to different sets of facts. So while both strive for similarity in the basis of the study, they could both end up overlooking pockets of difference. The more we approach macrocomparisons—involving entire legal systems, or even entire legal families or 'Legal Traditions of the World'[84]—the less significant the problem of the hidden pockets of differences in the basis of comparison becomes.

The basis of comparison also extends to sources: legislation, judgments, and other decisions as primary sources, academic legal writing as a secondary source, and additionally all other primary or secondary sources (including non-legal sources) which can throw light on the research question. The comparative researcher should also strive for similarity when selecting this part of the basis of comparison.

A typical beginner's mistake in Anglo-German comparisons is to compare a digest of English case law with a concoction of German legal doctrine on the chosen topic. But even experienced comparatists will sometimes find it difficult to adhere strictly to a common basis of comparison where the available sources for the systems under consideration show strong slants towards diverging bases. Not even a purely functional approach which uses sets of factual situations as a basis for comparison is immune to this problem. One possible way forward is to include those slants in the comparison—in our example by showing how different 'legal formants' interact, for example by evaluating the respective influences of academics on legal practice and the importance of case law for academic discussion.[85] More generally, where differences in the basis of comparison cannot be avoided, this should be addressed in the enquiry.

It is worth reflecting on the reasons why the basis of comparison should be similar. The commonplace assertion that one must not compare apples with pears is unhelpful,[86] not only because so many shoppers will do exactly that at the greengrocer's, but mainly because it offers no further explanation.

Why should we not compare rules as phrased in the original Napoleonic codes with twenty-first century English case law? It can be done. However, such a comparison would yield much lower potential for comparative analysis. The more common ground the researcher covers for the legal systems under consideration, the more numerous and richer will be the issues which lend themselves to a comparative analysis. Moreover, ensuring a common basis of comparison makes it less difficult to show possible links between rules and effects. No medical study would compare the occurrence of an illness amongst 18-year-old women from rural Iceland with its occurrence amongst 65-year-old male New Yorkers, because we would not know whether any differences were to be attributed to age, sex, climate, or the fact that one group lives in a city and the other in the country.

---

[84] Glenn (n 11); see Ch 12 of this book.   [85] See Sacco (n 33).
[86] See Haupt and Kocka (n 74), 24–5 for further explanation of why apples can indeed be compared with pears.

(b) Legal Systems

When choosing which legal systems are to be included in the comparison, the question of similarity or difference may often not be at the front of the researcher's mind. In the case of a single researcher, it is often simply his 'home law', and the law of another country which is linguistically accessible and with which the researcher may have some ties. Nevertheless, this choice is of central importance for our topic. On a very general level, if we choose similar systems, their descriptions will tend to be similar, and while it is easier to produce in the process of this description sufficient common ground for analysis, too much similarity will nevertheless mean that there is not that much to analyse. There must be a minimum of difference between the systems under consideration to make a comparative enquiry worthwhile. How much difference we need, and what type of difference, is closely linked to the purpose of the enquiry, and also to its methodological approach.

If unification or harmonization of rules is the main aim of the enquiry, it is important that the rules under consideration address similar or identical problems, so one would include only such countries where the same problems exist. To a certain degree, the exaggerated functionalist assumption that 'the legal problems of all countries are similar'[87] may have been nourished by the fact that most comparative legal enquiries which seek to unify or harmonize the laws of various jurisdictions have found similar problems in the countries they have examined because they have consciously or unconsciously chosen the topic and the systems under consideration to fit that bill. I suspect that there is little room in the chthonic legal tradition[88] for problems relating to intellectual property, in spite of the fact that we have witnessed major global unification in this area of law. And comparative studies on maritime law, where we have also seen unification efforts, will take little note of the law of land-locked states.

Unification will also be much easier if the economic, social, political, and cultural factors in which legal rules are embedded are fairly similar, so one would look for legal systems which are similar in these respects. Taken together with linguistic reasons and some other factors, this might help to explain why comparisons have been particularly popular between legal systems of modern industrialized nations with a population of predominantly European origin.

On the other hand, the legal rules under consideration must show some difference, at least in their black-letter form, in order for unification or harmonization to be an issue. Because unification is easier if the rules to be unified are relatively similar, one could be led to believe that comparative enquiries with a unification agenda would be well advised to stick to areas with limited differences between black-letter rules and legal institutions. Practice tells us otherwise. One might as

---

[87] Zweigert and Kötz (n 5), 46.   [88] Glenn (n 11), ch 3.

well tell a mountaineer to stick to hills. It has been noted above that difference is the spice of life also for those who follow the functional approach, and they like differences best if they can be observed between black-letter rules. This attractive combination of similarities in non-legal factors with substantial differences in legal norms and institutions is reflected in the rule of thumb proposed by Zweigert and Kötz, namely, that one should compare English (and United States), French (and Italian), and German (and Swiss) law.[89]

A different picture emerges for comparative enquiries which aim to resolve a particular problem by looking abroad for advice (see above Section III.3(b)). While for rules with low legal context (eg speed limits), difference or similarity between the legal systems observed is not a major factor, the resolution of problems with high context rules (eg the doctrine of privity in English contract law) would appear to require, primarily, the choice of legal systems which, although they have a different rule or at least a different application of the rule, are otherwise as similar as possible. The ultimate aim of such an enquiry is to borrow solutions from elsewhere, or to look for confirmation of intended solutions. Because such an enquiry is usually concerned with establishing causal links between rules and effects, any additional factor which might interfere with that link is a nuisance. This may explain in part why English courts have for long given preference to other common law systems when looking abroad for persuasive authority. The disadvantage of that approach is that it may be unduly restrictive for the purpose of finding new solutions, as in the case of the common law doctrine of privity of contract.[90]

Comparative enquiries in the context of applying foreign law in a given case (see above Section III.3(c)) have no choice: they have to compare the *lex fori* with the applicable foreign law, or a foreign law which has in other ways influenced the case. Additionally, there has to be substantial difference between those legal systems for the problem to arise in the first place. The latter also applies to academic enquiries which discuss on a more general level such problems of squeezing foreign law into domestic categories.

We will now turn to comparative enquiries which aim to facilitate the choice which a person or party may exercise between legal systems (see above Section III.3(d)). It was noted above that the emphasis of such an enquiry is on difference, in particular as far as results are concerned, because different results increase choice. This aim would call for a large and diverse array of legal systems to be included, with limitations being imposed for (often non-legal) reasons of practicality which are linked to the purpose of the particular enquiry. Practical commercial reasons may thus dictate that such an enquiry be limited to, for example, EU member states because of its internal market, or to countries with a major stock exchange.

---

[89] Zweigert and Kötz (n 5), 41. Countries in brackets are to be included for research into particular institutions or questions, whereas the other three suffice for research into more general questions.
[90] See above Section III.3.(b).

Comparative enquiries which are not primarily interested in direct application but which mainly aim at better understanding (see above Section III.3.(d)) have the greatest choice as to whether to look for similar or for different law and context when choosing the legal systems to be included in such enquiries. In application of what has been said above (Section III.2.), enquiries looking for common features should tend to choose similar systems, and enquiries aiming to gain a sharper image of individual systems and their paths of development should choose different systems.

One should therefore expect very different patterns of choice between those who advocate a search for similarity, and those who advocate a search for difference. This is, however, not the case.[91] Followers of both approaches show a strong tendency towards comparing one or more common law system(s) with one or more civil law system(s), and it is only recently that the call to look beyond Europe and America has been heeded by a growing number of researchers who have considerably enriched comparative scholarship by venturing into, for example, Islamic, Chinese, and Japanese law. It is not solely Eurocentric views which are to blame for this pattern. It may simply be an attractive combination of 'controlled difference' which allows some researchers to find similarity amongst differences, and others differences amongst similarity, in a fairly comfortable setting of widely accessible resources in widely accessible languages.

Comparative scholarship might profit from an approach which ventures beyond different legal systems with a similar context by adding at least one legal system with a different context. Such a triangular comparison would combine, for example, German, English, and Indian law for a civil law enquiry. This would allow the comparative researcher to test which similarities in the practical application are due to similar legal institutions (on a first axis formed by England and India), and which are due to similarities in non-legal context (on a second axis formed by Germany and England). Using the same matrix, one could extend this comparison to a square formed, for example, by Dutch and Indonesian, and English and Singapore law. Or one could add a fresh perspective to a popular choice by comparing, for example, French, English, and Chinese law. The additional contrast which such a combination of similarity and difference offers could well serve to show difference to those who tend to see global similarity, and to show, for instance, Anglo-French similarity to those who tend to see irreconcilable difference.

---

[91] On the contrary, two distinguished proponents of a difference-based view disagree on this issue. Gutteridge (n 19), 73 warns that a comparison of legal systems which do not share the same stage of legal, political, and economic development leads to illusory comparison, whereas Ancel (n 21), 75 suggests that comparing radically different legal systems would yield more results than comparing similar legal systems.

2. Description

(a) Legal Institutions and Rules

Any comparative enquiry will have to describe those rules, legal institutions, theories, or even entire legal systems which are the object of the enquiry. Should one look for similarity or for difference during this step, or for both?

It may well be that this is where Ancel's observation rings particularly true, namely, that difference will be the first thing which a comparative lawyer, trained in one system, will notice when encountering another.[92] On the other hand, the same comparative lawyer can fall for apparent similarities by slotting foreign law into home categories.[93]

Difference may, however, gain more emphasis during the process of description because a focus on describing similar features is likely to lead to repetition, whereas a focus on different features will not. Additionally, while those who generally look more for difference will have every reason to do so here, those who advocate similarity of problems and results will have no qualms if difference can be shown at the level of institutions and rules. The way in which, for example, Zweigert and Kötz or von Bar describe various domestic tort law rules[94] shows no less contrast than similarity, because the latter is only expected and found for problems and their solutions. Schlesinger, who was instrumental in the development of the functionalist approach, has expressed this as follows: 'It is a well known truism in comparative law that different legal systems, even in the countless instances in which they arrive at identical results, usually proceed along divergent conceptual routes'.[95]

As for the different types of comparative enquiries, none will push towards observing similarity at this stage, whereas at least one (solving a particular problem, Section III.3.(b)) will look for difference. All this will frequently add up to a slant in favour of observing differences in the description of legal institutions and rules. As not all of the factors mentioned above are based on conscious choice, less experienced researchers should perhaps be warned that they must also keep an eye open for similarities where they first see differences, and for differences where they first see similarity.

There has been some controversy as to whether each legal system should be described by a comparative lawyer as this system views itself,[96] or whether an effort

---

[92] Ancel (n 21), 67.   [93] Similarly Großfeld (n 38), 108–9.

[94] Zweigert and Kötz (n 5), ch VIII. E.; Christian von Bar, *The Common European Law of Torts* (vol I, 1998; vol II, 2000).

[95] Rudolf B. Schlesinger, 'The Common Core of Legal Systems: An Emerging Subject of Comparative Study', in *Twentieth-Century Comparative and Conflicts Law: Legal Essays in Honor of Hessel E Yntema* (1961), 65 ff, 73.

[96] Legrand (n 26), 289 ff.

should be made to present one legal system from the other's perspective,[97] or to present all systems from a 'neutral perspective' derived from a functional comparison.[98] The first can be seen as emphasizing difference, the second and third as emphasizing similarity. But that need not be true. There is not one right approach, and much will depend on the purpose of the enquiry.

The first approach may be more suitable for macrocomparisons, the second for making a foreign law accessible to less experienced readers, the third for enquiries aiming at harmonization. If the first approach is used for the second or third purpose, it will frequently fail to bring out differences. Instead, it will just make it more difficult for the reader to pick up on either differences or similarities because such a description is likely to make insufficient efforts to relate the different laws to each other. Little would be gained from a comparison which presents an excerpt from a leading textbook from country X next to an excerpt from a leading textbook from country Y—although this would do full justice to the demand that legal systems should be described as they view themselves. Such an approach would also be particularly prone to overlooking unwanted differences in the basis of comparison.

Conversely, the second and third approaches are less suitable for macrocomparisons, because they are prone to missing out on particular features which are not capable of being generalized or translated. For example, such a typical feature of the common law as the use of legal fictions[99] will go by unnoticed if those fictions are, in the process of 'translation' or generalization, converted into substantive rules.

(b) Legal Context

There is broad agreement that legal context is relevant for the proper understanding of particular rules. If we use again the example of the doctrine of privity in English contract law, it is difficult to understand how English law has for so long been able to cope with it, and why Continental legal systems have not been able to do so, without looking at the laws of agency, torts, and trusts.[100] Most legal rules and institutions operate in a context made up of other rules, institutions, and areas

---

[97] Basil S. Markesinis, Werner Lorenz, and Gerhard Dannemann, *The German Law of Obligations* vol I: *The Law of Contracts and Restitution* (1997), preface.

[98] Zweigert and Kötz (n 5), 44–5.

[99] 'Juries were first told that from user, during living memory, or even during 20 years, they might presume a lost grant or deed; next they were recommended to make such presumption; and lastly, as the final consummation of judicial legislation, it was held that a jury should be told, not only that they might, but also that they were bound to presume the existence of such a lost grant, although neither judge nor jury, nor any one else, had the shadow of a belief that any such instrument had ever really existed': Cockburn CJ in *Bryant v Foot* (1867) LR 2 QB 161, 181.

[100] Third parties who can claim in contract in a civil law system might in English law be able to claim as beneficiaries in trust, as undisclosed principals in agency, or as victims of a breach of duty in tort.

of law; substantive rules interact with rules of procedure, etc. Therefore, areas of law which initially fall outside the scope of a particular enquiry become relevant for the understanding of those rules which are within the scope.

This indicates that we are generally more interested in differences of legal context. If it is similar, it is less likely to impact on our main topic, and we can therefore keep discussion of context short. If we note differences, we will have to examine its impact on our main topic, and treat context in more detail. This built-in preference for difference in legal context cuts across all methodological approaches, and all types of comparative enquiries.

(c) Non-legal Context

There appears to be broad consensus within the modern debate that it is important to look beyond law for the context in which a rule, institution, or entire legal system operates, which may include economic, social, cultural, political, but also religious or geographical issues.[101] Should we look primarily for similarity, difference, or a balance of both?

To a certain degree, what has just been said about legal context applies also to non-legal context. We look at context in order to understand how this interacts with our main legal issues, so that context becomes particularly important if it differs, and does not require to be covered in detail if it is very similar.

There is, however, one particular aspect in which similarities in non-legal context are sought, and that is to explain similarities of problems and of solutions, the two areas in which the functionalist approach mainly sees or presumes similarity. For example, Christian von Bar has observed that the birth of the English tort of negligence occurred at the same time as French law was developing its *gardien* liability and German law its general duty of care in tort. He attributes these three major shifts to common developments in society, economy, and technology.[102] Similarity in context is thus used to explain both similarity of problems (more and new forms of accidents), and similarity of results (increased liability). Difference in non-legal context can be used for the corresponding purpose of explaining differences in problems or results. On an overall view, though, comparative enquiries are more concerned with difference than with similarity of non-legal context.

(d) Results

It is obvious that the results which different legal systems produce for similar or identical cases will sometimes be similar and sometimes be different. There can be

---

[101] But see Watson's (n 47) demonstration of how easily legal concepts have wandered between systems, leaving William Ewald, 'Legal History and Comparative Law', (1999) 7 *Zeitschrift für Europäisches Privatrecht* 553 ff, to reject both the contextual and what he calls Watson's textual approach in order to see non-legal context 'mediated through the realm of jurisprudential thought' (558).

[102] von Bar (n 94, vol I), 300.

no general answer to the question whether we are primarily interested in similarity, or in difference. This depends largely on the purpose of each comparative enquiry.

Enquiries aiming at unification or harmonization show a strong tendency towards looking for similarity—but should nevertheless be interested in difference, and not only as a matter of proper stock-taking: it is both difficult and unwise to unify or harmonize without being aware of the change which this would bring about (see above, Section III.3.(a)).

Enquiries aimed at solving particular problems are interested in different results. In exceptional cases, the problem may not be the results but the unsatisfactory way in which they are reached; such an enquiry would look for similar rather than different results (see above, Section III.3.(b)).

Enquiries made in order to apply foreign law properly will have to look equally for similarity and difference (see above, Section III.3.(c)).

Enquiries which aim to facilitate the choice between legal systems will primarily look for differences in results (see above, Section III.3.(d)).

The greatest diversity is shown, once again, with regard to enquiries which are not primarily interested in the practical application of these findings (see above, Section III.3.(e)). What has been said above (Section IV.1.(b)) about looking for difference or similarity when choosing the legal systems under consideration applies *mutatis mutandis*. In particular, it appears that similar results are most interesting if produced by legal rules, institutions, or systems which show considerable difference, and that different results are most interesting if produced by similar rules, institutions, or systems.

The above shows that, even within its limited sphere of application, the presumption of similarity of results cannot be maintained as a rule for comparative legal enquiries. This would entail that two of the types of comparative enquiries mentioned above are essentially a waste of time, because they are unlikely to unearth the differences we are looking for. Experience tells us otherwise. A dangerous and unintended side-effect of this presumption is that it would teach us legal fatalism, that it does not matter how we shape our rules and institutions, because the most appropriate results will find their way through those rules and institutions regardless of what they state or what they look like. I know from my teaching experience that the presumption can misguide students and lead them to believe in earnest that a German judge will do the same with the principle of good faith in § 242 BGB as an English judge will do with the principle that 'equity shall suffer no wrong without a remedy'.

So even within its limited sphere of application, the presumption of similarity must be downgraded to the observation that, given the considerable differences between some legal systems, it is noteworthy how often they nevertheless produce the same results in certain areas of law, in particular if the non-legal context is similar. Francis Reynolds, who is rather critical of those who predominantly see similarity, has used the following metaphor for this observation: '. . . legal systems come on to the stage from opposite doors, but then proceed to meet somewhere in the middle, with comparatively slight variations in marginal cases, resulting from the different starting points'.[103]

3. Analysis

Whereas differences and similarities are noted during the descriptive stage, it is within the analytical stage that one will seek to find explanations for those differences and similarities. In addition, comparative legal enquiries may investigate what (if anything) the legal systems could learn from each other.

(a) Explaining Differences and Similarities

Generally speaking, the analysis should seek to explain differences and similarities as they arise from the description of the legal systems under consideration, so that whoever has predominantly found similarity, will predominantly have to explain similarity, whereas those who have predominantly found difference, will predominantly have to explain difference. Nevertheless, some additional issues can surface in this context.

The issue of gaps is situated at the analytical end of the borderline between description and analysis. Comparative law is particularly useful for observing gaps in the law of one country which—almost like the blind spot in our eyes—can be difficult to detect from within. We will use the contractual capacity of minors to provide two examples. When struggling to balance the protection of minors with the need for minors to enter into contracts, the common law simply seems to have forgotten those whose main task it is to protect and advance children, that is, the parents, who are generally at least as good as judges, and certainly faster and less expensive, in finding out which contract is necessary for a child and which one is not. On the other hand, I am not aware of any German textbook which would have noticed that it is rather difficult for minors to give birthday presents to their parents, and that in principle they could vindicate those presents as their property at any time until their forty-eighth birthday.[104] Such blind spots can be revealed by

---

[103] Francis Reynolds, *The Diversity of the Common Law: A Warning for Unification Projects* (2000), 24.

[104] Minors cannot make gifts, or transfer property, without consent of their parents as statutory agents, § 107 BGB. § 181 BGB makes it impossible for an agent (including statutory agents) to enter into a legal transaction with himself on behalf of his principal (ie the child); parents can thus not give consent to a gift and transfer of property to themselves. As title does not pass, children can vindicate their presents, § 985 BGB. Limitation of children's claims against their parents runs from their eighteenth birthday (§ 207 I BGB), with thirty years as prescription period (§ 197 I no. 1). *Bona fide* acquisition by the parent might arguably be possible on the child's twenty-eighth birthday, §§ 937, 939, 206 BGB. Paucity in case law may simply signal that the result is so absurd that it has hardly ever crossed anyone's mind to make such a claim.

a comparison with another system which, due to its different rules, institutions, or legal thinking, has something for which there is no equivalent in the other legal system (in our examples, the Continental notion of parents as statutory agents, or the English notion of necessaries, which may include gifts made by a minor). In order to discover gaps, one needs to find a difference in the scope of particular rules, so this is an area in which we mainly look for difference.

Another situation where a comparative analysis can look for similarities or differences is the search for unformulated policies (or Sacco's 'cryptoformants'). As discussed above, similar results in spite of different rules indicate the presence of such unformulated policies. Conversely, where similar or identical rules produce different results, this also indicates the presence of unformulated policies. Thus, the search for unformulated policies will look for a combination of similarity and difference between rules and results: similar rules and different results, or different rules and similar results.

Such an enquiry may also take a comparison to a higher level of abstraction. For example, if English law pushes liability for pure economic loss into tort law, and German law into contract law, we can note as a similarity that they both push a difficult borderline area of law down the path which offers the least resistance, so that in both legal systems certain deficiencies in one area can and will be compensated by another—at a certain cost in terms of consistency and predictability for the recipient area of law.

(b) Learning between Legal Systems

Some comparative enquiries are simply not interested in legal systems learning from each other. Such learning is outside the scope of an enquiry which aims to facilitate choice, and the same can usually be said for enquiries made for the purpose of applying foreign law. On the other hand, learning between legal systems is the principal aim of comparative enquiries which look abroad in order to solve a problem at home. Many academic enquiries, although primarily aimed at better understanding, find it appropriate to use this understanding for the purpose of improving the law, and will formulate suggestions as to what the legal systems under consideration could learn from each other. Unification enquiries will also have to assess the potential for such learning. If they find different results, they must decide which result should be preferred. And if the results are similar, they will nevertheless have to assess which of those different rules that produce the similar result is best suited as a unified rule in terms of consistency or clarity. If rules and results are the same, there is not much left to unify.

Learning requires a legal system to take something on board which it does not have, but which another system has. Thus, those interested in legal systems learning from each other will primarily look for difference, and evaluate this difference by forming an opinion as to which rule, institution, theory, or result is to be preferred.

If and once this is clear, a comparative enquiry should examine whether the preferred rule, institution, theory, or result would work equally well in the different environment provided by the receiving legal system.[105] In this context, whereas similarity is important during the process of selection (providing an incentive to select legal systems which are generally similar), it is difference that is most important in this analytical part of the enquiry. In order to evaluate the likely consequences of such a transfer, a critical account must be made of the differences, and an assessment provided of how these differences are likely to impact on the rule, institution, theory, or result which is to be transplanted.[106] This involves enquiries into causal links, so what has been said above (Section III.1) applies *mutatis mutandis*.

4. Summary

Those engaged in comparative enquiries are generally well advised to look for both difference and similarity. The purpose of the enquiry will be the most important factor in determining where one should primarily look for difference, where for similarity, and where for both in equal measure. The second most important factor is the choice of the legal systems which are to be compared. The current debate between those who advocate a presumption of similarity, those who advocate a priority of difference, and the increasing number of those who occupy the middle ground, appears to have had no noticeable impact on the second factor, and a limited impact on the first. It is true that those who advocate a presumption of similarity are much more likely to engage in unification enquiries than those who advocate a priority for difference and who may quite generally be less interested in applied comparative law, or at least in those forms of it which aim to show how legal systems can learn from each other.[107] It is difficult to tell, though, whether the methodological standpoint is the cause, and an interest in certain types of comparative enquiries the effect, or whether it is rather the other way around. Those who want to unify might be naturally drawn towards searching for similarity, and those who want to limit influences between legal systems might be naturally drawn towards searching for difference.

If the last explanation is correct, the results of the step by step analysis (Section IV) might come as a surprise. While a clear priority for similarity exists across the board only for defining the basis of comparison, there are several steps

---

[105] See Ch 13 of this book.

[106] For an interesting account of an unsuccessful transplant of a legal theory, see David Ibbetson, *A Historical Introduction to the Law of Obligations* (1999), 220 ff: the English reception of the will theory in contract law overlooked that it was exceedingly difficult to reconcile with some particular features of English contract law.

[107] See eg Legrand (n 26), 295–6.

where there is a clear priority for difference, in particular during the description and analysis of legal as well as non-legal context. One also needs to search for differences, not similarities, in order to find gaps within legal systems.

We have noticed on several occasions (Sections II.4, III.3(e), IV.1(b), and IV.2(d)) that it is often the right mixture of difference and similarity which makes comparative enquiries particularly attractive, regardless of the methodological approach pursued. Finding difference in similarity can be as fascinating as finding similarity in difference. If any general advice is to be offered, it is to keep an eye open for both similarity and difference, be it to trace those hidden pockets of difference in the basis of comparison, or to make the search for causal links a little less difficult, or to increase the chance of successful learning between legal systems.

BIBLIOGRAPHY

Harold C. Gutteridge, *Comparative Law* (1946)

Marc Ancel, *Utilité et méthodes du droit comparé: Eléments d'introduction générale à l'étude comparative des droits* (1971)

Günter Frankenberg, 'Critical Comparisons: Re-thinking Comparative Law', (1985) 26 *Harvard International LJ* 411 ff

Rodolfo Sacco, 'Legal Formants: A Dynamic Approach to Comparative Law', (1991) 39 *AJCL* 1 ff and 343 ff

Bernhard Großfeld, *Kernfragen der Rechtsvergleichung* (1996)

Richard Hyland, 'Comparative Law', in Dennis Patterson (ed), *A Companion to Philosophy of Law and Legal Theory* (1996), 184 ff

Jürgen Osterhammel, 'Sozialgeschichte im Zivilisationsvergleich', (1996) *Geschichte und Gesellschaft* 143 ff

Vivian G. Curran, 'Cultural Immersion, Difference and Categories in U.S. Comparative Law', (1998) 46 *AJCL* 43 ff

Konrad Zweigert and Hein Kötz, *An Introduction to Comparative Law* (trans Tony Weir, 3rd edn, 1998)

Jaakko Husa, 'Farewell to Functionalism or Methodological Tolerance?', (2003) 67 *RabelsZ* 417 ff

Pierre Legrand, 'The Same and the Different', in Pierre Legrand and Roderick Munday (eds), *Comparative Legal Studies: Traditions and Transitions* (2003), 240 ff

James Q. Whitman, 'The Neo-Romantic turn', in Pierre Legrand and Roderick Munday (eds), *Comparative Legal Studies: Traditions and Transitions* (2003), 100 ff

CHAPTER 12

COMPARATIVE LEGAL FAMILIES AND COMPARATIVE LEGAL TRADITIONS

H. PATRICK GLENN

Montreal

I. INTRODUCTION

How should one think about the laws of the world? The simplest response would be to think about them as the laws of the world, with no further qualifications or categorizations. This option is sometimes used, but the number and diversity of our laws has led to an apparently irresistible process of aggregation or categorization. Amongst comparative lawyers over the last century the categorizing notion most frequently encountered has been that of 'families' of laws, and all of the laws of the world could thus be divided and understood as members of this (relatively limited) number of legal families. The law of France would belong to the civil law family, the law of England to the common law family, the law of Saudi Arabia to the Islamic law family, and so on. Some countries might fall within a socialist legal family, though today both the family and its members are questioned. René David's treatise was entitled *Les grands systèmes de droit contemporain* but in spite of its title the notion of legal systems was largely abandoned in favour of 'The Idea of a Family of Laws' and an ensuing discussion of 'Legal Families in the World Today.'[1] The notion of an existing family (as opposed to a dysfunctional or divided one) is a positive and constructive metaphor and unquestionably served a useful purpose in a time of radical legal nationalism. It reminded lawyers, and others, of forms of belonging which the state could not encompass, or avoid. At the same time, however, it was a product of its times and appeared to accept and even reinforce the idea of autonomous national legal systems, the relations of which could only be described in terms of international law or in terms of membership in larger, though non-normative, legal families.

The developments of the last few decades, however, have challenged the idea of autonomous national legal systems and their grouping into legal families. The state is said to be in decline, even to have failed entirely in some parts of the world, and both new and ancient forms of law are increasing in influence.[2] The conclusion has thus recently been drawn that '[t]he taxonomic orientation . . . largely spent itself' with the treatise of David and that of Zweigert and Kötz,[3] though it is said that the 'discourse of legal families still partly dominates the imagination of comparative legal studies today'.[4] So the notion of legal families would represent an ongoing important idea, though of declining influence. That of legal tradition would have

---

[1] René David and John E. C. Brierley, *Major Legal Systems in the World Today* (3rd edn, 1985), vii.

[2] See eg, H. Patrick Glenn, 'A Transnational Concept of Law', in Peter Cane and Mark Tushnet (eds), *The Oxford Handbook of Legal Studies* (2003), 839; H. Patrick Glenn *On Common Laws* (2005).

[3] John Langbein, 'The Influence of Comparative Procedure in the United States', (1995) 43 *AJCL* 545, 547, cited in Ugo Mattei, 'Three Patterns of Law: Taxonomy and Change in the World's Legal Systems', (1997) 45 *AJCL* 5, 10.

[4] Jaakko Husa, 'Classification of Legal Families Today: Is it Time for a Memorial Hymn?', (2004) 56 *Revue internationale de droit comparé* 11, 13.

become, however, in the last quarter century, the 'dominant paradigm' in understanding the world's laws and would look 'beyond . . . legal systems and families as static and isolated entities'.[5] It is therefore appropriate to attempt an assessment of these two large and apparently imprecise ideas. What can be said in favour of each of them? What difference will the use of one or the other make to the relations amongst the laws of the world?

II. THE TAXONOMIC PROJECT

The contemporary academic discipline of comparative law arose as a reaction to the decline of over-arching concepts of law in Europe in the nineteenth century. It was in some measure an antidote to the various forms of nationalization of law which were then taking place, largely through codification and the development of a national concept of *stare decisis*. Chairs and societies of comparative law were created throughout the nineteenth century and in 1900 a first International Congress of Comparative Law was held in Paris. It is important to situate the new discipline within larger intellectual and political movements which were then current.

The legal unification of the nation-states of Europe created new law and new legal institutions which were designed to overcome much of the corruption, imperialism, and imprecision of the earlier times. The new institutions and laws had widespread popular support, were meant to last, and were the result of some of the very best legal thinking of all time. They were, in short, irresistible, and notably irresistible through invocation of older ideas of Christian unity or universal natural law. If bridges were to be rebuilt, it could not be with the old stones, but with the techniques of modern law and modern science. So the new states had to be taken as cornerstones of the new science of comparative law and they had to be situated within a new, scientific cadre which would *describe* what was actually going on, in terms of the new, positive institutions, but which would also *surpass* them in indicating their relative characteristics. This scientific dimension of the new comparative law drew heavily from two related intellectual movements.

The first was that of comparison in the physical and notably biological sciences, a process begun by the taxonomy of Linnaeus in the mid-eighteenth century and

---

[5] Mathias Reimann, 'The Progress and Failure of Comparative Law in the Second Half of the 20th Century', (2002) 50 *AJCL* 671, 677; and see John H. Merryman, *The Civil Law Tradition*, (2nd edn, 1985); Mary Ann Glendon, Michael Gordon, and Christopher Osakwe, *Comparative Legal Traditions* (1994); Reinhard Zimmermann, *The Law of Obligations: Roman Foundations of the Civilian Tradition* (1996); H. Patrick Glenn, *Legal Traditions of the World* (2nd edn, 2004).

continuing in the nineteenth with the development of comparative anatomy (Cuvier), comparative biology, and comparative linguistics. Scientific progress here resulted from classification and systematization of entire fields of human knowledge, and the notion of families in science thus extended well beyond those of human beings. The process of classification initially requires the fixing of boundaries of various classes. There is then assignment or allocation of objects to the appropriate larger classes based on their patterns of observable characteristics. The emphasis is on the process itself and it is a given that there are objects of classification, objects found in the real world for the physical sciences and in the existence of particular laws for the new science of comparative law. The objects of classification find their true, and distinct, identity through their assignment to a particular class. A national legal system could thus be better understood, and its existence affirmed, through its classification as a common law system or a civil law system.

The second intellectual movement which influenced the new science of comparative law was that of social Darwinism. This idea has today been discredited in considerable measure but in the nineteenth century the progression of peoples through distinct, evolutionary stages of social organization was taken as a serious scientific hypothesis. The end point of the evolution coincided remarkably with the then present state of European society, such that other peoples were thought to be appropriately described as 'primitive' in some measure and there was a deep, underlying justification for the process of colonization, which could accelerate the process of evolution. The end of colonization brought about the end of the underlying theory, but it contributed greatly to the emergence of comparative law as a distinct academic discipline founded on scientific classifications.[6] Today the notion of progression through evolutionary stages of society has become very faint, but the underlying notion of taxonomy and classification is seen as separable and had vigorous defenders in the late twentieth century.[7]

The taxonomic project in comparative law was thus strongly influenced by developments in the physical sciences, as was law in general in the nineteenth century. In the physical sciences great efforts were made to extend classifications to the immense range of living and other objects. In contrast, and this is of interest for the entire taxonomic project, very little effort has been expended on the classification of national legal systems. It is generally recognized that it is national legal systems which are the appropriate objects of classification,[8] and it would be an

---

[6] David and Brierley (n 1), 4–5.

[7] Léontin-Jean Constantinesco, *Traité de droit comparé*, vol III: *La science des droits comparés* (1983), 55 ff.

[8] David and Brierley (n 1), 23; Husa, (2004) 56 *Revue internationale de droit comparé* 13; Esin Örücü, 'Family Trees for Legal Systems: Towards a Contemporary Approach', in Mark Van Hoecke (ed), *Epistemology and Methodology of Comparative Law* (2004), 359; Jacques Vanderlinden, *Comparer les droits* (1995), 309.

immense and difficult task, given the diversity of sources of national law in the world, to assign all national laws to particular legal families. Yet efforts of classification have been directed almost exclusively to definition of the legal families which should control the classification process and there has been very little agreement on the appropriate definitions. This problem will be returned to (see Section VI, below) but for present purposes it will suffice to observe that the taxonomic project in law, unlike that in science, never progressed much beyond debate as to the criteria for classification.

In contrast to the taxonomic objective underlying the concept of legal families, that of legal traditions has no explicit taxonomic purpose. Indeed, it may well be impossible to categorize national legal systems according to legal traditions, since the concept of tradition is simply that of normative information[9] and national systems may repose on different and varying amounts of (traditional) normative information. The concept of legal tradition thus suggests that one look for the *degrees* to which different traditions have been influential in the make-up of different national laws, and would be antithetical to exclusivist categorizations according to a limited range of criteria. Legal traditions would thus underlie and infiltrate national legal systems, which could no longer be taken as simple objects of classification and taxonomy.

It is true that one can still debate the manner of identification of legal traditions, and there could be perhaps as much disagreement on this question as there is on the definition of legal families. Moreover, many legal families (though not all, see Section V, below) reappear as legal traditions, such as those of the civil and common law. As normative information, however, legal traditions are largely self-identifying and need not answer to taxonomic requirements of providing the best means of understanding and structuring legal systems. The information of a legal tradition tells you that it is a common law tradition, or a romano-germanic tradition, or an Islamic tradition, and people and lawyers adhere to each tradition because of its content and identification. The boundaries of a legal tradition, moreover, are fuzzy. Since information is largely uncontrollable, the information at the core of every legal tradition will be complemented, in some measure and to some degree, by information drawn from other legal traditions. So legal traditions themselves are not exclusivist in character and debate as to their content and identity is essential and internal to them, not to be avoided through imposition of scientifically defined criteria. Debate is the normal state of things, and not an obstacle to scientific precision. If taxonomy and classification are effected through fixing the scientifically chosen boundaries of various classes, the nature and working of tradition is thus opposed to the fixing of boundaries and criteria for their fixation. Taxonomy and legal families have the task or objective of separation and distinguishing, whereas legal traditions have the task only of supporting their own

---

[9] Glenn (n 5), ch 1.

forms of normativity. This usually involves more art than science, more attempting to do justice than attempting to build and classify systems.

Of course, legal traditions antedate the nineteenth century and legal scientism, while legal scientism grew up within the Western legal traditions and even became a sub-tradition within them. So there is no fundamental antagonism between the idea of legal families and legal tradition. It is a question of age and generality rather than opposition. The idea of legal families would represent a particular legal tradition the influence of which is now in decline, leaving the older and more general idea of legal traditions to play a more obvious role. This appears to be recognized by those who have been most influential in developing taxonomic ideas and the concept of the legal family. René David thus concluded that legal families did not correspond to 'biological reality' and were no more than 'didactic devices' or means of understanding,[10] while the greater part of his treatise was given over to the explanation of what may be considered to be the major legal traditions of the world.

While the concept of legal families may thus be seen as a particular variant of legal tradition, there remain major differences in the methods and objectives of the two concepts. Families are distinct biological entities, inviting taxonomic determination of their members. A tradition is ongoing normative information, inviting compliance and not classification (least of all of itself). These underlying differences may be of consequence for the relations of the laws of the world, and our understanding of them.

III. Taxonomy and Stasis

In a world seen as fast moving, it is a major criticism to refer to a concept or idea as 'static'.[11] The criticism does not simply reflect a fascination with novelty, however, but is rather directed to the manner of understanding the world which the idea of legal families would represent. It would notably impede, or even prevent, any appreciation of change or variation in the course of human and legal life and would therefore constitute a major obstacle to human understanding. This point should perhaps be emphasized. It is often said that the taxonomic project is not driven by instrumental or other objectives but is simply a means of understanding law and therefore justifiable as such. To this is often added a defence of the

---

[10] David and Brierley (n 1), 21; cited approvingly in Hein Kötz, 'Abschied von der Rechtskreislehre?', (1998) 6 *Zeitschrift für Europäisches Privatrecht* 493, 494.

[11] Reimann (n 5), 677.

academic function as opposed to that of the legislator, judge, or legal professional. The criticism of stasis, however, is to the effect that the means of understanding which the concept of legal families provides is one which distorts or impoverishes our understanding of the legal world. Being free of instrumental objectives is not in itself a justification. Understanding of the legal world is not enhanced if major dimensions of it are excluded by the concepts employed. Legal families would thus conceal more than they reveal and are not justifiable as a means of understanding.

How exactly is the concept of legal families a static one? Like all means of classification it is inherently static by fixing, at least temporarily, the objects of classification for purposes of their classification. Where the objects of classification are not physical objects, but large amounts of legal information, the classification attempts to freeze the contemporary flow of information in the world, for purposes of the present classification. The process parallels the contemporary concept of the national legal system, which would exist not in enduring form but rather as a succession of 'momentary' legal systems, each one of which would represent the law in force at a given moment.[12] Each of these 'momentary' systems would be classified during the brief moment of its existence. Once the law is no longer in force by virtue of the present system, however, it is dead law, of no interest for purposes of the present system. More precisely, it becomes legal history, which thereby becomes the study of law which is no longer in force. So the process is inherently static because it has no means of assessing or appreciating what is often referred to as the 'development' of law or its variation over time. It is an entirely synchronic process, by itself. It tells us to understand law as though we were required to watch a film through looking first at one frame, then at another, with no necessary recollection of the previous frame.

The taxonomic endeavour in the physical sciences rested in large measure on the physical stability of the objects of classification. There is, however, no such stability of legal systems, which exist not as 'solid and sensible entities' but rather as 'thought-objects, products of particular discourses rather than presuppositions of them'.[13] If we fix them at particular times, we lose the flow of the discourse, the variation of the system over time and any sense of direction this may provide. We are unable to assess the extent of change or the extent of resistance to change. There is an inevitable loss of normativity, and it is an inherent element of the teaching of positivist legal systems that they are unable to create an obligation to obey the law.[14] They simply exist, at a given moment. The concept of legal families

[12] Joseph Raz, *The Concept of a Legal System* (1970), 34; Joseph Raz, *The Authority of Law: Essays on Law and Morality* (1979), 81.

[13] Neil MacCormick, *Questioning Sovereignty: Law, State and Nation in the European Commonwealth* (1999), 113.

[14] Raz, *Authority* (n 12), 242–5; M. B. E. Smith, 'Is There a Prima Facie Obligation to Obey the Law?', (1973) 82 *Yale LJ* 950 ff.

adds no normativity to this way of thinking, but would rather simply confirm the existence of these systems within the broader cadre of (descriptive) legal families.

In contrast to the inherently static character of legal systems and legal families, legal traditions exist as ongoing, normative information, and their normative force is drawn in large measure from their duration over time. This is not an obstacle to change, however, and resort to tradition is the primary justification for the most radical of changes,[15] as when those responsible for the 'revolutions' of the eighteenth century 're-volved' or returned to the tradition of Greek rationality as the most effective justification for their activity. Tradition thus provides justification for change and a means of measuring it, as actual, contemporary conduct can be evaluated against prior teaching. Legal traditions thus do not 'bind' but, as tradition, provide justification for conduct and may even be taken as the source of obligation. In this they surpass legal systems and families in terms of normative force.

How does a tradition function through time, such that it cannot be described as static? There must first be capture of information (which may be revelatory, decisional, legislative, or other). Capture is already an indication of normativity, since only information of particular value will justify the effort of capture, through memorization, writing, or recording in mechanical or electronic form. Most information relating to human or other activity simply disappears, and this is as true today as it was millennia ago, even with contemporary means of capture. Once captured in accessible form, information may become a standard of conduct, such that people purport to act in accordance with it. They will then seek to ensure that it remains available, through transmission, or *traditio*, to subsequent generations. These subsequent generations may or may not act in accordance with the particular tradition, or they may develop variations within the tradition, such that it must develop intellectual means of accommodating internal variation. Whatever is done, it will generate more information, and this information is then in turn subject to capture and subsequent transmission. Each generation thus represents a continuation of the tradition, if this is indeed the case, and a contribution to it in the form they have chosen. The mass of information of the tradition is then enhanced in terms both of its size and of its legitimacy. A living tradition thus functions by way of a continual reflexive process, through looping or feedback. We can observe it as we would a film. It is a process which is necessarily diachronic in character.

Different legal traditions may or may not insist on a formal definition of the legal. The tradition of Western legal systems has taught the necessity of formal definition over the last two centuries. Other legal traditions are less concerned with formal definition and have no pure concept of law. This is not considered a disadvantage. Identification of that which is law will therefore depend on the tradition, but in all cases it will be recognizable as law as a result of the working of tradition over time. The only instance of 'static' tradition which can be recognized

---

[15] Glenn (n 5), 23.

is in the case where the information of a tradition is no longer adhered to by a present group of people, though the information of the tradition may continue to be known and available. The tradition is then in a state of suspended animation, as Roman law is said to have become inoperative in the early middle ages, or as the law of the ancient Middle East, preserved on tablets or monuments, became literally covered over through the ages and now exists only in museum collections. To the extent that the information of the tradition remains available, however, it may be revived as a living tradition (as with the Hebrew and Welsh languages) and present adherents will thus continue and contribute to the revived tradition, revising it as they see fit. A living tradition thus represents a remarkable process of oscillation between stability and variation. It cannot be described as static.

The notion of static legal systems and families also raises major questions as to the relations betweeen them.

IV. Taxonomy, Comparison, and Conflict

The notions of categorization and comparison are well known in the sciences. Indeed, it was through borrowing from the physical sciences that the taxonomic project for legal systems was initiated. Yet the sciences also recognize a gradation in the power of explicative concepts, and categorization is at the lowest or least effective level of these concepts. Carnap thus distinguished between classificatory, comparative and quantitative concepts and saw classificatory concepts as the 'simplest and least effective kind of concept'.[16] Comparative concepts would be more 'powerful' in enabling 'a more precise description of a concrete situation' and they would allow this more precise description because they constitute a 'relation' as opposed to a 'property'.[17] 'Warmer' is thus more descriptive than 'warm' since it indicates a higher degree than the purely classificatory concept of 'warm'. We thus find that the degrees of analysis of legal systems provided by the concept of tradition (above Section II) correspond to a characteristic of a truly comparative concept, as opposed to a purely classificatory one. In expressing the *relationship* of two objects of comparison, and in variable degrees, the comparative concept is true to the underlying etymological origins of the word, derived from the Latin 'cum', or

---

[16] Rudolf Carnap, *Logical Foundations of Probability* (1950), 12. Quantitative concepts allow still further precision, if quantification is possible, and provide a more precise means of comparison.

[17] Carnap (n 16), 10, 12.

with, and 'par', or equal. So the comparative concept is inherently *relational* and involves a bringing together for purposes of evaluation or judgment.

There would be, of course, an element of comparison in the classification of legal systems, to the extent this process was actually undertaken. Each legal system would have to be compared to the criteria fixed for the definition of each legal family, and categorized according to the results of this comparison. Yet the comparison involved is not that of legal systems themselves, but that of a given legal system with a theoretical construct, and we have already seen that the construction of these theoretical constructs more or less exhausted the efforts of those involved in the taxonomic process. There was relatively little categorization actually undertaken and correspondingly little comparison of system to system, in terms of their ongoing relations and degrees of representation of theoretical models. The taxonomic project would thus have represented a relatively low-level project, in terms of scientific concepts, and would not have progressed very far in terms of implementation. There may be important, underlying reasons for this lack of progress in the scientific undertaking.

Léontin-Jean Constantinesco, in developing the taxonomic project, reflected contemporary teaching of the nature of the legal system in referring to it as a 'totality', or a 'tout' in the original French.[18] It is a bounded entity, characterized by the interaction of its internal elements. Systems are thus profoundly inner-directed and that which lies beyond their boundaries is in principle of no interest to them. The taxonomic process, in seizing systems as static entities according to their present characteristics, ignores their development over time but also, perhaps more fundamentally, ignores their reciprocal relations and reciprocal influence. In so doing it acts according to the teaching of the nature of legal systems, which by its nature can have very little to say about that which is beyond the system. Contemporary positivists are very explicit about this. Hart declared, for example, that '[t]he legal system of a modern state is characterized by a certain kind of *supremacy* within its territory and *independence* of other systems . . .'.[19] while Kelsen spoke of the relations between 'norm systems' as being either those of independence or subordination.[20] Legal systems thus do not give reasons for their own application, and provide no suggestions as to when they are open to external influence. They suggest their own incomparability, and Constantinesco acknowledged that intersystemic comparison appeared at first sight impossible, while eventually recognizing a process of 'osmosis' by which certain civilizations would see a decline in the 'pure' character of their values and characteristic institutions.[21] Underlying the teaching of legal systems and legal families there is therefore a profound epistemology of separation, which inevitably had its effect on the entire taxonomic project.

---

[18] Constantinesco (n 7), 241.   [19] H. L. A. Hart, *The Concept of Law* (2nd edn, 1994), 24.
[20] Hans Kelsen, *Pure Theory of Law* (trans M. Knight, 1967), 330, 332.
[21] Constantinesco (n 7), 245.

The taxonomic school of comparative law thus never reached the stage of actual comparison, or bringing together, of laws.[22] This appears paradoxical, but flows quite naturally from the underlying concepts, of legal systems and legal families, which were widespread in the nineteenth and twentieth centuries and with which comparatists had to work. The absence of actual comparison appears, however, undeniable. John Merryman thus concludes that '[m]ost comparative law teaching and scholarship could more accurately be called "foreign law" since its principal aim is to describe foreign legal systems'.[23] This general phenomenon is perfectly consistent with Constantinesco's claim that '[e]ach legal system must be judged in relation to its own frame of reference, but this frame of theoretical reference must first be confronted with its own practical reality'.[24]

The absence of active comparison was comprehensible at the time of the greatest legal nationalism which the world has known. Moreover, the debate about how to classify autonomous legal systems at least raised the question of how to think about the laws of other people. It may be too charitable, however, to think of the taxonomic project as simply benign and ineffectual. It may have contributed in a significant way to conflictual and antagonistic relations between peoples and laws. The nineteenth century was not only the century of the emergence of comparative law as a scientific discipline. It was also the century of the paramountcy of the notion of conflicts of laws, as a means of conceptualizing relations between legal systems. Differences between laws were thought of as necessarily involving conflicts, such that each legal case involving a 'foreign'element was seen as requiring a preliminary decision as to which legal system was to be controlling over it. This is still the positive law of some jurisdictions today. All cases thus had to be assigned to one or another paramount legal system, and since there was incompatibility between systems their nature was inherently conflictual. The taxonomic process would have reinforced the free-standing, autonomous, and conflictual nature of legal systems, and it has recently been stated that the process allows a better understanding of what Samuel Huntington has described as a 'clash' of civilizations.[25] If law is understood in terms of incompatible systems, grouped in families of greater or lesser size, it will be viewed as a primary weapon in conflictual relations between peoples.[26]

---

[22] The remark is limited, however, to the taxonomic school, and much distinguished comparison of laws has taken place in what is often referred to as 'micro-comparison', though the expression is not an entirely happy one.

[23] John Merryman, David Clark, and John Haley, *The Civil Law Tradition: Europe, Latin America, and East Asia* (1994), 1.

[24] Constantinesco (n 7), 423.

[25] Heinrich Scholler and Silvia Tellenbach (eds) *Die Bedeuting der Lehre vom Rechtskreis und der Rechtskultur* (2001), 11.

[26] Ibid.

Unlike the notions of legal systems and legal families, which involve categorization but little or no comparison, the notion of legal traditions would be characterized most of all by an absence of sharp boundaries and systemic features. This would not prevent the development of the particular tradition of legal systems, but the concept of tradition in itself provides no demarcation of its own limits. Conceived as normative information, moreover, tradition is difficult to reconcile with a notion of spatial or categorical limits. Information is difficult to control or limit, and attempts to do so can be derived only from particular traditions which tend to the systemic. So the notion of a legal tradition is one which by its nature facilitates comparison or bringing together. In a sense, the hypothesis is the reverse of that of the legal system, where the question is whether and to what extent there can be a bringing together. With the concept of legal tradition, the question is whether and to what extent there can be a keeping apart. Traditions by their nature rub against one another, and overlap. They are more, or less, influential, in different places and with different peoples. In that respect, they are insidious, since they will persist in spite of all efforts of exclusion and control. Above all, however, they involve constant comparison, since they speak constantly to the relations between the local and the less local, and even between the local and the distant. The other tradition must be evaluated, even implicitly, and its relation to local tradition will be seen as one of increasing, or decreasing, influence, however satisfying or infuriating this may be. All legal traditions thus necessarily contain teaching on their relations with other legal traditions. In the language of scientific concepts, they express relations, and not properties. They claim to represent the better, as opposed to the good, the bad, or the adequate, and thus lend themselves to more comprehensive forms of understanding. Even radical difference is no obstacle to the process of comparison inherent in the idea of legal traditions. This is recognized by basic works on language, if not in discussion of taxonomic comparative law. In the United States a standard work on synonyms and antonyms thus states, under the word 'Contrast', that '[t]o *compare* . . . is to place together in order to show likeness or unlikeness. We *contrast* objects that have already been *compared*. We must *compare* them, at least momentarily, even to know that they are different'.[27] The taxonomic process would thus have lent itself to a decline in understanding of the laws of the world, in attempting to reduce comparison between legal traditions through crystallization of them in the form of legal systems. The historical relations amongst legal traditions are today, however, in the process of restoration. There is a corresponding increase in the active process of comparison of laws.

Though the concept of legal systems has dominated western legal theory for the last two centuries, just as the concept of legal families has dominated that of the scientific discipline of comparative law, the comparative relations of legal

---

[27] James C. Fernald, *Funk & Wagnalls Standard Handbook of Synonyms, Antonyms, and Prepositions* (1947) (emphasis in original).

traditions remained vigorous at the level of judicial and legal practice in most of
the world. This is evidenced by the ongoing relations between European laws and
the laws of their former colonies. These relations were never adequately captured
by the idea of territorially paramount legal systems, since European laws have
never been able to impose themselves overseas, in a so-called 'binding' manner,
and it has always been a question of their relative influence in the face of local and
non-systemic forms of normativity. The process was the same as that of the spread
of the common laws of Europe, within Europe, as local law prevailed over expanding common laws, best conceived as normative legal traditions.[28] Comparison of
laws has thus been endemic in much of the world and much of legal practice, as
lawyers and judges constantly evaluated and appraised the suitability of application
of local or distant (metropolitan) law.[29] In so doing, they deployed a scientific
concept, that of comparison, which was more powerful than the concept of
categorization practised in the scientific discipline of comparative law.

There is a further dimension of the taxonomic process which is important for
the relations of laws in the world. As a descriptive enterprise, the classification of
legal systems into legal families concentrated on the dominant or leading characteristics of legal systems in order to assign them to the appropriate family. In so
doing it necessarily did away with the teaching inherent in all legal traditions on
the relations of each tradition to the other. Legal traditions are not autonomous or
independent, and in all cases they have developed means of reconciling their teaching with conflicting opinion, whether recognized as within or without the tradition. European legal history is particularly instructive in this regard, since for
centuries multiple legal traditions were applicable on particular European territories and a great deal of law was developed as to how to reconcile these different legal
traditions. The *ius commune*, the common law, and the other common laws of
Europe were thus reconciled for centuries, through various comparative processes
of interpretation, with the different particular laws, or *iura propria*, which accompanied them. The construction of autonomous legal systems, however, meant the
elimination of such practices of reconciliation and active comparison, while the
classification into legal families only reinforced an apparent lack of need for such
reconciliation. As exclusivist legal theories today decline in influence, we are in
great need of techniques of reconciliation of different laws which would be applicable on the same territory. The teaching of legal families cannot, however, by its
nature, provide such information. There must therefore be some measure of
revival of the teaching of legal traditions on their own mutual reconciliation.[30]

[28] Glenn, *Common Laws* (n 2).

[29] For the present acceleration of comparative legal practice, see H. Patrick Glenn, 'Comparative
Law and Legal Practice: On Removing the Borders', (2001) 75 *Tulane LR* 977 ff.

[30] For the teaching, see Glenn (n 5), chs 3–9, in the fourth section of each chapter.

The process of reconciliation of laws raises profound questions, however, as to possible bias in the process. To what extent do the concepts of legal families and legal traditions lend themselves to bias in the appreciation of the multiple laws of the world?

V. EUROCENTRISM

The expression 'Eurocentric' has recently become current. It appears to be closely related to the emergence of 'postcolonialism', which would be an intellectual movement in favour of a new equilibrium in world relations, as a present correct-ive to the European colonialism of the past. In itself, Eurocentrism is a perfectly normal and profoundly human attitude, for Europeans and those who admire European achievements. It is used as a mild pejorative, however, to describe European (and now more generally western) attitudes towards non-European phenomena, and more particularly where the persistence of European attitudes gives rise to distortion in the comprehension of the non-European. Reconciliation of the different laws of the world would therefore become difficult if Eurocentric attitudes prevented appreciation of the merits of non-European laws.

There is now widespread criticism of the notion of legal families, and the taxo-nomic process it entails, as being Eurocentric in character.[31] The notion of legal families would be Eurocentric because the work devoted to it has concentrated very largely on laws derived from Europe, with corresponding marginalization of the other laws of the world. This is not to say that the non-European laws of the world have been entirely ignored. They would rather have been treated in an essentially unsympathetic manner. Thus the treatise of René David famously dealt with civil, common, and socialist law, and then with all other laws of the world in a fourth section entitled 'Other Conceptions of Law and the Social Order'.[32] This was described by René Rodière as a 'pocket-emptier' ('vide-poche') and as making as much sense as a jurist from the islands of Touamoutou lumping together civil, common, and Islamic law in the same 'family'.[33] David's treatment was, however, broadly representative of the taxonomic school's representation of non-Western laws. This was on occasion defended. Rodière, in spite of his criticism of David, argued that the only 'true' comparison which was possible was that which took

---

[31] Glenn (n 5), 164, with referencess; Mattei, (1997) 45 *AJCL* 5, 8; Vanderlinden (n 8), 416; Husa (n 4) 579.

[32] David and Brierley (n 1), 453.

[33] René Rodière, *Introduction au droit comparé* (1979), 26, 27.

place within the 'christianized' or 'civilized' world,[34] reflecting the limited view that comparison is only possible of similar entities or concepts. David justified his exclusion of Jewish law on the basis that its sphere of influence was (even) 'incomparably' less than other laws, in spite of its 'historical and philosophical interest'.[35] Treatment should thus follow present demographic importance as opposed to intellectual and historical influence.

The explanations offered by the taxonomic school of their treatment of non-western laws did not acknowledge, however, the inherent bias of the concept of legal families in favour of western concepts of law, and notably in favour of the concept of the legal system. Western legal traditions are the only ones of the world which have developed the concept of a legal system, and the only ones of the world which purport to *describe* law, notably in terms of legal families, as opposed to simply living according to it. There are thus no candidates for inclusion in the legal families of the world other than the legal systems which western laws have inspired. The project of categorizing the laws of the world was in reality a project of categorizing nation-states and their legal systems, and all nation-states are conceived in terms of the sources of law recognized by western traditions. The *Rechtsstaat* or State of Law is one which is founded on western law. So it really was necessary to categorize states according to criteria of western law (civil, common, socialist) since there were no other types of state. States influenced by non-western forms of law could incorporate such laws into their structures in some measure but, as states, inevitably did so with western instruments of state law. Non-western laws were thus inevitably seen as non-law ('Other Conceptions . . . of Social Order') or as law which was relevant to the taxonomic process only to the extent it had received state approval. Since this was often not the case, appreciation of non-western law was rare and haphazard, essentially perceived as beyond the taxonomic process. Only the human importance of such laws favoured some measure of analysis of them.

It is possible to see this exclusionary tendency of taxonomic comparative law as a product of comparative law thinking of the nineteenth and twentieth centuries, but such thinking is itself rooted in profound tendencies of western law and western legal education. Since the origins of contemporary legal education and research, in the twelfth century, western lawyers have taught, and learned, only one law, originally the *ius commune* derived from Roman law, in the universities of both the continent and England, then the common law, in the Inns of Court, then the law of the state, in public institutions of education. This may be seen largely as the result of the joint influence of the Holy Roman Empire and the Church, both of which were oriented towards the idea of a single, universal law, the *ius unum*. There was thus little or no teaching of the *iura propria* of Europe, the laws of the people. Comparison was avoided, and it has been said recently that

---

[34] Rodière (n 33), 25, 30.   [35] David and Brierley (n 1), 29.

this was the case because of a widespread fear of 'contamination' through the process of comparison. To say that God was larger than the human person, even infinitely, was to measure God from the perspective of the human person.[36] It was therefore a major development when some formal teaching of 'comparative law' became recognized in the nineteenth and twentieth centuries, but this recognition and teaching of foreign law remained subject to profoundly anchored notions of the nature of law.

The movement away from the concept of legal families and towards that of legal traditions may thus be seen as a movement towards a more open and objective means of appreciation of diverse laws. The conclusion is itself a comparative one and there is no suggestion of objectivity in an absolute sense, which may be illusory. The concept of legal tradition would be less burdened, however, with the characteristics of western legal thought than that of legal families. Conceived as normative information, the concept of legal tradition would be broad enough to include all the laws of the world, while still allowing crystallization in the form of specific traditions corresponding to particular beliefs and circumstances. Religious laws thus rely explicitly on the notion of tradition, as do the infinitely varied forms of *lex non scripta*. Western lawyers also rely on the concept of western legal traditions, in spite of widespread notions in the contemporary western world of a 'modernity' somehow divorced from the long history of western thought. Nor would the notion of legal tradition be somehow antagonistic towards the idea of legal systems and legal families, since these represent particular traditions of western legal development. Western legal systems would thus rest, not on presumed basic norms or inexplicable general habits of obedience, but on a vast body of normative legal information which gave rise to the contemporary concept of a legal system.

The concept of legal tradition thus allows comparative appreciation of laws of the world which are non-systemic in character. They need not be filtered through state systems in order to be included in a taxonomic process of categorization, but may be appreciated as normative information with their own criteria for human grouping. Still more advantageously, they may be seen as influencing, in greater or lesser degree, the structures of contemporary states. The state and its legal system thus becomes no longer a positive construction, which either exists or does not exist according to criteria which are difficult to define, but a place of meeting and potential reconciliation of different laws.

The notion of legal tradition would thus be more apt in conceptualizing contemporary legal relations than that of legal families, and this involves appreciation of these ideas in the contemporary state of the laws of the world.

---

[36] Xavier Thunis, 'L'empire de la comparaison', in François R. van der Mensbrugghe (ed), *L'utilisation de la méthode comparative en droit européen* (2004), 5 at 6.

VI. Legal Families, Legal Traditions, and the Laws of the World

It has been remarked (above, Section I) that both new and old forms of law are today of increasing influence, with a corresponding decline in influence of the formal law of the state. It is also the case that populations today are mobile as they have never been before, and that all states contain minorities who may be more or less constant in their adherence to one form or another of non-state law. All of the non-state laws in question are laws of great persuasive authority, and the older forms of them may have exerted this persuasive authority over millennia. The newer forms of transnational law find their justification in contemporary need, modern technology, and deliberate human collaboration. To what extent can the concepts of legal families and legal traditions speak to these contemporary circumstances?

The constant problem for the taxonomic project of classifying national laws into legal families has been the choice of criteria for classification. In the formal language of scientific taxonomy, it has not been the 'extension' of the classification which has created the difficulties, the listing of cases to be classified, but rather its 'intension', the listing of properties which characterize the cases.[37] Vanderlinden lists fourteen criteria which have been used, including race, culture, origins and history, sources, technique, structures, professionalization, doctrinal autonomy, and others, along with the authors who have deployed them.[38] It has been said that there are as many classifications as there are comparatists, and the number and variety of classifications is itself an indication of the failure of the enterprise. The legal families enterprise would thus have become the 'legal families trap', in the present circumstances of the world.[39] There appear to be two fundamental reasons for this.

The first is found in the persistent tendency of the taxonomists to classify according to a limited number of criteria and even a single criterion, however fluid it might be. The classification would tend to the 'monothetic' as opposed to the 'polythetic'. All laws of the world would thus speak in some measure to this limited number of criteria of classification. In a time of increasing multiplication of sources of law in a given territory, the nature of the classification process thus requires concentration on a limited range of explanatory concepts, to the necessary exclusion of others. Are the civil and common laws today 'hermetically sealed'

---

[37] H. Feger, 'Classification: Conceptions in the Social Sciences', in Neil Smelser and Paul Baltes (eds), *International Encyclopedia of the Social & Behavioral Sciences* (vol III, 2001) 1966, 1968.

[38] Vanderlinden (n 8), 328.

[39] Husa, (2004) 56 *Revue internationale de droit comparé* 32, citing Harding.

from one another, or converging? Is the United States of America a civil or common law jurisdiction? What of China? In what family should the law of the European Union be classified? Are rules of product liability the product of common or civil law thinking? Is there a socialist legal family today? To what extent can a legal system be said to have 'failed'? These are all questions which pose fundamental problems for the taxonomic project. It is not that no answers can be given. It is rather that the answers will not convince, since the entire enterprise appears too crude or simplistic to respond to the fluidity of present circumstances. This is inevitable with 'limited feature classification',[40] since the multiplication of characteristics in an object of classification results in the classification system losing plausibility and practicability.[41] The problem would not have been cured by the multiplication of criteria for classification, since this has resulted in a collapsing of the multiple criteria into a larger, composite factor.[42]

The second problem is a still larger one, and involves the entire project of submitting legal traditions to criteria imposed by the taxonomist. This problem remains whatever the criteria and whatever their number. The major legal traditions of the world are themselves encompassing phenomena. They deal with life, death, and all between, in a normative manner. They are all different from one another, from basic points of departure or world-views down to the most precise forms of day-to-day regulation. Yet they also speak and relate to one another, in comparative terms (above Section IV). What criteria can be constructed by a contemporary comparative lawyer, even drawing from knowledge of the traditions, which could encompass and order all of the laws of the world in a way which respected each of them and which also reflected the dynamic amongst them? No one has been able to do so because it is unlikely in the extreme that anyone could. No contemporary, constructed criteria can be imposed on such complex normative phenomena. The same conclusion has been suggested by some social science observers, expressing fundamental criticism of the possibility of classification of social phenomena. Any given system of classification would thus inevitably be arbitrary.[43] Such a conclusion would be devastating for classificatory social sciences and for the taxonomic project in comparative law, as suggested by taxonomic practice to date, but this would be without prejudice to the ongoing process of comparison of laws in the world.

This more advanced scientific process of comparing laws to one another is entirely compatible with the concept of legal tradition, which because of its non-positive character is suitable to the current flows of legal normativity in the world. Territory has become largely irrelevant to the relations of legal traditions, since a tradition other than one's own may provide a model over any terrestrial space, in

---

[40] Hiram Chodos, *Global Justice Reform* (2005), 39.
[41] Feger (n 37), 1968 ('comorbidity' in medical patients).   [42] Chodos (n 40), 39.
[43] Feger (n 37), 1972 (citing Galt and Smith).

societies now described as networked.[44] It is symptomatic of this state of affairs that a call has thus been made recently in Europe, home of the legal system, for admission of tradition as a source of law to complement the inevitable inadequacy of state law. Tradition would here include 'comparative law' and what is meant by this is not the macro-process of taxonomy, but the issue-by-issue bringing together (*com-parare*) of different solutions.[45] Legal traditions thus influence, though do not displace, one another. They may thus co-exist as a matter of degree and correspondingly provide a means of conceptualization of laws which overlap in some measure in their application in a given territory. They also provide a source of obligation and legitimation and are thus essential to the decisional responsibilities of the lawyer and judge.

VII. CONCLUSION

The concept of legal families maintained the law of other peoples in western view at a time of legal scientism and legal nationalism, in the nineteenth and twentieth centuries. It did so by accepting the idea of national legal systems and the possibility of taxonomic description of them. Legal comparison was thus undertaken at a so-called 'macro' level, but the efforts of taxonomic categorization foundered on the difficulty of fixing criteria for membership in the legal families and the difficulty of actually comparing legal systems perceived as autonomous and static. As communication between the peoples of the world accelerated in the late twentieth century it became more and more evident that national legal systems could no longer be treated as autonomous and sovereign, as both new and ancient forms of non-state law asserted themselves. The notion of legal traditions allows a conceptual understanding of the relations of laws conceived as normative information. There can thus be multiple laws applicable in a given territory, with varying degrees of influence, since the concept of legal tradition is one which accommodates multiple sources of law and gradations in the force of their normativity. The process of comparing legal traditions is the ancient one of bringing together (*com-parare*), without prejudice to the ongoing existence of that which is compared, in order to achieve the most just solution of whatever problem has arisen.

---

[44] Manuel Castells, *The Rise of the Networked Society* (2000).

[45] Eugen Bucher, 'Rechtsüberlieferung und heutiges Recht', (2000) 8 *Zeitschrift für Europäisches Privatrecht* 394.

BIBLIOGRAPHY

Marc Ancel, *Utilité et méthodes du droit comparé* (1971)

René Rodière, *Introduction au droit comparé* (1979)

Léontin-Jean Constantinesco, *Traité de droit comparé*, vol III: *La science des droits comparés* (1983)

René David and John E. C. Brierley, *Major Legal Systems in the World Today* (3rd edn, 1985)

Rodolfo Sacco, *La comparaison juridique au service de la connaissance du droit* (1991)

Jacques Vanderlinden, *Comparer les droits* (1995)

Ugo Mattei, 'Three Patterns of Law: Taxonomy and Change in the World's Legal Systems', (1997) 45 *AJCL* 5

Hein Kötz, 'Abschied von der Rechtskreislehre?', (1998) 6 *Zeitschrift für Europäisches Privatrecht* 493 ff

Konrad Zweigert and Hein Kötz, *Introduction to Comparative Law* (3rd edn, trans Tony Weir, 1998)

Heinrich Scholler and Silvia Tellenbach (eds), *Die Bedeuting der Lehre vom Rechtskreis und der Rechtskultur* (2001)

Mathias Reimann, 'The Progress and Failure of Comparative Law in the Second Half of the 20th Century', (2002) 50 *AJCL* 671

H. Patrick Glenn, *Legal Traditions of the World* (2nd edn, 2004)

Jaakko Husa, 'Classification of Legal Families Today: Is it Time for a Memorial Hymn?', (2004) 56 *Revue internationale de droit comparé* 11 ff

Esin Örücü, 'Family Trees for Legal Systems: Towards a Contemporary Approach', in Mark Van Hoecke (ed), *Epistemology and Methodology of Comparative Law* (2004), 359 ff

Hiram E. Chodosh, *Global Justice Reform: A Comparative Methodology* (2005)

H. Patrick Glenn, *On Common Laws* (2005)

CHAPTER 13

....

COMPARATIVE LAW AS THE STUDY OF TRANSPLANTS AND RECEPTIONS

....

MICHELE GRAZIADEI

*Alessandria**

* The author expresses his gratitude for comments and editorial assistance to Jane Bestor, James Gordley, Nancy Paul, Mathias Reimann, and Reinhard Zimmermann. The usual disclaimer applies.

I. INTRODUCTION

THE comparative study of transplants and receptions investigates contacts of legal cultures and explores the complex patterns of change triggered by them. While transplants and receptions have played an important part in shaping the world's legal systems since antiquity, even in the cosmopolitan world of comparatists, the subject of this chapter is a relatively new field of inquiry. Indeed, while the reception of Roman law in Europe has been an academic subject at least since the nineteenth century, the treatment of transplants and receptions as general phenomena became a major topic in comparative law only in the last three decades of the twentieth century, after the publication of pioneering studies that appeared before the 1970s.[1]

In 1970, the International Academy of Comparative Law dedicated a section of its Congress to 'The global reception of foreign law'.[2] Four years later, Alan Watson's *Legal Transplants* singled out that theme as a major subject for comparative legal studies.[3] In the same year, general methodological issues of comparative law were linked to the study of legal transplants and receptions by Rodolfo Sacco.[4] In the following years, the notion of legal transplants rapidly

---

[1] See eg the literature cited in Max Rheinstein, Hans-Eckart Niethammer, and Reimer von Borries, *Einführung in die Rechtsvergleichung* (2nd edn, 1987), 124 ff (quoting contributions by Max Rheinstein, Andreas B. Schwarz, and Imre Zajtay).

[2] The important precedent was the conference on the 'Reception of Foreign Law in Turkey', held by the International Association of Legal Sciences in Istanbul in 1955. See the *Annales de la Faculté de droit de Istanbul*, n 6, (1956) and Unesco, *International Social Science Bulletin* (1957), IX n 1.

[3] Alan Watson published widely on the topic since the first edition of this title. For a discussion of the first twenty years of his work on transplants see William Ewald, 'Comparative Jurisprudence (II): The Logic of Legal Transplants', (1995) 43 *AJCL* 489. Watson's latest book on the subject is *Law Out of Context* (2000).

[4] Rodolfo Sacco, 'Les buts et les méthodes de la comparaison du droit', in *Rapports nationaux italiens au IX Congrès international de droit comparé, Téhéran 1974* (1974), 113 ff, at 127–31.

became a central 'paradigm' in comparative law. None the less, the very possibility of legal transplants was also contested and various essays by Pierre Legrand animated a lively controversy about transplants, attracting even more attention to the topic.[5]

Most of these contributions advanced theoretical reflections unconnected to actual projects of legal change, such as those promoted by the earlier American law and development movement.[6] None the less, in a shrinking world, those reflections were long overdue. Today, the importance of the topic is still growing. One sees it, for example, in law reform programmes adopted or supported by international institutions that promote legal change on a global scale. It is also prominent in the law and economics literature that investigates the relevance of transplants to economic performance.

II. Terminology

Possibly due to its rapid growth, the terminology of the field is still surrounded by some uncertainty. The term 'transplant' is based on a metaphor that was chosen *faute de mieux*, ill-adapted to capturing the gradual diffusion of the law or the continuous nature of the process that sometimes leads to legal change through the appropriation of foreign ideas. Alternative terminology that has gained acceptance (especially outside the common law world) is 'circulation of legal models'. Thus, the Thirteenth Congress of the International Academy of Comparative Law discussed the topic to which this chapter is dedicated under that title. The *Association Henri Capitant* dedicated one of its annual meetings to the circulation of the French legal model abroad. More recent contributions speak of the 'transfer' instead of 'transplant' of law. The term 'reception' is sometimes used as a synonym for any and all of the above, though it also has a specific denotation referring to global legal transfers. In this sense, the most important case of 'reception' in the history of Europe is the diffusion of Roman law that occurred when the subject was taught in universities during the medieval and early modern ages. 'Reception' as a synonym for global legal transfer is not limited to this case. Indeed, the first legislative acts of the newly independent American States enabling their courts to receive and develop the English common law are known as 'reception statutes'. And the list of terms used to identify legal change by legal transfer goes on. Generic

---

[5] See below, Section VI.2.

[6] For an overview and a full bibliography, see David M. Trubek, 'Law and Development', in *International Encyclopaedia of the Social and Behavioural Sciences* (2004), at 8443.

expressions such as 'influence' or 'inspiration' are also in use, while other terms, for example, 'cross-fertilization', are gaining currency. All these variations subtly qualify the study of the main theme, but may also denote phenomena similar to those covered by a different terminology.

This contribution will take the terminological couple transplant/reception to be all-embracing for present purposes and will speak of 'transfer' where a generic term is suitable. It will not adopt further distinctions because it does not aim to develop a typology of the available materials, but rather to address some fundamental issues of this field of study. This approach does not pre-empt the question of the borders of the relevant phenomena, nor does it deny the variety of approaches and problems inherent to the study of legal transplants and receptions. In fact, the current debates over terminology reflect the open character of the debates over the law's mobility. The following pages will map them and assess them critically.

III. SOME CLASSICAL CASES

An overview of the transplants and receptions that have changed (or are changing) the legal landscape of the world is a task that exceeds the ambitions of this piece. A brief presentation of some legal transfers that have acquired historical prominence is none the less helpful to understand the scale of the phenomenon and the complexity of the issues involved. Accordingly, this section covers the reception of the Roman law from the Middle Ages up to the epoch of the national codifications, the diffusion of some influential national codifications both inside and outside Europe, the expansion of the common law across the world, and the interaction between common and civil law in mixed legal systems. The last part of this section concerns the transfer of specific institutions in several places, as opposed to the reception of an entire legal system.

Inevitably, the cases considered below constitute a very small sampling of examples of legal transplants and receptions. The general character of both phenomena should alert the reader to the fact that the dynamics triggered by transplants and receptions are not unique to the geographical areas covered by the following survey, nor to the fields of law touched by it. There is, indeed, no lack of evidence that transplants and receptions have taken place in geographical areas and fields of law outside the reach of Roman, civil, or common law. An interesting case is the influence of traditional Chinese law outside China, notably in Japan before the Meiji era. Japan first borrowed Chinese characters in the early centuries of the Christian era, many centuries after their first use in China. The influence of China's literate culture in Japan produced the reception of the T'ang (AD 619–906)

Codes by the imperial court during the eighth century AD. After that, Japan was exposed to neo-confucian ideas of family and governance that were adapted to the local situation. Even in the Tokugawa period (AD 1603–1867), which was marked by a relative isolation, Chinese influence in Japan was at work in the shogunate and daimyo domains.[7] The diffusion of Islamic law in the world is another major example of legal modelling on a large scale that has been studied in depth and deserves attention.[8]

1. The Reception of Roman Law in Europe and in Other Parts of the World

The re-birth of Roman law in the Middle Ages and its spread to most parts of continental Europe and Scotland probably represents the best-known case of diffusion of a legal model across the European space.[9]

This gradual process started in Bologna, the first centre of university learning, around the year AD 1070, as an intellectual attempt to bring to life an ideal model of law, out of force and not sanctioned at first, by any political power. The lawyers involved in this enterprise, with the notable exception of the Humanists, were not philologists. They tried to elucidate the meaning of their sources, but they looked at them primarily from the perspective of their contemporary reality. This fundamental attitude persisted until the end of the *ius commune* in Europe and explains the subsequent transformations of the interpretation and application of the Roman sources during that epoch. The lawyers involved in the reception of the Roman law felt free to adapt and reinterpret it whenever they had sufficient reasons to do so.[10] This was hardly an original sin, however, as Justinian's compilation itself

---

[7] Dan Fenno Henderson, 'Chinese Legal Studies in Early Eighteenth Century Japan—Scholars and Sources', (1970) 30 *Asian Studies* 21. For a study concerning Vietnam, see Nguyên Ngọc Huy and Tạ Văn Tài (eds), *The Lê Code: Law in Traditional Vietnam: A Comparative Sino-Vietnamese Legal Study with Historical-Juridical Analysis and Annotations* (1987).

[8] One could cite an entire library on this topic. Abdullahi A. An-Na'im (ed), *Islamic Family Law in a Changing World: A Global Resource Book* (2002) surveys the state of affairs in the field of family law. The *Studies in Islamic Law and Society* edited by Ruud Peters and Bernard Weiss and the volume by Michael Kemper and Maurus Reinkowski (eds), *Rechtspluralismus in der islamischen Welt. Gewohnheitsrecht zwischen Staat und Gesellschaft* (2005), explore the interaction between Islamic law and local laws. On the relationship between religious and secular laws today in general, see Andrew Huxley (ed), *Religion, Law and Tradition: Comparative Studies in Religious Law* (2002).

[9] Franz Wieacker, *A History of Private Law in Europe* (trans Tony Weir, 1995); Manlio Bellomo, *The Common Legal Past of Europe, 1000–1800* (trans Lydia Cochrane, 1995) are the principal reference works in English. Peter Stein, *Roman Law in European History* (1999) provides a brilliant introduction to the topic, starting from the Roman foundations. Kenneth Reid and Reinhard Zimmermann (eds), *A History of Private Law in Scotland* (2000) covers the reception in Scotland.

[10] Indeed, since the codification of the civil law eventually rescued the study of the Roman law sources from their troubling association with contemporary legal practice, nineteenth-century

had seen the light thanks to the selective appropriation and the interpolation of the original sources.

As mentioned above, the story of this long love affair with Roman law had its initial centre of gravity in the universities. The universities adopted the study of Roman law as a proper object of learning. From the eleventh century onwards, Roman-law-based education at the universities prepared a whole class of learned lawyers who practised law as administrators, judges, and advocates. The Roman law revived by the universities eventually received political sanction from the Emperor, but sometimes met resistance even within his realm.[11] To be sure, the Roman law never completely prevailed, nor was it uniformly received throughout Europe even in the lands that today form part of the civil law world. Canon law, feudal law, and the law merchant evolved in parallel and were also part of the European landscape together with local legislation and the customary laws of each region. None the less, they too were often infiltrated by Romanist learning because of the common Roman-law-based education of the lawyers who dealt with them.

It is often claimed that Roman law was received in most European countries because of its superior quality but this point has been disputed too. Paul Koschaker, for example, held that this claim was at odds with the historical reality—the reception of Roman law in Europe was not the result of free choice, but of historical necessity.[12] To be sure, the occasional presence of strong central institutions antedating the triumph of the Roman law tradition at the universities may explain patterns of resistance to its reception. The growth of English law provides indirect support to this argument, which is also illustrated by several chapters of the history of French law.[13]

English common law developed on the foundations of the institutional structures provided by a set of centralized courts staffed by lawyers who were mostly trained as practitioners and not as doctors in civil law. To be sure, this is not to say that England remained completely isolated from the continent or that it ignored the Romanist legal heritage for most of its history. There are simply too many pages of English legal history that reveal contacts with that tradition to adopt this simplistic point of view.[14] In fact, over the centuries, the Romanist legal heritage

German legal historians noticed that, as a result of codification, the Roman legal sources could be subject to a properly historical scrutiny. On this episode, see Reinhard Zimmermann, *Roman Law, Contemporary Law, European Law* (2001), 44 ff.

[11] See eg Gerald Strauss, *Law, Resistance, and The State: The Opposition to Roman Law in Reformation Germany* (1986).

[12] Paul Koschaker, *Europa und das Römisches Recht* (2nd edn, 1953), 79–81, 137–8, where he expresses the opinion that 'the question of the reception of a legal system is not a question of quality' with reference to the reception of laws in general.

[13] John H. Baker, *The Oxford History of the Laws of England (1483–1558)*, vol VI (2003), 3 ff. On the French scenario, see John P. Dawson, *The Oracles of the Law* (1968), 262 ff.

[14] For an overall view of the links between English law and the civilian tradition see Reinhard Zimmermann, 'Der europäische Charakter des englischen Rechts', (1993)1 *Zeitschrift für europäisches*

repeatedly attracted attention in England. It inspired the elaboration of specific rules and eventually offered the opportunity to organize the structure of major subjects, such as contracts and torts.[15] Indeed, some institutions that are often thought to be specifically English, such as trusts, are, on closer examination, part of a wider European picture.[16] Even the sharpening perception of the distinctive features of the English legal tradition owes much to the comparison between the laws of England and the laws of continental Europe.[17] Until the twentieth century, American law was also exposed to the influence of the civil law, which began to decline only with the outbreak of World War I.[18]

For better or for worse, during most of its history, the system of origin of one of the world's main legal traditions developed along a path that was quite separate from the teaching of the Roman law in the universities so that the impact of civilian learning remained much more limited than on the continent.

Outside Europe, the initial spread of the Romanist learning in Central and Latin America and elsewhere, for example, South Africa, was an effect of the expansion of colonial powers. The Roman law tradition was the legal tradition of the colonizers and, thus, became one of the sources of the local law.

2. Some Civil Codes and their Diffusion

The period of the *ius commune* on the European continent came to an end when the movement to codify the law produced a wave of legal change. The most

---

Privatrecht 4 ff; *idem*, 'Roman Law and the Harmonisation of Private Law in Europe', in Arthur Hartkamp, Martijin Hesselink, Carla Joustra, Edgard du Perron, and Muriel Veldman (eds), *Towards a European Civil Code* (3rd edn, 2004), 21 ff, at 34 ff. See also the series Comparative Studies, **Continental and Anglo-American Legal History.**

[15] David J. Ibbetson, *A Historical Introduction to the Law of Obligations* (1999); *idem*, ' "The Law of Business Rome": Foundations of the Anglo-American Tort of Negligence', (1999) 52 *Current Legal Problems* 74 (with important final remarks).

[16] Richard Helmholz and Reinhard Zimmermann (eds), *Itinera Fiduciae: Trust and Treuhand in Historical Perspective* (1998); Michele Graziadei, Ugo Mattei, and Lionel Smith (eds), *Commercial Trusts in European Private Law* (2005), with further references.

[17] For an illustration of this point, see Michele Graziadei, 'Changing Images of the Law in XIX Century English Legal Thought (The Continental Impulse)', in Mathias Reimann (ed), *The Reception of Continental Ideas in the Common Law World 1820–1920* (1993), 115 ff.

[18] This issue is best analysed by distinguishing its different aspects. See Mathias Reimann, 'Continental Imports: The Influence of European Law and Jurisprudence in the United States', (1996) *The Legal History Review*, 391 ff; *idem*, *Historische Schule und Common Law: Die Deutsche Rechtswissenschaft des 19. Jahrhunderts im amerikanischen Rechtsdenken* (1993). Michel H. Hoeflich, 'Translation and the Reception of Foreign Law in the Antebellum United States', (2002) 50 *AJCL* 753. A different story concerns the heritage of Spanish and French law derived from early settlers and conquerors: Rudolf B. Schlesinger, Hans W. Baade, Peter E. Herzog and Edward M. Wise, *Comparative Law: Cases—Text—Materials* (6th edn, 1998), 16 ff.

influential codification in Europe was the French civil code enacted in 1804. Its model was widely imitated throughout the world.[19]

The diffusion of the French civil code was at first linked to the military success of the Napoleonic army. The civil code was initially enacted in countries annexed by France or brought under its rule. Thus, it entered into force in the Netherlands, first in a slightly altered version and then in its original form, when it was annexed in 1809. Belgium and Luxembourg were French territories when the code was introduced there. In Germany, the code was enacted in the territories beyond the Rhine that were annexed. Moving further east, the Napoleonic code entered into force in Poland where, as in some other countries, the code was not translated but simply enacted in French. In Switzerland, the Canton of Geneva and the Bernese Jura (both parts of the French Republic) had the code. But the French code was also imitated without being imposed. An early example of this different dynamic is found in the Louisiana Digest of 1808. This text followed the plan of the French civil code and was largely influenced by it, though Spanish civil law was also very influential in Louisiana at first.[20] The French legacy in Lower Canada was also apparent in the civil code of Lower Canada of 1866, effective until it was superseded by the Quebec civil code of 1994.[21]

The restoration following Napoleon's fall did not generally lead to the repeal of the civil code. In the countries where the original version of the code was repealed, modified versions were subsequently enacted. In the Netherlands, the *Burgerlijk Wetboek* of 1838 (recently repealed with the entry into force of the new Dutch civil code)[22] was essentially a translation of the French codification.[23] The Italian civil code of 1865, applicable until superseded by the *Codice civile* of 1942, was also by

---

[19] Konrad Zweigert and Hein Kötz, *Introduction to Comparative Law* (trans Tony Weir, 1998), 100–22, provide an excellent overview in English. The following volumes collect important contributions: Barbara Dölemeyer, Heinz Mohnhaupt, and Alessandro Somma (eds), *Richterliche Anwendung des Code civil in seinen europäischen Geltungsbereichen ausserhalb Frankreichs* (2006). Jean-Philippe Dunand and Bénédict Winiger (eds), *Le code civil français dans le droit européen* (2005); various authors, *Le code civil 1804–2004: Livre du bicentenaire* (2004); various authors, *1804–2004: Le code civil* (2004); various authors, *La circulation du modèle juridique français, Travaux de l'Association Henri Capitant* (1993). Paolo Cappellini and Bernardo Sordi (eds), *Codici: Una riflessione di fine millenio* (2002). For a brilliant short piece, see Michel Grimaldi, 'L'exportation du code civil', *Pouvoirs* (2003), 80 ff.

[20] On the legacy of the French code in Louisiana: Vernon V. Palmer, 'Concernant le 200 anniversaire du Code Napoléon: son importance historique et contemporaine sur la codification du droit en Louisiane', in various authors, *Le code civil* (n 19), 575 ff.

[21] Jaen-Louis Baudouin and Pierre-Gabriel Jobin, 'Le Code Civil Français et les codes civils québécois', in various authors, *Le code civil 1804–2004* (n 19), 630 ff.

[22] Ewoud Hondius, 'Le code civil et les néerlandais', in various authors, *Le code civil 1804–2004* (n 19), 612 ff discusses the relationship between the new code and the French tradition.

[23] Indonesia and Suriname did not repeal the Dutch code after independence. Hence, the Dutch civil code of 1838 is still in force in both countries. Cp Jan M. Smits, 'Import and Export of Legal Models: The Dutch Experience', (2003) 13 *Transnational Law & Contemporary Problems* 551.

and large a translation of the French model.[24] The French civil code and the project of the first Italian civil code were in turn the basis of the Romanian codification that entered into force in 1865.[25]

The diffusion of the French *Code civil* outside Europe is remarkable as well. In Central and South America, its advent was facilitated by the fact that most countries achieved independence when the French civil code was practically the only model available (other than the Austrian codification of 1811). The Dominican Republic, Haiti, and Bolivia replicated the original text most closely. Many of the subsequent codifications are indebted to the civil code of Chile (1855) and show a tendency to draw from more recent codes as well, such as the German (1900), the Swiss (1912), and the Italian (1942).[26]

In Asia, the Japanese civil code of 1898 is largely indebted to the German model, though it also includes features of the French.[27]

With the exception of Turkey and Israel, the *Code civil* reached Africa and the Middle East as well. African law students from francophone countries still often approach the law through the provisions of the *Code civil*.[28] Another vehicle of (indirect) French influence was the Egyptian civil code of 1949, which sought to knit together Islamic and Western law.[29]

While this diffusion of the *Code civil* was often imposed by force, the initial imposition was not the key to its final success. Its acceptance after Napoleon's defeat calls for further explanation.[30] In many European countries, the content of

---

[24] Stefano Solimano, '*Il letto di procuste': Diritto e politica nella formazione del codice civile unitario. I progetti Cassinis (1860–1861)* (2003). The Italian civil code of 1865 is still in force in the Vatican State.

[25] Valentin A. Georgescu, 'Rumänien—Sources et literature du droit privé (1800–1914/1918)', in Helmut Coing (ed), *Handbuch der Quellen und Literatur der neueren europäischen Privatrechtsgeschichte* III.2 (1988) 214 ff, 220–1.

[26] Alejandro Guzmán Brito, *La codificación civil en iberoamerica. Siglos XIX y XX* (2000); Gustavo Bossert, 'Bicentenaire du code civil: L'Argentine', in various authors, *Le code civil 1804–2004* (n 19), 539 ff. Bartolomé Clavero, Ama Llunku, Abya Yala, *Constituyencia indígena y codigo latino por América* (2000), discuss the fate of indigenous customs under the code both before and after independence. The Spanish civil code (1889) influenced the codes of Nicaragna (1904) and Panama and it entered into force in Cuba and Puerto Rico.

[27] Eiichi Hoshino, 'L'influence du code civil au Japon', in various authors, *1804–2004 Le code civil* (n 19), 871 ff. For a detailed analysis accessible in English, see Wilhelm Röhl (ed), *History of Law in Japan since 1868* (2005), 166 ff.

[28] See Kéba Mbaye, 'Le destin du code civil en Afrique', in various authors, *Le code civil 1804–2004* (n 19), 515 ff; Etienne Le Roy, 'Le code civil au Sénégal ou le Vertige d'Icare', in Michel Doucet and Jacques Vanderlinden (eds), *La réception des systèmes juridiques: implantation et destin (1994)*, 291 ff. What Le Roy writes about Senegal is true for other francophone countries in the same area.

[29] The key figure behind this code was 'Abd al-Razzāq al-Sanhūrī, who worked with Eduard Lambert on the codification project. Cp *Actes du congrès international du cinquantenaire du Code civil égyptien (1948–1998)* (1998). For a general view, see Pierre Gannagé, 'L'influence du code civil sur les codifications des états du proche orient', in various authors, *Le code civil 1804–2004* (n 19), 597. The Egyptian precedent was influential in Lebanon, Syria, Iraq, Libya, Algeria, Qatar, Kuwait, and Bahrain.

[30] James Gordley, 'Myths of the French Civil Code', (1994) 42 *AJCL* 459.

the civil code was not entirely novel. In fact, it rested to a great extent on the foundation of a common legal heritage. Though the *Code civil* could claim to be the first codification in the world to herald the ideals of a bourgeois society, the most radical ideas aired during the French Revolution were not incorporated into it. Furthermore, the rather loose character of several of its provisions made it a flexible and adaptable text. Indeed, its acceptance did not always mean a departure from the local legal culture. Finally, the introduction of the code (or some version of it) was often accompanied by reforms that excluded parts of it, such as the articles on marriage and divorce. Other parts that were considered defective from a technical point of view were also often rejected by the importing countries (eg the regulation of mortgages).

All in all, even when no legislation intervened to adapt the code to local circumstances, the application of the civil code in foreign lands made it part of, and influenced by, local history. Outside the European continent, the code has been simply one of the many components of a local legal order that was (and largely remains) pluralistic (see below, Section V). But, even in Europe, the fate of the code was more complicated than one would at first imagine. Neither Italy nor the Netherlands, for example, let liability for damage caused by things in someone's custody grow into a comprehensive system of strict liability, as it did in France on the unlikely textual basis of Art 1384 *Code civil*. In fact, the interpretation of the code outside France often stuck more closely to its letter than was the case at home. Thus, the course of the code's interpretation was no more predictable in France than abroad.

While no other civil code has matched the French *Code civil* in terms of foreign influence, the project of the German civil code became a source of inspiration for the Japanese civil code, which also bears traces of the French model. In turn, the Japanese codification provided the basis for the draft civil code of 1911 prepared in China during the last years of the Qing dynasty.[31] South Korea, while under the direct rule of Japan, also came into contact with the German model via the Japanese civil code. In Europe, the German codification influenced the present Greek civil code. But the history of the influence of the German model abroad is a complex matter because that code was heavily indebted to the German legal science of its epoch. The influence abroad of German legal science from the middle of the nineteenth century through the first three decades of the twentieth century was simply immense. For example, virtually every twentieth-century civil code that

---

[31] According to Zhiping Liang, 'Law, Politics and Social Change: Codification in China since 1902', in Cappellini and Sordi (eds), (n 19), 401 ff, 410 ff, that text was a direct response to the extraterritorial jurisdiction of foreign powers in China at the time, and the fruit of the conviction that the Japanese turn towards Western law provided a model for the modernization of China as well. On this, see also Philip C. C. Huang, *Code, Custom, and Legal Practice in China: The Qing and the Republic Compared* (2001).

has a general part is indebted to the German model of private law, in code form or otherwise.[32]

As another example, the Swiss civil code and the Swiss code of obligations[33] provided the substance for the Turkish civil code, enacted in 1926 after the creation of the Republic of Turkey by Kemal Atatürk. This transplant has been repeatedly investigated in the last century because of the remarkable differences between Switzerland and Turkey. The official demise of Islamic law and the adoption of a secular order as a consequence of the choice to modernize Turkey met resistance from the majority of the population. Today, the coexistence of official and unofficial law in Turkey offers a typical example of legal pluralism (see below, Section V).[34] Currently on its way to accession to the European Union, Turkey has recently amended its Constitution and changed the code to promote gender equality in family matters and to modify parts of its patrimonial law.

3. The Diffusion of the Common Law

The presence of the common law across the globe owes much to the growth of British trade and of Britain as a world power. At the heyday of its expansion, in 1921, the British Empire included almost a third of the world's lands and about a quarter of its population. After World War II, decolonization brought the empire to an end. The last significant British colony, Hong Kong, returned to Chinese sovereignty in 1997.

The British colonies comprised a variety of territories. Some lands were acquired by conquest or cession, others, such as the Australian continent, by right of first possession because they were considered to be unoccupied (*terra nullius*), although the factual premises of this distinction were sometimes false or dubious.[35]

The territories the English settlers colonized without recognizing prior sovereignty were brought under the rule of the common law unless the local circumstances rendered this solution inappropriate. This qualification was often more

[32] The influence of German scholarship in its heyday was so great that even where the law in force owed nothing to the German code the works of German jurists guided its commentary. Cp Ugo Mattei, 'Why the Wind Changed: Intellectual Leadership in Western Law', (1994) 42 *AJCL* 195.

[33] The Swiss codification itself was drafted in the light of the German and French experience with the codes: Bénédict Winiger, 'Le Code suisse dans l'embarras entre BGB et Code civil français', in Dunand and Winiger (eds), (n 19).

[34] Esin Örücü, 'Comparatists and Extraordinary Places', in Pierre Legrand and Roderick Munday (eds), *Comparative Legal Studies: Traditions and Transitions* (2003), 467, 477 ff. This is especially true in the field of family law: *idem*, 'Turkish Family Law', (2003) 18 *Migrantenrecht* 4; Ihsan Yilmaz, 'Non-recognition of Post-modern Turkish Socio-legal Reality and the Predicament of Women', (2003) 30 *British Journal of Middle Eastern Studies* 25. On the relationship between the code and the previous sources, see Ruth A. Miller, 'The Ottoman and Islamic Substratum of Turkey's Swiss Civil Code', (2000) 11 *Oxford Journal of Islamic Studies* 335.

[35] Cp *Mabo and others v Queensland* (No. 2) (1992) 175 CLR 1.

important than the rule itself. The sources of law in each colony varied because each settlement could be treated differently in consideration of the nature of the venture and pursuant to the applicable legislation. By contrast, the British policy concerning conquered or ceded colonies was to leave the law that was previously applicable in force, unless it was undesirable or repugnant from the British point of view.[36] Thus, the local court system, and the traditional mechanisms of dispute resolution in accordance with customary law, often continued to operate. Pursuant to this general policy, family and succession matters in the Indian subcontinent remained subject to Hindu or Muslim law.[37] However, during the nineteenth century, the common law effectively became the applicable law most other regards. This was camouflaged by the general principle that, specific enactment aside, the courts of British India adjudicated cases according to 'principles of justice, good conscience and equity' if found applicable to Indian society and circumstances.[38] When the British Crown itself took over the administration of India from the East India Company after 1857, it pursued a programme of codification and consolidation of law along the lines of English law. Over a period of fifty years, a number of Acts prescribed rules for civil and criminal procedure, contracts, the sale of goods, partnerships, succession, and other matters. After the fall of colonial rule this legislation was not repealed wholesale and the common law legacy became part of the legal system of India.

A similar pattern of transition was apparent in the United States. After the creation of the Union, many of the federated States adopted 'reception statutes' receiving the English common law and Acts of Parliament as they existed as of a certain date (usually 1507, 1620, or 1776), provided that they were not contrary to federal or state constitutions or statutes.

The formal recognition of the link between the law of newly independent entities and English law has not been universal but, even where it has not occurred, the English legal heritage remained part of the newly established legal system. Therefore, today the laws of jurisdictions once under British control still share many distinctive common features. The role of the judiciary, the relationship between bench and bar, the methods of legal education, and the style and substance of the legislation make the impact of the common law tradition

---

[36] On the situation in Canada, see Jacques Vanderlinden, 'La réception des systèmes juridiques européens au Canada', in *Revue d'histoire du droit* (1996), 359 ff. With respect to British colonies in Africa, see Gordon R. Woodman, 'The Peculiar Policy of Recognition of Indigenous Laws in British Colonial Africa: A Preliminary Discussion', in *Verfassung und Recht in Übersee* (1989), 273; Robert B. Seidman, 'The Reception of English Law in Colonial Africa', in Yash Ghai, Robin Luckham, and Francis Snyder (eds), *The Political Economy of Law* (1987).

[37] Werner Menski, *Hindu Law beyond Tradition and Modernity* (2003), 131 ff illustrates the impact of English rule on Hindu law. Muslim law was subject to similar pressure.

[38] *Waghela Rajsanji v Shekh Masludin* (1887) 14 Ind. App. 89, 96 (PC). The High Courts in Bombay, Calcutta, and Madras had original jurisdiction to apply the common law directly. See Martin Lau, 'The Reception of Common Law in India', in Doucet and Vanderlinden (n 28), 266 ff.

immediately clear to the foreign observer. Indeed, one could argue that some features of the original model are better preserved abroad than in England. But such a view of the matter is somewhat partial and superficial.

4. Mixed Legal Systems

Transplants and receptions have taken place across different legal traditions. In some cases, they have created mixed legal systems, that is, systems that exhibit features commonly associated with different legal traditions. Generally speaking, legal systems come in a variety of blends, for example, those produced by the influence of religious laws on secular regimes (and vice versa). In this sense, most legal systems are the result of mixing and show a motley composition. But the term 'mixed legal system' is commonly employed in a much narrower sense, that is, to denote legal systems in which the Romano-Germanic tradition (or, rather, a branch of that legal tradition, eg Spanish law, Roman Dutch law, etc.) has become suffused to some degree by English or United States law.[39]

Notable mixed jurisdictions in the latter sense include the Republic of South Africa, Scotland, Louisiana, Quebec, Puerto Rico, The Philippines, and Israel. All these legal systems have distinct foundations containing elements of both civil law and common law, though they sometimes include other components as well, depending on the circumstances. They imply a kind of pervasive duality that goes beyond mere acknowledgement of the historical origins of a specific rule or institution. For a variety of historical reasons, these systems are often indebted primarily to their civilian heritage for the foundations of their private laws and to the Anglo-American legal tradition for their constitutional and public law, including court structure and procedure. Mixed legal systems thus show that the same legal order may be open to what is now often called 'bijuralism'.[40]

5. Specific Examples

Is it possible to transfer a specific legal institution from one legal system to another? If wholesale transfers can take place, one can easily see why transfers

---

[39] For a general view of mixed jurisdictions (and a complete list of them), see Vernon V. Palmer (ed), *Mixed Jurisdictions Worldwide: The Third Legal Family* (2001). See also the papers presented to the first worldwide congress on mixed jurisdictions: (2003) 78 *Tulane LR* 1–501. For an in-depth study concerning South Africa see: Reinhard Zimmermann and Daniel Visser (eds), *Southern Cross: Civil Law and Common Law in South Africa* (1996) and the more recent essay by François du Bois and Daniel Visser, 'The Influence of Foreign Law in South Africa', (2003) 13 *Transnational Law & Contemporary Problems* 593.

[40] Nicholas Kasirer, 'Bijuralism in Law's Empire and in Law's Cosmos' (2002) 52 *Journal of Legal Education* 29.

concerning specific elements of law are possible as well. Indeed, there are countless examples. They are so numerous that one is tempted to conclude that nobody really likes to re-invent the wheel.

Transfers are easy to trace where they involve institutions that were introduced in rapid sequence in various places. If the national parliaments of several countries have, one after another, introduced workers' compensation schemes, compulsory insurance for automobile accidents, no-fault divorce, or antitrust legislation, we may rightly suspect that all these changes are somewhat related. The local law often evolves by learning from, or at least by being exposed to, other experiences.

Quite often, however, it is not easy to determine who produced the initial innovation that becomes the model. A vivid illustration of this point is provided by the diffusion of the system of land transfer that takes its name from Sir Robert Richard Torrens. Torrens was an Irish emigrant to South Australia in the nineteenth century. He claimed to have invented a system of land registration modelled after Lloyd's of London's method for keeping track of maritime insurance. He success-fully campaigned for its introduction and was eventually appointed chief land registrar under the newly established system. However, the reform he promoted was not original. In South Australia, title registration had been an issue for more than twenty years before Torrens became involved. Several bills had already been presented to Parliament before Torrens actually took up an earlier project, the handiwork of a German immigrant, Dr Ulrich Hübbe, who had modelled it on the system operating in the German Hanseatic cities, and managed to have it enacted. But wherever similar legislation was introduced, the terms 'Torrens Act' and 'Torrens titles' were employed to refer to the innovation. Its intellectual prece-dent thus fell into obscurity. For more than a century, the Australians, who knew better, insisted on speaking of their 'Real Property Act titles', rather than 'Torrens titles' but since the 1970s, they too have accepted the general terminology. The history of the diffusion of the Torrens type of land registration is noteworthy because it also shows that some innovations may cross the boundaries of legal traditions that are usually considered to be far apart. Notably, the French colonizers introduced versions of that system in Tunisia, Madagascar, French Congo, West Africa, and Morocco, though the system of land registration in France was very different (except in Alsace-Lorraine).[41]

Even today transplants tend to be eclectic—they are often no more 'coherent' than those occurring in the past. Croatia's law on company groups followed the German model, but its tender offer rules are inspired by the American model.[42]

---

[41] John Bell, 'Property and Legal Culture in France', in Peter Birks and Arianna Pretto (eds), *Themes in Comparative Law in Honour of Bernard Rudden* (2002), 83 ff, 95.

[42] Siniša Petrovic, 'The Legal Regulation of Company Groups in Croatia', (2001) 2 *European Business Organization LR* 285.

The Italians looked to American law when they reformed their criminal justice system in the 1980s, but failed to adopt several crucial aspects of it.[43]

Two general remarks are appropriate here. First, transfers are often shrouded in ambiguity. The intellectual means deployed to carry them out and their material conditions and purposes often generate this lack of clarity. Usually, each player in the game has different stakes in it, different motivations, and different (eg linguistic or conceptual) means at hand.[44] Second, a new law enacted as a consequence of a transplant cannot be considered proof that the same economic, political, or social conditions prevail in both the giving and the receiving system. Thus, one country may enact legislation strongly protective of human or consumer rights in response to human or consumer rights movements, and such legislation may become the model for the law in another country where such movements are completely absent.

IV. FACTORS OF CHANGE

Legal change is caused by a variety of factors. Historically, the migration of a population often explains transfers of law.[45] Political decisions influence law making and sometimes lead to transplants or receptions. Religious, moral, or philosophical influences have produced changes across vast geographical areas. Technological change is often at the root of similar laws in different countries. Comparative law itself is sometimes involved in the transformation of the legal system. The abundant literature on the use of comparative law by legislatures and courts shows this possibility, though legal change inspired by the example of foreign models is seldom carried out on the basis of in-depth comparative legal studies. In the last decades, the production of uniform or harmonized legal norms at the international level has become a major force stimulating legal transplants across the world. Legal instruments providing uniform rules for several jurisdictions are usually adopted in the form of international treaties and conventions. Recourse to soft law texts, pursuing substantially the same ends, is becoming increasingly common. In the public law sphere, the ongoing elaboration of human

---

[43] Elisabetta Grande, 'Italian Criminal Justice: Borrowing and Resistance', (2000) 48 *AJCL* 227.

[44] The history of the enactment of the present constitution of Japan illustrates the point: Kyoko Inoue, *MacArthur's Japanese Constitution* (1991).

[45] Rheinstein (n 1), 126, rightly notes that the law of the English colonies in America was at first the law practised in the English villages and towns that the settlers had left. On this theme see eg David Grayson Allen, *In English Ways: The Movement of Societies and the Transfer of English Local Law and Custom to the Massachusetts Bay in the Seventeenth Century* (1981).

rights instruments is a fundamental aspect of this general movement and touches upon constitutional law at the national level. Uniform and model laws are parts of the same trend with regard to private and commercial laws. Institutions such as UNCITRAL and UNIDROIT have been very active in this field and their work has a truly global dimension. Today various other entities compile and draft texts that help to disseminate uniform or harmonized models across the world.[46] Some of these organizations have a regional dimension. Thus, for example, the *Organisation pour l'Harmonisation en Afrique du Droit des Affaires* is working to reform the contract and commercial laws of sixteen African countries. Many public and private initiatives target specific geographical areas or sectors.[47] Projects of regional integration often involve the enactment of uniform or harmonized legislation, as is the case under the European Community Treaty.

Confronted with the problem of understanding legal change, comparative law, of course, pays attention to these factors and initiatives. For example, comparative law is sometimes employed to gauge how much uniformity or harmonization is actually achieved by enacting uniform or harmonized norms, or to construe the respective instruments. Yet, the study of transplants and receptions should focus particularly on three factors of legal change that feature prominently in the analysis of these phenomena. These are: imposition of law through violence in one form or another; change produced by the desire to follow prestigious models; and reform for the purpose of improving economic performance. These factors accordingly receive special attention in the following pages.

1. Imposition

Transplants and receptions have often been the result of military conquest or expansion. During the twentieth century, the extension of German law to Austria after the *Anschluss* of 1938 is a notable example. The Sovietization of the law in Central and Eastern Europe after World War II is another case in point. The growth of colonial empires in Africa, the Americas, Asia, and Oceania brought with it the importation of Western models, which were the only ones familiar to the colonizers.[48] In

---

[46] John Braithwaite and David Drahos, *Global Business Regulation* (2000) show how this is occurring across many fields.

[47] Like those that have worked to advance legal reforms in central and eastern Europe, the ABA promoted the Central European and Eurasian Law Initiative (CEELI) to advance the rule of law and the legal reform process in that area. The Center for International Legal Cooperation (based in the Netherlands) supports legal reform in developing countries and in Central and Eastern Europe as well. The German Foundation for International Legal Cooperation is active in the same area. Cp more generally John C. Reitz, 'Export of the Rule of Law', (2003) 13 *Transnational Law and Contemporary Problems* 429.

[48] See M. B. Hooker, *Legal Pluralism: An Introduction to Colonial and Neo-Colonial Laws* (1975) (reviewing the impact of British, French, and Dutch colonial laws in various areas of the world).

the Middle Ages, military expansion by Islamic rulers extended the reach of Islamic law. Contemporary military operations in different parts of the world still trigger legal transplants affecting various dimensions of the law.

However, the landscape is not uniform. On the one hand, the imposition of foreign legal models can be a dramatic but transitory experience. In that case, there is ample opportunity for the ultimate rejection of the model imposed. On the other hand, the imposition of foreign law may be backed by the permanent political or military control of the dominating power. The regime thus established often generates dual and contradictory notions of legality.[49] This happens, for example, when the law in force grants rights to only part of the population while denying equal treatment to the rest.[50] Such a strategy of differentiation was characteristic of colonial rule but by no means limited to it and shows how oppressive legal regimes may enforce exclusion and produce alienation.[51]

Domination carried out by the application of force often requires the use of local skills and abilities. It is no wonder, therefore, that the colonial rulers invested so much energy in the creation of the stereotype of the loyal colonial subject.[52] Recourse to violence has also contributed to the diffusion of law in an altogether different way, that is, by causing lawyers to emigrate to a different country where they then contribute to the development of the domestic law. The intellectual history of comparative law in the twentieth century is a testimony to this phenomenon: jurists escaping Nazism and fascism had to abandon their homeland and start a new life abroad.[53]

2. Prestige

Although legal change can be brought about by outright imposition, most often receptions and legal transplants have occurred without violence. The desire to have what others have, especially if it is deemed superior, may be enough to trigger

[49] Upendra Baxi, 'The Colonialist Heritage', in Legrand and Munday (eds) (n 34), 46 ff, 48 ff; Laureen Benton, *Law and Colonial Cultures* (2002).

[50] There are abundant illustrations of the policy mentioned in the text. See eg Bartolomé Clavero, 'Minority-Making: Indigenous People and Non-Indigenous Law between Mexico and the United States (1785–2003)', in *Quaderni fiorentini per la storia del pensiero giuridico* (2003), 175.

[51] For a broad reflection on this theme, see Sally Falk Moore, 'Certainties Undone: Fifty Turbulent Years of Legal Anthropology, 1949–1999', (2001) 7 *The Journal of the Royal Anthropological Institute* 95, 104–5 (referring the reader to the works of Richard Abel, Laura Nader, and Sally E. Merry); Jean Malaurie, 'Droit et logique coloniale', in Doucet and Vanderlinden (n 28), 449; Bernard Grossfeld, 'Comparatists and Languages', in Legrand and Munday (n 34), 154 ff, 168–9.

[52] Baxi (n 49).

[53] See eg Jack Beatson and Reinhard Zimmermann (eds), *Jurists Uprooted: German-Speaking Émigré Lawyers in Twentieth-Century Britain* (2004). On German emigré lawyers in the USA see Marcus Lutter, Ernst C. Stiefel, and Michael H. Hoeflich (eds), *Der Einfluss deutscher Emigranten auf die Rechtsentwicklung in den USA und in Deutschland* (1993).

transplants or receptions. Thus, 'prestige' motivates imitation.[54] While some have objected, describing prestige as a 'largely empty idea',[55] that objection fails to recognize that prestige is a well-known social fact.[56]

Generally speaking, prestige, like dominance, is normally associated with social stratification. Yet, as a factor of change, prestige differs from dominance in many respects. In contrast to prestige, dominance does not produce spontaneous adherence to cultural models. Furthermore, dominance is clearly dependent on the application of force and often disappears with it. Prestige does not display this dynamic. Though dominance and prestige are often joined, there are many examples of legal imitation driven by prestige alone. For example, the influence of German criminal law thinking among American scholars in recent decades can be explained only in terms of prestige.[57]

Legal change induced by the influence of a prestigious source often involves a variety of elements. A prestigious model may influence the development of the law by shaping legal ideals, institutions, categories, and rules. At least at the initial stage, those who are trying to replicate a prestigious model may be tempted to identify themselves with its authors. Thus, in the last quarter of the nineteenth century, the German professoriate became a role model for top legal academics in the United States.[58] Innovation brokers can also positively influence the diffusion of innovation associated with prestige. An innovation strongly supported by an opinion leader will spread much more rapidly than one that fails to enlist such support.[59]

Who governs the diffusion of an innovation supported by prestige? To be sure, the source proffered for imitation may provide incentives. Yet, the originators of the innovation may be unaware, or only dimly aware, of its impact elsewhere. They may know nothing (or very little) about the influence of their new model abroad and the local actors at the receiving end will manage the process of change. Their choice about what to do with the imported model can include options that would leave the authors of the original model baffled, surprised, or disappointed. An instance of this productive mismatch is the complex pattern of reception of the jurisprudence of Kelsen, Hart, and Dworkin in South America.[60]

---

[54] Rodolfo Sacco, *Introduzione al diritto comparato* (5th edn, 1993), 148 ff; Alan Watson, 'Comparative Law and Legal Change', (1978) *Cambridge LJ* 313.

[55] Ugo Mattei, 'Efficiency in Legal Transplants: An Essay in Comparative Law and Economics' (1994) 14 *International Review of Law and Economics* 3. See also *idem, Comparative Law and Economics* (1999). Later works by the same author represent a different phase of his thought.

[56] The nature of social facts like prestige has been clarified by John Searle, *The Construction of Social Reality* (1997).

[57] Elisabetta Grande, *Imitazione e diritto: ipotesi sulla circolazione dei modelli* (2000), 43 ff.

[58] Mathias Reimann, 'A Career in Itself: The German Professoriate as a Model for American Legal Academia', in Reimann (ed) (n 17).

[59] William Twining, 'Social Science and Diffusion of Law', (2005) 32 *Journal of Law and Society* 203, 217–23.

[60] Diego Eduardo Lopez de Medina, *Teoría impura del derecho: La transformación de la cultura jurídica latinoamericana* (2004) illustrates this point with respect to Colombia.

3. Economic Performance and the Transplant of Legal Institutions

Some of the most ambitious programmes of legal reform in the last decades have been launched by international financial institutions (in the first place the World Bank), or within the framework of international trade law agreements. Since 1990, the World Bank alone has supported 330 rule-of-law projects and spent almost $3 billion to fund them. The World Trade Organization agreements required legal changes on a massive scale in many countries. Many of these changes broadly qualify as legal transplants, or raise issues related to this topic. Quite often, the question is whether the transplanted law will function as expected by its supporters or merely constitute a deceptive façade behind which other arrangements prevail. The answer to this question is rarely an unqualified yes or no.

This aspect of the study of legal transplants involves an analysis of the relationship between economic performance and legal institutions. The question is whether legal transplants can improve economic performance by leading to the adoption of more efficient legal institutions. In other words, is the search for economic efficiency a major factor in producing legal transplants?

One thesis is that transplants often do facilitate the development of efficient legal institutions.[61] At first glance, this claim has some merit. The rise of similar legal institutions in different societies may be related to their capacity to lower transaction costs. The modern corporate form, trusts and other asset-management techniques, as well as negotiable instruments, among others, have replaced earlier legal forms that generated higher transaction costs. The inference is that their diffusion must be linked to their competitive advantage over alternative institutions associated with higher transaction costs.[62]

Yet, the notion that the efficiency of an institution or a rule explains its diffusion remains problematic. The idea that competition among legal institutions explains legal transplants (and more generally legal change) is questionable because of the assumptions on which it rests. The nature of decision-making under conditions of uncertainty and imperfect rationality in a world where 'ideas, ideologies, myths, dogmas, and prejudices matter',[63] suggests prudence. Nor can one ignore that vested interests play a major role in any battle for or against

---

[61] Mattei (n 55). Cp Chapter 26 of this *Handbook*.

[62] The features of these institutions in different places show significant variations, however. See eg Curtis Milhaupt (ed), *Global Markets, Domestic Institutions: Corporate Law and Governance in a New Era of Cross-Border Deals* (2003); John C. Coffee Jr, 'The Rise of Dispersed Ownership: The Roles of Law and the State in the Separation of Ownership and Control', in Klaus J. Hopt and Eddy Wymeersch (eds), *Capital Markets and Company Law* (2003), 663. On the gap that may exist between transplanted law and everyday practice, see the case study by John Gillespie, 'Transplanted Company Law: An Ideological and Cultural Analysis of Market-Entry in Vietnam', (2002) 51 *ICLQ* 641.

[63] Douglas C. North, *Economic Performance through Time* (Nobel prize lecture, 1993).

change.[64] The crucial factor in evaluating the chances of success for a proposed legal change seems to be the character of the transfer process rather than the nature of the law at stake.[65]

This is, of course, not to deny that the study of economics can provide empirical evidence about the effects of legal transplants. Thus, it is a welcome addition to the stock of tools usually employed by comparative legal studies for that purpose. Still, the quality of the economic indicators used to prove a correlation between economic performance and the law remains a persistent problem. None the less, projects pursuing reform through legal transfers are increasingly frequent. These transfers are usually supported by the promise of benefits designed to reward positive responses to the proposed changes.[66] As a consequence, governments come under pressure to introduce changes that conform to predetermined conditions. The accession to the European Union of the countries in Central and Eastern Europe is a case in point.[67] At the international level, the imposition of particular conditions promoted by donors or lenders has an impact on the respective legal systems. More than ever, reform projects based on conditional access to resources affect the respective domestic institutions.

This tendency is the result of a conscious effort to develop a new approach to economic policy-making. During most of the twentieth century, economic policy in pursuit of economic growth was designed without paying much attention to institutional settings. With respect to the countries outside the socialist block, the assumption was that once the choice of a market economy was made, the market itself would create the conditions necessary for its own success. According to this logic, it was quite enough to remove the obstacles hindering the working of the market and ensure an appropriate level of investment. The approach changed after some notable failures, for example in the countries belonging to the Commonwealth of Independent States. More sophisticated theories of economic development began to acknowledge how important the quality of the institutions available on the ground was for promoting economic growth. Eventually, a richer view of the meaning of development emerged as well.

Somewhat paradoxically, economic approaches to development have thus highlighted the importance of some factors that mainstream economics has traditionally

---

[64] See eg Michael Heller, 'A Property Theory Perspective on Russian Enterprise Reform', in Peter Murrell (ed), *Assessing the Value of Law in Transition Economies* (2001), 288 ff

[65] Cp Daniel Berkowitz, Katharina Pistor, and Jean-Francois Richard, 'The Transplant Effect', (2003) 51 *AJCL* 163; Daniel Berkowitz, Katharina Pistor, and Jean-Francois Richard, 'Economic Development, Legality, and the Transplant Effect', (2003) 47 *European Economic Review* 165–95.

[66] Cp The World Bank, *Review of World Bank Conditionality: Issues Notes* (2005). For a view from the trenches, see Sally Falk Moore, 'An International Legal Regime and the Context of Conditionality', in Michael Likowski (ed), *Transnational Legal Processes: Globalisation and Power Disparities* (2002), 333 ff

[67] Frank Schimmelfennig and Ulrich Sedelmeier, 'Governance by Conditionality: EU rule Transfer to the Candidate Countries of Central and Eastern Europe', (2004) 11 *Journal of European Public Policy* 661.

ignored, such as the quality of the legal system. Thus, international actors who have a stake in these projects now turn to the study of themes concerning legal transfers that have long been discussed in legal scholarship. It is true that interventions aimed at improving economic performance still run the risk of ignoring local knowledge. Still, the prescription of models and practices adopted in the most industrialized countries for less developed regions is now widely regarded as unsuitable and discredited.[68]

Of course, institutional change aimed at improving economic performance has a political dimension. The actors with global ambitions and powerful means are best placed to shape the politics of development. Their use of vague notions, such as 'good governance', is instrumental to these ends.[69] But orthodoxies designed for export may well be controversial at home.[70] Within this uncertain landscape, it is not easy to find a reliable standard by which to measure the legitimacy of legal transfers. Of major importance, it seems, are the accessibility of the information concerning the proposed change, the disclosure of its potential impact on the interested parties, and the degree and kind of the actors' involvement in the project.[71]

V. What Change?

Transplants and receptions have been mentioned above as a source of 'legal change' but this term itself is so vague that it invites critical scrutiny. Upon closer inspection, it turns out that transplants and receptions coexist with patterns of change and continuity in various ways.

First, new meanings can be attached to old institutions and rules. The well-known expression: *plus ça change, plus c'est la même chose*, captures the irony of the situation. Sovietologists have often investigated the degree to which soviet law relied on pre-revolutionary law. Students of French law have done the same with

---

[68] Yves Dezalay and Bryan G. Garth (eds), *Global Prescriptions: The Production, Exportation and Importation of a New Legal Orthodoxy* (2002). See also the bibliography on the law and development movement cited by Trubek (n 6).

[69] Alvaro Santos, 'The World Bank's Uses of the "Rule of Law" Promise in Economic Development', in David Trubek and Alvaro Santos (eds), *The New Law and Economic Development: A Critical Appraisal* (2006); Gianmaria Ajani, 'The Transplant of Vague Notions', in I. H. Szilágyi and M. Paksy (eds), *Ius Unum—Lex Multiplex–Festschrift in Honour of Zoltán Péteri* (2005).

[70] Yves Dezalay and Bryan G. Garth, *The Internationalization of Palace Wars: Lawyers, Economists and the Contest to Transform Latin American States* (2002).

[71] Cp Gianmaria Ajani, 'By Chance and by Prestige: Legal Transplants in Russia and Eastern Europe', (1995) 43 *AJCL* 93, on the debates concerning transplants in post-soviet regimes.

respect to the law before the French Revolution. Obviously, innovations introduced through legal transplants may show similar patterns of continuity and change.

Second, the appropriation of foreign elements may be disguised by dressing them in familiar clothes. The invocation of ancient precedents or apparently similar local practices is a strategic move that renders familiar and customary what is truly alien and novel. Such strategies help to forestall adverse reactions to change and to facilitate its acceptance. Yet, they also betray the difficulty of understanding change in its own terms. *Plus c'est la même chose, plus ça change* could be the paradoxical motto showing how innovation proceeds in this case.

Overcoming the vagueness of the notion of 'legal change' is a major goal of comparative law as a study of transplants and receptions. Any such study should begin with an enquiry about what exactly is changing. Does the change in question involve only the operative rules of the legal system? Does it affect the level of operative rules and other levels of the legal system as well? By focusing on these questions, comparative law facilitates our understanding of how continuity and change are often interwoven.[72]

An additional approach that helps us understand the variety of elements involved in legal change is the notion of legal pluralism. It was first developed to describe the coexistence of customary law, religious law, and state-sponsored law in societies where the state was confronted with instances of alternative normativity.[73] Today we need to recognize that theories of legal pluralism are also relevant to contemporary legal systems, including those in which traditional customary laws or religious laws occupy a marginal place.[74] Such theories provide a broad framework within which to discuss legal transplants that may entail a certain degree of diversity among different elements of the same legal system. Contact among different legal orders can result not only in pluralism but also in hybridization when different elements are combined into new phenomena that cannot be entirely ascribed to any single point of origin. Legal systems commonly described as 'mixed' testify to this possibility.

In all these instances, the language of the law is transformed. The appropriation of foreign elements and their introduction into the local context often requires the invention of new terminology. Sometimes the reception or transplant of foreign law generates a new legal style. Ultimately, it may bring about a new legal consciousness. The difficulty of translating legal terminology into the vernacular as well as the existence of multiple vocabularies to express new and old concepts

---

[72] A good example of this dynamic is the present influence of American law in Europe: Symposium 'L'Américanisation du droit', (2001) 45 *Archives de philosophie du droit* 7–271.

[73] Cp Hooker (n 48).

[74] Cp Moore (n 51); Jacques Vanderlinden, 'Trente ans de longue marche sur la voie du pluralisme juridique', in *Cahiers de l'anthropologie du droit* (2003), 21; Norbert Rouland, *Legal Anthropology* (trans Planel, 1994). The works of scholars like Franz and Keebet Benda-Beckman, Nicholas Kasirer, Ichiro Kitamura, Roderick Macdonald, Laura Nader, and Gunter Teubner come to mind here.

may well produce bewilderment and perplexity.[75] These are symptoms of the challenges encountered when accommodating different frames of reference within a single language. Linguists who study code-switching could find an ideal field of study here.

VI. LEGAL TRANSPLANTS AND RECEPTIONS AS UNSETTLING TOPICS

No matter how often transplants and receptions have occurred over time, the recognition of their contribution to the evolution of the world's legal systems still runs counter to some deeply held convictions about law. One of these convictions concerns the relationship between law and state authority. For a positivist, law is the expression of the will of the state. It can be unsettling to realize that law often comes from outside the state and that its adoption may have little to do with any express decision by state authority. Another conviction concerns the relationship between law and society. According to a long-standing and influential tradition of legal thought, law must reflect the mores and culture of a particular society. For adherents of that tradition, it can be unsettling to recognize that much of the law in one society is imported from another. Each of these convictions will be examined in turn.

1. Law and Authority

The recognition of legal transplants and receptions as proper objects of study has been hindered by adherence to legal positivism. Legal transplants and receptions challenge the notion that sovereign power determines legal change in all respects.[76] One response to that challenge might be that the transplants themselves occur because the sovereign power has made a decision about what the law should be. From this standpoint, the legislative adoption of a foreign code, for example, is merely legal positivism writ large. As mentioned above, some transplants do indeed occur because those in authority wish to adopt a solution that has proven itself elsewhere.

---

[75] For an excellent study concerning the Japanese situation, see Ichiro Kitamura, *Problems of the Translation of Law in Japan* (1993).

[76] The point is forcefully made by Alan Watson, *Roman Law and Comparative Law* (1991), 97.

Nevertheless, this view attributes more control over the law to those in authority than they commonly possess. It also fails to recognize that legal transplants concern not only rules enacted by the sovereign but also ideals and modes of thought that are highly influential without being formally sanctioned.

It is true that even borrowing elements beyond positive rules can be the result of a rational decision by those in authority. Careful evaluations are sometimes made of the content of what is borrowed along with forecasts of the outcome of the experiment triggered by the transplant. There is something reassuring in knowing that others have already experimented with the element under consideration for adoption. Most transplants, however, are not the result of such conscious decisions nor are they supported by superior knowledge of what is imported. Historically, even proponents of transplants have rarely claimed perfect knowledge of what is eventually transplanted, nor have they necessarily evaluated it thoroughly. In fact, recourse to a legal transfer can be an open admission of weakness or lack of expertise. This raises the question to what extent even a transplant sanctioned by authority is a clear-sighted decision about what the law should be. How much understanding do lawmakers around the world have regarding the implications of their actions? How often do they act in clear recognition of the alternatives? In short, to what extent do those vested with authority really determine the content of the law?

Moreover, many legal transplants are neither mandated by those in authority nor concerned with any practical changes which might be of interest to them. Jurists have developed models of how people might live in society by choosing to work with a great variety of sources, many of which are remote or obscure. Often, they have not done so because their aims are realistic or practical or focused on the need to replace one legal rule with another. Thus, borrowings may reflect the desire to realize a certain ideal more than a realistic assessment of what can or should be done. When Roman law was revived by university teaching in the Middle Ages, it was at first simply a grand ideal. In a similar vein, natural law was developed as an ideal model to which actual legal orders did not necessarily conform. Even today, the best law students are required to learn not only positive laws but also to reflect upon what the law should be. Academics regularly develop purely theoretical perspectives in their publications that are completely unrelated to the practice of law in their jurisdiction (or, indeed, in any jurisdiction). These are not anomalies—there are countless legal norms across the world that set ideals or goals to be attained rather than rules to be followed. The law is deeply involved with matters of principle,[77] as well as with more mundane considerations. The study of legal transplants and receptions highlights this reality, and it is important to understand it if we are to grasp the way in which legal transfers change the law. They

---

[77] This is why prices should not be confused with sanctions, and vice versa. They do not work the same way: Robert Cooter, 'Prices and Sanctions', (1984) 84 *Columbia LR* 1523.

need not do so because sovereign authority mandates some specific change, and they also highlight the gap between transplanting formal legal sources and transmitting tacit assumptions about law.

Even when those vested with authority have decided what law to import, the process of adaptation to the local environment will often add new and unexpected elements to the import. This is inevitable. It makes little sense to view these additions as distortions of the original model that would inexplicably fail to be reproduced locally. Although we commonly speak of 'adaptation' to denote this process of transformation, the expression must not mislead us. Sometimes these 'adaptations' actually increase the functionality of the import, but there are also 'adaptations' that are not 'functional' at all. Some reflect resistance to the import while others simply result from quirks of history. Be that as it may, imports are rarely received passively and any innovation faces challenges by forces that may resist change. In the world of law, just as in the physical world, there is no action without reaction.

Thus, those in authority are limited in their control of what the law is. That they are limited in these ways is perfectly consistent with the role a positivist ascribes to them: they possess authority and, indeed, sovereign authority. If that is all a positivist claims, legal transplants should not be unsettling. But they are unsettling if the positivist claims that the content of the law is merely what the sovereign has decided it should be. Transplants and receptions prove otherwise.

2. Law and Society

Legal transplants can also be unsettling to those who believe that law must reflect the mores and culture of a particular society. When law is transplanted, it passes from one society to another. To be sure, if all one believes is that the culture of a society is one force among many that influence the law's contents, there is nothing unsettling about that. But if law is considered inextricably bound and determined by social and cultural factors, transplants and receptions become a problem.

The common stock of ideas that most lawyers share about the relationship between law and society has been shaped by some grand narratives. Montesquieu's classical work on *The Spirit of the Laws* (1748) is a work that has foundational value for comparative law studies as well as for sociology. It is often cited to support the view that legal transplants and receptions have no influence on the evolution of legal systems. The conventional account of the work is that, for Montesquieu, it was 'a great coincidence' if the laws of one nation actually suited another. This has lead to the conclusion that the factors shaping the evolution of the law are inextricably linked with forces at work on the local level, which Montesquieu duly listed.[78] But

---

[78] Charles de Secondat, Baron de Montesquieu, *The Spirit of the Laws* (4th edn, T. Nugent trans, 1766) Book I, Chapter 3, p 7.

when reading Montesquieu, it is important not to miss a point often overlooked by his commentators. His argument against transplants was just that: an argument. Montesquieu was *arguing* against the advisability of legal transplants rather than coldly observing their failure or denying their possibility. His point was normative, not descriptive. When Montesquieu wrote, Roman law was still applicable in much of France, and his approach tended to undermine the universal claims of Roman law as *ratio scripta*.[79]

In the first half of the nineteenth century, Savigny conceptualized the relationship between law and society along similar lines but he added a romantic twist and effectively presented Roman law as an inextricable part of the German legal tradition.[80] After Montesquieu and Savigny, the idea of an organic connection between the law and the particular character of the people gained immense popularity. It became standard fare in European legal thought.[81] Incredibly, this idea won recognition just when the world was experiencing waves of legal transplants on an immense scale—without the paradox being noticed.

In due time, sociology, emerging from the tradition inaugurated by Montesquieu, embraced the notion that law reflects the constitution of society. Thus, in his classic work on the division of labour in society, Emile Durkheim argued that the law is an index or mirror of society.[82] Again, the claim of congruence and consistency between the law and society featured in Durkheim's work, just as in the grand narratives of Montesquieu and Savigny, required his readers to remain blind towards the reality around them. Eventually, the inconsistencies, contradictions, tensions, and vagaries in the law-and-society story were too obvious to go unchallenged. For a while, facts that did not fit the model could be explained away as due to time-lag or transition, or as peculiar to a particular historical period of development. In the end, however, the disparity between model and fact could no longer simply be ignored or side-stepped.

Thus today, the explanatory power of that model is doubtful.[83] This is partially due to the fragmentation of our notions of 'society' and 'community', which is now a common theme among anthropologists and sociologists investigating law.[84] By now, it is also clear that the law makes communities and societies just as it, in turn, is made by them. Legal institutions matter, and traditions can be 'invented'.

It is also notoriously difficult to make precise empirical claims about the

[79] See Robert Launay, 'Montesquieu: The Specter of Despotism and the origins of Comparative Law', in Annelise Riles (ed), *Rethinking the Masters of Comparative Law* (2001), 22, 23 ff.

[80] Peter Stein, *Legal Evolution: The Story of an Idea* (1980), 56 ff.

[81] Jhering was not convinced, however: cp Stein (n 80), 65–6.

[82] Emile Durkheim, *The Division of Labour in Society* (1893, W. D. Halls trans, 1984). In later works Durkheim softened his position.

[83] See Chapter 24 of the present *Handbook*.

[84] Cp Roger Cotterell, 'Is there a Logic of Legal Transplants?', in David Nelken and Johannes Feest (eds), *Adapting Legal Cultures* (2001), 71 ff.

relationship between law and society.[85] Even quantitative studies on specific issues are facing the proverbial chicken and egg question.[86] It would be naïve to assume that whatever keeps society together is always disturbed by the changes triggered by transplants and receptions, at least when they are not imposed. If those changes are a regular occurrence in the history of mankind, they cannot be thought of as more 'artificial' than the supposedly 'organic' ones. It is also naïve to think that a legal innovation is bound to take firmer roots where it was first produced, rather than elsewhere. Countless legislative projects abort in their country of origin but succeed abroad. Conversely, in some places, local innovations improve their chance of acceptance when they come dressed up in foreign clothes. Indeed, comparative studies often show that 'function' is the most elusive concept in the law and society discourse.

In recent years, Pierre Legrand has challenged the idea that legal transplants and receptions play a major role in producing legal change.[87] Legrand rests his claim not on a theory of how societies are constituted but on a denial that law can move from one society to another without a change in content. For Legrand, law does not have a determinate content apart from a given culture. Therefore, it cannot have the same content outside the community that first establishes it; thus it makes no sense to speak of legal transplants. Legrand argues that every language and every culture produces indigenous systems of meaning and world-views. These are bound to interfere with the very attempt to transfer law and will ultimately render such a transfer impossible. If comparative law ignores the significance of cultural diversity and difference, it can only approach the matter in a bookish or technical fashion, which is what Legrand sees in Watson's work on transplants.[88] Moreover, Legrand claims, Watson's approach is inherently conservative because it 'lacks any critical vocation'.[89]

---

[85] Lawrence Friedman, 'Some Comments on Cotterell and Legal Transplants', in Nelken and Feest (eds) (n 84), 93, at 94.

[86] Erhard Blankenburg, 'Patterns of Legal Culture: The Netherlands Compared to Neighboring Germany', (1998) 46 *AJCL* 1.

[87] Legrand's many contributions on legal transplants cannot all be cited in the space of a footnote. A representative sample includes at least: Pierre Legrand, 'What Legal Transplants?', in Nelken and Feest (eds) (n 84), 54 ff, first published under the title 'The Impossibility of Legal Transplants', (1997) 4 *Maastricht Journal of European and Comparative Law* 111; *idem*, 'The Same and the Different', in Legrand and Munday (eds) (n 34), 240 ff; idem, 'Issues in the Translatability of Law', in Sandra Berman and Michael Wood (eds), *Nation, Language and the Ethics of Translation* (2005). Mitchel de S.-O. l'E. Lasser, 'The Question of Understanding', ibid 197 ff provides a helpful reading of Legrand's work. What follows in the text is my attempt to offer a concise critical discussion of his work on transplants, rather than a surrogate of it.

[88] See also Charles Donahue, 'Comparative Legal History in North America', (1997) 65 *Tijdschrift voor Rechtsgeschiedenis* 1, 15. For Watson's rejoinder, see Watson, 'Legal Transplants and European Private Law', (2000) 4.4 *Electronic Journal of Comparative Law*, <http://www.ejcl.org> (*Ius Commune Lectures on European Private Law*, 2).

[89] Legrand, 'What Legal Transplants' (n 87), 65–6. In the same sense, see Richard L. Abel, 'Law as Lag: Inertia as a Social Theory of Law', (1982) 80 *Michigan LR* 785, 803.

The argument that Watson's approach is conservative and may, therefore, promote undesirable political agendas can be dismissed rather quickly. The argument can simply be turned on its head: one can use Watson's approach just as well to develop a democratic critique of ruling elites.[90] Indeed, the study of transplants and receptions adds leverage to comparative law as a tool to debunk ideological perceptions of legal orders on a world scale.[91]

Closer consideration is owed to Legrand's larger claim that law does not have a determinate content apart from a given culture. It is true that when cultural differences are ignored, the focus on receptions and legal transplants can lead to facile conclusions about differences and similarities among legal systems. Here, comparatists should be mindful of a simple truth: 'Once everything is the same, comparison will be impossible, or at any rate impossibly boring'.[92] All comparatists whose motto is *vive la difference!* will welcome Legrand's resistance to such an approach.

Nevertheless, it is far from clear that the transfer of law from one community to another is impossible (incidentally making the topic of this very chapter illusory). Ultimately, such a view rests on a claim about language and a claim about culture, both of which need to be examined more closely.

The claim about language is that it is so bound to culture that the terms of one language cannot have the same meaning in another. It is true that natural languages to some extent divide the world in different ways, as many have noticed. Still, languages have an open and evolving character that allows for linguistic change and cross-cultural communication.[93] Several legal systems have adopted multilingual laws. This shows that the same norms can, in principle, be expressed in several languages. The question whether cross-border communication can ever be 'complete' assumes that there can be 'complete' communication within any single linguistic system. But this assumption is questionable to begin with because it sets an impossible ideal standard. Our everyday life is a monument to misunderstanding, no matter what language we speak. On the other hand, the linguistic systems of individuals are often far more complex than the linking language, culture, and the law are willing to admit. Whole communities of individuals use different languages, spoken and written, for different purposes and in different contexts. This is not a recent phenomenon, that is, a by-product of modernity or of post-modernity. These facts are irreconcilable with a romantic view in which

---

[90] Pier Giuseppe Monateri, 'Everybody's Talking: The Future of Comparative Law', (1998) 21 *Hastings International and Comparative Law Review* 825, 840, advances this reading of Watson's work.

[91] Cp Duncan Kennedy, 'Two Globalizations of Law and Legal Thought: 1850–1968', (2003) 36 *Suffolk University LR* 631; Lopez de Medina (n 60).

[92] Tony Weir, 'The Timing of Decisions', (2001) *Zeitschrift für Europäisches Privatrecht* 678, 685.

[93] More generally, research on cognition mechanisms contradicts the idea that cultures are cages: Raffaele Caterina, 'Comparative Law and the Cognitive Revolution', (2004) 78 *Tulane LR* 1501. On the possibilities of legal translation see Legrand's 'Issues' (n 87), but also Susan Šarčević, *New Approaches to Legal Translation* (1997).

there is an indissoluble bond among law, language, and culture. Communication that takes place across linguistic or cultural boundaries is neither flawed nor doomed by definition. In short, there are problems with Legrand's claim about language.

His claim about culture is that each culture represents a unified and indigenous system of meaning. But this claim is problematic as well. If law is culture, we should be open to the idea that law, like culture, is the outcome of mishmash, borrowings, mixtures that have occurred, though at different rates, ever since the beginning of time.[94] If we view culture in this way, we can make sense of the opposing claims made by Watson and Legrand about legal transplants. According to Watson, 'the transplant of legal rules is socially easy'.[95] The difficult task is the intellectual work that transplantation or reception requires. Students may have to learn Justinian's Institutes, read cases in law reports, or familiarize themselves with the civil code (and perhaps even all these things at once). Legislators, judges, lawyers, and commentators may draw inspiration from an extraordinary variety of sources while doing their jobs. It is not self-evident that when they do so, they will accord primacy to local sources rather than the ones they seek to borrow. At the same time, however, the meaning of the import will be determined by the sense that the local user gives it. The transfer of law (just like that of other cultural elements) involves the reproduction of certain elements across time or space. This is not a mechanical process. It involves human learning, and learning cannot take place without improvization and experimentation. Learning is both imitative, as it requires following a model, and improvisational and experimental because the model must be tested. Needless to say, this process is rather creative, as any teacher knows. But creative interpretation does not take place in a vacuum—it takes place in a cultural context. Consequently, it is idle to ask if there can be perfect imitation because such perfection is simply not the point. To be sure, this cultural dynamic may involve the sacrifice of autochthonous elements of culture. But it does not imply a passive attitude by the culture that is exposed to change.[96]

Hence, there is some truth in Legrand's claim that 'the transplant' cannot survive the change of context. The essential point is that the law is a product embedded in the specific culture of the local actors, a culture that is usually

---

[94] Claude Lévi-Strauss, *Race and History* (1952), 28. Cp Ulf Hannerz, *Cultural Complexity: Studies in the Social Organization of Meaning* (1990). To be sure, as Legrand himself illustrates, the local community can be unwilling to concede that its identity (like all identities) is syncretic: Pierre Legrand, 'Comparative Contraventions', (2005) 50 *McGill LJ* 669, 672–3.

[95] Alan Watson, *Legal Transplants: An Approach to Comparative Law* (2nd edn, with an afterword, 1993), 95.

[96] For this reason Esin Örücü, 'Law as Transposition', (2002) 51 *ICLQ* 205, proposed a new metaphor to speak of legal transplants. I do not know if the metaphor will stick, but the point is well taken.

different—and sometimes radically different—from the culture that produced the imported law. This is not an endorsement of the extreme view that law has no determinate content apart from a given culture. It is simply based on the familiar view that the meaning of law is not fully determined, and that each interpreter will influence how it is understood. Consequently, although the meaning of law, like any other cultural element, may be manipulated, rearranged, transformed, and distorted as it is passed on, the transmission of law from one culture to another can still take place. Thus, it is wrong to claim that '[a]t best, what can be displaced from one jurisdiction to another is, literally, a meaningless form of words'.[97] That would be true only if cultures were so totally distinct that the law of one culture meant nothing in another. But cultures are not that distinct. Although they are unique configurations produced by the individuals who share them, cultures interact and change through the transmission of cultural elements—every day and throughout the world. The identity of a cultural group is not compromised by change through contact with another culture, except in tragic cases.[98] On the contrary, the selective appropriation of foreign cultural characteristics is often crucial to the maintenance of a living culture.

Legrand does not deny this.[99] He is simply strongly objecting to the urge to make comparative law the white knight in the quest for the unification of different legal systems in Europe as elsewhere and, thus, to the strait-jacket that such an approach imposes on comparative legal research. When Legrand's claims are understood in this, qualified, manner, the existence of legal transplants need not be unsettling to those who believe that law indeed reflects the culture of a particular society.

VII. Lessons

We can now ask what the study of legal transplants can teach us about law. We have seen that in order to understand transplants, we must not regard them simply as expressions of sovereign authority. Instead, we must consider the variety of roles played by those who initiate them, be they state authorities, interest groups, or academic or professional elites. We can also see that we must consider how law is transformed when it is transplanted.

---

[97] Legrand, 'What Legal Transplants?' (n 87), 63.
[98] See on this point the seminal contribution by Fredrik Barth (ed), *Ethnic Groups and Boundaries* (1969).
[99] See eg Pierre Legrand, 'Issues' (n 87), 48 n 47: 'It seems pertinent to repeat that I should not be understood as arguing that communication across legal cultures is absolutely impossible'.

Neither of these considerations is directly related to the law's overall intellectual coherence, rationality, and responsiveness to society's needs. Some scholars regard these factors as essential to any intellectually satisfactory account of law and they criticize studies of legal transplants for neglecting them. Yet, such criticism is ultimately misconceived. Legal transplants are winning increasing attention in comparative law circles precisely because they challenge the philosophical emphasis on the law's overall intellectual coherence, rationality, and responsiveness to society's needs.

The distorting effect of this philosophical emphasis on theories which propose unified generic concepts of 'the law', 'legal culture', and 'society' becomes obvious here. One can also see this effect in studies that try to explain successful transplants in terms of their 'fit' with the society that adopts them. And can see it in the efforts of comparative law scholars to classify legal systems into legal families. As we will see, each of these approaches misunderstands how and why transplants occur because they have all been led astray by the emphasis on coherence, rationality, and responsiveness to society's needs.

In short, legal theories proposing generic concepts of 'law', 'legal culture', and 'society' and stressing the law's coherence and consistency lead to stereotypes when the true issue is what, exactly, travels across time and space. Thus, such theories are part of the problem, rather than a key to the solution.[100]

To understand legal change in a comparative perspective, one must recognize that law in society is not the coherent and consistent object described by these generic concepts. 'The law' is really a generalization denoting a collage of legal artefacts.[101] Thus, within the same legal system, a multiplicity of factors can be at work. It may well happen that the application of the provisions of the French civil code falls into the hand of lawyers steeped in German legal thinking, who will read these provisions through the lenses of German legal categories. It may also happen that the structure of Justinian's Institutes is adopted to expound the common law, though the relationship between the two is, at best, elusive. Such odd combinations are rather common. Soviet lawyers could employ the notion of a legal act (*Rechtsgeschäft*)—the very symbol of private autonomy throughout the nineteenth century—while developing socialist law under a system of central planning. Islamic law may well accommodate customary elements of law which do not fully accord with, or indeed contradict, its sacred principles.

When we recognize this multiplicity, we can see that what crosses boundaries is highly diverse in both substance and form, even though it may simply be 'the law' to the untrained eye. Unified visions of legal cultures and legal orders should

---

[100] Cp Stig Strömholm, 'Comparative Legal Science—Risk and Possibilities', in Marku Suksi (ed), *Law under Exogenous Influences* (1994), 5 ff.

[101] Rodolfo Sacco, 'Legal Formants. A Dynamic Approach to Comparative Law', (1991) 39 *AJCL* 1; Alan Watson, 'From Legal Transplants to Legal Formants', (1995) 43 *AJCL* 469.

thus be replaced by a more analytic, dynamic, and realistic picture of the local law, which also comprises that law's interaction with other legal orders. Comparative law, as the study of legal transplants and receptions, shows that mismatch and contradiction are as much features of law as are consistency and coherence.

The process of transplantation and reception is often explained in terms of the supposed 'fit' between the transferred law and the local context. Scholars who take this approach often distinguish between autonomous and semi-autonomous institutions, or between self-contained and non-self-contained transplants, and so on.[102] Such distinctions are drawn in order to show which elements of the law can be transplanted (because they are rather loosely connected with their place of origin) and which cannot. It is commonly assumed, for example, that law governing economic matters (such as contracts) is rather easily transplanted while law pertaining to more culture-bound matters, such as family or succession law, is more resistant to reception. This approach, again, seeks consistency and rationality but by doing so, it distorts reality. One problem is that it pays insufficient attention to the reasons why transplants succeed or fail. They may fail on rather specific grounds, rather than simply on lack of 'fit', for example, because they are opposed by vested interests that would be adversely affected by legal change.[103] Another problem is that this approach does not explain how transplants actually occur. That law reflects or constitutes many of society's arrangements is beyond doubt. But the law may exhibit no obvious connection with those arrangements. The claim that legal transplants occur because they 'fit' rests on broad generalizations about what is, and what is not, resistant to transplants and receptions. These generalizations are not supported by the study of the actual transplants themselves. The evidence advanced to support them is usually anecdotal and thus hardly compelling.[104] Indeed, there are glaring examples which run completely counter to the explanation of transplants by virtue of 'fit' with the recipient culture. Up to this day, for example, the English and the Scottish laws of contracts exhibit a number of significant differences that would be difficult to explain from the standpoint criticized here.

---

[102] See the classic article by Otto Kahn-Freund, 'On Uses and Misuses of Comparative Law', (1972) 37 *Modern LR* 1.

[103] Compare the explanation of English resistance to good faith advanced by Hein Kötz, 'Towards a European Civil Code: The Duty of Good Faith', in Peter Cane and Jane Stapleton (eds), *The Law of Obligations: Essays in Celebration of John Fleming* (1998), 243 ff (most English precedents concern commercial cases; the litigation raising issues of good faith in other jurisdictions is of a different nature), with that advanced by Gunter Teubner, 'Legal Irritants: Good Faith in British Law or How Unifying Law Ends up in New Divergencies', (1998) 61 *Modern LR* 11 (the type of capitalism prevailing in Britain would be the key to understanding English resistance to that notion. But what about Scotland then?).

[104] Cotterell (n 84), 71 ff, 80 ff, gives many examples of similar anecdotal evidence. David Nelken, 'Comparatists and Transferability', in Legrand and Munday (eds) (n 34), 446 ff, 457, rightly notes that: 'Legal transfers are frequently—perhaps predominantly—geared to fitting an imagined *future*' (emphasis in original).

Yet another problem is that the approach of explaining transplants by their degree of 'fit' disregards the actors who effect transplants. Who these actors are affects what is transplanted. The study of legal transplants and receptions shows that networks of individuals and sub-communities have a conspicuous part in the diffusion of legal models across the world. Detailed investigations conducted at this level demonstrate who does what and for what purposes. Such investigations reveal more about the relationship between law and society than any broad generalization about the mutual 'fit' between them.

As we have seen, the sheer application of force has been a formidable engine of legal transfer. History also shows that change through transplants and receptions has often been produced by subtler means. The role of university teaching in the production and diffusion of legal innovation has been historically prominent. Today, transplants are regularly undertaken in the belief that imitation reduces the costs of legal innovation, at least in the short term.[105] Imitation based on this motivation need not ascribe prestige to its sources and may depend on circumstances that are entirely fortuitous. Private actors, such as global law firms, or organizations that receive governmental support, are also promoting the diffusion of legal models on a scale that was unknown before.[106] These global actors are actively pursuing strategies of legal change based on the mobility of law. The contemporary dynamics of legal change across the world can simply not be understood without attention to the global and international dimension of the subject. In short, 'fit' may matter, but so do the mechanisms of change. To be sure, to explain transplants in terms of 'fit' is attractive because it asserts coherence with pre-existing law. But reality is less coherent and more dynamic. Perhaps the limits of cultural transmission are ultimately only those set by our genes.[107]

Yet another way in which those who study comparative law have sought coherence is by attempting to divide the world into separate legal families and legal traditions. Comparative law assigns local law to such families and traditions by recording legal patterns that cross political boundaries. But these patterns are mostly the effect of transplants and receptions, rather than of independent parallel evolution caused by the uniform agency of extra-legal factors.

We are not concerned here with a general critique of such taxonomic exercises. Suffice it say that they are of little help for the study of legal transplants themselves. This study has shown that the boundaries of the world's legal systems are not

---

[105] Alan Watson, 'Aspects of Reception of Law', (1996) 44 *AJCL* 335; Jonathan M. Miller, 'A Typology of Legal Transplants: Using Sociology, Legal History and Argentine Examples to Explain the Transplant Process', (2003) 51 *AJCL* 839, 845, notes that transplants with this motivation 'may appear to have ludicrously little link to the drafter's society'.

[106] Yves Dezalay, *Marchands de droit: la restructuration de l'ordre juridique international par les multinationales du droit* (1992).

[107] Natural sciences define cultural transmission as the transmission of information between individuals by non-genetic means.

watertight. Legal transfers regularly take place across those boundaries, irrespective of what comparative lawyers think about legal families and legal traditions. Indeed, transfers occur even while boundaries between one legal system and another are being drawn and where the significance of law for the identity of a society is emphasized. Therefore, the study of transplants and receptions shows that many qualifications are in order when presenting the world's legal systems as a group of legal families. This study also provides a better account of the resemblances among these families.

VIII. Conclusion

Comparative law studies tell us that legal orders owe their existence to both original innovation and borrowing. This mix produces a variety of unique legal experiences.

The study of legal transfers offers considerable intellectual rewards. It shows that the law is a complex phenomenon and corrects simplistic views regarding what law is and how it develops. The spread of legal institutions, ideals, ideologies, doctrines, rules, and so on, is often in the hands of professional elites. The study of transplants and receptions demonstrates that the knowledge and standing of those elites comes from interactions between the local and non-local dimensions of the law, that is, between the national and international spheres. This picture is true in Berlin and in New York, in London and in Lima, but it is also true in less cosmopolitan environments. The conditions under which this interaction takes place deserve careful study.

Students of legal transplants have often emphasized that the correlation between law and society is not self-evident as the law migrates. Here, we also need to take into account the communities and individuals involved in the transfer. As we have seen, to understand transfer, one must first consider the role of those who bring it about, whether they are state authorities, individuals, groups, global actors, or members of the academic or professional elite. One must also examine the ways in which what is borrowed is not lost in the process, but nevertheless transformed.

The study of legal transplants has sometimes been accused of embracing a conservative orientation. Yet, ultimately this study simply subjects the law's pretensions concerning its origins and ends to critical analysis. Doing so is not inconsistent with advancing progressive goals at all; in fact, it may actually be vital to a progressive agenda.

BIBLIOGRAPHY

The literature on legal transplants and receptions is large and fragmented. Most comparative law handbooks contain helpful references, as do the footnotes of this chapter.

Edward M. Wise, 'The Transplant of Legal Patterns' (1990) 38 *AJCL* 1 ff (Supp)

Rodolfo Sacco, 'La circulation des modèles juridiques', in *Rapports géneraux au XIII Congrès International de droit comparé—Montreal 1990* (1992), 1

Mathias Reimann (ed), *The Reception of Continental Ideas in the Common Law World 1820–1920* (1993)

Mathias Reimann, *Historische Schule und Common Law: Die Deutsche Rechtswissenschaft des 19. Jahrhunderts im amerikanischen Rechtsdenken* (1993)

Alan Watson, *Legal Transplants* (1974; 2nd edn, 1993)

Michel Doucet and Jacques Vanderlinden (eds), *La réception des systèmes juridiques: implantation et destin* (1994)

Ugo Mattei, 'Efficiency in Legal Transplants: An Essay in Comparative Law and Economics', (1994) 14 *International Review of Law & Economics* 3

Pierre Legrand, 'The Impossibility of Legal Transplants' (1997) 4 *Maastricht Journal of European and Comparative Law* 111

Pier Giuseppe Monateri, 'The Weak Law: Contaminations and Legal Cultures', Global Jurist Advances : 1(3), Article 5

David Nelken and Johannes Feest (eds), *Adapting Legal Cultures* (2001)

Erin Örücü, 'Law as Transposition' (2002) 51 *ICLQ* 205

Daniel Berkowitz, Katharina Pistor, and Jean-Francois Richard, 'The Transplant Effect', (2003) 51 *AJCL* 163

Jonathan M. Miller, 'A Typology of Legal Transplants: Using Sociology, Legal History and Argentine Examples to Explain the Transplant Process', (2003) 51 *AJCL* 839

Inga Markovits, 'Exporting Law Reform—But Will It Travel?', (2004) 37 *Cornell International Law Journal* 95

William Twining, 'Diffusion of Law: A Global Perspective' (2005) 49 *Journal of Legal Pluralism* 1

Gianmaria Ajani, 'Transplants, Legal Borrowings and Reception', in David S. Clark and Bertha Wilson (gen eds), *Encyclopaedia of Law & Society* (2006)

CHAPTER 14

COMPARATIVE LAW
AND THE STUDY
OF MIXED
LEGAL SYSTEMS

JACQUES DU PLESSIS

Stellenbosch

I. INTRODUCTION

LEGAL systems generally are 'mixed' in the sense that they have been influenced by a variety of other systems.[1] However, traditionally the term 'mixed' is only used to describe a relatively small group of legal systems or jurisdictions[2] which have been shaped so significantly by both the civil law and common law traditions that they cannot be brought home comfortably under either. Thus, as far as their substantive law is concerned, key areas of the private law in many of these systems are predominantly civilian (in some it is even codified), whereas commercial law quite often strongly bears the imprint of the common law. And while public law in general has been strongly influenced by the common law, aspects of the criminal law, and more recently even constitutional law, at times display civilian features. Procedurally, these systems have in turn generally adopted a common law approach to adjudication: the judge is at the forefront of legal development, and precedent is generally regarded as binding and as more authoritative than academic writings.

The origins of this narrow approach to the notion of a 'mixed legal system' are at least as old as the subject of comparative law itself. Already in 1899, one year before the World Exhibition in Paris, which heralded the dawn of comparative law as a modern discipline, Frederick Parker Walton of McGill University pointed out that the legal systems of Scotland, Louisiana, and Québec defy classification by occupying a position 'midway' between the common law and civil law.[3] That the emergence of an awareness of these systems is closely linked to the rise of

---

[1] See Vernon Valentine Palmer, 'Introduction to the Mixed Jurisdictions', in Vernon Valentine Palmer (ed), *Mixed Jurisdictions Worldwide: The Third Legal Family* (2001), 3, 11; on the 'mixed' nature of the civil law and common law of obligations see Reinhard Zimmermann, *Roman Law, Contemporary Law, European Law: The Civilian Tradition Today* (2001), 159.

[2] The term 'mixed jurisdiction' describes the political unit, such as a country or province, in which a 'mixed legal system' applies; see William Tetley, 'Mixed Jurisdictions: Common Law v Civil Law (Codified and Uncodified)', (1999) 3 *Uniform LR* 591, 593; reprinted in (2000) 60 *Louisiana LR* 678, 685.

[3] F. P. Walton, 'The Civil Law and the Common Law in Canada', (1899) 11 *Juridical Review* 282, 291; see further Kenneth Reid's pioneering study of the origin of mixed legal systems, 'The Idea of Mixed Legal Systems', (2003) 78 *Tulane LR* 5, 8 ff.

comparative law is neither surprising nor coincidental: from the outset, one of the main interests of comparative lawyers has been to classify legal systems into families. When the civil law and common law came to be viewed as dominant categories—indeed, Walton even went so far as to refer to them as 'the two great legal systems of Christendom'[4]—it was inevitable that some label would be invented to describe systems that were strongly influenced by both these traditions.

Yet the circumstances surrounding the birth of the awareness of mixed systems cannot be described as particularly fortunate. First, the dominant spirit was still that of legal nationalism.[5] It may have been recognized that these systems had a separate identity from those of their parents, but they were rather neglected and lonely children—for a very long time scant attention was paid to any special characteristics which would make it worthwhile to study them in their own right. To make matters worse, this lack of attention was not only from the side of the parents. The siblings hardly seem to have been aware of each other's existence. It has even been said, with some parody, that the protracted isolated development of these culturally and geographically diverse regions resembled a 'grandiose and perverse experiment of legal science'.[6] Second, mixed systems were not generally formed by free, autonomous selection from the civil law and common law. They were almost all the product of colonialism—more specifically, successive waves of colonization by powers governed by the civil law and the common law. The pressure to conform to foreign influence could therefore be a more powerful determinant of change than a balanced weighing up of the merits of rules from these respective traditions. Furthermore, colonial power also resulted in the suppression, and even virtual obliteration of the customary law of indigenous populations.[7] Where the customary law did remain in force, it generally had to conform to the Western law, and was not regarded as a prominent feature of the legal landscape.

However, over the past decade, there has been a remarkable reversal of the fortunes of mixed jurisdictions. Lawyers working within them have acquired a sense of self-worth, and are displaying greater interest in each other's experiences. The parochialism which has characterized so much traditional legal analysis is subsiding in light of the demands of greater regional and global cooperation. This development has been characterized by an increased appreciation of the value of comparative analysis, which in turn has heightened the relevance of the experiences of mixed systems in blending civil law and common law. This renders it opportune to consider the relationship between the study of these systems and

---

[4] Walton, (1899) 11 *Juridical Review* 282.
[5] See Reinhard Zimmermann, 'Savigny's Legacy: Legal History, Comparative Law, and the Emergence of a European Legal Science', (1996) 112 *LQR* 576.
[6] Reid, (2003) 78 *Tulane LR* 7–8.   [7] See Palmer (n 1), 5.

comparative law. This chapter will especially focus on what these studies reveal about the broader comparative themes of the classification of legal systems, whether and how borrowing can take place, the quality of the law to which borrowing gives rise, the connection between civil law and the common law in the European context, and the role which language can play in comparative analysis and legal development. But to further this goal, it is first necessary to get a firmer grasp on the concept of the mixed legal system itself.

II. The Concept of the Mixed Legal System

Legal families are essentially groups of legal systems with certain shared features. Given that comparative lawyers may have different aims in grouping together legal systems, they can understandably differ about what these features should be, and consequently can come up with various classifications. Traditionally, the most prominent families have been configurations of the civil law and common law, whereas other families (eg those of customary or religious law) had to be satisfied with more modest positions. This relative prominence reflects the traditionally Eurocentric and private law-biased outlook of the classifiers. However, whatever the differences in detail may be, all these classifications have to deal with the phenomenon that a system can display the features of more than one family to the extent that it cannot easily be brought home under any one of them.[8] Comparative lawyers can deal with this phenomenon in a variety of ways.

The first is simply to concede that nothing can be done to attribute these systems to the 'right' family.[9] Until such time as these systems acquire characteristics that align them more closely to one group rather than another, they remain in a classificatory limbo. But, as Kenneth Reid has pointed out in the context of the traditional mixed systems, where these systems enjoy political autonomy and a developed legal literature, they can achieve a certain 'equilibrium', which means there is no

---

[8] This is also true of some modern classifications that differ quite radically from the traditional approaches: cf Ugo Mattei, 'Three Patterns of Law: Taxonomy and Change in the World's Legal Systems', (1997) 45 *AJCL* 5, 40.

[9] Systems which have been mentioned in this regard include Scotland, South Africa, Lousiana, Québec, Israel, the Philippines, Puerto Rico, Greece, the People's Republic of China: Konrad Zweigert and Hein Kötz, *An Introduction to Comparative Law* (3rd edn, 1998, trans Tony Weir), 72–3; for criticism of the treatment of the mixed system as an anomaly, see H. Patrick Glenn, 'Quebec: Mixité and Monism', in Esin Örücü, Elspeth Attwooll, and Sean Coyle (eds), *Studies in Legal Systems: Mixed and Mixing* (1996), 1.

reason to believe that they will necessarily proceed in the direction of any of their constituent systems.[10] Given that mixed systems may remain part of the legal landscape for quite some time, they should therefore not be regarded as anomalies or misfits, but rather as symptoms of the need to re-assess the criteria used to define the various groups, as well as the need to redefine the groups derived from these criteria.

This brings us to the second approach. According to Esin Örücü, the existing classifications of legal systems into legal families are no longer tenable, partly due to their inability to deal satisfactorily with mixed systems. Her remedy for this problem is that these classifications of legal families should be abandoned in favour of a new 'family trees' approach, which takes as its point of departure that all legal systems are regarded as mixed and overlapping to various degrees. These systems then have to be regrouped according to the predominance of the 'ingredient sources' from which they are formed.[11] The mixed or hybrid system is therefore no longer the troublesome exception, as the first approach would have it, but the rule. It is therefore clear that Örücü is not demanding the recognition of a distinct new legal family with the name of 'mixed jurisdictions', alongside the civil law and common law families. Any such notion is clearly rejected on the basis that 'not all "mixes" can be pooled together, and not all the existing members of such a family would have the same or similar ingredients'.[12] The point is that *all* systems are mixed; it is only the nature of the mix that varies.

A benefit of this general emphasis on variety is that it does not suffer from the rigidity of some current approaches to legal families, which tend to gloss over or even to deny the complex origins of systems when locating them in a specific legal family. However, it is a matter of some difficulty to determine how this approach, whereby all legal systems have to be realigned and placed on 'family trees' in accordance with criteria such as parentage and the constituent elements, is to be applied. The challenge of determining differences in the proportions of the elements, from which the various mixtures are formed, appears to be formidable. A potentially serious drawback is therefore that the resulting 'family trees' may be so complex and varied that their usefulness as classificatory tools, which should facilitate understanding, can be seriously undermined.[13]

This brings us to the third approach. Its answer to the problem that certain systems cannot easily be located within established legal families is neither to ignore them, nor to devise a whole new set of classificatory criteria based on the notion that all systems are mixed. The answer is to recognize that the phenomenon of extensive mixture is such a distinctive feature of certain systems that they

[10] Reid, (2003) 78 *Tulane LR* 20, in response to Robin Evans-Jones, 'Civil Law in the Scottish Legal Tradition', in Robin Evans-Jones (ed), *The Civil Law Tradition in Scotland* (1995), 3, 9.

[11] Esin Örücü, 'Family Trees for Legal Systems: Towards a Contemporary Approach', in Mark van Hoecke (ed), *Epistemology and Methodology of Comparative Law* (2004), 362, 363.

[12] Örücü (n 11), 367.   [13] See Palmer (n 1), 3, 11–12.

deserve to be regarded as a family in their own right. The scope of such a new category then of course depends on how strictly the criteria for admission to the other families from which the mixes derive are applied: the stricter the application of these criteria, the greater the number of systems that would have to be brought home under the family of mixed systems. This is illustrated by a study conducted at the Law Faculty of the University of Ottawa, which has described almost half the legal systems of the world as 'mixed'.[14] The difficulty with such a large grouping, though, is that the systems it comprises only share the feature of being mixed, and do not meet any of the other popular criteria for classification, such as a shared historical development, or specific techniques of adjudication and legal doctrines. This lack of a common core in turn means that the category does not give rise to the benefits normally associated with classification.[15] However, this problem does not imply that the category itself has to be discarded. It can be overcome, to some extent at least, by recognizing certain sub-groupings of mixed systems, defined according to the particular families which have influenced them.[16] The Ottawa study, for example, has identified the following ten sub-groupings of mixed systems:

(i)   civil law and customary law (26 jurisdictions)
(ii)   civil law and common law (15 jurisdictions)
(iii)   common law and customary law (15 jurisdictions)
(iv)   civil law and Muslim law (11 jurisdictions);
(v)   common law and Muslim law (8 jurisdictions)
(vi)   common law, Muslim law, and customary law (6 jurisdictions)
(vii)   civil law, common law, and Muslim law (5 jurisdictions)
(viii) civil law, common law, and customary law (5 jurisdictions)
(ix)   civil law, Muslim law, and customary law (4 jurisdictions); and
(x)   civil law, common law, and Talmudic law (1 jurisdiction).

But care must be exercised even on this more specific level not to assume that the sub-groupings necessarily share significant common features. Notable differences can exist between the representatives of the families that make up these groupings.

---

[14] <http://www.droitcivil.uottawa.ca/world-legal-systems/eng-monde.html> (accessed 4 July 2005). A total of 232 jurisdictions globally were divided into five main families. The mixed legal systems formed the largest family (96 jurisdictions), followed by the civil law (89 jurisdictions), common law (42 jurisdictions), customary law (3 jurisdictions), and Muslim law (2 jurisdictions). For broad approaches to the notion of mixed or hybrid systems, see further Joseph McKnight, 'Some Historical Observations on Mixed Systems of Law', (1977) 22 *Juridical Review* 177; L. G. Baxter, 'Pure Comparative Law and Legal Science in a Mixed Legal System', (1983) 16 *Comparative and International Law Journal of Southern Africa* 84, 92.

[15] See further Derek van der Merwe, 'Property in Mixed Legal Systems: South Africa', in G. E. van Maanen and A. J. van der Walt (eds), *Property Law on the Threshold of the 21st Century* (1996), 355.

[16] The divisions of mixed system on the site vary somewhat according to the context in which they are used. The particular division above was used in presenting the jurisdictions according to their populations.

For example, while the Ottawa study places Japan and Swaziland in the specific mix of civil law and customary law ((i) above), their customary components vary substantially. Similar arguments can be made with regard to Nepal and Uganda, which appear in the specific mix of common law and customary law ((iii) above), or India and The Gambia, which appear in the specific mix of common law, Muslim law, and customary law ((vi) above).

Furthermore, there may also be important differences in the degree of inter-action between the respective components of the sub-groupings. In this regard a distinction can be drawn between jurisdictions characterized by a true mix of some or all of its components, as opposed to jurisdictions characterized by 'legal plural-ism'. The latter concept, which originally was developed by sociologists and only recently has gained currency amongst lawyers, can be used to describe the situation where different legal systems are simultaneously in force in a single society or geographical area, but one of them applies only to specific groups or individuals. This phenomenon is particularly prevalent in jurisdictions that have been sub-jected to colonial rule, and the one component is customary or religious in nature, while the other derives from the civil and/or common law families.[17] An important feature of these jurisdictions is that the components often only interacted to the extent that customary law had to conform to colonial law.[18] For present purposes it is especially significant that two systems which contain comparable mixes of civil law and common law could be spread over different subdivisions, because the one, in addition, recognizes indigenous or religious law (and is characterized by plural-ism), while the other does not. For example, while Louisiana, Sri Lanka, and Zimbabwe all share the characteristic of containing mixes of the civil law and common law, the Ottawa study places Louisiana in category (ii), and Sri Lanka and Zimbabwe, which further recognize indigenous systems, in category (viii). When dealing with classifications of mixed systems it is therefore important not to overlook important similarities between systems because of a failure to appreciate the significance of legal pluralism.

This brings us to the last and narrowest meaning of the concept of a mixed legal

[17] cf Peter Newman (ed), *The New Palgrave Dictionary of Economics and the Law* (Macmillan, New York, 2002), vol 2, s.v. 'legal pluralism' (entry by Marco Guadagni). When legal pluralism is defined broadly as the 'situation in which two or more laws interact' (see Michael B. Hooker, *Legal Plural-ism—An Introduction to Colonial and Neo Colonial Laws* (1975), 6), it essentially absorbs the concept of the mixed system.

[18] On the distinction between 'weak pluralism', whereby the state affords some formal recogni-tion to indigenous legal systems, and 'strong legal pluralism', whereby even the unofficial social structures of certain groups are to be regarded as law, see J. Griffiths, 'What is Legal Pluralism?', (1986) 24 *Journal of Legal Pluralism* 1; for a general overview and critique, see T. W. Bennett, *Customary Law in South Africa* (2004), 30. On the limited degree of interaction between the various compo-nents in South Africa, see Reinhard Zimmermann and Daniel Visser, 'Introduction', in Reinhard Zimmermann and Daniel Visser (eds), *Southern Cross—Civil Law and Common Law in South Africa* (1996) 1, 12–15.

system. As we have seen in the introduction, it is traditionally used to describe systems that have been influenced significantly by the civil law and common law families. It is a matter of some difficulty, though, to determine how strong this influence must be before a system is regarded as mixed in this sense. Consequently, there is also no unanimity about the jurisdictions which fall under it.[19] Most commentators would accept that it at least includes Scotland,[20] Louisiana, Québec, Sri Lanka, and South Africa. Many probably would add Puerto Rico, the Philippines, Israel, and the other Southern African countries of Botswana, Lesotho, Swaziland, Namibia, and Zimbabwe. Less clear is the status of systems which also contain mixes of civil law and common law, but which thus far have not generally been described as 'mixed'. These include Cyprus, Malta, the Channel Islands (Jersey, Guernsey, Alderney, and Sark), Cameroon, Guyana, Mauritius, the Seychelles, California, Texas, Iran, Jordan, Saudi Arabia, Somalia, Yemen, Saint Lucia, Thailand, and Vanuatu.

No doubt out of concern that even this narrow notion of the mixed legal system may lose value as a classificatory tool if the net is cast too widely, Vernon Palmer has identified certain minimum characteristics that justify inclusion in the grouping (it is even called the third legal family) of 'mixed jurisdictions'.[21] The first characteristic relates to the specificity of the mixture: even though there may be other mixed elements (eg customary law in the case of South Africa), Palmer requires that the civil law and common law have to be the dual 'foundations' or building blocks of the systems. A positive feature of this requirement is that it accommodates pluralism, and thus avoids the obscuring effect of simply grouping together systems according to the number of components without in any way taking into account the degree of interaction between them.

The second characteristic is 'quantitative and psychological': the civil law and common law elements have to be obvious to an ordinary observer, which presupposes that they have to be of a sufficient magnitude. Thus, Texas and California, whose civil law components are rather obscure, do not warrant inclusion. A slight difficulty with requiring this characteristic is that it is not quite clear why such a subjective appreciation of a system being mixed is so important. If it is established that a system has been influenced fundamentally by the civil law and common law,

---

[19] For lists, see Reid, (2003) 78 *Tulane LR* 7; Zimmermann and Visser (n 18), 2 f; Palmer (n 1), 3–15; Appendix B, in Palmer (n 1), 479–84, and the systems listed in sub-groupings (ii), (vii), (viii), and (x) in the Ottawa study referred to at n 14 above. The list drawn up by Zweigert and Kötz is not restricted to systems that have been influenced by the civil law and common law (see n 9 above).

[20] For a firm rejection of the view that Scots law belongs to the common law family, see Niall R. Whitty, 'The Civilian Tradition and Debates on Scots law', (1996) *Tydskrif vir die Suid-Afrikaanse Reg* 227, 233 ff.

[21] See Palmer (n 1), 14. Palmer only refers to the systems of Scotland, Louisiana, Québec, South Africa, Botswana, Lesotho, Swaziland, Puerto Rico, the Philippines, Sri Lanka, Mauritius, Seychelles, Saint Lucia, and Israel.

even though observers have not traditionally appreciated that it displayed this characteristic, why should it not be included in the list?

More problematic, though, is Palmer's third characteristic, which relates to the structural allocation of content: the private law of mixed systems is predominantly civilian while the public law is predominantly Anglo-American. The first two characteristics are narrowly linked in that both presuppose a substantial blend of civil law and common law elements. Although, as with any classification, there may be some uncertainty about where exactly the line should be drawn (for example, it is not clear why Palmer apparently excluded Namibia and Zimbabwe from his list),[22] the sharing of these features appears to be a valuable ground for grouping systems together. The same type of criteria used to distinguish between the families from which these systems are derived (eg shared history, techniques of adjudication, etc.) could be applied to them. However, it is less clear why mixed systems have to display the characteristic of a specific allocation of material in public law and private law. As Daniel Visser has pointed out with reference to South African law, important aspects of its criminal law are civilian, while the post-apartheid constitutional law is the result of a complex blending of civil law (German law in particular) and common law.[23] It would therefore perhaps be safer to regard such an allocation of public law and private law as an incidental feature which the various systems display to a varying degree.

From the above, it is apparent that a broad consensus exists that certain core systems are 'mixed' in the narrow sense, but that the position is less clear with regard to other systems which have in some way been influenced by the civil law and common law. Such uncertainty is understandable for any classification of systems, but it is unfortunate that commentators have thus far generally avoided articulating more precise criteria, which are to be used in such a classification, and indicating why specific systems meet these criteria. This consequently makes it difficult to determine to what extent the 'non-core' systems listed above should be regarded as mixed in the narrow sense.

A further unfortunate aspect of the current position is that, when used in this narrow sense, the label of 'mixed legal system' is rather misleading. It only relates to a specific type of mix, namely that of the civil law and common law, whereas, as we have seen, many mixes do not contain both of these components.[24] It may well be, as Kenneth Reid has pointed out after considering alternatives such as 'Anglo-civilian' or 'Romano-English' systems, that it is at present unlikely that there will

---

[22] See Palmer (n 1), Appendix B, 479 ff; but see also at 4 n 3.

[23] Daniel Visser, 'Cultural Forces in the Making of Mixed Legal Systems', (2003) *Tulane LR* 41, 48–50.

[24] It is further not clear why this particular mix should lay claim to being described as the 'third legal family', as opposed to other families which traditionally have featured in classifications in addition to the civil law and common law.

be a change in the established usage.[25] But in due course some of the systems which contain blends other than that of substantial parts of civil law and common law may also go through a process of increased appreciation that they share features which make their mixes special. Ultimately, the label of the 'mixed legal systems' could perhaps be more usefully and sensitively employed in a broad sense to describe one family which contains all these various types of mixes. The 'mixed legal systems' defined in the traditional, narrow sense would then be only one, albeit important, sub-grouping in this family.

III. The Relevance of Mixed Legal Systems to Comparative Law

In 1949, exactly fifty years after Walton indicated that some systems occupy a position midway between the civil law and common law, Frederick Lawson gave his inaugural lecture as the holder of the newly established Chair in Comparative Law at the University of Oxford. His purpose was to identify certain areas that particularly merited comparative analysis. His conclusion was simple: '[f]or the moment, it seems to me that the most fruitful field to till is to be found in comparing the private law of the civil law and common law systems, and more especially in the marginal and hybrid laws where the two come into contact and perhaps conflict'.[26]

However, despite such a clear signal that the time was ripe to for a closer examination of mixed or hybrid systems (in the narrow sense), the comparative community only took up this challenge much later. Although the redoubtable T. B. Smith led a lone crusade between the mid-1950s and mid-1960s to advance the study of mixed systems, especially inasmuch as this might help to counteract the perceived subversion of the civil law by the common law,[27] comparative study of mixed legal systems only really commenced in earnest in the last decade of the twentieth century.[28] Serious claims have now been made about the merits and broader comparative significance of these systems, and serious reservations have been expressed about the tenability of such claims. This section will examine some of these claims in the light of certain aspects of the mixed jurisdiction experience. The conventional, narrow conception of mixed jurisdictions referred to in the

---

[25] Reid, (2003) 78 *Tulane LR* 20.

[26] 'The Field of Comparative Law', (1949) 61 *Juridical Review* 16, 35.

[27] As to his contribution, see generally Elspeth Reid and David L. Carey Miller (eds), *A Mixed Legal System in Transition—T B Smith and the Progress of Scots Law* (2005).

[28] On possible causes of this 'sudden flurry of activity', see Reid, (2003) 78 *Tulane LR* 17–19.

previous section, namely that of the civil law/common law mix, will be regarded as paradigmatic. However, it may well be that some of the experiences of this particular mix may also turn out to be relevant when dealing with mixes that have not been influenced by both these traditions.

1. The Possibility of Mixed Legal Systems: Legal Borrowing and Legal Transplants

It may at first seem rather obvious that mixed systems have been formed through a process of transplantation or borrowing from the civil law and the common law. However, some controversy exists about whether legal transplants are at all possible, and if so, of what value their study is to comparative law. Over three decades, Alan Watson has argued strongly that both these questions should be answered in the affirmative: transplants do not only take place, but are the most important source of change in the Western legal tradition. As far as their relevance to comparative law is concerned, he is quite direct:[29] 'as a practical subject Comparative Law is a study of the legal borrowings or transplants that can and should be made; Comparative Law an academic discipline in its own right is the other side of the coin, an investigation into the legal transplants that have occurred'.

Dramatically different, in turn, is the approach of Pierre Legrand.[30] To him, there is no such thing as a 'legal transplant'. Consequently it makes no sense for comparative lawyers to examine such 'transplants'. The basis for this view is the notion that one cannot think of the law as rules which take the form of 'propositional statements' that are not socially connected in any meaningful way. A meaningful 'legal transplant' can only occur '. . . when both the propositional statement as such and its invested meaning—which jointly constitute the rule—are transported from one culture to another'.[31] Given that the meaning of the rule is specific to a particular culture, the meaning therefore stays behind if the culture itself cannot be transplanted as well. And if the meaning stays behind, the transplant never happened—all that was displaced from the one jurisdiction to the other was 'a meaningless form of words'.[32] In fact, it does not even help the comparative lawyer to examine the displacement of the words.[33]

All that one can see is that law reformers (or other jurists) on occasion find it convenient, presumably in the interests of economy and efficiency, to adopt a pre-existing form of words which may happen to have been formulated outside their

---

[29] See Watson's summary of his own approach in Rudolf B. Schlesinger, Hans W. Baade, Peter E. Herzog, and Eduard M. Wise, *Comparative Law—Cases, Text, Materials* (6th edn, 1998), 13–14.

[30] See Pierre Legrand, 'The Impossibility of "Legal Transplants" ', (1997) 42 *Maastricht Journal of European and Comparative Law* 111; *idem*, 'What "Legal Transplants"?', in David Nelken and Johannes Fest (eds), *Adapting Legal Cultures* (2001), 55.

[31] Legrand, in Nelken and Fest (n 30), 60.   [32] Ibid 63.   [33] Ibid 64.

jurisdiction—not unlike the way writers on occasion find it convenient to quote from other authors, some of whom will be foreigners.

In dealing with this debate, it is necessary at the outset to consider the possibility that the protagonists may be talking at cross-purposes.[34] If legal transplants have to be defined in the way proposed by Legrand, then the fact that the contexts of the donor and recipient jurisdictions invariably are different indeed implies that legal transplants are impossible. Some change in meaning will take place. The difficulty, though, is that Watson is not saying that a transplant has to be an exact copy of the original.[35] The more foreign the new cultural environment (and especially legal culture), the greater the possibility that a rule will lose its meaning in such a new environment. But where the cultural conditions—and especially legal cultures—are similar, the argument that only a 'meaningless form of words' is transplanted, loses force. Furthermore, as will be argued below it is also possible that some form of cultural transfer could take place. If this happens, the changed recipient culture may be particularly receptive to transplantation.

It is at this juncture that we can introduce mixed legal systems into the discussion. By definition, they are the result of some process of introduction of foreign law. Lawyers in these jurisdictions generally have no great difficulty with identifying the foreign origins of their laws. They also do not deny that the law derived from a foreign law acquires new meaning in its new environment.[36] If a change in meaning implies that the term 'legal transplant' should not be used, because that which is transplanted by definition may not change in the process of transplanting, then another term should be used, such as 'legal borrowing'. The debate would then only be one of terminology.

The real difficulty with Legrand's view, however, is that it is not clear why some (even minor) change in meaning has to have the radical consequence that only a 'meaningless form of words' remains, and that the process of influencing consequently is not worthwhile examining at all. The notion that due to the difference in context, and especially culture, the lawmakers from the recipient country only imitate formulations used elsewhere is particularly troublesome. The compatibility of cultures is a matter of degree, and not of absolutes. As pointed out earlier, where cultural differences are extreme, it may be difficult to speak convincingly of a transplant taking place. However, it is quite significant from the perspective of

---

[34] This possibility is also recognized by Watson, 'Legal Transplants and European Private Law', *Ius Commune Lectures on European Private Law No. 2* (2002), 13. This may also have been the problem with an earlier debate between Watson and Sir Otto Kahn-Freund.

[35] See Alan Watson, *Law out of Context* (2000), 1. On the change in meaning of transplanted signs, see Bernhard Großfeld, 'Comparatists and Languages', in Pierre Legrand and Roderick Munday (eds), *Comparative Legal Studies: Traditions and Transitions* (2003), 154, 182. For a critical perspective of the limitations of the transplantation debate, see especially David Kennedy, 'The Politics and Methods of Comparative Law', in Legrand and Munday, 345, 361 n 15.

[36] cf Vernon Valentine Palmer, 'A Descriptive and Comparative Overview', in Palmer (n 1), 59–62.

mixed systems that when the civil law and common law traditions are measured in accordance with a number of key dimensions of culture, they score very similarly when compared to indigenous cultures.[37] Furthermore, culture is not genetic, and can be learnt.[38] This means that not only rules, but also legal culture itself, can be transplanted. In this regard the historical record of mixed jurisdictions reveals large-scale adoptions of foreign institutions and structures, such as new court procedures and (even) the importing of lawyers more familiar with the donor than donee system.[39] Where such crucial aspects of the legal culture of the donor are taken over, the idea that the donee merely replicates the wording of the donor's rules loses much of its force. In short, the experiences of mixed legal systems point in a direction opposite to that of regarding cultures as mutually incompatible, and legal transplants as inherently impossible.[40]

2. The Formation of Mixed Legal Systems: Factors which Influence Change through Borrowing

Given that some, albeit imperfect, form of legal transplanting or borrowing is possible, we can now proceed to a matter which has not only been of concern to lawyers in mixed systems, but also to the broader comparative community. The question essentially is what factors influence legal change, and more specifically, change through borrowing. Although all systems which borrow may be regarded as 'mixed', the focus here will only be on mixed legal systems in the narrow sense, where borrowing from the civil and common law traditions has been extensive, and further only those mixed systems which first adopted civil law and subsequently borrowed extensively from the common law.[41]

Traditionally, the most important instruments used to effect legal change in mixed legal systems are the legislature and the judiciary. As far as legislative change is concerned, the prime targets for change have been public law and commercial law. In the public law domain, legislative activity was particularly strong in constitutional and administrative affairs, the structure and operation of the judiciary,

[37] See Visser, (2003) 78 *Tulane LR* 71 ff.

[38] See Visser, (2003) 78 *Tulane LR* 44; see further H. Patrick Glenn, 'Mixing it up', (2003) 78 *Tulane LR* 79, 80 f.

[39] Palmer (n 36), 38.

[40] Watson may at times over-estimate the extent to which transplantation is possible, but this does not imply that transplantation and transcultural change itself is impossible: see James Q. Whitman, 'The Neo-Romantic Turn', in Legrand and Munday (n 35), 342. For an empirical study stressing the importance of the transplant taking place in a receptive environment, see Daniel Berkowitz, Katharina Pistor, and Jean-Francois Richard, 'The Transplant Effect', (2003) 51 *AJCL* 163.

[41] It therefore does not take into account developments in Israel, where the common law influences preceded that of the civil law. See generally Stephen Goldstein, 'Israel', in Palmer (n 1), 448.

civil and criminal procedure, and, to a lesser extent, substantive criminal law.[42] Statutory reform of commercial law, in turn, mainly concerned negotiable instruments, shipping, insolvency, insurance, intellectual property, corporate law, and, to a lesser extent, sale.[43] The policy goals pursued by these reforms were often to strengthen colonial rule and governance, and to facilitate economic interaction between the colony and the dominant economic power. Civil law rules which were regarded as barriers to trade could therefore easily fall prey to statutory reform aimed at harmonizing the law of the colony with that of the colonial power.

Whereas legislative change was prominent in the public and commercial law, the judiciary was especially influential in introducing common law elements into the private law. The processes whereby these changes took place have enjoyed considerable attention. Of particular interest has been the extent to which the mixed systems have adhered to the common law doctrine of precedent or *stare decisis*, which was introduced with the reform of the judicial system.[44] Although this doctrine basically required that courts, in the absence of statutory reform, should honour previous decisions, which in turn may have drawn on civil law sources, the courts in fact resorted to various techniques to justify borrowing from the common law. The tenability of some of these justifications has been heavily disputed in some systems, the main antagonists in this *bellum juridicum* being 'purists', who generally wanted the civil law to be untainted by a common law perceived to be disorganized and lacking in principle, and 'pollutionists', who, despite the constraints of *stare decisis*, had few qualms about supplanting civil law, which they often regarded as antiquated and obscure, by common law rules.[45] The tensions between these approaches underlie much of the formative years of mixed legal systems.

The first justification for judicial change represents an extreme form of the 'pollutionist' approach. It entails that the local law could simply be disregarded

---

[42] See the following national reports in Palmer (n 1): Paul Farlam and Reinhard Zimmermann, 'South Africa Report 1', 84–6; C. G. van der Merwe, J. E. du Plessis, and M. J. de Waal, 'South Africa Report 2', 148–9; Vernon Valentine Palmer and Matthew Sheynes, 'Louisiana', 258–9; John E. C. Brierly, 'Quebec Report 1', 329–30; Ennio Colón et al, 'Puerto Rico', 366–70; Pacífico Agabin, 'The Philippines', 426–7.

[43] See Palmer (n 36), 66–76, 80; Van der Merwe, Du Plessis, and De Waal (n 42), 172 ff.

[44] See Palmer (n 36), 44–53. On the role of precedent and its relationship to codification in mixed jurisdictions, see Vernon Valentine Palmer, *The Louisiana Experience—Critiques of Codification in a Mixed Jurisdiction* (2005); Ryan McGonigle, 'Role of Precedents in Mixed Jurisdictions', (2002) 6(2) *Electronic Journal of Comparative Law* (<http://www.ejcl.org/62/abs62-1.html>, accessed 4 July 2005).

[45] See generally Palmer (n 36), 31–5; Reinhard Zimmermann, 'Synthesis in South African Private Law: Civil Law, Common Law and Usus Hodiernus Pandectarum', (1986) 103 *South African LJ* 259; Eduard Fagan, 'Roman-Dutch Law in its South African Historical Context', in Zimmermann and Visser (n 18), 33, 60–4. For Scots law, see Whitty, (1996) *Tydskrif vir die Suid-Afrikaanse Reg* 227–39, 442–56. On the role of principle in Scots law, see, in this context, Niall R. Whitty, 'From Rules to Discretion: Changes in the Fabric of Scots Private Law', (2003) 7 *Edinburgh LR* 281.

where it was contrary to the principles of foreign law.[46] This phenomenon is illustrated by the following oft-quoted *dictum* by the notorious Sir John Wylde in the nineteenth-century Cape decision of *Letterstedt v Morgan*:[47] 'Quote what Dutch or Roman books you please—musty or otherwise—and they must be musty if they lay down such doctrines. I belong to a higher court than they refer to . . . My Queen has sent me here to administer justice under the Royal Charter'.

Thus, whether due to ignorance or bias, Wylde simply failed to take into account that the Charters of Justice at the Cape required that courts should administer justice according to the laws already in force in the Cape, that is, the Roman-Dutch law, unless subsequently amended. However, at times judges felt the need to provide at least some further rationalization for selecting the common law. They could for example attempt to forge a rule out of the best elements of the civil law and common law, but in practice select the common law rule,[48] or they could reinforce the introduction of the common law through linking it with notions of 'natural equity' or 'universal law'.[49] Courts further resorted to the device of stating that the civil law and common law were similar on a particular point, and that it would therefore be in order to make use of the common law.[50] These assumptions of similarity could at times be quite generous—somewhat contentious examples include the reception of common law rules on the cancellation of contracts due to breach, which were regarded as similar to civilian sources, and attempts to assimilate the civilian notion of *causa* with the common law doctrine of consideration, or the doctrine of estoppel with the *exceptio doli*.[51]

[46] The late Chief Justice of Puerto Rico, José Trías Monge, referred in this regard to the 'fantasy of the superior law', which is regarded as one of five 'fantasies' which influenced the introduction of common law: *El Choque de dos Culturas Juridicas en Puerto Rico* (1991; for a summary, see *idem*, 'Legal Methodology in Some Mixed Jurisdictions', (2003) 78 *Tulane LR* 333, 347 ff; see further Palmer (n 36), 54. The use of the word 'fantasy' in describing these influences suggests that the judges were somewhat naïve and even irrational in introducing the common law. However, as indicated above, the record is more complex, and this terminology is consequently avoided. The imagery of the 'fantasy' has also been used to criticize purists; see Alan Rodger, '"Say Not the Struggle Naught Availeth": The Costs and Benefits of Mixed Legal Systems', (2003) 78 *Tulane LR* 419, 422.

[47] (1849) 5 Searle 373. Wylde was Chief Justice of the Cape from 1827–1859. It should not be forgotten, though, that the introduction of the civil law in some mixed jurisdictions was in turn often characterized by scant regard for the indigenous or customary law.

[48] Monge, (2003) 78 *Tulane LR* 348–9.

[49] See Monge, (2003) 78 *Tulane LR* 348; Anton Cooray, 'Sri Lanka: Oriental and Occidental Laws in Harmony', in Örücü *et al* (n 9), 71, 77. This practice could have perverse consequences. Monge refers to the Puerto Rican case of *Dottin v Rigo & Co*, 22 Puerto Rico Supreme Court Reports 378, 383–4 (1915), where a San Juan restaurant's refusal to serve a black person was upheld on the basis that the equality of the races was not regarded as a principle of Natural law (348). In Louisiana the provision of the code justifying recourse to equity has apparently not been used as a portal for introducing common law: cf Palmer and Sheynes (n 42), 307.

[50] See generally Palmer (n 36), 56.

[51] See Farlam and Zimmermann (n 42), 120 f, Elspeth Reid, 'Scotland Report 1', in Palmer (n 1), 226; Palmer and Sheynes (n 42), 308–10; Jacques du Plessis, 'Common Law Influences on the Law of Contract and Unjustified Enrichment in Some Mixed Legal Systems', (2003) 78 *Tulane LR* 219, 222–4.

Nowadays, mixed jurisdictions tend to avoid these more robust techniques. Justifications which have proven to be more lasting deal with alleviating uncertainty in the existing law and with the promotion of uniformity. Typical situations of such uncertainty have been where the court regarded the local law as silent, or too insufficiently developed to deal with the problem at hand. For example, where the law of Louisiana did not expressly determine a prescriptive period for the action of the biological father to have his paternity recognized, the court resorted to the common-law inspired doctrine of laches in holding that his action was estopped after a six-year period.[52] Uncertainty could also flow from the use of open-ended concepts in the local law, which required further interpretation.[53] Judicial borrowing from the common law to counter this problem is, for example, reflected by the South African experience with fleshing out the broad requirements of delictual liability—an old battleground between purists and pollutionists. Finally, uncertainty could also arise from contradictory strands of thinking within the local law, as is illustrated by different constructions of the *condictio indebiti* in South African and Scots law. Here the common law influenced the direction of development, rather than supplanting the existing law.

The justification of resorting to the common law in order to promote uniformity between the local law and foreign law has been quite influential in the statutory reform of public and commercial law. But, even though the end of colonial rule in a number of mixed jurisdictions has reduced the need for conformity with the laws of the colonial power, this justification still enjoys popularity with the judiciary in some jurisdictions. Nowadays, the need for uniformity may flow from commercial considerations and the demands of regional and international cooperation. A notable recent example is the decision of the House of Lords in *Smith v Bank of Scotland*,[54] whereby Scots law was brought into line with English law by requiring that banks under certain circumstances have to warn potential sureties about the consequences of their actions and to take independent advice. An important feature of this decision, though, was that the court did not directly import a common law concept to effect the change, such as the common law doctrine of constructive notice, but rather based these duties on the open-ended concept of good faith, which had already enjoyed some recognition in Scots law. This reflects a more careful approach to borrowing than that experienced by many mixed systems at times when the influence of the foreign power was more pervasive.[55]

---

[52] See the discussion of *T. D. v M.M.M.*, 703 So. 2d 730 (La. App. 4th Cir. 1997) in Palmer and Sheynes (n 42), 308. For further examples of this justification see Farlam and Zimmermann (n 42), 120; Du Plessis, (2003) 78 *Tulane LR* 248; and Cooray (n 49), 77.

[53] See Du Plessis, (2003) 78 *Tulane LR* 248.   [54] 1997 SC (HL) 111, esp 118, 122.

[55] As champions of the civil law in mixed systems have pointed out, uniformity usually was achieved by making the local (civil) law adapt to the common law—not the other way round. Traditionally, the Supreme Court of Canada made the law of Québec conform to the other Canadian jurisdictions. Similar criticism about a lack of reciprocity has been expressed in regard to the harmonizing of Scots law and English law (see generally Robin Evans-Jones, 'Receptions of Law, Mixed Legal

Against this brief overview of justifications for change,[56] a few final words will be said about the relative ease with which foreign law at times was introduced, compared to the more inward-looking approach adopted by many modern jurisdictions. French, German, or (non-Louisianian) American jurists may, not without some justification, shake their heads in disbelief and puzzlement at the way in which local was displaced by a foreign import. However, the more extreme examples of this phenomenon date from an age when many of these systems were struggling to forge their own identities. Nowadays, there is still frequent recourse to the common law in some systems, but this mainly takes place in areas where layers of case law have been built on statutory foundations constructed in accordance with common law plans.[57] The common law influences are also often 'indirect', or amount to 'soft borrowing', in the sense that they are used to support or illustrate a position adopted with regard to the existing law, and not to supplant it. To comparative lawyers who may believe that foreign law can generally only influence local legal development via the statutory route, the mixed jurisdiction experience shows that the judiciary, given the appropriate conditions, can be a significant source of borrowing. Of course, this neither means that the borrowings necessarily improve the quality of the local system, nor that optimal use is made of the opportunities to adopt a comparative perspective. To these matters we shall now turn.

3. The Quality of Mixed Legal Systems: Borrowing as a Process of Selecting the Best Rules?

The quality of mixed legal systems has been the subject of diverse views. It has been suggested for some time that mixed systems, due to their unique location between the civil law and common law traditions, can be regarded as 'laboratories of comparative law', the implication being that they are able to experiment in selecting the best rules that these traditions can offer. The argument further has been made that they consequently may guide other systems, and even point the way to a 'universal

---

Systems and the Myth of the Genius of Scots Private Law', (1998) 114 *LQR* 228; but cf Tony Weir, 'Divergent Legal Systems in a Single Member State', (1998) 6 *Zeitschrift für Europäisches Privatrecht* 564, 570–4).

[56] The overview is not exhaustive. Other justifications include 'established usage' (see Farlam and Zimmermann (n 42), 121–2; Van der Merwe *et al* (n 42), 181; Palmer and Sheynes (n 42), 310–11), and the duty to apply the common law where questions of sovereignty were involved (see Palmer and Sheynes (n 42), 310).

[57] On the requirement in South African law that statutes be construed against their common law background, see L. M. du Plessis, 'Statute Law and Interpretation', in W. A. Joubert (ed), *The Law of South Africa*, vol 25, part 1 (1st reissue, 2001), para 360. On the position in the Phillipines see the cases quoted by McGonigle, (2002) 6(2) *Electronic Journal of Comparative Law* notes 118 ff.

law'.[58] For example, in 1925 the famous French comparative lawyer Henri Lévy-Ullmann (referring specifically to Scots law), wrote that it '. . . gives us a picture of what will be, some day (perhaps at the end of this century), the law of the civilised nations, namely a combination between the Anglo-Saxon and the continental system'.[59] Nowadays, it is especially within the context of discussions about the development of a European legal scholarship and the harmonization or unification of European private law that comparative lawyers draw attention to the blending of civil law and common law in mixed legal systems.[60]

But these systems have also had their detractors. Scepticism has existed for some time. Thomas Jefferson (President of the United States, 1801–9), for example, stated in the context of the law of Louisiana that even though he admitted the superiority of the Civil Law over the Common Law, '. . . yet an incorporation of the two would be like Nebuchadnezzar's image of metal and clay, a thing without cohesion of parts'.[61] More recently, scepticism about the value of mixed systems has been expressed by Robin Evans-Jones. According to him, receptions happen when strong legal systems come up against weak legal systems, and the former overwhelm the latter; the resulting mix is then not the product of critical choice, but 'often worse than the alternatives from which it is drawn'. The notion that Scots law is characterized by a particular 'genius' is therefore simply to be regarded as a myth.[62] In this section it will be attempted to shed more light on these markedly different appraisals of the value of mixed legal systems by focusing on certain of their experiences.

(a) Creating Quality: Factors which Influence the Value of the Mixes

A rather obvious observation which should be made at the outset is that mixed legal systems do not form a monolithic group which provide uniform answers to legal problems. Although, at times, they adopt remarkably similar positions, and have also experienced similar patterns of development, they can also diverge considerably in their approaches to specific situations. There is no single 'mixed legal systems laboratory'; there are a number of laboratories which, in response to the same problem, may chose different substances with which to experiment, may use

---

[58] See Palmer (n 1), 4.

[59] 'The Law of Scotland', (1925) 37 Juridical Review 370, 390 (trans Walton).

[60] See Zweigert and Kötz (n 9), 212; Reinhard Zimmermann, ' "Double Cross": Comparing Scots and South African Law', in Reinhard Zimmermann, Daniel Visser, and Kenneth Reid (eds), Mixed Legal Systems in Comparative Perspective—Property and Obligations in Scotland and South Africa (2004), 1, 32; Zimmermann (n 1), 126 ff; Hein Kötz, 'The Value of Mixed Legal Systems', (2003) 78 Tulane LR 435; Jan Smits, 'Scotland as a Mixed Jurisdiction and the Development of European Private Law', (2003) 7(5) Electronic Journal of Comparative Law (<http://www.ejcl.org/75/art75–1.html>, accessed 4 July 2005).

[61] Quoted in Vernon Valentine Palmer, 'Two Worlds in One', in idem (ed), Lousiana: A Microcosm of a Mixed Jurisdiction (1999), 23.

[62] See Evans-Jones, (1998) 114 LQR 228, especially at 247–8.

different techniques of experimentation, and may consequently produce different results. While some systems, for example, adopted the postal rule or the doctrine of consideration, others did not. Arguments that mixed systems generally select the 'best' rules have some difficulty accommodating such diverse results.

The second initial observation relates to the variety of factors which may have influenced a specific instance of borrowing. It has been shown in the previous section that receptions sometimes took place by force, or were the product of bias against one approach and ignorance of another. In making general claims about the quality of mixed legal systems, it therefore cannot be assumed that those responsible for the choice necessarily deliberated upon the merits of various approaches in an informed and objective manner. This undermines the credibility of claims that these systems generally produce 'superior' law.[63] However, the record also does not reflect, as Evans-Jones suggests, that the mixture was 'often' worse than the alternatives from which it was drawn.[64] While certain experiences with the development of the law of unjustified enrichment in Scotland may indeed be unfortunate, they do not provide sufficient support for a general thesis that receptions take place when a strong system overwhelms a weak one. As we have seen, the processes of reception are too multi-faceted to be captured in such a single formula.

Ultimately, though, perhaps too much attention is paid to the question whether mixed systems *generally* get it right or wrong. One will simply have to accept that mixed systems, like other systems, at times may get it right, and at times may get it wrong, and that the most value, especially to the comparative lawyer, is to be gained from examining concrete experiences of mixing on their own merits. In this regard it may be useful to focus on a specific example to provide some impression of how good quality mixes can be created. The example, which is probably most prominent in literature on mixed jurisdictions, is that of the trust.[65]

It may at first appear quite strange that a quintessentially common law construct like the trust could find a home in systems which have more civilian-based laws of contract, property, and succession, and which do not know the traditional common law distinction between legal and equitable title. However, the experiences of a number of mixed systems reveal that the trust is not such an inadaptable alien creature after all. The South African trust can serve as an example.[66] When the first

[63] Palmer (n 36), 57 ('The fantasies of the mixed-jurisdiction judges, then, are more than idle dreams. The uses and abuses of comparative law that they engage in are in fact, if one stands back as a neutral observer, a significant part of legal development. The familiar view that such countries are laboratories of comparative law usually suggests only the benefits and none of the hazards of their experiments').

[64] Evans-Jones, (1998) 114 *LQR* 228, 247 f.

[65] See generally M. J. de Waal and R. R. M. Paisley, 'Trusts', in Zimmermann *et al.* (n 60), 819; J. M. Milo and J. M. Smits, *Trusts in Mixed Legal Systems* (2001).

[66] On the reception of the trust in other mixed jurisdictions, see A. N. Yiannopoulos, 'Trust and the Civil Law: The Louisiana Experience', in Smits and Milo (n 65), 67 ff; Madeleine Cantin Cumyn, 'The Quebec Trust: A Civilian Institution with English Law Roots', in Smits and Milo (n 65), 73 ff; Colón

British settlers in the beginning of the nineteenth century began to refer to the 'trust' in the Cape, it did indeed have little meaning in terms of the existing Roman-Dutch civil law, which only knows one form of ownership, namely *dominium*. But over time a South African trust developed which, despite this difference in environment, fulfilled functions similar to the English trust and shared some of its features.[67] In the words of Kenneth Reid: '[I]t is possible to have the trust and yet still remain virtuous. To adopt the trust is not, or not necessarily, to sink into the arms of equity'.[68] Looking back, it has been said that the South African trust is 'all the stronger' for being able to draw so widely on English law, Roman-Dutch law, and its own distinctively South African rules.[69] This does not mean that after this gradual process of blending the South African trust is now some sort of *Übertrust*, superior to the English trust and comparable civil law constructs. The point is simply that the South African experience, as well as that of some other mixed systems, has shown that it is possible to recognize the trust, with some adaptation, within a civil law environment, and consequently to contribute to the overall quality of these systems.

It is worthwhile to reflect on possible reasons for the success of this process of reception and adaptation. There may be many, but two in particular stand out, namely the ability of the transplant to respond to a felt need, and its 'fit' with the existing law and legal culture. In the case of the trust, civilian constructs like the *fideicomissum* were not suited to meeting the practical needs fulfilled by the trust. And through shedding some of the trust's common law features, no violence was done to established civilian principles relating to property and contract. The experiences show that where an import meets a felt need, the system may at first tolerate an initial lack of fit. This is not only supported by experiences with the trust, but also by some other imports such as the law of undue influence as a factor vitiating contractual consent,[70] and repudiation as a form of anticipatory breach.[71] In both instances, there was a need to fill gaps in the existing law, and in both

et al. (n 42), 396 ff; the Scottish trust is apparently essentially civilian, but has been subjected to common law influences—see Reid (n 51), 233, Robert Leslie, 'Scotland Report 2', in Palmer (n 1), 240, 253.

[67] See M. J. de Waal, 'The Core Elements of the Trust: Aspects of the English, Scottish and South African Trusts Compared', (2000) 117 *South African LJ* 548; *idem*, 'In Search of a Model for the Introduction of the Trust into a Civilian Context', (2001) 12 *Stellenbosch LR* 63.

[68] 'National Report for Scotland', in *Principles of European Trust Law* (1999), 67; see further Bernard Rudden, 'Things as Things and Things as Wealth', (1994) 14 *Oxford Journal of Legal Studies* 81, 89.

[69] Edwin Cameron, Marius de Waal, Basil Wunsh, Peter Solomon, and Ellison Kahn, *Honoré's South African Law of Trusts* (5th edn, 2002), para 8.

[70] On the position in Scotland and South Africa, see Zimmermann (n 1), 136 ff; Jacques du Plessis and Reinhard Zimmermann, 'The Relevance of Reverence: Undue Influence Civilian Style', (2003) 10 *Maastricht Journal of European and Comparative Law* 345, 358 ff; J. E. du Plessis and W. W. McBryde, 'Defects of Consent', in Zimmermann *et al* (n 60), 117, 128 ff.

[71] On the position in Louisiana, South Africa, and Scotland, see Du Plessis, (2003) 78 *Tulane LR* 239–42; Eric Clive and Dale Hutchison, 'Breach of Contract', in Zimmermann *et al* (n 60), 176, 180–3.

instances the constructs found their niche in the established law.[72] On the other hand, when the import does not respond to a felt need, or is in serious structural conflict with the existing law, as was the experience of South African law with the doctrine of consideration, the prospects of successful reception are diminished.

In the light of these observations, the extent to which some commentators have downplayed the importance of 'fit' when seeking guidance from foreign jurisdictions seems to be problematic. Joe Thompson, for example, has argued in the Scottish context that it is simply unnecessary for statutory rules to be consistent with established legal principle to be transplanted successfully.[73] In this regard he points to experiences in Scotland, where statutory reform of family law was supposedly aimed at introducing the 'best' rules, and was not concerned with whether these rules 'fit'. This approach has a certain affinity with that of Peter Birks, who has stressed the importance of the 'rational', rather than the 'national', in legal development.[74] The difficulty with these analyses, though, is that they tend to view matters as contradictory when they are not: while it may be quite possible, through the exercise of legislative or judicial power, to introduce a rule which meets a felt need but does not 'fit', that rule could conceivably have been made even better had it been made to 'fit'.[75] Furthermore, an absence of fit could even direct one to problems with the rule itself. The supposedly 'rational' unjust factors approach to liability for unjustified enrichment which Birks developed in the context of the English common law, but also proposed for the civilian-based Scots law, failed to accommodate an established feature of the latter system, namely that enrichment had to be without legal ground. Nowadays, the taxonomical approaches proposed for Scots law are much more rationally aligned with, and sensitive to, its historical structure, while Birks, under the influence of civilian perspectives of the common law enrichment cases, abandoned the unjust factor approach. Ultimately, it may in fact be irrational not to take into account the national. This point is also reflected in George Gretton's analysis of the relationship between pragmatism and coherence. Gretton has argued forcefully that sensitivity to structural coherence is of crucial importance, and does not stand in opposition to pragmatism, but is in fact

[72] On the role which good faith can play in facilitating common law influences see Reinhard Zimmermann, 'Good Faith and Equity', in Zimmermann and Visser (n 18), 217; for a practical example in modern Scots law see *Smith v Bank of Scotland* 1997 SC (HL) 111.

[73] 'Legal Change and Scots Private law', in John W. Cairns and Olivia F. Robinson (eds), *Critical Studies in Ancient Law, Comparative Law and Legal History* (2001), 379.

[74] Peter Birks, 'The Foundation of Legal Rationality in Scotland', in Robin Evans-Jones (n 10), 82. For criticism, see Niall R. Whitty, 'Rationality, Nationality and the Taxonomy of Unjustified Enrichment', in David Johnston and Reinhard Zimmermann (eds), *Unjustified Enrichment—Key Issues in Comparative Perspective* (2002), 658, 660 f.

[75] In South Africa, for example, the common-law inspired Sectional Titles Act 95 of 1986 (based on the New South Wales Conveyancing (Strata Titles) Act of 1961), was 'almost seamlessly fitted' into civilian property law (see C. G. van der Merwe, 'Interpenetration of Common Law and Civil Law as Experienced in the South African and Scottish Law of Property', (2003) 78 *Tulane LR* 257, 272 f).

strongly linked to it. As he puts it: '[O]ther things being equal, the incoherent must be the unpragmatic. And so, other things being equal, receptions should be integrative'.[76]

The difficulty, of course, is where to draw the line. This brings us back to the *bellum juridicum*. It was stated earlier that, especially in the earlier phases of development of some mixed legal systems, conflicts existed between purists and pollutionists. Nowadays, purists and pollutionists are relatively rare breeds—mixed system jurists generally recognize that their systems have their own identity, and their mood is one of 'pragmatism'.[77] But the label of pragmatism covers a variety of views regarding the question to what extent, rather than the question whether, foreign influences are desirable. This is graphically illustrated by debates in Scots law about the 'floating charge'—a type of floating equitable security over assets introduced by the Companies (Floating Charges) (Scotland) Act 1961. Both George Gretton and Lord Rodger of Earlsferry recognize the importance of pragmatism, but they have markedly different views about how it should be displayed. While Gretton has recognized that some theoretical incoherence may be a price worth paying for the importation of a useful legal idea, he points out that the floating charge after forty years has still not been made to fit the existing law, and will probably remain an 'alien' institution unless revised by legislation. Lord Rodger, in turn, while admitting that the legislative introduction of the floating charge might have been accomplished more skilfully, has maintained that 'we live in a flawed world and cannot always expect the tedious joys of perfection'.[78] The challenge to him is not to bemoan its introduction, but rather to make it work. It is therefore clear that even in these more settled stages of the development of mixed legal systems, opinions can still differ quite strongly on the importance of structural coherence, and especially the extent to which it should be sacrificed in the name of pragmatism.

---

[76] George L. Gretton, 'Reception without Integration? Floating Charges and Mixed Systems', (2003) 78 *Tulane LR* 307, 308. On the importance of the nature of a specific area of law in which a development is to take place, see Niall R. Whitty, 'The Scottish Enrichment Revolution', (2001) 6 *Scottish Law and Practice Quarterly* 167; Jacques du Plessis, 'The Promises and Pitfalls of Mixed Legal Systems: The South African and Scottish Experiences', (1998) 9 *Stellenbosch LR* 338, 344 ff; Monge, (2003) 78 *Tulane LR* 351 f.

[77] It must be pointed out, however, that even the staunchest purists were pragmatic enough to recognize that the influence of English law has to some extent been beneficial: see T. B. Smith, 'Mixed Jurisdictions', in *International Encyclopedia of Comparative Law*, vol VI, 2 (1975), para 228; J. C. de Wet, 'Gemene reg of wetgewing?', (1948) 11 *Tydskrif vir Hedendaagse Romeins-Hollandse Reg* 1, 3. The label 'antiquarian' should be reserved for jurists who adopt a truly static or passive approach in favour of the retention of the civil law initially received by the system: see Farlam and Zimmermann (n 42), 137 f; C. F. Forsyth, *In Danger for their Talents—A study of the Appellate Division of the Supreme Court of South Africa from 1950–1980* (1985), 183 f.

[78] Rodger, (2003) 78 *Tulane LR* 423 ff.

(b) Improving Quality: The Role of a Historical and Comparative Perspective

In the light of these remarks on the exciting, but at times also frustrating, processes of blending which have characterized mixed legal systems, their future development can now be considered. This is of course a complex matter, given the notable differences in the extent to which their laws have been codified, their approaches to precedent and interpretation, the demands of regional interaction, and constitutional imperatives. Here the emphasis will only be on two techniques which, in view of certain unusual features, are of particular interest.

The first technique is especially significant in the uncodified mixed systems. Although some comparative lawyers assert the contrary, being aged does not automatically mean being dated. Recent experiences of mixed legal systems have confirmed that even though a significant part of their law of civilian origin is to be found in the modern case law, it may still be profitable to re-examine the earlier civil law to advance legal development. For example, in both the Scottish and South African contexts the courts recently have made great strides in the development of the law of unjustified enrichment by re-evaluating older authorities. In this regard the Scottish experience with the rule barring recovery of a payment made in mistake of law is of particular interest. Although this rule did not enjoy support among the seventeenth-century Institutional writers or case law, it became an established feature of Scots law as a result of common law influence. However, recently the Court of Session re-examined the cases which subsequently accepted the rule, and found that they were wrongly decided.[79] It must be emphasized that the result was not reached in order to champion the cause of purism—this is clear from the fact that the same rule has also been rejected in the common law.[80] In the South African context, in turn, the courts were unwilling, for a long time, to recognize that Roman-Dutch law recognized a general enrichment action. But, after some academic studies revealed the existence of a sufficient number of old authorities recognizing such an action, the Supreme Court of Appeal has now held that it is ready to place its stamp of approval on its reapperance in the modern law.[81] This has opened up the way for a re-assessment of the structure of enrichment liability, in which the relative merits of the civil law and common law approaches can be contrasted.

The second technique, which is narrowly linked to the first, is the creative use of the comparative method. The common law and civil law received by mixed systems obviously only represent certain stages in the development of these two traditions.

[79] In *Morgan Guaranty Trust Company of New York v Lothian Regional Council* 1995 SC 151.
[80] *Kleinwort Benson v Lincoln City Council* [1999] 2 AC 349.
[81] *McCarthy Retail Ltd v Shortdistance Carriers CC* 2001 (3) SA 482 (SCA). The more recent lack of imaginative interpretation and development of the civilian notion of good faith, by contrast, has been lamented (see Zimmermann (n 72), 235, 254 ff).

Due to the inherently dynamic nature of law, the donor systems inevitably re-assess their old positions and adopt new ones. It is therefore incumbent on mixed systems not to fall prey to an antiquarian approach, whereby they remain focused on the state of the law at the time of reception. The problem can be described as one of 'lagging behind', and the solution is the consistent re-examination of further developments in comparable modern systems with shared roots. One can even go as far as saying that, due to their origins, mixed systems have no choice but continuously to adopt a comparative perspective.

Unfortunately, even though mixed systems are traditionally open to foreign influences, they have not been particularly good at this process of updating. In fact, the patterns of citation of foreign materials by the courts in some systems seem to be quite skewed: for example, the judicial practice in both Scotland and South Africa has largely been to focus on modern common law jurisdictions.[82] This is partly explicable by their reception of large tracts of statutory commercial and procedural law, and because the common law materials are in English.[83] But, given the extent of civilian influences especially in private law, it is regrettable that the case law in mixed legal systems has not more rigorously attempted to benefit from following developments in modern civilian jurisdictions with similar founda-tions.[84] That such a practice could be of value is not only apparent from some experiences in statutory law reform[85] but also from academic contributions which make use of foreign civilian insights to order and re-interpret the existing case law. This practice is illustrated by South African criminal law, as well as its laws of contract and delict, and is also reflected in recent expositions of the Scots law of contract and unjustified enrichment.[86] In fact, given the practical constraints on the ability of practitioners and the judiciary to access foreign materials, academics appear to be the best situated to influence legal development in this manner. It must be emphasized, however, that the acknowledgement of the need for proper

---

[82] Hector L. MacQueen, 'Mixing it? Comparative Law in the Scottish Courts', (2003) 11 *European Review of Private Law* 735.

[83] cf section III.4 below.

[84] In South African private law, reference is relatively seldom made to modern foreign civil law. It has been said that a 're-civilianization' is apparent in Scots law (Hector L. MacQueen, 'Looking Forward to a Mixed Future: A Response to Professor Yiannopoulos', (2003) *Tulane LR* 411, 415), but the impact has been limited. Québec, where recourse is had to modern French law, is a notable exception.

[85] One of the most prominent modern civilian influences in the statutory reform of a mixed jurisdiction has been the adoption of aspects of German law in South African constitutional law: see Johan de Waal, 'A Comparative Analysis of the Provisions of German Origin in the Interim Bill of Rights', (1995) 11 *South African Journal on Human Rights* 1.

[86] See eg Whitty (n 74); *idem*, (2001) 6 *Scottish Law and Practice Quarterly* 167; Hector MacQueen, 'Glory with Gloag or the Stake with Stair? T B Smith and the Scots Law of Contract', in Elspeth Reid and David L. Carey Miller (eds), *A Mixed Legal System in Transition: T B Smith and the Progress of Scots Law* (2005), 138, 169.

presentation of foreign materials does not imply that the quest for insights from historical materials should be neglected.

Thus far the focus has been on the need for mixed jurisdictions to heed changes in the civil law and common law systems which have influenced them. But, as indicated in the introductory remarks, it is increasingly appreciated that these jurisdictions may also learn from each other.[87] What started as a 'one man band',[88] when T. B. Smith advocated contact between Scotland, South Africa, Québec, and Louisiana, has now expanded to an orchestra. There has, however, been a shift in the motive behind this cooperation: whereas Smith was essentially concerned with forging alliances against common law domination,[89] cooperation nowadays usually takes place in the spirit of pragmatic acceptance of the mixed nature of the systems, and the absence of a general agenda in favour of ridding these systems of either civil law or common law influences. The established view is that mixed systems have largely acquired their own identities, although opinions may of course differ on the relative importance of structural fit in certain areas of law. Prominent examples of this type of cooperation in recent times are the First Worldwide Congress on Mixed Jurisdictions at Tulane University in Louisiana in 2002, the founding of a World Society of Mixed Jurisdictions,[90] as well as the publication of *Mixed Jurisdictions Worldwide: The Third Legal Family*[91] and *Mixed Systems in Comparative Perspective—Property and Obligations in Scotland and South Africa*,[92] which are volumes of essays by academics and judges from these jurisdictions.

To conclude these views on the future development of mixed jurisdictions, and especially the value of adopting the comparative method, a few remarks should be added on how the use of this method may be given further impetus by recent developments on the constitutional front. Given the experience mixed systems traditionally have had in dealing with a variety of legal materials, there is something to be said for the view, expressed by President Barak of the Supreme Court of Israel and others, that these systems possess a certain flexibility which is particularly valuable when dealing with human rights issues.[93] Such flexibility in turn facilitates the introduction of foreign law through the conduit of a bill of rights—

[87] See eg Whitty, (1996) *Tydskrif vir die Suid-Afrikaanse Reg* 442, 457; Alan Rodger, 'Roman Law in Practice in Britain', (1993) *Rechtshistorisches Journal* 261, 271; Du Plessis, (1998) 9 *Stellenbosch LR* 338.

[88] Reid, (2003) 78 *Tulane LR* 11, 15.

[89] See eg his 'Strange Gods: The Crisis of Scots Law as a Civilian System', (1949) 61 *Juridical Review* 119 (= T. B. Smith, *Studies Critical and Comparative* (1962), 72); *idem*, 'The Common Law Cuckoo—The Problems of "Mixed" Legal Systems with Special Reference to Restrictive Interpretations in the Scots Law of Obligations', (1956) *Butterworths South African LR* 147 (= *Studies Critical and Comparative*, 89).

[90] Most of the papers presented at this conference have been published in (2003) 78 *Tulane LR*. The website of the Society is <www.mixedjurisdiction.org>. It contains *inter alia* a bibliography of legal materials on mixed jurisdictions.

[91] Palmer (n 1).   [92] Zimmermann *et al.* (n 60).

[93] See Hector L. MacQueen, 'Human Rights and Private Law in Scotland: A Response to President Barak', (2003) *Tulane LR* 363, 364.

especially where there are gaps, or the established routes of development have proven to be inadequate.[94] The rights and values in these bills generally transcend the traditional divisions between civil law and common law, and opportunities exist to reinvigorate the system by a renewed selection from civil law as well as common law sources. This flexibility does not imply that these systems have to embark on a wholesale constitutional reshaping of every aspect of the existing law. In fact, in mixed systems where a measure of horizontality is accorded to instruments containing basic rights, the experience thus far has been one of incremental change.[95] But that some renewal is necessary, and that a comparative perspective will be especially valuable to promote this end, cannot be doubted. The scope of the challenge has been elegantly summarized by Gerhard Lubbe in the context of South African law:[96]

The impression is that rather than being at the culmination of its growth, the mixed system of Private law in South Africa stands at the beginning of further development and renewal informed by the impulse emanating from the Bill of Rights. This will not only necessitate a review and development of the substance of Private law, but also of its methodology in precisely those areas in which it has been found deficient and outdated. The need for renewal in both the substance and method of the mixed system will inevitably bring about further borrowing from the legal traditions that inspired its development in the first place . . .

(c) Exporting Quality: Mixed Systems and the Development of Private Law in Europe

As indicated earlier, the possibility has been raised for some time that the experiences of mixed jurisdictions in blending civil law and common law may conceivably be of great significance for the development of private law in Europe. In this regard Reinhard Zimmermann has commented as follows:[97]

The establishment of an intellectual connection between civil law and common law is widely regarded as the most important prerequisite for the emergence of a genuinely European legal scholarship. Thus, it should be of the greatest interest for legal scholars in Europe to see that such connection has already been established, on an intellectual as well as practical level, in a number of 'mixed' legal systems. They provide a wealth of experience of how these two branches of the European legal tradition may be accommodated within

---

[94] On possible constitutional impetus for further reform of South African law to protect weak parties to a contract, see R. H. Christie, 'The Law of Contract and the Bill of Rights', in *Bill of Rights Compendium* (loose-leaf, 1998–), para 3H–13, 14; Gerhard Lubbe, 'Ex Africa semper aliquid novi?— The Mixed Character of Contract Law in the New South Africa', in Jan Smits (ed), *The Contribution of Mixed Legal Systems to European Private Law* (2001), 78–9. However, on the somewhat limited scope for such intervention in Scots law, see MacQueen, (2003) 78 *Tulane LR* 378.

[95] See generally MacQueen, (2003) 78 *Tulane LR* 363; Gerhard F. Lubbe, 'Taking Fundamental Rights Seriously: The Bill of Rights and its Implications for the Development of Contract Law', (2004) 121 *South African LJ* 395.

[96] Lubbe (n 94), 80.   [97] Zimmermann (n 1), 126 f.

one legal system. . . . Some members of that family have codified their private law. Others are still largely based today on common (in the sense of uncodified) law. They present the particularly fascinating picture of courts and legal writers still having to grapple with the historical sources of the ius commune and of the English common law and thus being faced with the specific problems and challenges arising from a living interaction between civil law and common law.

To illustrate this point, Zimmermann refers to a number of instances from the law of contract and delict which demonstrate that South African or Scottish private law have managed to establish such a 'special connection' between civil law and common law.[98] The background to these and many other instances of blending in the fields of property and obligations has been examined in two collections of historical essays on South African and Scots law,[99] which in turn have been followed by a further collection in which jurists from both jurisdictions compare the positions to which their respective experiences in blending have led.[100] At present we therefore have a fairly comprehensive picture of how the two uncodified systems of Scots and South African law have mixed elements of civil law and common law in key areas of private law. However, scholarly studies such as these run the risk of having limited impact in the European context if they are not linked more explicitly to the broad range of initiatives currently aimed at developing a common private law in that region. It is therefore of particular interest that the positions reached by the two mixed jurisdictions in the field of contract law have recently been compared to the respective provisions of the *Principles of European Contract Law*.[101] It is, however, still too early to predict what benefit may be derived from studies such as this for the interpretation and evaluation of the Principles of European Contract Law.

Zimmermann's focus has been on developments in substantive private law which show that an intellectual connection exists between civil law and common law.[102] However, the experiences of mixed jurisdictions may also be relevant for the implementation of measures in order to bring about a harmonization of private law in Europe. For example, Mathias Reimann has argued that the experiences of Lousiana and Québec can be particularly instructive as far as the codification of European private law is concerned. The reasoning behind this view is that jurists in these systems 'do essentially what the Europeans are now planning to do:

---

[98] Zimmermann (n 1), 129 ff, 151 ff.

[99] Zimmermann and Visser (n 18); Kenneth Reid and Reinhard Zimmermann, *A History of Private Law in Scotland*, vol I, Introduction and Property; vol II, Obligations (2000).

[100] Zimmermann et al. (n 60).

[101] Hector MacQueen and Reinhard Zimmermann (eds), *European Contract Law: Scots and South African Perspectives* (2006).

[102] For a further example of how civil law and common law experiences in blending can be instructive in the European context, see Kötz, (2003) 78 *Tulane LR* 436–9. According to Kötz the use in Israel of more civilian styles of legislative drafting demonstrates that adopting it is not incompatible with the common law tradition.

Codifying private law in a mixed jurisdiction in which the civil law predominates, the common law must receive its due, and the rules must be compatible with both traditions'.[103] Again, the point is not that these systems are instructive because they have always got it right; it is rather that an examination of their actual experiences in the blending of civil law and common law rules is likely to benefit those who are faced with a very similar task.

Another area in respect of which the mixed jurisdiction experience may be relevant for European legal harmonization is the role of the judiciary. Let us recall the circumstances surrounding judicial blending of the civil law and common law in mixed systems: first, the conviction at times existed that an import was necessary because the existing law was regarded as inferior, some social or economic goal had to be pursued, or uniformity was perceived to be a value in its own right. Second, the judiciary (sometimes aided by the academic community) had a variety of techniques and opportunities which could be used to justify borrowing. These included having to deal with statutes that already introduced foreign law, making use of the facilitative influence of assumptions of similarity, and taking advantage of the existence of gaps and open-ended norms in the existing law. Finally, judges were often motivated to introduce the new rule because, by virtue of their training and cultural background, they found it to be more comprehensible and accessible than the domestic law.

If these experiences are anything to go by, the judges in the various European states do not seem to be well situated at present to contribute in any meaningful way to harmonization. The most obvious consideration is the still essentially nationalistic approach adopted by them: judges are generally constrained by law and practice to look at and apply local sources, and there is no widespread conviction that it may be necessary or worthwhile to seek assistance elsewhere. It is therefore difficult to conceive how the judiciary, especially in codified systems, could attempt to blend civil law and common law in the absence of legislative changes investing them with greater powers to further this end. However, even if these powers were granted, formidable practical obstacles would remain. Unlike their mixed jurisdiction colleagues, judges in Europe are faced with a great variety of jurisdictions. Given that mixed systems have often come up with different blends, even though their sources of borrowing were limited, it is possible that European jurisdictions, faced with the greater variety of possible influences, could through selective borrowing move toward greater diversity rather than greater uniformity. Ultimately, it seems that a crucial determinant of the harmonization of private law in Europe—whether by way of statute or increased judicial discretion—is the development of materials which point out the existing communalities and differences and then show how harmonization may be best effected.

---

[103] Mathias Reimann, 'Towards a European Civil Code: Why Continental Jurists Should Consult their Transatlantic Colleagues', (1999) 73 *Tulane LR* 1337, 1341 ff; see especially 1343 f for examples.

Ideal instruments which can be used towards this end are sets of principles, commentaries, and treatises.

(d) Predicting Patterns of Change: Mixed Systems and Determining in What Areas Private Law in Europe Could be Harmonized

The final respect in which the mixed jurisdiction experience may be relevant in the development of private law in Europe deserves separate treatment. In essence, it concerns the areas where harmonization is most likely to take place.

As indicated earlier, mixed jurisdictions have generally experienced similar patterns of common law influence in private law: whereas contract and especially delict have been most affected, the influence was much less pronounced in property and succession, as well as unjustified enrichment. These patterns may be coincidental, but the more probable explanation is provided by some of the factors that contributed to legal change in mixed systems.[104] These include the relative ease with which similarities could be identified in certain areas of law compared to others, which in turn was often determined by the uniqueness or otherwise of certain legal institutions and the quality of the sources. Where civil and common law institutions share the same structural roots, as in certain areas of contract law, the possibility of borrowing is greater; and where the sources are relatively undeveloped, as was the case of the common law of property and 'quasi-contract', as it was called for some time, the possibility is reduced. Further factors include social, cultural, and economic considerations. It can, for example, be expected that a particular system would be more 'culturally attached' to its law of succession and family law than to more 'neutral' areas such as contract and delict. As far as economic considerations are concerned, there can be no doubt that powerful mercantile interests have backed the pursuit of greater uniformity in the commercial law of mixed systems—a phenomenon that is familiar in the modern European context. It must be emphasized again, though, that these processes of selection did not necessarily reveal the best that these traditions had to offer. As indicated before, the conditions accompanying reception in these systems and the variety in blending do not justify such generalizations about their overall quality.[105]

However, there is another point of view. According to Jan Smits, the mixed legal systems of South Africa and Scotland demonstrate how a free movement of legal rules can lead to the best rules being chosen, and how a 'mixed' European private law can emerge. In this regard he has resorted to a 'Law and Economics' perspective, whereby the most efficient rules, as determined in a 'market of legal culture',

---

[104] See section III.2 above; Du Plessis, (2003) 78 *Tulane LR* 247 ff.

[105] cf also the review by John Bell of Jan Smits, *The Making of European Private Law* (2003) 119 *LQR* 330.

are supposed to prevail.[106] More recently, he has adopted an 'evolutionary perspective', and has argued that mixed systems such as Scots law show which areas are most likely to be harmonized.[107] It is not possible to deal with these views in great detail here, but, given the key role which mixed jurisdictions play in Smits's thinking, a few remarks are called for.

The first concerns the transferability of economic and evolutionary models to the legal context. As far as the economic model is concerned, it seems rather doubtful whether some sort of 'invisible hand' guides legal systems to chose optimal rules in a way similar to the choices economic actors make when transferring value. The mixed system experience demonstrates that there has often been no free 'selection' of rules, but direct imposition. This resembles the heavy-handed approach of a centrally run economy rather than the multitude of discrete rational transactions that are supposed to characterize the free market. Furthermore, even when the choice was exercised freely, it cannot be said that the 'best rule' was chosen. Unlike the economic actor, who is primarily interested in maximizing wealth, the legal reformer in mixed systems may be influenced by a variety of irrational considerations, such as an ideological bias in favour of the civil law or common law. This does not mean that efficiency-related concerns cannot play some role in legal development and harmonization; but such a view does not require us to embrace a model which works with general processes of market-style selection.

Second, as far as the evolutionary approach is concerned, it is difficult to appreciate how a model which explains the natural processes of selection of physical, living entities can readily be transposed to the legal environment, where the very notion that some rules can 'survive' while others become 'extinct' is jurisprudentially questionable. Apart from the broad patterns of penetration referred to above, the present record of mixed systems does not reflect any general 'organic' overall process whereby the best rules survive. On the contrary, mixed systems vary, and continue to vary in terms of the specific blends they come up with. Due to political and linguistic variables, some mixed systems, like Scotland and Louisiana, have gravitated towards the common law tradition, while others, like Cyprus and Québec, still hold on strongly to the civil law. In sum, while the mixed jurisdiction experience can be instructive in showing how some specific forms of mixing may

---

[106] See Jan Smits, 'A European Private law as a Mixed Legal System', (1998) *Maastricht Journal of European and Comparative Law* 328–40.

[107] Smits, (2003) 7(5) *Electronic Journal of Comparative Law*; and generally, 'The Harmonisation of Private Law in Europe: Some Insights from Evolutionary Theory', (2002) 31 *Georgia Journal of International and Comparative Law* 79, 81.

[108] Thus, for many centuries, civil law countries also made use of sources in Latin, while Law French was written in England. See generally Celia Wasserstein Feinberg, 'Language and Style in a Mixed System', (2003) 78 *Tulane LR* 151.

take place, it does not lend itself to analysis in terms of economic and evolutionary theories about legal harmonization.

4. Mixed Legal Systems and Language

Comparative lawyers have long had to grapple with the intricate relationship between law and language. One situation where this relationship has proven to be particularly problematic is where more than one language is used in a single legal system. Such a system need not necessarily be 'mixed' in the sense of being significantly influenced by two or more systems,[108] but, given that the phenomenon of multilingualism is pervasive in mixed systems, their experiences may be particularly instructive.[109]

The influence of language on the initial phase of a process of reception is an obvious point of departure. In a number of systems, the decision to retain the existing law seems to have been influenced strongly by linguistic considerations: where a population did not understand English, the wholesale introduction of the common law was hardly feasible. However, as indicated earlier, certain legal elites, and judges in particular, were often more at home with common law sources than with the civil and indigenous law. This was due, in part, to the relative accessibility of these sources, compared to those in Latin, French, Spanish, or Dutch. This experience again substantiates the observation that considerations other than the relative merits of rules can influence the process of mixing.

However, language has not only influenced the initial processes of reception, but also the continued development of mixed legal systems. The more widespread use of English has, for example, been accompanied by a decline in the capacity to understand civilian sources. Conversely, the spread of the common law has apparently been inhibited where the local language is not English.[110] One way of overcoming this decline has been to translate these sources into English, and thus make them more accessible. In Louisiana, for example, the Civil Code has for long appeared in English. Even though very few lawyers speak the original source language of French, the civil law lives on. In fact, it has even been said that one of the factors contributing to the civilian renaissance in Louisiana has been the proliferation of civilian doctrine through English translations.[111] In Israel and Cyprus, in turn, the promotion and recognition of Hebrew and Greek, respectively, has led to the need to translate civil as well as common law materials into those

---

[109] For a general overview, see Palmer (n 36), 41–4.

[110] On the position in Québec, see William Tetley, 'Nationalism in a Mixed Jurisdiction and the Importance of Language (South Africa, Israel and Quebec/Canada)', (2003) 78 *Tulane LR* 175, 215 f.

[111] See Mack E. Barnham, 'A Renaissance of the Civilian Tradition in Louisiana', (1973) 33 *Tulane LR* 357, 360.

languages.[112] And in South Africa, Afrikaans has been a successful medium for presenting civilian sources—for example, J. C. de Wet's masterly analysis in Afrikaans of the civilian sources formed the foundation for the modern South African law of contract.[113] However, nowadays the general legal environment is much less receptive to Afrikaans contributions, and the harsh reality is that the survival of the civilian component of South African law may increasingly depend on its being accessible in English. Likewise, its indigenous or customary component appears to have little chance of generally influencing the civil law and common law mix if it is not made more accessible by being presented in English.[114] The point, ultimately, is that translation can be crucial for the survival of sources expressed in languages which are incomprehensible to the vast majority of those who have to use them. The Louisiana experience, in particular, shows that while it might have advanced the future development of the civilian component if French were still widely spoken today, it has not been essential for its survival.[115] However, these remarks essentially relate to the need for translation to ensure the preservation and greater accessibility of legal sources. They do not imply that there should also be a move towards the dominance of one standard language in daily legal practice. Here practical as well as constitutional considerations may well require the protection of greater linguistic diversity.[116]

[112]   See Celia W. Fassberg, 'Language and Style in a Mixed System' (2003) 78 *Tulane LR* 151; Symeon C. Symeonides, 'The Mixed Legal System of the Republic of Cyprus', (2003) 78 *Tulane LR* 441, 450; Max Loubser, 'Linguistic Factors into the Mix: The South African Experience of Language and the Law', (2003) 78 *Tulane LR* 105. In Puerto Rico, Spanish apparently still has a strong standing in legal practice: Colón *et al* (n 42), 417.

[113]   J. C. de Wet and A. H. van Wyk, *Kontraktereg en Handelsreg* (vol I, 5th edn, 1992) (ed G. F. Lubbe). De Wet, who was Professor of Private Law and Roman Law at the University of Stellenbosch from 1942 to 1972, was the most influential South African legal academic of his time: Reinhard Zimmermann and Charl Hugo, 'Fortschritte der südafrikanischen Rechtswissenschaft im 20. Jahrhundert: Der Beitrag von J. C. de Wet (1912—1990)', (1992) 60 *Tijdschrift voor Rechtsgeschiedenis* 157.

[114]   The position of the African languages appears to be even more precarious than that of Afrikaans. Judge President John Hlope of the Cape Provincial Division of the High Court of South Africa has argued in favour of more widespread use of indigenous languages in the courts (Visser, (2003) 78 *Tulane LR* 75–6). However, in *S v Matomela* 1998 (2) All SA 1 (Ck), Judge President Vuka Tshabalala of the Natal Provincial Division of the High Court favoured the use of only one official language for all courts.

[115]   But cf Tetley, (2003) *Tulane LR* 187 f, 218. Further see Claire L'Heureux-Dubé, 'Bijuralism: A Supreme Court of Canada Justice's Perspective', (2001) 62 *Louisiana LR* 449, 451.

[116]   On the measures taken to protect Gaelic in the West of Scotland, subsequent to the ratification of the European Charter for Regional or Minority Languages (ETS No 148), see Hector MacQueen, 'Laws and Languages: Some Historical Notes from Scotland', *Ius Commune Lectures on European Private Law No 5* (2002), 4–5. In South Africa, language rights are also constitutionally protected, but it is unclear how this is to be effected. Loubser favours an approach of 'non-diminution', which '. . . could leave room for language diversity and the further development of languages by extended translation services, so that black languages may be used as languages of record where required, without diminution of the use of Afrikaans for legislation and as a language of record': (2003) 78 *Tulane LR* 148.

The focus thus far has been on language and established sources. But language can also play an important role in the continued development of a system through borrowing from modern common law and civil law systems—in other words, in the improvement of the quality of the system through acquiring a comparative perspective. And here again we see how language can act as conduit or as barrier: for example, in Anglophone countries, recourse to modern foreign civilian sources can be hampered by linguistic constraints, rather than some inherent bias against them,[117] and conversely, common law sources can enjoy an automatic advantage because they are in English, and not because they are necessarily more valuable. Again, there is nothing inevitable about this position. As in the case of retaining the existing civil law, experience has shown that even a limited number of jurists who can use foreign sources and present them in an accessible format can be quite influential.

In conclusion, it is tempting to reflect briefly on whether the mixed jurisdiction experience with language is relevant to the problem of European legal unification. The first observation is perhaps the most obvious: where political power is sufficiently strong, a significant degree of harmonization of the civil law and common law is possible, despite linguistic differences. As Hector MacQueen has stated, 'a common language is not a prerequisite of a common law'.[118] However, the mixed jurisdiction experience shows that language can have a constraining effect on the extent and duration of such an endeavour. Here the challenge was usually only to harmonize one representative of the civil law with one of the common law tradition, with the relevant sources also only being in a limited number of languages. The greater number of systems and languages in the European context indicate that formidable practical challenges lie ahead for those committed to the ideal of harmonization.

---

[117] On the inaccessibility of analyses of the civil law by South African academics in Afrikaans see eg T. B. Smith, 'Scots Law and Roman Dutch Law: A Shared Tradition', 1959 *Acta Juridica* 36 (= *Studies Critical and Comparative* (n 89), 46); Rodger, (1993) *Rechtshistorisches Journal* 261, 271. In Israel the promotion of Hebrew may have removed an advantage automatically enjoyed by English law, but it has also entailed a dwindling knowledge of civilian sources: see Goldstein (n 41), 467 f. According to Jean-Louis Boudouin, 'Quebec Report 2', in Palmer (n 1), 347 at 359, the use of French in Québec, in turn, has meant that it was never really cut off from continental European and French sources, and 'goes a long way to explain why civil law is really alive and well, and not threatened, in Quebec'.

[118] MacQueen (n 116), 16.

IV. CONCLUSIONS

Although legal systems generally are 'mixed' in the sense that they have been influenced by other systems, this label traditionally is only attached to those systems which represent a mix between the common law and the civilian tradition. Even though these systems occupy only a modest place among the legal systems of the world in terms of their number and the size of their populations, their experiences are highly stimulating when considering some of the most vital problems in modern comparative law.

First, the phenomenon of mixing poses significant challenges to those concerned with the classification of the world's legal systems. Where legal systems reflect strong influences from more than one tradition, it does not seem helpful to wait for them to move in the direction of one of the constituent legal families, or to accommodate them in classifications based on the fact that all systems are mixed. The preferable approach is to accept that they are sufficiently different to warrant independent recognition as a separate family.

Second, the experiences of mixed jurisdictions are relevant to debates on legal transplants. In the process of transplanting there is inevitably a change of context, so that the transplanted rule can never be identical to the one operating in its original habitat. However, the mixed jurisdiction experience does not substantiate the conclusion that a legal transplant is nothing more than a meaningless form of words. Mixed systems, on the contrary, do not only demonstrate that the donor and donee contexts may be quite compatible, but also how aspects of the donor legal culture itself can be adopted, thereby facilitating the borrowing of rules.

Third, mixed jurisdictions illustrate what practical techniques may be used to adopt rules from various foreign jurisdictions and what motivations may underlie the use of these techniques. Of particular interest from a comparative perspective is the role which the judiciary, in conjunction with the academic community, can play in gradually incorporating foreign law—for example through the filling of gaps, the interpretation of open-ended norms, or the exploitation of similarities between the local and the foreign law. These experiences suggest that there may be greater scope for comparative material to influence legal development than is usually appreciated.

Fourth, as far as the quality of the mixture is concerned, there is no firm indication that the processes of borrowing in mixed jurisdictions have *generally* given rise to law which is particularly good or particularly bad. In assessing the quality of the mixture, care must be taken not to ascribe change to a single factor, such as foreign dominance. It can be highly instructive, though, for comparative lawyers to examine specific instances where a doctrine from one legal background has been introduced into an ostensibly new, and incompatible, environment. Positive as well as negative experiences with these instances illustrate the importance of taking steps to ensure that the import fits in sufficiently with the existing law—even though such a development may take some time. This sensitivity to the question of the right fit is not in conflict with the dominant spirit of pragmatism: in fact, there is much force in the view that it is a key requirement for a rational, pragmatic development of the law. It is further suggested that it is crucial for jurists in mixed systems to be constantly alert to changes in the systems which have influenced them, as well as other systems with which they share the same foundations. The failure to engage in such a continuous process of comparative re-evaluation can lead to stagnation or decline.

Fifth, an examination of the mixed jurisdiction experience may be relevant for those engaged in developing private law in Europe. The track record in blending civil law and common law can assist in the development of a European private law, as well as in the evaluation of the instruments available for harmonization. It does not, however, appear to be particularly fruitful to examine these experiences through the lenses of economic or evolutionary theory.

Sixth, mixed systems demonstrate the crucial role that language can play in the initial processes of reception, as well as in subsequent legal developments. While the continued use of the original language of a particular component of the mix may strengthen its recognition and development, such use is not essential, as long as accessibility is ensured through appropriate translation. Language also has a crucial impact on the use of the comparative method in mixed systems. Although linguistic constraints may render jurists in mixed systems less able to draw fully on a variety of other legal systems in order to improve the quality of their own, they have at times proven to be remarkably resilient in overcoming these obstacles. Hopefully, they will continue to be so in future. What comparative lawyers may do as a matter of interest, jurists in mixed systems have to do as a matter of necessity.

BIBLIOGRAPHY

Esin Örücü, Elspeth Attwooll, and Sean Coyle (eds), *Studies in Legal Systems: Mixed and Mixing* (1996)

Vernon Valentine Palmer (ed), *Louisiana: A Microcosm of a Mixed Jurisdiction* (1999)

—— (ed), *Mixed Jurisdictions Worldwide—The Third Legal Family* (2001)

Reinhard Zimmermann, *Roman Law, Contemporary Law, European Law: The Civilian Tradition Today* (2001)

J. M. Smits (ed), *The Contribution of Mixed Legal Systems to European Private Law* (2001)

—— *The Making of European Private Law—Toward a Ius Commune Europaeum as a Mixed Legal System* (2001)

First Worldwide Congress on Mixed Jurisdictions—Salience and Unity in the Mixed Jurisdiction Experience: Traits, Patterns, Culture, Commonalities (2003) 78 *Tulane LR* 1 ff

Reinhard Zimmermann, Daniel Visser, and Kenneth Reid (eds), *Mixed Legal Systems in Comparative Perspective—Property and Obligations in Scotland and South Africa* (2004)

Elspeth Reid and David L. Carey Miller (eds), *A Mixed Legal System in Transition—T B Smith and the Progress of Scots Law* (2005)

Hector MacQueen and Reinhard Zimmermann (eds), *European Contract Law: Scots and South African Perspectives* (2006)

CHAPTER 15

COMPARATIVE LAW AND ITS INFLUENCE ON NATIONAL LEGAL SYSTEMS

JAN M. SMITS

Maastricht

I. INTRODUCTION

THIS contribution does not deal with comparative law as an academic discipline, but focuses on some of its more practical applications.[1] It is well known that, alongside the scholarly pursuit of knowledge of similarities among and differences between legal systems, comparative law may also fulfil a role in national legal practice. The most obvious example of this is the use of comparative law by national legislatures and courts in creating, reforming, and interpreting national law.[2] This practical use of comparative law by national institutions has increased considerably over the last few decades. Particularly in Europe, comparative reasoning seems to play an ever larger role in drafting statutes and deciding cases. Still, in legal systems that have been mainly national in outlook and character over the last two centuries, many aspects of this recourse to foreign law are far from clear. One of the key questions is the extent to which it is legitimate for a court to refer to foreign law in a purely domestic dispute. While in Europe the drawing of comparative inspiration in such cases is usually met with enthusiasm, this is different in the United States, where it is keenly debated whether such 'comparative reasoning' is allowed, particularly in constitutional cases.

In this chapter, the scholarly state of affairs regarding the influence of comparative law in national systems is critically assessed. In so doing, emphasis is put on private law and constitutional law, as these are the two areas where comparative inspiration is discussed most vigorously. The structure is as follows. In Sections II and III, several types of use of comparative law by national legislatures and courts are distinguished and various examples of such influence are given. This provides the background for a critical evaluation of this influence in the subsequent sections. Apart from the legitimacy question and the question of how to categorize the different uses of foreign law (both discussed in Section IV), two other important points need to be addressed. The first is why a legislature or court actually refers to foreign law: is it always to find a better solution or are there more strategic reasons? The second is how to explain the different extent to which countries are open to foreign influence. Both questions are discussed in Section V. It then remains to consider what the exact influence of comparative law arguments on the legislature's or court's reasoning is. Despite sometimes abundant references to foreign

---

[1] See, on the various functions of comparative law, Konrad Zweigert and Hein Kötz, *An Introduction to Comparative Law* (trans Tony Weir, 3rd edn, 1998), 13 ff; René David and Camille Jauffret-Spinosi, *Les grands systèmes de droit contemporains* (11th edn, 2002), 4 ff.

[2] This topic was discussed several times at the meetings of the International Academy of Comparative Law (at the Seventh Congress in Uppsala in 1966, at the Eleventh Congress in Caracas in 1982, at the Fourteenth Congress in Athens in 1994 and at the Fifteenth Congress in Bristol in 1998). In this contribution, no attention is paid to comparative reasoning by European courts; on which see eg Markku Kiikeri, *Comparative Legal Reasoning and European Law* (2001).

law in explanatory memoranda to legislation or in court decisions, the true effect of comparative reasoning remains somewhat unclear. By way of a summary, Section VI addresses this point.

II. COMPARATIVE LAW AND THE NATIONAL LEGISLATURES

The use of comparative law while drafting new legislation is as old as the phenomenon of statutory law itself. It is well known that the law of the Twelve Tables (450 BC) was influenced by Roman visits to foreign (in particular Greek) cities and even the Code of Hammurabi (1700 BC) is presumably based upon the laws then prevailing in the Near East. In fact, the modern science of comparative law was primarily provoked by the wish to look at foreign law to improve national legislation. This discipline of 'législation comparée', as propagated by the *Société de Législation Comparé* (founded in 1869), led to the study of foreign codes not only in France but also in other countries. Famous examples of drawing inspiration from foreign law are to be found in Germany, where the Prussian company law of 1843 was partly based upon the French Commercial Code of 1807 and where the large nineteenth-century unification projects in the areas of private law, procedural law, and criminal law were inspired by extensive comparative research as well.[3] There is also abundant evidence of such influence of foreign law on national legislation in other countries. When Alan Watson held that the migration of ideas between legal systems is 'the most fertile source of (legal) development',[4] he referred mainly to legislation being adopted by countries other than those for which it was originally passed. More examples include income tax, which was imported from England to the European Continent around 1800, Austrian competition law, which formed the basis for the German *Kartellgesetz* of 1923, the Swedish institution of the ombudsman, which was taken over in many countries, and the French *Loi Badinter* (1985), which regulates the compensation of victims of traffic accidents and which was itself based upon comparative research and subsequently influenced other European countries' legislation. The wholesale importation of civil codes into other countries is also a well-known phenomenon. Thus, not only did the French *Code civil* serve as a model for many countries in Europe

---

[3] See, for such examples, Ulrich Drobnig and Peter Dopffel, 'Die Nutzung der Rechtsvergleichung durch den deutschen Gesetzgeber', (1982) 46 *RabelsZ* 253 ff.

[4] Alan Watson, *Legal Transplants* (2nd edn, 1993), 95.

and South America, the Swiss Civil Code of 1907 was taken over in Turkey (1926), and the drafts of the 1900 German Civil Code, together with French law, played a large role in the drafting of the Civil Code of Japan (1896). The new civil codes of the Netherlands (1992) and Québec (1994), and the new German law of obligations of 2002, were also based upon extensive comparative reasoning. Likewise, it is no coincidence that most European countries have enacted rather similar laws in the fields of environmental liability, company law, social security, and family law. Sometimes it seems as if one can meticulously trace the migration of an institution from one country to another: thus, same-sex marriage was first recognized by statute in the Netherlands in 2002, subsequently accepted in Belgium and most of the Canadian provinces in 2003 (followed by the whole of Canada in 2005), accepted in the state of Massachusetts (2004) and Spain (2005), and its introduction is now being discussed in many other countries. Of special importance is the influence of Western law on the former communist countries of Central and Eastern Europe: the new codes in the areas of civil, commercial, and criminal law were usually based upon extensive comparative considerations. The same is true for China, which also based its new contract code of 1999 on comparative research.

In most of the above examples, the respective governments had resources available to integrate comparative law findings into the drafting of new legislation. In civil law countries such as Germany and France this has even become routine: in the drafting of any major new statute, the ministry of justice usually looks for inspiration to the laws of other countries. In this respect, it sometimes solicits opinions on foreign law from comparative law research centres, but not infrequently it relies on research by its own civil servants. This is different in many common law jurisdictions, where a ministry of justice in the Continental style does not exist.[5] However, one cannot say that there is less influence of foreign law on these countries' legal systems, only that such influence takes a different form. In the United Kingdom, it is through the English and Scottish Law Commissions that comparative law finds its way into legislation. Section 3(1)(f) of the Law Commissions Act 1965 states that one of the functions of the Law Commissions is 'to obtain such information as to the legal systems of other countries as appears to the Commissioners likely to facilitate the performance of any of their functions' (ie systematically developing and reforming the law of England and Scotland). An example is the (English) Law Commission's report on 'Privity of Contracts: Contracts for the Benefit of Third Parties'. It not only discussed the laws of other common law jurisdictions, but also stated that a factor in support of reform of the third party rule in English law was that 'the legal systems of most of the member states of the European Union recognise and enforce the rights of third party

---

[5] Rudolph B. Schlesinger, Hans W. Baade, Peter E. Herzog, and Edward M. Wise, *Comparative Law* (6th edn, 1998), 15.

beneficiaries under contracts'.[6] The report led in the end to the Contracts (Rights of Third Parties) Act 1999.

In the United States, the American Law Institute (founded in 1932) makes use of comparative law in drafting the Restatements of Law. Model codes (like the Model Penal Code) are also inspired by other legal systems, and even in the field of competition law the federal legislature benefited from European experience in reviewing the Sherman Antitrust Act of 1890.[7] Generally speaking, however, the American debate is less enlightened by foreign law than is the case in Europe: reference to foreign law is made, but it seems to play a less important role than in European countries. This may be linked to the fact that inter-state comparison (ie among the fifty-three American jurisdictions) is much more important than comparison with legal systems outside the United States. 'The American common law', as Zaphiriou states, 'contains contrasts that are almost as instructive and often more constructive than any comparison with the law of a foreign country'.[8]

When confronted with these examples, one can only agree with Schlesinger:[9] little new legislation is enacted, in Europe and elsewhere, without at least some comparative research, and *every* legal system contains imported elements. The above examples raise several questions. One is what the *exact* influence of the comparative argument has been on new legislation: it is often very difficult to establish the extent to which foreign law was decisive for the way in which a national statute was drafted. Same-sex marriage offers a good example of this: the mere fact that the Dutch recognized this type of marriage in a statute is not likely to have played as important a role as prevailing societal and cultural opinion in the Belgian, Canadian, and Spanish decisions to adopt this institution as well. In other words: these 'importing' countries would probably have accepted same-sex marriage even *without* the Dutch example. It is also important to note that the most common way in which foreign law permeates national law is through national legal writing; for often legal academics take up a point from some foreign legal system, make it part of the national discourse, and thus bring it to the notice of the legislatures of their respective countries. Ludwig Raiser's book on standard contract terms of 1935,[10] based upon comparative considerations, was received in German doctrine and this in turn influenced the German legislature to introduce, in 1976, a special statutory regime on this topic.

In the literature on comparative inspiration of the legislature, one finds few attempts to categorize different types of foreign influence. One may distinguish between the wholesale importation of large pieces of law (like a complete civil code)

---

[6] Law Commission, 'Privity of Contracts: Contracts for the Benefit of Third Parties', (Law Com No. 242, 1996), 41.

[7] cf George A. Zaphiriou, 'Use of Comparative Law by the Legislator', (1982) 30 *AJCL* 71 ff for these and other examples.

[8] Zaphiriou, (1982) 30 *AJCL* 91. Also see Section V, below.   [9] Schlesinger *et al.* (n 5), 13.

[10] Ludwig Raiser, *Das Recht der Allgemeinen Geschäftsbedingungen* (1935).

and the adoption of specific rules. One might also distinguish between the voluntary and mandatory borrowing of foreign law. In instances of mandatory borrowing a state is obliged to adopt a foreign statute, as in the case of the importation of a civil code by way of colonization or conquest. In most cases, however, the national legislature's reasons for drawing inspiration from foreign law are far more subtle; indeed, they may not differ fundamentally from those explaining why national courts look at foreign law. These reasons are being explored in Section V below.

III. COMPARATIVE LAW AND THE NATIONAL COURTS

1. Introduction

A national court making use of foreign materials is often considered to be far more exciting than a national legislature doing the same thing. The reason for this is probably that in the traditional view a court, unlike the legislature, has to *apply* national law, not to *create* it. At the same time, however, this statement makes clear that there can be very good reasons for a court to look at foreign law, in particular where national law does not offer a solution to the case at hand, either because the applicable rule is unclear or because there is no rule available at all. It is the famous Art 1 of the Swiss Civil Code which relates the task of the court to that of the legislature by stating that: 'If no relevant provisions can be found in a statute, the judge must decide in accordance with customary law, and, in its absence, according to the rule which he would, were he the legislator, adopt. In so doing he must pay attention to accepted doctrine and tradition'.

In principle, this opens up the national debate to foreign influence and in Swiss practice the *Bundesgericht* does indeed often refer to comparative law in difficult cases. In other countries courts are more reluctant to do so, but there, too, the use of comparative law by courts is on the rise.

Before an overview of national court practice in respect of this 'voluntary' or 'optional' recourse to foreign law is given, it is useful to remember that there are also cases in which it is mandatory, or highly desirable, for a court to look at law of foreign origin.[11] The most obvious example is when conflict of laws rules oblige the

---

[11] For the common distinction between mandatory and voluntary recourse to foreign law see eg Raymond Legeais, 'l'Utilisation du droit compare par les tribunaux', (1994) 46 *Revue internationale de droit comparé* 348; Ulrich Drobnig, 'The Use of Comparative Law by Courts', in Ulrich Drobnig and Sjef Van Erp (eds), *The Use of Comparative Law by Courts* (1999), 6 ff.

court simply to apply another country's legal system, for example because of a choice of law by the contracting parties. But it can also be that private international law requires some sort of comparison with the court's own national law, as in cases of *qualification*: if a foreign rule that does not have an equivalent in the forum state needs to be applied, it must first be compared with the law of the *lex fori*.[12] Another example in which a court is obliged to compare legal systems with each other is offered by Arts 5 and 6 of the Rome Convention of 1980,[13] which protect the consumer and the worker by offering them the minimum protection of their own legal system in cases where a less favourable legal system is declared to be applicable. And since Art 288(2) EC Treaty on the delictual liability of the European Union and its agents prescribes that this liability is to be determined 'in accordance with the general principles common to the laws of the member states', the court can only derive such principles from a comparison of the laws of the member states.

There are also cases in which a court is not required to take account of foreign law, but in which it seems highly desirable to do so. This is the position if the field of law is so international that reference to foreign authorities is natural. Obvious examples are maritime law and transportation law, both of which are greatly influenced by international treaties. If national law is based upon such a treaty, a proper 'uniform' interpretation should take into account the way in which other countries implement its provisions. Many treaties[14] therefore state that the international character of the treaty is to be taken into account in interpreting its provisions. The same is true for the interpretation of European law: even though it is the European Court of Justice that is to supervise the proper interpretation of EC law, the contribution by national courts in interpreting provisions of national law based on European legislation in a European spirit is vital. Finally, there is an extra reason to look at foreign law if a statute has a foreign origin. The idea behind the American 'borrowed statute' doctrine, which allows a court to interpret the statute in accordance with the foreign source, is also accepted in many other countries. Thus, Australia adopted a constitution after the American model and Australian courts are therefore keen to look at American law when interpreting it.

2. Voluntary Recourse to Foreign Law in Domestic Disputes

When the influence of comparative law on national courts is discussed, it is often the *voluntary* use of foreign law in purely *domestic* disputes that forms the centre of attention. There are now examples of such influence in almost every legal system, even though important differences between various countries are to be appreciated.

---

[12] Drobnig (n 11), 8.

[13] Convention on the law applicable to Contractual Obligations (Rome, 1980).

[14] See eg Art 17(1) 1 CISG.

Concerning this voluntary recourse to foreign law, it should always be kept in mind that it is a 'luxurious' form of legal analysis[15] that cannot be expected from every judge. One may even wonder whether it is permitted. Some countries (particularly in South America) explicitly prohibit the application of foreign law, while in other (mostly European) countries it is not formally forbidden but not done very often. The truth is that recourse to foreign law is not so much the application of a foreign legal regime in a national context, but usually only the taking over of a foreign *argument* if it fits in with the national legal system and if this is found necessary. It is thus of persuasive rather than formal authority.[16]

When is there a need in a domestic dispute to find persuasive authority elsewhere? The reasons already mentioned—national law has a *lacuna* or is unclear—are not completely convincing as these problems have always existed and can also be solved within the purely national context by using techniques which courts have used time and again. The increasing use of comparative arguments has more to do with the growing feeling among many (in particular supreme) courts that it may be counter-productive *not* to benefit from foreign experience. This is all the more so if similar problems arise in different countries. Koopmans[17] points out that many countries face identical legal problems caused by the pollution of air, water, and soil, new (bio-)technology, an emerging claim culture, migration, urban decay, and so on. For a variety of reasons, political institutions often do not enact legislation to deal with these problems, thus leaving a large burden on the courts.

It is therefore no surprise that most cases in which a court looks at foreign law[18] concern controversial new issues for which no solution can be found in the existing national law (be it statute or precedent). Thus, the question whether 'immaterial damages' should be awarded in cases of infringement of privacy (which at the time was denied by the German Civil Code) was answered affirmatively by the highest German civil and constitutional courts, and by both of them with reference to foreign law.[19] In the Netherlands it was debated whether damages for pain and suffering may be allowed at all, a question on which the civil code was silent at the time. The Dutch Supreme Court awarded damages, also drawing upon the law of neighbouring countries.[20] Likewise, the question whether actions for wrongful

---

[15] cf N. S. Marsh, 'Comparative Law and Law Reform', (1977) 41 *RabelsZ* 655.

[16] cf H Patrick Glenn, 'Persuasive Authority', (1897) 32 *McGill LJ* 261 ff. and Basil Markesinis, 'Comparative Law in Search of an Audience', (1990) 53 *Modern LR* 1.

[17] T. Koopmans, 'Comparative Law and the Courts', (1996) 45 *ICLQ* 549.

[18] For more extensive surveys, see Drobnig and Van Erp (n 11); Guy Canivet, Mads Andenas, and Duncan Fairgrieve (eds), *Comparative Law before the Courts* (2004); Bernhard Aubin, 'Die rechtsvergleichende Interpretation autonom-internen Rechts in der deutschen Rechtsprechung', (1970) 34 *RabelsZ* 458 ff; Ulrich Drobnig, 'Rechtsvergleichung in der deutschen Rechtsprechung', (1986) 50 *RabelsZ* 610 ff; Legeais, (1994) 46 *Revue internationale de droit comparé* 347 ff; Hein Kötz, 'Der Bundesgerichtshof und die Rechtsvergleichung', in *idem, Undogmatisches* (2005), 120 ff.

[19] BGH 5 March 1963, BGHZ 39, 124 and BVerfG 14 February 1973, BVerfGE 34, 269.

[20] HR 21 May 1943, *Nederlandse Jurisprudentie* 1943, 455 (*Van Kreuningen v Bessem*).

birth or wrongful life should be allowed was answered in the 1980s and 1990s by highest courts throughout the world, most of them making use of the decisions of their foreign colleagues.[21] Furthermore, in deciding whether land rights should be given to aboriginals the Australian High Court relied heavily on arguments taken from other legal systems, citing fourteen cases in favour of its decision, only three of which were Australian.[22] The same is true for the Supreme Court of Canada, which made extensive use of American case law in deciding which rights aboriginals should have.[23] In South Africa and in the United States foreign material has been used to analyse arguments for and against the death sentence.[24]

One should not derive from these examples the conclusion that voluntary recourse to foreign law is now common in controversial cases. It is far from that. There are many cases that do not refer to foreign law at all, even though this would have been fruitful and legal counsel explicitly referred to it. In this respect, it may be useful to look at four countries in more detail. France, Germany, England, and the United States differ considerably in the extent to which their courts take foreign law into account when deciding purely domestic cases.

In Germany it is not uncommon for the highest court to refer to foreign law in order to support its arguments, but the number of cases in which this actually happens is limited. Not surprisingly, most of the references are to other countries within the Germanic legal family, such as Switzerland and Austria, and there are only a few cases in which English, American, or French law is cited. Some examples in the field of private law have already been given above. In criminal law, the German Supreme Court decided that statements made by a defendant during a police interview were not admissible as evidence if the defendant had not been informed of his right to remain silent and of his right to legal representation. In doing so, the Court referred to the famous American case of *Miranda v Arizona* of 1966 and to French, English, and Dutch law.[25]

The situation in France is very different. In French case law there are hardly any references to foreign law. This is not surprising as the decisions of the French *Cour de cassation* in particular are not extensively reasoned and usually do not even contain references to French case law or legal doctrine. The same is true for the Netherlands and Belgium, where the sparse references to foreign law are only in the most general terms (eg that the outcome is in accordance with legislation and case

---

[21] For an overview of these cases, see Walter van Gerven, Jeremy Lever, and Pierre Larouche (eds), *Cases, Materials and Text on National, Supranational and International Tort Law* (2000), 114 ff; and Christian von Bar, *The Common European Law of Torts* (vol I, 1998), 601 ff. The most recent summary of common law cases on this issue is given by the High Court of Australia in *Cattanach v Melchior* [2003] HCA 38.

[22] High Court of Australia, *Mabo & Others v State of Queensland* (1992) 107 ALR 1.

[23] *Inter alia* in *Van der Peet v The Queen* (1996) 2 SCR 507.

[24] cf *State v Makwanyane*, 1995 (3) SA 391 (CC) and below text to n 42 and n 60.

[25] BGH [1992] *Neue Juristische Wochenschrift* 1463.

law in neighbouring countries). One should however be careful not to draw the general conclusion that foreign law has no influence at all on the court's reasoning in these countries. In civil law countries which have a system of Advocates-General who advise the Supreme Court, it is in the opinion (*conclusion*) of the Advocate-General that one often finds elaborate comparative considerations. In many cases the decision of the court can be related to parts of the Advocate-General's opinion, although it is, of course, difficult to accept a clear relationship between foreign law and the court's decision if the court does not make an explicit reference to the corresponding part of the Advocate-General's opinion.[26] But sometimes the influence cannot be coincidental: in a decision of 1991, the French *Cour de cassation*[27] held that Art 1384 of the *Code civil* entailed a general liability for other people's acts. In 1920, the Privy Council had applied the same reasoning in a Québec decision on the similar provision of the Québec Civil Code. This decision probably influenced part of French legal doctrine, which in turn influenced the Advocate-General in the *Cour de cassation* case. This led, in the end, to the court's following its Advocate-General and thus, indirectly, the law of Québec.

The most spectacular development has taken place in England in this respect. It was, and still is, common for an English court to refer to other common law jurisdictions: thus, even after the abolition of appeals to the Privy Council, English law influenced Australian and Canadian law (and vice versa). This is quite logical in view of the shared legal heritage in these countries, which makes it difficult even to say whether a specific rule is 'foreign'. Although during the nineteenth century, and particularly in the field of contract law, civil law exerted quite a strong influence on the common law, during the twentieth century it became almost unheard of to derive arguments from civil law countries. Even in 1978 Lord Diplock stated that it would not be consistent with English law 'to attempt to incorporate holus-bolus from some other system of law, even so close as that of Scotland, doctrines or legal concepts that have hitherto been unrecognized in English common law'.[28] At best, civil law was mentioned in passing when brought to the attention of the court and certainly did not guide the court's decision.[29] But this changed in the 1990s, a period described by Lord Bingham as 'the time when England . . . ceased to be a legal island'.[30] The turning point was the decision of the House of Lords in *White v Jones*.[31] A testator had asked his solicitor to change his will to the benefit of some of

---

[26] See Drobnig (n 11), 5.

[27] Cour de cassation, Ass plén 29 March 1991, *Jurisclasseur périodique* 1991.II.21673, on which Legeais, (1994) 46 *Revue internationale de droit comparé* 358.

[28] *MacShannon v Rockware Glass Ltd* [1978] AC 795, 811.

[29] Örücü demonstrates that between 1972 and 1995, little has changed in English courts looking for guidance in the civil law: Esin Örücü, 'Comparative Law in British Courts', in Drobnig and Van Erp (n 11), 253 ff.

[30] T. H. Bingham, ' "There is a World Elsewhere": The Changing Perspectives of English Law', (1992) 41 *ICLQ* 514.

[31] *White and Another v Jones and Others* [1995] 2 AC 207.

his descendants. The solicitor failed to execute these instructions before the testator died. The intended beneficiaries were successful in claiming their loss from the solicitor. In his leading speech, Lord Goff relied heavily on comparative law arguments from civil law systems (in particular German law), even though these arguments were not directly influential for the outcome.[32] The case was followed by several others in which comparative reasoning played an even larger role, such as in *Greatorex v Greatorex*,[33] in which the High Court allowed a claim for psychiatric damage on the basis of arguments derived from a similar German case, and *Fairchild v Glenhaven Funeral Services*,[34] in which the normal rules of causation were not applied in a case where a person suffering from a disease caused by exposure to asbestos dust would otherwise not have been able to show which of several employers had caused his illness. Alongside common law authority, the House of Lords quoted civil law sources from Germany, Norway, France, and the Netherlands. Sometimes the House of Lords also refers to a lack of international consensus, as in the *Pretty* case[35] where the right to assisted suicide was denied.

It is clear that references to civil law cases by the House of Lords are usually based on legal literature and not so much on a reading of the foreign cases themselves: it is through the 'filter' of comparative literature[36] that foreign law enters a decision. In the wrongful birth case of *McFarlane v Tayside Health Board*, the House of Lords referred to precedents from civil law systems, basing itself on the *ius commune* casebook on tort law[37] and other literature. It is quite likely that the growing interest in foreign law among English courts would not have originated without such comparative legal literature.

In the United States foreign law does not play an important role in court decisions. Although in the past there have been considerable civil law influences on American law, in particular in the early nineteenth and mid-twentieth centuries as a result of émigré lawyers who influenced legal practice through their writings,[38] the

---

[32] See the criticism of Lord Rodger of Earlsferry, 'Savigny in the Strand' (First John Kelly Memorial Lecture, Dublin 1995), 24 ('only rather limited and inconclusive assistance from looking at Civil Law material').

[33] [2000] 1 WLR 1970, on which see Basil Markesinis, 'Foreign Law Inspiring National Law: Lessons from Greatorex v. Greatorex', in *idem*, *Comparative Law in the Courtroom and Classroom* (2003), 157 ff.

[34] [2003] 1 AC 32, on which see Jens M. Scherpe, 'Ausnahmen vom Erfordernis eines strikten Kausalitätsnachweises im englischen Deliktsrecht', (2004) 12 *Zeitschrift für Europäisches Privatrecht* 164 ff.

[35] *Regina (Pretty) v Director of Public Prosecutions* [2002] 1 AC 800.

[36] Bernhard Grossfeld, 'Vom Beitrag der Rechtsvergleichung zum deutschen Recht', (1984) 184 *Archiv für die civilistische Praxis* 295.

[37] 2000 SC (HL) 1. The reference was to the first edition (1998) of the Casebook mentioned in n 21.

[38] See Marcus Lutter, Ernst C. Stiefel, and Michael H. Hoeflich (eds), *Der Einfluß deutscher Emigranten auf die Rechtsentwicklung in den USA und Deutschland* (1993); Schlesinger *et al* (n 5) 9 ff; for England, see now Jack Beatson and Reinhard Zimmermann (eds), *Jurists Uprooted: German-Speaking Émigré Lawyers in Twentieth-Century Britain* (2004).

present situation can be characterized as parochial. On the whole, the conclusion which Levasseur drew in 1999 still stands: with the exception of Louisiana, 'the relevance of foreign . . . comparative law in American courts is almost nil'.[39]

This is not to say that there are no examples of state courts or of the United States Supreme Court referring to foreign law; in the field of constitutional law there are even signs indicating a significant change. A famous old example is *Muller v Oregon*,[40] in which the Supreme Court had to decide the constitutionality of Oregon's 'maximum hours for women' law. Counsel for the state of Oregon was the later Supreme Court Justice Louis D. Brandeis; he referred to a whole range of foreign statutes (including those of France, Germany, Austria, Italy, and the Netherlands) that restricted the working hours of women. Justice Brewer did not consider these to be authorities in a technical sense, but did consider them to be 'significant of a widespread belief that woman's physical structure, and the functions she performs in consequence thereof, justify special legislation . . .'. In *Roe v Wade*[41] Justice Blackmun also referred to historical and comparative materials on abortion.

As to the interpretation of the Eighth Amendment to the Constitution of the United States, comparative reasoning is on the rise. The Amendment prohibits 'cruel and unusual punishments'. There are now several cases in which the Supreme Court refers to international opinion to find out what is a cruel and unusual punishment in view of 'the evolving standards of decency that mark the progress of a maturing society'. In the 2005 case of *Roper v Simmons*,[42] for example, the Court held that the execution of offenders who were under the age of 18 when they committed their crimes was a violation of the Eighth Amendment. The majority of the Court found confirmation for its view in the fact that executing juveniles violated several international treaties and that 'the overwhelming weight of international opinion [was] against the juvenile death penalty'. This reliance on foreign materials provoked fierce reactions that may be typical of the American attitude *vis-à-vis* foreign law. I will come back to this in Section IV, below.

This short survey reveals that the exact role of the reference to foreign law in a purely domestic case is often not very clear. The above evidence merely suggests that courts (like legislatures) do sometimes refer to foreign law, but we are in need of an analytical structure to categorize these cases and to explain why these references, by both courts and legislatures, are justified. These questions are addressed in the next section.

---

[39] See Alain A. Levasseur, 'The Use of Comparative Law by Courts', in Drobnig and Van Erp (n 11), 333.
[40] 208 US 412 (1907).   [41] 410 US 113 (1972).   [42] 543 US 551 (2005).

IV. The Legitimacy of Comparative Law Influence: Why Comparative Inspiration?

1. A Categorization of Types of Comparative Influence

Legislatures and courts can make use of comparative law for a variety of reasons. It seems useful to distinguish these into three different groups, whilst recognizing that this is not the only possible categorization. In the American literature in particular one can find a whole range of possible categorizations, ranging from the very practical to the very sophisticated. Thus, Tushnet makes a distinction between functionalism, expressivism, and bricolage,[43] and Choudry distinguishes between universalist, dialogical, and genealogical comparative interpretation.[44] The distinction adopted here is a more practical one, based on the criterion of whether or not the legislature or the court uses foreign law as a normative argument.

First, legislatures and courts can make use of comparative law as a source of fresh ideas and, particularly, in order to find a solution to a given problem. It is this type of reasoning that comes closest to the idea of comparative inspiration, of comparative law as a means for the legislature or the court to inform itself about other countries' solutions and to gather ideas from this 'fund'. Thus, the legislature may want to know which new topics to address; or if it already knows the topics to be placed on the legislative agenda, it may want to know how to draft rules to address the issues which they raise; or, if it already knows how to draft such rules, it may want to know how they will operate in practice. In all these cases foreign law may offer inspiration. Similarly a court that does not know how to solve a case, how to interpret a national rule, or how to deal with a certain argument, may look for inspiration elsewhere. There is no need for the legislature or court to give any justification for looking at foreign law at this stage. Often the use of foreign law will be 'hidden'[45] in the sense that it does not show in the explanatory memorandum or in the court decision. In other cases the fact that foreign law has been consulted will be mentioned 'in passing'. But this is not important because no normative weight is attached to the foreign law.

---

[43] Mark Tushnet, 'The Possibilities of Comparative Constitutional Law', (1999) 108 *Yale LJ* 1225.

[44] Sujit Choudhry, 'Globalization in Search of Justification: Toward a Theory of Comparative Constitutional Interpretation', (1999) 74 *Indiana LJ* 819 ff. For more distinctions, see Taavi Annus, 'Comparative Constitutional Reasoning: The Law and Strategy of Selecting the Right Arguments', (2004) 14 *Duke Journal of Comparative and International Law* 307 ff.

[45] This term is used by J. H. M. Van Erp, 'The Use of Comparative Law in the Legislative Process', in Ewoud H. Hondius (ed), *Netherlands Reports to the 15th International Congress of Comparative Law* (1998), 34.

Second, legislatures and courts may refer to foreign law as a normative argument. This means that foreign law plays a role in justifying a court decision or a statute: it is at least one factor which favours a particular result. It is of course not the only such factor: its importance is still to be decided and it may well be that the comparative argument is overridden by others, with the result that the foreign example is not followed.

There are two types of such 'normative' use of foreign law. It may be that foreign experience is looked to as an illustration of how a certain rule is applied in practice, turning foreign experience into an empirical argument for the legislature or court. When the American Supreme Court decided against the legality of assisted suicide,[46] it took the Dutch experience into account and considered the (albeit contested) evidence that the Dutch guidelines had in practice failed to protect patients from involuntary euthanasia. Annus rightly observes that foreign countries may thus serve as a laboratory:[47] their experiences may help legislatures and courts to avoid mistakes made elsewhere, and possibly also to convince a national audience of the utility of a foreign institution. In this respect, it was helpful that countries wanting to introduce an ombudsman could point to the success of the Swedish example.

But it may also be that the content of foreign law itself is a normative argument to adopt a certain solution. In such cases, foreign law contributes directly to the court decision or legislation and thus possesses authority for the court or the legislature: it is *because* a particular solution has been adopted elsewhere that the court or legislature wants to do the same. This argument may still have to be balanced against others, but it *does* have normative weight as an authority-based argument. The best examples of such 'hard' use[48] of foreign law are cases in which a certain international consensus, or a foreign solution, is explicitly used as an argument for adopting the same solution at the national level. The argument then is simply that the mere fact that the world community, or a foreign state, adopted a particular solution is (co-)decisive for the outcome in one's own country. The American cases on the proper interpretation of the Eighth Amendment are—highly criticized— examples of this approach. Another example is the case law of the various courts within the Commonwealth in which a solution is sometimes adopted *because* it is in line with the law of other jurisdictions. This type of argument functions at the same level as the argument that a certain outcome is in line with legal history and should *therefore* be adopted.

It is not always easy to establish whether a legislature or a court uses foreign law as a normative argument. Often, the method of reasoning is far more subtle because it is not the foreign decision or statute as such that is used as the basis for

---

[46] *Washington v Glucksberg* 521 US 702 (1997).

[47] Annus, (2004) 14 *Duke Journal of Comparative and International Law* 337.

[48] Annus, (2004) 14 *Duke Journal of Comparative and International Law* 312.

the reasoning, but rather the *argument* used in it which is taken over by the national court or legislature. Adopting the underlying reasoning may, however, be characterized as falling under the first category of the use of foreign material, that is, its use as a source of inspiration. In most of the examples discussed above under the heading of voluntary recourse to foreign law by courts, this is what has happened. But as soon as legislatures or courts use foreign law to *control* an outcome on the basis of 'national' arguments, they do use foreign law in the normative sense.[49] And this is in fact how foreign law is used in many cases. In the *Fairchild* case,[50] for example, Lord Bingham stated that:

if . . . a decision is given in this country which offends one's basic sense of justice, and if consideration of international sources suggests that a different and more acceptable decision would be given in most other jurisdictions, whatever their legal tradition, this must prompt anxious review of the decision in question.

Third, foreign law can be used for 'ornamental purposes'.[51] If references to foreign law are used in explanatory memoranda or court decisions without any visible connection with the statute or court decision, such references are obviously superfluous. They demonstrate the learning of civil servants or judges, but do no more than that. The drafters of the new Dutch Civil Code of 1992, and in particular its original draftsman, Eduard M. Meijers, took pride in citing the (black-letter) law of more than forty countries (including the civil codes of Brazil, Egypt, and Chile), but the exact relationship of these citations with the adoption of a particular rule often remained unclear. The normative weight of such ornamental references is nil, but there can be other reasons why they are used. Thus, they may contribute to the draftsman's prestige: by demonstrating his learning in the field of comparative law, the draftsman can try to convince others (like Parliament) of the high quality of his work in general.

2. The Legitimacy of Comparative Reasoning

The question whether it is legitimate for a national legislature or court to undertake voluntary comparative reasoning only arises when foreign law is used as a normative argument (the second type of use of foreign law described in the previous subsection). It has not been discussed very often in the European literature. The obvious answer is that the use of foreign law is permissible as it would be counter-productive to deal with a (new) problem without taking into account the experiences elsewhere. This answer presupposes that law is not national in nature,

---

[49] This 'control function' goes back to Konrad Zweigert, 'Rechtsvergleichung als universale Interpretationsmethode', (1949–50) 15 *(Rabels) Zeitschrift für ausländisches und internationales Privatrecht* 17 ff.

[50] [2003] 1 AC 32, 66.   [51] Drobnig (n 11), 17.

but that there is an international common 'fund' of solutions from which anyone may draw. Both Portalis and von Savigny knew this: they were convinced that a national code needed to be based on a legal scholarship which was not limited to national materials; and that while interpreting such a code it would be important to benefit from a European legal scholarship.[52] In their times, the international stock of solutions was made up largely of Roman law, but that does not matter. What does matter is finding a good solution, which does not depend on the nationality of the respective legal system. If this argument is taken to its extreme, it leads to Konrad Zweigert's far-reaching idea of comparative law as a 'universal method of interpretation': even in cases where clear national rules are available, these rules should be interpreted in line with foreign law.[53]

We should be aware that, underlying this view, there must be some more fundamental reason why it is legitimate to regard foreign authority as important. In fact, there are two such reasons. First, one may find an argument in the promotion of uniformity. If one sees the attainment of uniform law as a desirable goal, the justification of the use of comparative reasoning by legislatures and courts is that it may help to achieve this aim. The former president of the German Federal Supreme Court, Walter Odersky, wrote that 'the national court is entitled to take note of the fact that a particular solution is conducive to the harmonization of European law. . . . It is an argument that he should use with increasing frequency as the integration of Europe proceeds.'[54] This is a strong argument: it fits in with the idea that competition of legal systems is one of the best ways to promote uniformity without, at the same time, sacrificing national legal culture, and that of the protagonists of legal development the courts are best able to perform this job.[55]

There is a second reason that may explain the legitimacy of using foreign law in a national context.[56] It is that all legal systems share the common goal of finding and applying the best and most just legal rules. All legal systems try to approximate this goal, and it is likely that some of them will have succeeded earlier or more convincingly than others. This means that it is useful to compare the solutions reached elsewhere with domestic solutions in order to develop one's own law in accordance with that of other legal systems. Essentially this justification is based on the theory of Natural law. Legal rules are treated as if they are all cut from a universal cloth and each court is trying to identify the same set of norms.[57] The argument is

---

[52] James Gordley, 'Comparative Legal Research: Its Function in the Development of Harmonized Law', (1995) 43 *AJCL* 555 ff.

[53] Zweigert, (1949–50) 15 (*Rabels*) *Zeitschrift für ausländisches und internationales Privatrecht* 5.

[54] Walter Odersky, 'Harmonisierende Auslegung und europäische Rechtskultur', (1994) 1 *Zeitschrift für Europäisches Privatrecht* 1 ff.

[55] cf Jan Smits, 'A European Private Law as a Mixed Legal System', (1998) 5 *Maastricht Journal of European and Comparative Law* 328 ff.

[56] See Jens C. Dammann, 'The Role of Comparative Law in Statutory and Constitutional Interpretation', (2002) 14 *St Thomas LR* 525 ff.

[57] Choudhry, (1999) 74 *Indiana LJ* 825.

particularly strong in the context of human rights, but it may also be extended to private law. In the debate on European harmonization of private law there is an important line of thought taking this view as a (sometimes implicit) starting-point: legal diversity is merely coincidental and the main task of European legal scholarship is to unveil the principles that European legal systems have in common.

It is important to note that both theories are based on the idea that national laws are not something unique. This view is as contested in the United States as it is popular in Europe. The argument against the value of comparative reasoning is best presented by the United States Supreme Court Justice Antonin Scalia, who wrote extrajudicially:[58]

We judges of the American democracies are servants of our peoples, sworn to apply . . . the laws that those peoples deem appropriate. We are not some international priesthood empowered to impose upon our free and independent citizens supra-national values that contradict their own.

In other words: courts have to apply *national* law. In particular the national constitution is an expression of a uniquely national character and courts should help to constitute the nation by respecting this character.[59] When the United States' Supreme Court had to decide about the constitutionality of the death penalty for juvenile delinquents in *Roper v Simmons* (see Section III, above), the reference to international opinion by a majority of the court ('The United States now stands alone in a world that has turned its face against the juvenile death penalty') as a confirmation of a national consensus was fiercely attacked by Scalia. In a dissenting opinion he rejected the use of international or foreign law with the following words:

I do not believe that the meaning of . . . our Constitution should be determined by the subjective views of five Members of this Court and like-minded foreigners. . . . 'Acknowledgement' of foreign approval has no place in the legal opinion of this Court. . . .

The decision of the Court even led to a proposal by some Republican congressmen for a 'Constitution Restoration Act', prohibiting an American court from relying upon any foreign law in interpreting and applying the Constitution.[60] It should be added that, on this view, drawing inspiration from foreign material is less problematic for the legislature. In *Printz v United States*, Justice Scalia said that 'comparative analysis [is] inappropriate to the task of interpreting a constitution, though it was of course quite relevant to the task of writing one'.[61] This is quite logical as in a democratic society the legislature is permitted to do what a court cannot do: to implement whatever legal rule it chooses, and on whatever basis.

It is clear that there is a fundamental difference between Europe and the United

---

[58] Antonin Scalia, 'Commentary', (1996) 40 *St Louis University LJ* 1122.
[59] Tushnet, (1999) 108 *Yale LJ* 1228.
[60] Senate 520 (2005). Also see House of Representatives 1070 (2005).
[61] 521 US 898, 921 (1997).

States in valuing the role of foreign law. It is too easy simply to refer to American 'parochialism' and to the European belief in 'universality' in order to explain this difference. There must be underlying reasons why some countries invoke foreign law more readily than others. These reasons are discussed in the next section.

V. Motives, Strategies, and Differences among Countries in Valuing Foreign Law

1. Introduction

There are still two questions which need to be answered. The first is why a legislature or a court voluntarily refers to foreign law. Obviously in most of the well-known examples of voluntary use of foreign law, the court or the legislature would have reached the same result had it not referred to foreign law. Lord Goff's speech in *White v Jones* is usually considered to be one of the highlights of comparative reasoning in English law, but it has been sceptically remarked that the decision was, in the end, purely based on English law.[62] It is a truism that gaps or unclear rules in national law can always be, and in the past often were, remedied other than by reference to foreign solutions. This suggests that the use of comparative law arguments often has not so much to do with substance as with other motives. It seems useful to pay attention to these motives.

The second, related, question is how to explain the differing extents to which various countries are open to foreign influence. Why is it that some legislatures and courts engage more readily in comparative reasoning than others? It was made clear above that American courts are less open to foreign influence than English or German courts. Countries like Turkey and Japan were once willing to import foreign civil codes, but are now far less receptive. How can this be explained?

2. Motives and Strategies in Comparative Reasoning

There is a large literature which attempts to explain legal transplants in general. Most of this literature is about why national *legislatures* take over foreign law.

---

[62] Lord Rodger of Earlsferry (n 32). On *White v Jones*, see above, text to n 31.

Without going into details,[63] there seems to be a consensus that the legislature often borrows law for reasons other than mere inspiration or the mere *quality* of a foreign rule.

One reason is that it simply saves time and money to use a solution which is already in operation abroad. A frequent example of such a 'cost-saving transplant' is the adoption by developing countries of Western environmental or health and safety legislation. In the end it is simply efficiency and not the search for the 'best' rule that is decisive: it saves (information) costs to adopt something which has been proved to work elsewhere. Another reason for a country's legislature to take over foreign law can be that it adds to the 'prestige' of that country in the rest of the world. That is why developing countries often introduce human rights charters into their constitutions, even if these are not complied with in practice.

The most important reason for a country to take over foreign law, however, is that it is often more or less compelled to do so: the adoption of a foreign model can be made a condition for giving loans (as is the case with the International Monetary Fund) or for granting political autonomy. Western countries often make their financial aid to the Third World dependent on the respect for human rights. After World War II General Douglas MacArthur imposed a Western-based constitution on Japan; Eastern European countries, on the other hand, faced a 'Sovietization' of law. In both cases this was part of a policy to 'assist' these countries to adapt to a prevailing ideology. In the 1990s Russia abolished the (execution of the) death penalty so as to be able to join the Council of Europe. Such 'dictation' can also be far more subtle. Many European countries have adopted legislation for new types of contracts such as franchising, leasing, and factoring. In doing so, they created legal certainty for contracting parties who wanted to base their dealings on these new contractual concepts developed in American law. There was thus an economic interest to borrow from a foreign system. When China adopted its new Contract Code in 1999, it did so to enhance the market economy by attracting foreign investment. In today's world, political and economic pressure and commercial dominance are far more important explanations for legal transplants than the mandatory adoption of foreign institutions.

Unlike legislatures, courts are not primarily driven by political or economic considerations. It may be that courts look elsewhere for inspiration in cases where there is either no domestic rule or the domestic rule is unclear, because they think that this will save time and money or will provide prestige, but it is probable that there is also a different mechanism at work. As was mentioned in Section III, courts are particularly keen to refer to foreign law when they have to deal with a controversial new issue. It is likely that the more controversial or novel an issue is, the more the court feels obliged to convince its audience of the correctness of its

---

[63] For an overview, see Jonathan M. Miller, 'Typology of Legal Transplants', (2003) 51 *AJCL* 839 and Chapter 13 of the present book.

decision. To convince outside observers that its decision is correct, the court can seek support in legal systems where a similar issue has been decided before. Thus, courts can use references to foreign law strategically to improve the acceptance of their decisions by the legal community of their own country.

This thesis was advanced by Walsh, and tested by Smithey, for Canadian and South African constitutional law.[64] Both Canada (in 1982) and South Africa (in 1996) adopted a new charter of fundamental rights and created a system of constitutional control by the courts. Both countries lacked any tradition in constitutional review, and yet the Supreme Court of Canada and the Constitutional Court of South Africa have had to decide very controversial cases, such as on the 'horizontal effect' of the new constitution in relationships among citizens, or the acceptability of the death penalty. Justice Beverly McLachlin of the Canada Supreme Court put it like this: 'Consider . . . the sinking feeling that besets a common lawyer upon finding himself or herself confronted by a new document, an amalgam of unfamiliar American and European and who-knows-what-other ideas, without so much as a case to show the way'.[65] This is why Section 39 of the South African Constitution explicitly declares that courts 'may consider foreign law' when interpreting the Bill of Rights. In post-apartheid South Africa reference to foreign law also served the purpose of showing the world that the country was able to catch up with international human rights standards. Walsh's thesis was indeed supported by evidence: in the first seventy-five cases decided by the two courts, abundant reference was made to foreign law. The Canadian court cited foreign precedents in 64 per cent of the cases and the South African court in 68 per cent.[66]

The idea that legal uncertainty produces greater reliance on external sources also seems to be evidenced by most of the private law cases mentioned in the previous sections. When there is no guidance in national law, the use of foreign law increases, but as soon as one knows how to deal with an issue, the need to find guidance abroad is less obvious and reliance upon foreign law decreases again. A study in which this thesis is empirically tested for countries other than Canada and South Africa is still lacking.

We should, however, not forget that this motive does not explain everything. Often, the influence of foreign law is a result of coincidence. The most famous example is probably the introduction of the Swiss Civil Code and the Code of Civil Procedure of the canton of Neuchâtel in Turkey in 1926. It is safe to say that this would not have happened if the then Turkish minister of justice had not studied law in Neuchâtel. In a similar vein, without the influence of German émigré lawyers like Friedrich Kessler, Albert Ehrenzweig, and Stefan Riesenfeld, American

---

[64] David J. Walsh, 'On the Meaning and Pattern of Legal Citations', (1997) 31 *Law and Society Review* 337 ff; Shannon Ishiyama Smithey, 'A Tool, Not a Master', (2001) 34 *Comparative Political Studies* 1188 ff.

[65] McLachlin, cited by Smithey, (2001) 34 *Comparative Political Studies* 1194.

[66] Smithey, (2001) 34 *Comparative Political Studies* 1198.

contract law would have looked different. Likewise, if Andreas von Tuhr had not taught law at various German universities, his textbook on the Swiss law of obligations, and, indeed, Swiss law itself, would not have been as greatly influenced by German law as it is today.[67] As far as courts are concerned, much depends on legal counsel, or on the judges' linguistic knowledge, or on the availability of a good library.

3. Differences in the Extent to which Different Legal Systems are Open to Foreign Influence

How may the differences in the extent to which various legal systems are open to foreign influence be explained? As far as legislation is concerned, several factors have already been mentioned above: apart from political and economic considerations, the extent to which the legislature of a particular country has access to comparative materials plays an important role. If the drafting of legislation is left to a special branch of government or to a Law Commission, these bodies can make it a matter of course to refer to comparative law. This may partly explain why foreign materials play a less important role in American legislative practice: comparative resources are often not available at the state level, and at the federal level all energy is put into comparing the fifty-three American jurisdictions. The differences in court practice are caused by similar factors. The aim of this section is to identify some of them.

A first factor is the amount of national materials available. We just saw that a court is more likely to refer to foreign law if the question before it does not receive a clear answer in national law. As a consequence, the more material that is available within the court's own jurisdiction, the less likely it is that the court will need to refer to foreign law. 'New' questions are simply less frequent in large jurisdictions. This may explain why foreign law does not play a large role in deciding cases in the United States, with its enormous amount of case law. The theory is confirmed by the experience of small countries such as Luxembourg, where courts are obliged to refer to foreign law far more often.[68]

It is important to note that the greater the sense of national lawyers that they are part of some larger legal tradition, the bigger the chance that they will refer to countries which are also part of that tradition. This is very obvious within the

---

[67] cf Jutta Klapisch, *Der Einfluss der deutschen und österreichischen Emigranten auf contracts of adhesion and bargaining in good faith im US-amerikanischen Recht* (1991) and Ingeborg Schwenzer, 'Rezeption deutschen Rechtsdenkens im Schweizerischen Obligationenrechts', in *eadem* (ed), *Schuldrecht, Rechtsvergleichung und Rechtsvereinheitlichung an der Schwelle zum 21. Jahrhundert* (Schlechtriem Symposium) (1999), 59 ff.

[68] See Drobnig (n 11), 21.

British Commonwealth. As noted above, the laws of the Commonwealth countries are widely seen to belong to one and the same tradition, which means that cases from other jurisdictions within the Commonwealth are frequently cited. In *R v Kingston*, Lord Mustill said: 'In the absence of guidance from English authorities it is useful to inquire how other common law jurisdictions have addressed the same problem . . .'.[69] Typically, an English judge once apologized to his New Zealand friends for using the word 'foreign' when referring to New Zealand law.[70] This point is confirmed by statistical analyses. Between 1983 and 1994, 85 per cent of the foreign cases referred to by Australian courts were English cases.[71] In England, approximately 70 per cent of the references to foreign law concerned common law jurisdictions.[72] In a similar vein, though on a much smaller scale, Austrian and Greek courts often seem to be inspired by German law. If the Swiss *Bundesgericht* cites foreign law, in 90 per cent of cases it is German law.[73]

Frequent recourse to foreign law may be expected in mixed jurisdictions.[74] Thus, Scottish and South African courts are able, in principle, to rely on materials from both the civil law and the common law traditions in finding the best solution to a problem. This is consistent with what, for example, the Scottish judge Lord Cooper of Culross said about drawing inspiration from abroad.[75] However, statistics show that the reality is different. Between 1920 and 1997, 25 per cent of the case law cited in judgments of the Scottish Court of Session was English. Only 5 per cent of the case law cited was of other origin, most of it probably coming from common law jurisdictions. The only change since 1997 seems to be that the case law of the European Court of Human Rights is increasingly cited.[76]

A second factor which explains differences between courts has to do with the political constellation of a country. As mentioned above, courts in countries undergoing political transition seek to legitimize their decisions by reference to case law of more experienced courts. This is what happened in South Africa and Canada. It is likely that the general lesson to be learnt from this is that young constitutional courts engage more readily in comparative reasoning than more established ones. This can be part of a strategy to convince the legal community

---

[69] [1995] 2 AC 355

[70] *Attorney General of New Zealand v Ortiz and Others* [1982] 3 WLR 570, cited by Örücü (n 29), 257.

[71] Jianfu Chen, 'The Use of Comparative Law by Courts: Australian Courts at the Crossroads', in Drobnig and Van Erp (n 11), 27.

[72] Örücü (n 29), 263 ff.

[73] David Gerber, 'Der Einfluss des ausländischen Rechts in der Rechtsprechung des Bundesgerichts', in *Perméabilité des ordres juridiques* (1992), 141 ff.

[74] On which, see Chapter 14 of the present book.

[75] Lord Cooper of Culross, 'The Importance of Comparative Law in Scotland', in *idem, Selected Papers 1922–1954* (1957), 145.

[76] Claire McDiarmid, 'Scots Law: The Turning of the Tide', [1999] *Juridical Review* 156 ff; Hector L. MacQueen, 'Mixing it? Comparative Law in the Scottish Courts', (2003) 6 *European Review of Private Law* 735 ff. For South Africa, see the figures provided in Reinhard Zimmermann, 'Roman Law in a Mixed Legal System', in Robin Evans-Jones (ed), *The Civil Law Tradition in Scotland* (1995), 55 f.

that a legal system is distancing itself from the past. This need not be a past of human rights violations, as was the case in South Africa. When Australia finally abolished appeal to the Privy Council in 1986, this was part of a desire to develop an autonomous Australian law. It was obvious that 'autonomy' in this context meant first and foremost autonomy from England. As a result, Australian courts began to cite other foreign sources more often than before. A similar development can be expected in Scotland, where, as a result of devolution, the civil law aspect of its legal system may be emphasized more strongly than in the past, simply to demonstrate its independence from England.

As a third factor, it should be mentioned that the receptiveness in Europe towards comparative law arguments increased because of the process of Europeanization.[77] It is not only the influence of the European Convention on Human Rights, and EC law, or of the 'transnational law explosion'[78] as such, that has led to a Europeanization of national law. Perhaps even more important is the fact that the process of European integration provoked a profound interest in the law of other countries generally. The European Court of Justice itself shows the way as it often bases its judgments on comparative research. This may explain why within Europe legal borrowing takes place on a larger scale than in other parts of the world. Of course, a common legal history is very helpful in this respect, and the role of academia should not be ignored either: the development of a European legal scholarship that we have witnessed since the beginning of the 1990s, has proven to be immensely useful for the courts. It has already been mentioned that it is often through legal literature that judges get to know about foreign solutions.

There is also a fourth factor. Receptiveness towards foreign law may also have to do with the way in which the law in a country is formed. If this is on a case by case basis, as in common law countries, it is easier to refer to similar foreign case law than in countries where the law is primarily formed by statute. The reason for this is simply that it is easier for a judge to compare similar situations decided in foreign cases than to compare abstract statutes. Basil Markesinis puts it like this:[79] "The full benefit of comparing systems comes ... when one compares factually equivalent litigated circumstances. The immediately obvious similarities encountered when one is comparing similar litigated situations makes the "foreign" reader feel reassured by what he is discovering rather than put off.' This may indeed explain the influence of one common law country on another and also why civil law courts seem to refer more readily to foreign case law than to foreign legislation. It does not explain, however, the minor role of foreign case law in the American discussion.

---

[77] On which, see Chapter 16 of the present book.
[78] Hans W. Baade, 'Comparative Law and the Practitioner', (1983) 31 *AJCL* 507.
[79] Basil Markesinis, 'Judicial Style and Judicial Reasoning in England and Germany', (2000) 59 *Cambridge LJ* 295. Also see 'Judge, Jurist and the Study and Use of Foreign Law', (1993) 109 *LQR* 622 ff.

If Markesinis is right, this also casts doubts on the practical usefulness for courts of 'restatements' such as the Principles of European Contract Law and the UNIDROIT Principles of International Commercial Contracts. These cannot take the place of reference to foreign case law. It is more likely that such principles can offer important guidance in the drafting of national legislation. Both in the recent modernization of the German law of obligations and in the drafting of the new Chinese Contract Code, the UNIDROIT Principles of International Commercial Contracts were cited.

Again, these factors do not explain everything. There are many other, often more practical, factors which may determine the use of foreign law in domestic disputes. Knowledge of foreign languages, the availability of foreign material, intellectual curiosity, the time available to decide a case, and mere coincidence also play a role. If Markesinis had not advised counsel in *White v Jones* to refer the Court to comparative materials, Lord Goff's opinion would have looked different. More formal incentives play a role as well. Article 1 of the Swiss Civil Code was often interpreted by Swiss courts as an invitation to incorporate foreign law in their decisions. Section 39 of the South African Constitution is even more explicit.

VI. Finally: The Influence of Comparative Reasoning on National Law

The title of this chapter suggests an influence of comparative law on national legal systems. In the end, it is clear that such influence does exist, but also that it is often difficult to measure. One reason why the causal link between foreign and national law cannot easily be established is that it is not so much foreign law as such that is taken over by a national lawmaker or court, but the *argument* expressed in foreign legislation, or in a foreign court decision. That argument itself, however, is not specifically 'foreign': it has persuasive authority because of its inherent quality, not because it is used in another country. Whether there should be liability in tort for pure economic loss does not depend on English or French law allowing this, but on the substantive arguments in favour and against such a claim, arguments that may, of course, have been discussed in an enlightening way in a foreign case or explanatory memorandum. But when it comes down to weighing these arguments, every legal system has to make its own choice. In the *McFarlane* case, Lord Steyn puts it like this:[80] 'The discipline of comparative law does not aim at a poll of solutions adopted in different countries. It has the different and inestimable value of sharpening our focus on the weight of competing considerations.' This means that the influence of comparative law in this type of case is, at most, one of finding inspiration in the process of weighing the arguments in favour or against a particular solution.

This is different if comparative law is used in a normative way. A certain international consensus, or a foreign solution, *as such* is then used as an argument for adopting the same solution at the national level. In this situation, foreign law influences national law more directly. If the legislature or court explicitly states that it has made use of comparative arguments there is little doubt that there *is* influence, but the problem then is that it is difficult to establish exactly what this influence has led to. It is banal to state that that the foreign solution may have a very different impact on the legal system of the importing country.[81] Present-day Turkish private law is very different from Swiss private law, even though Turkey took over the Swiss Civil Code. This also means that, if one's goal is to promote uniformity among legal systems (see above, Section IV.2), the mere adoption of foreign law will not achieve this aim. One need not agree with Montesquieu's famous statement that the laws of each nation 'should be closely tailored to the people for whom they are made, so that it would be pure coincidence if the laws of one nation would meet the needs of another';[82] but it is clear that diverging legal cultures often do stand in the way of the unifying effect of legal borrowing.[83]

Despite these doubts about the unifying effect of recourse to foreign law, it is certain that the continuing Europeanization and globalization will lead to a further increase of comparative reasoning in the years to come. As a result, the store of legal arguments to be considered in deciding hard cases, or in drafting new legislation, will become more and more similar across the world. This is likely to lead to a higher quality of legislation and court decisions: important arguments are less likely to be overlooked. This alone should make the drawing of comparative inspiration an indispensable part of present-day legal practice.

BIBLIOGRAPHY

Konrad Zweigert, 'Rechtsvergleichung als universale Interpretationsmethode', (1949–50) 15 (*Rabels*) *Zeitschrift für ausländisches und internationales Privatrecht* 5 ff

---

[80] *McFarlane v Tayside Health Board* 2000 SC (HL) 15.

[81] Cf Drobnig (n 11), 5 and recently eg Daniel Berkowitz, Katharina Pistor, and Jean-François Richard, 'The Transplant Effect', (2003) 51 *AJCL* 163 ff.

[82] *De l'Esprit des Lois* (1748).

[83] On the factors decisive for the 'success' of legal transplants, see Chapter 13 of the present book.

Bernhard Aubin, 'Die rechtsvergleichende Interpretation autonom-internen Rechts in der deutschen Rechtsprechung', (1970) 34 *RabelsZ* 458 ff

Otto Kahn-Freund, 'On Uses and Misuses of Comparative Law', (1974) 37 *Modern LR* 1 ff

H. Patrick Glenn, 'Persuasive Authority', (1987) 32 *McGill LJ* 261 ff

Raymond Legeais, 'L'utilisation du droit comparé par les tribunaux', (1994) 46 *Revue internationale de droit comparé* 347 ff

T. Koopmans, 'Comparative Law and the Courts', (1996) 45 *ICLQ* 545 ff

Mathias Reimann, 'Continental Imports: The Influence of European Law and Jurisprudence in the United States', (1996) 64 *Tijdschrift voor Rechtgeschiedenis* 391 ff

Basil Markesinis, *Foreign Law and Comparative Methodology: A Subject and a Thesis* (1997)

Ulrich Drobnig and Sjef Van Erp (eds), *The Use of Comparative Law by Courts* (1999)

Mark Tushnet, 'The Possibilities of Comparative Constitutional Law', (1999) 108 *Yale LJ* 1225 ff

Hector L. MacQueen, 'Mixing it? Comparative Law in the Scottish Courts', (2003) 6 *European Review of Private Law* 735 ff

Esin Örücü, *Judicial Comparativism in Human Rights Cases* (2003)

Taavi Annus, 'Comparative Constitutional Reasoning: The Law and Strategy of Selecting the Right Arguments', (2004) 14 *Duke Journal of Comparative and International Law* 301 ff

Guy Canivet, Mads Andenas, and Duncan Fairgrieve (eds), *Comparative Law before the Courts* (2004)

Sofie Geeroms, *Foreign Law in Civil Litigation: A Comparative and Functional Analysis* (2004)

CHAPTER 16

COMPARATIVE LAW AND THE EUROPEANIZATION OF PRIVATE LAW

REINHARD ZIMMERMANN

Hamburg

I. Prologue: Unification of Private Law as a Task for Comparative Legal Studies

THE International Congress for Comparative Law, organized in Paris in 1900, is widely regarded today as having stimulated the emergence of comparative law as a specific branch of legal scholarship. The congress was masterminded by two French scholars, Edouard Lambert and Raymond Saleilles, who were inspired by the idea of a *droit commun de l'humanité civilisée*.[1] Comparative law, in their view, had to resolve the accidental differences which divide the laws of the various modern nation states. The international unification of law was thus, from its inception, taken to be a key task for comparative legal scholarship. This impulse was to lead, if only after the end of the First World War and under the umbrella of the League of Nations, to the creation of the International Institute for the Unification of Private Law (UNIDROIT) in Rome. In the 1960s a second organization devoted to the international unification of law was founded under the name of UNCITRAL (United Nations Commission on International Trade Law). The

---

[1] See the account by David S. Clark, 'Nothing New in 2000?: Comparative Law in 1900 and Today', (2001) 75 *Tulane LR* 871 ff: a paper presented at the Centennial World Congress on Comparative Law in New Orleans.

impact of both bodies on the development of law has remained limited.[2] Their most significant achievement, so far, has been the preparation of the Convention on Contracts for the International Sale of Goods, an instrument covering a key area of private law that has entered into force in more than sixty states—among them twenty-one of the EU member states—and, as a result, has become increasingly important in legal practice.[3] It has also become highly influential in the field of national and supranational law reform. The driving force behind the unification of international sales law was Ernst Rabel, one of the greatest comparative lawyers of the twentieth century. His two-volume treatise on the law of the sale of goods today still represents a model for comparative scholarship in the field of private law.[4]

Legal unification on a global level presents problems in view of the invariably Eurocentric (including the offshoots of European law in other parts of the world) character of this enterprise. Legal differences between the laws of different nations, or peoples, are not necessarily attributable to historical accident or contingent circumstances; they may be based on fundamental cultural, economic, or political differences. Legal unification, therefore, is a much more promising project if it focuses on the laws of nations at a broadly similar stage of cultural and economic development which, moreover, share the same historical experiences and political philosophy. When such nations embark on the project of creating an economic community, the unification of the legal regime concerning business transactions is bound, sooner or later, to become an issue of considerable political importance.[5] This is what has happened in Europe after the Second World War. The gradual emergence of a European private law is one of the most significant contemporary legal developments. Comparative law scholarship has played an important role in this process and will continue to do so. The Europeanization of private law as a new and challenging task for comparative law: that is the topic of the present chapter.

---

[2] Herbert Kronke, 'Ziele—Methoden, Kosten, Nutzen: Perspektiven der Privatrechtsharmonisierung nach 75 Jahren UNIDROIT', [2001] *Juristenzeitung* 1149 ff. Kronke is presently the secretary general of UNIDROIT.

[3] Kurt Siehr and Reinhard Zimmermann (eds), Symposium: 'The Convention on the International Sale of Goods and its Application in Comparative Perspective', (2004) 68 *RabelsZ* 427 ff; Franco Ferrari (ed), *Quo Vadis CISG?* (2005).

[4] Ernst Rabel, *Das Recht des Warenkaufs* (2 vols, 1936 and 1958). See Gerhard Kegel, 'Ernst Rabel— Werk und Person', (1990) 54 *RabelsZ* 1 ff.

[5] See generally Arnold J. Kanning, *Unifying Commercial Laws of Nation-States: Coordination of Legal Systems and Economic Growth* (2003).

II. The Europeanization of Private Law

1. From Rome to Laeken: The Creation of the European Union

The devastations of the two world wars were very widely taken to mark the ultimate failure of an era of aggressive nationalism. Thus, the (three) European Communities were designed as a cornerstone for a peaceful and politically unified Europe.[6] This is evident, for instance, from the determination in the preamble of the European Economic Community Treaty of 1957 'to lay the foundations for an ever closer union among the peoples of Europe'. The intention of the founding fathers, in this respect, reflected the ideas expressed by Winston Churchill in his famous Zurich speech of September 1946 and, already in the early 1930s, by Aristide Briand.

Actual progress, however, turned out to be slower than originally envisaged. For a long time, the European Economic Community remained, essentially, what its name indicates: an economic community between a number of sovereign European states. It was only in the 1970s that the movement towards integration gained new momentum. It led to the adoption of the Single European Act of 1986, which not only expanded the Community's range of competences, but also contained a commitment to 'adopt measures with the aim of progressively establishing the internal market' by the end of 1992. The (Maastricht) Treaty on European Union, which was signed in February 1992, took matters further by laying the foundation for a monetary union (this led to the introduction of a common currency in 1999) and by creating a European Union based on the three established European Communities as well as two new 'pillars' of common policy areas: foreign and security affairs on the one hand, and police and judicial cooperation in criminal matters on the other. The Amsterdam Treaty of 1999 brought the third major revision of the legal foundations of the European Union and further advanced the process of integration in the non-economic area. The Treaty of Nice (December 2000) gave rise to a number of institutional reforms. Finally, the Declaration of Laeken on the future of the European Union (December 2001) established a Convention charged with the preparation of a European Constitution. The document drawn up by that Convention was signed by the governments of the member states of the European Union in June 2004. It was subsequently ratified by a number of member states but failed to gain a majority in the referenda held in the Netherlands and France. Whether this is merely a temporary set-back in the process of constitutional

---

[6] For details, see the documentation edited by Reiner Schulze and Thomas Hoeren, *Dokumente zum Europäischen Recht* (2 vols, 1999 and 2000).

consolidation of the European Union (which today numbers twenty-five as opposed to the original six member states) remains to be seen.

2. A Patchwork of Directives

In spite of the fact that Walter Hallstein, the first President of the European Commission, had called attention to the necessity of harmonization in the area of private law as early as 1964,[7] the challenge was only taken up, in earnest, by private law scholarship in the 1990s. Up until then, the European Economic Community was widely perceived to be dealing with agricultural subsidies and import duties, and to be regulating the shape of tractor seats or the size of cucumbers. European Community law became a specialized field of study and was regarded, very widely, as a branch of public law. Even when European Community legislation did indeed start to affect (or, as it was often perceived: encroach upon) private law, it tended to do so in specialized areas such as competition law or intellectual property law. A particularly ambitious harmonization programme has been undertaken in the area of company law.[8] The first two Directives in the core area of traditional private law date from 1985: the Product Liability and the Doorstep Selling Directives. But it was only the Unfair Terms in Consumer Contracts Directive of 1993 that brought home to every lawyer the clear message that private law in Europe had acquired a new dimension. For some time, the introduction of a fairness control for all provisions contained in consumer contracts had even been considered, no matter whether they were standardized or not. Vociferous protests, particularly from Germany,[9] eventually forced the European Commission to back down in this respect. Another major step in the Europeanization of private law by means of European Community Directives was the enactment of the Consumer Sales Directive in 1999. The contract of sale, after all, has always been the central type of transaction in commercial life; moreover, the Directive was envisaged as a general model for the modernization of the national sales laws as well as a first building block for a European codification of sales law.[10] In Germany it has triggered the most sweeping reform ever to have affected the BGB since it entered into force.

---

[7] Walter Hallstein, 'Angleichung des Privat- und Prozessrechts in der Europäischen Wirtschaftsgemeinschaft', (1964) 28 *RabelsZ* 211 ff.

[8] See today Mathias Habersack, *Europäisches Gesellschaftsrecht* (2nd edn, 2003); Stefan Grundmann, *Europäisches Gesellschaftsrecht* (2004).

[9] See eg Claus-Wilhelm Canaris, 'Verfassungs- und europarechtliche Aspekte der Vertragsfreiheit in der Privatrechtsgesellschaft', in *Wege und Verfahren des Verfassungslebens: Festschrift für Peter Lerche* (1993), 873 ff.

[10] Stefan Grundmann, in Stefan Grundmann and Cesare Massimo Bianca (eds), *EU-Kaufrechts-Richtlinie: Kommentar* (2002), Einleitung, n 19.

Today we have close to twenty Directives within the area of traditional private law and many others outside it.[11] They constitute a patchwork of individual legislative measures that has been added to the tapestry of private law. However, they are not always well adjusted to that general tapestry or to each other. The confusion surrounding the key concept of 'consumer' provides an example.[12] The common denominator of these Directives is that they have, or are supposed to have, some bearing on the proper functioning of the internal market. This gives them a certain policy bias. Yet, the institutions of private law do not derive their significance only from their contribution to the creation or maintenance of free markets; contract law, for example, is more than a mere corollary of, or appendage to, the free movement of goods, persons, services, and capital (ie the four basic economic freedoms enshrined in the EC Treaty). Directives have to be implemented; this means that the member states have to bring into force the laws necessary to comply with the Directive. Whether they do so by way of piecemeal legislation, the drafting of part codifications (such as consumer contract acts), or incorporation into the general Civil Code, the national legal systems thereby inevitably acquire a new dimension of complexity, and often also internal fragmentation. The development of consumer law, in particular, has been dominated over the past twenty-five years by the European Union. Yet, it is still far from clear how consumer law and general contract law are supposed to relate to each other.[13] At the same time, all pertinent Directives have been based on Art 95 EC Treaty; or, more precisely, and in the words of the Directives themselves, 'in particular' Art 95. In its decision on the Tobacco Advertising Directive, the European Court of Justice has, however, emphasized that the European Union may only adopt measures for the approximation of the laws prevailing in the member states if they aim at improving the functioning of the internal market. This can only be the case if the divergence of the respective national rules constitutes an impediment for free trade or leads to noticeable distortions of competition.[14] In view of these strict standards, many provisions of the consumer protection Directives rest on fragile foundations. The

---

[11] For an overview, see Peter-Christian Müller-Graff, 'EC Directives as a Means of Private Law Unification', in Arthur Hartkamp, Martijn Hesselink, Ewoud Hondius, Carla Joustra, Edgar du Perron, and Muriel Veldman (eds), *Towards a European Civil Code* (3rd edn, 2004), 77 ff. The Directives in the core areas of private law are conveniently available in Oliver Radley-Gardner, Hugh Beale, Reinhard Zimmermann, and Reiner Schulze (eds), *Fundamental Texts on European Private Law* (2003), 3 ff.

[12] Wolfgang Faber, 'Elemente verschiedener Verbraucherbegriffe in EG-Richtlinien, zwischenstaatlichen Übereinkommen und nationalem Zivil- und Kollisionsrecht', (1998) 6 *Zeitschrift für Europäisches Privatrecht* 854 ff; Karl Riesenhuber, *System und Prinzipien des Europäischen Vertragsrechts* (2003), 250 ff. Generally, see Thomas M. J. Möllers, 'Europäische Richtlinien zum Bürgerlichen Recht' [2002] *Juristenzeitung* 121 ff.

[13] For an approach based on the self-determination of the consumer, see Josef Drexl, *Die wirtschaftliche Selbstbestimmung des Verbrauchers* (1998); Reinhard Zimmermann, 'Consumer Contract Law and General Contract Law', in *idem, The New German Law of Obligations: Historical and Comparative Perspectives* (2005), 159 ff.

[14] Case C–376/98 *Germany v European Parliament* [2000] ECR I–8419.

real aim pursued by the European Union appears to be the promotion of a certain minimum level of consumer protection across all member states rather than the removal of supposed trade barriers resulting from a diversity of levels of protection in the member states.[15]

3. The Role of the European Court of Justice

If, therefore, the present state of legal harmonization within the European Union by legislative means is unsatisfactory for a number of reasons, the activity of the European Court of Justice does not very much improve the general picture. For while it is true that that Court fashions concepts, rules, and principles which are relevant for the law of the Union and, to an increasing degree, also for the laws of its member states, it also remains true that its opportunities to do so are restricted by the provisions of Arts 220 ff EC Treaty.[16] The European Court of Justice is not a Supreme Court for private law disputes in the European Union. It has jurisdiction in disputes relating to compensation for damage caused by the Community, and, as far as non-contractual liability is concerned, Art 288(2) EC Treaty specifically refers the Court to 'the general principles common to the laws of the Member States'.[17] Apart from that, the main avenue for the European Court of Justice into private law matters is paved by Art 234 EC Treaty on preliminary rulings, the aim of which is to ensure uniformity of interpretation of legal acts of the Community. Thus, for example, the Court has held that the right of revocation concerning doorstep transactions applies to contracts of suretyship, provided that the main obligation which the surety is supposed to secure has also been concluded away from the business premises of the entrepreneur; that a purchaser who has concluded a doorstep transaction must be able to revoke the contract even after the lapse of six months if he has not been duly informed about his right of revocation; or that the term 'damages' in the Package Travel Directive (and possibly beyond?) includes non-pecuniary loss.[18] These are, no doubt, important questions affecting the application of private law in all twenty-five member states of the European Union. Still, however, they only lead to a harmonization of a limited and piecemeal nature.

---

[15] Wulf-Henning Roth, 'Europäischer Verbraucherschutz und BGB' [2001] *Juristenzeitung* 477 ff.

[16] Walter van Gerven, 'The ECJ Case-Law as a Means of Unification of Private Law', in Hartkamp *et al* (n 11), 101 ff.

[17] For a detailed discussion, see Wolfgang Wurmnest, *Grundzüge eines europäischen Haftungsrechts: Eine rechtsvergleichende Untersuchung des Gemeinschaftsrechts* (2003), 13 ff.

[18] Case C–45/96 *Bayerische Hypotheken- und Wechselbank AG v Edgard Dietzinger* [1998] ECR I–1199; Case C–481/99 *Heininger v Bayerische Hypo- und Vereinsbank AG* [2001] ECR I–9945; Case C–168/00 *Simone Leitner v TUI Deutschland GmbH & Co KG* [2002] ECR I–2631.

4. Improving the Present and Future *Acquis?*

The opposite to piecemeal harmonization is comprehensive and systematic harmonization. This cannot be achieved by the courts but only by way of legislation. A comprehensive and systematic piece of legislation is normally referred to as a code. The codification of European private law has been championed, consistently, by the European Parliament, first in a resolution of May 1989.[19] The Council of the European Union took up this theme at its meeting in Tampere in October 1999 by requesting 'an overall study . . . on the need to approximate Member States' legislation in civil matters in order to eliminate obstacles to the good functioning of civil proceedings'. Contract law, obviously, is of key significance in this respect. The Commission of the European Union has thus issued an action plan for a more coherent European contract law[20] which, *inter alia*, aims at the development of 'a common frame of reference'. This frame of reference is supposed to provide the basis for further deliberations on an optional instrument in the field of European contract law. Essentially, therefore, the Commission endorses the second option put up in its communication of July 2001[21] and evaluated positively by the great majority of the reactions received: the preparation of non-binding common principles of contract law which would be available as a model instrument in business life and for the purposes of dispute settlement and law reform.[22] The Principles of European Contract Law, drawn up by the so-called 'Lando Commission', tie in with this description. They are available as a blueprint for an optional instrument and also serve as the basis for the work of the Study Group on a European Civil Code.

III. EUROPEAN LEGAL SCHOLARSHIP

The 'Lando Commission' and the Study Group are private initiatives, without official status and without any form of political legitimation. They constitute specific forms of international academic cooperation and can thus be seen as manifestations of a Europeanization of legal scholarship.[23] But they are not the only

---

[19] On which see Winfried Tilmann, 'Entschließung des Europäischen Parlaments über die Angleichung des Privatrechts der Mitgliedstaaten vom 26.05.1989', (1993) 1 *Zeitschrift für Europäisches Privatrecht* 613 ff.

[20] COM (2003) 68, [2003] OJ C 63/1.   [21] COM (2001) 398, [2001] OJ 2001 C 255/1.

[22] For further discussion, see Christian von Bar, 'Ein gemeinsamer Referenzrahmen für das marktrelevante Privatrecht in der Europäischen Union', in *Festschrift für Erik Jayme* (vol II, 2004), 1217 ff.

[23] See below, Section IV.8 and 11.

such manifestations. Konrad Zweigert had reflected on fundamental questions of European legal harmonization as early as 1963 and had recommended to the European Court of Justice the elaboration of general principles of law on the basis of an evaluative comparison of the legal systems of the EC member states.[24] Hein Kötz, in a contribution in honour of Konrad Zweigert from 1981, had mapped the various ways of how comparative legal scholarship might advance the attainment of a common private law for Europe.[25] And in 1990 Helmut Coing had pointedly called for a Europeanization of legal scholarship as a precondition for a European private law.[26] In that article, he had referred to the Roman-Canon *ius commune* as having been based on a truly European legal scholarship and as having established a European legal culture of which the modern national legal systems were merely specific manifestations. The medieval and early modern *ius commune* did not, therefore, merely constitute an historical example of European unity on the level of legal scholarship but could still be drawn upon as a point of departure for overcoming the national particularization of private law and private law scholarship. Helmut Coing's *opus magnum* on the historical *ius commune*, which had appeared in two volumes in 1986 and 1989, had been given the title 'European Private Law'.[27] Others had referred to a civilian, or Western, legal tradition as being subject to constant change and adaptation but still intellectually related to the same body of sources, values, rules, and concepts.[28] Previously, Paul Koschaker had already drawn attention to Roman law as an essential foundation of European legal culture.[29] This was the intellectual soil for the first textbook on European Contract Law which, freed from any particular national system or systematics, ventured to take account of national legal rules only as local variations of a European theme.[30] In the meantime, a considerable body of academic literature has been published, and a great number of academic projects have been launched which have contributed significantly to the emergence of a European legal scholarship. Which role does comparative law play in this process?

---

[24] Konrad Zweigert, 'Grundsatzfragen der europäischen Rechtsangleichung, ihrer Schöpfung und Sicherung', in *Vom deutschen zum europäischen Recht: Festschrift für Hans Dölle* (vol II, 1963), 401 ff.

[25] Hein Kötz, 'Gemeineuropäisches Zivilrecht', in *Festschrift für Konrad Zweigert* (1981), 481 ff.

[26] Helmut Coing, *Europäisierung der Rechtswissenschaft*, [1990] *Neue Juristische Wochenschrift* 937 ff.

[27] Helmut Coing, *Europäisches Privatrecht* (vol I, 1985; vol II, 1989).

[28] Harold J. Berman, *Law and Revolution: The Formation of the Western Legal Tradition* (1983). Reinhard Zimmermann, *The Law of Obligations: Roman Foundations of the Civilian Tradition* (1990).

[29] Paul Koschaker, *Europa und das römische Recht* (1st edn, 1947; 4th edn, 1966).

[30] Hein Kötz, *Europäisches Vertragsrecht* (vol I, 1996, English trans under the title *European Contract Law* by Tony Weir, vol I, 1997).

IV. The Contribution of Comparative Law

1. Legal Training

It is widely accepted today that the Europeanization of private law decisively depends on a Europeanization of the legal training provided in the various universities throughout Europe.[31] For if students continue to be taught the niceties of their national legal systems without being made to appreciate the extent to which the relevant doctrines, or case law, constitute idiosyncracies explicable only as a matter of historical accident, or misunderstanding, rather than rational design, and without being made to consider how else a legal problem may be solved, a national particularization of legal scholarship that takes the mysteries of the owner-possessor relationship (§§ 987 ff BGB) or the abracadabra of conditions, warranties, and intermediate terms for granted, threatens to imprint itself also on the next generation of lawyers. Europeanization of the legal training, therefore, requires the strengthening of subjects which are not only of a foundational character but also inherently international in nature: Roman law, the history of private law and constitutional law in Europe, comparative law, and jurisprudence. Sadly, however, in the law curricula of virtually all European countries these common elements tend to be reduced rather then enhanced in importance.[32] A much more positive development has been the introduction of the Erasmus/Socrates programme by the Commission of the European Communities as a result of which the mobility of students across Europe has been very significantly increased. Every year, thousands of law students spend at least one semester at a university in another EU member state;[33] and even if that period is not normally a fully integrated part of their degree programme, it encourages the kind of distance from the respective student's own legal system that is required for an interest in comparative law. Ideally, of course, the comparative approach should be an integral part of the teaching of private law at the various law faculties in Europe: be it in the normal diet of courses on German, French, or English private law, or by way of special courses on European private law.

---

[31] Hein Kötz, 'Europäische Juristenausbildung', (1993) 1 *Zeitschrift für Europäisches Privatrecht* 268 ff; Michael Faure, Jan Smits, and Hildegard Schneider (eds), *Towards a European Ius Commune in Legal Education and Research* (2002).

[32] On the decline of Roman law in Britain, see, by way of example, Peter Birks, 'Roman Law in Twentieth-Century Britain', in Jack Beatson and Reinhard Zimmermann (eds), *Jurists Uprooted* (2004), 249 ff.

[33] The mobility of German students has increased from 657 in 1987–8 to 18,482 in 2002–3. Of the 18,482 German 'outgoings' in 2002–3 1,341 were law students: information kindly supplied by the German Academic Exchange Service.

2. Making the Legal Materials Readily Accessible

For courses of this kind, teaching materials are required which make the relevant sources readily accessible. A series of 'Casebooks on the Common Law of Europe', initiated by the former Advocate General at the European Court of Justice, Walter van Gerven, has appeared over the past few years. To date, it covers the fields of contract law, tort law, and unjustified enrichment.[34] These casebooks are designed 'to familiarize future generations of lawyers with each other's legal systems' and, at the same time, to explore the extent to which, in spite of differences in approach, concepts, and terminology, common principles underlie the European legal systems. They contain the relevant provisions of the national codes, important decisions by the national courts, extracts from textbooks, commentaries and other forms of national legal literature, introductory texts, commentary, and explanation. At the same time, genuinely European texts are integrated, particularly the Principles of European Contract Law (in the casebook on contract law) and the case law of the European Court of Justice (in the casebook on tort law). The casebooks are thus comparative in the sense of making available the most important legal materials from a number of EU member states, so as to provide a basis for a common understanding of the essential features of private law in Europe. The authors of the casebooks do not normally proceed to a critical assessment and comparative evaluation of the materials presented. Nor do they aim at legal harmonization. They merely want to portray the existing situation as accurately as possible.

Very similar, in these respects, is the approach pursued by the author of a casebook covering the European law of obligations.[35] A comparison between the van Gerven series and Ranieri's book also, however, reveals a number of differences. Three of them are particularly interesting, in the broader context of the development of European private law. While van Gerven and his team of authors focus on the laws of England, France, and Germany as main exponents of the three major legal families traditionally distinguished in Europe (the casebook on unjustified enrichment, however, also includes Dutch law as well as the two 'mixed' jurisdictions of Scotland and South Africa), Ranieri incorporates materials from across Europe, including Poland, Portugal, and Switzerland. This difference, turning, essentially, on the related questions of practicability and comprehensiveness of coverage, is a recurrent theme in comparative legal literature concerning European private law. Second, while all the materials presented in the van Gerven books have been translated into English, Ranieri cites them in their original language

---

[34] Hugh Beale, Arthur Hartkamp, Hein Kötz, and Denis Tallon (gen eds), *Cases, Materials and Text on Contract Law* (2002); Walter van Gerven, Jeremy Lever, and Pierre Larouche, *Cases, Materials and Text on National, Supranational and International Tort Law* (2000); Jack Beatson and Eltjo Schrage (gen eds), *Cases, Materials and Texts on Unjustified Enrichment* (2003).

[35] Filippo Ranieri, *Europäisches Obligationenrecht* (2nd edn, 2003).

(though he adds German translations in the case of languages not widely known in Germany). Undisputedly, the perception of peculiar legal styles prevailing in Europe today is facilitated by reading all sources in their language of origin. Again, however, it is not always easy to determine how much may realistically be expected of lawyers and law students in Europe. Translation into an easily accessible language (or even the native language of the reader) can advance the process of familiarizing young lawyers with each other's legal systems more effectively than insistence on reading legal texts in foreign languages. The dangers of distortion and misunderstanding, incidentally, appear to be evenly balanced between both approaches. This leads to the third important difference. It concerns the sensitive question in which language (or languages) European private law presents itself. Do all European languages have the same standing, as far as European private law is concerned, or does English (or possibly: do French and English) enjoy precedence? Not accidentally, the van Gerven casebooks appear to be much better known for they are written in English. The use of Ranieri's book, a German language teaching tool, is confined, essentially, to Germany, Switzerland, and Austria. The rise of English as the primary medium of international communication affects law as much as most of the other academic disciplines; and this has led most contemporary comparative lawyers who wish to contribute to the debates surrounding European private law to resort to English. The alternative of making available important works in several different language versions is, in most cases, practically not feasible. What can sometimes be achieved is the translation into English of a work originally written in another language—which, in turn, reinforces the practical precedence of English.

3. Disregarding the National Boundaries: The Case of Contract Law

A work originally written in German, and shortly thereafter translated into English, is Hein Kötz's European Contract Law.[36] Just like the van Gerven and Ranieri casebooks, it has been written, in the first place, for students. It goes, however, a crucial step further in that it does not merely present the laws, as they actually prevail in different parts of Europe, but provides a (largely) integrated account by adopting a vantage point situated beyond, or above, the national legal systems. Thus, the European private law described by Kötz is not 'in force' anywhere and is not 'applied' as such by any court in Europe: its reality is virtual rather than actual. But it establishes an intellectual framework for discussing, developing, and teaching contract law in Europe. By conceiving European contract law as a

---

[36] Kötz (n 30). vol II, to be written by Axel Flessner, has not yet appeared.

subject ready to be treated in its own right, and consisting of rules either corraborated or modified by the rules contained in the national legal systems, Kötz has pioneered a new type of legal literature. This was possible as a result, first, of the fact that the material to be used for writing *European Contract Law* was readily available in Konrad Zweigert's and Hein Kötz's textbook on comparative law:[37] a work which is firmly based on the functional approach and very widely regarded today as the classic restatement of methodological orthodoxy in comparative legal scholarship. Very pointedly, one might say that the textbook on European contract law merely presents the material collected in (the third part of) the textbook on comparative law under different auspices, which is indicative both of the Eurocentricity of traditional comparative law discourse and of the potential inherent in the functional approach even for the constitution of a European contract law.

This brings us to a second point. If Kötz in his new work has merely taken further what he had set out to do in his earlier book, his task was facilitated by the fundamental unity of European contract law, based on its long, and largely common, tradition. It is not, therefore, without good reason that most chapters of *European Contract Law* set the scene by giving an overview of the historical developments of the legal problems to be discussed, thereby alerting the reader to the fact that the solutions adopted in the modern codes, or espoused by modern courts, are products of the same historical experience or, so to speak, fruits of the same tree. Modern contract law in Europe is based on the same philosophical origins,[38] and the hypothetical will of reasonable parties to a contract has usually been the focal point in the evolution of its doctrines.[39] The stock of fundamental concepts and common evaluations has not been deeply affected by developments during the age of legal nationalism; and so it is still possible to identify common problems and to strive for reasonable solutions on the basis of a common understanding. Significantly, therefore, Kötz tends to formulate such common problems before discussing legal doctrine. An agreement cannot be contractual unless it is sufficiently definite. But when can it be said to be sufficiently definite? All legal systems subscribe to the principle of *pacta sunt servanda* but still agree that not every informal agreement can be treated as binding. But which is the most appropriate *indicium* of seriousness to distinguish enforceable from non-enforceable agreements? Words are not always understood as they have been intended. Which perspective determines the interpretation of a contract: that of

---

[37] Konrad Zweigert and Hein Kötz, *Einführung in die Rechtsvergleichung auf dem Gebiete des Privatrechts* (1st edn in two vols, 1971, 3rd edn in one vol, 1996, English trans under the title *An Introduction to Comparative Law* by Tony Weir, 3rd edn, 1998).

[38] James Gordley, *The Philosophical Origins of Modern Contract Doctrine* (1991).

[39] On the use of the device of implying conditions into the contract, see Reinhard Zimmermann, ' "Heard Melodies are Sweet, but those Unheard are Sweeter . . .": Conditio tacita, implied condition und die Fortbildung des europäischen Vertragsrechts', (1993) 193 *Archiv für die civilistische Praxis* 121 ff.

the person making a promise or of the one receiving it? Contract law in Europe is based on freedom of contract in the sense that the parties are free, in principle, to determine the content of their transaction. Nowhere may a judge treat a contract as invalid merely because he does not regard it as fair. However, certain additional factors can indicate that the contract may not be accepted as an expression of *both* parties' self-determination. How can these additional factors best be formulated? This way of proceeding enables Kötz to embark on the task of critical evaluation wherever he finds divergence in detail. Ultimately, therefore, it is the comparative method[40] which also allows him to create European law where it cannot merely be uncovered.

4. Common Conceptual Structures? The Cases of Delict and Unjustified Enrichment

In a number of places in Kötz's work the presentation reverts to the traditional mode of country reports before it is steered back onto a genuinely European track. Kötz, in fact, himself stresses that his book constitutes but a first attempt to conceive of European contract law as a uniform discipline. None the less, the kind of integration achieved in it has not, so far, been emulated in any other field, not even the two most closely related ones, that is, delict and unjustified enrichment. For both, treatises have been written which, in their own way, are as pioneering in nature as Kötz's *European Contract Law*. Also, like Kötz's work, they are products of the classical tradition of comparative legal scholarship, initiated in Germany by Ernst Rabel. Still, however, they cannot really claim to reveal a fundamental legal unity of which the existing legal systems can be regarded as national manifestations. This is immediately obvious in Peter Schlechtriem's work which is, significantly, entitled 'Restitution and Recovery of Enrichment *in Europe*' (rather than European law of restitution) and which carries the subtitle: a comparative exposition.[41] The discussion of the individual problems arising in this area of the law is conducted, essentially, by way of country reports (which, in turn, are structured according to the well-known 'legal families'). But it is also true of Christian von Bar's ambitious study on the Common European Law of Torts.[42] In its first volume we find chapters on 'Continental Europe's Codified Law of Delict', 'Scandinavian Liability Laws and the Common Law of Torts', or 'Unification and Approximation of the Law of Delict within the European Union', that is, on

---

[40] As restated authoritatively in Zweigert and Kötz (n 37), 31 ff (32 ff of the English edn).

[41] Peter Schlechtriem, *Restitution und Bereicherungsausgleich in Europa: Eine rechtsvergleichende Darstellung* (vol I, 2000; vol II, 2001).

[42] Christian von Bar, *Gemeineuropäisches Deliktsrecht* (vol I, 1996; vol II, 1999; English translation under the title *The Common European Law of Torts*, vol I, 1998; vol II, 2000).

individual constituents of a European law of torts. Volume II is structured not by countries, or groups of countries, but by requirements for, or typical forms of, delictual liability. A closer look, however, reveals that nearly every important conceptual issue, or policy decision, is heavily disputed, often even within one and the same legal system, or legal family. The notions of wrongfulness and fault provide prominent examples, and so do the issues of pure economic loss, the recoverability of 'immaterial' damage, or the proper scope of fault and no-fault liability. This is why von Bar constantly has either to make choices between the views prevailing in Europe, even on the most fundamental conceptual level, or to construct new devices or solutions. Thus, while he is certainly making true his promise not to portray a single national law in comparison with other laws, or to fashion a European approach on an individual, national pattern, his system of European tort law is both decidedly less 'European' (in the sense of reflecting an existing uniformity of approach) and less concrete than the European contract law we find in Kötz.

This is not, of course, the fault of the author. It follows from the state of development of the discipline itself. For while it is true that the continental law of delict rests on the same historical foundations (in the era of the *ius commune* it constituted an *usus modernus* of Aquilian liability which was reconceptualized under the influence of Natural law theory),[43] and that the ideas prevailing in Continental Europe have also influenced the development of English law,[44] it is equally true that in the eighteenth and nineteenth centuries the modernized version of Roman law was no longer really modern. In its basic structure it was still essentially geared towards the sanctioning of private wrongs rather than the reasonable allocation of losses.[45] This was a problem which European legal systems only started to grapple with in the course of the nineteenth century, by which time the first wave of codifications had contributed to a national isolation of the legal discourse. Particularly, therefore, every national legal system had to devise its own way of dealing with the problem of strict liability. As a result, the European legal landscape became considerably more patchy in this field than in that of contract law. The development was similar only in so far as it was attempted, in England as much as in France or Germany, to supplement, rather than to challenge, the conceptual structure of a law of delict still revolving around the notion of wrongful behaviour. This has led to a situation which is characterized, at least in some respects, by a lack of fundamental concepts which are both common to the various legal systems and teleologically satisfactory.[46] It is highly significant, in this respect, that the

---

[43] Zimmermann (n 28), 1017 ff; Nils Jansen, *Die Struktur des Haftungsrechts* (2003), 271 ff.

[44] David Ibbetson, 'Harmonisation of the Law of Tort and Delict: A Comparative and Historical Perspective', in Reinhard Zimmermann (ed), *Grundstrukturen des Europäischen Deliktsrechts* (2003), 133 ff.

[45] The point is made, and substantiated, by Jansen (n 43), 181 ff. Jansen's own re-conceptualization (389 ff) is predicated on this analysis.

[46] Nils Jansen, *Binnenmarkt, Privatrecht und europäische Identität* (2004), 33 ff.

draftsmen of the first set of 'Principles of European Tort Law'[47] to have been published have essentially dodged the thorny issue of 'wrongfulness', and that they were unable to reach agreement on the equally difficult problem of strict liability (see Art 5:102 Principles of European Tort Law).

The recovery of enrichment is governed, in all European legal systems, by rules which are based on a common stock of concepts and ideas. Most prominently, this common stock comprises the different types of *condictiones* inherited from Roman law (these, however, were not enrichment actions in the modern sense of the word), Pomponius' famous general precept, based on natural justice, that nobody should be allowed to enrich himself at the expense of another person, and the late scholastic restitution doctrine (which attempted to conceptualize cases of wrongful interference with, and of unjustified retention of, somebody else's property under the auspices of *iustitia commutativa*).[48] But the configuration of these elements in the modern national systems varies considerably and, as a result, some basic questions have remained disputed, particularly whether the recipient is liable for enrichment received or enrichment surviving, and whether a claim based on unjustified enrichment requires not only the recipient to have been enriched but also the claimant to have been impoverished. As a result, no unanimity has yet been reached as to whether this branch of the law ultimately serves to protect a person whose rights or interests have been impaired, or whether it merely looks at the position of the recipient and aims to skim off an enrichment which it regards as unjustified.[49]

In both fields the search for doctrinal structures which are recognizably European has only just started. Methodologically, the concept of a flexible system as well as the theory of legal principles appear to be of key significance.[50] Concerning the substance of the law, it is easier, so far, to state which doctrinal devices are unsuitable on the European level: the German concept of unlawfulness in the law of delict, the English unjust-factor approach in enrichment law, or the two-track model (fault-based liability and no-fault liability) of extracontractual liability prevalent in many modern legal systems. A positive assessment must remain more tentative. But if account is taken of the way the European legal systems have in fact developed during the twentieth century, it appears reasonable to accept a discrimination, in principle, between financial loss and physical injury.[51] This

---

[47] Below, n 87.

[48] Reinhard Zimmermann, 'Bereicherungsrecht in Europa: Eine Einführung', in *idem* (ed), *Grundstrukturen eines Europäischen Bereicherungsrechts* (2005), 22 ff; Nils Jansen, 'Die Korrektur grundloser Vermögensverschiebungen als Restitution? Zur Lehre von der ungerechtfertigten Bereicherung bei Savigny', (2003) 120 *Zeitschrift der Savigny-Stiftung, Romanistische Abteilung* 106 ff.

[49] Jansen (n 46), 40 ff.

[50] Axel Flessner, 'Juristische Methode und europäisches Privatrecht', [2002] *Juristenzeitung* 14 ff.

[51] Gerhard Wagner, 'Grundstrukturen des Europäischen Deliktsrechts', in Reinhard Zimmermann (n 44), 229 ff.

has been one of the most hotly debated issues in European tort law.[52] As far as unjustified enrichment is concerned, cogent arguments can be advanced for the recognition of a uniform regime governing the restitution of benefits exchanged under a contract that turns out to have failed (no matter whether it is invalid, has been rescinded, or terminated).[53] Apart from that, we witness a growing awareness of the distinction between enrichment by transfer (in a wide and untechnical sense of the word) and enrichment as a result of a wrong, or an encroachment.[54] And the reappearance of the *condictio indebiti* in English law[55] marks the end of a particularly obstructive structural difference (or rather: the perception of such difference) between the common law and the civilian systems. The latter development, in particular, can be seen as a triumph of comparative law scholarship.

It may be remarked in passing that the tendency to look at contract, delict, and unjustified enrichment in isolation has tended to leave a number of important topics common to all three branches of the law (set-off, prescription, plurality of parties, and so on) in the no-man's land of scholarly neglect, at least as far as comparative law and comparative doctrinal history are concerned.[56] The same applies to *negotiorum gestio*.

5. Establishing Networks: The New Law Journals

Comprehensive treatises which aim at compiling and analysing the legal material from as many European jurisdictions as possible can hardly be written today by a single author, working in the solitude of his office. This is apparent from the works by Schlechtriem and von Bar, both of which are based on the successful establishment of, and cooperation with, a team of young scholars. The van Gerven casebooks, too, are based on international cooperative efforts. International cooperation has, in fact, become a key feature of the growing Europeanization of private law. International initiatives, working groups, and networks have shot up like mushrooms over the past fifteen years. Merely by virtue of their composition,

[52] See, apart from Wagner (ibid) and Jansen (n 43), 524 ff, Mauro Bussani and Vernon Valentine Palmer (eds), *Pure Economic Loss in Europe* (2003); Willem H. van Boom, Helmut Koziol, and Christian A. Witting, *Pure Economic Loss* (2004).

[53] The point is substantiated in Phillip Hellwege, *Die Rückabwicklung gegenseitiger Verträge als einheitliches Problem* (2004); Reinhard Zimmermann, 'Restitutio in integrum', in *Privatrecht und Methode: Festschrift für Ernst A. Kramer* (2004), 735 ff.

[54] See Christiane Wendehorst, 'Die Leistungskondiktion und ihre Binnenstruktur in rechtsvergleichender Perspektive', and Thomas Krebs, 'Eingriffskondiktion und Restitution for Wrongs im englischen Recht', both in Zimmermann, *Grundstrukturen* (n 48), 47 ff, 141 ff.

[55] Sonja Meier, *Irrtum und Zweckverfehlung* (1999); Peter Birks, *Unjust Enrichment* (2nd edn, 2005), 101 ff.

[56] But see now Part III of the Principles of European Contract Law; below, n 73. A comprehensive historical and comparative monograph on set-off has now been published by Pascal Pichonnaz, *La compensation* (2001).

the work carried out by these bodies is comparative in nature. Each of the members tends to bring along his own national preconceptions, and an important aspect of the cooperation consists in an effort to find a common basis for mutual understanding and rational discussion. This, in my own experience, is one of the greatest benefits involved in these exercises: a partial change of frame of mind. It is an educational process which the more widely shared it is among the protagonists of legal development in Europe, will significantly contribute to the Europeanization of private law. Some of the more important of these initiatives will be mentioned in the following section of this chapter.[57]

One of the earliest such international networks was established by the founding editors of the *Zeitschrift für Europäisches Privatrecht*: one of the first two law journals devoted to the newly emerging field of European private law. The editorial of the first issue in 1993 stresses the importance of comparative law (apart from the common basis in the old *ius commune*, European community law, and the law contained in international conventions) for the development of the new *ius commune* and for the editorial policy of the journal. The editors, corresponding editors, and members of the advisory board have, at regular intervals, met for symposia in order to discuss how best to implement this policy. The journal, *inter alia*, makes available, and comments upon, the texts which have come to constitute essential threads within the tapestry of European private law; it looks at important decisions by national courts of law in a comparative and European perspective; it attempts to stimulate interest in the new discipline among students by means of an essay competition; and it has published, over the years, a large number of individual studies putting the comparative method into the service of European private law. The other journal in the field, established at about the same time under the name of *European Review of Private Law*, has introduced comparative case notes as a new type of European legal literature, and it regularly features special issues on subjects like comparative property law, the constitutionalization of private law in Europe, or the comparative implementation of the Consumer Sales Directive. Just as the *Zeitschrift für Europäisches Privatrecht*, the *European Review of Private Law*, has created an international network of editorial and advisory board members. The same is true of other journals which have, in the meantime, been founded (*Europa e diritto privato*, *Maastricht Journal of European and Comparative Law*, etc; most recently, a *European Review of Contract Law* has been established). A comparison between *Zeitschrift für Europäisches Privatrecht* and *European Review of Private Law* reveals a characteristic difference in language policy: the one journal is published largely in German but also accepts contributions in English and French (and places great emphasis on making available, in its section on annotated

---

[57] cf also Wolfgang Wurmnest, 'Common Core, Grundregeln, Kodifikationsentwürfe, Acquis-Grundsätze—Ansätze internationaler Wissenschaftlergruppen zur Privatrechtsvereinheitlichung in Europa', (2003) 11 *Zeitschrift für Europäisches Privatrecht* 714 ff.

case law, extracts of court decisions in their original language of publication), the other is officially trilingual but effectively constitutes an English-medium publication (with abstracts being provided also in French and German). Both alternatives have their specific drawbacks: on the level of the circulation of the journal in the one case, and on that of the linguistic quality of some of the contributions and the abstracts in the other.

6. Finding the Common Core

The biggest existing network in Europe today, as far as the sheer number of participants is concerned, is the one created around the (Trento) Common Core of European Private Law Project.[58] Its origins are fairly humble: they reach back to a meeting of five persons at the University of Trento in the summer of 1993. At that meeting it was decided to make the analysis of specific sets of facts by a number of reporters from various European legal systems the key feature of the project: a manner of proceeding which had previously been used by a team of scholars led by the late Rudolf Schlesinger in relation to the formation of contracts[59] and which, it was hoped, would shed light on the practical significance of specific legal notions and doctrines, place them in their context, and clear away some of the misunderstandings and misinformation which had often, in the past, prevented unbiased comparative evaluation. Apart from that, the case study approach was supposed to provide interesting insights into the different ways in which the analysis of cases is conducted in the various European states. The aim of the Trento project is descriptive: it is designed to establish how much common ground there actually exists among the private laws of the member states of the European Union. The individual volumes appearing under the aegis of Trento thus attempt to provide a map of the private law as it is rather than a blueprint for legal harmonization. The first sub-project to be completed dealt with Good Faith in European Contract Law:[60] a topic of considerable practical significance at a time when every legal system within the European Union had to implement the Directive on Unfair Terms in Consumer Contracts and was thus facing the challenge of coming to terms with a general notion of good faith. All contributors to the good faith sub-project were asked to address the thirty cases chosen for comparative investigation at three different levels. In the first place, they were requested to provide a purely legal, or doctrinal, analysis,

---

[58] Mauro Bussani, ' "Integrative" Comparative Law Enterprises and the Inner Stratification of Legal Systems', (2000) 8 *European Review of Private Law* 85 ff; Mauro Bussani and Ugo Mattei (eds), *The Common Core of European Private Law* (2002).

[59] Rudolf Schlesinger (ed), *Formation of Contracts: A Study of the Common Core of Legal Systems* (vols I and II, 1968).

[60] Reinhard Zimmermann and Simon Whittaker (eds), *Good Faith in European Contract Law* (2000).

pointing out the practical result and explaining the way in which it was reached, some indication as to significant differences of opinion which might exist in the respective legal systems, and a discussion of the underlying policy concerns. Second, this analysis was to be placed in its legal context; and third, account was to be taken of institutional, procedural, or cultural features that might be pertinent to a proper understanding of the approach adopted. Each case study was rounded off by the editors' comparative observations which, in turn, provided the basis for general comparative conclusions. What emerged was a considerable harmony of result, with a great variety of doctrines being applied in cases which, in some systems, are thought of as involving the general notion of good faith. Contrary to a widely held opinion, differences both in result and approach were seen to cut across the civil law/common law line. In the meantime, a number of similar studies have been published in the fields of contract, delict, and property law.[61] The work of many other subgroups established under the umbrella of the Trento project is in progress.

7. Bridging the Channel

The great gulf supposedly existing between the civilian systems on the one hand and the English and Irish common law on the other[62] is taken by many to constitute a major obstacle within the process of harmonization of European private law. This traditional perception, widely shared on both sides of the Channel, has prompted a significant amount of literature attempting to find common ground and to specify and critically evaluate the existing differences. This literature has been both historical and comparative in nature, it has focused on substantive private law and legal methodology, and it has contributed both to a growing awareness of existing connections between common law and civil law[63] and to the process of a growing convergence.[64] James Gordley has even declared the

---

[61] James Gordley (ed), *The Enforceability of Promises in European Contract Law* (2001); Mauro Bussani and Vernon Valentine Palmer (eds), *Pure Economic Loss in Europe* (2003); Eva-Maria Kieninger (ed), *Security Rights in Movable Property in European Private Law* (2004); Ruth Sefton-Green (ed), *Mistake, Fraud and Duties to Inform in European Contract Law* (2005).

[62] It has sometimes even been elevated to the level of a *summa differentia*, or of an irreducible 'epistemological chasm'; see Pierre Legrand, 'Legal Traditions in Western Europe: The Limits of Commonality', in R. Jagtenberg, E. Örücü, and A. J. de Roo (eds), *Transfrontier Mobility in Law* (1995), 63 ff.

[63] Reinhard Zimmermann, Der europäische Charakter des englischen Rechts: Historische Verbindungen zwischen civil law und common law, (1993) 1 *Zeitschrift für Europäisches Privatrecht* 4 ff; David Ibbetson, *A Historical Introduction to the Law of Obligations* (1999); Richard H. Helmholz, *The Ius Commune in England: Four Studies* (2001); Harold J. Berman, *Law and Revolution II: The Impact of the Protestant Reformations on the Western Legal Tradition* (2003), 201 ff.

[64] Basil S. Markesinis (ed), *The Gradual Convergence: Foreign Ideas, Foreign Influences and English Law on the Eve of the 21st Century* (1994); *idem, Foreign Law and Comparative Methodology: A Subject and a Thesis* (1997); *idem* (ed), *The Clifford Chance Millennium Lectures: The Coming Together of the Common Law and the Civil Law* (2000).

distinction to be obsolete.[65] And indeed, it must be obvious to anyone who has cooperated in one or more of the projects on the harmonization of European private law that the diversity existing among the civilian systems may be as great, and sometimes greater, than the differences between French and English, or German and English law. Specific attention has been devoted, over the past ten or fifteen years, to the topics often emphasized by those who see the world in terms of a civil law/common law dichotomy; among them good faith, the law of trusts, unjustified enrichment, and statutory interpretation. On the latter topic Stefan Vogenauer's great study has revealed that England was for many centuries a province of the *ius commune*.[66] The trust, on closer historical analysis, appears to be the specifically English variation of a common European theme. Common patterns of the development, similar social conditions, use of the same legal sources, a coincidence of purposes pursued: it can hardly be maintained that a wall of incomprehension separated the English trust from the law of the Continent.[67]

Again, occasionally, new forms of international cooperation have been tested. Thus, for example, civilian and common lawyers got together to identify the twelve key issues arising in the law of unjustified enrichment and to subject them to comparative scrutiny. Each topic was dealt with by two papers, one by a representative of a common-law system, the other by an academic with a civilian legal background.[68] Another example concerns legal systems, which are placed historically at the intersection of common law and civil law, and have, therefore, started to attract the attention both of scholars of comparative law, and of those concerned with the development of a European private law.[69] Pre-eminent among these 'mixed' legal systems are the uncodified ones of South Africa and Scotland. A recently concluded project has attempted to establish whether and to what extent Scots and South African law have been able to advance towards coherent and rational solutions of problems on which civil law and common law legal systems take a different view. Teams of leading experts from both jurisdictions have examined, collaboratively and comparatively, key topics within the law of property

---

[65] James Gordley, 'Common law und civil law: eine überholte Unterscheidung', (1993) 1 *Zeitschrift für Europäisches Privatrecht* 498 ff.

[66] Stefan Vogenauer, *Die Auslegung von Gesetzen in England und auf dem Kontinent* (2 vols, 2001).

[67] Richard Helmholz and Reinhard Zimmermann (eds), *Itinera Fiduciae: Trust and Treuhand in Historical Perspective* (1998).

[68] David Johnston and Reinhard Zimmermann (eds), *Unjustified Enrichment: Key Issues in Comparative Perspective* (2002).

[69] Vernon Valentine Palmer, *Mixed Jurisdictions Worldwide: The Third Legal Family* (2001); Jan Smits, *The Making of European Private Law: Towards a Ius Commune Europaeum as a Mixed Legal System* (2002), 107 ff; *idem* (ed), *The Contribution of Mixed Legal Systems to European Private Law* (2001); Reinhard Zimmermann, *Roman Law, Contemporary Law, European Private Law: The Civilian Tradition Today* (2001), 107 ff; Kenneth G. C. Reid, 'The Idea of Mixed Legal Systems', (2003) *Tulane LR* 5 ff.

and obligations.[70] The individual chapters, in a number of fields, reveal an emerging and distinctive jurisprudence of mixed systems, and thus suggest viable answers to some of the great questions which must be answered on the path towards a European private law. Trust law provides a prominent example. Neither Scots law nor South African law knew the institutional separation of law and equity. Both have a law of property based on Roman legal concepts. None the less, both Scots law and South African law have developed a vigorous law of trusts—true trusts, without being English trusts.[71] They have been an important source of inspiration for a set of Principles of European Trust Law.[72]

8. Principles of European Contract Law

The elaboration of such 'Principles' has become very much *de rigueur* among lawyers in Europe. The Principles of European Trust Law provide but one example. The trend was set by the Principles of European Contract Law, published in three parts in 1995, 2000, and 2003.[73] They constitute today the most advanced, and internationally most widely noted, project on the way towards the harmonization of a central branch of European private law.

(a) Scope, Approach, Characteristic Features

The Principles of European Contract Law have been prepared by a 'Commission on European Contract Law', a body without any official status which originated in a private initiative of Professor Lando of Copenhagen (hence also: 'Lando Commission'). It consisted of academics from all member states of the European Union. The growth of the Commission paralleled that of the EU. In the end it had twenty-three members; three of them came from Germany, two each from France, Italy, England, and Scotland. All in all, preparation of the Principles took more than twenty years, for the work on them began as early as 1982. Part I contains fifty-nine articles which deal with the modalities of performance, non-performance, remedies for non-performance, and a number of general questions such as

---

[70] Reinhard Zimmermann, Daniel Visser, and Kenneth Reid (eds), *Mixed Legal Systems in Comparative Perspective: Property and Obligations in Scotland and South Africa* (2004).

[71] For details, see M. J. de Waal, 'The Core Elements of the Trust: Aspects of the English, Scottish and South African Trusts Compared', (2000) 117 *South African LJ* 548 ff; G. L. Gretton, 'Trusts without Equity', (2000) 49 *ICLQ* 599 ff.

[72] D. J. Hayton, S. C. J. J. Kortmann, and H. L. E. Verhagen (eds), *Principles of European Trust Law* (1999).

[73] Ole Lando and Hugh Beale (eds), *Principles of European Contract Law* (Part I, 1995); Ole Lando and Hugh Beale (eds), *Principles of European Contract Law* (Parts I and II, 2000); Ole Lando, Eric Clive, André Prüm, and Reinhard Zimmermann (eds), *Principles of European Contract Law* (Part III, 2003). French, German, Italian, and Spanish versions of these works have been published, or are in preparation.

application, general duties of behaviour in the course of a contractual relationship, and terminology. The seventy-three articles of Part II cover the formation of contracts, authority of agents, validity (including vices of consent but excluding illegality), interpretation, and contents and effects (including contracts in favour of a third party). The third, and final, part of the Principles comprises sixty-nine articles on plurality of parties, assignment of claims, substitution of new debtor and transfer of contract, set-off, prescription, illegality, conditions, and capitalization of interest. Unlike Part II, Part III has not been integrated with the existing set of Principles but has been published separately, for the time being.

The long gestation period, as well as the fact that the work has been split into three stages, have left their trace on the substance of the Principles. The basic conception (preparation of a set of principles covering the general law of contract) dates back to a time before the EC had embarked on the regulation of an ever wider range of issues concerning consumer contracts. As a result, the *acquis communautaire* has largely been ignored in the Principles. In particular, the Lando Commission never addressed the difficult question of the way in which the mandatory rules on consumer protection can be integrated into a set of principles of general contract law.[74] In another respect the scope of application of the Principles has come to be extended over the course of time. For whereas their first two parts do indeed only deal with the law of contract, the first four chapters of Part III relate to all types of obligations. They thus constitute core components of a general law of obligations for Europe. A certain change of conception also appears to have occurred with regard to the character of the provisions contained in the Principles. Originally, as is apparent from the title chosen for their work, the members of the Lando Commission do not appear to have aimed at drafting a system of specific rules which might immediately be applied by courts of law. Yet, the rules contained in a number of the later chapters (such as those on plurality of parties, assignment, set-off, and prescription) attain a level of specificity emulating that of any of the existing national codes of private law. The term 'Principles' thus appears to be used, very largely, as a convenient smokescreen for a model code of legal rules.[75] And finally, the preparation of the Principles in three different stages has led to certain deficiencies of coordination. Thus, for example, all three parts contain rules dealing with the restitution of benefits. Article 5:114 PECL refers to situations where a contract has been avoided, Arts 9:305 ff PECL deal with the consequences of termination of contract in cases of non-performance, and Art 15:104 PECL covers the restitution of benefits received under a contract that has turned out to

---

[74] Hans-W. Micklitz, 'Verbraucherschutz in den Grundregeln des Europäischen Vertragsrechts', (2004) 103 *Zeitschrift für vergleichende Rechtswissenschaft* 88 ff. Generally on the relationship between consumer contract law and general contract law, see Reinhard Zimmermann, *The New German Law of Obligations: Historical and Comparative Perspectives* (2005), 159 ff.

[75] On the use of the term 'principles' as opposed to 'rules' in methodological discourse, see Ronald Dworkin, *Taking Rights Seriously* (1977), 22 ff.

be invalid because of illegality. This triplication of rules as well as the differences between them is not justifiable. It is one of a number of issues on which the Principles still need to be refined and revised.

The Principles of European Contract Law are the product of an international comparative and collaborative effort. Of course, one or two 'reporters' were responsible for the individual chapters. They had the task of preparing comparative position papers and draft articles and commentaries. However, a number of different members of the Commission served as reporters. The position papers and successive drafts were presented to the Commission as well as to a 'Drafting Group' and were discussed, criticized, refined, and referred back to the reporters several times by both bodies; finally they were passed in two 'readings' by the Commission and subsequently checked again by another body, the 'Editing Group'. All in all, the Commission met twenty-six times; each meeting, as a rule, lasted one week. Great efforts were made to achieve a consensus even if on a number of issues, eventually, a vote had to be taken. Also, every effort was made by the draftsmen of the Principles not to base their work on any individual legal system. Their approach was comparative in nature. They attempted, as far as possible, to identify the common core of the contract law of all the EU member states and to create a workable system on that basis. Thus, in a way, they aimed at a restatement of European contract law. At the same time, however, they realized that they were confronted with a more creative task than the draftsmen of the American Restatements. Divergences had to be resolved on the basis of a comparative evaluation of the experiences gathered in the national legal systems, by assessing and analysing European and international trends of legal development, or by employing other rational criteria.[76]

The Principles are also inspired by the Restatements of American Law, as far as the style and structure of their publication are concerned. Each volume contains the text of the articles which the Commission has agreed upon. In addition, for every article there are a commentary (including illustrations) and comparative notes; the latter inform the reader about the pertinent legal rules applicable in the EU member states but also take account of other sources of law, such as international Conventions. The articles contained in the Principles of European Contract Law have immediately been published in a French and an English version, even though English has otherwise been the language of publication. In the course of the deliberations of the Lando Commission great emphasis was placed on the possibility of expressing every term and concept used in the Principles in both French and English; the Commission was thus constantly aware of the danger of using a terminology indelibly shaped by the peculiarities of individual legal systems.

---

[76] For practical examples of the types of arguments to be employed in the process of drafting 'principles' of European contract law, see Reinhard Zimmermann, *Comparative Foundations of a European Law of Set-Off and Prescription* (2002).

(b) Purposes and Perspectives

Generally speaking, I think, that the Principles of European Contract Law can be regarded as the product of a long tradition, distinguished by its inherent flexibility and capacity for development,[77] and as a contemporary manifestation of a genuinely European law of contract (even in places where an unconventional solution has been found and adopted).[78] Which contribution are they, in turn, able to render to the Europeanization of contract law? The authors of the Principles themselves mention a number of purposes for which the Principles are designed.[79] They want to facilitate cross-border trade within Europe by making available to the parties a set of neutral rules, detached from the peculiarities of any one national legal system, to which they can subject their transaction. Moreover, the authors of the Principles regard their work as a modern formulation of a *lex mercatoria* which can be referred to, for instance, by arbitrators who have to decide a case according to 'internationally accepted principles of law'. These are very practical purposes. But the Principles are also seen by their authors in a less immediately practical, but rather longer-term perspective. They provide a conceptual and systematic infrastructure for community legislation concerning contract law; at the same time they can be taken to constitute a first step towards a European Civil Code.

Of central significance in the immediate future appears to be yet another aspect: the Principles as a source of inspiration for national legislation, courts of law, and legal doctrine.[80] For the foreseeable future we will still be faced with the coexistence of several national systems of private law in Europe. Much would, however, be gained if these could be assimilated gradually, or organically. The Principles of European Contract Law can play a key role within this process. For they provide a compass, established on the basis of comparative research and international cooperation, which can serve to guide the interpretation and development of the national legal systems. Comparison with the Principles will reveal the quirks and idiosyncrasies of the latter and will lead to their reappraisal. Unfortunately, in Germany, the Principles have not yet worked their way into the general textbooks and commentaries on private law. Dutch writers, on the other hand, refer to the Principles almost as a matter of routine even when they merely deal with a question of Dutch contract law. A recent collection of texts, cases, and materials on English contract law invokes the Principles on a number of occasions even

[77] Berman, *Law and Revolution I* (n 28), 1 ff; Reinhard Zimmermann, 'Roman Law and the Harmonisation of Private Law in Europe', in Hartkamp *et al* (n 11), 21 ff.

[78] The point is developed, and substantiated, in Reinhard Zimmermann, 'Ius Commune and the Principles of European Contract Law: Contemporary Renewal of an Old Idea', in Hector MacQueen and Reinhard Zimmermann (eds), *European Contract Law: Scots and South African Perspectives* (2006), 1 ff, 12 ff.

[79] Lando/Beale I and II (n 73), xxi ff.

[80] cf also Jan Smits, 'PECL and the Harmonization of Private Law in Europe', in Antoni Vaquer Aloy (ed), *La Tercera Parte de los Principios de Derecho Contractual Europeo* (2005), 567 ff.

although it specifically does not describe itself as a book on comparative law.[81] Another very interesting initiative has been taken in the Netherlands. Five authors have systematically examined their own legal system from the point of view of the Principles and have thus, by using a supranational frame of reference, made Dutch law more easily accessible to foreign lawyers.[82] As far as national legislation is concerned, the Principles have been taken into consideration in the final stages of the so-called 'modernization' of the German law of obligations; the new law of prescription has been based, in its general outlines, on the model proposed by the Lando Commission.[83] National courts of law, however, have not yet started to use the potential inherent in the Principles for what may be termed a 'harmonizing' method of interpretation.[84]

9. Principles of European Tort Law

The successful cooperation within the Lando Commission has inspired similar initiatives in other fields. One of them is the Group on European Tort Law, originally also referred to as 'Tilburg Group' but now based in the European Centre of Tort and Insurance Law in Vienna. Since its establishment in 1993, this group has endeavoured to survey tort law on a comparative basis and has published individual volumes devoted, *inter alia*, to wrongfulness, causation, damages, strict liability, liability of damage caused by others, contributory negligence, and multiple tortfeasors.[85] In addition, members of the group have been involved in a number of other comparative projects run by the Centre, such as those on medical malpractice, compensation for personal injury, damages for non-pecuniary loss, the impact of social security on tort law, and pure economic loss.[86] All these books contain country reports, based on questionnaires which usually consist of a mixture of abstract questions and cases. The country reports, in turn, provide the basis for a general comparative report by the editors of the respective volumes. In addition, in 2001, the European Centre of Tort and Insurance Law (through

[81] Ewan McKendrick, *Contract Law: Text, Cases and Materials* (2003).

[82] Danny Busch, Ewoud Hondius, Hugo van Kooten, Harriet Schelhaas, and Wendy Schrama, *The Principles of European Contract Law and Dutch Law: A Commentary* (vol. I. 2002; vol. II, 2006). For Germany, see Jürgen Basedow (ed), *Europäische Vertragsrechtsvereinheitlichung und deutsches Recht* (2000).

[83] See Zimmermann (n 74), 122 ff.

[84] Walter Odersky, 'Harmonisierende Auslegung und europäische Rechtskultur', (1994) 2 *Zeitschrift für Europäisches Privatrecht* 1 ff. Odersky is a former president of the German Federal Supreme Court.

[85] The most recent volume is Pierre Widmer (ed), *Unification of Tort Law: Fault* (2005). It is the tenth volume in the series.

[86] The most recent volume is Gerhard Wagner (ed), *Tort Law and Liability Insurance* (2005). This is the sixteenth volume in a series devoted to Tort and Insurance Law.

Helmut Koziol and Barbara C. Steininger) started to publish a yearbook on the development of European Tort Law. These activities have helped to pave the way towards the achievement of the main aim on the agenda of the Group on European Tort Law: the elaboration of a set of Principles of European Tort Law. These Principles were published in the second half of 2004.[87] In most respects, they resemble the Principles of European Contract Law. Like the Lando Commission the Group on European Tort Law did not choose one or two of the existing codes or draft codes as a model system on which to base its work. The approach adopted was essentially comparative in nature. Like the Lando Commission, the Group on European Tort Law has not drafted 'Principles' in the technical sense of the word but legal rules (even if sometimes extremely broad ones). Both sets of rules are characterized by a considerable amount of built-in flexibility. But whereas the Principles of European Contract Law tend to operate with open-ended standards such as 'reasonable', 'good faith', or 'proportional', the Principles of European Tort Law employ the technique of a flexible system:[88] they provide a basic rule and then attempt to specify the various elements which have to combine in various degrees and configurations in order to found liability. Apart from that, both sets of Principles are drafted in a similar style: an effort has been made to formulate rules which are short, general, and as easily comprehensible as possible. The draftsmen have also endeavoured to avoid concepts which carry a doctrinal connotation specifically related to the one or other national legal system. Unlike the Lando Commission, however, the Group on European Tort Law appears to have operated exclusively in English, which is also the original language of publication. Both groups were working groups; they were originally fairly small and have grown in the course of time. Both attempted to secure a broadly based international membership. But whereas the Lando Commission had at least one member from each member state of the European Union, and none from outside, the Group on European Tort Law also included members from Switzerland, Israel, South Africa, and the United States; on the other hand, it did not have members from all EU member states. The composition of the Tort Law group appears to be a better reflection of the idea that the members of the two groups were not supposed to be, and were not chosen as, representatives of the state from which they came. Moreover, it takes account of two related facts: private law that can historically be described as 'European' also exists

---

[87] (2004) 12 *Zeitschrift für Europäisches Privatrecht* 427 ff; and see now Group on European Tort Law, *Principles of European Tort Law: Text and Commentary* (2005). For comment, see Helmut Koziol, 'Die "Principles of European Tort Law" der "European Group on Tort Law" ', (2004) 12 *Zeitschrift für Europäisches Privatrecht* 234 ff; Reinhard Zimmermann, 'Principles of European Contract Law and Principles of European Tort Law: Comparison and Points of Contact', in Helmut Koziol and Barbara C. Steininger (eds), *European Tort Law 2003* (2004), 2 ff.

[88] On which see Walter Wilburg, *Entwicklung eines beweglichen Systems im bürgerlichen Recht* (1950); for an overview in English, see Bernhard A. Koch, 'Wilburg's Flexible System in a Nutshell', in Helmut Koziol and Barbara C. Steininger (eds), *European Tort Law 2001* (2002), 545 ff.

outside Europe;[89] and the boundaries of the European Union appear to be somewhat artificial when it comes to assessing the international (even the European!) development of tort law.[90]

10. More Principles

Other initiatives of a similar kind are the Principles of European Trust Law (drafted by an international working group based in Nijmegen and published in 1999),[91] the Principles of European Insolvency Law (drafted by an international working group also based in Nijmegen and published in 2003),[92] and, most recently, the Principles of European Family Law regarding Divorce and Maintenance between Former Spouses (drafted by an international Commission on European Family Law based in Utrecht and published in 2004).[93] The latter Commission had previously published two comparative studies devoted to grounds for divorce and maintenance between former spouses[94] and will in future explore other topics within the field of family law. An international project group Restatement of Insurance Contract Law, founded in 1999 and based in Innsbruck and Hamburg, has yet to publish the results of its deliberations.

The drafting of Principles has even become fashionable in the field of global legal harmonization. Thus, internationally the Principles of European Contract Law compete with the UNIDROIT Principles of International Commercial Contracts (published originally in 1994 and in an extended version in 2004).[95] Both

[89] Reinhard Zimmermann, 'Europäisches Privatrecht und Europa', (1993) 1 *Zeitschrift für Europäisches Privatrecht* 439 ff; Eugen Bucher, 'Zu Europa gehört auch Lateinamerika!', (2004) 12 *Zeitschrift für Europäisches Privatrecht* 515 ff.

[90] See Pierre Widmer, 'Reform und Vereinheitlichung des Haftpflichtrechts auf schweizerischer und europäischer Ebene', in Zimmermann (n 44), 147 ff.

[91] Above, n 72.

[92] W. W. McBryde, A. Flessner, and S. Kortmann (eds), *Principles of European Insolvency Law* (2003); and see Axel Flessner, 'Grundsätze des europäischen Insolvenzrechts', (2004) 12 *Zeitschrift für Europäisches Privatrecht* 887 ff.

[93] Katharina Boele-Woelki, Frédérique Ferrand, Cristina Gonzalez Beilfuss, Maarit Jänterä-Jareborg, Nigel Lowe, Dieter Martiny, and Walter Pintens (eds), *Principles of European Family Law Regarding Divorce and Maintenance between Former Spouses* (2004).

[94] Katharina Boele-Woelki, Bente Braat, and Ian Sumner (eds), *European Family Law in Action*, vol I: Grounds for Divorce (2003); vol II, Maintenance between Former Spouses (2003). Cf also Katharina Boele-Woelki, 'Comparative Research-Based Drafting of Principles of European Family Law', in Michael Faure, Jan Smits, and Hildegard Schneider (eds), *Towards a European Ius Commune in Legal Education and Research* (2002), 171 ff.

[95] UNIDROIT (ed), *Principles of International Commercial Contracts 2004* (2004); for comment, see Michael Joachim Bonell, UNIDROIT Principles 2004—The New Edition of the Principles of International Commercial Contracts, adopted by the International Institute for the Unification of Private Law', (2004) 9 *Uniform LR* 6 ff; Reinhard Zimmermann, 'Die UNIDROIT-Grundregeln der internationalen Handelsverträge 2004 in vergleichender Perspektive', (2005) 13 *Zeitschrift für Europäisches Privatrecht* 268 ff.

works are comparable in many respects. Thus, in particular, they have been prepared in a similar manner, they pursue similar aims, and they have been drafted in a similar style. The style and structure of the presentation are also very similar (even if the UNIDROIT Principles do not contain comparative notes). There are two major differences in that (i) UNIDROIT pursues the aim of a global rather than European harmonization of contract law and (ii) the UNIDROIT Principles specifically deal with international commercial contracts while the 'Lando' Commission has formulated principles of general contract law. In view of this it may appear surprising that the individual solutions proposed by both sets of Principles do not very much differ from each other; in a number of areas they are virtually identical.[96] The dominance of European legal thinking patterns even outside of Europe may provide an explanation, as far as the first point is concerned. With respect to (ii) it may perhaps be said that what is regarded as fair and reasonable for commercial contracts can very largely also be regarded as fair and reasonable for consumer contracts, and vice versa. This confirms an observation on the development of modern sales law: the provisions in the Consumer Sales Directive 1999/44, particularly those concerning the concept of conformity and the remedies in case of non-conformity, very largely mirror the rules contained in the UN Convention on the International Sale of Goods, even though the latter instrument specifically excludes consumer sales from its range of application.[97] The correspondence between these two international instruments will significantly contribute to the emergence of a common framework of reference for the discussion and development of the law of sale in Europe.[98] The same can be said, on the basis of a comparison between the UNIDROIT and the Lando Principles, for many central areas of the general law of contract.

European and international legal unification often go hand in hand and influence each other. This is one of two reasons why initiatives which aim at legal unification beyond the boundaries of the European Union (such as CISG, the Geneva Agency Convention, the Ottawa Factoring Convention, or the Cape Town Convention on International Interests in Mobile Equipment) have to be kept in mind when analysing the harmonization of private law in Europe.[99] The other is the simple fact that international unification also often, implicitly, brings about legal unification in Europe. Another potentially important document also for

[96] Arthur S. Hartkamp, 'Principles of Contract Law', in Hartkamp *et al* (n 11), 125 ff; Michael Joachim Bonell, *An International Restatement of Contract Law* (3rd edn, 2005), 335 ff.

[97] Stefan Grundmann, 'Verbraucherrecht, Unternehmensrecht, Privatrecht—warum sind sich UN-Kaufrecht und EU-Kaufrechts-Richtlinie so ähnlich?', (2002) 202 *Archiv für die civilistische Praxis* 40 ff.

[98] See Viola Heutger, 'Konturen des Kaufrechtskonzeptes der Study Group on a European Civil Code—Ein Werkstattbericht', (2003) 11 *European Review of Private Law* 155 ff; Viola Heutger and Christoph Jeloschek, 'Towards Principles of European Sales Law', in Hartkamp *et al* (n 11), 533 ff.

[99] cf also Harry M. Flechtner, 'The CISG's Impact on International Unification Efforts: The UNIDROIT Principles of International Commercial Contracts and the Principles of European Contract Law', in Franco Ferrari (ed), *The 1980 Uniform Sales Law* (2003), 169 ff; Bonell (n 96), 301 ff.

Europe are the Principles of Transnational Civil Procedure, a project jointly run by UNIDROIT and the American Law Institute. It was finalized in 2004 and published in 2005.[100] A European working group under the chairmanship of Marcel Storme had presented a report on the Approximation of Judiciary Law in 1994.[101] The recommendations contained in this report have not, however, been acted on by the European Commission.

11. Moving towards a Code? Study Group and Avant-Projet

A growing number of comparative and European lawyers today regard the preparation, and introduction, of a European Civil Code as both feasible and desirable. Two international initiatives have embarked on an attempt to elaborate draft codes. The one is the *Avant-projet* of a European Contract Code, published in the name of an *Accademia dei Giusprivatisti Europei*, with its seat in Pavia.[102] In spite of (or probably rather: in view of) the fact that that Academy consists of close to 100 members, the *Avant-projet* is the work, very largely, of one man: Giuseppe Gandolfi, described on the title of the publication with too much modesty as 'coordinator'. The academy did not have much more than a consultative function: it gave suggestions, commented on preliminary drafts, and met occasionally in plenary sessions as well as national subgroups. Its members do not appear to have been involved in the actual drafting of the rules. Moreover, the *Avant-projet* takes its cue from two models. These are the Italian *Codice civile* (since it combines elements of French and German law) and a Contract Code drawn up on behalf of the English Law Commission at the end of the 1960s (which, however, has neither been implemented nor even been published in England).[103] Another notable difference to just about all the other projects presented thus far is that the *Avant-projet* is published in French. While the *Avant-projet* offers interesting material for reflection and discussion, it is doubtful whether a draft which is neither based on detailed comparative research into the contemporary sources of national law nor the product of genuine international collaboration will commend itself to many objective observers as a model European Code.[104]

[100] See Rolf Stürner, 'The Principles of Transnational Civil Procedure: An Introduction to their Basic Conception', (2005) 69 *RabelsZ* 201 ff.

[101] Marcel Storme (ed), *Rapprochement du Droit Judiciare de l'Union Européenne—Approximation of Judiciary Law in the European Union* (1994).

[102] Giuseppe Gandolfi (*coordinateur*), *Code Européen des Contrats: Avant-projet* (2000); for an English translation, see Harvey McGregor, 'European Code of Contract', (2004) 8 *Edinburgh LR*, Special Issue.

[103] Harvey McGregor, *Contract Code drawn up on behalf of the English Law Commission* (1993), published by Giuffré, Milano.

[104] For more detailed criticism, see Reinhard Zimmermann, 'Der "Codice Gandolfi" als Modell eines einheitlichen Vertragsrechts für Europa?', in *Festschrift für Erik Jayme* (vol II, 2004), 1401 ff.

The other initiative is the Study Group on a European Civil Code, established in 1998 at the inspiration, and under the chairmanship, of Christian von Bar.[105] The Study Group has become an enormous international network consisting of individual working, advisory, coordinating, steering groups and specialized 'task forces'; it is financed, very largely, by a number of national research organizations. In a way, the Study Group is carrying on the work of the Lando Commission by drafting sets of model rules for adjacent areas of the law: delict, unjustified enrichment, *negotiorum gestio*, sales, services and long-term contracts, insurance contract law, credit securities and the transfer of movable property. The working groups are based in Osnabrück, Hamburg, Salzburg, Utrecht, Tilburg, and Amsterdam. A number of preliminary drafts have been published; and for insurance contracts a comprehensive comparative study in three volumes has been edited by Jürgen Basedow and Till Fock.[106] The first completed results of the work of the Study Group will be published in the course of 2006. These publications will probably be very similar in style and structure to those of the Lando Commission.

V. WHERE WE STAND TODAY

1. Obligations—and beyond?

If account is also taken of the large number of comparative studies on individual topics of European private law to have appeared since 1990,[107] and of initiatives like the creation of a Society of European Contract Law (Secola) and of a Study Group on Social Justice in European Private Law,[108] it will be apparent that

---

[105] Christian von Bar, 'Die Study Group on a European Civil Code', in *Festschrift für Dieter Henrich* (2000), 1 ff.

[106] Jürgen Basedow and Till Fock, *Europäisches Versicherungsvertragsrecht* (vols I and II, 2002; vol III, 2003).

[107] Many of them have been published in series of monographs specifically devoted to European private law; see, *inter alia*, *Schriften zur Europäischen Rechts- und Verfassungsgeschichte* (Duncker & Humblot, since 1991), *Europäisches Wirtschaftsrecht* (C. H. Beck, since 1992), *Ius Commune Europaeum* (Intersentia, since 1993), *Europäisches Privatrecht* (Nomos, since 1996), *Grundlagen und Schwerpunkte des Privatrechts in europäischer Perspektive* (Nomos, since 1999), *Untersuchungen zum Europäischen Privatrecht* (Duncker & Humblot, since 1999), *Salzburger Studien zum Europäischen Privatrecht* (Peter Lang, since 1999), *Private Law in European Context Series* (Kluwer, since 2002), *Europäisches Privatrecht* (Stämpfli, since 2002); *Schriften zur Europäischen Rechtswissenschaft* (Sellier European Law Publishers, since 2005).

[108] See, for the former, Stefan Grundmann, 'Die Gesellschaft für Europäisches Vertragsrecht (Secola)—und eine Tagung in Leuven zum Europäischen Vertragsgesetzbuch', (2003) 11 *Zeitschrift*

comparative law has eagerly embraced its new task. In fact, one can sometimes gain the impression that hardly any project, or study, in the field of comparative private law in Europe is launched today without at least a reference to its utility within the process of Europeanization of private law or private law scholarship. Thus, the time may have come occasionally to emphasize that comparative law may also legitimately serve other purposes. Originally, Europeanization of private law as a scholarly enterprise was promoted particularly forcefully by German authors. In the meantime it has caught on in many countries across Europe, among them Italy, Spain (particularly Catalonia), Scotland, and, above all, the Netherlands. Other countries, most notably France, have displayed considerable reserve. The move- ment has been strongly stimulated by a process of legal unification 'from above', that is, by way of central legislation within the European Union, which was widely perceived to be selective, uncoordinated, and detrimental to the integrity of private law. A broadly based Europeanization of private law was seen by some as a strategy to check, by others as the appropriate way to bolster, these developments. Within the traditional core areas of private law, contract law has been at the centre of attention. The internal market provides the most powerful motivation, and driving force, for legal harmonization within the European Union, and contract law, obvi- ously, is particularly closely related to the internal market. This is the reason why a considerable number of Directives have been enacted in this field. Moreover, in spite of two hundred years of legal nationalization, contract law is still more international in substance and character than tort law, property law, or family law. However, in the tradition of European private law (including England), contract is only one component of a larger systematic entity: the law of obligations.[109] The second main pillar of the law of obligations is the law of delict. Other non- contractual obligations can arise from unjustified enrichment and (in the conti- nental legal tradition) *negotiorum gestio*. Contract, delict, unjustified enrichment, and *negotiorum gestio* are, however, interrelated with each other in so many ways that the isolated consideration of merely one of these components is bound to lead to a distorted picture. Thus, it was to be expected that, sooner rather than later, the law of obligations in general would be caught up in the surge of Europeanization. This is what has actually happened, even though contract law has remained the most advanced, and most meticulously scrutinized, subject, by far. Property law, family law, and the law of succession have only marginally been affected. Whatever attention has been given to property law has largely been confined to movable property. This is as true of the comparative study edited by Eva-Maria Kieninger

---

für Europäisches Privatrecht 189 ff, and, for the latter, Study Group on Social Justice in European Private Law (ed), 'Social Justice in European Contract Law: A Manifesto', (2004) 10 *European LJ* 653 ff.

[109] Peter Birks (ed), *The Classification of Obligations* (1997); *idem*, 'More Logic and Less Experience: The Difference between Scots and English Law', in David L. Carey Miller and Reinhard Zimmermann (eds), *The Civilian Tradition and Scots Law: Aberdeen Quincentenary Essays* (1997), 167 ff.

within the framework of the Common Core Project[110] as it is of the two property law-related working groups of the Study Group (transfer of property and securities on movables), or of Willem Zwalve's pioneering historical and comparative work.[111] Christian von Bar, however, has edited a series of books offering a systematic introduction to the national property laws in Europe at large.[112] In the field of family law the (self-appointed) Commission on European Family Law has been mentioned. In Regensburg, Dieter Henrich and Dieter Schwab started to survey and till the field of European family law in the middle of the 1990s.[113] Considerable attention has been devoted to the comparative study of trust law. Recently a large-scale research project has been launched in Hamburg on the law relating to non-profit organizations in Europe.[114] Hardly more than one or two programmatic articles have, so far, been devoted to the Europeanization of the law of succession.[115]

2. An Educational Process

Europeanization of private law has been on the agenda of comparative law scholarship for about fifteen years. Over that period a number of new approaches have successfully been tried, though hardly any of the work surveyed in this chapter has fundamentally challenged the conventional 'method' of comparative law, as set out in standard works like Zweigert and Kötz.[116] The work done, so far, has either been of a descriptive nature in that it attempts to survey the European legal landscape as accurately as possible, or it has also had an evaluative, or normative, component suggesting the best, or most appropriate, solution to a problem on a European level. The arguments advanced in the latter context can be of an economic character, based on past experience, related to systematic concerns, and so on; ultimately, '(t)he comparatist uses just the same criteria as any other lawyer who has to

[110] Above, n 61.

[111] Willem Zwalve, *Hoofdstukken uit de geschiedenis van het Europese privaatrecht*, vol 1: *Inleiding en zakenrecht* (2nd edn, 2003).

[112] Christian von Bar (ed), *Sachenrecht in Europa* (vol I, 2000; vol II, 2000; vol III, 1999; vol IV, 2001). Cf also G. E. van Maanen and A. J. van der Walt (eds), *Property Law on the Threshold of the 21st Century* (1996) and the contributions by Ulrich Drobnig, Roy Goode, and Hans G. Wehrens, in Hartkamp *et al* (n 11), 725 ff., 741 ff., 757 ff., 769 ff.

[113] The first volume in the series, *Beiträge zum europäischen Familienrecht*, appeared in 1994 (edited by Dieter Schwab and Dieter Henrich, and containing country reports and comparative conclusions).

[114] Klaus J. Hopt and Dieter Reuter (eds), *Stiftungsrecht in Europa* (2001).

[115] Dieter Leipold, 'Europa und das Erbrecht', in *Festschrift für Alfred Söllner* (2000), 647 ff; Walter Pintens, 'Die Europäisierung des Erbrechts', (2001) 9 *Zeitschrift für Europäisches Privatrecht* 628 ff. Alain Verbeke and Yves-Henri Leleu, 'Harmonisation of the Law of Succession', in Hartkamp *et al* (n 11), 335 ff. But see Murad Ferid, Karl Firsching, Heinrich Dörner, and Rainer Hausmann (eds), *Internationales Erbrecht* (loose-leaf, since 1974); David Hayton (ed), *European Succession Laws* (1998); Rembert Süß and Ulrich Haas, *Erbrecht in Europa* (2004).

[116] This is also the view taken by Mathias Reimann, 'The Progress and Failure of Comparative Law in the Second Half of the Twentieth Century', (2002) 50 *AJCL* 671 ff.

decide which of two possible solutions is more suitable and just'.[117] Comparative
law scholarship has often been closely associated with historical legal studies.[118]
Legal historians have, in fact, been among the first to point out that the national
particularization of private law and private law scholarship in Europe is both
unnatural and anachronistic; and they have demonstrated that an awareness of the
common past can facilitate the path towards a common future. The real hallmark
of comparative law scholarship under the auspices of Europeanization has been the
astonishing proliferation of international working groups. The interaction
engendered by them has led to a significant change of mentality and has therefore
been of great value in itself. But it has also led to results. Occasionally, merely the
smallest common denominator between divergent traditions and solutions has
been established. Sometimes a very considerable amount of common ground has
been found. In other cases lawyers from many different countries have, on rational
grounds, been able to reach agreement that one approach to a legal problem is
superior to the other. From time to time new solutions have even been developed
which fit prevailing legal thinking better than the established ones. In some
instances the new solutions can be seen as a 'progressive development' within the
European legal tradition, in others they herald the recovery of ideas prevailing in
the past that had subsequently come to be suppressed.[119] It is, in other words,
an educational process which, in addition, sometimes produces excellent results;
and these results, in turn, can guide and stimulate the development of national
private law.

VI. Looking into the Future

1. The Right Time for a Code?

What is the future going to bring? Some will say (or hope) a codification of
European private law. The main proponent of this view is the European Parliament.[120] The Commission of the European Union, more cautiously, envisages the
preparation of a 'common frame of reference' for European contract law, with the
aim of improving the coherence of the existing and future *acquis*; the frame of

---

[117] Zweigert and Kötz (n 37), 46 (47 of the English edn).

[118] Hein Kötz, 'Was erwartet die Rechtsvergleichung von der Rechtsgeschichte?' 1992 *Juristenzeitung* 20 ff; Axel Flessner, 'Die Rechtsvergleichung als Kundin der Rechtsgeschichte', (1999) 7 *Zeitschrift
für Europäisches Privatrecht* 513 ff.

[119] See the illustrations in Zimmermann (n 78), 29 ff.   [120] Above, n 19.

reference may then serve as the basis for an 'optional instrument'.[121] It is likely that the Principles of European Contract Law of the Lando Commission will play a key role in this process. That the possibility of codifying European private law, or even of part of it, is seriously discussed today is nothing less than astonishing if account is taken of the lame and incredulous reactions with which the first steps towards a Europeanization of private law were received in the early 1990s. Yet, among academics across Europe the desirability of a European Civil Code is a hotly contested issue.[122]

The discussion today has obvious parallels to the great codification debate in early nineteenth-century Germany when A. F. J. Thibaut argued that a General German Civil Code, modelled on the French *Code civil*, would facilitate the emergence of an undivided German nation. It was to have a symbolic, apart from its practical, value. Thibaut's ideas, however, had been decisively rejected by Friedrich Carl von Savigny, soon to emerge as the patron saint of German legal scholarship, who had insisted on the necessity of establishing an 'organically progressive legal scholarship that may be common to the whole nation'.[123] Savigny's Historical School led to German legal unification on a scholarly level and, eventually, even to the drafting of a Civil Code—a code, however, which, rather than constituting a watershed in German legal development, bore certain characteristics of a restatement; and which was described by one of its principal architects, Bernhard Windscheid, as 'merely a ripple in the stream' within the development of the law by courts and legal scholars.[124] In a similar vein, the establishment of a legal scholarship 'which may be common to the whole of Europe' is widely seen as one of the great challenges of our time:[125] a scholarship which may, eventually, pave the way towards a codification as widely accepted in Europe as the *Code civil* in France or the BGB in Germany. Today we only see the beginnings of such development. For it must not be forgotten that, in spite of the developments analysed in this chapter, national courts, as well as legal literature and legal training regulations

---

[121] See, most recently, the Communication from the Commission to the European Parliament and the Council on 'European Contract Law and the revision of the acquis: the way forward', COM (2004) 651 final.

[122] The parameters for the academic discussion are analysed by Stephen Weatherill, 'Why Object to the Harmonization of Private Law by the EC?', (2004) 12 *European Review of Private Law* 633 ff; and see the survey by Ewoud Hondius, 'Towards a European Civil Code', in Hartkamp *et al* (n 11), 3 ff.

[123] Friedrich Carl von Savigny, 'Vom Beruf unserer Zeit für Gesetzgebung und Rechtswissenschaft', easily accessible today, in Hans Hattenhauer (ed), *Thibaut und Savigny: Ihre programmatischen Schriften* (2nd edn, 2002), 126.

[124] Bernhard Windscheid, 'Die geschichtliche Schule in der Rechtswissenschaft', in *idem*, *Gesammelte Reden und Abhandlungen* (ed Paul Oertmann) (1904), 76; and see Zimmermann (n 74), 5 ff.

[125] James Gordley, 'Comparative Legal Research: Its Function in the Development of Harmonized Law', (1995) 43 *AJCL* 555 ff; Reinhard Zimmermann, 'Savigny's Legacy: Legal History, Comparative Law, and the Emergence of a European Legal Science', (1996) 112 *LQR* 576 ff; *idem*, *Roman Law, Contemporary Law, European Law: The Civilian Tradition Today* (2001).

have, so far, predominantly retained their fixation on national codes of private law (or on the national common law).

Apart from that, the scope of an optional (or binding?) 'instrument'[126] is far from clear. Very few would argue that it should immediately include rules on immovable property, family law, or succession upon death. But should it be confined to general contract law? That is what the European Commission appears to envisage. Or will it have to cover closely related subjects such as those already tackled by the Study Group on a European Civil Code? It is equally unclear whether European Community Law provides a legal basis for the enactment of such an instrument.[127] This question, in turn, is closely linked to the issues of the legal form and scope of the instrument. Finally, it is open to doubt whether, apart from political considerations (a European Civil Code as a symbol of European unity), economic arguments can be advanced in favour of legal unification. This is regularly done. Still, however, leading European law and economics scholars have challenged the assumptions on which these arguments rest.[128]

2. Comparative Law and Legal History

Whatever the answers to these questions may be, the process of a Europeanization will continue, and even accelerate. Evidently, also, comparative law scholarship will continue to be crucially important. This is contested only by those who, oddly, equate legal culture essentially with national legal culture and who, equally oddly, wish to focus scholarship in comparative law on the investigation (or as it is sometimes put: the celebration) of *differences* in mentality, style, or approach.[129] Comparative law will continue to derive great benefit from its cooperation with legal history. Historical scholarship helps us to map out, and to become aware of, the common ground which still exists between our national legal systems as a result of a common tradition, of independent but parallel developments, and of

---

[126] For a discussion of the options (European Code replacing national laws versus an optional European code supplementing, not replacing, national laws), see the contributions to Stefan Grundmann and Jules Stuyck (eds), *An Academic Green Paper on European Contract Law* (2002), 131 ff; and see the reflections by Jürgen Basedow, 'Das BGB in künftigen europäischen Privatrecht: Der hybride Kodex', (2000) 200 *Archiv für die civilistische Praxis* 445 ff.

[127] See, most recently, Ulrich G. Schroeter, 'Europäischer Verfassungsvertrag und europäisches Vertragsrecht', (2006) 14 *Zeitschrift für Europäisches Privatrecht* 515 ff.

[128] For contract law, see Claus Ott and Hans-Bernd Schäfer, 'Die Vereinheitlichung des europäischen Vertragsrechts—Ökonomische Notwendigkeit oder akademisches Interesse?', in Claus Ott and Hans-Bernd Schäfer (eds), *Vereinheitlichung und Diversität des Zivilrechts in transnationalen Wirtschaftsräumen* (2002), 203 ff; for the law of delict: Michael G. Faure, 'How Law and Economics May Contribute to the Harmonization of Tort Law', in Zimmermann (n 44), 31 ff.

[129] Pierre Legrand, *Fragments on Law-as-Culture* (1999); *idem*, 'The Same and the Different', in Pierre Legrand and Roderick Munday (eds), *Comparative Legal Studies: Traditions and Transitions* (2003), 240 ff.

instances of intellectual stimulation or the reception of legal rules or concepts. At the same time, it will be able to explain discrepancies on the level of specific result, general approach, and doctrinal nuance. It is this kind of comprehension that paves the way for rational criticism and organic development of the law. The past, of course, does not justify itself; nor does it necessarily contain the solutions for present-day problems. But an understanding of the past is the first and essential prerequisite for devising appropriate solutions for the present day. This is as true within a given legal system as it is for the formation of European law. And just as legal history informs the development of private law doctrine in the one case, so it constitutes the basis for comparative legal scholarship in the other.[130]

3. The Communitarization of Comparative Private Law

One dimension of comparative law scholarship within Europe that will have to be considerably strengthened is the one concerning European Community private law. For just as we witness a growing process of Communitarization of the national private laws, so the European Community private law will have to play a vital role in the process of developing model rules or principles of private law in Europe. The European Community enactments in the field of private law are too scattered and too ill-coordinated to serve, on their own, as a basis for the elaboration of model rules of general contract law or tort law. But Principles of European Contract Law or Tort Law such as those prepared by the Lando Commission or the Group on European Tort Law can hardly be called 'European' in the true sense of the word, if they fail to take account of pertinent EC Directives (as well as of the relevant case law of the European Court of Justice). The neglect of these genuinely European sources of law is one of their most serious shortcomings. Likewise, other research initiatives will have to further the process of what may be called a Communitarization of comparative private law.[131] At the same time, however, comparative law

[130] Eugen Bucher, 'Rechtsüberlieferung und heutiges Recht', (2000) 8 *Zeitschrift für Europäisches Privatrecht* 394 ff; James Gordley, 'Why Look Backward?', (2002) 50 *AJCL* 657 ff; Nils Jansen, ' "Tief ist der Brunnen der Vergangenheit": Funktion, Methode und Ausgangspunkt historischer Fragestellungen in der Privatrechtsdogmatik', (2005) 27 *Zeitschrift für Neuere Rechtsgeschichte* 202 ff.

[131] Among the research activities focusing, primarily, on European Community private law are: Peter-Christian Müller-Graff (ed), *Gemeinsames Privatrecht in der Europäischen Gemeinschaft* (2nd edn, 1999), 9 ff; Stefan Grundmann, *Europäisches Schuldvertragsrecht* (1999); Nicolo Lipari, *Trattato di Diritto Privato Europeo* (2nd edn, 4 vols, 2003); Karl Riesenhuber, *System und Prinzipien des Europäischen Vertragsrechts* (2003); Martin Gebauer and Thomas Wiedmann (eds), *Zivilrecht unter europäischem Einfluss* (2005); the casebook series *Entscheidungen des EuGH* (Nomos, since 1999); the European Research Group on Existing EC Private Law ('Acquis Group') (on which see Wurmnest, (2003) 11 *Zeitschrift für Europäisches Privatrecht* 740 ff); a series of monographs called 'Ius Communitatis' (gen ed Stefan Grundmann, pub C. F. Müller, since 2004); and a new journal under the title *Zeitschrift für Gemeinschaftsprivatrecht* (Sellier European Law Publishers, since 2004).

scholarship has to contribute to what may equally be referred to as a Europeanization of Community law: a process by means of which a firm foundation for
Community law is established in the concepts and principles which the legal
systems of the EU member states have in common.[132] Even in the past, of course, the
Commission of the European Union commissioned comparative studies before it
issued a new Directive.[133] It is not always clear, however, what role these studies
have played in the actual drafting of the legislation. And while it may not be
necessary to bring books to Brussels,[134] there does appear to be room for a supply
of comparative information that is both more transparent and more comprehensive. The same can be said about the decisions of the European Court of Justice. In
the field of extra-contractual liability of Community institutions the Court has to
establish 'the general principles common to the laws of the Member States',[135] and
the search for such common principles, or critical comparative evaluation of the
rules found in the various national legal systems, is also of considerable importance in other fields. But the use of the comparative method is not readily apparent
since it does not normally leave its traces in the reasoning of the Court. Not rarely
the Court appears to ask its research service for comparative studies on specific
points of law. But since these are never published it is impossible to assess their
scope and quality.[136]

Comparative law scholarship in Europe should not, however, even if it is
engaged in the great task of Europeanization of private law, confine its attention
exclusively to Europe. There is much to be learnt from experiences gathered in
other parts of the world.[137] The American Restatements have already been a valuable source of inspiration in the search for 'Principles' of European law. Casebooks
are in the process of becoming an established form of European legal literature.
The creation of a European Law Institute on the model of the American Law

---

[132] Renaud Dehousse, 'Comparing National and EC Law: The Problem of the Level of Analysis',
(1994) 42 *AJCL* 761 ff; Walter van Gerven, 'Comparative Law in a Texture of Communitarization of
National Laws and Europeanization of Community Law', in *Judicial Review in European Union Law:
Liber Amicorum in Honour of Lord Slynn of Hadley* (2000), 433 ff.

[133] By way of example, see Norbert Reich and Hans-W. Micklitz, *Consumer Legislation in the EC
Countries: A Comparative Analysis* (8 vols, 1980).

[134] Thomas Hoeren, 'Bringt Bücher nach Brüssel—Überlegungen zur Informationskultur bei den
Europäischen Gemeinschaften', [2000] *Neue Juristische Wochenschrift* 3112 f.

[135] Above, n 17 and the text relating to it.

[136] Thijmen Koopmans, 'The Birth of European Law at the Crossroads of Legal Traditions', (1991)
39 *AJCL* 493 ff; C. N. Kakouris, 'L'utilisation de la Méthode Comparative par la Cour de Justice des
Communautés Européennes', in Ulrich Drobnig and Sjef van Erp (eds), *The Use of Comparative Law
by Courts* (1999), 97 ff; Markku Kiikeri, *Comparative Legal Reasoning and European Law* (2001).

[137] See Richard Hyland, 'The American Experience: Restatement, the UCC, Uniform Laws, and
Transnational Coordination', in Hartkamp *et al* (n 11), 59 ff; Mathias Reimann, 'Towards a European
Civil Code: Why Continental Jurists Should Consult Their Transatlantic Colleagues', (1999) 73 *Tulane
LR* 1337 ff who accuses European lawyers of a certain parocialism; but cf also Mathias Reimann,
'Amerikanisches Privatrecht und europäische Rechtseinheit—Können die USA als Vorbild dienen?',
in Reinhard Zimmermann (ed), *Amerikanische Rechtskultur und europäisches Privatrecht* (1995), 132 ff.

Institute has been proposed.[138] And even in the art of codification European lawyers can learn from their transatlantic colleagues: unification of private law through uniform (model) legislation provides one example, the codification experience in mixed systems (Louisiana, Québec) another.

4. Beyond Comparative Law?

The traditional 'comparative method', based on a functional approach, will probably continue to play a significant role for the further Europeanization of private law. Economic analysis can be useful for the evaluative part of comparative studies; for the more efficient solution will often be the better, or more appropriate, solution to a legal problem. But this type of argument is not specifically related, or conducive, to the Europeanization of private law. The same is true of other non-conventional forms of legal scholarship (critical legal studies, *autopoiesis* theory): as far as they are valid, they are valid for legal discourse in general; and if they have implications for comparative law, these implications have to be considered for comparative law in general. It is impossible to predict whether the new approaches will have an impact on the process of Europeanization of private law by means of comparative law. The application of the traditional comparative method may, however, run into difficulties in areas where we still have to devise adequate conceptual tools which are both common to the national legal systems and teleologically satisfactory (such as the law of delict). This is a constructive enterprise the dimensions of which are only beginning to be explored today.[139]

BIBLIOGRAPHY

Reinhard Zimmermann, 'Savigny's Legacy: Legal History, Comparative Law, and the Emergence of a European Legal Science', (1996) 112 *LQR* 576 ff

Martin Gebauer, *Grundfragen der Europäisierung des Privatrechts* (1998)

Stefan Grundmann (ed), *Systembildung und Systemlücken in Kerngebieten des Europäischen Privatrechts* (2000)

Mark van Hoecke and Francois Ost (eds), *The Harmonisation of European Private Law* (2000)

Jürgen Basedow (ed), *Europäische Vertragsrechtsvereinheitlichung und deutsches Recht* (2000)

Reinhard Zimmermann, *Roman Law, Contemporary Law, European Law: The Civilian Tradition Today* (2001)

[138] Werner F. Ebke, 'Unternehmensrechtsangleichung in der Europäischen Union: Brauchen wir ein European Law Institute?', in *Festschrift für Bernhard Großfeld* (1999), 189 ff.

[139] Nils Jansen (n 46) 64 ff; *idem*, 'Dogmatik, Erkenntnis und Theorie im europäischen Privatrecht' (2005) 13 *Zeitschrift für Europäisches Privatrecht* 750 ff.

Jan Smits, *The Making of European Private Law: Towards a Ius Commune Europaeum as a Mixed Legal System* (2002)

Mauro Bussani and Ugo Mattei (eds), *The Common Core of European Private Law* (2002)

Martijn W. Hesselink, *The New European Private Law: Essays on the Future of Private Law in Europe* (2002)

Hein Kötz, 'Alte und neue Aufgaben der Rechtsvergleichung', [2002] *Juristenzeitung* 257 ff

Mathias Reimann, 'The Progress and Failure of Comparative Law in the Second Half of the Twentieth Century', (2002) 50 *AJCL* 671 ff

Mark van Hoeke (ed), *Epistemology and Methodology of Comparative Law* (2004)

Arthur Hartkamp, Martijn Hesselink, Ewoud Hondius, Carla Joustra, Edgar du Perron, and Muriel Veldman (eds), *Towards a European Civil Code* (3rd edn, 2004)

Nils Jansen, *Binnenmarkt, Privatrecht und europäische Identität* (2004)

Reiner Schulze and Reinhard Zimmermann (eds), *Europäisches Privatrecht: Basistexte* (3rd edn, 2005; English edn, based on 2nd German edn, by Oliver Radley-Gardner, Hugh Beale, Reinhard Zimmermann, and Reiner Schulze, *Fundamental Texts on European Private Law*, 2003)

CHAPTER 17

GLOBALIZATION AND COMPARATIVE LAW

HORATIA MUIR WATT

Paris

To the extent that it affects the paradigm within which comparative law emerged as a discipline, globalization inevitably raises new challenges for comparative law. Comparative legal studies grew up within a vision of the world as divided into water-tight 'legal systems' attached to, and contained within, the various sovereign states. Profound changes affecting the fabric of the international environment, particularly the progressive decline of the descriptive and normative significance of traditional geo-political divisions of the world, tend to reveal as irrelevant certain often unacknowledged assumptions on which mainstream legal comparison has long rested and call for rethinking its ideological stance and methodological agenda. The emergence of new spheres of normativity distinct from the nation state, the appearance of powerful private or transnational actors in the public international arena, and novel configurations of relationships between polities challenge trad-itional representations of law itself, blur distinctions between the public and private spheres, and call into question western representations of centre and periphery of the globe which have been foundational until now for comparative research.

In this respect, while globalization can best be seen as a process, involving the deconstruction of space and state,[1] it is also the seat of profound tensions and contradictions. Triumphant economic liberalism, which reduces law to the status of product, encounters the new universalism of human rights.[2] Thus, globalization may mean the 'dédoublement du monde'.[3] In this respect, David Nelken warns against making one-sided assumptions about what is meant by globalization and the way it affects the law, since it comprises multiple and contradictory aspects (social, cultural, technical, political, economic) and is moreover a label often used to cover developments which could be understood in other terms. Changes may indeed be attributed misleadingly to globalization which in fact result from parallel but indigenous processes affecting national laws.[4] And of course, globalization is not in itself a new phenomenon, at least in so far as it signifies the hegemony of a given legal tradition.[5] The Roman Empire carried a process of world-building through the law, while the rediscovery of the *ius commune* in medieval Europe exemplifies a similar culture-driven, rather than political, phenomenon. Be that as it may, the various upheavals which are occurring today in the wake of these developments on a world scale affect the very definition of the law, its relationship to state and society, and the patterns of mutual encounter and reaction between different legal traditions, and cannot therefore leave comparative law indifferent or unscathed.

Not the least challenge faced by comparative law in this context is the fact that globalization is to a large extent itself a narrative, projecting a world-view that is only partially shared by the world it aims to include. It may be no more than neo-liberal policy choices clothed in the language of economic inevitability,[6] a

---

[1] Jean-Bernard Auby, *La globalisation, le droit et l'Etat* (2003).

[2] Michael Likoksy (ed), *Transnational Legal Processes. Globalisation and Power Disputes*, (2002); Mireille Delmas-Marty, 'La mondialisation du droit: chances et risques', (1999) *Recueil Dalloz* 2 ff.

[3] Auby (n 1), § 18.

[4] David Nelken, 'Comparatists and Transferability', in Pierre Legrand and Roderick Munday (eds), *Comparative Legal Studies: Traditions and Transitions* (2003), 437 ff at 460 ff.

[5] See Duncan Kennedy, 'Two Globalizations of Law & Legal Thought, 1850–1968', (2003) 36 *Suffolk University LR* 631 ff.

[6] Allan Scott, 'Globalization: Social Process or Political Rhetoric?', in Allan Scott (ed), *The Limits of Globalisation: Cases and Arguments* (1997), 1–24 ff.

purely western artefact.[7] Indeed, the rhetoric of globalization partakes no doubt of the continuous massive efforts deployed by the western legal tradition to export western rationality, but, like colonial law, it may well be used to sustain other visions of the world, just as the western concept of state was turned against colonial states.[8] As Lawrence Rosen explains, the reason why the rhetoric of globalization developed in western legal culture is deceptive—and why comparison becomes so crucial—is the common tendency of the west to see directionality where there is in fact variation.[9] Outside the western tradition, globalization may be perceived as partaking of a 'white mythology', harnessing the colonial legacy to iconic images of democracy and good governance[10] or alternatively, as a neo-liberal slogan.[11] But comparative legal studies themselves are in turn perceived as the narratives of the making of 'modern' law, serving a certain vision of the world and comforting Euro-American images of progress and 'developmentalism'.[12] From all these angles, the question is squarely raised as to the relationship of comparative law to global governance.

The fate of comparative law can obviously give rise to debate outside the context of contemporary economic globalization; indeed, comparison as a legal discipline was initially associated with ambitious projects for international uniformity of law. As Roderick Munday puts it, the purpose of the 1900 Paris Congress was to discover an 'objective, international "legal science", which if properly applied, was to reveal the deepest secrets of legal existence and ultimately lead to ever-greater uniformity among legal systems',[13] and might thus contribute to fostering peace and understanding among nations. However, the relationship of comparative law to global governance is posed with particular acuity in the present context. Indeed, as a product of western legal thought, and clearly bound up with a scientific conception of the law specific to the civilian tradition of continental Europe, where it became inseparable from the comparison of 'legal systems',[14] legal comparatism prospered in an environment composed of various legal traditions loosely identifiable with the nation states. It has long remained Eurocentric, focusing essentially on the respective characteristics of common law and continental civilian legal thinking, the post-war renewal of comparatism in the United States having prompted it to expand so as to include common law jurisdictions other than England. Comparative law thus shared many features with contemporaneous

---

[7] M. Mahmoud Mohamed Salah, 'La mondialisation vue de l'Islam', (2003) 47 *Archives de Philosophie du Droit* 27, 37 ff.

[8] H. Patrick Glenn, *Legal Traditions of the World* (2000), 49 ff.

[9] Lawrence Rosen, 'Beyond Compare', in Legrand and Munday (n 4), 502 ff.

[10] Upendra Baxi, 'The Colonialist Heritage', in Legrand and Munday (n 4), 51 ff.

[11] Salah (n 7), 29 ff.

[12] Baxi (n 10), 49 ff, citing Patrick Chabal, 'The African Crisis: Context and Interpretation', in Richard Werbner and Terence Ranger (eds), *Post Colonial Identities in Africa* (1996), 45–6 ff.

[13] Roderick Munday, 'Accounting for an Encounter', in Legrand and Munday (n 4), 3, 5.

[14] Glenn (n 8), 151 ff.

international law, both public and private, which similarly projected a view of the world according to the aspirations of European colonial powers. However, while the latter dealt with an international legal order composed of sovereign states, subordinating the private sphere, comparatism concentrated on the study of the private laws thus enclosed within the state, perceived in accordance with the epistemological tradition of the great civilian codes as sheltered from the intrusions of politics and thus amenable to scientific study as a system and ultimately to unification. The shadow of the nation state made itself felt nevertheless through the fact that the legal traditions under comparison were each assumed to be coextensive with the territory of a given community to which they were historically linked, while sources of law were in the main official sources, with judicial decisions in the fore as comparative legal studies began to flourish in the Anglo-American legal world.

While neither the figure of the state nor the normative authority of formal sources of law have disappeared under the pressure of globalization, fundamental shifts have occurred in the international landscape, favouring the emergence of concurrent actors and law-makers, unsettling the territorial jurisdiction of states so as to include some sort of recognition of community responsibility extending beyond national borders,[15] spreading human rights discourse, generating transnational norms and dehierarchized networks, and to a certain extent substituting markets for law.[16] 'Third spheres' constituted by international commercial arbitration and the emergence of the *lex mercatoria* are progressively dissolving the link between law and territory. Naturally, the challenges facing comparative law are not unlike those which affect international law, both public and private, which developed under analogous premises. Public international law has similarly to deal with international 'governance without government', while private international law has to grapple with the declining significance of territory. Comparative law is faced in turn with the issue of what makes up a tradition disconnected from state or irreducible to the concept of a national 'legal system'. It is equally clear that the resources of traditional comparative law alone are insufficient to take in the multiple dimensions of globalization and its effects on local legal traditions and that interdisciplinary approaches associated with these and other fields, such as political science, economics, and sociology of law, must all be invoked for a more complete standpoint.

Of course, even qualified as 'traditional', 'comparative law' is not in itself an ethically and methodologically homogeneous discipline. Thus, pioneering prewar comparatists did not share the same ideological agenda as their post-war

---

[15] Paul Schiff Berman, 'The Globalization of Jurisdiction', (2002) 151 *University of Pennsylvania LR* 311 ff.

[16] William Bratton and Jospeh McCahery, 'The New Economics of Jurisdictional Competition: Devolutionary Federalism in a Second Best World', (1997) 86 *Georgetown LJ* 201 ff.

successors[17] and today mainstream comparatism, which remains Eurocentric even if methodologically eclectic, diverges considerably from concurrent contextualist voices, which challenge more or less overt presumptions of commonalities between diverse laws and focus on otherness and respect for difference. However, even in relation to the 'neo-Romantic turn' of contemporary comparatism,[18] the question arises as to the sustainability of comparative studies which are ontologically linked to context and society, in an environment which is undergoing profound changes on both counts. What seems clear is that if comparative legal studies are to retain their relevance in understanding the impact of global changes on existing local traditions, their modes of interaction and influence, and their strategies for survival, their focus certainly needs adjusting. This chapter will attempt to examine the ways in which comparative law as a discipline is affected by the changes wrought by globalization, and in particular the challenges which such changes imply for the methodological agenda of comparative legal studies (Section I) and for its ideological commitments (Section II). More pragmatically, it may also be useful to envisage the impact of increased access to information on foreign laws, and the growth of trans- or international sources of uniform law, on the practical usefulness of comparative law (Section III).

I. The Methodological Challenge

The exact methodological implications of globalization for the agenda of comparative law are controversial. The issue here is whether, in a global context characterized by the decline of the nation state, or at least the resettling of the concept of state sovereignty, and producing novel polycentric forms of normativity, legal comparison is still a sustainable project, and to what extent, in order to remain a significant source of reflection on the nature of the law and its relationship to society in an extended and increasingly cosmopolitan world, comparative law must adjust its methodological agenda. First, there is a need to adjust the focus of comparison from nation states to traditions or epistemic communities (Section I.1). At the same time, there is a new awareness that only a dynamic perspective can make a useful contribution to comparative legal knowledge (Section I.2). It also appears necessary to revise some of the deep assumptions of the traditional comparative approach, overly concerned with 'private law' (Section I.3).

---

[17] David Kennedy, 'The Methods and the Politics', in Legrand and Munday (n 4), 345 ff.
[18] See James Q. Whitman, 'The Neo-Romantic Turn', in Legrand and Munday (n 4), 312 ff.

1. From Nation States to Epistemic Communities

Comparative legal studies are certainly linked ontologically to the existence of diverse local legal traditions, or at least to different societies. The lenses through which these diverse traditions have been viewed by successive generations of comparatists have differed, however. The unifying project borne by mainstream pre-war comparative law concerned the laws, or 'legal systems', of nation states. The links are patent between the world-views offered respectively by comparative law and public international law, which shared a vision of the international order divided into territorial polities each in charge of a specific legal system. While these links were later blurred through the decline of the unification project, the move to functionalist methodology, and the creation of a specific agenda for comparative law, it nevertheless remains the case that the representation of the object of this discipline as regards the various laws of nation states was still implicitly reproduced and reinforced. First, by philosophical representations as to the nature of the law, perceived either as expressive and coextensive with the territorial power of the sovereign, or alternatively as constitutive of a 'system' whose *grundnorm* was to be found in a national constitutional norm, the state appeared as the ascendance of a form of individualized, formal, rationality.[19] Second, on an epistemological level, a distinctive bias towards rule-based knowledge of the law indeed continues to a certain extent to push the emphasis in comparative work towards legal rules.[20] Thus, 'nationalistic perceptions have wielded enormous influence over the shape and direction of comparative studies'.[21]

Contemporary contextualist approaches to comparison tend to reject both the assimilation between law and rules, and law and state. The emphasis of this strand of research tends to lie on the link between law and community, de-emphasizing official or formal sources of law and privileging socio-cultural rather than geo-political divides. Sociology becomes a privileged partner in comparative studies,[22] which favours a focus on traditions rather than polities as an object of comparison.[23] Nevertheless, even according to this conception, history is perceived to play an important role in the constitution of a sense of community and identity, so that the link between tradition and polity is not wholly severed. While non-state local or nomadic communities secreting their own normativity belong to the field of comparative studies, it is also true that comparing, say, different spheres of transnational normativity is not comparative law, at least as we know it, even if novel issues of conflicts of law appear at times to overlap with areas of comparative

---

[19] Glenn (n 8), 132 ff.
[20] Geoffrey Samuel, *Epistemology and Method in Law* (2002), at 15 ff.
[21] Munday (n 13), 12 ff.
[22] See Roger Cotterell, 'Comparatists and Sociology', in Legrand and Munday (n 4), 131 ff.
[23] H. Patrick Glenn, 'The National Heritage', in Legrand and Munday (n 4), 76 ff.

knowledge, confirming the idea that understanding globalization requires an interdisciplinary approach.[24]

Is the comparative project sustainable in a global context of increasing inter-dependencies between national systems and emerging spaces of transnational normativity? Such claims have been made.[25] The intermingling of national laws, the interconnectedness of markets, the emergence of 'third legal spheres' such as the *lex mercatoria* and the growth of uniform international state sources including human rights would tend either to generate a world differently configured from the traditional juxtaposition of national legal cultures, or to lead to a progressive erosion of diversity, thereby depriving comparative legal studies of their object or interest. At the same time, such changes suggest multiple polyvalent perspectives from which law can be perceived: beyond the perspective of the national court, law is evolving, being concurrently under the impetus of private arbitrators, mobile capital seeking to invest, transnational communities of interests, international courts, or non-governmental organizations. Law can alternatively be seen as a mere product on a global market, or on the contrary as the ultimate vehicle of funda-mental values, defying national frontiers. Fischer-Lescano and Teubner see a global fragmentation of the law, due to profound collisions between colliding sectors of transnational society. Hierarchical solutions are no longer possible, any more than are sustainable static monodimensional visions of the world. Warning against reductionist perspectives, these writers observe that '. . . the fragmentation of global law is not simply about legal norm collisions or policy-conflicts, but rather has its origin in contradictions between society-wide institutionalised rationalities, which law cannot solve . . .'.[26]

Thus, the static interpretative approach represented as characteristic of trad-itional comparative law is claimed either to be no longer relevant for the 'dynamic longitudinal project',[27] or pointless in view of common causes and concerns, risk-ing a turn to occidentalism or orientalism.[28] Although such claims may in fact be demonstrative less of the essential irrelevance of comparative law, than of the need to revise its methodological agenda, which would require adjustment to grasp the dynamics of globalization and its impact on local systems, they must be taken seriously. Just as the expansion of democracy, following the vision of Fukuyama, would herald the end of history; similarly, it might be supposed that the diffusion of human rights would herald the end of comparative law, in the sense that it

---

[24] See Andreas Fischer-Lescano and Gunther Teubner, 'Regime Collisons: The Vain Search for Legal Unity in the Fragmentation of Global Law' (2004) 25 *Michigan Journal of International Law* 999 ff.

[25] Reported by Nelken (n 4), 462 ff.

[26] Fischer-Lescano and Teubner (n 24), 5 ff.

[27] Wolf Heydebrand, 'From Globalization of Law to Law under Globalization', in David Nelken and Johannes Feest (eds), *Adapting Legal Cultures* (2001), 117 ff.

[28] Maureen Cain, 'Orientalism, Occidentalism and the Sociology of Crime', (2000) 40 *British Journal of Criminology* 239; Nelken (n 4), 460 ff.

announces an a-historical society based on universal standards.[29] The question, then, is whether, despite globalizing trends towards transnational normativity and convergence through increased proximity, there are still distinct legal traditions, linked to stable communities (whether territorial or otherwise, connected or not to nation states), which are worth comparing, and, if the comparative project remains sustainable despite the changes involved in the process of globalization, what impact such changes are nevertheless likely to bring about to the way comparison is done.

Undeniably, diversity may be threatened by globalization in several ways. Pressure towards convergence may be induced variously through both public and private channels. Thus, the emergence of common global problems such as cross-environmental pollution or international money-laundering call for cooperative responses on the part of states. Self-regulation of global markets secretes trans-national uniform rules. The initiatives of various non-state transnational actors such as multinational firms spreading codes of conduct to level the global playing field, or NGOs fighting for transnational standards, also contribute to uniformity. Universalizing narratives such as human rights discourse tend to spread ideas and ways of thinking about the law. Various forms of legal transplants appear to take place at an accelerated rate, whether through imitation generated by cultural prestige,[30] or through the dominance of a given legal system with economic leverage.[31] Hegemony of one particular legal tradition is established through the creation of zones of influence. A particularly fascinating example of the contemporary Americanization of the law might be found in the exercise of universal jurisdiction in human rights cases under the Alien Torts Claims Act, whose potential effect could be to export American procedural concepts worldwide; one writer even considers that its effect is to invest the American judiciary with a mission to rewrite world politics.[32] Similar patterns of dominance can be found in all previous examples of globalization, such as in the Romanization of the laws of Europe, and later in the proselytizing tradition of the great civilian codes, which appear as the predecessors of contemporary Americanization.

Network effects such as exchanges among members of the judiciary of different countries or courts are yet another example of increased proximity and dialogue between epistemic communities, further enabled by information technologies,

---

[29] See Bernard Bourgeois, 'La fin de l'histoire, aujourd'hui?', (2003) 47 *Archives de Philosophie du Droit* 141 ff.

[30] Rodolfo Sacco, 'La comparaison juridique au service de la connaissance du droit', (1991) *Economica* 122 ff.

[31] Ugo Mattei, 'Why the Wind Changed: Intellectual Leadership in Western Law', (1994) *AJCL* 195 ff.

[32] Ugo Mattei, 'A Theory of Imperial Law: A Study on US Hegemony and the Latin Resistance', (2003) *Indiana Journal of Global Legal Studies* 383 ff. However, extreme prudence is requisite here. In an overwhelming number of cases brought under the Alien Tort Claims Act, the concept of universal jurisdiction is not needed because jurisdiction over the defendants can be based squarely on other grounds.

which are of course another important factor in facilitating the free exchange of ideas. The progressive creation of a transnational public space in which cross-fertilization regularly occurs is taking place through the use of comparative law in judicial decisions. The rise of the idea of due process (*procès équitable*) in European legal culture is an excellent example of a legal concept which has gained momentum and substance through a certain 'globalization of the judiciary'.[33] As other systems become better known, they may even constitute persuasive authority before foreign courts. Heightened opportunities for application of foreign law in national courts in conflicts of law cases or recognition of foreign judgments increasingly confronts national systems with otherness and provides important insights into the ways in which other systems work. The role of supranational courts in diffusing ideas among participant states, as in the case of the European Court of Human Rights, has obviously enhanced this phenomenon.

However, whether exchange and dialogue lead ultimately to uniformity is entirely debatable. And while the existence of centrifugal and universalizing pressures conducive to legal uniformity are undeniably at work, it remains a moot question as to whether they are of a kind to deprive comparative legal studies of their object and point. Although globalization brings heightened exchange in certain fields, its real impact on local legal culture remains to be seen. Empirical research appears to show that global pressure can actually strengthen the local. 'Despite a world with globalizing pretensions, [comparatists] would discover that intensity of contact actually emphasizes a sense of difference, not of sameness.'[34] It may be that accelerated exchange actually accentuates local particularisms; it does not appear, at any rate, that the world is becoming more homogeneous.[35] Increased awareness of alterity may generate a need for identity and tradition, while accelerated contact and juxtaposition with other traditions may mean that all sides develop a sharper sense of identity.[36] The turn to tradition and local anchorage may mean that universalizing pressures are neutralized by fragmentation or 'glocalization'.[37] It may be that the effect of interconnectedness is to institute a dialectic relationship between the global and the local. Even on a political level, a displacement of governance towards the global level may be compensated by the revalorization of the local.[38]

One of the reasons for the perennity of the local anchorage of legal traditions seems to lie in their efforts to reappropriate the global. This phenomenon is not new to contemporary developments, since it was apparent in previous forms of globalization: colonial law was used by local groups to strengthen diversity, even

---

[33] Julie Allard and Antoine Garapon, *Les juges dans la mondialisation* (2005); dialogue between Justice Breyer and President Canivet, (2005) *Culture Droit* 16 ff.

[34] Munday (n 13), 21 ff.   [35] Nelken (n 4), 460 ff.   [36] Glenn (n 8), 30 ff.

[37] Pierre Legrand, 'The Same and the Different', in Legrand and Munday (n 4), 240 ff; 'L'hypothèse de la conquête des continents par le droit américain', (2003) 45 *Archives de Philosophie du Droit* 37 ff.

[38] Auby (n 1), at § 106.

against the interests of the colonial state.[39] The same phenomenon may exist too when the ideas peddled by a certain form of globalization encounter other, concurrent globalizations. In the case of Islam, for example, a certain reappropriation of western ideas, if not ideals, seems to be taking place to a certain extent, resulting in a compromise between the Islamic ethic and market economy.[40] The axiological content of globalization is neutralized or channelled when it is represented as having an essentially economic-technical content. Interestingly if not unexpectedly, to the extent that globalization involves a certain recomposition of spheres of identity, the impact of external global pressure on local traditions varies according to the capacity of local culture to accommodate multiple affiliations. As the example of India indicates, such accommodation is easier, without loss of identity, in traditions with fuzzy or multiple identities.[41] The shock that globalization represents for French legal culture would tend to confirm this conclusion.[42] Be that as it may, the extent of local resistance to global pressures in the direction of uniformity, strategies of reappropriation of the global by local traditions, and more generally the meaning of legal culture and the ways in which traditions maintain their distinctiveness, should all now be put squarely on comparative law's methodological agenda.

2. From a Static to a Dynamic Perspective

Indeed, if globalization does not mean the end of comparative history or at least of diversity in the legal sphere, it must inevitably impact on the way in which comparison is undertaken. What is it that is compared? In the first place, the assault of globalization on state sovereignty means that the identity of cultural or epistemic communities needs to dissociate from geo-political divisions of the globe.[43] Their increasing irrelevance leads to comparing legal cultures which find expression in fora which are wider than mere states.[44] Similar difficulties arise for private international law, which will henceforth be required to think in terms of communities rather than territories, while ultimately, statehood and national identity will be redefined. From this standpoint, it has been suggested that 'tradition' may well be a more promising concept with a view to defining the object of comparative law in a global context than that of a 'legal system', which is linked to

---

[39] Glenn (n 23), 84 ff; on previous globalizations, see Duncan Kennedy, 'Two Globalizations of Law & Legal Thought, 1850–1968', (2003) 36 *Suffolk University LR* 631 ff.

[40] See Salah (n 7), 44 ff, observing 'la tentative ambigüe d'une réappropriation de la mondialisation par l'Islam'.

[41] François Chenet, 'La mondialisation vue de l'Inde', (2003) 47 *Archives de Philosophie du Droit* 55 ff.

[42] Antoine Garapon, 'French Legal Culture and the Shock of "Globalization" ', (1995) 4 *Social and Legal Studies* 493.

[43] Nelken (n 4), 445 ff.   [44] Glenn (n 8), 49 ff.

an outdated scientific approach to comparison, suggests a rational, rule-based model of legal knowledge and remains inextricably bound up with the pre-eminence of the 'frozen accident' of state. However the political concept of state sovereignty is affected by globalization, comparative law must ask whether and to what extent legal traditions can retain their sense of identity or distinctiveness in the face of change.[45] Much of course depends upon what is meant by tradition, which may itself be no more than 'imagined community'.[46] According to Patrick Glenn:

Once tradition is seen as transmitted information, an ongoing bran-tub churned by new generations, with no inherent elites or hierarchy, the linking of tradition with stability becomes less obvious and less defensible. Tradition becomes rather a resource from which reasons for change may be derived, a legitimating agency for ideas which, by themselves, would have no social resonance.[47]

Comparative law then should harness its agenda to the question of how, if law fits society, this could be changing, or on the contrary consolidating, under globaliza-tion.[48] Heydebrand's point[49] is that mainstream comparative methodology tends to be static. Whether functionalist or contextualist, it tends to focus primarily on an internal historical link between law and tradition, whereas the important questions raised by globalization processes are essentially dynamic and concern the impact of these changes on the configuration of legal traditions, on how they adapt or maintain their distinctiveness, on how they reinterpret their foundational myths, how they make strategic use of law in relationships with other cultures, whether law itself is a vehicle or a factor of resistance to global pressure, what is special about current developments attending legal transfers.

Among the formidable challenges which await tomorrow's comparatist . . . are the tasks of tracing the sometimes improbable paths taken by migrating laws, of investigating the ways in which they come to be assimilated, rejected or refashioned within the host system, of analysing the consequences that flow from this process of transplantation and adapta-tion, and finally of assessing the inevitable conceptual implications inherent in these phenomena.[50]

Mainstream functionalist methodology[51] may not be sufficient to apprehend these impacts and interactions. Indeed, as Lawrence Rosen points out, static method-ological approaches may actually downplay change.[52] For this writer, comparatists create categories that tend to neutralize direction, whereas human society is best characterized by variation: '(i)t's context that matters'.[53] The methodological focus should be on interpenetration of ideas and reciprocal influence, on change and

---

[45] Nelken (n 4), 445   [46] Glenn (n 8), 78 ff.   [47] Glenn (n 8), 22 ff.   [48] Ibid.
[49] See n 27.   [50] Munday (n 13), 9 ff.
[51] On which, see Michele Graziadei, 'The Functionalist Heritage', in Legrand and Munday (n 4), 100 ff.
[52] Rosen (n 9), 503 ff.   [53] Rosen (n 9), 505 ff.

resistance to change. The theoretical and political dangers of the functionalist approach are pointed out by Pierre Legrand, in so far as such an approach assumes that all societies face the same problems. As Nelken emphasizes in turn, there is considerable variation as to how problems are conceived. And even whether given situations are treated as problems, varies.[54] It may well be that one of the main errors of dominant comparative law lies in its reluctance to question its own methodological and culturally embedded assumptions about what law is and how it is structured. Similar conclusions are being reached in neighbouring disciplinary fields, particularly in private and public international law,[55] which have traditionally shared some of the entrenched assumptions of comparative law.

3. Abandoning the Private Law Focus

A certain conception of comparative law defines its task as identifying an 'unspoken body of assumptions' within a given tradition.[56] Comparative methodology itself, emerging in a given cultural context, also rests on unacknowledged assumptions which its confrontation with narratives of globalization may contribute to calling into question. While the traditional focus on Euro-American legal traditions is clearly ideologically conditioned (see below, Section II), what of the fact that comparative legal studies have also tended, as a methodological matter, to privilege private law? It is remarkable that much of comparative legal theory has referred to private law, and that current projects of harmonization of law using comparative legal knowledge, whether in a global or European context, tend to focus on the central Roman categories of obligations or property law, with rarer incursions into family law or procedure. The *corpus iuris* project, designed to harmonize aspects of criminal law, is a notable exception. Moreover, such projects appear to entertain little doubt as to how to identify or delineate 'private law' and what it actually comprises. This methodological stance, and its apparent inevitability, appear to result from the conjunction, on the one hand, of the influence of systematic legal thinking on the initial methodological options of comparative legal studies, and on the other, of the epistemological signification of the private/public divide in the civilian tradition.

On the first point, Patrick Glenn explains:[57]

With the growth of systematic thinking, the idea began to take hold that comparison also had to be systematic. If systems were to be built, systematic comparison was essential to the construction, and thereafter to their refinement. So the process of comparison, the

---

[54] Rosen (n 9), 443 ff.

[55] S. Hobe, 'Globalisation: Challenge to the Nation State and to International Law', in Michael Likosky (ed) *Transnational Legal Processes. Globalisation and Power Disputes* (2002), 378 ff.

[56] Whitman (n 18), 315 ff.   [57] Glenn (n 8), 151 ff.

intellectual process of keeping traditions in touch with one another, itself became subject within the civil law tradition to the characteristics of the tradition itself. If the civil law was to be rational and systematic, things could get all mixed up again by just allowing other ideas or concepts to wander in. The tradition's definition of system could be called an open one, but it had to be a controlled openness . . .

Thus, comparison was 'co-opted to the rationalist effort' and thereafter, comparative law had a formal structured place in civilian legal thinking. A close look naturally traces this influence on the deep assumptions behind the fundamental choices of comparative methodology. The scientific neutrality of post-war comparatism, its detachment from distributional effects—and later also the legal transplant thesis, although easily overturned when considering civil law as the private law constitution of society—have all been reinforced by the fact that private law is traditionally perceived in codified civilian thinking as strictly non-political and non-distributional. For scientific comparative law, private law epitomized the 'grammar of the law'.[58]

The separation between public and private law crystallized with the great civilian codes. The law of the codes is by essence systematic, de-contextualized, a-historical.[59] As the constitution of civil society, it encloses inter-individual relationships in a hermetic, private, and a-political sphere.[60] The codified form of private law was a guarantee of no return to the secrecy and mystification of *l'Ancien droit*, while the separation of the private from the public meant protection for individuals from the arbitrariness of sovereign will. However, this separation also favoured the emergence of the dogma of the neutrality of private law, which was long sustained despite acute disharmony with the rise of the regulatory and post-regulatory state, and the correlative transformation of the function of the law of property, contract, or torts, henceforth deeply involved in the management of the complex, the massive, and the prospective.

Now, current comparative projects focusing on private law tend to imply that the scope, function, and content of that category are to a large extent determinate.[61]

---

[58] Pierre Legrand, 'The Strange Power of Words: Codification Situated', (1994) *Tulane European and Civil Law Forum* 1 ff, at 16 ff.

[59] On the intemporality of the codes, see Legrand (n 61), 16 ff. The Romanist Peter Stein traces this idea back to Justinian: 'Certainly Justinian decreed that his Corpus Iuris contained the whole law and that no reference should be made to earlier sources. The idea, therefore, that the code wipes the slate clean and offers a new beginning to the law may be traced to him'. 'Roman Law, Common Law and Civil Law', (1992) 66 *Tulane LR* 1591 ff.

[60] Denis de Béchillon, 'L'imaginaire d'un code', (1998) 27 *Droits* 173 ff at 175 ff; Geoffrey Samuel, 'English Private Law in the Context of the Codes', in Mark Van Hoeke and Francois Ost (eds), *The Harmonisation of European Private Law* (2000), 47 ff; Guy Canivet, 'Preface', in François Ewald (ed), *Naissance du Code civil* (2004) at xxxvi. ('l'institution d'un droit civil est faite pour sinon dépolitiser, du moins dépubliciser la vie des citoyens').

[61] Fabrizio Cafaggi, 'A Coordinated Approach to Regulation and Civil Liability: Rethinking Institutional Complementarities', in F. Cafaggi (ed), *The Institutional Framework of European Private Law* (2006), 191.

However, projects which claim to identify private law through the identity of actors or subject-matter will be communicating only an incomplete picture of legal reality. Indeed, one of the most spectacular effects of globalization is to blur the distinction between the public and private spheres. While some of these changes might be due to parallel indigenous movements of national legal systems moving out of an overly restrictive formal structure, it is clear that international developments have had much to do with the new fuzziness of the public/private divide. First, the emergence of a competitive paradigm of international relations linked to globalizing markets transforms law into product and puts an end to the monopoly of states as providers of public goods.[62] Second, the rise of the regulatory function of private law and of modes of regulation involving a plurality of both public and private actors is equally linked to developments involving interconnected markets, although the influence of the European law may be more obvious for the time being than global pressure. The retirement of the regulatory state, the declining significance of territory, the growth of spheres of self-regulation, and increasing involvement of private actors in the regulatory process mean that the conventional view of the state and the normative process is changing profoundly, and calls for a rethink of the governance structures associated with regulatory processes and the interaction between private and public governments.[63] As Fabrizio Cafaggi states, 'the major phenomenon we are witnessing at a global level, but to different degrees, is a move from a world in which public and private regulators occupy different and independent spaces of the regulatory domain to a world in which they coordinate through hierarchy, cooperation and/or competition'.

Here, comparative law needs to be sensitive to these new modes of governance and to the gradual mixing and redefining of private and public spheres. The redefinition affects diverse legal traditions differently, if only because it has been more or less culturally entrenched. In this respect, on the level of comparative legal epistemology, Geoffrey Samuel observes that the unscientific culture of the common law, which had never lent itself to a scientific division between public and private law, is better equipped to embrace complexity in a globalizing world than the more systematic civilian ways of acceding to legal knowledge.[64] Be that as it may, the example of the private law focus of dominant comparative methodology shows that certain entrenched assumptions are therefore severely challenged by the pressure of globalization. Predictably, such assumptions also have an ideological resonance, which is perhaps the second main challenge globalization poses to comparative law.

---

[62] See below, section II.2.

[63] Cafaggi (n 61), 195; Colin Scott, 'Regulation in the Age of Governance: The Rise of the Post-regulatory State', in Jacint Jordana and David Levi-Faur (eds), *The Politics of Regulation* (2004).

[64] Geoffrey Samuel, 'Epistemology and Comparative Law: Contributions from the Sciences and Social Sciences', in Mark van Hoecke (ed), *Epistemology and Methodology of Comparative Law* (2004), 35 ff.

II. The Ideological Challenge

A study by David Kennedy of 'The Methods and the Politics' of post-war comparatism has shown it as adhering to a certain ideological agnosticism.[65] David Kennedy has shown that post-war comparatists, unlike their pre-war predecessors, have been careful in the main to distance themselves from the sphere of governance and the choices of political life.[66] Curiously, this ideological agnosticism and a certain 'retreat to the academy' came about at a time when sociological jurisprudence had become mainstream in most other fields, connecting law to politics and social realities.[67] Indeed, their pre-war forerunners had played a significant role in the methodological assault against parochialism and formalism, spreading socially orientated ideas about the law.[68] Comparative law had come to stand for an opening up to values outside formalism. While serving the cause of legal realism, comparatists eschewed neither philosophical debate about the law nor ideological commitment to projects of world-building. Despite certain methodological differences,[69] the shared vision of international governance of Lambert, Pound, or Rabel tended to be cosmopolitan, humanist, and progressive.[70] Whatever the reasons behind the ostensible political detachment of contemporary mainstream comparative law (Section II.1), it seems that that it has never in fact been innocent of a world-vision (Section II.2), while today globalization clearly raises issues of governance on which it is now difficult for comparatism not to take a stance (Section II.3).

1. The Contemporary Academic Retreat

As observed by David Kennedy, mainstream comparatism in the latter half of the twentieth century has self-consciously asserted political agnosticism, retreating in acute discomfort from the sphere of ideology and projects of governance.[71] The widespread acceptance of functionalism as mainstream comparative methodology has reinforced the idea that comparison consisted essentially in the 'mapping' of commonalities and differences between legal systems, and that the knowledge thus produced was itself independent of policy choices and governance projects.[72] Revealing the existence of a common core of European legal principles might then leave the legislator free to codify or not. Mauro Bussani thus describes the Trento

---

[65] Kennedy (n 17), 345 ff.
[66] Ibid. See too William Twining, 'Comparative Law and Legal Theory: The Country and Western Tradition', in Ian Edge (ed), *Comparative Law in Global Perspective* (2000), 47 ff.
[67] Kennedy (n 17), 414 ff.   [68] Ibid.   [69] On which, see Kennedy (n 17), 374 ff.
[70] Kennedy (n 17), 414 ff.   [71] Kennedy (n 17), 349 ff.   [72] Graziadei (n 51).

Common Core project as aiming to 'produce reliable information', which may then be used to unearth features that hitherto remained obscure or provide a useful instrument for legislative harmonization. 'But this has nothing to do with the common core research itself'.[73] Thus distributional consequences are down-played, while the choice of private law regimes for privileged study is that of regimes apparently 'innocent of distribution'.[74]

An explanation for this paradoxical escape to political limbo might lie, it has been suggested, in 'academic post traumatic stress disorder',[75] in which pre-war comparatism is remembered as entangled in ideological debates as to the nature of law. This traumatic memory may in fact distort the reality of pre-war compara-tism, where ideological disagreement was no doubt more limited than it was later represented, particularly by European refugee academics in the United States.[76] These comparatists were keen to turn a world-weary page, leaving ideology behind them for the comfort of agnosticism and science. Be that as it may, 'com-pulsive hand-washing is still traumatic':[77] methodological eclecticism and political agnosticism undeniably obscure comparative law's contribution to global govern-ance, but do not eliminate it. Indeed, asserted apolitical sensibility may well have its own politics.[78] It has been suggested in this respect that functionalism may well postulate commonalities, and conceal a desire to assimilate the 'other'. Thus, for Pierre Legrand, dominant epistemological discourse has operated an 'institutional-ization of sameness', comparatists having made it their collective and coercive purpose to proscribe disorder and to invalidate dissonance.[79] Difference then appears as a disturbance of the universal, inciting comparative projects to 'take the law in hand, lay claim to it'.[80]

Ideological agnosticism in comparative law is less easy to sustain today, simply because the world, or rather the categories hitherto used to represent it, is becom-ing progressively less compartmented. Even in a domestic setting, private law which constituted the privileged field of comparison cannot be held aloof from politics and social realities; within Europe, Community law contributes actively to the blurring of the public/private divide. Transborder politics are not only the realm of public international law, but find expression in transnational public interest litigation initiated by private parties through ordinary courts.[81] Legal plur-alism finds expression in private transnational norms with contractual fora. The spread of human rights discourse means that reflection on the universality of rights and the relativity of cultures cannot be avoided, even as the increase in economic and social exchange generates multiple occasions for contact with pro-foundly different legal cultures outside the western orbit and brings home the

---

[73] Mauro Bussani, 'Current Trends in European Comparative Law: The Common Core Approach', (1998) *Hastings International and Comparative LR* 78, 787 ff.

[74] Kennedy (n 17), 415 ff.   [75] Kennedy (n 17), 353 ff.   [76] Ibid.   [77] Ibid.

[78] Kennedy (n 17), 345 ff.   [79] Legrand (n 37), 249 ff.   [80] Legrand (n 37), 250 ff.

[81] Harold Konju Koh, 'Transnational Public Law Litigation', (1991) 100 *Yale LJ* 2347 ff.

reality of 'extraordinary places' in the legal world.[82] Multiple standpoints become simultaneously valid and equally worthy of respect. At the same time, contemporary jurisprudence has opened increased opportunities for reflection on the deep assumptions of law as narrative.[83] Just as comparative law contributed in the pre-war period to the spread of ideas about law as social reality,[84] more recent currents in law and literature, and law and development, focus on the metalanguage of legal and cultural traditions, so that the ideologies involved respectively in the globalization process and in the politics of comparative law cry out for analysis in these terms.

2. The Unacknowledged World Vision of Comparative Law

As David Kennedy has again shown, comparative law, while ostensibly neutral, often supports ideological projects developed in other disciplinary fields, particularly in international law, where it has been used to promote projects of international unification of private law. Indeed, the methodological agenda of comparative law can then be seen to carry an implicit world-view. In particular, choices as to the traditions to be compared or the disciplinary field of comparison, the emphasis laid on commonalities or differences, the conception of law as instrumentality or as narrative, may all contain hidden assumptions concerning the globe's cultural or economic centre and periphery, the relationship between the legal and economic spheres, the way in which economies develop, theories of dominance, the relationship between public and private spheres. It is therefore important to think about the role comparative law might be playing within the contemporary global context, in constructing and promoting a vision of the world. In this respect, dominant comparative theory has served a particular narrative of the relationship between the centre and the periphery.

Indeed, it seems clear that comparative legal theory, which can be seen as a 'narrative of the making of modern law',[85] has actively contributed to the 'exoticization of legal cultures'.[86] It has been instrumental in the construction of a deliberate view of 'us and them', of the world's centre and its relationship to the periphery. Thus, P. G. Monateri explains, the beginnings of comparative legal theory in civilian legal thinking should be repositioned in the context of the cult of Roman law and Roman specificity in German legal history, which were in turn linked to the great civilian codifications of the nineteenth century.

---

[82] On this concept, particularly adapted to comparative law in a global setting, see Esin Örücü, 'Comparatists and Extraordinary Places', in Legrand and Munday (n 4), 467 ff.

[83] For an example of such reflection, see Baxi (n 10), 46 ff.   [84] Kennedy (n 17).

[85] Baxi (n 10), 49 ff.

[86] P. G. Monateri, 'Black Gaius: A Quest for the Multicultural Origins of the "Western Legal Tradition" ', (2000) 51 Hastings LJ 479 ff.

The stress on the overall importance of Roman Law led to a conception of Roman Law as something more than just positive law. Roman Law came with an implied intellectual history, but it was a peculiar history. In order to build a new German law on its basis, Roman Law had to be studied as a complete and autonomous system which in turn could be elaborated and developed according to scientific principles into a modern legal system. It is not hard to see at work here the theory of the renewal of the old, and an eye towards the projects of governance that are reaffirmed today. This approach produced an 'ideology' of Roman uniqueness which entails an almost total exclusion of all other laws' importance.[87]

Similarly, the French *Code civil* constitutes the divisions and categories of Roman law in products of natural reason. This crystallization of Roman ideas and classifications in the Code was clearly part of the construction of the specific identity of civilian systems.[88]

According to parallel schemes in law and linguistics, the world was divided into legal 'families'. The ideological thrust of these classifications, carrying a hidden agenda of governance, appears with the realization that the trend to demonstrate the intellectual purity of Roman culture serves to divide the world into a centre and periphery.

In fact, in this project, Comparative Law assumes the typical function of depicting the frame of diversities between an 'us' and a 'them,' a centre and a periphery, a West and an East. What is peculiar is that this theory entails a devaluation of the classical Common Law/Civil Law distinction, in favour of a convergence among 'modern' Western systems which ultimately depicts a more unitary Western legal family resting on the Roman pillars of Roman jurisprudence, superior to all the other world legal cultures.[89]

In the centre, the Roman tradition is presented as organic, conserving its essence despite inevitable borrowing from elsewhere. The mythology of the codes were in turn to inherit this metaphysical transcendence or integrity.[90] But the civilian 'family' has clearly multicultural origins. Monateri suggests a

shift in approach [which] has various consequences for the 'ideology' of Western law. The first is that Western law is a patchwork no less exotic than others. The second is that Western law is derived not only from Roman Law, but from other ancient laws as well. This suggests a more globalized view of Western institutions, and of their origins. Indeed, it intimates that 'Western' law is not nearly so 'Western' as we have been led to believe.[91]

Was Gaius black? (One recognizes the figure of 'Black Athena'.) Rome itself was the projection of a myth. 'Historical consciousness and genealogies associated with it have a political dimension which cannot be underestimated: there is something worth fighting for'.[92] And again,

if modern Western law is to be rooted on Roman uniqueness, we can still perceive Western legal history as a unit evolving from Roman times through the Middle Ages to its actual

---

[87] Monateri (n 86), 592 ff.   [88] Stein (n 59).   [89] Monateri (n 86) 485 ff.
[90] De Béchillon (n 60), 178 ff.   [91] Monateri (n 86), 514 ff.   [92] Monateri (n 86), 515 ff.

predominance as 'the' modern law par excellence . . . From this point of view it is true that Comparative Law, coupled with traditional Roman-based legal history, becomes a project of global cultural governance in the field of law. A major strategy of this project is the exoticization of legal cultures different from the Western one.[93]

The 'epistemological racism' of mainstream comparative legal theory has further been emphasized by Upendra Baxi. For this writer, the choice of the *genre* of comparative legal studies clearly determines what can meaningfully be said about the colonialist heritage.[94] Thus, the positivistic genre strictly addresses forms of normative or institutional diffusion of global legal reality; instrumentalist approaches, including Old and New 'law and development', remain concerned with issues of efficient management of transitions from non-modern to modern law; the sociological genre explores productions of difference within, between, and across legal cultures, while the critical comparative genre provides frameworks for understanding the spread of dominant legal-ideological traditions and the transformations within them. 'Each of these and related genres develops its own kind of (pre-eminently Euro-American) epistemic communities sustaining the practice of inclusion/exclusion that define the distinctive domain of comparative legal studies.'[95] And further

Comparative legal studies, understood as the narratives of the making of 'modern law', still stand marked by the 'Caliban syndrome', the construction of colonial/post-colonial narrative voices in ways that comfort the Euro-American images of progress and 'developmentalism'. Caliban is the history of exclusion and exploitation for the purposes of another's development.[96]

For Upendra Baxi, the dominant tradition of comparative law

reproduces the binary contrasts between the common and civil law cultures or the bourgeois and socialist ideal-types, thus reducing the diversity of the world's legal systems to a common Euro-American measure.[97]

A Jurgen Habermas, a John Rawls or a Ronald Dworkin thus remains able to expound theories of justice, public reason and judicial process *as if* the *living law* of the third World or the south, transcending colonial inheritances, simply does not exist or is supremely irrelevant to theory construction.[98]

The perspective of the excluded Other can be seen as part of the 'colonial inheritance'. As Upendra Baxi puts it,

in every sphere, the 'modern law' remains the 'gift' of the west to the rest. The large processes of 'westernisation', 'modernization', 'development' and now 'globalization' of law present the never-ending story of triumphant legal liberalism . . . Thus emerges a history of a mentality that maps unidirectionality of legal 'development'. Unidirectionality leads to perfectibility of global epistemic hegemonic practices which consolidate the view

---

[93] Monateri (n 86), 469 ff.   [94] Baxi (n 10), 46 ff.   [95] Baxi (n 10), 46 ff.
[96] Baxi (n 10), 49 ff.   [97] Ibid.   [98] Baxi (n 10), 53 ff.

that the masters and makers of modern law have nothing worthy to learn from the discursive tradition of the Euro-American tradition's other . . .[99] 'It becomes the mission of the laws' late modernity to arrest deflections from the path of legal liberalism by persuasion when possible and through justified arms intervention when necessary'.

In this context, globalization is a narrative which perpetuates the mythology of the modern law, which Upendra Baxi depicts as an aspect of the wider phenomenon of 'White Mythologies'. This discourse presents the progress of modern law in terms of foundational and reiterative violence of 'modern law'.[100]

A similar ethnocentric world vision supported by comparative law can be found in connection with human rights discourse. The potential for universalization of human rights lies squarely in the idea that if a right is a fundamental attribute of humanity, it must necessarily be of universal relevance. However, this conception tends to rest upon an essentialist vision of humanity which leaves little place either for the diverse histories of peoples or for the concurrent conception of a reciprocal relationship between the individual and the community.[101] Human rights discourse contains both the potential for a 'flattening effect' of abstraction and an ideological project presented as having universal, objective validity. Positing individual rights free from all duties to the community, it creates an obvious risk of arbitrariness and conflict, for the solution of which the same rights are then required to intercede. Hence criticism of its auto-referential character, which tends to reinforce its propensity to reduce diversity.[102] From the Islamic perspective, the apparent neutrality of human rights discourse occults a certain conception of social structures, in which the relationship between power and society, religion and politics, are clearly marked by western modernity, long since rejected by the Arab-Muslim world.[103] Indeed, a similar weakness affects more generally 'civilizational' approaches to globalization,[104] which rest on the premise that democracy itself is essentially a western political and cultural phenomenon. But the democratic ideal can have western origins without necessarily being anchored in a substantive conception of human dignity indissociable from Christianity.[105]

Thus, the patterns of dominance carried by the world-view supported by comparative legal theory are sufficiently clear. They can easily be linked up today to the narrative of globalization itself. Comparison of different visions of human dignity reveal the strong cultural dimension of the world vision projected by the western rhetoric of globalization, which 'reworks and harnesses the colonial legacy and the post-colonial experience in the pursuit of visions of the globalising world's iconic images of democracy, good governance, economic rationalism'.[106] Is there any way

---

[99] Baxi (n 10), 50–1 ff.   [100] Ibid.

[101] A. Papaux and E. Wyler, *L'éthique du droit international* (1997).

[102] Papaux and Wyler (n 101), 102 ff.   [103] See Salah (n 7), 32 ff.

[104] See S. P. Huntingdon, *The Clash of Civilisations and the Remaking of the World Order* (1996).

[105] René Sève, 'Introduction', (2003) 45 *Archives de Philosophie du Droit* 3, 7 ff.

[106] Baxi (n 10), 49 ff.

out of this hermeneutic conundrum? It could be that comparatist reflection on difference or otherness can provide enlightenment. For Pierre Legrand, the function of comparative law, far from imposing one's own vision on the Other, is to 'organise the diversity of discourses around different cultural forms'.[107] 'The notion of relation must be at the heart of any comparative endeavour'.[108] His plea for differential thinking takes on a particular significance in a globalizing context, echoing that of Papaux and Wyler in favour of an ethic of international law founded on the respect of the self-hood of the Other. Citing Hamacher, the author goes on to say,

the point is to avoid cultural fusionism which permits the other ... 'to be perceived no longer in its alterity but only a variant of one's own culture and further permits treating one's own culture as homogeneous, given fact, ignoring its internal tensions, contradictions and struggles and giving oneself over to the fantasy that it is a logical continuum without history and does not always *also* contain the demand to transform that history'.

The point, then, 'is to impel the comparatist toward an ethical encounter with the other-in-the-law'.[109] That the ethics of comparative legal studies in a globalizing world should be founded on a respect of otherness seems particularly apt. It remains to be seen how far from this ideal is the strategic use of comparative knowledge in the world today.

3. Comparative Knowledge and Issues of Global Governance

Mainstream post-war comparatism, as David Kennedy points out, cultivated aloofness from the distributional consequences of particular policy choices or institutional arrangements. Contemporary comparative projects purport to map differences and commonalities between national laws, without pre-judging the pragmatic use to which such knowledge could be put. It is deemed futile to attempt to discover the practical usefulness of comparative knowledge, which certainly provides a better understanding of the Other, and no doubt a sharpened awareness of what law is, but does not in itself carry a political or strategic agenda. However, as the study of the colonial heritage in comparative law has shown, this stance of neutrality towards the strategic indifference of comparative law is hardly credible.

In this respect, globalization entails deep implications for the relationship between law and market. The triumph of economic liberalism means that there is a global market for laws based on difference, which not only reverses the traditional articulation between markets and laws, but also impacts on the mutual interaction between different laws, which henceforth interact according to a competitive model. Private international law and economics are best equipped to highlight

---

[107] Legrand (n 37), 299 ff.   [108] Legrand (n 37), 301 ff.   [109] Legrand (n 37), 303 ff.

the paradigmatic changes wrought by globalization concerning the relationships between legal systems. Thus, for the best part of the twentieth century, despite cultural cleavages concerning the proper place of politics in the regulation of private relationships between private actors, certain postulates tended to be shared. Conflicts law purported to define the thrust of law and judicial decisions concerning persons, activities, or things geographically dispersed; independently of the methods used to get there, it supposed that transactions between individuals were subjected to law and not the other way round. While the distinction between the public and private spheres on an international level was growing increasingly indeterminate, it was generally accepted that there was an important difference between rules which, from the standpoint of a given state organ, could be set aside by the parties to an international transaction and those which carried fundamental state policies which necessarily trumped individual arrangements. Generally the latter category was perceived to comprise rules addressing both market organization and market failures, through mandatory protection for weaker parties. But these shared assumptions were bowled over by the globalization of markets, which signalled a new paradigm under which national law-makers were henceforth subjected to the arbitrage of consumers on product markets and mobile capital looking for immediate profit. As essential actors in these changes and the main beneficiaries of the deregulation which accompanied the decline of the state, multinational firms pursue purely financial strategies, looking for the highest rate of return on investment without regard to the geographic location of their activities. Protective legislation is seen as having a cost. In many cases, mechanisms of private international law ensure juridical 'lift-off' of these actors from legal regulation.[110] Such changes impact directly on the relationship between law and market.

Under the new competitive paradigm, national laws are themselves the object of a globalizing market, of which the regulation is the sole province of interjurisdictional competition and not of mandatory state intervention, which is powerless to prevent international arbitrage linked to the lifting of restrictions on free movement and trade barriers. Henceforth, state policies are to a large extent tributary to either consumers' market decisions or investment decisions of private capital. This means the state is no longer the monopolistic provider of public goods, but is itself subject to competition: 'Former monopolistic states seem to change into mere "locations" that must compete with each other for public goods and services. The monopoly paradigm of economic policy, therefore, tends to be replaced by a competition paradigm of economic policy'.[111] According to the

---

[110] Robert Wai, 'Transnational Liftoff and Juridical Touchdown: The Regulatory Function of Private International Law in a Global Age', (2002) 40 *Columbia Journal of Transnational Law* 209 ff.

[111] Wolfgang Kerber, 'Interjurisdictional Competition within the European Union', (2000) *Fordham International LJ* 217, 248 ff.

teachings of economic federalism, competition between legal systems in a borderless economy would be an alternative mode of governance to centralized regulation: the global market would determine the optimal intensity of state regulation across the board. The development of third spheres of normativity such as international arbitration contributes to the reversal of the relationship between law and market, since ever-more liberal rules on the free choice of law and forum allow parties to move freely from one system to another, evading mandatory rules when desired. This phenomenon of 'barrier-crossing' is then consolidated by increasingly generous rules for enforcement of arbitral awards, according to which the violation of state public policy is no longer necessarily a cause of non enforcement.[112]

Under the competitive paradigm, differences between sets of legal rules and institutions are part of the make-up of the law as product. In theories of global economic federalism, differences are generally supposedly healthy as they will generate emulation through consumer or investor arbitrage and lead to specialization of legal systems across the board.[113] Such an effect will only take place if the legal product is heterogeneous, creating winners and losers likely to vote with their feet and thereby create pressure on the legislator: private law rules may arguably be excluded.[114] The strategic importance of comparative law appears in the evaluation of the economic attractivity of given regulations and their institutional setting: 'Doing business' abroad means choosing the most efficient, but also the least costly, legal system.[115] However, there are times when the global market fails to regulate. While capital crosses boundaries freely, arbitrage between various legal environments tends to take place at the expense of the immobile local workforce. States desirous of capturing capital engage in a race to the bottom, lowering standards and thereby costs to the point of depriving the local population of conditions which in other parts of the world are considered as prerequisites to human decency. Comparative law can serve to highlight the private international law mechanisms which then come into play to lock a population into the lower standards. The doctrine of *forum non conveniens*, for instance, as practised in the United States, may lead to depriving victims of industrial accidents or environmental harm of their access to the forum of the state where the multinational defendant is domiciled.

Comparative law could step in here to help understand these mechanisms of 'global liftoff'.[116] To what extent is regulatory competition transposable to fields of

---

[112] Luca G. Radicati di Brozolo and Horatia Muir Watt, 'Party Autonomy and Mandatory Rules in a Global World', (2004) 6 *International Law Forum* 88 ff.

[113] Stephen Choi and Andrew Guzman, 'Portable Recognition: Rethinking the International Reach of Securities Regulation' (1998) 71 *Southern California LR* 903 ff.

[114] See Anthony Ogus, 'Competition between National Legal Systems: A Contribution of Economic Analysis to Comparative Law', 48 *ICLQ* 405 ff.

[115] See the criteria used by the World Bank, 'Report on Doing Business, Eliminating Obstacles to Growth' (2004).

[116] Wai (n 110).

private law? Is private law homogeneous or does it contain 'implicit regulatory schemes'.[117] What are the unacknowledged assumptions made by studies such as that of the World Bank as to the elements which make up the economic attractiveness of a given law? Why are civilian systems deemed less competitive? What are the regulatory fields in which competition leads to the sacrifice of standards? What would the effect of raising minimum standards be on economic development? The answers to these questions are all essential to global governance, and it is difficult not to involve comparative law in them. As David Nelken points out,

many of the governmental and international agencies which promote legal change in developing countries focus on formal as opposed to informal institutions. These are easier to identify, analyse and engineer in ways by which such bureaucracies justify their existence. Yet there are likely to be informal institutions, less amenable to change by external interventions, which already carry out many of the tasks of the formal institutions whose performance the agencies are seeking to improve.[118] The 'Doing Business' Report of the World, which purports to measure economic attractiveness in a global setting, is a case in point.

The necessary implication of comparative knowledge in issues of world governance is confirmed by recent reflection on the effects of the expansion of the rule of law and the separation it supposes of law and market, in a global setting. Globalization in western narrative comprises a tendency to spread democratic ideals.[119] Economic leverage tends to be used by powerful agencies such as the World Bank to export democratic institutions, and among them, particularly the concept of the rule of law. William Scheuerman argues that the political and legal infrastructure of globalization bears little resemblance to the liberal model of the rule of law.[120] The rule of law was useful to business when it created certainty, making distance in time and space manageable in contexts of commercial exchange. Private international law contributed to the reduction of uncertainty by allowing binding party choice of the applicable law. But compression of time and space means that there is 'less of an elective affinity between capitalism and the rule of law'.[121] The risks which the rule of law was designed to manage are better dealt with directly through technology. Law loses its autonomy. Moreover, the rule of law was valued because it protected private transactions from the arbitrariness of the state. But now private actors frequently have at least as much leverage as the states themselves, the balance of power is no longer to their advantage. As seen above,

---

[117] On which, see Hugh Collins, 'Regulating Contract Law', in Christina Parker, Colin Scott, Nicola Lacey, and John Braithwaite (eds), *Regulating Law* (2004), 23 ff.

[118] Nelken (n 4), 465 ff.

[119] See Michael Likoksy, 'Cultural Imperialism in the Context of Transnational Commercial Collaboration', in Likoksy (n 2), 221 ff; Baxi (n 10), 49 ff.

[120] 'Globalization and the Fate of Law', in David Dyzenhaus (ed), *Recrafting the Rule of Law: The Limits of Legal Order*, (1999), 243, discussed in Nelken (n 4), 465 ff.

[121] Nelken (n 4), 466 ff.

there is considerable evidence that economic globalization flourishes where lower standards in health, labour, and environment are exploited by powerful multi-national firms. 'It would be misleading', opines David Nelken, 'to ignore these and other similar factors when assessing the likely outcomes of introducing the type of separation between state and market as identified with the classical (but now some-what dated) idea of the rule of law'.[122] Thus, comparative legal knowledge clearly has a role to play in global governance. Here, the challenge which globalization presents to comparative legal studies lies in understanding the effects of paradigm changes in the relationship between local laws and global markets and in highlight-ing ways, in conjunction with neighbouring disciplinary fields, in which a global race to the bottom could be countered.

III. The Practical Challenge

On a practical level, the changes wrought by globalization, including new infor-mation technology, interconnectedness of national economies, and the emergence of transnational norms and practices, raise two different and apparently contra-dictory challenges to comparative law. On the one hand, the ever-widening access to data about foreign laws, as well as the expansion of transnational or international sources of uniform law might appear to make comparative law obsolete. What need is there of comparative scholarship if information on foreign law is readily available or if the applicable rule is a rule of substantive uniform law? However, comparative scholarship still has an important rôle to play, albeit in novel forms. An increase in the available volume of information renders all the more necessary a comparative legal grammar capable of converting bare data on a national legal system into an understandable form for the foreign user (Section III.1). At the same time, uniform law requires, for both its elaboration and its interpretation, a comparison of possible alternative solutions (Section III.2).

1. Increased Information and Interconnectedness

First and most obviously, increased access to knowledge of foreign law through new information technology has important implications for the usefulness of comparative law as a source of information about foreign laws. Traditionally, as

---

[122] Ibid.

David Gerber has pointed out, one of the main functions of comparative law was to provide information about other, different, legal cultures.[123] Indeed, comparative studies often tended to be descriptive or 'anatomical', concentrating on the assembling of stark data about a foreign law which was otherwise unobtainable. As access to information improves, this particular function of comparative legal scholarship is no doubt becoming redundant.

While essential in this respect, new information technologies are not the only reason for the increase in widespread knowledge about foreign legal cultures. The existence of supranational courts such as the European Court of Human Rights, for instance, inevitably feeds a common core of knowledge about the legal systems of the other contracting states. Its case-law, binding all the legal communities within the ambit of the Convention it applies, acts inevitably as a vector of information on the content and functioning of neighbouring national laws. Much cross-border knowledge has been created in this way about the criminal and procedural laws of the various states party to the European Convention on Human Rights, or, similarly, about various aspects of civil procedure and jurisdiction in civil and commercial matters among the states of the European Union.

At the same time, increased contacts between legal systems through the rise of international travel and transactions make such knowledge all the more important for the practising lawyer. Legal advice and litigation involve increasingly cross-border elements—from products liability to investment choices to car accidents abroad—which may require making decisions in the light of foreign law or which call for the application of foreign law under conflict of laws principles. The easy availability of information about foreign law is obviously likely to enhance cross-border legal practice. However, comparative law as a disciplinary field is far from obsolete in this context.

As David Gerber has emphasized, while significant data about foreign law is directly and rapidly available via the Internet, it is generally both unstructured and decontextualized.[124] Available information may be increasingly dense, but it may be becoming more opaque. It may be creating a new, double problem of understanding, since bare data such as texts may be undecipherable to the uninitiated and even in the clearest form are unlikely to provide insights as to how they fit within the foreign legal system or how the latter actually works in practice. Much of comparative scholarship has been devoted in recent years to uncovering the hidden formants which cement and drive a given legal community, and clearly, bare access to data cannot replace this type of reflection but on the contrary makes it increasingly indispensable. Language may also be a barrier to access. 'Knowing foreign law means crossing a linguistic border' even when a language base is shared.[125] It would

---

[123] David Gerber, 'Globalization and Legal Knowledge: Implications for Comparative Law', (2001) 75 *Tulane LR* 949, 969 ff.

[124] Ibid 953 ff.   [125] Gerber (n 123), 967 ff.

seem then that, more than ever, a common conceptual language, a comparative legal grammar, will be necessary to maximize the benefits of increased information and make them significant to the foreign user.

Beyond the difficulty of access to significant knowledge of other legal cultures, Gerber warns too of the increased risk of distorted perceptions which may be the price of the new proximity between legal cultures induced by availability of information.[126] Stereotyped assumptions about other systems which tend to shape the perception of legal knowledge may well be intensified by increased contact. Globalization, he warns, may influence the accuracy of knowledge of foreign law by intensifying the impact of such distorting factors. Thus, twin illusions of 'similarity' (differences are negligible) and ease (any differences there are may easily be overcome), which are recurrent temptations within comparative scholarship itself, are likely to be fostered as information moves more rapidly and becomes more dense. Relying on ready-made assumptions is a cognitive strategy likely to develop as the user is subject to increased time pressures and the need to simplify the task of processing information. Clearly, such pressures generated by the ready availability of information need to be counteracted by strong intellectual efforts to structure knowledge about foreign law and maintain the awareness of otherness.

A related issue concerns the impact of available information on the question of judicial notice of foreign law in conflicts of laws cases.[127] Since heightened cross-border contacts generate more conflicts of laws, greater ease of access to information about other legal cultures raises the question of the status of foreign law before the national courts. At a time when the availability of reliable information about foreign systems remained extremely difficult, the courts of most countries traditionally avoided direct involvement with the determination of the content of foreign law, relying in the main upon the parties and the adversarial process to bring convincing proof of the substance of applicable foreign rules. The quasi-universal subterfuge used here was to consider foreign law as fact to be proved to the satisfaction of the court. Supreme courts thereby avoided the embarrassment of committing themselves to a faulty version of another state's law. However, improved access to information lessens the need for such prudence, and in various countries, and to varying degrees, courts must now take notice of foreign laws. This is of course particularly so among the sister or member states of federal or quasi-federal systems, where, in addition to constitutional requirements of equality of treatment or full faith and credit between the laws of the various states before each other's courts, there exist both heightened judicial cooperation and a common body of rules. However, even outside such a context, changes are taking place, with

---

[126] Ibid 968 ff.
[127] See the various contributions in Guy Canivet, Mads Andenas, and Duncan Fairgrieve, *Comparative Law before the Courts* (2004).

the result that courts will increasingly be acceding directly to data about the foreign law governing a given case. Indeed, progressively, they may well be ready to cite available foreign sources as persuasive authority in hard cases. But, once more, in either case, the usefulness of comparative legal methodology and insights are in no way obsolete. Here again, easily obtained information as to the content of a given statute does not tell how that statute is actually applied by the courts of the foreign country, nor indeed whether judicial decisions bear weight, nor how that particular solution fits into the foreign law as a whole.

2. The Rise of Transnational Uniform Law

A second practical challenge for the comparative lawyer in a global context stems from the changes affecting the sources and nature of applicable legal rules. These will frequently be contained in international conventions bearing uniform rules, or will consist in commercial customs and practices assembled under the banner of the new law merchant or *lex mercatoria,* or indeed in various forms of trans-national soft law such as the UNIDROIT or Lando principles. Once more, in view of this trend towards unification, the question arises as to whether comparative law is becoming redundant through the lack of national, local laws to compare. But once again, the answer appears to be that comparative law retains all of its usefulness, albeit in new ways.

First, at the outset, comparative legal scholarship can contribute to the improved content of transnational uniform rules, whether these are negotiated at a diplomatic conference or chosen by a single arbitrator invested by contract with a mission to apply a better rule. A uniform rule is always to some extent the product of competition between diverse legal rules. Preparatory comparative studies should therefore be, and frequently are, systematically undertaken in both a diplomatic and private context. At a later stage, similar comparative knowledge remains essential when courts and arbitrators are called upon to interpret uniform rules in a given case. When a given uniform rule is clearly borrowed from a given national legal culture, insights as to the difficulties it raises and its mode of functioning are clearly useful even if national case-law or doctrinal constructions can clearly have no more than persuasive authority in such a context. Quite frequently, too, international instruments appeal to common principles of national law to fill the gaps in its own provisions. A variation on this theme appears in the 1980 Vienna Convention on the international sale of goods that requires courts to take account of its international character and of the need to reach uniform results in its application (Art 7). This means that courts may need to look at foreign case-law, applying the convention itself when in doubt as to its meaning. A similar appeal to principles common to different legal systems may be found in international commercial arbitration agreements. In all these contexts, comparative law as a way of structuring knowledge about foreign laws, and translating it into a comprehensible form for the user, retains real practical usefulness.

BIBLIOGRAPHY

Antoine Garapon, 'French Legal Culture and the Shock of "Globalization" ', (1995) 4 *Social and Legal Studies* 493

A. Papaux and E. Wyler, *L'éthique du droit international* (1997)

Mireille Delmas-Marty, 'La mondialisation du droit: chances et risques', (1999) *Recueil Dalloz* 2 ff

H. Patrick Glenn, *Legal Traditions of the World* (2000)

P. G. Monateri, 'Black Gaius: A Quest for the Multicultural Origins of the "Western Legal Tradition" ', (2000) 51 *Hastings LJ* 479 ff

William Twining, 'Comparative Law and Legal Theory: The Country and Western Tradition', in Ian Edge (ed), *Comparative Law in Global Perspective* (2000)

David Gerber, 'Globalization and Legal Knowledge: Implications for Comparative Law', (2001) 75 *Tulane LR* 949

Michael Likoksy (ed), *Transnational Legal Processes. Globalisation and Power Disputes* (2002)

Geoffrey Samuel, *Epistemology and Method in Law* (2002)

Jean-Bernard Auby, *La globalisation, le droit et l'Etat* (2003)

Duncan Kennedy, 'Two Globalizations of Law & Legal Thought, 1850–1968', (2003) 36 *Suffolk University LR* 631 ff

Pierre Legrand and Roderick Munday (eds), *Comparative Legal Studies: Traditions and Transitions* (2003)

Ugo Mattei, 'A Theory of Imperial Law: A Study on US Hegemony and the Latin Resistance', (2003) *Indiana Journal of Global Legal Studies* 383 ff

'La mondialisation entre illusion et utopie', (2003) 47 *Archives de Philosophie du Droit*

Guy Canivet, Mads Andenas, and Duncan Fairgrieve, *Comparative Law before the Courts*, (2004)

CHAPTER 18

COMPARATIVE LAW AND THE ISLAMIC (MIDDLE EASTERN) LEGAL CULTURE

CHIBLI MALLAT

*Beirut**

* Many thanks to my colleagues John Donohue at Saint Joseph's University and James Whitman at Yale Law School for their most helpful comments on the draft of this chapter. All shortcomings naturally remain mine.

I. Islamic Law and Civilization: The Comparative Framework

In a posthumous publication on 'Law and Justice' in the Islamic world, Joseph Schacht (d. 1969), the leading twentieth-century Western scholar in the field, underlined the unique importance of law in defining Muslim (or Islamic) civilization:

The sacred law of Islam, the *Shari'a*, occupies a central place in Muslim society, and its history runs parallel with the history of Islamic civilization. It has often been said that Islamic law represents the core and kernel of Islam itself and, certainly, religious law is incomparably more important in the religion of Islam than theology. As recently as 1959, the then rector of al-Azhar University, Shaykh Mahmud Shaltut, published a book entitled 'Islam, a faith and a law' (*al-Islam, 'aqida wa-shari'a*), and by far the greater part of its pages is devoted to an exposé of the religious law of Islam, down to some technicalities, whereas the statement of the Islamic faith occupies less than one-tenth of the whole. It seems that in the eyes of this high Islamic dignitary the essential bond that unites the Muslims is not so much a common simple creed as a common way of life, a common ideal of society. The development of all religious sciences, and therefore of a considerable part of intellectual life in Islam, takes its rhythm from the development of religious law. Even in modern times, the main intellectual effort of the Muslims as Muslims is aimed not at proving the truth of Islamic dogma but at justifying the validity of Islamic law as they understand it.[1]

While this statement is true with respect to the fourteen-century-long history of Muslim civilization (the Muslim calendar starts at CE 622, the year of the Prophet Muhammad's flight from his home town Mecca to the neighbouring city of Medina), the period between World War I and the early 1970s was anything but a moment of glory for the *shari'a*, 'the sacred law of Islam'.[2] Most of Islamic law as it had come down over the centuries was displaced by Western-style legislation. With the exception of ritual observances, few Muslims were conducting any of their legal business in open reference to *shari'a* precepts, and the place of religious law receded considerably in the Muslim world. Politically, the rise of socialist ideologies was rightly considered by Muslim religious leaders to represent a clear and present threat to their way of life. It undermined what little power they retained in their communities: except for rules bearing on marriage, divorce, inheritance, and family life generally, few laws in the various modern nation-states

---

[1] Joseph Schacht, 'Law and Justice', in *The Cambridge Encyclopedia of Islam* (vol 2, 1974), 539. Note that in the following text and footnotes, references are to both the Christian and the Muslim calendars. Where only one date is mentioned, it refers to the CE (Christian or Common Era); where two dates are listed, the first gives the year according to the Muslim calendar, the second according to the Christian (Common) calendar.

[2] *Shari'a* or *shar'* are used as generic terms for Islamic law. *Fiqh* is the classical term. *Qanun* is used nowadays for positive law, as well as more specifically for statute law.

were rooted in the millennium-deep legal tradition of the *shari'a*. The classical jurists of the law, *imams, sheikhs, muftis, fuqaha', mujtahids*, and *'ulama*,[3] when they survived, dispensed knowledge which, to the chagrin of such religious leaders as the Azhar *sheikh* Mahmud Shaltut, had little impact on the daily transactions of the citizen. The degrees they granted did not even entitle their holders to become lawyers or judges. Islamic law and Islamic law-trained lawyers remained peripheral to public life.

The revolution in Iran, led by Islamic jurists, changed the scene. In 1979, the world awoke to the victory of the *shari'a's* exponents, who had toppled one of the most powerful regimes in the Middle East. Iranian revolutionaries rallied behind the call for 'the rule of the (Islamic) jurist' (in Persian, *velayat-e faqih*), as the most famous pamphlet of *Ayat Allah*[4] Ruhullah Khumaini (d. 1989) came to be known. The advent of *Islamic government* (another title of the same pamphlet) in Tehran followed an Islamic renaissance across the Shi'i world that had started in response to the rise of communism amongst the more deprived sectors of Muslim societies. Islamic law had 'regained the high ground in disciplines which had seemed only a few decades ago beyond its pale: constitution, economics and banking'.[5] By the beginning of the twenty-first century, the *shari'a* was back at centre stage of the political life of most countries with a sizeable Muslim majority. The advocates of its relevance and implementation challenged the established legal order across the world, including a Western world which, for the first time in its history, had large, and increasingly self-assertive Muslim communities in its midst. The more radical proponents of the return to the *shari'a* focused the world's attention on their agenda with the violence unleashed in New York on 11 September, 2001. While the revolution in Iran was arguably Shi'i (the second largest community in a Muslim world that is predominantly Sunni—there are some 1.2 billion Muslims, with about a billion Sunnis and 200 million Shi'is), the call for the establishment of Islamic states, defined as states observing Islamic law, had by then become universal among Muslims.

In this context, comparative law is an essential component of the contemporary Muslim world, because the enactment and interpretation of all 'modern' legislation in every Muslim country is subject to scrutiny for its compatibility with Islamic law. Between the quasi-total displacement of the *shari'a* and its vigorous return, almost every legal issue has become comparative. This pervasive comparative aspect

---

[3] An *imam* is a leader of the prayer, as well as generally the leader of the community, including the eponym of a law school. In the Shi'i tradition, he is also one of the recognized historic leaders who took on the mantle of the Prophet through his daughter Fatima. *Sheikh* (or *shaykh*) is also generically a respected community leader. A *mufti* is a jurist who issues *fatwas*, normally non-binding legal opinions. *Mujtahid* is a generic term for jurist, as is *'alim*, plural *'ulama* (literally scholar) or *faqih*, *fuqaha'* (expert on *fiqh*).

[4] *Ayat Allah* (literally sign of God), known as Ayatollah in the west, refers to a religious 'degree' achieved by a scholar in the Shi'i hierarchy.

[5] Chibli Mallat, *The Renewal of Islamic Law* (1993), 189.

of the *shari'a* is complicated by the fact that a historical axis brings an immense cultural perspective to the field that goes well beyond law to encompass religion, arts, literature, and sciences, all under the rubric of Islamic 'civilization'.

In fact, Islamic law is only a small, discrete component of a larger frame of reference within Islamic culture. The civilization built by Muslims prided itself also on military prowess. Consider the early period of the Conquest that brought it all the way to Poitiers in the eighth century, the protracted and ultimately successful battle against the Crusaders, and the European military expansion of the Ottoman Empire which twice brought Islam to the gates of Vienna. On the other hand, Islamic art and architecture have given the world monuments of exquisite refinement, from the Taj Mahal in India to the Alhambra in Spain, and, in literature, texts from the tenth and eleventh centuries, such as Mutanabbi's (d. 965) *Diwan* (collection of poetry), or Firdawsi's (d. 1020) epic poem of *Shahnameh*, are considered world-class writings and are revered to this day as the most impressive literary legacy in the Arab and Persian-Iranian worlds.

That said, Islamic law is increasingly all-encompassing and, in fact, is equivalent to the rule of law in the modern state. Every aspect of life is regulated by (Islamic) law. Indeed, every subject in the thematic area of the present *Handbook* could include a specific section on the ways Islamic law deals with it. Such is the wealth of material in the field that it has branched out in recent years into disciplines, including environmental law and economics, where no identifiable corpus of law could previously be found.

Before comparing the Islamic nomocracy and the rule-of-law states in modern democracies, it is helpful to draw certain distinctions. One consideration has to do with the arbitrariness that prevailed in many parts of the Islamic world during its history. Not only would an attempt to apply the model of a modern democracy to pre-modern times in the Middle East or South East Asia constitute a grave anachronism, but the absence of a central power structure in many countries where Islam was the predominant religion meant that the operation of the law in those lands was enormously complex. There was simply no unifying and exclusive power at the top to bring all its strands together. Perhaps Islamic law, in historical perspective, can best be described through the metaphor of the French philosophers Deleuze and Guattari, as *Mille Plateaux*, a 'thousand plains' where various levels and intensities of authority and legitimacy operate.[6]

Besides constituting a special type of nomocracy and operating at a multi-level order in society, Islamic law is also unique in that it represents a personal, rather than a territorial, system of law. It thus stands in sharp contrast to the post-Westphalian order that dominates the rest of the world. This characteristic,

---

[6] Chibli Mallat, 'From Islamic to Middle Eastern Law: A Restatement of the Field, Part 1', (2003) 51 *AJCL* 699 ff; 'From Islamic to Middle Eastern Law: A Restatement of the Field, Part 2', (2004) 52 *AJCL* 233, 281–6. Gilles Deleuze (d. 1995) and Félix Guattari (d.1992) published *Mille Plateaux* in Paris in 1980.

which is typical of any religious-based social order, is also typically Middle Eastern. The application of law to a person on the basis of religious affiliation is an increasingly important source of tension in the world order, one that is based on personal, or communitarian, law, as opposed to the territorial law that dominates the rest of the world. This contrast is possibly the most pervasive and divisive issue that arises when regarding the different legal systems and cultures at play from a comparative perspective.

From a historical perspective, Islamic law consistently elicits an array of autonomous references. Looking at its uninterrupted flow since the Muslim revelation in the seventh century, the *shari'a* appears as the common law in the region and beyond, reaching Mauritania and West Africa on its western fringes and Indonesia to the east. Beyond its textual differences with other major legal systems, the *shari'a* is increasingly studied for its immense diversity across history. In the early period, the Qur'anic text, the *hadiths* (aphorisms attributed to the Prophet) and the *sira maghazi* literature (the *sira* consists of biographical accounts of the Prophet, the *maghazi* of the early conquests), were all elaborated upon in many legal genres after the death of the Prophet Muhammad (d. CE 632). Added to this legacy were the classical age books of doctrine (*fiqh*), the customary rules, the case law available from extant archival courts, the literature on the art of judgments, the *fatwas* (individual legal opinions), formularies, deeds and contracts, the statute law (*qanun*) since the fifteenth century, as well as the relevant histories and literature at large, such as chronicles or *belles letters*. Recent scholarship brings all these genres within the purview of Islamic law. This has led to profound changes in the appreciation of the concept of sources, the development of law and its interpretation, the phenomenon of the Islamic legal 'schools' or *madhhab*s (there are four central Sunni schools—Shafi'i, Hanafi, Maliki, Hanbali—and one main Shi'i school, called Ja'fari), all the way to the emergence of codified national laws in the nineteenth and twentieth centuries.[7]

Before addressing public and private legal disciplines where the *shari'a* has become relevant once again, we should note some important avenues which will *not* be followed in this chapter.

First, as the title indicates, the focus is on the Middle East rather than on the much larger Muslim world. This chapter generally covers jurisdictions extending from Mauritania in the west to Pakistan in the east. It does not include India, which has a large Muslim minority of over 150 million, or Indonesia, which has the largest Muslim population in the world (about 200 million). Occasionally, we look at Israel even though it is not a Muslim country, because some of its public law reflects a 'personal legal pattern' that is parallel to that of Islam.

In terms of method, several options for approaching the field in a comparative

---

[7] The footnotes in this chapter have been restricted to a minimum and seek to offer a representative sample of the large variety of classical and modern sources available in the field.

manner could be fruitfully adopted. We could, for example, carefully examine Islamic law as it exists in various nation-states. We shall not pursue such a course here for several reasons. First, it would amount to no more than a survey of the black-letter legal developments in each jurisdiction. Second, it would simply result in the description of judicial systems that are overwhelmingly Western in form, as is the case regarding the hierarchy of courts, the right of appeal, and the professional lawyers who represent litigants exactly as they would in the West. Finally, the *shari'a* appears to have minimal influence over statutes and codes of Western inspiration in practically all fields except matters of personal status. Instead of a jurisdiction-by-jurisdiction approach, therefore, this chapter examines the rule of law *lato sensu*, from the angle of the legal professions in the classical and modern age (Section II), to be followed by some comparative reflections in public and private law (Section III).

II. The Rule of Law in the Prism of the Legal Profession

Looking at the legal profession, or the ensemble of professions for which law is a full-time bread-winning activity, offers a particularly useful way to assess the rule of law in society. On the contemporary side, practical experience trumps any amount of scholarly writing. Books on the legal profession are even less common in Islamic countries than in European or American jurisdictions. While one occasionally finds memoirs by the odd lawyer or judge written in the 'life in the law' style, legal practice tends to be dwarfed by the political imprint of the author. On the classical side, in contrast, a unique Islamic genre known as *adab al-qadi* (literally manners, or literature, of the judge) features manuals left by judges that show how they viewed their job and exercised their responsibilities. One finds here an unusual paradox: more pointed material on the 'real' life of the law exists in the classical age than in the modern world.

1. The Classical Legacy

In order to ascertain patterns in the authority of the law as it operated in the classical age, we use here the manual for judges of Ibn Abi al-Dam, a judge (*qadi*) who lived in Syria from 583 to 642/1244, together with some material from the classical age as reflected in archival sources. We know little about the judge himself, but his book on *adab al-qadi* offers some remarkable comments on the profession.[8] The manual is particularly important in light of its extraordinary documentation speaking *against* the infamous image of *Kadi-Justiz*, which remains associated with an idea of 'Oriental despotism' dominant in the Western perception of the Islamic 'Middle Ages'.

'Oriental despotism', as it appears in Karl Wittfogel's seminal book,[9] describes societies where arbitrariness prevails due to a mode of economic production dominated by the scarcity of water. In these societies, the state assumes a dominant role which, in the end, destroys individual autonomy for the sake of organizing water resources. Wittfogel extends the concept far beyond the Middle East to encompass totalitarian states such as China and the then Soviet Union, but it is the original Near Eastern model of the 'hydraulic state' that stands at the core of his argument. Such absoluteness, steeped in the characteristic absence of the rule of law and the dominance of a behemoth state, mirrors Max Weber's image of the *qadi* dispensing arbitrary justice under the proverbial tree. Extant *qadi* manuals and archives of courts recently researched belie both negative images.

Ibn Abi al-Dam's manual is long and detailed. Conceived to guide both judges and lawyers, it covers the essentials a practitioner on the bench or on the court floor would need to know. This book, like others in the same vein,[10] offers a comprehensive image of the world of judges and litigants at the time. The exposé is eminently practical: 'What we have mentioned in this book is common in the court of the judges as between litigants. . .'. Although some of the issues are elusive and may be somewhat complicated for a modern reader, it is clear that the book was intended as an aid for practising jurists. It is divided into six long chapters which the author presents in the introduction to the work, and is interspersed with models and case studies covering the appointment of judges, court set-up, trials and procedures, the taking of testimony, relations among judges, and typical contracts and formularies. The outline of the book, presented in the introduction, is repeated at the end of Book 5:

This then is the concluding word on the nature of judgeship, the rules and art of judges, what they must do, what they may do, what is forbidden to them and what is abhorred, the rules of trial and evidence, the trial sessions and the conduct of litigation between the parties, testimonies and the like, judicial referrals from the sitting *qadi* to other judges.

---

[8] Muhammad 'Ata (ed), Shihab al-Din Ibn Abi al-Dam, *Kitab adab al-qada'* (1987). Full references are omitted in the present chapter, but detailed annotation can be found in Mallat, (2004) 52 *AJCL* 209, 233–40 (section on 'Qadi literature').

[9] Karl Wittfogel, *Oriental Despotism* (1957).

[10] See for instance the book by another famous Shafi'i, al-Mawardi (d. 450/1058), M. Sirhan (ed), *Adab al-qadi* (2 vols, 1971). Comprehensive *fiqh* treatises invariably include long books on *adab al-qadi*, for instance in vol 16 of Sarakhsi's (d. *c.*1090) *Mabsut* for the Hanafis (*Al-Mabsut* was published at the turn of the twentieth century in Cairo in 30 vols), and vol 14 of Muhammad Hasan al-Najafi (d. 1266/1849), *Jawahir al-kalam* (Beirut edn, 1992), for the Shi'i Ja'faris. (*Jawahir al-Kalam* published in 15 vols).

The book is eminently didactic. It is 'especially intended for the lawyers who have set themselves out to defend their clients', and it offers explanations on various 'common practical issues'. This focus is important. It shows that a specialization had occurred over the years, and that a 'profession' of legal counsel-representatives was alive and well at the time of Ibn Abi al-Dam. It also suggests that, at one point, lawyers constituted 'a profession' in classical Islam, though not a recognized 'corporation'. On the other hand, judgments we have from the eleventh/seventeenth-century Tripoli (Syria) court show that most litigation was carried out either by the parties themselves, or by family representatives, rather than by paid professional lawyers. This was also clearly the case in other parts of the Ottoman Empire, as substantiated by scholarship covering Turkish courts in the first part of the seventeenth century, but not in the Syria-Egypt of Ibn Abi al-Dam's thirteenth century.[11] Although this disparity calls for a reassessment of the ebb and flow in the advocacy profession through an immense stretch of Islamic/Middle Eastern history, Ibn Abi al-Dam's manual is nevertheless important for the wealth of material it offers the practitioner in terms of both procedure and substance.

It is actually possible to revise the whole field of Islamic law from the perspective of the practitioner as it appears in *qadi* literature, and this revision is supported by the emergence of a series of court reports which had until recently remained in closed or unknown archives.[12] In this literature, we find not only the natural intermingling of sources, a phenomenon not unique to the Islamic tradition though perhaps more pronounced there than elsewhere, but also delightful evidence of the social mores of the time, viewed in the context of court proceedings. For instance, we have in Ibn Abi al-Dam evidence of widespread lies in court, the taking of oaths by all kinds of people with various religious backgrounds, including those one would identify today as agnostics or atheists, and warnings from the judge against the propensity of court scribes to write at length. For all these problems, the judge tries to offer solutions.

This description of justice in the courtroom raises the question of how *Kadi-Justiz*[13] should be viewed in an age when people were convinced, with some legitimacy, that the rule and authority of the law in their world was far superior to that in any other conceivable contemporaneous society. A complete answer would require investigation into the state of adjudication in thirteenth-century China or India, but it is certain that Ibn Abi al-Dam did not give much thought to possible

---

[11] Ronald C. Jennings, 'The Office of Vekil (Wakil) in 17th century Ottoman Sharia Courts', (1975) 42 *Studia Islamica* 147–69.

[12] We have translated in full one of these judgments (n 6 at 213–15), 'The Franjiyyeh case', original Arabic in 'Umar Tadmuri, Frederic Ma'tuq and Khaled Ziadeh (eds), *Watha'eq al-mahkama al-shar'iyya bi-Tarablus* (Documents of the shar'i court of Tripoli, Lebanon, full facsimile of the 1666–7 register) (1982), 153.

[13] Max Weber, in Guenther Roth and Claus Wittich (eds), *Economy and Society* (1968), 976: '*Kadi*-justice knows no rational "rules of decision" whatsoever'.

examples from systems outside the boundaries of a Muslim world that was rather closely knit in terms of legal scholarship and interaction.

That provincialism, however, is not present in the world of modern-day *qadis*, whether they studied French law in Egypt, Morocco, or Lebanon, Egyptian or US law in the Gulf, or indeed just their traditional *fiqh* texts. Their societies have all come under severe scrutiny regarding the rule of law as perceived under today's standards, and they themselves know perfectly well what judicial review and a truly independent judiciary mean. Unlike Ibn Abi al-Dam, however, contemporary judges are understandably defensive about their own authority. In light of the systematic adversity endured under authoritarian governments across the Muslim world since national independence was achieved by most countries in the 1950s, a subdued profession of judges and lawyers keeps hauling the Sisyphian rock of the rule of law, while governments fight it directly, stonewall its decisions, stack the judicial system, or simply replace the rule of law with rule by law. It is telling that we do not have manuals such as Ibn Abi al-Dam's in the twentieth century. In the absence of such reflections from the bench, we shall now illustrate the fight for the rule of (Islamic) law on the contemporary scene from a legal practitioner's perspective.

2. The Contemporary Scene

In *Democracy and the Rule of Law*, a wide-ranging volume on the rule of law from a comparative and multi-disciplinary perspective, the editors concluded their introductory remarks by reflecting on '[t]he preconditions that make the rule of law possible'.[14] These include 'a functioning, independent judicial system [as] a key element in the maintenance of civil society and the possibility of non-military settlement of disputes'.[15] Although one might lose sight of this underlying truth, the judge is the main repository of adjudication, and this accounts for the centrality of 'the judge as metaphor' for the stability and fairness of all contemporary societies.[16] While the stability of some pre-modern societies does not necessarily conform to that metaphor—for instance, judges and courts seem far less important in pre-modern East Asia or Central Africa—this is not the case in the classical Arab-Muslim world where the importance of the judge, and the law in general, can hardly be doubted. Ibn Abi al-Dam's manual for judges and attorneys offers an important contrast to the everyday life of his successors in the modern Arab world.

The judge, as opposed to other legal professionals, is central in the Arab-Islamic tradition. Amongst the many professions connected in some way to the law—the

---

[14] Norman Dorsen and Prosser Gifford (eds), *Democracy and the Rule of Law* (2001), xv.

[15] Ibid.

[16] Chibli Mallat, *Democracy in America* (in Arabic, 2001), 147, developing a concept coined by Anthony Kronman.

main three being law teacher, lawyer, and judge—the metaphor of the judge is the most compelling because decision-making about matters of importance to parties in conflict rests with him. As Anthony Kronman has noted,

[T]he priority of the judicial form of dispute resolution is a function of the fact that it is judges who must ultimately define the authority that mediators, arbitrators, and special masters exercise—not the other way around—and so long as this remains true, judges and the work they do are bound to retain the position of dominant importance they have occupied in our [US] legal culture from the start.[17]

This is not unique to the American context. The judge as metaphor is a universal image, at least in civilizations where law is recognized as an autonomous, if not separate, discipline.

In reflecting on the better part of two decades of the rule of law in the Middle East, one must look past many false starts and discouraged hopes. Sobering conclusions must be drawn about the effectiveness of the judge and the court over which he presides as a means of keeping peace among litigants in the contemporary Muslim world. Looking at the 'noblest' dimension of judgeship—constitutional review—there is the disconcerting example of Egypt.

In 1980, for the first time in Egypt's history, a Supreme Constitutional Court began operating as an institution, with a recognizable leadership, serious case-law, and judicial checks on executive and legislative acts. At last, citizens were seeing some of their fundamental rights recognized and defended in court.

A quarter of a century later, accumulated case-law is now available. It testifies to a good day for the Supreme Constitutional Court. Unfortunately, the Court today acts less and less as a decisive voice in the Egyptian public place. In other countries in the region, the drive towards constitutional review has continued and expanded, but the latest experiment in establishing judicial review of laws under the constitution collapsed soon after it had begun in the mid-1990s in Lebanon.

Constitutional review has also been attempted in Iran and Israel, but the results have been equally disappointing. In the least known experiment, that of Iran, review of legislation and electoral processes, which had formally started in 1979, was undermined by the members of the Council of Guardians (*shura-ye negahban*, roughly equivalent to the French Constitutional Council) over the following two decades. The Council acted outside its proper authority to prevent a reformist president and Parliament from yielding to the popular demand for freedom and participation. The most recent victim of once high expectations is the Israeli Supreme Court, which has not only proved incapable of responding to legitimate demands for minimal protection by the non-Jewish minority in Israel, but has also managed to write *into law* the authoritarian behaviour of the executive branch in ways that neither international standards nor natural law can condone. Considering

---

[17] Anthony Kronman, *The Lost Lawyer* (1993), 317–18.

the decades-long battle between Palestinians and Israelis, this collapse does not come as a surprise, and few would be shocked by the retreat of law in the face of open and sometimes systematic violence on both sides.

Similar failures appear across the Arab and Muslim world. In Algeria, the Constitutional Council and the courts at large are meaningless in an environment of daily ruthlessness by both the military government and the Islamic extremist groups. In Yemen, the reliance on the judiciary collapsed after the civil war in 1994.

The name of the game has therefore been changed from the rule of law to rule by law, and the problem is not merely the undermining of constitutional review. Lack of independent judicial review operates at all levels, and it is mainly a function of a lack of free political representation. The disappointment in this area is strongest for rule-of-law advocates who have become frustrated that their call for democracy has gone unheeded. This was a universal call which they had hoped would extend throughout the Middle East after the collapse of the Berlin Wall and the democratization of many parts of the world.

Muslim states remain, by and large, notable exceptions to the rise of democracy across the planet. Beyond the understandable dejection resulting from the collapse of legal and democratic processes across the world of Islam, the loss of faith in the judiciary underlines the graver dimension of this downward trend. Hopes have been raised only to be betrayed, and the executive power has systematically and skilfully stacked the top judiciary with people whose allegiance is not to independence, but to their patrons. This has not been limited to public prosecutors or their equivalents in the various institutions constituting the criminal arm of the state. It extends to the supreme court judges within each jurisdiction and to judgeships down the ladder. Reversing that process may take years. Meanwhile, the authority of the law is undermined in its most 'central and decisive branch of the profession as a whole', judgeship.[18]

Undermined judges have so widely become the norm that the whole legal profession is forced to reconsider its bread-winning activities and its daily dedication in an existential manner. While faith in the authority and fairness of the law may re-emerge in response to the sudden courage of one court or the occasional heroic judge, the reality of arbitrariness and executive fiat is daunting. As a result, practitioners fight a disheartening (and so far losing) battle to protect the authority of the law, in the hope that one day a John Marshall-like judicial phoenix will rise. Such a figure will have to escape the safety nets devised by executive power, be it by stealth through the ruse of reason (see Hegel's *Philosophy of History*), or, also in a Hegelian metaphor, by the necessity of the 'rule of law-State', understood as the ultimate historical embodiment of the Spirit (see Hegel's *Philosophy of Law*).

Meanwhile, other soothing considerations operate to mitigate daily disappointments on a number of temporal and spatial lines. Some are monetary, when the

---

[18] Ibid 318.

use of law is managed to enhance the lawyer's financial well-being with some crafty commercial settlements. Some are geographic, both horizontal and vertical. Horizontally, loss of faith on the Egyptian stage, for example, is redeemed with a sudden opening in Bahrain, in Morocco, or even in Indonesia. This goes beyond the Muslim world. Since notions of universal jurisdiction have been pursued on the European and other Western stages, vindication of rights can also be sought in new contexts, such as in the International Criminal Court and other instances of universal jurisdiction, in an experience which is halting yet hopeful.

Vertically, the judiciary offers occasional successes to the cause of individual human rights. The successful fight for the right to a passport in Morocco, the failure of blasphemy cases in Yemen and Lebanon, the occasional check on the executive in Egypt, and the first *Katzir* ruling in Israel, all paint a judicial picture that is not entirely dark. In the first case, a plaintiff whose right to a passport had been stonewalled for years by the administration was vindicated by a decision of the Supreme Court.[19] In Yemen and Lebanon, courts were able to undermine complaints against authors and singers accused of blasphemy; with the result that, after years of harassment, the accused were deemed innocent.[20] In Egypt, the Court of Cassation eventually quashed the abusive jailing of the leading dissident Saadeddin Ibrahim, but only after he had spent two years in prison.[21] In Israel, the Supreme Court acknowledged the right of non-Jews to rent a flat in a compound owned, like 90 per cent of the land, by a Jewish public authority.[22] Unfortunately, these cases rarely become benchmarks, and the rule of law soon relapses to the ultimate discouragement of the legal profession as well as the public at large.

The rule of law often takes one step back for every two steps forward, but the pattern over the past four decades has more often been inverted, so that one step forward is followed by two steps back. Cycles being what they are, it is logically possible that a legal 'critical mass' might suddenly revitalize the rule of law in a given jurisdiction. Alternatively, and perhaps more likely, systematic degradation of the law and legal process may unleash violence. The resulting downward spiral could reach cataclysmic proportions, the harbingers of which one saw in Halabja, Iraq, on 16 March 1988, when some 5,000 villagers were gassed to death by their

---

[19] *Echemlal* case, Morrocan Supreme Court, 11 July 1985, reported in (1988) 20 *Revue Juridique Politique et Economique du Maroc* 42–3.

[20] In Yemen, *al-'Udi* case, Supreme Court, Criminal and Military division, 7 May 1992, reported in (1995) 2 *Islamic Law and Society* 87–91; in Lebanon, the singer Marcel Khalifeh was acquitted on 14 December 1999 of blasphemy for using passages from the Qur'an in a song. Full report carried by the daily *al-Nahar* (Beirut), 15 December 1999.

[21] Decision of the Egyptian Court of Cassation, 18 March 2003, dismissing accusations of using foreign funds to 'discredit the reputation of Egypt'. A comment on the case before that final decision can be found in Curtis Doebbler, 'The Rule of Law v. Staying in Power: *The State of Egypt v. Saad Eddin Mohammed Ibrahim*', (2001–2) 8 *Yearbook of Islamic and Middle Eastern Law* 353–63.

[22] Katzir (*Adel Qa'adan et al v Israel Land Authority et al*), High Court of Justice 6698/95.

own government, and in New York on 11 September, 2001, when militants claiming Islamic legitimacy killed 3,000 people in a blatant crime against humanity.

What might, in a brighter alternative, constitute a critical mass that would allow the rule of law to blossom? Looking at the failed cases and failed states of the recent and not-so-recent past, how is it possible to avoid disaster and secure those critical junctures where the machine of justice regularly breaks down?

As a rule of thumb, the elusive answer might best be sought in those countries where the rule of law functions reasonably well—for example, in the UK, Sweden, or New Zealand. There, the people lawyering *feel* that the adjudication of cases is based almost entirely on legal and judicial independence and fairness, with the remaining uncontrolled factors being 'politics', luck, quality of legal representation, and an 'X' factor, sometimes referred to as the 'length of the judge's foot'. In the Muslim world, by and large, the picture is exactly the opposite, with law *stricto sensu* comprising perhaps no more than 20 per cent of the factors underlying a judicial decision. The remaining factors are a combination of will-power, corruption, and executive intervention. When lawyers finally believe their cases will be decided more by law than by politics, then the threshold for confidence in the system will be close at hand. In the Middle East, we are far from that mid-range percentile. If British or French lawyers felt that half of their cases were decided mostly by politics, they would not feel proud of their 'rule of law' or 'Etat de droit' societies.

Another way of looking at law's authority considers the judge less as a metaphor than as a professional recruit. This perspective focuses on the judiciary's composition, education, and background, and these factors vary widely in the Islamic/Middle Eastern world. In most countries of the Middle East, the legal system follows a French model in which a career in the judiciary is embarked on early in life. The candidate attends a special magistrates' school between the ages of 25 and 30, and slowly ascends the ladder of judicial accomplishment and authority until retirement at around age 65. In Saudi Arabia, Iran, and Yemen, one finds this French system married to a strong reliance on the traditional *'ulama*, but the judiciary in all three countries is a mixture of the traditional and the 'modern'. Additionally, the ministries of justice tend to supplement the bench with appointees from outside the hierarchy of the French model, partly due to the lack of qualified people, but more disconcertingly in efforts to stack the courts with judges who have a particular political point of view. The result is a judiciary that is structurally flawed from a societal perspective. Joining the profession is not prestigious enough to attract the most qualified candidates because the judiciary is not perceived as being sufficiently independent from executive power. A critical criterion will be met in the Arab-Muslim world when the best lawyers begin actively seeking judicial appointments. Unlike Britain and the United States, where judicial positions stand as the crowning jewel in a legal career, few successful attorneys in the Arab-Muslim world are prepared to give up their legal practice for a position in the judiciary.

Perhaps the sole exceptions to this rule are the very top judicial positions—heads of cassation courts and constitutional councils as end-of-career honorific titles.

Alternatively, and until some more scientific indicators are developed, the rule of law can be gauged through the perception of the courts from the outside—from the perspective of the litigant and his or her lay surroundings. Ultimately, law produces a good, however intangible, which is 'justice' from a macroeconomic viewpoint, and 'the fair and firm settlement of a dispute' in a microeconomic perspective. In both cases, the 'judicial product' is an alternative to the sometimes violent self-help that would otherwise ensue.

The performance of that function—producing justice and hence peace—is deficient across the Arab-Muslim region. Naturally, this problem is not limited to the judiciary. All the branches of the legal profession—judges, lawyers, and law professors—are subject to various forms of degradation, and that degradation varies in intensity depending on the nature of the cases addressed. More demanding expectations operate on the higher level, which may be called 'constitutional' for short. Here the typical cases concern freedom of expression, fairness of the electoral process, accountability for abuse of power, protection of the marketplace from executive corruption (including confiscation of property and the forcing of commissions on state contracts), and finally, the accountability of top officials for war crimes and crimes against humanity. The quality of decisions reached in these cases varies considerably. The conclusions reached by George Sfeir in a comprehensive survey of Arab legal systems summarize the problem at hand:

If one were to apply Mellwin's criteria, that the essential quality of constitutionalism has been the legal limitation on government, the excessive authority of the Executive and the personality of power with which it is commonly identified represent, together with judicial review, the two main problems of constitutionalism in the Arab states.[23]

Worse, rule by law, rather than the rule of law, is increasingly the name of the game. The result is the manipulation of 'due process' to advance clearly illegitimate goals of government. Examples of rule by law run a wide gamut. Sometimes they seem trivial: a note under a hotel door signed by 'the secret services (*mukhabarat*)' asking the guest to vacate the room within two hours because it is needed for some high-level delegation visiting the country. Sometimes they are grave: the closure of a television station in Lebanon because it was alleged to have violated electoral advertising rules in a recent political campaign, concurrent with a decision of the Constitutional Council appointing a candidate who received 2 per cent of the vote to the parliamentary seat under dispute.

[23] George N. Sfeir, *Modernization of the Law in Arab States* (1998), 227.

III. Public and Private Law:
Select Comparative Issues

While the contemporary scene appears discouraging, the search for the rule of law and democracy continues. Decency in the public place as well as honest, courageous leaders—whether legal scholars, attorneys, or judges—are recognized and saluted. Assessment of these developments is best left to the sociologists and political scientists. We shall turn now to a survey of some of the important legal fields in public and private law.

The thread running through the following comparative argument—that 'Middle Eastern (or Islamic) law is distinct in terms of style'—derives from the classic *Introduction to Comparative Law* by Konrad Zweigert and Hein Kötz.[24] For this argument to hold, it must go beyond *Kadi-Justiz* and constitutional law to include contracts, torts, and family law. Before delving into these central private law disciplines, we need a brief review of administrative and criminal law, as well as procedure and property, from a comparative perspective.

Administrative law is an important element in the daily life of the citizen in any country. Across the Muslim world, a French-style administrative court is the rule. The lack of effective judicial checks on administrative courts makes their power overwhelming in modern-day Islam, and the fact that the state was a far more imposing factor for citizens in the heyday of classical Islam does not minimize the importance of this conclusion.

From a comparative perspective, Middle Eastern criminal law is both tedious in its straightforward copying of Western-style codes and elusive in terms of the exact interaction between traditional legal theories and contemporary societies. The recent revival by some excessive governments of classical law practices such as cutting off the thief's hand, beheading the murderer or rapist, and stoning an adulterer, is intolerable as well as untenable in any twenty-first-century society. Such practices have been resurrected as part of a provocative political message and, for that reason, it is difficult to make any constructive comments about them. Criminal law is important and may be more alluring than other legal fields from a historical perspective, especially with respect to countries that continue to apply tribal or communal traditions. However, the field is understudied, and sociological and anthropological work may well produce more interesting and informative results than purely legal study. All in all, there is too little by way of an 'Islamic/Middle Eastern style' in contemporary criminal law to warrant a more developed discussion.

---

[24] First German edn (vol 1, 1969, vol 2, 1971). English translation by Tony Weir at Oxford University Press, in two volumes, later in one, starting 1992.

Understanding procedure requires considerable practical experience with a number of legal systems across the Muslim world. A collaborative effort at the bar association or university level may someday flesh out this important subject but, at present, it is difficult to draw any conclusions or propose any theories about the character of legal procedure in the Muslim world.

Property law also demands practical experience because the law as it appears in the statutes is quite different from the law as it is applied in everyday life. One characteristic found in many Middle Eastern countries is the dominant position of the Cadastre (Arabic *sijill ʿiqari*). The Cadastre derives from an Australian system developed around 1860 to scientifically map the newly colonized continent. It was slowly introduced in the Near and Middle East to bring stability and order to legal ownership of land and has no known antecedent in the laws of the region.

Turning now to three core legal disciplines, we shall examine the degree to which a specific Islamic/Middle Eastern style can be identified from a comparative perspective in constitutional law, obligations arising from contracts and torts, and family law.

1. Constitutions: Personal versus Territorial Models

Since 1992, all countries in the modern Muslim world, including the Kingdom of Saudi Arabia, have adopted constitutions or basic laws. Useful comparisons regarding the place of Islam in these constitutions were recently carried out, especially with regard to such basic questions as 'the reference to Islam in the constitutional text'.[25] When looking at comparative public law, it is more interesting to compare the Westphalian 'territorial model' of nation-states with what we can describe as the Islamic 'personal model', in which the application of law to an individual depends more on membership in a given religious sect than on citizenship in a nationally defined territory. The system of nation-states is well entrenched in all Muslim countries with sizeable Muslim populations, but it does not function well. Here, comparative law yields a powerful contrast: the overarching system of Islamic law as a 'personal model' versus the dominant system of Western law described as a 'territorial model'.

Although this distinction became fashionable after the publication of Samuel Huntington's *Clash of Civilizations* (1996), it requires an initial caveat: the comparison is uneven by nature, especially for lawyers. The depiction of a clash between two world patterns may have broad-brush merits, but it breaks down when we look

---

[25] United States Commission on International Religious Freedom, *The Religion-State Relationship and the Right to Freedom of Religion or Belief: A Comparative Textual Analysis of the Constitutions of Predominantly Muslim Countries*, released 8 March 2005, available on the Commission's website, <http://www.uscirf.gov/countries/global/comparative_constitutions> (last visited April 2005).

at the details. In the first place, the concept of civilization is vague. Second, Islamic law is based in a religion and several countries with a Muslim majority seem to have little in common despite a shared religion. Third, while the dominant subject on the international scene remains the nation-state, Tunisia, Nigeria, and Indonesia hardly appear as a common legal bloc. Conversely, 'Western civilization' is rarely defined in terms of religion, even though the concept of 'a Judaeo-Christian culture' has been stretched considerably since Nietzsche's devastating critiques in *Genealogy of Morals* (1887) and *Beyond Good and Evil* (1886).

That said, law in the modern nation-state is eminently territorial: within a country's boundaries, there is one legal system that is, by definition, exclusive. All citizens in the state are bound by that system, and they become bound by the system of an adjacent country as soon as they cross an international border. In contrast, the classical divide in Islamic law between *dar al-harb* and *dar al-silm* or *dar al-islam*—the war territory as opposed to the peace territory—creates relationships and obligations that tend to be far more personal than territorial. Thus, a citizen's legal relationships follow her wherever she goes. While this is not completely unknown to an American or a French national who may, for example, be bound by the tax laws of her country anywhere in the world, personal law is not the dominant consideration when travelling abroad.

While this sort of generalization may seem trite or over-broad, it is valid and useful as it relates to the issue of personal law versus territorial law in the context of a typical Middle Eastern constitutional system and arguably beyond as in Pakistan, India, Malaysia, and now Europe (because of the emerging and self-defining Muslim communities there). This issue may also be framed as communitarian versus territorial federalism and it is at the root of the difficulty confronting nation-states in the Muslim world. Three pressing constitutional examples from the beginning of the twenty-first century illustrate the difficulties surrounding this issue.

Lebanon is a good example with which to begin. Its population is divided more or less evenly between Christians and Muslims. The Lebanese Constitution, originally passed in 1926, is now the dean of the constitutions in the region. Its longevity is due in part to its recognition and formalization of an important structural characteristic of Lebanese society derogatorily known as sectarianism or communitarianism (*confessionalisme* in French, *ta'ifiyya* in Arabic). It often appears in the political science literature as 'consociationalism' and describes a relationship between the citizen and the state that is not an immediate or direct one; it is filtered, or mediated, by the citizen's community. In Lebanon, eighteen or so sects make up the country resulting in a complicated set of constituencies. These may be simplified by considering a general line separating Muslims and Christians and, further, the no less powerful lines separating Muslim Sunnis, Muslim Shi'is, and Christian Maronites, the three larger communities in the country. In this setting, communitarian privilege derives from the personal scheme harking to the *shari'a* as the millennium-guiding model: a person is Muslim or Christian or Jewish before she is

Lebanese, French, or Saudi. The great historian of tenth- to thirteenth-century Egypt, Samuel Goitein, describes this model as 'medieval religious democracy ... Law in those days was personal rather than territorial'.[26]

Although communitarianism is at odds with the concept of the equality of citizens as individuals, it can be viewed as a positive step toward the Western goal of individualized justice. However frustrating to the Western constitutionalist, one should approach communitarianism *positively*. As in Egypt or Morocco in the classical age, the system in Lebanon is not necessarily inappropriate; people who question it may find reasons to reconsider it in the worldwide debate over the emerging Iraqi Constitution. It is a correct assumption, widely held and well-founded, that the government in Iraq cannot be stable (ie fair) if the Sunni community is not represented in the decision-making process. This is actually the Lebanese constitutional litmus test: regardless of how a community may be perceived, it nevertheless retains its constitutional right to be represented in government. Nor is this concept exclusively Lebanese. It has deep roots in the Near East. In Karl Marx's words, the puzzling nature of Near or Middle Eastern history is that it has always taken the *appearance* of religion.[27] The Lebanese Constitution thus offers a blueprint of the personal, as opposed to the territorial, model for the rest of the region.

It may not be out of place to discuss Palestine and Israel as a *negative* counter-example. In Israel, a discrete, insular, and historically victimized minority of Israeli Arabs, representing a fifth of the population, has never had significant executive representation in Israel's government. Under a Lebanese-style constitution, non-Jewish Israelis would be entitled to five central cabinet posts out of twenty. The issue of legal protection and representation for the indigenous Palestinian (mainly Muslim) community, which lies at the root of a century-old conflict, is the same issue facing Christians and Muslims in Lebanon, or Shi'is and Sunnis in Iraq, except that the two groups in Israel are Jews and non-Jews. In the legal and sociological study of Israel, 'Jewishness' is deemed to be the defining characteristic of the country, in the same way that 'Muslimness' would be emphasized in Iran or Pakistan. Because of the obvious historic legacy of the Holocaust, this is an issue that is overwhelmingly seen as the essence of Israel as a state.

Throughout the history of the State of Israel, the central legal question has always been: 'Who is a Jew?' It figures prominently in the current debate regarding the latest waves of immigrants from Ethiopia and Russia and, for Christians and Muslims directly affected by the emergence of Israel, it is central because its answer, by definition, places them outside the legal order of a state defined by its Jewishness.

---

[26] S. D. Goitein, *A Mediterranean Society: The Jewish Communities of the Arab World as Portrayed in the Documents of the Cairo Geniza* (5 vols, 1967–85), vol 2, *The Community* (1971), 5, 2.

[27] Letter to Friedrich Engels, 2 June 1855, cited in Mallat, 'Du fait religieux dans les institutions', in Mallat (ed), *L'Union Européenne et le Moyen-Orient: Etat des lieux* (2004), 83.

In particular, three groups of non-Jews have been impacted by this structural discrimination. First, those who were evicted from their homes when Israel was formed, and never allowed to return, simply do not exist in the eyes of Israeli law. They are the refugees of 1948, defined by Israeli law as perpetual and irrevocable 'absentees'. Second, those who were subjected to occupation beginning in 1967 have experienced a four-decade long domination coupled with slow and relentless expropriation of their land. And third, there is the one-tenth of the native population that was not evicted in 1948. These 'Israeli Arabs' (or, more properly, 'Palestinian Israelis') grew to number about a million by the turn of the twenty-first century. While their constitutional participation is guaranteed by an absolute right to vote, the Jewishness of the State of Israel has meant that their participation in the government or judiciary has remained tightly constrained by a combination of harsh legal rules and overt discrimination.

One now better understands Lebanon's constitutional structure as defining what might be called a 'counterconstitutional' model, that is, counter to the one dominant in the West since Montesquieu and the *Federalist Papers*. In the spring of 2001, drafts of the 1926 Lebanese Constitution were released, and they are sobering. Two texts stand in apparent contradiction. In Art 7 of the draft constitution, all citizens are declared equal, just as would be expected in any Western country. In Art 95, however, the communities are designated as legal agents or intermediaries for those very citizens. This has not changed almost a century later, except that the present Art 95 has established parity between Christians and Muslims in Parliament, moving away from multiples of the six–five formula (six Christians to five Muslim MPs) that prevailed until the so-called Taef Agreement in 1989 and the Amendments which that Agreement introduced in the text of the Constitution a year later.

In fact, Lebanese constitutionalism predates 1926. The earliest extant prototype of the Lebanese Constitution, a text that goes back to 1836, established municipal councils, that is, representation plus executive power, in the major cities (then Sidon and less prominently Beirut), on the basis of parity between the number of Christian and Muslim councilmen. By any historical measure, parity in representation between Muslims and Christians from 1836 to 2005 is significant, but that model may also be seen in the so-called Ottoman Millet system, which is itself rooted in the medieval religious democracy portrayed by Goitein. Therefore, any effort to enhance individual equality by jettisoning communitarianism may be both unwarranted and impracticable, regardless of any advantages it may offer.

Federalism offers one way forward, as may be seen in Muslim countries such as Nigeria and Malaysia where the federal model has increasingly taken root. The problem is that federalism, at least as it has been implemented to date, is inevitably territorial. For instance, in the United States, with federalism following territory (and history), one has senators from Rhode Island and California coexisting happily as equals. California uses the fact that it has a greater population to disadvantage Rhode Island in other ways, but the territorial model remains the rule. When it comes to the executive branch, the majority of votes tends to bring the person chosen by the majority of people to the presidency, with individual Californians and Rhode Islanders counting almost equally at the polls.

At this point, the challenge of adapting federalism as it appears in Western democracies to Middle Eastern communitarian states becomes clear. Federalism, to be meaningful, would have to allow corrective representation of communities standing in lieu of states, and this is by and large a non-territorial scheme.

It is also a difficult scheme to implement. Populations are interwoven and people move about. While a majority may dominate a given territory, cities and the trend towards urbanization, a universal sociological trait by the end of the twentieth century, tend to blur the boundaries between groups. Rarely if ever is there territorial 'purity', and this compounds the problem because communitarian federalism requires territories that are homogeneous. Homogeneous territories are not readily available in most of the Muslim world, and when they are, it may be the result of forms of ethnic cleansing that no one wants to validate in law. Even when territories appear to be homogeneous in terms of their population, they are subject to shifting or fluid borders, as one can see at the turn of the twenty-first century in Kirkuk between Arab and Kurdish Iraqis, in Jerusalem between Jews and non-Jews (or Israelis and Palestinians, or Muslims and non-Muslims), and in Southern Beirut between Shi'i and non-Shi'i Lebanese.

The central problem for federalism in Iraq, Lebanon, or Israel is also thornier than elsewhere in the world. The issue tends not to be separation of powers in three branches of government, but the fight in the centre over executive power. Executive power is a difficult issue by nature. As Robespierre noted 200 years ago, you cannot have executive power if you have only part of it. Executive power requires, by definition, one chief executive chosen by universal suffrage; one chief executive whose power to rule is granted by the majority.

There is no readily available answer to this conundrum, although various possible solutions, such as the presidential triumvirate of Iraq that emerged in 2004, are being examined and tested. Such power-sharing solutions tend to become bewildering and unduly complex for the pervasive quotas they encourage, and multi-religious and multi-ethnic mosaics should not be allowed to cloud one's moral principles on basic equality among citizens. The problem is the essential dualism of the region. To put the issue simply, it appears that each individual's allegiance in all the countries of the Muslim world is dual in law. A person operates nationally, as a constitutional citizen in a Habermas way, but also relates to public affairs through religious or sectarian affiliation, which makes the (religious) community a constitutional agent recognized in law.

For the Muslim world, bringing the two allegiances together into one functional framework is the challenge of constitutionalism for the twenty-first century.

2. Contracts and Torts: Defining an Islamic Style

Like many pre-modern legal systems, classical Islamic law did not include a comprehensive theory of obligations and contracts. The formation of the law as a distinct discipline, with the rise of the long treatises of *fiqh* after the ninth century in a common-law style of jurisprudential accretions, meant that a comprehensive system had to wait for the modern period. Only in the middle of the twentieth century did individual authors from Egypt and the Levant (notably ʿAbdul-Razzaq al-Sanhuri, d. 1971, and Subhi Mahmasani, d. 1986) develop an integrated theory of obligations and contracts in well-constructed treatises.[28] This coincided with or followed the effective codification of the law of contracts, some of it in the form of private restatements, but most by legislation. The codification of the law of obligations was achieved in most countries in the late nineteenth and early twentieth centuries.

A decisive change in the legal systems of the Muslim world took place when the expansion of colonial rule spread the French Napoleonic Code through the world. At that time, the Muslim tradition, then vesting in the Ottoman Empire and to a lesser extent in Persia (later Iran), began seriously to consider the codification of the law of obligations.

The result was the celebrated *Majalla* (Ottoman *Mecelle*), enacted between 1869 and 1876, which in turn became the model for widespread codification of the law of contracts in the Muslim world. Codification of the Islamic law of obligations then took place in North Africa (Tunisian *Majalla* of 1906, Moroccan Code of 1912) and in the private compilations of the Egyptian scholar Muhammad Qadri Basha (flourished late nineteenth century) and his Saudi colleague Ahmad ibn ʿAbd Allah al-Qari (d. 1940). In Iran, a similar process, completed in the mid-1930s, produced the Iranian Civil Code. In other countries of the Muslim world, especially in those under British or Dutch influence (India, Pakistan, Indonesia), legislation was more piecemeal and tended to be less attentive to the Islamic legacy.

Another major phase of the codification of the law of contracts was completed when the Egyptian Civil Code was enacted in 1949, under the impressive editorship of ʿAbd al-Razzaq al-Sanhuri. The Egyptian Civil Code was the model for the Syrian, Kuwaiti, and Libyan contract codes. In Egypt, Sanhuri was careful to incorporate both *fiqh* principles and Egyptian case-law precedents, but the language he and his fellow drafters used featured a comparative element that diluted the more classical terminology of the Ottoman *Majalla*. Later civil codes (in Jordan, a new code was passed in 1976; in Kuwait in 1980; in the United Arab Emirates in 1985; and in the unified Yemen in 1990) paid more attention to *fiqh* terminology, following the Iraqi

---

[28] ʿAbd al-Razzaq al-Sanhuri, *Masader al-haqq fil-fiqh al-islami* (Sources of law in Islamic *fiqh*), (6 vols, 1954–9); Subhi Mahmasani, *Al-Nazariyya al-ʿamma lil-mujibat wal-ʿuqud fish-shariʿa al-islamiyya* (General theory of obligations and contracts) (2 vols, 1948).

Civil Code of 1953, which appeared to be a compromise between Sanhuri's code and the *Majalla*. There are jurisdictions such as Saudi Arabia where a unified civil code has not yet been enacted and the law must still be ascertained in light of the common law represented by classical *fiqh*. However, most countries have preferred the simplicity of an integrated text for the law of obligations and contracts.

This area has been the locus of the most heated debate over the comparative dimension of positive law in the modern Islamic/Middle Eastern world, and it continues to incite polemics across the region. Before the Civil Code, the Ottoman *Majalla* had successfully combined the format of the Napoleonic codes with both the structure and vocabulary of classical Islamic law. Despite declared efforts by Sanhuri that 'we did not leave a single sound provision of the *shari'a* which we could have included in this legislation without doing so',[29] the Civil Code of Egypt has been repeatedly attacked for its alleged ignorance of the classical Islamic law of obligations. Recent scholarship ranges from support for the view that the Code is generally 'not Islamic'[30] to a reading of the corpus as hybrid, and even eclectic.[31] Sanhuri himself does not deny this eclecticism. In fact, he declared the need for Egyptian law to rise to universalism 'in order to pay its own tribute to humanity for the advancement of law in the world, that is what the doctrine calls comparative law'.[32] Our own conclusion on this never-ending debate regarding the debt of the Egyptian (and many other Arab) codes to Islamic law highlights vocabulary and structure over substance. The codifiers of the *Majalla* were far more interested in their own tradition as Islamic lawyers than in any foreign system. Sanhuri's scholarly upbringing, on the other hand, was wider, but his enrichment of the Code with foreign and comparative material diluted the Islamic flavour that might otherwise have been evident in its arrangement and terminology.[33]

What are the rules of obligations in the Islamic tradition? In the classical system, the general law of a contract falls under the twin headings of Qur'anic injunctions and *fiqh* principles. Qur'anic injunctions require contracts to be entered into and applied in good faith, to be preferably in writing, and to avoid including *riba* (interest, usury, though the definition of *riba* remains controversial to date). At

---

[29] From *al-Qanun al-madani: Majmu'at al-a'mal al-tahdiriyya* ([Egyptian] Civil Code, collection of preparatory works) (1950), i, 20, cited in Norman Anderson, *Law Reform in the Muslim World* (1976), 83.

[30] Bernard Botiveau, *Loi Islamique et Droit dans les Sociétés Arabes* (1993), 150.

[31] Kilian Bälz, 'Europäisches Privatrecht jenseits von Europa? Zum fünfzigjährigen Jubiläum des ägyptischen Zivilgesetzbuchs (1948)', (2000) *Zeitschrift für Europäisches Privatrecht* 51–76; Amr Shalakany, 'Sanhuri and the Historical Origins of Comparative Law in the Arab World', in Annelise Riles (ed), *Rethinking the Masters of Comparative Law*, (2001), 152.

[32] 'Abd al-Razzaq al-Sanhuri, *Al-Wasit fi sharh al-qanun al-madani al-jadid* (Middle-length [in fact extensive] commentary of the new Civil Code) (10 books in 12 vols, 1952–70), vol i, *ha'* (page 'e' or 5 in Arabic), citing another book of his on 'the theory of contract' (*nazariyyat al-'aqd*), published in 1934.

[33] Developed in Mallat, *Droit Civil au Moyen-Orient: Essai de Théorie Générale* (forthcoming).

best, the principles of contract law in the Qur'an are sketchy. The classical law of obligations as developed in the jurists' work was elaborated upon over the subsequent centuries in the texts that form the large corpus of *fiqh*. There is, however, no book devoted to contracts in general in the great treatises of *fiqh*. The core model is the contract of sale, upon which a number of other less important contracts are modelled. While these are sometimes discussed in minute detail, they lack the clear sense of structure required by the modern age. Contractual models can also be found in the literature of *shurut* (literally, 'conditions'). *Shurut* are legal formulas developed by notary-publics and judges. They varied over time and geographical area and were followed by judges and legal specialists in the course of their practices.

The place of the Islamic legal tradition in the modern period becomes evident in the survival of some of its more specific rules of contract. For instance, Article 3 of the Ottoman *Majalla* specifies that 'in matter of contract, intention and meaning have priority over wording and syntax'. This establishes the importance of intent over formal expression, and it is derived from a saying ascribed to the Prophet that acts derive from intent. Similarly, many jurisdictions in the Middle East have introduced the principle of the unity of *majlis al-ʿaqd* ('the contractual session'), which classical jurists define as an integrated session of negotiation for the contract, limited in time and place. The theory is described by the Hanafi jurist Kasani (d. AH 587/1191 CE) as 'offer and acceptance in the same session: if the session varies, the contract does not take place'.[34] While the term is common in several modern Muslim jurisdictions, contracts on future things and variations on the obligations in more complex cases have forced some flexibility on both the codes and the courts alike.

Contracts, when valid, are binding. Flaws of form and consent are known in Islamic law and their treatment does not differ in any major way from the civil and common law systems. Some tenets of the classical theory have been revived to allow revision of a contract when some of the obligations have become too onerous on one of the parties. This principle has been formalized in several codes, notably in Egypt and Iraq, but revision of a contract that has become too onerous on the debtor has been generally restricted in the decisions of contemporary Muslim jurisdictions.

The law of torts offers a useful illustration of modern law's failure to bring the traditional and the modern together.

There is a significant difference in the comparative genesis of contracts and torts. The law of contracts, even if only recently systematized, is readily identifiable in classical works where it is elaborated upon with great sophistication and acumen by the jurists of the high classical age. In the modern Islamic world of contract law,

---

[34] ʿAlaʾ al-Din al-Kasani (d.1191), *Badaʾeʿ al-sanaʾeʿ fi tartib al-sharaʾeʿ* (7 vols, Cairo edn, 1328/1910), vol 5, 136.

these jurists' successors have managed to bridge the gap in legislation, in doctrine, and in the court. While some efforts have been more successful'than others, the law as found in the *Majalla* and its equivalents across the Muslim world offers the best example of a genuine achievement in terms of preserving the classical *acquis* while adapting it for application in the modern world. Where codification was less successful in a country like Egypt for the *aggiornamento* of classical law, it was more an issue of style than of content.

In a field such as torts, however, the gap between the classical and the modern is structurally resistant to adaptation. Just as there was no theory of contracts in classical Islamic law, there was no readily recognizable theory of torts. But the problem is not one of systematization and there is a comprehensive compendium of torts written by one classical author.[35] The problem is that compensation resulting from a tort is not treated as *sui generis* in classical law. The victim of a tort is entitled to compensation much as the debtor is entitled to compensation as the victim of the other party's breach of the contract. The principle is that 'any tort must be compensated'.[36] This prevents the operation of negligence as found in the common law system, or *faute* in the civil law system. The victim is entitled to compensation on a strict liability basis, irrespective of the other party's negligence or fault.

Some codes sought to incorporate the classical system and one will find an attempt to include the *shari'a*'s tort system in the Civil Code of Jordan. Article 256 establishes the principle of no-fault liability: 'Any damage caused to another engages the responsibility of its author, irrespective of discernment'. The problem is that courts are unwilling to apply that principle because judges remain attached to the concept of '*faute*'. In a recent decision of the Cassation Court in Jordan, the application of the no-fault system recognized in principle by the Code was simply rejected: 'Responsibility in tort rests on three pillars: fault, damage and the causality relation between the fault and the damage'.[37] This formulation is typical of a jurist imbued by the celebrated interpretation of Art 1382 of the French Civil Code.

3. Family Law: The Search for Gender Equality

Family law is best understood from the point of view of legislative reform and the position of women in the legal system. Mirroring what Alexis de Tocqueville called

---

[35] Abu Muhammad al-Baghdadi (eleventh century), *Majma' al-damanat* (Compendium of torts) (1987).

[36] *al-darar yuzal*, Ottoman *Majalla* art 20.

[37] Jordanian Court of Cassation, decisions of 16 May 1987 and of 28 May 1988, reported in *Naqabat al-muhamin* (Bar association), *al-Mabade' al-qanuniyya li-mahkamat al-tamyiz, mundhu bidayat sanat 1989 hatta nihayat sanat 1991* (Judicial principles of the Court of Cassation, from the beginning of 1989 to the end of 1991), vol 7, ii, 1000 and 1007 respectively.

the 'age of equality', the development of family law across the Muslim world has been driven by legislative efforts to increase equality between men and women, set against an overwhelmingly non-egalitarian classical age.

Like most other pre-modern societies, the classical Islamic age was fundamentally impervious to gender equality. Classical law systematically relegated women to a status we perceive nowadays as inferior or secondary to men. In most family-related laws, a woman was entitled to only a fraction of the rights recognized for her male counterpart. What follows is a discussion of the central rights pertaining to women that are addressed in classical law.

Marriage

Only the woman who has reached majority and has already been married (that is, divorced or widowed) can get married without first 'consulting' her guardian. In most other cases, the male guardian chooses for her, and he may 'overcome' any resistance she has to his choice.

The Muslim husband can take up to four wives and can marry a non-Muslim woman belonging to one of the other world religions. The Muslim woman can only marry or be married to one man, and he must be Muslim.

While married, the wife owes obedience to her husband. If she violates one or more of the numerous duties that apply to wives, she is placed in the penalized position of disobedience, *nushuz*. *Nushuz* is exclusively associated with women.

Termination of marriage

In the law of separation, repudiation, *talaq*, is the prerogative of the husband. This is a unilateral right which is not granted to the wife.

Upon termination of marriage, classical Islamic law does not recognize 'alimony' or 'ancillary relief' as an entitlement of the repudiated or divorced wife. Under classical law, the end of marriage stops any payment of maintenance to the wife by the husband in the absence of children. When there are children, any money which the husband may pay to his divorced wife is directly connected to her status as caretaker of the broken marriage's children. Although the right to 'ancillary relief' does not strictly pertain to the sphere of equality, it has become a key indicator of women's rights in contemporary Muslim societies.

Custody

Custody of a child is entrusted to either the mother or father, depending on age and sex. Young children tend to be placed in the mother's care, but the father takes custody of them when they reach a given age. The father has an overall right to guide the child's education as he is considered 'the head' of the family and its ultimate guardian, even after divorce. There is therefore a difference between custody and guardianship, and the father is invariably the guardian of the child after separation, even if the mother is granted the right to custody up to a certain age.

Succession

The law of succession is characterized by a few cardinal principles. The first principle governs *ab intestatio* inheritance through a refined and complex system of arithmetic equations derived from the Qur'an. According to those equations, women—whether wives, mothers, or daughters—receive half of the share prescribed for the corresponding men in the family structure (husbands, fathers, sons). The relevant formula is repeated twice in the Qur'an: 'To the male twice the share of the female'.[38]

Upon the death of the husband, in the simplest figures, the surviving wife receives one-quarter of the estate if there are no children, and one-eighth if there are. Upon the death of the wife, the husband receives one-half and one-quarter in the corresponding scheme. In the presence of a brother, the daughter never receives more than half of his share. The share of father and mother is more complicated, but the mother never receives more than her husband's share in Sunni law, though there are cases when she might inherit the same amount he does.

The second principle, 'no will for more than one third of the estate',[39] means that *ab intestatio* inheritance governs at least two-thirds of the deceased's property.

The third cardinal principle, which is limited to Sunnis, prohibits a will in favour of an heir receiving a share in the estate under the following rule: 'No bequest in favour of an heir'.[40] The combination of these limitations on free wills and the rigid system of *ab intestatio* rules renders variations of the Qur'anic rules of succession extremely limited.

At this very general level, Shi'i law includes an important variation on the Sunni system. In the Sunni law of succession, the importance of *'asaba*, or male agnates, is paramount. This concept, arguably a calque of the Syro-Roman Code of the fifth century of the Christian Era, stands in contrast to an equally ancient Persian legacy. That legacy seems to be at the root of the Shi'i rejection of the agnates as the repository of succession law. Sunni law establishes the entitlement of the male kin, however distant from the deceased, to such part of the estate as might not have been distributed under the Qur'anic shares. This portion can be significant,[41] and it is crucial for inheritance when considered from the perspective of equality between men and women.

The Sunni principle of 'the remainder to the agnates' is bluntly rejected in Shi'i law by the rule of 'nothing to the agnates', which is 'graphically expressed

---

[38] Qur'an, iv, 11; iv, 176.

[39] '*Al-wasiyya bith-thulth, wal-thulth kathir* (and the third is too much)'. Bukhari (d. 256/870), *Sahih* (9 vols, Cairo edn, 1376 AH), iv, 4.

[40] *La wasiyya li-warith*. Ibid.

[41] In an extreme instance, a man dies leaving his wife and a distant cousin on the male side of the family. The widow gets one-eighth and the cousin the remaining seven-eighths. For examples and further illustrations, including on the influence of ancient Syro-Roman and Persian legal systems, see Mallat, (2003) 51 *AJCL* 708 ff.

in the dictum of the Shi'i *Imam* Ja'far al-Sadeq (d. 147/165): 'As for the *'asaba* (the agnates), dust in their teeth'.[42] The consequences can be significant, as the Shi'i system can turn out to be much more favourable to a daughter than the Sunni system. For instance, if a deceased father leaves one daughter and no son, the Shi'i system allows her, as the father's closest kin, to receive his entire estate. The Sunni system, on the other hand, restricts the daughter's share to the portion established in the Qur'an—one-half. The remainder goes to the nearest male kin. So if the deceased is survived by an agnatic uncle or cousin, however distant, the remaining half goes in its entirety to that relative. There is no way for the Sunni father to increase his daughter's share by will because of the second and third principles mentioned above (no bequest to an heir, and no bequest for more than a third). The difference between the two systems has prompted a number of *causes célèbres* in which prominent male Muslims changed their allegiance from Sunni to Shi'i law in order to take advantage of the Shi'i inheritance rules.

It is important to note that this advantage in Shi'i succession law only marginally advances the cause of gender equality because it applies only in the absence of a son. Whether in Sunni or Shi'i law, if the daughter has a brother, the Qur'anic rule of half the share applies so that she receives merely half of what her brother inherits. Thus, in both Shi'i and Sunni law, the woman (daughter, sister, wife, or mother) tends to receive less than her counterpart on the male side of the family.

Variations in the law of succession can lead to further systemic inequalities. This occurs most notably in the *mut'a* or temporary marriage for the Shi'is, and the slave law of the classical age, which introduces elements of unequal treatment between the male and female slaves. If slavery as a legal category has all but disappeared in the twenty-first century, temporary marriage, an institution open to men only, is still known in a large country like Shi'i Iran. It allows a married or single man to contract *mut'a* for a stipulated amount of time—it could be several years or a few hours—with any number of women he may wish. Once the 'contractual time' has lapsed, the *mut'a* marriage is automatically dissolved. A married woman cannot contract *mut'a*, and, in theory, a virgin woman who is single is also barred from contracting *mut'a*.

Overall, the woman is clearly disadvantaged at law. None the less, it should be noted that the absence of equality can actually benefit married women in two fairly narrow respects. The first benefit involves the payment of the dowry on the occasion of or after the marriage. Unlike the 'Western' dower (which the wife brings

---

[42] Al-Hurr al-'Amili (d. 1104/1693), *Wasa'el al-Shi'a*, xxvi, 85 (*al-mal lil-aqrab wal-'asaba fi fihi al-turab*: property to the closest relative, and dust in the mouth of the agnates).

from her family property upon marriage), the *mahr*, the sum of money paid by the bridegroom to his wife upon marriage, is owed by the husband to his wife. In return, there is no dower owed by the wife to the husband. The second benefit arises from the husband's duty to provide maintenance and non-monetary forms of protection during marriage. A husband is required to pay his wife's usual expenses as well as those of the household as a whole. Even if the wife has considerable means, the classical age did not impose on her any duty of reciprocal treatment towards her husband. These 'benefits' are another illustration of the difference between the classical and modern outlooks. Again, we must guard against projecting our contemporary notions of gender equality backwards into the past.

The rise of women's awareness and their struggle for equal rights has forced the legal system to take into account the demands of 'the age of equality' for men and women, and both legislation and the courts have tried, with varying degrees of success, to close the legal gender gap. Codification of family law started towards the end of World War I and continues to date. The pattern of reform, with little variation, has affected the core of the rights discussed above without confronting the issue head-on with a principle of equality. While men and women are sometimes formally declared equal, in constitutions or in family acts, the core principles and institutions of the classical age are never formally jettisoned. Even in exceptional instances such as the family code of South Yemen during its 'socialist egalitarian' period, family law retained the hallmarks of the classical inegalitarian system.

The current reform effort can be illustrated, in matters of marriage, divorce, and custody, by the latest such effort, enacted in Morocco in 2004. This reform consists of a list of amendments to the family code of Morocco known as the *Mudawwana*. Here, the central rights of classical law have been modified as follows.

Marriage

Women and men are 'consecrated' equal in the law, and the family is placed 'under the joint responsibility of the spouses'. The age of marriage for women is raised to 18, which makes male guardian control over them inapplicable. 'Obedience' to husbands is no longer required, so *nushuz* becomes irrelevant. Polygamy remains possible in theory, but it is subject to so many procedural constraints that it becomes extremely difficult in practice. The first wife can make it a condition of her marriage that the husband shall not marry another wife, and both the first and a subsequent wife must be informed about the polygamous situation. Their express assent is required for the husband to get married again. In addition, a judge oversees the capacity of the husband to be 'fair' to his wives and to the children of a subsequent marriage, should the husband contract several marriages with the consent of all the wives. As a consequence, polygamy is both discouraged and controlled. In Morocco, as in other Muslim countries, it has therefore become rare.

Termination of marriage

Repudiation, *talaq*, gives the right to divorce to both spouses, and repudiation can no longer be exercised unilaterally. In addition, repudiation can no longer be made verbally and must take place under the control of a judge. Dissolution of marriage is made possible for the two spouses by the 2004 Amendments, again under judicial control.

Upon termination of marriage, the judge is asked to control the distribution of assets in a way that takes into account the rights of the divorced woman. While 'alimony' is not a recognized right, the law grants the divorced wife and her children the right to the marriage home. A separate regime for assets tends to protect the wife from the husband taking over her property; but assets acquired during marital life are subject to redistribution under the control of the judge, who may grant them in part or in totality to the divorced wife.

Custody

Custody of a child no longer depends on age and sex. The right to custody over a child is the mother's as a matter of principle, then the father's, until the child reaches the age of 15, whereupon the child can choose the guardian. No longer is the father, as 'head of the family', the automatic guardian of the child, and the distinction between custody and guardianship in the classical law has become effectively moot. Nor does the wife lose her right to custody if she remarries or relocates. Morocco now includes open reference to international conventions on the rights of children. In addition, the 2004 Amendments significantly enhanced the rights of children born out of wedlock.

These amendments to the marriage, divorce, and custody laws offer a paradigmatic example of family law reform across the Arab and Muslim world over the past half-century. Many similar egalitarian dispositions can be found in other jurisdictions. But there is virtually no egalitarian or corrective trend in the case of succession. The Moroccan amendments on that score are restricted to allowing grandchildren issuing from the deceased person's daughter to inherit in the same way as grandchildren issuing from the deceased person's son. Beyond that, equality between men and women in succession law is not acknowledged in any Muslim jurisdiction. The last attempt to establish equality in inheritance, enacted in Iraq in 1959, was reversed in an amendment passed four years later.[43]

---

[43] For details, see Chibli Mallat, 'Sunnism and Shi'ism in Iraq: Revisiting the Codes', in Chibli Mallat and Jane Connors (eds), *Islamic Family Law* (1990), 71–91; 'The Search for Equality in Middle Eastern Family Law', (2000–1) 48–9 *al-Abhath* 7–63.

IV. Epilogue

In his *Summa* on Mediterranean society as seen through the Cairo Geniza documents of the tenth to thirteenth centuries, Samuel Goitein includes a notable passage:

At the root of all this was the concept that law was personal and not territorial. An individual was judged according to the law of his religious community, or even religious 'school' or sect, rather than that of the territory in which he happened to be. Perhaps it would be even more exact to say that, with the exception of some local statutes, promulgated and abrogated from time to time, the states as such did not possess any law.[44]

A millennium and a half after the Islamic revelation, unrest and violence associated with the Islamic/Middle Eastern world make one wonder, from a comparative perspective, whether West and East are not on a collision course precisely because of their diametrically opposed concepts of law. On the Western side, law is associated with nation-states and their territory; on the Islamic/Middle Eastern side, law is dominated by the personal dimension, defined on the basis of religion and even sect within that religion.

It may be a broad generalization, but at the turn of the twenty-first century, one can only acknowledge the failure of the rule of law in the modern Islamic/Middle Eastern world, in terms both of the protection it should offer the individual and of the control of government under a working constitution.

In the field of obligations and family law, a pattern of differences, if not of confrontation, seems to have prevailed, albeit with the occasional success of a Code such as the Ottoman *Majalla*. But even in the field of contracts and torts, separate systems of superimposed (or intermingled) laws make it difficult to achieve coherence and stability: the Islamic legal system starts with no-fault compensation, and then makes exceptions to the principle for both contracts and torts. This is the reverse of the Western system, where the individual's responsibility needs to be proven as starting-point. Civil codes in the modern Middle East have had difficulty accommodating both approaches simultaneously. Courts tend to abide by the Western system without adjusting its standards to the millennium-deep Islamic tradition.

In family law, social pressure and an increasing search for equality between men and women have improved the classical system, which was inherently inegalitarian. However, the success is neither total nor uniform, and the contradictory systems of Western and Islamic law remain apparent in the field's most recent legislative reform.

For the comparatist reader, this chapter may not answer legitimate questions

---

[44] Goitein (n 26), (1967) vol 1, 66.

pertaining to the classification of Islamic law as 'religious' or 'sacred', or the question of foreign influence or transplants, among others. But with the pronounced ascendance of Islamic law as the defining feature of militant Muslim states and groups since the revolution in Iran, the personal/territorial dichotomy may ultimately prove more important than any traditional classification familiar to comparative jurisprudence. Meanwhile, the comparative tradition remains strong: legislatures hardly ever pass a law without first examining foreign precedents and examples, whether they come from France, as in the case of amendments to civil or criminal law, or from a neighbouring Arab/Muslim state, as in the case of family law. Even judges are affected by the increasingly international and global nature of legal matters, and the Supreme Constitutional Court of Egypt does not shy away from citing long excerpts drawn from cases decided by the US Supreme Court. Within this worldwide phenomenon of growing attention to foreign and comparative law, the Islamic law tradition itself is increasingly drawn into the discussion. As a result, the comparative experience is enriched even though this often makes debates more acrimonious than they are in less tension-ridden contexts.

BIBLIOGRAPHY

Joseph Schacht, *An Introduction to Islamic Law* (1964)

Noel Coulson, *A History of Islamic Law* (1964)

—— *Succession in the Muslim Family* (1971)

Norman Anderson, *Law Reform in the Muslim World* (1976)

Chibli Mallat, 'Constitutional Law in the Middle East: The Emergence of Judicial Power', (1994) 1 *Yearbook of Islamic and Middle Eastern Law* 85–108

—— 'Islamic Law: Reflections on the Present State in Western Research', (1995) 43 *al-Abhath* 3–34

—— 'The State of Islamic Law Research in the Middle East', (1998) 8 *Asian Research Trends* 109–36

—— 'Commercial Law in the Middle East between Classical Transactions and Modern Business', (2000) 48 *AJCL* 81–141

—— 'The Search for Equality in Middle Eastern Family Law', (2000–1) 48–9 *al-Abhath* 7–63

Nathan Brown, *Constitutions in a Nonconstitutional World* (2001)

Chibli Mallat, 'From Islamic to Middle Eastern Law: A Restatement of the Field, Part 1', (2003) 51 *AJCL* 699–750

Sami Zubaida, *Law and Power in the Islamic World* (2003)

Chibli Mallat, 'From Islamic to Middle Eastern Law: A Restatement of the Field, Part 2', (2004) 52 *AJCL* 209–86

—— *Droit Civil au Moyen-Orient: Essai de Théorie Générale* (forthcoming)

CHAPTER 19

COMPARATIVE LAW AND AFRICAN CUSTOMARY LAW

T. W. BENNETT

Cape Town

I. Customary Law in Comparative Studies

CUSTOMARY law grows out of the social practices which a given jural community has come to accept as obligatory. It is a pervasive normative order, providing the regulatory framework for spheres of human activity as diverse as the family, the neighbourhood, the business of merchant banking, or international diplomacy. Because custom is so diverse and so wide-ranging, it is clearly impossible to consider all possible systems. Instead, this chapter looks only at the customary laws of sub-Saharan Africa.

In certain legal systems, custom has been elevated to a position of honour, respected by courts and law-makers as a national tradition; the laws of Maoris in New Zealand and Aboriginals in Australia are recent examples. For the most part, however, lawyers pay custom little attention. It will be no surprise then, to discover that customary law is a latecomer to the discipline of comparative law. Even René David, whose vision was more expansive than most, subsumed custom under civil, common, and socialist law, systems which he regarded as the world's main legal families.[1]

The main reason for this neglect would seem to lie in the fact that lawyers take as their model for law the system that evolved in Europe. On this understanding, they believe that the primary sources of law are those endorsed by the state—legislation and precedent—and not the potentially anarchic social practices of local communities. Hence, legal scholars everywhere tend to regard custom as a somewhat primitive regime, one less worthy of study than 'law'.

The history of comparative law has, in fact, been markedly eurocentric. It was only in the fifteenth and sixteenth centuries that lawyers in Europe started looking to the wider world. Initially, their interest was sparked by the conquest of the Americas and the opening of trade routes to the East, events which aroused a taste

---

[1] As an afterthought, he added an assorted group of 'other' laws—Jewish, Hindu, Asian, and African: René David, *Major Legal Systems in the World Today* (1985), 18, 27, 28.

for the exotic and a self-conscious reflection on European culture. Attention was drawn to the indigenous laws of sub-Saharan Africa only very much later, once the scramble for colonies was over, and the colonial powers were confronted with the problem of governing their possessions.

Eventually, all the European administrations had to recognize the unwritten laws of their subject peoples for the simple reason that they suffered chronic shortages of personnel and finance. Because lawyers lacked the skills necessary to determine the content of these laws, however, the job was relegated to anthropologists. Thus, as will be apparent below, the study of custom has been dominated by social anthropology.

In so far as comparative lawyers were prepared to consider customary law, they dwelt on the substance of the rules. By dint of liberal generalizations, they provided accounts of the law governing marriage, succession, land tenure, and so on, on the assumption that they were describing features typical of African life and thought. According to this approach, although differences in detail were to be noted, the many indigenous laws of the Continent could be treated as a single entity.

While it is, of course, true that common socio-economic conditions do work to produce similar legal forms, the economies and cultures of Africa were far from being uniform. Broad similarities no doubt existed, as they do in any 'family' of laws, but African societies were continually changing, in response to forces both internal and external, and these changes were occurring at different rates and in different places. Even if resources had been available, no one could have kept abreast of the infinite variations and fluctuations. Moreover, because customary laws are confined to small, more or less self-contained, communities, they are not immediately accessible to outsiders. Hence the great problem with customary law: ascertaining the rules.

From what has been said thus far, it will be evident that no comprehensive account can be given of the substance of sub-Saharan customary laws. This chapter is therefore concerned, instead, with matters of form and development, namely, the preservation of the law in an oral tradition and how it has been influenced by certain social, economic, and political structures. This focus requires, in turn, that particular attention be paid to factors influencing the production of texts on customary law. Because information on the subject is, for most people, available only in books, and because so many of these books are now criticized for being out of date and lacking in objectivity, readers must be made aware of how changes in the theories of jurisprudence and anthropology have affected the authors' ideas and preconceptions.

II. THE COLONIAL ENCOUNTER

The European powers had a curious relationship with their African colonies, one that has been described as an unhappy blend of tyranny and paternalism. Because all major decisions were made by absentee sovereigns, far removed from the sites of implementation, relations between rulers and subjects were, at best, a 'working misunderstanding'.[2] Even today, this phrase would be an apt description of customary law.

The first written accounts of the subject were produced by outsiders, initially the teachers of Islam and, later, officers of colonial government. With hindsight, it now seems inevitable that these works would be biased, occasionally in favour of Africa, but mostly against. Some writers were captivated by qualities that had been lost in their own cultural histories—the nobility of warrior nations, such as the Ashanti, Herero, and Zulu, or the primordial purity of cattle-keepers, such as the KhoeKhoe, Masai, and Nuer[3]—but, by and large, most of those reporting on Africa saw only barbarism and backwardness.[4]

The following account of customary marriage is typical. Survivors of a seventeenth-century Portuguese shipwreck on the coast of South Africa remarked, disparagingly, that:[5]

[t]he women bring no dowry in marriage, on the contrary the husband pays the bride's father with cattle, and they become as slaves to their husbands . . . The kings have four, five, and seven wives. The women do all the work, planting and tilling the earth with sticks to prepare it for their grain. Cows are what they chiefly value.

Even much later, at the opening of the twentieth century, a British court could declare that indigenous land tenure in Zimbabwe was incompatible with 'the legal ideas of civilized society'.[6] The Ndebele knew only precarious possession, not ownership, the *sine qua non* of civilization.[7] (The consequences, of course, were serious: whatever lands were not 'owned', were open to British occupation.)

By its very nature, customary law stood condemned. As a pre-legal order, custom was said to be no more than mindless conformity to tradition.[8] Hence, an early anthropologist could claim that: '[n]o-one dreams of breaking the social

---

[2] Paul Bohannan, *African Outline* (1966), 22.

[3] See eg François le Vaillant, *Voyages de M. le Vaillant dans l'Intérieur de l'Afrique par le Cap de Bonne-Espérance dans les années 1780–85* (1790).

[4] See Adam Kuper, *Invention of Primitive Society: Transformations of an Illusion* (1988), 2–3.

[5] Cited in George McCall Theal, *Records of South-Eastern Africa* (vol VIII, 1898–1903), 205.

[6] *Re Southern Rhodesia* [1919] AC 211 (PC) at 233–4.

[7] Martin Chanock, 'Paradigms, Policies, and Property: A Review of the Customary Law of Land Tenure', in Kristin Mann and Richard Roberts (eds), *Law in Colonial Africa* (1991), 62.

[8] Edwin Hartland, *Primitive Law* (1924), 2, 5, and 8.

rules. Custom is King, nay tyrant in primitive society.'[9] Implicit in this view was a particular conception of the 'primitive' mind: 'spontaneous, traditional, personal, commonly known, corporate, relatively unchanging . . .'.[10] Derogatory adjectives abounded: primitive society was irrational, emotional, incapable of objectivity or individual thought. By contrast, the laws of Europe stood for all that was rational and impartial. Backed by the structures of organized state, they were instrumentalities, which could be used to achieve reasoned and predetermined ends.

During the nineteenth century, positivism reached its height in Europe, and, from a positivist perspective, rules derived from custom could not be a truly 'legal' order. According to Austin, whose teaching left a long-lasting impression on British jurisprudence, law 'properly so called' emanated from the commands of a sovereign. Because the decentralized polities of Africa did not comply with European ideas of statehood, they could not be considered sovereign, and, in consequence, they could have no law. As a body of habits, conventions, or moral standards, customary law was not fit for legal analysis. Rather, it was consigned to the study of anthropologists, whose interests lay in whatever was alien or secondary.

Colonialism has imprinted its values on custom, and these have proved difficult to shake. Throughout Africa, European laws, whether French, English, Portuguese, Belgian, or Roman-Dutch, have constituted the basic laws of the land. Customary laws were applied only as matters of exception. This situation still pertains. In consequence, European law stands as the comparator for customary law, as the ideal to which custom is always expected to conform.

III. The Transformation into Western Forms

For the sake of the orderly administration of justice, however, the colonial powers had to overcome their misgivings about customary law. Because they lacked the resources needed to impose their laws on large and potentially hostile populations, they were forced to compromise and recognize indigenous laws—provided, however, that these laws were suitably 'civilized'.[11] Thus, courts could refuse to apply

---

[9] Robert Marett, *Anthropology* (1912), 183.

[10] Stanley Diamond 'The Rule of Law versus the Order of Custom' (1971) 38 *Social Research* 42 ff.

[11] The British principle, established in *Campbell v Hall* (1774) 1 Cowper 204 at 209, was in fact similar to that applied elsewhere in Africa. For general accounts of the administration of justice in the colonies, see Lord Hailey, *African Survey* (1945), ch 7 and Jeswald Salacuse, *An Introduction to Law in French-Speaking Africa* (vol IV, 1969), 43 ff.

customary law if they found it incompatible with natural justice, equity, morality, or public policy. While the exact terms of these provisions varied from colony to colony, the general idea remained the same: the fundamental rights and freedoms of Europe were to be the basis of the colonial legal order.[12]

1. The Reduction of Oral Traditions to Writing

Politically, the decision to recognize customary law was fraught with difficulties. So, too, was its application. With a few exceptions,[13] customary law existed in oral form only. Although an absence of writing was clearly no problem for indigenous tribunals, it presented a formidable challenge to the Western idea of justice, which was predicated on an assumption that courts applied a fixed and certain code of rules known to the whole population in advance.

Colonial courts could, of course, treat the unwritten laws of Africa in the same way as the customs with which all systems of European law were already familiar. This approach required an evidentiary fiction that the customary rule was a matter of fact, to be proved by calling witnesses in each case in which it was alleged.[14] When custom was the rule rather than the exception, however, courts could not operate on this basis. Not only was the need to determine rules on a case-by-case basis simply too time-consuming, but the potential for change and local variation undermined the overall values of colonial justice, which considered certainty and uniformity essential. Hence, in order to overcome the problem of proof and to provide the courts with a single authoritative set of rules, the business began of reducing oral custom to writing.

In anglophone Africa, one of the first official projects was launched in the mid-nineteenth century, when the colonial administration of Natal drafted a code of Zulu laws. Shortly thereafter, the Cape administration established commissions of inquiry to gather information on the customary laws of Basutoland and the Transkeian Territories. Independent texts also proliferated. A famous example, considered a model of its type, was Isaac Schapera's *Handbook of Tswana Law and Custom* (1938), which was commissioned by the administration of the Bechuanaland Protectorate. Even the post-colonial period saw the production of restatements of customary law, notably, those undertaken by the School of Oriental and African Studies at London University.

---

[12] In the post-colonial period, the human rights movement has provided a similar, supervening code of values: Thomas W. Bennett, *Human Rights and African Customary Law* (1995), ch 1.

[13] In some cases, local customs had been incorporated into Islamic law, which was then written down. In Madagascar, the Merina began to codify their customary laws from 1828 onwards, mainly in order to stave off colonization by France.

[14] Moreover, whoever alleged a custom had to establish that it was reasonable, certain, and had existed from 'time immemorial': *Angu v Attah* (1916) Gold Coast Privy Council Judgments (1874–1928), 43.

All of these works were driven by a belief that the written word is of greater authority and durability than the spoken word. The authors paid little attention to the effect that writing was having on the data recorded. It was commonly believed that, through the pen, readers acquired unhindered access to the information being described. In reality, however, the reduction of oral law to writing effects a change not only to form but also to content.[15]

2. The Nature of Oral Law

Oral laws are vague and indeterminate. Because the creator is usually an anonymous being, lost in the past, there is no possibility of referring back to an authoritative original. What is more, when people talk about this law, they present new accounts, each one being only a partial representation of the original, since it is limited to what the speaker can remember. The way in which information is expressed is then influenced by the occasion for talking and the composition of the audience. Whether consciously or otherwise, speakers place on their materials personal interpretations. So it happens that, as an item of information is passed from one generation to the next, it is continually being recreated.[16]

In any organized social order, however, the applicable rules must be sufficiently stable and certain if they are to function effectively. In oral cultures, these requirements are met by the use of various social and stylistic controls on speech. First, in order to keep information alive, it is repeated on all possible occasions (which results in a conservative, rather than an experimental, attitude to knowledge). Second, only certain people are allowed to speak, and then only at particular times. The social conventions of Africa, for example, generally allow only senior males to expound the law, and then only on the occasion of formal trials or council meetings. Third, stylistic devices give speech a fixed framework, which serves as a useful aid to memory. Myths and proverbs provide commonly understood genres for presenting rules. Assonance, alliteration, and rhythm contribute to the creation of pithy maxims, such as *mekgwa le melao* (customs and laws) and *morena ke morena ka batho* (a chief is a chief by the people).[17] Hence, although oral laws do not appear as systematic abstractions, they are nevertheless formulaic and structured.

Oral communication does not lend itself to conveying a long chain of abstract reasoning. Instead, the language tends to be conversational, and, as a result, consists of short sentences, a readily understandable vocabulary, and many deictic markers, which serve to link information to its social context. Oral cultures therefore rely

[15] See Thomas W. Bennett and Thuys Vermeulen, 'Codification of Customary Law', (1980) 24 *Journal of African Law* 206 ff.

[16] Jan Vansina, *Oral Tradition, A Study in Historical Methodology* (1965), 76.

[17] Isaac Schapera, 'Tswana Legal Maxims', (1966) 36 *Africa* 121 ff.

heavily on the mnemonics of physical objects and topographical features. Rights to land, for instance, are marked by trees, streams, hills, and gullies, and by the location of ancestral graves. The existence of a marriage may be determined by the presence of livestock as bridewealth, and a wife's status in the family may be visibly fixed by the position of her house in a homestead.

3. The Effects of Writing

When an oral tradition is written down, the rules are inevitably transformed. On a macro-scale, it is immediately apparent that highly localized customs tend to be generalized and applied in a range of new situations. As authors accept international boundaries, rather than particular social groups, for defining the limits of the subject, customary laws expand to fill the states and provinces created by colonialism.

Together with generalization comes system. Laws preserved in an oral tradition lack precision and definition. Such rules are difficult to differentiate, and, without differentiation, it is impossible to begin the job of classification into different types. If rules cannot be classified, they cannot be organized into a system, and, without system, redundancies and contradictions are bound to occur. (It is no accident that logical coherence is a cardinal value of written rather than oral law.) In fact, it might be said that oral versions of customary law are not systems at all. They are better described as *repertoires*, or loose collections of similar, though varying, types of norm, from which discerning judges select whichever rule best suits the needs of a particular case.[18]

Another consequence of writing is specialization, and hence legal science. Writing makes possible sustained reflection and abstract analysis, conditions that favour the development of a specialist profession. In oral cultures, however, it would be unusual to find a particular group of people dedicated to the application, interpretation, or making of the law. Thus, in Africa, customary law was never regarded as an esoteric discipline, beyond the reach of ordinary people. Every adult male was expected to be familiar with the laws of the community, and thus competent to argue them in court.

Writing has effects even more profound, however, than the creation of system and science. In almost every case, it involves translation from a vernacular into a European language. Although this process is generally regarded as little more than a matter of form, it has significant implications for content.

This proposition is most vividly illustrated by the search for an appropriate European word to denote the common African rule that a husband is obliged to give livestock or some other form of consideration (here termed 'bridewealth') to his

---

[18] See John Comaroff and Simon Roberts, *Rules and Processes* (1981), ch 3, esp 70.

wife's family in order to conclude a marriage. In the lusophone and francophone colonies, the seemingly obvious choice was found in the word 'dowry', which is a familiar practice in Mediterranean countries. Notwithstanding associations with marriage, however, dowry and bridewealth have little in common. The most obvious difference lies in the identity of the duty-bearer: dowry is a payment by the wife's guardian to the groom, whereas bridewealth requires payment by the groom.

In anglophone colonies, the giving of livestock is often termed 'brideprice', because the husband appears to be paying a purchase price for his wife's services.[19] Due in large part to this interpretation, colonial governments disapproved of the practice, and, in certain countries, the courts refused to enforce bridewealth agreements on the ground that they were repugnant to 'general principles of civilization'. Although wives are never treated as slaves or chattels under customary law, and the courts' interpretation was eventually discredited as a complete fallacy, colonial policy had, in effect, 'bastardised almost the entire Native population . . . deprived practically every Native father of guardianship or other rights to his children . . . [and] destroyed any equitable claim to property'.[20]

The very use of a noun to describe bridewealth obscures the fact that certain vernaculars use verbs, thereby suggesting a sense of process rather than a material object or a completed event. As fieldwork on the Tshidi people in Botswana showed, customary marriages are not defined by the performance of single acts or ceremonies. Instead, the Tshidi regard marriage as a process.[21] It begins with a series of meetings between senior representatives of the bride and groom's families, at which the parties settle the terms and conditions of the union.[22] When agreement is reached on the amount of livestock or cash to be paid, the Tshidi allow the future husband to take up residence with the bride's family, where he may start cohabiting with his wife. After a period of time, the couple moves to the husband's homestead, and the bridewealth is formally handed over. Although payment of the full amount is usually delayed, the wife's guardian has justification for demanding more with the birth of each child. Not until all marital obligations are fulfilled, however, can a couple be considered fully married.

The above example illustrates another significant feature of nearly all systems of customary law: jural relationships are determined without reference to outside authority. Marriages are concluded by the families concerned. In the absence of serious disagreement between the families, there is no need to involve outsiders,

[19] See generally Adam Kuper, *Wives for Cattle* (1982). See the brief account of the function of bridewealth in Daniel Nsereko, 'The Nature and Function of Marriage Gifts in Customary African Marriages', (1975) 23 *AJCL* 682 ff.

[20] (1929) 1 Native Appeal Court (Natal & Transvaal) 1.

[21] See Simon Roberts, 'The Kgatla Marriage: Concepts of Validity', in Simon Roberts (ed), *Law and the Family in Africa* (1978), 241 ff. More generally on customary marriages, see Arthur Phillips (ed), *Survey of African Marriage and Family Life* (1953), Introduction.

[22] See John Comaroff (ed), *The Meaning of Marriage Payments* (1980), 168 ff.

and the parties are free to waive or re-negotiate the applicable rules. It follows that customary law is always 'adaptable, and situational',[23] qualities which contribute to a sense of process and transaction rather than one of irrevocable acts and events.

4. Legal Terminology

A major reason why writers on customary law so often use inappropriate translations is a predisposition to use Western legal terminology. All too often, the authors of early texts were officials in the colonial courts or administration. Partly because of their training and partly because the rules were written with the needs of practising lawyers in mind, Western concepts were used to describe the data. This tendency is most obvious in titles: chapters in textbooks are headed with terms familiar to Western legal systems, such as marriage, succession, property, contract, crime, and delict.

The use of these specifically legal terms was not always inadvertent, however, because certain authors believed in the universality of legal concepts. Gluckman, one of the great theorists on customary law, is a case in point. He argued that the concept of ownership exists in all cultures; it is merely manifested by different words. Max Gluckman could therefore say that the Barotse word *bung'a* should be translated by the English term 'ownership'.[24]

Today, few people would support this argument without major qualifications. It takes no great linguistic insight to realize that terms and concepts are historically and culturally specific. In other words, words have no metalinguistic meanings. Once we accept that the concept of ownership is generated by a particular culture, then it is clear that the English word cannot be expected to give an accurate reflection of how proprietary relationships are regulated in Africa.

Paul Bohannan was a decided opponent of Gluckman's approach. He argued for the use of vernacular terminology, saying that this was the only way to understand the nuances of African thought systems. By implication, he accepted the unique quality of all cultures,[25] and, in his own work, *Justice and Judgment among the Tiv* (1957), Bohannan was able to expose the distinctive character of indigenous institutions to great effect. Given the dominance of European languages in all official contexts in Africa, however, vernaculars have seldom been used.

[23] Sally Merry, 'Anthropology, Law and Transnational Processes', (1992) 21 *Annual Review of Anthropology* 365.

[24] Max Gluckman, *The Ideas in Barotse Jurisprudence* (1972), xxiv, 254 ff. See more generally, Sally Falk Moore, 'Comparative Studies: Introduction', in Laura Nader (ed), *Law in Culture and Society* (1969), 340–2.

[25] Bohannan was influenced by the Whorf-Sapir school of ethno-linguistics, which maintained that language users were predisposed to think in categories which had been encoded in their vocabulary and grammar.

The use of European terms and concepts has operated, at many levels, to transform indigenous laws into something more amenable to a Western way of thinking. When colonial authors wrote about family relationships, for example, they tended to discount the rights and duties of family members *inter se* as irrelevant to a legal text. Notwithstanding the fact that these rights and duties form a critical component of customary law, they were demoted to mere morality or convention.[26]

Western lawyers have also found it difficult to accept the fundamentally asymmetrical nature of African legal relations. For instance, in customary law, the powers of the head of a household are general and diffuse. He is expected to judge disputes fairly, to provide his subordinates with food and shelter, and to make appropriate decisions on their behalf. However, in keeping with the image of a wise care-giver, customary law emphasizes responsibility, not rights and powers.[27]

The same sense of asymmetry is true of laws about children. Claims for support—at least in the past—were less significant than a child's responsibilities to contribute to the welfare of the family, whether by bringing in bridewealth or by providing labour in the fields.[28] These duties persist, whatever the age of the child. Indeed, the idea of any member of a family enjoying special rights (as is implied by the best interests of the child rule in Western systems of law) is at odds with the African legal tradition. Nevertheless, texts on customary law tend to gloss over the emphasis on responsibility. Instead, authors describe the law in terms of rights and duties, a framework which better suits the Western demand for balanced legal relations.

IV. THE DEVELOPMENT OF LEGAL ANTHROPOLOGY

Social anthropology has always been a major source of information about customary law. Not only did anthropologists have the job of gathering data,[29] but they were also responsible for much of the theory on the subject. As a result, shifts in thinking have had a strong influence on perceptions of customary law and the ways in which it has been studied.

---

[26] See Martin Chanock, *Law, Custom and Social Order* (1985), chs 10 and 11.

[27] This emphasis was considered sufficiently important to warrant a special chapter on duties in the African Charter on Human and People's Rights (1982), ch 2.

[28] Welshman Ncube, 'The African Cultural Fingerprint?', in Welshman Ncube (ed), *Law, Culture, Tradition and Children's Rights in Eastern and Southern Africa* (1998), 21–2.

[29] They were described as the 'intelligence department' of colonial government: Robert Rattray, *Ashanti* (1923), 8.

1. Evolutionism

The term 'anthropological jurisprudence' was coined in 1886 by the German jurist, Albert H. Post, but it is Sir Henry Maine who has the reputation of being the 'founding father', largely because of his book *Ancient Law* (1861). Anthropologists of the mid-nineteenth century—many of whom also happened to be lawyers and active contributors to the discipline of comparative law—had already extrapolated the theory of biological evolution to human society. In an application of evolutionism to law, Maine argued that all legal systems progressed through clear and inescapable stages, from a lower, primitive, to a higher, more civilized, state. By comparing various archaic systems—Roman, Hindu, English, and Celtic—he claimed to have detected universal patterns in the development of legal institutions.

While evolutionism was responsible for many thought-provoking ideas about the relationship between law and society, the method was highly questionable. One problem was a lack of empirical data to back up the theory. Another was an implicitly ethnocentric bias, for evolutionism rested on a belief that European society represented the apogee and object of all social change, a belief conveniently endorsed by the racism endemic in European colonialism. However, in spite of its shortcomings, evolutionism proved extremely persuasive, and, long after it had been discredited in anthropology, it continued to influence policy-making in the colonial administration, not to mention the thinking of many writers on customary law.

2. Functionalism

In the 1920s, the emergence of the rival theory of functionalism began to challenge evolutionism. Exotic data were no longer to be explained by comparison with notionally superior, Western cultural systems, but rather with reference to the native systems themselves. It followed that, if the meaning of an item of information was to be properly understood, then that item had to be considered in relation to all other items in the culture under study. The practice of giving bridewealth, for example, was no longer viewed from a European perspective—which might suggest the purchase of a wife—but rather from the perspective of a participant in the system. From this angle, the institution appeared less as a social evil and more as a means for protecting wives and providing them with a public measure of their reputation.[30]

A separate branch of functionalism grew out of the work of a group of British anthropologists working mainly in Africa, notably, Radcliffe-Brown, Evans-Pritchard, and Gluckman. They were concerned with the network of relations and

---

[30] Hence, John Soga, *The Ama-Xosa* (1931), 274–5 described lobolo as 'the Bantu woman's charter of liberty'.

institutions which together constituted the structure of society, and the way in which these institutions functioned to maintain a stable and harmonious unit. *Structural*-functionalism heralded a period of great activity in legal anthropology. At that time, the policy of indirect rule was the established dogma of colonial government, and authorities were in urgent need of more and better information about their subjects. Research projects therefore received generous government sponsorship, and the number of ethnographies grew accordingly.[31]

Gluckman can still be considered one of the chief theorists on customary law. From his research among the Barotse, a people in the south-western area of Zambia, he used both evolutionism and structural-functionalism to produce a series of provocative ideas about legal development. In formulating these ideas, Gluckman attributed a decisive influence to the structures of Barotse society.[32]

This society was composed of small, self-contained settlements, each inhabited by one or more closely related families, who supported themselves from subsistence agriculture. The people produced little beyond what they could consume, and, from a restricted range of material goods, it followed that everyone had a similar standard of living. There could be no distinct class, marked by wealth and power.

'Tribal' societies, such as the Barotse, were described as 'status dominated'. This term means that the imperatives of material support and reproduction were realized through the performance of duties attached to an individual's status within a family system. Thus, kin (and neighbours) were responsible for performing such critical tasks as rearing children, caring for the sick, and propitiating the ancestors. Rights and duties derived from contract were of peripheral importance. Hence, Gluckman could confirm Maine's famous dictum that the progress of society was 'a movement from Status to Contract'.

On the basis of the 'tribal' nature of Barotse society, Gluckman constructed a theory about property and social relations in customary law. He observed that, because rights to property were constantly being overridden by the support claims of kin, no individual could 'own' food, cattle, or land absolutely. Admittedly, this proposition is also partially true of Western societies, for a parent's responsibility towards children requires the constant provision of food, shelter, and support, and parents who fail to discharge these duties are liable to legal action. An individual's right to property, in other words, is superseded by duties to the family.

Similarities between Western and customary law end at this point, however, because, in the Western world, an individual's survival is never totally dependent on the support of kin. Instead, adults are expected to earn their living from relationships formed by contracts in the labour market, and their economic security is underwritten by ownership of their acquisitions. In Africa, on the other hand, the duties arising out of social relationships always take precedence. Gluckman

[31] See Adam Kuper, *Anthropology and Anthropologists* (1983).
[32] See Gluckman (n 24), 4–5.

therefore says that '[p]roperty law in tribal society defines not so much rights of persons over things, as obligations owed between persons in respect of things'.[33]

Customary conceptions of property were conditioned not only by the nature of social relationships but also by a critical economic factor: scarcity. Whenever goods are freely available, they have little economic importance; access and control then require no legal protection. Regulation becomes necessary only when there is competition for resources. It is at this stage that the law begins to focus on the individual's right to property rather than relations with other people.

This development was confirmed by a study of customary-law rights to land in two Malagasy cultures.[34] The Merina, whose agriculture was based on a shortage of land but an abundance of labour, especially slave labour, conceived of proprietary rights as a person's right to his land. The Zafimaniry, on the other hand, had an abundance of land but a shortage of labour. Their law emphasized the relationship between persons; the land was a secondary consideration.

Regular trade is the final determinant of a fully-fledged concept of ownership. Before its advent, economically valuable property tends to attract many highly specific rights, each of which may potentially vest in a different person. Commerce can flourish, however, only when these goods are loosened from the specific rights of particular interest holders so that they can circulate freely in the market. Once every commodity bears an easily measurable exchange value relative to all others, ownership emerges.

This highly abstract concept can be applied to any type of commodity, and it can be made available to any trader. Ownership has the distinctive feature, especially in civilian systems of law, of being 'absolute', a quality which implies the concentration of all entitlements in one person—usually the possessor—who, in consequence, is free to use and dispose of property at will.

In summary, and following Gluckman's theory, since most systems of customary law are rooted in a pre-trade era, proprietary rights to such economically important property as land and livestock can be distinguished from the Western concept of ownership by the fact that customary law allows a number of specific interests to vest in various different holders. The typically capitalist legal system, by contrast, allows a collection of interests to vest in a single holder.[35]

Wills appeared at the same time as ownership. Because customary law had less concern with property than with support obligations, death raised no particular questions about the disposal of the deceased's assets. Instead, the issue was one of succession, namely, the transmission of the deceased's duties of support, together with concomitant powers of control over the family estate, to a suitable heir. In

[33] Gluckman (n 24), 163.
[34] Maurice Bloch, 'Property and the End of Affinity', in Maurice Bloch (ed), *Marxist Analyses and Social Anthropology* (1975), 203 ff.
[35] Edward Thompson, 'The Grid of Inheritance: A Comment', in Jack Goody, Joan Thirsk, and Edward P. Thompson (eds), *Family and Inheritance* (1976), 341.

systems of Western law, on the other hand, because individuals owned their property and were free to decide how it should be used and disposed of during their lifetimes, the same power extended to disposal on death. Wills were therefore believed to be the best and the most natural way of transferring property to the next generation.

Contract is yet another institution associated with property. In the pre-colonial period, with the exception of certain cultures in West Africa, commerce in sub-Saharan Africa was neither regular nor general. In consequence, few systems of customary law had any clear concept of contract. This is not say, however, that contract-like institutions were lacking.

Promises, for instance, were taken very seriously. In fact, European observers remarked that pledges had a sacramental quality, which was signified by the performance of rituals. A typical example would be a pact of brotherhood, which was sworn by members of age sets as part of their initiation. The importance ascribed to such pledges can be explained by the effect they had on the parties' relationship: they established long-term bonds, equivalent to those of close kin.

Gift-giving was also a great feature of African cultures, but it, too, bore little resemblance to a contractual relationship, because it lacked a specifically economic purpose. Instead, gifts were given by people already bound to one another as kin or close friends in order to strengthen relationships or discharge the obligations attached to them.

Barter was also common. Households in most parts of Africa were self-sufficient subsistence units, but they might well produce surpluses which could then be bartered in order to procure some particularly sought-after product. Unlike gift-giving, barter did not imply a prior social relationship. Once the transfer of goods had occurred, the parties had no further obligations towards one other.

Gluckman studied equivalent relationships among the Barotse.[36] The undertakings which interested him were in the nature of partnerships. They involved specialist hunters and craftsmen, who traded their products with the local farmers. After a series of transactions between the same parties, a pledge of friendship would ensue. Thereafter, the relationship ceased to be predominantly economic, as each partner strove to outdo the other in generosity. In this way, a series of isolated transactions between two strangers would be recast as a deeper and more complex relationship between kinfolk, a transformation which was usually signified by the parties' adopting kinship nomenclature. They would now talk about one another as 'brothers', with the implication that fraternal standards of behaviour were expected.

These partnerships were still not the same as commercial contracts. On the one hand, their purpose soon ceased to be purely economic, and, on the other, a bare promise was not considered binding. Gluckman noted that Barotse courts were prepared to enforce agreements only when property had been conveyed or

---

[36] Gluckman (n 24), ch 4.

when the parties had performed some formality specific to the transaction, such as the clapping of hands or the drinking of palm wine. Although the purpose of these preliminaries was obviously to provide evidence of a serious intent, more was at stake, because, even if both parties clearly wanted a binding agreement, the courts would not hold them to it unless they had observed the formalities. Gluckman concluded that Barotse law endorsed Maine's thesis that, in early legal systems, contract consisted of incomplete conveyances of property.[37]

V. The Shift to Process and Disputes

1. Acephalous and State Societies

Anthropologists working in the structural-functionalist tradition tended to follow one of two approaches. The first, led by Radcliffe-Brown, concerned itself with rules and the maintenance of order in society. As might be expected, such a concern meshed readily with Western legal scholarship, which also regarded rules as the key element of any social order.[38] The research methods and interests of this branch of anthropology therefore complemented the needs of colonial lawyers and administrators.[39] The second approach was derived from Bronislaw Malinowski's concern with mechanisms of social control. From the 1960s onwards, a group of writers, dissatisfied with the preoccupation with order and rules, turned instead to consider disputes.[40]

In what became a classic work on the comparison of legal cultures, *Justice and Judgment among the Tiv* (1957), Bohannan revealed how differently the British and Tiv in Nigeria viewed the function of rules in disputes. From the British perspective, courts were there to apply rules to facts, whereas, from the Tiv perspective, the *jir* (a more inclusive institution, since it embraced both courts and family councils) was there to counteract breaches of social norms.

The Tiv expected the *jir* to settle disputes in order to restore social harmony. A settlement might be achieved by application of rules to facts or by the elders

---

[37] Anthony N. Allott, Arnold Epstein, and Max Gluckman, 'Conceptions in Substantive Law', in Max Gluckman (ed), *Ideas and Procedures in African Customary Law* (1969), 71 ff.

[38] Indeed, social order was a value built into the disciplines of law and anthropology: Paul Bohannan, 'The Differing Realms of the Law', in Paul Bohannan (ed), *Law and Warfare* (1967), 44–6.

[39] See Richard Abel, 'A Comparative Theory of Dispute Institutions in Society', (1973) 8 *Law & Society Review* 217, 221–32 and Comaroff and Roberts (n 18), 5–17.

[40] eg Arnold Epstein, *Juridical Techniques and the Judicial Process* (1954) and Max Gluckman, *The Judicial Process among the Barotse of Northern Rhodesia* (1967).

performing an appropriate ritual. The Tiv saw no significant difference between these interventions. Bohannan therefore concluded that the Tiv would not have shared the British idea that customary law consisted of a body of known and certain rules. Rather, the Tiv believed that there was a right answer to any dispute, and that the task of a *jir* was simply to find that answer.

Bohannan's work suggested that, if legal cultures in Africa were to be properly understood, the focus should be shifted from rules to the methods and procedures for dealing with disputes. Indeed, as this idea took root, it became apparent that a concern with rules is a specifically Western cultural value.[41]

Through the study of process, it also appeared that adjudication, although a procedure central to the Western concept of justice, is only one of a variety of different methods for settling disputes. Customary courts, for instance, are less likely to adjudicate, in the sense of pronouncing one party right and the other wrong. They are more likely to seek compromise solutions, often a simple reconciliation of the parties. In fact, for a time, it was assumed that reconciliation was the dominant value of litigation in Africa. While this view was later shown to be something of an exaggeration, customary courts in Africa are still less likely than their Western counterparts simply to apply rules to facts in order to achieve win-or-lose solutions.

The interest in process did more than merely shift the attention of legal anthropology away from rules and adjudication. It also involved the study of power, and hence politics. A considerable body of literature was then directed at explaining how political and social institutions influenced methods of dealing with disputes.

The small-scale, close-knit nature of so many African societies obviously influenced the manner in which disputes were settled. Of particular interest was the degree of political centralization, and, for this purpose, anthropologists distinguished between acephalous and state societies.[42] Although now considered too categorical and too eurocentric, this dichotomy still proves useful as a general analytical framework.

In state societies, rulers could rely on organized force to sanction their commands and prerogatives. Such societies were therefore likely to have a permanent judicial system, in the sense of an organ of government dedicated to hearing disputes both between subjects and between the state and its subjects. In acephalous societies, on the other hand, although tribunals of a sort existed, they did not have the backing of organized force to carry out their decisions.

Where a society had no supra-familial authority, the only method for dealing with disputes was self-help. Aggrieved parties then had the option of resorting to an outright contest of strength (although ritualized procedures usually mitigated the damaging effect of physical violence) or a process of negotiation.[43] In either

---

[41] Simon Roberts, *Order and Dispute* (1979), 45–7.

[42] See Myer Fortes and Edward Evans-Pritchard (eds), *African Political Systems* (1940), Introduction.

[43] Bohannan (n 38), 'Introduction' poses the two poles of conflict resolution, namely, law and violence. See, too, Roberts (n 41), ch 9.

case, rules were of little relevance to the final outcome. The dispute would be settled either by superior physical prowess or the arts of persuasion.[44]

In centralized societies, on the other hand, the state can compel parties to submit their disputes to its courts. Hence, the less power at the state's disposal the more likely that a tribunal's jurisdiction will depend on voluntary submission, in which case it can do no more than persuade the parties to accept a compromise solution.[45] When a tribunal has the backing of police, a sheriff, and prison service, however, it can compel submission, and the disputants will be forced to accept whatever judgment is handed down. In order to legitimate its exercise of power, however, state courts must comply with a code of predetermined rules. Impartial application of these rules on terms of strict equality is therefore the basis of adjudication.

Acephalous and state societies were ideal types, seldom realized in their pure forms. Nevertheless, the political structures typical of most parts of Africa suggest that courts would be more inclined to mediate or arbitrate than to adjudicate. In a classic study of dispute settlement in rural Zimbabwe, for example, Johan Holleman showed that the people of the small community in question would not consider the strict and impartial application of rules to be 'justice'. Rather, the law served as 'a broad and flexible basis for discussion'. It was never considered 'inviolable and imperative'. The satisfactory solutions to problems lay in a process of persuasion, with an emphasis on the spirit of give and take.[46]

2. The Importance of Social Relationships

This study was borne out by Gluckman's work on the Barotse.[47] Because Barotse social structure consisted of intricate networks of status obligations, relationships were highly complex. It followed that disputes were equally complex. What might seem a petty quarrel about the infringement of a mere courtesy could well be the surface manifestation of a simmering conflict, fuelled by years of grievance. Moreover, because relationships were so intimate, disputes between kin generated intense emotion, and were quite likely to erupt into public displays of anger. In these circumstances, Barotse courts were expected to untangle all the complaints with a view to convincing the disputants that they ought to sink their differences so that social harmony could be restored.

The litigants' relationship has an important bearing not only on the nature

---

[44] See Peter Gulliver, *Social Control in an African Society* (1963), 297 and 'Negotiations as a Mode of Dispute Settlement: Towards a General Model', (1973) 7 *Law & Society Review* 667 ff, Lloyd Fallers, *Law without Precedent* (1969), 11–12 and Ian Hamnett (ed), *Social Anthropology and Law* (1977), 15.

[45] See Peter Gulliver, *Disputes and Negotiations* (1979), 271.

[46] Johan Holleman, *Issues in African Law* (1974), 18.   [47] Gluckman (n 40).

of a hearing but also on the type of rules applied, a point John Comaroff and Simon Roberts demonstrated in their study of courts in Botswana.[48] The authors showed that the broad notion of customary law embraced both general and specific rules. The former were associated with disputes about relationships, while the latter were associated with particular rights or values. If a dispute was about a specific value, as might arise between persons associated for a limited purpose, such as a loan of cattle, specific rules were invoked, and strict procedures had to be followed. On the other hand, if a dispute was about a generalized relationship, such as a father and son arguing over the duty of filial support, the obligations would be equally general, and the court's aim more likely to effect a reconciliation.

The nature of the dispute and the parties' relationship also had a marked influence on the scope of the hearing. When disputes flared up between close kin, the court made no attempt to pare down the facts to fit a predetermined normative category. In other words, it did not insist on the parties defining the nature of the claim before the trial began. What is more, during the hearing, the court did not extract certain issues from the complex of facts out of which the dispute arose as being 'relevant'. Hence, the dispute was defined by the parties' relationship rather than a legal category.[49]

In fact, the very measure of an effective court in Africa is its willingness to engage in a thorough inquiry. The latitude allowed, however, is qualified by the court's overall purpose. The more distant the parties' relationship, the more likely that the court's purpose will be straightforward adjudication, and thus the less detailed the investigation. Hence, if a person suffers injury at the hands of a stranger, the inquiry is aimed at simply assessing compensation, and a strict procedure is followed. Conversely, where a court seeks to reconcile the parties, the immediate 'legal' issues that might have precipitated litigation have little significance for the eventual outcome. The court must consider the parties' full relationship over a long period of time.

3. Wrongdoing in Customary Law

These considerations have a direct bearing on the treatment of wrong-doing in customary law. In societies lacking centralized structures of power and authority, no absolute distinction can be drawn between private wrongs and public crimes. Hence, unlike Western systems of law, which are careful to classify offences as crimes or delicts, customary law deems any act or omission wrongful, if it is in breach of a general duty to avoid doing something which might reflect on the reputation of others, harm their persons, or damage their property.

---

[48] Comaroff and Roberts (n 18), 115–17.   [49] See Gluckman (n 24), ch 7.

According to popular wisdom in the colonial service, which (predictably) can be traced back to Maine, Africans dealt with wrong-doing on the basis of collective responsibility, an inquisitorial procedure, strict liability, and a 'thirst for vengeance'.[50] None of these propositions does justice to the reality. The first, collective responsibility, can only be understood in the context of property management. When property is administered by the most senior member of a family, individuals have no means of satisfying their debts. Whatever liabilities they incur have therefore to be satisfied from the family estate. The fact that the tortfeasor does not personally make reparation gives the impression that responsibility is collective.

As for the idea of inquisitorial procedure, it was often said that customary courts presume guilt and that judges question defendants on an assumption that they are lying.[51] This portrayal was also something of a misconception. In Western systems, plaintiffs bear the onus of proving their rights, but, in Africa, where the emphasis falls on duty rather than right, the onus is not so clearly located. Because defendants must avoid harming others, once the fact of damage is established, the likely offender has to convince the court that he or she had no responsibility for its cause.

The connection between damage and an offender cannot always be determined through observable facts, for many offences are committed secretly. Through a belief that the ancestors, spirits, or witches have the power to influence events in the physical world, however, misfortune may be attributed to an individual's breach of rules of good conduct, without any specific evidence of factual causation. If sickness suddenly spreads among the cattle, for example, the reason might lie in a family's failure to propitiate its ancestors. Similarly, if a person is killed by lightning, although the physical cause of death is quite obvious, the malign activities of a witch may explain why that particular person had to die at that particular time.[52]

Because it is impossible to prove a factual connection between the agent and the misfortune, a court has to draw inferences from evidence indicative of the practice of witchcraft. This evidence includes bearing the stigmata of a witch, such as warts, blemishes, and other physical abnormalities, an unnatural association with animal familiars, or, even more telling, the culprit's aberrant and antisocial behaviour. Thus, although witchcraft is usually invoked as an explanation for extraordinary misfortunes, it is pertinent only if the misfortune was preceded by bad relationships within small, close-knit communities.

In everyday inquiries, motive, intention, and negligence may seem irrelevant. If liability is collective, and, if reparation is the aim of a trial, then it is true that a tortfeasor's state of mind can be of little importance. But more thoughtful writers

---

[50] See Sally Falk Moore, 'Legal Liability and Evolutionary Interpretation: Some Aspects of Strict Liability, Self-Help and Collective Responsibility', in Max Gluckman (ed), *The Allocation of Responsibility* (1972), 51 ff.

[51] See Gluckman (n 40), 94–7 and (n 24), 10–11.

[52] See Edward Evans-Pritchard, *Witchcraft, Oracles and Magic among the Azande* (1937), esp 63–83.

on customary law produced much evidence, especially in cases of witchcraft, to show that state of mind might be critical to an inquiry.

In fact, Gluckman showed that the idea of strict liability had to be understood within the context of particular social relationships. Western systems of law can be distinguished by an assessment of *mens rea* independently of the parties' relationship or the nature of an offence. In Africa, however, the closer the relationship between the wrongdoer and the aggrieved party, the more likely that fault will be investigated. Within a family, for example, motive and intention are highly relevant to the process of reconciliation.

Finally, the 'thirst for vengeance' is, in reality, restricted to politically decentralized societies, such as that of the Nuer in Sudan, who are often taken to be archetypically acephalous. With the Nuer, a wrong against one family entitles it to seek retribution from the offender's family. Unless a compromise can be agreed upon, a sense of unrequited wrong leads to a feud, which might persist from one generation to the next. Even Nuer families, however, usually decide to negotiate, and, if it can be shown that a killing was accidental, compensation may be accepted instead of blood.[53]

VI. Decolonization and its Aftermath

1. Decolonization

In the 1960s and 1970s, the study of disputes came to dominate legal anthropology, an emphasis which led to a concentration on the pathological at the expense of the ordered and the everyday.[54] An even more serious problem, however, was the ahistorical approach typical of all functionalism. Anthropologists had tended to neglect the socio-economic upheavals caused by colonization.[55]

Independence from colonial rule, and the awakening of a new national consciousness, provided the occasion for a major change of attitude towards customary law. African writers, such as the distinguished Nigerian judge, T. O. Elias, in his work *The Nature of African Customary Law* (1956), were at pains to show that customary law was every bit the equal of European law. It was now claimed as an

[53] Edward Evans-Pritchard, *The Nuer* (1940), 150 ff.

[54] Johan Holleman, 'Trouble Cases and Troubleless Cases in the Study of Customary Law and Legal Reform', (1973) 7 *Law & Society Review* 585 ff.

[55] Francis Snyder, 'Anthropology, Dispute Processes and Law: A Critical Introduction', (1981) 8 *British Journal of Law and Society* 141 ff.

African cultural heritage, in line with the doctrine of *négritude*, and thus worthy of serious attention and respect.

In spite of a rediscovered sense of pride and self-confidence, however, the newly independent states generally resisted the temptation to Africanize their legal systems.[56] Custom was all too often seen as an obstacle to the two great imperatives of the age: national unity and modernization.

Because customary law stood for an ethnic diversity, it was at odds with the principle of equality and the drive to forge a new national identity.[57] Customary law also connoted a rural conservatism. Because its source of legitimacy lay in tradition, custom was not an appropriate medium for producing goal-oriented enactments, and hence could not function as an instrument for achieving pre-determined ends. Custom was perceived as a restraint on action rather than a catalyst for new patterns of behaviour. In short, customary law was considered antithetical to contemporary ideas of social change and individual initiative.

The response of certain states, especially those which had inherited a civil-law regime, was either to exclude customary law from the national legal system or to restrict its scope of operation. According to the former approach, which was epitomized by the codification projects in Ivory Coast and Ethiopia, the entire legal system had to be rewritten in order to meet the demands of a modern state.

René David, drafter of the Ethiopian civil code, thought that custom varied too much from place to place, was too unstable, and lacked a true juridical character. He said that Ethiopia was in no position to wait for centuries until the legal system had evolved to the required level. Instead, 'ready-made' laws were to be imported from Europe. For this reason, 'ce n'est pas d'une évolution, que le pays a besoin, c'est d'une révolution'.[58]

A less radical approach was to draft new laws based on European models, but moulded to fit the contours of traditional custom. The Malagasy codification project was an example. Here the legislature decided that the nation should be given 'une législation unifiée, adaptée aux usages des différentes populations de Madagascar et acceptées par elles'.[59] For instance, in a telling blend of tradition and modernity, the code preserved the customary practice of *misintaka* (which is common to most parts of Africa), whereby a wife may return to her natal family if her husband is not performing his marital duties. Although *misintaka* had been condemned by the colonial authorities for violating the marital consortium, it was now reinterpreted as desirable, because it conformed to the principle of female independence.[60]

[56] Kwame Nkrumah, 'Law in Africa', (1962) 6 *Journal of African Law* 103 ff.

[57] See Anthony Allott, 'Towards the Unification of Laws in Africa', (1965) 14 *ICLQ* 366 ff.

[58] '*La Refonte du Code Civil dans les Etats africaines*', (1962) *Annales Africaines* 161. See, too, René David, 'A Civil Code for Ethiopia: Considerations on the Codification of the Civil Law in African Countries', (1962–3) 37 *Tulane LR* 188 ff.

[59] Resolution of the Malagasy Legislative Assembly, 2 June 1959.

[60] Article 55 of *Ordonnance* 62–056 of 1960.

2. Disillusionment and Marxist Theory

However, neither the francophone codes nor the many other legal reforms enacted in post-independent African states fully achieved their goals. Inspiration for legal change tended to come from urban elites, and, as a result, had little support from the majority of the population. Hence, by the 1970s, it was evident that the bold attempts to transform African society were not succeeding, and customary law still held sway. Concern about this state of affairs, and dissatisfaction with the answers provided by orthodox scholarship, prompted new directions in research.

Closer collaboration between lawyers and sociologists opened one avenue of inquiry;[61] changes in anthropology opened another. The static vision of society implicit in structural-functionalism (and legal positivism) had yielded curiously one-dimensional results. In the 1980s, a new generation of anthropologists, inspired by theoretical Marxism, brought both history and the political economy directly into their work.

Francis Snyder's *Capitalism and Legal Change* (1981) was shaped by these concerns. From his work in the Casamance region of Senegal, the author set out to explain both change in customary institutions and their extraordinary degree of persistence. He based his explanation on the interaction of a dominant capitalist mode of production and one or more indigenous, pre-capitalist modes. Customary law was clearly embedded in the subordinate, pre-capitalist mode, but it had been transformed to serve interests that were dictated, ultimately, by world capitalism. Indigenous institutions of marriage and family, for instance, provided long-term support for migrant labourers who were forced to work for mines, industries, and farms in the capitalist enclave. The persistence of customary law therefore worked to the advantage of capitalist enterprise, because it served to subsidize low wages and provide workers with a refuge in times of unemployment, sickness, or old age.[62]

3. Ideological Functions of Customary Law: Culture and Tradition

Apart from explaining the persistence of customary law, neo-Marxist theory prompted inquiry into the ideological dimension of professional and academic writing. Anthropologists had long criticized jurisprudence for its subservience to state interests, but now they turned their attention inwards to their own work.[63] Were anthropological representations of data as objective as the writers claimed?

---

[61] See eg Sandra Burman and Barbara Harrell-Bond (eds), *Imposition of Law* (1979).

[62] Claude Meillassoux, 'From Reproduction to Production', (1972) 1 *Economy & Society* 102 ff.

[63] James Clifford and George Marcus (eds), *Writing Culture* (1986).

How did ethnographies contribute to the maintenance of government and its policies?

The critique targeted culture and tradition, two concepts which functioned to define the very subject-matter of anthropology, and, indirectly, customary law. Laws were deemed co-extensive with cultures, and the notion of custom implied a normative order legitimated by tradition. A re-examination of these concepts therefore had profound implications for understanding customary law and its position in modern legal systems.

Culture was a particular casualty. As the new school of anthropology demonstrated, culture had never been of much value in explaining the workings of society. In fact, when called upon to account for the lives of people suffering poverty and oppression, which was the fate of most people living in developing countries, it seemed quite meaningless. Culture nevertheless served useful political functions. In South Africa under apartheid, for example, the government had divided the population into separate 'cultural' units, simultaneously depriving them of the benefits of national citizenship, on the ground that it was doing no more than realizing their right to cultural self-determination.

As the political manipulation of culture was exposed, legal anthropology began discarding ideas previously considered part and parcel of the concept, namely, that cultures were pure, discrete units, consisting of fixed values, norms, and institutions. Hence, today, culture is regarded as a much more porous concept,[64] as a repertoire of signs culled from a group's beliefs, values, laws, artefacts, and behaviour, whereby members of the group can distinguish themselves from members of other groups.[65] Once these possibilities were accepted, it followed that customary law, a prime manifestation of culture, also had to be regarded as both permeable and malleable.

Researchers are now far more willing to acknowledge the diversity of forces active in the creation of customary law. For example, since the eleventh century, from origins in the Sahel, disciples of Islam had taken the Shari'a deep into Africa, with obvious implications for the customary laws of the converts. It was not so obvious, however, how to label the result. While it could be said that the laws of such peoples as the Hausa and Wolof had been Islamicized, it could equally be said that they had Africanized Islamic law. Christianity had produced similar effects, and raised similar questions: had customary marriages been Christianized or had the so-called independent African churches Africanized Christian marriage?

Both culture and custom are intimately linked to tradition, an institution which functions to give people a sense of continuity and security in circumstances

---

[64] See Eugeen Roosens, *Creating Ethnicity* (1989), 12.

[65] At the heart of any analysis of culture is power. In their struggles to gain power, both groups and individuals exploit culture as a resource to build hegemonic relationships. See Mandy Lazarus-Black and Susan Hirsch (eds), *Contested States* (1994), 9–13.

of disruptive social change. As far as culture is concerned, tradition connotes the means whereby thoughts, values, and institutions are transmitted from one generation to the next. As far as custom is concerned, it connotes a basis of legitimacy.

The social practices on which all custom rests are, in the nature of things, continually changing. The volatility of this normative order is balanced, however, by a belief that the rules are derived from the past, a belief which gives legitimacy to the novel and unexpected. Hence, the paradox: while forgotten rules of customary law are constantly sinking into oblivion and new rules are rising to take their place, it is always understood that the new is old and deserving of respect.[66]

These propositions were borne out by Sally Falk Moore's study of the Chagga, a people who live on the slopes of Mount Kilimanjaro in Tanzania. Falk Moore showed that, with the introduction of coffee as a cash crop, and a steady decrease in the amount of land available for agriculture, rights of access had to be reformulated to meet changed social and economic conditions. Although the rules at the time of the study were certainly not those of the pre-colonial past, the people still regarded them as traditional customary law.[67]

It becomes apparent from such studies that tradition, like culture, is a resource to which people appeal in struggles for power. Colonial, and then post-colonial, governments reconstituted existing institutions to achieve new policies, but then returned these same institutions to the people as if they were unchanged. In this process, 'history was denied and tradition created instead'.[68] The people subjected to these changes also invoked tradition, however, partly to resist the imposition of new laws and partly to make sense of new situations.

Acknowledgement of human agency in the creation of culture and tradition has had a profound effect on our understanding of customary law. A noticeable scepticism pervades the attitude to earlier literature, for readers are now aware that authors give particular representations of their subjects, ones shaped by contemporary intellectual trends and the authors' own interests. Such is the level of doubt that the term customary law is now frequently qualified to signal its degree of legitimacy.

Especially suspect is 'official' customary law. This version is found in texts used by the state judiciary and official administration. Because it appears in the form of statutes, codes, restatements, and precedents, it is most likely to have strayed from an authentic tradition, and, in fact, may well have been produced by government to serve some ulterior purpose. Academic versions of customary law are also available, but they, too, are not considered totally reliable, given the theoretical and other preoccupations of the authors.

---

[66] Michael Clanchy, *From Memory to Written Record* (1979), 233.
[67] Sally Falk Moore, *Law as Process* (2nd edn, 2000).
[68] Peter Fitzpatrick, 'Is it Simple to be a Marxist in Legal Anthropology?', (1985) 48 *Modern LR* 479.

Scholars, and even courts and law-makers would now be ready to concede that the only truly authentic version of customary law is the 'living law', which is the law in fact being observed by its subjects. By definition, however, this law is not directly available to outsiders. It may still be adduced in court by way of evidence, but the procedure is costly and time-consuming. Hence, the unhappy situation, that, for better or for worse, people needing to refer to customary law are usually forced to make do with official or academic versions.

VII. Legal Pluralism

1. Centralism and the Pluralist Critique

The dichotomy between official and living law forms the basis of legal pluralism, a perspective that now dominates the study of customary law. Pluralism grew out of a profound sense of dissatisfaction with legal positivism, which, in pluralist terms, is called 'legal centralism'.

Centralism assumes that the state has a monopoly of all legal institutions. It follows that legal and non-legal norms must be clearly distinguished and that legal norms have an overriding authority. Centralism also assumes the logical coherence of the legal system,[69] and, perhaps most important, it accepts the main tenets of legal liberalism, namely, that state institutions operate according to strict principles of equality and neutrality: all individuals are equal before the law, and, to reach decisions, courts must impartially apply rules to the facts.

Over the years, however, anthropological fieldwork had produced abundant evidence to show that none of these assumptions was being realized in fact. The reach of the state was not nearly as extensive as centralism might suggest. To the contrary, research showed that, in everyday life, the formal legal system was often treated as a secondary, not a primary, source of regulation. Moreover, courts, especially those in states with poorly developed infrastructures, seldom realized the requirements of impartiality and equal treatment. Instead, fieldwork showed a multiplicity of different normative regimes in operation: the law being applied in the courts and the various other laws associated with distinctive social units.

In 1986, John Griffiths set out to debunk legal centralism, and to proclaim the

---

[69] Gordon Woodman, 'Ideological Combat and Social Observations: Recent Debate about Legal Pluralism', (1998) 42 *Journal of Legal Pluralism & Unofficial Law* 51.

manifesto of legal pluralism.[70] He denounced centralism as a myth and an ideal, and he rejected, as pure ideology, the proposition that 'law is and should be the law of the state, uniform for all persons, exclusive of all other law, and administered by a single set of state institutions'.[71] Admittedly, both colonial and post-colonial states formally recognized the operation of indigenous systems of law, but Griffiths described this phenomenon as 'weak' pluralism.[72] He said that it was no more than legal centralism in a different guise, for the state, in its discretion, had decided whether to take cognizance of these subordinate systems.

In place of weak legal pluralism, Griffiths advocated what he called the 'strong' variety, namely, a frank acceptance of the fact that people's lives were regulated by various independent but related legal orders, each valid in its own terms. Griffiths's proposal was an elaboration of earlier works, notably, Eugen Ehrlich, *Fundamental Principles of the Sociology of Law* (1936), Leopold Pospisil, *Anthropology of Law* (1971), and Sally Falk Moore, *Law as Process* (1973). Ehrlich had claimed that true, 'living law' was the actual conduct of people in associations, such as factories, religious communities, or political parties. Pospisil had viewed society as a constellation of groups and sub-groups, the higher groups containing the subordinate, and each group distinguished by its own legal order. For her part, Moore claimed that law emerged from semi-autonomous social fields, each of which was 'defined . . . by the fact that it can generate rules and coerce or induce compliance to them'.[73]

From these works, Griffiths extracted a common theme: that the unofficial normative orders operating within discrete social groups were as valid for the subjects as state law. Hence, unlike the former weak legal pluralism, strong pluralism regards all law-like behaviour as worthy of study. Griffiths's contention rested on what he said was the self-evident fact that people within semi-autonomous social fields actually observe the normative orders of those fields, often in contravention of state law. To say that the state has exclusive jurisdiction over social life is, therefore, to endorse an ideology, since the claim is not borne out by the reality.

The keystone of legal pluralism is the semi-autonomous social field, a concept developed by Sally Falk Moore. It can be defined as any social entity, whether village, family, church, or workplace, with the capacity to create rules and induce compliance. Because individuals may simultaneously be members of two or even more semi-autonomous social fields, they will be subject to concurrent and

---

[70] John Griffiths, 'What is Legal Pluralism?', (1986) 24 *Journal of Legal Pluralism & Unofficial Law* 1 ff. A similar manifesto had in fact appeared earlier in an analysis of methods of dispute processing in the United States: Mark Galanter, 'Justice in Many Rooms: Courts, Private Ordering and Indigenous Law', (1981) 19 *Journal of Legal Pluralism & Unofficial Law* 1 ff.

[71] Griffiths, (1986) 24 *Journal of Legal Pluralism and Unofficial Law* 3.

[72] See the accounts by John Gilissen (ed), *Le Pluralisme Juridique* (1971) and M. B. Hooker, *Legal Pluralism* (1975).

[73] Moore (n 67), 57.

contradictory obligations. For legal pluralists, this situation is to be expected, because pluralism is always present whenever two or more normative orders overlap.

This potential for overlap is significant in two respects. In the first place, it implies that individuals located at the intersections of semi-autonomous social fields have choices as to which rules they will invoke and abide by. In the second place, it suggests that social fields do not function in isolation but in interaction. Those responsible for applying a particular normative order will be constantly influenced by other norms, either formally, as when judges in state courts acknowledge new rules of customary law, or informally, as when customary tribunals take account of state laws.

Legal pluralism insists that we pay careful attention to the way people behave, because it is only from actual behaviour that a 'true' version of the law can be discovered. Seen in these terms, much of the customary law applied in the higher courts is of dubious validity. It is at this point that legal pluralism converges with the critique of culture and tradition, because both acknowledge the need to distinguish the living from the official versions of customary law.

2. The Value of Pluralist Research

Legal anthropologists were quick to adopt Griffiths's thesis, which they hailed as a key to 'reconceptualising the relationship between law and society'.[74] Pluralism has therefore exerted a considerable influence on research into customary law. A good example is the work being done by Women and Law in Southern Africa (WLSA), a private NGO which is conducting a series of studies in several southern African states to discover how women are affected by the interaction of official and living law.[75]

WLSA employs an eclectic range of data-gathering techniques. Its preferred method is a 'grounded process', which can be described, in an appropriately African image, as that of the 'dung beetle'.[76] Thus, WLSA researchers start their work with the subject's 'lived reality', namely, his or her perceptions of rules and courts, and how tribunals deal with problems. Careful attention is paid to the intersections of semi-autonomous social fields, together with structures of gender, generation, and culture to show how overlapping normative orders affect individual

[74] See Gordon Woodman, 'Unification or Continuing Pluralism in Family Law in Anglophone Africa: Past Experience, Present Realities, and Future Possibilities', (1988) 4 *Lesotho LJ* 40–1 and Sally Merry, 'Legal Pluralism', (1988) 22 *Law & Society Review* 869 ff.

[75] Another excellent example is Anne Griffiths, *In the Shadow of Marriage* (1997), a book derived from the author's fieldwork on property claims made by women of the Bakwena group in Botswana.

[76] See Agnete Weis Bentzon, Anne Hellum, and Julie Stewart (eds), *Pursuing Grounded Theory in Law* (1998), 178 ff.

choice. Like other, similar research agencies, WLSA favours an action-oriented approach, whereby field workers actively assist vulnerable groups, especially women, to improve their position in law and society.

WLSA's work on succession is an excellent example of its approach. The project revealed that well-meant legislative reforms were not necessarily being implemented in people's lives. Hence, although heirs might be entitled, under statutory rules, to specific fractions of an estate, social practice dictated that the surviving spouse simply took over the whole estate.[77] Predictably, WLSA reported a divergence between the approaches of higher and lower courts towards customary law. The lower courts, including those of traditional rulers, responded to perceived social needs regardless of the strict rule, whereas higher courts applied only the official version of customary law. Hence, although the original purpose of customary law was to create an environment conducive to the care and protection of a deceased's family, the law applied by the higher courts very often had the opposite effect.

WLSA also noted the emergence of new rules of succession, which go unmentioned in the upper courts. Throughout southern Africa, it is an accepted rule of official customary law that only males can succeed as heirs. According to this strongly patriarchal system, the heir is supposed to succeed to the deceased's status and obligations in order to care for the widow and the deceased's immediate dependants. WLSA research, however, revealed strikingly different patterns of practice.

The position of widows, for instance, is both better and worse than is apparent in the official version. On the one hand, they are generally involved in family decisions about the estate, and heirs regularly consult them. Moreover, widows, especially those with young children to raise, often take control of their husbands' lands and movable assets in order to secure maintenance of the surviving family unit. On the other hand, it is also true that widows regularly suffer at the hands of the deceased's male relatives, who readily exploit their patriarchal privileges to seize whatever property they can find in the estate.

WLSA research has shown dramatic departures from the principle of primogeniture, which has always been assumed to be a cardinal rule of customary law in southern Africa. The oldest son may still inherit the largest portion of the estate, on the ground that he has responsibilities for maintaining the family, but other children also take a share. Moreover, several field studies have shown that last-born sons inherit the family homestead. The practice of ultimogeniture is based on the fact that the oldest son is normally the first to marry, leave home, and start a new family. The youngest son is left behind to assume responsibility for his parents in their old age. Inheritance of the family land and house gives him both the means and the incentive to do so.

---

[77] See generally Welshman Ncube and Julie Stewart (eds), *Widowhood, Inheritance Law, Customs and Practices in Southern Africa* (1995).

Litigants naturally make the most of the opportunities offered by contradictory laws. Throughout Africa, society is in a state of constant change, and WLSA shows how people invoke either the old or the new orders, depending on which affords the greater advantage. Courts and state officials, too, are alive to the differences between the official and unofficial systems, and, to a limited extent, they are prepared to use the one to modify the other.

Reservations about legal pluralism have only recently begun to emerge. First, pluralists, like the functionalists before them, took it for granted that their perspective would be more objective than what had gone before. In common with others who insist on empirical observation, they seemed to think that they had emancipated themselves from all value systems.[78] In fact, however, pluralist writing—following a long tradition in anthropology—shows a predisposition to favour the underdog.

Second, legal pluralists refuted any hierarchy in their units of study—the semi-autonomous social fields—and by implication in the normative orders of those units. This stance followed from the argument that the state is not in exclusive control of law. Although the pluralist viewpoint is understandable, it obscures the fact that state law can and often does exert a considerable power, which in many situations will prove to be decisive. Thus, treating state law as a superior order is certainly not blind obedience to ideology.

Third, and related to the last point, is the assumption in pluralism that all normative orders are equally valid. While the pluralists' original intention was to rescue indigenous and other normative orders from a position of inferiority, they have succeeded in elevating mere social practice to the same status as law. The logical consequence is, paradoxically, to deny customary law much of its current status. If it enjoys a rank equal to that of the normative orders observed in factories or the banking industry, then it loses its value as an African cultural heritage.

3. Customary Law in a Pluralist Age

Over the last twenty or so years, research into customary law has declined—most texts are produced in and with reference to southern Africa, especially South Africa—and many of the new works have turned from the task of recording law to the job of reflecting critically on existing texts. Indeed, awareness of the ambiguity of customary law has made study of the subject much more difficult than in the heyday of the functionalist ethnographies in the 1950s and 1960s.

---

[78] For the critiques of pluralism, see: Brian Tamanaha, 'The Folly of the "Social Scientific" Concept of Legal Pluralism', (1993) 20 *Journal of Law & Society* 198 ff and 'A Non-essentialist Version of Legal Pluralism', (2000) 27 *Journal of Law & Society* 298 ff. For an excellent summary of the history and current state of legal pluralism, see Anne Griffiths, 'Legal Pluralism', in R. Banakar and M. Travers (eds), *An Introduction to Law and Social Theory* (2002), 289 ff.

Customary law can no longer be treated as if it were a neatly contained system, locked in a rural tradition. Instead, field workers must take account of the normative systems developing in Africa's sprawling urban areas, where approximately 40 per cent of the sub-continent's population now lives. The heterogeneity of this unit of study implies the need to take account of the many forces shaping people's lives, whether work, religion, new forms of residence, or HIV/AIDS. Urban thinking and behaviour have, in turn, exerted an influence far beyond the confines of towns and cities, as urban dwellers commute to families in the country.

What is more, throughout Africa, reforming governments have contrived to change people's lives. Bills of rights are probably the most dramatic example, although family relationships regulated by customary law were usually shielded from their effects. None the less, reform legislation is challenging entrenched traditions, notably the privileges enjoyed by senior males and traditional rulers. The social effects of these laws vary considerably, however, and not always in ways that legislators would like.

Because written laws are now the basis of all African legal systems, the survival of customary law is coming to depend increasingly on its being recorded. The process of documenting custom generally requires at least three shifts of register. The first is a shift from everyday to legal terminology. The second is a change of language, because most texts are written with a view to use in courts and organs of state, where the use of European languages still prevails. (An attempt in Tanzania to use only Swahili eventually had to be partially abandoned.) The third is a shift from a loose repertoire of rules to a structured system.

Each of these changes entails a move farther away from the living law. Hence, the mere fact of writing about customary law constitutes the creation of a new and somewhat artificial product. It must be accepted, however, that this construct is the outsider's only access to the subject.

VIII. Legal Anthropology in Comparative Law

Lawyers have dictated the scope of comparative legal research, and, with characteristic conservatism, the normative orders they selected for comparison have been remarkably similar. Custom poses a much more challenging venture.

Customary laws operate most effectively in close-knit, homogeneous communities, whose members share common values and goals. Both the nature of these rules (and the methods developed for their study) stand in sharp contrast with the laws typical of heterogeneous societies. Hence, study of custom requires a radical shift in thinking.

In the first place, law existing only in oral tradition has features which distinguish it markedly from written laws, notably, a lack of system and a high degree of particularity (whereby laws are linked to specific peoples, events, or places). In the second place, the relatively weak degree of political control in customary communities precludes any notion of central authority over juristic acts. Legal relations are classically transactional and open-ended. As a result, law—the corpus of abstract rules—carries far less importance than processes for dealing with dispute.

Breaking into the tight-knit communities of custom, with their unwritten, and sometimes even unspoken, laws is far from simple, and it is certainly not possible using the traditional methods of legal research. Instead, the techniques developed by legal anthropology are essential. Moreover, because of its long association with marginal social groups and because its method demands direct questioning of informants and on-the-spot observation, anthropology has much to teach the conventional lawyer about the efficacy of the law. The legal practitioner's view is formed by statements in legal texts and pronouncements in court rooms. Legal anthropology, however, and, in particular, legal pluralism give the recipient's rather than the law-giver's point of view. This grass-roots perspective reveals the law as observed by its subjects, and the ways in which rules and processes are manipulated.

What is more, the anthropologist's interest in methods of social control and in the ideological functions of law have produced new perspectives on key concepts, in the case of customary law, culture, and tradition. Thus, anthropology would ask us to question closely the implications of ascribing the qualities of a distinct culture or tradition to a particular body of rules. Who ascribes these qualities and why? How does a cultural tradition strengthen the validity of a rule?

Once comparative lawyers are prepared to consider the social basis of law, then legal anthropology becomes an invaluable adjunct to their research. Indeed, the intimate connection between the two disciplines is not something new: Oliver Wendell Holmes remarked that '[i]t is perfectly proper to regard and study the law simply as a great anthropological document'.[79]

BIBLIOGRAPHY

Arthur Phillips (ed), *Survey of African Marriage and Family Life* (1953)
Max Gluckman, *The Judicial Process among the Barotse of Northern Rhodesia* (1955; 2nd edn, 1967)
—— *The Ideas in Barotse Jurisprudence* (1965; reprinted 1972)

---

[79] (1899) 12 *Harvard LR* 444.

Lloyd A. Fallers, *Law without Precedent* (1969)

Laura Nader (ed), *Law in Culture and Society* (1969)

Max Gluckman (ed), *Ideas and Procedures in African Customary Law* (1969)

Ian Hamnett (ed), *Social Anthropology and Law* (1977)

Peter H. Gulliver, *Disputes and Negotiations: A Cross-cultural Perspective* (1979)

Simon Roberts, *Order and Dispute: an introduction to legal anthropology* (1979)

John L. Comaroff and Simon Roberts, *Rules and Processes* (1981)

Martin Chanock, *Law, Custom and Social Order, the Colonial Experience in Malawi and Zambia* (1985)

John Griffiths, 'What is Legal Pluralism?', (1986) 24 *Journal of Legal Pluralism & Unofficial Law* 1

Thomas W. Bennett, *A Sourcebook of African Customary Law for Southern Africa* (1991)

Kristin Mann and Richard Roberts (eds), *Law in Colonial Africa* (1991)

Sally F. Moore, *Law as Process: An Anthropological Approach* (2nd edn, 2000)

CHAPTER 20

COMPARATIVE LAW AND LANGUAGE

VIVIAN GROSSWALD CURRAN

Pittsburgh[*]

[*] For their helpful thoughts on some of the issues discussed in this chapter, sincerest thanks to John Allison, Sir Franklin and Lady Berman, Cécile Desandre, Dan Simpson, and Phil Watts. Unless otherwise noted, translations are mine.

> [T]he suggestion that inquiries into the meanings of words merely
> throw light on words is false.
>
> (H. L. A. Hart)

I. INTRODUCTION

AT the simplest level of observation, language issues arise in connection with comparative law because people in different countries speak in different languages, producing legal texts in foreign languages that become the target of comparative legal studies. At the same time, English is gaining ascendancy, if not dominance, with international exchanges in the field increasingly conducted solely in that single language, whether in scholarly conferences, in journals targeting an international readership, or in university classes where professors and students do not share a native language. These matters of simple observation will be discussed in Section II, with some suggestion of how they relate to a deeper link between comparative law and language that is a principal subject of this chapter: namely, the study of language as a cognitive model for comparative law.

Section III discusses language's dependence on translation inasmuch as translation is the mechanism central to meaning construction, even within a given language. Section IV links translation to comparative law as a model for the study of similarity and difference, of the universal and the particular, and discusses them in terms of the contrasting categories that undergird the civil and common law legal systems. It also discusses how post-war comparative law scholars analysed these subjects, explaining their rejection of the legal positivism that increasingly had marked legal theory from the nineteenth century until the Second World War.

Section V examines the post-war émigré comparative law scholars' immersion in a new language and legal culture, and how that experience informed their scholarly theory on issues of sameness and difference across legal orders. It then progresses to the generation that followed, whose divergence from the post-war perspective has reflected an increasing incorporation of postmodernist influences. The debate in comparative law over the relative importance of similarity and difference among legal systems has its counterpart in linguistics in conflicting views about whether commonalities among languages are fundamental or merely marginal. Section VI shows that these issues situate comparative law between deeply entrenched, mutually contradictory aspirations of universalism and pluralism which have stalked the evolution of both language and legal studies.

Universalism may seem to be on the ascendancy today, due to the globalization that vastly increases contacts in law without impediments from geographical distance; the widespread use of English as a means of facilitating communication throughout the world; and the increasing importance of non-national structures in law. Section VII discusses these phenomena in order to demonstrate that former *domains* of pluralism and difference indeed are receding, but that difference itself remains undiminished. Rather, its nature and provenances are changing, due to rapidly multiplying reconfigurations that characterize our time. Comparative law's challenge lies in deciphering significance amid reconstituting categories so as to unravel deceptive appearances, whether of unchanged legal significance surviving under a mask of change, or, conversely, of changed legal significance evolving under a surface that appears to remain static (Section VIII). In this task, comparative law's effectiveness as a translator of the foreign will depend on how well its acquired skills and methods can be adapted to new kinds of foreignness.

Section IX offers a concrete application of comparative law analysis as translator of current European legal developments, and shows why comparative law is needed urgently today in a world in which law increasingly absorbs influences and ideas that have crossed national borders and have blurred traditional legal classifications.

The concluding section discusses comparative law's need for fluctuating methods and resistance to formulaic approaches as the field continually must re-establish its equilibrium in changing contexts. Comparative law's continuity is in the permanence of its location between the same and the other, an attribute it shares with language. This necessitates ongoing reconnoitring as the poles of sameness and otherness shift in form and substance, elusive to detection and prediction, requiring comparative law to undergo internal methodological metamorphoses in keeping with the metamorphosing world.

II. Simple Observations

Comparative law's most visible connection to language is due to different legal systems' legal texts being in different languages. Issues of foreign law's accessibility arise where comparatists are not fluent in the relevant foreign languages. If translations exist, corollary issues arise, such as whether a legal text can be studied productively in any language but the original.

If fluency in the language of the target legal order is a prerequisite for comparative studies, comparatists necessarily will be limited in the range of legal cultures they can study by the foreign languages they know. Moreover, if foreign language knowledge is crucial, then even a polyglot comparative law scholar may not be able to communicate successfully to students who are unable to read foreign texts except in translation, thus reducing comparative law's educational potential.

To the extent that translation is considered to be a viable option, how should translations be elaborated where a legal phenomenon has no exact equivalent in two languages? It is common in comparative law to translate certain words by approximation, so that, for example, the French word 'procès' generally is translated into English as 'trial', even though innumerable attributes associated with the French 'procès' are not attributes of 'trials'. Some authors add explanations to such effect in footnotes. The problem with this solution is that lengthy explanations will be necessary for a great many terms, making the translation of even a short legal text so cumbersome that it cannot be achieved without an encyclopaedic volume of explanation in footnotes.

One need only consider that if the French 'procès' is not a 'trial', it is in part that the French '*juge*' is also not a 'judge', or at least that, if she is a 'judge', she is only so in some ways, but not in others. Further, if the French 'juge' is not entirely a 'judge', it is in part because the relevant 'cour' or 'tribunal' is not exactly a 'court', and so on and so forth, with virtually limitlessly connected concepts that are not quite equivalent when any word is translated. Thus, the explanatory footnotes will be unwieldy unless drastic short-cuts and omissions are made, which in turn, however, would leave readers with an exaggerated and misleading impression of similarity to their own legal systems.

An alternative approach is to leave in the original language words that translate poorly. The appearance of a word or phrase in a foreign language and in italics will alert the reader to the irremediably foreign nature of the underlying concept. The obvious disadvantage of this technique, however, is that an untranslated word is not accessible to the reader in the absence of explanatory references. Thus, by leaving a word in a foreign language, a comparatist will succeed in conveying that the concept at issue is foreign and without exact equivalence, but will not in this manner transmit the concept.

Translation may appear to be a decreasing problem to the extent that English emerges as the single, dominant language of the field, with increasingly accomplished levels of fluency among those for whom it is not a native language. This would be an incorrect conclusion, however. The language of law is bound to the inner grammar of legal systems, cultures, and mentalities, which in turn impede communication in words that are borrowed from another legal system, culture, and mentality. As the rest of this chapter seeks to show, the complex comparative nature of language also characterizes law, making comparative law of paramount importance as a translator of law, but only so long as comparative law remembers that the comparative undertaking remains one of translation.

III. Plurilinguism, Imagination, and Comparative Law

As Chapter 24 ('Comparative Law and Socio-legal Studies') discusses, comparative law scholars today generally agree that the field encompasses the exploration of the nature of law in society, such that the examination of foreign law is an aspect of comparative legal scholarship, rather than its defining attribute. The more reconfigurations law undergoes in its dynamic interaction with a world in transition, the more comparative law must become a process of decoding legal presences that are like languages whose connotations change just as they begin to acquire meaning, languages in which all of the speakers are among the uninitiated.[1]

As this section discusses, the decoding process, whether of foreign language or law, is a process of translation. Understanding translation's mechanisms thus illuminates the processes of comparative law. Translation is both de-coding and re-coding, identifying and constructing meaning. Translating between languages involves vast networks of associations of a word in one language that cannot all be transposed into the other, such that there must be loss of connotative significance in the process. At best, translation achieves an overlap of some meanings between two domains, as in an intersection of sets, but not total overlap, as in a union of sets. The extent to which translation can succeed is a matter of debate.[2] Similarly, the extent to which comparative law can succeed in communicating the other in law is a matter of debate.

Linguists and philosophers of language diverge on how communication takes place, and on whether any communication means, or can mean, an exchange of equivalent concepts. Theories also range as to whether and to what extent all languages may share deep structures.[3] There is dispute as to how to define the concept of language.[4] Finally, and crucially, the status and role of language are not the same in every society and legal order.[5] In comparative law, analogously, theories

---

[1] This is the principal theme of Vivian Grosswald Curran, 'Re-membering Law in the Internationalizing World', (2005) 34 *Hofstra LR* 93 ff.

[2] Another debate concerns the legitimacy of undertaking translation between two domains of law. Neil Walker, 'Postnational Constitutionalism and the Problem of Translation', in J. H. H. Weiler and Marlene Wind (eds), *European Constitutionalism beyond the State* (2003), 27 ff.

[3] The term originated with Noam Chomsky. In his most recent book on linguistics, Chomsky has revised his theory to reject the term, but he continues to consider language structure as 'invariant'. Noam Chomsky, *New Horizons in the Study of Language and Mind* (2000), 7 ff.

[4] Donald Davidson, *Inquiries into Truth and Interpretation* (1994), 186 ff.

[5] Bernhard Grossfeld, *Core Questions of Comparative Law* (trans Vivian Grosswald Curran, 2005); Bernhard Grossfeld and Josef Hoeltzenbein, 'Globalization and the Limits of Language', in Werner Krawietz (ed), *Rechtstheorie* (2004), 87 ff. Bernard Hibbitts, 'Making Sense of Metaphors: Aurality and the Reconfiguration of American Legal Discourse', (1994) 16 *Cardozo LR* 229 ff.

range as to how to define law; whether too little equivalence links legal orders, such that they are not mutually communicable; or whether, on the contrary, law shares deep structures throughout the world. Also analogously to language, the status and role of law are not the same in every society.

For present purposes, it is sufficient to posit that there are irreducible untranslatables between languages. A vast and varied literature links the phenomenon of untranslatability to the conclusion that language uniqueness arises from, and in turn also fortifies, a unique world perspective, an irreproducible manner of seeing and understanding.[6] This attribute of language has significance for comparative law beyond the similarity of the field to translation. It means that knowing a second language allows entry into another world, a way of seeing through another lens, into 'incommensurable systems of concepts'.[7] Consequently, for comparatists, knowing the languages of legal systems they study signifies access to all that the texts of law imply and connote, but do not state, to their infinity of links to the contexts that spawned them and that they also affect. It has been suggested that communication always lies beyond language.[8] The kind of openings to perspective, to ways of thinking and feeling, that an additional language offers, also allows one to intuit the *nature* of the closures and barriers to intercontextual understanding that are comparative law's greatest challenges, even before one locates, identifies, and learns to overcome the particular impediments in the particular study at hand.

The polyglot knows that much alterity is not apparent. The polyglot legal comparatist knows that legal orders reside as much beneath and aside from words as they do in the words that purport to embody them. Ernst Rabel's insistence on multilinguism for legal comparatists, like George Steiner's for literary comparatists, stems from the premise that, since knowing another language is a powerful and crucial entry into another world vision and universe of thought, it more importantly indirectly transmits the fact that other world visions and universes of thought exist and are to be apprehended.[9] Beyond the particulars of two differing underlying networks of meaning, knowing another language expands one's imaginative capacities to encompass an understanding of the nature of differences, the

---

[6] Support for this may be found throughout the Romanticist movement and the field of semiotics. In legal literature, see eg H. L. A. Hart, *Definition and Theory in Jurisprudence* (1953).

[7] Davidson (n 4), 186.

[8] George Steiner, *Language and Silence: Essays on Language, Literature and the Inhuman* (1967), x ff; Vivian Grosswald Curran, 'Metaphor is the Mother of All Law', in Roberta Kevelson (ed), *Law and the Conflict of Ideologies* (1995), 65 ff.

[9] On Rabel, see Gehard Kegel, 'Ernst Rabel (1874–1955): Vorkämpfer des Weltkaufrechts', in H. C. Helmut Heinrichs, Hans-Harald Franzki, and Klaus Schmalz (eds), *Deutsche Juristen jüdischer Herkunft* (1993), 571 ff, at 585; David S. Clark, 'The Influence of Ernst Rabel on American Law', in Marcus Lutter, Ernst C. Stiefel, and Michael H. Hoeflich (eds), *Der Einfluß deutscher Emigranten auf die Rechtsentwicklung in den USA und in Deutschland* (1991), 107 ff, at 113. On Steiner, see George Steiner, *No Passion Spent: Essays 1978–1995* (1996), 142 ff. Accord, Ernst Cassirer, *Language and Myth* (trans Susanne K. Langer, 1946).

imperfections of translation, the pitfalls to constructing equivalences, and the like-lihood that newness and difference will have unexpected locations and provenances in another system of thought.

Immersion in more than one language, and the struggle to translate between languages, highlights tapestries of interlinking threads that are woven into infinity, connections between past and present, and among spiralling associations inspired by words and phrases in a unique syntax, endless links of threads to connecting ties. It is a messiness that one can approach but not reduce without distortion. Just as comparison is an act of translation, so too translation is an act of comparison, and the word 'comparison', after all, admits of being less than exact correspondence. Comparison is of the order of simile, not metaphor.

The process of translating from one language to another is the basic pattern not just of comparative law, but of all analysis, of cognition.[10] Thus, the monoglot also engages in the same process within a given community of signs, or semiotic system, for translation is

formally and pragmatically implicit in every act of communication, in the emission and reception of each and every mode of meaning . . . To understand is to decipher. To hear significance is to translate. Thus the essential structure and . . . means and problems in the act of translation are fully present in acts of speech, of writing, of pictoral encoding inside any given language. Translation between different languages is a particular application and model fundamental to human language even where it is monoglot . . . [One should] con-sider . . . the teeming difficulties encountered inside the same language by those who seek to communicate across spaces of historical time, of social class, of different cultural and professional sensibility.[11]

The passage between discourses of difference that comparative legal analysis demands will be less well performed by monoglots because monolinguism deprives one of a rigorous training and insight into both detecting and conveying alterity that conscious translation endows.

Roland Barthes said that 'language is fascistic'.[12] In advocating the search for a 'hazy polylinguism' ('un polylinguisme flou'), rather than a single perfect, or even imperfect language, Umberto Eco notes that 'a language always is a prison . . . because it imposes a certain vision of the world'.[13] A language imprisons thought and understanding. Many languages liberate them.

---

[10] George Lakoff, *Women, Fire and Dangerous Things: What Categories Reveal about the Mind* (1987); George Lakoff and Mark Johnson, *Metaphors We Live By* (1980).

[11] George Steiner, *After Babel: Aspects of Language and Translation* (2nd edn, 1992), xii. One who considered those 'teeming difficulties' was Isaiah Berlin throughout his life's work, and in particular in Henry Hardy (ed), *Concepts and Categories: Philosophical Essays* (1999).

[12] '*La langue est fasciste.*' Roland Barthes, 'La leçon', in *Leçon inaugurale au Collège de France* (1978).

[13] Umberto Eco, interview by Bernard Pivot, *Double je*, TV-5, broadcast on 25 July 2005.

Automatic understanding accompanies immersion in another society: 'Imagination conforms on its own to the customs of a country in which one is located'.[14] Knowing the language of others brings such an intuitive, automatic understanding of the other. It enables polyglots to gain insight into foreign ways of being foreign, and to bend their cognitive grids, so as to be more open to absorbing data that monoglots will be unable to process. Language pluralism locates one elsewhere. For comparative law, language knowledge not only is part of foreign legal systems under examination; it is the most efficient shortcut to understanding how to understand.

IV. The Universal and the Particular in Post-War Comparative Law and Language

We have suggested through the translation metaphor that comparative analysis cannot be valid unless it is keenly attuned to elements and domains of difference and, most fundamentally, unless it is attuned to expect changes from unexpected provenances and kinds of difference. If plurilinguism, multiplicity, and the detection of alterity are comparative law's trump cards, then it may seem as though comparative law should choose difference over sameness. This section shows that, for comparative analysis, those attributes are not crucial because difference is an ultimate goal, but, rather, because it is only by identifying difference that one can identify both difference and its equally important counterpoint, similarity.

Somewhat paradoxically, western comparative law was steered towards the identification of similarity after the Second World War by those whose plurilinguism attuned them to the importance of difference. The field since then experienced a reaction, tending increasingly towards privileging difference. This section shows some striking parallels between the fields of comparative law and language concerning the issue of sameness versus difference. It first discusses the issue in terms of the contrasting conceptions that undergird the civil and common law legal systems.

In western legal discourse, historically and traditionally the common law perspective was primed on the particular and specific, on cases, the accumulation of facts within each, and the mosaic which cases create as a *pointilliste* composite.

---

[14] Charles Louis de Secondat, baron de la Brède et de Montesquieu, and 'Usbek à Rhédi', in *Lettres persanes* (1721), LXXX ('L'imagination se plie d'elle-même aux mœurs du pays où l'on est').

Continental European civil law traditionally embraced the universal and general, and marginalized the particular. In this one may see a link between civil law and the Enlightenment, with its premises of overarching coherence and unity; and between the common law and Romanticism, with its focus on the particular, the individual, and, therefore, the different.[15]

Spinoza, whose work arguably is far more crucial to understanding the Enlightenment than generally has been credited,[16] believed in universals. He wrote, however, that because of the human incapacity to apprehend more than a few of the links of causality in the concatenation or great, overarching chain of events, humans must act as though the world were one of contingencies rather than universals.[17] As we will see below, comparative law scholars after the Second World War inverted Spinoza's admonition, acting as though the world were one of universals, regardless of their personal experiences of a world governed by turbulent contingencies. They believed that in universals lay whatever hope there might be for preserving civilization.

The identification of core human similarities as a hallmark of post-war comparative legal studies and theory derived from several sources. Some of the reasons were unrelated to the Second World War, and included Enlightenment-inspired views. Other reasons did relate to the war, shaped by a reaction against fascism's legalized persecution of those it had defined as different.[18] Along with racism, nationalism, with its concentration on differentiating an in-group from an out-group, was seen as having been the scourge implicated in Hitler's rule, to be repudiated in favour of a tolerance based on human-wide commonality.[19]

Post-war comparative law, like much western political thinking, urged not just non-nationalistic, universalist concepts, but, more particularly, it urged law itself as the remedy to political terror and ideology. The post-war generation of comparatists, including those who had not known exile personally, was undeterred by the spectacle of law's degradation in Hitlerism and Stalinism. On the contrary, their position was substantially Gustav Radbruch's, who elevated law to having a powerful redemptive capacity for self-perpetuation and for creating enduring civilization by excluding as non-law such measures as a state may issue that violate the

---

[15] Vivian Grosswald Curran, 'Romantic Common Law, Enlightened Civil Law: Legal Uniformity and the Homogenization of the European Union', (2001) 7 *Columbia Journal of European Law* 63 ff.

[16] Jonathan I. Israel, *Radical Enlightenment: Philosophy and the Making of Modernity 1650–1750* (2001); Stuart Hampshire, *Spinoza and Spinozism* (2005).

[17] Benedict de Spinoza, 'Natural Laws and Human Laws', Section 4:1 ff in *Ethics* (trans R. H. M. Elwes, 1883).

[18] This is a principal theme of Vivian Grosswald Curran, 'Cultural Immersion, Difference and Categories in U.S. Comparative Law', (1998), 46 *AJCL* 43 ff, discussing the work of Ernst Rabel, Konrad Zweigert, Hein Kötz, Edgar Bodenheimer, Max Rheinstein, Rudolf Schlesinger, and some others.

[19] Ibid. The word 'nation' derives from *natio*, originally used to signify the 'other'. Amos Elon, *The Pity of it All: A Portrait of the German-Jewish Epoch 1743–1933* (2002), 23.

most fundamental values of civilized society.[20] The theoretical underpinnings for this stance have roots in natural law, thereby marking a reversal of course from the increasingly positivistic legal perspective of the pre-war era.[21]

As Nathaniel Berman has recounted,[22] faith in law as the primary, ultimate, and durable solution to age-old barbarism also had inhabited the legal scholars of the interwar years, following the First World War. After the Second World War, it was revived by some of the very scholars who had had an opportunity to observe the fallibility of their views. Hans Morgenthau described this phenomenon of repeat mistake with prescient irony as he observed the renewed article of faith taking form in the 1940s yet again, calling it an 'inveterate tendency to stick to . . . assumptions and to suffer constant defeat from experience rather than to change . . . assumptions in the light of contradicting facts . . .'.[23]

The Nobel laureate René Cassin may be said to have been one of the clearest incarnations of this phenomenon, having been active and prominent in international law circles both in the interwar and the post-World War II periods. His writing reflects his unchanged faith in the power of law, and he became a principal drafter of the Universal Declaration of Human Rights.[24] His unflagging courage, dedication, humanity, and brilliance more than explain his reputation and the honours heaped upon him. One may wonder, however, if his post-war eminence may not in some measure also have been due to the tenacity of his refusal to sink into disillusion with the law despite a life of much personal hardship that included confrontations with law's darkest potentials to enable and execute abject state terror. That such a man could maintain his lifelong faith in law's capacity to become a nearly universal panacea may have held great appeal for those whom his example enabled to credit law in similar fashion, allowing them to keep intact a cherished ideal that history otherwise might have compelled them to consider an illusion.

Post-war comparative law tended to assume that a perception of others as different invariably is the first step towards hatred and discrimination, which in turn may culminate in legalized persecution, as had been the case in Nazi Europe and as legal theorists such as Carl Schmitt, Julius Binder, and Karl Larenz, among others,

---

[20] Gustav Radbruch, 'Gesetzliches Unrecht und übergesetzliches Recht', (1946) 1 *Süddeutsche Zeitung* 105 ff, translated in Stanley L. Paulson, 'Lon L. Fuller, Gustav Radbruch and the "Positivist" Theses', (1994) 13 *Law and Philosophy* 313 ff.

[21] It is in viewing law as inseparable from morality that Radbruch shares natural law roots, but the general agreement to categorize his position simply as one of natural law is problematic, in part reflecting the overlap between positivism in many versions with natural law. I especially like David Dyzenhaus's characterization of Radbruch's theory as being sufficiently distant from natural law to be, rather, 'positivism with a minus sign'. David Dyzenhaus, 'The Juristic Force of Injustice', in David Dyzenhaus and Mayo Moran (eds), *Calling Power to Account: Law's Response to Past Injustice* (2005).

[22] Nathaniel Berman, 'But the Alternative is Despair: European Nationalism and the Modernist Renewal of International Law', (1993) 106 *Harvard LR* 1792 ff.

[23] Hans J. Morgenthau, 'Positivism, Functionalism, and International Law', (1940) 34 *AJCL* 260 ff.

[24] René Cassin, *La Pensée et l'action* (1972).

had supported. The link between otherness and hatred has not been indissociable throughout history, however. René Girard argues that, contrary to general belief today, it is sameness, rather than difference, which elicits visceral hatred, as illustrated among others in antiquity's violent discrimination against twins.[25] Vladimir Jankélévitch coined the term 'le presque-semblable', 'the almost-the-same', in arguing, based on Freudian theory, that the greatest hostilities in society arise neither from sameness nor difference, but from *minimal otherliness*.[26]

Nor has the assessment of sameness and difference been a matter necessarily dependent on the historical era in question. An insight that captured a great deal about Rousseau and Diderot, who were contemporaries, suggests that, while Rousseau feared the other, Diderot feared the same: 'Rousseau's savage evolved the concept of "man" to fix and stabilize the gnawing anxieties stemming from his fear of the *other*, [while] Diderot's *moi* ["I," by contrast] . . . fear[ed] the *same*'.[27]

Language studies have their own version of comparative law's intense focus on whether legal systems throughout the world are (1) fundamentally similar, such that apparent differences are superficial in nature, justifying universalist conclusions; or (2) fundamentally different, such that apparent similarities are misleading, and universalist conclusions unwarranted. Noam Chomsky views language principally as universal, such that the differences are relegated to a marginal role. In his most recent book on linguistics, he writes: '[W]e know that the diversity and complexity [of language] can be no more than superficial appearance[;] that all languages are variations on a single theme[; and that] language structure [is] invariant, except at the margins'.[28]

Chomsky therefore situates the unshared, individual, internalized aspects of language, which he calls 'I-language', at the periphery. One might derive from the very concept of 'I-language' a diametrically different picture of the nature and constituent elements of language, however. Accordingly, both Willard van Orman Quine and George Steiner create an ultimate portrait of language as primordially *non-universal*, dominated by Chomskian 'I-languages' that are fundamental, not marginal, thus particularizing language, and rendering particularity essential.[29] Where Chomsky sees the defining attributes of language in universals, they emphasize that assumptions of universality and similarity are unwarranted, and that they obfuscate barriers to communication which result from language particularities.[30]

On the other hand, according to Wittgenstein, an entirely private language must

---

[25] René Girard, *La Violence et le sacré* (1972).

[26] Vladimir Jankélévitch and Béatrice Berlowitz, *Quelque part dans l' inachevé* (1978), 69 ff.

[27] Arthur Goldhammer, 'Man in the Mirror: Language, the Enlightenment and the Postmodern', in Daniel Gordon (ed), *Postmodernism and the Enlightenment: New Perspectives in Eighteenth-Century French Intellectual History* (2001), 31 ff, at 38.

[28] Chomsky (n 3), at 7.

[29] Willard van Orman Quine, *Word and Object* (1960); Steiner (n 11).

[30] Steiner (n 11); Willard van Orman Quine (n 29); Davidson (n 4).

be a conceptual incoherency,[31] since, as Charles Taylor has put it, '[t]he genesis of [language] . . . is not monological . . . but dialogical'.[32] Notwithstanding all of the problems relating to verifiability in semantics, language is meaningless and even inconceivable in complete isolation because it cannot exist without community and communication. This conclusion need not contradict the importance of particularity and difference to language. It indicates, rather, that for language, as for comparative law, the issue is one of balance.

V. RECENT HISTORY

1. Languages and Comparative Law Theory in the Post-War Generation

The generation of comparatists immediately following the Second World War was steeped in many languages, products of classical educations strong in the tradition of multilingualism, including Greek and Latin. Those who left Nazi Europe further perfected their knowledge of the languages of new host countries. Since many emigrated to common law nations, their immersion also was into the 'other' of the legal culture and mentality from the ones in which they had been trained.

Reading legal texts in their original languages was an obvious practice that did not figure as an explicit preoccupation of their scholarly writing about comparative law. Post-war comparative law thus was conducted by those who were well equipped to understand the nature of translation, the challenges to conveying meaning from one community to another, the disguises of the seemingly similar, and the depth and nature of differences.

Rudolf Schlesinger's memoirs, a book not intended either for publication or for a legal audience, was written to tell his American children and grandchildren of the trajectory their grandparents and great-grandparents had undergone, and to describe a European 'otherness' to American progeny.[33] It recreates the world of those whom Victor Klemperer in his diaries so aptly called 'Goethedeutsch'.[34] It also

---

[31] Ludwig Wittgenstein, *Philosophical Investigations* (1953); Saul A. Kripke, *Wittgenstein on Rules and Private Language* (1982), 68–9: '[T]he skeptical solution does not allow us to speak of a single individual, considered by himself and in isolation, as ever meaning anything'.

[32] Charles Taylor, 'The Politics of Recognition', in Amy Gutmann (ed), *Multiculturalism* (1994), 25 ff, at 32. Taylor refers to 'the genesis of the human mind', not just of language, as being dialogical.

[33] Rudolf B. Schlesinger, *Memories*, Ugo Mattei and Andrea Prodi (eds) (2000).

[34] Victor Klemperer, *Ich will Zeugnis ablegen bis zum Letzten: Tagebücher 1933–1945* (2 vols, 1995 and 1996).

is a subtextual story of the legal translating which informed his methodological approach, and provides a glimpse into the generation of dual-identity comparatists that followed the Second World War.

Schlesinger conveys his youthful adventures with practising German law under Hitler, a narrative of many social and legal metamorphoses, including the struggle to persuade legal authorities to treat previously established principles of traditional, unrepealed German law as though they were printed in an ink stronger than that of Hitler's superimpositions in the ever-changing palimpsest that constituted law in Germany from 1933 to 1945.[35] It was a losing battle, as the government had foreseen the contest between the two legal regimes vying for supremacy, and had mandated that the palimpsest be construed exclusively through the ink from the Nazi presses if the texts that might seep through from the past otherwise would thwart political ideology.[36]

Schlesinger was experiencing a dual existence as an outsider permitted until 1939 to be a lawyer on the inside of the system that was starting to erase his own legal existence.[37] He had become a foreigner-native, advocating a law whose meaning was disappearing as it became an unintelligible archaism, cluttered with newly enacted contradictory principles, and as unchanged legal texts from the past transmogrified when they became subject to an altered system of judicial interpretation and definition.[38]

Schlesinger then recounts his steps in absorbing the common law and its bewildering language as a much confused '1-L' student at Columbia Law School after emigration to New York. One watches the seeds of understanding a new law and world germinating in a mind whose initial methodological approach mirrored the twin tenets of his native German legal training and mathematical mindset.

Schlesinger later was to develop the 'common core' approach to law, reflecting

[35] Schlesinger's memoirs are a rare first-hand account of the practice of law in Nazi Germany by one who was not an apologist for the system. Other first-hand accounts by those deemed non-Aryans may be found in Ernst Fraenkel, *The Dual State: A Contribution to the Theory of Dictatorship* (trans E. A. Shils, 1941); and Yves Ternon, 'La Robe brune—les juristes allemands et le national-socialisme (1933–1936)', (2000) *Revue d'histoire de la Shoah*, 68 ff (summarizing the book of a German-Jewish lawyer who practised until 1936 in Germany, less long than Schlesinger, and who adopted the pseudonym of 'Timoroumenos' ('I avenge'). The only known surviving copy of the book is located in Paris, *Centre de documentation juive contemporaine*).

[36] Bernd Rüthers, *Die unbegrenzte Auslegung: Zum Wandel der Privatrechtsordnung im National-sozialismus* (1968), 70 ff; Ingo Müller, *Hitler's Justice: The Courts of the Third Reich* (trans Deborah Lucas Schneider, 1991); Michael Stolleis, *The Law under the Swastika: Studies on Legal History in Nazi Germany* (trans Thomas Dunlap, 1998).

[37] The legal theory pursuant to which Jews lost legal rights was founded on a new interpretation of Art 1 of the civil code, such that 'legal capacity' (*Rechtsfähigkeit*) was no longer to benefit those deemed outside the German *Volk*. Rüthers (n 36), 323 ff.

[38] Ibid; Fraenkel (n 35); Ternon (n 35).

his dedication to human-wide universals as central to his vision of a transcendent tolerance.[39] Numerous post-war comparatists shared this outlook.[40] That his analytical approach did not ignore differences of context as he engaged in finding commonalities that unite systems may be seen between the lines of his autobiography; in the enthusiasm with which he embraced and added to his common core theory Sacco's legal formants, those icons of contextual difference that are latent and elusive to detection;[41] and by his own statement at the end of his career that the search for differences also was crucial to the 'common core' project.[42]

As was the case for many of his colleagues of similar age and education, plurilinguism, both literally and figuratively, informed Schlesinger's scholarship and was central to it, without being an explicit part of the scholarly comparative project he elaborated.[43] This meant, however, that the superb comparative skills of the polyglot and dual-identity comparatists were an unspoken component of their methodology, and that their comparative law scholarship transmitted ideas the next generation of students would be less well equipped to execute, other than those whose life experience had replicated immersion in more than one language and society.

Imre Kertesz wonders if one can get an idea of water from those who drink it.[44] The post-war generation drank directly from the sources. The challenge for comparative law is to convey the tastes and textures of the sources to those who have not drunk from them. The problem is acute in the classrooms of the United States,

---

[39] Rudolf Schlesinger, 'The Common Core of Legal Systems. An Emerging Subject of Comparative Study', in Kurt H. Nadelmann, Arthur T. von Mehren, and John N. Hazard (eds), *XXth Century Comparative and Conflicts Law. Legal Essays in Honor of Hessel E. Yntema* (1961), 65 ff.

[40] Ernst Rabel fits in this group, based on his writing during and after the war. See eg Ernst Rabel, 'Private Laws of Western Civilization', (1950) 10 *Louisiana LR* 431 ff; Edgar Bodenheimer, *Jurisprudence* (1940); Konrad Zweigert and Hein Kötz, *An Introduction to Comparative Law* (trans Tony Weir, 1977); Gustav Radbruch, in Erik Wolf and Hans-Peter Schneider (eds), *Rechtsphilosophie* (1973). For an extended discussion of post-war comparative law as a search for commonalities, see Curran (n 18).

[41] Rudolf B. Schlesinger, 'The Past and the Future of Comparative Law', (1995) 43 *AJCL* 477 ff; Rodolfo Sacco, 'Legal Formants: A Dynamic Approach to Comparative Law', Parts I and II, (1991) 39 *AJCL* 1 ff; 343 ff.

[42] Schlesinger, ibid.

[43] Ugo Mattei also has suggested that Schlesinger may have considered Sacco's legal formants initially to have 'been in the background at Cornell [ie the common core project], but in a sense was taken for granted and so was never actually discussed'. Ugo Mattei, 'The Comparative Jurisprudence of Schlesinger and Sacco', in Annelise Riles (ed), *Rethinking the Masters of Comparative Law* (2001), 238 ff, at 249.

[44] 'Peut-on se faire une idée de la source d'après ceux qui y boivent?', Imre Kertesz, *Un autre: Chronique d'une métamorphose* (trans Natalia and Charles Zaremba, 1999), 62. Kertesz echoes Quine's more philosophical articulation: 'It is misleading to speak of the empirical content of an individual statement—especially if it is a statement at all remote from the experiential periphery of the field'. W. V. O. Quine, *From a Logical Point of View* (1980), 43.

a country whose educational system has yet to wage a war against pervasive mono-linguism. If there was failure of imagination on the part of the post-war gener-ation, it was in not envisaging the order of limitation the single-identity monoglot faces.

The substantive objective of detecting commonality and unifying human-wide legal principles was challenged by the next generation of comparative law scholars.[45] It is the issue of the universal versus the particular, the same versus the different. As others have argued, however, the 'core' of law is both common and distinct.[46] Comparative law's modes of analysis should enable it to shed light on how to take in the image of the world with as little preconception as can be mustered: '[T]he world is not to be narrowed till it will go into the understanding . . . but the understand-ing is to be expanded and opened until it can take in the image of the world . . .'.[47] In this task, it is helpful to remember Wittgenstein's caution that '[t]he limits of my language are the limits of my world'.[48]

2. The Next Generation

The recent history of comparative law has seen changes that have mirrored intel-lectual trends since the Second World War. Western intellectual discourse gradually espoused group claims as postmodernism and multiculturalism gained ascend-ancy, and a new generation turned its attention to the national, contextual, and linguistic differences that are irreducible, and that conflict with the idea of a search for commonality.[49]

The idea of a common core to law still can be seen in many comparative law undertakings today, from the Trento Common Core of European Private Law project that adopts Schlesinger's approach as a model, to the proposals for a

---

[45] The Trento project, in reaction to such criticism, has explicitly rejected an a priori objective of finding commonalities. Ugo Mattei, 'Hard Code Now!', (2002) 2 *Global Jurist Frontiers*; see (n 48) and surrounding text.

[46] Rodolfo Sacco, 'Diversity and Uniformity in the Law', (2001) 49 *AJCL* 171 ff.

[47] Francis Bacon, 'Preparative towards a Natural and Experimental History', in James Spedding, Robert Leslie Ellis, and Douglas Denon Health (eds), *Collected Works of Francis Bacon: Translation from the Philosophical Works* (1976) (vol IV, reprint of the 1875 edn), 255 ff. I am grateful to Professor Freeman Dyson for introducing me to this passage and directing me to its source.

[48] Wittgenstein, *Tractacus Logico-Philosophicus*, Proposition 5.6 (1933).

[49] Sacco gives an account of 'the ideology of diversity' in Rodolfo Sacco, 'Diversity and Uniformity in the Law', (2001) 49 *AJCL* 179 ff; see generally also Günter Frankenberg, 'Critical Comparisons: Re-thinking Comparative Law', (1985) 26 *Harvard International LJ* 411 ff; Richard A. Hyland, 'Babel: A She'ur', (1990) 11 *Cardozo LR* 1585 ff; Pierre Legrand, 'Comparative Legal Studies and Commitment to Theory', (1995) 58 *Modern LR* 262 ff (1995); Rodolfo Sacco, 'Legal Formants: A Dynamic Approach to Comparative Law', (1991) 39 *AJCL* 1 ff; 343 ff; Vivian Grosswald Curran, 'Cultural Immersion, Difference and Categories in U.S Comparative Law', (1998) 46 *AJCL* 43 ff; Teemu Ruskola, 'Legal Orientalism', (2002) 101 *Michigan LR* 179 ff.

European Civil Code and a common contract law. Opposition to such projects sometimes has stemmed from considerations such as maintaining national traditions deemed essential to cultural identity,[50] and has included the argument that differences trump similarities, such that a project of legal unification is doomed to remain illusory.

The postmodern tendency has been to debunk universals, in keeping with Lyotard's view that western postmodernism is coterminous with loss of belief in any of the metanarratives that claim universalism, such as religion, socialism, or the Enlightenment.[51] The proponents of difference in comparative law are part of the pendulum swing away from the post-war generation. It has been suggested recently that '[t]o accord difference priority is the only way for comparative legal studies to take cognizance of what is the case'.[52] As Derrida signalled, however, neither identity nor difference is foundational, nor either derivative of the other, because they are interdependent, each conceptually incoherent without the other.[53]

Martti Koskenniemi has summarized the debate in similar terms of an interdependence in which the universal depends on the local for its expression, and is unintelligible without it, such that one can consider the particular to be a channel for the universal, a means of its expression.[54] Habermas envisions fusion of the universal and particular in law: 'The universalism of legal principles is reflected in a procedural consensus, which must be embedded in the context of a historically specific political culture through a kind of constitutional patriotism'.[55] He criticizes postmodernism for its 'suspicion of an indiscriminately assimilating and homogenizing universalism [and for] ... obliterat[ing] the relational structure of otherness and difference that universalism, properly understood, precisely takes into account'.[56]

---

[50] Yves Lequette, 'Quelques remarques à propos du projet de code civil européen de M. von Bar', (2004) 28 Le Dalloz 2202 ff.

[51] Jean-François Lyotard, The Differend: Phrases in Dispute (trans Georges van den Abbeele, 1988). Already in 1947, the American Anthropological Association criticized the Universal Declaration of Human Rights on the basis that '[s]tandards and values are relative to the culture from which they derive ...'. The implication was that the Universal Declaration was not universal, but the reflection of one culture only. American Anthropological Association, 'Statement of Human Rights by the Executive Board', (1947), 49 American Anthropologist 543 ff.

[52] Pierre Legrand, 'The Same and the Different', in Pierre Legrand and Roderick Munday (eds), Comparative Legal Studies: Traditions and Transitions (2003), 240 ff, at 279 (emphasis omitted).

[53] Jacques Derrida, Writing and Difference (trans Alan Bass, 1978), 278 ff; Jacques Derrida, Margins of Philosophy (trans Alan Bass, 1982), 3 ff.

[54] Martti Koskenniemi, 'International Law in Europe: Between Tradition and Renewal', (2005) 16 European Journal of International Law 113. Koskenniemi is in the tradition of Hegel, for whom different particularized forms in law carry within them an objective generalization, thereby transcending themselves. Georg Wilhelm Friedrich Hegel, Hegel's Philosophy of Right (trans T. M. Knox, 1967).

[55] Jürgen Habermas, 'Struggles for Recognition in the Democratic Constitutional State', in Gutmann (n 32), 107 ff, at 135.

[56] Jürgen Habermas, 'Preface', in Ciaran Cronin and Pablo De Greiff (eds), The Inclusion of the Other: Studies in Political Theory (1999), xxxv.

The historian John Higham said that the refugees from Hilter's Europe were America's first multiculturalists.[57] The comparative law scholars following the Second World War in the United States and Great Britain were no exception, but their scholarship did not make this evident. Their collision with multiculturalism and postmodernism derived from both a failure to elaborate explicitly what remained an unspoken attention to difference, context, and incommensurables, and from the fact that they revived universalist claims incompatible with most renditions of postmodernism and multiculturalism. To the extent that contemporary comparative law's postmodernist tendencies cause it to apprehend the world as consisting of 'structures of otherness' that consign us to coexistence without the possibility of mutual understanding or meaningful communication across legal communities, implicitly the field would consider legal communities to be divided not just by incommensurables, but also by a Tower of Babel.

VI. BABEL

Comparative law has experienced the debate over universalism and pluralism as consisting of mutually contradictory aspirations. As we have seen, the post-war generation put its plurilinguism at the centre of its search for a universal language of law, an Esperanto to reconcile all of humanity. In this, it echoed the goal of a single law for all of civilization that Saleilles expressed during the first modern international congress of comparative law in 1900.[58]

Historically, language and law both have known relentless human aspirations towards a universalist perfection that would eliminate disorder. These continue today. In law, some of this may be viewed as the 'legocentrism' Günter Frankenberg coined to denote the perils of a field that inflates its own importance.[59] Those immersed in law have a tendency to suggest political and social solutions based on law. The principles of translation evoked above imply that comparatists will convey law poorly if they view it in isolation from the social, political, historical, and cultural influences that inform it, and that create the environment of the humans

---

[57] John Higham, in Carl J. Guarneri (ed), *Hanging Together: Unity and Diversity in American Culture* (2001).

[58] Édouard Lambert, 'Rapport', in *Congrès international de droit comparé réuni à Paris du 31 juillet au 4 août 1900. Procès-verbaux des séances et documents* (1907), 39 ff. (summarizing Lambert's urging a common law for humanity).

[59] Günter Frankenberg, 'Critical Comparisons: Re-thinking Comparative Law', (1985) 26 *Harvard International LJ* 411 ff.

who people its institutions.[60] Plurilinguism in the figurative sense requires interdisciplinariness.

Legocentrism may explain why legal scholars and legal actors exaggerate law's capacity, tending to view it as an ideal and universal panacea, but universalist aspirations for law are widespread also in the larger population. More generalized than legocentrism within the field is an urge, as intense among the lay population as among legal specialists, to believe that law represents a solution to the problems of human conflict and a potential remedy to past barbarism, if only the right law and legal order can be identified, codified, and enacted.

Universalist claims both fortify this perspective, and ensue from it. To view law as subject to the vicissitudes of transitory human perceptions and contemporaneous values, as are all other social institutions, is to recognize that there are no final solutions to barbarism that law can provide in a reliable and durable way. As Nathaniel Berman has put it, however, in a title that explains the strength and tenacity of the refusal to acknowledge the full measure of law's limitations and vulnerabilities, '*But the Alternative is Despair . . .*'.[61]

Language has inspired similar hope and faith in its perfectibility. George Steiner's *After Babel*[62] and Umberto Eco's *The Search for the Perfect Language*[63] tell the tale of the age-old anguish born of earth's many mutually incommunicable languages, and of each individual human language's incapacity to achieve a transparent reflection of the world through the medium of words. The despair that no spoken language can match signifier to signified in a one-to-one correspondence has been linked to the biblical message that such a perfect language existed before God created the confusion at Babel to punish man. By the twentieth century, one sees in Gottlob Frege's work, and the beginning of modern philosophy of language, that the ideal of an entirely unambiguous language also is considered to be the key to discovering the nature and functioning of thought.[64] Eco tells us that an obsession with finding a single, redemptive, perfect, universal language is to be found in every culture in the world.[65]

---

[60] This should not be interpreted as contradicting the view of Luhmann and Teubner that the field of law is to be understood as an autopoietic system. I mean, rather, that those who project law as a solution in areas to which law is not relevant ignore other fields at their peril precisely because of law's limitations. Eg Niklas Luhmann, 'Operational Closure and Structural Coupling: The Differentiation of the Legal System', (1992) 13 *Cardozo LR* 1419. Günther Teubner, 'The Two Faces of Janus: Rethinking Legal Pluralism', (1992) 13 *Cardozo LR* 1443.

[61] Nathaniel Berman, 'But the Alternative is Despair: European Nationalism and the Modernist Renewal of International Law', (1993) 106 *Harvard LR* 1792 ff.

[62] Steiner (n 11).

[63] Umberto Eco, *The Search for the Perfect Language: The Making of Europe* (trans James Fentress, 1995).

[64] Gottlob Frege, 'The Thought: A Logical Inquiry', in P. Strawson (ed), *Philosophical Logic* (1967).

[65] Eco (n 63), at 1 (citing Arno Borst (1957), *Der Turmbau von Babel. Geschichte der Meinungen über Ursprungen und Vielfalt der Sprachen und Völker*).

Steiner, like the postmodern legal comparatists, turns the Babel story on its head, seeking to resolve the mystery of the incommunicable. He explores how it is that many mutually incomprehensible languages persisted within geographical areas too small for distance to explain their multiplicity, and concludes in the tradition of Romanticism that language profusion is metaphoric of a human-wide desire to develop individual worlds of difference in which the enduring and productive richness of imagination can best flourish and be preserved for future fertility.

Steiner suggests that the value of particular languages is in being *untranslatable*, in not being subject to communication to the 'other'. Since to translate is possible only to the extent of shared elements in more than one language, in the measure that translation is successful, languages are not unique. If unicity is the goal, then the chaos of Babel can become more desirable than its alternative of communication. If one finds Steiner's thesis improbable, one may wish to reflect on the fact that Heine was reproached in Germany for having written poetry *which translated too well* into other languages. According to Amos Elon, it was in Heine's having crafted a German that could be communicated easily outside German that his critics charged him with treachery to the language.[66]

In Steiner's work, language multiplicity incarnates the value of the particular and the local. A more recent study, *Vanishing Voices*,[67] the collaboration of a linguist and anthropologist, analyses the vastly accelerated rate at which languages are dying across the planet today, and likens the phenomenon to an irremediable loss in biological species. It raises the spectre of a sterile world converging towards one language, an 'after Babel' monolinguism of loss. *Vanishing Voices* argues the irreplaceable nature of loss when the number of languages diminishes in the world; *After Babel* allows one to divine the measure of loss in the degradation and death of any one language.

It should be remembered, however, that no matter how immeasurable losses in difference prove to be, difference itself does not diminish. Rather, the terrains of difference shift, such that the importance of some of the differences that have mattered most in the past will recede. For comparative law, as the world globalizes, it is foreseeable that the field's traditional skills for grasping the nature of national, including language, contexts will be of decreasing usefulness in their particulars. The acquired skills will retain value to the extent that having developed those skills allows the field to adapt so as to perceive and interpret new orders of difference.

---

[66] Elon (n 19), 128 ff.
[67] Daniel Nettle and Suzanne Romaine, *Vanishing Voices: the Extinction of the World's Languages* (2000).

VII. Language Deflation and the Growth of the Non-national

Ours is an era of simultaneous language deflation and law inflation (see Section IX), both of which are eliciting considerable anxiety.[68] The increased dominance of English is a much debated topic in comparative law; in law; and in many other fields. Efforts to reverse or even halt the trend to use English seem to be as ineffective as efforts to defend any one language from foreign importations within it. Even autocratic rulers lack power to control language evolution. Bernhard Grossfeld tells us how Marcellus is reputed to have instructed the Emperor Tiberius that, no matter how great the ruler's power, it extended over people only, but not over words.[69]

On the other hand, English is changing as it enters other languages. Inexorable as language evolution may be, where host languages absorb foreign words, the foreign imports are altered in a highly complex process of assimilation reminiscent of the transformation process Watson describes for legal transplants.[70] Conversely, an accumulation of imported words affects and alters the host language. In law, the limitations of the English legal language to express concepts that extend beyond the boundaries of its underlying common law context have led to a modification of English in the form of new words spawned by concepts of civilian origin.[71] Thus, where many languages cede to a dominant single one, the ascendant language must expand to accommodate to difference, transforming itself in the process.

Just as Steiner wondered at the evolutionary significance of language multiplicity where geographical distance did not provide an adequate explanation, today one can wonder at the evolutionary significance of language diminution, including the extraordinary rate of English importations into European languages where the imported vocabulary seems to replace words already in existence, rather than to add new meanings.[72] There is little doubt of an ultimate language impoverishment as one language emerges to dominate others, but the wealth of subtleties lost in the ascendancy of English is part of those kinds of distinctiveness that are dissolving around the world. Their disappearance is a scent on the trail comparatists

---

[68] For a recent discussion of the language issue, see Ewoud Hondius, 'The Impact of American Law and American Legal Theory: Threat or Incentive?', in *De Tous horizons: Mélanges Blanc-Jouvan* (2005), 271 ff.

[69] Grossfeld (n 5), 91.

[70] Alan Watson, *Legal Transplants: An Approach to Comparative Law* (2nd edn, 1993).

[71] Nicholas Kasirer, 'The Common Core of European Private Law in Boxes and Bundles', (2002) 10 *ERPL* 417 ff.

[72] Umberto Eco, 'Le populisme menace l'Europe', *L'Express* (14 June 2004), 37 ff; Umberto Eco, 'Méconnaître les langues produit de l'intolérance', *L'Express*, (22–8 avril 1999), 12 ff.

can follow in detecting new subtextual changes as old divisions and categories reconfigure.

One such reconfiguration is the contemporary trend away from the national. The transformation of the national into the non-national is most striking when even efforts originally dedicated to reinforcing national strengths are subsumed into detracting from them. Today, measures designed to preserve linguistic plural-ism, including those measures intended to do so, no longer principally reinforce nation states. Thus, in the EU, support for linguistic diversity originally was centred on the preservation and flourishing of member state national languages, but now has transmuted into support for the rescue and even renaissance of subnational languages, some already moribund, in the name of 'Europe's cultural wealth and traditions',[73] and pursuant to the European Charter for Regional and Minority Languages.[74]

France provides an example of a state which throughout centuries and in various ways undertook to develop, preserve, and promote French as the exclusive language of the nation through legal regulation. Until recently, this meant discouraging the use of languages other than French, including its own territory's ancient regional languages. As recently as 1992, the French Constitution was amended to state that French is the nation's language.[75]

As English came to be considered a greater threat to French than its own regional languages,[76] and pursuant to EU policies, France reversed course in favour of the very linguistic pluralism it traditionally repressed as subversive to the national.[77] The French government's current promotion of subnational languages whose sur-vival minority populations consider threatened is in a relation of paradox, if not complete contradiction, with its objective of protecting the national language.

This tangled web is the latest in a history of efforts to define, preserve, and purify French over centuries, from errors in philology that once caused clerics to attempt

---

[73] Preamble, European Charter for Regional and Minority Languages, ETS no. 148 (1992). On the original EU purpose to support national languages, see 'The EU's Commitment to "Linguistic Diver-sity" ', in Richard L. Creech, *Law and Language in the European Union* (2005), 49 ff. It has been pointed out that EU texts in support of national languages have been sufficiently vague as to lend themselves to being interpreted as supporting not necessarily just the language of each nation state, but also the many languages within states. Bruno de Witte, 'Language Law of the European Union: Protecting or Eroding Linguistic Diversity?', in Rachael Craufurd Smith (ed), *Culture and European Union Law* (2004), 205 ff, at 206.

[74] ETS no. 148 (1992) (ibid).

[75] Marc Frangi, 'État, langue et droit en France', (2003) 119 *Revue du droit public*, 1607 ff, at 1612.

[76] The *loi Toubon* had English as its target, not regional languages. *Loi no. 94–98 du 1er février 1994,* analysed in Frangi, ibid 1616 ff.

[77] In April 2001, then Minister of Education, Jack Lang, publicly acknowledged that the French government historically had maintained an active policy of repressing regional languages. 'Les annonces que le ministre Jack Lang a faites devant la presse, le 25 avril 2001, représentent une évolution très sensible et dans le bon sens', in *Union démocratique bretonne*, available at <http://www.udb-bzh.net/ Brezhoneg/com-lang–0401.htm> (last visited 6 August 2005).

to freeze the language in illogical spelling,[78] to endowing the *Académie française* with legal authority to define and regulate French. The country's history of projects to govern language among others testifies to the indomitable force of language in resisting direction and governance.[79] Language traditionally has emerged as stronger than any law purporting to control it, like a butterfly escaping from its chrysalis in colours impossible to predict and flying in unknown directions. Current evidence suggests the towering difficulties of regulating language either by positive measures, such as financial support, or by interdictive measures, such as legal regulation of linguistic criteria.[80]

In their ungovernable and independent paths, languages resemble nothing more than law, whose history also is one of resistance to stasis in meaning. As the humans who operate legal institutions change in beliefs and values over time, the subtextual meaning of law drifts with them. When such 'ideological drift'[81] occurs despite unchanged, unamended language in legal texts, it may be due to conscious subversion, but equally often to innocent, unknowing shifts reflecting an ever-changing 'constitution . . . written in the citizens minds' that, according to Ernst Cassirer, inevitably, perpetually, and always changeably, determines law's meaning.[82] The variables that affect the evolution of both language and law are innumerable, and originate in many non-linguistic and non-legal sources. Comparative legal analysis therefore cannot help but be interdisciplinary if it is to be effective in understanding and conveying law.[83] The extent to which law's transitions elude

---

[78] Spelling was fixed so as to reflect what were thought to be the relevant Latin or Greek derivations, but mistakes were made as to the etymology of many words, such as where the French term had an apparent similarity with Latin, but in fact was derived from Greek.

[79] See Eco, '*Le populisme menace l'Europe*' (n 72), 37 ('No power on earth can impose a national or vehicular language. Languages are in a way biological forces.'). Recently, French courts occasionally have felt themselves called upon to declare that language must be controlled by usage, not law. Frangi (2003), 119 *Revue du droit public* 1612 ff.

[80] Nettle and Romaine (n 67). At least one recent survey indicates moderate success recently in reviving languages newly used in schools, although the results are inconclusive. 'Why the Welsh language is making a comeback', (13 August 2005) *The Economist* 31. De Witte reports mixed success in reviving dying minority and regional languages. De Witte (n 73), 211 ff. Some of France's more recent legal measures have been compared to a new Maginot line. Frangi, (2003) 119 *Revue du droit public* 1611 ff.

[81] J. M. Balkin, 'Ideological Drift and the Struggle Over Meaning', (1993) 25 *Connecticut LR* 869 ff.

[82] Ernst Cassirer, *The Myth of the State*, (1946), 27. Very much in line with Cassirer, who was a political philosopher, were his contemporaries Hermann Kantorowicz and Eugen Ehrlich of the Free Law School, who emphasized the inevitable role of community values on the meaning of law due to, *inter alia*, textual gaps in the law, and language indeterminacy.

[83] To put this in Luhmann's terms (n 60), such interdisciplinariness refers to elements that the autopoietic system of law has absorbed, or others on which it depends. On the latter, see Gunther Teubner, 'How the Law Thinks: Toward a Constructivist Epistemology of Law', (1989) 23 *Law and Society Review* 727, at 742 ('The dynamics of social differentiation force legal discourse to produce reality constructions of its own, but the very same dynamics make law dependent upon a multiplicity of competing *epistèmes*').

detection is the extent to which they also preclude reaction and direction by legislators, regulators, and educators.

VIII. Familiarity and Foreignness

Translating the foreign into the familiar ends by clarifying the familiar that one discovers also to be foreign.[84] For comparative law, this means clarifying one's own legal framework through perspectives the foreign adds to one's lens of vision. As Arthur Rimbaud, one of France's nineteenth-century 'accursed/wretched poets', *poètes maudits*, said with metaphoric prescience and alienation a century later, 'je est un autre', 'I is another',[85] a theme Franz Kafka renewed in the twentieth century ('I have hardly anything in common with myself')[86] and that Imre Kertesz generalized beyond the personal to the whole of the human race ('we have nothing in common with ourselves'),[87] as well as by scholars including Julia Kristeva in *Strangers to Ourselves*.[88] As a field that has specialized in examining the outside, the other, comparative law is situated to see the foreign in the familiar, so as to elucidate the familiar.

The divided self that confronts its own 'other' was the basis for Rousseau's social contract between the self-individual and the self-citizen.[89] It also became the foundation for Stuart Hampshire's conception of justice in heterogeneous western constitutional democracies. Hampshire posited that no set of substantive values would be shared by all populations within the ever more diverse national communities of western democracies, such that justice systems cannot legitimately impose any single set of substantive norms. Rather, the fair hearing should serve as the cornerstone of justice inasmuch as each individual has conducted internal hearings when in inner conflict, thereby creating ubiquitous recognition of the value and fairness of a system based on listening to each side.[90]

---

[84] This was the fascination that Montesquieu's *Persian Letters* exerted on French readers in the eighteenth century, in the epistolary novel featuring visitors from Persia who described French mores. cf Goethe: 'He who does not know foreign languages knows nothing of his own', quoted in George Steiner, *What is Comparative Literature?* (1995), 5.

[85] Arthur Rimbaud, in Jean-Marie Carré (ed), *Lettres de la vie littéraire d'Arthur Rimbaud (1870–1875)* (1931) (Lettre à Paul Demeny, 15 mai 1871).

[86] Franz Kafka, in Max Brod (ed), *The Diaries* (1976), 169.

[87] '[N]ous n'avons rien de commun avec nous-mêmes', Kertesz, (n 44), 73.

[88] Julia Kristeva, *Strangers to Ourselves* (trans Leon Roudiez, 1991).

[89] Jean-Jacques Rousseau, *Du contrat social* (1762) (Flammarion, 2001).

[90] Stuart Hampshire, *Justice is Conflict* (2000).

For Hampshire, the experience of the foreign 'other' within a fragmented, con-flicted self is a defining human attribute, and a cause for celebration. Both Kristeva and Edward Saïd have suggested beauty in the further identity disruption experi-enced by those who undergo physical exile from their country of birth. Kristeva equates it with a 'weightlessness in the infinity of cultures [that] gives [the exiled] the extravagant ease to innovate'.[91]

Unlike the nineteenth-century *poètes maudits* who lived in an inner exile, exiles from lands of birth know language displacement and disruption as part of their experience of the foreign. Some, like Theodor Adorno, emigrate from their home-land because it is the unpleasant price they must pay for physical survival. Exile was so bitter for Adorno that he returned to Germany after the Second World War, explaining his return as the longing to be reunited with the language of his birth.[92] In this, he was in a tradition of German-Jewish writers starting with Heine, who declared that his fatherland was not Germany, but German, the language.[93] Adorno most famously said that the holocaust had transformed poetry, that ultimate trib-ute to the power and beauty of language, into barbarism.[94] Barbarism was the Greek word for foreign. For him, the familiar had become the foreign, irremediably altered in his manner of experiencing it. Adorno's remark was reminiscent of Walter Benjamin's view that barbarism is embedded in the very concept of cul-ture,[95] and a forerunner of still others who foresaw the legacy of twentieth-century totalitarianism's abuse of language as the beginning of the end of language itself.[96]

According to Adorno, it is in the foreign and barbaric only that one can see the familiar: 'He who wishes to know the truth about life must scrutinize its estranged form'.[97] Only the estranged, the barbaric, the 'other', can be noticed because the familiar, taken for granted, becomes invisible. The estranged is a conduit to noticing the familiar because it is that which we are able to see. Zygmunt Bauman extends Adorno's and Benjamin's ideas by suggesting that estranged forms do not just show us sameness through showing us difference. Rather, what appear to be differ-ences may be the germinated form of unsuspected seeds long implanted and

---

[91] Kristeva (n 88), 13.

[92] Christian Joerges, '*La langue de l'étranger*', Observations on the Need to Observe and Under-stand Discourses on Foreign Territories', available at <http://www.europeanlawbooks.org/>, citing Jacques Derrida, *Fichus: discours de Francfort* (2002).

[93] Heinrich Heine, *Sämtliche Schnitten*, (1975–85), 55, quoted in Elon (n 19), 118.

[94] Theodor Adorno, *Negative Dialectics* (trans E. B. Ashton, 1973) (1966), 360 ff.

[95] 'Die Barbarei steckt im Begriff der Kultur selbst', Walter Benjamin, 'Das Passagen-Werk', in Walter Benjamin, 5 *Gesammelte Schriften* (Rolf Tiedemann and Hermann Schweppenhäuser eds, 1977), 584.

[96] Jean-Pierre Faye, *Langages totalitaires: la raison, critique de narrative, l'économie* (1967); Steiner (n 8). For a more optimistic view, implying that language remains redeemable, see John Wilson, *Language and the Pursuit of Truth* (1967), viii ff.

[97] Theodor Adorno, *Minima Moralia: Reflections from Damaged Life* (tran E. F. N. Jephcott, 1974), 15.

embedded within the familiar.[98] Just as the study of metastasized cells can reveal previously unperceived functions of the normal, we can see in 'estranged forms' how the familiar carries the potential for its own dramatic metamorphoses, and thereby better identify the development of those potentials.

Once we understand that even the familiar is foreign, we also see that it is not just the 'other' which requires translation: so does sameness, since sameness masks alterity ('I is another'). Visible otherness merely renders visible the need for translation, and permits one to observe its processes. Those processes of translation also are the ubiquitous mechanisms of meaning construction and comprehension. Thus, translation always is at work, even within the apparently same system of signs, only less easily observably so when interlocutors are not aware of what communication and exchange imply.[99]

If comparative law is the translator of the law of others and otherness, but if translation is not the making equivalent of foreign languages, only a lantern that makes visible how 'every mode of meaning'[100] signifies, then, by extrapolation, what can comparative law have to offer? If everything is foreign because, ultimately, the self is another, then in deciphering the officially, visibly foreign, and also the foreign that is masked by the familiar, does comparative legal analysis do something that is not being done through legal analysis *tout court*? Is comparative law a fraud in posing as something different from the regular run of legal analysis?

In its essence, comparative legal analysis *is* just legal analysis, since comparison is not unique to the field of comparative legal analysis, since, rather, all analysis, legal and other, is comparative at heart.[101] Comparative law is merely an 'estranged form' of the familiar. Comparative law remains key to understanding law, our own and others', because of its habits and history, its accoutrements, because it is conversant in otherness, in approaching and dealing with the alterities of languages, histories, and legal mentalities. It is our best bet today, because it is the field with the biggest head start towards deciphering the peculiar newnesses of the contemporary legal world, in which law has become mobile and, it has been suggested, a product of exchange.[102] Comparative law can begin the process of detecting the unseen that lurks beneath the seen if it can put to fruitful current uses its own history of venturing into contexts that enlarge the practitioner's cognitive grids, enabling the assimilation of information that can be processed in no other way than by extending the limitations of imagination.

---

[98] Bauman writes of the inner logic of the modern nation state that consists of structures which load the dice towards genocidal conduct. The structures he identifies are not in and of themselves culpable, making their innocuous appearance all the more dangerous, since they relate causally to destructive state practices without being necessarily ill-intentioned. Zygmunt Bauman, *Modernity and the Holocaust* (1989).

[99] Steiner (n 11), xii.   [100] Ibid   [101] Lakoff (n 10).

[102] Julie Allard and Antoine Garapon, *Les juges dans la mondialisation: La nouvelle révolution du droit* (2005), 5.

Law's messiness cannot be reduced. If comparative law can be an effective trans-lator, it may be by conveying messiness more accurately, thereby allowing for a deeper understanding of the ways in which law is changing, the subtle new associations and linkages occurring as old distinctions give way to new ones. In our globalizing world, the distinctions associated with geography, including statehood and language differences, are fading as English becomes ubiquitous and even nation states that have not restructured officially are dealing with non-national normative claims, entailing legal changes of a non-national nature. The struggle to understand legal phenomena that do not fit within the traditionally exclusive categories and nomenclatures of law: namely, the national or the international, extends to trying to identify a new vocabulary capable of encompassing the novelties, tentatively termed by some as 'transgovernmental'; by others as 'post-national', as unfamiliar phenomena continue to unfold in a dynamic of mutual interaction with the words that name them.[103]

Comparative law is the sleuth of significance, of legal meaning, and its old antennae, so carefully and painstakingly attuned to the sorts of hidden change that challenged past generations, now need to be adapted to unearthing new configurations. Its objective should be to become so pervasive that it disappears. Its greatest contribution would be to convince all those who analyse law today that comparative law must be part and parcel of their undertakings, and consequently to merge into invisibility by making itself part of a familiar that it permeates, shedding its own distinctiveness in a globalizing world which needs the methods and skills the field has developed to be infused into all forms of legal analysis.

IX. TRANSLATING EUROPEAN LAW: EXAMPLES

Europe today is one of many arenas of legal change in need of comparative analytical methodology. The difficulties of perceiving how law is transforming in Europe are magnified still further on the world scale, where legal encounters involve states and sources less connected by history and geography than are the current European member states. Even in Europe, like silences between words, a host of legal changes are passing unobserved under the mantle of observable change. Conversely, unchanged legal concepts persist under misleading guises of change.

---

[103] 'Transgovernmental' is Anne-Marie Slaughter's term, 'post-national' Jürgen Habermas's. See Curran (n 1).

European institutions such as the European Court of Justice and European Court of Human Rights (ECHR) are spaces of encounter and exchange that have become more than the sums of their parts, having developed considerable legal convergence in a distinctive emerging culture. National legal publications purporting to report their decisions often fail to include much-needed comparative analysis, however, filtering the foreign aspects of European court decisions through domestic legal frames of reference that result in distortion.

The failures of translating legal meaning in renditions of European court decisions tend to be exacerbated when the national legal publication and the country whose law was analysed by the European court are not from the same legal system, as could be observed when a major French legal publication excerpted and analysed an ECHR decision in a case on assisted suicide that had originated in the United Kingdom.[104] The choice of which excerpts to reproduce from the lengthy European decision was the first step of inadvertent transformation of the European court decision in its presentation to the French reader, who typically would be following European law to the extent it is likely to impact a domestic legal practice, and would read European decisions only in the versions national legal publications publish.

In its manner of abridging the ECHR decision, the French publication did not just shorten the original; it expurgated the ECHR's common law analysis, thus omitting those portions of the ECHR decision that would have been inhabitual in a French court decision.[105] These included ECHR reasoning by analogy among cases in their factual contexts. The French rendition preserved ECHR references to cases through factually decontexualized, normative principles more familiar to civilian legal thinking.

The scholarly analysis which followed the French rendition of the ECHR decision further magnified the failure to translate legal meaning from the European context to the domestic one, as it portrayed aspects of the court's decision as being substantively defective when in fact they reflected a common law manner of reasoning. Notably, the French scholar in civilian manner was indignant that the ECHR had referred with approval to UK policy that not every defendant whose conduct violated the relevant statute against assisted suicide need be prosecuted. There was no discussion of the UK policy as rooted in a systemically different legal approach, nor of the possibility of latitude for the ECHR to approve of it.[106] The result of such purported domestic republication and explanation is a rendering familiar of European law to a national legal community through use of the legal

[104] *Pretty v United Kingdom* (2002) App No. 2346/02, 35 EHRR 1. '*La Cour EDH ne reconnaît pas l'existence d'un droit à la mort*', (2003), 15–16 *La Semaine juridique*, 676 ff.

[105] For a more detailed discussion, see Curran (n 1).

[106] *La Semaine juridique* (n 104), 682. For a fuller explanation of the civilian approach as withholding punishment but not prosecution, see Antoine Garapon, 'French Legal Culture and the Shock of "Globalization" ', (1995) 4 *Social & Legal Studies* 500 ff.

code of the home mentality, freeing European law from confusing foreignness by recoding it according to the categories of the reader's member state legal order.

Conversely, symbols of new legal convergence throughout Europe by means of an apparently common vocabulary also can be deceptive and illusory, and perpetuate legal differences that remain unrecognized. Assumptions in both civil and common law systems that European law today has adopted the common-law concept of case law are widespread but largely erroneous. The acceptance by civil law states of European court decisions as a source of law appears to be a change towards legal convergence because it sounds reminiscent of common law methodology and practice, and because the common law term 'case law' is used extensively by civilians.

For the civilian, the concept of 'case law' is the validation of court decisions as a source of law, but such decisions then are reduced to what, in common law parlance, is only one component part of a court decision: the 'rule' of the case, a normative principle from which future case solutions will be deducible.[107] For the common law lawyer, however, 'case law' is an intricate network of significance in which legal principle is fused indissociably with particular, contextualizing facts from a host of cases. In the common law, an individual court decision becomes the basis for future detailed inductive reasoning, to be conducted by comparisons among multifarious aspects of other cases that fit within an arguable, and to-be-argued, range of similarity. For the civilian, even the court decision that has acquired the stature of law is understood as a normative rule resembling a code provision. The civilian conception of 'case law' thus has not assimilated cases-*qua*-law in the common law manner, which would require not just recognizing court decisions as a source of law, but also would require a fundamentally altered understanding of the nature of law when cases are its source.

A common law feature has penetrated the EU, however, in the piecemeal pattern of change increasingly characterizing legal development in all EU member states. The evolution proceeds from detailed directive, or other individual European institutional command, to the reactive changes in member state domestic law in order to become compliant with new European law. It is a direction antithetical to the civilian pattern of legal change emanating from an initial, a priori, overarching coherence associated with the very idea of law and legal legitimacy.[108]

This pattern of change in Europe, coupled with the principle of subsidiarity, has led to a particularized drafting style, inhabitual and discomfortingly unfamiliar to the civilian legal public in its expectations of such language.[109] It is reminiscent of

---

[107] Curran (n 1).

[108] Antoine Garapon and Ioannis Papadopoulos, *Juger en Amérique et en France* (2003); Christophe Jamin, 'Un modèle original: la construction de la pensée juridique française', (2004) *Bulletin d'information Cour de cassation*.

[109] Christian von Bar, 'Le groupe d'études sur un code civil européen', (2001) 53 *RIDC* 127, 138 ff; *Bulmer Ltd v Bollinger SA.* (1974) All ER 1226.

the detailed common law statute that similarly arose from a piecemeal system: namely, from the common law tradition of courts creating unenacted law by means of cases, and of the legislature's interference as being the exception rather than the rule, occurring only where the legislature wrests control over particular matters it deems necessary to take into its own hands from the a priori accepted ubiquity of judicial governance.[110] Part of the civilian frustration with perceived 'legislative inflation' in European member states today can be explained by its association with this suspect pattern of legal change that is experienced as the reverse of law's proper course from the whole to the particular.

Law profusion also recalls the fascist period, in which there was an explosion of statutes that undermined the prior rule of law through outer garments of legality veiling profound change and, as was later judged, abdication rather than preservation or promotion of law and rule of law.[111] The association between statutory abundance and the subversion of law also has roots that go back further in modern civilian legal thinking, as Portalis's explanation of the drafting of the French Civil Code reveals.[112]

Along with an ideal of keeping laws few in number, the sparse style of the civilian legal norm is considered inseparable from law and the rule of law because it is considered to have proven its ability to withstand changed circumstances. As exemplified by the Prussian code that failed before Napoleon's succeeded,[113] abundant language and abundant law are deemed fated to outlive the problems they address, entrapping society by legal texts that eventually bind senselessly, because they become helpless to resolve future problems time-bound legislators inevitably fail to foresee.[114]

The civilian view that legal quantity and linguistic specificity in enacted law cause injustice, law subversion, and social mayhem may owe more to historical contingency than to causality, however.[115] The lessons Continental European nations learned that caused national codifications to espouse a general, loose style of language, widening future interpretive potential, do not take into account the alternative possibilities for balancing legal stability with societal changes that the

---

[110] Felix Frankfurter, 'Some Reflections on the Readings of Statutes', (1947) 47 *Columbia LR* 527, 532 ff; John Chipman Gray, *The Nature and Sources of the Law* (1909), 164 ff; Roscoe Pound, 'Common Law and Legislation', (1907–8) 21 *Harvard LR* 383, 389 ff.

[111] Stolleis (n 36); Rüthers (n 36).

[112] Portalis, *Discours préliminaire au premier projet de code civil* (1999, Firmin Didot frères 1841).

[113] *Allgemeines Landrecht*, Prussian General Territorial Law of 1794, discussed in James Q. Whitman, *The Legacy of Roman Law in the German Romantic Era: Historical Vision and Legal Change* (1990), 55 ff.

[114] 'Dossier spécial.: législation; Inflation législative galopante', (10 November 2004) *La Semaine juridique*.

[115] This is a principal theme of Vivian Grosswald Curran, 'Fear of Formalism: Indications from the Fascist Period in France and Germany of Judicial Methodology's Impact on Substantive Law', (2002) 35 *Cornell International LJ* 101 ff.

common law developed in a much different pattern, one that has included narrowly drafted legal norms arising as circumstances in society were deemed to justify their enactment. Unreflective associations arising from particular historical trajectories confuse the issues today as Europe seeks to reconcile two substantially different legal traditions and mentalities within a single supranational judicial system.

X. CONCLUSION

Comparative law as translator can be envisaged as cybernetics for the irreducible messiness of legal concepts that are wedded to the language which encases them and to the connotations which adhere to them. The physicist Freeman Dyson describes cybernetics as '*a theory of messiness*',[116] and its Greek etymology as evoking one 'who steers a frail ship through stormy seas between treacherous rocks'.[117] According to Dyson, the founder of cybernetics, Norbert Wiener, was a former child prodigy who became immersed in the cultures and languages of both pure and applied mathematics, engineering, and neurophysiology, and translated among all of them. Wiener determined that 'the messiness of the real world was precisely the point at which his mathematics should be aimed'.[118]

As this chapter has discussed, comparative law and its practitioners have long been interpretants attempting to steer through the messiness of the foreign by reordering it into the language of the familiar without betraying the original. Today's world of dizzying legal changes, and the accelerated rate at which changes are occurring, heighten comparative law's difficulties, even as the field increasingly finds itself implicated in world events. Comparatists have ceased being remote from reality like the philosophers an empress once envied: 'You philosophers are fortunate. You write on paper, and paper is patient. I unlucky empress write on the sensitive skin of people'.[119]

As Ugo Mattei has been exhorting his colleagues to remember, scholarship is an important influence on European legal and political decision-making in this

---

[116] Freeman Dyson, 'The Tragic Tale of a Genius' (14 July 2005) *New York Review of Books* 10
[117] Ibid.   [118] Ibid.
[119] 'Ihr Philosophen habt es gut. Ihr schreibt auf Papier und Papier ist geduldig. Ich unglückliche Kaiserin schreibe auf der empfindlichen Haut von Menschen.', *Nachrichtendienst für Historiker*, <http://www.nfhdata.de/premium/index.shtml>. (*Spruch des Tages*, 5 June 2005). David Kennedy disagrees: 'Comparative law today is about knowing, not doing'. David Kennedy, 'The Methods and the Politics', in Legrand and Munday (n 53), 345 ff, at 346.

foundational period, and will affect millions of people for a long time to come.[120] In other parts of the world, new encounters of laws and legal norms occur, crossing borders of geography, statehood, and, most confusingly, crossing traditional categories for law and legal meaning.[121] Analyses and interpretations of interlocking, often mutually irreconcilable claims will affect decision-making as the reshaping world seeks to solidify emerging concepts of legitimacy and legality.

Comparative law tends to be least acknowledged and most often absent where legal analysis does not involve visibly divergent legal orders. It is needed urgently in contexts of unrecognized metamorphosis, however, and today metamorphoses are burgeoning in murky areas outside of the traditional rubrics of either national or international law.[122] The less apparent, the less visibly foreign, the foreign is, the more comparative law's task of translation involves finding and forming the vocabulary to transmit new configurations that resist detection and articulation. The field is acquainted with the uneasy transitions of words and concepts from foreign legal contexts to a targeted audience's frames of reference. This acquaintance is its arsenal for discerning new manifestations of legal significance.

However much comparative legal analysis can clarify, the process itself is not amenable to scientific method. Like language, inevitably imprecise and perpetually in flux, comparative law cannot be frozen once and for all, to be captured for future application if only it is developed with sufficient acuity and insight. It shares what Isaiah Berlin attributed to philosophy and distinguished from the scientific: it does not carry within itself the way or method of its own solution, and therefore does not lend itself to formulaic approaches.[123] This means that comparative law cannot be transmitted from one generation to the next. Each generation bears the task of developing methods that will allow the field to remain an effective interpretant of contemporaneous legal meaning.

Great scientists show how generalizations can be integrated into formulae that become the basis for future scientists of lesser abilities to use, in order to make deductions in what Berlin called 'uninspired progress'.[124] Comparative law evolves differently. Its progress cannot be accomplished in such small linear advances, but requires changing the very perspective from which problems are conceived, and debunking entrenched, established orthodoxies:

---

[120] Ugo Mattei, 'Hard Code Now!', (2002) 2 *Global Jurist Frontiers*, Art 1, 3 ff, available at www.bepress.com/gi/frontiers/vol2/iss1/art1.

[121] Mireille Delmas-Marty, *Les forces imaginaires du droit. Le relatif et l'universel* (2004); Anne-Marie Slaughter, 'The Real New World Order', (1997) 76 *Foreign Affairs* 183 ff; Anne-Marie Slaughter, *A New World Order* (2004); Julie Allard and Antoine Garapon, *Les juges dans la mondialisation: La nouvelle révolution du droit* (2005), 5 ff.

[122] Slaughter (n 121); Delmas-Marty (n 121). They agree that new configurations of legal significance are emerging, but interpret them differently.

[123] Isaiah Berlin, *The Sense of Reality. Studies in Ideas and their History* (1996), 58 ff.

[124] Ibid 60.

To take so vast a step as to liberate oneself from the incubus of an entire system of symbols—and it is scarcely possible to distinguish symbols from thoughts—to shake oneself free of so obsessive a framework, requires genius and intellectual strength and independence of the highest order. The new construction, if it is created by a man of creative as well as destructive talent, has an immense and liberating effect upon his contemporaries, since it removes from them the weight of a no longer intelligible past, and a use of language which cramps the intellect and causes the kind of frustrating perplexity which is very different from those very real problems which carry the seeds of their own solution in their own formulation. The new system, born of an act of rebellion, then becomes a new orthodoxy, and disciples spring up on all sides, eager to apply the new technique to new provinces to which the original man of genius had perhaps not conceived of applying them. This is sometimes successful, [but] sometimes leads to a new and equally arid and obfuscating scholasticism. Once the new orthodoxy has won the day, this in its turn, by making concepts rigid, by creating an ossified system of symbols no longer flexible in response to the situations which had originally led to the revolt, creates new frustrations, new insoluble problems, new . . . perplexities.[125]

As translator of legal meaning, comparative law always has had to invent and reinvent tools with which to translate. The paradox is that this undertaking, however descriptive in nature its ultimate objective may be, requires the ability to destroy its own past rigidities and manners of perceiving, its own methods of decoding and transmitting, in order to construct a new modality of analysis, a new vocabulary better adapted to changed contemporaneous meaning in the perpetually chameleon-like world of new presences, claims, standards, and influences, in which the legal and extra-legal increasingly criss-cross to the point of becoming indistinguishable, and whose junctures are the more difficult to perceive to the extent that they are unexpected.[126] Comparative law, like Berlin's rendition of philosophy, can and must maintain logical rigour, but it is the antithesis of final answers, of absolute truths, such that, in comparative legal analysis, there can be 'no final method of dealing with problems'.[127]

The field's strength lies in exposing law's complexities, and its tentacles lodged in every aspect of life. Comparative law's fragility is the fragility of law, a concept no sooner defined than changed in meaning. The discourse of law has been characterized as 'a creative language, which gives existence to that which it articulates'.[128] Like the law of the 'other' it seeks to transmit, comparative law ultimately also is subject to the language in which it is couched, that gives it sense, and that, as Paul de Man believed to be the distinctive privilege of all language, is equally adept at hiding as at bestowing meaning.[129]

---

[125] Ibid 62.   [126] Delmas-Marty (n 121).   [127] Berlin (n 123), 63.

[128] Pierre Bourdieu, *Ce que parler veut dire* (1982), 21 ('Le discours juridique est une parole créatrice, qui fait exister ce qu'elle énonce'.)

[129] Paul de Man, *Blindness and Insight: Essays in the Rhetoric of Contemporary Criticism* (1983) (1st pub 1971) 11 ('It is the distinctive privilege of language to hide meaning behind a misleading sign.'). Kertesz (n 44), 121, has gone a step further: 'Language indicates something that the understanding is not able to follow: is language also an illusion of the senses?' ('La langue indique quelque chose que la connaissance est incapable de suivre: la langue est-elle aussi une illusion des sens?')

It has been said that the distance 'between the same and the other [is] the gap in which language stands . . .'.[130] This does not make language transparent or efficacious, honest or able. Rather, it situates language and evokes its pitfalls and potentials. Like language, comparative law also stands in the gap between the same and the other. Like language, comparative law faces the stark pitfalls of miscommunication and misunderstanding, but, also like language, it possesses the unique and breathtaking potentials of learning to see, to communicate, and to shed light in that elusive, inevitable, shifting, and ever-reconfiguring gap between the same and the other.

BIBLIOGRAPHY

Eva Hoffman, *Lost in Translation: A Life in a New Language* (1988)

James Boyd White, *Justice as Translation: An Essay in Cultural and Legal Criticism* (1990)

George Steiner, *After Babel: Aspects of Language and Translation* (2nd edn, 1992)

Umberto Eco, *The Search for The Perfect Language* (trans James Fentress, 1995)

William Bragg Ewald, 'Comparative Jurisprudence (I): What Was it Like to Try a Rat?', (1995) 113 *University of Penusyluania LR* 1889 ff.

Bernhard Großfeld, *Kernfragen der Rechtsvergleichung* (1996), available in English as Bernhard Grossfeld, *Core Questions of Comparative Law* (trans Vivian Grosswald Curran, 2005)

Günter Frankenberg, 'Critical Comparisons: Re-thinking Comparative Law', (1998) 26 *Harvard LR* 411 ff

Daniel Nettle and Suzanne Romaine, *Vanishing Voices: The Extinction of the World's Languages* (2000)

Donald Davidson, *Inquiries Into Truth and Interpretation* (2nd edn, 2001)

Marc Frangi, 'État, langue et droit en France', (2003) 119 *Revue du droit public* 1607 ff

Pierre Legrand and Roderick Munday, *Comparative Legal Studies: Traditions and Transitions* (2003)

Neil Walker, 'Postnational Constitutionalism and the Problem of Translation', in J. H. H. Weiler and Marlene Wind (eds), *European Constitutionalism beyond the State* (2003), 27 ff

Mireille Delmas-Marty, *Les forces imaginantes du droit. Le relatif et l'universel* (2004)

Bruno de Witte, 'Language Law of the European Union: Protecting or Eroding Linguistic Diversity?', in Rachael Craufurd Smith (ed), *Culture and European Union Law* (2004), 205 ff

Maximo Langer, 'From Legal Transplants to Legal Translations: The Globalization of Plea Bargaining and the Americanization Thesis in Criminal Procedure', (2004) 45 *Harvard International LJ* 1 ff

---

[130] Emmanuel Levinas, *Entre nous: Thinking-of-the-Other* (trans Michael B. Smith and Barbara Harshav, 1998), 32.

CHAPTER 21

COMPARATIVE LAW AND LEGAL CULTURE

ROGER COTTERRELL

London

I. Introduction

AN interest in understanding law in its various cultural settings might be thought to underlie all imaginative comparative law scholarship. In the past this has often been merely implicit. However, since the early 1990s, an explicit concern with law's relation to culture, and especially with the concept of legal culture, has become much more prominent in comparative legal scholarship. In particular, the idea of legal culture has had an important place in major recent debates about the nature and aims of comparative law. Indeed, it has been taken up by some comparatists as a tool to try to reorient the entire field of comparative legal studies.

The idea of legal culture entails that law (as rules, practices, institutions, doctrine, etc.) should be treated as embedded in a broader culture of some kind. This culture may, but need not necessarily, be seen as wider than the lawyer's or lawmaker's professional realm of law. Certainly, elements that make up the 'official' world of law (for example, lawyers' and lawmakers' practices, traditions and professional understandings) may be seen as themselves comprising a culture—some kind of complex totality of meaning and experience. Often, however, conceptions of legal culture encompass much more than this professional juristic realm. They refer to a more general consciousness or experience of law that is widely shared by those who inhabit a particular legal environment, for example a particular region, nation, or group of nations.

Whatever approach to fixing the scope of legal culture is taken, the basic message which the use of the concept of legal culture gives is clear: much more than legal rules needs to be subjected to comparison, even if advocates of cultural approaches to comparative law may disagree about what exactly the additional elements are. In emphasizing legal culture, these advocates often suggest that much of previous, mainstream (especially positivist or functionalist) comparative legal scholarship has been wrongly focused; that it has studied only limited or surface aspects of legal reality.

Thus, for comparatists who emphasize culture, a positivist focus on legal rules alone misses much that—while not expressed in rule-form—is important about law and should be taken into account in any worthwhile comparison of legal phenomena. Such non-rule elements might include underlying values or principles of a legal system, as well as traditions, shared beliefs, common ways of thinking, constellations of interests or patterns of allegiances of lawyers, lawmakers, and citizens.

Functionalist approaches, identifying criteria of comparison in terms not of rules but of problems, tasks, or societal needs to be met by law, are usually held by cultural comparatists to be no less deficient.[1] Functionalist approaches are seen as

---

[1] Pierre Legrand, 'The Same and the Different', in Pierre Legrand and Roderick Munday (eds), *Comparative Legal Studies: Traditions and Transitions* (2003), 240, 292; Vivian Grosswald

failing to recognize that purposes and tasks of law are inevitably defined using the terms of reference provided by particular cultures, and cannot be satisfactorily generalized or abstracted from these.

Culture, therefore, appears fundamental—a kind of lens through which all aspects of law must be perceived, or a gateway of understanding through which every comparatist must pass so as to have any genuine access to the meaning of foreign law.

II. LAW INSIDE CULTURE

The concept of legal culture has been invoked for a wide range of purposes in comparative legal studies. Prominent among recent advocates of a cultural focus have been scholars who argue that comparative legal studies should devote much more attention to exploring and appreciating differences, rather than similarities, between legal ideas, legal systems, and legal traditions. For Vivian Curran, for example, 'different categories [of thought] undergird each legal culture'.[2] Culture marks important cognitive boundaries. A recognition that law inhabits different cultures must, in Pierre Legrand's view, require the comparatist to develop an 'empathy for alterity',[3] an interest in and appreciation of differences in legal experience in different cultural environments—a shift away from the comparatist's more traditional focus on trying to remove legal differences and disagreements between jurisdictions.

If law is embedded in culture it may be that the study of law can be undertaken realistically only by adopting the standpoint of someone 'inside' a culture, by a kind of 'immersion'[4] in it. According to this approach, the comparatist must understand law in the same way that people who participate in its culture do. Such a study must recognize the integrity, identity, or coherence of the culture in which law exists, and the interwoven characteristics that make that culture unique and distinguish it from others. To understand law, the scholar will try to operate, as far as possible, in the thought patterns of that law's particular culture.

Law cocooned inside a culture, it might be claimed, is *necessarily* different from law that exists in another culture. If each culture has its own identity, it will be different from all others. This radical differentiation of cultures entails the radical

Curran, 'Cultural Immersion, Difference and Categories in U.S. Comparative Law', (1998) 46 *AJCL* 43, 66, 71.

[2] Curran, (1998) 46 *AJCL* 43, 45.   [3] Pierre Legrand, *Fragments on Law-as-Culture* (1999), 11.
[4] Curran, (1998) 46 *AJCL* 43 ff.

differentiation of the laws that exist within them. So, an attempt to compare the law embedded in one culture with the law embedded in a different one (even if the legal rules appear to be the same) might pose particular difficulties. The reason is that, as suggested earlier, legal rules alone can never tell us all we need to know. The meaning of the law may not be revealed 'on its face', in the letter of the law. Deeper inquiries may be needed to discover this meaning—inquiries about established practices, traditions, implicit assumptions or preconceptions that will colour the way rules are understood and applied—in short, inquiries about aspects of the law's cultural setting. The claim of most of the leading advocates of a cultural approach is that the letter of the law can *only* be read in the cultural context that gives it meaning. Read in a different cultural context it will simply be different law.

In the view of many cultural comparatists comparative law has devoted too much attention to seeking similarity between the legal phenomena (usually rules) that it sets out to compare. Its overwhelming focus has been on harmonization or unification of law between jurisdictions, and this has tended to be a superficial, technical focus, rather than an effort to understand law in depth. An appreciation of difference may be more intellectually justifiable than a search for similarities, where the latter relies on finding a sort of 'lowest common denominator' of legal doctrine in different systems. Sometimes the claim is that, for moral or political reasons, it is imperative to celebrate legal differences rather than to minimize them. On this view, promoting legal harmonization or unification between different legal systems or doctrines may be far from a self-evidently good thing, although comparatists have usually thought of it in this way. For many cultural comparatists there are important virtues in 'sustainable diversity' in law.[5]

Thus, behind the efforts of at least some cultural comparatists a powerful agenda can often be seen: comparative law must become a more useful enterprise than it has been in the past; a more effective agent for promoting mutual understanding; a voice against the undermining, ignoring or domination of cultures. It must not just tolerate but appreciate legal difference, no less urgently than it seeks similarity between the laws of different systems. This outlook easily connects with wider political or reformist positions. As will appear, these include positions on multiculturalism, European legal integration, and globalization.

Often explicit among cultural comparatists generally, and particularly those who stress 'difference', is a claim that mainstream or traditional comparative law scholarship has simply lost its way. It suffers from a deep 'malaise',[6] having failed to link with wider currents of non-legal scholarship (especially in philosophy and history) and having set its goals in too limited a manner. Most fundamentally, the claim is made that, because of its narrow conception of law and its consequent

---

[5] cf H. Patrick Glenn, *Legal Traditions of the World: Sustainable Diversity in Law* (2nd edn, 2004).

[6] See, especially, William Ewald, 'Comparative Jurisprudence I: What was it Like to Try a Rat?', (1995) 143 *University of Pennsylvania LR* 1889, 1961–65.

misunderstanding of what legal comparisons involve, mainstream comparative law has undermined its intellectual promise as a field of social inquiry as well as its practical promise to promote effective communication between lawyers and lawmakers in different nations and cultures.

While the focus on 'difference' has been prominent among some leading cultural comparatists, it is important to stress that legal culture has also been an important idea in other contributions to comparative legal scholarship that do not have this focus and seem motivated by completely different concerns. In what follows, I shall look first at these other developments involving the concept of legal culture, and at some general considerations about its use, before returning to consider the multi-faceted argument that, above all, comparatists 'must learn to detect, to understand, to value, indeed, to cherish difference'.[7]

III. Cultures as Fields of Similarity

If invoking legal culture has appealed to some scholars as a basis for emphasizing 'difference' in law, other uses of the concept have been in a seemingly opposite cause: to promote or celebrate a growing harmony in law across large cultural spaces. Using an idea of legal culture, one can look *outwards* at other cultures, perhaps stressing cultural difference and the need to respect it. But one can also look *inwards*, at the common experience within a culture, the shared points of reference that culture gives to those who inhabit it. A cultural approach might show that seemingly similar rules are actually different when understood in the context of their different cultural settings. But, conversely, recognition of law's roots in culture might make it possible to show profound *unities* between the laws of different legal systems that inhabit a common legal culture even where legal rules differ between these systems.

1. European Legal Culture

For example, if it can be shown that a common European legal culture exists, linking the different national legal experiences of Europe, it may be possible to recognize deep links between, say, French and Italian law, or even between English common law and German civil law; links that are important despite differences between legal

---

[7] Legrand (n 3), 10–11.

rules in those systems, or even despite differences in legal styles that comparatists associate with contrasting 'families' of law (such as common law and civil law).

Thus, in contrast to cultural approaches that emphasize legal difference, there can certainly be cultural approaches that stress similarity and seem to offer bases on which legal harmonization or unification might be extended and enriched in a certain cultural area. The most important example of such a postulated cultural area in recent comparative legal studies is, indeed, 'Europe'. The idea of a European legal culture, with deep roots in partly common, and partly parallel, legal histories of the major Western European nations, has provided both an inspiration and a kind of template for recent efforts towards harmonizing European private law.

Franz Wieacker's identification of elements of European legal culture has been influential here. He emphasizes three elements that may together indicate the essence of this culture.[8] Thus, 'Personalism' refers to the 'primacy of the individual as subject, end, and intellectual point of reference in the idea of law', but it implies also a balance and tension between individual freedom and social duty, and an emphasis on both liberty (of individuals and groups) and sovereignty (of state, monarch, or people). 'Legalism' indicates decision-making through general rules of law not dependent for validity or acceptance on some moral, social, or political value or purpose. It points to a positivistic separation of law and morals, and of law and politics; and ultimately (by expressing collective social responsibility in statutory form) to the legal framework of a welfare state. Finally, 'intellectualism' indicates a general, intellectually orderly, systematic way of thinking about law that, for Wieacker, strains towards 'thematization, conceptualization and contradiction-free consistency'.

Presented at such a level of abstraction ('a first draft' of 'a synopsis') these markers take us only a short distance. The paleness of their generalizations is a reminder that culture is primarily something lived in and experienced. It does not lend itself to neat summary but needs complex description, evocation, and exploration 'from within', from 'the centre or root of the system'.[9] Wieacker himself offers this, from one perspective, in his own rich historical narrative of European private law.[10]

Cultural comparatists have noted that intellectual inspirations for this kind of exploration can be traced to Johann Gottfried Herder's late eighteenth-century romantic nationalism which emphasizes the particularity of cultures as a source of meaning and as a framework for common history.[11] Links can also be made particularly with Friedrich Carl von Savigny's early nineteenth-century romantic

---

[8] Franz Wieacker, 'Foundations of European Legal Culture', (1990) 38 *AJCL* 1, 20–5.
[9] Giorgio Del Vecchio, 'The Crisis of the Science of Law' (1933), in Ralph A. Newman (ed), *Man and Nature: Selected Essays by Giorgio Del Vecchio* (1969), 171, 180.
[10] Franz Wieacker, *A History of Private Law in Europe* (trans Tony Weir, 1995).
[11] Ewald (n 6), 2004–12; Legrand (n 1), 266–71.

nationalist view of law as tied to culture rather than to political organization,[12] so that, for him, it could make good sense to consider the evolution and internal coherence of a distinctively German law founded on inherited Roman sources, even in the absence of a unified German polity. In other words, culture could be envisaged as unifying and giving meaning to law, and perhaps inspiring its future development in ways that would be justified by the sense of a cultural heritage in which changing positive law finds secure moral and emotional foundations.

It is not surprising, then, that Reinhard Zimmermann calls for the development, in a Europe-wide context, of what Savigny called an 'organically progressive' legal science, and for the reconstitution of Savigny's German historical school of jurisprudence on a European level.[13] Implicit in this is the idea that legal culture itself cannot be codified but has to grow from diffuse sources, hard to define or categorize. If, in reality, a European legal culture hardly exists as a strong feature of contemporary legal experience, or exists only sketchily in history, tradition, emotional allegiances, and certain complex beliefs and values that resist final specification in neat formulae, the idea of such a culture might nevertheless provide inspiration and direction for legal integration, and a promise of an ultimate harmonization of law. This kind of argument is now familiar among many European comparatists.

2. Components of Culture

Yet, because the components of culture are hard to specify, or at least to agree on, much controversy is likely to accompany any attempt to claim the existence or explain the nature of cultural unities. Social scientists, who use the concept of legal culture in empirical research and have produced a large literature on the subject, often demand unambiguous specification of its components.

On this basis, the German legal sociologist Volkmar Gessner, noting Wieacker's claims, declares bluntly that no common European legal culture exists. 'As long as patterns of interpretation (values, attitudes) and behavioural routines with respect to law as well as social institutions which form part of the legal implementation process are not integrated, a common or even similar legal practice cannot be expected.'[14] For Gessner, 'important indicators for a comparison of European legal cultures are goal attainment of public administrations, degree of legalization of state activities, frequency of illegal (corrupt) behaviour of public officials, knowledge of law in the general population, attitudes towards state regulation,

---

[12] Friedrich Carl von Savigny, *Of the Vocation of Our Age for Legislation and Jurisprudence* (trans Abraham Hayward, 1831).

[13] Reinhard Zimmermann, 'Savigny's Legacy: Legal History, Comparative Law and the Emergence of a European Legal Science', (1996) 112 *LQR* 576 ff.

[14] Volkmar Gessner, 'Global Legal Interaction and Legal Cultures', (1994) 7 *Ratio Juris* 132, 134, 135–6.

preferences for formal vs. informal dispute resolution and the ideological position of judges'.[15] What is at issue here is not the hardly fathomable working of a diffuse cultural force like Savigny's postulated 'national spirit' (*Volksgeist*) in law but a set of concrete behavioural and attitudinal indicators, detectable in the activities and opinions of lawyers and other citizens.

James Gibson and Gregory Caldeira, following a similar kind of approach, predict, on the basis of a survey of popular attitudes to law among European citizens, that 'differences in legal cultures [within Europe] will play an even greater role in the ways in which EC law gets implemented within each of the member states'.[16] Studies of this kind at least illustrate that legal culture can mean many things. For some scholars, especially comparatists, it exists primarily in the outlook and practices of legal professionals. For other scholars, including many social scientists, it exists, most significantly, in wider, probably very varied, popular attitudes to and experiences of law.

Some social scientific approaches, such as those of Gessner and Gibson and Caldeira, adopt a very different way of studying legal culture from that of many cultural comparatists. The cultural comparatist, using 'a capacity for imaginative projection',[17] may try to see legal culture through the 'habits of thought'[18] of those (especially lawyers) who inhabit it. This is not a matter of using social scientific indicators but of 'feeling oneself into' the experience characteristic of a particular culture.[19]

Perhaps these kinds of approaches that advocate an immersion in culture, an empathetic exploration of the meaning it has for those who participate in it, will tend to emphasize the irreducibility of cultural differences to a greater extent than approaches that focus on identifying precise cultural indicators. The close definition of such indicators to make them usable in cross-cultural research allows them to act as foci for broad generalization or abstraction from experience. Indicators select particular points of comparison, suggesting common reference points—in a sense, meeting-points between the particularities of environments, histories, or lives. But immersion in culture, as a kind of hermeneutical method, is likely to emphasize the irreducible uniqueness of the experience of that culture and the inevitable strangeness and 'otherness' of what lies outside it.

Those invocations of legal culture that have accompanied the most sweeping claims about a growing uniformity or harmonization of law between legal systems have usually focused on specific indicators of legal convergence or uniform traits of law.

Thus, the American legal sociologist Lawrence Friedman sees a vast '*modern*

---

[15] Gessner, (1994) 7 *Ratio Juris* 135.

[16] James L. Gibson and Gregory A. Caldeira, 'The Legal Cultures of Europe', (1996) 30 *Law and Society Review* 55, 80.

[17] Legrand (n 3), 64.   [18] Ewald (n 6), 2045.   [19] cf Ewald (n 6), 1942.

legal culture: the legal culture of modern, industrial, "advanced" societies' as being in process of formation.[20] Modern law in general, as Friedman sees it, is characterized by rapid change. It is 'dense and ubiquitous', notable for the increasing bulk of legal doctrine and law's pervasiveness in more and more areas of life. It is instrumental—a mere tool for achieving social and economic aims—but is also expected to be an expression of human rights. What links these instrumental and expressive aspects of law is legal individualism, with the idea of 'right' or 'entitlement' at its heart. Modern law 'presupposes a society of free-standing, autonomous individuals'. Finally, modern law exists in the shadow of economic globalization and so tends towards convergence, harmonization, and the elimination of differences between legal systems and national legal cultures; towards 'a certain melting together of world cultures' that finds expression in law.[21]

No less ambitiously than Friedman, the sociologist Philip Selznick refers to a broad 'rule of law culture' founded in 'the Western legal tradition' and an emerging 'post-modern legal culture' that promises to extend the rule of law 'to all spheres in which power is exercised and may be abused'.[22] A focus on legal culture can thus inspire a search for increasing similarity and convergence in law no less than an appreciation of difference.

3. Who Defines Culture?

No doubt, the canvas on which images of law can be painted is greatly enlarged when culture is brought into the discussion, but there is always a danger of reading into legal culture what one wishes to see. Friedman finds rights and entitlements fundamental to his, admittedly tentatively sketched, overarching modern legal culture. Wieacker, however, emphasizes a balance of freedom and responsibility—a different conception of individualism in a specifically European context.

The primary difficulties, which affect all uses of the concept of legal culture, are twofold. First, how are components of legal culture to be identified in an acceptable way? (Whose acceptance matters? Those who see themselves as inhabiting the culture? Those who observe it as outsiders?) Second, how are the boundaries of legal culture to be recognized? Friedman is prepared to recognize innumerable legal cultures, overlapping and interacting. For comparatists who start from an idea of national legal cultures, the presumption will be of common legal experience within nation states and different experiences between them. But a recognition

---

[20] Lawrence M. Friedman, 'Is There a Modern Legal Culture?', (1994) 7 *Ratio Juris* 117, 119. Emphasis in original.

[21] Friedman, (1994) 7 *Ratio Juris* 125, 126.

[22] Philip Selznick, 'Legal Cultures and the Rule of Law', in Martin Krygier and Adam Czarnota (eds), *The Rule of Law after Communism: Problems and Prospects in East-Central Europe* (1999), 21, 26, 29, 34.

of European, Western, modern, or post-modern legal cultures (and many other possible varieties) will indicate other boundaries, other parameters, determining when and where similarity, on the one hand, or difference, on the other, will be the governing presumption about legal experience.

It can, at least, be said that to invoke legal culture is *always* to imply both similarity (within) and difference (between) cultures. Culture is invariably invoked *against* something, however much it is used to emphasize the common interests, beliefs, values, traditions, or allegiances of those who share the culture. Vivian Curran has noted that the European *émigrés* who became leading figures in developing comparative law in the United States after World War II tended to seek legal similarity—the unification or harmonization of law between nations as the objective of comparative legal scholarship—although many of them naturally and unostentatiously informed their legal studies with a broad awareness of the diverse cultural roots of law, grounded in their own cosmopolitan experience.[23] She sees some of these pioneer modern comparatists as subscribing to a vision of a single humanity and of a law that could express universal human attributes—in short, a Natural law. Yet this vision is set up, she plausibly suggests, at least partly in reaction against the Nazi *inhumanity* which many of them fled.

Somewhat similarly, the Italian legal philosopher Giorgio Del Vecchio, writing soon after World War II, saw the 'unity of the human mind' as a basis for comparative law, so that this field is 'as large as that of the history of man' and 'the greater part of legal principles and institutions form a common inheritance of humanity at all times'.[24] For Del Vecchio, the best way for the comparatist to treat 'barbaric forms' of law that 'sometimes reappear among so-called civilized countries' is to see them as regressions to a historical phase already past.[25] Thus, in this case, the 'other' against which a common humanity is set is its own past—a different (more primitive) culture.

IV. LEGAL CULTURE AND LEGAL CHANGE

One very influential body of recent work in comparative law relies heavily on an idea of legal culture but does not initially seem to fit into the picture so far sketched. Alan Watson's work does not focus directly on either similarity or

---

[23] Curran, (1998) 46 *AJCL* 43 ff.
[24] Giorgio Del Vecchio, 'The Unity of the Human Mind as a Basis for Comparative Legal Study', (1950), in Newman (n 9), 31, 32, 33.
[25] Del Vecchio (n 24), 35–6.

difference between legal ideas, systems, or traditions. Instead, it treats culture as a filter for legal change or development. A consequence of Watson's researches, he remarks, has been 'my appreciation of the enormous power of the legal culture in determining the timing, the extent, and the nature of legal change'.[26]

Perhaps surprisingly, Watson's view of the nature and effects of legal culture is much closer to Lawrence Friedman's than to that of most contemporary cultural comparatists. Like Friedman, Watson sees culture as an *agent*, a major cause of legal change or legal inertia. He is less concerned to explore, evoke, and describe cultures as ways of thinking about, practising, and experiencing law, than to ask how culture works on law, sometimes impelling its development, sometimes slowing or preventing it, but always shaping it. This is also Friedman's concern.

But Watson the comparatist and Friedman the legal sociologist disagree strikingly about the location of the power of legal culture. Friedman distinguishes 'internal' (or mandarin) legal culture (the culture of lawyers and those who professionally manage, maintain, and develop the legal system) from 'external' (lay or popular) legal culture—the law-related attitudes and beliefs of citizens at large. He sees external legal culture as ultimately much more powerful than internal culture; the latter will adapt to the former.[27] Watson, by contrast, is almost entirely concerned with internal legal culture in Friedman's sense. The occupational culture of lawyers and lawmakers is crucial and, in Watson's view, operates largely autonomously of 'external' social forces in shaping legal change.

This is not the place to attempt a detailed evaluation of Watson's claims about the causal power of legal culture,[28] which he sees primarily as the outlook, traditions, values, and interests of legal elites. But it is important to note that Watson's approach raises the same kind of serious problems of proving cause and effect, and determining the boundaries and content of legal culture, that have been identified in relation to Friedman's use of the concept.[29] If culture is a variable in explaining legal change, it is essential to be able to define this variable precisely—that is, to identify the exact components of legal culture and their relative weight in influencing change in law.

Watson is better placed than Friedman in that his conception of legal culture as an effective cause is narrower and more focused than Friedman's. Watson is almost entirely concerned with the effects of identifiable legal elites. For Friedman, by contrast, significant legal cultures of many different kinds are found anywhere and everywhere in society. Nevertheless, a focus on the effects of legal elites demands

[26] Alan Watson, 'Legal Change: Sources of Law and Legal Culture', (1983) 131 *University of Pennsylvania LR* 1121, 1154; *idem*, 'From Legal Transplants to Legal Formants', (1995) 43 *AJCL* 469, 470.

[27] See especially Lawrence M. Friedman, *The Legal System: A Social Science Perspective* (1975).

[28] For a recent evaluation see Roger Cotterrell, 'Is There a Logic of Legal Transplants?', in David Nelken and Johannes Feest (eds), *Adapting Legal Cultures* (2001), 71 ff.

[29] Roger Cotterrell, 'The Concept of Legal Culture', in David Nelken (ed), *Comparing Legal Cultures* (1997), 13 ff.

empirical study of those elites and an identification of which cultural components, from among their interests, values, beliefs, traditions, and allegiances, are more or less important in producing effects on law.

Without such a study, Watson's appeal to legal culture explains very little. It does not enable us to predict *how* legal elites will shape law in any particular context or period. It would allow us to say only that, *whatever* change occurs or fails to occur in law, the (main) cause will always be (in some unknown way, and to some unknown extent) legal culture. Watson's work points inescapably to a need for sociological inquiries about the forces that shape law. It should direct him to the terrain that Friedman occupies—that of sociology of law. But Watson's use of the concept of legal culture is a sociologically oriented one—without any sociology.

In fact, what is most intriguing about the way Watson's ideas on legal culture have been applied in some recent comparative legal studies is the effort, based on them, to *marginalize* the contribution of sociological and anthropological studies to comparative law, and to argue for the centrality of philosophy and history in the comparatist's enterprise.[30] Legal culture is seen not only as fundamental in determining most legal change but as something that develops with a kind of inner dynamic and a substantial autonomy from 'external' social forces.

In the understandings of Watson and his sympathetic interpreter William Ewald, legal culture is to be understood historically (as a matter of the shaping by legal elites of their practices and traditions over time) and philosophically (as a matter of the shaping by these elites of the ideas and values that inform law). Yet given the focus of this approach on culture's causal significance in explaining legal change, there is still a need—seemingly unrecognized by Watson and Ewald—to examine how and under what conditions general philosophical currents influence legal elites (or are transformed by them) and what social forces in history are significant in shaping the experience of legal elites. Social scientific inquiries addressing these matters cannot realistically be excluded; they should be central to the Watson–Ewald use of the concept of legal culture.

This unjustified (and rare) attempt explicitly to marginalize sociological or anthropological perspectives in comparative law is intriguing because it shows that ultimately Watson's and Ewald's invocation of legal culture is indeed, like all other uses of the concept by comparatists, closely associated with the similarity–difference axis. In this case, legal culture is a means of differentiating the culture of legal elites—often 'distant from social reality'[31]—from the social world at large. *Similarity* exists, for Watson, between the practices and experiences of legal elites: indeed, to 'a considerable degree, the lawmakers of one society share the same legal culture with the lawmakers of other societies'.[32] *Difference*, however, exists in the

---

[30] Ewald (n 6); William Ewald, 'Comparative Jurisprudence II: The Logic of Legal Transplants', (1995) 43 *AJCL* 489 ff.

[31] Watson, (1995) 43 *AJCL* 469.   [32] Watson, (1983) 131 *Univ Pennsylvania LR* 1157.

form of a clear distinction between the typical power of these elites to shape legal change and the typical powerlessness of society at large to do so. Crudely, we might say, it is a postulated (but entirely undemonstrated) almost absolute difference between the world of jurists and the world of sociologists. Thus, Watson's view of legal culture celebrates both similarity and difference, in a strikingly different way from that of most cultural comparatists.

V. IDENTIFYING AND INTERPRETING LEGAL CULTURES

We have noted that legal culture can mean various things in its different uses in comparative legal studies. And it can be understood in different ways—from the 'inside', by trying to appreciate the thought processes and experience of participants in a culture, and from the 'outside', as observable indicators of culture. Either of these approaches (or a combination of them) could be congenial to comparatists. An immersion in the legal experience of a foreign legal system is likely to involve many of the interpretive techniques that lawyers use in relation to their own legal systems. Equally, identifying various indicators of legal culture might be close to lawyers' everyday positivistic identification of sources of law and of valid legal rules in their own legal system. In either case, however, it may be natural for lawyers—concerned with law as ideas embodied in practices—to focus on cultures as ways of thinking, on the one hand, and traditions of practice, on the other.

For Pierre Legrand, culture is 'the framework of intangibles within which an interpretive community operates' and it refers to 'ways of organising one's place in the moral universe through commitments to standards of reference and rationality'.[33] Legal culture is a matter of *mentalité*, an entire distinctive way of thinking about law and legal experience, 'a particular epistemological framework'.[34] It is a cognitive structure that allows individuals to make sense of the legal world in which they exist.

What are the boundaries of any particular *mentalité*, or legal culture? The answer is not clear but often the assumption is that national legal systems have their distinctive cultures. Beyond that, the common law tradition has its *mentalité*, as does that of the civil law. For Legrand, however, delineating boundaries is not important, except, as will appear, when he addresses particular issues about the

---

[33] Legrand (n 3), 19, 27.
[34] Pierre Legrand, 'What "Legal Transplants"?', in Nelken and Feest (n 28), 55, 65.

transferability or influences of legal ideas, especially in the European context. What counts—the fundamental message of cultural comparison—is that those who participate in law, especially lawyers, look out at the world from inside a legal culture that shapes all their legal perceptions and differentiates these from the perceptions of people who are not a part of the same culture. Legrand very often couples references to legal tradition with references to legal culture but he discusses culture mainly as ways of thought and modes of understanding, rather than traditions of practice. William Ewald has a similar view of legal culture: 'what we need to understand is neither law in books nor law in action but law in *minds*'.[35] Watson adopts the view that 'the essential core of culture consists of traditional (i.e. historically derived and selected) ideas and especially their attached values'.[36]

Some of these formulations (perhaps especially Legrand's and Ewald's) are reminiscent of much older appeals to the 'spirit' of legal systems, and a lineage of ideas traceable from Montesquieu, via Vico, Herder, and others,[37] through to the preferences of legal philosophers such as Del Vecchio for 'the intrinsic spirit of the [legal] system', extending far beyond the 'almost invariably imperfect' letter of particular rules.[38]

The claim of the cultural comparatists is typically that comparative law fails to understand the nature and meaning of foreign law unless it can appreciate legal culture conceptualized in some such way.[39] Unless comparatists understand the culture which foreign law inhabits they are fated to misinterpret or underestimate this law. Even when foreign legal rules seem familiar, easily intelligible in terms of comparatists' experience of their own legal system, problems of translation remain. These may be problems of translation in the most obvious sense—the language of foreign law may itself be foreign to the comparatist. But there may be more profound problems of translation in so far as language is only one aspect of culture. Thus, between, say, English law and American law, sharing the same language, it is easy to fail to recognize important differences of legal outlook that, even when not unambiguously signalled on the face of rules, reside in deeper differences in, for example, patterns of values and beliefs, historical experience, and national outlook. These kinds of influences colour law and provide its 'self-understood',[40] its unstated, taken-for-granted, yet vital elements.

---

[35] Ewald (n 6), 2111. Emphasis added.

[36] Watson, (1983) 131 *University of Pennsylvania LR* 1152–3.

[37] See eg James Q. Whitman, 'The Neo-Romantic Turn', in Legrand and Munday (n 1), 312, 315–26.

[38] Del Vecchio (n 9), 179, 180.

[39] The same claim can be made with regard to legal historians' efforts to understand the law of distant eras; on this, see Ewald (n 6), discussing medieval trials of animals.

[40] David Daube, 'The Self-Understood in Legal History', (1973) 18 *Juridical Review* 126 ff. The important idea here is that law relies on understandings (including specific rules) that are not expressed in legal doctrine because they are generally self-evident to both the regulators and the regulated. Sacco's notion of 'cryptotypes' or non-verbalized rules seems closely related. See Rodolfo

We might say that the primary warning which many cultural comparatists seek to give by emphasizing legal culture is: prolong your puzzlement!—do not jump to easy or convenient conclusions about the nature of foreign law and those who use it; and never try to explain foreign laws and societies using criteria that reflect only your own cultural experience.

How, then, is legal culture as ideas, ways of thinking, an epistemological framework, to be grasped by the comparatist? One might say, defensively, that the cultural comparatist's warning is unnecessary; that immersion in the whole context of foreign law is what a good comparatist will obviously seek. Curran asks American comparatists 'to beware of avoiding truths and the complexities of truths, of losing the gist of attributes of other legal cultures by overlooking the untranslatables'.[41] The comparatist should understand not merely rules but also underlying principles. Curran gives, as an example, the principle of the binding character of contractual obligation in German contract law.[42] That such an exhortation needs to be made seems odd, but some cultural comparatists might see the necessity as arising from a legacy of a narrowly technical positivism and functionalism in comparative legal studies.

If we look for more incisive and elaborate statements of what is needed to engage with culture in comparative law the literature seems disappointing. Legrand often refers to a need for 'thick or deep understanding', a formula reminiscent of Clifford Geertz's method of thick description[43] in anthropology, the detailed recording and in-depth empathetic interpretation of experience in the culture being studied. While Curran uses the term 'cultural immersion', it is not clear how deep this immersion need be. 'It contemplates a slow pushing against cultural barriers towards an ideal of mutual comprehension . . . and a recognition that some distances will remain.'[44] Legrand rejects the idea of 'immersion' because, for him, it suggests trying to be a part of the foreign culture, which he thinks impossible: 'one cannot "be" the other'; any interpretation will be an 'intervention' with the comparatist maintaining 'critical distance'.[45] For Nora Demleitner, more than

---

Sacco, 'Legal Formants: A Dynamic Approach to Comparative Law II', (1991) 39 *AJCL* 343, 384–6. A legal system that cannot rely on an extensive 'self-understood', in this sense, will presumably be wracked by uncertainties and interpretive difficulties and will often have the appearance of arbitrariness.

[41] Curran, (1998) 46 *AJCL* 43, 85.   [42] Curran, (1998) 46 *AJCL* 43, 78–83.

[43] Clifford Geertz, 'Thick Description: Toward an Interpretive Theory of Culture', in *idem, The Interpretation of Cultures* (1973), 3 ff. Geertz writes that the comparative study of law should be 'an attempt . . . to formulate the presuppositions, the preoccupations, and the frames of action characteristic of one sort of legal sensibility in terms of those characteristic of another. Or, slightly more practically, to bring off this hermeneutical *grand jeté* with respect to some more focused problem . . .': see Geertz, 'Local Knowledge: Fact and Law in Comparative Perspective', in *idem, Local Knowledge* (1993), 167, 218–19.

[44] Curran, (1998) 46 *AJCL* 43, 91.   [45] Legrand (n 1), 251–2, 253.

tolerance of the unfamiliar is required; there must be 'a commitment to find common ground and to put our most deeply held beliefs at risk'.[46]

Apart from a degree of vagueness at the level of general methodological prescription, there seem to be differences of emphasis in these views. For Legrand, it would take something comparable to a religious conversion to be able to think in terms of a different *mentalité*. A common lawyer, for example, can never think like a civil lawyer, and vice versa.[47] On the whole, Legrand's emphasis is on the formidable difficulties of cultural translation. For Curran, Ewald, and Demleitner, by contrast, there is much emphasis on communication and the need to increase and improve it between cultures, even though there will always be 'distortion', and 'perfect comparison' is impossible.[48]

While these variations in expression should not be exaggerated, their importance may be primarily as a reflection of differences in political uses of the concept of legal culture in recent comparative legal scholarship. A relatively negative focus on the difficulties of understanding another culture in anything like its own terms may be particularly important for a writer, such as Legrand, who has argued for the importance of protecting the separate integrity of legal cultures (eg the legal culture of English common law in Europe) against what he sees as a process of undesirable homogenization. By contrast, a positive, even optimistic, emphasis on the possibility of overcoming inter-cultural interpretive difficulties and extending communicative possibilities between cultures might be especially significant for writers, such as Curran and Demleitner, worried by a perceived parochialism in aspects of their own American national legal culture and seeking means to overcome it. The positive emphasis might also be significant for efforts to equip comparative law to deal sensitively and progressively with differences between local cultures *within* the nation state, and so to link with movements in legal and social theory that are already engaging with pressing problems of multicultural communication.

How should the analytical significance of the concept of legal culture (as contrasted with its possible political usefulness) be judged? When we ask how far the concept of legal culture helps comparatists *directly* in obtaining reliable knowledge of foreign legal systems and especially in making comparisons between them, the answers are not necessarily encouraging. The same is true when we ask how useful the concept of legal culture is in unambiguously identifying and organizing objects of study in comparative law.

It has often been claimed that, as Geoffrey Samuel puts it, culture 'is too weak a concept to act as an epistemological model in itself'.[49] It seems impossible to

---

[46] Nora V. Demleitner, 'Challenge, Opportunity and Risk: An Era of Change in Comparative Law' (1998) 46 *AJCL* 647, 655.

[47] Legrand (n 3), 77.   [48] Curran, (1998) 46 *AJCL* 43, 45, 49.

[49] Geoffrey Samuel, *Epistemology and Method in Law* (2003), 50.

specify the content, scope, or power of legal culture with clarity. Samuel asks: if (as Legrand implies) an Italian lawyer cannot think like an English lawyer, why should it be assumed that a lawyer from Welsh-speaking North Wales can think like an English lawyer born and bred in London? If, however, these can indeed be considered to share a legal culture, do lawyers in parts of Belgium and France also share one? What are the important boundaries and essential elements of culture for purposes of comparison?

There is no problem as long as culture is used without any implication that it refers to a *bounded unity* of some kind which can be distinguished absolutely from others. There is no difficulty as long as culture remains just a portmanteau term for a more or less arbitrarily assembled aggregate of phenomena, and a means of referring provisionally to a compendium of bits of social experience whose inter-relations are not yet known. Used in this way culture is a highly convenient idea: like a box in which a miscellany of objects can be kept safe and together, until at some later time they can be examined, sorted, and stored individually.

There may, indeed, be no problem as long as culture is not seen as a unified *cause* of legal or social effects: for example, as long as it is not seen as an impediment to or facilitator of legal harmonization or legal change. To have any prospect of evaluating such causal claims it would be necessary to know what 'it' is. But that would involve disaggregating culture—breaking it up into precisely defined components that can be linked to specific consequences. How it might be possible to disaggregate culture is a matter to return to later, but it is hard to see that much would be lost if we were to speak only about the various disaggregated elements; for example about such matters as inherited traditions and customs, shared beliefs and values, common allegiances and emotional attachments, or convergent interests and projects. The main loss would be the convenience of an evocative and familiar idea that links in fuzzy, indeterminate fashion many features of life and law that seem important.

This negative view of legal culture's usefulness is not the final conclusion I want to reach. A far more positive evaluation of the concept is possible. And it is no slight to cultural comparatists to suggest that the most powerful impact of the idea of legal cultures is a political or even a moral one. The demand that cultures be understood from 'the inside' can, indeed, produce inquiries that, to some extent, avoid the intellectual difficulties just mentioned. This is possible when these inquiries entirely avoid issues about the boundaries or unity of legal cultures, their exact delineation from other cultures or their causal significance; instead, they set out to explore the meaningfulness, emotional power, and everyday appropriateness of cultures for those who inhabit them and find identity in them.

These kinds of inquiries (and the advocacy of them by cultural comparatists) can have powerful *political* significance by suggesting the *moral* legitimacy of different ways of life and law, and the corresponding illegitimacy of efforts to eliminate or undermine these without recognizing and respecting the security and identity that they can give to those who share participation in a culture that they regard as their own.

VI. CELEBRATING DIFFERENCE

How far does the literature of comparative law emphasize these moral-political aspects of the use of the concept of legal culture? Certainly, there are efforts to give the prioritization of difference an intellectual rather than a moral-political basis. Thus Legrand sees a logical necessity for this priority: 'How, ultimately, could the self exist if the other were reconcilable with it? . . . Only the existence of non-identity allows identity to exist as identity . . . identity owes its existence to non-identity . . . it takes its being from non-identity or difference.'[50] Difference, he thinks, is more fundamental than similarity; it is the foundational concept. 'To accord difference priority is the only way for comparative law to take cognisance of what is the case'; comparatists should 'privilege alterity at all times'.[51]

Curran takes a more moderate and defensible position. For her, 'difference . . . is *equally* as foundational a concept as identity'; Western thought has erred in treating difference as a derivative concept 'such that one can say that two things are different only if one can say that they are not the same'.[52] Both Legrand and Curran cite Jacques Derrida's work, which would seem to support Curran's position that each concept (similarity and difference) must presuppose the other, its excluded opposite. But Legrand's apparent claim for some kind of philosophically necessary priority of difference seems merely an effort to disguise the essentially moral and political character of the argument that comparatists have been too concerned with seeking harmonization and unification of laws and too little with appreciating law's cultural foundations and the benefits of cultural diversity. Curran's disagreement with Legrand is clear: she states that her 'aim is not to promote a search for differences', nor to reverse functionalist emphases 'by presuming difference. Rather, I am anxious for comparatists to beware of avoiding truths and the complexities of truths, of losing the gist of attributes of other legal cultures by overlooking the untranslatables.'[53] The message is exhortatory: look more deeply, avoid conclusions based only on the doctrinal surface of the law; discover the common-sense assumptions and shared understandings that do not need to be expressed in legal rules but colour all understanding of them.

---

[50] Legrand (n 1), 245, 263.   [51] Legrand (n 1), 279; *idem* (n 34), 67.
[52] Curran, (1998) 46 *AJCL* 43, 46. Emphasis added.   [53] Curran, (1998) 46 *AJCL* 43, 85.

1. Multiculturalism and Legal Pluralism

Once the claim to some logically necessary priority of difference over similarity is rejected, it becomes possible to concentrate on moral-political reasons for advocating special attention to legal difference in comparative law. These include a call 'for the voice of the other and, specifically, for the voice of the other-in-the-law to be allowed to be heard above the chatter seeking to silence it'.[54] Legrand's terminology here calls to mind feminism's demand that 'different voices' of women's experience be heard, as well as efforts to raise the voices of (eg ethnic, racial, sexual, or religious) minorities in and through law. Cultural comparatists who emphasize difference often contrast what they see as the moribund state of comparative law as a critical discipline with vital recent critical movements in legal and social theory. Among these movements they cite feminism, critical legal studies, critical race theory, legal semiotics, and economic analysis of law.[55]

A focus on celebrating cultural difference is a way of trying to link comparative law with a recent but well established 'jurisprudence of difference'[56] which questions in a host of ways the focus of much mainstream legal theory. Traditionally, mainstream legal theory has set out to demonstrate unity or system in legal doctrine and legal thought, and to portray legal regimes as relatively comprehensive, unified, and integrated normative structures. The new jurisprudence of difference emphasizes the significance of different understandings of law among law's various professional interpretive communities in so far as these are linked to different social constituencies. The prioritizing of difference in comparative law is potentially allied with this jurisprudence of difference in legal theory in so far as both of these aim to highlight the diversity of the *social*—that is, the social environment in which law exists and from which it receives its meaning and moral force. The plea to celebrate diversity wholeheartedly is, in one of its aspects, a plea to rethink radically law's relation to the social, and to recognize that legal analysis can no longer take the social for granted, leaving it to social scientists to study.

In particular, legal analysis can no longer treat the social as made up only of interchangeable 'abstract individuals', 'citizens', or 'subjects'—persons uniformly addressed by law, owing allegiance to it, and 'owning' law jointly and severally through democratic processes. The question of what law means in different parts of the social, among different population groups, and in the context of different cultures is one that needs to be addressed in legal thought. Curran suggests that comparatists may need to reject an old assumption that recognizing difference

---

[54] Legrand (n 1), 250.

[55] Legrand (n 3), 20; Curran, (1998) 46 *AJCL* 43, 84; Nora V. Demleitner, 'Combating Legal Ethnocentrism: Comparative Law Sets Boundaries', (1999) 31 *Arizona State LJ* 737, 738.

[56] Roger Cotterrell, *The Politics of Jurisprudence: A Critical Introduction to Legal Philosophy* (2nd edn, 2003), ch 8.

necessarily goes along with social exclusion of the 'differentiated'.[57] Perhaps, when twentieth-century European *émigré* comparatists in the United States favoured seeking similarity over appreciating difference in law, they were indirectly reflecting their cultural assumption that *assimilation* of minorities was the only way to minimize the threat of repression of these minorities by the majority.[58] Now, assimilation (as opposed to integration) is no longer perceived to be desired by many minorities, nor necessarily by majorities who value the cultural richness and inventiveness that diversity can offer. In general, the often brief and undeveloped references by cultural comparatists to countering ethnocentricity, responding to the challenges of multiculturalism, and recognizing legal pluralism[59] (the idea of a diversity of official and unofficial legal regimes negotiating their coexistence in a single social environment), all point to a need to bring comparative legal studies into areas of debate that have become familiar and fundamental in contemporary legal theory.

It might be thought that some of these concerns are far removed from comparative law, with its familiar focus on the study of foreign legal systems. After all, multiculturalism is primarily a challenge *within* legal systems. And legal pluralism, in so far as it focuses on various kinds of unofficial 'law' which many lawyers might not recognize as law at all, is a special concern of legal sociologists and legal anthropologists rather than comparative lawyers. But the appeal in comparative law to ideas of culture and legal culture directs attention far beyond the boundaries of legal positivism's view of law. As noted earlier, the cultural approach understands legal phenomena as including much more than positive law. Even Watson's relatively narrow view of legal culture at least recognizes the existence of a popular (non-lawyers') legal culture, although it puts almost exclusive emphasis on the cultures of legal elites. As we have seen, one of its deficiencies is its failure to understand those elites sociologically and so to see the continuities between lawyers' legal cultures and popular legal cultures.

Thus, the appeal to culture in comparative law denies any strict limitation of comparative law's concerns to the positive law of nation states. It makes possible a recognition that different legal cultures can exist inside the boundaries of a single nation state,[60] and that legal cultures may transcend these boundaries—as in the idea of European, Western, or 'modern' legal cultures. To this extent, the idea of legal culture (whatever problems there are in making it analytically rigorous) points clearly to a far wider and more flexible view of law than the one that positivist lawyers typically adopt. Hence the work of cultural comparatists has the

---

[57] Vivian Grosswald Curran, 'Dealing in Difference: Comparative Law's Potential for Broadening Legal Perspectives', (1998) 46 *AJCL* 657, 665–7.

[58] See Curran, (1998) 46 *AJCL* 43, 66–78.

[59] Demleitner, (1999) 31 *Arizona State LJ* 737 ff, offers one of the fullest discussions of these matters.

[60] See eg Prakash Shah, *Legal Pluralism in Conflict: Coping with Cultural Diversity in Law* (2005).

potential to move comparative legal studies towards a legal pluralist understanding of the scope of law that is close to that of many legal sociologists and legal anthropologists. While legal pluralism is far from universally accepted in sociology of law or legal anthropology, it is nevertheless a familiar, much discussed idea in these fields and has been since their modern beginnings.[61]

2. European Legal Integration

In a very different field, that of European legal integration, the politics of legal culture and of difference in comparative law seem no less significant. Pierre Legrand has argued, in many publications, against a general harmonization of European private law—a process of legal change that is, however, well under way and has been gathering pace. He writes that 'Europe's cultural heterogeneity' must not be jettisoned 'in the name of an instrumental re-invention of Europeanism dictated by the ethos of capital and technology'.[62] He opposes the 'frenetic and hasty search' for common doctrinal roots of European law in various fields as 'irresponsible simplification'[63] and sees a tendency by Continental civil lawyers to minimize the real differences between English common law and Continental civil law. In fact, Legrand insists, each of these 'must be seen as a discrete epistemological construct' and 'such difference is irreducible so that is not possible for a civilian to think like a common lawyer' or vice versa.[64] A civil lawyer might see English common law's 'casuistic nature', 'bizarre traditionality', and 'peculiar interlocking' of law and equity,[65] while English lawyers see not casuistry but practicality and flexibility, not traditionality but secure rootedness in aspects of national culture, and a conceptual separation of (but intimate interaction between) law and equity as natural and productive.

Legrand is concerned at what he sees as a bowdlerization of Continental civil law in pragmatic, patronizing, and culturally myopic technical expositions for English audiences. But his main fear is of misunderstandings from the other direction, and a politics of European legal integration that makes them dangerous. Thus, in Europe, 'the common law is being squeezed out of significant existence'[66] and 'the civilian must resist the urge to dismiss the common law as unsophisticated or primitive'.[67] Common law is not a deviation from the civilian tradition which will be reabsorbed into it; rather it represents a separate legal culture that reflects distinctive national traditions, a culture formed from a collective will to express a unique and complex historical and social experience in law.

[61] For a convenient survey see Jørgen Dalberg-Larsen, *The Unity of Law: An Illusion? On Legal Pluralism in Theory and Practice* (2000).

[62] Legrand (n 1), 294.   [63] Pierre Legrand, 'Book Review', (1999) 58 *Cambridge LJ* 439, 442.

[64] Legrand (n 3), 64.   [65] Zimmermann, (1996) 112 *LQR* 587.

[66] Legrand (n 1), 311 (quoting Tony Weir).   [67] Legrand (n 3), 79.

These positions have much merit in insisting on the positive benefits of a sensitive recognition of Europe's legal and cultural richness and diversity. But the controversial political impulsions behind them are shown by the extremes to which Legrand takes his arguments. It seems that, for him, *any* significant moves towards a convergence between common law and civil law in Europe are misguided (despite much evidence that they are happening and producing effects). Legal transplants—the carrying of legal ideas, rules, or institutions—from one legal system to another are, in his view, not merely difficult but *impossible*[68] because any legal import (eg the Continental notion of 'good faith' in contracts, carried into English law by European Directive) will be transformed into something different from what it was in the legal system from which it was imported. It will therefore not be a 'transplant' but something new and perhaps unpredictable.[69]

Legrand's outlook has been termed 'naïve epistemological pessimism'[70] because of its seemingly dogmatic negativity, which nevertheless is motivated by a passionate commitment to protect the autonomy of cultures. The flaw in his thinking that leads to his extremes of view is his reification of legal culture, his tendency to assume that cultures are integrated, well-bounded, and homogeneous totalities, either immune from external influence (so that it will be futile to try to exert it) or vulnerable to disruption from it (in which case it must be prevented or resisted). Legrand's writings remain ambiguous as to which of these two conditions of legal culture he accepts.[71] Either of them, however, provides a superficial, but ultimately insecure, basis for arguing against efforts to integrate or unify European private law.

No less extreme arguments can be found for the opposite position (ie that legal convergence in Europe is easy and painless). Thus, Alan Watson sees the creation of a European code of private law as mainly a matter of technical problems, which concern only lawyers and can be dealt with by having them talk things out together as professionals. No profound difficulties stand in the way since to 'a considerable degree' lawmakers in different European societies all share the same legal culture.[72]

But, if we recognize law as having roots in beliefs, ultimate values, national sensibilities and traditions of thought, this view is no less simplistic than 'naïve epistemological pessimism' (and not unrelated to the kind of narrowly technical thinking that surely contributed to the débâcle of the European draft constitution

---

[68] Legrand (n 34).

[69] See Gunther Teubner, 'Legal Irritants: Good Faith in British Law or How Unifying Law Ends Up in New Divergences', (1998) 61 *Modern LR* 11 ff.

[70] Mark Van Hoecke, *Deep Level Comparative Law* (2002), 8.

[71] David Nelken, 'Towards a Sociology of Legal Adaptation', in *idem* and Feest (n 28), 7, 37–8.

[72] Alan Watson, 'Legal Transplants and European Private Law', (2000) 4 *Electronic Journal of Comparative Law*, no. 4 <http://www.ejcl.org/44/art44–2.html>; *idem* (1983) 131 *University of Pennsylvania LR* 1157.

in 2005). To be able to say how much legal convergence in Europe is possible it is necessary to ask: *which aspects of culture, including legal culture, favour convergence and which aspects hamper it?* Culture needs to be disaggregated to examine how its different facets relate (perhaps in contrasting ways) to law. This is a matter to be addressed in the final part of this chapter.

3. Globalization and Legal Parochialism

A broader but related expression of the politics of difference among cultural comparatists is in arguments about globalization. Homogenizing tendencies of economic and cultural globalization (eg through the internationalization of trade and mass media, and the worldwide extension of communication and travel) may make 'cultural difference' specially relevant and attractive as a rallying cry. Nora Demleitner writes that: 'The on-going globalization of all aspects of life has led to increasing cultural penetration': populations move more extensively than in the past and 'the same geographical space is inhabited and shared by groups with diverse cultural and legal backgrounds'. Thus, 'new identities of hybridity' have replaced national identities. But 'there is reluctance to recognize, let alone accept, such changes politically, economically, socially and legally'.[73] It may be doubted how far actual replacements of national identity have taken place. Much more important is an ongoing, gradual reshaping of these identities, as a result of the interplay of internal and external cultural influences, as well as external pressures for national economic reforms or transnational economic harmonization.

In this situation, the issue of celebrating cultural difference can easily become one of protecting an assumed *integrity* of cultures—by, on the one hand, denying the need for a thoroughgoing cultural assimilation within nation state populations that contain cultural minorities (protecting cultural difference within the nation state); and, on the other, by resisting cultural influences from abroad that seem hostile to cherished aspects of existing national culture (protecting the cultures of the nation state from external colonization). The enemy in both cases is seen as bland cultural homogenization or, worse, the substantial repression of some cultures in favour of others. Here the politics of difference becomes a politics of resistance to standardization and a fierce assertion of identity: 'the other refuses to disappear: it subsists, it persists; it is the hard bone on which reason breaks its teeth'.[74]

Is this politics, then, one of *un*reason? One might see it as a politics that opposes merely *instrumental* reason. It notices something far more important in culture than that which can be reduced to efficiency requirements. I mean by efficiency

---

[73] Demleitner, (1999) 31 *Arizona State LJ* 737, 745.
[74] Antonio Machado, quoted in Legrand (n 1), 301.

requirements, on the one hand, the perceived requirements of optimal economic performance, including the effective organization of an emerging global economic order (with its legal supports); and, on the other, the perceived requirements of governmental control and of a national (and transnational) rule of law that demands similarity (legal uniformity) as a bureaucratic convenience, rather than purely as a support for personal and group freedoms and for autonomous ways of life.

Matters such as these clearly provoke much passion. The Hungarian legal scholar Csaba Varga has described bitterly some mechanisms by which legal similarity as a servant of globalizing efficiency has been pursued in Central and Eastern Europe. Since the fall of communism, 'an army of dandies, arrivists, fantasizers, dreamers and easy experts of international agencies' has 'flooded the region to give hope for remedy' by 'hammering in magic [legal] words. . . . [U]nknown "civilisators" . . . arrive uninformed of the region with a few weeks' commission and leave still uninformed, without having even learnt about its varied historic past and culture, customs and potentialities.' After the local translation 'of laws taken out of their pockets' they 'return home with the epoch-making news: "By giving them a (New) World I acted as their transformation's Madison!" '[75]

Appreciating difference here, therefore, means bothering to learn about foreign 'others'; respecting them and taking them seriously as people with *different*, no less valid, understandings, expectations, ambitions, allegiances, and memories. But it should be remembered that these 'unknown civilisators' do not arrive uninvited. They are either Watson's law-creating legal elites, or are brought in to cooperate with these elites. For those who see cultural realities as primarily a matter of modernization and reform according to more or less uniform economic and governmental templates, the conversation of legal elites alone may be adequate to address all important relationships of law and culture. But, for others, harmonization or reform in ignorance of the 'varied historic past and culture, customs and potentialities' is a moral and political affront. They are likely to see it as a recipe for disaster unless cultural conditions, ignored by the harmonizers or reformers, are eventually addressed.

This kind of outlook in the politics of difference in comparative law suggests a close connection between charges of insensitivity in the pursuit (perhaps, the engineering) of legal similarity between countries, and charges of *parochialism* in the outlook of some comparatists—complaints that they judge foreign legal experience through the criteria provided by their own local legal culture. The charge of parochialism has been made especially in relation to recent American comparative legal scholarship.[76] Curran associates a retreat to parochialism with

---

[75] Csaba Varga, 'Comparative Legal Cultures: Attempts at Conceptualization' (1997) 38 *Acta Juridica Hungarica* 53, 58.

[76] Ugo Mattei, 'Why the Wind Changed: Intellectual Leadership in Western Law', (1994) 42 *AJCL* 195 ff.

the passing of the old generation of Continental European *émigré* comparatists in the United States and a relative lack of foreign language competence among more recent American comparatists.[77] Demleitner claims that, increasingly, 'American society and academia have become inward looking even though much lip service is being paid to the global society and the internationalization of markets and societies'.[78] The more general point is that parochialism, wherever found, tends to go along with an assumption that similarity is more desirable than difference.

In a sense, perhaps, appreciating difference, in law and culture, requires more effort than assuming or seeking similarity. One's 'home' culture is almost inevitably privileged through familiarity and the reinforcement of comfortable myths. Demleitner makes the powerful point that, because of this, comparisons with foreign cultures will frequently be to their disadvantage; 'the reality of the "other" will be disappointing, open to criticism and even rejection while the domestic system and its values will provide (unsubstantiated and undeserved) cause for celebration and even glorification'.[79] Comparative study, as part of legal education, can do something to counter this tendency, but only where legal cultures, not just rules of law, are compared.

VII. DISAGGREGATING CULTURE

One does not need to accept the various positions that have been taken, in the politics of difference in comparative law, to recognize that the call to appreciate difference has the capacity to reinvigorate aspects of comparative legal scholarship, merely by emphasizing aspects of culture that raise issues about non-instrumental objectives of legal comparison. The dominant trend in modern comparative law scholarship has been to assume that unification or harmonization of law is a primary objective of comparative legal studies. While many reasons for valuing the search for similarity in law have been given, the main one has surely been to foster trade and transnational commerce, and more generally to facilitate international legal communication and cooperation—a more effective use of law in regulating relations between individuals and corporations in different jurisdictions. Thus, a primary focus has been on law's role in regulating instrumental relations, the relations of people engaged in convergent or common projects.

The emphasis on legal culture in recent comparative law can be understood as,

---

[77] Curran, (1998) 46 *AJCL* 43, 54–9.   [78] Demleitner, (1998) 46 *AJCL* 647, 648–9.
[79] Demleitner, (1999) 31 *Arizona State LJ* 737, 761.

in part, an effort to bring into sharp focus law's contributions to many other kinds of relations apart from instrumental ones. Law is not merely valuable as a facilitator of contractual, commercial, and corporate relations. It is also a protector and shaper of traditions, an expression of shared beliefs and ultimate values, and—in much less definable ways—an expression of national expectations, allegiances, and emotions. Savigny tried to grasp this elusive aspect of law in the *Volksgeist* idea, which threatens always to slide into a dangerous mysticism. Nevertheless, the suggestion that law has an important role in expressing or recognizing aspects of emotional experience in personal or collective life is not absurd. While at one level this focus on affective relations is extremely abstract—for example, on the nation, or even on 'Europe' or the 'West'—at another it is found in everyday aspects of the regulation of domestic, fiduciary, or caring relations at interpersonal level.

As regards law's relation to tradition we should not just think in terms of custom as a source of law, or of the contradictory relations between law and time—for example, law enshrining in normative form accepted practices of the past until they are changed by new positive law, but able also to delegitimize those practices instantaneously in an essentially political process by a stroke of the lawmaker's pen. We should think rather of a very diverse set of links between law and tradition— including the protection of national heritage in the form of architecture, national monuments, historic sites, and cultural artefacts; the protection of historical memory (eg in laws that criminalize denials of the historical reality of the Holocaust); attempts to protect by law various aspects of national language, or to promote and preserve minority languages; and laws to protect the natural environment, as well as the conditions of everyday neighbourly relations. One aspect of the legal expression of culture is the promotion by law of all of these diverse aspects of tradition—understood as the inherited environment of coexistence. Legal action in these areas—essentially *conservation* action—is very different from law's involvement with the promotion and guarantee of commercial or other projects, in which people are engaged in activities which they understand as instrumental in a direct and obvious sense: producing or building things, trading or negotiating to increase wealth, or developing economic networks.

The linking of law and culture also emphasizes law's relation to beliefs and ultimate values. But here it highlights some of the most elusive of law's regulatory contributions. Ultimate values are easily recognized, for example as 'liberty', 'human dignity', 'equality', or 'justice'. Yet, clarifying them poses difficult philosophical problems. In a given cultural environment certain values or beliefs may be familiar and seen as generally accepted, yet their interpretation may vary significantly among participants in the culture. Nevertheless, it is not a pointless exercise to try to understand common beliefs and shared ultimate values that animate a culture. Thus, James Whitman has tried to contrast a Continental European ultimate value of 'human dignity', with a fundamental American value of 'liberty'.[80] By their nature, however, the exact meaning of these values in a culture will be hard for outsiders to appreciate.

Even more difficult will be any attempts to link conclusively particular legal *rules* with ultimate values or beliefs, so that the former can be considered to express the latter. Because of the ambiguity and complexity of these values and beliefs, they will rarely be expressed in any simple way in law. Often they will not be directly expressed at all, merely taken for granted as part of the 'self-understood', the unstated intellectual context in which legal rules are given meaning and purpose. All of these matters of value-invocation or value-expression resist conclusive interpretation. It will be difficult for the comparatist to talk about them without stirring fierce controversy.[81] By contrast, law's link to instrumental social relations may seem relatively straightforward: a matter of technical drafting and precise specification of appropriate legal frameworks for social relations that are relatively limited in scope. Law's relation to values and beliefs poses much harder problems since, while law reflects values and beliefs, it rarely tries to codify them and almost always runs into problems if it tries to do so.

The primary importance of the legal culture literature in recent comparative law is that it reminds us of law's significance in addressing social relations shaped by tradition (in the sense referred to above), ultimate values and beliefs, and elusive affectual or emotional elements. Cultural comparatists' critique of mainstream comparative law's strong focus on legal harmonization or unification may be driven by a wish to emphasize non-instrumental or expressive aspects of law, and by a desire to focus attention on aspects of culture that go beyond economic or other instrumental social relations.

Patterns of instrumental social relations are certainly a part of culture. Anthropologists speak of *material* culture in discussing such matters as the level of technological or economic development of a society. But material culture alone is a thin, limited indicator of culture. Social relations based solely on instrumental benefits (utility) to the participants are typically weak social relations, lasting only as long as the convergent or common projects continue. Nevertheless, the law that expresses and guarantees these relations is often relatively strong (ie it produces the main regulatory results intended), and it may be unusually well-defined and precise in its aims. This is because it addresses relatively well-defined, limited social relations. Because they are typically limited or 'thin', compared to social relations based on affection, shared beliefs, or common ultimate values, instrumental social

---

[80] James Q. Whitman, 'The Two Western Cultures of Privacy: Dignity Versus Liberty', (2004) 113 *Yale LJ* 1151 ff.

[81] See eg Gerald L. Neuman, 'On Fascist Honour and Human Dignity: A Sceptical Response', in Christian Joerges and Navraj Singh Ghaleigh (eds), *Darker Legacies of Law in Europe: The Shadow of National Socialism and Fascism over Europe and its Legal Traditions* (2003), 267 ff, rejecting (as unfounded or too ambiguous to assess) Whitman's controversial claims about the contribution of Nazi policies and 'old norms of social honour' to modern European conceptions of human dignity.

relations lend themselves to relatively precise technical regulation, and perhaps to regulation that can be more or less the same in many different societies where these social relations exist. Much of the basic law relating to traditional relations has some similar characteristics. Hence it may be unsurprising that an emphasis on unification or harmonization of law has often been typical of private law comparatists who focus attention on such fields as contract and tort/delict that can be considered basic to instrumental and traditional social relations, respectively.

The analytical separation of instrumental, traditional, affective, and belief-based social relations is a first step towards *disaggregating culture*, and so towards understanding more precisely law's relations to culture.[82] As this chapter has sought to show, culture and legal culture are full of problems, as concepts used to designate a distinct component of the social. Yet the appeal to ideas of legal culture in recent comparative law remains important and valuable. It emphasizes moral imperatives to recognize and understand the integrity of the 'other', and political imperatives to accept the legitimacy of diversity and conflict in beliefs, ultimate values, traditions, national allegiances, and worldviews. Culture should be understood not merely in terms of indicators that can be proposed (controversially) at a relatively abstract level, but also as far as possible in terms of its intimate meaning for those who participate in it. That is, culture should be seen as the basis of participants' moral and cognitive experience. Because of this, the appeal to culture, despite its problems, has a moral and political force that may vitalize comparative legal studies as an agent of good in a contemporary world wracked by dangerous misunderstandings, suspicions, and intolerances.

BIBLIOGRAPHY

Csaba Varga (ed), *Comparative Legal Cultures* (1992)

Clifford Geertz, 'Local Knowledge: Fact and Law in Comparative Perspective', in *idem, Local Knowledge* (1993) 167 ff

William Ewald, 'Comparative Jurisprudence I: What was it Like to Try a Rat?', (1995) 143 *University of Pennsylvania LR* 1889 ff

William Ewald, 'Comparative Jurisprudence II: The Logic of Legal Transplants', (1995) 43 *AJCL* 489 ff

Antoine Garapon, 'French Legal Culture and the Shock of "Globalization" ' (1995) 4 *Social and Legal Studies* 493 ff

David Nelken, 'Disclosing/Invoking Legal Culture: An Introduction', (1995) 4 *Social and Legal Studies* 435 ff

Pierre Legrand, 'European Legal Systems are not Converging', (1996) 45 *ICLQ* 52 ff

David Nelken (ed), *Comparing Legal Cultures* (1997)

---

[82] For further discussion see, generally, Roger Cotterrell, *Law, Culture and Society: Legal Ideas in the Mirror of Social Theory* (2006).

Vivian Grosswald Curran, 'Cultural Immersion, Difference and Categories in U.S. Comparative Law', (1998) 46 *AJCL* 43 ff

Gunther Teubner, 'Legal Irritants: Good Faith in British Law or How Unifying Law Ends Up in New Divergences', (1998) 61 *Modern LR* 11 ff

Nora V. Demleitner, 'Combating Legal Ethnocentrism: Comparative Law Sets Boundaries', (1999) 31 *Arizona State LJ* 737 ff

Pierre Legrand, *Fragments on Law-as-Culture* (1999)

David Nelken and Johannes Feest (eds), *Adapting Legal Cultures* (2001)

Pierre Legrand, 'The Same and the Different', in Pierre Legrand and Roderick Munday (eds), *Comparative Legal Studies: Traditions and Transitions* (2003), 240 ff

Roger Cotterrell, *Law, Culture and Society: Legal Ideas in the Mirror of Social Theory* (2006)

CHAPTER 22

COMPARATIVE LAW AND RELIGION

HAROLD J. BERMAN

Harvard

The law is holy . . . the law is spiritual. . . .
(St Paul, Romans 7: 12, 14)

I. OVERVIEW OF THE LITERATURE

THE scholarly literature on interrelationships of comparative law and religion is skimpy, to say the least. Classical writings on comparative law hardly mention relationships between law and religion in various cultures. This may have been partly because such writings were focused largely on contrasts between the Anglo-American 'family' of common law systems and the continental European 'family' of civil law systems, and it was apparently assumed that religious beliefs embodied in both types of legal systems were fundamentally the same, namely, Christian. Some exceptions were recognized. Thus differences within a given Western type of legal system concerning marriage and divorce, rights of adopted children, and other aspects of family law and inheritance were attributed to differences in religious affiliations, as were differences in constitutional relations between church and state. The main emphasis of most comparatists, however, throughout the nineteenth and twentieth centuries, was on features of legal method, or legal science, that distinguish different families of Western legal systems from each other, especially in fields of private law such as contracts, torts, and property. Only in the last decades of the twentieth century did comparative law texts begin to include short chapters on Islamic law, Judaic law, Hindu law, Buddhist law, and other types of non-Western religious legal traditions, usually, however, without drawing specific comparisons and contrasts between them and religious aspects of Western legal systems.[1]

Indeed, the fact that the various Western legal systems are themselves derived historically from religious sources and have a religious dimension does not appear in the standard classical works on comparative law. Instead, it is generally considered that each of the major Western legal systems is fundamentally secular in nature, except for those special parts of them that are explicitly religious, such as the Canon law of the Roman Catholic and the Anglican churches. Indeed, until the late twentieth century the Canon law was only occasionally included in standard comparative law studies, although historically it was a fundamental source of development of Western secular legal systems. Moreover, it was hardly noted by comparatists that the distinction between secular law and religious law is itself based historically on Western Christian religious concepts, as is the sharp distinction between the respective roles of the church and of the state.

Like most classical works on comparative law, so most classical works on comparative religion have also ignored or minimized connections between various types of religious belief and various types of law. Just as one who looks in the indexes of leading works on comparative law for the word 'religion' will find few entries, so one who looks in the indexes of leading works on comparative religion for the word 'law' will be equally disappointed.

In the first decade of the twenty-first century the separation of the comparative study of law from the comparative study of religion has begun gradually to change, as legal scholarship and religious scholarship have begun to find mutual

---

[1] Thus a leading text, Konrad Zweigert and Hein Kötz, *An Introduction to Comparative Law* (trans Tony Weir, 3rd edn, 1998), as in earlier editions published in English translation in 1977 and 1987, devotes less than twenty pages to the topic of religious legal systems, namely, the Hindu and the Muslim; ibid at 303–22. See also Rudolf B. Schlesinger, Hans W. Baade, Peter E. Herzog, and Edward M. Wise (eds), *Comparative Law: Cases, Text, Materials* (6th edn, 1996), which, like earlier editions, focuses almost entirely on a comparison of the continental European civil law and Anglo-American common law systems. The same is true of other leading course books and treatises on comparative law.

connections with each other. A scholarly literature has begun to be created on the interaction of law and religion, which has come to include the study of legal and religious theories and practices both in Western and in non-Western cultures. Examples of the latter type of book are Werner F. Menski's *Comparative Law in a Global Context: The Legal Systems of Asia and Africa* (2000; 2nd edn, 2006), which, in addition to comprehensive chapters on religious dimensions of Hindu (Indian), Muslim (including Turkish and Pakistani), African and Chinese law, contains an extensive jurisprudential critique of the failure of comparative legal scholarship to accept 'a truly global legal perspective' that includes the interaction of law and religion; H. Patrick Glenn's *Legal Traditions of the World: Sustainable Diversity in Law* (2000; 2nd edn, 2004), which compares not only the civil and common law traditions of the West but also the Talmudic, Islamic, Hindu, Asian, and indigenous African legal traditions, emphasizing fundamental differences in religious beliefs that account for fundamental differences in legal method and legal values; and Andrew Huxley (ed), *Religion, Law and Tradition: Comparative Studies in Religious Law* (2002), which, again, contains chapters on Canon law, Judaic law, Islamic law, early Chinese law, Hindu law, and Buddhist law, and which also emphasizes the interaction of religious and legal concepts. Also volume II of the *Encyclopedia of Religion* (2nd edn, 2005) contains extensive entries on religious dimensions of law in various cultures.

II. Religious Influences on Diverse Families of Law

One might forgive scholars of comparative law for failure to compare diverse systems of religious law, such as the Talmudic law of Judaism, the Canon law of the Roman Catholic Church, and the Shariah of Islam, since one might count on scholars of comparative religion to undertake that responsibility. Students of comparative law have typically been lawyers—jurists—by profession, not theologians or religious scholars. Less forgivable, however, is the failure of most comparatists of law to explore the influence of Christianity on various Western families of law, or the influence of Islam on the legal systems of Middle Eastern and other countries whose population is largely Muslim, or the influence of Hinduism on the legal systems of India and other countries whose populations are largely Hindu, or the influence of Buddhism on the law of a country such as China where for centuries Buddhism was the predominant belief system.

It may be useful to indicate briefly some insights that can be derived from studies of the influence of various religions on various prevailing families of legal systems. Regarding the impact of Christianity on secular Western legal systems, it has been noted above that the distinction between secular law and religious law is itself derived historically from Western Christian religious beliefs. In the twelfth to the sixteenth centuries the Canon law of the Roman Catholic Church was distinguished as 'spiritual law' from the 'secular' or 'worldly' law of kings, feudal lords, merchants, and cities, and in Europe in those centuries not only matters directly affecting the church as such and the clergy and the sacraments but also matters of family law, education, relief of poverty, and care of the sick were within the ecclesiastical jurisdiction. With the Protestant Reformation of the sixteenth century, when princes and kings became heads of the church in Protestant lands, what had been Canon law became combined with other branches of law under princely or royal authority. Thus more comprehensive national legal systems emerged in which secular authorities regulated in diverse ways matters that had previously been considered to be subject to spiritual law. The degree and character of such secularization in the various families of Western legal systems is an important key to the differences and similarities among them.

Moreover, in the comparison of contemporary Western legal systems with contemporary legal systems of countries in which the predominant religion is Islam or Hinduism or Buddhism or Judaism, it is important to consider to what extent a distinction between 'secular law' and 'religious law' has come to be accepted in each of the various countries. Earlier comparatists such as Zweigert and Kötz, in short chapters on Hindu and Buddhist and Muslim law, emphasized the extent to which the secular law of countries in which those religions predominated had superseded the older religious law. Indeed, most writers on the law of India, for example, treat it as an offspring of British law. More recent scholarship, however, such as that of Werner Menski, has uncovered strong Hindu influences on the contemporary law of India. Likewise Islamic belief has been shown to have strong influence on the contemporary law of countries such as Turkey, whose official law is now secular but whose populations are largely Muslim. Thus in Turkey, despite the adoption in the 1920s of a civil code closely modelled on the Swiss, provisions on marriage and the family retain important features of Islamic customary law. Moreover, in many Turkish villages polygamy is tolerated in practice despite the code's requirement that only monogamous marriages are valid. The study of the impact on official law of Hindu and Muslim concepts, with the internal diversities of each, can, as Menski writes, 'teach us a lot about law itself'. Above all, it can teach comparatists about the impact of social custom on official law when the two diverge.

III. The Impact of Civil
Religions on Law

Definitions of religion are at least as numerous and as varied as definitions of law. Writers on the Abrahamic religions Judaism, Christianity, and Islam tend to define religion in theistic terms, as belief in a God who created the world and governs it. This, however, would exclude other recognized world religions such as Hinduism and Buddhism as well as so-called Deism, the eighteenth-century Enlightenment belief in a God who created humanity and gave it reason but then left it to govern itself—a belief-system that still prevails among many people of Europe and North America.

Both Hinduism and Buddhism, the religious belief-systems that prevail among hundreds of millions of persons living in India and in east and southeast Asian countries, share a belief in 'dharma', a word that is often translated as 'law' but should be understood as sacred law or, more particularly, the spiritual precepts through which persons can achieve enlightenment and ultimate rebirth ('nirvana'). Ancient collections of Hindu laws, called 'dharmasastras', did indeed contain detailed rules relating to sales, to property, to work relations, to family relations, to crime, and to other matters; today, however, what remains of ancient Hindu positive law in India and other countries where most Hindus live consists largely of some aspects of family law and inheritance. Yet the natural-law concept of dharma as spiritual precept continues to be important, and also the ancient caste system associated with it survives, although the prevailing official law of India is in the tradition of the English common law that was introduced by the British conquerors and occupiers.

Buddhism, on the other hand, although it retains the belief in dharma, emphasizes the supreme value of withdrawal into spirituality, other-worldly contemplation, and inner peace.

Thus the official law of most Asian countries, like the official law of countries of Europe and America, is for the most part no longer religious law in the conventional sense of the word 'religious'; that is, it is not 'Hindu law' or 'Buddhist law', although it is the law of peoples that adhere to Hindu or Buddhist belief systems. What, then, gives it its authority over those peoples and what inspires them to adhere to it?

Patrick Glenn states that '[p]robably the greatest traditional source of [the] normativity [of law] in Asia is Confucianism, which is not a religion, while Asian religions ... have concerns which are largely other than legal'.[2] Confucianism, Glenn says, as do most other Western scholars who have written about it, is not a

---

[2] H. Patrick Glenn, *Legal Traditions of the World: Sustainable Diversity in Law* (2nd edn, 2004), 302.

religion but a philosophy. But that characterization seems to assume that a religion must contain a belief in a God or gods or other spirits to whom prayers are offered and from whom rewards and punishments are received. What is it, one may ask, other then a religious impulse, that makes Confucianism an 'ism' and a 'source of normativity'? May we not say, at least, that Confucianism is a 'religious philosophy'—one that propounds a set of beliefs that command the loyalties and passions and sacrifices of its adherents?

Some five centuries before Christ, the great Chinese sage Confucius taught the primacy of interpersonal relations of compassion and harmony and goodness and love—all of which he summed up in the Chinese world 'li'—over regulations, general standards, formal sanctions, legality, which he summed up in the Chinese word 'fa'. Thus Confucianism, like both Hinduism and Buddhism, minimizes the value of law. Law, indeed, must exist and must be observed; no society can long exist without it; it is not, however, for followers of Confucius, a lofty ideal.

The impact on law of traditional religious belief-systems—Hindu, Buddhist, Christian, Muslim, Judaic—must be juxtaposed with the impact of philosophical belief-systems, such as Confucianism, which have the force of religion. In the words of a leading twentieth-century theologian, Paul Tillich, religion may be defined as a person's or a community's 'ultimate concern', that is, those fundamental convictions for which people are willing to make sacrifices and, indeed, if necessary, to give their lives.

At the end of the eighteenth century the name 'civil religion' was given by Jean-Jacques Rousseau to such belief-systems—social and political doctrines which people not only believe to be true but also believe *in*, that is, accept as unquestionable as a matter of faith, devote themselves to, and will make sacrifices for. Rousseau's 'social contract' rested, he wrote, on 'a purely civil profession of faith', whose dogmas, established by the sovereign, excluded orthodox Christianity but included belief in an 'intelligent, beneficent divinity that foresees and provides' as well as belief in 'the happiness of the just, the punishment of the wicked, [and] the sanctity of the social contract and of the laws'.[3] The concept of 'civil religion' has been applied by twentieth-century scholars to the belief-system of a large proportion of the American population who, in Robert Bellah's words, from the earlier years of the republic have had a 'collection of beliefs, symbols, and rituals with respect to sacred things and institutionalized in a collectivity. This religion— there seems no other word for it . . . was neither sectarian nor in any specific sense Christian.' America's civil religion, Professor Bellah adds, 'has its own prophets and its own martyrs, its own sacred events and sacred places, its own solemn rituals and symbols'.[4] It includes faith in individualism, democracy, and the rule of law.

---

[3] Jean-Jacques Rousseau, *On the Social Contract* (1762, trans Donald A. Cress, 1983), 102.

[4] Robert N. Bellah, 'Civil Religion in America', in William G. McLaughlin and Robert N. Bellah (eds), *Religion in America* (1968), 10, 20.

It is noteworthy, in this connection, that after World War II the study of comparative law in the West was transformed by the emergence of what was called by its authors a 'new type of law', namely, Soviet socialist law, based on Marxist-Leninist doctrines of law as an instrument of class domination and of the transformation of law in the progression from socialism to communism. In the 1950s and 1960s, Western comparatists began to count not only the traditional two major families of legal systems, the common law family and the civil law family, but also a third family, socialist law, whose character was determined by a new belief system. In earlier works, Western comparatists had tended to neglect 'ideological' differences among different legal systems. Analysis of legal systems of the Soviet Union and other countries governed by Communist Parties, however, challenged comparatists to examine more closely differences among legal systems based on differences in underlying theories of the relationships of law to fundamental belief systems. Indeed, Soviet law purported to be based on atheism, which raised sharply the question on what religious beliefs, if any, other families of legal systems were based.[5]

With the collapse of the Soviet Union in December 1991, coupled with the end of Communist Party rule in countries of Eastern Europe, analysis of the 'socialist family of legal systems' virtually disappeared from texts on comparative law in the West, as did what little had been included on the impact of fundamental belief-systems on legal institutions.

IV. Religious Dimensions of Law

If religion is defined broadly to signify 'ultimate concern', fundamental convictions concerning the nature and the purpose of life, that for which a community is willing to devote its life, that which it not only believes but believes *in*—then the belief in law may itself constitute a religious belief, and the comparatist of different legal systems may consider to what extent and in what ways each legal system reflects, rests on, and depends for its vitality on, such ultimate concerns and such fundamental convictions.

The secular-rational model of law, which dominated Western comparative legal scholarship in the nineteenth and twentieth centuries, tends to neglect elements of law that transcend secular rationality, elements that law shares with

---

[5] In the mid-1930s Anglican Archbishop William Temple characterized Soviet Marxism-Leninism, with its belief in the fundamental goodness of human nature, corrupted only by economic class conflict, as a Christian heresy.

religion. Like religions, law everywhere communicates its values (a) through *ritual*, that is, formal procedures of legislation, adjudication, and administrative regulation that symbolize its objectivity, (b) through *tradition*, that is, distinctive legal language and practices handed down over generations and centuries that symbolize its continuity with the past and its ongoingness into the future, (c) through *authority*, that is, reliance upon written or spoken sources that effectively symbolize its binding power, and (d) through *universality*, that is, justification of itself in axiomatic terms as the embodiment of universally valid principles and concepts—that contracts should be kept, that wrongful injuries should be compensated, that crimes should be punished, that property rights should be protected, that one accused of an offence is entitled to a hearing, and the like. These characteristics of law tend to give it a sacred quality. They support basic legal emotions that also have a religious component—feelings of responsibility and obligation, feelings of satisfaction and gratitude when justice is done. These religious aspects of law are concealed by the distinction between the spiritual and the secular.

In contrast to Western Christianity, both Roman Catholic and Protestant, other religious traditions make no such distinction. Talmudic and Islamic law give religious authorities competence over what non-Jews and non-Muslims would call 'secular' matters—the food one eats, for example, or the clothing one wears. Likewise, other religious cultures—Hindu, Buddhist, and indigenous African—do not distinguish the legal from the moral or the moral from the religious. 'Torah' in Judaism and 'Shariah' in Islam mean both moral principles and legal principles, both divine law and human law, just as 'dharma' in Hinduism and in Buddhism means both spiritual precept and legal precept.

V. WORLD LAW AND WORLD RELIGION

Comparative law studies have only begun to take seriously the positive impact of religion on official law in Islamic cultures and the negative impact of Confucian religious philosophy on such law in the Hindu and Buddhist cultures. The impact of Roman Catholicism and of Protestantism on the Western legal tradition has also only begun to be studied by scholars in the field of comparative law. It is perhaps presumptuous, then, to ask them to take an even greater leap—to explore the common features of the major legal systems of the world in order to determine their source in common features of the major belief-systems of the world.

That a common law of humankind has begun to emerge in connection with the emergence of an integrated world economy and instantaneous transnational communications is undeniable. A crucial question for comparatists is whether the emerging common features of the major legal systems of the world are founded on common beliefs concerning the nature and functions of law, and beyond that, whether the major cultures of the world share a common faith in law as a process of just and orderly resolution of conflicts.

Among people who adhere to a belief in God as the ultimate source of law, especially among believers in Judaism, Christianity, or Islam, faith in law is part of religious faith. In cultures that adhere, on the other hand, to non-theistic religions, including Buddhism and Hinduism, or to humanist philosophies such as Confucianism, which do not share a belief in divine law, it is nevertheless generally accepted that conflicts that are not resolved through reconciliation, submission, self-denial, or other spiritual means should be resolved by law rather than by force. In such cultures, when Buddhist enlightenment or Confucian harmony or other spiritual values have not succeeded in overcoming conflict or deterring anti-social acts, resort is to be had to formal institutional procedures of settlement. Faith in such procedures when less formal, more personal modes of settlement fail is, in fact, common to the operative belief-systems of virtually all the world's various cultures. Legal systems, to be sure, vary widely among the peoples of the world, but all complex societies have some forms of legislation, administration, and adjudication, and everywhere these are accepted as authoritative. It is a thesis of this essay that the universal belief in law constitutes an important element of the fundamental belief system—in that sense, the religion—of the emerging world society.

The development of a body of world law is sustainable only if the belief-system that underlies it and nourishes it also continues to be sustained and to develop. Such a world belief-system does not include a common belief in a transcendent or ultimate divine being or beings. It shares, however, important features of the world's major religions. These include fundamental moral beliefs—that it is wrong to murder or to steal or to lie or to break one's promises, that one should act responsibly toward others, that children should respect parents and parents should care for children, that it is right to aid persons in distress, that the dignity of all persons should be respected, that every human being should be treated humanely, and that (as summarized in the Golden Rule) 'you should do unto others what you would want them to do unto you'. These and similar moral principles are reflected in all the cultures of the world; they constitute a global ethic, endorsed not only by Judaism, Christianity, Islam, Buddhism, Hinduism, and other religions but also by Confucianism and other humanist philosophies. Such moral principles form a part of the foundation on which all social cohesion is built. In the words of Hugo Grotius, traditionally considered to be the founder of modern theories of international law, the universal law of nations is based on the existence of a fundamental quality of sociability that is inherent in human nature itself and that is a fundamental source of all law.[6]

It is true, of course, that in practice these ethical principles have repeatedly been violated by adherents of the various religious faiths, just as fundamental principles of law have repeatedly been violated by persons subject to the various legal systems. How can one speak, for example, of Christian or Muslim love of neighbour, let alone love of enemy, in view of violent attacks upon each other by Christians and Muslims in the name of their respective faiths? Yet these are distortions of the basic doctrines of all the major religions, and not only of their doctrines but also of their basic spirit. At the heart of all the major religions is the same faith in peace, in sociability, that is at the heart of all the major legal systems. It is this faith that is exploited by extremists who invoke divine support for war and enmity.

A common faith in law adds to the common ethical principles of the world's religions a commitment to formal institutional settlement of conflicts that disputing parties are unwilling or unable to settle amicably by mutual accommodation, including conflicts that arise from criminal acts as well as from civil offences. The foundational ethic of such institutional settlement is the ethic of the hearing: a person charged with violation of a legal obligation has a right to be heard. A hearing, in law, must be a fair hearing; that is, it must be before an impartial tribunal, with the opposing parties given full opportunity to present evidence to support their arguments pro and con. This often means that the parties should be represented by persons capable of eliciting such evidence and presenting such arguments. The decision of the tribunal must be based on general principles applicable to the issues in dispute. Time must be taken for such procedures and time must be taken for deliberations by the tribunal. These and other fundamental principles of law are applicable not only in judicial proceedings but also in legislative and administrative proceedings. Moreover, they are applicable, in different forms, not only in official proceedings before official bodies but also in the unofficial settlement of conflicts within and between associations of all kinds—within and between families, neighbourhoods, workplaces, or professional associations, within and between religious societies, within and between diverse ethnic groups, nations, cultures, and civilizations. It is out of the universal ethic of a fair hearing that substantive legal rights and duties—of contract, of property, of civil liability for injury, of punishment of crime, of business associations, of taxation and other public controls of the economy, of constitutional liberties, and the rest—have emerged in one form or another in virtually all cultures.

It is true that some of the world religions and philosophies, such as Buddhism and Confucianism, as well as certain branches of Christianity, have minimized the

---

[6] Hugo Grotius, *Prolegomena to the Law of War and Peace* (1625, trans Francis W. Kelsey, 1957), section 6. Cf Cornelius F. Murphy, 'The Grotian Vision of World Order', (1982) 76 *American Journal of International Law* 477 ff.

spiritual value of law, with its emphasis on formal procedures, on objective application of general principles of justice and order, and on the enforcement of rights. Yet no large complex society that adheres to a Buddhist or Confucian or other anti-nomian religious or philosophical faith has been able to survive without some forms of legal regulation of conflict. In that respect, the legal traditions of the world transcend orthodox religious traditions. The global ethic of a fair hearing, expressed in the ancient Latin legal maxim *audiatur et altera pars*, 'let also the other side be heard', is a common article of faith among all the cultures of the world—often, to be sure, disregarded or abused in practice, but nevertheless believed in as a sacred instrument of peaceful resolution of conflict.

A universal faith in law shares with religious faith not only a body of moral principles but also the element of faith itself. Faith adds to ethics a sense of commitment. Faith involves feelings of dependence, gratitude, and humility, and of purpose, obligation, and responsibility. It comes not only from the mind but also from the heart. It is our willingness to live out our beliefs, to sacrifice for them if necessary. Also, as the theologian H. Richard Niebuhr emphasized, faith brings human beings together in communities of trust and loyalty. It has a social dimension. 'Faith', Niebuhr wrote, 'is embodied in social institutions as well as in private intuitions, in corporate endeavors as well as in individual activities, in secular pursuits as well as sacred expressions'.[7] World faith in law shares with world religions not only their ethical dimension but also their commitment to a common future of universal peace and universal justice. Faith in law is, indeed, more universal in its acceptance by world society than either Rousseau's civil religion of individualism, democracy, and civil rights, or the twentieth century's civil religions of collectivism and state programmes of social welfare.

If one thinks of law only in positivist terms as a body of rules laid down by political authorities and backed by coercive sanctions, one will not naturally be led to connect law with faith. Starting from such positivist assumptions, most legal scholars in recent generations, including most comparatists, have stated that connections between law and religion that existed in earlier societies have been severed in modern times. Yet law itself, in all societies, encourages the belief in its own sanctity. It puts forward its claim to obedience in ways that appeal not only to the material, impersonal, finite, rational interests of the people who are asked to observe it but also to their faith in a system of justice that transcends social utility—in ways, that is, that do not easily fit the image of instrumentalism presented by the prevailing theory.

William George has called attention to the challenge that much international legislation presents to the world's religious communities:

---

[7] H. Richard Niebuhr, *Radical Monotheism and Western Civilization* (1960), 38–48.

to transcend the boundaries of their own belief systems, to reassess their views of women, of cultures and races, of global banking and finance, of nonhuman species, of outer space and celestial bodies, of the deep seabed, of migratory bird and fish populations, of the ozone shield, of radio frequencies, of the sun's radiation, of polar icecaps, of future generations, of intellectual property—all current or potential topics of international law . . .

'This suggests,' Professor George states, 'that international law has . . . a transcendental or religious dimension or capacity'.[8]

The fact that theological references have largely dropped out of international legal discourse does not mean, he adds, that religious persons cannot recognize the religious dimensions of much of the recent international legislation. He gives the striking example of the 1970 declaration of the United Nations General Assembly, quoted in the 1982 UN Convention on the Law of the Sea, that the open seas are 'the common heritage of mankind', and that the exploration of the open seas and the exploitation of its resources shall be carried out 'for the benefit of mankind as a whole'. 'If the earth, or a part thereof, is the heritage of humankind,' Professor George asks, 'then what—or who—is the primordial benefactor? . . . And if the claim is that the goods of the earth are given to humankind as a whole, from what vantage point do people regard the whole if not from a transcendent viewpoint . . .? Common heritage of humankind, it seems, points to an "Ultimate Reality".'[9]

Similarly, as Michael Perry has shown, the provision in the human rights covenants of the United Nations that those rights are based on 'the inherent dignity' of all persons presupposes a universal source of such rights that transcends political authority.[10]

Comparative law—the scholarly discipline of comparison of legal systems—has the capacity to show that a common faith in law among the various cultures of the emerging world society constitutes an essential element of a world civil religion. Though not universal among transcendental religions, faith in law is common to all civil religions. It offers hope for establishing world channels of cooperation and resolving world conflicts when less formal and more amicable means fail.

It is not too much to ask of scholars of comparative law that they go behind the rules and techniques and concepts of diverse national legal systems to identify and explore the transnational belief systems, the religions or religious philosophies, that underlie them, and in doing so, to identify what they have in common that will support the development of world law.

---

[8] William P. George, 'Looking for a Global Ethic? Try International Law', in Mark W. Janis and Carolyn Evans (eds), *Religion and International Law* (1999), 488.

[9] Ibid. 490–1.

[10] Michael J. Perry, 'The Morality of Human Rights: A Nonreligious Ground?', (2005) 54 *Emory LJ* 97 ff.

BIBLIOGRAPHY

Harold J. Berman, *Law and Revolution: The Formation of the Western Legal Tradition* (1983)

International Encyclopedia of Comparative Law, vol II, chapter 3: 'Sources of Law' (1984)

Konrad Zweigert and Hein Kötz, *Introduction to Comparative Law* (3rd edn, trans Tony Weir, 1998), chapters V and VI ('Law in the Far East' and 'Religious Legal Systems')

Mark W. Janis and Carolyn Evans (eds), *Religion and International Law* (1999)

Werner R. Menski, *Comparative Law in a Global Context: The Legal Systems of Asia and Africa* (2000; 2nd edn, 2006)

Andrew Huxley (ed), *Religion, Law and Tradition: Comparative Studies in Religion and Law* (2002)

Harold J. Berman, *Law and Revolution II: The Impact of the Protestant Reformations on the Western Legal Tradition* (2003)

H. Patrick Glenn, *Legal Traditions of the World: Sustainable Diversity in Law* (2nd edn, 2004)

Encylopedia of Religion, vol 2 'Religion and Law' (2nd edn, 2005)

Mark Juergensmeyer (ed), *Religion in Global Civil Society* (2005)

CHAPTER 23

COMPARATIVE LAW AND LEGAL HISTORY

JAMES GORDLEY

Berkeley

I. Introduction

MATHIAS Reimann has said that there should be no question that legal history can support the study of comparative law, and comparative law that of legal history.[1] Yet there has been. Legal historians have sometimes studied the law of one place and time while disregarding that of others. Comparative lawyers have sometimes compared the law of different jurisdictions while ignoring the historical reasons they are alike or unlike. The consequences have been unfortunate. Historians have often explained rules which are ubiquitous by the circumstances peculiar to one time and place. Comparative lawyers have often explained the similarities and differences among laws with a blind eye to how they arose.

To understand how these problems came about, we should examine the origins of legal history and comparative law. We can then describe, more concretely, why these disciplines need each other.

II. Origins

1. Legal History

In the Middle Ages, university study of law centred on Roman texts. The professors commenting on these texts knew that they had been written by many jurists over centuries. Yet they interpreted them as a unified whole and tried logically to reconcile each text with every other. Reconciliation was not purely a matter of logic. They read the texts, in so far as possible, to meet the needs of their times. But still, the texts had to be logically squared. Medieval historians call this the scholastic method. One historian has noted its similarity to the efforts that lawyers make today to reconcile their cases and code provisions and concluded that law is inherently scholastic.[2]

Legal history was born when the Renaissance humanists found another way to deal with texts. They used the methods of philology to determine what words originally meant to their authors. In 1340, Petrarch, one of the founders of humanism, concluded that the scholastic method was deeply flawed. 'I regret and will

---

[1] Matthias Reimann, 'Rechtsvergleichung und Rechtsgeschichte im Dialog', (1999) 7 *Zeitschrift für Europäisches Privatrecht* 496.
[2] Charles H. Haskins, *The Twelfth Century Renaissance* (1957), 204–5.

regret, as long as there is breath in me, so large a part of my life passed' studying law in Bologna. 'The greater part of our legists . . . care nothing for knowing about the origins of law and about the founders of jurisprudence . . .'. In the fifteenth and sixteenth centuries, Alciatus and Cujas and other able writers applied humanistic methods to Roman law generally.

The humanists regarded Roman law as a model not only for classical times but also for their own. Their objection was that the scholastics had distorted it. Petrarch complained that it 'never occurs to [our legists] that the knowledge of arts and of origins and of literature would be of the greatest practical use for their very profession'.[3] Nevertheless, humanist aspirations led to problems. What was to be done about contradictions and gaps in the texts and problems that the Roman jurists had not expressly confronted, after the scholastics' innovations were condemned? The seventeenth-century scholar Bodin denounced the humanists and praised Bartolus, perhaps the greatest of the scholastic jurists: 'We cannot hope for assistance', he said, 'from those whom no one wants to consult in matters of law, who prefer to consider themselves grammarians rather than jurists . . .'[4] In early modern times, a new school of jurists arose, now called the *Usus modernus pandectarum*, who were concerned less with what the texts meant to classical jurists and more with their practical application. Still, unlike the medieval jurists, and perhaps because of the humanists, they did not regard the texts as unquestionably authoritative and ultimately reconcilable. For example, they disregarded the Roman rules that limited when a contract was formed.[5] The scholastics had accepted them reluctantly. The humanists endorsed them as authentic Roman law.[6]

Moreover, the humanists believed that recovering authentic Roman law would elevate legal thought. The Romans, however, were poor philosophers, albeit excellent lawyers. In part because of the work of the humanists, some jurists now recognized that Roman texts expressed only partial truths which philosophical analysis could elucidate. That task was undertaken by the so-called natural law schools of sixteenth-century Spain and seventeenth- and eighteenth-century northern Europe. Thus, in early modern times, there were three approaches: that of the humanists which sought the original meaning of the texts; that of the *Usus modernus* which applied them to practical legal disputes; and that of the natural law schools which used them as examples of larger philosophical principles.

In the nineteenth century, these schools died out in most of Europe as many countries codified their law and natural law fell into disrepute. By way of exception,

---

[3] Petrarch, *Epistolae de rebus familiaribus et variae* (ed J. Fracassetti, 1859–63, vol III), 14–15, quoted in Myron Piper Gilmore, 'The Renaissance Conception of the Lessons of History', in Myron Piper Gilmore, *Humanists and Jurists: Six Studies in the Renaissance* (1963), 30.

[4] Jean Bodin, 'Praefatio', *Methodus ad facilem historiarum cognitionem* (1610), 11.

[5] Klaus-Peter Nanz, *Die Entstehung des allgemeinen Vertragsbegriffs im 16. bis 18. Jahrhundert* (1985), 85.

[6] Helmut Coing, *Europäisches Privatrecht* (vol I, 1985), 401.

the so-called *Pandektenschule* emerged in Germany. Members of the school wanted to preserve the Roman texts, to be faithful to their historical meaning, and yet tried to fit them into a conceptualist system that no Roman could have imagined. Some historians have said that the historical study of Roman law truly began when the German Civil Code came into force in 1900, and the texts were no longer in force. Finally, historians could simply try to understand what the texts meant to the Romans without the qualms that even the humanists had felt.

Unfortunately, for some historians, this task meant, not only reading the texts in historical context, but reading them to mean no more than their Roman authors consciously understood. One result was a rupture between the study of classical Roman law and the study of the later Continental tradition. Any innovation or new use of the texts could only be a distortion, and not a development, of their true meaning. Dieter Simon has claimed that the very effort of jurists such as Reinhard Zimmermann to study how Roman law shaped modern law means the end of legal history as we know it.[7]

Another unfortunate result was to dismiss much of what the Romans had glimpsed but not expressly said. As my late colleague David Daube has shown, to do so was to misunderstand the texts themselves. When an older author used a word, according to Daube, 'we have to ask whether the uniform use of the word was actually due to an inherent limitation in its meaning. It may be due to external factors such as the great importance for the lawgiver of a particular type of [case] ... not because it can denote nothing except that type...'.[8] When an earlier author reached a conclusion which a later author explained by a principle the earlier one did not distinctly grasp, 'the generalization may or may not involve actual innovation in doctrine'. That is to say, 'the substance of the principle may be new—or it may be classical, only that the classics took it for granted and, therefore, did not bother to set it down'.[9] Indeed, they may not have set it down, not because they did not grasp the principle, but because they thought it should not be invariably applied. For example, in Roman law, not all contracts were binding on consent. That does not mean the Roman jurists did not believe that in principle contracts rest on consent. '[I]s it likely', Daube asked, 'that the men who created the much admired system of Roman law did not see what was known to any witch-doctor before, and to any pedant after, namely, that a contract normally involves mutual understanding between the parties—otherwise it would be meaningless?'[10] Indeed, 'the ordinary function of any contract, whether consensual or

---

[7] Dieter Simon, 'Zwillingsschwestern oder Stammesbrüder oder What is What?', (1992) 11 *Rechtshistorisches Journal* 574, 579.

[8] David Daube, '*Nocere* and *Noxa*', (1939) 8 *Cambridge LJ* 23, 26.

[9] David Daube, 'Generalisations in D. 18.1, *de contrahenda emptione*', in *Studi in onore di Vincenzo Arangio Ruiz* (vol I, 1952), 185.

[10] David Daube, '*Societas* as Consensual Contract', (1938) 6 *Cambridge LJ* 381, 396.

non-consensual, is to produce exactly that "objective" situation which is "subject-ively" desired by the parties'.[11]

If so, the historians Daube criticized both misunderstood their texts by ignoring principles the Roman authors actually did glimpse, and made it impossible to see the later constructions of Roman law as clarifications and developments of these principles rather than misunderstandings of texts. The central error is to think that the law of a particular time and place, or the law of a particular people, is an independent object of study, so that what happened elsewhere or later can be ignored. We will see later that that error survives and is an obstacle to a fruitful partnership between legal history and comparative law.

For now, we will simply note that many legal historians now avoid it. Alan Watson has shown that one cannot understand modern legal history while ignor-ing the weight and influence of Roman texts throughout history.[12] John Dawson and Peter Stein have written excellent general studies of how the Roman legal tradition shaped modern law.[13] Detailed work has been done on medieval and early modern Roman law: for example, in Helmut Coing's multi-volume survey,[14] and by Stephan Kuttner's[15] and Gero Dolezalek's[16] indices of medieval manu-scripts. Their work enables one to ask how the substantive law changed and why. Both Coing[17] and Franz Wieacker[18] have investigated the origins of particular modern doctrines although they were not always clear about the relative influence of the early modern schools: the *Usus modernus* and the late scholastics and north-ern Natural lawyers. The influence of these schools has been studied in more detail by historians such as Reinhard Zimmermann, Paolo Grossi, Robert Feenstra, and others.[19] Harold Berman has stressed that the Roman texts were not read in isol-ation but in conjunction with others, particularly those of Canon law.[20] It is hard to understand key notions of fault that have shaped modern criminal and tort law,

---

[11] Ibid 397.   [12] Alan Watson, *The Making of Civil Law* (1981).

[13] John P. Dawson, *Oracles of the Law* (1968); Peter Stein, *Roman Law in European History* (1999).

[14] Helmut Coing, *Handbuch der Quellen und Literatur der neueren europäischen Privatrechtsges-chichte* (1973).

[15] Stephan Kuttner, *A Catalogue of Canon and Roman Law Manuscripts in the Vatican Library* (1986).

[16] Gero Dolezalek, *Repertorium manuscriptorum veterum Codicis Iustiniani* (1986).

[17] Helmut Coing, *Europäisches Privatrecht* (vol I, 1985; vol II, 1989).

[18] Franz Wieacker, *Privatrechtsgeschichte der Neuzeit unter besonderer Berücksichtigung der deut-schen Entwicklung* (2nd edn, 1967; English trans under the title *A History of Private Law in Europe* by Tony Weir, 1995).

[19] Paolo Grossi organized a conference on the Spanish scholastics in Florence, October 1972. One of the most notable papers was by Robert Feenstra, 'L'influence de la scolastique espagnole sur Grotius en droit privé', in Paolo Grossi (ed), *La seconda scolastica nella formazione del diritto privato moderno* (1973), 377. See also Stein (n 12), 94–6; James Gordley, *The Philosophical Origins of Modern Contract Law* (1991), 69–111.

[20] Harold J. Berman, *Law and Revolution: The Formation of the Western Legal Tradition* (1983); see Stein (n 12), 49–52.

without reading, not only the Roman sources, but Stephan Kuttner's classic on *Schuldlehre* in medieval Canon law.[21] These historians see development where others saw distortion.

So far we have spoken of Continental law. English legal history does not go back to the Renaissance. Only in the nineteenth and twentieth century, a gifted group of scholars, led by Frederic William Maitland, applied the historical methods pioneered on the continent to study English law.[22] Unlike the humanists, Maitland had no desire to rediscover a pristine English common law supposedly corrupted by later interpreters. He described how the writs of the common law came into being and changed over time. Different and brilliant as Maitland's work was, it was flawed by an error like the one just discussed. He assumed that English law possessed a unity over time much as some Roman historians assumed that classical Roman law possessed a unity at a particular period of time. In a famous speech, 'Why the History of English Law is Not Written', he claimed that although the English judges did not have distinctly in mind 'the great elementary conceptions, ownership, possession, contract, tort, and the like', these concepts had somehow emerged from English law although he admitted he could not explain how.[23] We now realize he was wrong. As Charles Donahue has said, 'We know a considerable amount more today than we did when Maitland wrote. . . . Relatively little of the history of the forms of action has to do with "the great elementary conceptions" like ownership, possession, tort and contract.'[24]

The answer, as legal historians increasingly recognize, is that English law is not an independent object of study any more than classical Roman law. A. W. B. Simpson and others have shown that in the nineteenth and early twentieth centuries, the English borrowed these 'great elementary conceptions' from Continental law.[25] Until then, the English organized their thinking in terms of the rules governing particular writs such as trespass and assumpsit. In the nineteenth century, for the first time, they developed a systematic doctrinal structure, borrowing much from the Continent. If that is true, the history of English law cannot be read, nor modern English law understood, apart from the history of Continental law.

To conclude, a persistent problem in legal history has been to try to understand

---

[21] Stephan Kuttner, *Kanonistische Schuldlehre von Gratian bis auf die Dekretalen Gregors IX: systematisch auf Grund der handschriftlichen Quellen dargestellt* (1935).

[22] Frederick Pollock and Frederic William Maitland, *The History of English Law before the Time of Edward I* (2nd edn, 1898) (written largely by Maitland).

[23] Frederic William Maitland, 'Why the History of English Law is Not Written', in Herbert A.L. Fisher (ed), *The Collected Papers of Frederick William Maitland* (vol I, 1911; reproduction Buffalo, 1981), 480, 484.

[24] Charles Donahue, *Why the History of Canon Law is Not Written* (1986), 6.

[25] Alfred William Brian Simpson, 'Innovation in Nineteenth Century Contract Law', (1975) 91 *LQR* 247; Gordley (n 18), 134–60; James Gordley, 'The Common Law in the 20th Century: Some Unfinished Business', (2000) 88 *California LR* 1817.

the law of a time or place or nation as an independent object of study. We will now see that, while the historical reasons are different, a similar problem has plagued comparative law.

2. Comparative Law

The study of comparative law has a shorter history. It began in the nineteenth century and, according to some, matured only in the twentieth. As René David noted, comparative law emerged as an independent discipline only because of the nationalization of law on the European continent.[26] The Bavarians codified their law in 1756; the Prussians in 1794; the French in 1804, and the Austrians in 1811. Belgium and the Netherlands adopted codes much like that of the French. The Italians adopted a similar code in 1865, the Portugese in 1888, and the Spanish in 1889. In Germany, as we have noted, codification was delayed. Savigny argued that the law of each nation reflected a national spirit, a *Volksgeist*, and therefore could not be made by legislative fiat. The *Geist* of German law was to be found, of all places, in the Roman texts. Still, German law was codified in 1900. Swiss law was codified in 1907–12.

At the same time, the idea of what a code meant changed. A code came to be regarded as the exclusive source of law within the jurisdiction that enacted it. Cases were to be decided by an exegesis of its texts or by grasping a system immanent in them. The result was positivism in practice: the study of one's national code became—and still remains—the prime object of legal education and academic commentary. Part of the reason may have been the rise of positivism in theory: the idea, opposed by Savigny, that law was the will of the legislator. Be that as it may, this conception of a code was a nineteenth-century innovation. Portalis, the architect of the French Civil Code, had warned that the texts of the French Civil Code could not decide all cases, and perhaps, not any that came before the courts. 'No one pleads against a clear statutory text.'[27] 'Few cases are susceptible of being decided by a clear text. It has always been by general principles, by doctrine, by legal science, that most disputes have been decided. The Civil Code does not dispense with this learning but, on the contrary, presupposes it.'[28] Portalis was not speaking of some future doctrine or legal science to be founded on the texts of the Code. He was speaking of the legal scholarship already in place, scholarship as it

---

[26] René David and John E. C. Brierley, *Major Legal Systems in the World Today: An Introduction to the Comparative Study of Law* (2nd edn, 1978), 2–3.

[27] Corps législatif, 'Discours prononcé par Portalis, séance du 23 frimaire, an X' (14 December 1801), in Pierre Antoine Fenet (ed), *Recueil complet des travaux préparatories du Code civil* (vol VI, 1827), 269.

[28] 'Discours préliminaire prononcé lors de la présentation du projet de la Commission du gouvernement', in Fenet, *Recueil complet des travaux* (n 27, vol I), 471.

had developed in Europe over the centuries.[29] He certainly did not think there was some French spirit animating the Code that would guide future jurists.

Actually, all European codes were amalgams of rules, some Roman, some elaborated over centuries, and some adopted by drafting committees because they were then popular. Yet jurists came to regard the codes as unified statements of law that could be understood without looking elsewhere. Teaching and academic writing in Europe focused on the texts of the national code. Students still study, and academics write, about German law, French law, Italian law, and so forth as though each were an independent object of study.

By and large, comparative lawyers assumed this approach was legitimate. That assumption shaped their understanding of their own discipline and severed it from the study of legal history. If each nation had its own law, the job of comparative lawyers was to compare the law of one nation with another. The question was how to do so.

That question permitted only a limited range of answers. Mittermaier and Zachariä founded one of the first journals of comparative law in 1829: the *Kritische Zeitschrift für Rechtswissenschaft und Gesetzgebung des Auslands*. Zachariä introduced the first volume by explaining[30] that while the old unity of European law, supplied by Roman texts, was gone, a new unity was possible based on the ideals of codification accepted in France and on the political ideal of a liberal state. The purpose of the journal was to help to frame new national legislation. In other words, the point of comparative law was to help draft national legislation, and once it was drafted, there was no need for comparative law.

Franz Bernhöft and Georg Cohn founded the *Zeitschrift für vergleichende Rechtswissenschaft* in 1878. Bernhöft explained that comparative law would 'teach how peoples of common origin worked independently with the legal concepts they took over, how a people borrowed the institutes of another and reworked them according to its own national outlook (*Anschauung*), and finally how each factual tie between legal systems of different nations was constructed according to common laws of development'.[31] The result, Zweigert and Kötz point out, was a journal 'primarily devoted to comparative legal history'.[32] But it was legal history of a strange sort. It assumed each jurisdiction's law was constructed according to 'its own national outlook', whatever that meant. It was like the approach of those legal historians who looked for the unity of the law of a given nation or of a given time and place.

---

[29] See James Gordley, 'Myths of the French Civil Code', (1994) 42 *AJCL* 459, 484–92.

[30] 'Über den Zweck dieser Zeitschrift', (1829) 1 *Kritische Zeitschrift für Rechtswissenschaft und Gesetzgebung des Auslands* 1.

[31] 'Über Zweck und Mittel der vergleichenden Rechtswissenschaft', (1878) 1 *Zeitschrift für vergleichende Rechtswissenschaft* 1, 37–8.

[32] Konrad Zweigert and Hein Kötz, *An Introduction to Comparative Law* (trans Tony Weir, 3rd edn, 1998) 58.

Nevertheless, by the mid-twentieth century, the idea that each nation's law formed a 'system' was widely accepted among comparative lawyers, although they were unclear as to what a 'system' meant: did it mean rules that were logically coherent, or rules that reflected a 'national outlook' or common ideals, or rules that reflected common methods and values? Many have dated the emergence of comparative law to the work of these twentieth-century scholars who defined their task as the comparison of legal 'systems'.[33] The archetypical work was by René David: *Les grands systèmes de droit contemporains*.[34] According to David, '[e]ach law constitutes in fact a system: it employs a certain vocabulary, corresponding to certain legal concepts; it uses certain methods to interpret them; it is tied to a certain conception of social order which determines the means of application and the function of law'.[35] These systems can then be grouped into families according to two criteria: if 'someone educated in the study and practice of one law will . . . be capable, without much difficulty, of handling another', and 'if they are founded on opposed philosophical, political or economic principles, and if they seek to achieve two entirely different types of society'.[36] On that basis, David divided law into three families: romano-germanic, common law, and socialist.[37] Others have distinguished legal families differently. The classification that Zweigert and Kötz find 'most penetrating'[38] is that of Arminjon, Nolde, and Wolff who identified seven legal families: French, German, Scandinavian, English, Russian, Islamic, and Hindu.[39]

The problem is that it is hard to think that French law or German law, let alone Russian, Islamic, or Hindu law, constitutes a 'system'. The French and German codes incorporate a conglomerate of ideas, developed over centuries, some incorporated because they had been traditionally accepted, some at the whim of the drafters. But that hardly makes them a system in the sense of an ideological or philosophical system, in which each part is intelligible only in terms of every other part. Is there anyone conversant with the history of the French and German codes who would make such a claim? Or such a claim about the Soviet Russian Code, which was an imitation of those of France and Germany, and then declared to be socialist? Or about Islamic or Hindu law?

As in the case of legal history, recent writing is liberating the discipline. Scholars such as Rodolfo Sacco have shown that much of the law is not national. He speaks of legal 'formants'—institutions, concepts, or rules—that pass from one nation to another while retaining their content. They do not make sense, nor do they originate, in the context of a national system.[40] He is surely right as an historical matter.

[33] David and Brierley (n 26), 3.   [34] (7th edn, 1978).   [35] Ibid 20.
[36] David and Brierley (n 26), 21.   [37] David (n 34), 22.
[38] Zweigert and Kötz (n 32), 64.
[39] Pierre Arminjon, Boris E. Nolde, and Martin Wolff, *Traité de droit comparé* (vol I, 1950), 47.
[40] The most accessible source is Rodolfo Sacco, 'Legal Formants: A Dynamic Approach to Comparative Law', (1991) 39 *AJCL* 1.

Consequently, one cannot accept the premise from which comparative law began: that one is comparing a domestic law contained in domestic sources with foreign law. If Sacco is right, domestic law includes in large part ideas or 'formants' taken from abroad. One has to study them, and what they meant abroad, even to understand domestic law.

A. W. B. Simpson and others have shown us how much of the common law is neither national, nor an organic growth from English judicial decisions. Before the nineteenth century, the English organized their thinking by writs such as assumpsit and trespass. These writs and their rules were not the result of systematic thought based on any system of concepts. In the nineteenth century, Anglo-American treatise writers tried to systematize the common law, organizing it around concepts such as contract and tort rather than traditional writs, and in the process, borrowing heavily from the continent.[41] It is not clear how this amalgam of traditional rules and Continental borrowings can be described as a system.

Alan Watson has shown us how the influence of Roman texts and Roman rules has persisted and shaped modern law. If he is right, modern law does not consist of national systems each intelligible in its own terms. The differences depend on what was borrowed.[42] In Reinhard Zimmermann's nuanced account, Roman law is like a trunk and modern legal systems like branches. One cannot understand why the French or even the English have a rule without looking at problems that perplexed a civilian author long ago.[43]

The law of a given country, then, is not a unified system but an amalgam of solutions to problems faced in the past. If so, then an historical critique of the concept of 'legal systems' and 'legal families' joins hands with another kind of modern critique: one that takes a functionalist approach. The law of any country is a series of solutions to problems it confronts and that may have arisen in other places as well. If so, one cannot understand the law without understanding the problem, and to do so, one might do well to see how different countries deal with it.

The value of this approach is illustrated in the findings of the Trento project on the Common Core of European Law. Experts from different jurisdictions in the European Union are asked how their law would resolve cases that could arise anywhere. The solutions are often the same, despite a diversity of doctrines. When they are not, some of the discrepancies are matters over which reasonable people might differ. Others are due to historical circumstance: for example, a drafting committee enacted some solution popular in its time but since rejected by other jurisdictions. A similar comparative but functional approach has influenced the UNIDROIT Principles, a restatement of international commercial law, and the

---

[41] Simpson, (1975) 91 *LQR* 247; Gordley (n 19), 134–60.   [42] Watson (n 12).
[43] Reinhard Zimmermann, *The Law of Obligations: Roman Foundations of the Civilian Tradition* (1990; paperback edn, 1996).

Principles of European Contract Law, which hope to pave the way for a common European law of contract.

Indeed, leading comparative law scholars have moved in a similar direction. The classic work on comparative law by Zweigert and Kötz pays tribute to the older idea that there are 'systems' and 'families'. But it describes the functional approach, in this sense, as the hallmark of the comparative method.[44] Indeed, much of their book treats legal problems individually and functionally, and describes how different nations have handled them. A further and important step was taken in Kötz's later book, *European Contract Law*.[45] Here, the law is described problem by problem with an eye to the value of opposing solutions. One must sometimes look at the footnotes to see which legal 'system' endorses one solution or the other.

III. THE COMMON MISTAKE

If what has been said so far is correct, then past failures to integrate the study of legal history with that of comparative law are not due to a difference in subject-matter but to a common mistake. The mistake for legal historians is to assume that the law of a given time and place develops in its own way which can be studied without regard to how the law developed elsewhere. The corresponding mistake for comparative lawyers is to assume that the law of each modern jurisdiction forms a coherent system rather than an amalgam of solutions developed over time.

These mistakes are not historical relics. In the next section we will examine some of the forms they now take. We will then suggest more concretely how legal history and comparative law can be brought to bear on some common problems.

1. The Existence of a 'Legal System'

I think that few today would defend the idea that French or German law forms a coherent system rather than an amalgam of historically inherited rules, influenced by decisions about appropriate solutions made over the centuries. French courts recognize a law of nuisance, or, as they would say, of *troubles de voisinage*, even though no text of their Code covers the matter. They do not recognize relief in contract for changed circumstances or, as they say, for *imprévision*, supposedly because no text of the Code provides for relief.[46] Both omissions are the result of

---

[44] Ibid 33–4.   [45] Hein Kötz, *European Contract Law* (vol I, 1997).
[46] See James Gordley, 'Impossibility and Changed Circumstances', (2004) 52 *AJCL* 602.

historical accidents. Napoleon gave the drafters little time to work, and so they did not address some problems, such as *troubles de voisinage*, even though they were mentioned in sources on which they chiefly drew: Jean Domat and Robert Joseph Pothier. They did not address others, such as relief for *imprévision*, probably because Pothier and Domat did not happen to mention them, even though their failure to do so was presumably an accident, since most jurists of their day accepted relief for changed circumstances. Thus the Code is not a system. Its texts depend on the historical accident of which problems the drafters addressed, and their application depends on choices made, not by the drafters, but by French courts.

The same can be said of the German Civil Code although thirty years went into its drafting. Still, much of it consists of last minute improvisations by the drafters or the legislature rather than a systematic working out of principles. In any case, few today would claim the principles of the drafters govern the very creative use courts have made of rules they understood quite differently, such as the 'good faith' principle of § 242 of the German Civil Code.

2. The Search for Principles Unifying Legal Systems

(a) Unity of Philosophical Principle

While both legal historians and comparative lawyers have looked for unity in the law of a given time and place, or in that of a nation, modern philosophers have aggravated the problem by suggesting that there can be no unity beyond that of the spirit of a *Zeit* or *Volk*. Fichte, Hegel, and their successors wanted to reject both the position that a person's sense of justice and morality was arbitrary, and the position that it was grounded in universal truths about how people should behave. They concluded that a person's judgments had meaning only in the context of some larger system of ideas. Fichte was the first to call it a *Weltanschauung*, a world view. Within a world view, each conviction made sense but only in relation to the larger whole, without which it would lack meaning.

This approach once had more influence among historians than among comparative lawyers. It inspired *Geistesgeschichte* in which the events and cultural accomplishments of the renaissance or the baroque era were understood in terms of the world view of the Renaissance Man or the Baroque Man. By and large, philosophers and historians have rejected any pure form of this approach. It imagines an implausible degree of coherence among the values of those who shared an historical period, and an implausible lack of coherence between their values and those of other eras. It also cannot explain how different features of the same world view are supposed to be interconnected, since they do not flow logically from given axioms as in mathematics nor are they related teleologically or purposefully like the organs of the body or the parts of the machine. But again, the approach lingers.

Strangely enough, it lingers among comparative lawyers. Michele Graziadei has described it as 'holism' by which he means 'any theory by which an account, or an interpretation of a part is impossible, or at least inadequate, without reference to the whole to which that part belongs'.[47] The 'holists' he is describing do not relate the parts of a legal system to a whole either logically or teleologically. They claim there is some other relationship which they often call 'cultural'.

Consequently, as Graziadei observes, the 'radical version of holism holds that it is impossible to know what it is like to think like an American or an Italian lawyer unless that condition is experienced in the first person, that is to say, unless one actually becomes an American or an Italian lawyer'.[48] That, he notes, is the position of Pierre Legrand who typically uses the example of French law.[49] The provisions of the French Civil Code, however, have been enacted in many countries and many languages. Did they then change their meaning *ipso facto*? Moreover, even if French courts interpreted them differently, what evidence is there, or could there be, that the reason they did so is characteristically French? Traditionally, under French law, lunatics and children were not held liable for harm they could not have prevented. Now they are, due to recent legislation and case law.[50] Should the old rule or the new rule or the change in rules be understood as characteristically French? If so, why?

A more moderate thesis is defended, for example, by William Ewald. He believes we should seek 'not the law in books nor the law in action but the law in minds' and so understand the law as a 'style of conscious thought'.[51] His position is like that of the German historian Franz Wieacker:

Virtually every great age of technical legal studies has had its background in generally recognized social and ethical doctrine: that of classical Rome in the philosophy of the Academy, the Peripatics, and above all the Stoa; that of the Glossators, Canonists and Post-Glossators in the moral philosophy and social teachings of the medieval church; the *Pandektenwissenschaft* of the nineteenth century in Kant's ethic of freedom and duty.[52]

Similarly, Ewald believes that one must understand the German Civil Code in terms of the influence of 'Kant, Herder and the German Idealists'.[53] These claims

---

[47] Michele Graziadei, 'Comparative Law, Legal History, and the Holistic Approach to Legal Cultures', (1999) 7 *Zeitschrift für Europäisches Privatrecht* 531, 538.

[48] Ibid.

[49] See Pierre Legrand, 'European Systems are not Converging', (1996) 46 *ICLQ* 52, 78; Pierre Legrand, 'The Same and the Different', in Pierre Legrand and Roderick Munday (eds), *Comparative Legal Studies: Traditions and Transitions* (2003), 240.

[50] Law of 3 January 1968, now Art 489 al 2 *Code civil* (lunatics); Cour de cassation, Ass plén, 9. 5. 1984 (4th case), D 1984, Jur, 29 (minors).

[51] William Ewald, 'Legal History and Comparative Law', (1999) 7 *Zeitschrift für Europäisches Privatrecht* 553, 556.

[52] Wieacker (n 18), 249.

[53] Ewald, (1999) 7 *Zeitschrift für Europäisches Privatrecht* 556. He develops this position at length in William Ewald, 'What Was It Like to Try a Rat?' (1995) 143 *Pennsylvania LR* 1189, although I think the

should be regarded with care. One cannot assume that thinkers of the same age must have reflected each others' views because they shared the same age. One needs evidence as to whether one thinker influenced another and how. Wieacker should explain how medieval moral philosophy influenced Commentators such as Bartolus or Baldus. They approved of Thomistic moral philosophy, but, as I have tried to show, they used it only occasionally.[54] Unlike the late scholastics of the sixteenth century, they did not try to synthesize Roman law and Thomistic philosophy. Similarly, Ewald should describe whom the nineteenth-century German philosophers influenced and in what way. We can then determine how German philosophers influenced the jurists and how they did not. For example, Savigny claimed that law comes from the *Volksgeist*,[55] an idea he owed to Hegel. He said that law gave each person a realm of freedom in which he could flourish,[56] an idea which, as Wieacker notes, he probably took from Kant.[57] But Savigny broke with Hegel and Kant by denying that law governing the Germans followed from the philosophical concept of the *Volksgeist* or from that of freedom. Jurists had to find it in the Roman texts which, curiously enough, Savigny claimed, expressed the German *Volksgeist*.[58] Savigny thus neutralized the philosophers and left the jurists free to do the job they loved, which was interpreting these texts, without philosophical advice. Their interpretation had little to do with Herder, Kant, or Hegel. When a philosophical concept like 'freedom' bore on a legal problem such as consent, Savigny claimed that the philosophical concept was irrelevant to the work of a jurist.[59] Mutual influence should be demonstrated, not postulated.

(b) Unity of Economic Purpose

In the case we have just considered, historians have imagined that because certain philosophical ideas were influential at a certain time, they shaped the law of that time. A similar mistake is to assume that because a given rule leads to a certain result, and that result furthers someone's economic interest, the rule was made to promote that interest. Sometimes, of course, it may have been. But to show that requires evidence of the intent of those who promoted the rule. At one time, it was common for anthropologists and political scientists to explain social institutions— even witchcraft—by identifying some psychological or societal need that they might unwittingly satisfy. Since one could always dream up some such need, 'functionalism' of this kind is now viewed by many social scientists as tautological.

---

example of trials of animals is not well chosen. The few references to such trials may have been elaborate jokes. In any case, to deem an animal guilty of a crime was contrary to the moral and theological conceptions of the time.

54 Gordley (n 19), 30–68.
55 Friedrich Carl von Savigny, *System des heutigen Römischen Rechts* (vol I, 1840), § 8.
56 Ibid, § 52.   57 Wieacker (n 18), 353, 387, 431.
58 See Gordley (n 19), 226–7.   59 Savigny (n 55, vol III), § 114.

In law, the fallacy is exemplified by the work of the law and economics movement. Many of its practitioners are Americans who have not studied the law of other countries. Yet because they claim that economic considerations explain law in modern societies, they are making comparative claims, and so doing comparative law, albeit in an odd way. They try to show that a legal rule could promote 'efficiency' and conclude that they have thereby identified the purpose of the rule. For example, there is a rule in admiralty law that a ship that rescues another cannot claim more than a fair amount for doing so. The purpose of the rule, it is claimed, is to optimize investments in rescue equipment.[60] The law of nuisance typically prevents a cement plant from polluting neighbouring land without paying compensation. The purpose is supposedly to optimize the production of farm products and cement.[61] In many legal systems, courts strike down an unfair term of a contract. The purpose, supposedly, is not to prevent unfairness but to minimize the cost of drafting contracts. One member of the movement even claims that the reason the law of unjust enrichment will not let me keep one million dollars accidentally deposited in my bank account is to avoid the inefficiency of extra paper work at the bank to prevent such a mistake.[62] The rules to which they refer are ancient and framed by jurists who could not possibly have had these purposes in mind. Indeed, the proponents of some economic explanations congratulate themselves on their ingenuity in discovering purposes for rules that never occurred to anyone else before, even to their colleagues who study law and economics. If so, one wonders why they think their explanations shaped these rules.

One would expect better of legal historians who, after all, should be acquainted with the minds of the people they are studying. Yet many of them write as though once they have shown that a rule benefits a certain group, they can conclude that the purpose of the rule was to benefit that group. An example is Morton Horwitz's claim that nineteenth-century American law was 'transformed' in order to favour industrialism and a rising class of entrepreneurs. That is why courts rejected traditional ideas about the fairness of prices,[63] enforced contracts for the future delivery of goods,[64] developed a law of nuisance,[65] and so forth. No doubt, some measures were enacted in the nineteenth century to support industrialism. The enactment of tariffs to support New England mills was the subject of bitter debate between Northerners and Southerners. Those who debated tariffs spoke frankly about the legitimacy of laws that helped industry, and yet the jurists and judges whose work

---

[60] William M. Landes and Richard A. Posner, 'Salvors, Finders, Good Samaritans and Other Rescuers: An Economic Study of Law and Altruism', (1978) 7 *Journal of Legal Studies* 83; Francis H. Buckley 'Three Theories of Substantive Fairness', (1990) 19 *Hofstra LR* 33, 40–8.

[61] See Ronald Coase, 'The Problem of Social Cost', (1960) 3 *Journal of Law and Economics* 1, and the endless discussion that article triggered.

[62] Saul Levmore, 'Explaining Restitution', (1985) 71 *Virginia LR* 65, 69.

[63] Morton J. Horwitz, *The Transformation of American Law 1780–1860* (1977), 164–9.

[64] Ibid 920   [65] Ibid 31.

Horwitz describes were unaccountably shy. Rarely if ever do they mention industrialism, and Horwitz finds their silence sinister. For him, if rules helped industrialists, they must have been adopted to do so, and if no one said so, it shows that the real purpose was concealed.

Much the same can be said of James Willard Hurst's classic essays on nineteenth-century American law.[66] The purpose of the law, he said, was to 'unleash energy'. His evidence is that Americans of the period liked energy, and they unleashed a lot of it. Supposedly, that explains a multitude of rules which, so far as one can tell from the evidence, were not adopted with any such purpose in mind.

The mistake here is like the one we have seen with positivism and 'holism'. It is the assumption that the law of a time or place, or of a particular nation, is an independent subject of study, with its own unity, which is to be explained without looking elsewhere.

If we avoid that mistake, however, legal history and comparative law can be of use to each other.

IV. The Need for Mutual Support

1. Legal History in the Service of Comparative Law

A comparative lawyer may find differences in the rules of the legal systems he studies which puzzle him. He may assume they are due to a difference in 'system'. He may find similarities and assume that because certain rules are ubiquitous, they result from common needs. In each case, he can be helped by knowing the history of the rules. The mistakes he might otherwise make can be best shown by example.

An illustration of the first difficulty is the way in which comparative lawyers usually characterize the difference between ownership and possession in common and civil law systems. According to Beekhuis in the *International Encyclopedia of Comparative Law*, a basic structural difference is that unlike common law, '[C]ontinental law makes a sharp distinction'[67] between these concepts. English authors typically say that there is no real distinction at all, except that the owner has rights against all the world, and the possessor has rights against everyone except the

---

[66] James Willard Hurst, *Law and the Conditions of Freedom in the Nineteenth-Century United States* (1956).

[67] Jacob Houdyn Beekhuis, 'Civil Law', in *International Encyclopedia of Comparative Law*, vol VI, chapter 2 (1973), 3, 18.

owner.[68] In contrast, Continental authors typically explain that the difference between the owner and the possessor is that the latter has no rights, and then discuss why he is protected anyway.[69] Yet, if one traces the history of the English approach, one discovers that it was not rooted in traditional English case law.[70] It was advanced by Sir Frederick Pollock in the late nineteenth century as the most plausible response to the debate among Continental jurists as to why, if the possessor had no rights, he ought to be protected.[71] Pollock concluded that he must therefore have rights, although rights inferior to those of the owner. He claimed this theory explained both common law and Roman law:

[T]he relations of possession and ownership in Roman and English law, the difficulties arising out of them, and the devices resorted to for obviating or circumventing those difficulties, offer an amount of resemblance even in detail which is much more striking than the superficial and technical differences. We cannot doubt that these resemblances depend on the nature of the problems to be solved and not on any accidental connection. One system of law may have imitated another in particular doctrines and institutions, but imitation cannot find place in processes extending over two or three centuries, and whose fundamental analogies are externally disguised in almost every possible way.[72]

Thus we are not dealing with structural features that distinguish common and civil law. We are dealing with a response, which English authors endorsed, to a Continental debate, a response intended to explain both Roman and English law. We are less likely to misinterpret differences among legal systems if we see how they arose.

Comparative lawyers may make a different mistake when different systems adopt a similar rule. Unless the rule is puzzling on its face, scholars are likely to assume it was adopted on its merits. Common law courts,[73] the French Civil Code,[74] and codes elsewhere[75] have adopted the rule that a party in breach of contract is liable only for damages he could foresee when the contract was made. The rule was incorporated in

---

[68] Michael Harwood, *Modern English Land Law* (2nd edn, 1982), 503; Edward Hector Burn, *Cheshire and Burn's Modern Law of Real Property* (16th edn, 2000), 26–7; Robert Megarry and HenryWilliam Rawson Wade, *The Law of Real Property* (5th edn, 1984), 104, 106.

[69] See eg Gabriel Marty and Pierre Raynaud, *Droit civil: Les Biens* (2nd edn, 1980), § 14, 14–15; Alex Weill, François Terré, and Philippe Simler, *Droit civil: Les Biens* (3rd edn, 1985), § 54, 63–4; § 55, 64–5; Henri Mazeaud, Léon Mazeaud, Jean Mazeaud, and François Chabas, *Leçons de droit civil*, vol II: *Biens Droit de propriété et ses démembrements* (8th edn, 1994), §§ 1413–14, 190–1. Elmar Bund, in *J. von Staudingers Kommentar zum Bürgerlichen Gesetzbuch* (rev edn 2000), vor § 854 n 36; Detlev Joost in *Münchener Kommentar zum Bürgerlichen Gesetzbuch* (vol VI, 4th edn, 2004), vor § 854 n 10; Karl Heinz Schwab and Hanns Prütting, *Sachenrecht* (31st edn, 2003), para 49.

[70] James Gordley and Ugo Mattei, 'Protecting Possession', (1996) 44 *AJCL* 293, 319–29.

[71] Frederick Pollock and Robert S. Wright, *An Essay on Possession in the Common Law* (1888) (Pollock wrote Parts I and II in which this theory is presented; Wright wrote Part III).

[72] Frederick Pollock, *A First Book of Jurisprudence for Students of the Common Law* (1896), 179.

[73] *Hadley v Baxendale* (1854) 9 Ex 341.   [74] Art 1150 *Code civil*.

[75] See Art 1225 *Codice civile*; Art 1107 (Spanish) *Código civil*.

early drafts of the German Civil Code,[76] although the final draft merely provided that the failure to acquaint the other party with the otherwise unforeseeable consequences of his breach could be contributory negligence.[77] Because of its ubiquity, the rule that damages must be foreseeable has been endorsed by projects that rely heavily on comparative law to recommend rules: for example, the Convention on the International Sale of Goods,[78] the UNIDROIT Principles of International Commercial Contracts,[79] and the Principles of European Contract Law.[80] But if one looks backward in time, the rule is no longer ubiquitous and its spread seems largely a matter of chance. It was proposed by the sixteenth-century French jurist Dumoulin, not as a rule, but as an explanation of a Roman limitation on disproportionately high damages: in certain contracts, a party could recover no more than twice the contract price. According to Dumoulin, the reason was that such damages were unforeseeable. In the eighteenth century, Pothier presented this explanation as a rule in its own right. French drafters and English judges, in the famous case of *Hadley v Baxendale*,[81] took the rule from Pothier.[82] The rule might be unknown today if Dumoulin had made a different conjecture or Pothier had been less influential. Might it be, then, that the rule has less merit than its ubiquity suggests? That is a definite possibility. Indeed, one can find cases in which modern common law and civil law courts deny recovery by claiming damages were unforeseeable when, in fact, what seems to have bothered them was that the damages, however foreseeable, were disproportionate to the contract price.[83] The history of the rule alerts one to the possibility that the Romans may have been right all along.

---

[76] *Protokolle der Kommission für die zweite Lesung des Entwurfs des Bürgerlichen Gesetzbuchs* (vol II, 1897), 292 (relating to § 218 of the First Draft).

[77] § 254 II BGB.   [78] Art 74 CISG.   [79] Art 7.4.4 PICC.   [80] Art 9:503 PECL.

[81] (1854) 9 Ex 341.   [82] Zimmermann (n 43), 829–30.

[83] *Hadley v Baxendale* may itself have been such a case. According to the headnote, the shipper, hired to transport a broken mill shaft, had been told that he must do so quickly since the mill was shut down. For an American example, see *Lamkins v Internat'l Harvester Co*, 182 2d 203 (Arkansas 1944), where a farmer was denied lost profits when an inexpensive device designed to allow him to harvest at night malfunctioned. Interestingly, while the foreseeability rule is endorsed by the Restatement (Second) of Contracts (1981), the Restatement explains both this case and *Hadley* by mentioning 'the extreme disproportion' between the 'loss of profits' and 'the [contract] price'. Ibid, Illustrations 17 & 18 to § 351. French courts say that there is no liability if the kind of harm that might occur can be foreseen but its extent cannot. Significantly, they have done so in cases in which the harm greatly exceeds the contract price. See eg Cass civ, 3. 8. 1932, D 1932.572 (racehorse dies); Cass civ, 7. 7. 1924, D 1927, I, 119 (contents of lost box particularly valuable); Cass civ 1re, 11. 5. 1982, Gaz Pal 1982, 2, 612 (owner loses rentals when contractor's employee sets fire to his roof with a blowtorch). For German cases in which disproportion, rather than foreseeability, seems to matter, see OLG Hamm, 28 February 1989, [1989] *Neue Juristische Wochenschrift* 2006 (a translator supposedly could not foresee that his error would make the translation unusable, yet the court noted the damages were forty times his fee); BGH, 29 January 1969, [1969] *Neue Juristische Wochenschrift* 789, translated in Basil S. Markesinis, Werner Lorenz, and Gerhard Dannemann, *The German Law of Obligations*, (vol I, 1997), 320–3 (hotel garage not liable for theft of jewellery in trunk of car, although, had the owner said that it was there, the theft would have been even more likely). See James Gordley, 'The Foreseeability Limitation on Liability in Contract', in Arthur S. Hartkamp and Christian von Bar (eds), *Towards a European Civil Code* (3rd edn, 2004), 215.

It is also possible that a rule which is widely adopted is puzzling because it seems inadequate to the problem it is supposed to address. An example is the definition of the defects against which the seller must warrant his goods. In the United States, Germany, and other legal systems, a defect is defined as a characteristic which makes the goods unsuitable for the purpose for which they were sold. That definition is not of much use in determining, for example, whether a lawn-mower is defective because it could have had a guard that better protects the user's fingers, or, to use Reinhard Zimmermann's examples, whether paintings are defective if they are spurious or pearls if they are imitations.[84] As Zimmermann points out, the definition was formulated that way by Roman jurists in a context in which it worked quite well. It applied to sales of animals and slaves. One could not sue for a scratch on a slave as long as he could do his work. No wonder, as Zimmermann points out, the rule doesn't work well when it is applied to the design of man-made things.[85] The rule's history explains why it is unsatisfactory although ubiquitous.

In cases like these, it is hard to see how a comparative lawyer could adequately explain the differences and similarities among rules without the help of legal history.

2. Comparative Law in the Service of Legal History

A legal historian attempting to relate a rule to the circumstances of a given time and place can yield to the opposite temptation. He may take a rule which, if not ubiquitous, has flourished in other circumstances, and explain it by those of the time and place he is studying. The cure is a comparative look at law elsewhere.

To pick an extreme example, Grant Gilmore claimed in his book, *The Death of Contract*, that the idea of a general law of contract 'never . . . occurred to the legal mind until [Christopher Columbus] Langdell somehow stumbled across it' in the nineteenth century.[86] He reached this conclusion because he knew that common lawyers, before the nineteenth century, organized their thinking in terms of writs such as assumpsit and covenant rather than by means of concepts such as contract, and that American lawyers only began to systematize contract law with the work of Langdell and contemporaries such as Oliver Wendell Holmes. Had he taken even a brief look at the law of other times and places, he could not have thought that the idea of a general law of contract was a nineteenth-century invention.

Morton Horwitz, in my judgment, yielded to the same temptation when, as described earlier, he argued that American law was 'transformed' in the nineteenth century to favour industrialization and a new class of entrepreneurs. The problem is not merely the assumption that whatever favoured that class was adopted in

---

[84] Zimmermann (n 42), 327.   [85] Ibid.
[86] Grant Gilmore, *The Death of Contract* (1974), 6.

order to do so. The problem is also that, if one looks at other times and places, one can see that rules such as those mentioned earlier, which he offers in support of his thesis, do not support it. American courts did reject traditional ideas about just prices. But as A. W. B. Simpson pointed out, that fact does not support Horwitz's thesis since, traditionally, the just price had been identified with the market price under competitive conditions.[87] Entrepreneurs would not have found that idea constraining. Horwitz claims that because of nineteenth-century economic conditions, people for the first time made contracts for the future delivery of goods. But they had done so for centuries.[88] The law of nuisance arose in the nineteenth century, according to Horwitz, because for the first time people were living in close enough proximity to bother each other. But, for centuries, English law protected neighbours from breweries and pigsties,[89] and Roman law protected them against the smoke from a nearby cheese shop.[90] Comparison with other times and places would have allowed Horwitz to separate out features which really were unique to the nineteenth century such as the development of corporate law.

V. Conclusion

Legal rules acquire their structure over time. Thus even if a comparative law scholar were only interested in the structure of modern rules, he would need the help of history. Some rules are characteristic of a given time and place and others are not. Thus even if an historian merely wanted to understand the law of a given time and place, he would need a comparative approach to see which rules are characteristic of it.

As noted, the problem was caused, in part, because of the way in which legal history and comparative law emerged as separate disciplines. To some extent, this was the result of an undue willingness to treat the law of a given time or place or country as a unity, and therefore an independent object of study. In all honesty, it may also have been due to the human temptation of every scholar to imagine himself as the master of a given subject, needing no help from subjects he has not mastered. Be that as it may, more scholars are recognizing that one cannot

---

[87] A. W. B. Simpson, 'The Horwitz Thesis and the History of Contracts', (1979) 46 *University of Chicago LR* 533, 536–8.

[88] Indeed, the generic sale of goods had been recognized for centuries. Wolfgang Ernst, 'Kurze Rechtsgeschichte des Gattungskauf', (1999) 7 *Zeitschrift für Europäisches Privatrecht* 583.

[89] *Aldred's Case* (1611) 9 Coke's King's Bench Report 57 (b), 77 ER 816; *Jones v Powell* (1628) Palmer's King's Bench Reports 536, 81 ER 1208.

[90] Ulpian D. 8, 5, 8, 5.

understand the rules of the past without looking beyond the period he is studying, or those of the present without looking at those of the past. Certainly, that is a change for the better.

BIBLIOGRAPHY

René David, *Les grands systèmes de droit contemporains* (7th edn, 1978)

Alan Watson, *The Making of the Civil Law* (1981)

Reinhard Zimmermann, *The Law of Obligations: Roman Foundations of the Civilian Tradition* (1990; paperback edn, 1996)

Rodolfo Sacco, 'Legal Formants: A Dynamic Approach to Comparative Law', (1991) 39 *AJCL* 1 ff

Hein Kötz, 'Was erwartet die Rechtsvergleichung von der Rechtsgeschichte?', [1992] *Juristenzeitung* 20 ff

Dieter Simon, 'Zwillingsschwestern oder Stammesbrüder oder What is What?', (1992) 11 *Rechtshistorisches Journal* 574 ff

Alan Watson, *Legal Transplants: An Approach to Comparative Law* (2nd edn, 1993)

William Ewald, 'What Was It Like to Try a Rat?' (1995) 143 *Pennsylvania LR* 1189 ff

Konrad Zweigert and Hein Kötz, *Einführung in die Rechtsvergleichung* (3rd edn, 1996; English translation under the title *An Introduction to Comparative Law* by Tony Weir, 3rd edn, 1996)

Reinhard Zimmermann, 'Savigny's Legacy: Legal History, Comparative Law, and the Emergence of a European Legal Science', (1996) 112 *LQR* 576 ff

Albrecht Cordes, 'Was erwartet die (mittelalterliche) Rechtsgeschichte von der Rechtsvergleichung und anderen vergleichend arbeitenden Disziplinen?', (1999) 7 *Zeitschrift für Europäisches Privatrecht* 545 ff

William Ewald, 'Legal History and Comparative Law', (1999) 7 *Zeitschrift für Europäisches Privatrecht* 553 ff

Michele Graziadei, 'Comparative Law, Legal History, and the Holistic Approach to Legal Cultures', (1999) 7 *Zeitschrift für Europäisches Privatrecht* 531 ff

David Johnston, 'Roman Law, Comparative Law and Legal History', (1999) 7 *Zeitschrift für Europäisches Privatrecht* 560 ff

Klaus Luig, 'Was kann die Rechtsgeschichte der Rechtsvergleichung bieten?', (1999) 7 *Zeitschrift für Europäisches Privatrecht* 521

Matthias Reimann, 'Rechtsvergleichung und Rechtsgeschichte im Dialog', (1999) 7 *Zeitschrift für Europäisches Privatrecht* 496 ff

Reinhard Zimmermann, *Roman Law, Contemporary Law, European Law: The Civilian Tradition Today* (2001)

James Gordley, 'Why Look Backward', (2002) 50 *AJCL* 657 ff

Michele Graziadei, 'The Functionalist Heritage', in Pierre Legrand and Roderick Munday (eds), *Comparative Legal Studies: Traditions and Transitions* (2003), 100 ff

Pierre Legrand, 'The Same and the Different', in Pierre Legrand and Roderick Munday (eds), *Comparative Legal Studies: Traditions and Transitions* (2003), 240 ff

James Gordley, *The Foundations of Private Law* (2006)

CHAPTER 24

COMPARATIVE LAW AND SOCIO-LEGAL STUDIES

ANNELISE RILES

Cornell

I. Introduction

THE tradition of socio-legal studies in comparative law has an eminent pedigree. Among its antecedents, Rousseau's early thought experiments concerning the character of life in the state of nature and the devolution from the world of the Noble Savage toward a system of private property rights[1] demonstrate an early curiosity about how the character of one's own legal system might be illuminated by thinking comparatively about other regimes separated from one's own by time or space. Montesquieu's writings on the American, English, and Roman legal traditions anticipate anthropological modes of inquiry with their focus on the place of courts, judges, lawyers, and legal knowledge in mentality and social life.[2] Many of the luminaries of comparative law, from Max Weber[3] to Karl Llewellyn,[4] and from Henry Maine[5] to Lewis Henry Morgan,[6] straddled the fields of law and social science and are actively revered in both fields today. As David Clark has noted, it was largely agreed at the founding 1900 Paris International Congress of Comparative Law by Raymond Saleilles, Edouart Lambert, and others that 'social science would establish general laws that show how legal institutions appear, develop, and disappear'.[7] And yet, in recent decades, the precise territory and stakes of engagement

---

[1] J. J. Rousseau, *The Social Contract* (orig 1743) (1968); *idem*, *A Discourse on Inequality* (orig 1758) (1984). For an interesting discussion of the legacy of Rousseau in dialogues between lawyers and anthropologists, see Karen Sykes, *Arguing with Anthropology: An Introduction to Critical Theories of the Gift* (2005).

[2] See Charles Montesquieu, *The Complete Works of M. de Montesquieu* (orig 1777), (2003).

[3] Max Weber, *Max Weber on Law in Economy and Society* (1966); *idem* and Edward Shils, *Max Weber on the Methodology of the Social Sciences* (1949).

[4] Karl N. Llewellyn and E. Adamson Hoebel, *The Cheyenne Way* (1941).

[5] Henry Sumner Maine, *International Law: A Series of Lectures Delivered before the University of Cambridge 1887* (1888); *idem*, *Ancient Law* (orig 1861) (1986)

[6] Lewis Henry Morgan, *Ancient Society* (1985).

[7] David S. Clark, 'Nothing New in 2000? Comparative Law in 1900 and Today', (2001) 75 *Tulane Law Review* 871, 895.

between socio-legal studies and comparative law have often seemed somewhat unsettled.

Nevertheless, one finds everywhere today signs of a new rapprochement. First, a new series of shared topics engage both comparative lawyers and socio-legal scholars. These include, in particular, questions surrounding the character of law in transnational or globalized conditions, and the consequences of the exportation or importation of doctrines, practices, and institutions associated with the 'Rule of Law' from one jurisdiction to another. Second, the emergence of concerns among mainstream comparative lawyers about the consequences of new legal orthodoxies for the national differences that traditionally concerned comparative lawyers has created new points of normative alliance between comparative lawyers and more critically minded socio-legal scholars. Third, a series of methodological shifts in both fields—shifts emblematic of wider epistemological realignments in law, the humanities, and the social sciences more broadly—has rendered some of the old fault lines between socio-legal studies and comparative law increasingly obsolete.

In this chapter, I begin by describing some shared ancestral figures of both comparative law and socio-legal studies, and the conundrums they have left to both fields. I then turn to the divisions between socio-legal studies and comparative law. I qualify this account of disciplinary division with a description of two important areas of research—non-European comparative law and legal pluralism—in which there has been long-standing collaboration between comparative lawyers and socio-legal scholars. Next, I describe the new rapprochement between the fields, and outline a series of foci of active debate. These include the nature of legal pluralism under conditions of globalization, the character of legal culture, the causes and prospects of legal transplants, and the consequences of legal harmonization. From this point of view, I outline a number of points of general agreement between comparative lawyers and socio-legal scholars—what I term consensus items—in hopes that the debate on these particular points can now be put to rest. Finally, I conclude with some thoughts on future directions for research.

One introductory caveat: The field of socio-legal studies is by its very nature highly heterogeneous. It encompasses a range of methods and projects, from qualitative to quantitative research methods, from social science to social activism, from American anthropology and sociology to British social anthropology, Continental critical sociology,[8] and more. Due to space constraints, I have confined the discussion to those aspects of socio-legal studies that are not covered in other sections of this volume. Hence I will not discuss legal history, law and economics, law and religion, critical legal studies, Islamic legal studies, or law and language,

---

[8] For insights into the differences between American and French socio-legal studies traditions, see Bryant Garth and Joyce Sterling, 'From Legal Realism to Law and Society: Reshaping Law for the Last Stages of the Social Activist State', (1998) 32(2) *Law and Society Review* 409–72; Pierre Noreau and André-Jean Arnaud, 'The Sociology of Law in France: Trends and Paradigms', (1998) 25(2) *Journal of Law and Society* 257–83.

and will treat the legal transplants debate only in so far as it touches directly on methodological questions relevant to socio-legal studies.

II. Labouring in the Long Shadow of Weber

In the late nineteenth century, with the increasing differentiation of the social sciences into distinct disciplines, each with their own provinces of methodological and subject-matter expertise, one begins to find legal scholars turning to these nascent disciplines for comparative insights. A good example is Henry Maine's historical jurisprudence.[9] Like Rousseau, Maine sought to answer specific questions about the character of law in modern England—in particular he sought to qualify some of the more universalizing arguments of Jeremy Bentham and the positivists concerning the superiority of legislation over judge-made law, the nature of law as the command of the sovereign, and the useless and obfuscating quality of legal expertise—by thinking comparatively and historically about the differences between modern English law and the legal systems of other places and times. Working from an evolutionary paradigm, Maine described the role of legal innovation in the evolution of 'the progressive societies' from regimes in which rights and obligations flowed from status relationships (as for example in Roman law) to regimes in which rights and obligations attached purely to anonymous and individualized contractual relations (as in modern English commercial relations). This 'status to contract' model of legal evolution continues, for better or worse, implicitly to sustain many law and development projects around the world that place contract law at the centre of efforts to spur legal evolution.

But to foreshadow the argument that follows, there are perhaps other aspects of Maine's work that we might wish to reclaim as an antecedent for contemporary socio-legal approaches to comparative law. In his account of the distinctiveness of the legal systems of the progressive societies, Maine emphasized the character and effects of legal knowledge—the devices used by judges such as arguments in equity or legal fictions that enabled the law to change gradually and almost imperceptibly. It is without a doubt a common lawyer's vision of legal change, but whether or not the particular devices Maine emphasizes have universal applicability, it remains a fruitful direction for inquiry. It includes the attention to how legal experts do their knowledge work, to the devices they deploy, to what

---

[9] Maine, *Ancient Law* (n 5).

constitutes legal creativity, to the problems legal knowledge encounters in confronting new social political or economic phenomena, and the effects of legal creativity on the development of the law but also on larger social phenomena, from the market to the nature of personhood.

As we move forward in time to the twentieth century, without a doubt the most important ancestral figure for the contemporary socio-legal approach to comparative law is Max Weber. Unlike other intellectual antecedents, Weber remains very much an interlocutor for many contemporary comparative lawyers and socio-legal scholars alike although, as we will see, what each takes from Weber often differs dramatically and even pits the disciplines against one another. Weber's most important text on law, *Economy and Society*, was translated into English by none other than the celebrated comparatist Max Rheinstein,[10] who had attended Weber's lectures.[11] Weber's ideal typic approach—his focus on categories of social and legal phenomena that set typological differences into relief—continues to serve as a methodological model in comparative law. Ugo Mattei, for example, has proposed a new classification project in comparative law 'based on the role of law as a tool of social organization in the Weberian sense'.[12] In the branch of comparative law concerned with issues of law and development, likewise, Jonathan Miller has produced a Weberian style 'typology' of the motivations for legal actors in a developing country to accept imports from abroad, including time and cost saving, the influence of external bodies such as international financial institutions, 'entrepreneurial' objectives of particular actors, or the prestige or international legitimacy of the state whose legal institutions are emulated.[13] In Law and Society scholarship, it is rather Weber's emphasis on the character of the social,[14] and of its generative consequences for legal arrangements, coupled with his appreciation (contra Marx) of the sociological autonomy of legal actors and legal development from the market, that continues to inspire. Weber's own ambivalent endorsement of the Western legal tradition and, with it, Western rationality, and his dual commitment to methodological rigour on the one hand and the impossibility of ultimately separating fact from value, or sociological inquiry from political inquiry on the other,[15] also remains a source of inspiration, not to mention fodder for conflicting interpretations of his text. As Tim Murphy puts it, '[t]o look "back" to Weber is one way of exploring the possibilities and the limits of the contemporary socio-legal imagination'.[16]

---

[10] Max Weber, *Max Weber on Law in Economy and Society* (1966).

[11] Pierre Legrand, 'John Henry Merryman and Comparative Legal Studies: A Dialogue', (1999) 47 *AJCL* 3–66.

[12] Ugo Mattei, 'Three Patterns of Law: Taxonomy and Change in the World's Legal Systems', (1997) 45 *AJCL* 12.

[13] Jonathan M. Miller, 'A Typology of Legal Transplants: Using Sociology, Legal History and Argentine Examples to Explain the Transplant Process', (2003) 51 *AJCL* 839.

[14] Max Weber, Guenther Roth, and Claus Wittich, *Economy and Society* (1968), at 26–8.

[15] Max Weber, *The Methodology of the Social Sciences* (1949).

[16] W. T. Murphy, *The Oldest Social Science? Configurations of Law and Modernity* (1997).

Weber's work on the character of modern law begins from the standpoint of what he sees as the uniqueness and particularity of the modern Western legal tradition, and he seeks to answer the question of what accounts for this uniqueness through a comparison of Western society and its laws with those of non-Western societies and legal traditions. Weber's answer, in a phrase, is a particular kind of knowledge, rationality: Modern Western societies are unique in their functioning according to rationalities of different kinds, whether in the spheres of religion, economy, government, or law, he argues.

In law as in other spheres of social and economic life, Weber differentiates two kinds of rationality. Action is 'instrumentally rational (*zweckrational*)' if it is 'determined by expectations as to the behaviour of objects in the environment and of other human beings; these expectations are used as "conditions" or "means" for the attainment of the actor's own rationally pursued calculated ends'.[17] Weber contrasts instrumentally rational action with action which is 'value rational (*wertrational*), that is, determined by a conscious belief in the value for its own sake of some ethical, aesthetic, religious or other form of behaviour, independently of its prospects for success'. Legal systems rooted in a religious tradition might therefore be substantively rational, in the sense that legal rules consciously promote a particular set of values, but are not formally rational in this view, because (according to Weber) such religious laws do not consciously treat the law as a means to some calculated social, political, or economic end.[18] Both forms of rationality in turn differ from action that is 'affectual (especially emotional), that is, determined by the actor's specific affects and feeling states' and action that is 'traditional, that is, determined by ingrained habituation'.[19]

For Weber, law differs from other aspects of social life such as custom or tradition. Unlike law, '"custom" refers to rules devoid of external sanction'. Only some customs evolve over time into enforceable law.[20] As we will see, this distinction between law and custom has fuelled entire disciplinary divides.

Although there are many types of instrumentally rational legal systems, the most advanced form of legal knowledge, he argues, is logically formal legal thought, which has the following features:

first, that every concrete legal decision be the 'application' of an abstract legal proposition to a concrete 'fact situation'; second, that it must be possible in every concrete case to derive the decision from abstract legal propositions by means of legal logic; third, that the law must actually or virtually constitute a 'gapless' system of legal propositions, or must, at least, be treated as if it were such a gapless system; fourth, that whatever cannot be 'construed' rationally in legal terms is also legally irrelevant; and fifth, that every social action of human beings must always be visualized as either an 'application' or 'execution' of legal

---

[17] Weber *et al* (n 14), at 24.   [18] Ibid at 875.   [19] Ibid.   [20] Ibid at 29.

propositions, or as an 'infringement' thereof, since the 'gaplessness' of the legal system must result in a gapless 'legal ordering' of all social conduct.[21]

As Lawrence Friedman puts it, this 'legalistic reasoning is reasoning that rejects the importation of new criteria, especially criteria from outside the law'.[22] Weber contrasts this form of legal knowledge to 'substantively irrational' legal reasoning— reasoning based on non-intellectual methods such as oracles—and to 'substantively rational' legal reasoning—what he terms 'kadi justice'—in which values such as equity, rather than the application of abstract rules to concrete facts, determine the legal outcome. In Weber's view, these latter systems are less advanced forms of law; the trajectory of progress is rather clearly oriented toward formal rationality. Weber's antipathy toward more equity and fact-based forms of adjudication was later picked up by conservative legal theorists from Carl Schmitt to Friedrich Hayek as a basis for their own attacks on the rise of the welfare state.

For our purposes, what is most relevant is Weber's approach to comparative analysis and its consequences. By his own admission, Weber was not at all an expert in the legal systems he uses as examples of substantively irrational law, such as those of Asia; in this sense, one could say that he is the forefather of a certain amateuristic approach to comparative law:[23] 'however objectionable it may be, such trespassing on other special fields cannot be avoided in comparative work. But one must take the consequences by resigning oneself to considerable doubts regarding the degree of one's success.'[24]

Weber's discussion of Asian law as the paradigmatic example of substantively irrational law almost has a legal hypothetical-like quality. It serves as a kind of foil, an example of the very opposite of the modern Western legal rationality that defines legal rationality through the contrast: Asian law, in direct contrast to modern Western law, is 'a featureless conglomeration of ethical and legal duties, moral exhortations, and legal commandments without formalized explicitness'.[25] Weber's claims about Asian law are now universally recognized to be highly problematic and uninformed at best and much ink has been spilled in refuting his claims point by point to demonstrate that, in fact, many aspects of Asian legal regimes shared far more with Weber's formally rational type than he recognized.[26]

[21] Weber *et al.* (n 14), quoted in Sally Ewing, 'Formal Justice and The Spirit of Capitalism—Max Weber's Sociology of Law', (1987) 21 *Law and Society Review* 487–512, at 491.

[22] Lawrence M. Friedman, 'On Legalistic Reasoning—A Footnote to Weber', (1966) 1966 *Wisconsin Law Review* 148–71.

[23] See Annelise Riles, 'Encountering Amateurism: John Henry Wigmore and the Uses of American Formalism', in Annelise Riles (ed), in *Rethinking the Masters of Comparative Law* (2001), 94–128.

[24] Max Weber, *The Protestant Ethic and the Spirit of Capitalism* [1930] (1992), at xli.

[25] Weber *et al.* (n 14), at 810.

[26] See R. M. Marsh, 'Weber's Misunderstanding of Traditional Chinese Law', (2000) 106 *American Journal of Sociology* 281–302.

Weber's grouping of the common law with 'kadi justice', as an example of law that is substantively rational but not formally rational, has also generated considerable debate among comparative lawyers. As Murphy summarizes Weber's view,

For Weber, the common law is essentially an 'empirical art' especially when compared with what he regards as the 'abstract logic' of civilian systems. Law finding, especially in America, has a charismatic quality—the 'concrete individual judge' stands in contrast to the 'impersonal District Court' of Continental systems. The civil jury and the 'patriarchal,' 'highly irrational' system of JPs is contrasted with the professionalization of continental adjudication.[27]

In response, Murphy seeks to show that the common law is far more decontextualized and routinized than Weber understood it to be. In another line of response, scholars in both comparative law and socio-legal studies have challenged Weber's evolutionary framework.[28] Duncan Kennedy emphasizes that Weber's view of formally rational law as the most advanced form of law is a product of the historical period in which he wrote. Weber worked in a context in which classical legal thought dominated, but found itself increasingly challenged by more 'substantively rational' approaches—approaches which, he argues, in retrospect have won the day.[29] Lawrence Friedman likewise has commented that the tendency of twentieth-century legal systems to move toward more substantive forms of rationality demonstrates at least that Weber's ideal types are best imagined as temporally coexisting alternatives rather than steps in an evolutionary progression toward formally rational law:

[L]egalism is not a particular evolutionary stage of development of legal systems, in Weber's sense. It is a feature which can and does appear whenever certain conditions prevail in a legal system—the duty to decide; the duty to give reasons; a closed canon of principles and rules; legal functionaries whose roles do not legitimately allow for the making of law.[30]

Whatever the problems with Weber's larger argument and comparative methods, certain distinctions, typologies, and themes in his work continue to influence disciplinary directions in both comparative law and socio-legal studies. In the pages that follow, I query whether further integration of comparative law and socio-legal studies does not demand stepping outside Weber's shadow in certain respects. And yet, we must wonder why Weber's work continues to fascinate and inspire such a range of scholars working at the interstices of comparative law

---

[27] W. T. Murphy (n 16), at 55–6.

[28] For a sociological critique of Weber's evolutionary scheme, see P. D. Jennings, M. Schulz, D. Patient, C. Gravel, and K. Yuan, 'Weber and Legal Rule Evolution: The Closing of the Iron Cage?', (2005) 26 *Organization Studies* 621–53.

[29] D. Kennedy, 'The Disenchantment of Logically Formal Legal Rationality, or Max Weber's Sociology in the Genealogy of the Contemporary Mode of Western Legal Thought', (2004) 55 *Hastings LJ* 1031–76.

[30] Friedman (n 22), at 161.

and socio-legal studies. I conclude by returning to some other aspects of the Weberian tradition and to how we might reclaim them for the future of socio-legal approaches to comparative law.

III. TRADITIONAL DISTANCE

The last three decades saw less dialogue between comparative lawyers and socio-legal scholars than might be ideal for both fields. Even to this day, a perusal of the pages of *Law and Society Review* or *Law and Social Inquiry* reveals relatively few articles concerning transnational, or even non-American subjects. Likewise, relatively little empirical and socio-legal work has appeared in the *American Journal of Comparative Law* or to date.

On the socio-legal side, one can point to a number of reasons for the lack of attention to comparative questions. In the United States the field of socio-legal studies is organized primarily through the Law and Society Association. This association (and the larger intellectual movement it represents) is the methodological and political heir to American Legal Realism. Despite its many contributions, Legal Realism was profoundly domestic in its focus. In the Conflict of Laws, for example, the Realist Revolution, as it is known, turned American Conflicts away from a transnational perspective to a more narrow focus on inter-state conflicts.[31] In both the United States and Europe, the relative marginalization of anthropology, as compared to sociology in socio-legal studies reflects the domestic focus of socio-legal studies in each region (where the traditional disciplinary division between sociology and anthropology has reflected a division of research subjects into domestic and foreign subjects). From this perspective, mid-twentieth-century socio-legal scholars saw little obvious overlap between their concerns and those of comparative lawyers.

A second reason relates directly to the Weberian legacy in comparative law. With certain important exceptions (discussed below under the topic of legal pluralism), comparative lawyers have largely followed Weber's definition of law as norms backed by the coercive force of the State. Yet the Realist commitments of American Law and Society scholars to focus on 'law in action' rather than 'law in the books'[32] translated into relatively little interest in state law and institutions, and hence to a certain distrust of what socio-legal scholars took as comparative lawyers' narrow

---

[31] On this history, see Annelise Riles, *Collateral Knowledge: Instrumental Reason, Market Sociality, Legal Subjectivity* (forthcoming).

[32] Roscoe Pound, 'The Scope and Purpose of Sociological Jurisprudence', (1911) 24 *Harvard LR* 591 ff.

and overly formalistic focus on state-sanctioned rules rather than wider social norms.[33]

A third reason traces to the very different Weberian legacy in socio-legal studies, and its consequences for socio-legal scholars' understanding of the subjectivity of the scholar and the nature of the scholarly project. As I have described elsewhere,[34] Law and Society scholars assumed a steadfastly 'outsider' perspective on the law. They sought to describe legal institutions from the perspective of the 'trenches' rather than the 'ivory towers'. On the whole, these scholars shared a set of normative commitments to critique the hierarchies and inequalities law produced, to describe 'how the legitimacy of law is maintained',[35] and to draw attention to social justice issues surrounding law that they felt were ignored in mainstream legal scholarship. From this perspective, comparative law seemed more like a potential target of critique than a potential ally.

Law and Society scholars also drew from the Weberian tradition a strong commitment to the separation of fact from value in empirical research. Social science was assumed to be descriptive, not normative. This commitment to empiricism, implicitly opposed to both 'theory' and 'doctrine', always sat somewhat uneasily with Law and Society scholars' own normative commitments to expose the limits and consequences of law. Nevertheless, this commitment to empiricism rendered comparative law's more normative, programmatic, doctrinal, and theoretical analyses less interesting to socio-legal scholars.

Finally, one important methodological and epistemological arbiter of modernism in the social sciences concerned attention to social context.[36] From this perspective, the grand comparative schemes of Morgan, Maine, and Weber seemed outdated and amateuristic. Hence socio-legal scholars tended to view comparative lawyers' efforts to compare the laws of numerous jurisdictions, to actually engage in ideal typic categorizations in the Weberian tradition, as lacking sufficient attention to context and hence partaking of the methodological amateurism of an earlier era.

For their part, comparative lawyers had their own reasons for keeping their distance from socio-legal studies. First, to the extent that comparative law focused

[33] For a more contemporary expression of this concern, see John Flood, 'The Vultures Fly East: The Creation and Globalisation of the Distressed Debt Market', in David Nelken and Johannes Feest (eds), *Adapting Legal Cultures* (2001), 257–78. Flood chooses to speak of 'normative transplants' in contrast to legal transplants although 'most comparative law scholars think in terms of law as their topic. Those of us who have been immersed in the anthropological and sociological debates on law regard this interpretation of law as restrictive and narrow'. Ibid 258.

[34] Annelise Riles, 'Representing In-Between: Law, Anthropology and the Rhetoric of Interdisciplinarity', (1994) *University of Illinois Law Review* 597–650.

[35] Yves Dezalay and Bryant Garth, 'Merchants of Law as Moral Entrepreneurs: Constructing International Justice from the Competition for Transnational Business Disputes', (1995) 29 *Law and Society Review* 27–64, at 29.

[36] See Riles, (1994) *University of Illinois LR* 597–650, at 639.

on state law, socio-legal scholars seemed to have relatively little expertise to contribute. Second, some comparative lawyers drew a distinction between 'comparative law', which they took to entail an explicit comparison of the rules or institutions of two or more jurisdictions, and 'the study of foreign law'—the more contextual, ethnographic, or historical studies of socio-legal scholars that usually focused on only one jurisdiction at a time. Finally, comparative law traditionally paid relatively little attention to non-European legal systems. From this perspective, the comparative or internationally focused work of socio-legal scholars, much of which concerned legal institutions in the developing world, held only marginal theoretical interest.

That said, comparative lawyers and socio-legal scholars collaborated actively in the second half of the twentieth century around two principal subjects—the study of legal institutions other than those of Europe, North America, and Latin America on the one hand, and the (often related) study of 'legal pluralism' on the other. Indeed, the current resurgence of interest in socio-legal studies among comparative lawyers (and vice versa) is owed in part to the growing prominence of both of these areas of research in both fields. Before going further, I provide a brief overview of the nature of the collaboration in these two areas.

IV. COMPARATIVE LAW BEYOND EUROPE AND THE AMERICAS

When comparative lawyers turned their attention to what René David unceremoniously termed 'other legal systems'—legal systems that were neither Civilian, Common Law-based, nor Socialist, that is, the legal systems of most of Asia, Africa, the Middle East, and the Pacific—they found it necessary to adapt the traditional methods of comparative law. A focus on 'law in action' often seemed more salient, from the social actors' point of view, than a more narrow focus on rules or legal cases.[37] The key questions became not so much the content of legal rules and their functions, but the relative significance of legal rules and institutions vis-à-vis other institutions for resolving disputes or expressing social norms,

---

[37] See Victor H. Li, *Law without Lawyers: A Comparative View of Law in China and the United States* (1978).

from bureaucracy[38] to gift exchange[39] to violence, apology,[40] or social protest,[41] as well as different epistemologies of legal reasoning and forms of jurisprudential debate.[42]

A deeply contextual approach informed by the methods of history, sociology, anthropology, and economics, and based on extensive, long-term contacts with the societies in question and analysis of materials in primary languages, has long been the dominant tradition of comparative law in these regions and, in fact, comparative lawyers working there often confess more affinity with regional specialists in other disciplines than with other comparative lawyers.[43] In particular, comparative legal studies focusing on African and Pacific legal systems have long been intimately engaged with legal anthropology, and many of the most prominent comparatists working in these legal systems have conducted ethnographic fieldwork co-authored with legal anthropologists, and contributed actively to theoretical debates in legal anthropology.[44]

Ironically, in the last ten years, as the legal institutions of some East Asian countries have developed increasingly in the direction of Euro-American legal institutions, East Asian comparative law has seen a small decline in engagement with socio-legal studies. However, the trend seems once again in the other direction as exemplified by the publication of a recent volume of essays on Chinese legal institutions edited jointly by a legal and socio-legal scholar and advocating a more empirical and methodologically sophisticated approach to the intersection of Chinese legal studies and Law and Society scholarship.[45] As the authors suggest, a socio-legal perspective is needed all the more in a period of legal growth in order to answer a key question: 'If law matters, then for whom does it matter most, and for what purposes is it used?'[46]

---

[38] Frank K. Upham, *Law and Social Change in Postwar Japan* (1987); John Owen Haley, *Authority without Power: Law and the Japanese Paradox* (1991).

[39] Andrew B. Kipnis, *Producing Guanxi: Sentiment, Self, and Subculture in a North China Village* (1997).

[40] Hiroshi Wagatsuma and Arthur Rosett, 'The Implications of Apology: Law and Culture in Japan and the United States', (1986) 20 *Law and Society Review* 461–507.

[41] Eric A. Feldman, *The Ritual of Rights in Japan: Law, Society, and Health Policy* (2000).

[42] Max Gluckman, *The Judicial Process among the Barotse of Northern Rhodesia* (1955); Max Gluckman, 'Concepts in the Comparative Study of Tribal Law', in Laura Nader (ed), *Law in Culture and Society* (1969). Clifford Geertz, *Local Knowledge: Further Essays in Interpretive Anthropology* (1983).

[43] See Annelise Riles, 'Wigmore's Treasure Box: Comparative Law in the Era of Information', (1999) 40 *Harvard International LJ* 221–83.

[44] See eg John L. Comaroff and Simon Roberts, *Rules and Processes: The Cultural Logic of Dispute in an African Context* (1981); Simon Roberts, *Order and Dispute: An Introduction to Legal Anthropology* (1979). Peter Fitzpatrick, 'Is it Simple to be a Marxist in Legal Anthropology?', (1985) 48 *Modern LR* 472–85.

[45] Neil Jeffrey Diamant, Stanley B. Lubman, and Kevin J. O'Brien, *Engaging the Law in China: State, Society, and Possibilities for Justice* (2005).

[46] Ibid 4.

V. Legal Pluralism

A second and often related area of long-standing debate between comparative lawyers and socio-legal scholars concerns the character of legal pluralism—'the situation in which two or more laws interact'.[47] In the early stages of the Law and Society movement, most internationally oriented work within that tradition emerged out of the experience of lawyers working on development and legal reform projects within colonial and newly independent states. These lawyers typically dealt with problems surrounding the superimposition of colonial law on regimes of religious or customary law. In many such contexts, a series of practical questions concerning the status that should be accorded to so-called 'customary law' emerged—for example, whether customary law should be recognized as a source of law in state courts or even codified, whether special institutions such as village-based dispute resolution institutions should be created to give effect to customary law and if so what kind of jurisdiction these institutions should have.[48]

At an early stage, it seemed that 'pluralism' was a progressive, reformist position—that a more pluralist legal system was prima facie a more just legal system. For example, Masaji Chiba, one of Japan's leading comparative lawyers and socio-legal scholars, deployed legal pluralism as a theoretical vehicle for confronting what he viewed as the hegemony of Euro-American legal theories and institutions. Chiba studied with the anthropologist E. Adamson Hoebel, Karl Llewellyn's collaborator on *The Cheyenne Way*.[49] As a result, Chiba began from the standpoint of a firm grounding in mid-twentieth-century 'structural functionalist' legal anthropology. In his youth, he had also defied conventional elite Japanese academic contempt for both empirical research and customary Japanese practices to conduct field research on dispute resolution in rural Japanese villages. Dismayed by what he viewed as the unwillingness of many non-Euro-American legal scholars to appreciate and work within their own legal traditions, but taking as a starting reality, also, the diffusion of European and American legal institutions in the post-war era, Chiba initiated a global comparative dialogue among legal scholars in the 'South' about the vitality of customary legal institutions and their interaction with state law.[50]

However, the foregrounding of pluralism in turn led to active comparative debates about the character of 'custom'. These debates soon turned from celebrating customary law and working to give it expression through pluralist legal institutions

---

[47] M. B. Hooker, *Legal Pluralism* (1975), at 6.

[48] Peter Fitzpatrick, *Law and State in Papua New Guinea* (1980).

[49] Karl N. Llewellyn and E. Adamson Hoebel, *The Cheyenne Way* (1941).

[50] See Masaji Chiba, *Asian Indigenous Law: In Interaction with Received Law* (1986); Masaji Chiba, *Legal Pluralism: Toward a General Theory through Japanese Legal Culture* (1989); Masaji Chiba, 'Islamic Law Transplanted in Asian Countries' (in Japanese), (1997) 32 *IUAES CFLLP* 41–6; Masaji Chiba, 'Other Phases of Legal Pluralism in the Contemporary World', (1998) 11 *Ratio Juris* 228–44.

to questioning its authenticity. By now, comparative lawyers and socio-legal scholars, working together on the process of 'discovering' customary law in diverse colonial and postcolonial states, have conclusively shown that 'custom' is often best understood as the artifact of (often well-meaning) colonial officers, working in collaboration with local elites who themselves often have little first-hand knowledge of customary practices, and sometimes harbour the worst stereotypes of local traditions.[51] Comparative lawyers, for example, have shown that the legal frame in which 'custom' must find expression in modern state legal systems already implies many unstated background Euro-American conceptions, such as assumptions about the nature of the individual or of time. Forcing customary practices to fit into these frames may undermine the very project of pluralism where the difference between state law and 'custom' inheres in different starting assumptions about such background matters as the character of the person or of time.[52]

Thus comparative lawyers and socio-legal scholars alike now treat customary law as a kind of 'invented tradition',[53] and one that ironically often lives on long after official decolonization and the reform of other legal institutions of the postcolonial state.[54] More recent anthropological work has exposed harrowing examples of legal deferrals to invented custom in contemporary times. James Weiner details the unwitting collusion of anthropologists in the fabrication of evidence of secret indigenous women's customary knowledge in a lawsuit against the Australian government's proposed construction of a bridge to Hindmarsh Island. His aim is not to accuse individual anthropologists, lawyers, or indigenous activists of bad faith but to point to the inherent tensions in the legal concept of custom:

[W]hat is in fact tested judicially is not strictly speaking 'Aboriginal culture' but some relational product of indigenous Aboriginal exegesis and Western notions of tradition. . . . the process by which this relational product emerges is masked by the current emphasis on contemporary versions of cultural significance insisted upon by indigenous communities (especially those engaged in confrontation with outside forces), by anthropologists' desire to authenticate and legitimate these versions, and by indigenous heritage protection legislation . . .[55]

---

[51] Martin Chanock, *Law, Custom and Social Order: The Colonial Experience in Malawi and Zambia* (1985); Sally Falk Moore, 'Treating Law as Knowledge: Telling Colonial Officers What to Say to Africans about Running "Their Own" Native Countries', (1992) 26 *Law and Society Review* 11–46; William L. Twining, *The Place of Customary Law in the National Legal Systems of East Africa: Lectures Delivered at the University of Chicago Law School in April–May, 1963* (1964).

[52] H. Patrick Glenn, 'The Capture, Reconstruction and Marginalization of "Custom"', (1997) 45 *AJCL* 613–20, at 617–18.

[53] John Borneman, *Settling Accounts: Violence, Justice, and Accountability in Postsocialist Europe* (1997), at 18.

[54] Daniel S. Lev, *Islamic Courts in Indonesia; A Study in the Political Bases of Legal Institutions* (1972).

[55] James F. Weiner, 'Culture in a Sealed Envelope: The Concealment of Australian Aboriginal Heritage and Tradition in the Hindmarsh Island Bridge Affair', (1999) 5 *The Journal of the Royal Anthropological Institute* 193–210, at 195.

VI. THE RAPPROCHEMENT

In the last ten years, a new conversation has begun to emerge between socio-legal scholars and comparative lawyers. New themes and concerns in each field now render the expertise of the other vital. On the one hand, socio-legal studies has seen a tremendous growth of interest in international and transnational subjects. On the other hand, comparative law has engaged more with empirical studies and with social theory. The following survey of some of these themes begins with those that resonate more with socio-legal scholars then moves to those whose centre of gravity is located more in comparative law.

1. Globalization of the Legal Profession

The sociology of the legal profession has long been a core subject in socio-legal studies. In recent years, however, socio-legal scholars working in this area have been forced to take note of the undeniably transnational character of much legal practice. Beginning with comparative studies of the professional cultures of legal practice in different jurisdictions,[56] socio-legal studies have moved to consider the effects of globalization on the practice of law. Topics range from new invocations of global human rights discourses by Israeli cause lawyers and the way engagement with such global discourses shapes the political agendas, legal strategies, and personal ambitions of such lawyers,[57] to the effects of foreign (principally American) models of legal education and practice on the changing character of legal education and legal practice in Asia.[58]

One important theoretical development for comparative law to come out of this work is the extensive empirical work conducted by Yves Dezalay, Bryant Garth, and others, concerning the role of legal actors in the global proliferation of American legal rules and practices. Drawing on the work of the sociologist Pierre Bourdieu, Dezalay and Garth have shown how ideas about law and legal institutions migrate from one jurisdiction and social context to another as a result of the efforts of individual legal actors working in the service of their individual interests—their personal career interests, the interests of their families or class, or of their firms and organizations. Adapting Bourdieu's vocabulary, Dezalay and Garth argue that the

---

[56] Richard L. Abel and Philip Simon Coleman Lewis, *Lawyers in Society: An Overview* (1995).

[57] See Lisa Hajjar, 'Cause Lawyering in Transnational Perspective: National Conflict and Human Rights in Israel/Palestine', (1997) 31 *Law and Society Review* 473–504.

[58] William P. Alford, Geraldine Chin, Laura A. Cecere and Emma Johnson, *Raising the Bar: The Emerging Legal Profession in East Asia* (2004); Setsuo Miyazawa, 'The Politics of Judicial Reform in Japan: The Rule of Law At Last?', (2001) 2 *Asian-Pacific Law and Policy Journal* 89–121.

growth of the influence of American law firms in the 'international legal field' and, by extension, of the evolution of international legal practice, from a more civilian system to a practice imbued with Anglo-American legal norms, resulted from the 'international strategies' of particular individuals seeking to augment their 'social capital'. Thus, legal change is a result of what they term these 'international palace wars'.[59] This approach has inspired a number of further empirical studies of the role of transnational legal elites in the transmission and transformation of legal norms.[60]

2. Law and Development/Rule of Law/ Harmonization Projects

A second area of dialogue between socio-legal scholars and comparative lawyers concerns the recent resurgence of interest in 'Rule of Law', 'Law and Development', and 'Legal Harmonization' projects. A new generation of legal scholars has taken on projects to promote the Rule of Law in the developing world—from legal codification projects in Vietnam to the training of judges and lawyers in Palestine. Cognizant of the failures of past generations of law and development projects, these lawyers seek to join forces with social scientists—primarily political scientists—to consider more carefully the conditions under which Rule of Law projects are most likely to prove successful.[61] For example, Tom Ginsburg brings together legal and political science perspectives to study the political conditions under which judicial review is most likely to develop as an institution.[62] Christian Joerges, likewise, has organized a collaborative research project with political scientists working on the conditions necessary for legal compliance to consider the prospects for harmonization of laws within the European community from a more empirical perspective.[63] This work expands the scope of comparative law to include

[59] Yves Dezalay and Bryant Garth, *The Internationalization of Global Palace Wars: Lawyers, Economists, and the Contest to Transform Latin American States* (2002); Yves Dezalay and Bryant G. Garth, *Dealing in Virtue: International Commercial Arbitration and the Construction of a Transnational Legal Order* (1996).

[60] See eg Flood (n 33); Larissa Adler Lomnitz and Rodrigo Salazar, 'Cultural Elements in the Practice of Law in Mexico: Informal Networks in a Formal System', in Yves Dezalay and Bryant G. Garth (eds), *Global Prescriptions: The Production, Exportation, and Importation of a New Legal Orthodoxy* (2002), 209–48.

[61] See Daniel Berkowitz, Katharina Pistor and Jean-Francois Richard, 'The Transplant Effect', (2003) 51 *AJCL* 163.

[62] Tom Ginsburg, *Judicial Review in New Democracies: Constitutional Courts in Asian Cases* (2003); See also Mark Findlay, 'Independence and the Judiciary in the PRC: Expectations for Constitutional Legitimacy in China', in Kanishka Jayasuriya (ed), *Law, Capitalism and Power in Asia: The Rule of Law and Legal Institutions* (1999), 281–99.

[63] See Michael Zürn and Christian Joerges, *Law and Governance in Postnational Europe: Compliance beyond the Nation-State* (2004).

a new series of cross-disciplinary and transnational subjects such as the regulatory practices of European Union committees and, by conditions outside the law that drive legal reform, such as the growth of popular commitment to democracy.[64] As mentioned earlier, much Law and Development work still proceeds very much under the sign of Weberian typologies and Weberian ideas about what constitutes legal progress. For example, deploying the Weberian typology discussed above, Jonathan Miller suggests that disaggregating the particular reasons for the acceptance of 'legal transplants' will help to specify the conditions in which particular legal reform projects are most likely to fail.[65]

For the most part, however, members of the Law and Society movement who write about law and development came into the movement as a result of their critiques of the law and development projects of the 1960s and 1970s.[66] Following in this tradition of critique, comparative lawyers and socio-legal scholars have been equally active in developing a critique of second generation Law and Development projects. Although a generation ago critics of law and development would not necessarily have sought allies among comparative lawyers, there is now increasing scepticism among mainstream comparative lawyers about the claims made by international aid agencies, First World governments, international legal institutions such as the European Union, and the legal experts they employ on behalf of these law and development regimes (see discussion of Legal Transplants below). Some comparative lawyers now routinely ask questions about 'who gets to define what is meant by success' in Rule of Law debates,[67] although as Nelken suggests, comparative lawyers bring to such questions an appreciation of the need 'to avoid romanticizing the idea of resistance'. Some comparative lawyers also express unease at the increasing global dominance of American legal norms and practice, and this unease has provided the ground for collaboration with socio-legal scholars, as exemplified by the work of Ugo Mattei and anthropologist Laura Nader on 'American legal hegemony'.

This less romantic perspective is something comparative lawyers share with a new generation of empirically grounded socio-legal scholars who focus on the disparate impacts of global legal structures but remain sceptical about the claims to moral high ground of non-governmental organizations, labour movements, and international development agencies. In a number of conferences held at Harvard, Wisconsin, Birkbeck College, Cornell, and elsewhere, veterans of the first wave of law and development projects have entered into conversation with socio-legal

---

[64] See Christian Joerges and Ellen Vos, *EU Committees: Social Regulation, Law and Politics* (1999).

[65] Jonathan M. Miller, 'A Typology of Legal Transplants: Using Sociology, Legal History and Argentine Examples to Explain the Transplant Process', (2003) 51 *AJCL* 839.

[66] See eg David M. Galanter and Mark Trubek, 'Scholars in Self-Estrangement: Some Reflections on the Crisis in Law and Development Studies in the United States', (1974) *Wisconsin LR* 1062.

[67] David Nelken, 'Towards a Sociology of Legal Adaptation', in David Nelken and Johannes Feest (eds), *Adapting Legal Cultures* (2001), 7–54, at 49.

scholars and comparative lawyers about the nature and consequences of contemporary law and development projects. What distinguishes this conversation from earlier critiques is its empirical grounding. Anthropologists working closely with the clients of law and development initiatives, for example, have shown precisely how such projects are misunderstood, misinterpreted, or unable to articulate local concerns. For example, Kimberly Coles's ethnographic study of Rule of Law projects in Bosnia-Herzegovina captures the distance between the culture of international development workers and the citizenry they ostensibly work with, and how the knowledge at issue in Rule of Law projects produces 'difference and exclusion' in the way it constructs an image of Europe and Europeanness.[68] This work in turn evokes comparisons between current Rule of Law projects and the legal projects of the colonial era. Darian-Smith and Fitzpatrick, for example, highlight the utility of postcolonial theory for contemporary Law and Development including ideas about Orientalism; that is, the way development projects serve to construct European understandings of the identity of the metropole through a negative contrast with the images they construct of the targets of development.[69]

3. National and Local Effects of Global Legal Forms

A third area of socio-legal engagement with comparative law concerns the effects of globalization on national and local regulatory practices, and the way transnational or global economic and legal forms are accommodated, resisted, or translated locally. Much of this work extends the Law and Society tradition of understanding legal issues in the context of market relations and of emphasizing the disparate social and economic consequences of regulatory structures. For example, a number of sophisticated socio-legal studies of immigration policies have tracked the legal instantiation of tensions between state interests in excluding migrants from the citizenry and the polity and state interests in including migrants in the market. Socio-legal scholars have argued that the particular *legal form* such expressions take has wide-ranging social consequences. For example, against the popular view that the law simply expresses popular antipathy towards immigrants found in the wider 'society', Calavita argues on the basis of extensive sociological research among Spanish immigration officials and immigrants that immigration law constructs migrants as outlaws and hence produces popular antipathy towards them.[70] Calavita points out that in the context of the New Europe, in which the

---

[68] Kimberly Coles, 'Ambivalent Builders: Europeanization, the Production of Difference, and Internationals in Bosnia-Herzegovina', (2002) 25 *Political and Legal Anthropology Review* 1–18.

[69] Eve Darian-Smith and Peter Fitzpatrick, *Laws of the Postcolonial* (1999).

[70] Kitty Calvita, 'Immigration, Law and Marginalization in a Global Economy: Notes from Spain', (1998) 32 *Law and Society Review* 529–66.

boundaries of the state now extend to include much of Western Europe, social marginalization does not necessarily map onto foreignness in simple terms. Rather, people turn to the law to define marginality, and the law maps particular identities of illegality onto particular persons 'based on the person's location in the global economy'.[71]

Socio-legal studies of the disparate effects of free trade regimes likewise show how integration in some spheres produces further differences in other spheres, or along other axes. For example, Ruth Buchanan's study of the effects of NAFTA on immigration and labour relations on the border between the United States and Mexico shows how reconfigurations of state sovereignty through international agreements, and the mundane harmonization of environmental, labour, shipping, packaging, and other laws they demand, as well as immigration policy, generates new differences—new forms of gender inequality, militarization of borders, and spatial divisions of labour. Susan Coutin, Bill Maurer, and Barbara Yngvesson have compared the regulatory practices in the global financial markets, global adoption markets, and immigration regimes (three areas where the individual authors had conducted extensive fieldwork) to propose a focus on regulation as the 'legitimation work of globalization'—that is, the work of delineating acceptable cross-border flows (of money, labourers, or babies, for example) from unacceptable ones. Their work points to the large jurisprudential and political questions at stake in such seemingly mundane regulatory practices as 'issuing and denying documents, sealing and opening records, regulating and criminalizing transactions, and repudiating and claiming countries and persons'.[72] All of these questions demand a careful and sophisticated understanding of the different regulatory regimes of different jurisdictions, and the different ways states accommodate or respond to globalization through law. From the socio-legal side, then, there are plenty of reasons to engage with comparative law. I now turn to some current topics in comparative law where the converse is just as true.

4. New Debates about Legal Pluralism

The questions discussed in the previous section have parallels in the resurgence of interest among comparative lawyers in legal pluralism. As mentioned above, some comparative lawyers have long had an interest in legal pluralism. However, recently comparative lawyers and socio-legal scholars have extended the concept to legal relations in Euro-American societies. Sally Merry's study of disputing in American society has shown that different communities and classes live with

---

[71] Ibid 560.
[72] Susan B. Coutin, Bill Maurer, and Barbara Yngvesson, 'In the Mirror: The Legitimation Work of Globalization', (2002) 27 *Law and Social Inquiry*, 801–43, at 804.

different normative regimes and actively navigate the institutions in which those regimes overlap.[73] Comparative lawyers have seized upon the concept as a tool for grasping the character of law under conditions of globalization. Specifically, legal pluralism seems to offer a way of describing globalized legal forms that is more subtle and accurate than traditional understandings of state legal regimes arranged within an international economic and public legal order. Boaventura de Sousa Santos, for example, has argued that 'a legal field is a constellation of different legalities (and illegalities) operating in local, national, and global time-spaces',[74] and has proposed that comparative lawyers focus on 'the intersubjective or phenomenological dimensions of legal pluralism I call interlegality'.[75] André-Jean Arnaud likewise has deployed the concept of legal pluralism to understand the character of European legal thought under conditions of postmodernity and globalization.[76]

One consequence of this work is that it demands that comparative lawyers rethink what comparison itself entails. A simple comparison of 'French Law' with 'American Law', for example, seems inadequate if one accepts that 'French Law' is actually many coexisting, fragmented, sometimes integrated, sometimes conflicting normative orders with different degrees of access to coercive authority and with different kinds of articulations with other cultures and with the global legal arena. Gunther Teubner, for example, has argued that the crucial legal differences in the contemporary world—the kinds of differences that presumably should lie at the heart of the comparative legal enterprise—are not those differences between systems of law delineated by state sovereignty (eg the difference between the law of France and of Germany) but rather between the legal orders attached to particular economic sectors (eg the private arbitration system for adjudicating disputes in the shipping industry versus the state-based judicial system for regulating drug cartels). From the point of view of this model of 'polycentric globalization', comparative lawyers should study these differences among sectoral legal systems, and also trace the interconnections between them, and they should do so without presuming, as in the old legal pluralism debates, that these systems are arranged in any given hierarchy (in which state law is the politically dominant and also more complex form of law).

In sum, the debate over state versus non-state law raises the question of the scope of law, that is, the breadth of phenomena we might want to catch within our subject. Santos, for example, argues for a broad understanding. Following the legal pluralist dogma, he suggests that we look beyond the regulation of State–citizen

---

[73] Sally Engle Merry, 'Legal Pluralism', (1988) 22 *Law and Society Review* 869–96; Sally Engle Merry, *Getting Justice and Getting Even: Legal Consciousness among Working-class Americans* (1990).

[74] Boaventura de Sousa Santos, *Toward a New Legal Common Sense: Law, Globalization, and Emancipation* (2002).

[75] Ibid at 97.

[76] André-Jean Arnaud, *Entre modernité et mondialisation: leçons d'histoire de la philosophie du droit et de l'état* (2004).

relations to relations within other institutions (the household, the workplace, even the global setting). But a broad and innovative interpretation of the scope of law can bely a quite traditional understanding of the character of that law, independent of its scope. For all its postmodern trappings, Santos's understanding of law is functionalist in a conventional sense: law for him is a set of (diverse and plural) regimes that serve the function of ordering social relations.

5. Legal Transplants

But the flashpoint for comparative law's engagement with Law and Society in recent years has been the debate about 'legal transplants', or the process of transmission of legal knowledge, practices, and institutions from one society or jurisdiction to another. Because this debate is the subject of another chapter in this volume, I will not summarize it here. Rather I wish to focus on only one issue, that of the status of 'society' and, hence, of socio-legal studies, in the transplant hypothesis.

In his original thesis about legal transplants, Alan Watson attacked the relevance of Law and Society scholarship to comparative law.[77] His argument, as elaborated in his own work and the work of William Ewald, suggests that legal reform takes place independently of social forces.[78] From this perspective, there is no need to inquire into the character of society or social change since the law is not a reflection of society. Watson and Ewald dismissed what they termed the 'mirror theory' of Law and Society in which, they argued, socio-legal scholars imagine law as simply a mirror of social conditions. It is important to recognize that Watson and Ewald were responding here to an equally absolutist claim on the part of some socio-legal scholars and comparative lawyers that law is a pure artifact of society and hence that legal differences should be studied purely from an 'external' perspective.[79]

Implicitly or explicitly, this debate about the relative autonomy of law from the social occurs in the long shadow cast by Weber over comparative law and socio-legal studies. And as usual, Weber's own text provides more than enough fodder for both sides. Weber's insistence, as against Marx, that the development of what he terms 'legal and formalistic perfection' has a certain autonomy that seems to support Watson's thesis:

Capitalistic interests have in turn undoubtedly also helped, but by no means alone nor even principally, to prepare the way for the predominance in law and administration of a class

---

[77] Alan Watson, *Legal Transplants: An Approach to Comparative Law* (1993).

[78] See William Ewald, 'Comparative Jurisprudence (II): The Logic of Legal Transplants', (1995) 43 *AJCL* 489–510. See also David Nelken, 'Towards a Sociology of Legal Adaptation', in David Nelken and Johannes Feest (eds), *Adapting Legal Cultures* (2001), 7–54.

[79] See Lawrence Friedman, *The Legal System: A Social Science Perspective* (1975).

of jurists specially trained in rational law. But these interests did not in themselves create that law.[80]

And yet Weber then turns around and describes this very autonomy as itself a product of Western 'culture' in the broadest sense:

For in all the above cases it is a question of the specific and peculiar rationalism of Western culture. . . . There is, for example, rationalization of mystical contemplation, that is of an attitude which, viewed from other departments of life, is specifically irrational, just as much as there are rationalizations of economic life, of technique, of scientific research, of military training, of law and administration. . . . Hence rationalizations of the most varied character have existed in various departments of life and in all areas of culture. . . . It is hence our first concern to work out and to explain genetically the special peculiarity of Occidental rationalism, and within this field, that of the modern Occidental form.[81]

In response to this first generation of starkly opposed and fairly extreme arguments, a number of comparative lawyers and socio-legal scholars produced more sophisticated and fine-grained accounts of the social dimensions of legal transnationalism and also of the impact of transnational legal influences on the character of local cultural and social life. Today, the consensus in both comparative law and socio-legal studies is that the division of the world into 'law' and 'society' has outlived its analytical utility.[82] A number of sophisticated comparative and socio-legal studies recently have begun to challenge the social determinist paradigm to suggest that legal knowledge is not just a by-product of social forces; that it is also a shaper of social forces. Understanding law as its own agent however demands a more subtle understanding of how aspects of law interact with one another and with other forms of knowledge than the crude 'transplant' metaphor allows. Gunther Teubner for example agrees with Watson that 'legal discourse is not an expression of society and culture tout court' although he also points out that transplants (which he prefers to term 'irritants') do not simply enter a new legal system as whole entities but rather set in motion a long and turbulent set of reactions within the host legal system that both reshape the host legal system and the transplanted law.[83]

6. Legal Culture

Comparative lawyers have also engaged socio-legal scholars around the question of the nature of 'legal culture'. Some comparative lawyers have treated culture as an

---

[80] Weber (n 24), at xxxviii.   [81] Ibid at xxxviii–xxxix.

[82] See Riles, (1994) *University of Illinois LR* 597–650.

[83] Gunther Teubner, 'Legal Irritants: Good Faith in British Law or How Unifying Law Ends Up in New Divergences', (1998) 61 *Modern LR* 11–32.

explanatory tool—they have explained differences among legal systems in terms of differences of 'legal culture'.[84] These scholars have made an important contribution to comparative legal theory and methodology by dislodging functionalist, instrumentalist understandings of law prevalent both in empirical social science and in technocratic projects, and by emphasizing instead a highly contextual, interpretive approach. More specifically, the cultural approach replaces instrumentalism and functionalism with a focus on meaning, as determined by context, and with a hermeneutic methodology. Perhaps because of the dominance of functionalism in an earlier generation of socio-legal studies, comparative lawyers who invoke the concept of legal culture tend to draw their methodological inspiration more from the humanities and from literary and linguistic theory than from anthropological and sociological debates about culture within the Law and Society movement.

More recently, the status of legal culture has become particularly prescient in the above-mentioned debate about legal transplants. Pierre Legrand borrows from literary and linguistic theory on the one hand and from Marcel Mauss's anthropological concept of the gift as a 'total social fact' on the other to argue that the very notion of a legal transplant is predicated on a formalistic understanding of law as a set of rules. This formalistic view of law and of legal transplants, Legrand argues, ignores the way law is given meaning by the context in which it is read. From this standpoint, a transplanted rule is no longer the same rule once it is embedded in a new context of meanings. 'A rule does not have any empirical existence that can be significantly detached from the world of meanings that defines a legal culture; the part is a synthesis and expression of the whole: it resonates'.[85]

Because of the implications of Legrand's critique for the now hotly debated topic of legal harmonization in Europe, Legrand's thesis about legal culture has been subjected to considerable caricature—by Legrand's critics, but also in my view by Legrand himself in his own rush to stake out a clear and singular position in the harmonization debate.[86] In its less dogmatic versions, Legrand's thesis adds a number of sophisticated angles to comparative legal theory. For example, he borrows from Gilles Deleuze to understand transplants as acts of repetition, as enunciations, acts of iteration 'conditioned by a particular epistemological

[84] Lawrence M. Friedman, 'Legal Culture and Social Development', (1969) 4 *Law and Society Review* 29–44; Henry Walter Ehrmann, *Comparative Legal Cultures* (1976). Mitchel de S. O. l'E. Lasser, *Judicial Deliberations: A Comparative Analysis of Judicial Transparency and Legitimacy* (2004); John Bell, *French Legal Cultures* (2001).

[85] Pierre Legrand, 'What "Legal Transplants"?', in David Nelken and Johannes Feest (eds), *Adapting Legal Cultures*, (2001), 55–70.

[86] There seems to be a contradiction, in particular, between Legrand's claim that legal transplants are impossible because of the robust character of cultural context on the one hand, and his claim that the harmonization of European law would destroy cultural difference on the other.

framework, by a specific mentalité'.[87] Others have built upon these insights, soften-
ing, qualifying and specifying where necessary. For example, Maximo Langer draws
on a similar cultural understanding of law as a system of meanings to propose that
we speak of 'legal translation' rather than legal transplants.[88]

However, as numerous comparative lawyers have observed, there are profound
problems with the cultural argument in its strong form. Indeed, one can take these
problems as indicative of the need for those working in this tradition to engage
more actively with sophisticated empirical studies of legal culture now prevalent
in socio-legal studies. First, to the extent that these culturalists invoke anthropology, they seriously mischaracterize contemporary anthropological claims about
culture. Legrand's appeal to Marcel Mauss's understanding of the 'total social fact',
or rich legal, economic, and moral events rolled into one which could not be
understood outside the particular social relations that constituted them, as a
description of each state's law, for example,[89] neglects to mention that Mauss
explicitly argued that such an understanding of transactions did not apply to
modern capitalist societies. Indeed, the point of Mauss's argument was to pose a
contrast between traditional pre-capitalist societies, in which persons were not
distinct from things and transactions were total social facts on the one hand,
and modern capitalist societies in which individuals possess things and legal
transactions became divisible from social relations on the other.

More importantly, to the extent that comparatists treat legal 'meanings' as
straightforward derivations of holistic cultural contexts, they argue for a view of
culture that has been soundly rejected in anthropology for at least twenty-five
years.[90] As Patrick Glenn has usefully detailed,[91] anthropologists since the 1960s
universally reject a concept of culture as an integrated, totalizing whole. This
totalizing understanding of culture fails to take into account the role of individual
actors in generating meanings and, in particular, fails to account for conflicting
understandings and views within every culture. It treats cultures as hermetically

[87] Ibid 65.
[88] Maximo Langer, 'From Legal Transplants to Legal Translations: The Globalization of Plea-
Bargaining and the Americanization Thesis in Criminal Procedure', (2004) 45 *Harvard International
LJ* 1–64.
[89] Marcel Mauss, *The Gift* (1990).
[90] John Bell's definition of legal culture, for example, tellingly cites to anthropological writings
from the 1950s that would not find a place in contemporary anthropological debates. Bell, (n 84), at 2
(citing Kroeber and Kluckholn's 1952 definition of culture).
[91] H. Patrick Glenn, 'Legal Cultures and Legal Traditions', in Mark van Hoecke (ed), *Epistemology
and Methodology of Comparative Law* (2004), 7–20. Glenn and others' proposal to replace 'culture'
with 'tradition' however raises further questions. The anthropologist Laura Nader points out that it is
precisely the association of culture with heritage, and in particular the impermeability of 'heritage' to
ideas of conflict and change, that is the problem with culture in the first place. Nader proposes the
exact opposite—a notion of culture that considers its hegemonic and counter-hegemonic pro-
pensities, its qualities as 'travelling ideologies' in a world that is 'always only partly integrated or
coherent or in effect only partly shared'. Laura Nader, 'Controlling Processes: Tracing the Dynamic
Components of Power', (1997) 38 *Current Anthropology* 711–37, at 721–3.

sealed units rather than pluralistic, intersecting, hybrid entities. And it fails to give sufficient attention to questions of hierarchy and power in the constitution of cultural meanings.[92]

This does not mean that socio-legal scholars would endorse either a purely doctrinal analysis or a purely instrumentalist or functionalist comparative law. Indeed, part of the problem with the culture concept in comparative law seems to rest with the limited range of methodological options on the table—to exaggerate slightly, too often it seems that either one is a culturalist, a doctrinalist, or a functionalist in comparative legal circles. Rather than choose between culturalist and rationalist explanations, socio-legal scholars would maintain that we need a more fine-tuned, specific, sceptical, and open-ended understanding of cultural practices, including a recognition that many such practices are not necessarily 'local' and not necessarily opposed to legal transplants or legal harmonization, as some advocates of a cultural approach to comparative law seem to assume.

VII. Consensus Items: Stepping Outside Weber's Shadow

As we have seen, comparative lawyers and socio-legal scholars now share a series of political, theoretical, and methodological agendas, as well as a new constellation of subjects of study and debate. Today, the divide between comparative law and socio-legal studies on topics of common interest is perhaps more a matter of relative emphasis than of basic ideology. As William Twining puts it, the differences between himself as a comparative lawyer and the sociologist Boaventura de Sousa Santos on the character of globalization are simply a matter of 'different starting points and concerns'.[93] At this stage, it is possible to identify a series of positions and conclusions that by and large garner consensus in both fields. In this section, I want to propose that we put debate about the following topics finally to rest.

1. A Transnational Focus is Indispensable

The reconfiguration of both fields around the transnational character of even the most local of regulatory practices, and the emerging consensus in both fields about

---

[92] Sally Engle Merry, 'Human Rights Law and the Demonization of Culture (and Anthropology Along the Way)', (2003) 26 *Political and Legal Anthropology Review* 55–76.

[93] William Twining, *Globalisation and Legal Theory* (2000), at 197.

the importance of studying new forms of legal orthodoxy and their local consequences provides ample space for dialogue. For comparative lawyers, this means that the debate over whether transnational phenomena should 'count' as a subject of comparative law, or whether comparative law can only include the comparison of two or more national legal systems should be regarded as closed. As Gunther Teubner points out, global law has its own qualities—it is not just an underdeveloped by-product of national law—and hence it deserves the kind of careful description that is the hallmark of comparative analysis. The descriptive treatment comparative lawyers will give such phenomena will be entirely different in character from the normative and doctrinal arguments of international lawyers and hence there is little need for concern about losing our disciplinary distinctiveness by expanding our subject-matter.

2. The Stark Distinction between Law and Society has Outlived its Utility

As we saw, empirical studies of the actual agents of legal transplants, their motivations, and their influence on the ultimate character of transplanted law exposed the false choice between 'social' and 'legal' explanations of legal change, since describing the actions of elite actors as either 'legal' or 'social' seemed to illuminate little. For comparative lawyers, one implication is that we need to set aside once and for all the insistence that the subject of study should be limited to normative orders backed by the coercive sanction of the nation-state, in the Weberian mold. As Teubner points out, much law-making takes place without the threat of state-backed coercion,[94] and as Dezalay and Garth show, global legal actors take this fact for granted as a starting assumption about their own legal field.[95] The notion of law as a coercive system of social control is equally problematic in the social sciences. As Laura Nader points out, the focus on law as a system of social control has dubious roots in efforts to enlist the social sciences in subduing social unrest.[96] From another point of view, the anthropologist Marilyn Strathern demonstrated a generation ago that focusing on social control obscures normative practices that do not begin from the standpoint of a central 'problem' of coercing and controlling individual behaviour.[97] This is not to suggest that the State is not important, or that comparative lawyers should ignore state-based law, but rather that the debate should shift from the question of whether to include non-state-based normative orders within the purview of comparative

---

94 Gunther Teubner, *Global Law without a State* (1997).
95 Dezalay and Garth, *Dealing in Virtue* (n 59).
96 Nader, (1997) 38 *Current Anthropology* 711–37, at 721–3.
97 Marilyn Strathern, 'Discovering "Social Control" ', (1985) 12 *Journal of Law and Society* 111–34.

law to understanding the character of such orders and their interaction with state-based regimes.

Another implication of the increasingly obsolete character of the distinction between law and society is that the distinction between 'insider' and 'outsider' perspectives that once defined the difference between comparative lawyers and socio-legal scholars no longer adequately characterizes the disciplinary divide. The division between participating in Rule of Law projects and observing or critiquing such projects, for example, is far too crude in a context in which the same scholars who engage in such projects also produce some of the most thoughtful critiques of them, and in which bureaucrats routinely appropriate 'objective' social science research in the service of their own ends. Comparative lawyers and socio-legal scholars increasingly understand that they are both insiders and outsiders, both participants and critics, at once.

Once we put this simple dichotomy behind us, a number of other intriguing questions come to the fore. For example, the sociologist John Hagan and legal scholar Ron Levi have taken Weber's argument that state law is norm backed by coercion as a starting-point for investigating how law comes to have coercive backing. Taking the development of international criminal law as a case study, they conducted extensive empirical research at the International Criminal Tribunal for the Former Yugoslavia to trace the precise social and material processes by which a court that began with relatively little authority to enforce its judgments came, over time, to command far greater coercive authority.[98]

3. The Distinction between Normative and Descriptive Argument is also No Longer a Fruitful Way of Delineating Disciplinary Boundaries

As we saw, following in the tradition of Weber's separation of fact from value, there was once a time when comparative lawyers distinguished their work from social science by arguing that their work was normative while the latter was empirical. But the incorporation of empirical research into mainstream legal studies has rendered this position increasingly untenable. Moreover, there is growing appreciation in comparative legal circles of our discipline's unique role in producing high quality descriptions of legal phenomena, whether or not these lead directly to policy recommendations or normative claims. From the other side, also, the advent of more reflexive and normative approaches to empirical research has made it a common place in most sectors of both comparative law and socio-legal

---

[98] J. Hagan and R. Levi, 'Crimes of War and the Force of Law', (2005) 83 *Social Forces* 1499–534.

research that all empirical description is, and indeed should be, also normative—an intervention in debates, not just a distanced observation.

Related to this, it is now generally agreed that we need not choose between 'theoretical' and 'empirical' work. Although Law and Society scholars have long shown some antipathy towards 'theory' and comparative lawyers have shown some antipathy towards empiricism, there is consensus now that scholarship in both fields needs to be both theoretically informed and empirically grounded—and that different mixes of these two elements should be encouraged and appreciated.

4. The Transplant Concept, at least in its Strong Form, is Too Crude

As we saw, it is widely accepted by both comparative lawyers and socio-legal scholars that legal arguments, actors, and institutions have some degree of agency and autonomy in the process of diffusion of legal practices, although Watson's own claims for the complete autonomy of law strike most scholars in both disciplines as overdrawn. Again, the interesting question then becomes what alternatives might better describe practices of transnational borrowing.

5. The Culture Concept, at least in its Strong Form, is also Too Crude

As we saw, a fourth legacy of the Weberian tradition in comparative law is the argument from culture—the claim that differences between legal systems are attributable to the character of the cultures in which the legal systems are situated, where, as with Weber, culture is defined in general and quite totalizing terms. Yet we are now at a point at which such generalized definitions of culture seem increasingly implausible and even theoretically suspect. The interesting question then becomes what alternative categories, questions, and approaches might occupy the same intellectual field.

In a brilliant essay on this topic, the comparatist Takao Tanase responds to an endless and sometimes tedious debate in Japanese legal studies on this point—a debate again framed by Weberian typologies, about the extent to which differences in Japanese culture account for unique aspects of Japanese law. In this debate, most American comparatists of Japanese law have rejected culturalist arguments and have sought to portray Japanese as 'rational'—in other words, following implicitly from Weber, they have treated rationality as the opposite of cultural difference. Tanase points out that these American scholars' arguments that the myth of Japanese cultural uniqueness is a kind of 'invented tradition'—an invention of the nineteenth-century Meiji government for its own ideological purposes—are hardly new; rather, these arguments were put forward by Japanese scholars themselves in the 1950s. However, Tanase wants to move beyond either defending Japanese cultural uniqueness, or attacking culturalist arguments with equally absolute claims about Japanese 'rationality', to consider why the 'culture question' is so profoundly fascinating to Japanese and foreign legal scholars alike.

Tanase diagnoses the obsession with Japanese legal culture in terms of the politics of legal modernization and its cognitive and emotional impact on the citizenry of modernizing states. Japanese citizens—like all citizens of modernizing states, he argues—live with profound self-doubt about whether, after all the modernizing effort, they truly are 'modern'. But this phenomenon is not 'cultural' (in the sense of something 'outside' of law): rather, he traces Japanese self-doubt to the way 'law talk' is 'loaded with the power of rationality, universality and the future while indigenous culture is declared irrational, parochial and backward'. And yet, through a strange twist, 'modernization, and law's reception as well, needs a simultaneous denial and affirmation of the society, which again necessitates the rhetoric of culture to construct an image of society for public consumption'. Culture, then, in Tanase's analysis, is an effect of law—or more precisely of law's own claims to rationality. Hence the debate about whether the Japanese are 'rational' or 'cultural' is more symptomatic of the enduring effects of the Weberian ideology than interesting as an empirical question.[99]

Interestingly, Tanase does not argue that this means that legal transplants are impossible. On the contrary, he points out, the law thrives on claims about the 'absence of the modern . . . The judiciary, legal professors, and even bureaucrats in Japan consciously or unconsciously exploit this authority of the modern to enhance their legitimacy.'[100] Yet his analysis does draw attention to an aspect of legal transplants that goes unrecognized in most comparative legal analysis— the cognitive or emotional toll of legal transplants, and associated ideologies of legal modernization that, in his view, constitute a culture of self-doubt, condemned to continually asking questions about one's 'culture'. Tanase's response to the question of what might come after cultural analysis is framed in terms of a very particular set of theoretical and political concerns. The next methodological task is surely to develop and gather together a broader diversity of alternative projects of this kind. In the section that follows, I want to conclude by describing one emerging body of work that seems particularly promising.

---

[99] Takao Tanase, 'The Empty Space of the Modern in Japanese Law', in David Nelken and Johannes Feest (eds), *Adapting Legal Cultures* (2001), 187–98.

[100] Ibid 196.

VIII. EMERGING WORK ON LEGAL KNOWLEDGE: RECLAIMING THE WEBERIAN TRADITION

In the previous section we considered some of the divisions and debates, often framed by the long shadow of Weberian thought, that have too long impeded conversation between comparative lawyers and socio-legal scholars. But at this stage we must ask, what is it about Weber that continues to inspire? Surely there is far more to the project than the typologies and evolutionary trajectories, the divisions of law and custom, the carelessness about the legal facts of non-Western legal systems—we need to account for our own fascination with Weber's text.

For Lawrence Friedman, it is Weber's focus on the 'overt use of reasoning processes'[101] that continues to inspire. Friedman points out that legal reasoning is all-too-little appreciated, as a serious topic of inquiry, in socio-legal studies:

Legalism, as a social phenomenon, has been more excoriated than studied. Indeed, neglect has been the destiny of legal reasoning generally, at least from the sociological standpoint. The great exception is found in the work of Max Weber. Weber studied and analyzed systems of legal reasoning and legal thought with particular emphasis on the relationship between types of legal reasoning and economic systems [citations omitted].[102]

As the Weber Scholar Rogers Brubaker notes, 'Weber was not, of course, the first to stress the unique rationality of the modern Western social order'. Writers from Montesquieu to Kant to Simmel had made similar claims. What differentiates Weber's account, however, is Weber's own ambivalence toward this rationality— his fascination with what it enables as well as his appreciation of its dark sides— and it is this ambivalence that continues to render Weber's work so 'challenging and evocative today'.[103] Tim Murphy likewise highlights scepticism as a tenet of the Weberian tradition: 'Modern law simultaneously enjoys a triumph ideologically and is exhausted epistemically. . . . Weber called this the loss of the "metaphysical dignity" of the law, so that in "the great majority of its most important provisions, it has been unmasked all too visibly . . . as the product or the technical means of a compromise between conflicting interests" (E & S 875).'[104]

I agree with Friedman: what is so useful for comparatists about Weber's discussion of law is his tackling of a subject almost entirely ignored in the social sciences—the technical quality of legal knowledge, as distinct from legal norms, legal processes, legal institutions, actors, or even legal language, the more traditional

---

[101] Friedman, (1966) *Wisconsin LR* 148, at 160.   [102] Ibid 149.

[103] Rogers Brubaker, *The Limits of Rationality: An Essay on the Social and Moral Thought of Max Weber* (1984), at 31

[104] Murphy (n 16), citing Weber *et al.* (n 14).

socio-legal subjects. But what remains delightfully fresh about Weber's treatment of the technical nature of modern legal reasoning is that it differs entirely from the kind of treatment a lawyer might give the subject—it is not an inquiry into the nature of particular rules or of the evolution of particular kinds of doctrines, nor is it even, as with Maine, a study of particular legal devices such as equity or the legal fiction. What Weber manages to do is to give us a sceptical cultural account of legal knowledge that remains internal to the culture of legal knowledge itself—that does not reduce legal knowledge to elements outside the law such as society, politics, or culture. Weber's work points to how, rather than treating 'law' and 'society' as distinct spheres of inquiry each with their own methods (legal, sociological), it is possible to understand legal activity in socio-legal terms as a realm of social and cultural practice in its own right. Indeed, a considerable body of exciting work at the intersection of comparative law and socio-legal studies is doing just this.[105] I now want to describe the gradual development of this line of work on the character of legal knowledge as an extension of Weber's own interest in the reflexive quality of legal knowledge.

As Rogers Brubaker notes, Weber's argument is that in the modern world, knowledge becomes increasingly important: 'the rise of systematic empirical science and of scientific technology gives knowledge an importance above and beyond its universal significance as a basis for individual rational action'. But what is most surprising in Weber's account is the way this valuing of knowledge in turn leads to a kind of turning of this knowledge on itself: 'Another aspect of intellectualization is the increasing tendency for individuals to act on the basis of conscious reflection about the probable consequences of their action'.[106] Indeed, it is precisely this self-reflexivity that enables the means–ends calculations of instrumental rationality. Murphy adds that self-reflexivity characterized Weber's own intellectual project as he made of his method, rationality, a subject of inquiry (rationality in the modern world): 'For Weber, then, what was, historically, the foundation of critique—rationality—slipped over into being the principal form of closure against which critique had to be directed'.[107]

The development of a new line of comparative and socio-legal work that builds on this reflexive aspect of the Weberian tradition begins with legal pluralism (see Fig 24.1, p 813). As we saw, legal pluralism provided an early point of dialogue between comparative lawyers and socio-legal scholars because it made room for

---

[105] See Bryant Garth, 'Comparative Law and the Legal Profession—Notes toward a Reorientation of Research', in John J. Barcelo and Roger C. Cramton (eds), *Lawyers' Practice and Ideals: A Comparative View* (1999), 227–40; Annelise Riles, 'Law as Object', in Sally Merry and Don Brenneis (eds), *Legal Legacies, Current Crises: Fiji and Hawaii* (2003); Annelise Riles, 'Property as Legal Knowledge: Means and Ends', (2004) 10 *Journal of the Royal Anthropological Institute* (NS) 775–95; Annelise Riles, *Documents: Artifacts of Modern Knowledge* (2006); Eric A. Feldman, *The Ritual of Rights in Japan: Law, Society, and Health Policy* (2000).

[106] Brubaker (n 103), at 3.   [107] Murphy (n 16), at 50.

each of their respective areas of expertise: both state law and customary law deserved exploration. However, as we saw, this project soon foundered on growing concerns about the inauthenticity of the customs comparatists were discovering. This realization about the inauthenticity of custom, and about the complicity of socio-legal scholars and comparative lawyers in its construction and institutional elaboration, was important not simply because of its practical consequences or because of the necessity to rectify false empirical claims. Rather, this debate in retrospect marks the beginning of an epistemological shift in comparative law methodology that continues to have profound consequences. What comparative lawyers active in customary law reform projects realized was that they were part of the story—that the object, customary law, and the nature of the difference between the two 'jurisdictions' compared (state law and customary law) was in a real, practical, and concrete way an effect of their own knowledge. It is no wonder, therefore, that so many of the discipline's most sophisticated theorizers of epistemological questions—William Twining,[108] Peter Fitzpatrick,[109] Masaji Chiba, for example—got their start in the legal pluralism debates.

This self-reflexive critique fed into wider currents in social, political, and legal thought of the time, from the same kinds of crisis of confidence in law and development projects to the loss of faith among many intellectuals in Marxist paradigms, to the rise of interest in the sociology and anthropology of knowledge and of new arguments in social theory that foregrounded questions of knowledge.[110] By the 1990s, a number of scholars had begun to look for a way to say something more about what they had learned from their own unwitting implication in legal practices they had sought only to critique or describe. How could one tell a more complicated story about how legal initiatives like law and development go 'wrong'—an account that would recognize that the errors of legal pluralism or law and development were the product of something far more subtle than simple bad faith on the part of policy-makers or their status as agents of colonial or capitalist power? It is in this context that legal knowledge emerges as a subject in its own right. In a parallel sense to sociological work on so-called 'cultures of expertise' in the sciences and technological fields, it began to seem worthwhile to inquire into the culture of expert legal knowledge to see what implicit assumptions, what social mores, what institutional constraints, what hierarchies accounted for how common sense was constructed there.

This work began by importing traditional sociological techniques into the study of elite legal knowledge. Chief among these was the notion that everything one took for granted about the way law worked should be open for empirical questioning. Take, for example, the definition of law. In their work discussed above, Yves

---

[108] See William L. Twining, *Globalisation and Legal Theory* (2001).
[109] See Peter Fitzpatrick, *The Mythology of Modern Law* (1992).
[110] Michel Foucault, *The Order of Things* (1970).

Dezalay and Bryant Garth treat law not as a set of institutions with functions but as a social field—an arena of action that is constructed and given legitimacy as a result of the competitive acts of particular individuals and groups. Arbitration, for example, is 'law' in their analysis to the extent that social actors, for their own reasons and in pursuit of their own strategies, manage to imbue it with legal attributes, that is, to convince disputing parties to 'invest' in granting this field the kind of legitimacy ordinarily reserved for state law. In this approach, the definition of law is a matter for the actors to decide, not an a priori analytical question.

In this work, therefore, the technicalities of law that so fascinated Weber re-emerge as a legitimate subject of empirical investigation: socio-legal studies is no longer confined solely to the 'trenches'—it takes on the 'towers'. Moreover, there is a marked reflexivity in the work of scholars like Garth and Dezalay: having learned the lessons of earlier débâcles, they are quite aware that sociologists and comparative lawyers are part of the story—that their own work is not just describing the field of international arbitration they write about, but helping to legitimize it. But the sociological hook of these sociological studies of cultures of legal expertise is that they find something akin to the social in the towers of modern law: For Garth and Dezalay, for example, legal knowledge is never interesting for its own sake, as it was for Weber. It is interesting only as a function of social forces—power politics, competition between different individuals and groups, social hierarchies within legal institutions.

Building on this first generation of work, more recent comparative work has sought to describe legal knowledge as something more, or other, than a function of social forces. The first of these, epitomized by the work of Gunther Teubner, treats law as a form of self-reflexive communication feedback. Teubner shares with Dezalay and Garth a view of law as what legal actors say it is. However, building on the sociology of Nicholas Luhmann, he treats law as a 'discourse' rather than an instrument of individual strategy—a realm of communication and description of a particular form: 'the idiosyncrasies of the profession seem to be to be a secondary phenomenon. It is the inner logics of the legal discourse itself that build on normative self-reference and recursivity and thus create a preference for internal transfer within the global legal system'.[111] Teubner's work brings even greater attention than the sociology of legal experts to the 'reflexive' character of legal systems—to their capacity for building their own autonomy by observing and commenting on themselves (as in legal debates about legal process, for example). Van Hoecke's 'communicative' theory of comparative law builds on the same understanding but from a Habermasian point of view.[112]

If Teubner begins from the standpoint of legal theory, another body of work describes the inner workings of legal knowledge from the standpoint of theoretical

[111] Teubner, (1998) 61 *Modern LR* 11, 16.
[112] Mark van Hoecke, *Law as Communication* (2002).

arguments drawn from the social studies of science and technology.[113] Building on his work on the construction of scientific facts within laboratories, the sociologist of science Bruno Latour has sought to compare scientific fact-making with legal fact-making by engaging in an extensive empirical study of the French Conseil D'Etat.[114] Like Teubner, Latour treats the law as a 'mode of enunciation' but he is interested in the material quality of this law-making—the mundane accumulation and circulation of documents, of drafts, of reports it takes to produce a judgment. His interest is in how complex social facts become calculable as a legal dispute through this internal process of producing chains of 'inscriptions': 'For both law-yers and scientists, it is possible to speak confidently about the world only once it has been transformed—whether by the word of God, a mathematical code, a play of instruments, a host of predecessors, or by a natural or positive law'.[115] Here again, legal knowledge and the process by which it comes to frame political, social, and epistemological conflicts is a central subject in its own right. Latour and colleagues describe legal knowledge as a phenomenon that is not simply reducible to social pressures and forces but has its own epistemological and material autonomy.

One way of thinking about this is to suggest that legal knowledge, far from just working 'on' social, political, or economic phenomena, or being shaped by them, actually serves to constitute these phenomena by providing the cognitive frames through which social actors, including legal and social scientific observers, apprehend social realities. In this respect, one particularly interesting conversation is emerging in diverse pockets of comparative law and socio-legal studies around the question of the *agency of legal form*: This work draws attention to the way legal categories function as constraints that shape actors' choices and even enable certain kinds of legal subjectivity. In this respect, we can speak of legal categories and techniques as *generative* of certain kinds of social, political, and epistemological realities.

The emerging interest in the agency of legal form takes up the critique of social determinism underlying the transplant thesis and reformulates it in more subtle and precise terms. As Geoffrey Samuel puts it, 'What is . . . interesting for the comparatist is the extent to which models of traditional legal concepts act as schemes for constructing the objects of legal science'. He gives the example of categories such as 'person', 'damage', 'thing', and 'fault' which the law treats as facts, and which social actors treat as social categories, but which are actually legal

---

[113] See Mariana Valverde, *Law's Dream of a Common Knowledge* (2003). R. Levi and M. Valverde, 'Knowledge on Tap: Police Science and Common Knowledge in the Legal Regulation of Drunkenness', (2001) 26 *Law and Social Inquiry* 819–46; Mariana Valverde, 'Authorizing the Production of Urban Moral Order: Appellate Courts and their Knowledge Games', (2005) 39 *Law and Society Review* 419–55; Susan S. Silbey, 'After Legal Consciousness', (2005) 1 *Annual Review of Law and Social Science* 323–68.

[114] Bruno Latour, *La fabrique du droit: Une ethnographie du conseil d'état* (2002).

[115] Ibid 96.

categories. Samuel terms these categories 'virtual facts' because 'they are factual modes which transcend actual factual reality. Some kinds of damage may not amount to 'damage', while some types of things may not amount to a 'thing'. In sum,

The idea that legal science is a discourse that has its object in actual factual situations is to misunderstand, fundamentally, legal thought . . . [Law] functions as much within the world of fact as within the world of law and it is this dual role that endows it with its capacity to create virtual facts. Lawyers, like scientists, do not work directly on reality but construct rationalized models of this reality, and it is these models that become the 'objects' of legal discourse.[116]

This focus in turn has engendered a new dialogue between comparative lawyers and socio-legal scholars about the global proliferation of neoliberal legal forms and the local responses they generate. A number of new empirical studies of the cultures of law and development, for example, have exposed some of the assumptions of law and development workers and contradictions in their ambitions. My ethnographic account of global issue networks, for example,[117] contradicts the enthusiastic claims made on behalf of such networks in the legal and political science literature.[118] Likewise, Bill Maurer's study of global due diligence regimes ostensibly intended to combat fraud in the global financial markets details how such regimes have spawned an elaborate industry of document production in which the content and original aims of due diligence are all but sidelined.[119] But what differentiates these studies from other critiques of law and development projects is that they go beyond pointing to contradictions in development agendas, or the bad faith of development agents, to focus on something more—the forms of knowledge at issue in Rule of Law projects that prefigure particular kinds of conclusions and outcomes.

Another project approaches the same questions of the agency of legal form from the standpoint of a kind of synthesis of the traditions of autopoesis, science studies, and the anthropology of knowledge. In a collection co-edited with anthropologist Martha Mundy, the comparatist Alain Pottage addresses 'the question of how legal techniques fabricate persons and things'. In spheres from biotechnology to agriculture, human rights to new reproductive technologies, Pottage points out, the divide between persons and things and, hence, the very definition of the person is actually produced as an effect of the technical workings of legal institutions.

---

[116] Geoffrey Samuel, 'Epistemology and Comparative Law: Contributions from the Sciences and Social Sciences', in Mark van Hoecke (ed), *Epistemology and Methodology of Comparative Law* (2004), 35–77, at 74.

[117] Annelise Riles, *The Network Inside Out* (2000).

[118] Margaret E. Keck and Kathryn Sikkink, *Activists beyond Borders: Advocacy Networks in International Politics* (1998); Anne-Marie Slaughter, 'The Real New World Order', (1997) 1997 *Foreign Affairs* September/October 183.

[119] Bill Maurer, 'Due Diligence and "Reasonable Man," Offshore', (2005) 20 *Cultural Anthropology* 474–505.

Pottage recognizes that the claim that what we take as a fundamental divide between persons and things is actually based in the mundane and technical workings of such doctrines as property law is liable to shock the sensibilities of many social scientists, and indeed many lawyers who wish to see law as simply a reflection of social values: 'Minimally and most importantly, this means that the legal person has no necessary correspondence to social, psychological, or biological individuality. In an age which still identifies personal fulfilment or emancipation with the acquisition and defence of legal rights, this might seem almost perverse.'[120] The innovation of this approach may become clearer by contrasting it with the work of Garth and Dezalay described above. The problem with Garth and Dezalay's focus on law as a social field is that it cannot explain why actors pursue the particular strategies the authors impute to them. Rather, it proceeds from a methodological individualist assumption of a self as possessing interests—and interests of a kind that happen to be characteristic of the late modern middle-class Euro-American societies in which the authors find themselves, such as getting ahead in one's organization or building up a high profile legal practice. Such transactionalist models were the subject of considerable critique in anthropology in the early 1980s. Although these assumptions survived longer in sociology—perhaps because sociologists have often focused on Euro-American societies where the assumptions in those models correlated better with the folk models of their subjects—they become increasingly problematic when transposed onto a comparative and global field that increasingly encompasses non-European actors (and when the researcher has only short-term, interview-based interactions with informants in which it is difficult to become aware of the problems with one's starting assumptions). Again, Weber serves as a kind of model for a different perspective; he very squarely recognizes that certain forms of legal knowledge are intimately tied to certain unique forms of personhood.

The question of the constitution of social facts by legal form opens up a new set of comparative questions. Bringing in new work in comparative law now gaining prominence in France,[121] as well as anthropological work on subjects ranging from Islamic jurisprudence to Melanesian ownership regimes, Pottage and Mundy's collection demonstrates the diversity of ways the work of legal forms is generative of forms of subjectivity. For example, Yan Thomas's research into the techniques of legal fictions for managing inheritance funds in Roman law shows how 'facts' such as whether there was indeed a corpse, and what counted as a dead person, were matters produced internally by legal argumentation, even as that argumentation itself turned on a divide between matters of fact and matters of law: 'The difference

---

[120] Alain Pottage, 'Introduction: The Fabrication of Persons and Things', in Alain Pottage and Martha Mundy (eds), *Law, Anthropology, and the Constitution of the Social: Making Persons and Things* (2004), 1–39, at 11.

[121] Yan Thomas, '*Fictio Legis*: L'empire de la fiction Romaine et ses limites Médiévales', (1995) 21 *Droits* 17–63.

between law and fact is not a difference of fact but one of law, and this is what defines the essence of the institution, and what makes fictions so revelatory of the artificiality of the institution'.[122]

All of these approaches significantly advance our appreciation of legal knowledge as a subject in its own right where comparative law and socio-legal studies might meet. However, it remains the case that most scholars in both camps continue to speak squarely from their own disciplinary perspective—and hence to limit their claims about law to what is intelligible within their own disciplinary communities. The sociological studies of the legal field remain grounded in a traditional social framework, in which legal knowledge is a function of social relations. Latour's work likewise draws its authority from a traditional empirical claim—'I was there inside the chambers of the Conseil D'Etat; I got the empirical facts on how law really works'—which does not seem to do justice to lawyers' own scepticism about such truth claims, and indeed seems at odds with his subtle account of how such truths are produced in science as in law. For his part, the lawyer Gunther Teubner ultimately settles for a surprisingly conservative normative argument for 'legal formalization', that is, a return to formal law as an arbiter of plurality. Law remains a device of systematization, in a quite conventional sense, even though the understanding of how law systematizes has shifted to include communicative practices and reflexivity.

This firm disciplinary grounding in given paradigms of comparative law on the one hand or socio-legal studies on the other is certainly understandable given disciplinary pressures to speak to one's peers in a familiar and recognizable vocabulary. But it stands in striking contrast to Weber's own refusal to settle in one disciplinary domain or the other. Indeed, what I would wish to reclaim as the Weberian tradition is precisely what has made generations of legal scholars and social scientists alike so uncomfortable as they seek to settle, in reading after reading of his text, whether Weber 'really' approached legal knowledge from a legal or social scientific point of view. Would it be possible, following Weber and building on the important traditions of legal knowledge discussed here, to develop a kind of scholarship that does not begin from the traditional premises of either comparative law or socio-legal studies, but that truly makes its home at the juncture of the two? Such work would finally and definitively move both fields beyond functions and systems, beyond law and society, beyond culture and transplants to a new set of concerns. In this respect, Pottage's new approach to comparative collaboration is exemplary for its refusal of a singular disciplinary paradigm; my work and the work of Maurer similarly tries, against the traditions of both comparative law and socio-legal studies, to generate 'epistemological limits' for the comparative project from within the parameters of the subject itself.

If, as Tim Murphy suggests, Weber's contribution was to make his own methods—rationality—into a subject of inquiry, and if recent work in the character of legal knowledge has sought to further explore and develop that subject through a variety of legal and sociological methods, the project now must be to turn the insights gained from our understanding of the subject of legal knowledge back into a method for comparative scholarship. Careful inquiry into the nature of legal technologies brings back to the foreground a set of subjects for comparative inquiry distinct from the traditional subjects of rules, norms, and functions. These subjects, from legal fictions to statutory drafting techniques to the analogical practices of civilian legal reasoning,[123] have, in fact, been on the table in comparative law since Weber and before. Foregrounded and reframed as sources of methodological innovation, not simply as subjects of study, they raise a number of fresh questions such as how law constitutes the 'facts' of the world it purports only to regulate, from the distinction between persons and things, to the nature of globalization, to the character of economic realities.[124]

Bibliography

Max Weber, Guenther Roth, and Claus Wittich, *Economy and Society* (1968)

Yves Dezalay and Bryant G. Garth, *Dealing in Virtue: International Commercial Arbitration and the Construction of a Transnational Legal Order* (1996)

Gunther Teubner, *Global Law without a State* (1997)

William Twining, *Globalisation and Legal Theory* (2000)

Boaventura de Sousa Santos, *Toward a New Legal Common Sense: Law, Globalization, and Emancipation* (2002)

Alain Pottage and Martha Mundy, *Law, Anthropology, and the Constitution of the Social: Making Persons and Things* (2004)

Annelise Riles, *Collateral Knowledge: Instrumental Reason, Market Sociality, Legal Subjectivity* (forthcoming)

---

[123] Riles (n 31).
[124] Bill Maurer, *Mutual Life, Limited: Islamic Banking, Alternative Currencies, Lateral Reason* (2005).

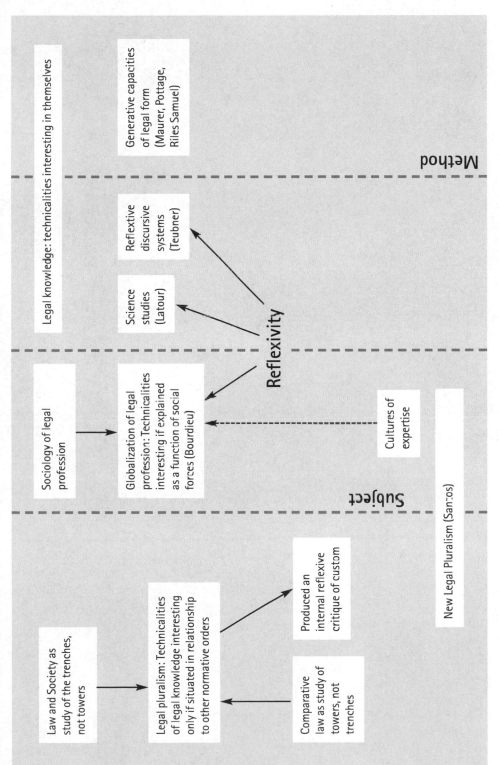

Fig. 24.1 The emergence of legal knowledge as a subject of comparative legal studies

CHAPTER 25

....

COMPARATIVE LAW AND CRITICAL LEGAL STUDIES

....

UGO MATTEI

Turin and Hastings*

* This chapter originated as a cooperative effort with my former student and now Critical Legal Studies scholar Anna di Robilant, whose invaluable help and contribution in data gathering I fully acknowledge here. Ultimately, she did not agree with my interpretation and selection of the materials. This makes it particularly true that responsibility for mistakes is *only* mine. Otherwise we would have co-authored the entry.

I. FOR STARTERS:
DEFINING THE KEY QUESTION

IN discussing the relationship between comparative law and critical legal studies, we must first clarify the topic. In particular, the meaning of 'critical legal studies' can be defined in various ways. One definition would encompass the whole, fairly rich, contemporary critical movement in comparative law; this movement includes voices from many places, especially various European countries (France, Germany, Italy and the United Kingdom) as well as the United States.[1] This chapter, however, defines the term more narrowly and looks at the relationship between comparative law and the specific network of scholars affiliated with the movement originating in the United States in the 1970s and known as Critical Legal Studies, or, more colloquially, CLS.

Critical Legal Studies, sometimes a political movement, today certainly a school of thought, and perhaps even a theory of law,[2] encountered comparative law in the early 1990s, that is, quite recently. This encounter created a fairly broad network of Critical Legal Studies scholars thinking and writing about foreign and comparative law. The contributions made by these scholars over the last decade or so are the focus of this chapter.

One must not overlook, however, that Critical Legal Studies has also had another, very different, relationship with comparative law, namely as an object of comparative study. In the last few decades, American law and legal scholarship have acquired a position approaching global hegemony. As a result, Critical Legal Studies, as one of the most important (post-realist) jurisprudential movements in the United States, has received its share of attention abroad as well. Thus, its critical agenda has influenced legal thought in many parts of the world. This contribution *through* comparative studies may well be as significant as its contribution *to* the discipline, but it is not my concern here.

The contribution of Critical Legal Studies to comparative law is a matter of considerable (international) interest, not only in light of the remarkable presence of the movement in several leading US-American academic institutions but also in view of the rather desperate need for comparative law as an academic discipline

---

[1] A non-affiliated and non-organized recent critical wave of writings in comparative law includes those of Bussani, Curran, Ewald, Feldman, Fitzpatrick, Grande, Hesselink, Legrand, Michaels, Muir Watt, Obiora, Reimann, Sefton Green, and many others. I offer this selection of names purely for the purpose of indicating the kind of work that can certainly be considered 'critical' of the comparative mainstream. It might even be possible that some scholars on this list consider themselves 'insiders' to the network, while others whose work I consider as 'insiders' might not like to be included.

[2] Duncan Kennedy, *A Critique of Adjudication* (1997), 8–10.

for theoretical revision and reorientation. The relationship between Critical Legal Studies and comparative law is also interesting from the institutional perspective. Critical Legal Studies has skilfully employed the international appeal especially of the Harvard Law School and its graduate programme to attract young, gifted scholars from all over the globe. Some of them were eager to enter academic life in the United States, while others have returned to their home country. The result is a global network of American-trained scholars working in the United States, Europe and the Mediterranean region, Latin America, and Africa, who affiliate themselves with Critical Legal Studies as a movement and as a critical and leftist agenda.

The encounter of Critical Legal Studies with comparative law has produced a variety of dissertations and law review articles in which the methodological postulates of (traditional) comparative law were scrutinized and criticized. This work has questioned the standard terms and concepts as well their meanings and implications. In particular, functionalism, perceived by Critical Legal Studies as the creed of the priestly caste of mainstream comparative law, has been criticized with the goal of exposing its underlying assumptions. As a result of such, and other, critiques, both comparative law and Critical Legal Studies have been reinvigorated. In particular, comparative law, a discipline which had already begun to overcome its former self-congratulatory mood, was infused with a healthy dose of criticism, for example, through the challenge that it fosters practices of hegemony and domination.

Yet, the relationship between Critical Legal Studies and comparative law raises some important questions. The Critical Legal Studies scholars' characterization of mainstream comparative law is not beyond challenge, the novelty of their critique is not always free from doubt, and their claims to new discoveries are not always fully convincing. This leads to the key questions pursued in this chapter: what are the contributions Critical Legal Studies has really made to comparative law, and how original are they?

We will first describe the emergence, as well as some of the work, of Critical Legal Studies comparative law (Section II), then pursue to what extent the Critical Legal Studies approach breaks with, or rather continues, the agenda of the discipline's mainstream (Section III), and finally arrive at a sympathetic critique of the critique (Section IV).

II. CRITICAL LEGAL STUDIES MEETS COMPARATIVE LAW: A TOUR D'HORIZON

The network of Critical Legal Studies comparative lawyers constituted itself as a visible group in the mid-1990s. But its beginnings really lie in a seminal article of the previous decade. In 1985, Günther Frankenberg, a scholar belonging to the German anti-formalist, critical, and leftist school of jurists at the universities of Bremen and Frankfurt, published an essay entitled 'Critical Comparisons: Rethinking Comparative Law'.[3] In this article, which the discipline's mainstream happily (and unfortunately) ignored, Frankenberg launched a full-scale attack on traditional comparative law primarily from two sides. He chastised the traditional approach for being ethnocentric and 'legocentric'; and he claimed that comparatists suffered from a 'Cinderella complex', that is, an imbalance between their perception of the discipline's great value and the very modest recognition it actually enjoyed in legal academia.

Frankenberg was well connected and highly respected at Harvard and it was no accident that his article appeared in the *Harvard Journal of International Law*. As a result, his ideas soon circulated widely among Critical Legal Studies scholars in the United States where they helped to stimulate the Crits' interest in comparative law. It is noteworthy that this occurred at a time when comparative law found itself in a rather paradoxical situation: on the one hand, it played a decidedly marginal role in American legal academia; on the other hand, it was just about to become a powerful agenda on the international level with the initial buzz about globalization.

The Harvard Critical Legal Studies group had generated a few students who were engaged in various non-domestic lines of scholarship, *inter alia*, at the University of Utah. Thus in 1996, Salt Lake City became the venue of a much-noted conference on 'New Approaches to Comparative Law'. The purpose of the conference was the presentation of Critical Legal Studies work on a panoply of issues transcending American boundaries.[4] In the years after the Utah Conference, annual meetings at the Harvard Law School, as well as in other venues, created a

---

[3] Günter Frankenberg, 'Critical Comparisons: Rethinking Comparative Law', (1985) 26 *Harvard Journal of International Law* 411. By 'legocentrism' Frankenberg means that 'law is treated as a given and a necessity, as the natural path to ideal, rational or optimal conflict resolutions and ultimately to a social order guaranteeing peace and harmony'. He further specifies that 'legocentric thinking and legalism, its political strategy, draw their strength from an idealized and formalized vision of law as a set of institutions, rules and techniques that function to guarantee and, in every possible conflict, to vindicate individuals' rights. If legal provisions do not live up to the promises inherent in the rule of law, this may be interpreted as an unfortunate and atypical accident, a singular event of justice miscarried. Thus the overall legitimacy and efficiency of the legal order remain intact' 445.

[4] See the Symposium, 'New Approaches to Comparative Law', (1997) *Utah LR* 255–663.

transnational network of loosely affiliated Critical Legal Studies comparatists. Membership is not limited, however, to those affiliating themselves professionally with comparative law as a discipline but instead rests on a common interest in exploring the formation and circulation of global 'modes of legal consciousness'. In other words, the major common denominator of the membership is the expansion of the Critical Legal Studies agenda beyond the domestic American legal system, which had hitherto been the sole target of Critical Legal Studies critiques.

Members of the network share an aversion against allegiances with any established professional discipline or vocabulary and they often create their own alternative terms and categories. Thus, they are active in various fields, ranging from international law and law and development to legal theory and legal history. They are drawn to the comparative method by its critical and de-mystifying potential. Network members are characterized by an (often moderate) leftist political orientation and, more importantly, a belief in the primary significance of critical scholarship. This critique is mostly directed at the implications of law for the reproduction of entrenched social hierarchies, and it usually entails a commitment to greater social and political equality and participation.

The critique has two major, interrelated, dimensions.[5] First, it views law as a hegemonic system legitimating direct forms of domination: legal rules shape and reproduce hierarchical structures of power (race, class, gender, etc.) by both forging legal identities and affecting the redistribution of social resources. Second, it regards the legal system as an instrument for the legitimization of the status quo: (false) legal consciousness is a cluster of beliefs shared by legal actors; it reinforces current power structures by mediating or denying contradictions, creating false necessities, and producing false justifications. While liberals and part of the traditional left attempt to pursue their goals by relying on political practice and seek to build on the (perceived) positive aspects of the rule of law, Critical Legal Studies scholars (and comparatists) subscribe to an agenda of liberation through disruption and disorientation. The goal is to illuminate the fallacies of legalistic strategies, the double-edged nature of our 'dearest treasures',[6] that is, fundamental rights, equality before the law and other such basic concepts, and the double-binds implicit in our political choices.

This intellectual approach is applied to a variety of geographic contexts. The chosen turf depends usually, but not necessarily, on the national origin of the respective scholar. A few examples might serve as a rough guide to this brand of scholarship.

Among Mediterranean comparatists, some are primarily interested in producing a plausible secular and modern account of post-colonial legal consciousness in the

---

[5] See Kennedy (n 2), at 6.
[6] Janet Halley and Wendy Brown, 'Introduction', in Janet Halley and Wendy Brown (eds), *Left Legalism/Left Critique* (2002), 6.

Arab World. Scholars pursuing this project are deeply influenced by Edward Said and his call for 'secular criticism'. They are thus 'fundamentally opposed to the idea of reserving to Islam any privileged space in the public sphere'.[7] They build on the notion of 'orientalism', exploring its implications for the law, and engage in an 'oppositional discourse seeking to transcend both Western hegemony and fundamentalist resistance through systematic critique'.[8] Their studies analyse post-colonial structures through the lens of critical scholarship and undertake to illuminate the relationship between the metropolis (or centre) and the periphery in all its complexity and ambiguity. In particular, by introducing notions such as that of the 'Muslim Cosmopolitan', they reject the categorical divide between East and West as a valid epistemological basis and expose the ambivalence of the idea of cosmopolitanism which itself is loaded with conflicting political projects.[9] Thus, a comparative study of violence against women in the Arab World and in the United States can challenge both the orientalist construct of how *the other* treats its women and the 'international feminism' approach.[10] Other scholars and writers are interested in exploring the biases and the deforming effects of nationalist projects in the Mediterranean area. For instance, they show how the nationalist narrative of the Greek state's creation elides the struggles of various actors with competing agendas for the political organization of the new state.[11]

Latin American Critical Legal Studies scholars use comparative law to cast light on both the fiction of the 'European-ness' of Latin American legal culture and on their distinctive 'Latin American-ness'. According to this approach, the Latin American periphery is trapped in a peculiar ambiguity. On the one hand, Latin American legal systems are not part of the (European, or at least Western) mainstream. On the other hand, Latin American law is 'not being exotic enough to claim the cultural exception'. Thus, Latin America is seen as a European appendix lacking a distinct legal culture that could serve as the 'basis of a genuine and exotic contribution to jurisprudence'.[12] Comparative law also proves to be a crucial tool for questioning the political implications of the trope of European-ness. As an early critical comparatist suggested, the fiction of European-ness serves the interests of Latin American elites, strengthening and supporting the liberal project of national governance by insulating the legal system from the input and interests

---

[7] Hani Sayed, 'Beyond the Old and the New: Engaging the Muslim Cosmopolitan', in ASIL Proceedings 1999 at 362.

[8] Ibid 362.   [9] Ibid 363

[10] Lama Abu-Odeh, 'Comparatively Speaking: The "Honor" of the "East" and the "Passion" of the "West" ', (1997) *Utah LR* 287.

[11] Philomila Tsoukala, 'Beyond Formalism in Greek Legal Thought: Re-thinking the Familiy Law Reforms', SJD dissertation, Harvard Law School (on file with author).

[12] Diego Lopez Medina, 'Comparative Jurisprudence. Reception and Misreading of Transnational Legal Theory in Latin America', SJD Dissertation, Harvard Law School (2001), 5. Now published as *Teoria Impura del Derecho* (2004).

of broader constituencies and particular local cultures.[13] Moreover, a critical-comparative investigation helps to formulate and test hypotheses concerning the distinctiveness of Latin American law. It sheds light on the dynamic of production and reception, on the relation between law and social change, and between law and economic development. Finally, critical comparative studies tackle the question whether there are any peculiarly Latin American modes of legal reasoning. Critical comparatists reject the widely held assumption that Latin American law belongs to the civil law family, and they explore the connection between modes of reasoning and particular institutional forms and practices.[14]

Critical comparative law also has an African spin-off, mostly active in Kenya. This work focuses on the devastating cultural and economic impact of international agencies, such as the World Bank and the IMF, on Third World countries, for example, by means of Structural Adjustment Programs targeting the legal system.[15]

Finally, 'metropolitan' Critical Legal Studies comparatists (ie those in the United States) are often interested in exploring the premises and political implications of the discipline's 'Western-ness'. They question the mainstream's methodological postulates and tacit assumptions and see comparative law as a 'Western' enterprise loaded with political projects and strategies.[16] Thus, they claim to detect and spell out the political implications of the comparative enterprise. In particular, they envision comparative lawyers, together with their fellow international lawyers, as prime actors in a project of cosmopolitan governance. But they also make a plea for rethinking comparative law more generally, claiming that for the comparative method to become a tool of critique, its ethnocentric and 'legocentric' biases must be exposed.[17] Critical Legal Studies comparatists approach the project of European integration in a similar vein, looking for blind spots and ambiguities.[18]

---

[13] Jorge Esquirol, 'The Fictions of Latin American Law (Part I)', (1997) *Utah LR* 425 (1997); *idem*, 'The Fictions of Latin American Law (Part II)', (2003) 55 *Florida LR* 41.

[14] These themes have been extensively discussed at the conference 'Thinking of Law in/and Latin America', Harvard Law School, 4 March 2005, organized by Alvaro Santos and Arnulf Becker. See <http://www.law.harvard.edu/programs/elrc/events/#mar4>.

[15] African Crits are James Gathii, Sylvia Kang'ara, Joel Ngugi, and Celestine Nyamu. See Joel Ngugi, 'Searching for the Market Criterion: Market-Oriented Reforms in Legal and Economic Development Discourses', (Phd Dissertation, Harvard Law School). See also Sylvia Kang'ara, 'When the Pendulum Swing too Far. Structural Adjustment Programs in Kenya', (1998) *Third World Legal Studies Journal* 109–51.

[16] See Lama Abu Odeh, 'The Politics of (Mis)recognition: Islamic Law Pedagogy in American Academia', (2004) 52 *AJCL* 789.

[17] Frankenberg, (1985) 26 *Harvard International LJ* 411; *idem*, 'Stranger than Paradise: Identity and Politics in Comparative Law', (1997) *Utah LR* 259.

[18] Daniela Caruso, 'The Missing View of the Cathedral: The Private Law Paradigm of European Legal Integration', (1997) 3 *European LJ* 3; *idem*, 'Comment: Lonchner in Europe', (2005) 85 *Boston University LR* 867, Fernanda Nicola, 'Asymmetry, Distribution and Local Governance in European Integration: A View from Private Law Theory', SJD dissertation, Harvard Law School (on file with author). Anna di Robilant, 'A Genealogy of Soft Law', (2005) 54 *AJCL* (forthcoming).

While this brief overview amounts to little more than a bibliographical guide, it shows that the Critical Legal Studies network points to many areas of the discipline, and to the global model of governance through law, inviting critique. In all this, Critical Legal Studies comparatists have spent considerable time in 'self reflection'[19] and have reached a remarkable degree of theoretical sophistication. Unfortunately, their contributions are sometimes difficult to fully appreciate and are easily misunderstood by individuals outside of the network. The main reason for the resulting miscommunication is that Critical Legal Studies comparatists often write and reason at high levels of abstraction and frequently borrow freely from particular intellectual traditions in neighbouring social sciences, putting the resulting scholarship well beyond the ken of many, if not most, readers.

An observer outside the network may be tempted to conclude that Critical Legal Studies comparatists chose, or at least imagined that they were choosing, to start their project from scratch and attempted to construct an entirely new canon for comparative law. Much of the Critical Legal Studies comparative scholarship, it seems, seeks to establish a dialogue with scholars other than (traditional) comparatists, especially with so-called 'area studies' (or, from a US perspective, scholarship on 'foreign' law and legal systems). Thus, Critical Legal Studies scholars often seem rather reluctant to engage in genuine comparison or to consider critical work carried on by 'professional' (ie mainstream) comparatists.[20] As a result, building an agenda common to Critical Legal Studies comparatists and their mainstream colleagues has proved to be difficult, at least in the beginning.[21] In fact, for years after the Utah conference, Critical Legal Studies comparatists and the discipline's 'establishment', institutionalized in the American Society of Comparative Law (the corresponding institution of the International Academy of Comparative Law), largely failed to communicate in the United States, possibly because of reciprocal suspicion. This situation has begun to change only very recently and today, a number of Critical Legal Studies comparatists are involved with the American Society of Comparative Law (ASCL), often offering outstanding contributions.[22]

[19] Karen Engle, 'Comparative Law as Exposing the Foreign System's Internal Critique', (1997) *Utah LR* 359.

[20] One can think of Annelise Riles (ed), *Rethinking the Masters of Comparative Law* (2001) as an exception.

[21] A full-scale critique of the discipline has been carried on for example in Mathias Reimann and UgoMattei (eds), Symposium, 'New Directions in Comparative Law', (1998) 46 *AJCL* 597.

[22] At the recent Ann Arbor Meeting of the ASCL leading comparative Crits such as Lama Abu Odeh, Annelise Riles, Daria Roithmayr, and Teemu Ruskola presented much applauded and important papers.

III. Disruption or Continuity?

Like all complex intellectual phenomena, the work of Critical Legal Studies comparative law scholars is susceptible to different interpretations. In particular, one can conceive of it primarily as the disruption of traditional comparative law assumptions, approaches, and methods, or one can emphasize the elements of continuity and connection with the discipline's mainstream. This leads to the question to what extent Critical Legal Studies comparative law can really be said to begin the comparative law enterprise 'from scratch'. There is no question that within the Critical Legal Studies network, the emphasis is all on rupture with the mainstream's professional project and ideology. This is signalled by the avoidance of the traditional, and the invention of a new, vocabulary, and it becomes evident in the rather eclectic references to, and use of, the existing (traditional) scholarship. Yet, an analysis of the relationship between the iconoclastic and the traditional for purposes of this *Handbook* requires a more detached perspective. We will look at a variety of contexts in order to observe the respective critiques of Critical Legal Studies comparatists and in order to gauge how revolutionary these critiques really are. As a result, this part of the chapter deals primarily with methodological issues rather than with actual comparative work.

1. The Assault on the Traditional 'Canon'

Critical Legal Studies comparatists are actively challenging what they regard as the traditional canon of the discipline's mainstream. From its early beginnings, Critical Legal Studies comparative law has critiqued the traditional discipline's tacit methodological and epistemological assumptions. The portrait of traditional legal scholarship in general as a powerful professional project legitimizing the status quo and reproducing hierarchical structures[23] has been extended to include comparative law in particular, thus, in a sense, expanding the critique from the domestic to the global sphere. This critical inquiry approaches comparative law as a canon consisting of interlocking texts and explores how structures of consciousness shape this canon, how it is formed, and which functions it serves. In Frankenberg's analysis, for instance, ethnocentrism, 'legocentrism', and cognitive controllability are among the central ideas informing the canon. Frankenberg thus questions the very epistemological operations by which comparative lawyers select and process their information. He argues that the mainstream has long relied on a mode of comparison that assures 'cognitive control' and that it is characterized

---

[23] See Kennedy (n 2) and *idem, Legal Education and the Reproduction of Hierarchy* (1983).

by the 'formalist ordering and labelling and the ethnocentric interpretation of information, often randomly gleaned from limited data'.[24] This critique suggests that comparative law ought to be envisaged primarily as a 'learning experience', involving two crucial epistemological paradigms: distancing and differencing. The former requires that we resist the power of prejudice and ignorance by casting aside settled knowledge and entrenched beliefs; the latter implies a conscious effort to foreground the observer's subjective perspective and experience.

Yet, when reflecting upon such a critique, one cannot but wonder whether its full-fledged assault on the entire mainstream tradition is really productive. Critical Legal Studies criticism often fails to distinguish the various elements within this tradition, synchronically, diachronically, as well as in terms of quality of the work. To be sure, there is a lot of bad comparative law out there, characterized by woefully limited efforts at data gathering and by a lot of speculation.[25] But considering that there are also outstanding examples of painstaking data gathering within the mainstream comparative law tradition,[26] the Critical Legal Studies critique appears to be too general as well as too extreme. Perhaps more importantly, the Critical Legal Studies critique, in a sense, misses the mark: the Critical Legal Studies revolt against mainstream liberal scholarship aims at what is constructed as an institution of power, whereas comparative law has always fought its battle against legal chauvinism and positivism from a weak, often marginal, position. If a canon existed at all[27] (eg one constructed in the 'European shadow'[28]), it consists of methods of inquiry across time and space.

It is true that some Critical Legal Studies-affiliated scholars go beyond methodological generalizations. They seek to explore the professional, political, or personal projects of actual comparatists rather than ascribing a monolithic attitude to a tradition that consists of many different individuals working in different times and spaces and that is in fact fairly rich in perspectives.[29] Thus, one Critical Legal Studies international law scholar detects, for instance, a variety of so-called 'comparativism(s)' (pointing at their nature as political and professional projects).

---

[24] Frankenberg, (1985) 26 *Harvard International LJ* 421.

[25] The point is made by anthropologist Laura Nader, 'Comments', (1998) 46 *AJCL* 751.

[26] For a classic example, well worth being carefully studied, Rudolf B. Schlesinger (n 34). For a recent example sharing the accuracy but employing an improved theory, see Mauro Bussani and Vernon Palmer (eds), *Pure Economic Losses in Europe* (2003).

[27] Note however, that the very lack of an agreed-upon canon has recently been offered as an explanation of the malaise of the field (at least in the US) by an editor-in-chief of the *American Journal of Comparative Law*, the official organ of the discipline's (US-American) mainstream; Mathias Reimann, 'The Progress and Failure of Comparative Law in the Second Half of the Twentieth Century', (2002) 50 *AJCL* 671, 695–8.

[28] See Mathias Reimann, 'Stepping out of the European Shadow. Why Comparative Law in the United States must Develop its Own Agenda', (1998) 46 *AJCL* 637.

[29] A good example is Annelise Riles, 'Encountering Amateurism: John Henry Wigmore and the Uses of American Formalism', in Annelise Riles (ed), *Rethinking the Masters of Comparative Law* (2001) 94.

He distinguishes multiple internal divisions of the discipline and invents a multi-layered complexity. While at one level, he finds 'historicists', 'functionalists', and 'idealists', at another level he identifies 'technocrats' and 'culture vultures'.[30] On the whole, this polemic assumes that professional comparatists wield considerable political power—a proposition which is surely open to doubt.

2. Functionalism and Structuralism

As mentioned before, Critical Legal Studies comparatists have aimed their critique, *inter alia*, at a basic method that has characterized mainstream comparative law for well over half a century, that is, functionalism.[31] Yet, this critique overlooks that functionalism is neither the unquestioned creed of the mainstream any more nor is it a method without alternatives.

Traditional comparative law can no longer be considered unambiguously functionalist.[32] Functionalism, though certainly an important (and arguably the dominant) approach in the second half of the last century, had long been hybridized by the time the Critical Legal Studies first turned to comparative law. As I have argued elsewhere,[33] even in the early 'Common Core' methodology developed by Rudolf Schlesinger,[34] the functionalist approach was clearly, though perhaps unconsciously, infused with structuralism. Moreover, beginning as early as the 1970s, the structuralist method developed by the Italian school of Rodolfo Sacco grew rather influential in Europe and, by the early 1990s, it became well known in the United States as well.[35] Thus, the Critical Legal Studies contribution in that regard may well be more mainstream than its young adepts are willing to acknowledge in their (academically mandatory) search for originality. It is a fact that the structuralist approach proved a powerful weapon in the hands of critical comparatists both belonging to the Critical Legal Studies network and outside of it. By abandoning the principle of the unity of the law, Sacco and his school demonstrated that legal 'rules' are really products of the competitive interaction between multiple 'legal formants'. Sacco's structural dissection of law is a powerful tool in

---

[30] David Kennedy, 'New Approaches to Comparative Law: Comparativism and International Governance', (1997) *Utah LR* 545, 594.

[31] On functionalism, see Chapter 10 of this *Handbook*.

[32] See Michele Graziadei, 'The Functionalist Heritage', in Pierre Legrand and Roderick Munday (eds), *Comparative Law. Traditions and Transitions* (2003), 100.

[33] Ugo Mattei, 'The Comparative Influence of Schlesinger and Sacco. A Study in Legal Influence', in Annelise Riles (ed), *Rethinking the Masters of Comparative Law* (2001), 238.

[34] Rudolf B. Schlesinger, '*Formation of Contracts. A Study on the Common Core of Legal Systems*'; conducted under the Auspices of the General Principles of Law Project of the Cornell Law School (2 vols, 1968).

[35] Rodolfo Sacco, 'Legal Formants: A Dynamic Approach to Comparative Law', (part I) (1991) 39 *AJCL* 1; (part II) (1991) 39 *AJCL* 343.

several respects. It sheds light on the gaps, conflicts, and ambiguities resulting from the clash between the multiple legal formants that constitute the rule, and it illuminates the role of ideology in reconciling conflicting formants and shaping legal outcomes. In emphasizing the disjuncture between the legal rule and the rhetorical justification for the rule devised by legal professionals, Sacco's structuralism showed remarkable similarity to Duncan Kennedy's contrast between the legal *parole* and the legal *langue*. These obvious methodological similarities between comparative structuralism and Critical Legal Studies work had been observed in Europe[36] long before the Critical Legal Studies comparative law network was founded at Harvard and launched at Utah in 1996. In particular, scholars have described the post-realist nature of both approaches and they have examined some of their common 'non legal', especially linguistic and anthropological, references. Thus it was not an accident that a significant contingent of European comparatists (including this author) travelled all the way to Salt Lake City to observe the first official Critical Legal Studies comparative conference. These Europeans considered themselves kindred spirits, trying to connect with the emerging critical movement in the United States.

Beyond structuralism, other approaches have played a significant role in mainstream comparative law as well. This is true, *inter alia*, for John H. Merryman's dense stylistic analysis[37] which carried Konrad Zweigert's notion of 'legal style' beyond the context of a general taxonomy of legal families. Merryman's analysis constituted a fairly radical departure from the socio-functionalist mode of inquiry and provided important insights for the Critical Legal Studies comparative project. In particular, the concept of 'legal style' (and many variations on this basic idea, such as *mentalité*) can be considered the ancestor of the critical concept of 'legal consciousness'. Embracing this concept is as crucial for the self-portrait of Critical Legal Studies network members as subscribing to the 'legal formants' approach is for members of the Sacco school.

Finally, even Critical Legal Studies comparatists should not overlook that historical-comparative analysis was part of mainstream comparative law long before the Critical Legal Studies network entered the scene. This analysis has generated a number of now classic studies on the formation and development of European legal systems[38] and provided the material for Alan Watson's theory of

---

[36] Elisabetta Grande, 'Ai confine delle responsabilità (Prime riflessioni per un programma di ricerca in diritto comparato)', in *Rassegna Diritto Civile* (1995), 857–97; Giovanni Marini, 'Ipotesi sul metodo del diritto privato: Piccola guida alla scoperta di altri itinerari', (1990) *Rivista Critica di Diritto Privato* 343.

[37] John Henry Merryman, *The Loneliness of the Comparative Lawyer and Other Essays in Foreign and Comparative Law* (1999).

[38] John Henry Merryman, *The Civil Law Tradition. An Introduction to the Legal Systems of Western Europe and Latin America* (2a, 1985); Alan Watson, *The Making of the Civil Law* (1981); R. C. Van Caenegem, *European Law in the Past and in the Future: Unity and Diversity over Two Millennia* (2001); *idem, An Historical Introduction to Private Law* (1992); Gino Gorla, *Il Contratto* (2 vols, 1955).

Legal Transplants[39] to which we turn in a moment. Thus, when Critical Legal Studies scholars generated their own studies on the historical contingency and sensitivity on law as well as on its development over time, they did not really transcend the mainstream of the discipline but rather enriched it—often with much needed critical bite.

3. Critiques of Transplants and Receptions

Just as Critical Legal Studies comparatists shift from the traditional concept of 'legal style' to the notion of 'legal consciousness', they also tend to replace the idea of 'legal transplants'[40]—which has become part of the general vocabulary within the mainstream[41]—with neologisms intended to emphasize various phenomena occurring in the process of transferring law from one context to another. While Alan Watson's legal transplants' paradigm receives credit for striking a full blow at functionalism, it is ultimately considered inadequate to capture the complexity of the phenomenon of legal exportation or importation. In order to overcome the deficiencies of the notion of legal transplants in explaining the circulation of legal ideas, Critical Legal Studies-affiliated comparatists turn to other disciplines, mostly literary theory and linguistics from which they try to derive new heuristic devices. Terms such as 'globalizations',[42] 'productive misreadings',[43] and 'translations'[44] are employed to effect a paradigm shift in theories of legal change that are capable of accounting for domination and power disparity. Some elements of the Critical Legal Studies critique are novel, while others resemble long-established notions. For example, Critical Legal Studies comparatists share with other critics the idea that the legal transplants metaphor is pre-realist, focuses exclusively on prestige, historical accidents, inertia, or internal characteristics of the legal profession, and thus obliterates the link between law and external political, social, and economic factors.[45] Nor is there much novelty in the Critical Legal Studies idea that the very notion of a 'transplant' obscures the creative, and sometimes very original, re-shaping of the transplanted element in the receiving

---

[39] See Alan Watson, *Legal Transplants* (1974); on this topic see Graziadei, Chapter 13 of this *Handbook*.

[40] Alan Watson, *Legal Transplants: An Approach to Comparative Law* (1974).

[41] See William Ewald, 'Comparative Jurisprudence (II). The Logic of Legal Transplants', (1995) 43 *AJCL* 489.

[42] Duncan Kennedy, 'The Two Globalizations of Law and Legal Thought 1850–1968', (2003) 36 *Suffolk University LR* 631.

[43] Lopez Medina (n 12).

[44] Maximo Langer, 'From Legal Transplants to Legal Translations: The Globalization of Plea Bargaining and the Americanization Thesis in Criminal Procedure', (2004) 45 *Harvard International LJ* 1.

[45] See Rudolf B. Schlesinger, Hans W. Baade, Peter E. Herzog and Edward M. Wise, *Comparative Law*, already in its 5th edn (1988).

context.[46] Still, both the notion of a 'productive-misreading' and the idea of 'translations' correctly emphasize the creatively transformative effect of receptions. In particular, the idea of misreading (a phenomenon similar to what is known in some non-affiliated circles as 'acoustic reception'),[47] is explored in a variety of ways and much debated within the network. It has recently been suggested, for instance, that excessive emphasis on the transformative power of peripheral misreading might itself hide a pattern of domination.[48] It is certainly an important contribution to emphasize the fact (in line with some anthropologists)[49] that Watson's paradigm fails to capture the complexity of the unequal power relations between the metropolitan centre, the semi-periphery, and the colonial periphery.[50] Here, Critical Legal Studies-affiliated comparatists have developed a more complex understanding of 'contexts of production and reception'.[51] This understanding has now gained considerable international currency. Important applications of this idea include Shalakani's work on Sanhuri's Egyptian civil code[52] and Duncan Kennedy's essay on 'Two Globalizations'.[53]

4. Exploring 'Legal Consciousness'

As already mentioned, an important activity of critical comparatists consists of exploring the structure and operation of different forms of what they call 'legal consciousness'. Of course, as suggested, notions of style, *mentalité*, or sensitivity, which were borrowed from anthropologists and other social scientists, have a distinguished pedigree even in the work of the mainstream. Nevertheless, Critical Legal Studies scholars have developed theories and ideas of 'legal consciousness' to a high degree. A brief description of these theories and ideas will allow the reader to judge their originality for him- or herself.

---

[46] Again this critique can hardly be considered entirely novel. Among 'non-affiliated' critical comparatists such observations have been around for quite a while. See eg Elisabetta Grande, *Imitazione e diritto. Ipotesi sulla circolazione dei modelli* (2000).

[47] See a variety of such uses in A. D'Angelo (ed), *Good Morning America* (2003).

[48] Arnulf Becker Lorca, 'International Law in Latin America or Latin-American International Law? Rise, Fall and Retrieval of a Tradition', (2006) 47 *Harvard International LJ* 283.

[49] See Sally Falk Moore, 'An International Legal Regime and the Context of Conditionality', in Michael Likosky (ed), *Transnational Legal Processes* (2002), 333–76.

[50] For instance, the 'Globalization' of Classical Legal Thought was 'a combination of influence within the system of autonomous Western nation states and imperialism broadly conceived'; Kennedy, (2003) 36 *Suffolk University LR* 640.

[51] The underlying ideas were more fully developed by the Colombian jurist Lopez Medina (n 12) who distinguished between 'hermeneutically rich' contexts of production and 'hermeneutically poor' contexts of reception.

[52] Amr Shalakany, 'Between Identity and Redistribution: Sanhuri, Genealogy and the Will to Islamise', (2001) 8 *Islamic Law & Society* 201.

[53] See Kennedy, (2003) 36 *Suffolk University LR* 631.

The notion of legal consciousness refers to a set of premises about the salient features of the legal order, especially the historical background of the legal process, the institutional apparatus, and the conceptual tools devised by lawyers, judges, and commentators. A number of those shared premises are so deeply embedded in the actors' minds that they are seldom acknowledged and tend to operate— in structuralist terminology—as cryptotypes.[54] Thus, legal consciousness is the cluster of beliefs held by the legal profession as a social group. To some extent, it operates independently, or in relative autonomy, from concrete economic or social interests. Such autonomy, however, is relative in the sense that the peculiar structure and operation of a certain mode of legal consciousness are intelligible only against the backdrop of larger patterns of social thought and action.[55] Like their more traditional fellow comparatists engaging in the study of legal trans- plants and legal change, Critical Legal Studies comparative lawyers are interested in how different modes of legal consciousness emerge, operate, and travel. For exam- ple, the network leader's ambitious effort consisting of a project analysing 'Three Globalizations'[56] is a sweeping study of the circulation of different transnational modes of consciousness. Here, 'Classical Legal Thought' and 'The Social' are con- ceived not only as two subsequent styles of legal scholarship but also as trans- national modes of thought, produced piecemeal in different civil law and common law countries and providing conceptual vocabularies, organizational schemes, modes of reasoning, and characteristic arguments. Within the network, studies now explore the operation of legal consciousness in foreign systems and expose these systems' self-critique; the respective study on France is almost a classic,[57] and there is also an important line of scholarship dealing with China and Japan.[58] A study of the *Juristes Inquiets*, for example,[59] challenges the dominant image of the French legal system as formal and positivist by emphasizing the existence and complexity of a vibrant critical tradition in France; ultimately, the analysis shows that the unitary and systematic nature of the *école de l'exégèse* is largely a result of the projections of the French antiformalist scholars.[60] Here, the close examination of a different legal system, in which a tradition is almost invented by subsequent

---

[54] Sacco, (1991) 39 *AJCL* 1.

[55] Duncan Kennedy, 'The Rise and Fall of Classical Legal Thought' (Harvard Law School, on file with author).

[56] So far only a discussion of the first two globalizations has been published. See Kennedy, (2003) 36 *Suffolk University LR* 640.

[57] Mitchel de S.-O.-l'E. Lasser, 'Judicial (Self-)Portaits: Judicial Discourse in the French Legal System', (1995) 104 *Yale LJ* 1325.

[58] See Teemu Ruskola, 'Legal Orientalism', (2002) 101 *Michigan LR* 179; Annelise Riles, *The Network Inside Out* (2003).

[59] Marie Claire Belleau, 'The "Juristes Inquiets": Legal Classicism and Criticism in Early Twentieth Century France', (1997) *Utah LR* 379.

[60] One can find similar observations in the work on the exegetic school of Carlo Augusto Cannata and Antonio Gambaro, *Lineamenti di Storia della Giurisprudenza Europea* (1983).

scholars, is employed as a powerful tool for questioning the observer's own system, where similar phenomena might have been produced by the legal realists in their (stereotyped) account of legal formalism.[61] One should note that a very similar function of comparative law was suggested in the structuralist canon of the 'Theses of Trent'.[62] Again, the question of rupture versus continuity between more mainstream and Critical Legal Studies comparative scholarship remains open.

5. Other Areas of Activity and Contexts of Critique

The topics explored above do not constitute a comprehensive summary of Critical Legal Studies comparative law scholarship but simply highlight some of the most important areas. An exhaustive survey is not possible here. Suffice it briefly to mention three other aspects of Critical Legal Studies comparative law: the effort to overcome the traditional West-centred perspective; the examination of the interface between comparative and international law; and the exploration of the 'dark sides' of particular phenomena which are usually seen in an unquestioned positive light.

Mainstream comparative law and its taxonomy have often been accused of being too centred on a Western perspective.[63] Critical Legal Studies comparatists have not only joined that critique but have also attempted to establish a genuinely global perspective by broadening the scope of comparative analysis both horizontally and vertically. They look at the East and the South and are concerned with the inter-action of multiple layers of regulation, for example, on the national versus the transnational level. In the horizontal dimension, they undermine the myth that the Western legal tradition is coherent or unique, unveiling non-Western roots, for example, by 'rehabilitating' multiple non-Roman 'legal imaginations'.[64] Moreover, they explore how the ethnocentricism of traditional comparative law has constructed a whole set of binary opposites (not only West versus East but also Us versus Them or Here versus There) through a careful policing of similarities and differences. In all this, the influence of mainstream anthropological ideas is evident. In the vertical dimension, Critical Legal Studies comparatists seek to dissect the coherence and unity of legal systems, emphasizing pluralism, 'interlegality', and legal 'policentricity'. In this, they again share with other comparatists a variety of approaches that appropriate and adopt sophisticated tools of social inquiry.[65]

Another interesting area of Critical Legal Studies critique entails the exploration of the uneasy relationship between comparatists and their fellow international

---

[61] Engle, (1997) *Utah LR* 366.   [62] See Grande, Chapter 3 of the present *Handbook*.

[63] See Ugo Mattei, 'Three Patterns of Law. Taxonomy and Change in the World's Legal Systems', (1997) 45 *AJCL* 5.

[64] Arnulf Becker Lorca, 'Mestizo International Law' (Harvard Law School, on file with author).

[65] See Mauro Bussani, ' "Integrative" Comparative Law Enterprises and the Inner Stratification of Legal Systems', (2000) 1 *ERPL* 83 ff.

lawyers. David Kennedy has investigated the role comparatists, as 'legal specialists in difference', play in the wider project of public and private governance.[66] He suggests that internationalists and comparatists share more than they realize: they ultimately deal with the same crucial problem—the problem of 'order above states and understanding between cultures'. Comparatists perceive themselves as concerned with culture and knowledge but assign to internationalists the terrain of (world) politics. However, if one sees both groups as partners and rivals in a project of cosmopolitan governance, they face and manage essentially the same threats and temptations. The diversity of the Critical Legal Studies network's constituency and the current collapse of disciplinary boundaries have made it clear that we need to rethink the relationship between comparative and international law—incidentally a view widely shared by scholars outside the network as well.[67] All this brings to mind the lesson taught by the late Rudolf Schlesinger who showed how differences and analogies in the law are a matter of emphasis, changing across time, space, and politics. In this (mainstream) light, the description of comparatists as 'specialists in difference' is clearly insufficient.

Finally, some Critical Legal Studies comparatists seek to shed light on the 'dark side' of phenomena that have traditionally been seen in a very positive fashion. This hermeneutic of suspicion can be very refreshing in a field that has too often revelled in self-congratulatory rhetoric (or that has been, if one prefers that point of view, suffering from a 'Cinderella complex'). For example, Jorge Esquirol's important study of René David's portrayal of Latin America exposes the dark side of David's anti-formalist and socio-historical approach.[68] When applied to the Latin American context, David's anti-formalist method with its emphasis on the social and material embeddedness of law ends up serving a neo-colonial project of liberal democracy. In a similar fashion, the Human Rights Movement has been subjected to critical scrutiny. If viewed pragmatically and comparatively, the human rights agenda is marked not only by humanitarian, progressive, and emancipatory characteristics but also by deficiencies, distortions, and dangers.[69] In a similar vein, the Western ideology of rights displays its dark side as well if it is applied to those lacking all power.[70] Interestingly, these very issues took centre-stage in the

---

[66] Kennedy, (2003) 36 *Suffolk University LR* 557.

[67] See Mathias Reimann, 'Beyond National Systems. A Comparative Law for the International Age', (2001) 75 *Tulane LR* 1103.

[68] Esquirol, (1997) *Utah LR* 425.

[69] David Kennedy, 'The International Human Rights Movement: Part of the Problem?', (2002) 15 *Harvard International LJ* 101.

[70] See Obioma Nnaemeka, 'If Female Circumcision Did Not Exist Western Feminism Would Invent It', in Susan Perry and Celeste Schenck (eds), *Eye to Eye. Women Practicing Development Across Cultures* (2001), 179. For a 'specialist in difference' approach to this issue following the 'integrative' lesson of Rudolf B. Schlesinger, see Elisabetta Grande, 'Hegemonic Human Rights and African Resistance: Female Circumcision in a Broader Comparative Perspective', (2004) 4 *Global Jurist Frontiers* art 3.

dialogue between Critical Legal Studies comparatists and the mainstream at the annual meeting of the American Society of Comparative Law in Ann Arbor in the fall of 2004.

IV. Conclusions: A Sympathetic Critique of the Critique

In summarizing this survey of select issues and materials, we need to evaluate the actual political and scholarly contribution of the Critical Legal Studies approach to comparative law. So far, the encounter between comparative law and Critical Legal Studies has proved productive and its potential is far from exhausted. Paradoxically one can regard the encounter between more traditional comparatists and Critical Legal Studies as the counter-hegemonic by-product of the present hegemonic state of American law. After all, at the core of the Critical Legal Studies network, comparative law is taken up by powerful academic superstars whose work enjoys worldwide attention because they operate from prestigious academic centres, such as the Harvard Law School and other elite institutions that reproduce academic hierarchies. Because of their power and prestige, comparative law, otherwise mostly relegated to peripheral or semi-peripheral contexts, suddenly becomes a hot topic.[71] Yet, its critique also construes the discipline's mainstream in a monolithic and simplified manner that obliterates the nuances, complexities, and the variety of voices. This not only hides the target's complexity from worldwide view, it also risks—ironically—empowering it. But despite the original sin of launching a counter-hegemonic critique from a highly hegemonic academic centre, the creation of the Critical Legal Studies network undeniably has its merits: it has institutionalized the encounter between critical legal studies and comparative law and thus moved the Crits' progressive legal agenda to a global level.

None the less, one must wonder about the counter-hegemonic nature of the network, that is, about the very possibility and efficacy of a leftist and critical comparative project from a geo-political point of view. In fact, the Harvard-centred network of critical comparatists can be seen as yet another instance in which a strong (herein: academic) metropolis colonizes weaker cultural contexts. In other words, one may question the Critical Legal Studies project's fundamental

---

[71] See Ugo Mattei, 'A Theory of Imperial Law. A Study on U.S. Hegemony and the Latin Resistance', (2002) 10 *Indiana Journal of Global Legal Studies* 404.

ambitions: can one really resist hegemony from a highly privileged position at the centre of the Western world?

Like the glossators and commentators from Bologna, the humanists from Montpellier, the natural lawyers from Salamanca, and the Roman-Dutch jurists from Leyden, Critical Legal Studies scholars have managed to spread their message from a remarkably influential venue. Critical Legal Studies comparative law is ultimately the product of a leftist elite born and developed at Harvard, a Mecca of Western academic culture. It is true that it has drawn considerable intellectual power from non-Western students but even they usually come from elite backgrounds and are often quickly seduced to become part of American legal academe. Given the complex structure of the new political, economic, and cultural world order,[72] a critical project that operates from the hegemonic metropolitan centre is easily susceptible to cooptation and neutralization by the very forces it seeks to oppose. True resistance, one may argue, can come only from oppression, not from privilege. It can thus hardly be expected from Critical Legal Studies comparatists who enjoy privileged mainstream career patterns and use elite venues of publication. Also, their Critical Legal Studies mentors have shown little concern for the consequences of the brain-drain they orchestrated at the expense of less privileged countries and for the need to create alternative patterns of academic communication. Other network members, however, have arguably made serious contributions to the counter-hegemonic project by returning to, and then operating in, subordinate contexts.[73]

Even observers who sympathize with the general political and critical stance of the Critical Legal Studies comparatists may also wonder about the negative tone and the dangerously self-indulgent character of the post-modernist critical exercise, which is so common in its metropolitan venue. At least at times, the Critical Legal Studies approach takes on features of a mere *divertissement*, played by ultra-theoretical scholars; such games, however, can easily deteriorate into mere aestheticism and entail the risk that all serious political struggle is abandoned. Especially in the choice of their tools and literary forms, Critical Legal Studies comparatists display a striking eclecticism, appropriating different genres and often crossing disciplinary boundaries. A now classic study, for example, presents an unofficial portrait of the French judge through the use of several lenses of literary criticism, borrowing from such disparate sources as Russian formalism and French post-structuralism.[74] It is true that unusual style can release valuable critical

---

[72] Seen as either a revived global form of Imperialism, Giovanni Arrighi, 'Hegemony Unravelling', (2005) 32 *New Left Review* 23, or a novel rhizomatic, de-territorialized and de-centred (though US-inspired) model of sovereignty, Antonio Negri and Michael Hardt, *Empire* (2000).

[73] See Lopez Medina (n 12). See also on African Crits n 15. Kang'hara, for example publishes a column in a daily periodical in Nairobi.

[74] Mitchel de S.-O.-l'E. Lasser, 'Lit. Theory Put to the Test: A Comparative Literary Analysis of American Judicial Tests and French Judicial Discourse', (1998) 111 *Harvard LR* 689; *idem*, 'Comparative Law and Comparative Literature: A Project in Progress', (1997) *Utah LR* 471.

energy but it can also lose touch with the underlying political concerns. All too easily, critique can turn from a means to a (political) end into an exercise just for its own sake. Thus, on some occasions, Critical Legal Studies authors use a theatrical,[75] *carnivalesque* language; on others, they create complex and suspenseful narrative structures.[76]

Critical Legal Studies comparatists often display an outright irony towards the discipline as a whole as well as an unfortunately condescending attitude towards what they consider the grandiosely overambitious understanding of its functions and aims by the mainstream. But if a scholarly agenda seeks to have a political impact, post-modernist irony is not sufficient; instead, a lot of real work must be done. Some of that work requires a real political struggle for the sake of freeing the subordinate elements of the (intellectual) world from present structures of domination. To be sure, critique may be the beginning of such work. But comparative law, in any form, remains elite business until one seriously tackles the problem of how to give voice to the subordinate contexts. In the interim, scholarly exercises like comparative law still have to be evaluated in scholarly terms.

Viewed from this perspective, the institutionalization (however loose) of a network may well present the dark side of the critical potential of the discipline. It is an almost invariable consequence of such institutionalization that the respective group needs to produce an identity, and that need, in turn, may in fact produce the canon against which the revolt is then directed. This can easily lead to a rather ungenerous and wholesale targeting of an entire scholarly tradition, notwithstanding the fact that many of its members share much of the critics' political and scholarly agenda—perhaps precisely because of earlier encounters with these critics and their work. Thus, the requisite process of identity creation leads various contributions of the Critical Legal Studies network to ignore previous work of non-affiliated scholars although this work may be fully in line with the Critical Legal Studies comparatists' own inquiry. At least occasionally, the result is the appropriation, and publication under the Critical Legal Studies logo, of critical insights that originated elsewhere and long before the Critical Legal Studies network ever came into being. This practice is itself essentially a form of hegemony.

Perhaps most importantly, some Critical Legal Studies comparatists portray the mainstream of the discipline, as well as its masters, in caricature form rather than trying to genuinely understand the tensions and nuances in the mainstream scholars' work. At least some of the reason for this problem may lie in the Critical Legal Studies comparatists' extensive use of anthropomorphic ideas, such

---

[75] Frances Olsen, 'The Drama of Comparative Law', (1997) *Utah LR* 275.
[76] Frankenberg, (1985) 26 *Harvard International LJ* 411.

as 'project' or 'strategy'; it is almost ironic that these terms are being applied to a scholarly tradition *that has never been the mainstream* to begin with.

All this being said, it remains true that the multiple projects pursued by Critical Legal Studies-affiliated comparatists help to nurture scepticism within the field, to open up space for critique, and to empower alternative voices. Constant critical scrutiny focusing on any claim of intellectual or political correctness is a source of creative energy and sometimes of relief. For example, Critical Legal Studies comparatists have challenged the myth of comparative law as a universal language. Jacques Derrida suggested that there would be no architecture if the Tower of Babel had been completed;[77] only the impossibility of the tower, the symbol of a logocentric ideal of a universal language, allows architecture to have a history. In comparative law, Critical Legal Studies-affiliated scholars and writers have the potential to draft such a history but they must recognize that just patting each other on the shoulder is dull business, both for the mainstream and for the Critical Legal Studies comparatists.

At the end of the day, the genuinely important contribution of Critical Legal Studies to the development of comparative law, both through the network and through previous encounters, consists not so much of a higher degree of theoretical sophistication which can easily end up in mere self-congratulation; instead, the network's most significant contribution to comparative law consists of two other elements: the systematic and collective attempt to include both the dimension of power and a theory of domination, and the relentless questioning of the 'dark sides' of apparently emancipatory and progressive agendas. These contributions are lessons likely to remain.

Bibliography

Günter Frankenberg, 'Critical Comparisons: Rethinking Comparative Law', (1985) 26 *Harvard International LJ* 411

Duncan Kennedy, *A Critique of Adjudication* (*Fin de Siècle*) (1997)

Symposium: 'New Approaches to Comparative Law, (1997) *Utah LR* 255

Stephen M. Feldman, *American Legal Thought from Pre-Modernism to Post-Modernism* (2000)

Horatia Muir Watt, 'La Fonction Subversive du Droit Comparé', (July–September 2000) 52 *Revue internationale de droit comparé* 503.

William Twining, *Globalization and Legal Theory* (2000)

Ugo Mattei and Anna di Robilant, 'The Art and Science of Critical Scholarship: Postmodernism and International Style in the Legal Architecture of Europe', (2001) 75 *Tulane LR* 1053–92

---

[77] Jacques Derrida, 'Architetture dove il desiderio può abitare', (April 1975) Domus, 671, reprinted in G. Chiurazzi, *Il Postmoderno* (1999).

Laura Nader, *The Life of the Law* (2001)
Annelise Riles (ed), *Rethinking the Masters of Comparative Law* (2001)
Janet Halley and Wendy Brown, *Left Legalism/Left Critique* (2002)
Teemu Ruskola, 'Legal Orientalism', (2002) 101 *Michigan LR* 179
Pierre Legrand and Roderick Munday, *Comparative Law. Traditions and Transitions* (2003)

CHAPTER 26

....

COMPARATIVE LAW AND ECONOMIC ANALYSIS OF LAW

....

FLORIAN FAUST

Hamburg

COMPARATIVE law and economic analysis of law—two legal disciplines, the first with a long tradition,[1] albeit not as an academic endeavour,[2] the second fairly modern,[3] although legal thinking has long involved economic considerations. Both allow lawyers 'a detached outside look at the actual dynamics of the law'.[4] However, this look comes from different perspectives.

Comparing two legal disciplines is like comparing apples and oranges: both are distinctly different members of the same category. One can state their respective characteristics, but a full-fledged comparison is probably a rather fruitless undertaking. Therefore, I will neither attempt such a comparison nor will I discuss the features of comparative law and of the economic analysis of law as such. The different aspects of, and approaches to, comparative law are examined in other chapters of this volume and a detailed description of the economic analysis of law would fill a volume of its own. Hence, I will outline the characteristics of the economic analysis of law only as far as is necessary for an understanding of the links between economic analysis and comparative law (Section I). For, despite—or perhaps even because of—the fundamental differences between the two disciplines, they complement each other and it is possible to connect them in various ways. Thus, I will discuss how one field can operate as an ancillary discipline to the other; this is what, in recent years, has been termed 'Comparative Law and Economics' (Section II). However, it is also possible to link the two disciplines in a different fashion, that is, by making one the subject-matter of the other. So far, little has been published on this subject and I will point out various possibilities demonstrating the potential for future research (Section III).

---

[1] See Konrad Zweigert and Hein Kötz, *An Introduction to Comparative Law* (trans Tony Weir, 3rd edn, 1998), 49 ff, who point out that the earliest comparative studies are to be found in Ancient Greece.

[2] Zweigert and Kötz (n 1), 2 explain that comparative law as it is known today started with the International Congress for Comparative Law in Paris in 1900.

[3] The early landmark essays date from the beginning of the 1960s. See eg Ronald H. Coase, 'The Problem of Social Cost', (1960) 3 *Journal of Law and Economics* 1 ff; Guido Calabresi, 'Some Thoughts on Risk Distribution and the Law of Torts', (1961) 70 *Yale LJ* 499 ff.

[4] Ugo Mattei, *Comparative Law and Economics* (1997), 10. See also Holger Fleischer, 'Die "Business Judgment Rule" im Spiegel von Rechtsvergleichung und Rechtsökonomie', in Rolf Wank, Heribert Hirte *et al* (eds), *Festschrift für Herbert Wiedemann zum 70. Geburtstag* (2002), 827, 846 f.

I. Economic Analysis of Law:
A Short Sketch

1. Positive Economic Analysis

There are two branches of economic analysis of law: the positive and the normative. The positive branch uses economic theory to explain or predict certain facts. Positive economic analysis may be employed retrospectively, that is, in order to explain why the law—be it statute law or case law—developed in a specific way. Thus, Richard Posner, one of the founders of economic analysis of law, proposed that 'the common law is best (not perfectly) explained as a system for maximizing the wealth of society'.[5] Yet, much more important, at least from a practical point of view, is the predictive value of positive economic analysis. For economists, the principal function of legal rules is not that they resolve conflicts after their occurrence but that they influence future behaviour. If, for instance, the law holds a person liable for a certain loss he or she causes to another, this person will prevent the loss if, and only if, the cost of prevention is lower than the cost of liability (the latter being the loss discounted by the probability (1) that—without preventive measures—the loss will actually occur and (2) that the person in question will in fact be held liable).[6] Consequently, the main concern in creating a legal rule has to be what kind of behaviour the rule will induce. Economic analysis offers a model for predicting this behaviour. Thus, positive economic analysis is used as a tool for rule-making: being able to predict the consequences of the possible alternative norms, the law-giver can select the rule which best serves to achieve the desired end.

In particular, legal rules have to address the fundamental problem of so-called externalities, that is, consequences of an action that are not borne by an actor himself but by others. The starting-point here is the idea that people will tend to take into account only those consequences that affect them personally and neglect the loss their actions cause to others.[7] For instance, a plant operator may not take the environmental pollution caused by his plant into consideration when he decides how to equip it and how much to produce with it. He will, therefore, make decisions based on his own (private) cost instead of the total cost and will take too few precautions against the adverse effects of the plant, running it too much or too intensely. One of the fundamental tasks of legal rules is to avoid this outcome by

---

[5] Richard Posner, *Economic Analysis of Law* (6th edn, 2003), 25. See also ibid at 249 ff and Richard Posner, *The Economics of Justice* (2nd edn, 1983), 4 f.

[6] Of course, this example is considerably simplified. For an exact analysis, for example, one would have to use marginal cost and marginal expected detriment.

[7] Conversely, they also neglect the benefits others derive from their actions.

making actors take into account the cost of their actions to others. Thus, the public cost has to be 'internalized', that is, converted into a private cost.

One fundamental insight offered by positive economic analysis is called the Coase theorem.[8] It suggests that, in many cases, the law need not worry about the internalization of externalities because people will actually take them into account by themselves (at least in theory). This is due to the fact that people are free to bargain in regard to the externalities and thus consider the price they have to pay or receive. Suppose that a night club has two neighbours who suffer from the club's noise emissions. Two possible property rules apply: either the club has a right to emit the noise or the neighbours have a right not to be affected by it. In the first case, the neighbours will be willing to pay the club a certain amount to reduce the noise; in the second case, the neighbours will be willing to surrender their right for the payment of compensation. In both cases, the amount of money will depend on the value the neighbours attach to their peace and quiet.[9] Consequently, in both cases the club will take the neighbours' need for quiet into account when deciding how late to stay open, whether or not to install noise protection, and so on. It will do so in the first case because it can be paid to reduce the noise and, in the second case, because it has to pay for noise emission. Thus, according to the Coase theorem, whatever the property rule is, the club will internalize the external cost of its activity and consequently make socially desirable decisions. The difference between the two property rules is ultimately distributional.

However, the assumption that property rules do not really matter with respect to influencing behaviour is true only if bargaining between the parties involved is without cost. As soon as bargaining causes transaction costs, and in reality, it always does, such costs can well prevent an agreement. In that case, the original entitlement remains the final entitlement, the external cost is not internalized, and the property rule becomes of crucial importance. The lesson economists draw from this is that legal rules should try to minimize transaction costs.[10] For instance, in order to induce negotiations between the parties involved, the property rules should put the pressure on the party in the better position to start the negotiations.[11]

In many cases, however, transaction costs are simply prohibitive. Typically this happens when the parties are strangers who have no reasonable opportunity to negotiate *ex ante* (as in car accidents) or when so many people are involved that cooperation is not practicably feasible (eg when factory emissions affect a vast area). In such situations, the law must intervene to make the actor who is favoured by the property rule internalize the external cost. In principle, there are two possible

---

[8] See Coase, (1960) 3 *Journal of Law and Economics* 1 ff.

[9] As to the difference between offer price and asking price, see n 26.

[10] Unless, of course, bargains are to be rendered more difficult, for instance in order to protect the parties against ill-considered contracts.

[11] Such rules are called 'penalty default rules'. See Ian Ayres and Robert Gertner, 'Filling Gaps in Incomplete Contracts: An Economic Theory of Default Rules', (1989) 99 *Yale LJ* 87 ff.

ways to accomplish this goal: liability and taxation. Thus, the law can subject the actor to liability for the external cost of his actions. For example, the law can place the plant operator under an obligation to compensate the plant's neighbours for the pollution damage they suffer. The operator will then take these liability costs into account when deciding whether or not to take precautions against pollution and how intensely to run his plant. Facing the total (both private and public) cost, the plant operator will act in a socially beneficial manner. The second method to internalize external cost is taxation. To determine a tax that equals the external cost of an activity is, of course, a very difficult task. However, in many cases a liability rule is inoperable because either the damage affects society as a whole rather than particular individuals or because the damage each individual suffers is so difficult to prove or so small that, in practice, the actor would not be held liable. In such cases, taxation is preferable to a liability rule. For instance, putting a tax on petrol is a means of internalizing the pollution caused by driving because it raises the cost of driving. As a result, people may choose to drive less, buy more fuel-efficient cars, or switch to public transportation altogether.

Positive economic analysis is, in principle, uncontroversial. It helps to explain rules and behaviour in the past and to achieve desired ends in the future while leaving the choice of the desired goals and of how to accomplish them to the decision-maker. Still, criticism is directed at the predictive value of specific behavioural assumptions.[12] For example, it has been widely acknowledged that the model of the rational, utility-maximizing individual[13] has to be refined.

The first important refinement relates to people's attitudes towards risk. Studies in economic analysis are greatly simplified by the assumption that people are risk neutral, that is, indifferent when the choice is between a change of wealth that is certain and a change of equal expected monetary value that is uncertain; for instance, a risk-neutral person is indifferent to a certain loss of £10 and a 10 per cent risk of losing £100. However, in reality most people tend to be risk averse, at least where large sums are at stake, and prefer a certain change to an uncertain change of equal monetary value. For example, they choose a certain loss of £10 (eg for the payment of an insurance premium) rather than a 10 per cent risk of losing £100.[14] More sophisticated studies in economic analysis take this risk aversion into account.[15]

---

[12] cf Posner, *Economic Analysis* (n 5), 17 f.

[13] See eg Posner, *Economic Analysis* (n 5), 1; H. Eidenmüller, *Effizienz als Rechtsprinzip* (3rd edn, 2005), 28 ff; Hans-Bernd Schäfer and Claus Ott, *Ökonomische Analyse des Zivilrechts* (4th edn, 2005), 58 ff.

[14] For risk-averse people, the marginal utility of money decreases. Therefore, if they pay £10, the loss of utility is smaller than one-tenth of the loss of utility caused by a payment of £100. Consequently, they maximize utility by preferring a certain payment of £10 to a 10 per cent risk of having to pay £100. See Robert Cooter and Thomas Ulen, *Law and Economics* (4th edn, 2004), 50 f; Posner, *Economic Analysis* (n 5), 10 f.

[15] See eg the introduction of risk aversion in studying breach of contract remedies by A. Mitchell Polinsky, *An Introduction to Law and Economics* (3rd edn, 2003), chs 5 and 8.

The second refinement is necessary because people are biased in their perception and judgments. For instance, it has been shown that people who have to make a numerical prediction tend to take a known value as an 'anchor' which they then adjust and that such an adjustment is typically insufficient. Therefore, people overestimate the probability of so-called conjunctive events that require each of a series of elementary events to occur. This is because they take the probability of one elementary event as an anchor and do not sufficiently take into consideration that *all* of the elementary events must occur to produce the conjunctive event.[16] Conversely, people underestimate the probability of disjunctive events (occurring when any one of several possible elementary events occurs) because they start from the low probability of each elementary event. This is why risks are often underestimated. Thus, when a machine malfunctions if one of ten components does not work properly and the probability of the failure of each component is 1 per cent, the probability of mishap is almost 10 per cent.[17]

Still, the existence of these biases does not destroy the predictive value of economic theory. Many studies have shown that the respective biases are systematic and persistent so they can be taken into account in predicting behaviour.[18] Individual instances of irrationality deviating from the norm do not seriously affect the ability to predict future behaviour because economic theory is not concerned with predicting how a specific individual will act in a specific situation, but rather with predicting behavioural tendencies in the aggregate.[19]

2. Normative Economic Analysis

Unlike positive economic analysis of law, normative economic analysis is highly controversial. It is based on the assumption that legal rules should prevent the waste of resources so that, with limited resources available, we can satisfy as many needs as possible. In short, legal rules should be designed to promote efficiency. It can hardly be doubted that it is desirable to 'increase the size of the pie'. However, increasing the size of the pie causes distributional problems if it cannot be carried out without diminishing anyone's share.

Uncontroversial increases, which do not diminish anyone's share, are called Pareto improvements. They make at least one person better off (by enlarging his slice) without making anybody worse off (ie nobody's slice is reduced). But Pareto

---

[16] If a conjunctive event requires ten elementary events to occur and the probability of each elementary event is 0.9, the probability of the conjunctive event is only 0.35.

[17] See Amos Tversky and Daniel Kahneman, 'Judgment under Uncertainty: Heuristics and Biases', (1974) 185 *Science* 1124, 1128 f.

[18] See eg Cooter and Ulen (n 14), web note 2.1. at <www.cooter-ulen.com>; Schäfer and Ott (n 13), 65 ff.

[19] Posner, *Economic Analysis* (n 5), 18; Eidenmüller (n 13), 40; Schäfer and Ott (n 13), 63 f.

improvements are extremely difficult to design in practice.[20] Therefore, an increase of the size of the pie very often will meet only the so-called Kaldor-Hicks criterion (and not the Pareto criterion). The Kaldor-Hicks criterion is satisfied if a change causes gains to one group of people and losses to another group but the overall gains exceed the losses. Of course, if the winners were to use part of their gains to fully compensate the losers, there would be a Pareto improvement. However, under the Kaldor-Hicks test, such compensation is not necessary; instead, it is quite sufficient that the losers *could* be fully compensated. For that reason, Kaldor-Hicks improvements are also called *potential* Pareto improvements.[21] Thus, the use of the Kaldor-Hicks criterion will further the welfare of society as a whole, but may lead to distributional consequences that are deemed inequitable. Hence, after increasing the size of the pie with Kaldor-Hicks improvements, it is necessary to modify the division of the pie according to other criteria.[22] At first sight, such a two-step approach seems to take care of all problems: first, the size of the pie is increased by making changes which satisfy the Kaldor-Hicks criterion, and then distributional goals are achieved by re-slicing it. The problem is that redistribution is not costless but may cause huge financial and non-financial losses if, for instance, the group whose share is to be diminished puts up strong resistance.[23] The losses caused by redistribution may well exceed the gains initially made. Therefore, it is highly questionable whether the two steps can really be separated. Instead, distributional issues may well have to be considered up front when deciding on a specific measure.[24] In the latter case, the Kaldor-Hicks criterion could still play an important part as the starting-point in deciding on a measure but it could not be the only criterion used.

Another, and perhaps even more troublesome, problem with the Kaldor-Hicks criterion is that it requires a comparison of gains and losses among different people. With regard to financial losses, such a comparison causes no severe problems.[25] With regard to other losses, however, it may well be impossible because the

---

[20] Posner, *Economic Analysis* (n 5), 13; Eidenmüller (n 13), 52 f.

[21] Cooter and Ulen (n 14), 48.

[22] Cooter and Ulen (n 14), 7 ff; Schäfer and Ott (n 13), 7, 30 f, 36 f.

[23] cf Eidenmüller (n 13), 287 ff.

[24] Whether or not distributive goals should be relevant in assessing legal rules is hotly debated among scholars of law and economics. See eg Chris William Sanchirico, 'Deconstructing the New Efficiency Rationale', (2001) 86 *Cornell LR* 1003 ff; Louis Kaplow and Steven Shavell, *Fairness versus Welfare* (2002); Steven Shavell, *Foundations of Economic Analysis of Law* (2004), 654 ff; Eidenmüller (n 13), 274 ff, 283 ff. In many instances, it will indeed be cheaper to first increase the size of the pie and then redistribute because specifically redistributive measures (like taxation) can precisely target the envisaged distributive goals and therefore be more effective than pursuing these goals already at the first step.

[25] Of course, the same sum of money may confer a different amount of utility upon different people. The amount of utility somebody gains from a certain sum of money is linked to this person's attitude towards risk. Cf n 14.

size of emotional or other non-financial losses is neither observable nor reliably measurable. For example, how could one ascertain whether the pleasure one group derives from participating in auto racing (or in watching it) exceeds the emotional distress caused to another group by the environmental damage the races entail?[26] Hence the Kaldor-Hicks criterion is operable only with regard to the maximization of overall wealth, not with regard to the maximization of utility (ie people's happiness or satisfaction). In a society that does not regard wealth as the only, or even principal, value, efficiency (in the meaning of wealth maximization) will lose much of its normative impact. It is merely one of several competing ends that must be weighed.

To be sure, few people will doubt that, *ceteris paribus*, a measure which maximizes wealth should be adopted. In this regard, economic analysis does have a normative claim. But it offers no help in solving the conflict between the maximization of wealth and other goals and, as long as this conflict is acknowledged, economic analysis can never claim final decision-making authority with respect to normative issues. Today, even the most ardent proponents of economic analysis concede that efficiency 'has limitations as an ethical criterion of social decision-making'[27] and that 'there is more to justice than economics'.[28]

---

[26] One possibility is to measure the value of a commodity to an individual by either his willingness to pay for it or the price for which he would give it up. The two sums need not be identical because of the so-called wealth effects: people normally demand more for giving up a commodity than they are willing to pay for it. This is due to the fact that the marginal utility of money decreases (ie the same sum of money conveys less utility to a rich person than to a poor person; see also n 14): If the price that people ask for a commodity is to be determined, it is assumed that they already own the commodity and therefore, *ceteris paribus*, are wealthier than in a situation in which the price they offer for the commodity is to be determined. Accordingly, in the first case the utility they attach to the commodity will correspond to a larger sum of money than in the second case. In any case, the problem is that pure willingness cannot be ascertained. Consequently, these criteria are only operable if one asks how much somebody would actually pay or accept for the commodity in question. Then, willingness to pay is limited by the ability to pay; see Posner, *Economic Analysis* (n 5), 11, 13 f. This inevitably results in a commodity being more valuable to rich people than to poor people, regardless of the amount of happiness the commodity confers upon them. Hence utility would be maximized by redistributing from the poor to the rich. See Eidenmüller (n 13), 142 f.

[27] Posner, *Economic Analysis* (n 5), 12. See also ibid at 13 ff; Schäfer and Ott (n 13), 6, 53 f.

[28] Posner, *Economic Analysis* (n 5), 28. But see Kaplow and Shavell (n 24), presenting the thesis 'that social decisions should be based *exclusively* on their effect on the welfare of individuals—and, accordingly, should not depend on notions of fairness, justice, or cognate concepts'. Ibid xviii (emphasis in the original).

II. One Discipline as an Ancillary
Discipline to the Other

Comparative law and economics, as the combination is understood today,[29] brings together comparative law and the economic analysis of law by using one discipline to fill a gap in, or cure a deficiency of, the other. Thus, the disciplines are ancillary to one another.

1. Economic Analysis as an Ancillary Discipline to Comparative Law

It is a truism that comparison is the essence of comparative law. A mere description and study of foreign laws in itself does not constitute comparative research, but only the preparatory work for it.[30]

(a) The Descriptive Approach to Comparative Law

Comparative research can take a theoretical-descriptive form, inquiring how and why certain legal systems are different or alike.[31] Economic analysis may enrich this branch of comparative law 'by the scientific rigour and explanatory power of modern economics'.[32]

With regard to the explanation of existing likeness or difference, economic analysis is very valuable because it offers a model for explaining human behaviour.[33] Economists will assume that a legal actor—be it the member of a legislative body or a judge—will adopt the rule from which he or she derives the greatest personal utility. Ideally, this personal utility will correspond to the utility of society as a whole because the person in question simply tries to 'do a good job'. However, neither economists nor comparative lawyers[34] may disregard the fact that legislators and judges are also motivated by other, purely egotistical, considerations. For instance, a judge may, consciously or unconsciously, tend to rule in favour of

---

[29] See eg Mattei (n 4); Gerrit De Geest and Roger Van den Bergh (eds), *Comparative Law and Economics* (3 vols, 2004).

[30] Zweigert and Kötz (n 1), 6, 43. See also Nils Jansen, in Chapter 9 of the present *Handbook*.

[31] Zweigert and Kötz (n 1), 11; Gerrit De Geest and Roger Van den Bergh, 'Introduction', in Gerrit De Geest and Roger Van den Bergh (eds), *Comparative Law and Economics* (vol 1, 2004), ix f.

[32] De Geest and Van den Bergh (n 31), ix.

[33] Anne Sophia-Marie van Aaken, 'Vom Nutzen der ökonomischen Theorie des Rechts für die Rechtsvergleichung', in Brigitta Jud, Thomas Bachner *et al* (eds), *Prinzipien des Privatrechts und Rechtsvereinheitlichung: Jahrbuch Junger Zivilrechtswissenschaftler 2000* (2001), 127, 146 f.

[34] Zweigert and Kötz (n 1), 11.

tenants because he is a tenant himself, or he may be influenced by his friendship with one of the attorneys. It is the achievement of legal realism to have pointed that out most clearly.

A frequent conclusion of comparatists—according to Zweigert and Kötz, 'one can almost speak of a basic rule of comparative law'—is that, except in areas heavily impressed by moral views or values, different legal systems tend to give similar solutions to the same problems of life, even if the means by which these solutions are attained may be totally different.[35] A possible explanation for this fact is efficiency.[36] We can probably presume that the increase of wealth is considered a worthwhile goal in most, if not all, modern societies, and that the importance of this goal increases as the influence of moral judgments in a certain area of law diminishes. Thus, in many contexts, legal rules all over the world will strive to increase wealth.[37] In countries with similar economic and social conditions, wealth will often be increased most effectively by the same or very similar solutions to specific legal problems. Hence, the similarity of solutions provided by different legal systems for a particular problem is not really surprising.

The ways the law arrives at these solutions, however, may be quite different. For instance, while the common law invokes the consideration doctrine to protect people from the consequences of ill-considered gratuitous promises, other systems, such as German law, use form requirements for that purpose. These different paths may be explained on grounds of efficiency as well. Thus, in order to achieve the desired result, a legal system will choose the means it can most easily integrate to save transaction costs; which means that is depends on the framework already in force. This phenomenon is called 'path dependence': the further a legal system has progressed on an initially chosen path, the higher the costs of exit. As a result, norms that were merely second best at the outset may become preferable later because they better fit the other rules adopted in the meantime.[38]

---

[35] See Zweigert and Kötz (n 1), 39 f. The so-called *praesumptio similitudinis* is highly controversial. See Ralf Michaels, 'The Functional Method of Comparative Law', Chapter 10 in the present *Handbook*, under Section III.3.

[36] De Geest and Van den Bergh (n 31), ix, xi; Ugo Mattei and Alberto Monti, 'Comparative Law and Economics: Borrowing and Resistance', (2001) 1 *Global Jurist Frontiers* no. 2, art 5, 5; Fleischer (n 4), 848. Cf Saul Levmore, 'Rethinking Comparative Law: Variety and Uniformity in Ancient and Modern Tort Law', (1986) 61 *Tulane LR* 235 ff and 'Variety and Uniformity in the Treatment of the Good-Faith Purchaser', (1987) 16 *J Legal Stud* 43 ff, who claims that more uniformity across legal systems is to be found when the content of a rule matters than when it is only the existence of the rule (regulating, for instance, on which side of the road to drive) that matters (ibid at 237 f and 44, respectively).

[37] Thus, Richard Posner has argued that 'the common law is best (not perfectly) explained as a system for maximizing the wealth of society'. See Posner, *Economic Analysis* (n 5), 25, 249 ff and *The Economics of Justice* (n 5), 4 f.

[38] Mattei (n 4), 219; Mattei and Monti, (2001) 1 *Global Jurist Frontiers* no. 2, art 5, 6 f; Fleischer (n 4), 849. A striking example is the use of the consideration doctrine in US law; see Ferdinand Fromholzer, *Consideration—US-amerikanisches Recht im Vergleich zum deutschen* (1997), 355.

Economic analysis can be particularly interesting for the study of legal trans-plants.[39] Why does a legal system copy certain legal rules from another system, and why are some rules transplanted but not others? Sometimes, the explanation may be purely incidental—if, for example, a judge has read a book on foreign law or studied abroad. More often, however, a transplant may be based on grounds of efficiency:[40] the transplanted rule probably filled a need in the adopting legal system and copying the rule from elsewhere was cheaper than developing an entirely new rule or 'reinventing the wheel'.[41]

(b) The Normative Approach to Comparative Law

Besides theoretical-descriptive comparative research, there is a 'normative' approach under which comparative law proposes solutions to specific problems under given social and economic circumstances.[42] This implies the evaluation of the various national solutions.[43] Therefore, a standard of evaluation is necessary and which standard is to be applied depends on the purpose for which the com-parative study is conducted. If the comparatist aims to find a solution to a specific problem of national law, that national law decides which result is desirable. For example, if the goal is to strengthen the position of consumers dining in restaur-ants, the chosen rule should offer consumers the best protection in that context. However, it will often be far from clear what the 'best' protection is; in this regard, economic analysis can be extremely helpful. It will point out, for instance, that consumer protection is not without cost. First, there is a trade-off between con-sumer protection and other goals such as retaining sufficient incentives for open-ing restaurants. Second, different ways of attaining a chosen level of consumer protection may cause different amounts of transaction costs (eg because they lead to a different level of litigation). Positive economic analysis is able to predict the consequences of the potential solutions for the competing goals and for the amount of transaction costs incurred so that the comparatist can make a more informed choice.

Furthermore, if the comparison reveals the superiority of a foreign rule, this rule cannot simply be introduced into domestic law. Instead, one must test whether the foreign rule will maintain its superiority within the context of domestic law and the domestic legal and social culture[44] because each transplantation of a rule from one legal system into another one causes transaction costs. Again, positive

---

[39] See Alan Watson, *Legal Transplants: An Approach to Comparative Law* (1st edn, 1974, 2nd edn, 1993); Michele Graziadei, 'Comparative Law as the Study of Transplants and Receptions', Chapter 13 of the present *Handbook*.

[40] Mattei (n 4), 123 ff; Mattei and Monti, (2001) 1 *Global Jurist Frontiers* no. 2, art 5, 5; Fleischer (n 4), 848.

[41] cf Mattei (n 4), 133.   [42] Zweigert and Kötz (n 1), 11.

[43] De Geest and Van den Bergh (n 31), ix, x.   [44] Zweigert and Kötz (n 1), 17.

economic analysis can help to predict the amount of these transaction costs and thus assist in deciding whether the transplantation makes sense.

Economic analysis can play an even greater role for normative comparative research if the goal is not to find a solution to a specific problem of national law but rather comparatively to evaluate different national solutions to a real-life problem.[45] This may be a purely academic enterprise, but frequently it is a necessary step in drafting uniform law such as the United Nations Convention on Contracts for the International Sale of Goods (CISG) or the Lando Principles. In these cases, the normative standard of evaluation cannot be taken from any particular national law. To be sure, the comparatist can simply rely on his own sense of fairness.[46] By pointing out the consequences of the different solutions, positive economic analysis at least enables the comparatist to substantiate why he deems one solution preferable to the other—and, even more importantly, forces him to do so and not to hide behind vague notions of 'fairness' or 'justice'.

Of course, with regard to problems involving moral judgments or important immaterial values, a reliance on moral values or a sense of fairness may be well-nigh inevitable. Yet, with regard to problems within an economic context, normative economic analysis offers a much more precise and widely acceptable standard of evaluation, to wit, efficiency. In such cases, it is obvious that legal rules must not neglect the goal of wealth maximization[47] because inefficient rules decrease the size of the pie that can be distributed, according to whatever criteria,[48] among the members of society. In other words, efficiency may not be the only goal, but it is probably the most important and, consequently, it can be used as normative standard for evaluating the available alternative rules.[49] An efficiency evaluation will be acceptable to most, if not all, modern societies. Admittedly, there will be disagreement about the role efficiency is to play in various contexts. But even if someone thinks efficiency not the most crucial criterion in a specific context, he will consider a ranking of the various national rules according to the relative efficiency enlightening: at minimum, such a ranking permits a comparison of the rules under a uniform standard, even if that standard is not the only one employed.

Thus, economic analysis may fulfil a double function in the most important and most difficult activity of comparative lawyers, that is, the evaluation of the various national rules in comparison to each other: positive economic analysis is a valuable

---

[45] On the importance of the principle of functionality, see Zweigert and Kötz (n 1), 34 ff; Ralf Michaels, 'The Functional Method of Comparative Law', Chapter 10 of this *Handbook*.

[46] cf Zweigert and Kötz (n 1), 46 f; De Geest and Van den Bergh (n 31), ix, x f.

[47] If efficiency were to be understood as the maximization of utility, it could *always* be used as the standard of evaluation. However, as explained above, Section I.2, in practice utility is not an operable concept.

[48] See above, text at nn 21–4.

[49] Mattei (n 4), 94; Mattei and Monti, (2001) 1 *Global Jurist Frontiers* no. 2, art 5, 4; Fleischer (n 4), 847 f. van Aaken (n 33), 146 n 90 rejects the use of efficiency as a normative standard for assessing the different rules.

tool for establishing the advantages and disadvantages of the rules in question and normative economic analysis allows the rules to be ranked according to a standard that can be universally acknowledged, even if there is no agreement whether it should prevail in a particular instance.

2. Comparative Law as an Ancillary Discipline to Economic Analysis

Economic analysis of law is a social science. Since both positive and normative economic analyses of law study the effect of legal rules, they need these rules as input. Comparative law can be invaluable in providing it.

Of course, a scholar of economic analysis can study imaginary, that is, invented, rules, or, more likely, prototypical rules such as a strict liability rule without any qualifications and exceptions. Studies based on such rules can provide valuable insights into the workings of different basic concepts. Indeed, such studies are often indispensable because their relative simplicity and their suitability to mathematical modelling facilitate an understanding of how legal rules work and what effects they produce. None the less, the practising lawyer may be at a loss in the face of such studies when he tries to solve a specific legal problem. Comparing the set of imaginary or prototypical rules examined by the economist to the set of real rules governing his problem, he will often find little similarity. Even if economic analysis examines the very same rule that governs the case in question, it often detaches this rule from its framework and therefore does not respond to the real-life situation. The practically minded lawyer will also wonder what the rational (or only systematically biased), wealth-maximizing, and perhaps risk-neutral, actors he finds in studies of economic analysis have in common with the people he encounters in his everyday life—and for whom the legal rules he is concerned with are designed.

Naturally, economic theory must make use of models and the essence of models consists in the reduction of complexity. After all, a model that exactly depicts reality would be neither feasible nor useful. However, if economic analysis is conducted not for its own sake but in order to assist in solving real-life problems, the models used must be as close to reality as possible. A legal scholar or practitioner who wants to make use of the insights of economic analysis would often gladly accept less precision and weaker mathematical underpinnings (which most often he does not understand anyway) in return for more realistic results. A statement of what *kind* of behaviour will *probably* be caused by a specific rule under real-life conditions, that is, within the existing legal framework and if applied to real people, is much more useful to him than an *exact* prediction of the behaviour of some hypothetical individual under the influence of one specific rule detached from interactions with the surrounding norms.

Thus, in order to be useful in practice, economic analysis, having gained fundamental insights into the working of legal rules by modelling, must come down to earth and sacrifice exactitude in order to get closer to real life. In this process, comparative law can be helpful in two regards: the choice of the rules to be examined and a prediction of how people will react to these rules.

Comparative law can provide economic analysis with the objects of study, namely a huge variety of rules within a realistic legal environment.[50] Note that, for that purpose, mere knowledge of foreign legal rules is not sufficient; instead, it takes the special expertise of the comparatist. This is so because economic analysis and comparative law share the same point of departure. They both start not with a specific legal rule but rather with a real-life problem and then examine various legal rules, perhaps belonging to radically different branches of the law, which may be used for solving that problem.[51] The major difficulty for the scholar of economic analysis is to identify the rules in question and that is the comparatist's field of expertise. He is trained in the functional approach. Hence, he knows, for instance, that some problems can be solved either by rules of procedure or by rules of substantive law, which, again, may belong to completely different areas. Thus, he can help the scholar of economic analysis to make full use of the actual solutions available.

For a positive economic analysis, this not only expands its range, it also increases its analytical capacity. As mentioned above, economic analysis must reduce complexity. Thus, it becomes necessary to decide how much of the regulatory framework in which a particular rule is embedded must be taken into account. Is it, for instance, necessary to consider the procedural environment or is it possible to focus exclusively on substantive law? If economic analysis neglects rules that influence the behaviour of people coping with the real-life problem studied, the results are likely to be seriously flawed. To be sure, there are no general standards determining on what portion of the vast body of rules in a legal system one must focus. In order to find the right answer in each individual case, one needs a fundamental understanding of the interaction between the different sets of rules. For a comparatist, it is routine business to make such choices: cutting sensible portions out of a legal system is part of his everyday work. Admittedly, the ends pursued by the comparatist and the economist are different: the comparatist wants to compare the portions taken from different legal systems, whereas the scholar of economic analysis seeks to examine how the selected rules interact to influence human behaviour. But the correct selection and size of the portions of rules does not

---

[50] cf De Geest and Van den Bergh (n 31), ix, xiv; Fleischer (n 4), 848. Mattei (n 4), 29, 54, 57, 63 accuses law and economics of being based on a natural law conception of property that has never been 'law in action' anywhere. He holds this flaw responsible for the critical attitude many traditional legal scholars assume towards law and economics. In addition, he criticizes law and economics for often presupposing the modern institutional background of US law (ibid at 69, 75).

[51] cf van Aaken (n 33), 148 f; Fleischer (n 4), 847.

depend on the end for which they are to be used. As a result, the scholar of economic analysis should rely on the help and expertise of the comparatist who is trained in 'carving up' legal systems for purposes of study.

For normative economic analysis, it is even more important to survey all possible solutions for a specific problem. Since the goal of normative economic analysis is to find the best solution, it must necessarily examine all options available. Even more importantly, normative economic analysis must focus on the correct portion of rules in a given system lest it misunderstands, and thus misjudges, how well a legal system copes with a given problem.[52] If, for instance, a scholar of economic analysis overlooks procedural rules that help to solve a problem, and if he thus focuses on substantive law only, he may well conclude—wrongly—that the respective system copes insufficiently with the problem at hand. For example, Michael Adams has demonstrated that many US-American law and economics scholars who sought to assess the efficiency of rules allocating litigation costs in the United States and Germany neglected highly important characteristics of German law, such as the determination of attorney fees by statute and the monitoring of costs by judges.[53]

The second kind of help comparative law may offer relates to the main task of positive economic analysis, that is, the prediction of how people will react to specific norms. In this regard, economic analysis operates with a set of plausible assumptions about human behaviour and modern scholars, such as the proponents of behavioural law and economics, take into account the systematic biases people have. However, the lawyer who wants to use economic analysis as a tool for solving a specific legal problem will immediately miss concrete empirical proof for many of these assumptions. Economic analysis mainly relies on empirical studies of human behaviour in general, not on knowledge about the effects of a specific legal rule. In addition, many of these studies have been conducted in a laboratory environment and it is doubtful to what extent their results can be transferred to human behaviour in so complex an environment as a whole legal system. To be sure, economic analysis has to rely on general empirical studies of human behaviour and to draw conclusions from these studies about the incentives provided by a specific norm. After all, the very point of positive economic analysis is to reach conclusions about human reactions to specific norms *without* empirically establishing this reaction in every case. Even so, for the statements to be as accurate as possible, positive economic analysis has to accumulate as many real data as possible, and preferably data about behaviour in real-life situations rather than under laboratory conditions. These data can often be gathered

[52] cf De Geest and Van den Bergh (n 31), ix, xiv.

[53] Michael Adams, 'The Conflicts of Jurisdictions—An Economic Analysis of Pre-trial Discovery, Fact Gathering and Cost Shifting Rules in the United States and Germany', (1995) 3 *ERPL* 53, 80 ff. See also Mattei (n 4), 69, 75.

without specially designed, expensive studies by simply observing[54] how people behave in a legal system containing the rule in question.[55] Thus, De Geest and Van den Bergh have aptly called comparative law 'a huge library of reported legal experiments'.[56]

To summarize, the great benefit comparative law offers to the economic analysis of law is that it brings economic analysis down from the clear, blue skies of economic theory to the varied and complex conditions on earth. In the process, economic analysis may lose some of its rigour and thus some of its appeal to economic theorists, but it becomes much more useful to the practitioner who has to cope with the real-life problems he confronts.

3. An Example

A problem every legal system is faced with is establishing a rule for assessing contractual damages. Some systems (eg German law) provide for full compensation for all consequences of the breach. Others limit the compensation to the damage the breaching party could have foreseen at the time of contracting. Historical comparative research has shown that the foreseeability rule is a typical example of a legal transplant. Its immediate precursor is a rule laid down by Pothier in the late eighteenth century, which found its way not only into the French *Code civil* (Art 1150) but also into Kent's *Commentaries* and into the works of Chipman and Sedgwick. In 1839, fifteen years before the English landmark decision in *Hadley v Baxendale*,[57] two American courts referred to that rule.[58] It was via the United States that the rule was finally adopted in England; Baron Parke, one of the judges who decided *Hadley v Baxendale*, explicitly stated that his attention had been 'drawn to the subject by reading Mr. Sedgwick's work'.[59]

(a) *The Comparatist's Perspective*

For a comparatist who wishes to explain the success of the foreseeability rule, the model of human behaviour offered by law and economics can be very

---

[54] Of course, these observations have to be conducted on a scientific level and therefore are not costless. But they are relatively cheap because one does not need to set up an experiment, and they are very reliable because they stem from real life.

[55] Mattei and Monti, (2001) 1 *Global Jurist Frontiers* no. 2, art 5, 4; Mattei (n 4), 28; Fleischer (n 4), 848; van Aaken (n 33), 149.

[56] De Geest and Van den Bergh (n 31), ix, xiii.   [57] (1854) 9 Ex 341; 156 ER 145.

[58] See Richard Danzig, '*Hadley v. Baxendale*: A Study in the Industrialization of the Law', (1975) 4 *J Legal Stud* 249, 257 f; Florian Faust, '*Hadley v. Baxendale*—An Understandable Miscarriage of Justice', (1994) 15 *Journal of Legal History* 41, 42 ff; A. W. B. Simpson, 'Innovation in Nineteenth Century Contract Law', (1975) 91 *LQR* 247, 274 ff = A. W. B. Simpson, *Legal Theory and Legal History* (1987), 171 ff.

[59] *Hadley v Baxendale*, 23 LJR (NS) Ex 179, 181 (1854).

helpful. What made, for instance, the judges of the Court of Exchequer adopt the rule Baron Parke had read in Sedgwick's book? What utility did they derive from that rule? The comparatist may recognize, *inter alia*, certain personal reasons, such as the connections of two of the judges to the defendant whom the rule allowed to win.[60] He can also see political motivations—the rule limited the discretion of juries and thus increased the power of the judges.[61] Of course, the comparatist will also think of reasons of plain justice, that is, that the foreseeability test was simply considered to provide a good and fair rule. Which factors really motivated the Barons of the Court of Exchequer will probably never come to light but the economic model of human behaviour ensures that all these factors are taken into consideration, especially the personal and political reasons which lawyers, at least if they are not proponents of legal realism, might otherwise neglect.

The reasons of justice are, of course, the most interesting ones. For even if these reasons were not the decisive factor driving the initial adoption of the foreseeability rule, they alone can explain why the rule has remained the standard for determining contractual damage recovery in legal systems as diverse as the French and the US-American. What is the appeal of the foreseeability rule? The legal literature proffers several explanations: the rule is considered a consequence of party autonomy or of fairness or a means to foster economic activity.[62] These explanations remain rather superficial and do not really allow a comparison of the foreseeability rule with other norms governing contractual damages.

To a comparatist who wishes to go into greater depth, economic analysis proves extremely useful. For economists, the limitation of liability created by the foreseeability rule is not an end but a means to achieve a desired result: the optimal allocation of risks. A risk should be borne by the party who can best control it— the so-called cheapest cost avoider. Therefore, the risk of breach of contract should, in principle, be borne by the debtor because he alone can take precautions against breaching. But determining the level of precaution the debtor should exercise requires knowledge of the magnitude of the risk. This magnitude depends on two factors: the probability of risk occurrence and the amount of damage caused should the risk occur. While the debtor normally will be able to assess the probability of risk occurrence fairly well, he often lacks the information for evaluating the amount of possible damage. If he underestimates it, he is likely to take too little precaution; if he overestimates it, too much. In both cases, resources will be wasted. Hence, from an economic point of view, the rule for assessing contractual damages should induce the creditor to provide the debtor with the information required to take the efficient level of precaution. This is just what the foreseeability rule does.

---

[60] Faust, (1994) 15 *Journal of Legal History* 41, 64.   [61] Ibid 41, 54 ff.

[62] See Florian Faust, *Die Vorhersehbarkeit des Schadens gemäß Art. 74 Satz 2 UN-Kaufrecht (CISG)* (1996), 198 ff.

The risk of damage normally to be expected is borne by the debtor because he can foresee such damage and therefore determine the efficient level of precaution against breach. The risk of damage beyond normal foreseeability is borne by the creditor because he can decide whether to take precautions against such damage himself (if he considers himself the cheapest cost avoider) or whether to make the damage foreseeable to the debtor by providing him with the relevant information. In the latter case, he makes the debtor liable for such damage but also enables him to charge a premium for the additional risk.[63] In short, an explanation for the great success of the foreseeability rule may be that it fosters an efficient allocation of risk.

But why is it that some legal systems, such as the German, do not exclude recovery for unforeseeable damage and allow for full compensation instead? In order to answer this question, we have to examine whether, in these systems, there are other means serving the same purpose as the foreseeability rule. Consequently, the comparatist must look more broadly for rules that ensure that the risk of certain damages is borne by the party who is in a better position to assess the risk that such damages will occur. In the German Civil Code, for instance, he will find § 254 II BGB. This provision contains a comparative negligence rule under which damages are to be reduced if the creditor negligently failed to inform the debtor that he might suffer an unusually high damage. Like the foreseeability rule, this forces the creditor to inform the debtor if he wants to hold him fully liable and so enables the debtor to take the efficient amount of precaution. In contrast to the foreseeability rule, however, this information may be given after the time of contracting. An advantage of the German rule over the foreseeability approach is that it induces a transfer of information with regard to risks that become apparent only after the conclusion of the contract.[64] A disadvantage is that information given after the conclusion of the contract does not allow the debtor to take the additional risk into account in setting the contract price. As a result, he cannot tailor the price to the risk the contract entails but can only charge an average price. Consequently, creditors who suffer more than the usually foreseeable damages will be cross-subsidized, which, in turn, may lead to distortions of demand.

This is not the place to decide whether the foreseeability rule or a full compensation rule is preferable. The point of the example is rather to demonstrate how a comparative lawyer can take advantage of economic analysis of law. First, economic analysis revealed the rationale of the foreseeability rule. From a descriptive

---

[63] See eg Cooter and Ulen (n 14), 265 f; Posner, *Economic Analysis* (n 5), 127. For an extensive treatment from the point of view both of comparative law and of the economic analysis, see Faust (n 62).

[64] Under the foreseeability rule, the creditor could gain nothing by unilaterally informing the debtor. Rather, the debtor would have to assume liability for the additional risk. But that would require a renegotiation of the contract and cause considerable—perhaps even prohibitive—transaction costs.

point of view, this helps not only to explain the rule's success in various jurisdictions, it also helps to identify the rules that should be included in the comparison, that is, all the rules that serve the same purpose as the foreseeability rule. Without the recourse to economic reasoning, the comparatist might not take into account the German comparative negligence rule in § 254 II BGB. Second, from a normative point of view, economic analysis allows an evaluation of the various rules by offering a standard for such evaluation, that is, whether or not they lead to an efficient allocation of risks. Economic analysis also helps to determine whether the rules compared will meet that standard because, in the absence of concrete empirical data, the economic model of human behaviour allows predictions about how individuals will react to the different rules, that is, how the parties will allocate risk in response to certain rules.

(b) The Perspective of Economic Analysis of Law

The starting-point of the scholar of economic analysis will be quite different from that of the comparatist: he will ask which legal rule leads to an efficient allocation of risks between contracting parties. In order to answer that question, he has to examine an array of possible norms. Comparative law can provide him with these norms and help him to better focus his research because the rules furnished by comparative law are not merely theoretical but have stood the test of time and are thus likely to produce at least an acceptable allocation of risks. Hence the economics scholar need not waste his time studying rules that ultimately turn out to be totally inappropriate.

Perhaps even more importantly, in order to evaluate a rule, the economics scholar must know how people react to it. The foreseeability rule, for instance, only leads to an efficient allocation of risk if, in appropriate circumstances, the information about otherwise unforeseeable damage is actually communicated. To be sure, we can predict behaviour by applying the assumptions normally used in economic analysis. But the data generated by observing real-life conduct are much more reliable. Thus, the comparatist can tell the economist that the German comparative negligence rule (calling for a reduction of damage recovery if the creditor negligently fails to inform the debtor of the risk of unusually high damages) is hardly ever applied in practice. Or that in systems with a full compensation rule, debtors tend to limit their liability contractually, thus inducing creditors who foresee unusually great damages to reveal this fact and to bargain for a full liability clause. Such observations, made by the comparatist while studying the law in action, will help the scholar of economic analysis to adjust his theories about the incentives created by the different rules and thus to identify which rule leads to the best risk allocation in practice.

4. Summary

The discussion of the foreseeability rule shows how enlightening a combination of comparative law and economic analysis can be. Whether one starts from the economist's or the comparatist's perspective, the ultimate issues are the same: which rules are to be examined? How will people react to them? Which rule is preferred? With regard to all these issues, the two disciplines can successfully cooperate. As to the rules to be examined, economic analysis can help to identify the 'larger questions' underlying specific legal rules and comparative law can then establish which other norms may be used to cope with the issue in question. With regard to the prediction of human behaviour, comparative law can supply real-life data whereas economic analysis allows predictions where such data are unavailable. And as to which rule is preferable, economic analysis proffers efficiency as a universally applicable standard while comparative law can help to determine the extent to which this standard is acceptable.

III. One Discipline as Subject-Matter of the Other

Beyond using one discipline to support the other, comparative law and economic analysis of law can be brought together by making one discipline the subject-matter of the other. Thus, one can study the economic analysis of law from a comparative perspective, in the same way one can study contract law or tort law comparatively. Alternatively, comparative law can be subjected to the tools of economic analysis. In the following sections, I will outline these possibilities. So far, they have not been studied in any depth. Here, I can only present some hypotheses as to what results such studies might produce. These hypotheses, however, indicate that a closer examination of the subject would be worthwhile.

1. Comparative Economic Analysis of Law

As comparative contract law consists of comparing different contract regimes, so comparative economic analysis of law means comparing the way economic analysis of law is employed in different legal systems or even in different areas within the same legal system. In that sense, it is really nothing out of the ordinary, the only peculiarity being that the object of comparison is not an area of law but a method of legal reasoning. That use of comparative law is far from revolutionary because comparative studies of legal methodology have long been an established part of the discipline.[65]

(a) Application of Law

It may well be worthwhile to examine the different roles economic analysis plays with regard to the *application* of law in various jurisdictions or areas of law. For instance, is economic analysis more often used in case law systems than in codified systems? There is a strong, albeit intuitive, case for such a proposition; after all, the law and economics movement in the United States may be considered an answer to the legal indeterminacy proclaimed by the legal realist movement.[66] Normative economic analysis, in particular, with efficiency as the leading criterion for decision-making, was a welcome means of filling the normative vacuum the realists found in US-American law. It is not surprising that legal scholars who were unwilling to content themselves with the role of mere commentators on an increasingly disparate body of case law eagerly seized the opportunity to regain their role as social engineers with authority to say how cases should be decided.[67]

In a case law system, economic analysis also promises to structure the vast body of decisions according to systematic criteria because economic analysis allows abstraction from the facts of the individual case. For instance, it looks at a conflict between a polluting plant and its neighbours not only with regard to the very specific circumstances in question (such as 'pesticide factory' releasing 'poisonous effluents') but also under the more general heading of externalities. In this way, connections with cases that appear completely different suddenly come to light, such as a case in which a child is injured in a neighbour's swimming pool that was not properly secured. Here, the risk created by the swimming pool constitutes an externality of the neighbour's activity in the same way the pollution constitutes an externality of the plant's activity. One may ask whether the interests of the child, like the interests of the plant's neighbours, should be protected by a property rule (ie an interdiction of swimming pools in private gardens), by a liability rule, or not at all. Note that in order to take advantage of this structuring and explanatory power of the discipline, positive economic analysis (which is uncontroversial) already does the job; recourse to the normative branch of the discipline is not necessary.

In short, economic analysis of law can be expected to enjoy a comparatively high degree of popularity in case law systems because it fulfils two important functions:

---

[65] See eg Zweigert and Kötz (n 1), 256 ff or Stefan Vogenauer's path-breaking study on statute interpretation in England and in continental Europe: Stefan Vogenauer, *Die Auslegung von Gesetzen in England und auf dem Kontinent: Eine vergleichende Untersuchung der Rechtsprechung und ihrer historischen Grundlagen* (2 vols, 2001).

[66] Mattei (n 4), 85.   [67] cf Mattei (n 4), 85.

it provides a normative standard in the absence of precedents and it helps to structure the vast body of case law.

In contrast, the code itself constitutes the basis for judicial decision-making in codified systems, providing also rules governing novel cases. Of course, economic analysis may still play an important part in applying the code and the more general a code provision is, the greater the need to render it more concrete by normative criteria that may be provided, *inter alia*, by economic analysis. In order to apply the standard of negligence, for instance, one may have recourse to the Learned Hand formula.[68] But, as the need for a normative gap-filler is likely to be much smaller than in case law systems, one may expect economic analysis to play a lesser role. The same is true with regard to its function as a tool for the systematization of the law. In codified systems, the code already provides the organizational framework so that the need for economic analysis as a structuring device is much smaller than in case law systems. Still, even here economic analysis may be useful. It can, for instance, demonstrate the similarities between the law of delict (tort) and the law of nuisance which may well be contained in parts of the code that are far apart. But again, this function is less important than in case law systems and therefore economic analysis is expected to play a lesser role.

To summarize, comparative economic analysis of law may entail comparing the utility of economic analysis in case law systems versus codified systems. Obviously, this can amount to a comparison between different national legal systems, such as US-American law (on the federal or state level) and German law. Less obviously, it may also mean comparing the use of economic analysis in codified and non-codified parts of the *same* system. Here as well, we may presume that economic analysis plays a lesser role in the codified parts, although one would expect the difference to be smaller than between different legal systems.

Perhaps the most interesting comparisons involve the codified and non-codified parts of systems, some of which are essentially based on case law (like much private law in the United States) and some of which are essentially based on codes (like most of German private law). Does the *general legal culture* of a country influence the way statutes are applied or the manner in which courts deal with case law? Do, for instance, American courts make greater use of economic analysis in applying the Uniform Commercial Code than German courts in applying the German Civil Code (BGB)? I would expect the answer to be yes because what judges do is, to a large extent, the result of their legal education, and legal education continues to be heavily influenced by the distinction between case law systems and code systems. This is true notwithstanding the fact that statute law is becoming increasingly important in common law countries and that case law has an enormous significance for the application of codified rules in the civilian tradition.

Another worthwhile study may be to explore the importance of economic

---

[68] See Cooter and Ulen (n 14), 333 ff; Posner, *Economic Analysis* (n 5), 167 ff.

analysis in the application of internationally uniform law, such as the United Nations Convention on Contracts for the International Sale of Goods (CISG). One could, for example, compare the use of economic analysis by courts of different Convention member countries. Uniform law offers a unique opportunity for a comparison of the methods used by courts in different countries because the courts apply the same written rules[69] and any methodological differences are likely to result from disparities between the legal cultures. One could also compare how national courts make use of economic analysis in applying uniform versus domestic norms. On the whole, the difficulties courts encounter in applying uniform law are greater because judges are often confronted with rules in several, equally authoritative, languages; because they have to consider decisions from foreign jurisdictions; and because they must be aware that a term may have one meaning in the uniform law and another in their domestic law.[70] One may speculate that, in this state of uncertainty, courts like to have recourse to the (at least seemingly) objective and internationally universal economic analysis of law. My guess would be, however, that there are no perceptible differences between the use of economic analysis in the application of uniform law and of domestic law by the courts of the same country, simply because courts tend to transfer their respective methodological traditions from domestic to international sources.

(b) Legislation

So far, I have discussed comparisons between different uses of economic analysis in *applying* norms and speculated that the main distinction may be between case law systems and codified systems and, further, that this distinction may well obliterate other distinctions within a national legal system. The situation may well be different with regard to the role of economic analysis in the process of *legislation*. Here, the distinction between systems of case law and codified law is not that essential. Furthermore, positive economic analysis may be extremely helpful in making good laws, even if one does not accept the normative side of the discipline. After all, every law provides incentives for future behaviour so that every lawmaker must care about how individuals will react to new norms (in the worst case scenario, the reaction can be the exact opposite of what was intended). As we have seen, positive economic analysis is a most useful tool for predicting how legal rules influence future behaviour. This could lead one to expect not only that economic analysis plays a major part in legislation but also that in this regard, there are no significant differences between case law and codified systems.

---

[69] Problems arise, however, if there are equally authoritative versions in different languages; as to the CISG, for instance, there are official versions in Arabian, Chinese, English, French, Russian, and Spanish. In this case, it must be ascertained that different applications of the same rule do not stem from differences of the texts.

[70] cf Zweigert and Kötz (n 1), 21.

Yet, a different hypothesis may be plausible and could be tested by a study in comparative economic analysis of law: the role of economic analysis of law varies greatly according to the *subject of legislation*, and this role is, by and large, more significant in case law systems than in codified systems. In this context, the following considerations come into play.

First, an understanding of law as a source of incentives for future behaviour is not nearly as widespread as may be desirable. Legislators will almost certainly consider the consequences of the laws they enact but, very often, they will focus much more on fairness or justice than on incentives. They will also think primarily about the solution of existing problems rather than about the prevention of future conflicts or costs. The abundance of consumer protection laws enacted by the European Community can hardly be explained otherwise. This legislation seems to presuppose either that consumer protection is costless (to consumers, at least) or that all consumers like to buy a form of insurance even against very slight risks (such as the risk of not being satisfied with a mail-order mouse-pad) or that consumers have to be mandatorily insured against such risks. This example suggests that the role of economic analysis is smaller than one might expect. It is also plausible to assume that it will differ according to the subject of legislation. Economic analysis is more likely to be employed in making economic regulations, such as antitrust laws, than in legislation concerning non-economic matters, such as family law. In fact, many people consider the very idea that individuals behave as rational and utility-maximizing actors repulsive in the context of predominantly personal affairs.

Second, the role of economic analysis in the *application* of law probably influences its role in the *making* of norms. A country's legal culture is largely shaped by the way lawyers are trained, and that training focuses on the application, not on the making, of rules. Since the role of economic analysis in applying law differs quite substantially from one country to the next, its role in lawmaking is likely to do so as well.

Once we understand the different roles of economic analysis in various contexts we can next, and perhaps more interestingly, ask: What are the reasons for these different roles? So far, I have relied quite heavily on the distinction between case law systems and systems of codified law. I have assumed that this distinction has shaped the respective methodological traditions and that these traditions have, in turn, influenced the use of economic analysis even in areas where the distinction between case law and codified law is irrelevant. Yet, there may be further reasons that account for the various applications of economic analysis. As to its normative side, the value attributed to the goal of efficiency probably varies among countries. Also, the value of positive economic analysis as a tool for predicting future behaviour may vary according to the subject-matter in question. For instance, the economist's conception of human behaviour may be more accurate with regard to market-oriented activities than with regard to conduct in strictly personal matters.

Thus, one explanation for the varying role economic analysis plays in different contexts may be that its utility depends on the context in which it is used, which in turn means that the incentives to use it are context-driven as well. Be that as it may, such considerations go beyond a comparative economic analysis of law and constitute an economic analysis of comparative economic analysis of law.

2. Economic Analysis of Comparative Law

Economic analysis of comparative law is the application of the tools of economic analysis to comparative law as a discipline.

(a) Positive Economic Analysis of Comparative Law

From the perspective of positive economic analysis of law, one can examine the role comparative law plays in different countries, in different fields of law, or even at different universities. Assuming that a lawyer is a rational, utility-maximizing individual, he or she will make use of comparative law whenever its utility is greater than that of an alternative discipline. Accordingly, lawyers are expected to engage in comparative research when they can gain better insights from such research than from using other legal methods (for instance, from economic analysis of law). Consequently, one may expect them to resort to comparative law more often when the law in force leaves more room for interpretation and development—where there is little leeway in these regards, comparative considerations, that is, seeking inspiration from other legal systems, are of little utility. This would suggest that comparative law is more frequently used in the preparation of legislation than in the application of existing rules.

As to legislation itself, recourse to comparative law can be expected to be more frequent when dealing with novel fields and issues (such as the regulation of the Internet) or with areas involving fundamental ethical decisions (such as the regulation of stem cell research) than in the modification of existing statutes. As to the application of law, recourse to comparative law is probably more frequent if the rule governing the problem at hand is similar to foreign rules. For instance, one would expect considerable comparative research with regard to the interpretation of a national statute transposing an EC directive because there will (at least eventually) be twenty-four other national laws doing likewise and thus dealing with the same questions. Similarly, if a certain national law is modelled on the law of another country, comparative research should be quite probable. Conversely, if a national law is rather unique (such as the German Civil Code's rules about the legal relations between the owner and the unlawful possessor), comparative research as to the application of this law seems pointless—and hence will be rare.

It would be a fundamental mistake, however, to suppose that the incentives to engage in comparative research depend exclusively on the insight one may gain from it. Such insight is just one motivating factor among others, and not necessarily the most powerful one. To be sure, there are certain personal incentives that economic analysis of comparative law cannot take into account. For example, a scholar may resort to comparative law because he was once impressed by a charismatic academic teacher or because an attractive fellow-student always works in the comparative law section of the library. But other non-academic concerns are more easily calculable. For instance, at some point in time, it may have been easier for scholars of comparative law to get tenure because there was a shortage of academics in that field; or the prospect of attending conferences in foreign countries and meeting foreign lawyers makes comparative law an attractive field of work; some scholars may also strive for the international reputation they can gain as comparative lawyers. While people with high ethical and scholarly standards may find such considerations inappropriate, positive economic analysis cannot disregard them. Any discipline that attempts to explain and predict human behaviour must acknowledge that people (including scholars) are motivated not only by noble ideals, such as striving for knowledge or serving the public interest, but also by prospects of power, fame, and wealth.

(b) Normative Economic Analysis of Comparative Law

Economic analysis of comparative law may also pursue a normative approach. From this point of view, comparative law should be used (only) if its study promotes efficiency. However, such a normative approach encounters considerable problems because scholarship is not necessarily designed to increase wealth (otherwise whole university departments ought to be shut down right away) and the utility produced by scholarship is often hard to measure.[71] Thus, normative economic analysis of comparative law makes sense only with regard to the choice between different legal methods for solving a specific legal problem. For instance, somebody drafting a statute and looking for the rules that best achieve certain ends may have to choose between doing comparative research and undertaking a positive economic analysis. The decision will turn on a cost-benefit analysis, that is, on whether comparative research or economic analysis offers the greater surplus. The cost will primarily consist of the time investment required, but the researcher may also incur financial costs for buying books or travelling to foreign libraries. The benefit each of the two methods produces will depend on the insight it conveys. With regard to a statute intended to regulate market behaviour, the benefit of economic analysis is likely to be great because market behaviour (especially of businesses) is fairly predictable so that economic analysis may be a more direct and therefore less costly help in drafting than comparative studies could offer. By

---

[71] cf n 26.

contrast, the predictive value of economic analysis in areas where people pursue goals other than wealth maximization may well be significantly lower so that comparative research may be the superior choice. The benefit of comparative research will depend quite heavily on the degree of freedom the drafter enjoys and on the similarity of the foreign law: the more the drafter is restricted by the regulatory framework of his national law, and the less similar foreign law is, the smaller the benefit of comparative research.

IV. COMPARATIVE LAW AND ECONOMICS—A NEW DISCIPLINE?

We have seen a number of ways in which comparative law and the economic analysis of law can be combined. The use of one discipline to assist the other, as explained in Section II, has become fairly common among a certain group of scholars. Does that mean that there is truly a new discipline emerging from such a combination? *Comparative Law and Economics* is the title of a book published in 1997 by Ugo Mattei which purports to introduce comparative law and economics 'as a discipline that aims to carry the economic approach to law a step forward'.[72] Seven years later, Gerrit De Geest and Roger Van den Bergh published a three-volume collection of essays on comparative law and economics; they, too, call comparative law and economics a 'discipline'.[73] Is that designation justified?

As we have seen, the connections between comparative law and economic analysis of law are very heterogeneous. Sometimes comparative law has the upper hand, sometimes economic analysis is leading, with the other discipline as either a subject-matter or an ancillary device. If one leafs through De Geest's and Van den Bergh's impressive anthology, one finds that the collected forty-six essays are extremely diverse with regard to both subject and methodology; their common denominator is merely that all involve elements of comparison and economic analysis. In a similar fashion, the nine chapters in Ugo Mattei's book are rather heterogeneous as their subjects range from 'Efficiency and Equity' to 'The Distinction between Common Law and Civil Law' to 'Tort Law in Less Developed Countries' and beyond. No doubt, these books are very valuable because they explain how nicely comparative law and the economic analysis of law complement each other and how profitable the combination may be. But is that enough to constitute a new discipline?

---

[72] Mattei (n 4), 6.
[73] De Geest and Van den Bergh (n 31), ix, xix. Fleischer (n 4), 849 speaks of a *Teildisziplin*.

Of course, whether an area of study is a discipline, an interdisciplinary research field,[74] or merely a way of thinking is primarily a question of words, and one may well deem it a waste of time to pursue the question. Yet, labelling reflects the way we perceive a matter. If an area of study is considered a discipline, then there are insiders and outsiders, scholars who 'work at the frontiers of contemporary legal research'[75] and scholars who suffer from a 'diffuse and substantial lack of comparative understanding'.[76]

In my view, the creation of boundaries between different approaches to legal research by establishing 'disciplines' is scarcely beneficial to legal scholarship as a whole. We need to break down the barriers between the various 'disciplines', 'approaches', 'schools', and so on. Our ideal should be the universally educated legal scholar or practitioner who resorts to systematic, historical, comparative, economic, or other arguments as the problem at hand requires. Thus, in resolving legal problems, comparative and economic considerations should become tools as normal as the systematic interpretation of a code. And, just as systematic interpretation is not perceived as a separate discipline, comparative law and economics should not be considered a discipline in its own right either.

Richard Posner speculated that economic analysis of law 'may one day become so deeply woven into the fabric of the law that it ceases to be visible as a distinct field'.[77] Konrad Zweigert and Hein Kötz advocated teaching comparative law not as a separate discipline, but integrated into the teaching of national law.[78] When new approaches are universally accepted and thus no longer considered special, their fathers are often forgotten. Yet, it is precisely their absorption into the mainstream that signals their fathers' ultimate victory.

BIBLIOGRAPHY

Ugo Mattei, *Comparative Law and Economics* (1997)

Anne Sophia-Marie van Aaken, 'Vom Nutzen der ökonomischen Theorie des Rechts für die Rechtsvergleichung', in Brigitta Jud, Thomas Bachner, Raimund Bollenberger, Verena Halbwachs, Susanne Kalss, Franz-Stefan Meissel, Helmut Ofner, and Christian Rabl (eds), *Prinzipien des Privatrechts und Rechtsvereinheitlichung: Jahrbuch Junger Zivilrechtswissenschaftler 2000* (2001), 127–49

Ugo Mattei and Alberto Monti, 'Comparative Law & Economics: Borrowing and Resistance', (2001) 1 *Global Jurist Frontiers* no. 2, art 5

Holger Fleischer, 'Die "Business Judgment Rule" im Spiegel von Rechtsvergleichung und Rechtsökonomie', in Rolf Wank, Heribert Hirte, Kaspar Frey, Holger Fleischer,

---

[74] De Geest and Van den Bergh (n 31), ix.
[75] Mattei and Monti, (2001) 1 *Global Jurist Frontiers* no. 2, art 5, 1.
[76] Ibid.   [77] Posner, *Economic Analysis* (n 5), 28.   [78] Zweigert and Kötz (n 1), 23.

and Gregor Thüsing (eds), *Festschrift für Herbert Wiedemann zum 70. Geburtstag* (2002), 827–49

Gerrit De Geest and Roger Van den Bergh (eds), *Comparative Law and Economics* (3 vols, 2004) (collection of 46 articles)

Peter Behrens, 'Ökonomische Wirkungsanalyse im Kontext funktionaler Rechtsvergleichung' (paper delivered at the 2005 Conference of the German Society for Comparative Law in Würzburg)

PART III

SUBJECT AREAS

CHAPTER 27

SOURCES OF LAW AND LEGAL METHOD IN COMPARATIVE LAW

STEFAN VOGENAUER

*Oxford**

---

* I am grateful to Dr Alexandra Braun of St John's College, Oxford, for helpful comments on an early draft of this chapter.

I. Introduction

SOURCES of law matter. They serve to separate the province of law from the realm of non-law. Only propositions that are derived from a valid source of law are genuinely *legal* propositions. Other commands and prohibitions, be they of a religious, moral, or other nature, may determine our daily lives to a much greater extent. Nevertheless, they are not legal commands and prohibitions, with all the consequences this entails for their use (or non-use) in the legal process and in other spheres of public discourse. Adultery, for instance, may be prohibited by a statute or by a religious text. It may also be habitually sanctioned by the members of a particular social group. Your neighbour may find it offensive. Sociologists and political scientists may point to the fact that it has subversive and detrimental effects on families and on society as a whole. However, whether adultery is a legal issue depends upon whether we accord statutes, religious texts, group practices, your neighbour's personal opinions, or the views of social scientists the status of 'sources of law' or not.

Questions as to sources of law are inextricably linked with questions of legal method. Whether a source of law is successful in producing a particular result, indeed, whether it makes any impact at all, depends to a great extent on the way it is applied and interpreted. In a given legal system, the law does not simply consist of the raw legal sources. The law in force is the product of their refinement by the competent authorities applying and interpreting them. Law without interpretation, as Frederick Pollock said, 'is but a skeleton without life, and interpretation makes it a living body'.[1] Take, for example, the sentence: 'Congress shall make no law . . . abridging the freedom of speech'. This is most certainly a legal proposition since

---

[1] Frederick Pollock, *A First Book of Jurisprudence* (1896), 226.

the United States Constitution and its amendments are regarded as sources of law in the United States. However, the actual content of the rights conferred and the duties imposed by the First Amendment depends on what the relevant interpretative authorities, ultimately the US Supreme Court, understand by, say, 'abridging', 'freedom', 'speech', or even 'Congress'.

The purpose of this chapter is to outline the role of sources of law and legal method in the study of comparative law. In Section II I will explain why these topics have been central to comparative legal scholarship from its very beginnings. In Section III I will attempt to clarify their ambit for the purposes of comparative study, and I will identify the pitfalls lurking for the comparative lawyer who wants to determine another system's sources of law and the methodological approach prevailing there. Section IV gives an overview of the most important comparative studies specifically dedicated to these matters, and in Section V I will map out some areas which merit further research.

II. The Significance of Sources of Law and Legal Method for the Discipline of Comparative Law

Comparative lawyers have always attached special importance to questions of legal sources and legal method. There are three reasons for this. First, these topics are highly significant for every comparative enquiry, whatever its subject-matter. Second, they are central to one of the most widely discussed structural or taxonomical theories of the discipline of comparative law, the theory of legal families. Third, they raise interesting methodological questions because it might be argued that sources and method are not only the object of comparative studies but that, conversely, comparative law in itself constitutes a source of law and an important tool for legal methodology. Thus it can be said that sources of law and legal method are of interest to comparative lawyers on three different levels: in what may be termed 'applied comparative law', in the theory of comparative law, and in comparative methodology. In the following three subsections I will refer to each of these levels in turn.

1. Importance for the Practice of Comparative Law

It is impossible to conduct a comparative study without knowing which sources of law are acknowledged and which methodological approaches prevail in the various legal systems concerned.[2] Any enquiry into the solutions provided for a specific legal problem in different legal systems has to take account of the law in these systems, and 'the law', as it has been said above, is constituted by the legal sources as they are applied and interpreted in a given system. Thus it does not come as a surprise that the leading textbook in comparative law exhorts the comparatist to 'treat as a source of law whatever moulds or affects the living law in his chosen system, whatever the lawyers there would treat as a source of law, and [to] accord to those sources the same relative weight and value as they do'.[3] And, it might be added, the comparatist has to apply and interpret these sources in the same way as the lawyers in his chosen system do in order to make sure that he gives them the same content and meaning which they are understood to have in that system. Of course all of this does not only hold true for comparative enquiries in the narrow sense, but also for the merely descriptive study of a foreign legal system without further comparison (*bloße Auslandsrechtskunde*).

By way of example, a particular fact pattern that is provided for by statutory default rules in the contract law of one system might be dealt with by trade usages in another system. A third and a fourth system might solve the problem by judicial implication of terms into the contract or by a 'supplementary interpretation' of the agreement. In a fifth system, finally, the issue might typically be dealt with by contractual standard terms. In order to assess the solutions provided for this fact pattern the comparatist does not only have to know whether statutory default rules, trade usages, judicial glosses of the content of contracts, or standard terms constitute a source of law in the respective system. He also has to explore their relationship to other sources of law and their status in the legal system seen as a whole. And, finally, he must be aware of the methodological approaches that are adopted in relation to statutes, trade usages, contracts, and contractual standard terms in the various legal orders.

There is, of course, the possibility that, in one or other of the legal systems analysed, the fact pattern in question is provided for by mechanisms which these systems do not regard as genuinely legal. Comparative lawyers frequently observe that some societies are juridified to a different extent.[4] One might, for instance, imagine that the situation envisaged in the previous paragraph is not subjected to legal devices, but dealt with by a consumer ombudsman, an assembly of *boni viri* or *prud'hommes*, or the members of the local Chamber of Commerce who make decisions according to their discretion. Examples could be multiplied, and they

---

[2] A good example of the relevance of these issues to applied comparative law is provided by their extensive treatment in chapters 6 to 8 of Harold C. Gutteridge, *Comparative Law: An Introduction to the Comparative Method of Legal Study and Research* (2nd edn, 1949).

[3] Konrad Zweigert and Hein Kötz, *An Introduction to Comparative Law* (trans Tony Weir, 3rd edn, 1998), 35 f.

[4] See eg John Bell, 'English Law and French Law—Not so Different?', (1995) 48 *Current Legal Problems* II, 63, 90 ff.

could be drawn from most areas of law and society. A comparison of the positions of the chairpersons of national parliamentary assemblies of, say, the United Kingdom and Germany would reveal that the status of the President of the *Bundestag* is mostly perceived as a matter of constitutional law, whereas the position of the Speaker of the House of Commons is essentially thought of as a political office, so that the rights and duties of the officeholder are primarily defined and shaped by purely political considerations. However, findings of this sort do not necessarily entail that a comparative enquiry is impossible or irrelevant. The enquiry just changes its character and requires an examination of the relevant extra-legal context. And it provokes further questions, such as why the society in question does not see the need to deal with the fact pattern in legal terms, whether the relegation of the issue to the sphere of non-law is advantageous or not, and whether other legal systems might benefit from this approach.[5] In any event, the knowledge of the system's sources of law remains vital to the comparatist because, without it, he would not be able to assess the legal or non-legal character of the solution provided.

2. Importance for the Theory of Comparative Law

Sources of law and legal method are important to comparative lawyers for another reason: they are central building blocks of various theories of legal families. These theories divide the various legal systems of the world into larger groups with a view to organizing and classifying them in a rational way. Traditionally, the prevailing legal sources and the methods of reasoning from them were seen as a defining, if not *the* defining, criterion of classification. Early comparative research was mostly confined to Western legal systems and the divide between the 'common law' world and the 'civilian' systems. The crucial difference perceived by comparatists was that the legal orders in the former group were mostly based on judge-made law that was applied according to an elaborate doctrine of precedent, whereas the systems in the latter group were essentially based on codes and other statutes which were interpreted in a relatively broad and liberal fashion.[6] These issues figure prominently in theories of legal families to this day.[7]

---

[5] See Otto Kahn-Freund, 'Comparative Law as an Academic Subject', (1966) 82 *LQR* 40, 55 f.

[6] See eg Henri Lévy-Ullmann, 'Observations générales sur les communications relatives au droit privé dans les pays étrangers', in Société de législation comparée (ed), *Les transformations du droit dans les principaux pays depuis cinquante ans (1869–1919): Livre du cinquantenaire de la Société de législation comparée* (vol I, 1922), 81 ff. Proposed as one of two defining criteria by René David, *Traité élémentaire de droit civil comparée: Introduction à l'étude des droits étrangers et à la méthode comparative* (1950), 223 ff.

[7] See eg Peter de Cruz, *Comparative Law in a Changing World* (2nd edn, 1999), 40; Raymond Legeais, *Les grands systèmes de droit contemporains: une approche comparative* (2004), 64–71, 88.

Their importance was somewhat downplayed by the theory of legal families that dominated the second half of the twentieth century, that is, that of Konrad Zweigert and Hein Kötz. However, even these authors included 'the kind of legal sources a legal system acknowledges and the way it handles them' in the list of five factors the interaction of which was said to constitute the 'style' of that system. This 'style', in turn, was seen as the decisive criterion for allocating a given system to a particular legal family.[8] In addition, at least two of the other four stylistic factors advanced by Zweigert and Kötz cannot be applied without reference to sources of law and legal method, namely the 'distinctive mode of legal thinking' and the system's 'historical development'.[9] The former, as explained by Zweigert and Kötz, depends to a large extent on whether the system is based on case law or on codes and on the ways lawyers reason from these sources. The latter cannot possibly be traced without looking at the sources and the methodological approaches prevailing at different stages of this development. This becomes particularly obvious once it is acknowledged that sources of law and the approach to legal method do not exist in a vacuum, but are the product of human beings, and, frequently, of groups of persons exerting a dominant influence in a given legal system. These can be, for instance, judges, legislators, scholars, mandarins, or a caste of high priests. If the focus is shifted to these principal actors in a legal system who shape the system's general character or 'climate' and who can be called either '*honoratiores* of the law', 'legal notables',[10] or 'oracles of the law'[11] a legal system's decision to acknowledge various sources of law and a hierarchy between them can be perceived as the result of power struggles between groups of persons, each representing certain political and social ambitions.[12] When comparative lawyers talk about 'sources of law', and about that other key concept of 'legal notables', they simply highlight opposite sides of the same coin.

For the theory of comparative law, questions of legal sources and legal method are thus of the utmost significance. It does not matter, incidentally, whether a particular theory of comparative law is built on the notion of 'legal families' or, as has become fashionable more recently, on the conception of 'legal traditions' or 'legal cultures'. Every attempt to separate, say, one 'legal tradition' from the other has to give prominent weight to the sources of law and legal methods prevailing in the respective traditions.[13]

---

[8] Zweigert and Kötz (n 3), 71.　　　[9] For these two criteria see Zweigert and Kötz (n 3), 68–70.

[10] Following Max Weber, cf Edward Shils and Max Rheinstein (trans), *Max Weber on Law in Economy and Society* (1954), 52, 199–223.

[11] Following John P. Dawson, *The Oracles of the Law* (1968), who takes up an expression used for the judges by William Blackstone, *Commentaries on the Laws of England* (vol I, 1765), 69.

[12] Raoul C. van Caenegem, *Judges, Legislators and Professors: Chapters in European Legal History* (1987), 67–9, 84–6, 108–9.

[13] See eg John Henry Merryman, *The Civil Law Tradition* (2nd edn, 1985), chs IV–X; Patrick Glenn, *Legal Traditions of the World* (2nd edn, 2004), 61–5, 93–7, 172–6 and in other passages introducing particular legal traditions.

3. Comparative Law as a Source of Law and as a Tool of Legal Method

Finally, there is a peculiar twist to the relationship between legal sources and legal method on the one hand and the discipline of comparative law on the other. It is not only that the latter takes the former as an object of its study. Quite the reverse, it can be argued that comparative law as such, or, more precisely, the results of comparative enquiries constitute a source of law and a tool for legal method. This is a question that is traditionally dealt with under the rubric of 'functions of comparative law' and that is thus raised and discussed in much more detail in other chapters of this book.[14] However, the issue should at least be flagged in the context of this chapter.

There are, broadly speaking, two conceivable aims of comparative law. One possibility is to see the accumulation of comparative knowledge as an end in itself without further need of justification.[15] Alternatively, comparative studies can be regarded as a means to another end, and a number of functions of comparative law are conventionally enumerated for this purpose.[16] Some of these, one might even argue the most important of these, are directly concerned with the creation, application, and interpretation of law. Thus it is widely acknowledged that comparative law can be a valuable aid in drafting and also—despite some recent sceptical *dicta* on the part of some Justices of the United States Supreme Court and a number of somewhat ill-informed statements in ensuing debates in Congress[17]—in interpreting both national and supra-national legislation. It can also serve as a tool for courts creating and refining case law. Thus, the person making or applying a legal provision may take into account the solutions other legal systems provide for a given problem, and comparative law may, therefore, be said to be a 'source of law' in a wider sense. Subsequently, both the substantive law that is enacted on this basis and the methodological approach, which (a) has been followed in doing so and (b) is followed in the application and the interpretation of the law, can in turn be subjected to further comparative enquiries.

Whilst most lawyers would probably be prepared to accept the role of comparative law in the process of creating and elaborating the law as described in the previous paragraph, they would almost certainly be reluctant to accord to

---

14 See particularly Chapters 15–17 above.

15 See eg Rodolfo Sacco, *Introduzione al diritto comparato* (1980), ch 1, § 1.

16 For an authoritative account see Zweigert and Kötz (n 3), 13–31. For comparative studies of the role of comparative law in the courts, see Ulrich Drobnig and Sjef van Erp (eds), *The Use of Comparative Law by Courts* (1999) and Guy Canivet, Mads Andenas, and Duncan Fairgrieve (eds), *Comparative Law before the Courts* (2004).

17 For the most recent summary of the issues raised in *Lawrence v Texas* 539 US 558 (2003) and *Roper v Simmons* 543 US 551 (2005), see Ruth Bader Ginsburg, ' "A Decent Respect to the Opinions of [Human]kind": The Value of a Comparative Perspective in Constitutional Adjudication', (2005) 64 *Cambridge LJ* 575 ff.

comparative law the status of a 'source of law'. The reason for this is, as will be seen in the next section of this chapter, that the phrase 'source of law' is frequently understood to include the notions of bindingness and authoritativeness. Now it is undoubtedly true that the persons making and applying the law in a domestic context usually do not regard themselves bound by the results of comparative enquiries. They rather seek to 'derive *support*' for one or the other conclusion 'from what has been done in other legal systems' and want to know what a 'cross-check with these systems *suggests*'.[18]

In the increasingly important supra-national context, however, the normative force of comparative law is much stronger. Article 288(2) of the Treaty Establishing the European Community explicitly provides that the non-contractual liability of Community organs is to be determined 'in accordance with the general principles common to the laws of the Member States', and the European Court of Justice has affirmed that, 'in the absence of written rules' on a given issue, it is prepared to draw 'inspiration' from such general principles 'in other areas of Community law' as well.[19] It has particularly done so in developing a set of fundamental rights of Community law on the basis of 'the indications provided by the constitutional rules and practices of the . . . Member States',[20] an approach that was codified in Article 6(2) of the 1992 Treaty on European Union. Obviously, the 'general principles common to the laws of the Member States' can only be traced by comparing the solutions of domestic legal systems. This also applies in the case of the International Criminal Court which, according to Article 21(1)(c) of its 1998 Statute, has to apply the 'general principles of law derived by the Court from national laws of legal systems of the world'.[21] The provision is modelled on Article 38(1)(c) of the 1945 Statute of the International Court of Justice which directs the Court to apply 'the general principles of law recognized by civilized nations'. It is widely accepted that these principles belong to the sources of international law,[22] and the Court has frequently drawn on them to develop rules of fair procedure and substantive concepts, such as estoppel or the prohibition of abuse of rights. Comparative law can thus legitimately be said to be a 'source' of international law.[23]

---

[18] *Fairchild v Glenhaven Funeral Services Ltd* [2002] UKHL 22 [156] and [168], [2003] 1 AC 32 at 113, 118 *per* Lord Rodger (emphasis added). Cf s 39(1)(c) of the 1996 South African Constitution: 'When interpreting the Bill of Rights, a court . . . may consider foreign law'.

[19] Case C–46 and 48/93 *Brasserie du Pêcheur SA v Germany* [1996] ECR I–1029 [41].

[20] Case 44/79 *Hauer v Land Rheinland Pfalz* [1979] ECR 3727 [20]; see already Case 11/70 *Internationale Handelsgesellschaft mbH v Einfuhr- und Vorratsstelle für Getreide und Futtermittel* [1970] ECR 1125 [4] and Case 4/73 *Nold KG v Commission* [1974] ECR 491 [13]: '. . . to draw inspiration from constitutional traditions common to the Member States'. Neither of the decisions explicitly refers to Art 288(2) of the Treaty.

[21] Rome Treaty of 17 July 1998, establishing the International Criminal Court. See, in the criminal law context as well, the reference to 'the general principles of law recognised by civilised nations' in Art 7(2) of the 1950 European Convention for the Protection of Human Rights and Freedoms.

[22] See eg Restatement 3d of the Foreign Relations Law of the United States, § 102(1)(c).

[23] L. C. Green, 'Comparative Law as a "Source" of International Law', (1967) 42 *Tulane LR* 52 ff.

III. Establishing the Sources of Law and the Legal Method of another System

So far in this chapter I have used the concepts 'source of law' and 'legal method' as if their meaning were clear. In fact this is symptomatic of the way lawyers tend to use these terms: a lawyer surely knows a source when he sees it, doesn't he? However, the issue is not entirely straightforward, as has already been seen in the previous two paragraphs, when the question whether comparative law constitutes a 'source of law' was discussed. It might therefore be helpful to define the two key concepts of this chapter more closely and to enquire how a comparative lawyer can actually determine another legal system's sources and the methodological approaches prevailing there.[24]

1. Sources of Law

(a) Terminology

Law does not just happen. Every rule of law has an origin. It can be said to 'flow', 'emerge', or 'descend' from this 'source'. Such metaphors were already used in ancient Rome, by lawyers and non-lawyers alike.[25] The expression *fons iuris* was coined in medieval Latin from where it found its way into the major Western languages ('sources of law', '*sources du droit*', '*Rechtsquellen*', '*fonti del diritto*', '*fuentes del derecho*', '*rechtsbronnen*', '*retskilde*'). However, the commonly shared metaphor conceals an extremely varied use of the term in different legal systems. Frequently it is not even employed consistently within one and the same system. Different definitions can be found in different areas of law, and similar phenomena are given different names by different authors. Thus 'formal sources' are distinguished from 'factual', 'material', or 'substantial' ones, 'legal' ones from 'historical' ones, 'binding' or 'authoritative' ones from 'persuasive' ones, 'written' ones

---

[24] The most comprehensive and systematic treatment of the issues raised in this section can be found in Léontin-Jean Constantinesco, *Rechtsvergleichung*, vol II: *Die rechtsvergleichende Methode* (1972), nos. 40–69; a French translation is available under the title *Traité de droit comparé*, vol II: *La méthode comparative* (1974).

[25] Pomponius, D. 1, 2, 2, 6: '. . . lege duodecim tabularum ex his fluere coepit ius civile'; Papinian, D. 1, 1, 7 pr.: 'Ius autem civile est quod ex legibus, plebis scitis, senatus consultis, decretis principium, auctoritate prudentium venit'; Cicero, *De legibus*, 1.5.16: 'fons legum et iuris'. Cf also Livius, *Ab urbe condita*, 3.34.6 who describes the Twelve Tables as the 'fons omnis publici privatique . . . iuris'.

from 'unwritten' ones, 'mandatory' ones from 'permissive' ones, 'sources of validity' from 'sources of knowledge', and so on.

Part of the terminological difficulty stems from the fact that the notion 'source of law' is used to designate related, but ultimately different objects. First, it is sometimes employed to refer to the institutions and groups of persons which create law, for instance 'the legislature', 'the judiciary', 'the courts', or 'legal scholars'. Second, the metaphor is frequently used to denote various forms of conduct which these institutions or persons engage in and which are generally accepted in a legal system as validly generating law, such as the enactment of a statutory provision by the competent legislative authority in conformity with certain formal requirements, a long-standing and generally approved practice, or the formulation of a legal rule by the competent judge. Thus 'the passing of legislation', 'customary behaviour', or 'rendering a judicial decision' are said to be 'sources of law'. Third, the expression 'source of law' is referred to in order to designate the wide variety of factors influencing these institutions and persons when they are creating law in one of the ways just mentioned: a particular fragment in the Digest, for instance, can be seen as the 'source' of a passage in a treatise of Pothier's which, in turn, can be called a 'source' of a rule in the French Civil Code; Aristotle's ideas might pass off as a 'source' of the legal principle that like cases are to be treated alike; the comparative observation that the doctrine of privity of contract had been abandoned in the United States and New Zealand and was out of step with the laws of most European countries was, together with many other factors, at the origin and thus a 'source' of the English Contracts (Rights of Third Parties) Act 1999 which abrogated the doctrine. Fourth, the term is widely used to designate the body of law resulting from one of the forms of conduct that are generally accepted as validly generating law. It is in this sense that lawyers speak of 'statute law', 'customary law', 'case law', or 'professorial law' as 'sources of law'. Fifth, the phrase is employed to refer to the instruments or documents from which lawyers obtain their knowledge of such law and which provide evidence for its existence, such as collections of statutory materials, case reports, records of customs, or legal treatises.

The terminological confusion is increased by the fact that, in some languages and legal systems, similar words are used to denote different objects that can be regarded as sources of law. The English expression 'legislation' is a good example. It designates both the action of giving laws and the resulting body of enacted laws. At least up to the late seventeenth century, it was also employed to refer to the legislative body that passed statutes. In the Romance languages the term '*la doctrine*' or '*la dottrina*' refers to the body of persons producing legal literature, the products of their writing, and the body of printed material that may be consulted to ascertain these products alike.

The most important terminological issue with respect to legal sources is that of bindingness. In some legal systems the predominant view is that one can only speak of a 'source of law' if the persons framing legal solutions to given fact patterns are under an obligation to take the relevant item into account. From this perspective, a precedent, an Act of Parliament, or a Constitution can only be regarded as a 'source of law' if, say, a police officer is under a duty not to disregard a precedent in point, a judge deciding a case is bound to attend to a relevant statutory provision, or the legislature is obliged to respect the pertinent constitutional norms. The binding, authoritative, or mandatory character thus becomes an integral part of the definition of the term 'source of law' itself. In other legal systems a greater readiness to adopt a broader understanding of the term prevails, and it is widely acknowledged that factors which do not *have to*, but *may be* taken into account when framing a legal solution constitute legal sources as well. A judge in such a system, who finds that no source of law in the narrower, 'binding' sense just mentioned determines the case before him, might base his decision directly on a passage from the Digest[26] or from a treatise of Pothier.[27] The proponents of the broader view are, as will be easily seen, those who embrace, *inter alia*, the third possible use of the term 'sources of law', whereas those adhering to the narrower approach reject it. The narrower perspective typically prevails in legal systems which are dominated by a positivist concept of law. The wider view is characteristically endorsed in legal systems with a strong Natural law or other non-positivist tradition.

The difference of opinion as to the bindingness of legal sources is but one example of the fact that different legal systems and even different people within one and the same system adopt diverging views as to what constitutes a 'source of law'. If the comparative lawyer analysing another system is required, as has been said above, to treat as a source of law 'whatever the lawyers there would treat as a source of law', he cannot neglect any of these views. 'For the purposes of comparative studies', as Konrad Zweigert wrote almost half a century ago, 'a legal source is everything that shapes or helps to shape the law'.[28] As a consequence, comparative lawyers have to understand the term 'sources of law' in its broadest conceivable meaning. As has just been shown, the phrase 'source of law' is used to give an answer to five different questions relating to the creation or production of law: (1) Who creates law? (2) How is it created? (3) Which factors are taken into account in

---

[26] cf famously, *Acton v Blundell* (1843) 12 M & W 324 at 353 *per* Tindal CJ, holding that the authority of Marcellus 'appears decisive': 'The Roman Law forms no rule, binding in itself, upon the subjects of these realms; but, in deciding a case upon principle, where no direct authority can be cited from our books, it affords no small evidence of the soundness of the conclusion at which we have arrived, if it proves to be supported by that law, the fruit of the researches of the most learned men, the collective wisdom of ages and the groundwork of the municipal law of most of the countries of Europe'.

[27] See eg *Smith v Wheatcroft* (1878) 9 Ch 223 at 229–30 *per* Fry J.

[28] Konrad Zweigert, 'Zur Methode der Rechtsvergleichung', (1960) 13 *Studium Generale* 193, 196: 'Rechtsquelle im Sinne rechtsvergleichender Forschung ist alles, was das Rechtsleben . . . gestaltet oder mitgestaltet'.

doing so? (4) What are the products of the lawmaking process? (5) From which documents can they be ascertained? The comparatist is thus concerned with the creators of law, the modes in which law is made, the factors taken into account in the lawmaking process, the body of law emerging from this exercise, and the documents providing evidence for the existence of this body of law.

(b) Legislation on Sources, Theories of Sources, and Social Reality

How then does the comparative lawyer find out what the sources of law in another legal system are? In some systems the range of sources is determined by legislation. The classic example is that of Roman law where the sixth-century emperor Justinian, in his *Corpus Iuris Civilis*, enacted a catalogue of sources, stating that 'our law is written and unwritten'. The unwritten law comprised usage and custom, whereas 'the written part consists of enactments of the assemblies of the people, enactments of the plebeian council, resolutions of the senate, determinations of the emperor, edicts of the magistrates, and the opinions of the learned'. These sources were then defined in more detail.[29] Similar catalogues were frequently included in nineteenth- and twentieth-century civil codes which assumed quasi-constitutional status. Article 1(1) of the Spanish Civil Code of 1889, for instance, states that the 'sources of the Spanish legal order are statute law, custom and the general principles of law'. The Italian Civil Code of 1942, in Article 1 of the 'Provisions on the Law in General' which precede its main body, accords '(1) statutes; (2) regulations; (3) corporative norms; (4) usage' the status of sources of law.[30] Similar provisions can still be found in the introductory chapters of the civil codes of Louisiana, California, Switzerland, and Greece.[31]

Some civil codes also determine a hierarchy of the acknowledged sources. A hierarchy can be established between different kinds of sources in the sense that the source that is lower in the hierarchy may not contradict the higher source. The Italian Civil Code can again serve as an example. It states that regulations 'cannot contain rules contrary to the provisions of statutes', that in 'matters regulated by statutes and regulations usage has effect only to the extent indicated by them', and that corporative norms 'prevail over usage'.[32] The well-known first article of the Swiss Civil Code of 1907 obliges the judge to decide, in the absence of an applicable

---

[29] Inst. 1, 2, 3–9.

[30] As to corporative norms, please see the text following on page 884.

[31] Art 1 of the Louisiana Civil Code of 1870 as revised in 1987 (legislation and custom); ss 22.1 and 22.2 of the California Civil Code of 1872 (Constitution, statutes, and common law); Art 1 of the Swiss Civil Code of 1907 (statute law, custom, approved legal doctrine, and judicial tradition); Art 1 of the Greek Civil Code of 1940 (statutes and custom). See also Art 1 of the 1980 Israeli Statute on Foundations of Law (statute law, case law, analogy, and 'principles of freedom, justice, equity and peace of Israel's heritage').

[32] Arts 4(1) and 8 of the 'Provisions on the Law in General'. See also Art 1(2)–(7) of the Spanish Civil Code.

statutory provision, 'according to customary law, and in the absence of a custom, according to the rules which he would establish if he were called on to act as a legislator', deriving, in the last-mentioned case, inspiration from 'approved legal doctrine and judicial tradition'. Some codes also establish a hierarchy with respect to sources of the same kind. Article 2(2) of the Spanish Civil Code, for instance, disposes that, in the case of conflict between two statutory provisions, the more recently enacted or more special rule takes precedence over the more ancient or more general provision.

More recently, catalogues of legal sources have been increasingly contained in constitutional documents. Article 11 of the Constitution of the Republic of Ghana of 1992, to take but one example, provides that the 'laws of Ghana shall comprise (a) this Constitution; (b) enactments made by or under the authority of the Parliament established by this Constitution; (c) any Orders, Rules and regulations made by any person or authority under a power conferred by this Constitution; (d) the existing law; and (e) the common law'. In a supra-national context, catalogues of sources of law can be found in the Statutes of international courts.[33] Other legislative texts are less comprehensive and single out just one or a few sources that are regarded as particularly important or as radically breaking with the past. Thus, Article 55 of the French Constitution of 1958 declares that, in principle, international treaties and agreements 'prevail over Acts of Parliament'. Article 2(2) of the 2005 Constitution of the Republic of Iraq highlights that 'Islam is the official religion of the State and it is a fundamental source of legislation'. According to Article 8 of the 1950 Civil Code of the Philippines '[j]udicial decisions applying or interpreting the laws or the Constitution shall form a part of the legal system'. The 1919 Mexican statute on the 'amparo', the most important action in the Supreme Court which includes, *inter alia*, a procedural mechanism similar to the French *cassation*, established the binding nature for inferior courts of *jurisprudencia* laid down by five consonant decisions of the Supreme Court.[34]

Other legislators do not positively enumerate the legal sources they acknowledge. They rather single out, *ex negativo*, certain forms of conduct that are not supposed to generate law. Article 5 of the French Civil Code of 1804 famously prohibits judges to enunciate decisions by way of general and regulative disposition in the cases which come before them, and thereby denies the existence of judge-made law. The Austrian Civil Code of 1811 contains a similar provision in its § 12 and, in addition, its § 10 denies all customs the status of sources of law as long as they are not explicitly endorsed by legislation. The Prussian *Allgemeines Landrecht* of 1794, in § 6 of its Introduction, ordered that the 'opinions of legal writers or

---

[33] Art 38 of the 1945 Statute of the International Court of Justice (international conventions, international custom, general principles of law, judicial decisions, teachings of publicists, equity). See also Art 21 of the 1998 Statute of the International Criminal Court.

[34] See now Arts 192–197B of the *Ley de Amparo*, as published on 16 August 2005.

previous decisions of the courts will be ignored in future decision-making'. Article 265 of the 'supplementary provisions' annexed to the 1865 Italian Code of Civil Procedure also prohibited the courts from 'invoking the authority of legal writers'. Recently, in the United States much debate has arisen with respect to various Circuit Rules which provide that unpublished judicial decisions 'are not precedent' or 'not binding precedent'.[35]

Most of the legislation pertaining to sources of law remains fragmentary, and many legal systems do not contain any legislative provisions of this kind at all. More importantly, it might be argued that the legislator cannot possibly determine the sources of law in a comprehensive fashion because this would presuppose that legislation itself, be it in the guise of a civil code or of a constitutional document, is a source of law. For all these reasons, in most systems the task of developing a comprehensive and coherent set of answers to questions on sources is assumed by theories of legal sources. These are elaborated by legal scholars. There are different kinds of theories produced by different groups of writers. One group of theories is of a universalistic nature. Such theories are advanced by jurisprudential writers who are primarily concerned with the nature of the rules which ultimately determine whether a certain form of conduct qualifies as validly generating law and whether a certain body of rules and principles qualifies as 'law'. These writers are mostly occupied with finding a solution to the problem just mentioned, namely, that neither legislation nor any other source of law can validly generate its own legal validity. They maintain, for instance, that every legal system contains a certain basic rule ('*Grundnorm*') from which the validity of all other legal rules can be derived[36] or that it comprises one or more specific 'rules of recognition' which enable lawyers to identify what the law is.[37] For the comparative lawyer's work these jurisprudential theories are usually only of limited assistance since they are, precisely because of their claim to be of universal applicability, detached from the sources of law actually acknowledged in a given legal system and do not tell him the actual content of that system's *Grundnorm* or rule of recognition.

Other theoretical writings are meant to apply only to a specific legal system. Some of them are of a purely normative nature. They advance views as to who *ought* to create law, which forms of conduct *ought* to qualify as validly generating law, or which factors *ought* to be taken into account in this process. Others are purely descriptive. They are usually found in the works of doctrinal writers of the respective jurisdiction. General texts of the 'Introduction to the legal system' type,

---

[35] See eg the Eighth Circuit's Rule 28A(i), the Ninth Circuit's Rule 36–3(b), and the Eleventh Circuit's Rule 36–2. The constitutionality of such rules (which may be regarded as 'legislation' in the wider and substantive sense given to the term in Section IV.2.(a) of this chapter) was discussed in *Anastasoff v United States*, 223 F3d 898 (8th Circuit 2000) and in *Hart v Massanari*, 266 F3d 1155 (9th Circuit 2001).

[36] Hans Kelsen, *General Theory of Law and State* (1945), 110–24, 131–4.

[37] H. L. A. Hart, *The Concept of Law* (1961), 97–120.

or textbooks on specific areas of law, normally contain a short account of the sources that *are* in fact accepted in that particular system or area of law. Again, an early example can be found in Roman law. The 'Institutes' of Gaius, an overview of the law of the second century BC, begins with an account of what the law of the Roman people consists of.[38] It is essentially the same catalogue that was later codified in the *Corpus Iuris*. More sophisticated theories of legal sources were developed from the Middle Ages onwards. Their importance increased as new bodies of law, such as Canon law or territorial statutes, emerged alongside Roman law and a need for the harmonization and ranking of the different sources arose. Similar catalogues and rankings have been established ever since and can be found in introductory texts all over the world up to this day.[39] However, on closer inspection most of the writings on sources in a given system turn out to be a rather curious mixture of normative and descriptive elements. On the one hand, normative theories frequently refer to the attitudes to sources that are prevailing in the system. On the other hand, the descriptive accounts often combine the author's perception of what is generally accepted as a legal source with his views as to what ought to be regarded as a source of law. This mixture is responsible for the fact that, in many legal systems, rather different accounts of the system's sources are rendered. Still, most legal systems have a prevailing theory of sources that is widely shared in the legal community.

The comparative lawyer who looks at another legal system has to be suspicious of both the legislation and the prevailing theories on legal sources which he encounters. Legal systems, as John Henry Merryman once wrote, operate

in an atmosphere of assumptions which, although demonstrably unsound, tend stubbornly to persist because they are firmly rooted in the culture. This kind of folklore serves a variety of functions, some laudable and others regrettable. Although it exists in most exaggerated form in the lay mind, it tends, somewhat refined, to dominate the thinking of the profession itself. Alternately idealized and caricatured, it becomes the starting point of much scholarly discussion.

The folklore has a certain grasp on legal thought because participants in the legal system tend, 'through operation of the principle of self justifying expectations, to conform to the folkloric model'. However, this model does not represent an accurate picture of the legal process, and there remains a 'tension between folklore and practice'.[40]

These observations are particularly apt in the context of legal sources. There is a

---

[38] Gai. 1, 1–7. Cf Inst. 1, 2, 3–9, Papinian, D. 1, 1, 7 pr. (nn 29, 25, above).

[39] See eg John Bell, 'Sources of Law', in Peter Birks (ed), *English Private Law* (vol I, 2000), 3 ff; Ludwig Enneccerus and Hans Carl Nipperdey, *Allgemeiner Teil des bürgerlichen Rechts* (vol I/1, 14th edn, 1952), 240 ff, 311 ff; François Terré, *Introduction générale au droit* (6th edn, 2003), nos. 147 ff, 360 ff. The classic common law account can be found in Blackstone (n 11), 63–92.

[40] John Henry Merrymann, 'The Italian Style III: Interpretation', (1966) 18 *Stanford LR* 583, 585 f, 589, 591.

difference between how people talk and think generally about the law and how they go about it. The orthodoxy on sources, as conveyed by legislation and theoretical writings, does not necessarily reflect the social reality in the respective legal system, but rather the ideology as to the propriety of lawmaking that was predominant at the time the legislation was enacted or the theory was developed. But often there are conflicting views in the legal community which cannot be entirely suppressed. The Italian legislator's attempt to exclude scholarly writings from the range of legal sources, for instance, was widely ignored by the courts of the day. For decades the French *Conseil d'Etat* famously disregarded Article 55 of the Constitution of the Fifth Republic and did not accept the precedence of European Community law over subsequent domestic legislation. Furthermore, the conventions accepted within the legal system and, ultimately, in society at large as to what counts as a source of law can change over time. Such changes can be brought about abruptly and as a deliberate break with the past. The enactment of the prohibition on judicial lawmaking in the French Civil Code is an example of a revolutionary repudiation of the approach that had previously prevailed. The 'corporative norms' mentioned among the legal sources at the outset of the Italian Civil Code of 1942 were relegated to insignificance almost instantly by subsequent legislation. They had been the brainchild of Italian fascism and its corporative system: generally applicable rules produced by a variety of bodies and affecting the organization and operation of the economy. With the downfall of fascism in 1944 the corporate system was abolished, and since then no further corporate norms have been issued. Today, the reference to these norms remains in the Civil Code, but it only applies to a few collective labour agreements adopted prior to 1944. Similarly sudden changes of direction which were not even initiated by legislation could be witnessed in 1966 when the House of Lords discarded the firmly established convention that it was bound by its own earlier decisions, and in 1989 when the *Conseil d'Etat*, in an equally spectacular U-turn, accepted the supremacy of Community law.

More frequently, however, changes in a legal system's attitude towards sources of law come about slowly. Thus, the French prohibition on judicial lawmaking has become increasingly contested from the late nineteenth century onwards. Today, most French lawyers are, in spite of Article 5 *Code civil*, prepared to accord decisive weight to court decisions. Similarly, case law is of the utmost importance in the German legal system, which lacks a statutory regime of sources, but where the prevailing theory, deeply steeped in nineteenth-century legal thinking, only acknowledges legislation and custom as sources of law. The Austrian views on custom have significantly changed since 1811 when an exclusion of this body of rules from the range of legal sources seemed vital for political reasons. Because of such evolutionary changes in the general attitude to lawmaking in a legal system, legislative enactments and theories on legal sources are frequently out of step with reality.

As a result, the comparative lawyer, in his attempt to ascertain what 'the law' of another system actually is, cannot rely on official or semi-official statements and doctrines of sources. He must, to speak with Merryman once more, look beyond the 'folklore' and develop a certain sensitivity as to what is regarded as a source of law and as to how various sources are perceived to be ranked in the other system. In most legal systems, a closer look will show that the conventions as to the determination of the sources of law are far from settled. In reality 'the law' or, indeed, any specific legal rule will be constituted by a blend of various factors. The solution to a fact pattern will emerge from the interplay of statutory texts, judicial glosses, and suggestions in, maybe even contradictory, academic writings. This observation has led one of the leading comparatists of the twentieth century, Rodolfo Sacco, to draw an analogy with phonetics: just as a full tone is made up by the entirety of various characteristic sounds, the so-called 'formants', so a full legal rule is constituted by different 'legal formants'.[41] Domestic lawyers learn to discern the different strength of the various formants, that is, the difference in weight that is accorded to the respective sources, by years of training and experience. To acquire this ability whilst lacking the same background is one of the greatest challenges the comparative lawyer faces when he encounters another system.

2. Legal Method

(a) Terminology

'Method', in its original Greek meaning (μέθοδος), connotes the 'path' or 'way to achieve an end'. In post-classical Latin the term 'methodus' was already used to denote a mode of proceeding, and at least from the sixteenth century onwards the French 'méthode' described a rational way of doing things, a particular mode of proceeding according to a defined and regular plan in an intellectual discipline or field of study. In the same sense the expression subsequently found its way into all the major European languages. In a legal context, the term 'method' is usually employed to refer to the 'path' or the 'way' from an existing source of law to the decision on a particular legal issue in a given situation. Understood in this sense, it concerns the application and the interpretation of the law and is a synonym for the expression 'legal reasoning' that is more frequently used in common law systems.

Today it is widely accepted that the application and interpretation of law is, at least in some instances, a creative process that generates new law. As a consequence, the legal method of a legal system necessarily affects the creation of law in that system. It is for this reason that, as has already been said in the introduction to this chapter, considerations of sources of law are inextricably linked with questions of

---

[41] Rodolfo Sacco, 'Legal Formants: A Dynamic Approach to Comparative Law', (1993) 39 *AJCL* 1 ff and 343 ff.

legal method. This becomes even more obvious if, as is frequently done, legal method is not confined to the modes of legal reasoning, but is understood to include the 'ways' of lawmaking in a general sense. Legal method, understood in this broader sense, is also concerned with the creation of law from scratch and the procedures followed in doing so. It comprises, for instance, the legislative techniques or the style of drafting judicial decisions. An important part of a legal method therefore gives an answer to the second of the questions generally associated with the concept of sources of law, namely 'How is the law created?' As opposed to the theory of sources of law, it does not only identify the various forms of conduct which are generally accepted as validly generating law, such as the enactment of a statute by the competent legislative authority in conformity with certain formal requirements. It adds information as to how these forms of conduct are pursued.

In sum, and taking into account the role of methodological issues in both the creation and the application and interpretation of the law, it can be said that a legal method typically answers the following questions: (1) What is the style of lawmaking? (2) Who applies and interprets the law? (3) Which factors are taken into account in the application and interpretation of the law? (4) How are these factors ranked?

In the context of comparative studies, the notion of a 'legal method' is not unproblematic. It presupposes that there is a rational and methodological approach to lawmaking and legal reasoning. Undoubtedly there are primitive legal systems that have not developed such modes. Anglo-American lawyers sometimes speak of 'palm tree justice' when they feel that the decision in a particular case was methodologically flawed, thereby invoking the idea of a *cadi* leisurely sitting in the shade and dispensing justice as he pleases. It is certainly possible to envisage a society where disputes are resolved by, say, the casting of a dice or an observation of how the crows fly. However, such a society would probably be studied by legal anthropologists or legal ethnologists rather than by comparative lawyers. The systems that are analysed in comparative studies usually operate on the basis of rational ways of lawmaking and legal reasoning, even if the views as to rationality may differ from one system to another.

(b) Legislation on Legal Method, Methodological Theories, and Practice

In some legal systems the legislator gives directions on legal method. Legislative pronouncements on the style of legislation are rare. The legislative organs of the European Communities, for instance, have formulated a number of guidelines for the quality of drafting of Community legislation in a series of inter-institutional agreements.[42] A legislative provision on judicial style can be found in section 313 of

---

[42] [1999] OJ C73/1, [2002] OJ C77/1, [2003] OJ C321/1.

the German Code of Civil Procedure which enumerates certain aspects that have to be contained in judgments of the civil courts.

Examples of legislative enactments on the question as to who is entitled to apply or interpret the law are more frequent. Most of them belong to legal history. Once more, Justinian can be regarded as the ancestor of this tradition. He tried to monopolize the authority to interpret the *Corpus Iuris* by requiring judges to submit difficult cases to him.[43] Many other rulers from the Middle Ages up to the early nineteenth century followed suit. Religious legal systems commonly reserve the interpretive function to their spiritual leaders or high priests, as can still be seen in canon 16 of the Catholic *Codex Iuris Canonici* of 1983. An even more recent example of legislation on the power of interpretation is contained in the 1997 Hong Kong Basic Law. Its Article 158 provides that, in certain circumstances, this power shall be vested in the Standing Committee of the National People's Congress of the People's Republic of China. Usually, of course, in modern legal systems based on the separation of powers, the interpretative function is allocated to the judiciary. Thus, Article 220(1) of the Treaty Establishing the European Community stipulates that the Community courts 'shall ensure that in the interpretation and application of this Treaty the law is observed'. According to Article 90(2) and (3) of the Iraqi Constitution of 2005 the Federal Supreme Court of that country 'shall have jurisdiction over the . . . [i]nterpretation of the provisions of the constitution [and settle] matters that arise from the application of federal laws'.

Furthermore, many legal systems contain legislative provisions on the factors to be taken into account in interpreting the law and how to rank them. Some rules on the interpretation of legislation were contained in the *Corpus Iuris Civilis*. The *Corpus Iuris Canonici* of the Catholic Church added others, and the first Continental codifications of Bavaria, Prussia, and Austria contained more or less elaborate sets of interpretative guidelines.[44] The draftsmen of the French *Code civil* devised a similar set of rules for the *livre préliminaire* they suggested, but this part of the draft code was ultimately not enacted. This may be seen as a first example of legislatures recognizing that it is virtually impossible to develop a coherent statutory regime capable of embracing all the aspects of statutory interpretation. This view continues to prevail in civilian systems where today the task is seen to be one that has to be solved by the courts and legal scholars acting in cooperation. Consequently, the draftsmen of more recent civil codes, such as the ones of Germany, Switzerland, or the Netherlands, refrained from drawing up rules on this matter. However, some systems still contain provisions in point. Apart from Austria, this

---

[43] *Constitutio Tanta*, 21 = *Codex* 1, 17, 2, 21.

[44] See §§ 9–11 of chapter I 2 of the *Codex Maximilianeus Bavaricus civilis* of 1756, §§ 46–50 of the Introduction to the Prussian *Allgemeines Landrecht* of 1794, and §§ 6–9 of the Austrian Civil Code of 1811.

category comprises the likes of Chile, Louisiana, Italy, or Spain.[45] A fairly recent instance can be found in section 39(2) of the 1996 South African Constitution which provides that when 'interpreting any legislation, and when developing the common law or customary law, every court, tribunal or forum must promote the spirit, purport and objects of the Bill of Rights'.

In the common law world there are rules on statutory interpretation as well, but they are usually judge-made. Yet some common law systems have statutory provisions dealing with the interpretation of statutes. These 'Interpretation Acts' can be of two kinds. Some of them exclusively contain legal definitions of frequently used words and expressions, for instance the Irish Interpretation Act 1937 or the UK Interpretation Act 1978. Others also comprise general rules on interpretation, such as sections 4, 5, and 13 of the California Civil Code or the provision on the use of legislative materials in section 15AB of the Australian Acts Interpretation Act 1901, as amended in 1984, which is mirrored in the legislation of some of the Australian States. An attempt to codify some rules of this sort in the United Kingdom failed when the House of Commons rejected the Interpretation of Legislation Bill 1981.

Given the pointillist treatment of legal method by legislators, comprehensive and coherent accounts of the topic can only be found in scholarly writings on the topic. As is the case with respect to legal sources, there are both universalistic theories which are not necessarily useful for the comparative lawyer and writings focusing on the legal method of a particular legal system, the latter group being divided into normative theories, descriptive studies, and a majority of works that blend normative and descriptive features. The comparatist, again as in the case of sources, has to be wary of the legislation and of theories containing a normative element. They represent the preferences of legislators and legal writers with respect to various approaches to legal reasoning and methods of lawmaking, and quite frequently these views have not been accepted in the legal community at large, or they have changed over time. Section 4 of the California Civil Code, for instance, which stipulates that the Code's 'provisions are to be liberally construed with a view to effect its objects and to promote justice' can hardly be said to have made a profound impact on the practice of the Californian courts. The core message of § 6 of the Austrian Civil Code, that is, that statutes are not to be interpreted against their express words, has been assiduously ignored by the Austrian judiciary for a long time.

Even the more general or programmatic pronouncements on methodological issues made by the courts themselves cannot always be taken at face value. It is well

---

[45] Articles 19–24 of the Chilean Civil Code of 1855, Articles 9–13 of the Louisiana Civil Code of 1870 as revised in 1987, Articles 12 and 14 of the 'Provisions of the Law in General' of the Italian Civil Code of 1942, Articles 3–5 of the Spanish Civil Code of 1889, and Article 10(2) of the Spanish Constitution of 1978.

known that there is a difference between 'saying' and 'doing' in that the courts frequently propagate rules of application and interpretation which conform to constitutional and political orthodoxy, but are disregarded if they lead to undesirable results. The famous doctrine of *acte clair* developed by the French Supreme Courts is a case in point. It contends that a need to interpret a statute only arises if the provision in question is 'unclear and ambiguous'. If this is not the case, the statute has to be applied strictly to the letter. Still, it is no secret that the courts are prepared to deviate from the seemingly clear wording of enactments if strong arguments militate in favour of another result. The Anglo-Saxon counterpart of the doctrine of 'acte clair', the so-called 'literal' or 'plain meaning' rule, has suffered a similar fate throughout the common law world: although it has remained intact on the surface, the courts have been increasingly ready to discard it in order to achieve what they perceive to be more appropriate results. Similarly, the staunch English doctrine of *stare decisis* might demand that lower courts meticulously follow the precedents of higher courts, but again every English lawyer knows cases where this has not been done.

As a result, the comparative lawyer who attempts to establish a foreign legal system's approach to methodological issues will find that the respective legislation and the prevailing theories and doctrinal writings only assist him up to a point. As with respect to ascertaining the legal sources, he will have to overcome the other system's 'folklore' and develop a certain awareness as to which kinds of argument and modes of legal reasoning are generally regarded as acceptable and feasible in that system. This can only be acquired by observing the interpretative practices of the persons and institutions engaged in the application and interpretation of the law, typically, but not exclusively, the courts of that system.

IV. COMPARATIVE STUDIES OF SOURCES OF LAW AND LEGAL METHOD

In Section II of this chapter it has been shown that sources of law and legal method are of central importance to the discipline of comparative law. Yet, as has been seen in Section III, these concepts are far from clear, and getting to grips with another system's sources and methods is fraught with difficulties. Small wonder that a huge body of comparative literature has been dedicated to these topics. It is the purpose of this section to give a, necessarily rather sketchy, survey of the relevant writings.

1. General Studies

Sources of law and legal method are treated extensively both in textbooks on comparative law[46] and in introductions to legal systems[47] or to legal families[48] aimed at foreign readers. However, only few publications have been exclusively devoted to a comprehensive treatment of these issues from a genuinely comparative perspective. In the early 1930s the International Academy of Comparative Law devoted a session to the problem of the 'diverse sources of law, their equilibrium and their hierarchy in the different legal systems'. The papers, some of them given by scholars of the calibre of Roscoe Pound and Giorgio Del Vecchio, were published in the Academy's Proceedings.[49] A monumental, five-volume study by Wolfgang Fikentscher was published in the 1970s.[50] Over the course of more than 2,500 pages of text the author, a distinguished German private lawyer and legal anthropologist, dealt extensively with sources and methodology both in a comparative and in a historical perspective. He considered early and religious laws, the Romanistic legal family, the common law, and the Germanic systems before going on to develop his own highly sophisticated theory of sources and methodology. Many chapters of this book have the character of free-standing articles, or even monographs, for instance a 180-page-long account of Rudolf von Jhering's legal theory, or a fifty-page overview of legal realism. Whilst some passages of the book are outdated today, it still remains unsurpassed as the authoritative account of the subject-matter of this chapter.

A slightly less ambitious, but still comprehensive treatment is provided in the chapter on 'Sources of Law' in the International Encyclopedia of Comparative Law which was published in 1981. Over more than 200 pages, the doyen of French comparative law, René David, dealt with both the sources and the way in which

---

[46] Some, but by no means all of them, are referred to in the first section of this chapter.

[47] See eg with special emphasis on sources and method, Ivy Williams, *The Sources of Law in the Swiss Civil Code* (1923); Henri Lévy-Ullmann, *The English Legal Tradition: Its Sources and History* (1935); René David, *French Law: Its Structure, Sources and Methodology* (1972); Dominique T. C. Wang, *Les sources du droit japonais* (1978); Eva Steiner, *French Legal Method* (2002).

[48] See eg with special emphasis on sources and method, John Burton, *The Sources of Islamic Law: Islamic Theories of Abrogation* (1990); Yasin Dutton, *The Origins of Islamic Law: The Qur'an, the Muwatta' and Madinan 'Amal* (2nd edn, 2002); Robert Lingat, *Les sources du droit dans le système traditionnel de l'Inde* (1967). For the 'family' of mixed legal systems see Joseph Dainow (ed), *The Role of Judicial Decisions and Doctrine in Civil Law and in Mixed Jurisdictions* (1974); Vernon Valentine Palmer (ed), *Mixed Jurisdictions Worldwide: The Third Legal Family* (2001), 31 ff, 44 ff.

[49] 'Les diverses sources du droit, leur équilibre et leurs hierarchies dans les divers systèmes juridiques', in (1934) II/2 *Actorum Academiae universalis iurisprudentiae comparativae* (= Mémoires de l'Académie internationale de droit comparé), cf Roscoe Pound, 'Hierarchy of Sources and Forms in Different Systems of Law', (1933) 7 *Tulane LR* 475 ff. See, more recently, Edgar Reiners, *Die Normenhierarchie in den Mitgliedstaaten der europäischen Gemeinschaften* (1971).

[50] Wolfgang Fikentscher, *Methoden des Rechts in vergleichender Darstellung*, vol I: *Frühe und religiöse Rechte. Romanischer Rechtskreis* (1975), vol II: *Anglo-amerikanischer Rechtskreis* (1975), vol III: *Mitteleuropäischer Rechtskreis* (1976), vol IV: *Dogmatischer Teil* (1977), vol V: *Nachträge. Register* (1977).

they are applied and interpreted in different legal systems.[51] The chapter's most important contribution is the strong emphasis on Marxist law and on non-Western legal traditions with frequent references to Muslim law, Hindu law, and Jewish law. An important comparison of English and American law which comprised thorough examinations of sources of law and legal reasoning was published by Patrick Atiyah and Robert Summers in 1987.[52] Another monograph which focused on the sources in the common law world and in codified systems appeared in Italy in the early 1990s.[53]

As has already been seen in the course of this chapter, questions of sources and method can hardly be understood without reference to the history of the legal system in question. For this purpose it is helpful to draw upon Jan Schröder's recent account on the theories of sources of law and legal method prevailing in Continental systems between 1500 and 1850.[54] A slightly older, but still magisterial equivalent for the common law tradition is Carleton Kemp Allen's *Law in the Making*.[55] In this context, two other studies have to be mentioned as well: both John Dawson's *Oracles of the Law* and Raoul van Caenegem's *Judges, Legislators and Professors* provide ample references to English, French, and German legal history.[56] They approach the topic by focusing on legal notables, which, as has been said before, changes the perspective, but not the field of enquiry.

2. Studies of Specific Legal Sources and the Methodological Approaches Pertaining to them

Apart from these general works, there is a multitude of studies focusing on specific legal sources and the methodological approaches pertaining to them. The following observations are not intended to give a comprehensive overview over the relevant literature, but rather to highlight the most important and influential writings. In order to limit the material, only genuinely comparative works will be mentioned, at the expense of neglecting studies on the sources and methods of a

---

[51] René David, 'Sources of Law', in *International Encyclopedia of Comparative Law* (vol II, ch 3, 1981).

[52] Patrick S. Atiyah and Robert S. Summers, *Form and Substance in Anglo-American Law: A Comparative Study of Legal Reasoning, Legal Theory, and Legal Institutions* (1987).

[53] Lucio Pegoraro and Antonio Reposo, *Le fonti del diritto negli ordinamenti contemporanei* (1993). A shorter version was published by Lucio Pegoraro and Angelo Rinella, *Le fonti nel diritto comparato* (2000).

[54] Jan Schröder, *Recht als Wissenschaft: Geschichte der juristischen Methode vom Humanismus bis zur historischen Schule* (2001).

[55] Carleton Kemp Allen, *Law in the Making* (7th edn, 1964).

[56] Dawson (n 11); van Caenegem (n 12).

particular system which were written with an eye to a foreign readership, but do not specifically engage in comparison with another system.[57]

(a) Legislation

Comparative studies have paid much attention to the archetypal form of legislation, statute law. Other types, such as regulations, by-laws, and so on have been somewhat neglected despite their huge quantitative significance. Even more strikingly, the phenomenon of Constitutions as sources of law has not been treated in depth. This might be explained by the fact that, in most legal systems, Constitutions are technically regarded as statutes with a constitutional content.[58] However, it may be suspected that the traditional bias of comparative studies towards private law can account for the lack of interest in both Constitutions and legislation that typically emanates from the executive.

As to statute law, a European research project of the 1980s which covered various domestic systems and European law looked at the legislative process through all its stages, from the first political initiative until the promulgation of the text.[59] Much attention has also been paid to the style of legislative drafting.[60] Early comparative writings highlighted the differences between Continental codes and the traditional English 'piecemeal' approach to legislation. The latter only aims to give a pointillist solution to a specific and narrowly defined problem. As opposed to this, a code is a statute which comprehensively governs the law, or a branch of the law, such as private law or a part of it, abrogating the previous law relative to the same

---

[57] Three prominent and influential examples would be Karl Nickerson Llewellyn, *Präjudizienrecht und Rechtsprechung in Amerika* (1933); Konrad Zweigert and Hans-Jürgen Puttfarken, 'Statutory Interpretation: Civilian Style', (1970) 44 *Tulane LR* 704 ff, and the trio of articles by John Henry Merrymann on 'The Italian Style I: Doctrine', 'The Italian Style II: Law', and 'The Italian Style III: Interpretation' in (1965–6) 18 *Stanford LR* 39 ff, 396 ff, 583 ff. See also some of the works cited in nn 46–8 and Marc Ancel, 'Case Law in France', (1934) 16 *Journal of Comparative Legislation* 1 ff; L. Neville Brown, 'The Sources of Spanish Civil Law', (1956) 5 *ICLQ* 364 ff; Yvon Loussouarn, 'The Relative Importance of Legislation, Custom, Doctrine, and Precedent in French Law', (1958) 18 *Louisiana LR* 235 ff; Gianmaria Ajani, *Le fonti non scritti nel diritto dei paesi socialisti* (1985); Reinhard Zimmermann and Nils Jansen, 'Quieta Movere: Interpretative Change in a Codified System', in *The Law of Obligations: Essays in Celebration of John Fleming* (1998), 285 ff; Stefan Vogenauer, 'An Empire of Light? Learning and Lawmaking in the History of German Law', (2005) 64 *Cambridge LJ* 481 ff and 'An Empire of Light? II: Learning and Lawmaking in Germany Today', forthcoming in (2006) 26 *Oxford Journal of Legal Studies*; Alexandra Braun, Giudici e Accademia nell'esperienza inglese: Storia di un dialogo (2006).

[58] See eg the last sentence of the Constitution of the French Fifth Republic: 'La présente loi sera executée comme Constitution de la République'.

[59] Alessandro Pizzorusso (ed), *Law in the Making: A Comparative Survey* (1988).

[60] William Dale, *Legislative Drafting: A New Approach. A Comparative Study of Methods in France, Germany, Sweden and the United Kingdom* (1977); Alain Viandier (ed), *Recherche de légistique comparée* (1988). For a historical comparison of the legislative styles in England and in the Germanic legal systems, see Bernd Mertens, *Gesetzgebungskunst im Zeitalter der Kodifikationen: Theorie und Praxis der Gesetzgebungstechnik aus historisch-vergleichender Sicht* (2004).

subject-matter. More recent works have rather tried to downplay the consequences of these differences and to dispel some myths that could be found in English and American writings on Continental codes.[61] One of the reasons for this is the change in the character of statute law. The golden age of legislation in general and of codification in particular is gone. As opposed to the eighteenth and nineteenth centuries, the legislature cannot reign supreme any-more, but has come under increasing constraints imposed by Constitutions and international obligations. Furthermore, the inflationary use of legislation as an instrument of social change has not only led to a certain trivialization and marginalization of this source of law, but also to a continuing deterioration of the quality of codes and other statutes alike. These observations apply to both common law and civil law systems.[62]

The application and interpretation of statutes (perhaps surprisingly not of Constitutions)[63] has also given rise to a large body of comparative literature,[64] although only a few attempts at a comprehensive comparison of the methodological approaches of two or more legal systems have been undertaken. A groundbreaking study was published by the so-called 'Bielefelder Kreis' under the auspices of Neil McCormick and Robert Summers in 1991.[65] On the basis of an elaborate questionnaire, and using a sophisticated methodological approach, the contributors analysed the rules and principles of statutory interpretation in nine legal systems. That study sparked further research. The 1990s saw a number of English-German comparisons of particular methodological problems related to legislation in areas such as tax law, family law, and the law of unfair competition.[66] In 2001, for the first time a comprehensive comparative and historical study of statutory

---

[61] Hein Kötz, 'Taking Civil Codes Less Seriously', (1987) 50 *Modern LR* 1 ff; James Gordley, 'Myths of the Code Civil', (1994) 42 *AJCL* 459 ff.

[62] For the influences of these developments on sources of law and legal method in a comparative perspective, see Mary Ann Glendon, 'The Sources of Law in a Changing Legal Order', (1983–4) 17 *Creighton LR* 663 ff and Mauro Cappelletti, *The Judicial Process in a Comparative Perspective* (1989).

[63] The study of Thierry Di Manno, *Le juge constitutionnel et la technique des décisions 'interprétatives' en France et en Italie* (1997) concerns primarily the interpretation of simple statutes, and not the Constitution. But see now Goldsworthy (n 73).

[64] Herbert A. Smith, 'Interpretation in English and Continental Law', (1927) 9 *Journal of Comparative Legislation* 153 ff; Harold C. Gutteridge, 'A Comparative View of the Interpretation of Statute Law', (1933) 8 *Tulane LR* 1 ff; Walter G. Becker, 'Rechtsvergleichende Notizen zur Auslegung', in *Festschrift für Heinrich Lehmann* (1956), 70 ff; Bernard Rudden, 'Courts and Codes in England, France and Soviet Russia', (1973) 48 *Tulane LR* 35 ff; Reinhard Zimmermann, 'Statuta sunt stricte interpretanda? Statutes and the Common Law: A Continental Perspective', (1997) 56 *Cambridge LJ* 315 ff.

[65] D. Neil MacCormick and Robert S. Summers (eds), *Interpreting Statutes: A Comparative Study* (1991).

[66] Karsten Nevermann, *Justiz und Steuerumgehung: Ein kritischer Vergleich der Haltung der Dritten Gewalt zu kreativer steuerlicher Gestaltung in Großbritannien und Deutschland* (1994); Harriet Christiane Zitscher, *Elterlicher Status in Richterrecht und Gesetzesrecht: Über Rechtsfindung in Deutschland und England—Rechtsetzung und richterliche Methode seit 1800* (1996); Ansgar Ohly, *Richterrecht und Generalklausel im Recht des unlauteren Wettbewerbs: Ein Methodenvergleich des englischen und des deutschen Rechts* (1997).

interpretation in four legal systems was published. It covered England, France, and Germany, and thus the major three jurisdictions of the three Western legal families, and it looked at the approach of the European Court of Justice as well.[67] Building on the methodological groundwork of the *Bielefelder Kreis*, and in accordance with the approach advocated at the end of the previous section of this chapter, this new study aimed to overcome the structural particularities of the national theories on legal method by focusing predominantly on court practice. The trend of comparative research on statutory interpretation resembles that on statute law in general. Whilst the early works highlighted the differences between the systems belonging to the common law and those pertaining to the civil law world, the more recent studies show that, at least for a couple of decades now, there have been more similarities than previously thought.

(b) Case Law

Judge-made law is a further preoccupation of comparative lawyers. The difference between the literary, discursive, and closely fact-related judicial style of the Anglo-American courts and the formal, austere, and abstract mode of writing judgments on the Continent has been noted again and again.[68] Even more importantly, the fact that the common law systems acknowledge precedent as a binding source of law was long taken to be the essential difference between the common law and the civil law. It does not come as a surprise therefore that comparative works on the status of case law on both sides of the Channel and/or the Atlantic abound.[69] Today

---

[67] Stefan Vogenauer, *Die Auslegung von Gesetzen in England und auf dem Kontinent: Eine vergleichende Untersuchung der Rechtsprechung und ihrer historischen Grundlagen* (2 vols, 2001); for summaries in English see the reviews by Hans W. Baade, (2005) 69 *RabelsZ* 156 ff and Horst K. Lücke, (2005) 54 *ICLQ* 1023 ff. See now also Mitchel de S.-O.-l'E. Lasser, *Judicial Deliberations: A Comparative Analysis of Transparency and Legitimacy* (2004), covering France, the United States of America, and the European Union, and Patrick Melin, *Gesetzesauslegung in den USA und in Deutschland* (2005).

[68] Jan Gillis Wetter, *The Styles of Appellate Judicial Opinions: A Case Study in Comparative Law* (1960); Folke Schmidt, *The 'Ratio Decidendi': A Comparative Study of a French, a German and an American Supreme Court Decision* (1965); Gino Gorla, 'Lo stile delle sentenze: Ricerca storico-comparativa', (1967) 90 *Quaderni del Foro italiano* 313 ff; Hein Kötz, 'Über den Stil höchstrichterlicher Entscheidungen', (1973) 37 *RabelsZ* 254 ff; J. L. Goutal, 'Characteristics of Judicial Style in France, Britain and the USA', (1975) 24 *AJCL* 43 ff; F. H. Lawson, 'Comparative Judicial Style', (1976) 25 *AJCL* 364 ff; Jutta Lashöfer, *Zum Stilwandel in richterlichen Entscheidungen: Über stilistische Veränderungen in englischen, französischen und deutschen Urteilen und in Entscheidungen des Gerichtshofs der Europäischen Gemeinschaften* (1992). See also the contributions in *La sentenza in Europa. Metodo, tecnica e stile. Atti del Convegno internazionale per l'inaugurazione della nuova sede della Facoltà, Ferrara, 10–12 ott. 1985* (1988).

[69] John Chipman Gray, 'Judicial Precedents: A Short Study in Comparative Jurisprudence', (1895) 9 *Harvard LR* 27 ff; Robert L. Henry, 'Jurisprudence Constante and Stare Decisis Contrasted', (1929) 15 *ABA Journal* 11 ff; Arthur L. Goodhart, 'Precedent in English and Continental Law', (1934) 50 *LQR* 40 ff; Francis Deák, 'The Place of the "Case" in the Common and the Civil Law', (1934) 8 *Tulane LR* 337 ff; Charles Szladits, 'A Comparison of Hungarian Customary Law with English Case Law', (1937) 19 *Journal of Comparative Legislation* 165 ff; Antoinette Maurin, *Le role créateur du juge dans les*

there is widespread agreement that, as with statute law, the perceived differences are rather due to diverging theories of sources and that there are, at least in this respect, no major differences of practical relevance between the legal families. If evidence had been needed it would again have come from the *Bielefelder Kreis*, which produced another authoritative study, this time on precedent, in 1997.[70]

That book also drew attention to a huge gap in comparative research on precedent: whilst there was and is a very significant body of literature as to whether judge-made law is or is not a source of law in different systems, almost no comparative analysis of the case law method has taken place. The highly developed case law theory of Anglo-American jurisdictions has no counterpart on the Continent. There, lawyers had been so busy pondering yet again whether precedent is a binding source of law that they overlooked that even a *de facto* source which is habitually followed needs to be, and indeed is, applied and interpreted according to certain methodological standards. How this is done in different jurisdictions is certainly a promising field for further comparative enquiry.

(c) Other Sources of Law

Beyond statute law and case law comparatists have rarely ventured. Sure, the question as to whether doctrinal writings of legal scholars constitute a source of law or not is a comparative evergreen. However, the debate is narrowed down to discussions of scholars' 'influence' on the judiciary and to statistical analyses of citation practices of the courts.[71] A thorough comparative study which would take account of the different character of legal learning in different systems and which would venture beyond simple causal models of influence is missing. Custom, its estab-

---

jurisprudences canadienne et française comparées (1938); Imre Zajtay, 'Begriff, System und Präjudiz in den kontinentalen Rechten und im Common Law', (1965) 165 *Archiv für die civilistische Praxis* 97 ff; Mauro Cappelletti, 'The Doctrine of Stare Decisis and the Civil Law: A Fundamental Difference—or no Difference at all?', in *Festschrift für Konrad Zweigert* (1981), 382 ff; Thomas Probst, *Die Änderung der Rechtsprechung: Eine rechtsvergleichende, methodologische Untersuchung zum Phänomen der höchstrichterlichen Rechtsprechungsänderung in der Schweiz (civil law) und den Vereinigten Staaten (common law)* (1993) and, taking into account German, Italian, and US-American law, Frank Diedrich, *Präjudizien im Zivilrecht* (2004). For mixed legal systems, see Palmer (n 48), 44 ff and Ryan McGonigle, 'The Role of Precedents in Mixed Jurisdictions: A Comparative Analysis of Louisiana and the Philippines', (2002) 6.2 *Electronic Journal of Comparative Law* <http://www.ejcl.org/62/art62-1.html>. For rare analyses of different approaches in civilian jurisdictions, see C.-N. Fragistas, 'Les précédents judiciaires en Europe continentale', in *Mélanges offerts à Jacques Maury* (vol II, 1960), 139 ff; Uwe Blaurock (ed), *Die Bedeutung von Präjudizien im deutschen und französischen Recht* (1985). As to the different approaches in common law jurisdictions, see Arthur L. Goodhart, 'Case Law in England and America', (1930) 15 *Cornell Law Quarterly* 173 ff.

[70] D. Neil MacCormick and Robert S. Summers (eds), *Interpreting Precedents: A Comparative Study* (1997), examining eleven legal systems.

[71] Hein Kötz, 'Die Zitierpraxis der Gerichte: Eine vergleichende Skizze', (1988) 52 *RabelsZ* 644 ff; Neil Duxbury, *Judges and Jurists: Essays on Influence* (2001), with chapters on English, French, and American law.

lishment, its proof, and its application never seem to have arrived on the radar screen of comparative lawyers. Whilst this might be legitimate to the extent that customary law is increasingly less important even in many non-Western systems, this cannot be said with respect to the abundance of trade usages that play a major role in domestic and international commerce. Similarly, there is no comparative discussion of the question whether contracts are sources of law. Finally, there is very little effort to compare the various forms of 'higher law' that continue to be acknowledged in many contemporary systems, particularly in the religious ones, with other phenomena that seem to be equally grounded in supra-legislative norms, such as the *principes généraux* of French administrative law[72] or the 'law' that, according to Article 20 III of the German Basic Law, is supposed to exist beyond legislation.

V. WHERE TO GO NEXT?

Sources of law and legal method will remain perennial themes for comparative law. As has been seen in the preceding part of this chapter, these issues have probably been explored more thoroughly than most other comparative topics. Still, it should have become obvious that there is more to be done.

First, the attention of comparative lawyers has so far been directed mostly at statutes and case law, and at the methodological issues surrounding them. Other sources—both in the narrower sense and in the wider sense used for the purposes of this chapter—have been neglected. As far as legal method is concerned, there is a surprising lack of a comprehensive comparative study on constitutional interpretation.[73]

Second, the focus has been on a comparison between the common law and the civil law and of the leading exponents of these legal families, that is, English, French, and German law. There is a conspicuous absence of genuinely comparative studies taking into account, say, Canadian, South African, or Spanish law, not to speak of the non-Western legal traditions. The reasons for this are fairly obvious: the much-maligned eurocentrism of the discipline of comparative law, practical issues like linguistic skills and accessibility of materials, and the disproportionately

---

[72] But see Josef Esser, *Grundsatz und Norm in der richterlichen Fortbildung des Privatrechts: Rechtsvergleichende Beiträge zur Rechtsquellen- und Interpretationslehre* (1955); Philippe Jestaz, *Les sources du droit* (2005), 11 ff.

[73] But see now Jeffrey Goldsworthy (ed), *Interpreting Constitutions: A Comparative Study* (2005).

bigger challenge presented by an attempt to compare a Western system's sources and methods to those of a non-Western jurisdiction.

Third, the legal systems hitherto compared have mostly been those of traditional nation states. There are only a few studies comparing the sources and methods of these jurisdictions with those of supra-national legal systems which pose new questions and problems. One of these problems is that much of their law is deliberately not binding. Such 'soft law', which is also increasingly found in domestic laws, cannot easily be reconciled with many of the prevailing conceptions on sources of law. The reactions of different systems to this phenomenon would certainly merit comparative study.

Fourth, and maybe most importantly for the comparative agenda in the near future, the sources and methods of many of the supra-national systems are still evolving and being shaped. They are therefore not only waiting to become the object of comparative enquiries, but are in dire need of preparatory studies by comparative lawyers which provide arguments for or against the acceptance of particular sources or the adoption of particular methodological approaches, and building blocks for a theory of sources and methods that suit their needs.[74]

BIBLIOGRAPHY

Alf Ross, *Theorie der Rechtsquellen: Ein Beitrag zur Theorie des positiven Rechts* (1929)

Carleton Kemp Allen, *Law in the Making* (7th edn, 1964)

John P. Dawson, *The Oracles of the Law* (1968)

Wolfgang Fikentscher, *Methoden des Rechts in vergleichender Darstellung*, vol I: *Frühe und religiöse Rechte. Romanischer Rechtskreis* (1975), vol II: *Anglo-amerikanischer Rechtskreis* (1975), vol III: *Mitteleuropäischer Rechtskreis* (1976), vol IV: *Dogmatischer Teil* (1977), vol V: *Nachträge. Register* (1977)

René David, 'Sources of Law', in *International Encyclopedia of Comparative Law* (vol II, ch 3, 1981)

Mary Ann Glendon, 'The Sources of Law in a Changing Legal Order', (1983–4) 17 *Creighton LR* 663 ff

Patrick S. Atiyah and Robert S. Summers, *Form and Substance in Anglo-American Law: A Comparative Study of Legal Reasoning, Legal Theory, and Legal Institutions* (1987)

Raoul C. van Caenegem, *Judges, Legislators and Professors: Chapters in European Legal History* (1987)

Mauro Cappelletti, *The Judicial Process in a Comparative Perspective* (1989)

D. Neil MacCormick and Robert S. Summers (eds), *Interpreting Statutes: A Comparative Study* (1991)

---

[74] See eg the suggestions by Jan Kropholler, *Internationales Einheitsrecht: Allgemeine Lehren* (1977), 258 ff; Frank Diedrich, *Autonome Auslegung von Internationalem Einheitsrecht* (1994); Urs Gruber, *Methoden des Internationalen Einheitsrechts* (2004); Stefan Vogenauer, 'A European Legal Method: Should We, Could We, Would We?', forthcoming in (2006) 55 *ICLQ*.

D. Neil MacCormick and Robert S. Summers (eds), *Interpreting Precedents: A Comparative Study* (1997)

Stefan Vogenauer, *Die Auslegung von Gesetzen in England und auf dem Kontinent: Eine vergleichende Untersuchung der Rechtsprechung und ihrer historischen Grundlagen* (2 vols, 2001)

Philippe Jestaz, *Les sources du droit* (2005)

CHAPTER 28

COMPARATIVE CONTRACT LAW

E. ALLAN FARNSWORTH

New York†

† This is the last contribution of one of the leading contract lawyers in the world. Allan Farnsworth died on 31 January 2005 while he was working on this chapter. Professor Larry T. Garvin of the Michael E. Moritz College of Law, Ohio State University, and the editors revised the essay for publication. They would like to thank Professor Muriel Fabre-Magnan of the University of Nantes and Professor Bernhard Schloh of the Free University of Brussels for their helpful comments. Sections I, II, and XI were added by the editors and Section X by Professor Garvin. The tentative conclusion under XI appears to be justified particularly in view of the fact that Allan Farnsworth was a key member of the UNIDROIT Working Group that prepared the Principles of International Commercial Contracts.

I. The Prominence of Contracts in Comparative Law

The law of contract has long been one of the core subjects of comparative law. Of all areas of law, perhaps none has been subjected to comparative study as consistently, frequently, and intensely as contract law. The *International Encyclopedia of Comparative Law* devotes two out of seventeen volumes to the topic;[1] contract law takes up more than half of the subject matter analyzed in the classic work of Konrad Zweigert and Hein Kötz;[2] it is by far the most prominent topic in the current debates about a European private law;[3] and it figures prominently in comparative law casebooks.[4] There are, of course, several other fairly standard topics of comparative law, such as torts (delict), domestic relations, criminal law, and procedure, as well as, more recently, constitutional issues. But if there is a classical subject-matter of comparative law, that title should be awarded to the law of contract. This prominent status is due to three main reasons.

First, the origins of modern comparative law lie in the civil law world (ie in

---

[1] Arthur von Mehren (chief ed), *International Encyclopedia of Comparative Law* (vol VII, since 1971); Konrad Zweigert (chief ed), *International Encyclopedia of Comparative Law* (vol VIII, since 1972). Neither of the two volumes, the one relating to contracts in general, the other to specific contracts, has been completed. So far, seventeen chapters consisting of more than 1,000 pages have been published.

[2] Konrad Zweigert and Hein Kötz, *An Introduction to Comparative Law* (trans Tony Weir, 3rd edn, 1998), part II, 323–708, of which pp 323–536 are devoted to contract law.

[3] See Chapter 16 in this *Handbook*.

[4] See eg Ingeborg Schwenzer and Markus Müller-Chen, *Rechtsvergleichung* (1996), 1–185; Arthur von Mehren and James Gordley, *An Introduction to the Comparative Study of Private Law: Readings, Cases, Materials* (2006), 413–551; cf also Hugh Beale, Arthur Hartkamp, Hein Kötz, and Denis Tallon (general eds), *Cases, Materials and Text on Contract Law* (2002).

Western Europe) of the late nineteenth and early twentieth centuries, and in that world, contracts have been widely considered the pre-eminent area of law. In part, this was due to the Roman law tradition with its emphasis on private law, especially the law of obligations and, more particularly, on contracts; note that in most of the classic civil codes, contracts hold a central position and are dealt with at greater length than virtually any other individual topic. In part, the eminent position of contracts is also due to their central role for the ordering of market relations, especially in the heyday of liberalism, and to the symbolic importance of private agreements for the ideology of individual autonomy. For many jurists in the for-mative age of modern comparative law, the predominance of private agreements illustrated, in Maine's famous phrase 'the movement of the progressive societies ... from Status to Contract'.[5]

Second, modern comparative law soon began to focus particularly on the study of the similarities and differences between the civil law and the common law, and contract law turned out to be an enormously fertile field for such studies. On the one hand, the civil and the common-law approaches to contracts were similar enough to be comparable because they both centred around common topics, such as contract formation (offer and acceptance), non-performance and remedies for non-performance, interpretation, change of circumstances, mistake, deceit and duress; on the other hand, they showed sufficiently substantial differences to make such comparison interesting and worthwhile, for example, regarding the doctrines of cause and consideration, the underlying conceptions of breach, and the emphasis on specific performance versus payment of damages. These similarities and differences were largely the result of historical developments. While the traditional conceptions of contract were, at least for some time, quite different (on the civilian side the idea of agreement, in the common law the idea of promise),[6] there was a substantial convergence especially in the later nineteenth century when the common law came under massive civilian influence.[7] As a result of this curious combination of similarities and differences, contract law became the major topic in the classic context of comparing civil and common law. Prob-ably the best illustration of this phenomenon is Gino Gorla's famous study *Il contratto*.[8]

Third, contract law is a favourite topic for comparative study because it is among the practically most salient areas of law, both in terms of economic importance

---

[5] Henry Sumner Maine, *Ancient Law* (1861), 100 (emphasis in the original).

[6] For details, see Max Rheinstein, *Die Struktur des vertraglichen Schuldverhältnisses im anglo-amerikanischen Recht* (1932); A. W. B. Simpson, *A History of the Common Law of Contract* (1975).

[7] A. W. B. Simpson, 'Innovation in Nineteenth Century Contract Law', (1975) 91 *LQR* 247 ff; James Gordley, *The Philosophical Origins of Modern Contract Doctrine* (1991), 134 ff; Reinhard Zimmermann, 'Der europäische Charakter des englischen Rechts', (1993) 1 *Zeitschrift für Europäisches Vertragsrecht* 43 ff.

[8] Gino Gorla, *Il contratto* (2 vols, 1954).

and in terms of the realities of international negotiation and litigation. Since international trade, and economic relations more generally, depend mainly on private contracts, understanding the similarities and differences among the various national legal systems is a matter of immediate practical relevance. Thus, law and policy makers, the bench and the bar, and the international business community have a strong interest in understanding contract law in a transboundary context and are often avid consumers of its comparative study. This, in turn, provides incentives (and promises rewards) for comparatists addressing contract law issues.

II. Approaches to Comparative Contract Law

Aside from occasional works on the historical background of modern contract law,[9] comparative studies in this area can be assigned to four main groups. Three are more specifically defined with regard to their approaches and agendas while a fourth may be considered a residual category.

One specific approach is the search for commonalities among the contract laws of various legal systems. The original project of this type had a global scope: in the 1960s, Rudolf Schlesinger at the Cornell Law School organized a large-scale study purporting to identify a 'common core' of rules on contract formation shared by most developed legal systems in the world. While its actual results, eventually published in two massive volumes,[10] are considered scarcely relevant today, the approach was pioneering. Its major successor is an initiative limited to the laws of Europe: in 1994, scholars at the University of Trento, Italy, launched the search for a 'Common Core of European Private Law'. While this so-called Trento Project encompasses other areas of private law as well, it has generated several volumes focusing particularly on (European) contract law. Each work is gauging the existence of a 'common core' in a specific context.[11] A related, though quite different, undertaking is the first treatise on European contract law: Hein Kötz's

---

[9] See eg Reinhard Zimmermann, *The Law of Obligations: Roman Foundations of the Civilian Tradition* (1990; paperback edn 1996), 34–833; Gordley, *Philosophical Origins* (n 7).

[10] Rudolf Schlesinger, *Formation of Contracts: A Study of the Common Core of Legal Systems* (2 vols, 1968).

[11] Reinhard Zimmermann and Simon Whittaker (eds), *Good Faith in European Contract Law* (2000); James Gordley (ed), *The Enforceability of Promises in European Contract Law* (2001); Ruth Sefton-Green (ed), *Mistake, Fraud and Duties to Inform in European Contract Law* (2005).

ground-breaking *Europäisches Vertragsrecht* describes and analyzes the subject along the lines of common problems and themes.[12]

It is only a small step from the search for a 'common core' to agendas of contract law harmonization and unification. Thus, this second branch of comparative contract law often builds on the search for commonalities. Yet, it also goes much further and seeks actively to establish compromises bridging the gap between the various systems' concepts and rules. Efforts to harmonize or even unify contract law are driven less by academic interest than by the practical (real or perceived) needs of the business community for internationally uniform contract rules. These efforts have a fairly long and chequered history, especially with regard to the law of sales. They go back at least to the work of Ernst Rabel in the first half of the twentieth century. Rabel pioneered the establishment of an internationally uniform sales law in his two-volume survey *Das Recht des Warenkaufs* (The Law of the Sale of Goods), published in 1936 and 1958 respectively.[13] In subsequent decades, various attempts to unify sales law through international conventions drafted by the Hague Conference of Private International Law engendered little success. Yet, Rabel's belated triumph came with the adoption of the United Nations Convention on the International Sale of Goods (CISG) in Vienna in 1980. The Convention has been ratified by more than sixty countries throughout the world and is undoubtedly the greatest success of international contract law unification to date.[14] Most other efforts in this area have resulted in so-called soft-law, that is, restatement-like 'principles'. On a worldwide scale, the UNIDROIT Principles of International Commercial Contracts (1994, amended 2004),[15] drafted at the International Institute for the Unification of Private Law in Rome, lack legislative force but are used increasingly in international commercial arbitration. In the European context, the most noteworthy success is the publication of the Principles of European Contract Law, drafted by a Commission on European Contract Law led by Ole Lando.[16] The Principles of this so-called Lando Commission have generated enormous scholarly interest and may serve as the blueprint for future legislation on European contract law. In addition, several other unification projects are currently under way.[17]

---

[12] Hein Kötz, *Europäisches Vertragsrecht* (vol I, 1996; English trans under the title *European Contract Law* by Tony Weir, vol I, 1997).

[13] Ernst Rabel, *Das Recht des Warenkaufs* (vol I, 1936; vol II, 1958).

[14] For details, see Chapter 29 in this *Handbook*.

[15] UNIDROIT (ed), *Unidroit Principles of International Commercial Contracts 2004* (2004); for comment, see Michael Joachim Bonell, 'Unidroit Principles 2004—The New Edition of the Principles of International Commercial Contracts adopted by the International Institute for the Unification of Private Law', (2004) *Uniform LR* 5 ff; Reinhard Zimmermann, 'Die Unidroit-Grundregeln der internationalen Handelsverträge 2004 in vergleichender Perspektive', (2005) 13 *Zeitschrift für Europäisches Privatrecht* 264 ff.

[16] Ole Lando and Hugh Beale (eds), *Principles of European Contract Law* (parts I and II, 1999); Ole Lando, Eric Clive, André Prüm, and Reinhard Zimmermann (eds), *Principles of European Contract Law* (part III, 2003).

[17] For details, see Chapters 16 and 29 in this *Handbook*.

A third major branch of comparative contract law is the study of the influence exercised by one country's (or tradition's) contract law on other legal systems. This approach is part of the comparative law genre focusing on legal transplants which is addressed in a separate chapter of this *Handbook*. Like comparative contract law generally, the tracing of transboundary influence has occurred mainly in the civil versus common-law context. It is widely known among comparatists today that civilian contract doctrine exercised considerable influence on the common law world. This is true not only for earlier English borrowings from Roman law but, as especially Brian Simpson has shown,[18] it is even more remarkable in the late nineteenth century when French and German doctrine had a significant impact on English contract law. In a similar vein, Stefan Riesenfeld has described the migration of certain German ideas to the United States in the early twentieth century.[19] Around the middle of the last century, several German and Austrian émigré scholars, notably Friedrich Kessler, exercised considerable influence on American contract law as well.[20] From a more current perspective, there is also the (still largely unexplored) question of the reverse influence of common-law contract types (such as leasing or factoring) and, more visibly, prolix drafting styles, on a worldwide level.

Beyond these three, fairly specific, approaches comparative contract law has traditionally consisted mainly in the general study of doctrinal similarities and differences between various legal systems, again largely with regard to the civil and the common law. In this, quasi-residual, category, some scholars have focused on individual topics,[21] others have sought to cut across a broader spectrum.[22] Their goal has been mainly to show how similar problems can be handled in different ways; how different approaches often lead to similar outcomes (or vice versa); and, occasionally, how comparing contract law leads to a better understanding of one's own regime and provides ideas for law reform.

The present chapter follows essentially the fourth, more general, approach and provides an overview of major issues in the civil versus common-law context. It focuses on general contract law, as opposed to specific contracts, and thus reflects the current state of international debate. Apart, of course, from the contract of sale which also always serves as the paradigm for debates on issues of general

[18] Simpson, (1975) 91 *LQR* 247 ff; see also above, n 7.

[19] Stefan Riesenfeld, 'The Impact of German Legal Ideas and Institutions on Legal Thought and Institutions in the United States', in Mathias Reimann (ed), *The Reception of Continental Ideas in the Common Law World 1820–1920* (1993), especially at 92 ff.

[20] Jutta Klapisch, *Der Einfluß der deutschen und österreichischen Emigranten auf contracts of adhesion und bargaining in good faith im US-amerikanischen Recht* (1991).

[21] A well-known example is Basil Markesinis, 'Cause and Consideration: A Study in Parallel', (1978) 37 *Cambridge LJ* 53 ff.

[22] See eg Donald Harris and Dennis Tallon, *Contract Law Today: Anglo-French Comparisons* (1989); P. D. V. Marsh, *Comparative Contract Law: England, France, Germany* (1994); a broader range of issues is covered in the Symposium, 'Contract Law in a Changing World', (1992) 40 *AJCL* 541 ff.

contract law, comparative discussion of specific types of contracts has remained very limited.[23]

III. INTERNATIONAL COMMERCIAL CONTRACTS

Exchange is the mainspring of any economic system that relies on free enterprise. Such a system allocates resources largely by exchanges arranged by bargaining between private parties. In these exchanges each party gives something to the other party and receives something in return in order to maximize its own economic advantage on terms tolerable to the other. Because of differences in value judgments and because of the division of labour, it is usually possible for each to gain.[24]

Many of the most important of these exchanges are between commercial parties. Others, however, involve consumers, friends, or family members. Although contract law governs the enforceability of their promises, that law is not unitary. When major efforts have been mounted to provide uniform rules for international contracts, they have tended to limit their reach to commercial contracts. Thus the widely adopted United Nations Convention on Contracts for the International Sale of Goods does not apply to consumer contracts, nor do the UNIDROIT Principles for International Commercial Contracts.[25] The discussion that follows will also emphasize commercial contracts.

Sophisticated systems governing such commercial contracts are found in a wide variety of legal systems around the world. Because of space constraints, this chapter will focus on the one hand on civilian systems, notably the Romanistic systems epitomized by France, together with the Germanic systems typified by Germany, and on the other hand common law systems, particularly those of England and the United States. Many civilian systems, including those just mentioned, recognize a distinction between 'commercial' contracts on the one hand and 'civil', or non-commercial, contracts on the other. In those systems, important practical

---

[23] But see eg Werner Lorenz, 'Contracts for Work on Goods and Building Contracts', in *International Encyclopedia of Comparative Law* (vol VIII, ch 8, 1980) and William B. Fisch, 'Professional Services', in *International Encyclopedia of Comparative Law* (vol VIII, ch 9, 1999).

[24] cf also Arthur von Mehren, 'A General View of Contract', in *International Encyclopedia of Comparative Law* (vol VII, ch 1, 1982); James Gordley, 'Contract in Pre-Commercial Societies and in Western History', in *International Encyclopedia of Comparative Law* (vol VII, ch 2, 1997).

[25] See Art 2(a) CISG; on which see Peter Schlechtriem, in Peter Schlechtriem and Ingeborg Schwenzer (eds), *Commentary on the UN Convention on the International Sale of Goods (CISG)* (2nd edn, 2005), Art 2, nn 5 ff; Preamble to PICC and comment 2 in UNIDROIT (n 15), 2 f.

consequences turn on whether a transaction is classified as commercial or civil. Rules for civil contracts are found in a civil code while special rules for commercial contracts are often found in a commercial code. In Germanic systems, the criterion for classification is subjective and depends on the quality of the parties as 'merchants' or 'mercantile enterprises'. In systems influenced by the French, the criterion for classification is objective and depends on whether the transaction involves a 'mercantile act'. No formal distinction between commercial and civil law exists in common-law systems. In the United States, the Uniform Commercial Code is not limited to commercial transactions, although it contains some special rules for contracts for the sale of goods involving parties designated as 'merchants' and for consumer leases of goods.[26] Even within the civilian systems the distinction between 'commercial' and 'civil' contracts has been criticized for some time. Much more important in modern discussions about contract law, and its integrity, is the related issue of consumer protection. Particularly in Europe, a great number of statutes in the area of consumer contract law, often based on EC Directives, have been passed in piecemeal fashion and the question has thus arisen how to resolve this unsatisfactory state of affairs. Some countries (among them France and Austria) have enacted consumer codes whereas others (among them the Netherlands and Germany) have attempted to integrate their consumer legislation into the general civil code. The question is hotly debated on both a national and European level, the answer depending largely on whether general contract law and consumer contract law are seen as serving the same, or different, aims.[27] This issue cannot be pursued here.

The discussion that follows concentrates on aspects of contracts relevant to international transactions. These are, for the most part, transactions in which promises are exchanged for other promises. From the standpoint of contract law, the decision to enforce such exchanges of promises, even before any performance by either party, opened a Pandora's box of problems. The questions that will be explored here are these: First, what basis or bases are recognized as justifying the enforceability of a promise and what are the conditions of enforceability? Second, how is it to be determined whether the parties have reached agreement? Third, how is the scope of a party's obligations under a contract determined? Fourth, how does the law ensure that the exchange of promises will be followed by performance of those promises? Fifth, when will changed circumstances be taken into account in determining the parties' obligations? Sixth, in the event of one party's non-performance, what remedies are available to the other party? And seventh, how do these promises affect the rights of third parties?

---

[26] For a detailed discussion, see Denis Tallon, 'Civil Law and Commercial Law', in *International Encyclopedia of Comparative Law* (vol VIII, ch 2, 1983); and see Francesco Galgano, 'Diritto civile e diritto commerciale', in *idem* (ed), *Atalante di diritto privato comparato* (1992), 35 ff.

[27] For a discussion, see, most recently, Reinhard Zimmermann, 'Consumer Contract Law and General Contract Law: The German Experience', (2005) 58 *Current Legal Problems* 415 ff.

IV. BASES FOR ENFORCEMENT

1. Historical Background in Roman Law

No legal system has ever been reckless enough to make all promises enforceable. One can, however, approach the question of enforceability from two opposite extremes—by assuming that promises are generally enforceable, subject to certain exceptions, or by assuming that promises are generally unenforceable, similarly subject to certain exceptions. Both civil-law and common-law courts have made this latter assumption.

With the development of competitive markets and the specialization of labour, it became essential to provide a general basis for the enforcement of promises, even before any performance by either party. Such transactions were a far cry from the simple credit transaction such as loan of money or sale of goods, for the primitive mind saw the resulting debt as recoverable not because of the debtor's promise to pay but because the debtor would otherwise be unjustly enriched.

The notion that a promise itself may give rise to an enforceable duty was an achievement of Roman law. But since the human mind is slow to generalize, it is not surprising that the history of contract law in Roman times is the account of the development of a number of discrete categories of promises that would be enforced, rather than the story of the creation of a general basis for enforcing promises.

'Consensual' contracts afforded a legal basis for enforcing purely exchanges of promises, even before any performance by either party, but in keeping with the pattern of evolution through the growth of exceptions, they were limited to four important types of contracts—sale, hire, partnership, and mandate.[28] In addition, unilateral promises were enforceable, provided a strict form of words was used.[29] Even as late as the time of Justinian in the sixth century, the most important expansion beyond the categories of classical Roman law was to recognize yet another category known as 'innominate' contracts.[30] Unlike consensual contracts, they were not confined to specified classes of transactions. But they were severely limited because they did not cover exchanges of promises even before any performance by either party, for they were binding only when one of the parties had completed performance. The development of a general basis for enforcing

---

[28] For details, see Zimmermann (n 9), 230 ff.

[29] On the Roman *stipulatio*, see Zimmermann (n 9), 68 ff. Apart from that four types of 'real' contracts were recognized (loan for use, loan for consumption, pledge, and deposit); in these cases, obligations only arose with the handing over of whatever object the contract was about; see Zimmermann (n 9), 153 ff.

[30] For details of the development, see Zimmermann (n 9), 532 ff; cf also 511 ff.

promises—the foundation of a general theory of contract—was therefore left to the great modern legal systems that arose in Europe during the Middle Ages: the common-law system that grew up in England and the civil-law systems that emerged on the European continent.

2. Common-Law and Civilian Solutions

Because the influence of Roman law in England had faded with the breakup of the Roman political system, the common law began at a less advanced stage than that attained by Roman law. English courts therefore painfully constructed such a basis beginning in the Middle Ages. That they succeeded in doing so was all the more remarkable in view of the fact that, when they began, the English law of contracts was little more advanced than that of many primitive societies. Like Roman law, they created categories of actionable promises.[31] One of the most important of these, the action of debt, was no better suited than were the innominate contracts of Roman law to exchanges before any performance by either party, because the action of debt also required that the promisee had actually performed. It was only at the end of the sixteenth century that, goaded by competition from the ecclesiastical courts, the common-law courts were prepared to enforce exchanges of unexecuted promises.[32]

The basis of enforcement developed by common-law courts came to be known as the 'doctrine of consideration'. At first, the word *consideration* had been used without technical significance, but during the sixteenth century it came to be a word of art that expressed the sum of the conditions necessary for an action for breach of contract. The word thus came to be used to identify those promises that in the eyes of the common law were important enough to society to justify legal sanctions for their enforcement. It was, not surprisingly, neither a simple nor a logical test.[33]

Conventional learning is that a promisor's mere promise to do something is not enforceable unless supported by consideration. The essence of consideration came to be an exchange in which a promise was made in order to obtain something—often called a *quid pro quo*—in return. What the promisee could give might be either a promise or a performance. It was often said that the consideration could be either a benefit to the promisor or a detriment to the promisee, which remains

---

[31] For details, see Simpson (n 6), 1 ff; David Ibbetson, *A Historical Introduction to the Law of Obligations* (1999), 24 ff; Gerhard Kegel, *Vertrag und Delikt* (2002), 35 ff.

[32] On the rise of the action of assumpsit, see Simpson (n 6), 199 ff; Ibbetson (n 31), 126 ff; Kegel (n 31), 51 ff.

[33] On the history of the doctrine of consideration, see Simpson (n 6), 316 ff, 375 ff; Ibbetson (n 31), 141 ff; Kegel (n 31), 66 ff; Jörg Benedict, 'Consideration: Formalismus und Realismus im Common Law of Contract', (2005) 69 *RabelsZ* 1 ff.

the general approach in England.[34] The Restatement of Contracts abandoned the historical requirement of a benefit or a detriment and in its place formulated a 'bargain' test, now widely accepted in the United States. Under this test, consideration must be something, either a promise or a performance, that is bargained for, that is, sought by the promisor in exchange for the promise and given by the promisee in exchange for the promise.[35]

The requirement of consideration took care of the bulk of economically vital commercial agreements, and found easy acceptance in a society entering a commercial age. In view of the difficulty that other societies have had in developing a general basis for enforcing promises, it is perhaps less remarkable that the basis developed by the common law is logically flawed than that the common law succeeded in developing any basis at all.

The doctrine of consideration is not a device for policing contracts to assure that they are fair to both parties. Consideration does not have to be 'adequate' or 'sufficient', though those adjectives are sometimes added by courts.[36] Nor does the consideration have to be substantial in value, though marked disparity in value may signal the absence of bargain—of merely 'nominal' consideration. Furthermore, the requirement of an actual bargain is not taken so seriously as to exclude routine transactions concluded on the basis of standardized agreements to which one party simply adheres without any real negotiation of terms.

One commercially significant area affected by consideration is contract modification. Under the pre-existing duty rule, a modification to a contract must itself be supported by consideration to be binding. The rule persists in common-law nations, though it has been limited by statute and by various judicial incursions, particularly in the United States.[37]

In the United States, spurred by the Restatement of Contracts, the doctrine of 'promissory estoppel' developed during the twentieth century as an alternative to the doctrine of consideration as a basis for enforcing promises. Under the doctrine of consideration, the promisee's unsolicited reliance is not consideration because it is not bargained for. Under the doctrine of promissory estoppel, however, the promisee's unsolicited reliance on a promise may preclude the promisor from asserting the absence of consideration for the promise if the promisor should have reasonably expected such reliance. The doctrine has been applied not only to

---

[34] See eg *Midland Bank Trust Co Ltd v Green* [1981] AC 513; G. H. Treitel, *The Law of Contract* (11th edn, 2003), 67 ff.

[35] Restatement (Second) of Contracts § 71.

[36] Restatement (Second) of Contracts § 79; E. Allan Farnsworth, *Farnsworth on Contracts* (vol I, 3rd edn, 2004), 124 ff. For a comparative evaluation, see Ferdinand Fromholzer, *Consideration* (1997); for an analytical evaluation, see Stephen A. Smith, *Contract Theory* (2004), 215 ff.

[37] Perhaps the most significant incursion is § 2–209(1) UCC, which abolished the pre-existing duty rule for goods contracts. On the pre-existing duty rule, see Farnsworth (n 36, vol I) 520 ff; Fromholzer (n 36), 131 ff.

donative promises but also to other unremunerated promises. It has not yet been generalized in England as it has in the United States.[38]

In many civil-law systems, including the Germanic, there is no requirement comparable to consideration and it is enough if a promise is made with an intention to be bound.[39] In French law and some related systems it is often said that for an obligation in a synallagmatic contract (a bilateral contract with reciprocal promises) to be enforceable it must have an underlying *causa* or *cause*.[40] Under such a contract, the *cause* is the reason that led a party to engage in the transaction. French courts do not engage in a subjective inquiry into the motivations of the parties, but if the performance to be rendered in return for an obligation is worthless, of no genuine importance, a court may decline to enforce the obligation on the ground that there is an absence of *cause*. This necessarily vague concept is not usually invoked by courts as a basis for insisting on equivalence in exchanges, though some recent cases suggest its potential use.[41] Today, *cause* is important largely in providing a basis for enabling a court to refuse to enforce a contract if it is legally or morally offensive.[42] In addition, donative promises in civil-law systems are enforceable, but typically require notarization as an authenticating formality.[43]

3. Bases for Refusing Enforcement

All legal systems impose threshold conditions for the making of enforceable contracts. Thus some classes of persons, often because of youthfulness or diminished or impaired mental ability, are denied the capacity to make contracts.[44]

---

[38] Restatement (Second) of Contracts § 90. For comment, see Farnsworth (n 36, vol I), 167 ff; English law does not recognize a cause of action based on promissory estoppel, instead limiting it to a purely defensive role: *Combe v Combe* [1951] 2 KB 215.

[39] For the historical development of the principle of *pacta sunt servanda* under the *ius commune*, see Klaus-Peter Nanz, 'Die Entstehung des allgemeinen Vertragsbegriffs im 16. bis 18. Jahrhundert' (1985); Zimmermann (n 9), 537 ff; John Barton (ed), *Towards a General Law of Contract* (1990); Kegel (n 31), 3 ff.

[40] For the historical development, see Zimmermann (n 9), 549 ff.

[41] See eg Cass com, 22 October 1996, D 1997, 121. For comment, see François Terré, Philippe Simler, and Yves Lequette, *Droit Civil: Les Obligations* (9th edn, 2005), no. 342.

[42] For a comparative evaluation of cause and consideration as 'indicia of seriousness' of a promise, see Zweigert and Kötz (n 2), 388 ff; Kötz (n 12), 52 ff; P. G. Monateri, Francesco Galgano, and Guido Alpa, in Galgano (n 26), 89 ff; and see the case studies and comparative comment in James Gordley (ed), *The Enforceability of Promises in European Contract Law* (2001). Neither PECL nor PICC recognize cause or consideration; see Art 2:201 (1) PECL and Art 3.2 PICC ('. . . without any further requirement').

[43] Melvin A. Eisenberg, 'Donative Promises', (1979) 47 *University of Chicago LR* 1; John P. Dawson, *Gifts and Promises: Continental and American Law Compared* (1980); Zimmermann (n 9), 477 ff; James Gordley, *The Foundations of Private Law: Property, Tort, Contract, Unjust Enrichment* (2006), 352 ff.

[44] Zweigert and Kötz (n 2), 348 ff; Kötz (n 12), 97 ff; for the United States, see Farnsworth (n 36, vol I), 442 ff.

Furthermore, even assuming competent parties, abuse of the bargaining process by one of them may impair the enforceability of the resulting agreement. The two most common kinds of abuse are those arising from conduct that is misleading and from conduct that is coercive. Protection against these two kinds of abuse is commonly afforded by allowing the abused party to undo the transaction by avoiding it, restoring both parties to their positions before their agreement.[45]

With the standardization of contract terms, courts and legislatures were faced with more subtle inroads on the integrity of the bargaining process. The typical agreement in a routine transaction came to consist of a standard form containing terms prepared by one party and assented to by the other with little or no opportunity for negotiation. Traditional contract law, designed for a paradigmatic agreement that had been reached by two parties of equal bargaining power by a process of free negotiation, was ill-equipped to meet the challenge posed by standard terms.

Standardizing terms has obvious advantages. It renders individual negotiations unnecessary, lowering transaction costs and thereby serving the interest of both parties. Furthermore, because a judicial interpretation of one standard form serves as an interpretation of similar forms, standardization facilitates the accumulation of experience and helps to make risks calculable. Dangers are inherent in standard-ization, however, for it affords a means by which one party may impose terms on another unwitting or even unwilling party. The standard form is typically proffered as a take-it-or-leave-it proposition, often called a *contract of adhesion,* under which the only alternative to complete adherence is outright rejection.

The traditional concern of courts in policing contracts has been with abuse of the bargaining process rather than with the fairness of the resulting bargain. Neither consideration in common-law systems nor *cause* in French systems polices the substance of a bargain. And the doctrine of *laesio enormis,* which at one time permitted avoidance of unequal contracts in civil-law countries, has been rejected save at most for a few vestiges.[46]

Courts steeped in traditional contract doctrine were therefore not receptive to the argument that a party should be relieved of an agreement on the grounds of imposition of standard terms. Nevertheless, in hard cases, courts strained to afford relief to the weaker party and, in doing so, developed several techniques. Some-times they held that the standard terms did not become part of the contract at all, as where the terms were in small print, located on the back of a form, or

---

[45] Zimmermann (n 9), 651 ff; Zweigert and Kötz (n 2), 424 ff; Kötz (n 12), 196 ff; Thomas Probst, 'Defects in the Contracting Process', in: *International Encyclopedia of Comparative Law* (vol XI, ch 11, III and IV, 2001); Thomas Schindler, *Rechtsgeschäftliche Entscheidungsfreiheit und Drohung* (2005); Smith (n 36), 315 ff; Arts 4:107 f PECL; Arts 3.8 f PICC.

[46] On the doctrine of *laesio enormis,* see Zimmermann (n 9), 259 ff; F. Willem Grosheide, 'Iustum Pretium Redivivum?', in: F. Willem Grosheide and Ewoud Hondius (eds), *International Contract Law 2003* (2004), 69 ff; Gordley, *Foundations* (n 43), 364 ff.

incorporated by an obscure reference. Sometimes they applied rules of strict construction, finding the terms unclear or ambiguous and then interpreting them *contra proferentem* ('against the profferer'). However, none of these traditional judicial techniques was adequate, at least in theory, to protect an unfortunate person who had actual knowledge and understanding of the terms.[47]

In the years following World War II, it was increasingly recognized that such judicial techniques were inadequate and that abusive clauses must be subjected to tighter legislative and judicial control. Much of the concern with standardized terms was everywhere directed at the protection of consumers, on the rationale that the consumer, presumably the weaker party, must be protected against terms favoring firms that abused their economic superiority. The result has been a plethora of legislative measures proscribing specific types of abuse or requiring clearer or earlier disclosure of especially important terms.[48]

German legislation automatically invalidates standard terms of business if, contrary to the precepts of good faith, they place the other party at an unreasonable disadvantage.[49] More generally, it provides that 'surprise' clauses do not become part of the contract if they are so 'unusual that the other party could not be expected to suppose that they would be there'.[50] This legislation applies even though both parties are merchants. In addition, consumers may invoke lists of standard terms that are either proscribed or that are proscribed if they prove disproportionately harmful.[51]

French legislation dating from 1978 empowered the government to issue decrees prohibiting specified clauses in contracts between merchants and consumers in so far as they gave the former an unfair advantage and seemed to have been imposed on the consumer by an abuse of economic power.[52] The commission set up to do this was inactive and in 1991 the Cour de Cassation held that it was open to the courts to do this.[53] *Clauses abusives* may also be invalidated under the general law of contract.

In England, following World War II, there grew up a judge-made rule that an exculpatory clause is no defense to a claim based on a 'fundamental breach of contract', for the reason that in case of such a breach the contract as a whole is at

---

[47] For a historical account of standard terms of business, and how to police them, see Sibylle Hofer, Phillip Hellwege, and Stefan Vogenauer, in Mathias Schmoeckel, Joachim Rückert, and Reinhard Zimmermann, *Historisch-kritischer Kommentar zum BGB* (vol II, in preparation), §§ 305–10; see also Farnsworth (n 36, vol I), 556 ff.

[48] For comparative accounts, see Zweigert and Kötz (n 2), 333 ff; Kötz (n 12), 137 ff; Karl-Heinz Neumayer, 'Contracting Subject to Standard Terms and Conditions', in *International Encyclopedia of Comparative Law* (vol VII, ch XII, 1999).

[49] § 9 AGBG (Standard Terms of Business Act) of 1976; now § 307 BGB.

[50] § 3 AGBG; now § 305 c I BGB.   [51] §§ 10 f AGBG; now §§ 308 f BGB.

[52] Art L 132–1 *Code de la consommation*.

[53] Cass 1e civ, 14 May 1991, D 1991, 449. The pertinent statute has been revised greatly in light of the EC Directive on unfair terms in consumer contracts of 1993.

an end and the clause disappears. However, the House of Lords closed the door on this rule in 1980.[54] In 1977, the Unfair Contract Terms Act gave judges wide power of control over unfair clauses that exclude or limit liability, particularly where consumers are involved.[55]

In 1993 an additional layer of European law was added by an European Community Directive requiring member states to introduce provisions applicable to a contract that, rather than being individually negotiated, has been drafted in advance so that the consumer has had no ability to influence its substance. Courts are to be permitted to hold a clause in such a contract invalid if, contrary to the requirements of good faith, the clause causes a significant imbalance under the contract.[56] The implementing legislation varied widely.[57] German law largely remained intact, as for the most part it already regulated standard terms as strictly, or more strictly, than did the Directive. French law changed materially, now incorporating the 'black list' of unfair terms contained in the EC Directive. England, in contrast, enacted the Unfair Terms in Consumer Contracts Regulations in 1999, which run alongside the 1977 Act. As in France, the English approach largely incorporates the Directive with no amendment.[58]

In the United States, the problem of abusive clauses is dealt with by the doctrine of unconscionability, which allows a court to refuse to enforce part or all of a contract should all or part of the contract be unconscionable. This doctrine is rooted in the practice of courts of Equity, which withheld equitable relief if a contract is so unfair as to shock the conscience of the court. It gained currency through its adoption in the Uniform Commercial Code, and since has become established in the common law.[59] The concept is largely undefined in the Code, but cases and commentators have filled that gap. Courts have characterized the presence of unreasonably favourable terms as substantive unconscionability and the absence of meaningful choice in determining those terms as procedural unconscionability. They weigh all elements of both substantive and procedural unconscionability and may conclude that the contract is unconscionable because

---

[54] *Photo Production Ltd v Securicor Transport Ltd* [1980] AC 827.

[55] For details, see Treitel (n 34), 246 ff.

[56] Council Directive 93/13/EEC of 5 April 1993 on unfair terms in consumer contracts, [1993] OJ L 95/93.

[57] See Jürgen Basedow, in *Münchener Kommentar zum Bürgerlichen Gesetzbuch* (vol IIa, 4th edn, 2003), Vor § 305, nn 18 ff.

[58] The Principles of European Contract Law (which do not contain provisions specifically dealing with consumer contracts) have a general provision, but no 'black list': Art 4:110 PECL. There is no equivalent in the UNIDROIT Principles of International Commercial Contracts.

[59] § 2–302 UCC; Restatement (Second) of Contracts § 208. See further Farnsworth (n 36, vol I), 577 ff.

of the overall imbalance. They have resisted applying the doctrine when there is only substantive and no procedural unconscionability.[60]

In addition to refusing enforcement in order to protect the interests of one of the parties, courts sometimes refuse enforcement in order to protect the interests of the public as a whole. In all legal systems, courts reserve this power to themselves. French law brings into play the concept of *cause* on the rationale that a contract cannot be based on a *cause illicite*. A court will examine not only the reason that led a party to engage in the transaction, for example, the expectation of acquiring land in return for a price, but also the party's ulterior motive, such as operating a casino or a bordello, and determine whether this motive is offensive to law or morals.[61]

4. Formalities Required for Enforceability

All legal systems make some use of formalities as conditions of enforceability.[62] Their functions may include facilitating proof and confirming seriousness of intention. Many civil-law systems, however, have no general requirement of a formality as a condition of enforcement, though a writing or other formality may be required for specific types of contracts. Thus German law requires a writing for suretyship provisions in contracts, and contracts for the sale of land must be in notarial form.[63] Such requirements as exist may not affect commercial transactions, as in the case of the French *Code civil*'s requirement of a writing for every non-commercial contract involving more than a trifling sum.[64] Furthermore, in systems following the French, when a formality is required the effect may be merely to limit the means of *proof*, as by witnesses, rather than to affect the *validity* of the agreement.

In contrast, a fear of false testimony regarding oral contracts prompted Britain to enact the Statute of Frauds in 1677. It provided that designated classes of

---

[60] For other devices policing contracts which are procedurally as well as substantively unfair (such as undue influence, or § 138 II BGB, ie the rule on 'usury'), see, against the general background of freedom of contract, Zweigert and Kötz (n 2), 323 ff; Kötz (n 12), 130 ff; Arthur von Mehren, 'The Formation of Contracts', in *International Encyclopedia of Comparative Law* (vol VII, ch 9, 1992), nn 62 ff; Jacques du Plessis and Reinhard Zimmermann, 'The Relevance of Reverence: Undue Influence Civilian Style', (2004) 10 *Maastricht Journal of European and Comparative Law* 345 ff; Art 4:109 PECL; Art 3.10 PICC.

[61] For historical and comparative discussion of illegality and immorality, see Zimmermann (n 9), 697 ff; Zweigert and Kötz (n 2), 380 ff; Kötz (n 12), 154 ff; Arts 15:101 ff PECL; this subject is not yet covered by the PICC; Farnsworth (n 36, vol II), 1 ff.

[62] Generally, see Zimmermann (n 9), 82 ff; Zweigert and Kötz (n 2), 365 ff; Kötz (n 12), 78 ff; Arthur von Mehren, 'Formal Requirements', in *International Encyclopedia of Comparative Law* (vol VII, ch 10, 1998); Paul Brasseur, 'Le formalisme dans la formation des contrats: Approches de droit comparé', in Michel Fontaine (ed), *Le processus de formation du contrat* (2002), 605 ff.

[63] §§ 311 b I and 766 BGB.   [64] Art 1341 *Code civil*.

contracts were not enforceable unless evidenced by a signed writing. The most important of these classes were contracts of suretyship, contracts for the sale of an interest in land, contracts not to be performed within a year from the time of their making, and contracts for the sale of goods. Most American states adopted similar statutes covering these classes.

In 1954, after 277 years, Parliament repealed most of the Statute of Frauds, retaining only the provisions for contracts of suretyship and contracts for the sale of an interest in land.[65] There has been no widespread movement of this kind in the United States, where the Statute of Frauds retains much of its vigour and has been retained in the Uniform Commercial Code, with some amelioration, for contracts for the sale of goods. Indeed, there is a tendency to require the formality of a writing as a means of protecting unsophisticated parties such as consumers. Many American courts have shown hostility to the one-year provision, however, and have limited it radically.[66]

V. Requirement of Agreement

1. Offer and Acceptance; Definitiveness of the Contract

Agreement is the basis of contract, and all legal systems impose two requirements in determining whether there has been legally binding agreement. First, the parties must have manifested their *assent* to be bound, a requirement that follows from the premise that contractual liability is consensual. Second, the agreement to which they manifested their assent must be *definite* enough to be enforceable, a requirement that is implicit in the premise that contract law protects the promisee's expectation. The focus here will be on the first of these requirements, where the differences among legal systems are sharpest.

Contract law characteristically envisions the process of agreement in terms of a discrete offer by one party and an acceptance by the other.[67] Once the offer is accepted, both parties are bound by the resulting contract. A major difference among legal systems goes to the revocability of the offer before a contract has resulted from its acceptance. Revocation by the offeror after the acceptance has

---

[65] The Statute of Frauds for real property was revised again in 1989, this time to strengthen the formal requirements: Hugh G. Beale (general ed), *Chitty on Contracts* (29th edn, 2004, vol I), 334 ff.

[66] § 2–201 UCC. On judicial hostility to the one-year provision, see Farnsworth (n 36, vol II), 129 ff. On the Statute of Frauds in general, see Farnsworth (n 36, vol II), 101 ff.

[67] For the history of the doctrine of offer and acceptance, see Zimmermann (n 9), 559 ff; Gordley, *Origins* (n 7), 45 ff, 79 ff, 81 f, 139 f, 175 ff.

reached the offeree is to be distinguished from withdrawal by the offeror before the acceptance has reached the offeree, as to which the offeror is free.[68]

In the common law an offer has no binding force and can be revoked at any time before acceptance. The hardship on the offeree is traditionally mitigated somewhat by the common law's 'mailbox' rule,[69] under which an offer received by mail is accepted as soon as the offeree has dispatched an acceptance. The offeree risks revocation only during the time between the arrival of offer and the dispatch of acceptance. Perhaps surprisingly, an offer is revocable even if it provides that it cannot be revoked for a stated period. This is a consequence of the doctrine of consideration, the provision for irrevocability being regarded as a promise not to revoke that is not binding if not supported by consideration. A common practice is for the offeree to pay a nominal sum as consideration, converting the offer into an irrevocable option. It is also possible that revocation of an offer may be precluded under the doctrine of promisory estoppel. Furthermore, in the United States an offeror can make an irrevocable 'firm offer' for the sale of goods under the Uniform Commercial Code.[70]

In French law, too, the offeror is generally free to revoke the offer at any time, although in some circumstances revocation may be regarded as a *faute* and therefore illegitimate if it is abusive and frustrates the offeree's legitimate expectations. In such a case revocation is sanctionable in damages. This is the case where the offer fixes a period of irrevocability or where the circumstances indicate a reasonable time for irrevocability. French law is unclear as to whether an acceptance is effective on dispatch or on receipt.[71]

German law takes a different position, under which, absent a provision to the contrary, every offer is irrevocable during a reasonable period, even if no period has been fixed. During that period revocation is impossible and a purported revocation has no legal effect. If the offer fixes a period of irrevocability, it cannot be revoked during that period. In any case, an acceptance is effective, not when it is dispatched, but when it reaches the offeree.[72]

---

[68] For comparative discussions, see Zweigert and Kötz (n 2), 356 ff; Kötz (n 12), 16 ff; Arthur von Mehren (n 60), nn 134 ff; Franco Ferrari, 'La Formazione del contratto', in Galgano (n 26), 67 ff; Catherine Delforge, 'La formation des contrats sous un angle dynamique: Reflexions comparatives', in Fontaine (n 62), 137 ff; Arts 14 ff CISG; Arts 2:201 ff PECL; Arts 2.1.1 PICC; for discussion of these international instruments, see Eva Luig, *Der internationale Vertragsschluss* (2002).

[69] Established in *Adams v Lindsell* (1818) 1 B & Ald 681, 106 ER 250; confirmed by the House of Lords in *Dunlop v Higgins* (1848) 1 HLC 381, 9 ER 805 and adopted generally in the United States, see Restatement (Second) of Contracts § 63.

[70] § 2–205 UCC; for other approaches to converting offers into option contracts, see Restatement (Second) of Contracts § 87. English law is less accommodating; see *Chitty on Contracts* (n 65, vol I), 321 ff.

[71] Terré *et al* (n 41), nos. 168 ff.

[72] §§ 145 ff BGB. Other civil law systems differ, with a few requiring actual notice. CISG and the UNIDROIT Principles separate acceptance from revocation; an acceptance is effective only upon receipt, as in Germany, but the offer may not be revoked after the acceptance has been dispatched.

Whether an agreement is sufficiently definite to display the requisite intent to be bound likewise varies among legal systems. Certainly an agreement can prove too indefinite to enforce. Romanistic systems generally require that a contract have an *objet*, a requirement absent elsewhere.[73] As will be discussed, missing terms can be supplied by the courts, or are supplied legislatively.

2. Precontractual Liability

If negotiating parties sign the documents at the closing they clearly have assented to the terms contained therein. But problems arise if the negotiations fail and the documents are not signed. The resolution of disputes arising out of the failure of negotiations has assumed increasing importance. Common-law and civil-law systems have arrived at different solutions.[74]

Common-law courts have traditionally accorded parties the freedom to negotiate without risk of precontractual liability. Before an offer is accepted, neither party is bound. This broad freedom of negotiation is subject to occasional exceptions if, for example, the aggrieved party has a claim in restitution for a benefit to the other party during the negotiations, has been harmed by a misrepresentation or, at least in the United States, has relied on a specific promise made by the other party during the negotiations.[75]

German courts have adapted the concept of *culpa in contrahendo* (fault in contracting) developed by Rudolf von Jhering after the middle of the nineteenth century[76] and now codified in § 311 II BGB, to hold that a party that fails to observe the 'necessary *diligentia*' in negotiations commits a breach of its contractual obligations and is accountable for the other party's reliance losses. Although the mere breaking off of negotiations does not constitute such a failure, a party may be liable if it refuses without an appropriate ground to conclude a contract after conducting itself in such a way that the other party justifiably counted on a contract coming into existence.

[73] Arts 1108, 1129, 1591 *Code civil*; but see now the developments sketched by Bertrand Fages, 'Einige neuere Entwicklungen des französischen allgemeinen Vertragsrechts im Lichte der Grundregeln der Lando-Kommission', (2003) 11 *Zeitschrift für Europäisches Vertragsrecht* 514 ff. For a comparative discussion, see Kötz (n 12), 42 ff; cf also Art 2:103 PECL.

[74] See Arthur von Mehren (n 60), nn 112 ff; Kötz (n 12), 34 ff; Gordley, *Foundations* (n 43), 297 ff; Zimmermann and Whittaker (n 11), 171 ff; Bertrand de Coninck, 'Le droit commun de la rupture des négotiacions précontractuelles', in Fontaine (n 62), 15 ff; Ewoud Hondius, 'Pre-Contractual Liability', in F. Willem Grosheide and Ewoud Hondius (n 46), 5 ff; Arts 2:301 f PECL; Arts 2.1.15 PICC.

[75] Farnsworth (n 36, vol I), 391 ff.

[76] Rudolf von Jhering, 'Culpa in contrahendo, oder Schadensersatz bei nichtigen oder nicht zur Perfektion gelangten Verträgen', (1861) 4 *Jherings Jahrbücher für die Dogmatik des bürgerlichen Rechts* 16 ff.

Early in the twentieth century, a French scholar, Raymond Saleilles, advanced the view that after parties have entered into negotiations both must act in good faith and neither can break off the negotiations 'arbitrarily' without compensating the other for its reliance.[77] French courts have imposed liability on a theory of tort, the wrong being viewed as an *abus de droit* for which bad faith even without malice will suffice. Bad faith may be found where a party has negotiated with no serious intention to contract or where a party breaks off negotiations abruptly and without justification.

Legal systems also differ as to the enforceability of an explicit agreement by the parties to negotiate in good faith. Such agreements are clearly enforceable in civil-law systems. However, English courts have been adamant in refusing to enforce such agreements[78] on two grounds: first, that the scope of such an obligation is too indefinite to be enforceable; and, second, that there is no way to calculate expectation damages for breach of such an obligation because there is no way to determine the terms of the contract that might have been reached. Many courts in the United States have rejected these arguments and have enforced agreements to negotiate, at least where they have been concluded after some significant terms have been agreed upon. In answer to the second argument, these courts have calculated damages not on the basis of lost expectation but on the basis of reliance, sometimes including lost opportunities to conclude other contracts. In answer to the argument of indefiniteness, the same courts have concluded that at the very least it is a breach of the obligation to negotiate in good faith if a party simply refuses to abide by a term on which agreement has been reached unless the other party makes a concession on some matter yet to be negotiated.[79]

VI. THE CONTENT OF THE CONTRACT

1. Introduction

Most of what we usually think of as 'contract law' consists of a legal framework within which parties may create their own rights and duties by agreement. Developed societies confer upon contracting parties wide power to shape their

---

[77] Raymond Saleilles, 'De la responsabilité précontractuelle', (1907) 6 *Revue Trimestrielle de Droit Civil* 697, 717 ff.

[78] See the references in Treitel (n 34), 59 ff.

[79] Farnsworth (n 36, vol I), 391 ff; *idem*, 'Precontractual Liability and Preliminary Agreements: Fair Dealing and Failed Negotiations', (1987) 87 *Columbia LR* 217, 264 ff.

relationships under the principle of party autonomy or 'freedom of contract', and many contract disputes relate not to this legal framework but rather to the rights and duties that the parties themselves have created. Such controversies over the 'interpretation' or 'construction' of the contract[80] represent a substantial fraction of all contract disputes.

Before a party can be charged with a breach, the scope of that party's obligation must be determined. To begin with, a court will look at the language of the contract itself. In addition a court will look to terms implied in law, terms that are read into contract—sometimes on the basis of statute and sometimes as a matter of judicial discretion—in order to fill gaps in the language of the contract.[81] With rare exceptions for fields such as insurance law and consumer protection law, these rules are not mandatory, that is, not impervious to the parties' attempts to change them; instead, the parties are free to contract out of them. In the United States, such rules are commonly known as *default* rules, in Germany as *dispositives Recht*, and in France as *lois supplétives*.

Most civil-law systems know a default rule of great importance and widespread impact that requires a contracting party to behave according to good faith, or what is in German *Treu und Glauben* and in French *bonne foi*.[82] The common law traditionally knows no such default rule. English courts have been adamant in refusing to accept such a vague restraint on the behaviour of a contracting party, though they sometimes achieve the same ends by fashioning more specific rules.[83] In the United States, a remarkable exception in the common-law world, courts generally recognize a default rule that requires a contracting party to behave according to *good faith and fair dealing*, a vague standard that may, nevertheless, be less broad than its civil-law counterpart.[84] Yet, many American courts do not allow an independent cause of action for lack of good faith, except in cases of bad faith denial of an insurance claim which may be actionable in tort.

[80] On which see Zimmermann (n 9), 621 ff; Zweigert and Kötz (n 2), 400 ff; Kötz (n 12), 106 ff; Arts 5:101 PECL; Arts 4.1 ff PICC.

[81] For example, in England many default terms are supplied by the Sale of Goods Act of 1979 and the Supply of Goods and Services Act of 1982, though the courts readily fill in remaining gaps. On implied terms in English law in comparative perspective, see Martin Schmidt-Kessel, 'Implied Terms—Auf der Suche nach dem Funktionsäquivalent', (1997) 96 *Zeitschrift für Vergleichende Rechtswissenschaft* 101 ff; Wolfgang Grobecker, *Implied Terms und Treu und Glauben* (1998); and see Smith (n 36), 280 ff.

[82] For comparative analysis, see Jack Beatson and Daniel Friedmann (eds), *Good Faith and Fault in Contract Law* (1995); Hein Kötz, 'Towards a European Civil Code: The Duty of Good Faith', in *The Law of Obligations: Essays in Celebration of John Fleming* (1998), 243 ff; Martijn Hesselink, *De redelijkheid en billijkheid in het Europese privaatrecht—Good Faith in European Private Law* (1999); Zimmermann and Whittaker (n 11), 7 ff.

[83] *Interfoto Picture Library Ltd v Stilletto Visual Programmes Ltd* [1989] 1 QB 433.

[84] See Robert S. Summers, 'The Conceptualisation of Good Faith in American Contract Law: A General Account', in Zimmermann and Whittaker (n 11), 118 ff; Steven J. Burton and Eric G. Andersen, *Contractual Good Faith* (1995); cf also the explicit reference to good faith in § 1–203 UCC and Restatement (Second) of Contracts § 205.

A vexing related problem is how to determine the terms of a contract when the offer and acceptance differ. The classic answer makes a non-conforming acceptance a rejection and counter-offer.[85] Especially for contracts created by the exchange of standard forms, this proves impracticable. French and German case law has tended to place the terms of the parties at parity, allowing formation and replacing terms in conflict with default terms.[86] English law normally treats the differing forms as creating no contract until one party expressly assents or until performance. In the latter case the final document provides the terms of the contract.[87] American law depends upon the context. At common law, the answer is very much along English lines. For the sale of goods, the Uniform Commercial Code provides a somewhat muddy answer that variously yields something like French and German law or something like a first-shot rule, subject to a materiality test.[88]

2. Integrity of the Writing

Common-law systems show great respect for the integrity of written contracts. After lengthy negotiations, contracting parties often reduce part or all of their agreement to writing in order to provide trustworthy evidence of the agreement and avoid reliance on uncertain memory. If litigation ensues, however, one party may seek to introduce evidence of the earlier negotiations in an effort to show that the terms of the agreement are different than those shown in the writing. Faced with such a possibility, the parties may prefer to facilitate the resolution of disputes by excluding from the scope of their agreement those matters not reflected in the writing.

In common-law systems, the integrity of the writing is assured by the 'parol evidence rule', a rule with little counterpart in civil-law systems.[89] This rule may bar the use of extrinsic evidence—evidence outside the writing—to contradict and perhaps even to supplement the writing. The name of the rule is misleading, for it is not limited to oral (or 'parol') negotiations and may exclude such writings as letters, telegrams, memoranda, and preliminary drafts. Nor is it a rule of 'evidence' but one of substantive law.

---

[85] See eg § 150 II BGB. This 'mirror-image' rule has been softened somewhat in many legal systems to allow for contract formation where the offer and acceptance differ immaterially.

[86] For comparative accounts, see Kötz (n 12), 32 f; von Mehren (n 60), nn 157 ff; Catherine Delforge, 'Le conflit né de la confrontation de conditions générales contradictoires et son incidence sur la formation des contrats', in Fontaine (n 62), 479 ff; Ernst A. Kramer, ' "Battle of the Forms": Eine rechtsvergleichende Skizze mit Blick auf das schweizerische Recht', in *Gauchs Welt: Recht, Vertragsrecht und Baurecht. Festschrift für Peter Gauch* (2004), 493 ff; and see Art 2:209 PECL; Art 2.1.22 PICC.

[87] *Butler Machine Tool Co Ltd v Ex-Cell-O Corp (England) Ltd* [1979] 1 WLR 401.

[88] § 2–207 UCC.

[89] Though French law, in Art 1341 *Code civil*, provides that parol may not vary or contradict certain writings. This provision has been relaxed judicially.

The rule is intended to give legal effect to the parties' intention to make their writing at least a final and perhaps also a complete expression of their agreement. If the parties had such an intention, the agreement is said to be *integrated* and the rule applies. If they intended the writing to be a final expression of the terms it contains, but not a complete expression of all the terms agreed upon—some terms remaining unwritten—the agreement is said to be *partially* integrated and evidence of prior agreements or negotiations is admissible to supplement the writing though not to contradict it. If the parties intended the writing to be a complete expression of all the terms agreed upon, as well as a final expression of the terms it contains, the agreement is *completely* integrated and not even evidence of 'a consistent additional term' is admissible to supplement the writing. These preclusions, however, generally do not extend to usage or course of dealing.[90]

In order to make it clear that a contract is completely integrated, agreements in common-law countries often contain what is commonly known as a 'merger clause', which merges prior negotiations into the writing by reciting that the writing contains the entire agreement. Courts have generally given effect to such clauses.[91]

When the interpretation of the language of a writing is in issue, an adjunct to the parol evidence rule known as the 'plain meaning rule' may protect the integrity of the writing. In determining the meaning of contract, courts in all legal systems generally consider themselves free to look to all the relevant circumstances, including evidence of prior negotiations, even if it shows that both parties attached to the contract language a meaning different from the one that would ordinarily be given to it. Under the plain meaning rule, however, a court may refuse to consider evidence of prior negotiations to interpret contract language in a completely integrated writing that the court considers unambiguous on its face. The essence of this rule is that there are some instances in which the meaning of language, when taken in context, is so clear that evidence of prior negotiations ought not to be used in its interpretation. Civil-law jurisdictions are less wedded to plain meaning.[92]

---

[90] Restatement (Second) of Contracts § 213; Farnsworth (n 36, vol II), 219 ff; *Chitty on Contracts* (n 65, vol I), 752 ff.

[91] cf also Art 2:105 PECL; Art 2.1.17 PICC.

[92] See Art 1156 *Code civil*; § 133 BGB; and see Stefan Vogenauer, in Mathias Schmoeckel, Joachim Rückert, and Reinhard Zimmermann, *Historisch-kritischer Kommentar zum BGB* (vol I, 2003), §§ 133, 157.

VII. PERFORMANCE AND BREACH

Legal systems show a wide variety of approaches with respect to the rights of a party that claims that the other party is in breach of contract. Two distinct questions may be posed. First, how is a court to determine whether there has been a breach of contract? Second, if there has been a breach, how is a court to determine whether that breach is serious enough to justify the aggrieved party in ending the contractual relationship?

1. Determining Whether There Has Been a Breach

As to the first question, there is an important difference between common-law and civil-law systems.[93] In common-law systems, the norm is that of strict performance. A party is expected to perform in accordance with the letter of the contract, and a failure to do so is actionable, without regard to the fault of the non-performing party. Furthermore, a failure to render strict performance is of itself actionable, with no requirement that the aggrieved party give any notice or make any protest.

Here civil-law systems often differ in two significant respects from their common-law counterparts. First, in some civil-law systems, notably those based on German law, fault helps determine whether there has been breach. In principle, a party can avoid liability for breach by proving that it used reasonable care under the circumstances; thus under German law, delay is not a breach unless the delay is due to some fact or behaviour on the part of the obligor for which the obligor is 'responsible'.[94] Second, unlike the common law, many civil-law systems are not unitary. The German system, for example, divides breaches into the categories of impossibility and delay, with a residual category of 'positive breach of contract'.[95]

---

[93] For comparative discussions, see Zweigert and Kötz (n 2), 486 ff; G. H. Treitel, *Remedies for Breach of Contract: A Comparative Account* (1988); Gareth H. Jones and Peter Schlechtriem, 'Breach of Contract (Deficiencies in a Party's Performance)', in *International Encyclopedia of Comparative Law* (vol VII, ch 15, 1999); for an analytical discussion of the common law approach, see Smith (n 36), 376 ff.

[94] For comparative discussion of the relevance of fault, see Treitel, *Remedies* (n 93), 7 ff; Jones and Schlechtriem (n 93), nn 203 ff. International instruments such as CISC, PECL, and PICC do not base liability for breach of contract on fault. German law, however, has retained the fault criterion (even if only for the claim for damages) also under the new regime introduced as a result of the Modernization of the Law of Obligations Act in 2002: cf § 280 I 2 BGB.

[95] For the law before 2002, see the overview in Zweigert and Kötz (n 2), 488 ff; Zimmermann (n 9), 806 ff. The different types of breach survive as significant elements for determining the debtor's liability details even under the new law, albeit under a uniform umbrella concept of breach of duty (*Pflichtverletzung*). For details, see Reinhard Zimmermann, *The New German Law of Obligations: Historical and Comparative Perspectives* (2005), 39 ff. The international instruments adopt a unitary approach; see Arts 45 ff, 61 ff (breach of contract); Chs 8 and 9 PECL (non-performance); Ch 7 PICC (non-performance).

Impossibility of performance will also be treated differently depending on whether it is original or subsequent.[96] German law treats delayed performance as a special instance of default, and may not afford the aggrieved party the remedies for default by reason of the mere fact that the obligor failed to perform at the maturity date. The aggrieved party must make a protest (*Mahnung*) to put the other party in default and start a default period running, unless a time for performance has been fixed with reference to the calendar, or thirty days have passed after invoicing.[97]

French law distinguishes between an obligation to achieve a specific result (*obligation de résultat*) and an obligation to use reasonable efforts to achieve a result (*obligation de moyens*), as would commonly be undertaken by a doctor or lawyer or a person agreeing to manage another's business. For the former the obligee need only prove non-performance, leaving the obligee to prove excuse (*cause étrangère*); for the latter the obligee must prove both non-performance and fault. In principle no claim for damages, whether for delay or non-performance, can ordinarily be brought until the other party has been put in default by a formal protest (*mise en demeure*), though this is unnecessary if, for example, there is a fixed period for performance.[98]

2. Determining Whether Breach Justifies Ending Relationship

A mere breach or other failure of performance does not necessarily entitle the aggrieved party to end the contractual relationship, at least in the absence of a specific cancellation provision. A serious failure of performance, however, generally allows the aggrieved party at its election to end that relationship. Legal systems differ with respect to how serious a default is required to justify ending the contractual relationship, with respect to the extent to which the aggrieved party is entitled to use self-help in ending that relationship, and with respect to the nature of the aggrieved party's rights when the relationship is ended.[99]

English courts often focus on the significance of the relevant term, holding that the term must be 'essential' in order to justify ending the contractual relationship. In dealing with contracts for the sale of goods, they distinguish between conditions

---

[96] §§ 283, 311 a BGB; see Zimmermann, *New German Law of Obligations* (n 95), 52 f, 62 ff.

[97] § 286 BGB. For comparative discussion, see Treitel, *Remedies* (n 93), 136 ff. CISG, PECL, and PICC do not recognize a requirement of notice.

[98] For an overview of the French system, see Zweigert and Kötz (n 2), 496 ff.

[99] For comparative discussion, see Treitel, *Remedies* (n 93), 318 ff; Axel Flessner, 'Befreiung vom Vertrag wegen Nichterfüllung', (1997) 5 *Zeitschrift für Europäisches Privatrecht* 255 ff; for the international development, see Peter Schlechtriem, 'Abstandnahme vom Vertrag', in Jürgen Basedow (ed), *Europäische Vertragsrechtsvereinheitlichung und deutsches Recht* (2000), 159 ff; Ingeborg Schwenzer, 'Rechtsbehelfe und Rückabwicklungsmodelle im CISG, in den European und UNIDROIT Principles, im Gandolfi-Entwurf und im deutschen Schuldrechtsmodernisierungsgesetz', in Peter Schlechtriem (ed), *Wandlungen des Schuldrechts* (2002), 37 ff.

and warranties. A condition is an important term, a breach of which may give a right to end the contractual relationship, while a warranty is a subsidiary term, a breach of which gives right to damages only.[100]

This distinction is unknown in the United States where the focus is generally on the magnitude of the breach and not on the significance of the term. When the parties have exchanged promises, courts generally regard substantial performance by each party as a 'constructive' (or implied) condition of the other party's obligation to perform. If a party's non-performance is significant enough to be characterized as 'material', the non-performance at least justifies the aggrieved party in invoking the constructive condition and suspending its own performance, giving the other party a chance to cure the non-performance. If the non-performance continues without cure for a significant time, the aggrieved party is entitled to end the relationship.[101]

In common-law systems, an aggrieved party that is justified in ending the contractual relationship is entitled to declare the contract cancelled by giving notice to the other party. Of course, an aggrieved party runs the risk of overstepping the bounds of the law, for ending the contractual relationship and refusing to perform without justification is itself a material breach.

Under German law, the other party's failure to perform does not, as a rule, itself entitle an aggrieved party to end the contractual relationship. If the debtor does not perform, or does not perform properly, at the time when he has to effect performance, the creditor must generally allow the debtor a grace period. If the debtor does not perform within that period, the creditor may terminate the contract, whether or not the debtor was at fault.[102] However, he is automatically released from his obligation in cases where the debtor becomes free as a result of the fact that performance has become impossible.[103]

Under French law, the right to end the contractual relationship follows from the

---

[100] For details, see Treitel, *Contract* (n 34), 788 ff; for the historical background, see Reinhard Zimmermann, ' "Heard Melodies are Sweet, but those Unheard are Sweeter . . .": Conditio Tacita, Implied Condition und die Fortbildung des europäischen Vertragsrechts', (1993) 193 *Archiv für die civilistische Praxis* 153 ff.

[101] Farnsworth (n 36, vol II), 470 ff. For the sale of goods, any departure from 'perfect tender' allows the buyer to declare total breach. This apparently harsh rule is mitigated by a broad cure right and by exceptions for installment contracts: §§ 2–508, 2–601, 2–612 UCC.

[102] § 323 BGB; for details, see Zimmermann, *New German Law of Obligations* (n 95), 66 ff. If it is kept in mind that there are exceptions to the requirement of fixing a grace period for certain cases of serious breach, the practical result will often be the same as under Arts 9:301 (1) PECL and 7.3.1 PICC. Here, termination is available in cases of fundamental breach of contract, but the creditor may elevate a non-fundamental delay of performance to a fundamental one by means of granting a grace period: Arts 8:106 (3), 9:301 (2) PECL, 7.1.5 (3) PICC; cf also Arts 47, 49, 63, 64 CISG. The notion of essential breach is defined in Arts 25 CISG and 8:103 PECL; cf also Art 7.3.1 (2) PICC and Gerhard Lubbe, 'Fundamental Breach under the CISG: A Source of Fundamentally Divergent Results', (2004) 68 *RabelsZ* 444 ff.

[103] § 326 BGB; for a comparable rule in the international instruments, see Art 9:303 (4) PECL.

view that every synallagmatic contract is regarded as concluded under a resolutive condition of proper performance of the reciprocal duties. As under German law, some obligations are characterized as 'ancillary' or 'secondary' and are sanctioned only by damages. The contract is not, however, 'resolved' as a matter of law by the other party's failure to perform its undertaking, and the aggrieved party can either claim performance or put an end to the relationship.[104] If the aggrieved party claims the latter, self-help is severely limited, for *résolution* can be sought only in legal proceedings.[105] It is for the judge, who has broad discretion, to determine the gravity of the breach and order *résolution*, grant a period of grace (*délai de grâce*) during which the other party must render performance, uphold the contract, or, in the case of a contract for the sale of goods, order price reduction for defects that are not serious. There are some exceptions, and legal proceedings are not required, for example, if the contract contains an express provision for termination on occurrence of a stated event. Furthermore, if a fixed time is provided for a buyer to take delivery of goods, the seller can regard the contract as terminated if the buyer does not take delivery within that time.[106]

Various terms are used for the aggrieved party's ending the contractual relationship: termination, cancellation, rescission, avoidance. Ending the relationship necessarily liberates the parties from their remaining obligations of performance. Like full performance, it results in the discharge of the aggrieved party.

The doctrine of anticipatory repudiation, which enables an aggrieved party to claim damages even before performance becomes due, is often regarded as an important common-law peculiarity.[107] If, before the time for performance of a party's obligations has arrived, that party repudiates by stating that it will not or cannot perform those obligations, the aggrieved party need not wait until the time for performance has arrived but can immediately terminate the contract and claim damages for total breach. Indeed, in the United States even insecurity as to performance allows the insecure party to demand adequate assurances of performance from the other party, suspend its own performance if it is commercially reasonable to do so, and, should the assurances not issue, declare the contract repudiated.[108] Anticipatory repudiation is also, however, known outside the common-law world. Thus, German law recognizes the possibility that an

---

[104] Art 1184 *Code civil*; for historical background, see Boyer, *Recherches historiques sur la résolution des contrats* (1924), 11 ff, 381 ff.

[105] The *Cour de cassation* has now, however, recognized the possibility of a unilateral, extrajudicial termination of contract in cases of serious breach: Cass 1e civ, 13 January 1998, D 1999, 197; Cass 1e civ, 20 February 2001, D 2001, 1568; and see Fages, (2003) 11 *Zeitschrift für Europäisches Privatrecht* 523 f; Terré *et al* (n 41), nos. 643 ff.

[106] Art 1657 *Code civil*.

[107] The doctrine dates back to the decision of *Hochster v La Tour* (1853) 2 El & Bl 678; cf Michael Mustill, *Anticipatory Breach of Contract: The Common Law at Work, Butterworth Lectures 1989–90* (1990), 1 ff.

[108] § 2–609 UCC; Restatement (Second) of Contracts § 251.

anticipatory repudiation may justify termination of the contract and/or may allow the aggrieved party to claim damages.[109]

VIII. CHANGED CIRCUMSTANCES—
SUPERVENING EVENTS

It was pointed out earlier that courts look to terms implied in law in order to fill gaps in the language of the contract. An important situation in which courts do this is when supervening events result in changed circumstances not dealt with in the parties' agreement. The implied terms used to fill such gaps are default rules, and the parties are free to contract around them. Legal systems agree that if the changed circumstances make one party's performance impossible, that party is discharged from its duty of performance, at least if the impediment is not that party's responsibility. Whether excuse will result from mere impracticability or from frustration of purpose is less uniform.[110]

In civil-law systems, the resolution of such matters is often viewed as a conflict between two polar positions—the principle of *pacta sunt servanda* (contracts are to be observed) and the doctrine of *clausula rebus sic stantibus* (a contract depends on the continuation of circumstances existing at the time of formation).[111]

In the middle of the nineteenth century, French law was crystallized in a series of decisions favouring the principle of *pacta sunt servanda*.[112] *Force majeure* as an excuse is limited to an event that is unforeseeable, irresistible, and that makes performance absolutely impossible. Under the doctrine of *imprévision* of French administrative law, courts have modified contracts in the face of profound and surprising hardship in order to maintain public services and financial equilibrium.[113] *Imprévision*

---

[109] See now §§ 281 II, 323 II no. 1, 323 IV BGB and Zimmermann, *New German Law of Obligations* (n 95), 75. For a detailed discussion of the legal position under the old law (ie before the reform of 2002), see Ulrich Huber, *Leistungsstörungen* (vol II, 1999), 565 ff. The problem of insecurity is dealt with in § 321 BGB (*Unsicherheitseinrede*). For French law, see Simon Whittaker, 'How does French Law Deal with Anticipatory Breach of Contract?', (1996) 45 *ICLQ* 662 ff; for comparative discussion, see F. Dawson, 'Metaphors and Anticipatory Breach of Contract', (1981) 40 *Cambridge LJ* 83 ff; Treitel, *Remedies* (n 93), 379 ff; Jones and Schlechtriem (n 93), nn 139 ff; and see Art 72 CISG; Art 9:304 PECL; Art 7.3.3 PICC.

[110] For comparative discussion, see Zweigert and Kötz (n 2), 516 ff; Gordley, Foundations (n 43), 347 ff; Case 25 in Zimmermann and Whittaker (n 11), 557 ff; and see now Art 6:111 PECL; 6.2.1–3 PICC.

[111] Zimmermann (n 9), 579 ff.

[112] See, in particular, Cass civ, 6 March 1876, D 1976, I, 193 (*Canal de Craponne*).

[113] *Conseil d'État*, 30 March 1916, D 1916, III, 25.

has lately made incursions into purely private transactions, however. This appears to be part of a more comprehensive re-orientation of French contract law under the aegis of good faith.[114]

German courts, on the other hand, accepted the principle that judges have the power within narrow bounds to release parties from their contractual obligations. This is so not only in cases of impossibility[115] but also for what has been termed *Störung der Geschäftsgrundlage* (disappearance of the foundation of the contract). Thus it was held that a lease can be adjusted by raising rent to take account of greatly increased cost to the landlord and that debts could be revalorized to take account of the severe inflation of the early 1920s.[116]

The common law also accepts the principle that courts have a power within narrow bounds to release parties from their contractual obligations. English courts ask whether as a result of the impediment performance would be 'fundamentally different'. American courts ask whether the non-occurrence of the impediment was a 'basic assumption' on which the contract was made. In the United States the term 'impracticability' rather than 'impossibility' is used to suggest that a party may be discharged if performance becomes much more burdensome even though not absolutely impossible.[117] Common-law courts have traditionally rejected the notion that they have any power to adapt or modify contracts in the light of supervening events. If those events satisfy the requirements of discharge, the contract is wholly discharged, though courts have been reluctant to do this if the parties could reasonably have dealt with the events expressly. English courts developed the doctrine of 'frustration of purpose', under which a party may be discharged if the other party's return performance has become so worthless as to frustrate the first party's purpose in making the contract. American courts have followed suit.[118]

---

[114] See Cass com, 3 November 1992, Bull civ IV, no. 338; Cass com, 24 November 1998, Bull civ IV, no. 277; and see Fages, (2003) 11 *Zeitschrift für Europäisches Privatrecht* 519 f.

[115] Here the claim for specific performance is excluded according to § 275 I BGB. In cases of 'practical impossibility' and 'moral impossibility' the debtor is given the right to refuse to perform (§ 275 II, III BGB). 'Practical impossibility' must be distinguished from 'economic impossibility'; for details, see Zimmermann, *New German Law of Obligations* (n 95), 43 ff.

[116] See eg RGZ 100, 129 ff; 107, 78 ff; Bernd Rüthers, *Die unbegrenzte Auslegung* (6th edn, 2005), 36 ff und 66; Klaus Luig, 'Die Kontinuität allgemeiner Rechtsgrundsätze: Das Beispiel der clausula rebus sic stantibus', in Reinhard Zimmermann, Rolf Knütel, and Jens Peter Meincke (eds), *Rechtsgeschichte und Privatrechtsdogmatik* (1999), 171 ff; Christian Reiter, *Vertrag und Geschäftsgrundlage im deutschen und italienischen Recht* (2002). This is a judge-made doctrine which has, however, recently been included in the code: § 313 BGB.

[117] Farnsworth (n 36, vol II), 632 ff.

[118] See eg *Taylor v Caldwell* (1863) 3 B & S 826; *Krell v Henry* [1903] 2 KB 740 (CA); Restatement (Second) of Contracts § 265. See Zimmermann, (1993) 193 *Archiv für die civilistische Praxis* 121 ff, 137 ff; G. H. Treitel, *Frustration and Force Majeure* (1994); *idem, Contract* (n 34), 866 ff; Martin Schmidt-Kessel, *Standards vertraglicher Haftung nach englischem Recht* (2003).

IX. REMEDIES

1. Damages

When one party breaches a contract, the central purpose of most legal systems is to put the aggrieved party in the position in which it would have been had the contract been performed. Often this is attempted by an award of money damages that, in effect, imposes a new obligation—one to pay money—for the breach of the old. The objective of money damages is to redress loss by compensating the promisee and not to deter breach by punishing the party in breach.[119] For this reason, punitive damages are generally not available for breach of contract. An aggrieved party will often be content with an award of monetary damages, as may be the case if that party can use the money to purchase substitute goods or services elsewhere. This does not, to be sure, take account of the costs of litigating the dispute which may be necessary to get an award of damages.

2. Stipulated Damages

In some cases, the parties will want to include in their contract a provision stipulating the sums payable as damages in the event of various possible breaches. Such a provision is commonly regarded as both a ceiling and a floor for recovery. The enforceability of such stipulated damage provisions varies among legal systems.[120]

Civil-law systems are generally receptive to such provisions. French law starts from a principle of literal enforcement of provisions stipulating damages. Some years ago, however, the *Code civil* was amended to allow the judge to reduce or increase stipulated damages if the clause is manifestly excessive or derisory, in order to deal with abuses in certain types of transactions.[121] In German law, stipulated damage clauses are generally enforceable, but if the amount is unreasonably high the court can reduce it to a reasonable sum.[122]

The common law takes a more restrictive approach. The most important restriction is the one denying the parties the power to stipulate in their contract a

---

[119] These damages include only foreseeable losses, though French law makes an exception in cases of fraud, for which causation is the only limit: Arts 1150 f *Code civil*. See further Zimmermann (n 9), 829 ff; Treitel, *Contract* (n 34), 965 ff; Gordley, *Foundations* (n 43), 395 ff; Smith (n 36), 409 ff; Art 74 CISG; Art 9:503 PECL; Art 7.4.4 PICC; Florian Faust, *Die Vorhersehbarkeit des Schadens gemäß Art. 74 S. 2 UN-Kaufrecht (CISG)* (1996).

[120] Zimmermann (n 9), 95 ff; Ralf-Peter Sossna, *Die Geschichte der Begrenzung von Vertragsstrafen* (1993); Treitel, *Remedies* (n 93), 208 ff; Harriet Schelhaas, *Het boetebeding in het Europese contractenrecht* (2004); Art 9:509 PECL; Art 7.4.13 PICC.

[121] Art 1152 al 2 *Code civil*.   [122] § 343 BGB.

sum of money payable as damages that is so large as to be characterized as a 'penalty'. If the stipulated sum is significantly larger than the amount required for compensation, the stipulation may have an *in terrorem* effect on the promisor that will deter breach, perhaps inefficiently, by compelling performance. Common-law courts therefore exercise a power to condemn stipulated damage provisions that depart from the compensation principle, that is, contractual clauses providing for what are called penalties rather than for what are called liquidated damages.

If a stipulated damage provision is condemned as a penalty, the remainder of the agreement stands, and the aggrieved party is remitted to conventional damages for breach of that agreement. Drawing a line between liquidated damages and penalties has proved no simple matter for common-law courts. Several factors may be relevant. The most important is that the stipulated sum must be a reasonable forecast of the presumed loss, viewed as of the time when the contract is made. A second factor is that the damages to be anticipated as resulting from the breach must be uncertain in amount or difficult to prove.[123]

3. Specific Relief

Sometimes the aggrieved party will not find monetary damages satisfactory and will prefer specific relief. Of course if the promise of the party in breach was simply to pay a sum of money, the effect of a judgment for monetary damages is to give the aggrieved party specific relief. But it is not always easy for a court to place a monetary value on the loss occasioned by a breach. The broken promise may be one to deliver goods that have special 'sentimental' value to the aggrieved party, or it may be one that requires performance over a long period of time so that it will be difficult to forecast damages.

It is everywhere agreed that a buyer of goods must not resort to self-help to seize goods from a seller or use similar private means to coerce performance. An aggrieved party must go to court to get specific relief. Civil-law courts start with the principle that specific relief for breach of contract is generally available. Common-law courts, on the other hand, start with the principle that specific relief for breach of contract is an equitable remedy that will only be ordered when damages or other common-law remedies afford inadequate protection to the aggrieved party.[124]

[123] For details, see Treitel, *Contract* (n 34), 999 ff; *idem, Remedies* (n 93), 228 ff; Farnsworth (n 36, vol III), 300 ff.

[124] For historical and comparative analyses, see Zimmermann (n 9), 770 ff; Zweigert and Kötz (n 2), 470 ff; Treitel, *Remedies* (n 93), 43 ff; Gordley, *Foundations* (n 43), 388 ff; Shael Herman, 'Specific Performance: A Comparative Analysis', (2003) 7 *Edinburgh LR* 5 ff, 194 ff; and see Smith (n 36), 398 ff; Melvin A. Eisenberg, 'Actual and Virtual Specific Performance, the Theory of Efficient Breach, and the Indifference Principle in Contract Law', (2005) 23 *California LR* 975 ff.

In German law, a contracting party is entitled to demand specific relief. The law subjects this to exceptions, as where specific relief is impossible. If the obligation is to deliver movable property, enforcement involves the aid of an official who takes the property from the party in breach and gives it to the aggrieved party. If the obligation is to do an act that can be performed by another person, as in the case of a contract to build or to deliver generic goods, the aggrieved party can ask the court for authorization to have the act done at the expense of the party in breach, who may be required to pay in advance. But personal constraint is not excluded, and if an act cannot be performed by another person, or where performance consists of forbearance, failing to comply with the court's judgment may be punished by fine and imprisonment.[125]

The French and related systems also recognize in principle the availability of *exécution en nature* or what is called 'direct' execution. French law, however, proceeds in a very grudging manner in enforcing judgments of specific relief and the general availability of such relief is subject to an important exception. The *Code civil* distinguishes between obligations to transfer property (*obligations de donner*) on the one hand and obligations to do or not to do (*obligations de faire ou de ne pas faire*) on the other hand. Obligations of the former kind may be specifically enforced by having an officer of the court put the aggrieved party into possession, though otherwise state actors will not use force in support of *exécution en nature*.[126] If the obligation is to deliver generic goods, the court may authorize the purchaser to buy replacement goods at the seller's expense.[127] Under the *Code civil*, however, obligations to do or not to do are sanctioned only by damages and cannot be directly enforced, at least in the realm of personal services.[128] To help enforce promises, whether those giving rise to specific performance or merely to damages, the courts also developed the *astreinte*.[129] It usually takes the form of a judgment for performance or damages, coupled with a condemnation by which the party in breach must pay a fixed sum for each day or other period that that party remains in default. If, at the end of the period, the party in breach has still not performed, the aggrieved party may apply for a liquidation of the *astreinte* and for the issue of a further *astreinte*. The *astreinte* is not available to compel the performance of personal services, though it may be used to enforce negative injunctions. In contrast to German law, the fine is payable to the breached-against party, not to the state.[130]

---

[125] §§ 883, 887, 888, 890 German Civil Procedure Act; and see Zweigert and Kötz (n 2), 472 ff; Treitel, *Remedies* (n 93), 51 ff.

[126] Art 826 *Code de procédure civile*.   [127] Art 1144 *Code civil*.

[128] Art 1142 *Code civil* (based on the maxim of 'nemo potest praecise cogi ad factum' of the *ius commune*).

[129] It has since been codified in Law No. 91–650 of 9 July 1991, Arts 33–7.

[130] For details of the French system, see Zweigert and Kötz (n 2), 475 ff; Treitel, *Remedies* (n 93), 55 ff; Oliver Remien, *Rechtsverwirklichung durch Zwangsgeld* (1992), 33 ff.

The common law takes a very different approach to specific relief, one shaped by history.[131] Save for exceptional actions like replevin for goods, the law courts granted only substitutional relief, and the typical judgment declared that the plaintiff recover from the defendant a sum of money. Aside from the law courts stood a separate and parallel system of courts of Equity, presided over by a chancellor, and claimants could proceed in either law or Equity. Courts of Equity, in contrast to courts of law, granted direct relief for breach of contract in the form of an order of specific performance. In addition, they might, instead of ordering specific performance, direct a party by means of an injunction to refrain from doing a specified act. Where the performance due under the contract consists simply of forbearance, the effect of an injunction is to order specific performance. Often, however, a negative injunction is used as an indirect means of enforcing a duty to act. Decrees in Equity came to take the form of a chancellor's personal command to the defendant to do or not to do something, on pain of being held in contempt—either criminal contempt, at the instance of the judge, or civil contempt, at the instance of the plaintiff. Either could subject the defendant to imprisonment or fine—drastic remedies, which yielded significant limitations on their employ.

The most important historical limitation grew up out of the circumstance that the chancellor had originally granted equitable relief in order to remedy the deficiencies of the common law. Equitable remedies were therefore readily characterized as 'extraordinary'. When, during a long jurisdictional struggle in England between the two systems of courts, some means of accommodation was needed, an 'adequacy' test was developed to prevent the chancellor from encroaching on the powers of the common-law judges. Equity would stay its hand if the remedy at law of an award of damages at law was 'adequate' to protect the injured party.

To the 'adequacy' test was added the gloss that damages were ordinarily adequate—a gloss encouraged by a confidence that a market economy ought to enable the injured party to arrange a substitute transaction. English courts came to regard money damages as the norm and specific relief as the deviation. Only for land, which English courts regarded with particular esteem, was a general exception made. Each parcel, however ordinary, was considered 'unique', and its value was regarded as to some extent speculative. American courts act similarly, though they are more willing to consider routine transactions in land fungible and susceptible to damages, rather than specific performance.[132] In addition, damages will not be adequate to protect the injured party's expectation if the loss caused by the breach cannot be estimated with sufficient certainty, as with contracts involving matters of taste or sentiment.[133] It may also be the case even concerning contracts

---

[131] For what follows, see Rheinstein (n 6), 138 ff; Zweigert and Kötz (n 2), 479 ff; Treitel, *Remedies* (n 93), 63 ff; *idem, Contract* (n 34), 1019 ff; Gareth Jones and William Goodhart, *Specific Performance* (2nd edn, 1996); Farnsworth (n 36, vol III), 161 ff.

[132] See eg *Van Wagner Advertising Corp v S & M Enters*, 492 NE2d 756 (New York, 1986).

[133] See eg *Falcke v Gray*, 4 Drew 651 (Ch 1859); Restatement (Second) of Contracts § 360.

of a more commercial character, where an extended period for performance renders impossible the accurate forecast of damages at trial.

A second historical limitation, or group of limitations, is based on the concept that equitable relief is discretionary, allowing the chancellor to withhold relief if considerations of fairness or morality dictated. Relief is sometimes refused on the ground that it would impose on the court burdens of supervision that are disproportionate to the advantages to be gained. Because the restraints on the availability of equitable relief have traditionally been viewed as limitations on the court's jurisdiction, it has been generally supposed that the parties cannot enlarge the availability of specific performance or injunction by contract.[134]

In practice, the difference between the availability of specific relief in common-law systems and in civil-law systems may not be as great as at first appears.[135] The contemporary approach in common-law nations is to compare remedies to determine which is more effective in affording suitable protection to the injured party. The concept of adequacy has thus tended to become relative, and the comparison more often leads to granting equitable relief than was historically the case. In civil-law countries, the theoretical availability of specific relief may have limited practical importance because of a preference for money damages. The buyer that fails to receive promised goods may well find it preferable to purchase substitute goods on the market and claim money damages from the seller rather than seek to compel the seller to provide the goods or ask for some other form of specific relief. Nevertheless the attitudes of civil-law and common-law systems toward specific relief remain fundamentally different.

X. RIGHTS OF THIRD PARTIES

So far the discussion has focused on the rights of the promisor and promisee. Many contracts, however, implicate the rights of others—insurance contracts most notably, but also contracts with attorneys to make wills, contracts between manufacturer and retailer to supply goods ultimately sold to consumers, and so on.

---

[134] Farnsworth (n 36, vol III), 181 ff.

[135] cf also the compromise solutions adopted by Arts 9:101–903 PECL; Arts 7.2.1–7.2.5 PICC; Alfred Cockrell, 'Breach of Contract', in Reinhard Zimmermann and Daniel Visser (eds), *Southern Cross: Civil Law and Common Law in South Africa* (1996), 325 ff; Eric Clive and Dale Hutchison, 'Breach of Contract', in Reinhard Zimmermann, Daniel Visser, and Kenneth Reid (eds), *Mixed Legal Systems in Comparative Perspective* (2004), 193 ff; and see Treitel, *Remedies* (n 93), 71 ff; Art 28 CISG.

How civil-law and common-law systems deal with third-party rights and remedies is far from uniform.[136]

In all systems, contracting parties may expressly grant rights to non-parties that allow the non-parties to enforce the contract. This departs from Roman law, but became necessary as the institution of insurance grew during the nineteenth century. English law lagged materially in this regard, though the Contracts (Rights of Third Parties) Act of 1999 brought England into conformity here.[137] Civil-law jurisdictions are also willing to extend third-party rights by implication;[138] thus, for instance, where the lease of one property provides that it cannot be used for the same purposes as another property, the proper construction of that agreement may lead to the conclusion that the lessee of the second property has a direct claim against the lessee of the first property. The same can be said of American law.[139] English law does not yet recognize implicit intent. Much the same effect can sometimes be reached through tort law, which cares less about issues of privity. In any case, the rights granted to the third party are subject to any defenses or limitations created under the original contract.[140]

Most systems agree that the parties to a contract may modify or rescind the rights of third parties until the third party notifies the contracting parties that he accepts the right. English and American law go further by allowing reliance to yield irrevocability, while German law looks more generally at the intent of the contracting parties.[141] Finally, there remains some difference as to the promisee's ability to enforce the promise made for the benefit of the third party. Civil-law systems and American law allow the promisee to enforce the promise specifically and to collect damages due to the third party.[142] In contrast, English law remains unclear, as the recent statute was silent on this issue.

---

[136] For historical and comparative discussion, see Zimmermann (n 9), 34 ff; Walter Beyer, *Der Vertrag zugunsten Dritter* (1995); Zweigert and Kötz (n 2), 456 ff; Kötz (n 12), 245 ff; Hein Kötz, 'Rights of Third Parties: Third Party Beneficiaries and Assignment', in *International Encyclopedia of Comparative Law* (vol VII, ch 13, 1992), nn 2 ff (though all of these have been written before the coming into force of the Contracts (Rights of Third Parties) Act of 1999 in England); Vernon Valentine Palmer, 'Contracts in Favour of Third Persons in Europe: First Steps Toward Tomorrow's Harmonization', (2003) 11 *European Review of Private Law* 8 ff.

[137] On the Contracts (Rights of Third Parties) Act of 1999, see Robert Merkin (ed), *Privity of Contract: The Impact of the Contract (Rights of Third Parties) Act 1999* (2000); Treitel, *Contract* (n 34), 651 ff; Hans-Friedrich Müller, 'Die Einführung des Vertrages zugunsten Dritter in das englische Recht', (2003) 67 *RabelsZ* 140 ff; Robert Stevens, 'The Contracts (Rights of Third Parties) Act 1999', (2004) 120 *LQR* 292 ff.

[138] cf also Art 6:110 (1) PECL; Art 5.2.1 PICC.

[139] Though the law of sales is unclear about questions of privity, with the Uniform Commercial Code permitting great variation among the states: § 2–318 UCC.

[140] Art 5.2.4 PICC.   [141] The issue is dealt with in Art 6:110 (3) PECL and Art 5.2.5 PICC.

[142] Kötz, 'Rights of Third Parties' (n 136), nn 54 ff.

XI. A TENTATIVE CONCLUSION

The overview provided in this chapter has revealed a number of differences between civilian legal systems and the common law, and also between French and German law as two main exponents of the civil-law tradition and, to some extent, even between English and US-American law. The same is true of other major issues in the field of general contract law that have not been touched upon: contractual capacity,[143] mistake,[144] agency,[145] or assignment.[146] But the overview has also shown that there is a gradual convergence.[147] It is due to developments in all of the four legal systems covered in this chapter: English, US-American, French, and German law. And it has enabled scholars from around the world to elaborate an international restatement of contract law (the UNIDROIT Principles of International Commercial Contracts) and scholars from all the member states of the European Union to formulate a restatement of European contract law (the Principles of European Contract Law). These documents, in turn, may provide guidance for the future development of the national contract laws. They are discussed in some detail in Chapters 16 and 29 in this *Handbook*.

BIBLIOGRAPHY

Arthur von Mehren (ed), *International Encyclopedia of Comparative Law* (vol VII, 1974 ff)
G. H. Treitel, *Remedies for Breach of Contract* (1988)
James Gordley, *The Philosophical Origins of Modern Contract Doctrine* (1991)

---

[143] See Zweigert and Kötz (n 2), 348 ff; Kötz (n 12), 97 ff.

[144] Zimmermann (n 9), 583 ff; Martin J. Schermaier, *Die Bestimmung des wesentlichen Irrtums von den Glossatoren bis zum BGB* (2000); Zweigert and Kötz (n 2), 410 ff; Kötz (n 12), 171 ff; Ernst A. Kramer, *Der Irrtum beim Vertragsschluss: Eine weltweit rechtsvergleichende Bestandsaufnahme* (1998); Melvin A. Eisenberg, 'Mistake in Contract Law', (2003) 91 *California LR* 1573 ff; Ruth Sefton-Green (ed), *Mistake, Fraud and Duties to Inform in European Contract Law* (2005); Gordley, *Foundations* (n 43), 307 ff; Art 4:103 PECL; Arts 3.4 f PICC.

[145] Zimmermann (n 9), 45 ff; Wolfram Müller-Freienfels, *Stellvertretungsregeln in Einheit und Vielfalt* (1982); Zweigert and Kötz (n 2), 431 ff; Kötz (n 12), 217 ff; Chapter 3 of PECL; Chapter 2, Section 2 of PICC.

[146] Zimmermann (n 9), 58 ff; Klaus Luig, *Zur Geschichte der Zessionslehre* (1966); Bruno Huwiler, *Der Begriff der Zession in der Gesetzgebung seit dem Vernunftrecht* (1975); Zweigert and Kötz (n 2), 442 ff; Kötz (n 12), 263 ff; Hein Kötz, 'Rights of Third Parties' (n 136), nn 58 ff; Chapter 11 of PECL; Chapter 9 of PICC.

[147] See, as far as the civil-law/common-law dichotomy is concerned, Basil Markesinis, *The Gradual Convergence: Foreign Ideas, Foreign Influences and English Law on the Eve of the 21st Century* (1994); James Gordley, 'Common Law und Civil Law: eine überholte Unterscheidung', (1993) 1 *Zeitschrift für Europäisches Privatrecht* 498 ff; Reinhard Zimmermann, 'Savigny's Legacy: Legal History, Comparative Law, and the Emergence of a European Legal Science', (1996) 112 *LQR* 576 ff.

Reinhard Zimmermann, *The Law of Obligations: Roman Foundations of the Civilian Tradition* (paperback edn, 1996)

Konrad Zweigert and Hein Kötz, *Einführung in die Rechtsvergleichung* (3rd edn, 1996; English translation under the title *An Introduction to Comparative Law* by Tony Weir, 1998)

Hein Kötz, *Europäisches Vertragsrecht* (vol I, 1996, English translation under the title *European Contract Law* by Tony Weir, 1997)

David Ibbetson, *A Historical Introduction to the Law of Obligations* (1999)

Reinhard Zimmermann and Simon Whittaker (eds), *Good Faith in European Contract Law* (2000)

James Gordley (ed), *The Enforceability of Promises in European Contract Law* (2001)

Michel Fontaine (ed), *Le processus de formation du contrat* (2002)

James Gordley, 'Contract', in Peter Cane and Mark Tushnet (eds), *The Oxford Handbook of Legal Studies* (2003), 3 ff

Ruth Sefton-Green (ed), *Mistake, Fraud and Duties to Inform in European Contract Law* (2005)

Reinhard Zimmermann, *The New German Law of Obligations: Historical and Comparative Perspectives* (2005)

Michael Joachim Bonell, *An International Restatement of Contract Law* (2005)

CHAPTER 29

COMPARATIVE SALES LAW

PETER HUBER

*Mainz**

* The author would like to dedicate this chapter to Professor Drh.c. Dieter Henrich (Regensburg)
on the occasion of his seventy-fifth birthday.

I. Introduction

THE story of comparative law in the field of sales contracts is inextricably linked to Ernst Rabel (1874–1955). Rabel not only prepared the basis for any comparative study of the modern law of sales in his epochal treatise *Das Recht des Warenkaufs*,[1] but also initiated the process of world-wide harmonization of the law of (international) sales. This process has not only led to one of the most important international conventions in the field of private law (the 1980 UN Convention on Contracts for the International Sale of Goods—CISG) but has also become one of the most influential factors in the field of comparative sales law in the twentieth century.

In fact, any comparative approach to sales law will nowadays have to give prime importance to the existing body of uniform sales law. There are three reasons for this submission. The first is obviously that these legal instruments exist and have to be applied under certain conditions. The second reason is that these instruments themselves were strongly influenced by comparative law; one could say that the CISG, for instance, is a product of applied comparative law. The third reason is that these instruments have had a considerable impact on reform projects in national legal systems and have thereby found another way to

---

[1] Ernst Rabel, *Das Recht des Warenkaufs* (vol I, 1936; vol II, 1958).

enter the scene of comparative sales law. The close interrelation between comparative law and uniform law is also apparent in the life and the work of Ernst Rabel as his treatise on the law of sales developed from the preparatory work he had done for the UNIDROIT project to create a uniform law for international sales in the 1930s.

As a result of the priority of international harmonization efforts, Section II of the present chapter will outline the most important projects in this area and their interaction with comparative law. Section III will discuss selected characteristic features of the law of sales which are interesting from a comparative point of view.

II. COMPARATIVE LAW AND THE DEVELOPMENT OF UNIFORM SALES LAW

Comparative sales law today is linked to and interrelated with the process of the international harmonization of sales law. The most significant document in this field is undoubtedly the 1980 UN Convention on Contracts for the International Sale of Goods (CISG). This convention will therefore be dealt with first (Section II.1). There are, of course, other projects which need to be mentioned in this respect. Most of them have a regional character, such as the remarkable activities which have been undertaken under the auspices of the European Union (Section II.2), the Uniform Act of the African OHADA-States (Section II.3) or the specific harmonization process in the Scandinavian states (Section II.4). On a global level, one has to mention the growing importance of the UNIDROIT Principles of International Commercial Contracts (Section II.5).

1. The UN Convention on Contracts for the International Sale of Goods and the Idea of a World-Wide Unification of the Law of International Sales

Today international sales contracts are frequently governed by the CISG. The CISG is in force in more than sixty states from all parts of the world, among them both industrial nations and developing countries. It has been widely applied in international commercial transactions over the past twenty years. More than 1,000 decisions by state courts and arbitral tribunals have been reported so far.[2] It is therefore fair to say that the CISG has in fact been one of the success stories in the field of the international unification of private law. This success is the result of a rather long process which started in 1928 and was initially guided by the International Institute for the Unification of Private Law (UNIDROIT) and the Hague Conference for Private International Law, then by the United Nations Commission on International Trade Law (UNCITRAL).[3]

(a) UNIDROIT and the Hague Uniform Law of International Sales (ULIS)

In 1928 Ernst Rabel suggested to the newly established (1926) UNIDROIT Institute that it should adopt the unification of the law concerning the international sales of goods as one of its first projects. One year later Rabel submitted a preliminary report to UNIDROIT, and in 1930 UNIDROIT set up a committee charged with the elaboration of a uniform law for international sales. Between 1930 and 1934 the committee, of which Ernst Rabel had since become a member, met eleven times, and in 1934 it submitted a preliminary draft[4] which was, of course, considerably influenced by the comparative studies on the law of sales which Rabel and his colleagues at the Berlin Institute for International and Foreign Private Law had undertaken. After comments from member states of the League of Nations, the Governing Council of UNIDROIT adopted a revised version of the draft in 1939.

World War II interrupted the work on the harmonization of international sales law, but in 1951 the government of the Netherlands convened a conference in the Hague which appointed a special Sales Commission. Ernst Rabel—now living in the United States—was a member of this Commission and again had a considerable impact on its work until his death in 1955. The Sales Commission produced two drafts which were on the whole favourably received by the interested authorities. In 1964 a Diplomatic Conference was convened in the Hague; it adopted two conventions: the Convention relating to a Uniform Law of International Sales (ULIS) and the Convention relating to a Uniform Law on the Formation of Contracts for the International Sale of Goods (ULF). Both Conventions entered into force in 1972. They proved, however, unsuccessful. Only a very limited number of (mostly European) states ratified them, and they were not widely applied in international trade.[5]

---

[2] See eg the following databases: <www.cisg.law.pace.edu/>; <www.unilex.info>; <www.cisg-online.ch>; <www.uncitral.org/uncitral/en/case_law.html>.

[3] For a short account, see Michael Joachim Bonell, 'Introduction', in Cesare Massimo Bianca and Michael Joachim Bonell, *Commentary on the International Sales Law* (1987), 3 ff.

[4] Rabel could not, however, attend the final session in 1934, because Germany had in the meantime left the League of Nations; cf Ernst Rabel, 'Der Entwurf eines einheitlichen Kaufgesetzes', (1935) 9 *RabelsZ* 3 f.

[5] Peter Schlechtriem, 'Introduction', in Peter Schlechtriem and Ingeborg Schwenzer (eds), *Commentary on the UN Convention of the International Sale of Goods* (2nd edn, 2005), 1; Bianca and Bonell (n 3), 4 f.

(b) UNCITRAL and the Convention of 1980

While the process of ratification of ULIS and ULF was still pending, a new player entered the field of the international harmonization of commercial law: the United Nations Commission on International Trade Law (UNCITRAL), which had been established in 1966. After consulting the member states of the United Nations on their assessment of both Hague Conventions, UNCITRAL decided in 1968 to set up a working group in order to modify the Conventions or to produce a new text which would have a better chance of being accepted world-wide. In 1978 the working group submitted a Draft Convention (the 'New York Draft') which covered both the specific rules on sales and the rules on the formation of a sales contract, and in the same year the United Nations decided to convene a Diplomatic Conference on this matter.

The Diplomatic Conference took place in Vienna in spring 1980. After intense deliberations and several modifications of the New York Draft, the Conference finally adopted the 1980 CISG, often also referred to as the Vienna Convention. The CISG entered into force in January 1988 for eleven states; since then the number of contracting states has been growing steadily.[6]

(c) Scope of the CISG

The CISG applies to contracts of sale of movable goods between parties which have their place of business in different states when these states are contracting states (Art 1(1)(a) CISG) or when the rules of private international law lead to the application of the law of a Contracting State (Art 1(1)(b) CISG).[7] Certain types of contract are excluded from its scope of application by virtue of Art 2 CISG. For instance, most consumer sales will not fall under the CISG (cf Art 2(a) CISG).

With regard to the substantive issues, the CISG basically governs three areas: the conclusion of the contract, the obligations of the seller (including the respective remedies of the buyer), and the obligations of the buyer (including the respective remedies of the seller). The CISG therefore provides both a substantial 'law of sales' and a regulation of certain issues of the general law of contract, albeit limited to those international sales transactions which fall under its scope of application.

(d) The CISG and Comparative Law

As the short outline of the history of the CISG has shown, comparative law and the international unification process in the field of sales law were inextricably linked from the outset. The best symbol of this close interrelation can be found in the life and work of Ernst Rabel, whose comparative studies not only laid the ground for

---

[6] For the history of the CISG, see Schlechtriem (n 5), 1 ff (with further references).

[7] Several states have, however, declared a reservation against the application of the rule in Art 1(1)(b) CISG under Art 95 CISG.

the work of the first UNCITRAL Commission in the 1930s, but also led to his famous treatise on the comparative law of sales, which is still the leading work in that field. Apart from these early comparative foundations, the long process of international working groups and conferences led to a constant comparative input.

The text of the CISG, therefore, is the result of a long process of comparative legal work, both on the abstract, academic and on the practical, political level. In particular, the CISG tries to combine concepts of the civil law tradition with elements from the common law. The results of such comparative conflict or compromise can easily be found in the CISG.

Thus, for instance, the fact that Art 46 CISG grants the buyer the right to require performance of any of the seller's obligations clearly has its roots in the civil law tradition, which considers claims for specific performance as the natural consequence of the rule of *pacta sunt servanda*, whereas the common law regards specific performance as a discretionary remedy which should only be granted in a very restrictive manner.[8] The common law position, however, also left its trace in the CISG: according to Art 28 CISG, the national court is not bound to enter a judgment for specific performance unless it would do so under its own law in similar cases; this provision is primarily a concession to the common law states.[9]

The rules on damages provide another example of the comparative influence on the CISG. The basic principle in Arts 45, 64, and 74 f CISG is modelled on the common law system, which regards claims for damages as the primary remedy for a breach of contract and which should therefore be easily available, not based on fault (as in several countries of the civil law tradition), and limited by the foreseeability rule. On the other hand, Art 79 CISG provides a detailed set of rules on the exemption from liability (for damages). This provision created a considerable amount of controversy at the Vienna Conference and finally led to a compromise between the proponents of a strict liability regime and the advocates of a less severe, possibly even fault-based, system.[10]

2. Harmonization of the Law of Sales within the European Union

The key player with regard to the harmonization of private law in Europe is the European Union. Its efforts are twofold: on the one hand, it has taken specific regulatory measures to harmonize the law of its member states in certain areas of contract law (subsection (a)). On the other hand, it has started a consultation

---

[8] See, in more detail, Guenter H. Treitel, *Remedies for Breach of Contract* (1991), paras 43 ff.

[9] For a further concession to the common law position (performance as a remedy for breach) see Marcus Müller-Chen, in Schlechtriem and Schwenzer (n 5), Art 28, nn 1 ff, 10 ff.

[10] See Hans Stoll and Georg Gruber, in Schlechtriem and Schwenzer (n 5), Art 79, nn 1, 4.

and research process on future steps towards a closer harmonization of European contract law (subsection (b)).

(a) Regulatory Measures

In the last twenty years the EU has made constant efforts to harmonize certain areas of the law of contract. The instrument used by the EU was the directive (Art 249(3) EC Treaty). A directive is not directly applicable in the member states, rather it has to be implemented into the respective national laws by the national authorities. When implementing a directive, member states are bound as to the result that the directive aims to achieve but are free to choose the form and methods of implementation. Therefore, the effects of any harmonization effort based on the use of directives will be limited in certain respects: the European Union will be able to set (and unify) the basic standards and fundamental policies, but it is up to the member states to transform these standards into black-letter rules and to decide on technical details. The provisions which will actually be applied in practice are the national rules and not the directives themselves. These national rules may vary in detail from one member state to another. However, the fundamental principles and standards will be the same in every member state.

Regulatory harmonization by way of directives has traditionally been limited to so-called sector-specific measures, that is, to measures which are limited to certain areas. Directives were adopted where a particular need for harmonization was identified, for instance, due to the characteristics of specific types of contracts or due to specific marketing techniques. With regard to the law of contract, the Community's main area of activity has been the law of consumer protection.[11] Several EC directives have, for example, strengthened the consumer's contractual position towards a professional by granting the former a 'cooling off period' (ie the right to withdraw from the contract within a specified period after its conclusion). This requires that the contract has been concluded by certain marketing techniques which the directives regarded as 'dangerous' for the consumer (such as contracts negotiated away from business premises[12] or organized distances sales or service provision schemes run by the professional supplier[13]). One directive aims at eliminating unfair terms from contracts drawn up between a professional and a consumer.[14] Others impose certain mandatory rules for specific

---

[11] Other directives have covered, for instance, certain legal aspects concerning financial services, intellectual property, or e-commerce.

[12] Council Directive 85/577/EEC of 20 December 1985 to protect the consumer in respect of contracts negotiated away from business premises, [1985] OJ L 372/31.

[13] Directive 97/7/EC of the European Parliament and of the Council of 20 May 1997 on the protection of consumers in respect of distance contracts [1997] OJ L 144/19; amended by Directive 2005/29/EC of the European Parliament and of the Council of 11 May 2005, [2005] OJ L 149/22.

[14] Council Directive 93/13/EEC of 5 April 1993 on unfair terms in consumer contracts, [1993] OJ L 095/29.

types of contract, such as package travel contracts,[15] consumer credit contracts,[16] or timeshare contracts.[17]

Many of the aforementioned directives also, under certain circumstances, apply to contracts of sale. Yet, they cover only a limited number of specific issues and do not affect the central elements and policies of the law of sales. In 1999, however, the law of sales came to be centrally affected when the Community issued the Consumer Sales Directive.[18] It applies to sales of movable goods from a professional seller to a consumer. Its central provisions concern the notion of conformity of the goods and the buyer's remedies for lack of conformity (with the exception of claims for damages). Furthermore, the Directive contains provisions on the seller's recourse against his suppliers and on the content of contractual guarantees. In principle (and subject only to very limited exceptions), the provisions of the Directive are mandatory: they cannot be derogated from to the disadvantage of the consumer.

The Consumer Sales Directive is a crucial step forward on the way towards a common European law of contract. With the Directive the European Union has left the wings and entered the centre-stage of contract law. Any future developments in this field will have to take into account the standards set by the Directive.

Furthermore, the Directive is also highly interesting from the perspective of comparative law. There are two reasons for that. First, its drafters were considerably influenced by the CISG—a fact that they openly admitted.[19] The CISG—and its comparative background—therefore significantly shaped the Directive. At first sight, this may come as a surprise as the CISG only covers commercial sales[20] whereas the Directive is limited to consumer sales. A closer examination, however, reveals that the similarities between the two instruments relate to general issues of sales law, in particular to the conformity of the goods and to the structure of remedies. They do not extend to those parts of the Directive which contain the typical instruments of consumer protection, such as the mandatory character of its provisions.

The second reason why the Directive is particularly interesting from a comparative perspective has to do with the process of its transformation into the national

[15] Council Directive 90/314/EEC of 13 June 1990 on package travel, package holidays and package tours, [1990] OJ L 158/59.

[16] Council Directive 87/102/EEC of 22 December 1986 for the approximation of the laws, regulations and administrative provisions of the Member States concerning consumer credit, amended in 1990 and 1998, [1987] OJ L 278/33.

[17] Directive 94/47/EC of the European Parliament and the Council of 26 October 1994 on the protection of purchasers in respect of certain aspects of contracts relating to the purchase of the right to use immovable properties on a timeshare basis, [1994] OJ L 280/83.

[18] Directive 1999/44/EC of the European Parliament and of the Council of 25 May 1999 on certain aspects of the sale of consumer goods and associated guarantees [1999] OJ L 171/12.

[19] COM (1995) 520 final, para 5, [1995] OJ C 307/8.

[20] Art 2(a) CISG stipulates that the Convention does not apply to sales of goods bought for personal, family, or household use, unless the seller, at any time before or at the conclusion of the contract, neither knew nor ought to have known that the goods were bought for any such use.

legal systems of the member states. In fact, the member states have chosen different approaches in that respect.

The majority took a narrow approach and limited the transformation process to consumer sales. They inserted the necessary provisions either in their existing consumer protection laws or created special chapters or provisions on consumer sales in the relevant sales texts. Italy,[21] for instance, inserted into the sales provisions of the *Codice civile* a separate chapter which more or less mirrors the Directive. As a result, the *Codice civile* now has two sets of sales regimes: the general regime and the specific rules on consumer sales which only cover the issues dealt with in the Directive. It is for the (consumer) buyer to choose whether he avails himself of the remedies of the general rules or of the remedies provided for by the consumer rules.

On the other hand, some member states have used the transformation of the Directive as an opportunity to bring their general (ie non-consumer) law of sales into line with the basic concepts underlying the Directive and—as a consequence—with the concepts of the CISG. This is true particularly of Germany, where the transformation led to a fundamental and highly controversial reform both of the law of sales and of general contract law of the *Bürgerliches Gesetzbuch* (BGB).[22] It was one of the explicit objectives of the German legislature to adapt the old law, which still, essentially, reflected its Roman roots and the doctrinal achievements of the nineteenth century, to the new developments of the twentieth century. As the Directive was regarded as embodying several of these developments, its transformation was not strictly limited to consumer sales contracts. In fact, central elements of the Directive, such as the notion of conformity of the goods and the system of remedies, were integrated into the general law of sales and therefore now apply to all sales transactions. Only those aspects of the Directive which contain typical consumer protection law (in particular the mandatory character of the buyer's rights) were dealt with in a special part of the BGB which only applies to consumer sales.

The transformation process therefore leads to the following pattern of sales laws in the European Union. First, all EU states now have an essentially uniform set of rules on (certain issues[23] of) consumer sales contracts. Second, most EU states left their general law of sales untouched. Some states, however, in particular Germany, Poland, and Hungary, also changed their general law along the basic structures of the Directive.

---

[21] Decreto Legislativo 2 febbraio 2002, no. 24, Gazette Ufficiale de la Repubblica Italiana no. 57 del 8 marzo 2002—Supplemento Ordinario no. 40.

[22] For details, see Reinhard Zimmermann, *The New German Law of Obligations* (2005); Peter Huber and Florian Faust, *Schuldrechtsmodernisierung* (2002).

[23] As pointed out above, the Directive only covers a limited number of issues, in particular the conformity of the goods, the buyer's remedies for non-conformity (excluding, however, claims for damages), and rules on guarantees.

(b) The Action Plan for a More Coherent European Contract Law

Parallel to the elaboration of sector-specific measures by the EU, a broader debate gained momentum in the 1990s: it turned on the question of whether it would be desirable to create or develop a general European contract law. The discussion was not confined to academic circles,[24] but also extended to the institutions of the European Union. The European Parliament on several occasions called for the preparation of a common European Code of Private Law.[25] In 1999 the European Council in Tampere requested a study on the need to approximate the member states' legislation in matters of private law.[26]

In response to these developments the European Commission in 2001 published a 'Communication on European Contract Law'.[27] The purpose of that Communication was to launch a process of consultation of, and discussion between, all interested parties as to whether the Community should go beyond its traditional sector-specific approach and take further-reaching steps to harmonize European contract law. In particular, the Commission asked for feedback on the questions of whether the proper functioning of the European Internal Market might be hindered by divergences between the national contract laws. It was also interested in whether different national contract laws increased the costs of cross-border transactions. A further concern of the Commission was that the sectoral harmonization of contract law might lead to inconsistencies within the existing body of European contract law instruments. In its Communication the Commission suggested four possible (non-exhaustive) solutions to any problems which might become apparent in the course of the consultation process. These suggestions were: (1) to do nothing and leave the solution to the market; (2) to promote the development of non-binding common contract law principles; (3) to review and improve existing EU legislation to make it more coherent; (4) to adopt a new instrument at the level of the European Union.

The 2001 Communication triggered an enormous volume of reactions from governments, practitioners, and academics.[28] A majority of them favoured options (2) and (3), that is, the improvement of the existing instruments and the elaboration of common principles of contract law.

In 2003 the Commission submitted as a follow-up to the 2001 Communication

[24] See eg Arthur Hartkamp, Martijn Hesselink, Ewoud Hondius, Carla Joustra, and Edgar du Perron (eds), *Towards a European Civil Code* (2nd edn, 1998; now 3rd edn, 2004).

[25] Resolution A2–157/89, [1989] OJ C 158/400; Resolution A3–0329/94, [1994] OJ C 205/518; Resolution B5–0228, 0229–2030/2000, [2000] OJ C 377/323.

[26] Presidency Conclusions, Tampere European Council 15 and 16 October 1999, [2001] OJ C 12/1.

[27] Communication from the Commission to the Council and the European Parliament on European Contract Law, COM (2001) 398 final, [2001] OJ C 255/1.

[28] Many of the contributions and a summary may be seen at <http://europa.eu.int/comm/con-sumers/cons_int/safe_shop/fair_bus_pract/cont_law/actionplan_en.htm> (accessed 9 January 2006).

an 'Action Plan on a more coherent European Contract Law'.[29] The Action Plan suggests a mix of regulatory and non-regulatory measures and calls for contributions by all interested parties. The European Parliament[30] and the Council[31] adopted resolutions welcoming the Action Plan. In the light of these reactions the Commission in 2004 published another Communication entitled 'European Contract Law and the revision of the acquis: the way forward', in which it gave more information about the measures planned. Broadly speaking, the result of the communications of 2003 and 2004 is that the Commission envisages three types of measures.

The first of them aims at increasing the coherence of the existing regulatory body of EC law in the field of contract law. Apart from improving the existing rules, where necessary, the Commission intends to take a further step by elaborating a so-called 'common frame of reference' which should—in the view of the Commission—provide for the best solutions to the core issues of contract law in terms of a common terminology and of common rules. The scope of the common frame of reference is defined broadly and explicitly covers contracts of sale. Its main purpose would be to serve as a 'toolbox' for the amendment of existing, or the drafting of future, legal instruments in the area of contract law.[32] With regard to the legal nature of the common frame of reference, the Commission at present seems to favour a non-binding instrument. In the meantime a research network has been awarded EU funds to elaborate—on the basis of comprehensive comparative research—a proposal for such an instrument. The Commission intends to adopt it in 2009.

As a second initiative the Commission intends to promote the elaboration of EU-wide standard contract terms by providing support and information to interested parties.

Finally the Commission calls for further reflection on non-sector-specific measures such as an optional instrument in the area of European Contract Law. The Commission does not try to give any definite answers here. Its main objective is to start a discussion about the matter. The optional instrument is supposed to 'provide parties to a contract with a modern body of rules particularly adapted to cross-border contracts in the internal market'.[33] One advantage, according to the Commission, is that this would provide the parties with a 'neutral' set of rules on which it may be easier for them to agree than one of their respective national legal

[29] Communication from the Commission to the European Parliament and the Council: A more coherent European Contract Law—An Action Plan, COM (2003) 68 final, [2003] OJ C 63/1.

[30] COM (2004) 651 final, available at: <http://europa.eu.int/eur-lex/lex/LexUriServ/site/en/com/2004/com2004_0651en01.pdf> (accessed 9 January 2006).

[31] <http://ue.eu.int/ueDocs/cms_Data/docs/pressData/en/intm/77295.pdf> (accessed 9 January 2006).

[32] For further purposes (eg role model for national legislation, use in arbitration), see COM (2004) 651, 2 ff.

[33] Action Plan (n 30), para 90.

systems. A second advantage is supposed to derive from the fact that the economic actors would become (more) familiar with the rules of the optional instrument, which would encourage them to conclude cross-border contracts thereby facilitating the cross-border exchange of goods and services.

The application of the instrument would be 'optional'. It would therefore depend on the will of the parties. This objective may be achieved in two ways: either by applying the instrument only if the parties choose it as the applicable law ('opt-in') or by objectively defining a set of circumstances in which the instrument would apply (for instance if both parties have their place of business in a member state of the European Union) and granting the parties the possibility to exclude the instrument's application to their contract ('opt-out').

The optional instrument is supposed to take the common frame of reference as a basis, but it does not have to cover all of the areas dealt with there. The 2003 Action Plan left open whether the instrument should cover only general contract law rules or also specific contracts. The consultation process, however, has shown that most contributors favour an instrument which also covers specific contracts.[34] It is therefore likely that any future optional instrument would also cover sales contracts. The Commission is aware that it will be necessary to ensure coherence between the optional instrument and the CISG, but the question of how to do so remains open.[35]

In its 2004 Communication the Commission pointed out that it intends to continue the discussion process parallel to the development of the common frame of reference. However, as the optional instrument is supposed to be based on the common frame of reference, it seems unlikely that any definite steps will be taken before 2009.

(c) The Principles of European Contract Law and the Comparative Work of European Research Groups

In addition to the measures taken by political authorities, several academic research networks have undertaken comparative work on the law of contracts.[36] Originally the focus was on the general law of contract. Recently, however, the law of sales has received more attention. This is true, particularly, of the work of the Study Group on a European Civil Code[37] under the direction of Christian von Bar (Osnabrück). The Study Group, which was founded in 1999, continues the work which the Commission for European Contract Law (the so-called Lando Commission) started in the early 1980s and which resulted in the well-known

---

[34] Communication 11.10.2004, COM (2004) 651, 19 ff.

[35] For further reflections on this issue, see Peter Huber, 'European Private International Law, Uniform Law and the Optional Instrument', in ERA-Forum 2/2003, 85 ff.

[36] See Chapter 16 of this work. For an overview of the several groups see www.ipr.uni-koeln.de/eurprivr/arbeitsgruppen.htm (accessed 9 January 2006).

[37] www.sgecc.net (accessed 9 January 2006).

Principles of European Contract Law.[38] While these Principles are limited to the general law of contract, the Study Group intends to develop rules for specific contracts, including sales contracts, and also for other areas of the law of obligations and property, such as tort, unjust enrichment, the transfer of movables, and securities. Preliminary drafts for a European law of sales have been published on the website of the Study Group.[39]

The work of both the Lando Commission and the Study Group is based on comprehensive research and has several objectives. On the one hand, it is supposed to serve as a model for future attempts to create a European Civil Code. On the other hand, as evidenced by Art 1:101 PECL, the principles elaborated by both bodies are intended to be applied as general rules of contract law in the EU, to provide a set of rules which parties may incorporate into their contract, to be applied as part of the 'lex mercatoria', and to provide solutions for issues which are not dealt with by the applicable (national) law.

(d) Comparative Law in the European Harmonization Process

If one looks at the European harmonization process it becomes obvious that the role of comparative law within this process is considerable. This is true in particular of the work which is presently undertaken with regard to the measures proposed in the 2003 action plan and with regard to the work of the Study Group on a European Civil Code.

3. Harmonization of the Law of Sales in Africa

Up to now only a few African states have acceded to the CISG.[40] However, a regional harmonization of the law of sales has been achieved by the *Organisation pour l'harmonisation en Afrique du droit des affaires* (OHADA).[41] OHADA was founded in 1993 and presently comprises sixteen member states, most of them from the French-speaking part of Africa. The objective of OHADA is to promote the 'harmonisation of business laws in the Contracting States by the elaboration and adoption of simple modern common rules adapted to their economies, by setting up appropriate judicial procedures, and by encouraging arbitration for the settlement of contractual disputes'.[42]

---

[38] Ole Lando and Hugh Beale (eds), *Principles of European Contract Law* (Parts I and II, 1999); Ole Lando, Eric Clive, André Prüm, and Reinhard Zimmermann (eds), *Principles of European Contract Law* (Part III, 2003).

[39] <http://ecc.uvt.nl>.

[40] As of 14 June 2004 there were less then ten African member states, cf <http://www.uncitral.org/uncitral/en/uncitral_texts/sale_goods/1980CISG_status.html> (accessed 9 January 2006).

[41] For further information see <www.OHADA.com> (accessed 9 January 2006).

[42] Art 1 OHADA Treaty, <www.OHADA.com> (accessed 9 January 2006).

In 1997 OHADA adopted a Uniform Act Relating to General Commercial Law which covers certain areas of commercial law, among them, in Book V (Arts 202–88), the law of commercial sales. The Uniform Act entered into force in the OHADA member states on 1 January 1998. Within its scope of application it replaces the respective national laws. Its rules on sales law apply both to domestic and to international transactions and thus constitute a genuine uniform law of sales for the member states.[43] With regard to cross-boarder contracts the relationship between the Uniform Act and the CISG may, in theory, lead to complex questions.[44] In practice, however, cases of conflict will be rare as only one of the OHADA states has acceded to the CISG so far.

The Uniform Act is to a considerable extent mandatory law. Unlike Art 6 CISG, the Uniform Act does not contain a general opting-out rule. There seems to be agreement as to the fact that the parties cannot exclude the application of the Uniform Act *in toto*. They can, however, derogate from specific provisions of the Act if this is expressly provided for in these provisions.[45]

In order to ensure the uniformity of the Act's application, OHADA has established a Common Court (*Cour Commune de Justice et d'Arbitrage*) which can issue preliminary rulings on matters referred to it by the courts of the member states and which also serves as a court of last instance for certain national proceedings.[46]

The sales law of the Uniform Act has been strongly influenced by the CISG and is to a large extent similar to it.[47] There are, however, certain differences between both instruments. For instance, the buyer's obligation to give notice of any non-conformity of the goods is stricter in the Uniform Act than in the CISG, which is rather surprising given that the African states had argued for a lenient notice regime at the 1980 Diplomatic Conference which led to the CISG.[48] Furthermore, there are differences with regard to the role of the courts: the Uniform Act follows the French tradition in requiring certain remedies to be exercised with court assistance. So Art 254 of the Uniform Act requires the buyer to petition the competent court to terminate the contract whereas under the CISG the contract can simply be avoided by a declaration of the buyer.

---

[43] Petar Sarcevic, 'The CISG and Regional Unification', in Franco Ferrari (ed), *The 1980 Uniform Sales Law: Old Issues Revisited in the Light of Recent Experiences* (2003), 13 ff; Gaston Kenfack Douajni, 'La vente commerciale OHADA', (2003) 8 *Uniform LR* 191; Franco Ferrari, 'International Sales Law in the Light of the OHADA Uniform Act relating to General Commercial Law and the 1980 Vienna Sales Convention', [2001] *Revue de droit des affaires internationales* 600.

[44] See Franco Ferrari, 'Universal and Regional Sales Law: Can They Coexist?', (2003) 8 *Uniform LR* 177 ff.

[45] Sarcevic (n 44), 15; Ulrich G. Schroeter, 'Das einheitliche Kaufrecht der afrikanischen OHADA-Staaten im Vergleich zum UN-Kaufrecht', [2001] 4 *Recht in Africa* 166; cf also Douajni, (2003) 8 *Uniform LR* 198.

[46] Sarcevic (n 43), 14.

[47] Ferrari, [2001] *Revue de droit des affaires internationales* 599 ff; Douajni, (2003) 8 *Uniform LR* 191.

[48] cf Ingeborg Schwenzer, in Schlechtriem and Schwenzer (n 5), Art 38 n 2.

Obviously, comparative law had a considerable impact on the OHADA harmonization process. On the one hand the model character of the CISG led to an indirect comparative input into the project. On the other hand the drafters had to accommodate the CISG rules within the French heritage of most of the OHADA states, as the above example of the rules on termination shows.

4. The Special Case of Scandinavia

Scandinavia achieved a considerable degree of uniformity in the law of sales at a comparatively early stage. Between 1905 and 1907 Sweden, Denmark, and Norway enacted Sales Acts which were drafted in close comparative cooperation and were therefore essentially uniform in character. Finland did not enact a similar statute, but its law of sales has been considerably influenced by the Swedish act.[49] The Sales Acts did not purport to be a complete codification of sales law, but were limited to specific areas, in particular the remedies for breach.[50]

A further step towards the harmonization of Scandinavian private law was taken between 1915 and 1926 when Sweden, Norway, Denmark, and Finland enacted Contract Acts which, again, were essentially uniform in character and covered general issues of contract law.

Although the Scandinavian uniform laws did have an impact on the drafting of the 1964 Hague Sales Conventions, the Scandinavian countries themselves did not in fact ratify these conventions. This reluctant attitude towards an international harmonization of sales law changed when the CISG came into existence. In fact, all Scandinavian states ratified the CISG in the late 1980s. They did so, however, in a rather restrictive way which allowed them to maintain the uniformity that they had already achieved among themselves: all Scandinavian States declared that the CISG would not apply to contracts between parties which have their places of business in a Scandinavian state and that they would not be bound by the CISG provisions on the formation of contract (Arts 14–24).[51]

Parallel to the process of ratification of the CISG, the Scandinavian countries considered a modernization of their domestic (but—as mentioned above—essentially uniform) Sales Acts. As a result of this process new Sale of Goods Acts were enacted in Finland (1987), Norway (1988), and Sweden (1990), but not in Denmark. Due to the fact that the domestic enactments were modelled on the CISG, they are closer to the CISG than to Danish law (which is essentially still

---

[49] cf Joseph Lookofsky, 'The Scandinavian Experience', in Ferrari (ed), *The 1980 Uniform Sales Law* (n 43), 95, 100 f.

[50] For further details see Lookofsky (n 49), 102.

[51] They were entitled to make those reservations by virtue of Art 94 and Art 92 CISG.

based on the 1906 Sales Act).[52] It would, however, be inaccurate to say that the new enactments are identical with the CISG. In fact they show certain specific 'Scandinavian' features, most strikingly in respect of the liability regime: the no-fault liability regime of the CISG (which grants a claim for damages simply as a consequence of the debtor's breach but exempts the debtor from liability in certain specified cases, Arts 45, 64, and 79 CISG) is mirrored in the new enactments only to a certain extent. In fact, it is restricted to damages for direct loss whereas the recovery of indirect loss depends on fault. The notion of indirect loss seems to be rather broad: it is supposed to cover loss resulting from the reduction of production or turnover, loss of profit, loss resulting from damage to goods other than the goods sold, and loss resulting from the goods being unsuitable for their intended purpose.[53] This split liability system has encountered severe criticism in legal literature.[54] It has actually been suggested that its introduction was one of the reasons why Denmark did not follow suit in enacting a new Sales Act at the end of the 1980s.[55]

Briefly, therefore, the situation in Scandinavia is as follows: domestic sales are covered by the national sales laws which can be classified in two groups: on the one hand, there are the modern Sales Acts of Finland, Norway, and Sweden, which are similar to each other and have been considerably influenced by the CISG, and on the other hand, there is the 'old' Danish Sales Act from 1906. With regard to international sales the CISG will apply, except for its rules on the formation of contracts (which must give way to the application of the Uniform Contract Acts) and except for transactions between parties from Scandinavia (which are covered by the respective national sales law as described above).

[52] Norway, however, is a special case as it used a rather special and highly controversial technique. Instead of simply applying the CISG (or a specific statute incorporating it) in international transactions and creating a 'national' sales act for other transactions (as Sweden and Finland did), Norway enacted one single instrument which covers both domestic and international sales but submits them in part to different regimes. With regard to international sales the applicable rules are, of course, derived from the CISG. Unfortunately, however, the CISG was not simply incorporated into this text but transformed, that is, rewritten, which may lead to discrepancies. What is more, the structure of the Act does not clearly distinguish between domestic and international sales. In fact, most of the provisions are supposed to apply to both types of transactions. In addition to these rules there are several specific provisions which apply either to domestic or to international sales. All in all, one has to distinguish between three different sets of rules, which makes the application of the Act rather difficult. As far as the legal content is concerned, it is probably fair to say that the provisions which will ultimately be applied to international sales closely resemble the CISG—one commentator called it the 'Norwegian version' of the CISG (Lookofsky (n 49), 119)—whereas the rules applied to domestic transactions will closely resemble the rules of the new Swedish and Finnish sales acts. For a detailed account see Lookofsky (n 49), 116 ff.

[53] Jan Ramberg, 'Unification of Sales Law: a Look at the Scandinavian States', (2003) 8 *Uniform LR* 201, 203; Lookofsky (n. 49) 115.

[54] See Ramberg, (2003) 8 *Uniform LR* 203; Lookofsky (n 49), 115 f.

[55] Lookofsky (n 49), 121 f.

5. The Wider Context: The UNIDROIT Principles of International Commercial Contracts

A further instrument which must be taken into account when discussing the international harmonization and unification of sales law are the UNIDROIT Principles of International Commercial Contracts. First published in 1994, and revised and extended in 2004,[56] they are not a binding legal instrument (such as, for instance, the CISG), but have to rely on their persuasive authority in order to be applied. Thus, the preamble states that the Principles shall be applied when the parties have agreed that their contract be governed by them and that they may be applied (*inter alia*) if the parties have chosen the *lex mercatoria* (or general principles of law) to apply to their contract or have not made any choice of rules at all. Finally the Principles are meant to serve as a model for national legislatures and to be used to interpret or supplement international legal instruments or domestic law. In fact, the principles have been applied in a considerable number of arbitration proceedings and also in several court decisions.[57]

The UNIDROIT Principles 2004 cover the most important areas of both general contract law (such as formation, validity, interpretation, and the authority of agents) and the law of contractual obligations (such as remedies for non-performance, assignment of claims and contracts, third party rights, and set off). They also provide rules on limitation periods.

It is true that the UNIDROIT Principles do not contain a specific chapter on the law of sales and on the specific problems arising in that field. They are, however, meant to apply to sales contracts as to any other commercial contract and provide a set of remedies which are suitable for dealing with these cases. Art 7.1.1 of the UNIDROIT Principles states that non-performance is the failure by a party to perform any of its obligations, including defective performance or late performance. By explicitly mentioning defective performance the Principles make clear that contracts of sales and cases of defective delivery can fall within their scope of application.

---

[56] Michael Joachim Bonell, 'UNIDROIT Principles 2004—The New Edition of the Principles of International Commercial Contracts adopted by the International Institute for the Unification of Private Law', (2004) 9 *Uniform LR* 5; Reinhard Zimmermann, 'Die Unidroit-Grundregeln der internationalen Handelsverträge 2004 in vergleichender Perspektive', (2005) 13 *Zeitschrift für Europäisches Privatrecht* 264 ff; and see now Michael Joachim Bonell, *An International Restatement of Contract Law* (3rd edn, 2005) (with the text of the Principles).

[57] For an overview see the Unilex-Database: <www.unilex.info>, and Bonell, (2004) 9 *Uniform LR* 5.

6. The Overall Picture: Uniform Law and National Law

As we have seen, a considerable level of uniformity has been achieved in the area of sales law over the last hundred years. Usually comparative law played—and still plays—an important role in this harmonization process.

In order to paint the overall picture it is helpful to distinguish between cross-border sales and domestic sales.

With regard to cross-border sales, the success of the CISG has led to estimates that up to two-thirds of world trade is or—rather—could be[58] covered by this instrument.[59] Outside the ambit of the CISG certain regional measures have led to uniform rules for cross-border sales. This is particularly true for the African OHADA Uniform Act which has created a truly uniform law for both domestic and international sales. A similar situation has been achieved in Scandinavia where Sweden, Finland, and Norway[60] have closely related national laws which bear the 'CISG imprint'. Of course, these enactments do not constitute a real 'Uniform Scandinavian Sales Law' as they are national in character, but in practice they will lead to similar consequences. In fact, the Scandinavian states themselves seem to perceive the situation in that manner, as is shown by their reservations under Art 94 CISG where they declared their intention to exclude the application of the CISG to inter-Scandinavian sales. Both the OHADA Act and the Scandinavian Acts, however, bear a rather close resemblance to the CISG, so that it is fair to say that a considerable part of world trade is nowadays based on the CISG. Those transactions which do not fall under any of the harmonized instruments will still be subject to a national sales law in accordance with the rules of private international law.

With regard to domestic transactions one has to distinguish between different levels. First, some of the harmonization measures, in particular the OHADA Act and the Scandinavian Sales Acts (but not the CISG), are not restricted to cross-border sales but also apply to domestic contracts. Second, on the European level, the EU has achieved a certain degree of harmonization with regard to certain aspects of consumer sales as a result of the 1998 Sales Directive. Here the CISG has also exerted considerable influence as several of the provisions of the Directive were modelled on those contained in the CISG. Finally, outside the scope of the harmonized instruments, the national sales laws will apply. This, at first glance, seems to lead to a patchwork of different legal systems. Upon closer inspection, however, certain common structures can be discerned (see Section IV below).

---

[58] The term 'could be' probably refers to those transactions which would fall under the CISG if the parties had not excluded its application by virtue of Art 6 CISG, which, in fact, happens quite frequently in practice.

[59] Schlechtriem (n 5), 27.

[60] In the case of Norway, one should, however, keep in mind the very special structure of the statute, as mentioned above.

III. Characteristic Comparative Features of Sales Law—As Evidenced by the Buyer's Remedies for Non-Conformity of the Goods

It would be impossible to try to present a world-wide comparative overview concerning the state of the law of sales within the present chapter. The following sections therefore simply attempt to highlight some selected features which in the author's view are particularly interesting from a comparative perspective. Probably the most characteristic feature of any law of sales is that which deals with the buyer's remedies for defective performance. The following considerations therefore concentrate on that area of the law.

1. The Way from *Caveat Emptor* to an Objective System of Seller's Liability

Most legal systems seem to have originated from the principle of *caveat emptor*: The law did not impose on the parties (or rather: on the seller) any 'legal' requirements as to the quality of the goods sold but left it to them to agree on certain standards if they so wished. If the goods turned out to be defective, the seller was therefore only liable if these standards explicitly agreed upon by the parties had not been met.[61] One might label such a system a 'purely subjective' one as it is exclusively based on the intentions of the parties.

Nowadays, the *caveat emptor* principle is no longer the standard rule in the law of sales. Every legal system needs to provide a structured system of obligations and remedies which is not solely based on explicit promises by the seller but also enables 'the law' to set certain 'objective' standards. Of course the development of such an objective system does not mean that party autonomy would be completely set aside. In fact, most legal systems will, in principle, allow the parties to derogate from the objective system laid down by the law (with possible exceptions in the area of consumer contracts). The transformation from a purely subjective system to an objective system simply leads to a shift in the burden of reaching an agreement: in a purely subjective, *caveat-emptor*-style system the seller's obligation as to conformity of the goods only exists if it has been specifically agreed upon by the parties, whereas in an objective system the obligation will exist unless the parties have specifically derogated from it.

---

[61] Jürgen Basedow, *Die Reform des deutschen Kaufrechts* (1988), 12.

Not every legal system, however, chose the same avenue when moving from the purely subjective system to the objective system. Traditionally, two different approaches can be distinguished in that respect, namely the 'Roman' model (which establishes a 'two-tier approach') and the 'English' model (which is based on a unitary approach).

(a) The Roman Model: The 'Two-Tier Approach'

In Roman law, the *caveat emptor* principle only gave the buyer a remedy (the *actio empti* sounding in damages), if the seller had acted fraudulently or had given specific promises regarding the quality of the object sold. It soon proved to be insufficient. Roman law therefore developed specific rules relating to the seller's liability. They covered latent defects of the goods even if no specific promise had been made with regard to them. The buyer in these cases was entitled to a reduction of the purchase price (*actio quanti minoris*) or to affect a termination of the contract (*actio redhibitoria*). The practical effect of these so-called aedilitian remedies was that there was a 'statutory' liability of the seller for latent defects. Apart from that, the buyer could still claim damages under the traditional *actio empti*, that is, if the seller had fraudulently failed to disclose a defect known to him or if he had specifically guaranteed that the object was free from certain defects or that it had certain qualities. Thus, under the Roman law approach the purchaser could comparatively easily avail himself of the remedies of price reduction and termination for latent defects of the goods. He could, however, only claim damages if there had been fraud, or a specific promise, on the part of the seller. This system of remedies became—albeit with certain variations—the characteristic feature of most of the Continental European legal systems for many centuries.[62] In recent years several states (such as the Netherlands and Germany) have broken with their Roman tradition in that respect, but France and Spain, for example, still have sales laws which closely resemble the original Roman model.

The Roman approach may have had its virtues and advantages, but it also had one particular disadvantage which has caused problems and debates continuing until today: it led to defective performance by the seller being regulated by a system of rules and remedies which had not developed out of the general law of breach of contract but instead remained distinct from it. This is why it may be seen to establish a 'two-tier approach'. As a consequence, the rules and policy considerations which apply, for example, to late performance or non-performance are different from the principles that govern the cases of defective performance. They are different not as a result of a conscious decision by a legislature or other protagonist of legal development, but as a result of historical accident. Furthermore, the practical differences between the two regimes could be substantial. This is true,

---

[62] cf Reinhard Zimmermann, *The Law of Obligations: Roman Foundations of the Civilian Tradition* (1996), 327 ff.

in particular, for the limitation periods. The previous German law, for instance, showed a discrepancy of more than twenty-nine years in this regard: the limitation period for the specific remedies in sales law was six months, but that for the general remedies for breach of contract was thirty years; in addition, both had different starting-points. Further examples are provided by the rules on termination of contract (whereas sales law did not recognize a *Nachfrist* requirement, ie a duty on the part of the buyer to fix an additional period of time for performance before terminating the contract, the general rules on breach of contract often did) or by the law of damages (in the law of sales, damages were limited to cases of fraud or specific promises whereas their availability was determined by a simple fault requirement in general contract law).

As a result, most legal systems which followed the Roman model experienced (and still experience) considerable problems in trying to draw a clear line between the two different regimes. For example: where, in the case of a sale of generic goods, can the line be drawn between the delivery of an *aliud* (which triggers the application of the general rules of non-performance) and the delivery of defective goods (which leads to the application of the specific sales rules)? In other words: when are the goods delivered by the seller so far removed from the contractual description that they can no longer be regarded as defective examples of the promised type of goods but as something entirely different, that is, an *aliud*? An enormous amount of ink has been spilled in attempts to determine this borderline.

(b) The English Model: A Unitary Approach

English law, on the other hand, took a different path from *caveat emptor* to the modern 'objective' system of remedies for non-conformity. It managed to perform the necessary changes within the system of the general rules on breach of contract; this is why one can speak of a unitary approach.

This system is based on the idea that one party will be liable to the other party if it breaches a term of the contract. The core concept therefore is the notion of the contractual 'term'. Traditionally English law distinguished between two different types of terms: whereas a breach of a warranty entitles the other party to damages, the breach of a condition gives the other party the right to terminate the contract (or to treat the contract as repudiated). Whether a contractual term is a condition or a warranty will depend on the interpretation of the contract in light of the circumstances of the case.[63] However, as a general rule, it is fair to say that only those terms, which 'go to the root of the contract', or which are so important that

---

[63] See s 11(3) Sale of Goods Act 1979: 'Whether a stipulation in a contact of sale is a condition, the breach of which may give rise to a right to treat the contract as repudiated, or a warranty, the breach of which may give rise to a claim for damages but not to a right to reject the goods and treat the contract as repudiated, depends in each case on the construction of the contract; . . .'.

their breach will deprive the other party 'of substantially the whole benefit'[64] that it was entitled to expect under the contract will normally qualify as a condition.[65]

The distinction between warranties and conditions is based on the assumption that every term can be classified according to its gravity at the time of the conclusion of the contract. This assumption, however, may not be correct in all situations. In a considerable number of cases the character of a term is such that it can be breached both with very small and with very grave consequences for the other party. In those circumstances it will be more reasonable to look at the consequences of the actual breach in question rather than to base the decision as to whether or not the contract can be terminated on a rigid classification made at the time it was concluded. This is why, in the twentieth century, the English courts fashioned a third group of terms, the so-called 'intermediate' or 'innominate' terms. These terms need not be classified as conditions or warranties from the outset. Whether their breach will give the other party a right to terminate the contract will depend instead on the gravity of the breach.[66]

The development in English law from the principle of *caveat emptor* to an 'objective' system of remedies for defective delivery was effected by means of the 'implied term'. Originally English law had required that 'terms' had to be expressly stipulated (*caveat emptor*). In the course of the nineteenth century (much later than the legal systems inspired by Roman law), however, English courts started to assume that there were so-called 'implied terms', which did not need to be expressly stipulated.[67] Nowadays it is generally recognized that contracts may contain implied terms and that the implication of the term in question may either operate by law or result from an analysis of the intentions of the parties. In the case of terms implied by law, the courts or a statute lay down a general rule whereby in all contracts of a specified type (eg a contract of sale), certain terms will be implied unless this would be contrary to the express wording of the contract.[68]

The implied term technique makes it possible to set up an objective system of obligations and remedies of the parties. This is true in particular of the law concerning defective performance under a sales contract.[69] Here the Sale of Goods Act 1979 provides an extensive set of implied terms concerning the conformity of the goods (cf ss 13 ff Sale of Goods Act 1979: implied terms in sales by description, implied terms about quality or fitness, implied terms in sales by sample). Most of these terms are classified as conditions so that their breach entitles the buyer to terminate the contract. Outside the scope of consumer sales, however, the implied

---

[64] cf *Hongkong Fir Shipping Co Ltd v Kawasaki Kisen Kaisha Ltd* [1962] 2 QB 26, 66 (*per* Diplock LJ).

[65] cf *Hongkong Fir Shipping v Kawasaki Kisen Kaisha* [1962] 2 QB 26, 64 (*per* Upjohn LJ).

[66] See *Chitty on Contracts* (2004), para 12–034; *Hongkong Fir Shipping v Kawasaki Kisen Kaisha* [1962] 2 QB 26, 70 (*per* Diplock LJ).

[67] cf *Chitty on Contracts* (2004), paras 13–001 ff.   [68] *Chitty on Contracts* (2004), para 13–003.

[69] cf Ewan McKendrick, 'Remedies of the Buyer', in Ewan McKendrick (ed), *Sale of Goods* (2000), paras 10–004 ff.

term may be treated as a warranty rather than a condition if the breach is so slight that it would be unreasonable to allow the termination of the contract (s 15A Sale of Goods Act 1979); this rule to a certain extent assimilates the implied condition to an innominate term.

The defining difference between the Roman model and the English approach therefore is that English law managed to develop the seller's liability for non-conformity out of the general rules of contract law. Defective performance is, in principle, merely one instance of breach of contract and leads to the normal remedies provided for by the rules on breach of contract. In other words: the English model is based on a unitary concept of breach of contract whereas the Roman approach follows a two-tier structure by placing a separate set of remedies next to (and to some extent even into) the general law of breach of contract.

It is true that the Sale of Goods Act 1979 does contain several rules on remedies. This does not mean, however, that the Act sets up a specific system of rules for defective delivery. In fact, most of the provisions on remedies simply restate the general rules on breach of contract. Others may modify those rules in specific points, but they usually do not restrict those modifications to cases of non-conformity. All in all, the English Sale of Goods Act 1979 is far from establishing a special remedial system for cases of non-conformity. As a consequence the English approach avoids most of the problems of delimitation which the Roman law-based systems encounter when they have to draw the line between the general contract law and the rules on defective delivery.

The English model has, by and large, been followed by most of the states of the Commonwealth, as they based their sales laws on the English Sale of Goods Act.

The situation in the USA is somewhat more complicated to assess. If one takes Art 2 of the Uniform Commercial Code (UCC) as a model for the sales laws of the vast majority of the individual states, it is probably fair to say that US law is much closer to the English model than to the Roman approach. Although the UCC does not follow the classification of terms as warranties and conditions (and—nowadays—intermediate terms), and the remedial consequences which English law derives from that classification, a look at the basic concepts of the law reveals a certain resemblance to the English solution: the remedial system of Art 2 UCC is in principle based on the general law of contract, although there are modifications with regard to the seller's duties (for instance with regard to the perfect tender rule of sales law which differs from the material breach concept of general contract law[70]) and with regard to the buyer's remedies (where § 2–711 ff UCC provide detailed provisions).

The unitary system which is characteristic of the English approach has also been

---

[70] It is true, however, that the practical differences between these two concepts may be much less considerable than one might think at first glance; cf James J. White and Robert S. Summers, *Uniform Commercial Code* (2000), 313 f.

adopted in recent national reforms of the law of sales, notably in the Netherlands and in Germany. For example, in 2002, German law made an abrupt turn from the Roman model to the unitary system.[71] In fact, it was one of the main objectives of the reform to integrate the seller's liability for defective performance into the general law of breach of contract. This objective was achieved to a large extent. Two of the main remedies of the buyer, that is, termination and damages, are now governed by the respective provisions of the general part of the law obligations. The relevant provision in the law of sale, which lists all of the buyer's remedies (§ 437 BGB), simply states that with regard to damages and termination the general rules (§§ 280 ff, § 311a II, §§ 323 ff BGB) will apply. It is true that the general rules are subject to certain modifications in the law of sales, but those concern details and do not disturb the overall picture of a uniform system of remedies. A further important consequence of the unitary approach is that the buyer now has a statutory right to claim performance of the seller's obligation to deliver conforming goods ('supplementary performance') which can take one of two forms: he may demand the supply of an object that is free from defects, or he may ask for removal of the defect. Under the old law, there was no such claim because it was widely held that the seller of a specific object was only obliged to deliver that specific object. If it turned out to be defective, this was not a case of non-performance; the seller was rather held to be liable as the result of an additional warrant imposed on him by the modern, statutory version of the aedilitian remedies. The most striking particularity of the law of sales, as opposed to the general law of breach of contract, continues to be the right to reduce the purchase price (§ 441). Here, the old *actio quanti minoris* of Roman law has been preserved even under the new law. It should be noted, however, that the modern, unitary concept considerably influenced the requirements which have to be met before the buyer can reduce the purchase price. In fact, § 441 BGB states that, as a rule, the requirements for termination of the contract have to be met, and these requirements are to be found in the general law of breach of contract.

2. The Role of Termination as a Remedy

If the seller delivers goods which do not conform to the standards contractually agreed upon or fixed by law, one of the possible reactions of the law consists in giving the buyer the right to terminate the contract. As a result the buyer will not have to pay the contract price (or can claim his payment back), and the seller will have to take back the non-conforming goods.

In fact, most legal systems will at some point or other allow the buyer to

---

[71] For details, see Zimmermann (n 22), 79 ff and Reinhard Zimmermann, 'Remedies for Non-Performance', (2002) *Edinburgh LR* 271 ff.

terminate the contract if the seller has delivered non-conforming goods. The crucial issue, therefore, is not *whether* there is a right to terminate the contract, but rather *when* it will become available to the buyer. In this respect, a comparative analysis reveals interesting differences and developments. At least originally, the Roman law-based legal systems regarded termination of the contract as a remedy that was easily available (cf subsection (a)). Nowadays, however, there is a clear international trend towards a more restrictive approach which instead regards termination of the contract as a last resort within the system of remedies (cf subsection (b)).

(a) Termination as a Readily Available Remedy

In the original aedilitian system of remedies, and in the legal systems following the Roman model, termination was readily available to the buyer. In fact, almost every non-conformity entitled the buyer to terminate the contract.[72] Termination and price reduction were the standard remedies for non-conformity. There was—at least in contracts for the sale of specific goods—no claim for substitute delivery, or for repair, which meant that the buyer could immediately terminate the contract. This was, for instance, the situation in German law before the reform of 2002. A similar situation still exists in French law (if one disregards the specific rules implementing the EC Consumer Sales Directive).

(b) The Modern Trend to Restrain the Scope of Termination

The twentieth century, however, brought a clear trend against the termination being readily available as a remedy for defective delivery. Several modern sales laws and international instruments regard the termination of the contract as a remedy of last resort which should only be granted if other remedies (such as performance, price reduction, or damages) will not lead to an adequate result.

There are several reasons and policy considerations for curtailing the availability of termination.[73] The first reason can be described by the old principle of 'pacta sunt servanda'. The agreement which the parties have reached by their free will should be honoured and enforced by the law as long as reasonably possible.

The second reason for being opposed to termination as a remedy is an economic one. Termination of the contract for defective delivery leads to a restitution of the goods originally delivered and possibly to a restitution of money paid by the buyer. Restitution of the goods in particular may entail considerable costs and risks which could be avoided were the contract not terminated and were the buyer's interest in

---

[72] However, under the *ius commune*, this was disputed; see Zimmermann (n 62), 325 f, 329.

[73] cf Hugh Beale, 'Remedies: Termination', in Arthur Hartkamp, Martijn Hesselink, Ewoud Hondius, Edgar du Perron, and Jan Vranken (eds), *Towards a European Civil Code* (2nd edn, 1998), 348, 350; Michael Joachim Bonell, *An International Restatement of Contract Law* (1997), 76 ff; Peter Huber, *Irrtumsanfechtung und Sachmängelhaftung* (2001), 248 ff; Guenter H. Treitel (n 8), para 241.

getting conforming goods accommodated either by repair or by way of a claim for damages. From an economic perspective, therefore, termination may prove to be an expensive remedy.

A third reason for restraining the scope of termination results from an analysis of the legitimate interests of the parties. The seller can in many cases legitimately claim that his efforts in order to effect performance should not be frustrated by a minor defect which can easily be cured at his expense. At the same time, it is often difficult to justify the buyer's refusal of the seller's offer to cure in such a situation, provided that he is granted damages for any loss suffered until the cure has been effected and that he does not have to bear the costs involved in such case. By insisting on termination, the buyer may be trying to use the non-conformity to disguise his real motives such as a fall in the market prices for the goods.

(c) The Instruments for Restraining Termination as a Remedy

A comparative analysis of the modern rules reveals three instruments which can—on their own or combined with each other—serve to restrain the scope of termination as a remedy.

(i) The first tool is the so-called *Nachfrist* procedure which, in principle, requires the buyer to fix an additional period of time for performance (ie for repair or supply of another object free from defect). Termination of the contract will only be available for the buyer if the *Nachfrist* has lapsed to no avail. The *Nachfrist* procedure therefore effectively gives the seller a second chance to perform, before the buyer can terminate the contract. From the buyer's perspective, this means that defective delivery by the seller usually does not by itself entitle him to terminate the contract; however he does have the chance to 'upgrade' even a minor breach by fixing the additional period of time and waiting for its expiry.

The *Nachfrist* procedure is a centrepiece of the new German sales law (cf §§ 437 No. 2, 323 BGB): the buyer may only terminate the contract after a reasonable additional period of time has been fixed and has lapsed to no avail. There are, of course, exceptions to this rule, for instance, if it appears from the contract that the buyer's interest in receiving performance is limited to receiving it in time, if supplementary performance would be inadequate or impossible. The basic rule, however, is that the buyer has to give the seller a 'second chance' by fixing the additional period of time. The notion of *Nachfrist* has also found its way into the UNIDROIT Principles of International Commercial Contracts (Arts 7.3.1(3), 7.1.5), the Principles of European Contract law (Arts 9:301(2), 8:106(3)), and the CISG (Art 49(1)(b)). In these instruments, however, it is limited to cases of non-delivery or late delivery whereas in German law it also extends to defective delivery.

(ii) The second tool can be labelled the 'seller's right to cure'. It is closely related to the *Nachfrist* procedure, but starts from a different angle. If the buyer complains about the non-conformity of the goods and announces that he wants to terminate the contract, the seller has the right to prevent the termination by performing properly (by means of repair or supply of another object free from defects) within a reasonable period of time and without undue inconvenience to the buyer. The difference to the *Nachfrist* technique lies in the fact that here the initiative does not lie with the buyer (who would have to fix a *Nachfrist*), but on the side of the seller, who may offer substitute performance if he wants to keep the contract alive.

A good example of this mechanism can be found in Art 7.1.4 of the UNIDROIT Principles of International Commercial Contracts, which reads:

The non-performing party may, at its own expense, cure any non-performance, provided that

(a) without undue delay, it gives notice indicating the proposed manner and timing of the cure;
(b) cure is appropriate in the circumstances;
(c) the aggrieved party has no legitimate interest in refusing cure; and
(d) cure is effected promptly.

The provision further states that the right to cure is not precluded by notice of termination and that upon effective notice of cure, rights of the aggrieved party that are inconsistent with the non-performing party's performance are suspended until the time for cure has expired.

A similar rule can be found in Art 8:104 PECL which gives the seller the right to make a new and conforming tender where the time for performance has not yet arrived or the delay would not be such as to constitute a fundamental non-performance.

The seller's right to cure also plays an important role in the law of the United States. § 2–508(2) of the Uniform Commercial Code (UCC) in its new version of 2003[74] gives the seller the right to cure the defect even after the agreed time for performance has expired provided (*inter alia*) that the seller has performed in good faith, that he has given reasonable notice to the buyer of his intention to cure, and that the cure is appropriate and timely in the circumstances. If the seller manages to cure the defect, the buyer's right to reject the goods (which comes close to a termination of the contract[75]) is excluded.[76] Under the 2003 version of § 2–508(2) UCC the same is true with regard to the buyer's revocation of acceptance whereas this issue was disputed under the earlier versions of the UCC.[77] The details are not of relevance in the present context. Suffice it to say that, in principle, the

---

[74] The wording of the pre–2003 version of § 2–508(2) UCC differs from the present provision at several points. In principle, however, and subject to possible modifications in detail, the seller's right to cure even after expiry of the agreed time for performance was also recognized; cf White and Summers (n 70), 334 ff.

[75] cf § 2–710 UCC 2003; White and Summers (n 70), 305 f.

[76] cf Official Comment no. 1 to § 2–711 UCC 2003.

[77] cf White and Summers (n 70), 332 ff.

buyer's right to get out of the contract due to a non-conforming delivery is to a considerable extent subject to the seller's right to cure.

The question of whether the CISG recognizes a seller's right to cure is difficult to answer. Under certain circumstances, Art 48(1) CISG gives the seller a right to remedy (at his own expense) a failure to perform his obligations. This right to cure is, however, 'subject to article 49', that is, subject to the buyer's right to avoid the contract, which, in turn, requires that the delivery of non-conforming goods amounts to a fundamental breach (Arts 49(1)(a), 25 CISG). The crucial question therefore is whether the curability of the defect should be taken into account when deciding whether the breach is fundamental. This issue has created a considerable amount of controversy since the enactment of the CISG. Nowadays, however, there seems to be growing support for the view[78] that, in principle, curability should indeed be taken into account unless the buyer has a particular and legitimate interest in being allowed to avoid the contract immediately (ie without waiting for cure). The buyer would have such a legitimate interest if, for instance, the basis of trust between the parties were destroyed or if it appears from the contract that both time and conformity were of the essence of the contract. If one follows this view, the CISG can be taken to recognize a seller's right to cure which can override the buyer's right to terminate the contract.

Both the *Nachfrist* procedure and the right to cure serve at least two of the three policy requirements mentioned above: they strengthen the principle of '*pacta sunt servanda*', in that the contract will not be set aside simply as a result of a defective delivery; and they are also consistent with the legitimate interests of the parties, provided that there are exceptions for cases in which immediate conforming delivery was essential to the buyer, or in which cure by the seller would be inappropriate or impossible. With regard to the economic argument for restraining the scope of termination, the situation is more complex. In fact, in cases of defective delivery, the economic objective mentioned above will only be achieved if the seller is only permitted to cure the defect by repair and not by substitute delivery. The reason for this is that substitute delivery will result in the need to transport the defective goods from the buyer to the seller and the new goods from the seller to the buyer. So, in fact, substitute delivery leads to the same results as termination with regard to the defective goods which had originally been delivered.

(iii) The third technique which is used in order to restrict the scope of termination as a remedy for defective performance is the doctrine of fundamental breach. It restricts the buyer's right to terminate the contract for defective delivery to serious

---

[78] cf, for instance, Peter Huber, in *Münchener Kommentar zum Bürgerlichen Gesetzbuch* (vol IV, 4th edn, 2004), Art 49 CISG nn 28 ff; Müller-Chen (n 9), Art 48 n 15. There is also case law which seems to go in this direction: Oberlandesgericht Köln of 14 October 2002, [2003] *Internationales Handelsrecht* 15 = CISG-online (n 2), no. 709; Oberlandesgericht Koblenz of 31 January 1997, (2003) *Internationales Handelsrecht (IHR)* 172 = CISG-online (n 2), no. 256.

cases. It is the guiding principle of the CISG,[79] of the UNIDROIT Principles,[80] and of the Principles of European Contract Law.[81] These texts, in principle, make the buyer's right to terminate the contract dependent on the requirement that the seller has committed a fundamental breach. It is only in cases of non-delivery[82] or of delay[83] that the fundamental breach requirement is not mandatory but can be replaced by the *Nachfrist* procedure. Today, the doctrine of fundamental breach is also part of the Scandinavian Sales Laws and of those legal systems which have taken inspiration from the CISG, such as the new Estonian law of obligations.[84] It is often said that the fundamental breach doctrine has its origins in English law.[85] At first sight, this appears to be a correct assumption. In fact, both the distinction between conditions and warranties and the doctrine of intermediate terms are based on similar criteria as the fundamental breach concept of the international texts. With regard to the cases of defective delivery by the seller, however, a caveat should be entered: many of those breaches are classified by the Sale of Goods Act (ss 13 ff) as conditions and may therefore lead to a right to terminate the contract without the need to take account of the criteria mentioned above.[86]

Both the appeal and the problems of the fundamental breach doctrine are readily apparent: on the one hand, it is a plausible rule to allow the most far-reaching remedy only in particularly 'grave' cases of breach; on the other hand, there are considerable difficulties in drawing the exact line between those breaches which are fundamental and those which are not. All of the texts mentioned above therefore provide a definition of the notion of fundamental breach.

According to Art 25 CISG a breach is fundamental if it results in such detriment to the other party as substantially to deprive him of what he is entitled to expect under the contract, unless the party in breach did not foresee and a reasonable person of the same kind in the same circumstances would not have foreseen such a result. From an abstract point of view this definition may sound perfectly acceptable. On its own, however, it will not enable judges and practitioners to draw the line between fundamental breaches and other breaches. In fact, most of the debate will simply be shifted onto the question of whether the detriment caused by the breach substantially deprived the other party of what he was entitled to expect under the contract. The criteria which may or have to be applied to answer this question will in the last resort have to be clarified by the courts and arbitral tribunals. Under the CISG, for instance, the following criteria may be taken into

---

[79] Art 49(1)(a) CISG.   [80] Art 7.3.1(1) PICC.   [81] Art 9:301(1) PECL.

[82] Art 49(1)(b) CISG.

[83] Art 7.3.1(3) PICC; 9:301(2) PECL.

[84] cf Paul Varul, 'CISG: A Source of Inspiration for the Estonian Law of Obligations', (2003) 8 *Uniform LR* 209.

[85] See eg Comments to Art 8:103 PECL, in Lando and Beale (n 38), 364 ff.

[86] For details, see Guenter H. Treitel (n 8), para 267.

account:[87] any agreement of the parties as to which clauses in the contract should be regarded as fundamental; the gravity of the breach; and—at least in the view of the German and Swiss courts—the question of whether the buyer can make reasonable use of the defective goods[88] (eg by selling them at a lower price and claiming the loss of profit as damages from the seller under Arts 45(1)(b), 74 ff CISG). As mentioned above (ii), it has been a matter of some controversy whether the possibility to cure should play a role in determining whether the breach is fundamental.

Both the UNIDROIT Principles and the European Principles provide a more detailed definition of the notion of fundamental breach. Art. 8:103 PECL regards a breach as fundamental if (a) strict compliance with the obligation is of the essence of the contract, or (b) the non-performance substantially deprives the aggrieved party of what it was entitled to expect under the contract, unless the other party did not foresee and could not reasonably have foreseen that result, or (c) the non-performance is intentional and gives the aggrieved party reason to believe that it cannot rely on the other party's future performance. Art 7.3.1 PICC gives a non-exhaustive list of factors to be taken into account which to a considerable extent resemble those in Art 8:103 PECL. The question of whether the possibility of curing the defect should be of relevance when deciding on the buyer's right to terminate the contract for defective delivery is clearly decided in both the UNIDROIT Principles and the European Principles: the seller has a right to cure which takes precedence over the buyer's right to terminate the contract.[89]

IV. Conclusion

The comparative picture of the law of sales has changed considerably since the days when Ernst Rabel wrote his fundamental treatise. The most important factor for these changes is the process of unification which has, in some form or other, reached most parts of the world. As a result, a great number of sales transactions—

---

[87] For further details, see Huber (n 78), Art 49 CISG, nn 36 ff.

[88] cf (German) Federal Supreme Court, [1997] *Praxis des Internationalen Privat- und Verfahrensrechts* 342, 344 = CISG-online (n 2), no. 135; (Swiss) Federal Supreme Court CISG-online (n 2), no. 413; Peter Schlechtriem, in Schlechtriem and Schwenzer (n 5), Art 25 n 21a. It is, however, not certain whether this approach will be universally accepted. There are court decisions in other contracting states which decide on the fundamental breach issue without discussing the reasonable use test: see eg *Delchi Carrier SpA v Rotorex Corp* 71 F3d 1024 (1995) (United States Court of Appeals, 2nd Circuit) = CISG-online (n 2), no. 140.

[89] Art 8:104 PECL, Art 7.1.4 PICC.

both national and international—will nowadays be governed by a set of rules which are based either on an international legal text (such as the CISG or the OHADA Uniform Act) or on national legal systems which have been shaped by a uniform model (such as the Scandinavian Sales Acts or the law of consumer sales within the European Union). The process of unification of sales law is closely interrelated to the discipline of comparative law. On the one hand, unification projects are usually based on comparative studies and analyses. On the other hand, the existing uniform texts have a considerable impact on national legislatures which intend to reform or modernize their national sales laws. In the light of these developments it is the author's view that Ernst Rabel himself would probably not have minded the way in which this area of the law has developed. In fact, Rabel himself was one of the fathers of the unification process which has proved so influential in the last hundered years.

BIBLIOGRAPHY

Ernst Rabel, *Das Recht des Warenkaufs* (vol I, 1936; vol II, 1958)

Guenter H. Treitel, *Remedies for Breach of Contract* (1991)

Reinhard Zimmermann, *The Law of Obligations: Roman Foundations of the Civilian Tradition* (1996)

Konrad Zweigert and Hein Kötz, *An Introduction to Comparative Law* (trans Tony Weir, 3rd edn, 1998)

Michael Bridge, *The International Sale of Goods* (1999)

Acts of the Congress to Celebrate the 75th Anniversary of the Founding of the International Institute for the Unification of Private Law (UNIDROIT), Session 2: 'The Sale of Goods: Do Regions Matter?', (2003) 1/2 *Uniform LR* 173–230

Franco Ferrari (ed), *The 1980 Uniform Sales Law, Old Issues Revisited in the Light of Recent Experiences* (2003)

'Symposium: The Convention on the International Sale of Goods and its Application in Comparative Perspective', (2004) 68 *RabelsZ* 427 ff.

Heinz-Peter Mansel, 'Kaufrechtsreform in Europa und die Dogmatik des deutschen Leistungsstörungsrechts', (2004) 204 *Archiv für die civilistische Praxis* 396–456

Peter Schlechtriem and Ingeborg Schwenzer (eds), *Commentary on the UN Convention of the International Sale of Goods* (2nd edn, 2005)

Reinhard Zimmermann, *The New German Law of Obligations* (2005)

CHAPTER 30

UNJUSTIFIED ENRICHMENT IN COMPARATIVE PERSPECTIVE

DANIEL VISSER

Cape Town

I. Introduction: When Worlds Collide

IT is difficult to overstate the importance for comparative law of the fact that unjustified enrichment burst forth in abundant life in the common-law world during the last decade of the twentieth century.[1] It confronted both civil and common lawyers with thinking which was often completely outside the paradigm to which they had become accustomed. Whereas both civil law and common law had always had contract and tort as primary forms of obligation and had also had, despite profound differences, a great deal of shared understanding in regard to these areas, the recognition of unjustified enrichment as a cause of action in its own right in English law (even though certain antecedents had always been understood to be the functional equivalent of unjustified enrichment) created a new arena of uncertainty between the systems. For civil lawyers, the initial encounter with the principles and remedies relating to enrichment in the common law was not unlike that of the palaeontologists who first came across earth's great experiment with the weird and wonderful alternative life-forms embedded in the late-Precambrian fossils of South Australia. What they saw clearly had much in common with life as they knew it, but at the same time a great deal also seemed very, very different and, above all, it was easy to misunderstand what specific bits of the creatures were for. A civil lawyer chancing for the first time upon, say, proprietary restitution and its manifestations in the form of equitable liens, constructive trusts, and tracing finds himself in a world which has no obvious counterpart in his own. The experience of Anglo-American lawyers with the civil law of unjustified enrichment is similar. Thus the mysteries of the German *Leistungskondiktion* seem, at first glance, to be unfathomable and the specificity with which so-called 'third-party

---

[1] 'The revival of unjust enrichment has been one of the most important developments of the twentieth century in Anglo-American private law': Stephen Waddams, *Dimensions of Private Law: Categories and Concepts in Anglo-American Legal Reasoning* (2003), 10.

enrichment' cases are dealt with seems, on the face of it, an unnecessarily complicated matter which the common law has managed to avoid completely. And the
mutual discovery of the distantly related, but very differently evolved, life-forms
led to more than mere observation. It spurred a debate in which common lawyers
took rather more notice than usual of the developments in Continental legal systems. Peter Birks's conversion (inspired by a number of German authors)[2] to the
'without legal ground' approach of the civil law in his book *Unjust Enrichment*[3] (in
which he abandons the traditional common-law approach of requiring a specific
reason or 'unjust factor' to brand the enrichment as unjustified), coupled with the
lively debate that both preceded and followed it,[4] is a dramatic illustration of this
fact. But, conversely, Continental European authors also took serious note of the
developments in common-law countries and a meaningful dialogue has developed
since 1990. The best examples of this conversation are the detailed comparative
analyses of specific aspects of enrichment law by a number of Dutch and German
scholars such as Scheltema,[5] Meier,[6] van Kooten,[7] Schäfer,[8] Rusch,[9] and Hellwege;[10]
the edited collections under the leadership of, respectively, Zimmermann[11] and
Schrage;[12] the general comparative studies such as the (shorter) works of Gallo[13]
and Verhagen[14] and the longer contributions of Schlechtriem[15] and Krebs.[16] And
the important role of Zweigert and Kötz's book in starting the conversation should
not be forgotten.[17]

---

[2] See eg Sonja Meier, *Irrtum und Zweckverfehlung* (1999) and Reinhard Zimmermann, 'Unjustified
Enrichment: The Modern Civilian Approach', (1995) 15 *Oxford Journal of Legal Studies* 404.

[3] (2nd edn, 2005).

[4] See Andrew Burrows, Kit Barker, Charles Mitchell, Sarah Worthington, Robert Stevens, Thomas
Krebs, Graham Virgo, William Swadling, Gerard McMeel, and Andrew Tettenborn, 'Review Article:
The New Birksian Approach to Unjust Enrichment', (2004) 12 *Restitution LR* 260.

[5] M. W. Scheltema, *Onverschuldigde Betaling* (1997).   [6] Meier (n 2).

[7] Hugo J. van Kooten, *Restitutierechtelijke Gevolgen van Ongeoorloofde Overeenkomsten* (2002).

[8] Frank L. Schäfer, *Das Bereicherungsrecht in Europa: Einheits- und Trennungslehren im gemeinen,
deutschen und englischen Recht* (2001).

[9] Konrad Rusch, *Gewinnhaftung bei der Verletzung von Treupflichten* (2003).

[10] Phillip Hellwege, *Die Rückabwicklung gegenseitiger Verträge als einheitliches Problem* (2004).

[11] David Johnston and Reinhard Zimmermann (eds), *Unjustified Enrichment: Key Issues in Comparative Perspective* (2002); Reinhard Zimmermann (ed), *Grundstrukturen eines Europäischen Bereicherungsrechts* (2005).

[12] Eltjo J. H. Schrage (ed), *Unjust Enrichment: The Comparative Legal History of the Law of Restitution* (1999); idem (ed), *Unjust Enrichment and the Law of Contract* (2001).

[13] Paolo Gallo, 'Unjust Enrichment: A Comparative Analysis', (1992) 40 *AJCL* 431–65.

[14] H. L. E. Verhagen, 'Ongerechtvaardigde Verrijking: Rechtsvergelijking en Internationaal
Privaatrecht', in *Op Recht: Bundel Opstellen, aangeboden aan Prof. Mr. A. V. M. Struycken* (1996),
367–401.

[15] Peter Schlechtriem, *Restitution und Bereicherungsausgleich in Europa: Eine rechtsvergleichende
Darstellung* (2 vols, 2000 and 2001).

[16] Thomas Krebs, *Restitution at the Crossroads* (2001).

[17] Konrad Zweigert and Hein Kötz, *An Introduction to Comparative Law* (trans Tony Weir, 3rd edn,
1998,), 537–94. Also important here are those contributions which seek to make the law of enrichment

For those who want merely to understand the differences, unjustified enrichment displays all the levels of difference that occur between common-law and civil-law systems; for those who are interested in the harmonization of the law of Europe, it stands as a true test case for the ability of the common law and the civil law to find common ground.

II. THE ANATOMY OF DIFFERENCE

When comparatists consider the differences and similarities in the various manifestations of the law of enrichment, it happens in a charged atmosphere. First, it happens against the background of dispute about what comparative research should do. The 'difference theorists'[18] pour scorn on those who seek to find common ground between the two legal families[19] (and indeed they even reject the very notion of there being enough commonality between legal systems to divide them into families). They, for their part, seek to place difference at the centre of comparative work in law.[20] They argue, to borrow Hyland's description, that attempts at the harmonization of the law in Europe could be likened to 'the extinction of animal and plant species that results from the destruction of natural habitat'.[21] This is a powerful analogy, but we should not forget that legal systems are not species of animals: because they are part of the culture of the community that they serve, and because culture can be unlearnt just as well and as quickly as it is learnt, new and healthy diversities can (and inevitably will) be created after the learning involved in growing together has been exhausted. On the other hand, those who seek to harmonize European law often do minimize the influence

of one particular country accessible to lawyers in other countries: Reinhard Zimmermann and Jacques du Plessis, 'Basic Features of the German Law of Unjustified Enrichment', (1994) 2 *Restitution LR* 14; Zimmermann (n 2); and Basil S. Markesinis, Werner Lorenz, and Gerhard Dannemann, *The German Law of Obligations*: vol I: *The Law of Contracts and Restitution: A Comparative Introduction* (1997).

[18] See generally the references in nn 19 and 20 below.

[19] See eg Pierre Legrand's ('The Same and the Different', in Pierre Legrand and Roderick Munday (eds), *Comparative Legal Studies: Traditions and Transitions* (2003), 240, 249 *in fine*, 250) reference to 'the control desks in Hamburg, Trento, Osnabrück, Maastricht, Rome, Utrecht and Copenhagen [whence] . . . the self-appointed spokesmen of reason . . . wage an unceasing campaign to smother difference . . .'.

[20] See Richard Hyland, 'Comparative Law', in Dennis Patterson (ed), *Blackwell's Companion to Law and Legal Theory* (1997), 193.

[21] The quote is from Hyland (n 20), 195.

of the 'unarticulated, taken-for-granted assumptions [that] underlie the law'[22] in different systems.[23]

In this contribution my approach is that it is important to take difference seriously—even if one is ultimately interested (as I am) in finding common ground. Even though case law plays an increasing—and an increasingly acknowledged—role in civilian systems; and even though we know that judges in, say, England and France do not work quite as differently as the stereotypes would have us believe;[24] and even though there has recently been more overt interest in the structure of enrichment law than in any other part of the common law (largely as a result of the influence of academic authors), much of the thinking which underlies the common law remains far removed from that in codified systems. Furthermore, much effort has been invested in the doctrinal structures relating to enrichment in various jurisdictions and they are often defended with a piety not seen since the demise of Marxism.

When thinking about the differences between unjustified enrichment in the common law and the civil law, it is useful to keep in mind the lesson that the experience in private international law has taught us about various levels of difference. Thus Kurt Lipstein[25] distinguishes between instances where legal institutions or rules in different systems are (i) identical in form, but different in substance, (ii) identical in substance, but different in form, (iii) partly identical in form and substance, and (iv) existent in both form and substance in one system, but completely absent in another. And to this one might add that institutions are sometimes identical or similar in form and/or substance, but are simply differently conceived at a conceptual level and thus explained in different doctrinal terms. We encounter all of these in the law of enrichment. Thus, as an example of (i), we see that the basic elements of unjustified enrichment are often stated in a similar way in the two families (enrichment of the defendant, which is unjustified, at the expense of the claimant), but that is only so on the surface: the substance of these requirements are not at all alike in common-law and civil-law systems (and are often not even alike within each of these families). Subrogation (of the non-contractual variety) and its functional equivalent in German law, *Legalzession*, again, provide an example of (ii): both allow a person who has conferred a benefit on another to rely, in appropriate circumstances, on a right which that other person originally had against a third party, but in English law it is held to be an

---

[22] James Q. Whitman, 'The Neo-Romantic Turn', in Legrand and Munday (n 19), 312, 336; and see also 315 and 327.

[23] It should also be noted, however, that the reductionist assumption that all those that work in, broadly speaking, the functionalist tradition are obsessed with similarity is misplaced. See generally Michele Graziadei, 'The Functionalist Heritage', in Legrand and Munday (n 19), 101 and 108 ff.

[24] See Mitchel de S.-O.-l'E. Lasser, 'Judicial (Self-)Portraits: Judicial Discourse in the French Legal System', (1995) 104 *Yale LJ* 1325.

[25] Chapter 5, 'Characterization', in the *International Encyclopedia of Comparative Law* (vol III, 1999), 9–21 (5–24 to 5–49).

instance of unjustified enrichment, and in German law not. An instance that could be said to fall under (iii) is the disgorgement of gain resulting from the act of the defendant: both German and English law allow such a claim, but not in the same circumstances. (German law works with a wide concept of an invasion of rights in this situation and does not insist, as does English law, that a tort must have been committed before such a claim is competent; and although the remedy in certain situations amounts to a personal claim in both systems, the fact that this area straddles law and equity in English law means that there are remedies in the latter—I have in mind constructive trusts, resulting trusts, and equitable liens— which simply have no equivalent in German law and indeed go against some of the most basic suppositions of civilian systems of law.) The rules governing the winding up of failed contracts also fall into this category. The question whether someone who benefits another without having been requested to do so deserves to be compensated is an example of (iv): while the civil law is traditionally sympathetic to such a remedy, the common law (or at least a part of it) is hostile.

The questions that form the background to this contribution are: 'what constitute the main differences between the common-law and civilian families of legal systems in this area?'; 'what are the factors that influence—and flow from—these differences?'; and 'what do we do with these differences: can we bridge them; and if we can, is it meaningful to do so?' For simplicity, I will not articulate them in each section, but I would like them to be kept in mind as we make our way through the various classes, orders, families, genera, and species that make up the law of unjustified enrichment in the two families of legal systems. The purpose of concentrating on these differences is to make a contribution to the dominant themes of current research in the area, namely: a better understanding of the investigator's own system; identifying foreign approaches that are usable where the home system is seen to offer less than optimal solutions; and investigating the possibility of the harmonization of the laws that form the object of the research.

To confine the discussion to the interface between common law and civil law might seem to some to be too narrow a focus. There are, after all, a host of other issues that legitimately demand attention if one is pursuing the goals just mentioned. As examples one might mention, first, the scepticism in regard to the very notion of enrichment liability, both within the common law (as epitomized by the Australian jurisprudence and writing)[26] and in the Nordic systems (as evidenced in the approach of Swedish law);[27] second, the enormous potential to influence

---

[26] See eg Paul Finn, 'Equitable Doctrine and Discretion in Remedies', in W. R. Cornish, Richard Nolan, J. O'Sullivan, and G. Virgo (eds), *Restitution: Past, Present and Future: Essays in Honour of Gareth Jones* (1998), 252.

[27] See eg the foundational work of Jan Hellner, *Om obehörig vinst* (1950) and the discussion thereof—and of the approach in Swedish law in general—by Mårtin Schultz, 'Unjust Enrichment— Sweden', available at <http://www.juridicum.su.se/user/masc/UNJUSTENRICHMENT.htm> (last

the future direction of unjustified enrichment inherent in the *Restatement of the Law of Restitution and Unjust Enrichment* (*Third*) currently being undertaken by the American Law Institute; and, third, the importance of exploring fully the differences between the different civilian systems. However, the sheer vigour of the current debate between the common law and the civil law has convinced me to choose it, rather than one of the many other legitimate focuses of attention. To find ways of crossing the divide between these two legal families—either to gain greater understanding of the other or to produce systems-spanning solutions— constitutes the great contemporary challenge for comparative work in the field of enrichment law. The main purpose of this contribution is to explore the contours along which such research might proceed.

III. FINDING THE CORE: WHAT IS ENRICHMENT LIABILITY ABOUT?

In all legal systems the law of enrichment is about removing gains which the legal order decrees that the defendant should not keep. There is even enough similarity between most common-law and civil-law systems that it is possible to identify a set of core elements of enrichment liability which are—at least at the level of semantics—common to most legal systems. But, as has been mentioned, below the surface, it is a different story and in this section I would like to highlight the extent of the differences (and similarities) under the headings of (a) the work that enrichment liability does in a legal system and (b) how it goes about doing that work.

1. What Work Does Enrichment Liability Do?

(a) Is the Reversal of an Unowed Payment about Unjustified Enrichment?

The first point that I should like to illustrate about enrichment liability in the common law and the civil law is that the specific differences with which scholars are preoccupied often obscure similarities, or push differences within the legal families into the background. Let us consider the paradigmatic example of enrichment liability as a manifestation of corrective justice: the principle that an

accessed on 16 June 2005). See also generally Schlechtriem (n 15), 49 ff in regard to the Nordic systems (Sweden, Denmark, Norway, and Finland).

unowed payment must be returned. The debate in this context is usually about whether the basis of the claim can be said to lie in 'mistake' as an unjust factor, or should rather be found in the fact that there is no legal basis for the transfer. However, if one scratches below the surface of what is widely considered to be the traditional enrichment claim, that is, the *condictio*, one finds certain unexpected similarities between the civil law and the common law, and equally unexpected differences between certain civilian systems.

Dutch law, reflecting an important strand in the family of European codifications, draws a sharp distinction between unjustified enrichment (embodied in the general action in Art 6:212 BW) and 'undue payment' (*onverschuldigde betaling*), which is interpreted widely to mean 'undue performance' (including not only the payment of money, but also the transfer of property and the rendering of services), as set out in Art 6:203 BW.[28] The reclaiming of undue performances (ie in traditional civilian parlance, the *condictio indebiti*) is *not* regarded as the restoration of an enrichment.[29] Although this dichotomy goes back to the influence of French law in the Netherlands, the line drawn between the two institutions is clearer than the French distinction between *paiement de l'indu* and *enrichissement sans cause* because there the former is, following Pothier, sometimes also explained in terms of the principle of unjustified enrichment, although there is no doubt that in French law the claimant is not restricted to the enrichment of the recipient.[30]

The notion that the *condictio indebiti* is not an enrichment action has very old roots.[31] Roman law decreed that the defendant's obligation in terms of a *condictio* was, in the first place, to return that which he had actually received. The *condictio* was an *actio stricti iuris* aimed at a specific object (*certa res*) and the obligation in the case of such a *condictio* was to return the object itself, irrespective of whether the recipient's estate as a whole had been increased by the transfer. In other words, the Roman law relating to the *condictiones* did not concern itself with the enrichment of the defendant.

In German law, on the other hand, the *Leistungskondiktion* embodied in § 812 BGB, into which the *condictio indebiti* has been absorbed, is considered to be part

---

[28] J. H. Nieuwenhuis, C. J. J. M. Stolker, and J. Valk (eds), *Nieuw Burgerlijk Wetboek: Tekst & Commentaar* (1990), 636; J. Spier, T. Hartlief, G. E. van Maanen, and R. D. Vriesendorp, *Verbintenissen uit de Wet* (1997), 254 ff.

[29] Scheltema (n 5), 138 ff, although some argue that Art 6:203 is also, in the final analysis, founded on the principle of unjustified enrichment.

[30] See John Bell, Sophie Byron, and Simon Whittaker, *Principles of French Law* (1998), 406. The same ambivalence is noticeable in Swedish law: the traditional view is that the *condictio indebiti* stands apart from the notion of unjustified enrichment. In a recent case (1999 *Nytt Juridiskt Arkiv* 575) the *condictio* was explained in terms of unjustified enrichment, which drew sharp criticism from Sweden's leading commentator on unjustified enrichment. See Jan Hellner, 'Betalning av mistag', (1999–2000) 11 *Juridisk Tidskrift* 409–15 and the discussion of the case as well as Hellner's criticism by Schultz (n 27), 5.1 and 5.2.

[31] Werner Flume, 'Wegfall der Bereicherung in der Entwicklung vom römischen zum geltenden Recht', in *Festschrift für Hans Niedermeyer* (1953), 103.

of the law of enrichment, but nevertheless the roots of the Roman system still survive in that, if the enrichment is concerned with the transfer of physical property, it obliges the enrichment debtor to restore that which he received and only if restoration proves to be impossible, its value.[32]

Interestingly, the English law is similar to Dutch and German law in respect of what may be claimed. Where property has been (mistakenly) transferred to the defendant, the claim is an enrichment claim and '[t]he benefit is established simply by showing the defendant has the particular property claimed: the defendant cannot validly refuse to give up the property on the ground that it is of no value to him'[33] or, one should add, because he prefers to keep the specific thing and would rather return the value. If the object of the claim is, for instance, an object which the claimant personally values very highly, it is not difficult to see why the distinction between a focus on *the return of that which was given* as opposed to a focus on *the amount with which the defendant's estate has been enriched* is of crucial importance.

Thus, although the claim is an enrichment claim in one of the systems, but not in the others and although one system requires mistake for a successful claim and not the others, all three systems substantively do the same thing where property is the object of the claim: it must be returned, leaving us with an unexpected commonality that cuts across the common-law/civil-law divide.

(b) Is the Disgorgement of Benefits Obtained by the Act of the Defendant about Unjustified Enrichment?

The next issue that I want to highlight is that of the situation in which both the common law and the civil law partly do the same thing from a substantive point of view (mainly, but not exclusively, because the work is allocated to different systematic niches), but share similar challenges to articulate a fully coherent basis of liability. I will do this by highlighting the notion of restitution following on the doing of a wrong (used in a very general sense), which has found a foothold in several legal systems. In some systems it is seen as being based on unjustified enrichment, in others on tort.

The obligation to return a benefit which the defendant obtained, not as a result of an act of the claimant (as in the case of the enrichment considered under the previous rubric) but as a result of his own act, is unambiguously labelled as being based on unjustified enrichment in German law. For instance, the defendant makes a profit-making unauthorized use of, say, the claimant's image or his patented invention, and by thus invading one of his rights. Such an act may amount to a tort, but it need not: relief is given whenever someone infringes the right of another and, in addition, the gains that emanate from that right are exclusively attributable to the claimant (*die Lehre vom Zuweisungsgehalt*, or the theory of

---

[32] Reiner Schulze *et al* (eds), *BGB Handkommentar* (3rd edn, 2003), § 818, nn 2 and 6.
[33] Andrew Burrows, *The Law of Restitution* (2nd edn, 2002), 16.

attribution of gain). This theory is a convenient umbrella principle for the policy considerations that are taken into account in the decision whether a specific benefit should be disgorged. Even though it is opaque on the face of it, as so often happens with general standards, the German courts have considerably specified it through their decisions.[34]

In England, on the other hand, the relationship between restoration of benefits obtained as a result of the invasion of someone else's rights and unjustified enrichment is controversial. The older consensus—in which Peter Birks played a substantial role[35]—has collapsed. This consensus was based on the assumption that the overarching notion of restitution can be divided into 'subtractive' or 'autonomous' enrichment (where enrichment provided both the cause of action *and* described the nature of the available remedies) and 'profit from wrongdoing' (where the wrong— a tort, equitable wrong, or breach of contract—provided the cause of action and enrichment described the available remedies: hence the alternative title of 'remedial unjust enrichment'). Birks retreated from this view in a famous article[36] and argued that restitution of profit from wrongdoing had nothing to do with unjustified enrichment, and that the cause of action is to be found in the law of wrongs.[37] Graham Virgo, though differing from Birks in many respects, agrees that restitution for wrongs is not concerned with unjustified enrichment, except in an inexact 'descriptive sense' (ie 'to describe a state of affairs where the defendant can be said to have obtained a benefit in circumstances of injustice').[38] I confess, however, to finding Andrew Tettenborn's response to Birks convincing: 'Proof of a wrong cannot indeed be a necessary condition to show unjust enrichment, but there is nothing to stop it being, on occasion, a *sufficient* one', he says, and continues to observe that:[39]

the fact that the defendant has committed a tort or other wrongful act, may be one way (though not, of course, the only one) of showing that his enrichment is unjust and ought to be reversed. And in cases where this is so, there is (it is submitted) no reason not to say that the analytical basis of the plaintiff's recovery is unjust enrichment.

Andrew Burrows[40] makes a similar point when he comments that Birks's argument,

[34] Ernst von Caemmerer, 'Bereicherung und unerlaubte Handlung', in *Festschrift für Ernst Rabel* (1954), 333, 352; Markesinis *et al* (n 17), 741 ff.

[35] Peter Birks, *An Introduction to Restitution* (1985), 39–44. See further Andrew Burrows, *Understanding the Law of Obligations: Essays on Contract, Tort and Restitution* (1998), 7; *Halifax Building Society v. Thomas* [1996] Ch 217. But see Jack Beatson, 'The Nature of Waiver of Tort', in Jack Beatson, *The Use and Abuse of Unjust Enrichment* (1991), 206 ff and Peter Cane, 'Exceptional Measures of Damages: A Search for Principles', in Peter Birks (ed), *Wrongs and Remedies in the Twenty-First Century* (1996), 312

[36] Peter Birks, 'Misnomer', in Cornish *et al.* (n 26), 1–29.

[37] But see now Birks (n 3), 83 ff, taking a somewhat more lenient view. This view had already been discernible in his *Introduction to the Law of Restitution* (1989 rev edn), 314–15.

[38] Graham Virgo, *The Principles of the Law of Restitution* (1999), 310.

[39] Andrew Tettenborn, 'Misnomer: A Response', in Cornish *et al* (n 26), 34.

[40] Burrows (n 35), 8.

'would be greatly enhanced by practical proof that, in a series—contract, wrongs and unjust enrichment—the *only possible* analysis of restitution for wrongs is that the wrong (and not the wrong plus the enrichment) is the cause of action'.[41]

In my view, part of the answer lies in analysing the situation not only in terms of event (the wrong) and response (restitution) as Birks does,[42] but in a way that takes account of *three* aspects of the typical enrichment situation: (i) the causative event, (ii) *the effect of that event*, and (iii) the law's response to the combination of (i) and (ii). Thus, if I use the image of a famous person in my advertising campaign without his knowledge, that act (causative event) may result in that person suffering loss (effect 1), which the law redresses with an award of damages (response 1) and/or it may result in my making a large profit (effect 2), which the law will take from me and give to the victim (response 2). It is imperative that the taxonomic map should include not only causes and responses but also the middle category of 'effect'. Without this category we are left with one causative event and two responses, and the conundrum—if we insist on classifying exclusively according to causative event—that there is no way to decide whether the causative event should be a wrong or unjustified enrichment. On the other hand, if we include the middle category, it is possible to construct a taxonomy which takes account of the complexities of the situation. By combining the cause, the effect, and the object that the law wishes to pursue,[43] we are able to reason thus: if a wrongful and culpable act causes harm to the claimant, the law would seek to compensate the harm and this particular concatenation of cause, effect, and response is said to be the province of the law of tort. If the same wrongful and culpable act happened to be a breach of contract, the aim of the law will be to do more than merely compensate the harm already suffered. That is to say, it would also seek to fulfil the objectives created by the parties' consensus: this juxtaposition of cause, effect, and legal response is said to be the province of the law of contract. Should the same breach of contract cause the breaching party to make a profit as well, the law might consider an ancillary response, namely to cause the breaching party to transfer the loss to the innocent party ('restitutionary' damages), which may be said to be part of the law of enrichment. If a wrong, other than a breach of contract, has the effect that the wrongdoer makes a profit, the response of the law could also be to require the wrongdoer to surrender (all or part of) the profit, which once again falls under the law of enrichment. If we accept this approach, we are able, I believe, also to

---

[41] It is interesting to note that the Study Group on a European Civil Code has included in its present draft the situation of 'enrichment by making use of another's assets'—with 'assets' broadly defined as including property rights and other rights such as the right to one's image. See Eric Clive, 'Unjustified Enrichment', in Arthur S. Hartkamp, Martijn W. Hesselink, Ewoud H. Hondius, Carla Joustra, and Edgar du Perron, *Towards a European Civil Code* (3rd edn, 2004), 585, 591; Stephen Swann, 'The Structure of Liability for Unjustified Enrichment: First Proposals of the Study Group on a European Civil Code', in Zimmermann, *Grundstrukturen* (n 11), 265, 271.

[42] Peter Birks (ed), *The Classification of Obligations* (1997), 20.

[43] The 'remedial interest', as it is termed by Burrows (n 33), 9.

see the disgorgement of profit from wrongdoing as part of the law of unjustified enrichment in England and so to leave the division of enrichment into autonomous (subtractive) enrichment and profit from wrongdoing intact.[44]

Thomas Krebs has expressed the view that the inability of English law fully to recognize a separate category of enrichment arising from wrongdoing is attributable to its insistence that enrichment liability can exist only where the defendant's enrichment is mirrored by the claimant's loss.[45] The approach in Canada (where this requirement is put in even stronger terms than in England) is captured in La Forest J's statement in *Air Canada v British Columbia*[46] that unjustified enrichment 'is not intended to provide windfalls to plaintiffs who have suffered no loss'. It is easy to see that, if there is a perception that loss is a requirement for enrichment liability, many of the instances of restitution for wrongs (eg where a director makes a secret profit, but the company is also better off because of it) would not seem to amount to enrichment liability. However, there is no reason why mirror loss should be insisted upon as an element of an enrichment action. It is certainly not dictated by the fact that enrichment liability is largely about corrective justice: it is important to remember that corrective or commutative justice presumes a correlative relationship between gain and some form of an injustice, which need not be economic loss. Thus Weinrib explains that 'restitutionary damages should be available when the defendant's gain is the materialization of a favorable possibility—the opportunity to gain—that rightfully belonged to the plaintiff'.[47] The injustice which correlates to the defendant's gain in these circumstances might be either that the defendant's gain *actually deprived* the claimant of an opportunity to gain (eg where I move into another person's property and prevent him from renting it out, which can be described as a loss in the ordinary sense) or that the defendant's gain involved merely *usurping the defendant's entitlement to gain*, which is part of his proprietary right (eg where I use someone's equipment that was in storage, which cannot be described as a loss in the ordinary sense). If English law were to adopt this approach to corrective justice it would be very close to the German notion of attribution of gain.[48] In the end the real challenge in this situation is to work out

---

[44] See also Robert Goff (Lord Goff of Chieveley) and Gareth Jones, *The Law of Restitution* (6th edn, 2002), para 1–050.

[45] Thomas Krebs, 'Eingriffskondiktion und Restitution for Wrongs im Englischen Recht', in Zimmermann, *Grundstrukturen* (n 11), 145, 163 ff. Other systems that insist on mirror loss and consequently do not have a category of enrichment based on encroachment—or only a very underdeveloped sense of it—include the Netherlands, France, Scotland, and South Africa.

[46] (1989) 59 DLR (4th) 161, 194.   [47] Ernest J. Weinrib, *The Idea of Private Law* (1995), 12.

[48] Indeed, as Krebs (n 45), 164, points out, there is nothing in English law which makes it inevitable that a claim for the surrender of profits should be limited to a corresponding impoverishment on the part of the claimant: although cases such as *Banque Financière de la Cité v Parc (Battersea) Ltd* [1999] 1 AC 221, 237 clearly state loss as an element of enrichment claims in the subtractive sense, several other cases, such as *Penarth Dock Engineering Co Ltd v Pounds* [1963] 1 Lloyd's Rep 359, show that it is not necessarily a requirement in the case of restitution for wrongs. (It is important also to keep in mind that English tort law, as a result of torts such as conversion and trespass to chattels—which require

which gains should be surrendered. Much work has been done on both sides: the German courts have identified policy factors that might have validity across systems[49] and theorists such as Weinrib,[50] Gordley,[51] and Dagan[52] have laid important parts of the foundation in the common-law world.

(c) Is the Winding Up of Failed Contracts about Unjustified Enrichment?

The winding up of failed contracts provides a further instance of common and civil law being (in a complex way) partly similar on a substantive level, but different on a formal level; and here systems within each family do not share the same approach either. Both common-law and civilian legal systems—and also the various international instruments aimed at the harmonization of contract law—tend to offer different solutions for the different situations in which contracts fail (that is to say where they are (i) void *ab initio*, (ii) voidable, (iii) frustrated by supervening impossibility, or have been (iv) terminated as a result of breach of contract).[53] The principles and policies behind the various approaches are difficult to identify; and inevitably one has to ask whether there is any justification for treating them differently and assigning to them different niches in the law of obligations. It has been argued elsewhere, in regard to the law of Scotland and South Africa respectively, that the winding up of such failed contracts should indeed be given the same treatment and in each case be seen as a remedy based on unjustified enrichment.[54] In an important study containing an exhaustive treatment of the problem in Germany, England, and Scotland, Phillip Hellwege, reaching back to the historical basis of *restitutio in integrum*, has recently made a convincing case that they should all be treated in the same way, but that it does not matter whether one places the remedy under the law of contract or under the law of enrichment.[55] Hellwege shows that the arguments in favour of maintaining different regimes in regard to

neither proof of damage nor fault—has a wider reach than the law of delict in German law. This means that in England 'enrichment by committing a tort' covers an area which is wider than that which would have been covered if German law had restricted the *Eingriffskondiktion* to gains resulting from delict. But German law does not restrict it in this way and achieves a similarly wide reach through its theory of the attribution of gain. See the text to n 34 above.)

[49] See the sources quoted in n 34 above.

[50] Ernest J. Weinrib, 'Restitutionary Damages as Corrective Justice', (2000) 1 *Theoretical Inquiries in Law* 1.

[51] James Gordley, 'The Purpose of Awarding Restitutionary Damages: A Reply to Professor Weinrib', (2000) 1 *Theoretical Inquiries in Law* 39.

[52] Hanoch Dagan *The Law and Ethics of Restitution* (2004), 210 ff.

[53] See Reinhard Zimmermann, 'Restitutio in integrum: Die Rückabwicklung fehlgeschlagener Verträge nach den Principles of European Contract Law, den UNIDROIT und dem Avant-projet eines Code Européen des Contrats', in *Privatrecht und Methode: Festschrift für Ernst A. Kramer* (2004), 735.

[54] Daniel Visser, 'Rethinking Unjustified Enrichment: A Perspective of the Competition between Contractual and Enrichment Remedies', [1992] *Acta Juridica* 203 and Hector MacQueen, 'Unjustified Enrichment and Breach of Contract', [1994] *Juridical Review* 137.

[55] Hellwege (n 10).

the various winding-up situations usually have nothing to do with the winding up itself, but rather pertain to other objectives, such as providing a doctrinal justification for damages claims after breach (through the device of 'keeping the contract alive' and transforming the primary obligations of performance into secondary obligations of paying damages) and to the need to allow provisions restricting a party's liability to continue to be relevant when such damages are determined.[56] Of course any legal system must provide a rational system in regard to damages claims in the wake of breach of contract, but that does not affect the winding up, which must happen in every case, whether or not damages are also payable. And the purpose of winding up always remains the same (accepting that damages might, in addition, be payable in appropriate circumstances): both parties are as much as possible to be placed in the position that they were in before the contract was entered into. And since the purpose is the same, one should not have different models for instances where a contract comes to an end as a result of frustration, or is avoided due to a defect of consent, or is cancelled for breach. As Hellwege demonstrates, having different models causes no difficulties where both parties are able to return what they had received: the problem arises when they cannot—and here the different regimes are based on different evaluations, which cannot rationally be defended.[57] Hellwege proposes a uniform model which essentially places the risk on the receiving party on the basis that risk should be coupled with control and insurability. Although he regards it as an open question whether this model should be classified as contractual or enrichment-based,[58] I think it is best classified as part of enrichment because the purpose of winding up so clearly tries to do the same thing as enrichment remedies (namely to put the parties in the position that they were in before), whereas contractual remedies (in so far as they do not deal with winding up) try to bring about the original or the economic equivalent of what the parties had bargained for.

Seen in this way, this is an area where, for all the seemingly impenetrable differences, a simple and elegant structure could take the place of the current jumble; and then we would have a clear answer to the question posed in the heading: yes, it is about unjustified enrichment. However, it must not be forgotten that many countries (on both sides of the common-law/civil-law divide, such as South Africa[59] and Australia)[60] have not conceded that this is indeed part of the province

[56] See eg Phillip Hellwege, 'Ein einheitliches Regelungsmodell für die Rückabwicklung gegenseitiger Verträge', [2005] *Juristenzeitung* 337, 340.

[57] Ibid.   [58] Hellwege (n 56), 344.

[59] See, generally, the description in Visser (n 54) and Saul Miller's recent plea for maintaining a differentiated approach: Saul Miller, 'Unjustified Enrichment and Failed Contracts', in Reinhard Zimmermann, Daniel Visser, and Kenneth Reid (eds), *Mixed Legal Systems in Comparative Perspective: Obligations and Property in Scotland and South Africa* (2004), 437.

[60] See generally the discussion by Michael Bryan, 'Unjust Enrichment and Unconscionability in Australia: A False Dichotomy?', in Jason W. Nyers, Mitchell McInnes, and Stephen G. A. Pitel (eds), *Understanding Unjust Enrichment* (2004), 47, 78.

of unjustified enrichment. The debate to determine the proper border between enrichment and contract has only just begun and constitutes one of the great tasks of comparative law for the immediate future.

(d) Is Obtruding a Benefit on Another about Unjustified Enrichment?

The next instance is one where an institution exists in the civil law, but is non-existent (or virtually non-existent) in the common law: making good the expenses of the good Samaritan. On the face of it, it would seem that, unlike in the previous category, the difference in approach here reflects different cultural approaches: the former recognizes a claim by a good Samaritan for his expenses, while the latter is hostile and brands him as an 'officious intermeddler' who cannot sue for his expenses except in certain specified exceptions. The sentiments in the two families are undeniably different,[61] but Niall Whitty and Deon van Zyl point out that the modern civilian approach does not mean that the values of the Roman patriciate[62] survived into modern law—only that the rules which these values inspired did.[63] But is this problem about unjustified enrichment? In civilian systems it is fairly generally accepted is that it is closely related to unjustified enrichment, but that it is not unjustified enrichment in the ordinary sense: the cause of action is to be found in the institution of *negotiorum gestio* and, in any event, the recovery of the expenses of the claimant is not limited to the amount of the defendant's enrichment. In some systems (such as that of South Africa), however, the claim of the *negotiorum gestor* is sometimes an enrichment action, for example, when it involves administering the affairs of a minor or the affairs of someone who has expressly forbidden interference in his affairs. Furthermore, if common-law systems were to overcome their antipathy towards claims by unauthorized administrators, they would need to categorize such claims—and in the absence of the institution of *negotiorum gestio*, would the most obvious niche not be unjustified enrichment? After all, if the law in certain countries can regard the claim under the *condictio indebiti* as an enrichment claim, even though it does not work with the measure of enrichment of the defendant, why can this instance not be dealt with in the same way? Hanoch Dagan has, however, argued that it is not particularly helpful to categorize the good Samaritan's entitlement against the beneficiary as unjustified enrichment. This is not because the *negotiorum gestor* is normally entitled to all his expenses even if he is unsuccessful (because one may postulate, as Dagan does, that the defendant would have paid for an *attempt* rather than a result, so that the attempt saves the beneficiary that hypothetical expense). Rather, it is because it is

---

[61] See J. P. Dawson, '*Negotiorum gestio*: The Altruistic Intermeddler', (1961) 74 *Harvard LR* 817, 1073.

[62] About which see Reinhard Zimmermann, *The Law of Obligations: Roman Foundations of the Civilian Tradition* (paperback edn 1996), 435.

[63] Niall R. Whitty and Deon Van Zyl, 'Unauthorized Management of Affairs (*Negotiorum* Gestio)', in Zimmermann *et al* (n 59), 366, 369.

not enough to categorize it in this way. The real challenge, he points out, is to find the appropriate balance between encouraging altruism and protecting personal liability.[64] (The position is similar, but not identical, in regard to mistaken improvements of the property of another: civilian system treat this as a separate category of enrichment liability, but English law normally does not give improvers an enrichment action—though here it is not a uniform common-law position, for claims of mistaken improvers are well-developed in the United States.[65])

(e) Is Subrogation about Unjustified Enrichment?

How does the institution of subrogation relate to unjustified enrichment? Subrogation might be available as a result of a contract, or by operation of law. The first category obviously falls four-square within the province of contract, and that kind of subrogation is not the concern of the present enquiry.[66] In the second category each legal system identifies—through either legislation or court decisions—which situations merit subrogation. English law has recognized subrogation in a variety of instances, the most important of which occur in relation to suretyship, bills of exchange, insurance, and trust law.[67] In English law the basis of this second category has been very firmly identified as being unjustified enrichment,[68] as it is said to 'nip in the bud any ambition to secure a double enrichment' by the insured who, but for the subrogation, would otherwise be able to sue the wrongdoer in spite of having been paid by the insurer.[69]

The concept of *Legalzession* is the functional equivalent in German law of the English doctrine of subrogation.[70] Whenever a law decrees that a claim will pass directly and automatically to another (as opposed to instances where a creditor is merely obliged by law to cede his claim) one has an instance of true *cessio legis*.[71] The question that arises is whether the subrogated claim can be characterized as an

---

[64] Hanoch Dagan, 'In Defense of the Good Samaritan', (1999) 97 *Michigan LR* 1152, 1183.

[65] Andrew Kull, 'Mistaken Improvements and the Restitution Calculus', in Johnston and Zimmermann (n 11), 369. See also generally, Dirk A. Verse, 'Improvements and Enrichment: A Comparative Analysis', (1998) 6 *Restitution LR* 85. One should also keep in mind that equitable liens, for instance, are really improvement claims that should be recognized as such in English law. (See generally the judgment of Lord Denning in *Greenwood v Bennett* [1973] 1 QB 195.)

[66] cf Virgo (n 38), 661 and Goff and Jones (n 44), para 3–002.

[67] Goff and Jones (n 44), para 3–002.

[68] See *Banque Financiére de la Cité v Parc (Battersea)* [1999] 1 AC 221 and Goff and Jones (n 44), para 3–005.

[69] Ibid; *Banque Financiére de la Cité v Parc (Battersea)* [1999] 1 AC 221; *Boscawen v Bajwa* [1996] 1 WLR 328.

[70] See *J. von Staudingers Kommentar zum Bürgerlichen Gesetzbuch* (13th edn, 1997), § 774, nn 2 and 42 ff. See also now the exhaustive treatment by Johann A. Dieckmann, *Der Derivativregreß des Bürgen gegen den Hauptschuldner im englischen und deutschen Recht: Eine rechtsvergleichend-historische Untersuchung* (2003).

[71] See Gunter H. Roth, in *Münchener Kommentar zum Bürgerlichen Gesetzbuch* (vol 2, 4th edn, 2003), § 412 n 2. See generally, too, Knut Wolfgang Nörr, Robert Scheying, and Wolfgang Pöggeler, *Sukzessionen: Forsteningszession, Vertragsübernahme, Schuldübernahme* (2nd edn, 1999), § 14.

enrichment claim in German law. In both the older and more recent literature, one finds statements which suggest that it may be. Thus Savigny, in the nineteenth century, described the purpose of the surety's right of recourse as being the prevention of the enrichment of the principal debtor at the expense of the surety,[72] while a recent work on German law also uses language which creates the impression that this falls within the area of unjustified enrichment (in the broad sense of the word, of course, since only claims in terms of §§ 812 ff BGB are strictly speaking enrichment claims in German law): Nörr *et al.*[73] state that the justification for most instances of *cessio legis* is that 'the creditor is given more than would in itself be justified in terms of the relationship between the debtor and the person entitled to recourse'.[74] The right of recourse in indemnity insurance is often explained in the light of a so-called *Bereicherungsverbot* ('rule against enrichment') in the law of insurance.[75] A careful analysis of the law in this regard reveals, however, that statements such as those just quoted do not reflect the reality of German law. This may be explained with the following example from insurance law:

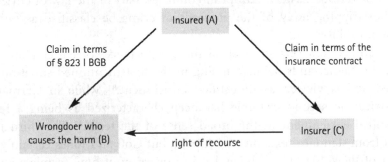

B wrongfully and negligently damages A's car, which costs R10,000 to repair. A now has a claim in delict. A claims this amount from C and C pays. The moment that C pays, A's claim in delict is transferred to C.[76]

A German lawyer would then argue that there is no period during which the two potential claims of A (in delict against B and in contract against C) overlap. There is, in other words, no period in which A has both claims and can thus be said to be enriched.[77] At most, then, the institution of *cessio legis* can be said to prevent what would otherwise have amounted to unjustified enrichment. Indeed, Gärtner goes further to state explicitly[78] that there is no necessary connection between the right of recourse in the law of insurance and a general rule against

[72] F. C. von Savigny, *Das Obligationenrecht* (1851), 226 ff, 229, and 243.

[73] Nörr *et al.* (n 71), § 14.   [74] Nörr *et al.* (n 71), § 14, 165, and 168.

[75] See, in this regard, the (critical) discussion of that view by Rudolph Gärtner, *Das Bereicherungsverbot; Eine Grundfrage des Versicherungsrechts* (1970), 1–19 (ch 1) and 141 ff (ch 6).

[76] See the decision in BGHZ 33, 97 and the *Münchener Kommentar/G. Roth* § 412 n 6.

[77] See Markesinis *et al* (n 17), 717.   [78] Gärtner (n 75), 160.

enrichment and the most authoritative sources[79] do not use the term 'unjustified enrichment'.[80]

Here we have an instance of a phenomenon that is for all intents and purposes the same thing in the two families, but which has been accorded a different formal place in the respective legal systems as a result of different formal reasoning.

(f) Is the Conferral of a Benefit in a Public-Law Context about Unjustified Enrichment?

The idea that economic benefits retained by someone without legal ground may be stripped away can, in addition to its traditional private-law application, also have a public-law dimension. For example, if legislation permits the government to de-contaminate, without permission, privately owned land, and the government does so—causing the value of the property to rise—should the government have an enrichment action against the owner? Is the restitution of property expropriated by inequitable past regimes in countries such as Germany and South Africa, as well as in various Eastern European countries, part of the law of enrichment? Might the stripping away of the proceeds of crime be classified as public-law enrichment liability?

Some authors view certain or all of these as instances of enrichment liability. Thus, in the Netherlands liability arising in the first-mentioned situation is well developed and is viewed as unjustified enrichment,[81] while in Germany and South Africa the second example has been characterized as being a response to unjustified enrichment in the broad sense of the term.[82] The third is often excluded from standard texts on enrichment, but Goff and Jones certainly regard it as part of the subject.[83] In the end it is a question of how seamless a web we want the law to be.

---

[79] See, generally, Nörr *et al.* (n 71).

[80] Although it is, without analysis, used sometimes in commentaries on the *Versicherungsvertragsgesetz*, eg Ralf and Katharina Johannsen (eds), *Bruck-Möller, Kommentar zum Versicherungsvertragsgesetz*, § 1 nn 24–5.

[81] See eg M. W. L. Simons-Vinckx, 'Ongerechtvaardigde Verrrijking door Bodemsanering', (1995) *Milieu en Recht* 56.

[82] See eg the discussion of Michael Heller and Christopher Serkin, 'Revaluing Restitution: From the Talmud to Postsocialism', (1999) 97 *Michigan LR* 1385; Daniel Visser and Theunis Roux, 'Giving back the Country: South Africa's Restitution of Land Rights Act, 1994 in Context', in M. R. Rwelamira and G. Werle (eds), *Confronting Past Injustices: Approaches to Amnesty, Punishment, Reparation and Restitution* (1996), 89 ff.

[83] Goff and Jones (n 44), paras 38–001 ff.

2. How Enrichment Liability is Given Effect: The Remedies and the Measurement of Enrichment

(a) The Remedies: Personal versus Proprietary

Both the common-law and civilian systems present us with a complicated set of remedies that are mainly explicable in terms of the heavy hand of history.

Let us start by considering the civil law. First, it must be said that there is no such thing as a 'civilian system' of unjustified enrichment, except in the broadest terms. We have seen, first, that a particular remedy can have the same name in two legal systems, but be branded as an enrichment action in one and as something else in another (cf the *condictio indebiti* in German and Dutch law). Second, we have noted that some systems recognize enrichment arising from encroachment on the rights of the claimant (eg German law), but that others do not (eg Dutch and French law).[84] Where a system does recognize such liability, different remedies sometimes exist for different situations, where logically we would expect only one. For instance, in German law the so-called 'owner-possessor' model[85] (a finely graded system which makes the measure of the liability dependent on the type, or quality, of possessor involved)[86] deals with enrichment that occurs as a result of one person possessing the property of another. The *Eingriffskondiktion*,[87] on the other hand, deals with these enrichment situations which do not fall under the first-mentioned model.[88] However, the owner-possessor model does not really do any work additional to what the *Eingriffs-kondiktion* could do, except in the case of the *bona fide* possessor[89] (by protecting the *bona fide* possessor for value against most claims). The German remedies just mentioned are personal claims (as are enrichment claims generally in civilian systems), but that does not prevent some of them from having a strong 'propri-etary focus'. The remedies under the owner-possessor model are clearly geared to protect and underscore the rights of the owner,[90] and so is the *Eingriffskondiktion*.

---

[84] Jack Beatson and Eltjo J. H. Schrage (eds), *Unjustified Enrichment: Cases, Materials and Commentary* (2003), 543 and 556 ff.

[85] On which see, above all, Dirk Verse, *Verwendungen im Eigentümer-Besitzer Verhältnis* (1999), and also generally Markesinis *et al.* (n 17), 741 ff.

[86] See, generally, von Caemmerer (n 34), 352; Markesinis *et al* (n 17), 741 ff.

[87] About which see the text following n 137 below.   [88] Markesinis *et al.* (n 17), 743.

[89] This is pointed out by Markesinis *et al.* (n 17), 742.

[90] Markesinis *et al.* (n 17), 742. Although a *bona fide* possessor for value (known as a *redlicher Besitzer*) is not obliged, in terms of § 988 BGB, read with § 993 BGB, to give up the gain which he has made except in so far as there has been unreasonable use of the object, a gratuitous *bona fide* possessor (a so-called *unentgeltlicher Besitzer*), on the other hand, must surrender (also in terms of § 988 BGB) his enrichment according to the ordinary principles of enrichment liability as found in §§ 812 ff BGB. A *mala fide* possessor (*bosgläubiger Besitzer*) must, as decreed by § 990 BGB, return that which he or she received (ie there can be no reliance on loss of enrichment).

Indeed Schlechtriem[91] has remarked that, in common with its Anglo-American counterparts, it has the function of protecting the property interests of the claimant. Indeed, the *Zuweisungstheorie* makes it clear that a benefit which 'belongs' exclusively to the plaintiff has accrued to the defendant and for that reason must be returned.[92] Essentially, then, the remedy has—perhaps even more explicitly than 'waiver of tort' in English law—a proprietary focus rather than a delictual/tortious one.

In English law, too, a salient feature is the fact that some remedies have a proprietary basis, while others do not. A fundamental distinction between civilian and common-law systems is that in the former enrichment remedies (whether or not they have a proprietary focus) are invariably personal claims, while in the latter they may be of either a personal or a proprietary nature. Where ownership has not passed, the position in all civilian systems is that a *rei vindicatio* (or its equivalent) provides the appropriate remedy. In common-law systems, too, a claim for the recovery of property to which the claimant has never lost title, is classified as a 'pure proprietary claim' and like a *rei vindicatio* it is not an enrichment claim.[93] Where ownership has passed, the remedy to recover that which had been so transferred—in both civilian and common-law systems—is normally a personal claim. However, in common-law systems this kind of claim can also be of a proprietary nature (known as a 'restitutionary proprietary claim'). Whereas the first kind of proprietary claim seeks to effect the return of the claimant's property which has never ceased to belong to him, this second kind of claim creates 'new proprietary rights in response to the defendant's unjust enrichment'.[94] The fact that this kind of claim is not proprietary in the German law sense of the word (ie 'supporting the law of property'), but brings actual property rights into being, represents the most profound difference between the common law and the civil law in the area of enrichment. The drawing of the boundaries in this way is, however, not free of controversy[95] and it demonstrates the truth of Dawson's remark that unjustified enrichment, like any other principle which is recognized only after a legal system has already matured, is not easily placed within that system because 'it cuts across other principles already expressed in doctrine and reinforced by rules'.[96] This distinction is tied up with the law–equity

---

[91] Peter Schlechtriem, 'Güterschutz durch Eingriffskondiktionen', in *Ungerechtfertigte Bereicherung: Grundlagen, Tendenzen, Perspektiven. Symposium zum Gedenken an Detlef König* (1984), 57 ff.

[92] See especially Schlechtriem (n 15), 59–61.

[93] Goff and Jones (n 44), para 1–011. This is, however, not an uncontroversial view. See, for instance, Peter Birks, 'Property and Unjust Enrichment: Categorical Truths', [1997] *New Zealand LR* 623.

[94] Andrew Burrows and Ewan McKendrick, *Cases and Materials on the Law of Restitution* (1998), 724; Burrows (n 33), 62.

[95] See eg Virgo (n 38), 8 ff and the judges in *Fosket v McKeown* [2001] 1 AC 102 (for a summary of which, see Burrows (n 33), 64–5).

[96] John Dawson, *Unjust Enrichment* (1951), 39–40, also quoted by Beatson and Schrage (n 84), 8.

dichotomy and the main restitutionary remedies are constructive trusts[97] and equitable liens.

The statement that constructive trusts and equitable liens are remedies can, however, be made only with a certain amount of caution. Burrows points out[98] that it is difficult to characterize them simply as remedies because 'normally one cannot cleanly separate the proprietary remedies from the proprietary rights that they protect'.[99] They arise, he says, 'irrespective of a choice exercised by the claimant or the court. They predate a court order or the issue of proceedings or a claimant's election'.[100] Here we see revealed a central aspect of the common-law approach to remedies. As Niall Whitty has argued, whereas in civilian systems it is not at all strange that the right (and the entitlement to the attendant remedy) predate the court order—*ubi ius, ibi remedium*—in some, if not all, common-law systems (and especially in the branch of those systems known as Equity) the correlation between the infringement of the right and the remedy tends to be looser: the remedy granted by the court is seen as being controlled, not by the nature of the right infringed or of the obligation which has been broken, but by the decision of the judge, who may have a very broad residual discretion in selecting the appropriate remedy—which in its most extreme form is known as 'discretionary remedialism'.[101] Whitty sees this as the juncture at which the difference between common law and civil law is particularly acute and suggests that in the different approaches to remedies lies perhaps the most fundamental difference between civil law and common law.

Without detracting from the validity of Whitty's valuable insight, I would like to suggest that perhaps the difference lies not so much in the degree of discretion about the remedy, but the kind of remedy that may be awarded in the exercise of that discretion. 'Discretionary remedialism', says Simon Evans, 'is the view that courts have a discretion to award the "appropriate" remedy in the circumstances of each individual case rather than being limited to specific (perhaps historically determined) remedies for each category of causative events'.[102] How far discretionary remedialism should be taken is uncertain in the common law, with different authors and judges in different jurisdictions taking very different views.[103] Ultimately it is a question of the proper measure of a judge's power—and the answer depends very much on the tenor the times. As Lord Goff's speech in

---

[97] It is important to keep in mind that the term 'constructive trust' is an uncertain concept in regard to which there is much confusion. See George L. Gretton, 'Constructive Trusts', (1997) 1 *Edinburgh LR* 281 (Part 1) and 408 (Part 2); *idem*, 'Proprietary issues', in Johnston and Zimmermann (n 11), 571.

[98] Burrows (n 33), 62.   [99] Ibid 64.   [100] Ibid 63.

[101] Niall R. Whitty, 'From Rules to Discretion: Changes in the Fabric of Scots Private Law', (2003) 7 *Edinburgh LR* 281 ff.

[102] Simon Evans, 'Defending Discretionary Remedialism', (2001) 23 *Sydney LR* 463.

[103] See eg on the one hand Peter Birks, 'Three Kinds of Objection to Discretionary Remedialism', (2000) 29 *Western Australian LR* 1 and, on the other, Evans (n 102), 463 ff.

Kleinwort Benson v Lincoln City Council[104] shows, the official and unofficial portrait of what common-law judges do has fluctuated over time, and that is true, too, in civilian jurisdictions. In German law the approach to judicial law-making is much closer to the common-law model than is often supposed, but it is fair to say that German law exhibits a disciplined approach to remedies.[105] In France, on the other hand, we know that, although historical forces—at least if we look at the 'official picture'—caused the *Code civil* to limit severely the freedom of French judges to make law,[106] 'unofficially' the judicial process in these systems is not so different from the common-law position after all. The forceful prohibition of judicial law-making in Art 5 of the *Code civil*, which was a reaction against the excessive powers which judges had arrogated to themselves in the pre-revolutionary period, has not prevented French judges from making law. Behind the terse, syllogistic judgments there is—mediated through the 'unofficial discourse' of the magistracy in the form of *conclusions* and *rapports*—a form of precedent[107] and, ironically, because they are forced to hide their judicial creativity, French judges in fact have a much greater latitude than judges in either Germany or England.[108] The breathtaking scope of the discretion of the French courts in creating torts under Art 1382 *Code civil* is a case in point.[109] It is true that the same has not happened in the law of unjustified enrichment in the wake of the *arrêt Boudier*[110] (the notion of subsidiarity has played an important limiting role in this regard), but the point is that it could have. Although the discretion exercised by the French courts in this respect is conceptually different from the kind of discretion exercised in the case of discretionary remedialism, the degree of discretion to create law without precedent is similar; and therefore dicretionary remedialism may not be quite as strange a concept to the French system as one might at first suppose.

The debate surrounding discretionary remedialism in common-law jurisdictions is about how much uncertainty a legal system can bear and is part of the wider (and evolving) debate about the limits of constitutional tolerance in respect of a judge's law-making powers. In the context of discretionary remedialism we begin to see where the limits of this tolerance might be: if the constraints on a court in regard to the kind of remedy it should afford the claimant are slight *and* the possible remedies include those that rearrange the property relations of the

---

104 [1999] 2 AC 349, 377–9.

105 See generally Reinhard Zimmermann and Nils Jansen, 'Quieta Movere: Interpretative Change in a Codified System', in Peter Cane and Jane Stapleton (eds), *The Law of Obligations: Essays in Celebration of John Fleming* (1998), 285.

106 See Lasser (n 24), explaining the 'unofficial portrait' of French judges, which is not as well-known as the 'official' one, as described eg by John P. Dawson, *The Oracles of the Law* (1968), 263 ff.

107 Lasser (n 24), 1355 ff.   108 Lasser (n 24), 1332; and see also Bell *et al.* (n 30), 25 ff.

109 See eg G. Viney, *Introduction à la responsibilité* (1995), 63–9 and 107–9, trans Tony Weir and reproduced in Beatson and Schrage (n 84), 59–60.

110 *Cour de cassation (Chambre de requêtes)* 15.6.1892; *Recueil Sirey* 1893.1.28; *Recueil-Dalloz* 1892.1.596 (Labbé).

litigants, we are entering an uncertain terrain where common lawyers are not unanimous and where at least some civil lawyers find themselves in a different world.

The creation of proprietary rights to combat unjustified enrichment places a very powerful remedy in the hands of the claimant, and working out when this kind of remedy is appropriate in common-law systems (which is tied up with the task of completing the fusion of law and equity) is an important challenge to comparative analysts in these systems. Burrows is adamant that proprietary remedies such as equitable liens and constructive trusts should not 'be rendered unacceptably uncertain' by making their existence depend on a broad judicial discretion, but that they should rather depend on rules that are set out as clearly as possible in advance.[111] It may be, though, that there is no one solution for the whole of the common-law world and that the approach will depend on how much a particular system values certain rights and how strongly it wants to protect them.

If the comparison of the law of enrichment in the common law and the civil law is motivated merely by a desire to understand the differences between the two, proprietary remedies can be seen as providing evidence of an interesting divergence between the two systems. If, on the other hand, harmonization is the issue, we have here a point of difference which is linked to the very essence of what history has made of the two legal worlds and on which a debate of the kind generated by the 'unjust factors'/'without legal ground' controversy will be needed to make any progress towards convergence.

(b) Measuring Enrichment: Value Received versus Value Remaining

In the civil law the influence of a general principle against enrichment gradually moved the focus of this area of law from effecting a return of that which had been transferred to effecting a return of the positive difference that the transfer produced in the defendant's patrimony as a whole. That is to say the law has moved from being concerned with the 'value received' to aimed at securing a disgorgement of the 'value remaining'.[112] The latter orientation is particularly strongly embedded in the BGB by § 818 III.[113] The recognition of the defence of change of position in *Lipkin Gorman v Karpnale* has meant that in English law, too, the value remaining can sometimes be the appropriate measure. The Study Group on a European Civil Code, on the other hand, wants to get rid of 'net enrichment' and favours an 'itemised . . . concept of enrichment'.[114] Particularly where 'value remaining' is the accepted measure of enrichment, but also to some extent where an itemized approach is followed, there must be a defence of 'change of position' (as it is designated in common-law countries; or 'loss of enrichment' in civil-law countries). But, however strongly change of position is embedded in a legal system,

---

[111] Burrows (n 33), 73–4.   [112] Flume (n 31), 103.
[113] See *Handkommentar/Schulze* § 818 nn 2 and 6; and Beatson and Schrage (n 84), 123–4.
[114] Swann (n 41), 279.

there are cases where the value received is the appropriate measure. For instance, in certain cases of failed reciprocal contracts it would be inequitable if one of the contracting parties could rely on change of position due to an inability to return what he had received.[115] For this reason German law developed the *Saldotheorie* and English law the rule that restitution can only be claimed if the claimant is able to offer to return what he has received. Determining the parameters of this defence is one of the central contemporary challenges of comparative law and thus studies such as those of Hellwege[116] and of Gordley[117] are enormously important. A corollary of this defence is that of 'passing on', that is to say a defence which draws attention to the fact that the claimant has not been impoverished by virtue of having passed on the loss to a third party such as an insurer. Ascertaining the existence and extent of this concept presents yet another contemporary task for comparative scholarship.

IV. Can Taxonomies Survive the Uncertainties of Multi-Party Enrichment?

The common law and the civil law have had very different experiences in regard to enrichment liability involving more than two persons. Typical instances are: a bank wrongly paying on the basis of an instruction that had been rescinded, or a subcontractor performing in terms of a contract with the main contractor, who subsequently disappears. Can the bank reclaim the amount directly from the payee, or is it limited to dealing with its customer? Can the subcontractor claim directly from the owner? The answers to these questions are complex. Should one seek to deal with the complexity by laying down detailed rules, or can one devise a flexible approach, which takes account of the typical policy factors (such as the possibility of insolvency or double jeopardy for the defendant)?

France is an example of a flexible approach that it would perhaps not be wise to emulate. The general enrichment action in *Boudier* was created in a multi-party

---

[115] See the discussion below.

[116] Phillip Hellwege, 'The Scope of Application of Change of Position in the Law of Unjustified Enrichment: A Comparative Study', (1999) 7 *Restitution LR* 93 and *idem*, 'Unwinding Mutual Contracts: *Restitutio in Integrum* v. the Defence of Change of Position', in Johnston and Zimmermann (n 11), 243.

[117] James Gordley, 'Restitution without Enrichment? Change of Position and *Wegfall der Bereicherung*', in Johnston and Zimmermann (n 11), 227.

enrichment situation without any restrictions. It has since been held to apply to a great many different situations involving more than two parties and, although the courts have now indicated that the principle will only be applicable if there is no contract between the claimant and the third party and that the principle of subsidiarity applies, the action comes close to the spectre of a general remedy based solely on the notion of equity. Indeed, the following statement in the first half of the twentieth century by Gutteridge and David remains essentially true: '[I]t is . . . impossible', they said, 'to state the doctrine in a form which is absolutely systematic, dominated as it is by the subjective and paramount notions of morality and fair play'.[118] In Germany, on the other hand, a detailed set of rules has been developed to deal with instances of multi-party enrichment and Whitty[119] has outlined a similar approach for Scots law. These detailed rules can work very well, but because of their complexity they tend to be difficult to digest, sometimes even in the domestic setting and certainly if they have to be imported into another system. The common law, again, has not to a great extent engaged with the issue of multi-party enrichment *eo nomine*,[120] but this does not mean that it has no solutions for these problems: For instance, a number of typical three-party enrichment situations are dealt with by the technique of tracing followed by either a personal claim or the imposition of a constructive trust.[121] Burrows and MacKendrick rightly point out that tracing is in essence about the 'at the expense of' requirement of enrichment liability.[122]

Although the multi-party problems and their solutions in different legal systems seem intractable, I believe that a case can be made for a flexible solution which could be adopted in both common-law and civil-law jurisdictions.[123] This should not follow the French approach, but rather seek to secure predictability by developing a set of policy factors—much as happens in the law of delict—which then incrementally create a set of stable situations in which indirect enrichment is

---

[118] H. C. Gutteridge and R. J. A. David, 'The Doctrine of Unjustified Enrichment', (1935) 5 *Cambridge LJ* 222–3, also quoted by Zweigert and Kötz (n 17), 562.

[119] Niall R. Whitty, 'Indirect Enrichment in Scots Law', [1994] *Juridical Review* 200.

[120] Contrast the contributions of Peter Birks, ' "At the Expense of the Claimant": Direct and Indirect Enrichment in English Law', in Johnston and Zimmermann (n 11), 493 ff and, in the same volume, Visser (n 123).

[121] Burrows and McKendrick (n 94), 664 point out that '[w]hile, no doubt, tracing is normally invoked by a plaintiff with the aim of obtaining a restitutionary remedy (whether an equitable lien or a declaration of a trust) over property retained by the defendant, tracing may also be invoked with the aim of seeking a personal restitutionary remedy (for example, an award of money had and received or equitable accounting) in respect of property *received* by the defendant (where property has reached the defendant from a third party)'.

[122] Burrows and McKendrick (n 94), 664; and see also Burrows (n 33), 79.

[123] See Daniel Visser, 'Searches for Silver Bullets: Enrichment in Three-Party Situations', in Johnston and Zimmermann (n 11), 526; and Daniel Visser and Saul Miller, 'Between Principle and Policy: Indirect Enrichment in Subcontractor and "Garage Repair" Cases', (2000) 117 *South African LJ* 594.

recognized. There is, however, likely to be considerable resistance to such a suggestion, because the following view expressed by Smillie is shared by many on both
sides of the civil-law/common-law divide: 'Substitution of vague discretionary standards and lists of relevant "factors" for firm rules means that litigation becomes
increasingly complex, protracted and expensive and the incentive to appeal an
adverse decision becomes stronger'.[124] But the experience in the law of delict shows
that standards which are applied by the manipulation of a reasonably contained set
of policy factors can in fact produce an acceptable standard of predictability. What
needs to be established is how much certainty a legal culture wants at a particular
stage: in the past the value of certainty had been so important that it was almost
axiomatic that individualized justice had to take a back seat. But the modern trend
is to sacrifice a certain amount of certainty for greater justice in individual
instances and the real question is: 'How should certainty and justice be balanced?'[125]

V. DRAWING IT ALL TOGETHER: WHICH TAXONOMY?

Can all of these diverse principles and institutions be arranged in a typology that
reaches across the common-law/civil-law divide? Civil lawyers spotted very early
on that the categories into which the law was divided by both Gaius and Justinian
contained a clear niche for the development of unjustified enrichment as an independent cause of action alongside contract and delict, with the result that its place
within the law of obligations was already settled by the Middle Ages. Although
there was the odd glimpse of this possibility in the common law—for instance by
Lord Mansfield (inspired by Roman law) in *Moses v Macferlan*[126]—the organizational structure of the common law obscured the emergence of this category until
the twentieth century, when, in 1937, the American Law Institute's *Restatement of
the Law of Restitution* (again drawing on Roman learning) brought the category
into the common-law consciousness.[127] Even then it did not take proper hold in the

---

[124] John Smillie, 'Certainty and Civil Obligation', (2000) 9 *Otago LR* 633, 635.

[125] See Whitty (n 101), 299 ff. Further important studies are: Meier (n 2); Simon Whittaker,
'Performance of Another's Obligation: French and English Law Contrasted', in Johnston and
Zimmermann (n 11), 433; Hector L. MacQueen, 'Payment of Another's Debt', in Johnston and
Zimmermann (n 11), 458; and Alexander Schall, *Leistungskondiktion und 'Sonstige Kondiktion' auf der
Grundlage des einheitlichen gesetzlichen Kondiktionsprinzips* (2003).

[126] (1760) 2 Burrow's King's Bench Reports tempore Mansfield 1005; 97 ER 676.

[127] David J. Ibbetson, *A Historical Introduction to the Law of Obligations* (1999), 264 ff.

United States,[128] while in English law it was only acknowledged in this sense in 1991; and some common-law jurisdictions (eg Australia) are still not fully convinced of unjustified enrichment being a 'determinant of liability' as opposed to being 'no more than a "unifying legal concept" which explains why the law recognises an obligation to make restitution in particular contexts'.[129] The fact that the very existence of unjustified enrichment as a cause of action is uncertain in the common-law world—and here the factual neglect of the concept in the United States[130] and the intellectual resistance to it in Australia[131] should not be underestimated—provides a special challenge to those who are interested in debating what its internal structure should ideally be. After all, it is difficult to consider the characteristics of the taxa of species and sub-species if there is no agreement on the overarching taxon of genus. Nevertheless, as long as one acknowledges the limitations that this broken reality imposes on the exercise, thinking about ideal structures can be an important catalyst to advancing the understanding of the proper role of unjustified enrichment in legal systems generally.

When one considers how to organize the law of unjustified enrichment, the influential classificatory model of the German-speaking legal world, namely the Wilburg/von Caemmerer taxonomy, immediately comes to mind.[132] According to the wording of § 812 BGB, enrichment liability rests on the general principle[133] of *something having been received without legal basis*; and this paragraph (which establishes a general enrichment action) is then followed in the ensuing paragraphs

---

[128] Andrew Kull, 'Rationalizing Restitution', (1995) 83 *California LR* 1191; Heller and Serkin (n 82).

[129] Finn (n 26), 251.   [130] See Heller and Serkin (n 82), 1385; Kull (n 128), 1191.

[131] Thus Bryan (n 60), 47 ff, in a considered and objective treatment of the doctrine of unconscionable dealings as it is understood in Australia, shows that it is not nearly as indeterminate as its opponents suggest, even though he pleads for a better understanding of the fact that many of the applications of the doctrine reverse unjustified enrichment.

[132] See Zimmermann and Du Plessis (n 17), 24 ff; and see Walter Wilburg, *Die Lehre von der ungerechtfertigten Bereicherung nach österreichischem und deutschem Recht* (1934); von Caemmerer (n 34), 333; see also *idem*, 'Problèmes fondamentaux de l'enrichissement sans cause', (1966) 18 *Revue internationale de droit comparé* 573.

[133] A great many civilian jurisdictions have accepted a general enrichment action: the *Cour de Cassation* developed a general action in the celebrated *Boudier* decision of 1892, utilizing the *actio de in rem verso*; Germany, having been in the position to survey a century of development after the enactment of the *Code civil* when it codified its law in 1900, immediately incorporated a general enrichment action in her BGB of 1900 (§ 812 BGB). The courts in Spain also developed a general action (where the *Código civil*, like its French counterpart, also did not contain a general action); Italy legislatively recognized a general action in Arts 2041–2 of its *Codice civile* of 1942, while the Netherlands did so in Art 6:202 of their new codification in 1992. Thus, during the course of the twentieth century the codified civilian systems saw a general movement towards the recognition of a general principle of liability based on unjustified enrichment. The uncodified mixed systems of Sri Lanka and South Africa have also moved towards a general enrichment action, on which see G. L. Peiris, *Some Aspects of the Law of Unjust Enrichment in South Africa and Ceylon* (1972), 401–2, and Niall R. Whitty and Daniel Visser, 'Unjustified Enrichment', in Zimmermann, *et al* (n 59), 406, while English law (even though the question is not much discussed there) effectively does recognize a general principle, capable of generating new instances of enrichment liability, as the recognition of new 'unjust factors' shows.

by what is essentially a rendition of the various Roman *condictiones*. However, the wording of the general principle allowed Wilburg to put forward his famous typology, in which he made a division between (a) *enrichment based on a performance, or transfer* (a transfer being, according to the predominant opinion, an intentional and purpose-oriented increase of the patrimony of the defendant by the plaintiff),[134] and (b) *enrichment 'in any other way'*.

The remedy in the first category is known as a *Leistungskondiktion* (claim based on a performance/transfer), which is available where the purpose of the transfer has failed (which may be for a variety of reasons, eg because it was never owed; or because the transfer was made in terms of an invalid agreement or in terms of a valid agreement that was subsequently rescinded; or because it was made in the hope that a particular consideration would follow from the other party, which never materialized). The thinking behind this arrangement is as follows: the purpose of a payment is usually to discharge a debt; if such a debt in fact exists, and if, therefore, the payment does indeed discharge the debt, the purpose of the payment is fulfilled by that payment and that fact creates for the recipient a *causa retinendi*; if, on the other hand, the debt does not exist—for any of the reasons listed above—the purpose cannot be fulfilled, with the result that the recipient has no cause for the retention of what he has received and that the payer can raise an enrichment action.[135] In terms of this approach it is not so much the absence of a legal ground, but rather the failure of purpose that forms the essence of the claim.[136] (There are, however, influential commentators who eschew the notion of purpose in determining the basis of this action.[137])

The remedies available to redress the second category were divided by von Caemmerer into (i) the *Eingriffskondiktion* (claim based on encroachment, ie where the defendant has been enriched as a result of his unauthorized interference with the rights of the plaintiff), (ii) the *Verwendungskondiktion* (claim based on unauthorized expenditure on the property of another), and (iii) the *Rückgriffs-kondiktion* (claim based on the discharge of another's debt).

This classification has several important characteristics. First, in its main sections it supports the classical division between a claim seeking to reverse undue payment and other forms of enrichment, which is inspired in many legal systems by French law, for the *Leistungskondiktion* broadly speaking mirrors the *répétition*

---

[134] See Werner Lorenz in *J. von Staudingers Kommentar zum Bürgerlichen Gesetzbuch II* (rev edn, 1999), § 812 n 4; Dieter Reuter and Michael Martinek, *Ungerechtfertigte Bereicherung* (1983), 106.

[135] Reuter and Martinek (n 134), 125; Zimmermann and Du Plessis (n 17), 26 n 102. This is often referred to as the 'subjective approach'. If the payer's purpose is indeed the determinative purpose, this is a correct appellation. It is suggested, however, that it would be more appropriate to postulate an objective intention, in the establishment of which the payer's intention is only one of the factors that must be taken into account. This was, incidentally, also the approach of the influential Dutch author Marcel Henri Bregstein, *Ongegronde Vermogensvermeerdering* (1927).

[136] Schlechtriem (n 15), 92.

[137] Karl Larenz and Klaus-Wilhelm Canaris, *Lehrbuch des Schuldrechts* (vol II/2, 13th edn, 1994), 137.

de l'indu. Second, it maps out the main ways in which enrichment can occur, highlighting that the law of enrichment functions in three different modes, with (a) enrichment due to transfer supplementing the law of contract; (b) enrichment due to unauthorized expenditure chiefly supplementing the law of property; and (c) enrichment due to encroachment mainly supplementing the law of delict or torts. Third, the *Leistungskondiktion* reaches back to the original basis of the *condictiones* with its notion that the essence of restitution in this kind of situation lies in the failure of the object, or purpose, of the performance or transfer.[138]

In the Anglophone world we find a different approach, which, as we have seen above, involves (a) dividing unjustified enrichment into 'autonomous unjust enrichment' and restitution for wrongs (or so-called 'remedial unjust enrichment'), while (b) emphasizing that the common law requires *a specific unjust factor* to found an unjustified enrichment claim. Unlike civilian legal systems, therefore, the common law does not work with the concept that enrichment is unjustified principally because it is *sine causa*: rather it is interested in a positive reason that makes the enrichment unjustified. Even though, as we have also seen, this taxonomy has come under fire in England, the rest of the common-law world has not abandoned it: the requirement of a specific ground to found an enrichment claim has old roots,[139] many authors in England are not ready to follow Birks,[140] and the broad axes of the common-law taxonomy also continue to be observed in the *Restatement of Restitution and Unjust Enrichment (Third)* in the United States.[141]

How different are these approaches? I think that they are less different than is sometimes assumed. Take, for instance, the defining characteristic of the common-law concept relating to the cause of action in unjustified enrichment, namely the fact that it insists on a specific reason to found an enrichment claim.[142] It is important to realize that the unjust factors are the common law's way of limiting liability, of avoiding saying that enrichment is reclaimable merely because it is 'unjust'.[143] Although the 'without legal basis' approach is often postulated as the opposite of this analysis, it must be kept in mind that the reason why an enrichment is without legal basis is also important in the civil law. Whatever we call it, the fact is that a benefit obtained by the defendant is without legal basis for some reason: because it was paid by mistake; or because it was transferred in terms of an illegal agreement; or because it was given in the knowledge that it was not owed but in the expectation of a counterperformance. Civilian lawyers would not want to

---

[138] Fritz Schwarz, *Die Grundlage der condictio im klassischen römischen Recht* (1952), 1 ff; but see, sceptically, Susanne Hähnchen, *Die Causa Condictionis: Ein Beitrag zum klassischen römischen Kondiktionenrecht* (2003).

[139] Dawson (n 96), 117.   [140] See Burrows *et al*. (n 4), 160 ff.

[141] Mark P. Gergen, 'Self-Interested Intervention in the Law of Unjust Enrichment', in Zimmermann, *Grundstrukturen* (n 11), 243.

[142] Dawson (n 96), 117.

[143] See in this regard eg *David Securities Pty Ltd v Commonwealth Bank of Australia* (1992) 175 CLR 353 (HCA) and the comments of Bryan (n 60), 52–3.

call these considerations 'unjust factors' because of the baggage associated with that concept, but they do not deny that each of these circumstances necessitates a different response. Indeed, there are many acknowledgements in civilian writing of the importance of the reason why an enrichment is *sine causa*. Thus Krebs reminds us that Wilburg himself stressed that, although enrichment brought about by a *Leistung* as well as that brought about in other ways share the characteristic of being *sine causa*, that, in itself, does not tell us much and therefore we need 'a reason rendering the enrichment unjustified'.[144] And Schlechtriem, although no true believer in the purpose-orientated 'subjective' approach of the prevailing opinion in Germany, acknowledges that the purpose with which a performance is made has a role in determining the validity or otherwise of a particular legal ground, for example where a transfer, which on the face of it is legal, has taken place for an illegal purpose.[145]

This does not, of course, imply that the common-law approach is the answer. Sonja Meier,[146] Reinhard Zimmermann,[147] Niall Whitty,[148] and Jacques du Plessis[149] have all pointed out very persuasively the defects of, especially, the English approach. However, in my view, the difficulties experienced with the 'unjust factor' approach are mainly attributable to its functioning in a context where, first, there is no acknowledgement that the main basis of enrichment liability is *the fact that the enrichment is sine causa* and where, second, the unjust factor is seen as *a requirement of liability*. This has led, on the one hand, to unjust factors being formulated too widely (eg not confining mistake to liability mistakes, but including any mistake even in situations where there existed a good legal ground for the enrichment);[150] and, on the other hand, to the law being paralysed when it could not easily articulate the reason for the enrichment being unjustified in a particular situation.[151] These pitfalls clearly have to be avoided. At the same time, however, it should be possible to accept, and preserve, the delimiting function of the circumstances in which an enrichment is *sine causa*. As Hamaker correctly observed, with regard to the formulation of the general enrichment action in the new Dutch civil code, to say that 'A may reclaim something which he gave "without legal ground" to B, says . . . nothing more than that A may claim *if* he may claim'.[152] Therefore,

---

144 Krebs (n 16), 210, explaining Wilburg (n 132), 14.   145 Schlechtriem (n 15), 192 n 722.

146 See her work cited in n 2 above.   147 See his contribution cited in n 2 above.

148 See especially Niall R. Whitty, 'Rationality, Nationality and the Taxonomy of Unjustified Enrichment', in Johnston and Zimmermann (n 11), 658.

149 Jacques du Plessis, 'Towards a Rational Structure of Liability for Unjustified Enrichment: Thoughts from Two Mixed Jurisdictions', in Zimmermann, *Grundstrukturen* (n 11), 175, 195 ff (also (2005) 122 *South African LJ* 142, 159 ff).

150 Reinhard Zimmermann and Sonja Meier, 'Judicial Development of the Law, Error Iuris, and the Law of Unjustified Enrichment—A View from Germany', (1999) 115 *LQR* 556.

151 See eg the discussion that followed *Westdeutsche Landesbank Girozentrale v Islington LBC*; *Kleinwort Benson Ltd v Sandwell BC* [1994] 1 WLR 938 (CA); [1996] AC 669 (HL).

152 G. Hamaker, *De Vordering uit Onverschuldigde Betaling naar Nederlands Recht* (1980), 66.

if one looks upon the relevant 'unjust factor' in a particular situation not as a 'requirement of recovery', but rather as a necessary further 'explanation of the defendant's restitutionary liability',[153] its proper function is revealed, namely to articulate the policy why this particular enrichment without legal ground is treated as recoverable.

Lord Rodger's approach in the Scottish case of *Shilliday v Smith*[154] seems to go in this direction. While it proceeds from the basic principle that enrichment liability is about reversing enrichment that has come about *sine causa*, that is to say, without legal ground, this approach also emphasizes the importance of taking note of the situation in which the enrichment arises in order to determine whether it should be labelled as being *sine causa*. (Such situations, Lord Rodger explains, are often described by reference to the *condictiones*, which represent a shorthand for some of the main kinds of situations that lead to enrichment liability.[155]) The judgment also highlights the necessity of keeping in mind the effect produced by a relevant event (eg that the defendant has received money, or property, or services), because that logically determines the nature of the law's response (ie the kind of remedy). The judgment, it seems to me, combines the various academic approaches to the division of the Scots law of unjustified enrichment: although it emphasizes the primary importance of the event which makes the enrichment unjustified, it does not accord an absolute quality to this aspect and thus emphasizes that a complex categorization, which incorporates the event, its effect, and the law's response thereto, is to be preferred. *Shilliday v Smith* shows, I think, that it is possible to fashion a classificatory system that is capable of bridging the civilian and common-law approaches: to take the *sine causa* approach of German law as worked out in the Wilburg/von Caemmerer typology (although not *in complexu*, but rather in broad outline) and to combine it with the common-law's emphasis on the reason why the enrichment should be returned (but without giving these reasons the rigidly controlling position that they have sometimes assumed in the common law).[156] It must be conceded, however, that the Wilburg/von Caemmerer model might, despite its intellectual attractiveness, be too much and too little to export (at least in its entirety). Too much, because the whole system fully makes sense only once the elaborate structure of the *Leistungskondiktion* is appreciated, which, however, is firmly based on a German conception of the law of obligations. Too much, also, because it includes enrichment resulting from encroachment, which many in England do not regard as part of the law of enrichment. And too little, because the *Eingriffskondiktion*

---

[153] Krebs (n 16), 217.   [154] 1998 SC 725.   [155] *Shilliday v Smith* 1998 SC 725, 727.

[156] See Daniel Visser, 'Unjustified Enrichment in Mixed Legal Systems', paper delivered at the Conference in Honour of Marcel Henri Bregstein on the European Law of Contract and Unjustified Enrichment at the University of Amsterdam in October 2000. This paper is unpublished, but its key sections are cited by Niall R. Whitty, 'The Scottish Enrichment Revolution', (2001) *Scottish Law and Practice Quarterly* 167, 185.

does not contemplate the proprietary restitutionary remedies available in English law (if these are indeed part of the law of enrichment). Be that as it may, Christiane Wendehorst,[157] setting out the strong and weak points of both the 'without legal ground' and the 'unjust factor' approaches, has demonstrated how they can be effectively combined in an attempt to harmonize the enrichment law of Europe.

Many would, however, prefer to have the one approach or the other. Both Whitty and Evans-Jones want Wilburg/von Caemmerer for Scotland; Du Plessis favours it as a basis for South Africa,[158] while Lionel Smith says that Canada must choose between the 'without legal ground approach' and the 'unjust factor' approach;[159] and Birks says the same now in regard to English law. These are formidable voices, but in my view a choice between merely relying on reasons why a particular enrichment may be claimed or adopting with the formula 'without legal ground' without any further adornment is impossible. The only realistic option seems to me to lie in an open acknowledgement of the policy considerations that dictate whether or not an enrichment is unjustified.

However, much remains to be done. It should not be forgotten that there is also little agreement at an even more basic level of taxonomy, namely as to what the elements of enrichment liability are. As we have mentioned, it is customary to say, in many jurisdictions, that enrichment liability exists when someone is (i) enriched, (ii) without legal ground, (iii) at the expense of another. But there is no unanimity on these elements. For instance, in Germany, the notion of a *Leistung*, or performance, has been defined with such precision that it takes care of all the causal concerns when it is applied, with the result that German authors have declared 'at the expense of' not to be a separate element of liability in the case of the *Leistungskondiktion*. In Canada, too, the causation element is not expressly articulated and the following formula for the existence of unjustified enrichment, as set out in *Pettkus v Becker*,[160] is authoritative: (i) an enrichment of the defendant, (ii) a corresponding deprivation of the plaintiff; and (iii) absence of a juristic reason for the defendant's enrichment. The express acknowledgement that enrichment must be balanced by a mirror loss is echoed in many countries (eg Holland, Scotland, and South Africa), but it is not a requirement in Germany, and probably not in England. Then again, as Michael Bryan points out, '[n]o restitution case in Australia has been analysed in terms of the trinity of enrichment, a

---

[157] 'Die Leistungskondiktion und ihre Binnenstruktur in rechtsvergleichender Perspektive', in Zimmermann, *Grundstrukturen* (n 11), 47.

[158] Du Plessis (n 149), 176; Whitty (n 148), 694; Robin Evans-Jones, *Unjustified Enrichment*, vol I: *Enrichment by Deliberate Conferral: Condictio* (2003), para 1.71.

[159] Lionel D. Smith, 'The Mystery of Judicial Reason', (2000) 12 *Supreme Court LR* (2d) 211.

[160] [1980] 2 SCR 834; (1980) DLR (3d) 257 (SCC). See also *Garland v Consumers' Gas* [2004] 1 SCR 629, where the elements listed in *Pettkus* were confirmed, but the court added the notion that, even if these three elements were satisfied, the defendant may show that the plaintiff should not be able to claim on the basis that it would go against the expectations of the parties and/or public policy.

corresponding deprivation and the absence of any juristic reason for the enrichment'.[161] All of this does not mean that convergence cannot happen; only that it will not happen without considerable effort.

As the work of Waddams shows, the experience of the common law with classification has not been a very happy one and, in fact, none of the attempts that have been made over the centuries has had lasting success.[162] This is the result, partly, of English lawyers—both judges and academic authors—having been hitherto largely indifferent to taxonomy. It was only with the open recognition of enrichment liability that a different pattern of thinking emerged. Enrichment liability is not just a new species of an existing genus, but rather a genus in its own right, and taxonomic issues therefore suddenly became important—hence the vigorous debate since 1990. The uncertainties surrounding classification in English law today should not come as a surprise. It is not as though the civil law had an easier path to traverse: civilians merely set out on it much earlier. The history of the classification of obligations from Gaius through Justinian, Donellus, and Grotius to the codifications was a continuously developing one. The profound revolution in thinking about enrichment liability that the Wilburg/von Caemmerer taxonomy brought about in the course of the twentieth century is ample evidence that there is never an end to the making and re-making of classifications. The lively debate in Scots law on the proper classification of enrichment further underscores this truth. However, this is the only 'truth' in classifications: none is ever perfect and when we engage in taxonomy we cannot do more than create aids to thinking.

VI. CONCLUSION

Comparative lawyers can make an important contribution to the future of the fractured and fractious world of unjustified enrichment. It will not be an easy task. As Robert Stevens points out:[163]

Comparative law is a dangerous business. Comparison of narrow legal rules may be misleading unless done in context as apparent inconsistencies may be explicable by more fundamental structural differences. Harmonisation of individual rules may increase rather than remove dissonance between different systems and runs the risk of creating incoherence within individual systems.

---

[161] Bryan (n 60), 53.   [162] Stephen Waddams (n 1), 1–22.
[163] In his section in Burrows *et al.* (n 4), 270.

But if the pioneering efforts of, for example, Christiane Wendehorst,[164] Thomas Krebs,[165] and Phillip Hellwege[166] in finding common ground and system-spanning solutions can be multiplied, and if the efforts of authors such as Weinrib,[167] McInnes,[168] and Dagan[169] to reveal the underlying foundations of the thinking behind the various solutions can be emulated, comparative law may help to uncover the enormous wealth of learning of which both the common law and the civil law are the repositories, and so bring the same level of understanding to the law of unjustified enrichment which has, over the years, been achieved between the systems in regard to contract and tort.

BIBLIOGRAPHY

J. P. Dawson, *Unjust Enrichment* (1951, reprinted 1999)

Reinhard Zimmermann, 'Unjustified Enrichment: The Modern Civilian Approach', (1995) 15 *Oxford Journal of Legal Studies* 404 ff

Basil S. Markesinis, Werner Lorenz, and Gerhard Dannemann, *The German Law of Obligations; vol I: The Law of Contracts and Restitution: A Comparative Introduction* (1997)

Lionel D. Smith, *The Law of Tracing* (1997)

Konrad Zweigert and Hein Kötz, *An Introduction to Comparative Law* (3rd edn, 1998, trans Tony Weir)

Eltjo J. H. Schrage (ed), *Unjust Enrichment: The Comparative Legal History of the Law of Restitution* (2nd edn, 1999)

—— (2000) 1 *Theoretical Inquiries in Law* 1 ff

Peter Schlechtriem, *Restitution und Bereicherungsausgleich in Europa. Eine rechtsvergleichende Darstellung* (2 vols, 2000 and 2001)

Thomas Krebs, *Restitution at the Crossroads* (2001)

Frank L. Schäfer, *Das Bereicherungsrecht in Europa: Einheits- und Trennungslehren in gemeinen, deutschen und englischen Recht* (2001)

David Johnston and Reinhard Zimmermann (eds), *Unjustified Enrichment: Key Issues in Comparative Perspective* (2002)

Jack Beatson and Eltjo J. H. Schrage (eds), *Unjustified Enrichment: Cases, Materials and Commentary* (2003)

Robin Evans-Jones, *Unjustified Enrichment*, vol 1: *Enrichment by Deliberate Conferral: Condictio* (2003)

Hanoch Dagan, *The Law and Ethics of Restitution* (2004)

Peter Birks, *Unjust Enrichment* (2nd edn, 2005)

Reinhard Zimmermann (ed), *Grundstrukturen eines Europäischen Bereicherungsrechts* (2005)

---

[164] See Wendehorst (n 157) above.   [165] See Krebs (n 16) above.
[166] See Hellwege (n 10).   [167] See Weinrib (n 50).
[168] Mitchell McInnes, 'Unjust Enrichment: A Reply to Professor Weinrib', (2001) 9 *Restitution LR* 29.
[169] See Dagan (n 52) above.

CHAPTER 31

....

COMPARATIVE
TORT LAW

....

GERHARD WAGNER

Bonn

I. INTRODUCTION

TORT law has always been one of the major areas of comparative law. Whereas the law of property, even today, remains on the outskirts of comparative learning, the law of extra-contractual liability has attracted much interest from comparative law scholars. The law of delict or tort constitutes the eleventh volume of the *International Encyclopedia of Comparative Law*. It was published between 1971 and 1981 and consists of no less than fourteen chapters totalling 1,489 pages.[1] Part of that interest may have a 'real' background in the sense that, particularly in modern times, an individual might be struck by an accident anywhere, for example during a business trip, while delivering goods to foreign markets, or while on holiday at distant shores. Another explanation certainly is that the law of delict or torts is particularly amenable to comparatist endeavour as the patterns of cases are almost identical across different societies, provided that they are at the same level of economic and technological development.

Endeavours in the comparison of the different systems of delict and tort have received a further boost from the objective of harmonizing European private law. In its Action Plan on European Contract Law submitted in February 2003, the Commission has embraced a multi-layered approach, combining elements of soft harmonization with the final goal of a European Civil Code.[2] Although

---

[1] André Tunc (ed), *International Encyclopedia of Comparative Law* (vol XI, 1971–81).

[2] *Communication from the Commission to the European Parliament and the Council: A more coherent European Contract Law—An action plan*, COM (2003) 68 final, 2.

it is impossible to predict the fate of this project, it is safe to assume that, in any event, contract law will be the pacemaker for tort law. If a European Code of contract law were enacted, the law of delict/torts would have to follow in the then-foreseeable future.[3] This development has been anticipated by scholars in several European countries but most thoroughly by Walter van Gerven and Christian von Bar, who have thrown themselves into the task of establishing the *acquis* of European Tort Law, either in the form of a case book or in the form of a treatise.[4] In addition, different groups have been struggling to come up with a set of 'Principles of European Tort Law', most prominently the Tilburg/Vienna group initiated and coordinated by Jaap Spier and Helmut Koziol.[5] Regardless of whether one agrees or disagrees with the solutions offered, the principles and the commentaries thereon certainly provide a valuable starting-point for further scholarly efforts and critical discussion.

II. General Clause versus Variety of Individual Torts

1. A Fundamental Difference in Style

An initial and significant schism within the law of extra-contractual liability is thought to be the one between the Continental European law of delict and the common law of torts. Accepting a certain degree of stylization and exaggeration, the two contrasting approaches parallel the distinction in modern legal theory

---

[3] cf Gerhard Wagner, 'The Project of Harmonizing European Tort Law', 42 *Common Market Law Review* 1269 ff (2005).

[4] Walter van Gerven, Jeremy Lever, and Pierre Larouche, *Cases, Materials and Text on National, Supranational and International Tort Law* (2000); Christian von Bar, *Gemeineuropäisches Deliktsrecht* (vol I, 1996; vol II, 1999); English translation: *The Common European Law of Torts* (vol I, 1998/2003; vol II, 2000).

[5] European Group on Tort Law, *Principles of European Tort Law* (2005); the preparatory works are: Jaap Spier (ed), *The Limits of Liability. Keeping the Floodgates Shut* (1996); *idem* (ed), *The Limits of Expanding Liability* (1998); *idem* (ed), *Unification of Tort Law: Causation* (2000); *idem* (ed), *Unification of Tort Law: Liability for Damage Caused by Others* (2003); Helmut Koziol (ed), *Unification of Tort Law: Wrongfulness* (1998); Ulrich Magnus (ed), *Unification of Tort Law: Damages* (2001); Bernhard Koch and Helmut Koziol (eds), *Unification of Tort Law: Strict Liability* (2002); Ulrich Magnus and Miquel-Martín Casals (eds), *Unification of Tort Law: Contributory Negligence* (2004); Horton Rogers (ed), *Unification of Tort Law: Multiple Tortfeasors* (2004); Pierre Widmer (ed), *Unification of Tort Law: Fault* (2004).

between rule-based and principle-based models of law.[6] At this point the focus of interest is not on substantive issues, such as the scope of protection, but rather on the basic structure and style of tort law, that is, on the contrast between the unitary law of delict and the pluralistic, fact-driven wrongs of the law of torts. As pointed out by Tony Weir:[7]

The systems *look* very different. . . . In France the law is laid out as a gloss on a central text, and a rule is found as easily and pleasantly as a flower in a formal garden set out along the path of principle. Not so in England, where one has to hack a way through a jungle of torts to find the relevant rule; once found, however, it is easier to apply, since it is at a lower level of abstraction.

A system of tort law which follows the style of a rule-based model operates with a multitude of causes of action, each of them geared to generic factual circumstances of a wrong and with the legal requirements for liability so exactly defined that it can be established by means of a simple subsumption, without any further evaluation being required. Such a particularistic approach to tort law also allows distinctions to be drawn when it comes to designating the consequences of responsibility in tort. Thus, the common law, for example, usually requires special damages, that is, proof of actual harm suffered, but under special circumstances the plaintiff is entitled to general damages even without proof of having suffered any loss.[8] In other circumstances, for example, in cases of misfeasance in public office or in defamation cases, even exemplary—that is, over-compensatory—damages may be awarded.

In sharp contrast to the plurality of the common law is the philosophy of the *Code civil*, whose short section on tort law begins with a general clause of rather emphatical formulation: 'Tout fait quelconque de l'homme, qui cause à autrui un dommage, oblige celui par la faute duquel il est arrivé, à le réparer'. This rule of Art 1382 *Code civil* is not quite as comprehensive as it appears because it only refers to intentional torts, as is made clear by the subsequent Art 1383. However, since the latter contains an identical rule for negligent acts, both can be combined to form a general clause for liability in tort.[9] As is well recognized, it does not follow from the broad and rousing formulation of Arts 1382 and 1383 *Code civil* that in France every loss caused through fault actually results in liability.[10] Rather, legal responsibility is subject to various qualifications, elaborated upon further below, which—

---

[6] Ronald Dworkin, 'The Model of Rules', (1967) 35 *University of Chicago LR* 14 ff = *Taking Rights Seriously* (1978), 15 ff. The comparison is somewhat strained because principles are thought to be subject to optimization which is obviously not the case with principle-style provisions like Arts 1382 and 1383 *Code civil*.

[7] cf John Antony Weir, in Pierre Catala and John Antony Weir, 'Delict and Torts: A Study in Parallel', (1965) 39 *Tulane LR* 701 ff, 781.

[8] cf Andrew S. Burrows, in John Frederic Clerk and William Henry Barber Lindsell (eds), *Clerk & Lindsell on Torts* (18th edn, 2000), para 29–04.

[9] Jacques Flour, Jean-Luc Albert, and Éric Savaux, *Les Obligations*, vol II—*Le fait juridique* (10th edn, 2003), nos. 110 ff.

[10] On this topic cf below, Section III.3(a).

and this is the crucial point—are not inherent in the application of these articles to the facts of an individual case but rather are extrinsic to them and must be sought in general legal principles or common-sense notions about what civil liability is about. In the course of legal history, precedent and jurisprudence have worked together to implant numerous distinctions into the French law of delict which are invisible on the face of the Code itself. In this sense Arts 1382 and 1383 *Code civil* do not supply the judge or attorney with rules capable of application but instead with a guiding principle, whose restriction by the operation of contrary principles is both possible in theory and common in practice.

2. Common Developments

(a) Roman Roots

In actual fact, the intricate differentiation of English tort law is not by any means based on insular peculiarities but is typical of case law systems, which derive their substantive rules from cases and therefore have a tendency to formulate them with regard to particular fact patterns.[11] The same traits, therefore, may be found in Roman law, with its menu of different delicts from *furtum* to *dolus*, and from the *lex Aquilia* to the *actio de deiectis vel effusis*.[12] However, even in the days of the Roman Empire the Aquilian action had developed a tendency to expand and to encroach upon the other heads of tort, developing at their expense. This tendency continued after re-discovery of the *Corpus iuris* in the twelfth century and culminated in the bold schemes of Natural law philosophers who worked to fuse the traditional learning into one general principle.[13]

(b) The General Clause of the Continent

Against this backdrop of legal development it does not come as a surprise that the general clause of Art 1382 *Code civil* and the following articles were by no means invented in 1804 but instead merely represent an adoption of the previous French customary law which, in turn, first and foremost in southern France, was greatly influenced by Roman law.[14] The leading authority on the French private law of the

[11] Pierre Catala and John Antony Weir, 'Delict and Torts: A Study in Parallel', (1963) 37 *Tulane LR* 573 ff, 605.

[12] Reinhard Zimmermann, *The Law of Obligations: Roman Foundations of the Civilian Tradition* (paperback edn, 1996), 922 ff.

[13] See generally Franz Wieacker, *A History of Private Law in Europe* (trans Tony Weir, 1995), 199; more specifically Reinhard Zimmermann, 'Christian Thomasius, the Reception of Roman Law and the History of the Lex Aquilia', in Margaret Hewett and Reinhard Zimmermann (eds), *Larva Legis Aquiliae* (2000), 49 ff, 60 ff.

[14] Catala and Weir, (1963) 37 *Tulane LR* 583; Henri and Léon Mazeaud and André Tunc, *Traité theorique et pratique de la responsabilité civile* (vol I, 6th edn, 1965), no. 36.

Ancien Régime was Jean Domat, who postulated the following principle in 1777, two decades prior to the French revolution:[15]

> Toutes les pertes et tous les dommages, qui peuvent arriver par le fait de quelque personne, soit imprudence, légèreté, ignorance de ce qu'on doit savoir, ou autres fautes semblables, si légères qu'elles puissent être, doivent être réparées par celui dont l'imprudence ou autre faute y a donné lieu.

To a large extent the development in Germany ran parallel to French law, as the practice of Roman law in Germany, the *usus modernus*, had already developed the Aquilian liability into a *de facto* general clause which dominated the field of delictual liability.[16] Therefore, it was not at all surprising that the editor appointed to draw up a preparatory draft of the part of the BGB containing the law of obligations, Franz Philipp von Kübel, expressly set himself the goal of making explicit what to a large extent was already common practice, that is, to embrace the general clause.[17] This approach was abandoned in the course of the legislative proceedings in favour of a compromise between the patchwork of specific torts and the solemn distance of a general clause.[18] The draftsmen of the so-called Second Commission, which rewrote substantial parts of the provisions of the First Draft of the BGB, did not intend to return to the old casuistic panoply of the ancient law of delict. Rather, they were worried about the uncertainty which a general clause would entail and tried to avoid these effects by specifying the scope of protection of the law of delict, in their own words, to 'provide the judge with a certain objective standard for his decision'.[19] The compromise achieved is the set of three 'small general clauses' contained in § 823 I, II and § 826 BGB.

(c) From Trespass to Negligence

Whilst on the Continent it was the legislators of the nineteenth century who took the step towards a general clause, this task was left to the courts in England, in accordance with the common law tradition. English tort law, in its regulatory style, corresponds to Roman law even though a wholesale reception has never taken place.[20] Much like the Aquilian action in the systems of the civil law tradition, in

---

[15] Jean Domat, *Les loix civiles dans leur ordre naturel* (1777), liv III, tit V; Mazeaud and Tunc (n 14), no. 36.

[16] Jan Schröder, 'Die zivilrechtliche Haftung für schuldhafte Schadenszufügung im deutschen Usus modernus', in Leticia Vacca (ed), *La responsabilità civile da atto illecito nella prospettiva storico-comparatistica* (1995), 144, 147 ff.

[17] Franz Philipp von Kübel, 'Unerlaubte Handlungen', in Werner Schubert (ed), *Die Vorlagen der Redaktoren für die erste Kommission zur Ausarbeitung eines Entwurfs eines Bürgerlichen Gesetzbuches, Recht der Schuldverhältnisse* (vol I, 1980), 659 ff.

[18] *Motive zu dem Entwurfe eines Bürgerlichen Gesetzbuchs* (vol II, 1896), 724.

[19] *Protokolle der Kommission für die zweite Lesung des Entwurfs eines bürgerlichen Gesetzbuchs* (vol II, 1898), 571.

[20] Zimmermann (n 12), 913; Catala and Weir, (1963) 37 *Tulane LR* 583; Frederick Pollock and William Maitland, *History of English Law before the Time of Edward I* (vol II, 2nd edn, 1968), 558.

England the writ of trespass, initially designed to safeguard the King's peace, and epitomized by the original requirement of conduct *vi et armis contra pacem regis*,[21] was expanded and supplemented by the so-called action of trespass on the case. Whereas trespass remained confined to directly caused infringements of a legally protected right,[22] the action upon the case was broader and also covered acts and omissions which only indirectly infringed a legally protected right.[23] It was the action upon the case which provided the basis for the development, over the course of centuries, of general negligence liability. By the early twentieth century Percy H. Winfield was able to remark that negligence was no longer 'simply a way of committing a tort; it *was* the tort'.[24]

Today, negligence liability outshines all of the other torts, and scholars have even raised the question whether in view of the dominance of negligence liability the numerous intentional torts warrant further care and attention.[25] Since its recognition in the early twentieth century, the tort of negligence has already assimilated a whole range of previously independent torts; 'its appetite to swallow up its satellites' is infamous.[26] Prominent examples of such victims are trespass to the person with its special forms of assault and battery, which nowadays has practically been merged into the tort of negligence,[27] or the erosion of the tort of deceit by negligence liability as a result of the rule in *Hedley Byrne*.[28] As a recent examination undertaken by David Howarth revealed, little would change in terms of practical outcomes if English law abandoned the menu of intentional torts and thereby openly and solemnly elevated the tort of negligence to a general clause.[29] After all, a tortfeasor sued in an English court cannot defend himself against a claim of negligence with the assertion that he acted intentionally, for then he is liable anyway.[30] Against this background, it is anything but contradictory to say that, 'actionable negligence can be a wilful act and the expression "wilful negligence" is well established'.[31]

To sum up, the contrast between the principled Continental law of delict and the casuistic common law seems to be exaggerated. In fact, the two systems could easily

[21] John G. Fleming, *The Law of Torts* (9th edn, 1998), 21; for more details cf David Ibbetson, *A Historical Introduction to the Law of Obligations* (1999), 39 ff.

[22] cf eg *Leame v Bray* (1803) 3 East's Term Reports, King's Bench 593, 599 ff; 102 ER 724, 726 ff; Fleming (n 21), 21.

[23] For details, see Ibbetson (n 21), 48 ff, 1159 ff; *Letang v Cooper* [1965] QB 232, 238 (Lord Denning).

[24] Percy Henry Winfield, 'The History of Negligence in the Law of Torts', (1926) 166 *LQR* 184 ff, 196.

[25] David Howarth, 'Is there a Future for the Intentional Torts?', in Peter Birks (ed), *The Classification of Obligations* (1997), 233 ff.

[26] Ibbetson (n 21), 200.   [27] Margaret M. Brazier, in Clerk and Lindsell (n 8), para 13–03.

[28] For details, see Howarth (n 25), 233, 242 ff.   [29] Howarth (n 25).

[30] Bramwell in *Emblen v Myers* (1860) 6 Hurlstone & Norman's Exchequer Reports 54, 59; 158 ER 23, 25.

[31] Christopher Walton, in Christopher Walton, Roger Cooper, Simon E. Wood, J. Charlesworth, and R. A. Percy (eds), *Charlesworth & Percy on Negligence* (10th edn, 2001), para 1–19.

be merged by simply abandoning the lush variety of intentional torts kept alive in England without much practical use.

3. The Relationship between Criminal Law and Tort

Just as the common law turns out to be more unitarian than widely thought, the Continental systems of delict are substantially more fragmented and casuistic than has generally been assumed. The key to a deeper understanding of the actual degree of generalization or, rather, differentiation, of the Continental legal regimes lies in their relationship to the criminal law and its enforcement through the criminal process.

(a) Continued Fragmentation of Criminal Law

A mere glance at the criminal codes of modern societies immediately reveals that they are a long way off a 'general clause' and show no signs of abstraction. Criminal law cannot but work with a multitude of wrongs because the sanctions imposed vary considerably from crime to crime and are never in line with an objective parameter like the value of the damage caused.[32] Instead, the graded system of criminal sanctions is sensitive both to the nature of the harm caused to the victim or to the public at large and to the degree of blame or guilt on the part of the offender.

(b) Criminal Law as a Blueprint for the Law of Delict?

For present purposes, the interesting question to ask is how criminal law and the private law of delict or torts interface in the various systems. As it turns out, the force of criminal law as an indicator of wrongful behaviour is much stronger in the rather general law of delict than in the common law of torts with its array of intentional wrongs.

Admittedly even English law allows the victim of a criminal wrong to claim damages from the offender-tortfeasor. The relevant tort of 'breach of statutory duty' supplements the statutory duty with a private duty to compensate the victim, but it does not integrate the statutory norm into the normative framework of the law of torts. Precisely for this reason, the English courts are reluctant to assume that a statute has a protective character and instead start from the reverse assumption that '[w]here an Act creates an obligation, and enforces the performance in specified manner . . . that performance cannot be enforced in any other manner'.[33]

---

[32] cf Geneviève Viney, *Introduction à la responsabilité* (2nd edn, 1995), no. 12.

[33] This quotation is from the leading case of *Lonrho Ltd v Shell Petroleum Co Ltd (No 2)* [1982] AC 173, 185 (Lord Diplock).

Since statutes introducing criminal offences by definition themselves stipulate a sanction, they fall entirely out of the field of application of the tort 'breach of statutory duty'.[34] On the other hand, the general duty of care enshrined in the tort of negligence is applied independently of legislation.[35] In this way, the large and ever-growing body of criminal law in the broad sense of the term is virtually off-limits and may not be used as a source of guidance in the development of new heads of liability.

The neglect of criminal law by tort law is not compensated for on the procedural level either, even although the English criminal courts since 1972 have had the authority not only to sentence the defendant to a criminal punishment but also additionally to order the payment of compensation for personal injury.[36] The award of damages simply runs with the criminal sanction and depends neither on whether the criminal offence can be regarded as a 'breach of statutory duty' in the sense of the relevant tort nor on the existence of any other private law tort.[37]

Not surprisingly, the legal systems going furthest in short-circuiting criminal law and tort law are those of France and its sister systems. The French law of delict—consistently and, so to speak, naturally—does not recognize a particular wrong of breach of a statute, or of a protective law. Nevertheless, a close link between the criminal code and the law of delict is provided by the French law of criminal procedure, which allows the victim of a wrong to join his damages claim to the criminal charge.[38] Prima facie the adhesive process appears merely to be a procedural institution,[39] but a comparative approach immediately reveals that the organization of French criminal procedure *de facto* supplements the casuistic wrongs of the French *Code pénal* with a civil duty to answer in damages. For all practical purposes, the crimes of the *Code pénal* are thereby converted into delicts. As such, they provide firm bases for the claims of victims.

This conclusion is supported by the fact that the victim cannot escape the dominance of criminal law by pursuing his damages claim in the course of civil litigation, because the civil court is barred from making any decision on delictual liability as long as the question of fault and the other requirements of the tortfeasor's responsibility have not been settled in criminal proceedings. The pre-emption of the issue by the criminal judge is succinctly expressed in the common saying that *le criminel tient le civil en l'état*.[40] The criminal verdict, once final in itself, is binding not only in the relationship between the prosecution and the

---

[34] W. V. Horton Rogers, *Winfield & Jolowicz on Tort* (16th edn, 2002), para 7.6; Tony Weir, *A Casebook on Tort* (10th edn, 2004), 178–9.

[35] *Morris v National Coal Board* [1963] 3 All ER 644, 647 ff; *Bux v Slough Metals Ltd* [1974] 1 All ER 262, 267 ff.

[36] Section 130 Powers of Criminal Courts (Sentencing) Act 2000; on this topic, see Basil Markesinis and Simon Deakin, *Tort Law* (5th edn, 2003), 50 ff.

[37] Rogers (n 34), para 1.13; Weir (n 34), 188.   [38] Viney (n 32), nos. 77 ff.

[39] Viney (n 32), nos. 131, 135.   [40] Viney (n 32), nos. 126 ff, 131.

offender but also in the relationship between the latter and all the victims of the act which was the subject of the criminal charge; the criminal verdict has an *autorité absolue de chose jugée*.[41]

It takes only a little exaggeration to conclude that the French general clause is both dissected and cushioned by the criminal law, in so far as it is for the criminal court to determine the scope of delictual liability whenever the behaviour complained of might give rise to public prosecution. Spanish law goes even further in this respect. Under Art 1092 *Código civil* the criminal law governs the issue of civil remedies wherever the behaviour complained of amounts to a crime or an administrative offence. This amounts to a 'dual-track' system of the law of delict, depending on whether the harmful conduct is a crime or not.[42]

(c) Conclusion

As a result, the Continental law of delict and English tort law are really much closer together than is commonly thought; there is no question of unbridgeable gaps and differences. On the one hand, within the common law, the wealth of nominate intentional torts is slowly fading away in the shadow of the ever-expanding tort of negligence, which amounts to a general clause for careless infringement of the rights of another. On the other hand, the experience of French law clearly confirms the view that a certain degree of concreteness, casuistry, and differentiation must not be renounced. This goal is accomplished by allowing the crimes of the penal code to be mirrored in the private law of torts. From this perspective, English law is framed even more generally than French or Spanish law because it dispenses with a strong link between criminal law and civil liability; the nominate tort of trespass to the person, for example, is framed considerably more generally than the special wrongs of the French *Code pénal* for the protection of physical interests of personality.

III. Scope of Protection

1. The Problem Defined

The substantive issue raised by the choice between a general clause and a multitude of different wrongs is the definition of the scope of protection which tort law provides. In order to see the choice more clearly it is helpful to imagine an individual seeking redress for damage suffered at the hands of another. Leaving aside

---

[41] Viney (n 32), nos. 134 ff.
[42] cf von Bar, *Common European Law of Torts*, vol I (n 4), no. 602.

problems of attribution, for example, of causation and of establishing whether the behaviour was wilful or careless, the question is whether any kind of interest is worthy of protection by the law of torts. As it turns out, the issue is more or less moot with regard to personal injury and damage to property because the underlying interests in one's life and limb as well as one's individual property rights clearly deserve protection against the tortious acts of another, and in fact they are so protected throughout the Western world. Once such interests have been infringed, full compensation of pecuniary losses and at least some compensation for non-pecuniary loss is provided.

There is no consensus, however, when one turns to pure economic loss and intangible personality rights. Pure economic loss is 'pure' in the sense that it is not the consequence of personal injury or damage to property, while 'intangible' personality rights form the counterpart of the 'physical' personality rights in the integrity and health of one's body. It is in these two areas that legal systems differ from each other, both with respect to the general approach adopted and with respect to the outcomes reached in particular cases.

2. Protected Interests versus General Clause

At first glance the several national systems of delict or tort law could not be more different. The general clause of the French *Code civil* requires *dommage* but not the infringement of a protected interest and thus seems to provide no basis at all for discriminating between economic loss consequential upon the infringement of bodily integrity and tangible property on the one hand and pure economic loss on the other. In this regard, a French commentator even remarked that '[l]e problème du dommage économique pur est difficile à traiter pour un juriste français, car celui-ci, a priori, ne connaît ni le problème, ni même l'expression!'[43]

At the other end of the spectrum, German law limits the scope of negligence liability to the infringement of protected interests which are specifically enumerated in the list of § 823 I BGB. The list is less interesting for what it contains than for its omissions, that is, purely economic interests in the patrimony as such, and intangible personality interests like honour, dignity, and privacy. Under the original scheme of delictual liability, as embodied in the Civil Code, these interests remained outside the scope of the general negligence liability of the 'small' general clause of § 823 I BGB and enjoyed protection only under § 823 II and § 826 BGB. These provisions require either the breach of a protective norm, that is, of a statutory duty meant to protect the victim (§ 823 II BGB), or the infliction of financial losses in a manner which is both intentional and *contra bonos mores* (§ 826 BGB).

---

[43] Christian Lapoyade Deschamps, 'La réparation due préjudice économique pur en droit français', in Efstathios K. Banakas (ed), *Civil Liability for Pure Economic Loss* (1996), 89.

The common law lacks a neat catalogue of protected rights and interests. Whereas systems like the German one set out with a definition of protected interests in order then to apply a 'general' duty of care, English law takes an alternative approach and limits the scope of the duty to take care to certain interests, thus integrating the issue of scope of protection into the concept of the duty to take care.[44] The crucial point, again, is that the individual actor is not obliged to prevent any kind of loss from being suffered by third parties but only to avoid causing certain types of harm; the protected interests are generally the same as in German law: personal integrity and tangible property.[45] Thus, the identical function of the German *Rechtsgüter* and the English duty of care is to define the scope of protection of delictual liability by discriminating against certain types of harm, that is, pure economic loss and infringements of intangible personality rights.[46]

With regard to the scope of protection, American tort law is more or less in line with its English counterpart. As Oliver Wendell Holmes explained in his decision in *Robins Dry Dock*, a victim who suffered pure economic loss and has no contractual relationship with the party responsible cannot sue in negligence even where the loss was consequential upon property damage to another party: 'The law does not spread its protection so far'.[47] Likewise, under the modern doctrine of product liability, a claim for compensation does not lie where the product damaged only itself and not 'other property' or the bodily integrity of a person, because the loss is thought to be 'purely economic'.[48] Thus, until today, 'the core of negligence law is about injury to persons and property'.[49] This limitation works to the detriment not only of pure economic losses but also of injuries to dignitary interests. The torts protecting these interests are 'disconnected from negligence law' and require intentional infliction of harm rather than mere carelessness.[50]

Upon first impression, the differences between jurisdictions operating with a general clause (France) and those limiting the scope of protection either through a list of protected interests (Germany) or limitations of the duty of care (England and the United States) appear fundamental. Whereas some legal systems discriminate against purely economic losses and dignitary injuries, others apparently do not. As economic and dignitary harms form important categories of losses which are of growing relevance today, it seems surprising that there is such a wide

---

[44] cf Frederick H. Lawson and Basil S. Markesinis, *Tortious Liability for Unintentional Harm in the Common Law and the Civil Law* (vol I, 1982), 99; as for South African law, see J. Neetling, J. M. Potgieter, and P. J. Visser, *Law of Delict* (3rd edn, 1999), 56.

[45] cf Fleming (n 21), 172 ff; Markesinis and Deakin (n 36), 95 ff.

[46] David Howarth, 'The General Conditions of Unlawfulness', in Arthur Hartkamp, Martijn Hesselink, Ewoud Hondius, Carla Joustra, Edgar du Perron, and Muriel Veldman (eds), *Towards a European Civil Code* (3rd edn, 2004), 607 ff.

[47] *Robins Dry Dock & Repair Comp v Flint et al* 275 US 303, 308 (1927) (Holmes J).

[48] *East River Steamship Corp v Transamerica Delaval, Inc* 476 US 858, 870 (1986); *Saratoga Fishing Co V J M Martinac & Co* 520 US 875, 879 (1997).

[49] Dan B. Dobbs, *The Law of Torts* (2000), 258.   [50] Dobbs (n 49), 1115.

gap between the legal systems of the Western world. This surprise grows when one considers that French and German law, though both based upon the civilian tradition, seem so radically different, whereas the common law seems to be very similar to German legal thought.

However, a deeper survey of the systems reveals that, in fact, the differences between the general clause and the protected interest approach are much smaller than at first appears, for the difference between the systems' 'façades' and their 'interiors' is considerable.[51] Whereas the restrictive systems have developed various institutions to take care of pure economic loss and dignitary harm, the general clause has been interpreted in ways that mirror the distinction between personal injury and damage to property on the one hand, and harm to economic and dignitary interests on the other. The following analysis will initially focus on pure economic loss and then turn to the problem of protection of intangible personality rights.

3. Pure Economic Loss

The scope of liability for pure economic loss certainly qualifies as the most intensely discussed subject-matter of comparative scholarship in the area of extra-contractual liability.[52] In spite of continuing ambiguities and differences of opinion, it is safe to say that these studies have revealed a high degree of convergence among the various legal systems in terms of the outcomes reached in particular cases.

(a) Restrictions on the Liability for Pure Economic Loss Employed by French Law

With regard to purely economic harm, the development of the French law of delict within the framework of the general clause of Arts 1382 and 1383 *Code civil* supports the conclusion that this kind of loss does not stand upon an equal footing with personal injury and damage to property. In France, too, important limits apply to liability for pure economic loss. However, French law achieves this result without explicitly distinguishing between different types of harm, but rather in indirect ways, namely by variations of the concept of *faute* as well as by restrictions within the concept of compensable damage. The requirement of *faute* has a different meaning depending upon whether injury to bodily integrity or tangible property

---

[51] This is essentially the upshot of the analysis of Mauro Bussani and Vernon Valentine Palmer, 'The Liability Regimes of Europe—Their Façades and Interiors', in *idem* (eds), *Pure Economic Loss in Europe* (2003), 120 ff.

[52] Willem van Boom, Helmut Koziol, and Christian A. Witting (eds), *Pure Economic Loss* (2004); Bussani and Palmer (n 51); Banakas (n 43); Gerhard Wagner, 'Grundstrukturen des Europäischen Deliktsrechts', in Reinhard Zimmermann (ed), *Grundstrukturen des Europäischen Deliktsrechts* (2003), 230 ff.

on the one hand, or pure economic loss on the other, is at stake. In relation to the former, more clear-cut interests, the potential tortfeasor is subjected to a general duty to take care, 'le devoir de prudence et de précautions': he must take all the safety measures required to avoid injury to the rights of third parties.[53] By contrast, in cases involving purely economic interests the examination of *faute* is organized differently. In this case, it is not to be taken for granted that the defendant tortfeasor should have taken appropriate precautions to avoid the harm complained of.[54] As in other Western countries, there is no automatic liability for the negligent or even intentional infliction of economic loss on competitors in the market-place. In this area, liability is contingent on breach of the rules of fair competition, on the conduct being 'déloyale', and upon its contravening the 'comportement d'un honnête commerçant'.[55] Only after this hurdle has been cleared does the duty to take care and to avoid the intentional infliction of harm apply.

Another important mechanism employed by French law to fence in liability for pure economic loss is, of course, the principle of *non-cumul des responsabilités*. Outside the scope of the EC Directive on products liability and its implementing legislation,[56] contract law takes priority over tort law in the sense that the existence of a contract between the parties precludes resort to Arts 1382 ff *Code civil*.[57] It is precisely because purely patrimonial interests are the main concern of contract law that tort law must pull back, as its cumulative application would undermine the bargain struck by the parties and the risk allocation provided by the default rules of contract law. To see why, imagine a case where a buyer contracts for a car coming with a two-year warranty covering engine defects. Two years and two days after delivery, a defect causes the car to break down on the road leading to the airport where the buyer wanted to depart for a business trip. As a result, he loses a deal worth €1 million. If purely economic interests were placed on the same footing as the rights to bodily integrity and tangible property, compensation could hardly be denied. However, not only the EC Directive[58] but also Anglo-American law would refuse to allow the compensation in tort of the economic loss described because otherwise, as the American Justice Blackmun has famously said, 'contract law would drown in a sea of tort'.[59] This danger may be avoided either by excluding pure economic loss from the scope of liability in negligence—or by a refusal to

---

[53] Geneviève Viney and Patrice Jourdain, *Les conditions de la responsabilité* (2nd edn, 1998), no. 477.

[54] Viney and Jourdain (n 53), no. 474.

[55] *Cour d'Appel de Paris*, 6.11.1989, D 1990, 564, 565 note Thouvenin.

[56] cf Art 1386–1 *Code civil*.

[57] Cass civ 11.1.1922, D 1922, I, 16; Cass req 21.1.1890, DC 1891, 380; Henri and Léon Mazeaud, Jean Mazeaud, and François Chabas, *Leçons de droit civil*, vol II/1: *Obligations, Théorie générale* (9th edn, 1998), no. 404.

[58] cf Art 9(b) of Council Directive 85/374/EEC of 25 July 1985 on the approximation of the laws, regulations and administrative provisions of the Member States concerning liability for defective products, [1985] OJ L210/29.

[59] *East River Steamship Corp v Transamerica Delaval, Inc* 476 US 858, 866 (1986) (Blackmun J).

apply tort law cumulatively to harm suffered within contractual relations.[60] In this sense, the principle of *non-cumul* is a necessary corollary of a general inclusion of pure economic loss in the protective perimeter of the law of torts,[61] as evidenced by the fact that the German and Anglo-American systems have no qualms about the cumulative application of tort law within contractual settings.[62]

Among the treatises on the law of obligations of the *Code civil*, the work of Starck *et al* stands out as the authors explicitly draw a distinction between harm to body and property—*dommages corporels et matériels*—on the one hand and the violation of non-physical interests of personality and pure economic loss—*dommages économiques ou morales*—on the other.[63] This differentiation has failed to win over the majority of French doctrinal thought.[64] It cannot be doubted, however, that it is the underlying rationale of the French law of delict as it is practised in the French courts and recorded in the relevant textbooks.

(b) Expansions of Liability for Pure Economic Loss in German and Anglo-American Law

On the other hand, both German and English law have found ways to allow for compensation of such losses even where they were caused negligently. The desire to expand negligence liability into this area explains why German courts have been prepared to stretch the concept of intention employed by § 826 BGB to its outer limits[65] and to develop a conceptual monster like the 'right of the established and operating commercial enterprise' (*Recht am eingerichteten und ausgeübten Gewerbebetrieb*).[66] Parliament has not been idle either, as it has introduced a general clause into the statute book with respect to the area of unfair competition back in 1909,[67] and in recent years it has been increasingly active in creating new statutory bases for liability for patrimonial losses, as the field of securities regulation shows most clearly.[68] In this respect, the German approach seems very much in line with the American one where 'the problem [of liability for pure economic loss]

---

[60] In the area of delictual products liability the French courts generously allowed contractual claims to be brought directly against the manufacturer by the buyer and even by successors in title: Cass civ 1re, 9.10.1979, Bull civ I, No. 241, p 192 = Gaz Pal 1980, 1, 249 note Planqueel.

[61] Tony Weir, 'Complex Liabilities', in Tunc (n 1), ch 12 (1976), nos. 54 and 55.

[62] Germany: RGZ 85, 185, 186; England: *Esso Petroleum Co Ltd v Mardon* [1976] QB 801, 819.

[63] Boris Starck, Henri Roland, and Laurent Boyer, *Obligations*, vol I: *Responsabilité délictuelle* (5th edn, 1996), nos. 69 ff, 80, 210 ff, 305 ff.

[64] cf Michel Puech, *L'illicéité dans la responsabilité civile extracontractuelle* (1973), nos. 324 ff. One reason for rejecting the distinction advocated by Starck seems to be that it is linked to and embedded in a theory of strict liability for personal injury and damage to property (*théorie de la garantie*; Starck et al (n 63), nos. 61 ff).

[65] Gerhard Wagner, in *Münchener Kommentar zum BGB* (vol V, 4th edn, 2004), § 826, no. 19 ff.

[66] *Münchener Kommentar*/Wagner § 823, no. 179 ff.

[67] cf Section 1 of the Unfair Competition Act ('Gesetz gegen den unlauteren Wettbewerb': UWG) of 1909; now § 3 UWG.

[68] *Münchener Kommentar*/Wagner § 826 no. 62 ff.

remains a backwater within the discourse of American tort law', as Gary Schwarz has observed.[69] The reason for this neglect may be that the most important cases have been taken care of by regulatory law, which brought with it statutory heads of liability. The most prominent example is, of course, securities fraud under Rule 10b–5 of the SEC Regulations.[70]

However, it is not the law of delict but contract law that has carried the main burden of expanding liability for pure economic loss. This drift towards contractual solutions was fostered by concurrent developments, namely that the German BGB of 1900 generally acknowledged contracts in favour of third parties (§ 328 ff BGB) and that German legal doctrine adopted the concept of contractual duties to protect life, limb, and property (*Schutzpflichten*—protective duties) which in fact create a mirror image within the domain of contract law of the established delictual duties to take care.[71] A combination of the principles underlying both institutions is the so-called 'contract with protective effect vis-à-vis third parties' (*Vertrag mit Schutzwirkung zugunsten Dritter*), which allows victims who have not been in privity with the negligent party to claim damages in contract from what would otherwise be an ordinary tortfeasor.[72] As the protective scope of contract law is not limited to bodily integrity and tangible property, the contract with protective effect for third parties allows for the compensation of pure economic loss. In other cases, the same function is maintained by the concept of *culpa in contrahendo*, which allowed contractual liability to blossom in areas where nobody had previously discerned anything like a contract.[73]

In England, liability for pure economic loss also saw considerable expansions, albeit only in the area of tort law itself and not under the guise of contractual—or, rather, quasi-contractual—liability. A major step in this direction was the landmark decision in *Hedley Byrne* where the House of Lords required a relationship of close proximity between the parties as a precondition for negligence liability for pure economic loss, namely a relationship 'equivalent to contract . . . in which, but for the absence of consideration, there would be a contract'.[74] Fourteen years later the famous decision in *Anns v Merton London Borough Council* came closest to

---

[69] Gary T. Schwarz, 'American Tort Law and the Economic Loss Rule', in Bussani and Palmer (n 51), 94, 96.

[70] § 10(b) of the Securities Exchange Act, 15 USCS § 78j (b), and SEC Rule 10b–5, 17 Code of Federal Regulations § 240.10b–5; cf *Superintendent of Insurance of New York v Bankers Life & Casualty Co et al* 404 US 6 (1971); for more details, see Thomas Lee Hazen, *The Law of Securities Regulation* (2002), 566 ff.

[71] cf § 241 II BGB; Günter H. Roth, in *Münchener Kommentar zum BGB* (vol 2a, 4th edn, 2003), § 241 no. 90 ff.

[72] Peter Gottwald, in *Münchener Kommentar zum BGB* (vol 2a, 4th edn, 2003), § 328 no. 96 ff; for a brief account in English, see Mathias Reimann in Bussani and Palmer (n 51), 396 ff.

[73] cf § 311 II BGB; Volker Emmerich, in *Münchener Kommentar zum BGB* (vol 2a, 4th edn, 2003), § 311 no. 50 ff; for a brief account in English, see Mathias Reimann, in Bussani and Palmer (n 51), 354 ff.

[74] *Hedley Byrne & Co Ltd v Heller & Partners Ltd* [1964] AC 465, 528 ff (Lord Devlin).

placing the patrimony as such on an equal footing with the traditional interests in bodily integrity and tangible property.[75] In his speech, Lord Wilberforce was not far from recognizing a general duty of care, which was not restricted to the protection of life, limb, and property.[76] The window flung open by *Anns* was later closed again by the equally seminal decision of *Murphy v Brentwood District Council*,[77] where the court once again insisted upon the differentiation of personal injury and damage to property on the one hand and pure economic loss on the other.[78] Since *Murphy*, it is clear again that where personal injury or damage to property is at stake, the broad neighbour principle as expounded in *Donoghue v Stevenson* is still good law. It excludes only the most capricious types of harm from the protective scope of the duty of care as it is enough for liability to attach that 'the plaintiff chances to be (out of the whole world) the person with whom the defendant collided or who purchased the offending ginger beer'.[79] With pure economic loss, matters are completely different as the mere foreseeability of the loss is not nearly enough to give rise to a duty to take care. Instead, protection of purely economic interests is to be established on a case-by-case basis, starting from the 'close proximity' requirement outlined in *Hedley Byrne*.[80]

From a comparative point of view it is notable that the test established in *Hedley Byrne* is hardly distinguishable from the requirements set up in German law for liability in *culpa in contrahendo* or for an implicit contract warranting the truthfulness of the information provided by a bank on the creditworthiness of a customer.[81] It is not in substance that German and English law differ but merely in categorization and classification. The interdependence captured in Markesinis's dictum: 'an expanding tort law—the price of a rigid contract law'[82] quite obviously cuts in the other direction as well: 'an expanding contract law—the price of a rigid tort law'. In any event, the partial 'opening of the floodgates' by the English and the German courts, whether orchestrated by tort or contract law, is a strong piece of evidence for the view that a full exclusion of negligence liability for pure economic loss simply goes too far.

---

[75] *Anns v Merton London Borough Council* [1978] AC 728

[76] *Anns v Merton London Borough Council* [1978] AC 728, 751 ff (Lord Wilberforce).

[77] Dale Hutchinson and Reinhard Zimmermann, 'Murphy's Law—Die Ersatzfähigkeit reiner Vermögensschäden innerhalb des 'negligence'-Tatbestands nach englischem Recht', (1995) 94 *Zeitschrift für Vergleichende Rechtswissenschaft* 42 ff.

[78] *Murphy v Brentwood District Council* [1991] 1 AC 398, 457 ff (Lord Mackay), 460 ff (Lord Keith).

[79] *Caparo Industries Plc v Dickman* [1989] QB 653, 686 (Bingham LJ).

[80] *Murphy v Brentwood District Council* [1991] 1 AC 398, 461; Markesinis and Deakin (n 36), 112 ff.

[81] cf the German decision BGH [2003] *Neue Juristische Wochenschrift* 1521, 1523 ff. This head of contractual liability was created by case law and flies in the face of § 675 II BGB (no liability for advice or recommendation).

[82] See the title of Markesinis's article in (1987) 103 *LQR* 354.

(c) Conclusion

What is the upshot of the preceding analysis? It would certainly be an exaggeration
to deny differences, even at the substantive level, between those systems which limit
the protective perimeter of negligence liability to personal injury and damage to
property, and those which work on the basis of a general clause which treats all
kinds of harm equally. It is, however, safe to contend that there is much less
diversity in outcomes than one would expect when looking at the several systems
of tort law or delict in the abstract and in isolation. Major areas where liability for
purely economic loss is particularly problematic—unfair competition and contractual relationships—reveal a high degree of convergence, even though the ways
and means employed by the several systems to reach the agreed outcomes are
different. A similar trend towards convergence may be found in other contexts. It
seems that the major difference between legal systems operating on the basis of a
protected interest approach and those embracing the general clause is the treatment of pure economic loss of primary victims suffered outside contractual or
quasi-contractual relationships. Pertinent examples are the power-failure cases, a
class of case whose attractiveness for academics stands in reverse proportion to
its practical importance. It is here that French law is effectively more generous
than German and English law in accepting the claim of the owner of a business
operation suffering loss due to the electricity being cut off.[83]

4. Dignitary Injuries

Roughly the same analysis also applies in the area of infringements of intangible
personality rights like defamation and intrusions upon the right of privacy. The
main particularity in comparison to pure economic loss is the fact that the protective perimeter of tort law is impossible to define in this area without taking into
account the guarantees of free speech and freedom of the press which feature in all
constitutions and bills of rights. Although the primary addressees of fundamental
rights such as freedom of speech are governments and their servants, and not
citizens, both the European Court of Human Rights and national supreme courts
have maintained the view that the civil judge hearing a claim sounding in tort or
delict must weigh the competing constitutionally protected interests, that is, freedom of speech and personal honour or the right of privacy.[84] In this sense, the

---

[83] England: *Spartan Steel & Alloys Ltd v Martin & Co (Contractors) Ltd* [1973] 1 QB 27, 38 ff;
Germany: BGHZ 29, 65, 67 ff; France: Cass civ 2e 8.3.1970, D 1970, *sommaires*, 203; see also the
discussions of 1, 2, and 3 in Bussani and Palmer (n 51), 171—221.

[84] For examples see European Court of Human Rights: *von Hannover v Germany* (2005) 40 EHRR 1
[57] with further references; House of Lords: *Campbell v MGN Ltd* [2004] 2 AC 457, 465, 485 ff; France:
TGI Paris, 21.12.1994 D 1995, 511; Germany: Federal Constitutional Court, BVerfGE 101, 361, 388 ff.

European Convention of Human Rights as well as the bill-of-rights sections of Western constitutions certainly have a 'horizontal effect'; even if they are not binding upon fellow citizens, they bind a judge exercising the judicial powers of the state.[85] By means of the court's weighing the competing interests, the protective perimeter of tort law is defined with respect to the particular case at hand. In 2004, the European Court of Human Rights, in a decision involving Caroline of Hannover (formerly Caroline of Monaco), decided to participate in this weighing exercise in order to lecture the German courts about how to strike the balance between the freedom of the press and the personality rights of celebrities and to urge them to abandon the concept of an all-purpose public figure (*absolute Personen der Zeitgeschichte*).[86]

The open-textured nature of the rights of privacy and of personal honour has been explicitly acknowledged in Germany where the concept of a *Rahmenrecht* (framework right) was coined to indicate that intangible personality rights do not enjoy the same level of general protection as the physical aspects of the person— life, body, health, freedom of movement. The codified German law of delict, of course, knows nothing of a general right of personality. It was only developed in the late 1950s and 1960s by the courts who regarded it as necessary in order to bring the law of delict in line with the requirements of the *Grundgesetz* (Basic Law) of 1949. In doing so, the German judges followed the example of their American brethren who, half a century earlier, did not hesitate to introduce the right of privacy in the face of a burgeoning tabloid press which Warren and Brandeis, in their seminal article, thought to be 'overstepping in every direction the obvious bounds of propriety and of decency' by disseminating gossip 'with industry as well as effrontery'.[87] In the United States, the 'constitutionalization' of tort law in the area of dignitary injuries was ushered in later, with the landmark case of *New York Times Co v Sullivan* of 1964 serving as the watershed.[88]

French law explicitly recognizes the *droit à la vie privé* in Art 9 *Code civil*, and, as a matter of course, grants protection within the framework of the general clause. But again, much like purely patrimonial interests, the intangible interests in one's personality do not command overall protection and thus are not protected by a general duty on others to take reasonable care to avoid infringements. On the contrary, establishing liability for infringement of the *droit à l'image* requires a

---

[85] The issue of 'horizontal effect' of fundamental rights is a major focus of German scholarly debate; see Claus-Wilhelm Canaris, *Grundrechte und Privatrecht—Eine Zwischenbilanz* (1999); *Münchener Kommentar/Wagner* Vor § 823 no. 57 ff.

[86] European Court of Human Rights in: *von Hannover v Germany* (2005) 40 EHRR 1; for details, see Gerhard Wagner, 'Country Report Germany', in Helmut Koziol (ed), *Protection of Personality Rights against Invasions by Mass Media* (2005), no. 43 ff.

[87] Samuel D. Warren and Louis D. Brandeis, 'The Right to Privacy', (1890) 4 *Harvard LR* 193 ff, 196; the current state of privacy law is expounded in Dobbs (n 49), 1197 ff.

[88] *New York Times Co v Sullivan* 376 US 254 (1964); for more details and subsequent developments, see Dobbs (n 49), 1169 ff.

balancing of the interests of the victim with the interests of the press protected under Art 10 ECHR.[89] Within this framework, the *Cour de cassation* has developed the principle that a photograph of a person may be published without his consent provided that the person was involved in some matter of public interest and that the publication does not infringe human dignity.[90] Likewise, the mere fact that a newspaper published an article containing information that is likely severely to damage the reputation of another is not sufficient to trigger the general duty to avoid this effect. Rather, the imposition of such a duty is subject to the requirement that the criticism is abusive, that is, amounts to *critique malveillante*.[91]

In the area of intangible personality interests, English law occupies a special position as, even today, it does not recognize a generic 'right of privacy'.[92] Intangible interests in personal integrity are protected only within the framework of specific torts, namely the defamatory wrongs of 'slander' and 'libel',[93] unless such interests can be brought within the protective scope of torts from other branches of the law, such as 'nuisance', 'breach of confidence', or 'passing off'.[94] It is not yet entirely clear what impact the Human Rights Act 1998, which gives effect to the European Convention on Human Rights in domestic English law, will have upon this state of affairs. From the latest decisions of English courts addressing this issue, it appears most likely that the legal landscape will stay roughly the same: a general right of privacy will continue to be rejected and instead the traditional heads of tort will be incrementally expanded in order to provide intangible personality interests with the protection they must receive in accordance with the European Convention on Human Rights.[95] This rather timid approach grows out of the perception that acknowledgement of a right of privacy would introduce a new 'blockbuster tort'[96] into the English legal system which has—of course—little to commend itself. From a comparative perspective, this view overestimates the impact and force which the recognition of the right of privacy would have and, at the same time, underestimates the uncertainty introduced into the English law of torts by the current theory, which treats the right of privacy as a benchmark for the evaluation of outcomes reached under established heads of liability. In practice, the

---

[89] Cass Civ 1re, 20.2.2001, D 2001, 1199 = Gaz Pal 2002, 641 ff; Cass Civ 2e, 24.4.2003, D 2003, Informations Rapides 1411; in essence, the balancing exercise is not different from the one carried out by German courts in cases involving limited purpose public figures; cf eg BVerfGE 35, 202, 224 ff, and Wagner (n 86), no. 35 ff.

[90] See previous note.

[91] Paris 14.3.1988, D 1988, Informations Rapides 104; Starck *et al* (n 63), no. 210; Philippe Le Tourneau, *Droit de la responsabilité et des contrats* (2004/5), no. 6769.

[92] Most recently *Campbell v MGN Ltd* [2004] 2 AC 457, 464; cf also *Wainwright v Home Office* [2004] 2 AC 406, 418 ff.

[93] On this topic, see Markesinis and Deakin (n 36), 648 ff; Patrick Milmo and Horton Rogers, *Gatley on Libel and Slander* (10th edn, 2004), ch 23.

[94] *Campbell v MGN Ltd* [2004] 2 AC 457, 465, 471.   [95] Ibid.

[96] *Wainwright v Home Office* [2002] QB 1334, 1351 (Mummery LJ).

outcomes reached by applying torts like breach of confidence in their traditional meaning are not really determinative in any given case but must be re-evaluated in light of Art 8 of the European Convention on Human Rights. This two-tiered approach keeps the blockbuster in the shadows but does nothing to strip it of its force. Would it not be better, then, to acknowledge the existence of a general right of personality, protected by a whole variety of torts, and to relegate invasion of privacy to the ranks of a specific wrong designed to protect the general right, much like the traditional heads of liability such as defamation and breach of confidence?[97]

IV. Liability for Fault

1. Liability for Moral Wrongdoing or Attribution of Risks?

In archaic law, commission of a delict invariably triggered the right to retribution in kind by the injured party or his family. In the course of development the *lex talionis* was replaced by a two-tiered approach to wrongdoing which combined the imposition of criminal sanctions by the government with a private action for compensation to be enforced by the victim.[98] Today, throughout the world, two major conceptions of the law of delict or tort may be distinguished, depending on whether liability in tort is thought to be a close sibling of criminal liability, aimed at deterrence of wrongful behaviour, or whether the law of delict is seen in parallel with the institutions of insurance and social security, as one of three systems which are primarily concerned with the compensation of victims. Although the schism goes to the normative foundations of the field, it is less troubling than one might expect because the choice between deterrence and compensation does not allow for a simple answer anyway. Rather, in every jurisdiction, there are two hearts of tort law—deterrence and compensation—beating simultaneously, albeit with varying strengths.

The concept of fault is one of the major battlegrounds where the rival perceptions of tort law lead to differing interpretations and results. The crucial issue here is whether fault requires a finding of personal blameworthiness, in the sense that the tortfeasor behaved in a morally reprehensible way, or whether fault in the area of the private law of delict or tort simply requires the violation of some legal

---

[97] cf Jonathan Morgan, 'Privacy Torts: Out with the Old, Out with the New', (2004) 120 *LQR* 393 ff, 397.

[98] Zimmermann (n 12), 969 ff.

standard, which itself may have been defined with respect to a whole set of factors, including the relative abilities of the parties to bear the risk of loss. It is impossible to give a short and direct answer to this question. In the common law world, the deterrence function of tort law has always been acknowledged more clearly than elsewhere but the leading textbook on the American law of torts still postulates somewhat emphatically that 'tort liability is not a criminal conviction or a badge of infamy'.[99] At the other end of the spectrum, French law certainly has gone furthest in its orientation towards the goal of compensation, but even in France scholars are divided, as is evidenced by the assertion in one of the popular treatises that 'il peut exister une responsabilité sans faute; mais il n'y a pas de faute sans faute'.[100]

2. Theory: The Dominance of the Objective Standard of Care

Upon a superficial examination of the major European legal systems the objective conception of the standard of care dominates everywhere and this is by no means a recent development. Roman law, as laid out in the *Corpus iuris*, saw *negligentia* as the reverse of *diligentia* and determined the latter with regard to the standard of the *diligens paterfamilias*.[101] This was also the point of view of the German pandectists on the eve of codification[102] and was then adopted by the drafters of the code and resulted in what is now § 276 II BGB.[103] The objective conception of fault also prevails in the French doctrine of *faute civile*, from which the so-called 'élement moral' has deliberately been purged in favour of an appreciation *in abstracto*.[104] The benchmark for the general legal duty to take care is the conduct of a ficticious reference person, the *bon père de famille*, not the actual person whose behaviour is evaluated.[105] Upon crossing the Channel, the continental *diligens paterfamilias* becomes the English 'reasonable man' who—in the age of anti-discrimination—has turned into the 'reasonable person':[106] 'Negligence is the omission to do something which a reasonable man, guided upon those considerations which ordinarily regulate the conduct of human affairs, would do, or doing something which a prudent and reasonable man would not do'.[107] It is thought that negligence has

---

[99] Dobbs (n 49), 287.

[100] François Terré, Phlippe Simler, and Yves Lequette, *Droit civil—Les obligations* (8th edn, 2002), no. 731.

[101] cf Zimmermann (n 12), 1008 f with n 69.

[102] Bernhard Windscheid and Theodor Kipp, *Lehrbuch des Pandektenrechts* (vol I, 9th edn, 1906), § 101, 3 with n 8.

[103] *Motive zu dem Entwurfe eines Bürgerlichen Gesetzbuchs* (vol I, 1896), 279; Protokolle (n 19), 604.

[104] Viney and Jourdain (n 53), no. 444–1; Mazeaud and Tunc (n 14), no. 390.

[105] Le Tourneau (n 91), nos. 6706, 6763; Mazeaud and Tunc (n 14), no. 417.

[106] Dugdale in Clerk and Lindsell (n 8), para 7–159; Rogers (n 34), para 5.52.

[107] *Blyth v Birmingham Waterworks Co* (1856) 11 Ex 781, 784 (Alderson B).

nothing to do with personal blameworthiness[108] but instead 'eliminates the personal equation and is independent of the idiosyncrasies of the particular person whose conduct is in question'.[109] The same is true with respect to the tort systems of the United States where the objective reasonable person standard has been famously proclaimed and justified by Oliver Wendell Holmes:[110]

The standards of the law are standards of general application. . . . [W]hen men live together in society, a certain average of conduct, a sacrifice of individual peculiarities going beyond a certain point, is necessary to the general welfare. If, for instance, a man is born hasty and awkward, is always having accidents and hurting himself or his neighbors, no doubt his congenital defects will be allowed for in the courts of Heaven, but his slips are no less troublesome to his neighbors than if they sprang from guilty neglect. His neighbors accordingly require him, at his proper peril to come up to their standard, and the courts which they establish decline to take his personal equation into account.

In addition to this eloquent defence of the objective standard,[111] American law has greatly contributed to the development of the negligence concept by giving it an economically inspired meaning. Under the formula developed by the eminent judge Learned Hand, negligence is economically unsound behaviour in the sense that the tortfeasor fails to take precautions that would have cost less than the injuries thereby avoided.[112] In retrospect, the *United States v Caroll Towing* decision of the late 1940s stands out as the starting-point for what has now become the intellectually fertile ground of economic analysis of tort law.[113]

Only a small number of jurisdictions, particularly Austria, defected from the club of the objectivists to form the camp of subjectivists which require personal blameworthiness for a finding of delictual liability.[114] Under this view, the benchmark for the standard of care is not the average behaviour of a reasonable person but the reasonable behaviour of the individual tortfeasor himself. Where the tortfeasor is simply not capable of living up to the standard of the reasonable person he will readily be excused because his behaviour is not blameworthy. The Principles of European Tort Law try to achieve a compromise between the objective majority approach and its subjective rival: Art 4:102(1) PETL employs the standard of the

---

[108] *Nettleship v Weston* [1971] 2 QB 691, 709 ff (Megaw LJ).

[109] *Glasgow Corp v Muir* 1943 SC (HL) 3, 10 (Lord Macmillan).

[110] Oliver Wendell Holmes, *The Common Law* (1881/1911), 108.

[111] For a modern account, see Richard A. Epstein, *Torts* (1999), 111 ff.

[112] Learned Hand J, in *United States v Caroll Towing Co* 159 F2d 169, 173 (1947): 'Possibly it serves to bring this notion into relief to state it in algebraic terms: if the probability be called P; the injury, L; and the burden, B; liability depends upon whether B is less than L multiplied by P: i.e., whether B is less than PL.'

[113] Richard A. Posner, 'A Theory of Negligence', (1972) 1 *Journal of Legal Studies* 28 ff; cf also *idem*, *Economic Analysis of Law* (6th edn, 2003), 167 ff.

[114] See Helmut Koziol, *Österreichisches Haftpflichtrecht* (vol I, 3rd edn, 1997), nos. 5/35 ff; *idem*, 'Objektivierung des Fahrlässigkeitsmaßstabes im Schadensersatzrecht?', (1996) 196 *Archiv für die civilistische Praxis* 593 ff.

reasonable person but Art 4:102(2) adds that 'the above standard may be adjusted when due to age, mental or physical disability or due to extraordinary circumstances the person cannot be expected to conform to it'.[115]

3. Reality: An Array of Mixed Systems

In fact, the situation is much more complex than the juxtaposition of objective and subjective standards suggests. At the outset, it is important not to confuse 'abstraction' from the idiosyncrasies of the individual tortfeasor with neglect of the factual circumstances of the situation in which the tortfeasor found himself when he caused the injury. In all jurisdictions adhering to the objective standard it is unanimously accepted that the *bon père de famille* or the reasonable person, respectively, must be put into the shoes of the tortfeasor in the particular historical situation *ex ante*.[116] Dangers that would have been invisible to a reasonable person in the situation of the tortfeasor before the accident occurred do not require precautionary measures, and measures of safety which were not (yet) available in the historical situation must be likewise ignored. In addition, the idiosyncratic properties of the historic situation—that may have been an emergency or even a catastrophe—have to be considered.[117] A rescue team of doctors will be held to one standard on an 'ordinary' day and to a different one on a day such as September 11, 2001.

Furthermore, the unanimous acceptance of the objective standard conceals the fact that there is much more subjectivity allowed than one would expect. In England,[118] on the one hand the courts have not hesitated to hold a learner-driver liable for the harm caused to her driving instructor[119] and to enter judgment against a driver who had suffered a heart attack at the wheel,[120] but on the other hand the Court of Appeal applied a clearly subjective standard of negligence in the *Weetabix* case.[121] There, a 38-ton lorry drove straight ahead on a sharp curve, crashed into and completely destroyed the plaintiff's shop in a Staffordshire village. The otherwise inexplicable behaviour of the driver had been caused by his having suffered a hypoglycaemic shock which, although it did not make him lose consciousness, made it impossible for him both to realize his own condition and to

---

[115] European Group on Tort Law (n 5), 75 ff.

[116] Le Tourneau (n 91), no. 6707; Dugdale (n 106), para 7–162; Hein Kötz and Gerhard Wagner, *Deliktsrecht* (10th edn, 2006), nn 113, 119; Josef Esser and Eike Schmidt, *Schuldrecht* (vol I /2, 8th edn, 2000), 82 ff (§ 26 II).

[117] Dobbs (n 49), 280 ff.   [118] For a historical account, see Ibbetson (n 21), 196 ff.

[119] *Nettleship v Weston* [1971] 2 QB 691; Markesinis and Deakin (n 36), 169 ff; Dugdale (n 106), para 7–163.

[120] *Roberts v Ramsbottom* [1980] 1 WLR 823, 832 (Neill J).

[121] *Mansfield v Weetabix* [1998] 1 WLR 1263.

react appropriately to the driving situation. Even though he had certainly breached the objective standard of negligence, the Court exonerated the driver by measuring his conduct against that of a reasonable person ignorant of his hazardous state of health: 'To apply an objective standard in a way that did not take account of [the driver's] condition would be to impose strict liability. But that is not the law'.[122]

In the various courts of the United States, it is well accepted that doctors are held to a different standard from the one applied to ordinary people, and that there are 'semi-subjective components', like additional knowledge, skill, and capability that the potential tortfeasor is bound to make use of in order to fend off liability.[123] At the other end of the spectrum, and contrary to the famous dictum of Holmes cited above, the substandard physical characteristics of the actor are in fact relevant to the negligence test, so that, for example, the behaviour of disabled persons is not to be measured against the behaviour of able-bodied people but compared to the performance of a reasonable person suffering from the same disability.[124] The same is true for children.[125] It is only where the handicap is of mental or psychological nature that American law insists on the objective standard of the reasonable person in a state of reasonable health.[126]

In Germany, likewise, the standard of care takes the personal characteristics of the acting party into account in a variety of ways. The BGB expressly places children under the age of 7 and persons in a state of unconsciousness or mental illness in a privileged position (§§ 827 and 828 I BGB), and makes the liability of minors above the age of 7 contingent upon proof of capacity in every single case (§ 828 II, III BGB). Where the tortfeasor is of above-average knowledge and abilities he must apply them in order to escape liability.[127] On the other hand, the driver of a motor vehicle is not liable for having run over an innocent bystander if he suffered a heart attack at the steering wheel and lost consciousness as a result.[128]

Among the major legal systems French law has clearly implemented the objective standard of care most rigorously, although scholars, even in france, have always remained divided.[129] In any event 1968 saw a triumph of the objectivists as the French legislature virtually adopted their approach in Art 489 *al* 2 *Code civil*, which imposes liability upon persons suffering from a mental disability: 'Celui qui a causé un dommage à atrui alors qu'il était sous l'empire d'un trouble mental, n'en pas moins obligé à réparation'.

In 1984 the *Cour de cassation* did not hesitate to apply the rationale of this provision to children and minors as well.[130] In the *arrêt Lemaire*, it was held that

---

[122] *Mansfield v Weetabix* [1998] 1 WLR 1263, 1268 (Leggatt LJ); for a similar American decision see *Hammontree v Jenner* (1971) 97 California Reporter 739.

[123] Dobbs (n 49), 280.   [124] Ibid 281 ff.   [125] Ibid 293 ff.   [126] Ibid 284 ff.

[127] BGH 1987 *Neue Juristische Wochenschrift* 1487, 1480; Erwin Deutsch, *Allgemeines Haftungsrecht* (2nd edn, 1996), no. 397 ff.

[128] BGHZ 23, 90, 92 ff.   [129] Le Tourneau (n 91), no. 6706.

[130] Cass ass plén 9.5.1984, D 1984, I, 525.

the defence of contributory negligence raised against a victim under the age of majority did not require that 'le mineur était capable de discerner les conséquences de son acte'.[131]

4. The Substantive Issues

From a comparative perspective it is evident that the rival schools of thought are much closer together than their respective adherents tend to think. In particular, there is unanimity across the jurisdictions that above-average information, intelligence, and skills will be taken into account in setting the standard of care. The differences concern the treatment of those tortfeasors who are not able to live up to the objective standard of care because they lack either the relevant information or the required skills or intelligence. With regard to most legal systems it is not easy to identify a principle governing this area of tort law; the US courts, for example, draw a difference between physical and mental handicaps.[132]

The many difficulties and ambiguities with defining normative standards of care stem from practical problems of the administration of justice. In theory, there is no point denying that a subjective standard should prevail because it makes no sense to impose duties which the addressee is incapable of performing and to ignore the fact that the costs of precautions vary from one actor to another.[133] However, a purely subjective standard would be unworkable in practice because 'quel juge pourrait sonder les reins et les cœurs?'[134] If one really wanted to be completely fair to the tortfeasor, there would be no rational reason why his difficult childhood, his disposition towards foolish conduct, or his generally aggressive and inconsiderate nature should not also be taken into account. In this way, the standard of care would cease to be a standard as 'tout comprendre c'est tout pardonner'.[135]

In order to avoid both the conceptual and the practical difficulties just described, the mixed solutions adopted by modern systems of tort law might be consolidated on the basis of a distinction between those personality traits that the individual is incapable of influencing and those which are generally within the control of the potential tortfeasor. Age and physical disabilities, like a missing joint or paraplegia, should be taken into account, because they cannot be made up by the defendant in order to escape liability, because the costs of verification are low and because, in many cases, the would-be victim will be able to discern the reduced capabilities of

---

[131] Cass ass plén, 9.5.1984, D 1984, I, 525; see also the critique of Viney and Jourdain (n 53), nos. 433–1, 593–1.

[132] Above Section, IV.3, especially text to nos. 124–6.

[133] Posner, *Economic Analysis of Law* (n 113), 171; Wagner (n 52), 265 ff.

[134] Le Tourneau (n 91), no. 6706.

[135] Philipp Heck, *Grundriß des Schuldrechts* (1929), 78 (§ 26); in the same vein Tony Honoré, *Responsibility and Fault* (1999), 34.

the other party and be able to adjust his own precautions accordingly.[136] Unfavourable character traits, like a strong taste for violence, a lack of a sense of responsibility, indifference towards the interest of others and the like, are at the other end of the spectrum. If such circumstances were allowed to exonerate the tortfeasor it would spell the end of fault-based liability as every tortfeasor would be tempted to plead his bad character as a defence. Mental illness is a category squarely on the borderline between the one category and the other. Where the illness may be diagnosed by medical experts with a sufficient degree of reliability it is hard to see any reason why it should not be treated like any other adverse medical condition capable of exonerating the tortfeasor. Of course, one would always have to keep in mind that a person knowing of his reduced capacity to take care must adapt his behaviour accordingly and avoid becoming involved in situations which overtax his capabilities.

V. STRICT LIABILITY

1. Historical Origins

Liability which is not based on the infringement of a duty has traditionally been the neglected child of tort law. Historically, its origins lie in the area of liability for animals, and for wild animals in particular. Large numbers of wild animals were kept in ancient Rome to supply the popular animal shows in circuses.[137] Although the circuses have now gone, strict liability for animals has been retained in the modern world and still forms the one case of broad similarity in this contested area of the law.[138]

Noxal liability of the *pater familias* was also strict,[139] vicarious liability of the principal within the common law still is,[140] and the same is true for the *responsabilité du commettant pour le fait de ses préposés* of Art 1384 *al* 1, 5, and 7 *Code civil*.[141] However, for reasons of conceptual clarity and normative consistency, liability for

---

[136] cf Posner, *Economic Analysis of Law* (n 113), 171.   [137] Zimmermann (n 12), 1105.

[138] There is only broad, not total, similarity, because the systems differ in the treatment of domestic animals (as opposed to those *ferae naturae* for which in Rome an *edictum de feris* was passed); cf England: Rogers (n 34), paras 16.3 ff; France: Art 1385 *Code civil*; Germany: § 833 BGB; USA: Dobbs (n 49), 942 ff.

[139] Zimmermann (n 12), 1118 ff; noxal liability was not the only head of liability for others, cf Lawson and Markesinis (n 44), 161 ff.

[140] Rogers (n 34), para 20.1; Dobbs (n 49), 905 ff.

[141] Viney and Jourdain (n 53), nos. 789–10, 808.

the torts of others should not be confounded with strict liability.[142] On the conceptual level it is obvious that strict liability on the part of the principal still requires the plaintiff to prove fault on the agent's part.[143] For this reason, the normative rationale underlying the 'true' cases of strict liability does nothing to illuminate vicarious liability, which must be explained and justified on the basis of principles of enterprise liability and not in terms of the 'source of danger' thinking that underlies strict liability proper.

2. The Diversity of Modern Law

In all Western nations strict liability expanded during the late nineteenth and twentieth centuries. It is legislatures, rather than courts, which have played the leading role in this area; however, the extent of legislative activity varies significantly from country to country.

The state of affairs in late nineteenth-century Germany provides a good illustration of the fact that the pandectists were more preoccupied with legal theory and the problems of ancient Rome than with the pressing practical needs of their own time. Even such an agile mind as Rudolf von Jhering's did not resist the temptation to greet the industrial revolution and its immediately obvious, and enormous, social problems by proclaiming emphatically that: 'It is not the occurrence of harm which obliges one to make compensation, but fault'.[144] This statement flatly ignored the fact that the great German scholar von Savigny, in his capacity as member of the Prussian government, had already proposed a bill in 1838 that subjected railway companies to strict liability.[145] The extent of von Jhering's misjudgment was made clear subsequently by nineteenth-century developments which saw the decline of the fault principle in German accident law: the liability of factory owners and operators of steam engines was established on the basis of strict liability as early as 1871, compensation for industrial accidents was taken out of the tort system completely in 1884, and strict liability for motor accidents was introduced by legislative fiat as early as 1909. During much of the twentieth century strict liability flourished, albeit in special statutes outside of the Civil code: it was extended to operators of aircraft, to those responsible for a whole range of installations dangerous to the environment, and was also enacted with regard to a number

---

[142] Wagner (n 52), 274 ff.   [143] Dobbs (n 49), 906.

[144] 'Nicht der Schaden verpflichtet zum Schadensersatz, sondern die Schuld': Rudolf von Jhering, 'Das Schuldmoment im römischen Privatrecht' (1867), in *idem* (ed), *Vermischte Schriften juristischen Inhalts* (1879), 155, 199.

[145] Theodor Baums, 'Die Einführung der Gefährdungshaftung durch F. C. von Savigny', (1987) 104 *Zeitschrift der Savigny-Stiftung für Rechtsgeschichte (Germanistische Abteilung)* 277.

of other activities.[146] Strict liability always, in a way, retained the proletarian and sooty face it had acquired in the early days of industrialization.

Nineteenth-century England was particularly affected by the heat of industrialization. The common law of England did not react by developing strict liability, but—much like von Jhering on the Continent—by vigorously emphasizing the fault-principle. This contributed to a considerable extent to the recognition of 'negligence' as a separate tort.[147] The decision which could have broken the ice for the principle of strict liability was *Rylands v Fletcher*. Characteristically it took place in the early days of industrialization, namely the 1870s, and involved a law suit between the operator of a coal mine and the proprietor of a mill. Lord Blackburn used the case as an opportunity to free strict liability from its existence on the fringes of the various categories of intentional torts:[148]

We think that the true rule of law is, that the person who for his own purposes brings on his lands and collects and keeps there anything likely to do mischief if it escapes, must keep it in at his peril, and, if he does not do so, is prima facie answerable for all the damage which is the natural consequence of its escape.

Whatever potential this principle might have had was squandered by English courts during the twentieth century. In the case of *Read v Lyons*, decided in 1946, the House of Lords refused to impose strict liability on the operator of a classic 'ultrahazardous activity', a munitions factory, for the simple reason that there was no emission of substances from one plot of land onto another.[149] The disparagement of strict liability as an institution of the common law was continued by the decisions in *Cambridge Water*, where Lord Goff referred the matter to Parliament,[150] and *Hunter v Canary Wharf*, where personal injuries were held to be excluded from the protective scope of the *Rylands* rule.[151] No wonder, then, that in the recent case of *Transco v Stockport* Lord Hoffmann found it 'hard to find any rational principle which explains the rule [in *Rylands v Fletcher*] and its exceptions'.[152] Although their Lordships shied away from explicitly overruling *Rylands*, the outcome is more or less the same: strict liability is dead within the common law, and the High Court of Australia has in fact had the courage to say so outright.[153] Although the English judges have hit the ball into the field of the legislature, Parliament has been

[146] *Münchener Kommentar/Wagner* Vor § 823 no. 16; *idem* (n 52), 275 ff.

[147] Winfield, (1926) 166 *LQR* 184 ff, 196.

[148] *Fletcher v Rylands* (1866) LR 1 Ex 265, 279 (Blackburn J); upheld by the House of Lords in *Rylands v Fletcher* (1868) LR 3 HL 330, 338 ff.

[149] *Read v Lyons & Co Ltd* [1947] AC 156, 165 ff.

[150] *Cambridge Water Co v Eastern Counties Leather Plc* [1994] 2 AC 264, 305 (Lord Goff of Chieveley): 'I incline to the opinion that, as a general rule, it is more appropriate for strict liability in respect of operations of high risk to be imposed by Parliament, than by the courts'.

[151] *Hunter v Canary Wharf Ltd* [1997] AC 655, 692, 696.

[152] *Transco plc v Stockport Metropolitan Borough Council* [2004] 2 AC 1, 20 (Lord Hoffmann).

[153] *Burnie Port Authority v General Jones* (1994) 179 CLR 520; (1994) 120 ALR 42.

reluctant to play with it. Most strikingly, motor accidents are not governed by strict liability but still constitute a domain of negligence law.[154] Even industrial accidents are dealt with on the basis of negligence principles,[155] at least to the extent that the losses are not covered by social insurance schemes.[156]

Ironically, strict liability as embraced in *Rylands v Fletcher* fared much better in the United States than in its country of origin. Whereas the English courts have deliberately relegated *Rylands v Fletcher* liability to a special remedy in settings close to nuisance, American courts have been prepared to generalize the decision towards a principle of strict liability for 'ultrahazardous' or 'abnormally danger-ous' activities.[157] Even this generalization was kept in narrow bounds, however: it was limited to explosives and toxic agents, in addition to the already-classic water reservoirs. Of course, the concept of strict liability also looms large in the modern law of product liability, but the career of the concept in this area is based upon a misunderstanding. As long as strict product liability remains limited to defective products, and as long as the concept of defect is more or less a reformulation of the negligence test, there is no strict liability in the true sense of the term. This is the state of affairs on both sides of the Atlantic as reflected, for example, by the American Restatement[158] and by Art 6 of the EC Product Liability Directive.[159] Within each of these systems, liability for design defects is in fact conditioned on some form of risk/utility test, which comes close to a reformulation of the Learned-Hand formula with regard to this area of the law. The only differences are that the 'alternative design' takes the place of precautionary measures and that liability may arise even in the absence of a reasonable alternative design if the risks inherent in the product outweigh the benefits derived from its use.

Whereas American, English, and German law share a somewhat tentative or even timid approach when it comes to the expansion of strict liability, French law is clearly different. Famously, the *Code civil* contains not only a general clause for fault-based liability but also one for strict liability.[160] Of course, this was not the original intention: Art 1384 *al* 1 *Code civil*, which provides that 'on est responsable . . . du dommage . . . causé par le fait de choses que l'on a sous sa garde', was

---

[154] Markesinis and Deakin, *Tort Law* (4th edn, 1999), 297.

[155] cf on this topic and on the concept of 'non-delegable duty' *Wilsons & Clyde Coal Co v English* 1937 SC (HL) 46, 60; David Howarth, *Textbook on Tort* (1995), 649 ff.

[156] Markesinis and Deakin (n 36), 560 ff; Peter Cane, *Atiyah's Accidents, Compensation and the Law* (6th edn, 1999), 282 n 4; see below, Section VI.3.

[157] Dobbs (n 49), 952 ff; cf Restatement of Torts (1938), § 520; Restatement of Torts, 2nd (1977), § 519 ff.

[158] The ALI, Restatement of the Law Third, Torts, Products Liability (1998), 19: 'traditional reason-ableness standard in negligence'.

[159] Council Directive 85/374/EEC of 25 July 1985 on the approximation of the laws, regulations, and administrative provisions of the Member States concerning liability for defective products, [1985] OJ L 210/29; cf also Rogers (n 34), para 10.19; *Münchener Kommentar/Wagner* Einl ProdHaftG nn 15 ff.

[160] cf Viney and Jourdain (n 53), no. 627: 'Originalité du droit français'.

originally intended to clarify that the keeper of a thing was under a duty to take care.[161] The conversion of Art 1384 *al* 1 *Code civil* into a general clause for strict liability was a feat of the courts, and counts among the 'constructions prétoriennes les plus célèbres du droit français'.[162] The starting signal for the establishment of an objective liability was the *arrêt du remorqueur* of 1896, where the *Cour de cassation* held an employer responsible for harm even though it could not be shown that he had violated a duty to take care.[163] Thirty-five years later, the *arrêt Jand'heur*, concerning a traffic accident, established the *gardien*-liability as an independent principle of liability (*responsabilité de plein droit*).[164]

In spite of the stunning career of Art 1384 *al* 1 *Code civil* during the last hundred-odd years, it would be wrong to think that the French law of strict liability is largely based on the French Civil code. On the contrary, French lawmakers have been no less active than their German and English counterparts in introducing *régimes spéciaux d'indemnisation* for various types of technical installations and operations.[165] In this way, liability for industrial accidents was taken out of the private law altogether and, following the German example, re-established as a branch of the social insurance system.[166] In addition, the *loi Badinter* of July 1985 introduced a special system of liability for traffic accidents which comes close to a no-fault compensation system but keeps the liability insurers in business.[167] Finally, the French version of strict liability is not really comparable to the respective concepts in the other countries as Art 1384 *al* 1 *Code civil* attaches liability to the keeper of a thing, regardless of whether that thing is particularly dangerous.[168] Consequently, strict liability also extends to a person who has a ladder or a cork, a wheelbarrow, a toy car, a bicycle, a sofa, or a rug *sous sa garde*.[169] An attempt to turn back the clock and restrict *gardien*-liability to dangerous objects, initiated by advocate general Charbonnier in 1984, was unsuccessful.[170] All in all, Art 1384 *al* 1 is not a case of liability for exposure to danger but rather a form of strict liability *sui generis*.

---

[161] Flour *et al* (n 9), no. 231; Viney and Jourdain (n 53), no. 628.

[162] Philippe Malaurie and Laurent Aynès, *Cours de droit civil, Les obligations* (10th edn, 1999/2000), before no. 187.

[163] Cass civ 18.6.1896 (Teffaine), D 1897, I, 433 note Saleilles.

[164] Cass ch réunies, 13.2.1930, p 1930.I.121 note Esmein.

[165] Le Tourneau (n 91), nos. 8051 ff.

[166] Yvonne Lambert-Faivre, *Droit du dommage corporel* (4th edn, 2000), nos. 16–2, 17.

[167] Flour *et al* (n 9), no. 361: 'rupture avec la responsabilité classique'.

[168] Cass ch réunies, 13.2.1930, S 1930, I, 121 note Esmein: 'qu'il n'est pas nécessaire, qu'elle ait un vice inhérent à sa nature et susceptible de causer le dommage'; cf Viney and Jourdain (n 53), no. 634.

[169] cf Cass civ 2e, 15.2.1984, Bull civ II, no. 29, p 19; Cass civ 1re, 28.4.1981, Bull civ I, no. 137, p 114; Geneviève Schamps, *La mise en danger: un concept fondateur d'un principe général de responsabilité* (1998), 645.

[170] Cass civ 15.11.1984, three decisions, in D 1985, I, 20, 25 ff.

3. Conclusions and Perspectives

The bird's eye view of the state of affairs in this area is dismaying. Obviously, there is no common core of strict liability, with the sole but somewhat sad exception of wild animals, who 'have [always] travelled in a compartment of their own'.[171]

In light of the developments referred to, it seems fair to conclude that a general clause of strict liability, although the beloved child of many scholars, is wrought with more problems than one might anticipate.[172] Even in France, the legislature has intervened time and again to set up special schemes for the most important areas of strict liability: industrial accidents and motor accidents. In the United States, the attempt to formulate such a clause with respect to abnormally dangerous activities resulted in the multi-factor test of § 520 of the Second Restatement, which has been rightly criticized for its ambiguity and vagueness.[173]

As things stand today, economic analysis is the only discipline that can offer a comprehensive and consistent explanation for strict liability. According to economic wisdom, strict liability achieves the same level of deterrence with regard to precautions, but goes further than that because it also affects the activity levels chosen by potential tortfeasors. Because, under strict liability, the tortfeasor must compensate even those losses that are impossible to avoid at a reasonable cost he has an incentive to balance the gains derived from the particular activity against its total cost. From there it follows easily that strict liability is the appropriate regime where the activity in question causes a substantial risk of harm even if all reasonable measures of safety have been observed.[174] In this sense, English, American, and German law are correct to limit strict liability to 'abnormal' activities, provided that this concept is understood in the sense just described. Richard Posner has nicely encapsulated the above reasoning in the following stylized example:[175]

Keeping a tiger in one's backyard would be an example of an abnormally hazardous activity. The hazard is such, relative to the value of the activity, that we desire not just that the owner take all due care that the tiger not escape, but that he consider seriously the possibility of getting rid of the tiger altogether; and we give him an incentive to consider this course of action by declining to make the exercise of due care a defence to a suit based on an injury caused by the tiger—in other words, by making him strictly liable for any such injury.

---

[171] *Read v J Lyons & Co* [1947] AC 156, 182 (Lord Simonds).

[172] For a more thorough treatment of the problem cf Wagner (n 52), 286 ff.

[173] Dobbs (n 49), 953 ff.

[174] Steven Shavell, *Economic Analysis of Accident Law* (1987), 29 ff; *idem, Foundations of Economic Analysis of Law* (2004), 206; Wagner (n 52), 273.

[175] *G J Leasing Co v Union Elec Co* 54 F 3d 379, 386 (7th Cir 1995) (Posner J).

VI. TORT LAW AND INSURANCE

1. A Patchwork of Systems

(a) Strict Liability and Liability Insurance Working in Tandem

The rise of strict liability during the twentieth century coincided with the rise of insurance, both in the form of private liability insurance and of social insurance. The combination of tort law, the civil justice system, and private liability insurance was increasingly seen as a mechanism to spread the cost of accidents across a wide range of people or even the public at large. As a consequence, private liability insurance, initially designed to protect risk-averse actors against high costs of liability, was refashioned as a device to protect victims against the risk of harm, or, more precisely, against the risk of being harmed by a judgment-proof tortfeasor. The clearest manifestation of this trend is motor accident insurance, which has been made mandatory in most countries of the Western world and allows the victim to assert his claim directly against the insurance carrier via the *action directe*. With these attributes, the combination of strict liability and liability insurance is moving in the direction of a social insurance scheme for the benefit of potential victims. The political potential inherent in this sort of institutional arrangement has been used quite vigorously by legislators and judges in some jurisdictions, with the Scandinavian countries and France serving as the primary examples.[176] The state of affairs in France has been succinctly summarized in the following observations:[177]

D'un côté la jurisprudence condamne d'autant plus facilement le responsable lorsque celui-ci est assuré, de l'autre l'assurance se développe pour prendre en charge des responsabilités devenues quasiment systématiques. La responsabilité se nourrit donc de l'assurance, et inversement. Et si, par cas, il n'y a pas de 'responsable', la loi crée des fonds de garantie! De sorte qu'on peut se demander si, insensiblement, le droit francais de la responsabilité civile ne devient pas un droit de la réparation.

(b) Social Insurance Schemes

More or less parallel to the rise of liability insurance, another institution took to the stage in the twentieth century, namely social insurance. During the late nineteenth century, Germany was the pacemaker among European nations in supplementing, or even replacing, the law of delict with social insurance schemes. In 1884 the Imperial German Chancellor, Otto von Bismarck, although a staunch

---

[176] Bill Dufwa, 'Country Report Sweden', in Gerhard Wagner (ed), *Tort Law and Liability Insurance* (2005), nos. 24 ff, 52 ff.

[177] Lapoyade Deschamps (n 43), 89.

conservative, introduced the system of workers' compensation, which converted what used to be fault-liability of individual employers into strict liability of public insurers funded by contributions of firms engaged in the particular industry.[178] This replacement of tort law by social insurance schemes served as a model throughout the Western world and is still in place in many countries today.[179]

Outside the area of industrial accidents, the European nations in particular, have developed comprehensive systems of public funds charged with the duty of compensating victims instead of fixing liability on individual tortfeasors responsible for the harm. In Europe these public insurance carriers internalize the bulk of losses from personal injuries, and, compared with the sums of money turned around by the various national health insurance systems, the 'turnovers' of tort law look modest indeed. Some numbers may be useful to put things in perspective: in Germany, for example, the total expenditure of public health insurance carriers in the year 2003 amounted to approximately €143 billion,[180] while the total payments of motor vehicle liability insurers were of the order of €13.8 billion, approximately 75 per cent of which was eaten up by compensation for property damage.[181]

2. The Rise and Decline of No-Fault Schemes

Compensation of victims of personal injury has in large part been taken care of by social insurance in Europe. This possibly explains why it was in the US that, in the mid-twentieth century, plans for a comprehensive replacement of private tort law by a system of no-fault insurance were developed, with motor accidents being the primary target area. The blueprint for such plans was supplied by Keeton and O'Connell's work entitled *Basic Protection for the Traffic Victim*.[182] In France, André Tunc sounded the same trumpet by pushing for the abolition of delictual liability for traffic accidents in favour of an insurance solution abstracted from individual

---

[178] Michael Stolleis, *Geschichte des Sozialrechts in Deutschland* (2003), 52 ff.

[179] cf the volume edited by Ulrich Magnus, *The Impact of Social Security Law on Tort Law* (2003). Workers' compensation schemes are continuing to replace tort law in Austria (p 11, nn 13 ff), Belgium (p 39, n 22), France (p 77, n 9), Germany (pp 97 ff, n 13), Greece (p 124, nn 35 ff), Switzerland (p 202, n 21). The situation in the United States is similar but for the fact that the institutional setting differs from State to State; in some States, the employer pays contributions into a public fund, in others he is under a duty to take out liability insurance; cf Dobbs (n 49), 1098 ff.

[180] Statistisches Bundesamt Deutschland, *Statistisches Jahrbuch für die Bundesrepublik Deutschland 2004* (2004), 190 n 7.2.3.

[181] Gesamtverband der Deutschen Versicherungswirtschaft e.V. (ed), *2004 Yearbook—The German Insurance Industry*, 90 ff (available at: <http://www.gdv.de/Downloads/Jahrbuch/Yearbook_Navi_2004.pdf>).

[182] Robert Keeton and Jeffrey O'Connell, *Basic Protection for the Traffic Victim—A Blueprint for Reforming Automobile Insurance* (1965), 5 ff, 273 ff; for a more recent and more comprehensive proposal, see Stephen D. Sugarman, 'Doing Away with Tort Law', (1985) 73 *California LR* 558 ff.

responsibility,[183] and in England Patrick Atiyah advocated an almost complete repeal of tort law in the field of bodily injuries in favour of insurance solutions that would have compensated every victim regardless of his share of causation and fault.[184]

The suggestion of abolishing tort law in favour of a no-fault insurance solution has not been realized in its pure form in any country in the world, but New Zealand moved close to full adoption when it introduced a comprehensive social insurance system for bodily injuries regardless of their cause.[185] Moreover, tort liability for road traffic accidents has at least been supplemented by no-fault regimes in sixteen US states, as well as in the Canadian provinces of Saskatchewan, Ontario, and Québec.[186] In France, the *Projet Tunc* has been pronounced dead[187] but before its demise it bore the fruit of the *loi Badinter,* which seized upon the core of the matter by largely detaching loss distribution in traffic accident cases from *faute civile* and by not only exposing liability insurers to the *action directe* of the injured party, but also placing them in charge of the compensation procedure.[188] In this way, 'la victime agit contre la collectivité des assurés, le véhicule impliqué désignant la compagnie débitrice'.[189] No wonder that in France some commentators regard this relegation of tort law to the role of a mere conduit which links a victim with an insurance fund as 'une tendance régressive dans l'evolution du droit contemporain'.[190]

In fact, the experience with no-fault schemes and their smaller siblings like the *loi Badinter* has been rather disappointing.[191] The incentive effects of such schemes were grossly underestimated because their proponents simply denied that tort liability served any deterrence function. The relatively few empirical studies that have been conducted have not, of course, remained uncontested; nevertheless, they suggest, at the very least, that pessimism concerning the deterrent effect of tort law is unwarranted. In France, which operates a quasi-no-fault system in the area of traffic accidents, the country's comparatively poor performance in terms of traffic

---

[183] André Tunc, 'Traffic Accident Compensation', in Arthur Hartkamp, Martijn Hesselink, Ewoud Hondius, Carla Joustra, and Edgar du Perron (eds), *Towards a European Civil Code* (2nd edn, 1998), 461, 462 ff.

[184] Patrick Atiyah, *Accidents, Compensation and the Law* (1st edn, 1970), 603 ff.

[185] Richard Mahoney, 'New Zealand's Accident Compensation Scheme: A Reassessment', (1992) 40 *AJCL* 159 ff.

[186] For an overview see Tunc, 'Traffic Accident Compensation: Law and Proposals', in *idem* (n 1), ch 14 (1971), paras 187 ff, paras 54 ff; as to the situation in the United States and Canada, see Don Dewees, David Duff, and Michael Trebilcock, *Exploring the Domain of Accident Law* (1996), 15.

[187] cf on this topic Viney and Jourdain (n 53), nos. 965 ff.

[188] cf Art L 211–8 ff, L–421–1 ff. *Code des assurances;* Simon Fredericq, *Risques modernes et indemnisation des victimes de lésions corporelles* (1990), nos. 48 ff.

[189] Terré *et al* (n 100), no. 935.   [190] Ibid.

[191] For a more comprehensive explanation, see Gerhard Wagner, 'Comparative Report and Conclusions', in *idem* (ed), *Tort Law and Liability Insurance* (n 176), nos. 108 ff.

accident-related deaths is noted with growing concern.[192] In fact, common sense suggests that firms will estimate the liability costs associated with various courses of action and behave accordingly. As far as individuals are concerned, it has always been implausible, on the one hand, to deny the deterrent effects of tort law, but then, on the other hand, to denounce the adverse effects of excessive tort liability (such as defensive medicine) or to put one's faith into administrative fines and the operation of the criminal law.[193] If drivers are responsive to the threat of being fined for violating a speed limit, why should they be irresponsive to the threat of being held liable in tort? Apart from this, an efficient law enforcement apparatus capable of reviving the incentive effects destroyed by no-fault schemes would be very expensive, which means that the perceived savings in terms of transaction costs are unlikely to be achieved.

In the same vein, the supporters of no-fault schemes tended to ignore the incentive effects which large funds providing generous compensation to accident victims have on victims of all kinds of diseases. It is primarily for this reason that the New Zealand scheme has run into financial difficulties: the costs have spiralled out of control as victims and private health insurance companies did their best to reframe all sorts of physical diseases and psychological harm as a consequence of some accident sustained during the victim's lifetime. As Patrick Atiyah, one of the early proponents of no-fault, succinctly observed:[194]

[National compensation plans] involve massive bureaucratic extensions of the welfare state of a kind which have gone out of fashion with governments and electorates. And they have gone out of fashion not just because of normal swings of public opinion, but because experience of similar bureaucratic schemes has been uniformly unsatisfactory in the modern world. . . . First, their cost estimates nearly always prove to have been too optimistic, as indeed has happened in New Zealand where their legislation has recently been cut down partly for reasons of cost.

In spite of these experiences, 'no-fault never seems to remain dead but repeatedly rises, ghoul-like, from the grave to walk the Earth anew'.[195] The current focus of the debate, both in Europe and the United States, is medical malpractice, with the Swedish patient insurance scheme serving as a model.[196] A switch to no-fault insurance in this area would be particularly problematic as the main practical hurdle that victims of iatrogenic injury have to overcome is not fault but causation. As it would be impossible to grant compensation to everyone leaving a hospital in

---

[192] Terré *et al* (n 100), no. 930.

[193] cf Stephen D. Sugarman, *Doing Away with Personal Injury Law* (1989), 18 ff.

[194] Patrick Atiyah, *The Damages Lottery* (1997), 183.

[195] Thomas Ulen, 'Tort Law and Liability Insurance in the United States', in Wagner (n 176), n 29; see also Wagner (n 191), no. 106 ff.

[196] For an overview, see Lotta Wendel, 'Compensation in the Swedish Health Care Sector', in Jos Dute, Michael G. Faure, and Helmut Koziol (eds), *No-Fault Compensation in the Health Care Sector* (2004), no. 28 ff; Dewees *et al.* (n 186), 139 ff.

another state than perfect health, patient insurance schemes could hardly econo-
mize on transaction costs to any considerable extent.[197]

3. Coordination of Tort Law with Social Security Systems

Whereas in the United States no-fault liability has seen its high watermark, it has
achieved a renaissance in some European jurisdictions. England, even back in 1948,
has abolished Bismarckian-style workers' compensation in order to integrate the
compensation function into the general system of social security benefits and to
reinstate the worker's private right of action against his employer for fault.[198] This
example was followed by the Netherlands in 1967,[199] and it might well be a model
for the other member states of the European Union. In fact, it is difficult to support
a system that distributes generous benefits to one particular class of victims—
employees suffering an accident, or contracting an occupational disease—and
refers the 'rest' to a social security system operating under dire financial constraints.[200] In principle, it seems preferable to operate a general, need-based social
security system which awards modest but equal benefits to all victims, regardless of
the source of their injury or disease, and to supplement this by a system of tort law
that is based on individual responsibility and that generates incentives to take care.

Vice versa, the interface between national systems of social security and the tort
system must be designed in a way that supports both the deterrent function of tort
law and the objective of a fair allocation of losses.[201] In this regard, the Continental
European systems have developed the institution of a claw-back from the tortfeasor of public monies paid to the victim. Both French and German law avoid the
alternatives of double compensation of the victim, or deduction of social security
benefits from the damages claim, by allowing the social insurer to step into the
shoes of the victim and to enforce any damage claims which the victim may have
against the third party tortfeasor.[202] With the help of this mechanism, the incentive

---

[197] Wagner (n 191), no. 109.   [198] Rogers (n 34), para 8.1.

[199] Edgar du Perron and Willem H. van Boom, 'Country Report Netherlands', in Magnus (n 179),
155 no. 21.

[200] This is upshot of Jane Stapleton's book, *Disease and the Compensation Debate* (1986), 142 ff,
150 ff; see also Wagner (n 191), no. 111. For an early account, see Jeremiah Smith, 'Sequel to Workermen's
Compensation Acts', (1913) 27 *Harvard LR* 235 ff, 251: 'If the fundamental general principle of the
modern common law of torts is intrinsically right or expedient, is there sufficient reason why the
legislature should make the workmen's case an exception to this general principle? On the other hand,
if this statutory rule as to workmen is intrinsically just or expedient, is there sufficient reason for . . .
refusing to make this statutory rule the test of the right of recovery on the part of persons other than
workmen when they suffer hurt without the fault of either party?'

[201] For a more thorough account, cf Wagner (n 52), 331 ff.

[202] Germany: § 116 Sozialgesetzbuch X (Social Security Act, part X); Wagner (n 52), 306 ff; France:
Art 29 ff *loi* 5.7.1985 (*loi Badinter*); Lambert-Faivre (n 166), no. 441 ff.

effects of tort law are fully restored, and the loss that has arisen is channelled towards those whose activities caused them.

In recent years, even England has broken with its tradition of either ignoring collateral sources of compensation altogether, which leads to double compensation, or of deducting social security benefits from any damages awarded against the tortfeasor. Instead, it now provides for the reimbursement of the collateral source.[203] In fact, the English solution goes one important step further in that claims for recoupment are not left in the hands of the various bodies of the social security administration but are transferred to a central authority, namely the Compensation Recovery Unit (CRU) in Newcastle.[204] By centralizing the recoupment procedure in this way, the English system is able to realize economies of scale and to harvest the efficiency gains from specialization and professionalization. It is no wonder, then, that the administrative costs of the CRU eat up less than 5 per cent of the monies recouped.[205]

4. Future Perspectives

In spite of what has been said above, collective solutions are not off the political agenda altogether. The collectivization of liability to the benefit of both victims and tortfeasors looms large in situations of major catastrophes, with the terrorist attack on the World Trade Centre on 11 September, 2001 serving as the most striking example. The US Congress reacted to that disaster by enacting the Air Transportation Safety and System Stabilization Act, Title 4 of which established The September 11th Victim Compensation Fund.[206] The Act does not foreclose resort to tort remedies but gives victims the option to claim from the Fund, which offers compensation on a no-fault basis and in a very generous amount. In fact, the September 11th Fund combines the low thresholds for liability typical of no-fault plans with the full compensation principle typical of tort remedies. Precisely for this reason, the Fund by no means signifies a revival of no-fault schemes but has to be explained as a result of shock and compassion in the aftermath of a disaster which profoundly affected the attitude of American citizens and politicians alike.

In the light of the foregoing analysis it is safe to predict that we will continue to see no-fault insurance schemes being implemented on an ad hoc basis in cases of

---

[203] As to the historical development in England, cf Richard Lewis, *Deducting Benefits from Damages for Personal Injury* (1999), paras 12.01 ff; Wagner (n 52), 314 ff.

[204] Lewis (n 203), paras 14.01 ff, 18.15 ff; see also Rogers (n 34), para 22.33.

[205] Lewis (n 203), para 14.03.

[206] cf Robert L. Rabin, 'Indeterminate Future Harm in the Context of September 11', (2002) 88 *Vanderbilt LR* 1831 ff; *idem*, 'The September 11th Victim Compensation Fund: A Circumscribed Response or an Auspicious Model?', (2003) 53 *DePaul LR* 769 ff; Marshall S. Shapo, *Compensation for Victims of Terrorism* (2005), 105 ff.

large-scale catastrophes, be they of human making or due to natural forces. In such instances, however, it is highly unlikely that compensation levels will ever again approach those of the September 11th Victim Compensation Fund.

With respect to the small catastrophes of everyday life, no-fault will not be an option in the foreseeable future. As a consequence, tort law is likely to gain in importance, rather than to lose further ground. In areas where losses are severe and frequent, and victims are able to generate enough political steam, a combination of strict liability and liability insurance is likely to play the role of a non-welfarist, market-style substitute for government-run no-fault schemes.

BIBLIOGRAPHY

Pierre Catala and John Antony Weir, 'Delict and Torts: A Study in Parallel', (1963) 37 *Tulane LR* 573 ff; (1964) 38 *Tulane LR* 221 ff and 663 ff; (1965) 39 *Tulane LR* 701 ff

André Tunc (ed), *International Encyclopedia of Comparative Law* (vol XI, 1971—81)

Frederick H. Lawson and Basil Markesinis, *Tortious Liability for Unintentional Harm in the Common Law and the Civil Law* (vol I, 1982)

Steven Shavell, *Economic Analysis of Accident Law* (1987)

Reinhard Zimmermann, *The Law of Obligations: Roman Foundations of the Civilian Tradition* (paperback edn, 1996), 902 ff

Christian von Bar, *Gemeineuropäisches Deliktsrecht* (vol I, 1996; vol II, 1999; English translation under the title *The Common European Law of Torts*, vol I, 1998; vol II, 2000)

Geneviève Viney and Patrice Jourdain, *Les conditions de la responsabilité* (2nd edn, 1998)

Dan B. Dobbs, *The Law of Torts* (2000)

Walter van Gerven, Jeremy Lever, and Pierre Larouche, *Cases, Materials and Text on National, Supranational and International Tort Law* (2000)

W. V. Horton Rogers, *Winfield & Jolowicz on Tort* (16th edn, 2002)

Basil Markesinis and Simon Deakin, *Tort Law* (5th edn, 2003)

Gerhard Wagner, 'Grundstrukturen des Europäischen Deliktsrechts', in Reinhard Zimmermann (ed), *Grundstrukturen des Europäischen Deliktsrechts* (2003), 189 ff

Gert Brüggemeier, *Common Principles of Tort Law: A Pre-Statement of Law* (2004)

European Group on Tort Law, *Principles of European Tort Law* (2005)

Hein Kötz and Gerhard Wagner, *Deliktsrecht* (10th edn, 2006)

CHAPTER 32

COMPARATIVE
PROPERTY LAW

SJEF VAN ERP

Maastricht

I. Introduction

UNLIKE the law of obligations, comparative lawyers seem to have avoided property law.[1] From the nineteenth century onwards, after the codification movement on the European Continent following the French Revolution, property law in civilian and common law systems was seen, in contrast to the law of obligations, as being of a national (local) character. Both in the civil law and the common law tradition, property law became a highly technical area of law. In order fully to understand property law a precise knowledge of the relevant statutory provisions was (and still is) required together with a thorough knowledge of case law and legal literature. This area of the law is, therefore, generally regarded as a set of national, fairly rigid, and technical legal rules, either in statutory or case law format, which are largely of a mandatory character, thus limiting the parties' freedom to shape their legal relations, at least as far as these relations may have an effect *vis-à-vis* third parties. As a result, property law became a rather petrified legal area, rooted in a desire for legal certainty.

This had a direct impact on the comparative study of property law. Property lawyers from both civil and common law, in spite of having realized that they share the same political and economic ideas with regard to the political and economic infrastructure, also, however, accepted that as a result of historical divergences their systems differed at a technical level. Thus, they became rather introverted. They tended to analyse problems in property law only from the perspective of their own tradition and sometimes declined to look even at other national systems within that same tradition. The focus was on the national system and not so much on developments outside that system. Comparative analysis of property law, for that reason, did not attract much attention and whatever comparative studies were undertaken took a divergence perspective as their starting-point. In other words, if a comparative lawyer did indeed look at property law, he usually took it for granted that the two major legal traditions of the Western world (civil law and common law) had fundamentally different historical roots and that the resulting conceptual

---

[1] Courses on comparative private law frequently focus on the law of obligations, because here, in spite of conceptual differences, convergence rather than divergence dominates the scene. This convergence-oriented comparative approach fits well into the growing tendency on a European as well a global level to harmonize or even unify large areas of the law of obligations, and particularly of contract law, to facilitate international trade. Within the framework of the European Union the first directives in the area of private law dealt with tort and contract law, rather than with property law. Even the European timeshare Directive—and timeshare is most certainly a property concept—only deals with pre-contractual information duties. Cf Directive 94/47/EC of the European Parliament and the Council of 26 October 1994 on the protection of purchasers in respect of certain aspects of contracts relating to the purchase of the right to use immovable properties on a timeshare basis, [1994] OJ L 280/94, p 83.

differences were so deeply entrenched that any convergence would be impossible. The study of comparative property law was therefore more a matter of *Auslands-rechtskunde* (ie the study of foreign law) rather than of comparative—let alone critical-comparative—analysis.

Remarkably enough, contract law and tort law (in other words, liability issues) have always been perceived in a different light. They are regarded as the dynamic areas of private law, full of fascinating developments. The law of obligations is characterized by fundamental debates at a legal, philosophical, and moral level on leading principles and on resulting new paradigms. Exciting new questions are raised, such as whether contract law is 'dead'.[2] The only statement that raised comparable emotions among property lawyers was the socialist view that 'la propriété c'rest le vol' (property is theft).[3] After communism became the leading ideology in, for example, Russia, China, and the states of Central and Eastern Europe, a growing interest arose in studies of property law focusing on a comparison between the so-called 'socialist legal systems', where private ownership had been banned, and the legal systems of Western Europe and the United States. With the decline of communism this interest, however, quickly vanished.[4]

Apart from the Marxist challenge to existing Western property concepts, a further issue that provoked—and still provokes—fundamental debates on the nature of property law are land claims by the autochthonous population in countries such as Australia, Canada, South Africa and the United States. These land claims are based on the presence of native people who used their land before Western property law was brought to them by Western settlers and who perceive relations between people and land in a very different light than the inhabitants of Europe or the United States. Such claims are now recognized at least to a certain degree. This acceptance raises questions concerning both the nature of, and justification for, the Western type of ownership as well as whether and, if so, in what way these land claims can be fitted into Western systems of property law.[5] In essence, these are questions of comparative property law.

Although comparative property law, except for the influence of communism on property rights and the land claims of autochthonous peoples, has not attracted as much attention from comparative lawyers as the law of obligations, there are notable exceptions. First of all, the *International Encyclopedia of Comparative Law*

---

[2] Grant Gilmore, *The Death of Contract* (1974).

[3] Pierre Joseph Proudhon, *Qu'est-ce que la propriété? Ou recherches sur le principe du droit et du gouvernement* (1848–9). Cf also the opposite view by Frédéric Bastiat, 'Propriété et Loi', [1848] *Journal des Economistes* (15 May): 'l'homme naît propriétaire' (a person is born being owner).

[4] For an analysis of modern Russian law see Evgueny A. Sukhanov, 'The Right of Ownership in the Contemporary Civil Law of Russia', (1999) 44 *McGill LJ* 301 ff.

[5] See, for Australia, the well-known case of *Mabo and others v Queensland (No 2)* [1992] HCA 23; and for South Africa, see *Richtersveld Community and others v Alexxor Ltd and another*, 2001(3) SA 1293 (LCC).

should be mentioned. This multi-volume work deals in volume VI with structural variations in property law, trust, apartment ownership, and recordation of interests in land.[6] Some ten years ago an international comparative property law colloquium was organized in Maastricht under the title 'Property law on the threshold of the twenty-first century'.[7] Also the collections of papers presented at biennial conferences on comparative property law, organized by the Centre for Property Law at the University of Reading, should be noted.[8] More recently, comparative property law has been at the heart of studies on mixed legal systems, such as the work collected in *Mixed Legal Systems in Comparative Perspective.*[9] The essays on property law in that volume concern, among other topics, acquisition of ownership, co-ownership, servitudes and real burdens, rights in security, assignation/cession, and trusts.

The number of studies in comparative property law has recently been growing as a result of efforts to harmonize, or unify, certain aspects of property law in areas crucial for international business transactions. Increasing regional and global economic integration has led to a growing awareness that the divergence of legal rules may lead to inefficiency and raise transactions costs. This is particularly true for the area of secured transactions.[10]

In Europe the four economic freedoms (free movement of goods, persons, services, and capital), laid down in the treaty establishing the European Community, have a growing influence on property law. This can be seen in the case law developed by the European Court of Justice.[11] The implementation of the economic freedoms demands increasing integration of the economies of the member states, and such economic integration is hardly possible without legal integration. As a result there is a growing need to understand the various property law systems in Europe, in order to pave the way towards harmonization or even unification of those areas of property law that are relevant for cross-border business transactions within the European Union and the European Economic Area. This has led to various comparative publications, such as, in particular, the studies by Eva-Maria Kieninger on security rights in movable property and by Graziadei *et al* on commercial trusts, published as the result of the Trento Common Core of

---

[6] Frederick H. Lawson and Athanassios Yiannopoulos (chief eds), *International Encyclopedia of Comparative Law* (vol VI, 1973 ff). For a recent comparative study, see Ugo Mattei, *Basic Principles of Property Law: A Comparative Legal and Economic Introduction* (2000).

[7] G. E. van Maanen and A. J. van der Walt (eds), *Property Law on the Threshold of the 21st Century* (1996).

[8] Elizabeth Cooke (ed), *Modern Studies in Property Law* (2001); *eadem, Modern Studies in Property Law* (vol II, 2003; vol III, 2005).

[9] Reinhard Zimmermann, Daniel Visser, and Kenneth Reid (eds), *Mixed Legal Systems in Comparative Perspective: Property and Obligations in Scotland and South Africa* (2004).

[10] cf Anna Veneziano, *Le garanzie mobiliari non possessorie: profili di diritto comparato e di diritto del commercio internazionale* (2000).

[11] cf case C–222/97 *Trummer v Mayer* [1999] ECR I–1661.

European Private Law project.[12] Then there is a comprehensive study by Christian von Bar and Ulrich Drobnig on the interaction of contract law and tort and property law in Europe.[13] In that study, von Bar and Drobnig discuss transfer of title in movables, contractual security rights in movables, contractual security rights in immovables (mortgages), and trust law.[14] Within the framework of the Study Group on a European Civil Code, which aims to draft a set of principles, *inter alia*, on core aspects of European property law, more publications in this area can be expected.[15] Finally, reference should be made to the contributions on property law in a collection of essays entitled *Towards a European Civil Code*.[16]

A further recent development that has led to a growing interest in comparative property law is the constitutionalization of private law. Human rights may have a direct impact also on property law, as can be seen in the case law developed by the European Court of Human Rights concerning the protection of ownership, as laid down in Article 1 of the first Protocol to the European Convention on Human Rights.[17] A striking example of the effect that the Court's case law may have on national property law can be found in the recent *Pye* decision.[18] This case demonstrates that national rules on prescription of a claim to ownership which may lead to acquisition of ownership at the expense of the original owner, can be qualified as a violation of the right of ownership of the original owner, as secured by Article 1,

---

[12] Eva-Maria Kieninger, *Security Rights in Movable Property in European Private Law* (2004); Michele Graziadei, Ugo Mattei, and Lionel Smith, *Commercial Trusts in European Private Law* (2005). On trust law, see also Richard H. Helmholz and Reinhard Zimmermann, *Itinera fiduciae: Trust and Treuhand in Historical Perspective. Comparative Studies in Continental and Anglo-American Legal History* (1998); D. J. Hayton, S. C. J. J. Kortmann, and H. L. E. Verhagen (eds), *Principles of European Trust Law* (1999).

[13] Christian von Bar and Ulrich Drobnig, *The Interaction of Contract Law and Tort and Property Law in Europe: A Comparative Study* (2004).

[14] See also Peter von Wilmowsky, *Europäisches Kreditsicherungsrecht: Sachenrecht und Insolvenzrecht unter dem EG-Vertrag* (1996); Eva-Maria Kieninger, *Mobiliarsicherheiten im Europäischen Binnenmarkt: Zum Einfluß der Warenverkehrsfreiheit auf das nationale und internationale Sachenrecht der Mitgliedstaaten* (1996); Jacobien W. Rutgers, *International Reservation of Title Clauses: A Study of Dutch, French and German Private International Law in the Light of European Law* (1999). For an earlier study, see Jean Georges Sauveplanne (ed), *Security over Corporeal Movables* (1974).

[15] More information can be found on the website of the Study Group: <http://www.sgecc.net/>. See also Christian von Bar (ed.), *Sachenrecht in Europa: Systematische Einführungen und Gesetzestexte* (vols I–IV, 1999–2001). With regard to European trust law, see also: Hayton *et al.* (n 12).

[16] Arthur Hartkamp, Martijn Hesselink, Ewoud Hondius, Carla Joustra, Edgar du Perron, and Muriel Veldman (eds), *Towards a European Civil Code* (3rd edn, 2004).

[17] Convention for the Protection of Human Rights and Fundamental Freedoms, Rome, 4 November 1950; Protocol to the Convention for the Protection of Human Rights and Fundamental Freedoms, Paris, 20 March 1952. Cf eg case 10/1993/405/483–484 *Holy Monasteries v Greece*; for an overview of relevant case law, see Barbara Mensah, *European Human Rights Case Summaries 1960–2000* (2000). See also Jan-Peter Loof and Hendrik Ploeger, *The Right to Property: The Influence of Article 1 Protocol no. 1 ECHR on Several Fields of Domestic Law* (2000).

[18] *J. A. Pye (Oxford) Ltd v the United Kingdom* (Application no 44302/02), to be found on the website of the European Court of Human Rights: <http://www.echr.coe.int/echr>.

Protocol 1 of the European Convention on Human Rights. Such loss would have to be adequately compensated. The full impact of this case is, as yet, unclear, but it is to be expected that it will lead to several comparative property law studies.

II. A View on the Future of Comparative Property Law

What this brief survey of the present state of affairs in comparative property law indicates is that, compared to the law of obligations, the number of studies devoted to the subject, although growing, is relatively small. In my view, a major reason for this is the still prevailing static approach to property law and, as a consequence, to comparative property law. The existing divergence between civilian systems and the English common law is seen as an historical accident that has led to the existence of two leading traditions in property law, coherent within themselves but difficult to reconcile. This approach to property law is the expression of a legal mentality that I would like to call technocratic conservatism. It is a legal mentality that aims at preserving the status quo and that accepts changes only when these are completely unavoidable. This mentality is also typical of the way in which property law is often taught, that is, as a coherent set of mandatory and technical rules from which by an almost logical reasoning answers to individual problems can be deduced.

Concerning the future of comparative property law I have asked myself the question whether the area is indeed still so static, or whether the underlying mentality is not beginning to change as a result of the regional and global integration of markets. Market integration is becoming a strong undercurrent in national economies, causing changes in the legal framework, including property law. What will be the impact of this undercurrent of regional and global economic integration on the comparative study of property law? In the next paragraphs I will show that a change of mentality is imminent, which will lead to a rapidly increasing role of comparative property law.

It can, of course, be doubted whether the static description of property law was at all ever fully justified. Systems of property law have been far more open to change than might appear at first glance. One clear example are the changes in Continental property law systems after the French Revolution and the ensuing abolishment of the feudal system of land holding. Furthermore, Scotland only recently abandoned the feudal system; and now even in England, where property law is still based on feudal property law notions, the Law Commission is considering how to abolish the remnants of feudalism.[19] These are very fundamental changes. In addition, it should be pointed out that, although in civilian systems property law is generally laid down today in statutory form, it has, to a considerable degree, been further developed by the courts, just as much as in common law jurisdictions case law has been reformed by statutes. In other words, although civilian property law is generally laid down in statutes, yet considerable changes take place through case law, whereas in common law systems, property law is often deeply affected by the enactment of statutes.

An example of the first phenomenon is the acceptance of a transfer of ownership for security purposes by the German and, inspired by them, also by the Dutch courts. This was done because the rules on pledge did not allow the creation of a non-possessory security interest. Grave difficulties were caused by these rules, especially for small and medium-sized businesses, which could hardly obtain credit, as the only real security they had to offer was usually their inventory. Pledging the inventory was only possible either by handing it over to the creditor (frequently a bank) or to a third person. Except for a few Italian banks that had cellars to store the wine from wine growers to whom they had given credit, banks were not interested in having their customers' goods in their possession. Pledging also prevented business people from selling the inventory freely and creating a cash flow, which would have allowed them to pay off the loan. The case law remedying the lack of non-possessory security interests in the civil codes of Germany and the Netherlands by allowing a transfer of ownership for security purposes changed the German and Dutch law on security interests in movables fundamentally.[20]

The other leg of our proposition above, that is, that property in the common law systems can be deeply affected by the enactment of a statute, can be illustrated by the English Law of Property Act 1925. This Act attempted to streamline English land law in the light of the introduction of land registration. A land registry does not function efficiently if the information that is made available is not—at least to a certain degree—standardized. The Law of Property Act attempted to do that by standardizing and limiting the number of common law 'estates' (property rights), thus effectively introducing a *numerus clausus* into English land law, a concept well-known in civil property law systems.[21]

---

[19] See the Abolition of Feudal Tenure etc (Scotland) Act, 2000, Acts of the Scottish Parliament 5, and the information on the website of the Law Commission for England and Wales: <http://www.lawcom.gov.uk/feudal.htm>.

[20] See, for the Netherlands, *Hoge Raad*, 25 January 1929, *Nederlandse Jurisprudentie* 1929, 616. Under the new Civil Code such a transfer of ownership for security purposes is no longer allowed, although it can be argued that under the pressure of European private law Dutch law has had to re-accept this type of transfer. See Directive 2002/47/EC of the European Parliament and of the Council of 6 June 2002 on financial collateral arrangements, [2002] OJ L 168/43–50. In English law the problems concerning the use of inventory and claims as non-possessory security were solved through the introduction of the so-called 'floating charge' in the case *In re Panama, New Zealand, and Australian Royal Mail Company*, (1870) LR 5 Ch App 318.

[21] Section 1 Law of Property Act 1925.

To show how dynamic property law, and hence also the comparative analysis of property law, have become I will, first of all, give a brief outline from a more static viewpoint of the two major Western property law traditions: civil law and common law. I will focus on the leading principles, underlying policies, fundamental concepts, and basic rules (in other words, the basic thought patterns) of these two traditions. It will be seen that these basic thought patterns, partly rooted in a common history, resemble one another quite closely. To demonstrate this at a more specific level I will then examine two related problem areas: (1) new objects of property rights and (2) new types of property rights. The two problem areas are related, because sometimes a new object of property law can only adequately be protected through property law by the creation of a new property right.

These more explorative paragraphs on new objects and new types of property rights will be followed by an attempt to place property law in a broader economic context and by examining the possible consequences for property law of economic, and the ensuing legal, integration. In this part the focus will be on movable and immovable real security. I will adopt what I would like to call an open critical-comparative approach. By 'open' I mean that it is not the aim and object of my research to reach specific results from a given limited policy perspective. Rather, I attempt to understand property law systems from the point of view of their historical development and their internal dynamics in the light of external influences coming, for example, from such supranational integration structures as the European Union. I do not intend to give an analysis guided by the policy perspective of harmonization, or unification. If the results of comparative analysis are that there is indeed a gap between various legal systems, particularly civil law and common law, then my follow-up question will not be how to bridge this gap. On the other hand, a critical analysis of the technical differences may show that similarities do exist at the level of underlying policies, leading principles, and basic rules, which would make convergence possible. My perspective, therefore, is not a priori the convergence paradigm. My approach is also not a priori the cultural diversity paradigm. A lawyer, of course, has to be very careful when studying a legal system in which he has not been educated. This does not, however, mean that it will never be possible to grasp a foreign legal system more than superficially. That quite the contrary can be true is demonstrated by the way in which German legal scholars who fled to the United States in the 1930s were able to become 'American' lawyers. It is from a critical-comparative perspective that in the final paragraph of this chapter the question will be revisited whether property law is of a static nature and, as such, will be resistant to calls for change. A negative answer to that question would mean that comparative property law has a bright future.

III. Property Law in Civilian Systems and in the Common Law: A Traditional Static Comparative Analysis

Comparative property law still frequently focuses on a description of the basic characteristics of civil law and common law, and such description is not usually followed by an open critical-comparative analysis. What I would like to demonstrate in this paragraph is how such a traditional, descriptive approach can and should be the basis of a truly comparative study, focusing on the search for common leading principles, policy choices, and concepts. I will start with a description of the basic features of civilian property law, followed by the basic features of common law property law. Based upon this description, an example of a traditional static comparative property analysis will be given. The example will be whether in the common law, as in the civil law, a *numerus clausus* of property rights can be found.

1. Civil Law

(a) Personal versus Real Rights

The *summa divisio* of civil law is the distinction between personal rights and real rights or, as they are also called, relative rights and absolute rights.[22] A relative right is a right that a specific person has against one or more specific other persons. This other person, or these other persons, are under a corresponding obligation. The name of this area of the law is based on the duty aspect of the legal relationship: the law of obligations. The most important sources of relative rights are contracts and torts. The content of the obligation and the freedom to shape that content vary. With regard to contractual obligations the parties have an enormous freedom, the so-called 'freedom of contract'. With regard to tort matters are different. What constitutes a tort is laid down by the law, and the resulting obligation is generally one to make good the loss that has arisen.

An absolute right is a right against the world or, as it is also called, a right *erga*

---

[22] cf Manfred Wolf, 'Beständigkeit und Wandel im Sachenrecht', [1987] *Neue Juristische Wochenschrift* 2647 ff; Wolfgang Wiegand, 'Die Entwicklung des Sachenrechts im Verhältnis zum Schuldrecht', (1990) 190 *Archiv für die civilistische Praxis* 112 ff. See also Vincent Sagaert, 'Les interférences entre le droit des biens et le droit des obligations: Analyse de l'évolution depuis le Code civil', in Patrick Wery (ed), *Le droit des obligations contractuelles et le bicentenaire du Code civil* (2004), 353 ff.

omnes.[23] This means that these rights are extremely strong. Interestingly enough, the area of the law dealing with rights *erga omnes* is called property law, meaning the law of property rights. The term, therefore, focuses on the right, not, as in the case of contract and tort, on the duty. It may be appropriate, at this point, to look at the duty side of absolute rights. The duty rests on everyone: he must not violate the absolute rights of others. If he does so, the person whose right has been infringed has an option. He can either demand to be restored in his right. If that right is a right of ownership, the claim is called the *rei vindicatio*. He can also claim that the violation of his right constitutes a tort, which entitles him to a personal damages claim. He can even bring both claims. An important difference arises in an insolvency situation. A claim based on an absolute right also binds the trustee in bankruptcy. The damages claim, on the contrary, is only a personal claim against the bankrupt. Whether it will be paid depends upon the funds available after the secured and preferential creditors have been paid.

Even in the civil law, as scholastic as it might appear at first sight, the *summa divisio* between real rights and personal rights is not absolute. An important example of this assertion is provided by the law of lease. According to the civilian tradition, lease is a contract from which mutual obligations arise. The lessor has to provide the lessee with the use of an object, and the lessee has to pay the price that has been agreed upon. However, the lessee is granted special protection in a situation where a lessor, who also owns the object of the lease, sells and transfers that object to a third party. According to general principle, the lessor would still be bound by the lease agreement, even though he is no longer able to perform. Only the new owner can provide the lessee with the use of the object. But then, he is not a party to the contract of lease and thus not bound by it. If the new owner were to use his right of ownership as the basis for a *rei vindicatio* to evict the lessee, the latter would only have a personal claim for non-performance against his lessor. Civilian systems have, however, protected the lessee against eviction by allowing him to assert his right even against the new owner. The legal maxim that has been coined in that respect is that 'sale does not break lease'.[24] Effectively, therefore the lease has been turned into a legal status. The moment someone other than the original owner/lessor acquires ownership of the object of the lease, the legal status of lessor also passes to the new owner. The latter will not only be bound by the contract of lease, but will also have the corresponding rights. That the contract of

---

[23] It may also be argued that a right *erga omnes* is the sum total of personal rights that, for example, the owner has against everyone. Cf Wesley Newcomb Hohfeld, *Fundamental Legal Conceptions as Applied in Judicial Reasoning and Other Legal Essays* (ed Walter Wheeler Cook, 1923). For a civilian analysis from the point of view of legal relationships, cf Friedrich Carl von Savigny, *System des heutigen Römischen Rechts* (vol I, 1840), 6 ff.

[24] See eg § 566 BGB (referring to the lease of residential space); Art 7:226 BW (also referring to movables); for the historical background, see Reinhard Zimmermann, *The Law of Obligations: Roman Foundations of the Civilian Tradition* (paperback edn, 1996), 377 ff.

lease has effectively turned into a status is, however, only true from the perspective of the lessor, not from that of the lessee. From the lessee's point of view his right to the object of the lease is still personal, and hence not freely transferable or otherwise marketable. English law has gone further and also given the lessee a legal status, resulting in a right that the lessee can transfer. The consequence is that under English law (as well as under other common law systems) lease has developed into an 'estate', a right that is not strictly personal, but valid 'against the world'.

The *summa divisio* of relative and absolute rights, therefore, is a convenient starting-point for legal analysis. It is an important distinction for civilian legal systems, but it is not a dogma. A further example are the so-called 'qualitative' rights and duties, also known as *Reallasten* or *Realobligationen*. These are rights and duties attached to, for example, the quality of being the owner of an object. The new Dutch Civil Code has introduced this concept as a special type of legal relationship that has effect against certain, but not necessarily all, third parties.[25] This effect can arise with respect to either the creditor's or the debtor's side of the relationship or sometimes both. An example of a qualitative right is a guarantee; an example of a qualitative duty is the duty not to build a brick wall to fence off one's land. Qualitative duties have been much restricted by the Dutch Code. They can only be created with regard to immovable property and can only be of a negative kind, that is, consist in a duty not to do something. Qualitative duties, therefore, closely resemble servitudes.[26]

(b) Numerus Clausus *of Absolute Rights*

Given the *erga omnes* effect of absolute rights, the civil law has set certain limits concerning the number and content of these rights. This is the so-called *numerus clausus* doctrine which is at the heart of civilian property law systems. It has various aspects. Most importantly, the number and content of absolute rights are limited by mandatory law. Absolute rights are, for example, ownership, mortgage (hypothec), pledge, servitude, usufruct, *superficies*,[27] *emphyteusis*,[28] or intellectual property rights, such as copyright. What is meant by 'ownership', 'mortgage', and so on is defined either by statute (ie a code or a so-called 'special statute') or by case law. This is what is called in German scholarship the *Typenzwang* and *Typenfix-ierung* of absolute rights. However, the *numerus clausus* doctrine does not mean that the parties do not have any freedom at all to determine the content of absolute rights, nor does it imply that the list is closed indefinitely. Let me first make a few

---

[25] See Arts 6:251 and 252 BW.
[26] cf Arts 5:70 ff BW. Contrary to servitudes (which only become binding after registration), a qualitative duty is immediately binding between the parties.
[27] The right to own a building on land that is owned by someone else.
[28] A long lease of land.

remarks about the nature of the closed list and about freedom of contract in civilian property law systems.

Although very important, the *numerus clausus* doctrine appears to function more as a frame of reference than as a stern guardian of civilian property law. According to a leading French case, the articles in the French *Code civil* on ownership do not have an absolute character.[29] The *Cour de cassation* has stated that 'ni ces articles [ie the articles on ownership], ni aucune autre loi, n'excluent les diverses modifications et décompositions dont le droit ordinaire de propriété est susceptible'. The Court concluded that certain feudal rights, governed by the customary law of Normandy, had remained valid after the enactment of the *Code civil*. Also in German law, the *numerus clausus* doctrine is not as absolute as it appears. Under German law the buyer under a retention of title clause is given a kind of property right with regard to the object bought, although ownership only passes after full payment of the purchase price. In spite of all doctrinal difficulties which resulted from the acceptance of such a new property right, German courts felt that the practical needs had to prevail. The right thus created (a so-called *Anwartschaftsrecht*, or expectation right) is now a well-established part of German property law, contested only by a few academic lawyers. How German courts have struggled with the recognition of such a right in the light of the *numerus clausus* doctrine becomes clear when one reads the definition of this right as being a 'wesensgleiches Minus' compared to ownership. This means that an *Anwartschaftsrecht* is less than ownership but still, essentially, the same.[30] Such a right comes very close to the beneficial ownership given by English Equity to the buyer of a piece of land.[31]

Even where the *numerus clausus* principle is adhered to strictly, parties are still given some freedom to shape their property relations. An example demonstrating that freedom of contract does, at least to some extent, exist in civilian property law is the right of *emphyteusis* as it can be found under Dutch law (a long lease of land, used in particular by local communities to control the use of land) and the right of servitude. Under Dutch law it is general practice that the right of *emphyteusis* is specified by including in the deed of establishment a set of general conditions, describing and limiting the use of the property which is to be burdened.[32] If the conditions do not violate the 'nature' of the right, their content becomes part of the real right and, therefore, binds third parties. This leaves the parties to the original deed of establishment a considerable—contractual—freedom to give 'real' effect to these conditions. Another example is servitudes. The degree of freedom that exists with regard to the creation of a servitude differs from country to country. In the

---

[29] *Caquelard v Lemoine*, 13. 2. 1834; D 1834, I, 218, S. 34, 1. 205.

[30] BGH, 24 June 1958, BGHZ 28, 16.

[31] *Rose v Watson* (1864) 10 HLC 672. Cf The Law Reform Commission of Ireland (LRC 49–1995), Interests of Vendor and Purchaser in Land during the Period between Contract and Completion (1995), to be found at: <http://www.lawreform.ie/>.

[32] Arts 5:85 ff BW.

Netherlands the concept is fairly open as long as no positive duty, that is, a duty to act, is created.[33] If such a positive duty is included in the deed creating the servitude, the provision only has *inter partes* effect and does not of itself bind third parties. A third party can only be bound if the provision is included in the deed of transfer of ownership to such a third party. The seller then imposes the duties contractually upon the buyer. Such provisions are known under the name of 'chain' or 'perpetual' clauses. Generally, it can be said that property law systems are very hesitant concerning the acceptance of positive duties having *erga omnes* effect. Burdens to do something can only be accepted by a legal system, as is frequently argued, if they are voluntary. Since the French Revolution freedom has become a basic human right; feudal burdens have been abolished, not least because they usually contain positive duties.

The parties' freedom to shape a property right depends upon the nature of the property right as defined by the legal system. In the case of ownership the nature of the right limits the freedom of the parties to a large extent, but not completely. Sometimes parties to a transfer of ownership can limit the effect of such a transfer. Although a transfer of ownership generally implies that the entire right as it existed before the transfer will pass, in some legal systems the parties to such a transfer are free to limit its effect by stating explicitly for which purpose the transfer takes place. Thus, German law accepts that the transfer of ownership may be limited in its effects by the promise of the new owner that his right of ownership will only serve to secure a claim he has against the former owner.[34] This is the transfer of ownership for security purposes. In such a case, the new owner is not as free as he would have been had the transfer been made without such a security purpose. This kind of transfer has an effect which resembles that of the creation of a common law trust, as the new (legal) owner has to take into account the interests of the former (now economic) owner. What is created is a 'civil law trust', such as the *Treuhand* under German law and the *fiducie* under future French law. Here one can see a basic thought pattern of the civil law shimmering through the technical rules: as a matter of principle the former owner has only a personal contractual right, rather than a real property right, against the new owner that the new owner will use his right of ownership for the purpose agreed upon. Otherwise, we would be faced with a fragmentation of the right of ownership. It is, however, a basic tenet of the civilian systems that ownership is unitary. It is not seen as a bundle of rights which can be divided over several persons.[35] Apart from that, accepting fragmented ownership would infringe the *numerus clausus* of absolute rights. Granting ownership

---

[33] See also the recent developments in Scots law, as laid down in the Title Conditions (Scotland) Act 2003, 2003 Acts of the Scottish Parliament 9, especially s 76.

[34] This may also, in the future, be allowed in French law; see the *Proposition de loi instituant la fiducie*, no. 178, Sénat, Session ordinaire de 2004–5, *Annexe au procès-verbal de la séance du 8 février 2005, présentée par M. Philippe Marini, Sénateur*.

[35] See, for the bundle of rights theory, Hohfeld (n 23).

rights to several people would effectively mean that new real rights could be created, and this is exactly what the *numerus clausus* doctrine wants to avoid.[36]

A final aspect of the *numerus clausus* doctrine that can only be touched upon here is the way in which a civilian system looks upon real rights other than ownership. These so-called limited real rights, as their name implies, limit the right of ownership and take away certain rights from the owner. In the civilian tradition two approaches can be found. A legal system may look upon a limited real right as a *démembrement* of ownership. Certain ownership rights are given to the person with the limited real right, such as a mortgagee. The very moment the limited real right vanishes, the owner regains his full position. This is the 'elastic' concept of ownership. A limited real right restricts the right of ownership 'from the inside'. The limited real right plus what remains of the ownership right amount to full ownership. On the other hand, a legal system may consider a limited real right as entailing limited powers, as compared to ownership, without, however, carving away any rights from the owner. Ownership and limited real rights are then seen as strictly separate rights. According to this approach the owner accepts that certain of his ownership rights can no longer be used, to the extent, and for the period, that a limited real right has been created. The right of ownership and limited real rights then cumulate 'externally'. This difference in view can have consequences in situations where one person obtains various property rights. In the external-cumulative approach, it is easier, for example, for a person to be mortgagor and mortgagee at one and the same time, as is possible in the case of the German *Eigentümergrundschuld*. In the internal-cumulative approach the first reaction will be that at the very moment when a limited real right passes to the owner, the latter regains all his rights with the result that the limited real right will vanish.[37] In that approach an *Eigenümergrundschuld* is a *contradictio in terminis*.

(c) Is the Civil Law as Dogmatic as it Seems?

It appears from the above that the civil law, though scholastic and dogmatic in its structure, also shows flexibility and openness. The civil law has been shaped by the doctrinal analysis and reinterpretation of Roman law by later writers who examined Roman legal texts from the perspective of their own times. Taking Roman law as their starting-point, they attempted to create an overall framework from which the existing reality could be explained in a coherent and systematic way. Hence the idea that it was a 'system of the *contemporary* Roman law' that had to be developed.[38] The influence of this school of thought differed from country to

---

[36] Co-ownership is an entirely different matter. In such a situation the co-owners share full ownership rights. However, the object of their right of ownership is an object that belongs to both of them.

[37] cf Wolfgang Wiegand, 'Numerus clausus der dinglichen Rechte: Zur Entstehung und Bedeutung eines zentralen zivilrechtlichen Dogmas', in *Wege europäischer Rechtsgeschichte: Festschrift für Karl Kroeschell* (1987), 623 ff.

[38] Friedrich Carl von Savigny, *System des heutigen Römischen Rechts* (vol VIII, 1849).

country, and it also sometimes differed within a country. It will be apparent from the above that this doctrinal nature of the civil law does not necessarily imply that civil lawyers would be rigid in their legal thinking and would exclude from their analysis social reality and the need to develop existing concepts to establish new categories. Reference can be made to the writings of Wouter Snijders, one of the leading Dutch civil lawyers responsible for the drafting of the new Dutch Civil Code in its final stages. In these writings Snijders reacts to criticism from Dutch legal practitioners and academics who regarded the property law provisions of the new Civil Code as being too strict and constituting an expression of legal thinking predating European and global economic integration. Snijders, in response, took the view that the text of the Civil Code should be approached in a flexible and not overly legalistic way, and that it should be taken as a source of reference and analogy. A civil code does not aim to stop further legal development but attempts to channel it in a rational, constructive, and consistent way. Snijders advocated these ideas particularly when he presented his views on problems concerning property law, such as the acceptance of new objects of property law.[39] According to this approach, therefore, a civil code is an interpretative framework, open also to solutions from other legal systems, that is not meant to limit, but to guide future developments.

2. Common Law

(a) Feudal Remnants: The Concepts of Tenure and Estate

In some respects the common law is still rooted in the feudal system as it developed in England after its conquest by William the Conqueror in 1066. Most importantly, however, the feudal system lives on through the use of feudal terminology. In other words, the survival of the feudal system is largely a matter of form. Examples of feudal terminology are the concepts of 'tenure' and 'estate'.

The term 'tenure' expresses that a person holds (French: 'tenire') rights from the Crown or from a lord. The King or Queen is in the feudal system the Lord Paramount. This can still be seen in section 79(1) of the (English) Land Registration Act 2002, which reads: 'Her Majesty may grant an estate in fee simple absolute in possession out of demesne land to Herself'.[40] What 'demesne land' is can be found in section 132(1). It 'means land belonging to Her Majesty in right of the Crown which is not held for an estate in fee simple absolute in possession'. In other words, the Crown is the sole holder of rights with regard to that particular piece of

---

[39] See eg Wouter Snijders, 'Ongeregeldheden in het vermogensrecht', (2005) *Weekblad voor Privaatrecht, Notariaat en Registratie* 6607, 79 ff and *Weekblad voor Privaatrecht, Notariaat en Registratie* 6608, 94 ff.

[40] Land Registration Act 2002 Chapter 9.

(demesne) land. Most land, however, is not held solely by the Crown. In fact, with regard to most land the Crown only has a nominal right and the idea of the Queen as the Lord Paramount is more an historical notion than legal reality. The rights of other persons holding land are called estates. The concept of estate denotes the length of time of a particular entitlement with regard to land. A right can be, as in the case of a freehold estate, of unlimited duration. In the case of a leasehold estate, the entitlement is limited in time.[41] The leasehold estate was not immediately developed under the feudal system, but was later fitted into the existing feudal land categories.

Nowadays, the feudal system, as it existed in the centuries after the Norman Conquest, of course no longer exists. It has developed, and it has been reinterpreted in a way that, drawing an analogy with the application of Roman legal concepts on the continent, may be said to constitute a 'system of *contemporary* feudal law'. Modern land law has been disconnected very largely from the original feudal system. It can, therefore, be no cause of surprise that the English Law Commission has started a project aimed at modernizing land law and doing away with long-gone feudal notions.[42]

Scotland has gone even further and abolished the feudal system altogether from 28 November 2004. To understand the changes in Scots law it should be realized that, unlike English law, the Scottish legal system was influenced, to a considerable degree, by Roman law. It is a mixed legal system in which two legal traditions (civil law and common law) have grown together. When, under the influence of Roman legal thinking, the feudal rights had to be categorized, a distinction was made, as in Continental Europe, between the property right of the lord (superior) who conferred feudal rights upon someone, and the property right of the person to whom these rights were conferred (vassal). The latter person *de facto* used the land, but had to acknowledge the superior rights of the lord. This is why the vassal was said to have the *dominium utile* and the lord the *dominium directum*. In this way a doctrine of *duplex dominium* was created. The purpose of this doctrine was to maintain a unitary concept of ownership (*dominium*) as it was thought to have been applied by the Roman lawyers, while at the same time adapting it to the existing legal reality. The Abolition of Feudal Tenure etc (Scotland) Act, after abolishing the feudal system in Section 1, provides in Section 2(1) that an 'estate of *dominium utile* of land shall . . . cease to exist as a feudal estate but shall forthwith become the ownership of the land'.[43] This is not unlike what can be found in the *Décret relatif à l'abolition des privilèges* of 4 August 1789, article 1, first sentence: 'L'Assemblée nationale détruit entièrement le régime feudal'.

---

[41] Frederick H. Lawson and Bernard Rudden, *The Law of Property* (2002), 79 ff.

[42] See the information on the website of the Law Commission for England and Wales: <http://www.lawcom.gov.uk/feudal.htm>.

[43] Abolition of Feudal Tenure etc (Scotland) Act 2000 (n 19).

In the light of the abolition of the feudal system on the European Continent as a result of the French Revolution, and in Scotland only a short time ago, it is remarkable to see that feudalism is still alive and well on the Channel Islands. The property law of Jersey and Guernsey is not only rooted in the ancient customs of the Duchy of Normandy—the same customs that were accepted as existing law in the above-mentioned *Caquelard* case—but these customs are even applied to this very day.[44] This means that the existence of feudalism as such does not prevent the law from developing into a modern legal system, particularly, if it is kept in mind that the Channel Islands are well-known centres of financial services.

(b) Personal Rights versus Real Rights

The distinction between personal (eg contractual) rights and real (property) rights is also known to the common law. At the same time, however, it must not be forgotten that the concept of absolute right in the civilian sense of that term does not exist in the common law, even with regard to that part of property law that was not directly affected by the feudal system, that is movables. What matters is the effect of a right *vis-à-vis* a third party. Such effect can be 'against the world', and then its effect resembles an absolute right in the civilian sense. But it can also be more limited in the sense that it is only effective against one or more specific (groups of) third parties. This is what is meant by the relative strength of title with regard to movables. What matters in that case is, who in legal proceedings has the better right.

(c) Common Law and Equity

A specific aspect of the common law, not directly related to the feudal system, is the existence of a *duplex ordo*: common law and Equity.[45] That there is no direct relation between the existence of a feudal system and this *duplex ordo* can be seen when studying the feudal system, as it existed on the European Continent before it was abolished as a result of the French Revolution. In the Continental feudal systems the English distinction between 'old' common law and 'new' Equity is absent. A consequence of the parallel existence of these two subsystems is that a person can have a property entitlement according to one of them, but not according to the other. A prime example is the trust. The trustee (manager of a fund) has a property entitlement at common law. The beneficiary, in turn, has a property

---

[44] See Henri Basnage, *Oeuvres de maître Henri Basnage: ecuyer, seigneur du Franquesnei, avocat au Parlement, contenant ses commentaires sur la coutume de Normandie, et son traité des hypothèques* (4th edn, 1778); and see the Privy Council Decision in *Snell v Beadle* (*né Silcock*) 2001 Jersey Law Reports 118.

[45] I cannot discuss here the ongoing debate concerning the so-called 'fusion' of common law and Equity. It does, however, seem correct to say that common law and Equity can be seen as subsystems (constitutive elements) of an overarching legal system.

entitlement in Equity. The position of the common law 'owner' (the trustee) is stronger than the position of the equitable 'owner' (the trust beneficiary).

The survival of thought patterns emanating from the feudal system and the existence of a *duplex ordo* of common law and Equity have led to what may be called a relational approach to property law. A civil lawyer is inclined to expect a clear-cut answer to the question whether a person is an owner or not. The answer is either yes or no, given the unitary concept of ownership. For a common lawyer it is not that simple. A common lawyer will want to know whether the question is asked according to common law or Equity. Furthermore, with regard to land law, a common lawyer will use the concepts of tenure and estate, and not the civil law concept of absolute rights.

3. Common Elements: Transparency Requirements, Transfer Systems

Because of the *erga omnes* effect of property rights, third parties must be aware of such rights. In order to provide a sufficient degree of transparency it must, first of all, be clear with regard to which object a property right is claimed and, second, that right must be visible to third parties. Visibility can result either from the exercise of factual power (possession) or of registration. These two aspects of the transparency principle are generally known as the principles of specificity and publicity. The transparency principle can be found in both civil law and common law.

Also in both civil law and common law the same types of transfer systems can be found. These are systems to regulate the creation, transfer, and termination of real rights. Two distinctions can be made, first, with regard to the property effect of a contract, and second, with regard to the property effect of rescission or annulment of the agreement that has led to a transfer. Concerning the former the consensual system and the *traditio* system are distinguished. I will take the property effects of a contract of sale as an example. Under the consensual system a contract of sale results in an immediate transfer of ownership, either merely between seller and buyer or, depending upon the type of object, also against (certain or all) third parties. This system is applied, *inter alia*, in France. Under the *traditio* system a contract of sale does not have any property effect. An act of delivery is necessary for the transfer of ownership, although in some legal systems a contract of sale concerning an immovable can be provisionally registered at the land registry for the protection of the buyer against, for example, the insolvency of the seller. The *traditio* system and its strict separation between contract and property can be found, among other jurisdictions, in Austria and Germany. The second distinction concerns the property effect of a defect with regard to the underlying agreement.

Again two systems can be distinguished, the causal and the abstract system. Under the causal system a defect in the underlying agreement means that there is no longer a justification for the transfer and that, for this reason, the transfer is invalid. The causal system can be found in Austria. Under an abstract system, the transfer of ownership is seen as a separate legal act, which is quite independent of the underlying obligatory relationship, and which is thus inherently protecting third parties. When under the abstract system a third party acquires the right of ownership or any other property right from the new owner whose contract of sale with the former owner has been dissolved or annulled, the third party will still get full and secure ownership because he acquires from the owner. The original owner will be able to claim back his object from the recipient. But since he has lost ownership, he cannot rely on the *rei vindicatio* but merely on the law of unjustified enrichment. In addition, sometimes a claim in tort may lie against the third party. However, in insolvency situations this will not really help the former owner, as these are only personal claims. Property law systems based upon the principle of abstraction, in order to counterbalance the overprotection of third parties, may therefore develop doctrines to annul the transfer as well. This is done in German law through the doctrine of the *Fehleridentät*: a vitiating factor that invalidates the underlying agreement may be so strong as to also invalidate the so-called 'real' agreement, that is, the agreement to transfer and, consequently, the transfer itself. Causal systems, on the other hand, tend to overprotect the original owner and therefore need special provisions to protect third parties in good faith.[46]

English law, unlike most civil law systems, does not follow a uniform approach with regard to transfer systems. Thus, the Sale of Goods Act of 1979 follows the consensual system. Transfer of a legal estate in land, however, requires a formal act. Also, it should not be forgotten that Equity may intervene; and the result may therefore be that while no transfer has taken place under the common law, it has taken place in Equity.[47]

4. An Example of a Static Comparison: The *Numerus Clausus* Debate in American Legal Literature

In a series of articles American authors have recently started a discussion on whether the common law knows a *numerus clausus* of absolute rights.[48] Their

---

[46] cf L. P. W. van Vliet, *Transfer of Movables in German, French, English and Dutch Law* (2000).

[47] See van Vliet (n 46), 91.

[48] Thomas W. Merrill and Henry E. Smith, 'Optimal Standardization in the Law of Property: The Numerus Clausus Principle', (2000) 110 *Yale LJ* 1; Henry Hansmann and Reinier H. Kraakman, 'Property, Contract, and Verification: The Numerus Clausus Problem and the Divisibility of Rights', (2002) 31 *The Journal of Legal Studies* 373; Henry E. Smith, 'Property and Property Rules', (2004) 79 *New York University LR* 1719.

arguments are mostly based upon notions of efficiency and not so much on a legal, or doctrinal, analysis. In defence of a *numerus clausus* theory they put forward legal policy arguments, such as the need for legal certainty and that it should not be too costly for third parties to obtain information concerning property rights. Too much freedom for the parties, according to this point of view, would lead to an increasing fragmentation of property rights which, in turn, would lead to legal uncertainty and increasing costs of information for third parties. Arguably, in this light, the English Law of Property Act 1925 created a *numerus clausus* of common law estates to provide the basis for the introduction of an efficient and cost-effective land registry. The same development can be observed in other common law jurisdictions whose courts have been reluctant to accept new property rights.[49]

The approach taken in American legal literature adds an interesting policy aspect to the more doctrinally oriented civilian debates on the *numerus clausus*. What is, however, to be regretted is that the focus is almost exclusively on legal policy aspects. Amercian authors seem to be unaware of the enormous body of civilian literature on the *numerus clausus*. They do not test their findings against the civilian experience which could have led to a fruitful dialogue between civilian and common law lawyers.

IV. CIVIL AND COMMON PROPERTY LAW: A DYNAMIC ANALYSIS

A dynamic approach to property law in the light of an open-critical comparative analysis can open up our minds and help us to find creative and workable solutions. I will demonstrate this assertion by discussing two questions which are just as pressing in civilian property law systems as they are in the common law. Both questions raise fundamental property law issues. Should the law recognize new objects of property law? And should it recognize new types of property rights?

In essence the law of property concerns legal relationships between people with regard to objects, from which rights ensue that may be invoked against more than one person, or a number of specific persons. We have already seen that the rights that may be invoked 'against the world' are generally limited. The same can be said about what qualifies as an object of property law. Whatever represents value, it has been argued, can as a matter of principle be an object of property law. Putting an

---

[49] See for the mixed jurisdiction of South Africa, Marius J. de Waal, 'Identifying Real Rights in South African Law: The "Subtraction from the Dominium" Test and its Application', in S. E. Bartels and J. M. Milo (eds), *Contents of Real Rights* (2004), 83–98.

object on the market means that its value can be measured. This implies that the question as to what constitutes an object of property law is closely connected with the transferability or marketability of such object. However, that does not always have to be the case. Something may be an object of property law in spite of not being alienable, at least not freely alienable. Examples are *res extra commercium* and the so-called 'public property'. Based upon the respect for the dignity of the human person, the human body is not normally regarded as 'property'. Legal systems try to prevent a commercial trade in organs of the human body. This is an issue that raises difficult legal as well as moral problems. To whom do parts of the human body 'belong'? In a large number of legal systems special statutory regimes apply. Public property (such as national parks and government buildings) is the object of property law, even though it is under the control of the state and may not be freely alienable. The rules of (acquisitive) prescription may also not be applicable. Public property still represents value, however, as can be seen when such property is privatized. Another example comes from space law. Article II of the Treaty on Principles Governing the Activities of States in the Exploration and Use of Outer Space, Including the Moon and Other Celestial Bodies, states that outer space 'is not subject to national appropriation by claim of sovereignty, by means of use or occupation, or by any other means'.[50]

Concerning what can constitute an object of property law new questions constantly keep coming up. Charles Reich asked himself the question whether 'new property' (entitlements created by the government) could be recognized, a question also asked outside the United States.[51] Who can own, and hence sell and transfer, or pledge, a domain name? Courts, faced with the question whether a domain name should be recognized as a new 'exclusive right', not yet recognized as an intellectual property right, have to balance various interests. First of all, there is the need to protect the value which a domain name represents for the person holding the right to use that name. Second, account must be taken of the quasi-monopoly in the hands of the holder of that right which comes into existence once the right has been given protection as an exclusive right, and of the resulting disadvantages that may arise for others. The development of digital technology also provides a further example of a possible new object of property law. Can the right to use a wireless network be regarded as an asset that can be the object of the law of property? When I have the right to use a wireless telephone or data network, is my right of such a nature that I can sell and transfer it to someone else? Is this not what an individual mobile phone user does when he sells and transfers his mobile phone with a prepaid sim card? Telephone companies that set up a mobile phone network and take care of maintenance may sell the right to use that network ('capacity') to other phone companies. Does the right to use the network thus become an object

---

[50] The Treaty was signed at Washington, London, Moscow, 27 January 1967.
[51] Charles A. Reich, 'The New Property', (1964) 73 *Yale LJ* 733.

of property law? A different species of new objects of property law consists of rights created by public authorities, such as licences. To implement the Kyoto Treaty, the European Union has created a system of trade in emission rights, following developments in the United States allowing such trade.[52] An emission right is defined as 'an allowance to emit one tonne of carbon dioxide equivalent during a specified period, which shall be valid only for the purposes of meeting the requirements of this Directive and shall be transferable in accordance with the provisions of this Directive'.[53] A public law licence ('allowance') is transformed into an object of private property law.

Of course, opinions will differ as to whether a new object of property law has to be accepted. A good example is the question whether the right to withdraw money under a given credit line can be seized by creditors. The German Federal Supreme Court has given a strongly affirmative reply; the Dutch *Hoge Raad* has given an equally strongly negative reply.[54] Various aspects were considered. What is the nature of a client's right to withdraw money? Is it really a full-fledged right, or merely the power to create such a right (what in German law is called a *Gestaltungs-recht*)? If it is merely the latter, than it has not reached the level of maturity required to be considered a right that someone might 'own' and thus could be seized by a creditor.

Once a new object of property law has been accepted the question arises how this new object can be fitted into the system of property law. Certain concepts and rules may be applied irrespective of the classification of the various objects (such as immovable, movable, a claim, intellectual property). With regard to the establishment, transfer, or termination of a property right, however, property law systems use requirements that differ according to the nature of the object. Delivery of an immovable is generally done by registration of a formal document of transfer, whereas delivery of a movable is performed by transfer of possession. The nature of the new object of property will thus play a prominent role. Licences, such as emission rights, originate in public law and have a very special content. This will influence the answer to the question which property concepts and rules should be considered applicable. It may even be that, if the new object cannot readily be fitted into the existing system of property law, new concepts and rules have to be developed. This can go as far as the creation of a new property right. 'Ownership' of

---

[52] Kyoto Protocol to the United Nations Framework Convention on Climate Change, signed in Kyoto on 11 December 1997. The treaty is a protocol to the United Nations Framework Convention on Climate Change (1992). As to European Union law, see Directive 2003/87/EC of the European Parliament and of the Council of 13 October 2003 establishing a scheme for greenhouse gas emission allowance trading within the Community and amending Council Directive 96/61/EC, [2003] OJ L 275/32.

[53] Article 3(a) of Directive 2003/87/EC.

[54] BGH, 29 March 2001, BGHZ 147, 193; *Hoge Raad*, 29 October 2004, Nederlandse Jurisprudentie 2006, 203.

emission rights does not necessarily have to mean the same as 'ownership' of a movable physical asset. Given the time limitation of such rights, it may be questioned, for example, whether the pledging or mortgaging of emission rights should be possible.

Whether a new property right has to be created is a question that does not only arise with regard to new, but also with regard to old and well-recognized objects of property law. Thus, the question is sometimes asked whether a special property right should be created giving ownership of a cable network, or a pipeline, to the person operating the cable network or pipeline. Generally, the law of servitudes is sufficiently flexible to accommodate the interests of the companies building and using cable networks or pipelines, *vis-à-vis* those who own the land through which or over which the network or pipeline passes. However, it may be extremely burdensome and expensive to agree on the creation of a servitude with all of the landowners involved. One way to solve this problem might be a reformulation of the law of servitudes, as can be found in the American Restatement on Property Third (Servitudes).[55] The restatement follows a pragmatic and non-formalistic approach. It leaves the parties involved all the freedom they need to pursue their individual interests, albeit within a mandatory framework aimed at protecting the general interest. The leading maxim seems to be: no more mandatory rules than needed. An alternative solution might be the creation of a new property right for the benefit of those who exploit a network or pipeline, entitling them to the network or pipeline irrespective of its location.[56] These questions have become very acute in jurisdictions where networks used to be in the hands of the government, but have subsequently been sold and transferred to private enterprises. In such circumstances it becomes important to know exactly what is sold and transferred, not just with respect to the physical aspects of the network, but also with respect to the property rights involved.

V. The Osmosis of National, Regional, and Global Property Law

The integration of markets has a growing impact on property law. Reference has already been made to the influence of European law on the property law regimes of the member states of the European Union. I have mentioned the EU directive on

---

[55] ALI, Restatement of the Law Third, Property, Servitudes (vols I and II, 2000).

[56] For the Netherlands, see Aart A. van Velten, 'Het zakenrechtelijk statuut van nutsleidingen in het Nederlandse recht', [2004] *Tijdschrift voor Privaatrecht* 1407 ff.

trading in emissions, which was enacted to implement the Kyoto Protocol. Whether a member state is willing to accept emission rights as a new object of property law or not has become irrelevant. European law obliges the member states to accept this. How these new rights are to be fitted into the various national legal orders is another matter. To some degree the directive gives guidance, but for the rest the solution depends on the various national legislatures. The result is a paradox. The EU emissions directive creates supra-national legal unity. At the same time, the result is fragmentation and inconsistency. The member states are free to fill the lacunae in the directive by national law. Consequently, divergence between the various national legal systems may increase rather than decrease. Furthermore, fragmentation is increasing at the national level because next to property law rules emanating from the national legislatures, those based on European law have to be applied.

The same phenomenon can be seen at a global level. The UNIDROIT Cape Town Convention on International Interests in Mobile Equipment introduces a uniform security interest for, among other objects, aircraft engines and railway rolling stock.[57] This interest has to be registered in a worldwide accessible computer registration system. Particularly for railway rolling stock this will be an innovation in many countries. Should national legal systems now treat a rail carriage as if it were registered immovable property? What are the consequences for other movable objects of great value, such as trucks? Should not trucks also become objects of registration, which can be mortgaged by way of entry of a mortgage deed in a computerized system? These matters are not resolved by the Convention and must therefore be settled at national level, with the risk of diverging national responses. A comparative analysis of the impact of the uniform regime may provide an insight into the problems caused by it, how the various legal systems have reacted, and in which way these problems can be solved uniformly and avoided in the future.

The preparation of a uniform regime and the analysis of the impact of such a regime on national law can only be done adequately on a comparative basis. In this way models can be discovered, compared, and evaluated, and their advantages and disadvantages can be assessed. In view of the pragmatic, flexible and open approach adopted by it, Article 9 UCC has become a leading model in the area of personal property security interests. The Cape Town Convention is clearly to a large degree inspired by Article 9 UCC. The same is true of the model law on secured transactions drafted by the European Bank for Reconstruction and Development, which has been designed for countries with economies in transition after the collapse of communism.[58] The European Bank for Reconstruction

---

[57] UNIDROIT Cape Town Convention on International Interests in Mobile Equipment (Cape Town, 2001).

[58] The model can be found on the website of the European Bank for Reconstruction and Development: <http://www.ebrd.org/>.

and Development model is also inspired by the English floating charge: a charge on the whole of a company's assets, both present and future. The latter aspect of that model, in particular, may create problems in civilian law systems that adhere strictly to the principle of specificity. A floating charge is essentially what was called before the French Revolution a general mortgage; it had been abandoned following the Revolution given its negative effect on economic life. The renewed acceptance of such mortgages (a phenomenon that can be described as *Wiederkehr der Rechtsfiguren*) does, however, fit in well with a broader global development towards acceptance of general security interests that rest on both present and future property to secure both present and future debt.[59] With regard to real security on immovables, German mortgage law is regarded as an interesting model. Under German law a mortgage over an immovable does not have to be accessory, which means that when the loan is repaid the mortgage is not automatically extinguished. This type of mortgage is referred to as *Grundschuld* and it has inspired proposals to introduce a European-wide uniform mortgage on real property, the so-called 'euromortgage'.[60] Also, recently a French working group chaired by Michel Grimaldi, which proposes a fundamental revision of the law on personal and real security interests and the addition of a new book on security interests to the French *Code civil*, suggested the introduction, in France, of a non-accessory type of mortgage (*hypothèque rechargeable*).[61] The new Dutch Civil Code has also acted as a point of reference, especially in countries with an economy in transition. To what degree Dutch property law can continue to be a model at the European level is unclear. Various fundamental policy choices made during the drafting of the Dutch rules on property law are now being questioned as a direct result of European and global developments. This is especially true for the ban on the use of ownership for security purposes, as laid down in Article 3:84(3) BW. Ownership is used very widely for security purposes and it can therefore cause no surprise that in the Grimaldi report this is accepted for France.

[59] cf for the *Wiederkehr der Rechtsfiguren* (return of legal models) Wiegand, (1990) 190 *Archiv für die civilistische Praxis* 112, 132; Theo Mayer-Maly, 'DieWiederkehr von Rechtsfiguren', [1971] *Juristen-zeitung* 1 ff; for the Netherlands, cf already J. P. A. Coopmans, *Renaissance van oud recht* (1965). With regard to the (renewed) acceptance of general security interests, reference can be made to the ten core principles for a secured transactions law, to be found on the website of the European Bank for Reconstruction and Development (n 58).

[60] See the report by the Forum Group on Mortgage Credit, *The Integration of the EU Mortgage Credit Markets* (2004) and, recently, the Green Paper, *Mortgage Credit in the EU* (presented by the European Commission), Brussels, 19.7.2005, COM (2005) 327 final, to be found at: <http://europa.eu.int/prelex/apcnet.cfm?CL=en>.

[61] Groupe de travail relatif à la réforme du droit des sûretés, *Rapport à Monsieur Dominique Perben, Garde des Sceaux, Ministre de la Justice and Avant-projet de texte issu du rapport Grimaldi* (2005), to be found at: <http://www.justice.gouv.fr/publicat/rapport/rapportgrimaldi.htm>. By Ordonnance no. 2006–346 du 23 mars 2006 relative aux sûretés, published in the Journal Officiel no. 71 of 24 March 2006, this non-accessory mortgage has now been introduced in French law.

I have only referred to a few legal systems that may be a potential model for a future uniform property law. Other legal systems could have been mentioned. An alternative would be not to take a particular national model as a starting-point for legal unification, but rather a truly international one that would have to be devised on the basis of thorough comparative analysis. That model would then be tested by making it compete with the existing (national) models. A European example in the area of private law is the so-called 'Common Frame of Reference' which is, as yet, in its drafting stage. It aims at establishing a system of principles and rules that can be used as a tool to analyse the existing European law (the *acquis communautaire*) from the point of view of consistency and effectiveness, and that can serve as a basis for future European law.[62] Based on this common frame of reference a so-called 'optional instrument' will be developed that may be chosen by contracting parties involved in European business transactions. This common frame of reference, although its focus is primarily on contract law, may also deal with certain property law issues such as personal property security interests, given the importance of security for intra-European trade.

VI. FINAL REMARKS

Property law, and hence comparative property law, once considered to be fairly static, is turning into an increasingly dynamic field of law. This is to a considerable degree a consequence of European and global economic integration, and the resulting legal integration.[63] The national property laws, whether belonging to the civilian or the common law tradition, will all be affected by this change.

The law on land registries provides a good example as to how the development may proceed. Here the impetus for unification is a desire to make information from a land registry that is available at the national level also accessible to others outside the boundaries of national jurisdiction. In this way foreign service providers, such as notaries and advocates, would have the same information as local service providers and could use that information to assist their clients more effectively when they want to enter the foreign real estate market. National land

---

[62] See, for more information, <http://europa.eu.int/comm/consumers/index_en.htm>.

[63] cf the paper published recently by Abraham Bell and Gideon Parchomovsky, 'Of Property and Federalism' (Bar-Ilan University Faculty of Law, Interdisciplinary Program for Law, Rationality, Ethics and Social Justice, Working Paper No. 06–85, and University of Pennsylvania Law School, Institute for Law and Economics, Research Paper No. 05–12, te be found at the webiste of the Social Science Research Network: <http://papers.ssrn.com/sol3/papers.cfm?abstract_id=709321>.

registries will then have become an international source of information.[64] The very moment when this happens, however, further steps will be required. Foreign lawyers will want to understand the information given to them. The mere translation of foreign legal terms (what does 'owner' mean?) will then hardly be sufficient. A simple translation can hide more than the original term. Also, it may lead the foreign lawyer to believe that he or she fully understands the foreign legal regime. To avoid misunderstandings, it will be necessary to draft not only a list of translations of legal terms, but to provide the context of these translations. In other words, multilingual glossaries will be needed. They cannot be written without in-depth comparative property law studies. The creation of an integrated market of legal services may, however, require even more. In order not only to understand the information available from the various land registries, but also to use it, pressure will arise to create a uniform legal regime, particularly with regard to security interests. This is the only way in which, at the end of the day, truly efficient access to other markets will be possible. In fact, this development has already started in Europe in the form of proposals concerning the euro-mortgage and worldwide through the creation of the (UNIDROIT) international security interest in mobile equipment.

My final conclusion, therefore, is that comparative property law has, for some time, been in the shadow of the more dynamic law of obligations. But this is now changing, and the comparative study of property law will rapidly gain importance.

BIBLIOGRAPHY

Frederick H. Lawson and Athanassios Yiannopoulos (chief eds), *International Encyclopedia of Comparative Law*, vol VI: *Property and Trust* (1973–present)

Jean Georges Sauveplanne (ed), *Security over Corporeal Movables* (1974)

G. E. van Maanen and A. J . van der Walt (eds), *Property Law on the Threshold of the 21st Century* (1996)

Peter von Wilmowsky, *Europäisches Kreditsicherungsrecht: Sachenrecht und Insolvenzrecht unter dem EG-Vertrag* (1996)

Richard H. Helmholz and Reinhard Zimmermann, *Itinera Fiduciae: Trust and Treuhand in Historical Perspective* (1998)

David J. Hayton, S. C. J. J. Kortmann, and H. L. E. Verhagen (eds), *Principles of European Trust Law* (1999)

Jacobien W. Rutgers, *International Reservation of Title Clauses: A Study of Dutch, French and German Private International Law in the Light of European Law* (1999)

---

[64] See the European Land Information Service (EULIS) project: <http://www.eulis.org>. Cf Sergio Camara-Lapuente, 'Registration of Interests as a Formality of Contracts: Comparative Remarks on Land Registers within the Frame of European Private Law', (2005) 13 *European Review of Private Law* 797–839.

Ugo Mattei, *Basic Principles of Property Law: A Comparative Legal and Economic Introduction* (2000)

Jan-Peter Loof and Hendrik Ploeger, *The Right to Property: The Influence of Article 1 Protocol no. 1 ECHR on Several Fields of Domestic Law* (2000)

Anna Veneziano, *Le garanzie mobiliari non possessorie: profili di diritto comparato e di diritto del commercio internazionale* (2000)

L. P. W. van Vliet, *Transfer of Movables in German, French, English and Dutch Law* (2000)

Christian von Bar and Ulrich Drobnig, *The Interaction of Contract Law and Tort and Property Law in Europe: A Comparative Study* (2004)

Eva-Maria Kieninger, *Security Rights in Movable Property in European Private Law* (2004)

Reinhard Zimmermann, Daniel Visser, and Kenneth Reid (eds), *Mixed Legal Systems in Comparative Perspective: Property and Obligations in Scotland and South Africa* (2004)

Michele Graziadei, Ugo Mattei, and Lionel Smith (eds), *Commercial Trusts in European Private Law* (2005)

James Gordley, *Foundations of Private Law: Property, Tort, Contract, Unjust Enrichment* (2006)

CHAPTER 33

COMPARATIVE SUCCESSION LAW

MARIUS J. DE WAAL

Stellenbosch

I. Introduction

ALL the chapters in this section of the book deal with one central question: what is the 'state of the art' of comparative law in a particular area? This central question, together with the more specific questions flowing from it, is also the focus of this chapter on the law of succession.

However, it can only be tackled against the background of a proper understanding of the true nature of the law of succession.[1] The primary function of the law of succession is to identify the persons entitled to succeed to the deceased and to identify the property they are to receive. From the perspective of the testator (if there is a valid will) it guarantees, as far as the law allows, that the property reaches the destination determined by him. From the perspective of the heirs it guarantees that the property is transferred to them in a lawful and orderly fashion.

Consequently, the law of succession facilitates continuity, prevents self-help, and ensures a smooth transfer of wealth upon death.

It will become readily apparent in the course of this chapter that the law of succession should always be analysed within a broader economic and social context.[2] This is because the law of succession fulfils both an economic and a social function. Its economic function is primarily to regulate the transfer of wealth upon a person's death. This function is supported by the principle of freedom of testation that holds that a person may, within certain limits, decide on the distribution of his property upon death. The social function of the law of succession is associated particularly with the maintenance and protection of the family as a social unit. As will be illustrated later,[3] this explains why the law of succession is influenced by social trends affecting the family.

---

[1] See M. J. de Waal, 'The Law of Succession and the Bill of Rights: Private Succession and Freedom of Testation in the Light of the Constitution', in *Butterworths Bill of Rights Compendium* (loose-leaf) (2003), para 3G3 with further references.

[2] See especially Section II below.   [3] See Section II.3 below.

A trite, though fundamental, feature of the law of succession is its subdivision into testate and intestate succession. Testate succession deals with the situation where a person has chosen to dispose of his property in a last will. More particularly, it deals with the execution, amendment, and revocation of wills as well as with the contents and interpretation of wills. Intestate succession, on the other hand, deals with the devolution of the property of a person who has died without leaving a valid will, or who has failed to dispose of all his property in a valid will. In this chapter the person whose property is the subject of distribution upon death will normally be referred to as the 'testator' in the context of the law of testate succession. In all other instances the term 'deceased' will be used.

It has often been stated as a piece of conventional wisdom that the law of succession is one of the most indigenous branches of the law and that it therefore does not ideally lend itself to comparative research. The law of succession is, as it were, a part of a country's cultural goods—like its monuments and museums.[4] This view has at least two general implications for comparative research in the field.

The first implication (an issue that will be revisited later)[5] is that it may lead to the premature conclusion that legal comparison with a view to the possible harmonization of the law of succession is in essence a futile exercise. This conclusion, in turn, is founded on two premises. First, legal comparison for this purpose cannot be successful because the law of succession is too much embedded in local culture and customs. And, second, harmonization in this area of the law is also not really desirable because it would inevitably lead to something akin to a loss of cultural goods.

The second implication is that it may inspire a tendency towards a potentially sterile form of 'micro'-comparison. For example, formalities for the execution of valid wills in different systems could be compared. The result would be the identification of an amazing variety of possibilities. Even in the European context comparative research has distinguished four broad types of will: (a) the holographic will (a will that must be written and signed personally by the testator); (b) the witnessed will; (c) the closed and international will; and (d) the notarial or public will.[6] Moreover, the specific requirements within each type may vary greatly. The notarial or public will can serve as just one example.[7] In most European countries this type of will is drafted by a notary but it must be signed by the testator. In Austria a notarial will can also be made by a judge. Belgian law and French law

---

[4] See Walter Pintens, 'Grundgedanken und Perspektiven einer Europäisierung des Familien- und Erbrechts—Teil 1', (2003) 50 *Zeitschrift für das gesamte Familienrecht* 329, 331.

[5] See Section II below.

[6] See eg Alain Verbeke and Yves-Henri Leleu, 'Harmonization of the Law of Succession in Europe', in Arthur Hartkamp, Martijn Hesselink, Ewoud Hondius, Carla Joustra, and Edgar du Perron (eds), *Towards a European Civil Code* (3rd edn, 1998), 335, 342.

[7] Verbeke and Leleu (n 6), 342.

require that the testator must dictate the will to the notary. In other countries, such as Germany and Austria, it is sufficient if the testator delivers the document to the notary with the confirmation that it is his will. This sort of exercise can be repeated with regard to, for example, capacity to make a will, amendment of wills, revocation of wills, condonation of formally defective wills, capacity to inherit, and so on. This type of comparison may be interesting; at the same time, however, its usefulness may be queried.

All of this relates to what has been called the 'postmodernist' approach to legal comparison: that is, the search not for points of contact between different legal systems and legal institutions, but the search for distinctions and differences between them.[8] This approach may have its value, but it entails the danger of stagnation and also the possible isolation from the advantages of legal comparison and harmonization.[9]

It is therefore worth observing right at the outset that relatively little has been written on the law of succession in a comparative perspective. In this regard the law of succession is certainly lagging behind many (if not most) other areas of private law. By way of example the very slow progress that has been made with the volume on the law of succession (vol V) in the *International Encyclopedia of Comparative Law* can be noted. Of the provisional nine chapters, only three have been completed to date. These are the chapters on the law of intestate succession, liability for obligations of the inheritance, and succession to agricultural property.

Against this general background we can now approach the more specific questions to which answers must be sought. What important comparative work has been done in the field of the law of succession? What are the achievements, if any, of this work? Are there particular difficulties facing comparative scholars in the law of succession? What are the important tasks to be fulfilled by comparative scholarship in this field? What is the future agenda for comparative scholarship?

It will be shown that answers to these questions can be sought in at least the following five contexts: (a) comparative law and the harmonization of the law of succession; (b) comparative law and private international law (conflict of laws); (c) freedom of testation and its possible limitations; (d) the example of the trust with reference to the contents of wills; and (e) the transfer of a deceased person's estate upon death.

---

[8] Pintens, (2003) 50 *Zeitschrift für das gesamte Familienrecht* 331.   [9] Ibid.

II. Comparative Research and the Harmonization of the Law of Succession

1. The Scope for Harmonization in the Context of the Law of Succession: The Traditional View

The concept of harmonization has been explained as the 'wide variety of methods and techniques which attempt to realize, to a variable degree, an approximation of differing national legislations in a certain area of law'.[10] Although the quest for harmonization (or, more ambitiously, unification) is not totally uncontroversial, its obvious advantages cannot be doubted. Chief among these would be the fact that it makes international legal dealings easier and also less risky by promoting predict-ability and security.[11] Further, in an era of globalization and greater mobility of people, the 'hazards of applying private international law and foreign substantive law' would be reduced.[12]

Although the advantages or otherwise of harmonization may be debatable, there seems to be general agreement as to what the starting-point should be. In order to find an answer to the question of whether or not the harmonization of a certain field of law is feasible, one has to start from comparative legal research. Zweigert and Kötz have stated that preparatory studies in comparative law are 'absolutely essential' here: 'without them one cannot discover the points of agreement or disagreement in the different legal systems of the world, let alone decide which solution is the best'.[13] And this research, it has been suggested, should be pursued according to the so-called 'functional-typological method'.[14] This means that, on the one hand, the function of a legal rule or institution is examined and that it has to be investigated whether the rule properly fulfils this function; on the other hand, 'typical solutions' to legal problems in different systems are to be identified.[15]

In general it would be true to say that in societies that are socially, economically, politically, and culturally comparable it is likely that the social problems to be regulated and solved by legal rules are more or less similar.[16] It is therefore also more likely that there should be 'typical solutions' to these problems. The social (and economic) problem to be addressed by the law of succession is, of course, the issue of how, when, and to whom property must be transferred at a person's death.

---

[10] Verbeke and Leleu (n 6), 335.

[11] Konrad Zweigert and Hein Kötz, *Introduction to Comparative Law* (trans Tony Weir, 3rd edn, 1998), 25.

[12] Ibid.   [13] Ibid 24–5.   [14] Verbeke and Leleu (n 6), 335.   [15] Ibid.

[16] Ibid 336.

However, as has been pointed out, there appears to be wide acceptance for the proposition that the law of succession is to a large extent influenced by local rules, customs, moral values, and cultural conventions. According to this view a (more) harmonized or unified law of succession is therefore neither feasible nor desirable.[17]

2. The Traditional View Challenged

In the broader context of comparative studies on the law of succession this general proposition has been challenged on a number of different grounds. First, the basic assumptions underlying it have been questioned. One of these assumptions is that the law of succession is characterized by its 'regionality'. This means that the legal relationships regulated by the law of succession are mostly localized. However, an author such as Dieter Leipold[18] has argued convincingly that this is a gross over-simplification. He indicates that such relationships can be manifold and that they often reach across borders. To mention only one common example (that will be expanded upon below in the discussion of private international law):[19] the testator is a national of one country but dies in another, leaving movable and immovable property in a third country. Regarding the European law of succession in particular, Leipold also questions another assumption, namely that its shape is necessarily dictated by different cultural, social, and religious considerations in different countries. In this connection he draws attention to the existence of a common legal tradition based on Roman law, Canon law, and the Roman-Canon *ius commune*.[20]

The general proposition has furthermore been questioned on the basis of historical research. A fascinating piece of historical evidence regarding the possibilities of harmonization in the law of succession is provided by the story of the creation of Book Five on the law of succession, in the German Civil Code. In order to create a unified law of succession for the whole of Germany it was necessary to harmonize at least four different succession regimes prevailing in different parts of Germany at the time: the *ius commune*, Saxon common law, Prussian *Allgemeinen Landrechts*, and French law.[21] Apart from these general regimes, there were more than 100 local laws applicable in certain parts of Germany. Despite the fact that it might at the outset have seemed to be a hopeless quest, unity was achieved even in the most sensitive areas such as the rules of intestate succession, forced succession, and formalities for the execution of wills.

More recently one can detect a momentum towards greater unity through common social and economic developments in different societies. And it is mainly through comparative research that these trends and their impact on the law of

---

[17] Verbeke and Leleu (n 6), 337.

[18] Dieter Leipold, 'Europa und das Erbrecht', in *Europas universale rechtsordnungspolitische Aufgabe im Recht des dritten Jahrtausends: Festschrift für Alfred Söllner* (2000), 647, 649.

[19] See Section III below.   [20] Leipold (n 18), 650.   [21] Ibid 655.

succession—predominantly in the spheres of intestate succession and forced succession—have been identified. In what follows these developments in, respectively, the social and economic spheres will be highlighted.

3. Social Factors Influencing the Law of Succession[22]

Reference has already been made to the important interplay between the broad areas of the law of succession and family law.[23] It is therefore not surprising that the social function of the law of succession is intimately linked with the family. The premise is that the family is an important social unit that needs to be protected and preserved. If a person dies, leaving a spouse and dependent children, the law attempts to ensure that the basic needs of the surviving family members will be provided for via the estate of the deceased. In intestate succession this is achieved by generally drawing the circle of potential heirs as small as possible and in testate succession by the numerous restrictions on the testator's freedom of testation.[24] Friedman[25] refers to this as the 'principle of forced succession':

The principle of forced succession we might call *social*. Practically speaking, forced succession means succession within the family—to the wife, children, or other dependants. Forced succession imposes upon the testator the obligation to care for members of his family before satisfying any other desires and needs. In a sense, it converts private property at death to family property.

The concept 'family' used thus far is the so-called 'nuclear' family that consists of married parents with dependent children. However, once a different or wider definition of 'family' is accepted, the succession rules aimed at the protection of the family may become different. And this 'redefinition' of the family is exactly what has been taking place due to social developments in many societies. These developments, and their influence on the law of succession, have been the focus of much of the more recent comparative research in the field. For purposes of this chapter it will have to suffice that some of these social developments are just mentioned:[26]

---

[22] See, in general, Marius J. de Waal, 'The Social and Economic Foundations of the Law of Succession', (1997) 8 *Stellenbosch LR* 162, 163–6 with further references.

[23] See Section I above.   [24] As to freedom of testation, see further Section IV below.

[25] Lawrence M. Friedman, 'The Law of the Living, the Law of the Dead: Property, Succession and Society', (1966) 29 *Wisconsin LR* 340, 366.

[26] See, especially, S. M. Cretney, 'Reform of Intestacy: The Best We Can Do?', (1995) 111 *LQR* 77 ff; De Waal, (1997) 8 *Stellenbosch LR* 162; Pintens, (2003) 50 *Zeitschrift für das gesamte Familienrecht* 329 ff; Walter Pintens, 'Grundgedanken und Perspektiven einer Europäisierung des Familien- und Erbrechts—Teil 2', (2003) 50 *Zeitschrift für das gesamte Familienrecht* 417 ff. As is evident from these references, important research regarding these developments has been done in the European context. For some developments in American law, see Paul J. Buser, 'Domestic Partner and Non-marital Claims against Probate Estates: *Marvin* Theories Put to a Different Use', (2004) 38 *Family Law Quarterly* 315 ff.

(a) a movement towards the strengthening of the position of the surviving spouse at the expense of children and further relations;

(b) the legal recognition of partnerships between persons (also of the same sex) who are not married;

(c) the legal recognition of adoption of children by partners of the same sex; and

(d) the general elimination of all discrimination against the extra-marital (illegitimate) child.

The effects of these developments on the law of succession are fairly obvious. First, the strengthening of the position of the surviving spouse at the expense of children has led to a shift in emphasis from a 'vertical law of succession' (succession between parents and children) to that of a 'horizontal law of succession' (succession between spouses).[27] Second, the legal recognition of partnerships between persons who are not married and the elimination of discrimination against the extra-marital child have an important impact on both the law of intestate succession and the system of forced succession.

Most of these developments have been brought about by the fundamental consideration of equality before the law (in other words, the abolition of all forms of discrimination). In South Africa, for example, the black customary law of intestate succession has always been founded on the basic principles of primogeniture (favoured treatment of the first-born) and preference to male heirs. Due to its inherently discriminatory nature this whole system has now been declared unconstitutional and has (at least as an interim measure) been replaced with the 'normal' regime of intestate succession as regulated by legislation.[28]

Another social factor that is relevant with regard to its effect on the law of succession is the steady increase in the rate of divorces. One issue is the difficult question whether a divorced spouse should be considered as a potential heir in terms of the law of intestate succession. Attention has been drawn to the 'bewildering range of possibilities' that have to be examined if the law is to cater for a situation where a deceased's surviving spouse is not the only person to whom he or she had been married.[29] A further issue concerns the impact of a divorce, or the annulment of a marriage, on the dispositions in a will that has been made before the divorce or annulment. Research on the legal position in the German, Spanish, Swedish, Portuguese, Dutch, and English law of succession has shown that, despite differences in approach, a common trend is noticeable,[30] for it is increasingly widely held that any bequest in the will in favour of the former spouse becomes

---

[27] Walter Pintens, 'Die Europäisierung des Erbrechts', (2001) 9 *Zeitschrift für Europäisches Privatrecht* 628, 629; Jean C. Sonnekus, 'The New Dutch Code on Succession as Evaluated through the Eyes of a Hybrid Legal System', (2005) 13 *Zeitschrift für Europäisches Privatrecht* 71, 76.

[28] See *Bhe v Magistrate, Khayelitsha* 2005 (1) SA 580 (CC).

[29] Cretney, (1995) 111 *LQR* 93–4; De Waal, (1997) 8 *Stellenbosch LR* 173.

[30] Antoni Vaquer, 'Wills, Divorce and the Fate of Dispositions in Favour of the Spouse: A Common Trend in European Succession Laws', (2003) 11 *European Review of Private Law* 782 ff.

ineffective. A further point worth noticing is that in all these systems that legal consequence is premised on the hypothetical intention of the testator.

In the final analysis it needs to be stressed that the general trend towards greater harmonization in the European law of succession, as described by comparative scholars, has not been the result of a deliberate policy of the different national legislatures. It may be explained by the common social developments intimately linked with the law relating to the family.[31]

4. Economic Factors Influencing the Law of Succession[32]

As indicated, the principle of forced succession within the family is based on *social* considerations. However, where a person is allowed to dispose freely of his property by will a different principle becomes relevant. Friedman[33] submits that the principle at work here is that of *gift*, an *economic* principle:

The principle of *gift*, since it exalts the volition of the property holder, is consistent with free market economics . . . Individuals as holders of private property may dispose of it as they see fit. The principle of gift can be called *economic*. Despite the paradox that a gift is not an economic transfer, the principle of gift is necessary to the economic system and is presupposed by it.

From forced succession the emphasis today has shifted to the principle of freedom of testation.[34] As this freedom is of vital importance in any developed system of testate succession, both its economic importance and its economic implications have received the attention of researchers in the field. At the same time, the principle and the limitations placed on it have received their fair share of attention by comparative scholars.[35]

As has been noted at the outset,[36] a will is an instrument by means of which wealth is transferred. Wills have therefore been described as 'economic documents of vital importance'.[37] However, John Langbein has convincingly demonstrated how the general importance of wills as means of wealth transfer has been considerably diminished in recent times.[38]

The first development in this context has been the emergence of so-called 'will substitutes'. In the United States of America, for example, forty-four states have enacted laws based on what is called the 'Uniform Non-Probate Transfers on Death Act' that is based on a model statute proposed in 1991. Non-probate transfers on

---

[31] Pintens, (2001) 9 *Zeitschrift für Europäisches Privatrecht* 628, 629.

[32] See, in general, De Waal, (1997) 8 *Stellenbosch LR* 166–9 with further references.

[33] (1966) 29 *Wisconsin LR* 353.   [34] See further Section IV below.

[35] See further Section IV below.   [36] See Section I above.

[37] Friedman, (1966) 29 *Wisconsin LR* 371.

[38] John H. Langbein, 'The Nonprobate Revolution and the Future of the Law of Succession', (1984) 97 *Harvard LR* 1108 ff.

death 'are "nontestamentary" in nature, meaning that the beneficiary takes the property outside the legal structure of probate court administration and law'.[39] Such transfers or 'will substitutes' include (but are not limited to):[40] (a) insurance policy benefits; (b) mortgages; (c) promissory notes; (d) securities; (e) deposit agreements; (f) deeds of gift; and (g) pension and retirement plans.

A second development concerns fundamental changes in the nature of wealth.[41] In the past *land* has been the dominant form of wealth. More recently, however, two new forms of private sector wealth have become increasingly important, that is, *financial assets* (such as stocks, bonds, bank deposits, shares, and insurance contracts) and *human capital* (the skills and knowledge forming the basis of advanced technological life). In particular, the importance of the latter—human capital—has increased the significance of lifetime transfers of wealth (such as expenditure on the education of children) as opposed to transmissions of wealth on death.[42]

And, finally, there is an important social fact with economic implications: many people live longer (and therefore outlive their period of productive employment) which means that a second 'great cycle of saving and dissaving' is being constituted (the first being the expenditure on children's education).[43] People live longer and through the system of annuitization much of their pension wealth (held in financial assets) is consumed during their lifetime. The result is that only a small fraction of pension wealth finds its way into intergenerational transfers.[44] However, one has to be careful not to over-generalize. For example, different factors may be relevant in societies with a strong social support system for the aged. With reference to the German situation, Walter Pintens points out how the average size of estates has increased over the last number of years.[45] One reason for this trend is the revalorization of pensions which resulted in a bigger income for retired people. This meant that savings could often be left untouched and could be allowed to grow through the capitalization of interest.

In general, however, one has to accept that changes in 'the timing and in the character of wealth transmissions'[46] have had an influence on the relative importance of wills as instruments of wealth transfer. There can be no doubt that this and other economic trends do and will have an influence on the law of testate succession. One possibility is, again, that common trends may result in the laws of different systems moving closer towards each other. There is still much scope for comparative work in this regard.

---

[39] Buser, (2004) 38 *Family Law Quarterly* 324.   [40] Ibid.

[41] John H. Langbein, 'The Twentieth-Century Revolution in Family Wealth Transmission', (1988) 86 *Michigan LR* 722, 723. See also Cretney, (1995) 111 *LQR* 91.

[42] Langbein, (1988) 86 *Michigan LR* 722.   [43] Ibid 743.   [44] Ibid 745.

[45] Pintens, (2001) 9 *Zeitschrift für Europäisches Privatrecht* 628.

[46] Langbein, (1988) 86 *Michigan LR* 723.

III. Private International Law (Conflict of Laws) and Comparative Research in the Law of Succession

1. The Typical Problems

The law of succession can, of course, generate numerous private international law (conflict of laws) problems. To give just one typical example: the testator, a national of country A, makes a will according to the law of country A; he then becomes a habitual resident of country B; and he eventually dies in country C, but with beneficiaries and property in countries A, B, C, and D. The law of which country will regulate the validity of his will? Under the law of which country will his estate be administered? Will the answers to these questions be dependent on the nature of the person's property, for example, whether it is movable or immovable property? Will the positions of the different beneficiaries differ depending on the particular country in which they find themselves? Of course, the dilemma is that there is not a single set of answers to these questions: it will all depend on which country's private international law rules are to be applied.

2. Important Public International Law Instruments

In order to address this dilemma a number of international instruments, dealing with a variety of issues, have been created. Examples include the following:

(a)   The Treaty of Washington of 26 October 1973 has created a so-called 'international will' in an attempt to regulate and unify the issue of the formal execution of wills. The bewildering number of variations possible in this context has already been pointed out.[47] The international will, as a device for unification, has not been as successful as was hoped since several states have simply added the international will to the number of their existing wills; and the rules for interpreting the Uniform Act are not identical in all the member states of the Treaty.[48] The Treaty goes one step further than the 1961 Hague Convention on the Conflict of Laws Relating to the Form of Testamentary Dispositions, the more modest aim of which was to establish common provisions on the conflict of laws relating to the form of testamentary dispositions.

(b)   The 1989 Hague Convention on the Law Applicable to Succession to the Estates of Deceased Persons allows a testator to choose either the law of his

---

[47] See Section I above.   [48] Verbeke and Leleu (n 6), 349.

nationality or the law of his habitual residence at the time of the making of the will to govern the succession to his estate.[49] This means that the testator's plan of succession will be unaffected, even if he subsequently changes his nationality or habitual residence.[50] The Convention also contains a chapter on 'agreements as to succession' (*pacta successoria*)[51] and a chapter with so-called 'general provisions'.[52]

(c) The 1985 Hague Convention on the Law Applicable to Trusts and on their Recognition does not introduce the trust into non-trust countries but creates a common set of conflict of law rules in terms of which trust problems can be dealt with. This Convention has been quite successful judged by the number of countries which have ratified it.[53] Comparative research has identified Italy and the Netherlands (two of the countries that have ratified the Convention) as civilian jurisdictions where the Convention may prove to be the catalyst for the development of an internal trust.[54]

(d) The 1973 Hague Convention concerning the International Administration of the Estates of Deceased Persons has not been a success. It has only been ratified by a small number of countries, and in the United Kingdom, for example, the Law Commission is believed to have concluded that the Convention's complexities make it impractical for implementation.[55]

3. The Role of Comparative Scholarship

As pointed out by Zweigert and Kötz, the areas of comparative law and conflict of laws are on the face of it entirely distinct, but they interact.[56] Indeed, according to these authors comparative law may be enormously valuable for private international law—'indeed so indispensable for its development that the methods of private international law today are essentially those of comparative law'.[57] The role of comparative lawyers in the creation of the instruments mentioned above is self-evident. And although such instruments must not be confounded with the whole harmonization enterprise, they can in themselves provide some momentum towards harmonization.

Closely linked with private international law problems in the law of succession is the practical issue of a lawyer of country A having to advise a prospective testator, a national of country B but habitually resident in country A, on succession issues regarding property situated in both countries A and B (and possibly also country C). In other words, lawyers are increasingly faced with the reality of people

---

[49] Art 5.
[50] David Hayton, 'The Problems of Diversity', in David Hayton (ed), *European Succession Laws* (1998), 1, 12.
[51] Ch III.   [52] Ch IV.   [53] Hayton (n 50), 15.   [54] See Section V.4 below.
[55] Hayton (n 50), 14.   [56] Zweigert and Kötz (n 11), 6.   [57] Ibid.

building up estates in more than one country, and with the task of advising such people during their lifetime, as well as their heirs, on complex and bewildering questions regarding the law of succession of more than one country. This has become a common scenario due to factors such as globalization, internationalization of businesses, mobility of people and jobs, increasing affluence, affordability of foreign travel, and so on.[58]

In order to meet the needs of lawyers faced with this sort of dilemma, a very specific type of comparative law project is required. An excellent example of such a project is the book *International Succession*.[59] It adopts a strategy of what may perhaps be referred to as 'vertical comparison'. The book contains chapters, or 'reports', in alphabetical order on more than forty different countries. The chapter on each particular country is based on responses to a uniform and very comprehensive questionnaire.

The questionnaire itself is divided into two sections. The first section deals with a 'brief survey of the local system'. Here questions such as the following are posed: (a) type of system ('civil law, common law or other'); (b) forms of wills (including questions relating to formalities, amendment, revocation, and revival); (c) the order of succession in cases of intestacy; (d) the importance of freedom of testation in the system (including the issue of forced succession); (e) matrimonial regimes; (f) capacity to make and witness a will and to be an heir; (g) grounds for invalidity of wills; (h) estate taxes; and (i) administration of estates. The second section of the questionnaire focuses on the 'applicable law/procedure where foreign elements are involved'. Questions dealt with here include those relating to: (a) questions relating to jurisdiction; (b) the applicable law (eg law of domicile or nationality); (c) the enforcement of foreign succession or inheritance orders; (d) the way expert evidence is dealt with; and (e) whether the formalities of a will executed in a foreign country must be the same as those in the local country for such a will to be recognized or submitted for a succession order.

A project altogether more ambitious than the one just described is *Internationales Erbrecht*, a long-established loose-leaf publication in eight volumes covering the law of succession of more than 60 countries.[60] The list includes a number of countries on which one does not often find comparative law material, such as Albania, Armenia, Ecuador, Morocco, Mongolia, Ukraine, and Uzbekistan. The standard pattern that is followed with regard to many countries is that of a detailed exposition of both the conflict of law rules with regard to the law of succession and the substantive law of succession. With regard to the latter, the focus falls on issues such as the general principles of succession, the rules of intestate succession, the

---

[58] See R. A. D. Urquhart, 'Introduction', in Louis Garb (ed), *International Succession* (2004), 1.

[59] Louis Garb (ed), *International Succession* (2004).

[60] Murad Ferid, Karl Firsching, Heinrich Dörner and Rainer Hausmann (eds.), *Internationales Erbrecht* (loose-leaf, starting in 1974).

important issues relating to testate succession (eg the capacity to make a will, the forms of will, formalities for the execution and amendment of wills, and revocation of wills) and, finally, administration of deceased estates. In most—though unfortunately not all—instances the country's relevant statutory texts are also included. In the case of some countries, however, only the statutory texts are provided. Despite its possible deficiencies—for a number of countries the information is out of date—one can only agree with the assessment of a prominent comparatist that this is a 'monumental' work.[61]

Of course, this 'vertical' type of comparison is not yet comparative research in the sense in which the term is understood most often. But, apart from providing the practical answers to questions asked by lawyers faced with the necessity of having to apply foreign law, projects such as these contain a mine of information for proper ('horizontal') comparative research.

IV. FREEDOM OF TESTATION AND THE LIMITATIONS PLACED ON IT

1. The Principle of Freedom of Testation

There can be no doubt that all developed systems of testate succession are based on the premise of freedom of testation: a testator can, in principle, decide who is to inherit his property. Equally, however, no developed system recognizes unlimited or unrestricted freedom of testation. Despite the validity of these basic propositions there remains a striking divergence between the ways this issue is approached, for example, in the Anglo-American common law systems and the civilian systems. And, again, it has been the task of the comparative researcher to analyse and describe these differences and to confront the question why these differences in approach exist and whether there is a trend towards common ground.

---

[61] See the review by Reinhard Zimmermann, [2003] *Neue Juristische Wochenschrift* 495 ff. For a further work of the same type as the two described above, but only focusing on Europe, see Hayton (n 50).

2. The Identification of Patterns: The Role of Comparative Research

The first important limitation that can be placed on freedom of testation are the potential claims of the spouse, the children, or even other relatives of the testator. In Anglo-American systems the point of departure has traditionally been (and to an extent still is) one of more or less unlimited freedom. In civilian systems, on the other hand, the notion of forced heirship (*Noterbrecht* or *Pflichtteil*, ie the legitimate portion) is recognized: certain family members are seen to have a natural and indefeasible claim to a part of the testator's wealth.

There appears to be scope for more research regarding the fundamental reasons underlying this difference in approach. In Continental Europe the notion that a person's property (or at least a part of it) in a sense belongs to his family still seems to be firmly entrenched. Therefore, forced succession is premised on the idea of 'solidarity between the generations'.[62] This gives a right to specific heirs not to be left unprovided for. Forced succession, therefore, has a maintenance function. Ethical, philosophical, and Natural law arguments are generally advanced in favour of rules on forced succession.[63] But even with reference to Continental Europe the danger of over-generalization has to be avoided. Comparative studies have shown, for instance, that the range of beneficiaries under the rules of forced succession is not the same everywhere.[64] To mention a few examples: (a) in France only the children and the parents of the deceased are forced heirs; (b) in Denmark it is the spouse and the children; (c) in Germany the descendants, the parents, and the spouse; and (d) in Sweden and Norway only the children.

Another explanation, coming from the common law side, is the 'lack of the concept of the trust in civil law systems and its presence in common law systems'.[65] The argument is that 'it makes dynastic and financial sense in one's lifetime to transfer majority shareholdings in companies to trustees to manage for the benefit of one's spouse and descendants rather than allow small minority shareholdings to pass absolutely to each of one's heirs'.[66] Such 'lifetime provision' would then be taken into account at a person's death.[67] However, in the light of the exposition below,[68] this view should be judged with scepticism.

While, therefore, at first blush there appears to be a wide gulf separating the two systems, on closer inspection it may not be all that wide—and it may indeed be narrowing. In common law systems the tendency has been to introduce the possibility of maintenance claims—in English law called 'family provisions'—in

---

[62] Pintens, (2001) 9 *Zeitschrift für Europäisches Privatrecht* 638.

[63] Pintens, (2003) 50 *Zeitschrift für das gesamte Familienrecht* 417, 423.

[64] Dieter Henrich, 'Familienerbrecht und Testierfreiheit im europäischen Vergleich', in Dieter Henrich and Dieter Schwab (eds), *Familienerbrecht und Testierfreiheit im europäischen Vergleich* (2001), 372, 380.

[65] Hayton (n 50), 8.   [66] Ibid.   [67] Ibid.   [68] See Section V below.

terms of which a discretionary allocation can be made in favour, especially, of the surviving spouse and dependent children. In Continental civilian systems the tendency has increasingly been to narrow the circle of relatives who have a fixed claim against the estate and also to limit the claim to one sounding in money (as opposed to a claim to a specific asset or assets).[69]

What is more, questions have been raised in Continental systems as to whether the whole concept of forced succession is not perhaps in need of a total revision.[70] A first consideration is that the idea of forced succession is based on outdated social premises (eg that children have a natural claim to their parents' wealth in order to give them a start in life). Another is the fact (also a social issue) that life expectancy has increased dramatically. This means that children now often inherit at an age when they have already built up their own estate. The 'maintenance function' of the law of succession has therefore become less convincing. Finally, there is the more fundamental question whether such a drastic curtailment of freedom of testation can at all be justified in modern times. Why should a person who can freely dispose of his property during his lifetime be curtailed so drastically in this freedom upon death?[71] Against the background of these considerations it is interesting to note that the common law approach of a flexible, discretionary maintenance claim is mentioned as a model for possible reform in the Continental systems.[72]

3. Other Focus Areas

There are at least two further areas of the law of succession where comparative research has focused on the principle of freedom of testation. They will be mentioned only briefly. The first is the issue of inheritance contracts (*pacta successoria*) where the principle of freedom of testation comes into conflict with another fundamental freedom, that is, the freedom of contract. Here comparative research has again shown two fundamentally different approaches.[73] In the Romanistic legal

---

[69] Verbeke and Leleu (n 6), 342–3; Pintens, (2003) 50 *Zeitschrift für das gesamte Familienrecht* 421–4.

[70] See, in general, Kurt Kuchinke, 'Über die Notwendigkeit, ein gemeineuropäisches Familien- und Erbrecht zu schaffen', in *Europas universale rechtsordnungspolitische Aufgabe im Recht des dritten Jahrtausends: Festschrift für Alfred Söllner* (2000), 589, 604–10; Pintens, (2001) 9 *Zeitschrift für Europäisches Privatrecht* 638–9; *idem*, (2003) 50 *Zeitschrift für das gesamte Familienrecht* 421–2; Sonnekus, (2005) 13 *Zeitschrift für Europäisches Privatrecht* 83–6.

[71] See eg for the discussion of this question in the context of the German law relating to the *Pflichtteil* Knut Werner Lange, 'Die Pflichtteilsentziehung gegenüber Abkömmlingen de lege lata und de lege ferenda', (2004) 204 *Archiv für die civilistische Praxis* 804 ff.

[72] Pintens, (2001) 9 *Zeitschrift für Europäisches Privatrecht* 638–9; Sonnekus, (2005) 13 *Zeitschrift für Europäisches Privatrecht* 83–6.

[73] See Pintens, (2001) 9 *Zeitschrift für Europäisches Privatrecht* 644.

family inheritance contracts are in principle invalid, since they are taken to be against public policy (*contra bonos mores*). In the Germanic legal family, on the other hand, such contracts are in principle valid. However, this seemingly stark difference is somewhat softened if account is taken of the exceptions to the principle of invalidity in the Romanistic legal family. For example, both testamentary provisions in an ante-nuptial contract and the so-called *donatio mortis causa* (a donation made in contemplation of the donor's death) are regarded as valid.

Another area where the principle of freedom of testation has featured in the context of comparative research is that of the possible limitations placed on this freedom by non-discrimination provisions in Constitutions and other human rights instruments. Among the questions that are relevant in this context are the following: (a) can a testator disinherit a potential beneficiary on grounds such as race, gender, sexual orientation, or religion?; and (b) can a testator institute a beneficiary but make the benefit subject to a condition that seeks to control the conduct of the beneficiary on grounds such as those just mentioned? South Africa provides a good illustration of a jurisdiction where comparative research has proved to be extremely useful in developing a rational approach to these types of questions that became relevant after the country had accepted a human rights dispensation in the mid-1990s.[74]

V. The Contents of Wills: The Example of the Trust

1. Introduction

Once one moves to the contents of wills, a vast vista for comparative research opens up. Obvious examples of testamentary institutions that can be the subject of comparative work include testamentary conditions, fideicommissary substitution, mutual wills, and the massing of estates. Another example is the trust—an institution that is also relevant in the context of the law of succession in view of the fact that it is often created in wills. For purposes of this chapter the focus will fall on some of the important work that has already been done by comparative researchers in the field of trust law, specifically regarding the introduction of the trust into

---

[74] See eg De Waal (n 1), para. 3G1 ff; Francois du Toit, 'The Limits Imposed upon Freedom of Testation by the *Boni Mores*: Lessons from Common Law and Civil Law (Continental) Legal Systems', (2000) 11 *Stellenbosch LR* 358 ff.

civilian and mixed jurisdictions. This particular topic illustrates the immense value of comparative scholarship in discarding mistaken assumptions and testing conventional wisdom.

2. The Trust as a Unique Institution of the Common Law?

It has long been accepted by many scholars in the field that the trust is a distinctive institution of the English common law. Typical assertions in this vein are that the trust is a 'uniquely Anglo-American institution' and that the 'Continental legal tradition did not develop the trust'.[75]

At the heart of this lies the insistence of many Anglo-American (and specifically English) lawyers that the trust should be defined in terms of a divided title between the trustee and the beneficiary.[76] The trustee has 'legal ownership' of the trust property and the trust beneficiary 'equitable ownership' or 'beneficial ownership'. The explanation for this is historical, for there is indeed a close link between the English trust and Equity, the system of law developed by the Chancellor in reaction to the more rigorous common law. The interest of the beneficiary under the use (the forerunner of the trust) could not be enforced under the common law. However, in Equity the Chancellor acknowledged the beneficiary's interest in the property. In due course it was recognized as a proprietary interest (ie equitable ownership) that could in general be enforced also against third parties. This was the origin of the distinction between the trustee's 'legal ownership' and the trust beneficiary's 'equitable ownership'—a distinction that was perpetuated in some British colonies, for example North America, Australia, Bahamas, Bermuda, and the Cayman Islands.[77]

However, more recent trust scholarship is critical of this inclination to define the trust strictly in terms of a divided title.[78] First, the assertion that the trust is completely foreign to the Continental legal tradition has been shown to be an over-simplification from an historical perspective. Although it is generally acknowledged that Roman law did not know the trust as such, research has indicated that there are signs in Roman law of 'trust-like' devices and 'trustee-like' persons.[79] This already tends to show that there are indeed links between the English trust and

---

[75] John H. Langbein, 'The Contractarian Basis of the Trust', (1995) 105 *Yale LJ* 625, 669.

[76] Marius J. de Waal, 'The Core Elements of the Trust', (2000) 117 *South African LJ* 548, 550.

[77] David J. Hayton and Charles Mitchell, *Hayton & Marshall: Commentary and Cases on the Law of Trusts and Equitable Remedies* (12th edn, 2005), 5.

[78] See eg Marius J. de Waal, 'In Search of a Model for the Introduction of the Trust into a Civilian Context', (2001) 12 *Stellenbosch LR* 63, 65; *idem*, 'Trust Law', in Jan M. Smits (ed), *Elgar Encyclopedia of Comparative Law* (2006) 755 ff.

[79] David Johnston, 'Trusts and Trust-Like Devices in Roman Law', in Richard Helmholz and Reinhard Zimmermann (eds), *Itinera Fiduciae: Trust and Treuhand in Historical Perspective* (1998), 45 ff.

Continental institutions such as *fideicommissum, fiducia,* and *Treuhand*—that there is a 'common core' that unites them.[80] Some researchers see an even stronger link. Maurizio Lupoi,[81] for example, argues that the English Chancellors (without mentioning their sources) drew on a wealth of thirteenth- and fourteenth-century civil law authority in their development of the English trust. For him it is therefore not far-fetched to refer to these civil law institutions as being the 'foundation' of the English trust.

Even though his research is conducted from a different angle, the conclusions of Patrick Glenn broadly echo those of Lupoi. Thus, according to him, the introduction of the trust into a civilian context is not a question of the importation of a foreign legal institution but rather of 'revivifying ideas of the common law of Europe'.[82]

Second, however, the issue can also be approached from an angle other than the historical one. According to Bernard Rudden[83] the orthodox explanation of the trust in terms of the distinction between law and Equity in any event provides only 'an historical [in terms of English law] and not a rational account of the trust'. Approached rationally, the question is therefore: can one have a 'proper' trust without such a divided title?

3. The Trust in Civilian and Mixed Jurisdictions

The question whether one can have a 'proper' trust in civilian and mixed jurisdictions where the law/Equity distinction is unknown has also received some scholarly attention in recent years. An analysis and a synthesis of research done especially in the context of the mixed jurisdictions such as Scotland and South Africa has shown that this question can be answered in the affirmative if the following 'core elements' are present:[84] (a) a trustee who fills a fiduciary position (meaning, among other things, that the trustee must act with scrupulous loyalty in the interest of the trust beneficiaries); (b) a separation between the trustee's personal estate and the trust estate; (c) the operation of real subrogation (meaning that the proceeds of a trust asset, if it has been sold, or of a substitute asset, if the proceeds have

---

[80] Richard Helmholz and Reinhard Zimmermann, 'Views of Trust and Treuhand: An Introduction', in Helmholz and Zimmermann (n 79), 27, 30.

[81] Maurizio Lupoi, 'The Civil Law Trust', (1999) 32 *Vanderbilt Journal of Transnational Law* 967, 975.

[82] H. Patrick Glenn, 'The Historical Origins of the Trust', in Alfredo Mordechai Rabello (ed), *Aequitas and Equity: Equity in Civil Law and in Mixed Jurisdictions* (1997), 749, 776.

[83] Bernard Rudden, 'Things as Thing and Things as Wealth', (1994) 14 *Oxford Journal of Legal Studies* 89.

[84] See, in general, De Waal, (2000) 117 *South African LJ* 548 ff with further references; *idem*, (2001) 12 *Stellenbosch LR* 63 ff with further references.

been used for its purchase, will also be subject to the trust); and (d) the construction of trusteeship as an office.

Lupoi is critical of this 'common core' approach. He prefers to define the trust in comparative law terms and to investigate whether the trust is to be found in civil law countries. For Lupoi an appropriate definition of the trust in comparative law terms would include the following elements:[85] (a) the transfer of property to the trustee or a unilateral declaration of trust; (b) the absence of 'commingling' between trust property and property in the trustee's personal estate (this corresponds with the second 'core element' above); (c) the loss of any power of the founder (or settlor) of the trust over the trust property; (d) the existence of trust beneficiaries or a trust purpose; and (e) the imposition of a fiduciary component upon the exercise of the trustee's rights (this corresponds with the first 'core element' above).

Once one has concluded on a rational level that the concept of a divided title is not a prerequisite for a proper trust, the focus can shift to the different possible ways in which the trust can be introduced into civilian or mixed jurisdictions. Here comparative research has shown that it is not possible, or indeed necessary, to identify one single model for such an introduction.[86] By way of illustration a few examples from some of the civilian and mixed jurisdictions can be given. Thus, the trust was introduced into Liechtenstein, Mexico, and Panama by way of specific legislation during the 1920s.[87] Interestingly enough the legislation in Mexico and Panama was inspired by civilian concepts (particularly the *fideicommissum*), while the Liechtenstein statute was drafted under the influence of Anglo-American law.[88] Lupoi[89] provides numerous further examples (such as Argentina, Colombia, Ecuador, Japan, and Israel) that are worth analysing from a comparative perspective. This work of Lupoi should ideally be read against the background of the earlier comprehensive comparative study by Fratcher.[90]

The introduction of the trust into some of the mixed jurisdictions also followed different patterns. In Scotland, for example, the trust emerged in the course of the seventeenth century. It is not clear exactly how this happened but it is possible that civilian concepts such as *depositum, mandatum*, and the *fideicommissum* did play a role.[91] However, the important point is that available evidence does not indicate anything like a reception of English trust law in Scotland.[92] Considerable English

---

[85] Lupoi, (1999) 32 *Vanderbilt Journal of Transnational Law* 970.
[86] De Waal, (2001) 12 *Stellenbosch LR* 63 ff.
[87] K. W. Ryan, 'The Reception of the Trust', (1961) 10 *ICLQ* 265 ff.   [88] Ibid.
[89] Maurizio Lupoi, *Trusts: A Comparative Study* (2000), 201 ff.
[90] William F. Fratcher, 'Trust', in *International Encyclopedia of Comparative Law* (vol VI, ch 14, 1973).
[91] George Gretton, 'Scotland: The Evolution of the Trust in a Semi-Civilian System', in Helmholz and Zimmermann (n 79), 507, 516.
[92] Ibid 511.

influence in the nineteenth century, and later, came only after the trust had established itself as an independent institution in Scots law.

The story of the introduction of the trust into South African law, another mixed system, is quite different. The trust that was introduced into South Africa by British settlers in the course of the nineteenth century was indeed the English trust.[93] However, it was quickly transformed into an institution that could be explained in civilian terms. This was done, again, by the extensive use of civilian concepts such as the *fideicommissum* (in the case of the testamentary trust) and the *stipulatio alteri* (in the case of the *inter vivos* trust). Thus, neither in Scotland nor in South Africa did legislation play a role in the initial introduction of the trust. In other mixed jurisdictions, such as Louisiana and Quebec, legislation was of central importance in this regard. The specific legislative histories fall outside the scope of this chapter but the final result is, in the case of Louisiana, a specific Trust Code and, in the case of Quebec, a number of chapters in its general Civil Code.[94]

4. Trust-Like Institutions in Continental Europe

With the exception of Liechtenstein a proper trust law has not been developed in Continental Europe. However, it has been noted that it would be wrong to conclude from this that the 'trust idea' is completely foreign to Continental legal thinking. A ground-breaking historical and comparative analysis of 'trust-like' institutions in Continental Europe has illustrated this convincingly.[95] For the purposes of this chapter a number of examples, taken from Dutch and German law and often used by comparative lawyers to indicate points of contact with the trust, will serve to demonstrate the point.

The Dutch legal institution that perhaps comes closest to the express *inter vivos* trust is the *fiducia cum amico*.[96] Assets are transferred to a manager (*fiduciarius*) who has to manage these assets for the benefit of one or more beneficiaries. Like the trustee, the manager becomes owner of the assets. However, unlike the beneficiary under the common law trust, the beneficiary under the *fiducia* has no real right ('equitable interest') to the assets. Another legal institution used under

---

[93] Tony Honoré, 'Trust', in Reinhard Zimmermann and Daniel Visser (eds), *Southern Cross: Civil Law and Common Law in South Africa* (1996), 849, 850.

[94] A. N. Yiannopoulos, 'Trust and the Civil Law: The Louisiana Experience', in Vernon Valentine Palmer (ed), *Louisiana: Microcosm of a Mixed Jurisdiction* (1999), 213 ff; Madeleine Cantin Cumyn, 'The Trust in a Civilian Context: The Quebec Case', (1994) 3 *Journal of International Trust and Corporate Planning* 69 ff.

[95] See Helmholz and Zimmermann (n 79).

[96] The exposition that follows is based on Sebastianus Constantinus Johannes Josephus Kortmann and Hendrikus Leonardus Engelbertus Verhagen, 'National Report for the Netherlands', in David J. Hayton, Sebastianus Constantinus Johannes Josephus Kortmann, and Hendrikus Leonardus Engelbertus Verhagen (eds), *Principles of European Trust Law* (1999), 195 ff.

Dutch law to create a trust-like relationship is the *bewind*. Under the *bewind* the *bewindvoerder* manages assets for the benefit of a beneficiary or beneficiaries. Unlike the trustee, the *bewindvoerder* is not the owner of the assets. Ownership vests in the beneficiary. In other words, the *bewindvoerder* only acts as the agent of the beneficiary. A third example that can be given from Dutch law is the foundation (*stichting*), an institution that fulfils a function much like that of the charitable trust. However, the obvious difference between a *stichting* and a trust lies in the fact that, unlike the trust, the *stichting* is a juristic person (ie an entity with legal personality).

In German law[97] a testator may provide in his will that his estate must pass to a particular person as 'provisional heir' (*Vorerbe*) and at that person's death or upon fulfilment of a specified condition to another person as 'subsequent', or 'reversionary heir' (*Nacherbe*). The testator can, however, exclude the provisional heir's limited power to dispose of the assets by appointing a testamentary executor (*Testamentsvollstrecker*) who will get the exclusive power to dispose of estate assets in accordance with the testator's instructions. The combination of *Nacherbfolge* and the appointment of a *Testamentsvollstrecker* will achieve practical results quite similar to those achieved by the common law testamentary trust. Note the similarity between this institution and the Dutch *bewind*: neither the *Testamentsvollstrecker* nor the *bewindvoerder* is owner of the assets. Under both institutions ownership remains vested in the beneficiary. The German institution that corresponds more closely to the trust is the *Treuhand*. Assets are transferred to a *Treuhänder*, coupled with a contractual agreement in terms of which he undertakes to manage the assets for the benefit of the beneficiary. Similarities between the common law trustee and the *Treuhänder* are that the latter becomes owner of the assets, that he fills a fiduciary position, and that he must keep the assets separate from his personal estate. On the other hand, real subrogation does not operate as it does in the case of the trust. Third, the German counterpart of the Dutch *stichting* is the *Stiftung*. The *Stiftung* is also a juristic person and it often fulfils a charitable purpose.[98]

Regarding the position of the trust in Continental Europe, interesting developments have taken place in Italy and in the Netherlands. They can only be properly understood against the background of the Hague Convention on the Law Applicable to Trusts and on their Recognition (1985). As indicated above,[99] the aim of this Convention is not to introduce the trust into the domestic law of states that do not already have it, but rather to establish a set of common conflict of law rules on the law applicable to trusts. Italy and the Netherlands are the only Continental

---

[97] The exposition that follows, is based on Hein Kötz, 'National Report for Germany', in Hayton *et al.* (n 96), 85 ff.

[98] For a historical and comparative study, see Andreas Richter, *Rechtsfähige Stiftung und Charitable Corporation* (2001).

[99] See Section III.2 above.

countries that have thus far ratified the Convention. In each case ratification has, however, actually set a process in motion which may eventually lead to the acceptance of the trust as a substantive institution.

Lupoi,[100] in particular, strongly argues that the Convention allows citizens of member states (such as Italy) to establish trusts governed by a foreign law. For example, a trust can be established in Italy by an Italian founder with an Italian trustee and beneficiary and with the trust property situated in Italy, but with English law governing it (if this was the founder's choice of law). Although there are those who disagree with Lupoi's interpretation of the Convention,[101] there are apparently numerous examples of this 'domestic trust' (*trust interno*) to be seen in Italian practice. In the Netherlands the ratification of the Convention was accompanied by special legislation. This statute, the *Wet Conflictenrecht Trusts* (1995), was thought necessary in order to reconcile some rules of Dutch domestic law with the obligations under articles 11 and 15 of the Convention. One of the main aims of the statute was to ensure, beyond any doubt, that 'the trust fund is regarded as a separate protected fund . . . and not part of the trustee's patrimony available to satisfy his creditor's claims . . .'.[102] This recognition of the concept of a separate trust estate can be seen as an important step on the way to a proper Dutch trust.

One of the objectives of the *Principles of European Trust Law*,[103] prepared by an international working group with a strong comparative focus, is to assist countries interested in implementing the Convention. The project has the further purpose of meeting 'the needs of those who have observed the usages to which the trust concept is put . . . but who find themselves puzzling over what exactly are the basic elements of the trust, and in particular of the common law trust'.[104]

---

[100] Maurizio Lupoi, 'Trusts and Civilian Categories (Problems Spurred by Italian Domestic Trusts)', in Helmholz and Zimmermann (n 79), 495 ff; *idem*, (1999) 32 *Vanderbilt Journal of Transnational Law* 967, 980.

[101] See eg Antonio Gambaro, 'Trust in Continental Europe', in Rabello (n 82), 777, 780.

[102] David J. Hayton, 'Trusts', in David J. Hayton, Sebastianus Constantinus Johannes Josephus Kortmann, André Johan Maria Nuytinck, Antoon Victor Marie Struycken, and N. E. D. Faber (eds), *Vertrouwd met de Trust: Trust and Trust-Like Arrangements* (1996), 3, 58.

[103] Hayton *et al.* (n 96).

[104] David J. Hayton, Sebastianus Constantinus Johannes Josephus Kortmann, and Hendrikus Leonardus Engelbertus Verhagen, 'Introduction to the Principles of European Trust Law', in Hayton *et al* (n 96), 3, 11.

VI. THE TRANSFER OF THE
ESTATE UPON DEATH

1. Introduction

Researchers in the law of succession often shy away from more practical matters such as the transfer of the deceased person's estate upon death, or the administration of the deceased estate. However, they can have a profound impact on a number of very fundamental issues, chief among them that of the vesting of rights. As far as could be established, the transfer of the estate upon death has only relatively recently been the subject of really comprehensive comparative research in the European context.[105]

2. Categorization

A central distinction that should be made is that between the transfer of the deceased's assets and the transfer of liability for the deceased's debts. Regarding the transfer of assets, two criteria are used to distinguish between three typical solutions. The first criterion concerns the *directness* of the transfer: do the assets pass to his heirs *directly* or *indirectly*, that is, through an intermediary? The second criterion concerns the *immediacy* of the heir's ownership: does he become owner immediately upon the deceased's death or is the transfer postponed to a later moment? Against this backdrop the following typical solutions have been identified:

(a) Ownership is transferred directly and immediately by operation of law (*ipso iure*) to the heirs. No intermediary is involved and no act of adiation or acceptance by the heirs is necessary. This is the system, for example, in Belgian, French, German, and Swiss law.

(b) Ownership is transferred directly to the heirs in the sense that no intermediary is involved. However, there is no immediate transfer of ownership because an act of adiation or acceptance by the heirs must first occur. Transfer of ownership is therefore deferred or postponed to a point in time after the deceased's death. This system prevails, for example, in Austrian, Italian, and Spanish law.

(c) Ownership is transferred indirectly through an executor or representative; again, an act of adiation or acceptance by the heirs is required before they can

---

[105] For the exposition that follows, see Verbeke and Leleu (n 6), 338–40.

become owners. This is the way succession upon death operates in English law
and other common law systems.

As regards the liability for the deceased's debts, the relevant criterion used relates
to the extent of such liability. Is the liability for debts restricted to property belonging to the estate or does it extend to the personal property of the beneficiary?
Once again, there are three typical solutions that have been identified:

(a) The first possibility is one that tends towards unlimited liability in the sense
     that the heirs can be held personally liable (ie with their personal property)
     for the debts of the estate. However, there are normally a variety of devices
     available that can be used by the heirs to protect themselves against such
     personal liability. French law provides an example of this type of regime.

(b) Other legal systems, such as the German one, tend to subscribe to a regime of
     liability where the personal estates of the heirs are somewhat better protected
     against debts that have been incurred by the deceased.

(c) The third possibility is the English system of executorship where an executor,
     or representative, administers the estate of the deceased before any transfer of
     property to the beneficiaries can take place. The administration of the estate
     primarily entails the settling of debts out of the property in the estate. The
     beneficiaries only have a claim (or personal right) against the executor or
     representative to transfer the property remaining in the estate after the debts
     have been settled. There is thus no question that they can ever be burdened
     with the deceased's debts. The worst thing that can happen to them is that
     they receive nothing.

3. The Role of the Executor, or Representative

The possibility of a direct transfer of the estate to the heirs upon death is based
on the concept of universal succession that prevails in civilian systems. This constitutes a fundamental contrast to the English system where the executor, or representative, acts as an intermediary between the deceased and the heirs. However, it does
not mean that the institution of executorship would be foreign to Continental
European systems. Quite the opposite is true. The following remark by Reinhard
Zimmermann encapsulates the reality:[106] 'The institution of executorship appears
to be an indispensable part of a modern law of succession and is known to all
modern European legal systems. It constitutes part of a contemporary European
ius commune.'

In other words, the appointment of an executor is also common in succession

---

[106] Reinhard Zimmermann, '*Heres Fidiciarius?* Rise and Fall of the Testamentary Executor', in
Helmholz and Zimmermann (n 79), 267 ff.

systems governed by the concept of universal succession. But there are significant differences between executorship in English law and that in Continental legal systems. And even in these Continental systems there are important 'national modifications'.[107] Zimmermann has subjected the institution of executorship to a very thorough historical and comparative analysis in order to explain, on the one hand, the fundamental difference between the English and Continental models and, on the other hand, the variations in the Continental models. In another comparative study on the topic it has been suggested that if a uniform law of succession and administration of estates is to be considered for a European private law, something along the lines of the English executorship would be worthy of closer scrutiny.[108]

The concept of universal succession was part of Roman-Dutch law and it was therefore received in South Africa. However, this changed when universal succession was replaced with the English model of executorship in the course of the nineteenth century. This may explain why, even today, there is still no clarity in South African law in connection with a number of important theoretical issues. Examples include the exact mechanism concerning the vesting of rights at the deceased's death and the question as to who is the owner of the property in the period between the deceased's death and the transfer of the property by the executor to the heirs. The latter question is also relevant in systems where there is a direct, but deferred, transfer of ownership to the heirs due to the fact that an act of adiation or acceptance by the heirs is first required. The comparative studies referred to above provide the framework within which answers to these kinds of questions should be sought.

VII. Concluding Remarks

It cannot be denied that the law of succession often projects a static—even a sterile—image. One possible explanation for this is the fact that certain areas of the law of succession are indeed somewhat technical. Here one thinks of the rules of intestate succession and the formalities required for the execution and amendment of wills. Another possibility is the perceived indigenous character of the law of succession which often translates into a reluctance to engage in comparative research.

---

[107] Zimmermann (n 106), 267.
[108] Sonnekus, (2005) 13 *Zeitschrift für Europäisches Privatrecht* 74.

However, this seeming tranquility is misleading. Already in the early 1980s John Langbein[109] wrote: 'Over the course of the twentieth century, persistent tides of change have been lapping at the once-quiet shores of the law of succession'. The central thesis of this chapter is that these changes have been detected and explained principally through comparative scholarship in the field of the law of succession.

On a more general level two issues have been identified. The first is the significance of common social and economic changes and their impact on aspects of the law of succession. In this regard the intimate relationship between the law of succession and family law has been stressed. These changes have also provided a common denominator between different national systems of succession which have previously been perceived as being indigenous in character and therefore hardly worth the effort of comparative research.

Second, the identification and analysis of these changes have also been the stimulus for a new 'mission' for comparative researchers in the field of the law of succession. This is the quest for greater harmonization, especially in the European context. The importance of harmonization has dawned on succession lawyers when it was widely realized that the law of succession cannot, in fact, exist in total national isolation. The realities of the modern world dictate the opposite. But they also emphasize the importance of conflict of law (or private international law) rules, and of comparative research in the area of the conflict of laws which, in turn, is intimately linked with the harmonization enterprise.

Comparative research has also proved extremely valuable in a number of more specific areas of the law of succession. This has been demonstrated with reference to principles of freedom of testation and its possible limitations, the institution of the trust, and, finally, the transfer of the estate upon death.

What about the agenda for the future? In the discussion of the various topics in this chapter a number of specific challenges for comparative scholars have been pointed out. Apart from that, however, it is to be expected that the general areas of the impact of social and economic changes on the law of succession, and the issue of harmonization, will remain a significant focus for comparative work. Another area will probably be the impact of constitutional provisions and human rights instruments on freedom of testation. The significant results yielded by comparative research on the trust should serve as a stimulus for similar research on other testamentary institutions. Here one thinks of the *fideicommissum*, other forms of substitution, mutual wills, and testamentary conditions. And finally, there can be no doubt that there is still a paucity of in-depth historical comparative research on the law of succession.

For a long time, the law of succession has led a precarious existence at the outposts of the comparative law landscape. However, there is every indication that this is going to change.

---

[109] (1984) 97 *Harvard LR* 1108.

BIBLIOGRAPHY

Murad Ferid, Karl Firsching, Heinrich Dörner, and Rainer Hausmann (eds), *Internationales Erbrecht* (loose-leaf in 8 vol, starting in 1974)

John H. Langbein, 'The Twentieth-Century Revolution in Family Wealth Transmission', (1988) 86 *Michigan LR* 722 ff

David Hayton (ed), *European Succession Laws* (1998)

Richard Helmholz and Reinhard Zimmermann (eds), *Itinera Fiduciae: Trust and Treuhand in Historical Perspective* (1998)

D. J. Hayton, S. C. J. J. Kortmann, and H. L. E. Verhagen (eds), *Principles of European Trust Law* (1999)

Kurt Kuchinke, 'Über die Notwendigkeit, ein gemeineuropäisches Familien- und Erbrecht zu schaffen', in *Europas universale rechtsordnungspolitische Aufgabe im Recht des dritten Jahrtausends: Festschrift für Alfred Söllner* (2000), 589 ff

Dieter Leipold, 'Europa und das Erbrecht', in *Europas universale rechtsordnungspolitische Aufgabe im Recht des dritten Jahrtausends: Festschrift für Alfred Söllner* (2000), 647 ff

Maurizio Lupoi, *Trusts: A Comparative Study* (2000)

Dieter Henrich and Dieter Schwab (eds), *Familienerbrecht und Testierfreiheit im europäischen Vergleich* (2001)

Walter Pintens, 'Die Europäisierung des Erbrechts', (2001) 9 *Zeitschrift für Europäisches Privatrecht* 628 ff

Karl Kroeschel and Wolfgang Winkler, 'Succession to Agricultural Property', in *International Encyclopedia of Comparative Law* (vol V, chapter 3, 2002)

Karl Heinz Neumayer, 'Intestate Succession', ch 3 in *Succession* (vol V), in *International Encyclopedia of Comparative Law* (2002)

Michael A. Schwind, 'Liability for Obligations of the Inheritance', in *International Encyclopedia of Comparative Law* (vol V, chapter 3, 2002)

Louis Garb (ed), *International Succession* (2004)

Alain Verbeke and Yves-Henri Leleu, 'Harmonization of the Law of Succession in Europe', in Arthur Hartkamp, Martijn Hesselink, Ewoud Hondius, Carla Joustra, and Edgar du Perron (eds), *Towards a European Civil Code* (3rd edn, 2004), 335 ff

Marius J. de Waal, 'Trust Law', in Jan M. Smits (ed), *Elgar Encyclopedia of Comparative Law* (2006)

CHAPTER 34

COMPARATIVE FAMILY LAW

PAST TRADITIONS
BATTLE FUTURE TRENDS
—AND VICE VERSA

HARRY D. KRAUSE

Illinois*

* Sincere gratitude is due the Alexander von Humboldt Foundation whose research prize awarded in 1992 afforded me numerous opportunities to visit Europe and pursue comparative family law studies. The generous hospitality of Dieter Giesen at the Free University of Berlin and of Hein Kötz and Reinhard Zimmermann at the Max Planck Institute in Hamburg has been wonderful over the years. Without the encouragement and help of my friend, colleague, and frequent co-author, David Meyer, I might not have finished this assignment. At the command of our (kind but firm) editors, footnotes and citations had to be held to an absolute minimum. My apologies, therefore, go to the enormous number of relevant authors and authorities in so many countries who have fertilized the many subjects here discussed but who thus cannot receive due credit. It may be a small comfort that boxes upon boxes of their work and words are in my office and have been of obvious value to me. Finally, Carrie May-Borich and Stacey Ballmes valiantly rescued my two-finger-self-typed-plus-handwritten manuscript from likely rejection by the editors—at least on technical grounds. Needless to add, my thanks are due to them all.

[T]here are two errors equally to be avoided both by writer and reader. One is that of supposing, because an idea seems very familiar and natural to us, that it has always been so. Many things which we take for granted have had to be laboriously fought out or thought out in past times. The other mistake is the opposite one of asking too much of history. We start with man full grown. It may be assumed that the earliest barbarian whose practices are to be considered had a good many of the same feelings and passions as ourselves. The customs, beliefs, or needs of a primitive time establish a rule or a formula. In the course of centuries the custom, belief, or necessity disappears, but the rule remains. The reason which gave rise to the rule has been forgotten, and ingenious minds set themselves to inquire how it is to be accounted for.[1]

---

[1] Oliver Wendell Holmes, *The Common Law* (1881), 2. Holmes was *not* speaking of family law, but his words fit.

I. Is Family Law Comparison
Impossible—or Useful?

EARLY in the development of comparative law as a distinct 'discipline', some scholars complained that family law could not be a fit subject for comparative study—simply because the cultural bases differ too greatly. Nor was there thought to be a compelling practical need for unification and access, nor would foreign family laws easily serve as models for transplantation.[2] These reservations retain some validity but scholars, judges, and practicing lawyers have expanded their horizons to take account of the family law of other nations. On a practical level, greatly increased mobility of individuals and families has resulted in a growing number of transnational family law disputes. These have spawned a proliferation of international legal instruments dealing with marriage, divorce, maintenance, child support, and child custody[3] and making lofty promises on individual and family rights.[4] Of necessity, lawyers and scholars now confront a wide range of questions relating to the conflicts and confluence of legal systems in family law.

Family laws are unfolding in similar directions. For all their very real differences, nations around the world find themselves facing fundamentally similar questions and dilemmas in defining and regulating the modern family. Accordingly, it makes sense to take stock of what has been tried and what has—or has not—worked elsewhere. Comparative family law's days as an unlikely pioneer are over.

---

[2] These concerns were not universal and did not deter some scholars: see eg Alexander Renton and George Phillimore (eds), *The Comparative Law of Marriage and Divorce* (1910). In the words of its own preface: 'This work forms the third volume of the second edition of *Burge's Commentaries on Colonial and Foreign Law*, originally published in 1838, which deals with the laws of Marriage and Divorce in the principal legal systems of the world. Those systems include the Roman Civil law, the Canon Law, the Roman-Dutch law, the ancient and modern French law, such typical modern systems as the Codes of Belgium, Italy, Spain, Germany, Austria, Hungary and Switzerland; the laws of the British Dominions and the United States, and such Oriental systems as the Hindu and Mahammadan laws in British India, the Buddhist law in Bermah, the laws of China, Japan and Siam; and the rules of Private International Law. As regards the British Dominions the common law is the main foundation of the law in the Colonies settled by Great Britain; the roman Civil law is the basis of the law of France, which still survives in the possessions originally French, such as the Coutume of Paris in Quebec and St Lucia, the Coutume of Normandy in the Channel Islands, and the Code Civil in Mauritius; the Roman-Dutch law continues in force in the Union of South Africa, Ceylon and British Guiana; the law of Spain (now to a very limited extent) in Trinidad; the Ottoman law in Cyprus; and the Italian law has been largely adopted in Malta'.

[3] See below (n 30).   [4] See below (nn 31–3).

II. WHAT HAS BEEN DONE, WHAT IS BEING DONE, WHO IS DOING IT?[5]

Much important work has been done to introduce comparative perspectives into family law.[6] First honourable mention goes to the International Society of Family Law. Founded in 1973, this group has been at the forefront of stimulating world-wide interchange and face-to-face contact between family law scholars, judges, and practitioners. Co-Founder Dieter Giesen[7] saved the young Society from likely oblivion by convening a first Congress in 1975 in (then West) Berlin. The Society has held regular congresses since then.[8] In the off-years between world conferences, regional conferences convene in Asia, Europe, and North America. The Society's *International Survey of Family Law* was modestly self-published until 1985. From 1986 until 1995, the Survey appeared as a yearly symposium issue of the *University of Louisville Journal of Family Law*.[9] After 1995 it was published by international publishing houses (Kluwer Law International and Jordan Publishing Ltd of Bristol) as a series of annual books.[10] This treasure of background materials chronicles developments in family law in many countries over recent decades, thanks to many authors and the dedicated editorships of Michael Freeman of London's King's College (until 1994) and Andrew Bainham of Christ College, Cambridge, (1994–2007).[11] In addition, the Society has produced special symposia of scholarly papers based on its conferences, exploring comparative themes.[12]

First place in the resource contest *should* have gone to the *International*

---

[5] The diligent reader must be tired after enduring thirty-three chapters of this volume. To avoid losing her or him before this essay really gets started, surveying this section may be deferred for now in favour of the substantive discussion in Sections III–VIII, below.

[6] Rainer Frank, 'Rechtsvergleichende Betrachtungen zur Entwicklung des Familienrechts', (2004) *Zeitschrift für das gesamte Familienrecht* 841.

[7] See Harry D. Krause, 'Dedication Essay: Professor Dr. Dieter Giesen', (1995)12 *Journal of Contemporary Health Law and Policy* ii–vii; Harry D. Krause, 'Nachruf: Professor Dr. Dieter Giesen', (1997) 52 *Juristenzeitung* 772–3.

[8] The Child and the Law (West Berlin, 1975); Violence in the Family (Montreal, 1977); Family Living in a Changing Society (Uppsala, Sweden, 1979); The Family, The State and Individual Security (Brussels, 1985); Issues of the Aging in Modern Society (Tokyo, Japan, 1988); Parenthood: The Legal Significance of Motherhood and Fatherhood in a Changing Society (Dubrovnik, 1991); Families across Frontiers (Cardiff, 1994); Changing Family Forms: World Themes and African Issues (Durban, 1997); Family Law: Processes, Practices and Pressures (Brisbane, 2000); Family Life and Human Rights (Oslo, 2002); Balancing Interests and Pursuing Priorities (Salt Lake City, 2005).

[9] See 'Annual Survey of Family Law', (1985–6 through 1995–6) 25–33 *University of Louisville Journal of Family Law.*

[10] *International Survey of Family Law* (1994–2005).

[11] Beginning in 2007, Bill Atkin of New Zealand's Victoria University will assume the editorship.

[12] Such as, *The Child and the Law; Violence in the Family;* and *Parenthood: The Legal Significance of Motherhood and Fatherhood in a Changing Society* (1991).

Encyclopedia of Comparative Law, self-described as 'one of the world's most ambitious comparative law projects'.[13] However, forty years after the individual chapters were assigned to internationally recognized scholars, the family law volume remains unpublished, as do volumes on other topics. This promising venture (originally sponsored by the International Association of Legal Science, UNESCO, and generous foundations) came out of the inspiration of Konrad Zweigert (as 'Responsible Editor'), Max Rheinstein (as the original chief editor of the family law volume) and others. For the first ten years, optimism and enthusiasm and accomplishments ran high.[14] Regrettably, long delays have all but foiled the project's lofty intentions.

Max Rheinstein's star student and the family law volume's final editor-in-chief, Mary Ann Glendon, ultimately recruited scholars from another generation who have worked generously to complete the volume.[15] All chapters (although one on the central topic of child support will not be written), along with Professor Glendon's introduction, are now in the hands of the general editor (Ulrich Drobnig), who promised in 2005 that the completed family law volume would be published in only two more years.

In the meantime, the comparatist seeking access to individually pre-published chapters may find these in libraries that have kept up their subscriptions to the *Encyclopedia*. While the rapid development of family life and law over four decades has rendered the older contributions more than a little out of date, even these chapters continue to provide valuable perspectives through richly detailed comparative analyses.[16]

Looking back once more as far as this unfinished *Encyclopedia*, one prior work is noteworthy: the *Rechtsvergleichendes Handwörterbuch für das Zivil- und Handelsrecht des In- und Auslandes*.[17] This seven-volume set is now cited very

---

[13] '[E]ine[s] der weltweit anspruchsvollsten Vorhaben der Rechtsvergleichung', <http://www.mpipirv-hh.mpg.de/deutsch/Institut/ProfilEntwicklung.htm>.

[14] Bernd Schulte, 'Buchbericht: Das Familienrecht der "International Encyclopedia of Comparative Law" ', (1978) *Zeitschrift für das gesamte Familienrecht* 285.

[15] Dagmar Coester-Waltjen and Michael Coester, 'Formation of Marriage', in Mary Ann Glendon (ed), *IV International Encyclopedia of Comparative Law* (1997); Andreas Heldrich, A. F. Steiner, W. Pintens, M. R. Will, and W. Zeyring, 'Persons', ibid (1995); Salvatore Patti, 'Intra-Family Torts', ibid (1998); Bea Verschraegen, 'Divorce', ibid (2004); M. Mladenović, M. Janjić-Komar, C. Jessel-Holst, 'The Family in the Post-Socialist Countries', ibid (1998).

[16] Max Rheinstein and René König, 'Introduction', in Max Rheinstein (ed), *IV International Encyclopedia of Comparative Law, Persons and Family* (1975); Max Rheinstein and Mary Ann Glendon, 'Interspousal Relations', ibid (1980). Samuel Stoljar, 'Children, Parents, and Guardians', ibid (1973); Harry D. Krause, 'Creation of Relationships of Kinship', in A. Chloros (ed), ibid (1976); Marko Mladenović, P. H. Neuhaus, Z. W. Falk, N. Anderson, J. D. M. Derrett, T. K. K. Iyer, and R. Verdier, 'The Family in Religious and Customary Laws', ibid (1983); see also Lennart Palsson, 'Marriage and Divorce', in Kurt Lipstein (ed), *III International Encyclopedia of Comparative Law* (Private International Law) (1978).

[17] Franz Schlegelberger (ed), *Rechtsvergleichendes Handwörterbuch für das Zivil- und Handelsrecht des In- und Auslanders* (1927–39).

rarely,[18] a fate that may be accounted for by the chief editor's career path.[19] Nevertheless, interesting articles on family law were produced by many scholars, some of whom have suffered undeserved obscurity. Historical value lies buried here, especially in the earlier volumes. Examples are entries on 'Adoption' and 'Ehe' (Marriage) published in 1929.

Further mention *might* go to the Académie Internationale de Droit Comparé (International Academy of Comparative Law) that was founded in 1924 in Geneva. The Academy typically assigns one family law topic at each of its quadrennial conferences. Over the years, these topics have ranged widely. To illustrate, at the 2002 Congress in Brisbane, the topic was 'What Family for the 21st Century?' The 2006 Congress in Utrecht will discuss 'Tensions Between Biological, Social, and Legal Conceptions of Parenthood'. For each Congress, General Reporters selected by the Academy solicit, synthethize, and review the work products of national reporters who are appointed by national committees. Regrettably, the sometimes undisciplined nature of individual country contributions—many of which remain unpublished and thus are all but unavailable—has led to General Reports that have all too often been sketchy and unsatisfactory.[20] In any event, even the General Reports are not readily available in most law libraries.

The International Association of Legal Science has discussed family law at its periodic Congresses. To illustrate, at its 1957 Congress, Max Rheinstein addressed 'The Stability of the Family'[21] and, as mentioned above, the Association helped launch the unfinished *Encyclopedia*.

---

[18] See eg the impressively comprehensive and panoramic study of comparative law and German civil law in the twentieth century by Filippo Ranieri, 'Die Rechtsvergleichung und das deutsche Zivilrecht im 20. Jahrhundert: Eine wissenschaftstheoretische Skizze', in Friedrich Ebel (ed), *Festschrift zum 70. Geburtstag von Knut Wolfgang Nörr* (2002), where there is just one incidental 'cf' citation in Ranieri's footnote 35 to Erich Hans Kaden's entry in the seven-volume compilation.

[19] In the words of the Nuremberg war crimes tribunal that sentenced him to life imprisonment in 1947 (Schlegelberger was released in 1951 with a large pension): 'Hitler ordered [Schlegelberger] in 1938 to join the NSDAP'. Subsequently, 'upon his retirement as Acting Minister of Justice on 20 August 1942, Schlegelberger received a letter of appreciation from Hitler together with a gift of 100,000 RM'. The Nuremberg Tribunal quoted him declaring as early as 1936: 'In the sphere of criminal law the road to a creation of justice in harmony with the moral concepts of the New Reich has been opened upon by a new wording of Section 2 of the Criminal Code, whereby a person is also (to) be punished even if his deed is not punishable according to the law, but if he deserved punishment in accordance with the basic concepts of criminal law and the sound instincts of the people. This new definition became necessary because of the rigidity of the norm in force hitherto'. Enough, said; this line of thinking is not a nice subject for comparative law, but it remains interesting.

[20] See eg Harry D. Krause, 'Property and Alimony in No-Fault Divorce', General Report, XIV Congress of the International Academy of Comparative Law, Athens 1994, published in K. D. Kerameus (ed), *Rapports Generaux XIVe Congrès International, Institute Hellenique de Droit International et Etranger* (1996) at 149–76.

[21] Max Rheinstein, 'The Stability of the Family: A Report to the Director of UNESCO', Paper No. 1, Part 2, Les Colloques de Chicago, L'Association Internationale des Sciences Juridiques (September 1957), reprinted at 6 *University of Chicago Law School Record* No. 2.

Many work products of national commissions contemplating the reform of particular areas of their laws are valuable sources of comparative family law. Significant works cover divorce,[22] assisted conception,[23] legal discrimination against non-marital children,[24] paternity and child support,[25] cohabitation,[26] legalized same-sex relationships,[27] and discrimination against women.[28]

The Hague Conference on Private International Law has produced a network of functioning treaties governing international concerns—such as international adoptions, child custody, child support enforcement, and marriage recognition—with each treaty based on careful comparative assessment and coordination of national laws, accompanied by carefully researched reports.[29] Several of these Hague Conventions, including prominently 'Civil Aspects of International Child Abduction' and 'Protection of Children and Cooperation in Respect of

---

[22] See eg Archbishop of Canterbury's Study Group, 'Putting Asunder: A Divorce Law for Contemporary Society', (1964); 'Report of the Governor's Commission on the Family', California (1966); Robert Levy, 'Uniform Marriage and Divorce Legislation: A Preliminary Analysis', prepared for the National Conference of Commissioners on Uniform State Laws (1968); 'Empfiehlt es sich, Gründe und Folgen der Ehescheidung neu zu regeln?', *Verhandlungen des achtundvierzigsten Deutschen Juristentages*, Teil M (vol II., 1970); *Law Commission (London), Reform of the Grounds of Divorce* (1966); *Facing the Future: A Discussion Paper on the Grounds for Divorce* (Law Commission No. 170, 1988).

[23] See eg the Warnock Report in the United Kingdom and the report of the Waller Committee in Australia. Department of Health and Social Security, *Report of the Committee of Inquiry into Human Fertilisation and Embryology* (1984) (Warnock Report); Committee to Consider the Social, Ethical and Legal Issues Arising from In Vitro Fertilization, *Report on the Disposition of Embryos Produced by In Vitro Fertilization* (1984) (Waller Report); see also Harry D. Krause, 'Artificial Conception: Legislative Approaches', (1985) 19 *Family Law Quarterly* 185.

[24] See Law Commission (London), *Family Law: Illegitimacy* (1982); Law Comm'n (London), *Family Law: Illegitimacy* (2nd Report, 1986); *Report of the Committee on One-Parent Families* (July 1974) (Finer Report).

[25] See Law Commission (London), *Blood Tests and the Proof of Paternity in Civil Proceedings* (1968); *A Maintenance Agency for Australia: The Report of the National Maintenance Inquiry* (Attorney-General's Office 1984).

[26] *See New South Wales Law Reform Commission, Report on De Facto Relationships* (1983).

[27] Jürgen Basedow, Klaus Hopt, Hein Kötz, and Peter Dopffel (eds), *Die Rechtsstellung Gleichgeschlechtlicher Lebensgemeinschaften* (2000) (containing numerous country reports mostly in German with several in English); Law Commission of Canada, *Beyond Conjugality: Recognizing and Supporting Close Personal Adult Relationships* (Ottawa, 2001) (surveying the legal regulation of intimate relationships and proposing a reorientation of family law away from its traditional focus on marriage and conjugal relationships more generally).

[28] See eg Australian Law Reform Commission, *Equality before the Law: Justice for Women* (1994) (recommending legal reforms to eliminate discrimination against women in Australian law, including family law); *Deutscher Bundestag, 8. Wahlperiode, Enquete-Kommission Frau und Gesellschaft, Stenographisches Protokoll der Oeffentlichen Anhoerung zum Thema Durchsetzung der Gleichberechtigung*, 5 September 1979, Harry D. Krause (oral testimony and response to questions supplementing written US national report) at 7–9, 13–14, 21–3, 40–4.

[29] See eg J. H. A. van Loon, *Report on Intercountry Adoption*, Hague Conference on Private International Law, Proceedings of the Seventeenth Session, Tome II (1993).

Intercountry Adoption' have been widely adopted and play a significant role in bringing international cohesion and cross-border enforceability to family law.[30]

Worldwide treaties, such as the United Nations' conventions on human rights, on women, and on the rights of the child, as well as certain regional conventions, such as the European Convention on Human Rights and the Organization of American States' American Convention on Human Rights, guarantee fundamental rights relating to family life.[31] Often recognizing rights only in highly abstract terms (consider the European Convention's 'right to respect for . . . family life'),[32] these conventions and pronouncements have a significant impact in encouraging commonalities in family law principles across national boundaries.[33] Opinions of the European Court of Human Rights regularly test the family laws of member states against European treaties and conventions. Scholars are now paying close attention to the Europeanization of family law.[34]

The United States' much-criticized reluctance to adopt international human rights instruments finds a benign explanation in the American tradition of respect for law.[35] Once a 'self-executing' treaty is ratified, US courts will apply it. And US

[30] See Convention of 19 October 1996 on Jurisdiction, Applicable Law, Recognition, Enforcement and Co-operation in Respect of Parental Responsibility and Measures for the Protection of Children (entry into force 1 January 2002); Convention of 25 October 1980 on the Civil Aspects of International Child Abduction (entry into force 1 December 1983); Convention on Protection of Children and Co-operation in Respect of Intercountry Adoption (entry into force 1 May 1995); Convention of 2 October 1973 on the Recognition and Enforcement of Decisions Relating to Maintenance Obligations (entry into force 1 August 1976); Convention Concerning the Recognition and Enforcement of Decisions Relating to Maintenance Obligations towards Children (entry into force 1 January 1962); Convention Concerning the Powers of Authorities and the Law Applicable in Respect of the Protection of Infants (entry into force 4 February 1969); Convention on Celebration and Recognition of the Validity of Marriages (entry into force 1 May 1991); Convention on the Recognition of Divorces and Legal Separations (entry into force 24 August 1975); Convention on the Law Applicable to Marital Property Regimes (entry into force 1 September 1992); Convention on the Recognition and Enforcement of Decisions Relating to Maintenance Obligations (entry into force 1 August 1976); The text of these conventions can be found at <http://www.hcch.net/index_en.php?act=text.display&tid=10#family>.

[31] The Convention for the Protection of Human Rights and Fundamental Freedoms, 213 UNTS 221 (4 November 1950), as amended by Protocol 11 (11 May 1994), Eur TS No. 155 (hereinafter 'European Convention'); American Convention on Human Rights, OASTS No. 36, 1144 UNTS 123 (22 November 1969); see below (n 33) (listing United Nations conventions).

[32] Article 8 of the European Convention, see Convention for the Protection of Human Rights and Fundamental Freedoms, 213 UNTS 221 (1950).

[33] Universal Declaration of Human Rights, GA Res 217, (1948); European Convention, above (n 29); Convention on the Elimination of All Forms of Discrimination Against Women, 1249 UNTS 13 (1980); Convention on the Rights of the Child, 1577 UNTS 3 (1989).

[34] See Reinhard Zimmermann, 'Civil Code and Civil Law—The "Europeanization" of Private Law and the Re-emergence of a European Legal Science', (1994/95) 1 *Columbia Journal of European Law* 63 ff, and the important works of Katharina Boele-Woelki and her associates, listed in the Bibliography.

[35] Having served in the early 1990s as a member of the US State Department's delegation to the Hague for the negotiation of the international adoption treaty and in 1998 on an ad hoc US State Department task group to decide whether President Clinton should be advised to sign the UN Convention on the Rights of the Child, this author experienced first-hand just how seriously treaties

constitutional litigation has shown what unexpected outcomes a generally worded provision may spawn.[36] Recently—and regrettably in strange contradiction to ever-increasing US involvements abroad—a certain hostility against international rules has invaded US foreign policy, extending from the executive branch to a reluctant US Senate, and to the US Supreme Court.[37]

At the level of federated or more or less closely aligned systems—such as the United States, Australia, Scandinavia, and recently the European Union—official and unofficial commissions, courts, and agencies have studied the laws of constituent jurisdictions for the purpose of unification or reform. Published work products of these bodies, in the form of law reform proposals, reports, and studies, identify shared principles and provide wide-ranging analyses of the ways in which family laws of related jurisdictions intersect, overlap, and might be brought more closely together.[38]

In the United States, a more diverse than commonly supposed federation of fifty-plus family-law-sovereign states,[39] prestigious law reform entities have offered visions of a future for family law. The American Law Institute's 'principles' may be ahead of our time.[40] More realistically, the National Conference of Commissioners

are taken at the highest US levels and what thorough analysis is made of a treaty before the State Department will recommend it be signed. President Clinton did sign, but the Senate did not ratify. At the time of writing, the Hague adoptions treaty is close to being ratified and detailed US implementing legislation and regulations are being completed. For a detailed legal analysis of the Convention in light of US (largely state) law, see eg Cynthia Price Cohen and Howard A. Davidson, *Children's Rights in America: U.N. Convention on the Rights of the Child Compared with United States Law* (ABA, 1990; summary, 1994).

[36] The abortion controversy is a good/bad example. See below (nn 84–92) and accompanying text.

[37] The willingness of some members of the Supreme Court, most prominently Justices Stephen Breyer and Anthony Kennedy, to consider judicial decisions from outside the United States in interpreting the US Constitution has provoked sharp rebukes from Justice Antonin Scalia. See *Lawrence v Texas*, 539 US 558 (2003); *Roper v Simmons*, 125 S Ct 1183 (2005); ibid at 1225–7 (Scalia J, dissenting); see 'The Relevance of Foreign Legal Materials in U.S. Constitutional Cases: A Conversation between Justice Antonin Scalia and Justice Stephen Breyer', (2005) 3 *International Journal of Constitutional Law* 519 (2005).

[38] See above (nn 22–9) (citing law reform reports).

[39] See Harry D. Krause and David D. Meyer, *Family Law in a Nutshell* (4th edn, 2003), 5–8.

[40] ALI, *Principles of the Law of Family Dissolution* (2002). This opinion is that of this author who served as an advisor to the project. Holmes's words suit: 'That is my outside thought on the present discontents. As to the truth embodied in them, in part it cannot be helped. It cannot be helped, it is as it should be, that the law is behind the times . . . It means that the law is growing. As law embodies beliefs that have triumphed in the battle of ideas and then have translated themselves into action, while there still is doubt, while opposite convictions still keep a battle front against each other, the time for law has not come; the notion destined to prevail is not yet entitled to the field. It is a misfortune if a judge reads his conscious or unconscious sympathy with one side or the other prematurely into the law, and forgets that what seem to him to be first principles are believed by half his fellow men to be wrong. I think that we have suffered from this misfortune . . . and that this is another and very important truth to be extracted from the popular discontent'. Holmes, 'Law and the Court', speech at Harvard Law School Association of New York, 15 February 1913, in *Collected Legal Papers*, 291, at 294–5.

on Uniform State Laws (NCCUSL) has drafted detailed, enactable, and often enacted laws that harmonize and improve scattershot or conflicting legal approaches that individual US states have taken.[41] More forcefully and forcibly, the United States Supreme Court has imposed federal constitutional mandates on topics ranging from illegitimacy to abortion and marital privacy, thereby 'unifying' often divergent state laws.[42]

Individual scholars from many nations have contributed to understanding family law across state and cultural boundaries. Max Rheinstein and Mary Ann Glendon have laid foundation stones[43] for comparative family law, and myriad others have contributed. A rich collection of comparative family law teaching materials was recently published in the United States.[44] For the English-language family law comparatist this work's comprehensive collection of international legal sources is indispensable. For those proficient in German, a remarkable work offers the verbatim translation into German of the texts of most family laws in the world, kept up to date in loose-leaf binders.[45]

III. What's to Compare—and How?

The substantive portion of this essay might have started with a comparison of traditional, state-decreed prerequisites for marriage. But it does not seem worth spending this scarce space on a review of what may be the minimum marriageable age in any number of systems—the general rule is puberty-plus, with a few child

---

[41] Again, this value judgment is that of this author, a former Commissioner on Uniform State Laws and reporter-draftsman for several uniform acts. NCCUSL's laws on family law topics include Uniform Adoption Act (1994); Uniform Child Custody Jurisdiction and Enforcement Act (1997); Uniform Marriage and Divorce Act (1970 & 1973); Uniform Marital Property Act (1983); Uniform Parentage Act (1973 and 2002); Uniform Premarital Agreements Act (1983); Uniform Probate Code (1969 and 1991); Uniform Marriage Evasion Act (1912); Uniform Disposition of Community Property Rights at Death Act (1971); Uniform Status of Children of Assisted Conception Act (1988); Interstate Family Support Act (2001). The text of these acts is available at <http://www.nccusl.org/Update/DesktopDefault.aspx?tabindex=0&tabid=65>.

[42] See Krause and Meyer, above (n 39), at 8–10, 16–30.

[43] A small sample of their work is Mary Ann Glendon, *The New Family and the New Property* (1981); Mary Ann Glendon, *Abortion and Divorce in Western Law* (1987); Mary Ann Glendon, *The Transformation of Family Law: State, Law and Family in the United States and Western Europe* (1989); Max Rheinstein, *Marriage Stability, Divorce, and the Law* (1972); Rheinstein and Glendon, above (n 16); Rheinstein and König, above (n 16).

[44] D. Marianne Blair and Merle H. Weiner, *Family Law in the World Community Cases, Materials, and Problems in Comparative and International Family Law* (2003).

[45] Alexander Bergmann, Murad Ferid, and Dieter Henrich, *Internationales Ehe und Kindschaftsrecht* (1976–2005 ff).

brides here and there, mostly there[46]—or what precisely the definition of pro-hibited incest may mean to eligibility for marriage—anything past first cousins generally goes, and first cousins may marry in many places. Indeed, incest—short of the element of abuse between brother and sister is no longer criminal in some European venues.

The essay might then have gone on with a side-by-side comparison of rules governing divorce, child custody, and child support as well as other subjects. For-tunately, recent studies by the (unofficial) 'Commission on European Family Law' under the leadership of Katharina Boele-Woelki provide such a side-by-side com-parison on numerous subjects.[47] Moreover, in her wide-ranging (though yet to be published) introduction to the Family Law Volume of the *International Encyclo-pedia of Comparative Law*, Mary Ann Glendon updates worldwide family law developments in admirable detail, with ample current citations, and with her usual insight.[48] My objective is more modest—even while the reader is invited to think beyond family law as he or she knew it.

After millennia of enduring similar conditions, the industrialized world has—in just a few centuries—moved far away from the economic subsistence model that still dominates the scene elsewhere. After millennia of relative isolation—not

[46] Some 250 years ago, Sir William Blackstone, *Commentaries on the Laws of England*, vol I, ch XVII. 2 (original 1765, new edn Chitty, London, 1826), dealt with this and related age questions in a compara-tive discussion: 'The ages of male and female are different for different purposes. A male at *twelve* years old may take the oath of allegiance; at *fourteen* is at years of discretion, and therefore may consent or disagree to marriage, may choose his guardian, and, if his discretion be actually proved, may make his testament of his personal estate; at *seventeen* may be an executor; and at *twenty-one* is at his own disposal, and may aliene his lands, goods, and chattels. A female also at *seven* years of age may be betrothed or given in marriage; at *nine* is entitled to dower; at *twelve* is at years of maturity, and therefore may consent or disagree to marriage, and, if proved to have sufficient discretion, may bequeath her personal estate; at *fourteen* is at years of legal discretion, and may choose a guardian; at *seventeen* may be executrix; and at *twenty-one* may dispose of herself and her lands. So that full age in male or female, is twenty-one years, which age is completed on the day preceding the anniversary of a person's birth; who till that time is an infant, and so styled in law. Among the ancient Greeks and Romans *women* were never of age, but subject to perpetual guardianship, unless when married, *"nisi convenissent in manum viri"*: and, when that perpetual tutelage wore away in process of time, we find that, in females as well as males, full age was not till twenty-five years. Thus, by the constitution of different kingdoms, this period, which is merely arbitrary, and *juris positivi*, is fixed at different times. Scotland agrees with England in this point (both probably copying from the old Saxon constitutions on the continent, which extended the age of minority *"ad annum vigesimum primum; et eo usque juvenes sub tutelam reponunt"*) but in Naples they are of full age at *eighteen*; in France, with regard to marriage, not till *thirty*; and in Holland at *twenty-five*'. Fast forward now to what is relevant in 2005: 'Legal Age for Tattoos Lowered to 18'. (*Champaign-Urbana News-Gazette*, 5 November 2005).

[47] Katharina Boele-Woelki, B. Braat, and I. Curry-Summers (eds), *Principles of European Family Law Regarding Divorce and Maintenance between Former Spouses* (2004), 1; see also Katharina Boele-Woelki (ed), *Perspectives for the Unification and Harmonisation of Family Law in Europe* (2002); Katharina Boele-Woelki, B. Braat, and I. Curry-Summers (eds), *European Family Law in Action: Volume I: Grounds for Divorce* (2003).

[48] Mary Ann Glendon, 'Introduction: Family Law in a Time of Turbulence', in Mary Ann Glendon (ed), *IV, International Encyclopedia of Comparative Law* (forthcoming).

always benignly alleviated by conquest, colonialism, and trade—the world is coming into close contact. On the surface, commonalities in terms of industrialization and global commerce nurture (and are nurtured by) a near-universal aspiration to material well-being. Where pragmatic objectives are largely the same, optimal solutions are bound to be similar or at least comparable. This makes a comparative discussion of commercial law relatively manageable, sensible—and instructive. In contrast to laws involving commerce, however, family law has resisted secularization and amalgamation. At its cultural foundations, humanity remains highly diverse. Universally, religions underlie and have set the tone of family law, and diversity of religions has continued to foster diversity of legal rules. Related cultural groupings have seen comparable family law developments, but comparison becomes ever less meaningful as we look farther afield. True, traditional cultures are meeting modern ones and sometimes not to their advantage, emulating behaviors which may or may not suit local conditions. True, many family life problems and outcomes remain similar and simple everywhere: Men and women join and have children. From earliest times, laws have regulated the framework for reproduction—records go back before Hammurabi's Code.[49]

The devil—and many believe that literally—is in the detail. In the 'West', relatively recent and liberated answers to many fundamental issues—ranging from individual freedom, to women's equality, to homosexual rights, abortion, even to the proper role of sexuality on television and in schools—are now perceived as necessary givens, sometimes as natural, universal human rights. This is not so elsewhere. Western notions, particularly of women's equality, are seen in many traditional cultures as the infidel's attack on millennia-old religious imperatives.

The West's newest 'enlightenments'—recognition of unmarried cohabitation, birth control, abortion, women's equality in the workplace and at home, legalized same-sex relationships, assisted conception, and soon, perhaps, human cloning— are fundamentally changing the traditional social order of sexual pairing, child-bearing, and child-raising. But the West's current moral certainties do not play well in the industrially 'developing' world—as indeed they would not have played well in the West a mere one hundred years ago. Worse, anti-modernist—thus all but automatically anti-Western—religions have been revitalized (especially in the Middle East, Pakistan, Afghanistan, and Indonesia) and now dominate even previously secularizing Muslim countries, as for instance Iran. Radical Islam finds political expression in extremes, including the Taliban, Al Qaida, and Saudi-nurtured Wahhabism. As much as these strains are violently forcing themselves into Western consciousness, they defy intelligent comparison because they defy what much of the economically developed world now perceives as universal human rights.

---

[49] My learned friend of Oxford days, Reuven Yaron, tells of *The Laws of Eshnunna* (2nd edn, 1988), ch 6 'Marriage and Divorce', comparing Hammurabi's Code, 172–222; see ibid at 165–71 (concerning the upbringing of children).

In the absence of common basic values, comparison of specific legal rules is a dangerous and likely fruitless exercise. There is thus considerable temptation to sort out cultures of family law in terms of levels of economic development and secular pragmatism. This essay will succumb to that temptation, but—as promised—resist the temptation of simply providing a side-by-side listing of Western 'accomplishments'. Instead, this essay takes a critical, even worried, look at Western lifestyles. In our era of diversity and respect for all lifestyles in the politically correct West, must we refuse to make value judgments? Can we afford not to?

Lest the 'West' be perceived as a monolithic culture, it should be noted that America is a place where politics in the sense of the wide European divergences between left and right, between democracy, dictatorship, and monarchy, or between socialism, communism, and capitalism, or extremist nationalism, have never played much of a role. Sex, however, and religion do—and ever more so with the current alliance between progressive feminists and ultra-conservative religions. The American 'sexio-political' atmosphere is characterized by reaction to the Clinton affairs. The growing influence of fundamentalist religion is obvious to the extreme of downgrading the teaching of evolution in schools.[50]

If Europeans loudly profess not to understand American (prudish?) attitudes regarding sex and the political power of fundamentalist (intolerant?) interpretations of religion, Americans do not understand the Europeans' preoccupation with ideology and their (mostly unpleasant) ethnic/nationalistic history. The conflict in the United States between traditional and modern lifestyles has aptly been termed the 'culture wars' and has rendered family law reform vastly more contentious and complex than it is in most of Europe where matters moral and sexual are rather more in the open, and religion is attended to on Sundays, if at all.

IV. FAMILY LAW

1. What is It?

Family law involves the rules by which men and women establish intimate relationships that have legal consequences. At the individual level, marriage imposes legal obligations that are enforceable even after the 'bliss phase' governed by continuing

---

[50] See Dennis Overbye, 'Philosophers Notwithstanding, Kansas Redefines Science', *NY Times*, 15 November 2005, at F1 (discussing decision of Kansas State Board of Education to revise the state's science curriculum to include criticism of the Darwinian theory of evolution). After voters in Dover, Pennsylvania, voted out of office local school board members who had backed instruction on

consent, has ended. Enforcement covers mutual economic responsibility and the support and upbringing of children. Obviously, fewer complications ensued in the days when each person had just one try at marriage. Then the regulation of entry into marriage was of the essence, few rules governed the ongoing marriage (not needed: the husband was in charge), and termination was unavailable in varying degrees (especially to women). Moreover, the incentive to end a relationship and to enter into a new one was cooled by the impossibility of remarriage. Marriage truly was for life, 'for better or for worse'. But the 'worse' became worse with increased emphasis on the individual and his (and more recently, her) right to happiness combined with lengthening life expectancies in general—and in particular through improved survival of wives in childbirth and through birth control.

2. The Social Purposes of Marriage

Marriage and the family served—and in many parts of the world continue to serve—as the sole legally and morally permissible harbour for sexual activity and child-rearing. This (1) assured the birth of children into two-parent families as the natural and then (pre-pill, pre-abortion) unavoidable consequence of sexual activity, (2) provided the structure for socializing children by means of role division between the marriage partners, (3) made parental role division possible by providing economic security for the stay-at-home partner through legal support obligations as well as through moral, social, and harsh legal strictures against divorce, and (5) assured old-age provision for parents through their children's reciprocal moral and legal support obligation.[51] Recognizing that traditional marriage is a good bargain for society, social customs, religious rites, and legal rules governing marriage were fairly tailored around these facts and goals, justifying a variety of legal and economic benefits and privileges for the partners to marriage. In the West, that bargain is now in question.

The chief trend that has transformed family life and law is the rapid acceleration of legal, social, and economic equality for women. Another vital trend is increasing recognition of children as separate legal actors independent from their parents.

'Intelligent Design', televangelist Pat Robertson warned town voters that they faced divine retribution: 'I'd like to say to the good citizens of Dover: If there is a disaster in your area, don't turn to God; you just rejected him from your city'. See 'Town Is Warned of God's Wrath', *NY Times*, 11 November 2005, at A16.

[51] See Karl L. Llewellyn, 'Behind the Law of Divorce', (1932) 32 *Columbia LR* 1281, 1288–94; Harry D. Krause, *Family Law in a Nutshell* (1977), 25–9; Elizabeth S. Scott, 'Marriage, Cohabitation, and Collective Responsibility for Dependency', (2004) *University of Chicago Legal Forum* 225; Michael S. Wald, 'Same-Sex Couple Marriage: A Family Policy Perspective', (2001) 9 *Virginia Journal of Social Policy & Law* 291; Brian H. Bix, 'State of the Union: The States' Interest in the Marital Status of Their Citizens', (2000) 55 *University of Miami LR* 1.

Children are now seen as entitled to their fair share of rights *vis-à-vis* their parents and society. A third factor is the modern welfare state. Society at large has ever more closely involved itself in social and economic functions that used to be the exclusive, private province of the family. The unintended side-effect is that the very act of seeking to help the family where it fails its functions or falls short, has made it less necessary for the family to fulfill its traditional tasks—such as socializing children and providing economic support for all its members, including the elderly.

Today a secular, pragmatic view of the family is spreading. An ever looser interpretation of marriage and family obligations along with decreasing everyday relevance of religions have brought similar, arguably more reason-based solutions. And as referred to above, numerous international conventions and declarations proclaimed by varying sources (such as the United Nations and the European Union), now express aspirationally universal views of what is 'good' and what is 'bad' and complement and accelerate worldwide secularization.

V. Yesterday's 'Great Debates'

In the last fifty years, reform efforts in country after country have departed from conditioning divorce on the commission by one marriage partner of a marital offense—such as adultery or cruelty—and have moved to an almost total disregard of marital fault. In the West, divorce has turned from being simply unavailable, to difficult (on fault grounds only), to easy to obtain (with uncontested and typically consensual faux-fault grounds), and now even past no-fault grounds. Today, as divorce plays in many courts, the State asks for little more than one party's unilateral decision to divorce the other. In consequence, the relevant focus of the divorce process has shifted almost entirely from status (*whether* divorce may be obtained) to the economic consequences (divorce is freely available, but not for free) and to allocating child custody and support. *Divorce, through its legal and social consequences, now all but defines the legal meaning of marriage and with that, Western family law.*

Western family law reforms of the last half century have achieved a more equitable allocation of the economic consequences of failed marriages. Between the spouses, the great shift was from periodic support (alimony) for a dependent ex-spouse to division between the ex-partners of marital property. But even in 'wealthy' countries, the problem remains that the typical marriage has produced little property to divide. And long-term, adequate spousal support is not only rarely granted but all too often beyond the obligor's capacity as he or she strives to support a new spouse, family, or lifestyle.

The second great reform has involved the proper allocation and enforcement of child support responsibility after divorce, as well as for the vastly increased numbers (and proportion) of children born outside of marriage. That debate too has succeeded in theory: and the absent parent is fully legally liable and increasingly held accountable for marital and non-marital children alike. Non-marital children are equal. Yet again, all too often he or she has inadequate resources to fulfill his or her responsibility. Society has not appropriately recognized its own stake in the future of its children.[52] Europe has done far more on this score than the United States—child allowances and tax benefits of varying generosity are the norm—but these efforts have not yet proved enough to stem dangerously falling birth rates.

VI. Today's and Tomorrow's 'Great Debates'

1. Downgrading Marriage and Upgrading Cohabitation Alternatives

Relaxed attitudes toward marriage, family formation, and sexual companionship have become socially and legally accepted in the West. This is reflected not only in high-flying divorce statistics, but in dropping marriage rates as well. Indeed, what optimists recently heralded as dropping divorce rates may simply reflect fewer marriages between less than totally committed partners—now that cohabitation options are available to them.

Certainly, an ever greater number of modern adults act on the realization that the commitments and burdens of formal marriage outweigh its advantages.[53] In the US, the number of cohabiting unmarried couples stands above four million. In many European countries much larger populations eschew formal marriage—the more, the farther north one looks. Scandinavia may still be on top, but with more than 40 per cent of births to unmarried mothers, France is holding its own.[54]

---

[52] See Harry D. Krause, 'Child Support Reassessed: Limits of Private Responsibility and the Public Interest', (1989) *University of Illinois LR* 367.

[53] See J. Rubellin-Devichi (ed), *Des Concubinages Dans Le Monde: Approche Socio-Juridique* (1990).

[54] See Jean-Marie Le Goff, 'Cohabiting Unions in France and West Germany: Transitions to First Birth and First Marriage', (2002) 7 *Demographic Research* 593, 594.

Matters have reached the point where many potential marriage partners—men and women—will not accept the risk of role division. In this new world, the attractions of unmarried cohabitation are (1) that potentially costly legal procedures are not needed to end the relationship, and the potentially considerable financial consequences of divorce are avoided. (2) Sophisticated unmarried couples have an opportunity to define the terms of their relationship by contract individually and more precisely if they wish to avoid the restrictions of laws that may still limit antenuptial contracts. (3) Income-tax-conscious two-earner couples may, typically in countries with joint return provisions for married couples, harvest income tax savings by cohabiting. (This advantage may be offset by preferences for surviving spouses in taxes levied at the partner's death.) (4) The feminist may see unmarried cohabitation as bringing—or in any event symbolizing—freedom from traditional male dominance in marriage. (5) For the unemancipated recipient of support derived from a first marriage or of welfare benefits, remarriage or marriage may be costly if, as is often the case, financial benefits are thereby terminated. (6) Finally, reduced relative[55] earnings have rendered marriage an all but unattainable aspiration for many in the lowest income groups.

These are the facts. Many complex *legal* issues have not been adequately addressed: Most jurisdictions have failed to put new partnership alternatives into a socially constructive and legally defined relationship to marriage.

If 'the life of the law has not been logic: it has been experience'[56]—occasionally logic has helped. When *logical* conclusions are drawn from our developing understanding that modern marriage is in need of far more individual ordering than traditional law allowed and that, conversely, supposedly 'free and open' intimate relationships are in need of more official supervision than some would like, rigid legal distinctions between marriage and informal intimate partnerships become less tenable.

Key questions are (1) how the law should define the legal position of unmarried partner *vis-à-vis* partner and that of unmarried couples *vis-à-vis* society? (2) Short of marriage, what level of marital-like rights and obligations should be imposed on, or granted to, unmarried partners? (3) Short of documented marriage, how may it be proved efficiently—both in terms of cost and predictability of consequences—that a legally significant, though not married, relationship exists or existed? (4) Must or should another country or a sister state that itself does not recognize a cohabitation status (or indeed, same-sex marriage or partnership) recognize a legal status created in another state or country?[57]

---

[55] 'Relative' in the sense of men compared with women, and high-income earners with low-income earners.

[56] Holmes's most quoted *bon mot*, Oliver Wendell Holmes, *The Common Law* (1881), 5.

[57] The authoritative study is Peter Hay, *Recognition of Same-Sex Relationships*, US National Report for XVIIth Congress of the International Academy of Comparative Law, to be held in *Utrecht* in July 2006, to be published in *AJCL* (forthcoming 2006); see also Peter Hay, 'The American "Covenant

2. Civil Marriage versus Religious Tradition

Modern realities call for a far-reaching 'decoupling' of the strictly legal meaning of marriage from the traditional legal-cultural-religious-historical significance of marriage.[58]

To make progress in any sensible adaptation of marriage and family to current conditions, civil marriage must be distinguished clearly from the continuing romance with religious images of 'marriage' as a status of supra-(or indeed super-) natural virtue. In the modern West, religions are free to define their own concepts of marriage in terms of their own and their believers' desired ends. Equally, so must the State. Religion has no role in secular affairs, just as the civil legislator has no role beyond proper civil business: 'Render therefore unto Caesar the things which be Caesar's, and unto God the things which be God's'.[59]

3. The State's Secular Interests in Civil Marriage

To adapt secular marriage to the modern world, the State's legitimate interests in marriage—as laid down in binding law—should be defined separately from the religious-personal meaning of marriage. The partners themselves are of course free to believe and do what their religions require—short of offending major state policies such as the prohibitions on polygamy and child abuse. But a pragmatic, secular concept of marriage should guide the legislator. In accordance with its legitimate interests, society should narrowly tailor legal default consequences of secular marriage to the realities of the life situation in question. The question should be 'What does this or that union do for Society, and what rights should Society provide in return?' The spotlight should be on the appropriate mix of *private* ordering (giving effect to the free will of the partners) and *public* ordering (based on social objectives that justify imposing limits on or providing incentives for the partners' choices).[60]

The first goal should be to ensure that predictable individual and social conse-quences follow from commitments that are efficiently provable. A prime practical function of formal marriage remains its capability of conclusively and efficiently

Marriage" in the Conflict of Laws', (2003) 64 *Lousiana LR* 43. A European Committee recently recommended that, within the EU, recognition should be extended to such partnerships even if local law does not recognize similar unions. A similar question arises on the opposite side of the spectrum, when a status of 'super marriage' (for instance difficult-to-divorce 'covenant marriage' that is now appearing in several US states) was created in one state and is up for adjudication in another.

[58] See Harry D. Krause, 'Marriage for the New Millennium: Heterosexual, Same-Sex—Or Not at All?', (2000) 34 *Family Law Quarterly* 271.

[59] Luke 20: 25, *The Holy Bible Newly Translated Out of the Original Tongues By His Majesty's Special Command* (John Baskett, Oxford, 1717).

[60] Compare text, above, Section IV. 2, p 1112.

proving that a legal relationship exists and what legal consequences it entails. This parallels the remaining relevance of marriage to children: While marriage of the parents no longer defines substantive parental rights and obligations (these are now essentially the same whether or not the parents are married), marriage importantly serves as the most expeditious method of establishing legal parentage.

Beyond the issue of proof and legal certainty, what are the public's proper concerns in this arena? What should be left to the private parties involved in a relationship, irrespective of whether they are formally married or not? Perhaps not surprisingly, many needed answers have not yet been found—even for hetero-sexual cohabitants. In that sense prematurely, today's discussion has skipped ahead to the next question: what about same-sex couples?

4. Same-Sex Relationships

Throughout the West, an emotional debate rages over the legal treatment of same-sex partners. That debate is taking place at national and supra-national legis-lative and judicial levels, as well as in an international market-place occupied by corporations seeking to steer a prudent course of business. Marriage or partner-ship rights for gay and lesbian partners have been debated or enacted in Australia, Brazil, Canada, Costa Rica, Israel, New Zealand, parts of the United States, and much of Europe.[61]

Should same-sex partners be permitted to marry? Should they be recognized as legal partners in what has sometimes been called a civil partnership or civil union? Should they have some, most, or all of the rights of married heterosexual couples? Or should same-sex partners—where they do not have a formal option—be allowed to contract into enforceable *private* cohabitation agreements, which—if and where enforceable—would offer them some help in legally ordering their mutual relationships? Answers so far given range from a flat 'no', to an unequivocal 'yes', to something in between.

To repeat, Brazil, Costa Rica, Israel, South Africa, and others are in the debate. In Europe, the Netherlands, Belgium, and Spain now provide same-sex marriage. But it gives pause to note that the Nordic countries—Europe's socially most lib-eral—have *not* provided gay marriage. Instead, Denmark, Finland, Greenland, Iceland, Norway, and Sweden recognize only a near equivalent, some with res-trictions on child-bearing and raising. Germany provides same-sex couples a

---

[61] See M. Andenas and R. Wintemute (eds), *Legal Recognition of Same-Sex Partnerships: A Study of National, European and International Law* (2001); Katharina Boele-Woelki and Angelika Fuchs (eds), *Legal Recognition of Same-Sex Couples in Europe* (2003); see also above (n 27).

near equivalent of marriage through 'domestic partnership' legislation.[62] France recognizes a contractually based legal status of cohabitation which is open to hetero- and homosexuals.[63] This contrasts with European countries that limit marriage substitutes to same-sex partners and relegate heterosexuals to 'regular' marriage.

Among common law countries, the United Kingdom is set to recognize 'civil partnerships' as of 2006. In 2005 Canada enacted legislation making full marriage rights available nationwide to same-sex couples, following court rulings that had legalized same-sex marriage in several provinces. Evading the 'technicality' that marriage is under the exclusive legal authority of the Australian federal government, Australian states enacted so-called 'De Facto Relationships Acts'. From New South Wales,[64] this type of partnership legislation has spread to other Australian states. It now covers same-sex cohabitants.[65] New Zealand has not legalized same-sex marriage, but recognizes legal effects in terms of property rights accruing from cohabiting relationships.[66]

In the United States, Massachusetts stands alone in recognizing actual marriage for same-sex couples. By court decision, this now is a state-constitutional mandate[67]—even while the voters may yet amend the Massachusetts Constitution to the opposite effect. Vermont, Connecticut, California, and Hawaii provide near-equivalents of marriage through 'civil union' or 'domestic partner' legislation that, in legal effects, run more or less parallel to marriage.[68] In September 2005, the California legislature sought to allow same-sex marriage, but that law was vetoed by Governor Arnold Schwarzenegger. He explained his decision on the ground that the legislation would conflict with a popular initiative approved by voters five years earlier stating that 'only marriage between a man and a woman is valid

---

[62] See Dieter Schwab, 'Eingetragene Lebenspartnerschaft', (2001) *Zeitschrift für das gesamte Familienrecht* 385–98; Robert Battes, 'Probleme bei der Anwendung des Gesetzes über eingetragene Lebenspartnerschafte', Teil 1 and 2, (2002) 2 *Familie und Recht* at 49–54, Teil 2 at (2002) 3 *Familie und Recht* at 113–22.

[63] See Xavier Tracol, 'The Pacte Civil de Solidarité (PACS)', in *Legal Recognition of Same-Sex Couples*, above (n 61), at 68.

[64] Reproduced in large part in Harry D. Krause, *Family Law: Cases, Comments, and Questions* (3rd edn, 1990), 162–7.

[65] Lindy Willmott *et al*, 'De Facto Relationships Property Adjustment Law—A National Direction', (2003) 17 *Austrian Journal of Family Law* 1.

[66] Bill Atkin, 'The Challenge of Unmarried Cohabitation—the New Zealand Response', (2003) 37 *Family Law Quarterly* 303.

[67] *Goodridge v Department of Pub Health*, 798 NE 2d 941 (Mass 2003).

[68] For a comprehensive state-by-state and country-by-country summary of laws recognizing same-sex partnership rights, see American Bar Ass'n Section of Family Law, 'A White Paper: An Analysis of the Law Regarding Same-Sex Marriage, Civil Unions, and Domestic Partnerships', (2004) 38 *Family Law Quarterly* 339 (hereinafter *ABA White Paper*).

or recognized in California'.[69] Schwarzenegger had previously gone on record favouring same-sex marriage—but only for heterosexuals.[70]

More than thirty US states, by sharp contrast, now provide by legislation or constitutional amendments that only heterosexual marriage is to be recognized. More constitutional amendments are on the way. For purposes of *all* US *federal* laws, from income tax to social security to welfare, the US Congress has commanded that only heterosexual marriage may be recognized.[71] US constitutional amendments have been introduced—but so far defeated—that would forestall any possibility of Congress' will being overridden.

In the United States, this highly charged struggle is not likely to calm down soon. And it is worth noting that until 2003—when the US Supreme Court invalidated such a law—about a dozen US states still *criminalized* homosexual conduct.[72] So divisive remains that struggle that (along with abortion—the other 'social issue' in the 'culture wars') same-sex marriage dominates US court appointments, political candidacies, and elections.[73] Indeed, many believe that it was Senator Kerry's provenance from same-sex-marriage Massachusetts along with his unwillingness to denounce gay marriage that helped defeat him in the 2004 US presidential race.

In short, the last words on the legalization of same-sex relationship have not been spoken everywhere. Whatever the future may hold, it would be good for both sides on this issue to go beyond raw emotion and try to think rationally.

5. The Future of Marriage—Is Legal Marriage Still Relevant?

Even opponents of same-sex marriage should ask why only heterosexual couples—simply through the formality of entering the legal institution of marriage—should be given a choice of legal consequences that is denied to others in essentially the same situation. Accordingly, an intelligent challenge to traditional marriage law

[69] 'Schwarzenegger Vetoes Bill Allowing Same-Sex Marriage', *Washington Post*, 30 September 2005.

[70] 'I think that gay marriage is something that should be between a man and a woman', said Governor Schwarzenegger being interviewed on CNN (<http://www.cnn.com/2003/ALLPOLITICS/08/27/schwarzenegger.views/index.html>). The Governor misspoke, but may also have had a linguistic problem inasmuch as good heterosexual marriages used to be gay—when as a first meaning 'gay' still meant 'joyous' and only as a fourth option—as few now recall—'dissipated, licentious'. See Clarence Barnhardt, *The American College Dictionary* (Random House, 1947). How that fourth option came to be today's preferred alternative to less offensive prior nomenclature is 'queer'—defined, in the same Barnhardt dictionary, as 'strange from a conventional point of view'.

[71] Defense of Marriage Act, 1 USC/7, 28 USC/1738C (1996); *see also* Harry D. Krause, 'US Law on Same-Sex Marriage, Formal and Informal Same-Sex and Heterosexual Cohabitation', in Basedow *et al*, above (n 27), at 187–273; *ABA White Paper*, above (n 68), at 403–5 (describing federal statute and proposed constitutional amendments).

[72] *Lawrence v Texas*, 539 US 558, 573 (2003).   [73] See text below, pp 1123–24.

should go well beyond whether and how the law should recognize unmarried heterosexual and/or gay and lesbian partnerships, or whether marriage, *qua* marriage, should be extended to the latter. Much of the current controversy over extending traditional marriage (with all its legal consequences) to same-sex couples may be quite misdirected. Full debate should include heterosexual marriage as a legal status: marriage itself, as a one-size-fits-all legal status, should be at issue: The rational test for providing legal preferences to intimate partners, whether heterosexual or homosexual, should be whether there is (1) a measurable gain for society or (2) a compelling social need for protective intervention.

The archetypal example of a life-style-changing intimate partnership bringing the greatest social gain, of course, is one where children are (or were) present. Clearly, the partners' costs as well as the social gain are much greater when partners raise children—and so is the risk of long-term spousal economic dependency. There is a social need to protect children as well as role-dividing marriage partners from undue economic dependency. This situation merits carefully tailored, multi-range, and long-term legal consequences, both in terms of a suitable default regime and in terms of rational restrictions on the partners' contractual freedom.

True, neither child-raising nor child-supporting is necessarily—though probably optimally, if only because of long-standing social convention—gender-based or partner-based.[74] That important topic may be better left to child psychologists than to the intuitions of lawyers. With all due respect, however, appropriate even obvious distinctions have not always been appropriately recognized: At least three broad categories of children that might be raised by same-sex couples, call for quite different answers: (1) The natural child of a divorced or unmarried parent; (2) a child brought forth by 'artificial conception' or 'surrogate' motherhood by agreement of same-sex partners; and (3) a child who is adopted by same-sex partners. All-or-nothing advocacy on the part of many self-appointed authorities on both sides of the controversy has left little room for the pragmatic view that, in a world overflowing with neglected or abandoned children who are in desperate need of home and care, the issue of the 'fitness' of a same-sex parents transforms itself to the simple question: 'compared to what alternatives?'

In addition to child-rearing, even the acceptance of a legally enforceable, long-term mutual support obligation is a suitable candidate for a social *quid pro quo* as well as equal outcomes for *any* two persons willing to enter into such a pact. After all, the assumption of a long-term partner-to-partner, spouse-to-spouse support obligation that is legally enforceable relieves the taxpayer of the risk of welfare expenditures. This merits some measure of '*quid*', whether the partners are

---

[74] For a pointed debate of the opposing points of view see Lynn D. Wardle, 'The Potential Impact of Homosexual Parenting on Children', (1997) *University of Illinois LR* 833 and the response by Carlos Ball and Janice Pea, 'Warring with Wardle: Morality, Social Science, and Gay and Lesbian Parents', (1998) *University of Illinois LR* 253.

heterosexual or homosexual. Sensibly, the social reward would be on a considerably lower level in the simple mutual support case of childless partners who, in the modern Western economy, realize not only enormous savings from not having children, but also may realize additional income from two unhindered careers.

In this day, a differentiated approach to imposing legal consequences on intimate partnerships—whether heterosexual or same-sex—seems appropriate. At least implicitly, rational distinctions between traditional marriage and newer lifestyles (even if still under the 'marriage' label) are already being made in the courts and some statutes. Consider the basic example of alimony: Not long ago, only the husband had a lifelong marital support obligation. Today, wives may be liable for alimony. More importantly, post-divorce spousal support generally is ordered only for limited periods and under special circumstances, such as the presence of children or a long-term, marriage-related impairment of a dependent spouse's earning capacity. This illustrates how many laws and courts already fine-tune (albeit implicitly and indirectly) the legal meaning of marriage in accordance with modern conditions as well as the specific circumstances of a particular relationship—thereby going beyond the traditional one-size-fits-all definition of marriage.

Across the board—for heterosexual as well as for same-sex couples—sensible law would result if the underlying social purposes of marriage and other intimate associations were more consciously, openly, and rationally defined and legal consequences tailored accordingly.[75]

6. Assisted Reproduction, Artificial Insemination; *In Vitro* Fertilization, Embryo Transplantation, Surrogate Motherhood

The West's newest enlightenments, such as recognition of unmarried cohabitation, birth control, abortion, women's equality in the workplace and at home, legalized same-sex relationships, same-sex marriage, and assisted conception, are fundamentally changing the traditional social order of sexual pairing, child-bearing, and child-raising. Even so, Western family law still struggles with conflicts between its own traditional ethics and religions and secular pragmatists. Nor have long-term viable approaches been found to deal responsibly with the sexual freedom that medical progress has brought and wrought, especially in the areas of assisted reproduction, contraception, and abortion. The common theme is that the law and traditional morality are struggling—but largely have failed—to keep up with medical capabilities.

In the realm of *assisted reproduction*, dramatic advances in medical technology have been of enormous benefit to many couples otherwise unable to conceive

---

[75] cf Section IV.2, above at p 112.

children. But they also have placed urgent demands on the law to define the respective rights and interests of the various parties involved. Relationships created by the modern techniques of artificial insemination, *in vitro* fertilization (IVF), and embryo transplantation stand somewhere in between what traditional law classified as legitimate, illegitimate, and adoptive relationships. These techniques challenge traditional definitions and understandings of what it means to be a parent.

Various possible claimants to family status in these cases include (1) the married mother's husband when the mother conceives a child by artificial insemination with semen donated by another man; (2) the woman (incorrectly called 'surrogate' mother) who carries a child through pregnancy and childbirth where the pregnancy resulted either from (a) her artificial insemination with the intending father's semen or (b) the transplantation of a fertilized ovum (embryo) stemming from another woman such as the wife of the intending couple; (3) the donor of the semen; and (4) the donor of the ovum or embryo. With human cloning in the future, perhaps the responsible scientists should be added into the picture.

Legal approaches to these possibilities have neither been uniform nor always optimal.[76] First, European law has been more willing to regulate access to reproductive technologies than United States law where regulation remains spotty and varies greatly.[77] In Europe and the United States it is now widely accepted that a child born to a married woman through artificial insemination is legally the husband's legitimate child.[78] Less widely, some US-American and European jurisdictions have applied the same rule to unmarried partners.[79] The unrelated sperm donor is generally dealt out of the picture, although not always.[80] One may generalise that the trend has been toward assigning parentage based on the parties' intent.

---

[76] See Harry D. Krause, 'Artificial Conception: Legislative Approaches', (1985) 19 *Family Law Quarterly* 185; Marsha Garrison, 'Law Making for Baby Making: An Interpretive Approach to the Determination of Legal Parentage', (2000) 113 *Harvard LR* 835.

[77] On the greater willingness of European law to regulate access, see Blair and Weiner, above (n 44), at 1018–22.

[78] In the United States and Europe, most jurisdictions have followed the approach of the Uniform Parentage Act of 1973, which provides that a husband who consents to the artificial insemination of his wife under the supervision of a licensed physician 'is treated in law as if he were the natural father'. Uniform Parentage Act/5(a) (1973). Similarly, '[m]ost European countries prohibit the husband who has consented to the use of AID from challenging paternity'. Blair and Weiner, above (n 44), at 1014.

[79] In 2002, the Uniform Parentage Act was revised to expand its coverage to unmarried couples but, as of 2005, that change has been adopted in only three states. See Uniform Parentage Act/703 (2002) (providing that '[a] man who provides sperm for, or consents to, assisted reproduction by a woman . . . with the intent to be the parent of her child, is a parent of the resulting child'). Some European countries, including France, Spain, and Sweden, similarly 'impose parental responsibilities on the mother's unmarried partner if there is consent to the procedure'. Blair and Weiner, above (n 44), at 1014.

[80] See Uniform Parentage Act/5(b) (1973); 'J.R.M. v. The Netherlands', (1993) 74 *European Commission of Human Rights Decisions & Reports* 120.

7. Contraception and Abortion

Effective *contraception* has long (actually, only since the latter half of the twentieth century) been available almost everywhere though not in Connecticut—even for married couples—until 1965.[81] Frighteningly in this day of HIV/AIDS (not to mention more traditional sexually transmitted diseases), contraception continues as a foreign aid policy issue. Worse, contraception is now merging with abortion in the US debate over 'Plan B', the 'morning after pill', also known as RU–486.

At the other end of the modern spectrum *abortion*—assisted *non*-reproduction—plays a particularly disputed and divisive role. US law—by *judicial* interpretation of a federal constitution entirely silent on the subject—generally allows for distinctly wider access to abortion than does European law.[82] United States law looks to 'viability' of the foetus, set at about two trimesters (six months). In starkest contrast, Germany's constitutional court has held that life begins at conception—but then has allowed substantial exceptions to be carved into that principle through legislation.[83] Other countries have taken a middle ground in the timeline leading to protected life.

In her thoughtful comparative study of abortion, Professor Mary Ann Glendon made the important point that the United States has 'less regulation of abortion in the interest of the foetus than any other Western nation, but we provide less public support for maternity and child raising. And, to a greater extent than in any other country, [US] courts have shut down the legislative process of bargaining, education, and persuasion on the abortion issue.'[84]

Indeed, on constitutional grounds, the US courts have shut down the *marital* process of bargaining on the issue as well. In 1976, the US Supreme Court answered in the negative the important question of whether state law might require the husband's consent to his wife's decision to have an abortion.[85] The next question was whether the State could require that the husband at least be *notified* if his wife wished to have an abortion. The US Supreme Court provided another negative answer, on the ground that even a notification requirement would deter women from seeking an abortion.[86] In 1991 US Court of Appeals Judge Samuel Alito (now a Justice on the US Supreme Court) would have upheld the notification requirement, given a violence escape clause in the Pennsylvania law at issue. In 2005, Judge Alito's dissent emerged as a major debating point in his nomination to

---

81 See *Griswold v Connecticut*, 381 US 479 (1965); *Eisenstadt v Baird*, 405 US 438 (1972).

82 See Blair and Weiner, above (n 44), at 1062–88.

83 BVerfGE 39 (1975), 1 (1–68) (Germany). Relevant parts of the lengthly opinion are translated at Harry D. Krause, *Family Law: Cases, Comments, and Questions* (3rd edn, 1990), 371–3.

84 Mary Ann Glendon, *Abortion and Divorce in Western Law* (1987), 2.

85 See *Planned Parenthood of Central Mo v Danforth*, 428 US 52, 71 (1976).

86 See *Planned Parenthood of Southeastern Pa v Casey*, 505 US 833, 896 (1992).

the US Supreme Court.[87] The vehemence and emotionality of the abortion debate in the United States becomes more understandable to outsiders in light of the fact that state statutes seeking to forbid the practice of so-called 'partial birth abortions' have so far failed the Supreme Court's constitutional muster.[88]

The question remains whether notification to the husband *after* an abortion takes place should be seen as an equally serious burden. Among husbands so predisposed, post-abortion notification may pose an even greater risk of violence. On the other hand, the wife's right to have the abortion should be balanced against the husband's procreative interest in knowing whether *this* wife is willing to bear his child—or whether he should seek one more willing.

On the question of spousal involvement, Europe has effectively arrived at the same balance point as the United States. The European Commission on Human Rights has held that a husband has no legal grounds under the European Convention to demand that his wife consult him before electing abortion.[89] Whatever right the potential father might have under Article 8's protection of family life was outweighed by the potential mother's superior interests in her private life and bodily integrity.[90]

VII. The Day after Tomorrow

It seems appropriate to remember that human rights and the ideal of democracy have in the West's own history come forward only slowly and gradually—and relatively recently. Anchor points range from the Magna Carta to the US American Constitution and the French revolution. Notably, some of the 'new enlightenment'

---

[87] Earlier in the US 'culture wars' appeals court Judge Robert Bork was defeated in his bid for a seat on the Court after he criticized the US Supreme Court's broad 1973 abortion decision.

[88] In *Carhart v Stenberg*, 530 US 914 (2000), the US Supreme Court held unconstitutional a Nebraska statute that prohibited 'partial-birth abortions', defined as 'deliberately and intentionally delivering into the vagina a living unborn child, or a substantial portion thereof, for the purpose of performing a procedure that the person performing such procedure knows will kill the unborn child'. Ibid at 922. The Court held that the statute placed an 'undue burden' on a woman's right to elect abortion because its language covered not only the rarely used 'dilation and extraction' (D & X) method of abortion, but also the 'dilation and evacuation' (D & E) method of abortion—the most common form of abortion used in the second trimester of pregnancy.

[89] 'Paton v. United Kingdom', (1981) 3 *European Human Rights Report* 408.

[90] The Commission wrote: '[A]ny interpretation of the husband's and potential father's right, under Article 8 of the Convention, to respect for his private and family life, as regards an abortion which his wife intends to have performed on her, must first of all take into account the right of the pregnant woman, being the person primarily concerned in the pregnancy and its continuation or termination'. Ibid, para 27.

views, especially on abortion and same-sex relationships, are increasingly under attack—particularly in the United States of America—by a resurgence of rightist and self-righteous Christians, aided by mainstream religions such as the Roman Catholic church. In the conflict between modernists and religious tradition—Christian, Jewish, and now very prominently Muslim—all sides see themselves as the true faith or even the only reality. Each denies the other's legitimacy—when actually only a few decades of time rather than universal legitimacy separate 'us' from 'them', and 'them' from 'us'. As wedded as much of the West now is to rational thought, family matters still go beyond pragmatic reason to the (irrational?) essence of existence.

The future will decide whether the current *laissez-faire* Western way of dealing with family life and law is viable over the long term. Evidence is developing that it may not be. The West's most pressing social problem is not its progress toward or decline into 'value-free' behaviour (seen by many as immorality) in the abstract. Very concretely, the West's crucial problem is a rapidly accelerating crisis in fertility. Modern lifestyles and attitudes—as well as inadvertent social policies that motivate ever more individuals and couples to opt against children—are bringing this crisis to a head. The dearth of children now threatens the survival of Western societies and cultures and economic lifestyles. Retirement outlays, elder-care obligations, and astronomically rising medical expenses may soon outstrip the productive capacity (and earlier than that, the good will) of a shrinking working population.[91] One might be pardoned for being concerned that modern Western reproductive behaviours put in question not only the much talked about survival of social security (and broadly, the social welfare state), but the very sustainability of Western civilization and culture.

A race is on between the soon-to-be elderly and ever-fewer children. To the extent state-provided social security retirement and private pension schemes (as well as health care) depend on ever-increasing numbers of working-age workers supporting the aged, well-intended inter-generational pyramid schemes will become unsustainable. For the time being, governments can print money to cover their health-care and pension obligations, but General Motors cannot.

The solution lies in productive capacity, both in human terms and in capital resources. Perhaps we will be rescued by the descendants of the robots that now make cars so much better than people used to make them—or by immigration. Recent events raise the prospect that the latter hope may founder on immigration-related unrest, resentment, and resulting violence as witnessed in France,[92]

---

[91] See Phillip Longman, 'The Global Baby Bust', *Foreign Affairs* (May/June 2004); 'Transitions in World Population', *Population Bulletin* (March 2004).

[92] 'M. Sarkosy demande l'expulsion des étrangers impliqué dans les violences urbaines', *Le Monde* (9 November 2005). 'Polygamy by Immigrants is Factor in French Riots', *NY Times*, at A12 (18 November 2005)—so say both the parliamentary leader of the Gaullist party and the permanent secretary of the Academie Francaise. See generally, 'Integrationskonflikte: Aufruhr in Eurabia', *Der Spiegel* 45/2005, (7 November 2005).

Germany, the Netherlands, the United Kingdom, Italy, Spain, Malta, and recent, illegal immigration-related chaos at the US borders.

It is 2006. Unprecedented socio-economic change has provided equality for women in most of the industrialized world. Equality with what? Equality in the workplace with the formerly exclusively male model of the full-time worker. But that work model had been reconcilable with the family's child-rearing function only through parental role division. Is there an unbridgeable conflict between the family with two full-time earners and the child-rearing function that formerly was performed by the one-earner, role-divided family? This concern stands above family *values*, it reflects the practical *reality* that for an overwhelming number of reasons—instability of marriage, easy divorce, professional fulfillment, economic independence—it has become all but necessary for both parents to be active in the 'paid' economy.

We have changed the way we live but have not changed the way we work. In a re-evaluation of its future, industrialized society must balance the cost of the possible work inefficiency of a family-friendly work environment against the cost of family disincentives created by a family-unfriendly work environment. Can work habits be adapted to the way we now live?

Paid family leave is widely available in Europe—again the Scandinavian countries are the most generous.[93] By contrast, limited *unpaid* family leave was enacted in the US only recently.[94] Part-time work, 'flexitime' jobs, 'telecommuting', day care, and year-around schools have been suggested as pieces of a possible answer. These and other schemes carry costs. But modern economies have been willing to swallow considerable economic inefficiencies by adjusting the workplace to the needs of the handicapped, by protecting the environment, by improving the safety of the workplace. Given the dire prospect of a collapsing social contract, child-raising (ie 'family') probably should rank at or near the top of the scale of values that transcend immediate, short-term work efficiency.

---

[93] See P. Moss and F. Deven (eds), *Parental Leave: Progress or Pitfall?* (Netherlands Interdisciplinary Demographic Institute, 1999) (surveying European policies); Anita U. Hattiangadi, *Bringing Up Baby: A Comparison on U.S. and European Family Leave Policies* (Employment Policy Foundation, 2000); Christopher J. Ruhm and Jacqueline L. Teague, 'Parental Leave Policies in Europe and North America', in F. Blau and R. Ehrenberg (eds), *Gender and Family Issues in the Workplace* (1997), 133.

[94] See Family and Medical Leave Act of 1993 (FMLA), 29 USC 2611 ff (2004); Hattiangadi, above (n 93); Patrick R. Hugg, 'Transnational Convergence: European Union and American Federalism', (1998) 32 *Cornell International LJ* 43, 65–6.

VIII. Judgment Day?

Current incentive structures discourage responsible people from fulfilling the social role—bearing and socializing children—that traditionally was performed by the rigidly regulated family at great individual cost, especially to women. Obviously, many modern Western values—uppermost women's equality—are sacrosanct. But another version of gender equality might be more seriously encouraged: Male equality in the tasks of child-rearing and the family home. Beyond that, the ever-increasing cost of rearing and educating the modern child must at least in part be borne by the childless segment of the economy. A revitalized, new contract between the generations needs to address the free-rider problem posed by the voluntarily childless and provide an equalization of burdens between parents and non-parents, whether by way of tax incentives or subsidy. A *new* contract? Plato suggested in 347 BC that 'he . . . that . . . does not marry when thirty-five years old shall pay a yearly fine . . . lest he imagine that single life brings him gain and ease'.[95]

The social contract must accept—and pay for—the basic value judgment that all children deserve a decent opportunity in home and school, in life and the economy. That is the individual human dimension. The social dimension is that children are the future's economic 'infrastructure'. In short, the cost of re-inventing a child-rearing incentive structure must be seen for what it is: a social investment, not a consumer expense.

Ironically, in poor countries, the sustainability of current family behaviors is also in question, but for the opposite reason: too many children. There the economic cost of an avalanche of children threatens progress and even survival. By contrast, China's road to almost immediate prosperity is being paved by the state-decreed one-child family. That saves the immediate expense of raising children and allows capital formation, but ignores the predictable reckoning that will come when the two parents of their one-child family will ask who will pay for their old age. In an immediate reaction to that concern, there already is a measurable preference in China for male offspring and, with the availability of abortion, the next generation of men will considerably outnumber females—thus further jeopardizing orderly social succession.[96]

Much more needs to be considered, but there is space only for one last caveat: Careful adherence to all necessary cultural and comparative considerations might have ensured success of this essay, but it would also have guaranteed its failure. Indecipherable chaos would have been the work product. The chief caveat must be

---

[95] Plato, *Laws*, Book IV, at 313 (trans R. Bury, 1926).
[96] See Wang Feng, 'Can China Afford to Continue its One-Child Policy?', Asia Pacific Issues, East-West Center Analysis No. 77 (March 2005) (unpublished paper available at <http://www.eastwestcenter.org/events-en-detail.asp?news_ID=275>).

that many caveats have been left aside in this evaluation of broad trends. If some of the notions here expressed sound naïve, utopian, and in any event unrealistic—it is clear that the future of intimate associations, reproduction, and children needs to be addressed beyond the level of academic writing.

The Grand Caveat is 'denn erstens kommt es anders und zweitens als man denkt'. This is not sensibly translatable, but may be nicely illustrated as follows: 'To wit, New York City made projections 150 years ago about its horse population. The population projections showed that the city would be under 300 feet of horse manure by the middle of the twentieth century'.[97]

I should like to end, as I began, with the words of Holmes (even at the risk of inviting a paraphrase of Senator Bentsen's classic put-down of Senator Quayle during the 1988 vice-presidential debates:[98] 'Professor, you are no Oliver Wendell Holmes').[99]

If I am right it will be a slow business for our people to reach rational views, assuming that we are allowed to work peaceably to that end. But as I grow older I grow calm. If I feel what are perhaps an old man's apprehensions, that competition from new races will cut deeper than working men's disputes and will test whether we can hang together and can fight; that we are running through the world's resources at a pace that we cannot keep; I do not lose my hopes. . . . I think it probable that civilization somehow will last as long as I care to look ahead.[100]

A Very Selective Bibliography

The worldwide literature on current family life and law is immense and multilingual. Listed below are a very few of the richest sources, mostly in the English language, all providing a variety of materials, individual essays, and articles. More may be found cited in the body of this chapter. Individual articles published outside compendia or symposia are not listed as they may readily be found in periodical indices.

Max Rheinstein, *Marriage Stability, Divorce, and the Law* (1972)

Alexander Bergmann, Murad Ferid, and Dieter Henrich (eds), *Internationales Ehe- und Kindschaftsrecht* (1926–2005 ff) (Frequently updated, worldwide country-by-country translations into German of family legislation)

Mary Ann Glendon, *The New Family and the New Property* (1981)

—— *Abortion and Divorce in Western Law* (1987)

---

[97] So cautioned Robert Reischauer, a former director of the US Congressional Budget Office, *Champaign-Urbana News Gazette*, (9 October 1996).

[98] Lloyd Bentsen to Dan Quayle: 'Senator, you are no Jack Kennedy'.

[99] And glad of it. See Liva Baker, *The Justice From Beacon Hill: The Life and Times of Oliver Wendell Holmes* (1991), 218–30 describing Holmes's childless and presumed sexless marriage. This seems the appropriate occasion to express my sincerest thanks to Eva, my wife of fifty-years seniority—and to our three wonderful sons!

[100] Holmes, above (n 40), at 296.

—— *The Transformation of Family Law: State, Law and Family in the United States and Western Europe* (1989)

Jürgen Basedow, Klaus Hopt, Hein Kötz, and Peter Dopffel (eds), *Die Rechtsstellung gleichgeschlechtlicher Lebensgemeinschaften* (2000) (numerous country-by-country reports on the legal position of same-sex partnerships—most are in German with several in English)

American Law Institute, *Principles of the Law of Family Dissolution: Analysis and Recommendations* (2002)

Katharina Boele-Woelki, B. Braat, and I. Curry-Summers, *Perspectives for the Unification and Harmonisation of Family Law in Europe* (2002)

Harry D. Krause, *Family Law: Cases, Comments, and Questions* (3rd edn, 1990; 5th edn with Linda Elrod, Marsha Garrison, J. Thomas Oldham, 2003)

—— *Family Law in a Nutshell* (3rd edn, 1995; 4th edn with David Mayer, 2003)

D. Marianne Blair and Merle H. Weiner (eds), *Family Law in the World Community, Cases, Materials and Problems* (2003)

—— —— (eds), *International Family Law: Conventions, Statutes and Regulatory Materials* (2003)

Katharina Boele-Woelki, B. Braat and I. Curry-Summers, *European Family Law in Action; vol I: Grounds for Divorce* (2003)

—— B. Braat, and I. Curry-Summers (eds), *Principles of European Family Law Regarding Divorce and Maintenance between Former Spouses* (2004)

International Encyclopedia of Comparative Law, Mary Ann Glendon (ed.) (predecessor eds: M. Rheinstein, A. Chloros), *vol. IV, Persons and Family* (briefly updated by Mary Ann Glendon, in *Introduction: Family Law in a Time of Turbulence* (forthcoming 2007?)). Most chapters constituting the family law volume were previously published in separate monographs, including Max Rheinstein and René König, *Introduction* (1975); Max Rheinstein and Mary Ann Glendon, *Interspousal Relations* (1980); Samuel J. Stoljar, *Children, Parents, and Guardians* (1973); Harry D. Krause, *Creation of Relationships of Kinship: Legitimacy, Illegitimacy, Adoption* (1976); P. H. Neuhaus *et al.*, *The Family in Religious and Customary Laws* (1983); Andreas Heldrich *et al.*, *Persons* (1995); Dagmar Coester-Waltjen and Michael Coester, *Formation of Marriage* (1997); Salvatore Patti, *Intra-Family Torts* (1998); Marko Mladenovic *et al.*, *The Family in the Post-Socialist Countries* (1998); Bea Verschraegen, *Divorce* (2004).

Conflicts of law (private international law) aspects of family relations are covered by Lennart Palsson, *Marriage and Divorce, International Encyclopedia of Comparative Law*, vol. IV (Kurt Lipstein (ed.), 1978).

International Society of Family Law: Annual surveys of world-wide family law (ed Michael Freeman 1986–93 in annual issues of the University of Louisville *Journal of Family Law* (1987–94), and by Andrew Bainham from 1994–2007 in separate volumes).

CHAPTER 35

COMPARATIVE LABOUR LAW

MATTHEW W. FINKIN

Illinois*

* The author wishes to express his appreciation to the Alexander von Humboldt Foundation whose financial support enabled an extended visit to the Max Planck Institute in Hamburg to research—and think about—this essay. A similar expression of gratitude is due to Reinhard Zimmermann for extending that invitation. The author wishes to acknowledge helpful suggestions from Rolf Birk, Roger Blanpain, Reinhold Fahlbeck, Richard Mitchell, Jacques Rojot, and Manfred Weiss.

I. Introduction

THE following proceeds in four stages. It will first take up the emergence of labour law and its comparative offspring as a discipline. It will next provide a crude taxonomy of comparative labour law scholarship. Third, it will treat the role comparativism has played in the development of national labour policy from the nineteenth century to the present. Fourth, and to come full circle, comparative study will be situated with respect to the contemporary quandary of labour law as a discipline.

Just a further word of introduction on the latter. Comparative labour law was born fast upon the construction of labour law as a subject of instruction and academic study. Even from the beginning, however, it was far from clear what labour law was. Today, that question has recrudesced: labour law is a discipline in search of an identity—and, to some, a future.[1] Consequently, attention rightly turns first to the root of which comparative study is a branch.

1. Labour Law

From the beginning of the species, work has had to be done to sustain life and, with adequate sustenance, to adorn and enrich it. How people are organized to produce goods and services for others is a distinctive feature in the history of civilizations, long a subject of academic study. How the law speaks to how people are to be organized for work, of how those who do it are regarded and treated, is an infant in the legal academy. As Georges Scelles observed in his little 1922 monograph, *Le Droit Ouvrier*, workers' law is 'the most recent of all our legal disciplines'.

In early modern times, workers, those who were not independent producers of goods or services, were governed by a variety of legal regimes most often involving

---

[1] See generally Richard Mitchell (ed), *Redefining Labour Law: New Perspectives on the Future of Teaching and Research*, University of Melbourne Centre for Employment and Labor Relations Law Monograph No. 3 (1995).

the lack of freedom—slavery, serfdom, apprenticeship, involuntary and voluntary servitude, or a master/servant relationship. Forms of unfree labour persisted in Europe and the United States into modern times, and persist still in some parts of the world. The free craftsmen of the Middle Ages and the journeymen they employed were often regulated by guilds (if they were able to gain entry) in almost every detail of their lives, and those systems of regulation persisted well into the nineteenth century. The laws that governed these multifarious relationships could be addressed as, if not labour law, then the proto-historical material out of which modern labour law emerged: If labour law's central concern is with the labour market, study could and, later, often did begin with the English Ordinance of Labourers (1349), the Statute of Labourers (1350–1), and the wealth of follow-on legislation regulating duration of employment, wages and wage payment, mobility of labour and choice of occupation, and the like. If the subject centres on how we are to deal with worker unrest, protest, and collective demands for better wages and working conditions, study could and, later, often did commence with the *Ordonnances* of the French King Charles VI (1382), of the *Reichpolizeiordnung* of 1530, 1548, and 1577, and other acts in Britain, Ireland, and on the Continent forbidding combinations of workers.

As a modern subject, however, labour law was created in consequence of industrialization and the widespread adoption of economic liberalism, starting with Britain in the eighteenth century and then accepted elsewhere, sometimes, as in the case of Germany, only in fits and starts. Industrialization, the creation of the factory system, drew enormous numbers of semi-skilled and unskilled workers from the hinterlands of the nation-state, that is, out of agriculture and from abroad into urban centres. As Sanford Jacoby explains, in the nineteenth century:

The urban population of Germany grew by more than nine times . . . and that of Britain by more than eight times . . . Vast numbers of Germans, Poles, Portuguese, Scandinavians, Irish, and Italians moved to North and South America in search of work. In the century following 1820, about 50 million Europeans set sail for the New World, with about three-fifths going to the United States . . . Gradually, disparate labour markets within and between countries were being knit more closely together.

As in the United States, 'extreme transience' characterized European cities in the nineteenth century and early twentieth centuries. Geographic mobility increased steadily between 1815 and 1914, peaking in the years before the First World War. Annual in-migration to German cities reached 18 percent in 1912, rising to above 25 percent in some German cities such as Düsseldorf and Duisburg. Instability characterized other European cities, such as Amsterdam, and these high rates of European mobility were on par with those of American cities like Boston.[2]

The social problems of industrialization would thus become inextricably linked to the problems of urbanization.

[2] Sanford Jacoby and Matthew Finkin, 'Labor Mobility in a Federal System: The United States in Comparative Perspective', (2004) 20 *International Journal of Comparative Labour Law & Industrial Relations* 313, 334–5.

Economic liberalism freed the labour market of governmental controls and guild restrictions. It also freed the worker, breaking the bonds of even voluntary servitude. The British Master and Servant Act of 1867 abolished imprisonment of employees who breached the terms of their employment, that is, by quitting prematurely; and the Industrial Code of the North German Federation did the same in 1869. The Thirteenth Amendment to the US Constitution (1865) had a like effect. In sum, the regnant ideology of the late nineteenth and early twentieth century was *laissez-faire*; its catchphrase, freedom of contract.

Robert Castel reminds us of how extraordinary was the shift from the security of tutelage to the precariousness of 'free' labour and of the inversion of values, built up over the centuries, this change worked:

We forget that wage-labour, which today occupies the vast majority of those who work, and to which most of our protections against social risk are inextricably tied, has long been among the most uncertain, as well as undignified and miserable, of conditions. One was a wage earner whenever he was nothing else, and had nothing to exchange other than the force of his arms. Someone fell into the position of wage earner when his conditions had deteriorated: the ruined artisan, the tenant whose land would no longer sustain him, the journeyman who could never become a master, and so on. To be or to fall to the level of wage labourer was to be put into a condition of dependency, to be condemned to live 'from day to day,' to find one's self subject to the empire of necessity.[3]

This historically unprecedented state of affairs summoned the modern idea of labour law into being. John R. Commons and John B. Andrews opened their seminal 1916 study, *Principles of Labour Legislation*, with a chapter, 'The Basis of Labor Law', that began with the words, 'Modern industry . . .'. More to the point legally are the introductory words of Arthur Stadthagen's *Das Arbeiterrecht* in 1904:

The characteristic of modern (capitalist) methods of production is that the worker, as a legally free actor, sells his power to work (*Arbeitskraft*) as a commodity, for another's business. Most labour contracts are such that the worker obliges himself to put a part of his mental or physical strength (*Arbeitskraft*) to the use of another's commercial or business enterprise.

The novelty of this arrangement instigated a great deal of serious doctrinal writing on the Continent about just what the contract of individual employment was in contrast to the treatment otherwise accorded by the civil law. The law of obligations rested upon the Roman law concept of *locatio conductio*—a lease, which, in terms of the labour contract, applied to, and some thought had derived from, the lease of a slave for the doing of work. If for that reason alone, *locatio conductio* was thought unsuitable for modern application, so, too, was the law of sale, the transfer of a

---

[3] Robert Castel, *From Manual Workers to Wage Laborers: Transformation of the Social Question* (trans Richard Boyd, 2003), xii.

commodity, a thing. The contract of individual employment came to be thought of as *sui generis*; it called for the creation of a body of law unto itself.[4]

Britain, its possessions, and the United States were spared this doctrinal agony for, as Otto Kahn-Freund so trenchantly critiqued, the British chose to take their cue from Blackstone, and Blackstone chose to ignore the Industrial Revolution altogether, chose, that is, to ignore the proletariat growing up all around him and to dress the relationship of these workers to their employers in the ancient and irrelevant garb of domestic service.[5] Just how ill the fit is illustrated, if unintentionally, in the Supreme Court of Tennessee's 1884 decision in *Payne v Western & Atl Rr Co*,[6] in which a shop owner contested the railroad's order to its employees not to shop at his store. What began as a commercial tort ended in a manifesto on labour law: 'May I not forbid my family to trade with anyone?,' the court's majority rhetorically questioned. 'May I not dismiss my domestic servant for dealing . . . where I forbid? And if my domestic, why not my farm-hand, or my mechanic, or teamster? And if one of them, why not all four? And, if all four, why not a hundred or a thousand of them?' The dissenters made short work of it: 'A father may well control his family in this but an employer ought to have no such right conceded to him'. American law refused, and continues to refuse, to see the difference, although the employer's power today is justified by the fiction of contractual consent in lieu of resort to domestic status.

Britain, as the most advanced of the industrializing countries of the early nineteenth century, took the lead as well in enacting legislation to deal with the asperities its economic and social system were creating: The earliest effort to deal with child labour was enacted in 1819—and was to be expanded and built upon over time. The first comprehensive Truck Act was enacted in 1831, to deal with the security of wage payment; 'comprehensive' because it swept away an accretion of piecemeal legislation from 1464 on down. These and later legislative proposals set the agenda of issues, clustered about the 'Social Question' in Europe or the 'Labor Question' in the United States, that so vexed industrializing countries in the last quarter of the nineteenth century and the first quarter of the twentieth: (1) exploitation of child and female labour; (2) wage setting and wage payment; (3) hours of labour; (4) accident, illness, and old age; (5) unemployment; and (6) the ability to bargain collectively and to strike, which opened in turn onto industrial dispute resolution and the status of collective agreements.

---

[4] eg Philipp Lotmar, *Der Arbeitsvertrag nach dem Privatrecht des deutschen Reiches* (vol 1, 1902, vol 2, 1908). The rich texture of German scholarship of the period is thoroughly discussed by Martin Becker, *Arbeitsvertrag und Arbeitsverhältnis in Deutschland: Vom Beginn der Industrialisierung bis zum Ende Des Kaiserreichs* (1995). See also Lodovico Barassi, *Il Contratto di Lavoro nel Diritto Positivo Italiano* (1901); Manuel Olea, *De la Servidumbre al Contrato de Trabajo* (1979); C. Perrau, *La Notion du Contrat du Travail* (1912); Simon Deakin and Frank Wilkinson, *The Law of the Market: Industrialization, Employment, and Legal Evolution* (2005).

[5] Otto Kahn-Freund, 'Blackstone's Neglected Child: The Contract of Employment', (1977) 93 *LQR* 508.

[6] 81 Tenn 507 (1884).

2. Labour Law as a Subject of Academic Instruction

Even as these economic and social problems came increasingly to demand that attention be paid, from the mid-nineteenth century on in Europe, North America, and the antipodes, the legal academy, such as it was, was slow systematically to address them. The first course to be offered in the United Kingdom, on 'Industrial Law', was in 1902, at the London School of Economics; but LSE was to be a lonely intellectual outpost for decades. In 1915, Professor Wolzendorf reported that he gave an annual lecture, 'The State and Social Interests in Modern Labour Law [*Arbeitsrecht*]' at Marburg, at which time both he and his colleague, Schücking, were arguing for a place for labour law in the German curriculum. They were joined by Potthof who, in 1918, reported that lectures on labour law were being given at Jena, Giessen, Kiel, and Leipzig as well as at Marburg and at various *Hochschulen*. The first attempt to lay a foundation for labour law in Sweden, as an aspect of the contract of employment, was in Jul Lassen's *Haandbog I Obligation-sretten, special Del*, in 1897, which was influenced by German writing. (The first full treatment of the law of collective bargaining agreements was Knud Illum's *Den Kollektive Arbejdsret* in 1938; it was to dominate Swedish thought for decades, though it drew on no outside comparisons. Paal Berg's *Arbeidsrett* (1930) commenced collective labour relations law in Norway.) A course in labour law was offered at the Harvard Law School by Francis Bowes Sayre from his casebook of that name, published in 1923; and in 1925, the University of Illinois' College of Law offered an elective in 'industrial relations' law. The first Dutch chair in labour law as created in 1936 (though M. G. Levenbach had lectured on labour law in Amsterdam as early as 1926). In 1919, 1920, and 1921, Barthélemy Raynaud lectured on industrial legislation at Aix-Marseille; his 1922 book, *Législation Industrielle*, included a chapter on international legislation and was dotted with references to foreign law throughout. But for much of the world, a law school offering in labour law was a phenomenon postdating World War II. R. W. Rideout, Professor of Labour Law at University College London, reported that when he introduced a course titled 'Labour Law' there in 1967, it was 'amidst much surprise'.[7]

Here, too, we witness a continental divide. The European concept of labour law—*droit de travail, Arbeitsrecht*—tends to encompass pretty much the whole of the employment relationship, individual and collective. Note, for example, the outline of Potthoff's fifteen lectures on German Labour Law given in 1913–14. These dealt with: (1) the fundamental concept of the contract of employment as distinct from sale, lease, and so on (and the treatment given by German law to distinct categories of employment); (2) the role of social politics; (3) the making of the employment contract; (4) the obligations of employees; (5) the obligations of

---

[7] R. W. Rideout, 'Labour Law in the United Kingdom', in W. E. Butler and V. N. Kudriavtsev (eds), *Comparative Law and Legal Systems* (1985), 101, 105.

employers; (6) work time; (7) methods of paying and computing wages; (8) wage security; (9) insurance and economic insecurity; (10) dissolution of the employment relationship; (11) employee competitive activity; (12) industrial strife; (13) the role of employee committees and commercial courts in achieving labour peace; (14) legal recourse; and (15) a unified law of service, dealing here with officials and white-collar workers.[8] In the United States, Sayre's casebook a decade later dealt almost exclusively with the law of unionization, collective disputes, and collective bargaining, with but a single, brief chapter given over to labour legislation and another to workers' compensation. A decade after that, James Landis's *Cases on Labor Law* (1934) dispensed with all but the treatment of unionization and collective bargaining. The rest, he opined, could 'with right claim shelter under such a term as labor law', but these—issues of contract, tort, and social legislation, that is, '[l]abor law broadly defined'—'already runs through the law-school curriculum'.

No sufficient reason exists for clustering these divergent subjects about the employer-employee relationship and divorcing them from the governing legal conceptions, which already take account in their application of the fact that 'labor' is concerned.

The stage was thus set for 'labor law' in America to become occupied exclusively with the law of collective bargaining.[9]

In Britain, Mansfield Cooper's *Outlines of Industrial Law* (1947) took a tack the exact opposite of Landis: Industrial Law is rooted 'in the law of contract and the law of tort. These topics must form the backbone of this book.' This is in keeping with the British attitude of legal voluntarism regarding collective labour relations. Samuel's *Factory Law* (1937) dealt only with labour protective legislation.

To get ahead of the story, Europe has continued to think in terms of a broad body of law and the United Kingdom has come 'round to this view'. Note the introductory to Simon Deakin and Gillian Morris's *Labour Law* (3rd edn, 2001):

The discipline of *labour law* is defined in part by its subject-matter, in part by an intellectual tradition. Its immediate subject-matter consists of the rules which govern the employment relationship. However, a broader perspective would see labour law as the normative framework for the existence and operation of all the institutions of the labour market: the business enterprise, trade unions, employers' associations and, in its capacity as regulator and as employer, the state . . .

---

[8] This fairly closely tracks the topics dealt with by Commons and Andrews in 1916, save that they place greater emphasis on workplace safety (while Polthoff treats it only as part of Lecture 5) and less on systems of wage accounting and payment; and, as they deal only with legislation, they are not concerned with the employee's duty of loyalty as it is a creature of the common law of master and servant.

[9] eg Walter Jaeger, *Cases and Statutes on Labor Law* (1939); Archibald Cox, *Labor Law* (1948). The remainder of the subject has been relegated to specialized or boutique offerings, eg on workers' compensation, on employee benefits or occupational health and safety, or on courses in civil rights legislation—with the law of employment discrimination destined to take on a robust and independent curricular life of its own.

The intellectual tradition to which we referred sees *labour law* as a unified discipline which has outgrown its diverse origins in the law of obligations and in the regulatory intervention of the state. As a subject with its own doctrinal unity and structure, it spans the divides between common law and legislation and between private law and public law. In Britain, as elsewhere in Europe, it has established itself as one of the principal branches of legal studies.

Today, with the decline of unions almost to the vanishing point in the private sector in the United States, a variety of teaching materials on 'Employment Law' have been published; and some effort at unification has been made. For example, recent casebooks are titled variously *Labor and Employment Law, Employment Discrimination and Employment Law*, and just plain *Work Law* (though the sacrifice of depth for coverage in offerings of the latter nature bids fair to approximate an undergraduate 'law appreciation' course). The appearance of these teaching materials hints at the manifestation of the discipline's identity crisis in the United States.

II. COMPARATIVE LABOUR LAW

If labour law came into its own in the decade or two running up to the turn of the twentieth century, comparative labour law was not far behind. In 1889, the Swiss Government proposed an international conference on labour standards in factory work. Kaiser Wilhelm II pre-empted the Swiss by holding a conference in Berlin in 1890. In 1901, an International Association for Workers' Statutory Protection was created. These efforts reflected not only a concern for what would today be termed a 'race to the bottom' in European labour standards, and a concern as well for how the citizens of one nation-state are treated in terms of conditions while working in another state, but also from the realization that, however variable economic, legal, and social conditions are from one state to another, fully portable means of capitalist production had the tendency to generate the same sets of issues wherever they were deployed. Each nation-state was therefore a potential laboratory from which other states could learn.

In 1894, Paul Pic, Professor of Workers' and Industrial Legislation of the Faculty of Law of the University of Lyon (occupant, it seems, of one of the earliest positions in the French legal academy devoted to professing the subject), published the first volume of his *Traité élémentaire de législation industrielle*, the third edition of which (1909) treats the laws of twenty-seven countries including the United States, Japan, Australia, New Zealand, Brazil, Chile, and Peru. In 1913, the Lawyers Co-operative Publishing Company in New York put out the eight-volume *Commentaries on the Law of Master and Servant Including the Modern Laws on Workmen's Compensation, Arbitration, Employer's Liability, Etc., Etc.*, compiled by C. B. Labatt and the staff of the Co-op, which, though drenched in British law—as was common for US jurisdictions at the time—dealt extensively with legal developments elsewhere in the English-speaking world—Australia, New Zealand, the Canadian provinces, and did not hesitate to treat the state of the law in Austria, France, Germany, Italy, Mexico, Spain, and Switzerland. In 1928, 1929, and 1930 respectively, the three volumes of Erich Molitor, Hans Carl Nipperdey, and Richard Schott, *Europäisches Arbeitsvertragsrecht* appeared, compiling the labour legislation in all of Western Europe, Central and Eastern Europe, and Turkey, with explanatory commentary. The Institut de Droit Comparé at Lyon published a series of comparative labour law studies in the 1920s and 1930s, doctoral dissertations of comprehensive design, if of narrow scope, were published, for example, Jean Desprez, *Le Délai-congé en Législation Comparée* (1929) (a comparison of the law governing the requirement of notice for the termination of the employment relationship); some on problems that vex us still, for example, Aline Vallée, *Le Consentement dans le Contrat de Travail* (1930). These were the precursors of what today is a library of comparative labour law. What fills these shelves is discussed next.

1. A Taxonomy of the Discipline

Comparative labour law can be categorized into several, sometimes overlapping genres: descriptive; purposive; predicative; theoretical; and, profound. As the preceding references indicate, these are found variously in books and monographs, articles in mainstream legal periodicals, and in specialized journals, of which there are four.[10]

(a) The Descriptive

By far, the vast majority of what is written, and sometimes just compiled, sets out what one state does on a legal issue or set of issues *vis-à-vis* another state or set of states. Material of this kind can be terribly superficial, the product, as Clyde Summers termed it, of 'academic tourism'. But it can also be finely textured,

---

[10] Two are in English: The *Comparative Labor Law & Policy Journal* and the *International Journal of Comparative Labour Law and Industrial Relations*. One in German: the *Zeitschrift für ausländisches und internationals Arbeits- und Sozialrecht*. One in French: *Bulletin de droit comparé du travail et de la sécurité sociale*. There are also two general compilations in English: the *International Encyclopedia of Labour Law and Industrial Relations*, a comprehensive multi-volume work whose entries are updated from time to time; and *International Labor Employment Laws*, a two-volume work annually supplemented.

attuned to the nuances of each jurisdiction, conveying a sense of how the law on the books derived from and plays out in the country's political, economic, and cultural context. The long-projected *International Encyclopedia of Comparative Law* included a volume on labour law, the several chapters of which have been printed as separate monographs, for example, Folke Schmidt and Alan Neal on *Collective Agreements and Collective Bargaining* (1984), Benjamin Aaron on *Labor Courts and Organs of Arbitration* (1985), Ruth Ben Israel on *Strikes, Lockouts, and Other Kinds of Hostile Actions* (1997)—that are models of the descriptive type. These monographs also underline the genre's short shelf life: the law may progress or regress, but it rarely stays still in any one jurisdiction let alone a constellation of them; and this is especially so of so volatile a field as labour law.

(b) The Purposive

Comparative description may be undertaken for the illumination it provides: to cause the reader to think and see outside his or her accustomed frame of reference; to learn that there are other ways for the law to deal with an economic or social question, ways that may actually be more protective of values the reader's system professes, that are more effective, that have lower transaction costs or fewer negative externalities. But comparative work is often undertaken less for enlightenment *per se* than in search of a better solution to a pressing problem than domestic law currently affords, which, on occasion, might well be no solution at all. That is, given the portability of modern methods of production and 'human resource management', what one country finds socially, and so legally, troublesome in consequence of a particular practice might well trouble another, and it is altogether rational to see how others have dealt with it.

For some, the outcome of comparative study may be pre-ordained. Referring to contemporary European infatuation with privatization, Colin Bennett noted that '[m]uch of the so-called fact-finding within the transnational policy community . . . can be attributed to a desire to reinforce conclusions already reached'.[11] But for others, the search can be more open-minded. The study, *Settling Labour Disputes in Europe* (Annie de Roo and Rob Jagtenberg, eds, 1994), a detailed four-nation comparison with comparative analyses, drafted with an eye on the prospect of labour dispute resolution in an integrated Europe, is a good example of this genre; so, too, is John Craig's *Privacy and Employment Law* (1999), a three-nation comparison looking toward the fashioning of a workable set of portable principles.

---

[11] Colin J. Bennett, 'How States Utilize Foreign Evidence', (1991) 11 *Journal of Public Policy* 31, 50. One would not ordinarily expect conservative American politicians to look to South America as a source of inspired policy, but that they did, to Chile, when it came to touting the privatization of social security.

(c) The Predictive

Labour law is a reflexive discipline: it responds to the changing demands of a socially dynamic aspect of modern capitalism. New problems, economic or social, may crop up earlier in one system than in another. The constant process of even descriptive comparison may, like the proverbial canary in the miner's cage, function as an early warning system as old problems are settled, more or less, and new ones appear. Note, for example, the series of editions put out by Roger Blanpain (possibly the century's most indefatigable missionary for comparative labour law) and his colleagues initially titled *Comparative Labour Law and Industrial Relations* and now *Comparative Labour Law and Industrial Relations in Industrialized Market Economies*. The first volume (1982) devoted five chapters to international labour law developments and included comparative studies of thirteen issues, the lion's share concerning aspects of unionization and dispute resolution and the remainder with workers' participation, prohibition of discrimination, and security of employment. The sixth edition (1998) expanded the coverage of international developments and, even as it reduced the number of topical comparative studies, it expanded the coverage accorded worker participation outside of collective bargaining, bolstered the development of anti-discrimination law and employment security, and added both working time (in a discussion by Jacques Rojot) and employee privacy (in a discussion by this author) as subjects calling for comparative treatment. A word on these.

One would have thought working time, a fulcrum of labour's struggles in much of the nineteenth century and carried on even into the early twentieth century, to have become a settled issue. It re-emerged in the United States, brought into the public forum by the appearance of Juliet Schor's *The Overworked American* (1991). In Europe, the obverse, of the underemployed, emerged as an issue. All manner of 'atypical' and 'nonstandard' work arrangements, especially part-time employment, had been gaining momentum; later, the question of excessive leisure time was to be vigorously disputed, on the economic terrain of productivity and competitiveness.

Worker privacy, rarely commented on heretofore, was brought to the fore by the enormous impact of information technology, of computerized work monitoring and record-keeping. It became the subject of two extensive International Labour Organization (ILO) reports in the early 1990s and a European Directive on data protection in 1995. Even in Japan, privacy, the very claim to which lacked deep cultural roots, has become a source of concern, with call upon a legal system that lacks a conceptual vocabulary to deal with it and is likely to turn to foreign models for guidance.[12]

---

[12] Ikuko Sunaoshi, 'The Legal Regulation of Disclosure of Personal Information of Employees or Prospective Employees to Employers or Prospective Employers in Japan', (2000) 21 *Comparative Labour Law & Policy Journal* 745.

(d) The Theoretical

A body of literature is devoted to legal borrowing and transplantation, of the portability of labour law from one country to another. The theoretical controversy is often sharp: of whether labour law is so autochthonous that, like a rare plant, it cannot take root elsewhere; or, if it can, of the circumstances that facilitate or obstruct transplantation; and, of whether it so undergoes mutation in the process of adaptation to the host's legal and cultural context as barely to be recognizable to its progenitor.[13] Some work seeks to examine if it is possible to develop a theory that will predict the circumstances under which transplantation is more likely than not to succeed.

(e) The Profound

Work of this kind is at once probing and insightful; it uses law as a lens through which an aspect of the object's, and the viewer's, society, sometimes heretofore obscured or unnoticed, is revealed. 'The law', Simon Deakin and Frank Wilkinson remind us, 'is just as much a product of a given society as an instrument for shaping it'.[14] This kind of work requires a near total mastery of two or more legal systems, in their vernacular; it tends to draw upon history, sociology, economics, or ancillary disciplines to illuminate and explore a legal concept, an economic trend, or a social state of affairs. Outstanding scholarship of this kind is consequently exceedingly rare. In recent years, the work of Spiros Simitis, for example, on 'juridification' and on the individual contract of employment, stand out as exemplars of the genre.[15]

Unlike the descriptive/prescriptive or even the predictive, work of this kind is not expected to have an immediate, or any, practical effect. That must be felt as it engages the thoughtfulness of policy elites—if, that is, they ever do engage. In fact, the influence of comparative labour law scholarship can only rarely be attributed to the work of any individual scholar. That there are exceptions—for example, Harry Arthurs in Canada, who successfully argued for the borrowing of the concept of 'dependent contractor' from Swedish usage ('worker-like persons'

---

[13] eg the debate between Tadashi Hanami, 'Japanization of Western Labor Law', in Helmut Coing (ed), *Die Japanisierung des Westlichen Rechts* (1990), 285 and Peter Hanau, 'Arbeitsrecht: mehr japanisch als westlich', ibid at 307, and Hanami's 'Comment,' on Hanau, ibid at 313. And on the highly variegated reception of British law even in its colonial sphere, see Douglas Hay and Paul Craven (eds), *Masters, Servants, and Magistrates in Britain and the Empire 1562–1955* (2004).

[14] Deakin and Wilkinson (n 4), at 9.

[15] Spiros Simitis, 'Zur Verrechtlichung der Arbeitsbeziehungen', in *Zacher, Simitis, Kübler, Hopt and Teubner, Verrechtlichung von Wirtschaft, Arbeit und Sozialer Solidarität—Vergleichende Analysen* (1984), 73; Sprios Simitis, 'The Case of the Employment Relationship: Elements of Comparison', in Willibald Steinmetz (ed), *Private Law and Social Inequality in the Industrial Age: Comparing Legal Cultures in Britain, France, Germany, and the United States* (2000), 181. Another such is Karl-Nikolaus Peifer, *Individualität im Zivilrecht* (2001).

(*Arbeitnehmerähnliche Personen*) being already a well-established category in German law) to ameliorate the asperities of the common law's rigid employee/independent contractor dichotomy[16]—only proves the rule. To borrow an analogy from James Crawford, '[A]rt critics may influence the development of painting in a variety of ways, but it would be misleading to write a history of art by reference to this work'.[17] Comparative labour law is a 'secondary literature'. The impact, if impact there be, would have to be found in the history of legal borrowing made possible by comparative study. An oversimplified outline is sketched below.[18]

III. THE INTERNATIONAL POLICY DIALOGUE

1. From Industrialization to the End of World War II

On all the socially contentious issues thrown up by industrialization, in which Great Britain, as the precursor, was to take the lead, there was intense agitation for legal reform that often took decades to achieve results politically, if at all. The search for solutions drove reformers to create indigenous, sometimes ingenious, sometimes ingenuous, solutions and to look elsewhere. The history of the period is characterized by a tenacious search for models worldwide, in reams of private and governmental comparative studies and reports, of efforts at legal transplantations and borrowing—sometimes with significant modification, sometimes with limited or no success—depending upon local political circumstances. Note Robert Castel's mordant observation on the ' "French model" ':

Eighteen years passed between the deposition of the first plan (1880) and the ratification of the law on workplace accidents (1898); it took twenty years to develop the first law on worker's and peasant's retirement that merits, as well it should, little more than a smirk. At

---

[16] Harry Arthurs, 'The Dependent Contractor: A Study of the Legal Problems of Countervailing Power', (1965)16 *University of Toronto LR* 89.

[17] James Crawford, 'Public International Law in Twentieth-Century England', in Jack Beatson and Reinhard Zimmermann (eds), *Jurists Uprooted: German Speaking Émigré Lawyers in Twentieth-Century Britain* (2004), 681, 692.

[18] It is drawn from numerous sources, the most prominent of which are: Bob Hepple (edn), *The Making of Labour Law in Europe: A Comparative Study of Nine Countries up to 1945* (1986); Daniel T. Rogers, *Atlantic Crossings: Social Politics in a Progressive Age* (1998); Sheldon Garon, *The State and Labor in Modern Japan* (1987); Kazuo Sugeno, *Japanese Labor and Employment Law* (trans Leo Kanowitz, 2002); H. D. Woods, *Labor Policy in Canada* (2nd edn, 1973); Folke Schmidt, *The Law of Labor Relations in Sweden* (1962); Stuart Macintyre and Richard Mitchell (eds), *Foundation of Arbitration: The Origins and Effects of State Compulsory Arbitration 1890–1914* (1989).

this date (1910), our great rivals of the time, the Germans, had already enjoyed for more than a quarter of a century a system of social assistance that covered the majority of workers against risks of sickness, accidents and old age. The English were [by then] in possession of unemployment insurance, which was not instituted in France until 1958.[19]

The focus here is less on the particular borrowings than in the transnational search for solutions, on the nature of the common 'social question', or questions, that had call upon the law.

Wage payment. The British Truck Act of 1831 required that wages be paid in 'the current Coin of this Realm only, and not otherwise'. It was widely followed in Europe—the Prussian law being adopted in 1844, though Belgian law, followed in Luxembourg, took a different turn. More than fifty years later, most of the United States adopted the British model, to require payment in US money and to prohibit payment in goods or in scrip redeemable only at the company's store, the US equivalent of the British 'tommy shop'.

Child and Female Labour. Britain's Factory Act of 1833, limiting work hours for children and, most importantly, creating a factory inspectorate, was widely emulated: A Swedish public report of 1877 singled the latter aspect of British law as especially worthy of emulation. Key bureaucrats in Meiji Japan, who had studied in both England and Germany, and were strongly influenced by the *Verein für Sozialpolitik*, pressed successfully for the passage of the analogous Factory Act of 1911. The United States Supreme Court, which had struck down a state law limiting bakers' hours to sixteen per day in 1905, as an infringement of freedom of contract, was persuaded three years later, in part by a brief submitted by Louis Brandeis incorporating extensive reference to European experience, to sustain a limit on women's work hours.

Unemployment insurance. In the 1890s, the Ghent plan, of municipal subsidization of union programmes paying benefits to out-of-work members, provided a model adopted in France, Norway, Belgium, and Denmark; and later, by the Netherlands, Spain, and Finland. But Britain proposed a broader model in 1911, of compulsory insurance, which was adopted in Germany and by other European states. The European experience in general and that of Britain in particular served as a stimulant for US legislation in 1935.

Industrial accident insurance. Bismark's 1884 legislation proved to be a model emulated throughout Europe, the United States, Japan, and elsewhere.

Labour rights adjudication. In 1806, legislation in Lyon created *conseils de prud-'hommes*, bipartite bodies of manufacturers and foremen that dealt with disputes

---

[19] Castel, above (n 3), at 260.

over payment for and work being done under existing agreements. These were transplanted into those German states along the Rhine occupied by Napoleon and remained even as the French retreated. They were modified into tripartite bodies with broader adjudicatory authority, as *Gewerbegerichte*, under the Commercial Ordinance of the North German Federation of 1869. The *conseils de prud'hommes* themselves went through metamorphoses in France, of expanded jurisdiction and membership in the period 1880–1907, which revised model was followed in Belgium. A parallel evolution of industrial *probiviri* took place in Italy. The German labour court system, of a tripartite body presided over by a professional judge, was enacted in the Weimar Republic (1926). The German labour court system has by now become widely emulated, most recently in Japan.

Arbitration and conciliation of interest disputes. Statutorily mandated arbitration systems can be traced back to the British Cotton Arbitration Act of 1800; from that, a texture of statutory law accumulated in Britain throughout the nineteenth century. Some of the American states and Canada enacted legislation based on the British model, as did Belgium. Some of the Australian states followed, as did New Zealand, and these, in the period 1894–1916, took on what Richard Mitchell has termed the 'classical form of Australian compulsory arbitration' as a unique, albeit much-studied system.

Collective bargaining. The one area where direct legal transplantation played almost no discernible role lay in the specifics of the regulation of unionization and collective bargaining. As Antoine Jacobs has pointed out, however, over the course of the nineteenth and into the twentieth century, Europe, and, it could be added, the United States and Japan as well, dealt with the demands of working-class militantcy in three phases—repression, toleration, and recognition[20]—but, except for the impact of British and Dominion law within its sphere of influence, there was little borrowing.[21] (Jacobs sees a missed opportunity in the Danish September Agreement of 1899, which 'could have become the Magna Carta of modern Western European industrial relations' but for the inaccessibility of the Danish language, political conditions elsewhere also permitting, though it was influential in Scandinavia.) The European countries, Britain included, dealt with unions that asserted the right to represent their members, to negotiate collectively on their behalf. The United States eventually opted for a different system, one of exclusive representation by a majority organization, overseen by an administrative agency; Canada and its provinces adopted this model.

---

[20] Antoine Jacobs, *Collective Self-Regulation*, in Hepple (n 18), at 193.

[21] South African collective labour law, starting with the Industrial Disputes Act (Transvaal) of 1909, surveyed the law elsewhere in the British Empire and borrowed most heavily from Canada. See Clive Thompson, 'Borrowing and Bending: The Development of South Africa's Unfair Labor Practice Jurisprudence', in Roger Blanpain and Manfred Weiss (eds), *The Changing Face of the Labour Law and Industrial Relations: Liber Amicorum Clyde Summers* (1993), 109.

Collective agreements. An issue common to all jurisdictions, once collective bargaining was not proscribed, concerned the legal status of a collective agreement, theretofore unknown in Continental legal systems or in the United States. On the Continent, legal scholars struggled to find a suitable framework into which these could be placed.[22] In 1900, Philip Lotmar published an article, 'Die Tarifverträge zwischen Arbeitgebern und Arbeitnehmern', in which he observed at the outset, 'The collectivity [*die Koalition*, of either workers or employers] is free, namely as free as a bird [*vogelfrei*], and a law governing the collectivization of the employment relationship has yet to be created'. (*Vogelfrei* was a play on words for, though it literally meant 'free as a bird', in usage it meant that which is outlawed.) His work influenced Barassi in Italy and provided the springboard from and against which Hugo Sinzheimer wrote his two-volume *Der Korporative Arbeitsnormenvertrag* in 1907–8.[23] Sinzheimer's working out of a theory of the normative effect of collective agreements had widespread influence in Europe: the concept of extension became law under the Weimar Republic, later to be emulated in several countries. According to Otto Kahn-Freund, the European lead on the enforceability of collective agreements was taken by the Swiss Code of Obligations (1912); other states followed.[24] Britain, however, was to persist in a policy of 'collective *laissez-faire*', strongly supported by Kahn-Freund, which took collective agreements legally to be unenforceable.

As some of the texts mentioned at the outset of Part II evidence, this period is rich in comparative study. The International Labour Organization, created in 1919, was both a stimulant to and a source of publication in comparative labour law. In the United States, the American Association for Labor Legislation was organized in 1906, as the US affiliate of the International Association for Labour Legislation, then composed of fifteen other national affiliates all in Europe. The US leadership was a 'who's who' of the Progressive movement: it included Louis Brandeis, then known as 'the people's lawyer', the labour economists John Commons and Richard Ely, Samuel Gompers, President of the American Federation of Labor, and Woodrow Wilson, who, less than a decade later, as President, would put Brandeis on the US Supreme Court. In 1910, the Association commenced publication of the *American Labor Legislation Review* as a vehicle for the aggressive promotion of labour law reform and in which reference to foreign developments were a regular feature.

In 1942, Sir William Beveridge produced the blueprint for the British welfare state, *Social Insurance and Allied Services*. It included an appendix surveying the

---

[22] Axel Adlercreutz, 'The Rise and Development of the Collective Agreement', in Folke Schmidt (ed), 2 *Scandinavian Studies in Law* (1958), 210.

[23] Helmut Isele, 'Philipp Lotmars und Hugo Sinzheimers Bedeutung für das Moderne Tarifvertragsrecht', in *Contratti Collettivi e Controversie Collettive di Lavoro: Studi in Memoria di Lodovic Barassi* (1965), 245.

[24] Otto Kahn-Freund, *Labour Relations and the Law* (1965), 11.

laws of thirty countries: as 'social security is a common interest of all peoples of the world', it had given rise to 'the development of national institutions of various kinds' from which the architects of the British system could profit. The report had a profound effect throughout Europe in the creation of a widely shared assumption that labour law and social security were integral elements of any society dedicated to social justice. By then, and subsequently, it had become an automatic reflex for policy-makers to acknowledge the approaches reflected in the laws of other nations—even as they might proceed to ignore them.

2. From the Philadelphia Declaration (1944) to the Treaty of Maastricht (1991)

These two documents bookend a period of the growth of labour law in the developing world, often by foreign borrowing or by reference to international labour standards;[25] of the intensive development of labour law and policy in Europe, mostly by domestic refinement but sometimes by comparative assimilation, and, importantly, of the nascence of European labour law; and, of growing disinterest in foreign labour law by policy elites in the United States. These themes are traced below.

In the wake of the war, the signatories to International Labour Organization called for a renewal and expansion of its 1919 mandate. The Philadelphia Declaration (1944) reiterated the rejection of the idea of labour as a commodity or article of commerce (so much for Stadthagen) and sought to establish more firmly an international commitment to common, if minimum, labour standards. Much of the developing world had borrowed or were given their labour laws by colonial powers: in 1952, France published a *Code du travail des territoires d'outre-mer* applicable to Francophone Africa, but inapplicable to Algeria, Morocco, and Tunisia. Latin America already had a texture of legislation, but Asia and much of the developing world elsewhere looked to International Labour Organization standards.

Japan was then a redeveloping country. It looked to the United States and Germany as a source of law; Korea, though freed of Japanese colonial rule, continued and continues to look to Japan for labour law and so, in turn, is influenced indirectly by those sources to which the Japanese have recourse.[26] The Soviet Union

---

[25] See generally, Efren Cordova, 'The Codification of Labor Law in Developing Countries', in Gerhard Müller and Franz Gamillscheg (eds), *International Society for Labour Law and Social Security, 9th International Congress, München 12–15 September 1978, Reports and Proceedings* (Band II/2, Heidelberg 1978), 817 ff.

[26] cf Ki Yop Lim, 'A Comparative Study of American and Korean Labor Laws' (1976) (unpublished SJD dissertation at the Stanford Law School).

and those states in its sphere of influence worked at generating a body of *sui generis* socialist labour law,[27] but only the Yugoslav experiment in worker management drew significant interest in the West.

The most significant development of the period in Europe was the first steps taken toward the creation of European labour law via the European Community—in the 1970s implementing principles of equal pay and non-discrimination against women, in regulating collective redundancies and transfers of undertakings. In this period, many European states also developed or refined their laws governing wrongful dismissal or requiring various forms of information sharing and consultation with workers—even co-determination of some issues with the workers' representatives: the *comités d'entreprise* in France, the *Betriebsräte* in Germany respectively. In general, the growth of law outside the context of EC law, the many paths to be taken toward achieving a social agenda, was more a matter of domestic refinement than the product of comparative borrowing. The singular exception to this generalization is Britain's experiment with the Industrial Relations Act of 1971, modelled on the United States' National Labour Relations Act, which experiment was short lived. Once burned but not twice shy, the Employment Relations Act of 1999 once again borrowed elements of US law regarding union recognition, thus far with greater success.[28]

The period is also rich in comparative work: The Swedish Work Environment Fund and the Centre for Working Life appointed a special Programme Group which supported research connecting labour law to other disciplines and in comparative perspective, for example, *Labour Law Research in Twelve Countries* (Sten Edlund, ed, 1986). Some of the monographs produced under the rubric of the *International Encyclopedia of Comparative Law* have been noted. Earlier, a series of comparative European studies were sponsored by the European Coal and Steel Community—on the contract of employment, dispute resolution, representation, strikes and lock-outs, and the like. The Institute of Industrial Relations at the University of California at Los Angeles put together a Comparative Labour Law Group that published comprehensive country studies, for example, *Labour Courts and Grievance Settlement in Western Europe* (Benjamin Aaron, ed, 1971) and *Discrimination in Employment: A Study of Six Countries* (Folke Schmidt, ed, 1978). A steady drumbeat of doctoral dissertations and *Habilitationsschriften* appeared in Europe, numerous studies by international bodies—International Labour Organization, OECD, World Bank—and a wealth of monographs and periodical treatment was published. In the United States, Derek Bok and John Dunlop's *Labor and the American Community* (1970), addressed to a popular audience, concerned the

---

[27] eg László Nagy, *The Socialist Collective Agreement* (1984); W. E. Butler, B. A. Hepple, and Alan Neal (eds), *Comparative Labour Law: Anglo Soviet Perspectives* (1987).

[28] Nancy Peters, 'The United Kingdom Recalibrates the U.S. National Labor Relations Act: Possible Lessons for the United States?', (2004) 25 *Comparative Labour Law & Policy Journal* 201.

future role of unions in the United States, drawing upon law, policy, and practice in Great Britain, France, Germany, and Sweden; Clyde Summers's comparative studies of worker participation in Sweden and Germany appeared in this period. In 1958, the International Society for Social Law and the International Congress of Labour Law merged to form the International Society for Labour Law and Social Security Legislation (ISLLSSL). The *American Labor Legislation Review* had ceased publication before the end of World War II; but, in 1976, the US International Society for Labour Law and Social Security Legislation Branch stimulated the creation of the *Comparative Labor Law Journal*. In 1983, apace with the growing social dimension of the European Community, the *Institut für Arbeitsrecht und Arbeitsbeziehungen in der Europäischen Gemeinschift* was founded in Trier, Germany.

However, labour law as a subject of instruction and practice continued to be largely local: as a general principle, domestic treatises and teaching materials, having now to deal with far more well-developed bodies of law, attended almost exclusively to the parochial.[29] The teaching materials produced early on in the United States by the Labor Law Trust Group sought a new approach, one that would introduce 'material from foreign countries as a basis for comparative study' as an integral part of a course of instruction in American labour law. The Group's book, *Labor Relations and the Law* (Robert Matthews, ed, 1953) and its second edition in 1957, edited by Donald Wollett and Benjamin Aaron, did just that; but the effort to integrate comparative material was not followed subsequently by the Group or emulated by others. In France, Pierre-Dominique Ollier's student text, *Le Droit du Travail* (1973), while parochial in substance, nevertheless set out a bibliography of relevant works in history, economics, sociology, and philosophy; it included works on international labour law and the then nascent idea of European labour law; but, on comparative labour law, he observed dryly that, apart from the publications put out by the International Labour Organization and the European Coal and Steel Community, 'studies of this nature in French are rare', though he did note Blanc-Jouvan's work on the law of collective agreements in the United States.

3. Maastricht to the Present

The past twenty years have witnessed three developments: the deepening of a body of European labour law that transcends national borders and that, of necessity,

---

[29] The trajectory of US teaching materials was noted earlier. In Germany, Alfred Hueck and Hans Carl Nipperdey's treatise, *Lehrbuch des Arbeitsrechts*, the seventh revised edition of which appeared in 1963 (the sixth in 1959) referenced no foreign material other than historical relevance. Some texts even urged extreme caution in the use of comparative law, eg Zöllner and Loritz, *Arbeitsrecht* (4th edn, 1992),123. (This was softened, slightly, in the 5th edn (1998), at p 138. I am indebted to Spiros Simitis for bringing this to my attention.) French treatises were similarly focused, eg Bernard Teyssie, *Droit du Travail* (1992). So, too, in the United Kingdom, eg G. H. K. Friedman, *The Modern Law of Employment* (1963).

tends to make comparativists of the European bench and bar; the continued exploration of foreign models in Asia and elsewhere in the developing world; and, in the United States, an increasingly sophisticated scholarly interest in the economic analysis of labour market institutions, including the law, there and abroad, that is paralleled by an expressed distaste for comparative legal resort by an influential element of the power elite.

(a) Europe

The time frame set out in the foregoing section is not quite as arbitrary as it might appear. The European Convention on Human Rights and Fundamental Freedoms was promulgated in 1950, but it required domestic enabling legislation, which was not always swiftly forthcoming or effective. Britain did not bring itself into compliance until the Human Rights Act of 1998, effective 2000. The European Social Charter came into force in 1965, but it, too, depended upon governmental compliance; provision for private complaint to the Committee of Independent Experts was not made until 1995. The potential of the European Community (EC) to generate a body of labour law binding upon the member states and enforceable domestically lay only modestly realized until 1991 when, it is generally recognized, a 'new social European dimension' came into being with the Treaty of Maastricht, to be extended by successor agreements.[30]

European labour law has now come to concern, among other things, free movement of workers, posting of workers, part-time work, fixed-term contracts, working time, parental leave, data protection, information sharing and consultation with worker representatives, and, at its most developed, the prohibition of discrimination against women, here drawing heavily on US law. The larger, if obvious, point is this: European labour law is now an integral element of instruction and practice: labour law in Europe is no longer local.[31] Consequently, it is natural to expect practitioners and judges to educate themselves about the gloss placed by sister states on common texts, that is, to become comparatively minded *malgré lui*, if only within the universe, a growing universe, of states included in the community. Note as only one, but nevertheless outstanding example, the papers put together by Silvana Sciarra, *Labour Law in the Courts: National Judges at the European Court of Justice* (2004).

---

[30] Roger Blanpain, *European Labour Law* (7th rev edn, 2000), para 26 at 29.

[31] Note, for example, the integration of European law into the treatise on UK law, Susan Deakin and Gillian Morris, Labour Law (3rd edn, 2001). Indicative of this sea change is a student-oriented summary of the key elements of the law in the United Kingdom, what in the United States would be called a student 'pony': Robert Upex, Richard Benny, and Stephen Hardy, *Labour Law* (2004), v, ('The other major contribution to the modern face of Labour Law is the United Kingdom's membership in the European Union'.).

(b) Asia and the Developing World

A virtual upheaval starting in the 1980s brought to the fore the relationship of labour standards to global trade: the International Labour Organization's declaration of four 'core' or fundamental labour rights in 1998, and the exponential growth in 'soft law'—of corporate codes, and even of framework agreements made by transnational corporations with international union federations.[32] Japan, Korea, and China, the former two by long tradition, the latter only recently, have explored foreign models for their potential adaptability; in China's case, the US model of labour arbitration and the British model of wrongful dismissal law are currently under examination. Similar movement elsewhere in the developing world, more often by resort to International Labour Organization standards, is being pursued as hand-in-glove with pressure from trading partners and non-governmental organizations connecting human rights to international trade.[33] India, however, appears to be at a remove.

Law as a subject of scholarly inquiry is of long standing in Japan and developing rapidly in Korea: both have governmentally supported institutes for labour policy studies. Moreover, '[i]t is common practice for Japanese law professors to engage in comparative studies of at least one or two foreign systems'.[34] Similar use of comparative study in parts of Latin and Meso-America, Africa, and elsewhere in Asia may have to await the development of commensurately sophisticated institutions of legal education and research.[35]

(c) The United States

Three points can be made about the United States. First, even as the tradition of descriptive studies in comparative labour institutions continues,[36] understanding of them has been enriched by having the perspectives of other disciplines brought to bear—economics primarily,[37] but also other of the social sciences.[38] Second,

[32] See generally Bob Hepple, *Labour Laws and Global Trade* (2005).

[33] For an assessment of the suitability of Western concepts of labour law for Asian countries see Sean Cooney and Richard Mitchell, 'Examining Labour Law Policy in the Countries of the Asian Region: Some Suggestions for an Approach', in Richard Mitchell and Jesse Min Aun Wu (eds), *Facing the Challenge in the Asia Pacific Region: Contemporary Themes and Issues in Labour Law* (1997).

[34] Takashi Araki, *Labor and Employment Law in Japan* (2002), 5.

[35] Luis Aparicio-Valdez and Juan Raso-Delgue, 'Teaching Labor Law in Latin American Universities', (2002) 23 *Comparative Labour Law & Policy Journal* 753.

[36] eg Wayne Vroman and Vera Brunsentsev, *Unemployment Compensation throughout the World: A Comparative Analysis* (2005).

[37] The body of writing in comparative labour economics is enormous. Note just two outstanding recent examples, Heckman and Carmen Páges (eds), *Law and Employment: Lessons from Latin America and the Caribbean* (2004); Francine Blau and Larry Kahn, *At Home and Abroad: U.S. Labor Market Performance in International Perspective* (2002).

[38] eg Frank Dobbin, 'Do the Social Sciences Shape Corporate Anti-discrimination Practice?: The United States and France', (2002) 23 *Comparative Labour Law & Policy Journal* 829.

doctrinal comparison at a deeper level than the descriptive, necessarily drawing from the vernacular of the legal systems compared, has largely languished. If, in practical terms, Europe has become eurocentric, its eurocentrism is multinational and multilingual; it builds necessarily upon knowledge of how other European systems work and in their vernacular. Unlike Japanese law professors, American law professors do not engage with the law of other systems as a matter of course; their monolingualism, which, in contrast to the 'teens and twenties, is now the norm, precludes it. As a result, conceptual divides between the United States and non-Anglophone law may become ever more difficult to bridge.[39] Third, at the level of the policy elite, general disinterest in foreign law has, in certain quarters, ripened into actual distaste.

This is not to suggest that legal xenophobia was never a player on the US stage. An opponent of a bill proposed in 1919 to limit office workers to eight hours a day, a bill whose supporters pointed to foreign legislation, testified in rebuttal before a New York legislative committee that, 'It is absurd and suicidal for America to ape Europe. These very laws have been the undoing of Europe and have helped surrender its separate governments to Bolsheviki.'[40] The then popular demand for reform and the obvious rationality of considering alternatives from whatever civilized source derived, legitimated by that powerful element of the policy elite identified with the Progressive movement, trumped the nativist challenge. (Eleven years before, the United States Supreme Court had already taken note of foreign law in sustaining the ability of the state, as against constitutional challenge, to adopt a protective law for women.) But, by 2004, American workers could be best described as docile; and the influence of politicians of a reformist stripe had evaporated. In that year, the US House of Representatives entertained a serious resolution declaring judicial reliance on foreign law to threaten the nation's very sovereignty;[41] and, in the year following, the nominee for Chief Justice of the United States, appearing before a committee of the United States Senate, was pressed publicly to assure his forbearance from any such reprehensible practice.

[39] eg Matthew Finkin, '*Menschenbild:* The Conception of the Employee as a Person in Western Law', (2002) 23 *Comparative Labour Law and Policy Journal* 577.

[40] Quoted in Susan Lehrer, *Origins of Protective Labor Legislation for Women 1905–1925* (1987), 214.

[41] H Res 568, 108th Cong, 2d Sess (17 March 2004).

IV. LABOUR LAW'S
CONTEMPORARY QUANDARY

In 1986, Gerard Lyon-Caen publicly inquired, *Quel avenir pour quel droit social?*,[42] which question was at once provocative and prophetic: it anticipated the 'Supiot Report' of 1999, on change in the nature of work and the future of employment law in Europe;[43] the Italian Ministry of Labour's 2001 White Paper, *The Labour Market in Italy*,[44] drawing deeply on European comparative law; of numerous engagements with workplace change in the United States,[45] and proposals for labour law reform there, and in Japan.[46] Whence the question noted at the outset of this essay: what *is* labour law today and is there any point in treating it as such?

As in Wagner's *Ring*, we are returned to the beginning. To James Landis, 'labor law' in 1934 was the law of unionization and collective bargaining; all the rest—contract, tort, even social legislation—had no claim for separate treatment merely because 'labor' was involved. To Sir Mansfield Cooper, the 'backbone' of 'industrial law' in that period was contract and tort. And to Walter Kaskel, writing his *Arbeitsrecht* in 1928, the subject demanded that it be treated as a totality, in connection to private law, public law, and civil procedure, and in all its aspects, individual, collective, legislative, and political. Even in the beginning, so to speak, there were critical differences in understanding what the subject was, and why.

This much seems clear: Labour law emerged as a response to economic liberalism and industrialization, to the factory system as it developed from the 1870s to the century's turn, and especially to the form industrialism eventually took to rationalize work and workers, loosely described today as 'Fordism'—in dubious honour of Henry Ford and his company's perfection of the assembly line in 1913. The elements of this system have been succinctly summarized:

(a) a male full-time breadwinner; (b) long-term service in the same firm, doing one or

---

[42] In Pierre van der Vorst (ed), *Ans de Droit Social Belge* (1986), 100.

[43] The English translation appeared as Alain Supiot (ed), *Beyond Employment: Changes at Work and the Future of Employment Law in Europe* (2001). Commentary from the perspective of Australia, Japan, and Latin America was published, ' "The Supiot Report" From a Non-European Perspective', (1999) 20 *Comparative Labour Law & Policy Journal* 621–714.

[44] Reprinted in Bulletin of Comparative Labor Relations No. 44, Roger Blanpain (ed) (2002). The White Paper was drawn up in part by Marco Biagi, for which effort he was assassinated by the Red Brigades.

[45] eg Stephen Herzenberg, John Alic, and Havarj Wial, *New Rules for a New Economy: Employment and Opportunity in Post Industrial America* (1998); Paul Osterman, Thomas Kochan, Richard Locke, and Michael Piore, *Working in America: A Blueprint for the New Labor Market* (2001).

[46] Kazuo Sugeno and Yasuo Suwa, 'Labour Law Issues in a Changing Labour Market: In Search of a New Support System', in Mari Sako and Hiroki Sato (eds), *Japanese Labour and Management in Transition* (1997), 53.

similar jobs; (c) homogeneous and standardized working style; (d) clear-cut separation of working time from leisure or private time, as well as collective and objective working time; (e) relatively short term of life expectancy after retirement; (f) predominantly industrial—sometimes enterprise—union and industrial collective bargaining.[47]

The economic and social, and so legal issues this system generated was the stuff of labour law, and so of comparative labour law, for nearly a century, with ever greater sophistication in advanced economies. In what is now loosely called a post-industrial world, almost all these elements have become or are becoming unpacked, albeit to lesser as well as greater extents. The challenges wrought by the dissolution of the Fordist model in the contemporary context can accordingly be gathered under four heads: (a) flexibilization; (b) individualization; (c) workforce heterogeneity and demographics; and, (d) governmental incapacity.[48]

1. Flexibilization

Employers have sought a variety of means nimbly to adjust and readjust work—wages and benefits, working time and tasks—to constantly shifting product or service demand. The result is the rise of 'contingent employment', what the Europeans call 'atypical' workers and the Japanese call 'freeters': temporary or leased workers, sometimes in lieu of the company's hiring of probationary workers; part-time workers; on-call or 'just-in-time' workers; workers classified as independent contractors; workers hired for the duration of a limited project or task, or for a limited time—all of which depart radically from the Fordist model of a full-time employee who has conceded to the employer the freedom to assign work within a mutually if roughly understood set of tasks in return for security of employment. To students of industrial relations, this arrangement had been understood to define what employment was in contrast to independent contractorship, that is, in contrast to a spot market for the sale of labour (a 'sales transaction') where each element of what is to be done and the price for it are to be agreed upon beforehand. As David Marsden explains:

[T]he advantages of the employment over the sales transaction to employers and workers are threefold. Employers gain flexibility and the knowledge that labour will be available to them when they know more precisely what their work requirements will be. Workers gain by the continuity of activity, an important benefit when their principal source of income is the sale of their labour. Finally, both sides benefit, as Coase stressed, by substituting a single transaction for what otherwise might have been many.[49]

---

[47] Takashi Iwagami, 'The End of Classic Model of Labor Law and Post-Fordism', (1999) 20 *Comparative Labour Law & Policy Journal* 691, 692.

[48] See generally Max Rood, 'Internationalization: A New Incentive for Labour Law and Social Security', in J. R. Bellace and M. G. Rood (eds), *Labour Law at the Crossroads: Changing Employment Relationships* (*Studies in Honour of Benjamin Aaron*) (1997), 139, 140.

[49] David Marsden, *A Theory of Employment Systems* (1999), 11.

Flexibilization raises the question, addressed more than a century ago, of how to define the employment relationship as distinct from sale or lease, and of what makes the sale or lease of labour worthy of treatment separate from the general body of law dealing with such transactions.[50] The common assumption undergirding the European concept of labour law, the thread that bound it together as an integrated body of law, is the subordinate nature of the relationship. Labour law is called into being by the need to protect the weaker party to the transaction, invariably the employee. But if there is no functional or economic difference between a worker and a petty entrepreneur, labour law should either expand to embrace a wider range of relationships or collapse into an aspect of commercial law.

Further, these new forms of work shift more of the risk—of the loss of employment and attendant benefits, of keeping job skills current—away from the employer and on to what might now be termed the seller of labour. For many, a life concern has become less for job security than for future employability. The question of who should bear these risks, and the capacity of the state to spread them, once largely settled, have been reopened. In Europe, that reopening is debated in the context of deep, long-term unemployment to which American-style economic analysts of labour market institutions have contributed a powerful critique of protective law.

2. Individualization

As we have seen, in the United States, labour law *was* the law of unionization and collective bargaining: the assumption was that, absent a union, an employee had few rights an employer need respect. But unions never achieved a private sector density greater than about 36 per cent, and then only in the 1950s. Great Britain, Australia, and Canada were not so single-minded conceptually, but collective bargaining as the primary means of ordering the employment relationship did occupy a prominent role. In Europe, the role of the 'social partners' was a critical feature as it fitted into the larger framework of the social state; and as much could be said for Japan. Only in Scandinavia could unionization be said to be *the* predominant form of workplace organization.

Today, union density has fallen in all but the Scandinavian countries:[51] in

[50] Peter Gahan and Richard Mitchell go further: labour law, as conventionally understood, addresses those who are already employed; it ignores (apart from elements of anti-discrimination law) those who are, or would be, in the labour market but who are without jobs. (However, some economists have argued for the 'insider-outsider' effects of job security and other protective law.) From this it could be argued that the subject should be expanded to grasp as a whole the law regulating the labour market—including, for example, availability of education and vocational training. Peter Gahan and Richard Mitchell, 'The Limits of Labour Law and the Necessity of Interdisciplinary Analysis', in Mitchell (n 1), 62.

[51] John Pencavel, 'Unionism Viewed Internationally', (2005) 26 *Journal of Labour Research* 65; *Japan Institute for Labour Policy and Training, Japanese Working Life Profile 2004/2005* (2004), 61.

Australia, from almost 50 per cent of the workforce in 1982 to perhaps 25 per cent in 2001; in Germany, from about 36 per cent in 1982 to perhaps 30 per cent in 1997; in Japan, from about 31 per cent in 1980 to under 20 per cent in 2003. In the United States, union density in the private sector is currently hovering around 8 per cent. This situation poses a major challenge: decline in union density may affect wage distribution, to contribute to greater wage inequality within a nation's workforce, as it has in the United States; and it has spillover effects, that is, contributing to a 'democratic deficit', a lessening of voice and of intramural institutions of countervailing power in the enterprise and in the larger body politic.

We are returned, again, to the beginning. In his 1913–14 lecture on labour law, Heinz Pothoff included, under the head 'Social Politics', the problem, identified as such, of exploitation and dependence, the latter raising the question of the '*Konstitutioneller Betrieb*'—of the workplace as a social realm where the liberal constitutional values of individual rights, including representational rights, need to be established. The decline of unions triggers the problem of how to secure these rights absent representation, of who can possibly speak for the unrepresented.

Europe has partially filled the representation gap on the shop floor with a directive calling for national legislation to create systems of information sharing and consultation with employees. The effectiveness of that measure will doubtless be the subject of extensive study. Given the political gridlock in the United States that has rendered the federal government incapable of effecting any significant change in the law of employee representation for more than four decades, the democratic deficit in the workplace, with its spillover into the political arena, will persist indefinitely.

Absent representation, employers are free unilaterally to adopt any employment policy, any working condition or human resource management policy believed to be economically beneficial, no matter how exploitative or invasive—unless a limit is imposed by law. Most if not all of these employer policies treat 'public goods': job security, benefits, the pace of work and work scheduling, job safety and health, employee privacy, and more. Inasmuch as the employer's policies on these subjects will affect a work group, or the entire workforce, no one employee or applicant is in much of a position to bargain about it. Thus the legal choices for the nation-state are three: (1) allow employers freedom of action as constrained only by market forces; (2) step in to legislate the terms—or minimum terms, the floor below which employers may not tread; or, (3) provide for systems of representation to require employers to negotiate these terms with their employees' representative. But, if German experience is a guide, its legal mandate of works councils with real, that is co-determinative statutory power, is realized in only half the workplaces where they are supposed to be; and, apropos of that, the use of contingent or atypical workers can be a means for an employer to avoid that obligation.[52] Thus, flexibilization and

---

[52] eg Tony Royle, *Working for McDonald's in Europe: The Unequal Struggle* (2000).

individualization can combine to conduce toward something like the US model of atomized, unrepresented workers; and the pressure of globalization—the fear of the loss of jobs to lower-wage countries—may reduce the capacity of the state to fill the gap with positive law. Even where positive law exists, individualization may enervate the individual's ability to vindicate his or her rights.[53]

3. Demographic Change

In terms of the distribution of workers, advanced economies have shifted from manufacturing to service economies. Moreover, the working force in most developed countries today is older than in the high-water-mark days of mass production. The aging of the workforce puts considerable pressure on social security systems; and the absence of younger male workers summons a need for alternative sources of labour. More women have entered the labour market in Europe and the labour force there has become more ethnically and religiously diverse as well. The former engenders tension between employer demands for productivity and the employees' family needs. The latter may make for a volatile mix. This combination of ingredients is not limited to Europe. The aging of the workforce is most acute in Japan, whose culture is notably resistant to the assimilation of non-native populations, that is, to filling the vacancies opened by a declining population of the young with immigrants. Special claims have also been made by the disabled for integration into the labour force, with divergent legal responses.[54]

4. The Capacity of the State

Some observers argue that the free flow of capital and jobs across borders enervates the power of the individual nation-state unilaterally to adopt measures to protect their citizen-workers against the asperities of such an economic regime. Whether that is so or not, four avenues better to level the labour playing field in a worldwide labour market have been essayed.[55]

First is the well-worn route of internationally negotiated standards. Second is the connection of labour standards to international trade or trade agreements. Third is the prospect, albeit remote, of multinational collective bargaining. Fourth, and the area drawing the most attention in the past decade, is of so-called 'soft law'—of unilaterally adopted corporate codes of good practice and, to a far lesser

[53] Anna Pollert, 'The Unorganized Worker: The Decline in Collectivism and New Hurdles to Individual Employee Rights', (2005) 34 *Industrial LJ* 217.

[54] See generally, 'Symposium: The Concept of Disability', (2003) 24 *Comparative Labour Law & Policy Journal* 533–667.

[55] These are treated comprehensively by Hepple (n 32).

extent, of international framework agreements with international union confeder-
ations, whereby the company asserts or agrees respectively that it, and, sometimes,
those it does business with, will observe certain fair labour standards. The domestic
legal effect of these codes and agreements, including the private international law
problems they will inevitably generate, have not yet emerged—but they will.

Moreover, in so far as power has arguably shifted away from government to
private actors, the whole area of corporate governance, in its relationship to worker
representation and protection, has been brought into question.[56] Even as students
of the employment relationship address the idea of convergence as well as borrowing
in labour standards as a result of globalization, so, too, have students of business
organization considered convergence or borrowing in corporate governance.

V. The Future of Comparative
Labour Law—in Hindsight

Nineteenth-century capitalism threw up a set of seemingly intractable problems
that vexed every nation-state hospitable to industrialization and economic liberalism. With hindsight, these proved amenable to meliorative legal resolution: child
labour could be prohibited, especially if public schooling could be made available;
working hours could be regulated, especially if technology could improve productivity; illness, accident, unemployment, and old age could be dealt with by insurance; the security of wage payment could be assured; income could be sustained
by a legislated floor on wages; and workers could be assured healthful and safe
working conditions and a right to be heard about the conditions under which most
of their waking lives would be spent by a mixture of legislated standards, administrative inspection, and workplace representation. All these measures required or
produced legally complex follow-on problems; each has engendered whole bodies
of law in themselves—reams of regulations and decisions, bodies of commentary,
separate courses of instruction. But the role of law has become largely settled.
That, with hindsight, these problems seem so soluble obscures the intense political
struggle over them, sometimes extending over decades, and the critical role com-
parativisim played in their resolution: comparative labour law provided not only
legal options capable of study in operation, but, and perhaps even more important,
it legitimated the very possibility of legal address.

---

[56] See generally, 'Symposium: Employees and Corporate Governance', (2000) 22 *Comparative
Labour Law & Policy Journal* 1–194.

Twenty-first-century capitalism is generating a fresh set of social problems. Some—the intermittency of work, alternative work forms such as reliance on contracting for services, the shifting of risk—actually resonate against pre-Fordist labour practices at the turn of the twentieth century, a period characterized by high labour turnover, the inside contractor system, and the total absence of any employment-related benefits. Other problems, the systematic invasion of personal privacy made possible by modern information technology, the demand for the full integration of women, ethnic and religious groups, older workers, and the disabled into the workplace, and the call for the exercise of corporate social responsibility in labour policies on an international scale, are new. And some have something old and something new in them: if unionism, in the form it has historically taken, is in decline, how should employees be represented? How are they to be represented if their ties are closer to an occupation than to any one employer, if, that is, their careers will take them through a series of employment relationships, for greater or shorter duration, with a number of employers? If history is a guide, it may take years before the law effectively comes to grips with these and other problems, even as a dynamic capitalism throws up new and as yet unforeseen issues.

In the resolution of the twenty-first century's *Labour Question*, or questions, comparativism can be expected to play much the role it played in the twentieth: to instigate thought outside one's accepted legal frame of reference; to present and dissect arguable alternatives; to examine the interplay of law and culture; where necessary—that is, in response to the challenge of neoclassical economics—persuasively to legitimate the law's role. As in the past, the use to which comparative work is put will lie in the hands of a political process over which the comparativist scholar has no control and little influence. (Even of the parochialism prevalent in the United States today, it is well to recall Derek Bok's admonition that it took the Great Depression, the total collapse of public confidence in the business order, for the political process to place into law the results of decades of comparative study theretofore languishing on the shelves.[57]) What able scholars can continue to do is to evidence the intrinsic intellectual worth of the comparative enterprise.

BIBLIOGRAPHY

Otto Kahn-Freund, 'Thoughts on Comparative Labor Law', (1974) 48 *Tulane LR* 894
Franz Gamillscheg (ed), *In Memoriam, Sir Otto Kahn-Freund: International Collection of Essays: Collections Internationale d'Études* (1980)

[57] Derek Bok, 'A Comment on American Difference and Indifference', (2000) 21 *Comparative Labour Law & Policy Journal* 391. Eg Daniel Nelson, *Unemployment Insurance: The American Experience, 1915–1935,* (1969), 220 ('While there was gradual progress in the general field of social insurance in the 1920s, only the devastating unemployment of the 1930's produced a feeling that the European approach to unemployment insurance should be reexamined'.).

Gerard Lyon-Caen, *La Crise de Droit du Travail* (1980)

Gian Guido Bilandi and Silvana Sciarra (eds), *Il Pluralismo e il Diritto del Lavoro: Studi su Otto Kahn-Freund* (1982)

Lord (Kenneth William) Wedderburn, *Employment Rights in Britain and Europe: Selected Papers in Labour Law* (1991)

—— (ed), *Labour Law in the Post-Industrial Era: Essays in Honour of Hugo Sinzheimer* (1994)

Christian Engels and Manfred Weiss (eds), *Labour Law and Industrial Relations at the Turn of the Century: Liber Amicorum Roger Blanpain* (1998)

Thomas Kohler, 'The Disintegration of Labor Law: Some Notes for a Comparative Study of Legal Transformation', (1998) 73 *Notre Dame LR* 1311

Dieter Simon and Manfred Weiss (eds), *Zur Autonomie des Individuums: Liber Amicorum Spiros Simitis* (2000)

Roger Blanpain and Manfred Weiss (eds), *Changing Industrial Relations and the Modernization of Labour Law: Liber Amicorum Marco Biagi* (2003)

Simon Deakin and Gillian Morris (eds), *The Future of Labour Law: Liber Amicorum Sir Bob Hepple QC* (2004)

Armin Höland, Christine Hohmann-Dennhardt, Marlene Schmidt, and Achim Seifert (eds), *Arbeitnehmermitwirkung in einer sich globalizierenden Arbeitswelt; Employee Involvement in a Globalizing World: Liber Amicorum Manfred Weiss* (2005)

Birgitta Nyström and A. Westergård (eds), *Liber Amicorum Reinhold Fahlbeck* (2005)

CHAPTER 36

....

COMPARATIVE COMPANY LAW

....

KLAUS J. HOPT

Hamburg

I. Introduction

COMPARATIVE company law is at once very old and very modern. It is very old because ever since companies and company laws first existed, trade has not stopped at the frontiers of countries and states. The persons concerned, practitioners as well as rule-makers, had to look beyond their own city, country, rules, and laws. This became even more true after the rise of the public company and the early company acts in the first half of the nineteenth century. Ever since, company lawmakers have profited from comparison.

But comparative company law is also very modern. Most comparative work has focused on the main areas of private law, such as contract and torts, rather than company law. While the law of business and private organizations was covered in the voluminous *International Encyclopedia of Comparative Law*,[1] and national company law books and articles occasionally also provided some comparative information, an internationally acknowledged standard treatise on comparative company law has not yet emerged. Company law and comparative company law work remained a task for professionals. The few academics who joined in this work tended also to be practitioners such as outside counsel, arbitrators, or advisers to legislators, who were less interested in theory and doctrine.

---

[1] Detlev Vagts (ed), 'Business and Private Organizations', in *International Encyclopedia of Comparative Law* (vol XIII, Tübingen, Dordrecht, 1972 ff) with more than a dozen instalments.

frames such scholarship, and it thereby colours and shapes it as well. A second is that the centrality of US law and experience divides the writing in the area and often distorts it. This dominance generates two fundamentally different perspectives on competition law. In one, US writers look out at the world and say 'follow us'. In the other, non-US writers ask, 'How do we assess the US experience and how do we respond to the US model and its supporters?' The third thread that runs through this chapter identifies the potential impact of economic globalization on the agenda of comparative competition law and the opportunities it creates for writers in the area to contribute to creating a sounder policy framework for transnational markets. Globalization can provide many benefits, but it can also cause much harm, and a clearer understanding of policy options and accumulated experience is critical in both promoting the former and impeding the latter.

I. Comparative Competition Law Scholarship—What is it?

'Comparative competition law' does not represent a clearly identifiable academic discipline. No specific methodology or body of works serves as a common reference point for writing in this area, and thus I need to clarify how I am here using the term.

Unlike most topics in this volume, the term 'competition law' itself requires clarification, because there are significant differences in the way it and its analogues in other languages are used. I use it here to refer to general laws whose primary objective is to combat restraints on the competitive process. In the US, this area of law is referred to as 'antitrust law'. Outside the US, the term 'competition law' is more commonly used to refer to laws with this function. One problem with the term 'competition law' is that it is often more broadly defined than 'antitrust', but there is no commonly accepted usage. In some countries, for example, it also refers to laws with other objectives (eg to protect competitors from 'unfair' competition). This discrepancy in usages can lead to serious misunderstandings and uncertainties. Here, however, I deal only with competition law in the narrower 'antitrust' sense just indicated.

Defining 'comparative scholarship' in this area is also a bit trickier than in most contexts. I am here concerned with writing about competition law that is comparative in that it seeks to *relate* material in two or more competition law systems to each other. My main focus here is on analytical and normative writing—that is, writing that is both explicitly comparative and that provides insights into the relevant differences and similarities or draws conclusions from them. I refer to this as 'analytical' scholarship. Included also, however, is the more common form of scholarship that looks primarily at the competition law of one foreign system, but in so doing may also identify differences between it and one or more other systems. I call this 'comparative descriptive' writing.

We will not, therefore, be concerned with material that merely describes some aspect of a foreign competition law system—for example, an article about how mergers are treated under the law of X. In one sense, comparison occurs wherever an observer from one system represents material from another system in the observer's language, but this 'implicit' comparison has been little studied and is beyond the scope of this essay.

II. Comparative Competition Law: A Global View

Comparative competition law calls for a global perspective because competition itself is increasingly global. In this section, therefore, I employ a wide lens to sketch an overview of comparative competition law writing. This task is made manageable by the relative paucity of relevant scholarship in countries outside the US and Europe. My objective here is to identify general patterns of comparative competition law scholarship, indicating the factors that influence such writing generally as well as those that distinguish among groups of writers and types of writing.

1. Shared Influences on Competition Law Scholarship

Several sets of factors shape comparative competition law scholarship everywhere. One is primarily domestic—or at least not directly transnational. Competition law systems operate under economic and often political pressure, because decisions in this area can directly shape the strategic and tactical choices of businesses, and they can also have significant impacts on national economic interests. Moreover, competition laws often impact large business firms in major decisions such as mergers and acquisitions, and such firms often have political influence. Such decisions are often also politically sensitive because they may impact national economic policies. These factors together tend in varying degrees to impact the operation of competition law systems everywhere.

They may also influence comparative competition law scholarship. They give practitioners significant incentives to write in the area, because it may attract or maintain clients. They may also tend to induce descriptive rather than analytical writing, because purely descriptive writing generally costs less to produce in terms of time and resources and because it tends to be 'safer' for practitioners to write, since it does not involve taking evaluative positions that might offend clients or potential clients. Finally, these considerations may tend to induce perspectives, values, methods, and conclusions that are likely to be rewarded by clients. For example, large businesses generally favour less stringent enforcement of competition laws, and thus tend to favour legal doctrines and procedures that make such enforcement less likely. The growth of very large, globe-spanning law firms intensifies these effects.

There are also transnational factors that influence comparative competition law virtually everywhere. One relates to the reach of national laws beyond borders. Because the process of economic competition often stretches beyond the borders of a single jurisdiction, the effects of anticompetitive conduct on a single market may involve many states. Since competition laws may be applied on the basis of the effects of conduct as well as on the basis of its physical location, numerous national laws may be applicable to the same conduct. This 'extraterritorial' effect of competition laws brings them into contact in ways that can bring much attention to the encounters, and comparative writing in this area is often associated with these issues. This writing generally focuses on the potential applicability of foreign law to particular conduct and possibly on its consequences. It seldom engages, however, in careful analysis of how foreign systems function.

Second, competition law is often associated with international trade issues. In this context, writing about a foreign competition law system is often part of a political battle about trade issues rather than an attempt to depict, much less understand, the foreign competition law. There was, for example, a spate of US writing about the Japanese antitrust system during the early 1990s, when the US sought to reduce the trade surplus with Japan by pressuring the Japanese to enforce their antitrust laws more forcefully (the so-call 'strategic impediments initiative'). Much of it was superficial and polemical, and it seldom enhanced understanding of the operation and influence of the Japanese antitrust system.

Another set of influences that operates 'universally' involves transnational cooperative efforts by states and international organizations to influence competition law developments. The US, the EU, Japan, and, to a lesser extent, Australia and others provide 'technical assistance' and other forms of aid to countries that are in the process of developing their competition law systems, often with the expectation that their assistance will give them influence on those developments. There are also transnational efforts to 'harmonize' competition laws.[1] The OECD seeks, for

---

[1] See, eg, Jürgen Basedow (ed), *Limits and Control of Competition with a View to International Harmonization* (2002). See also Eleanor M. Fox, 'Toward World Antitrust and Market Access', (1997) 91 *American Journal of International Law* 1 and Diane Wood, 'Soft Harmonization among Competition Laws: Track Record and Prospects', (2003) 48 *Antitrust Bulletin* 305.

example, to create greater uniformity in competition laws among its members (mainly developed countries). The International Competition Network, which was formed in 2001, pursues the same objective on a global level, primarily by developing 'best practice' guidelines. In these contexts, competition law officials and participating lawyers are the main players, while scholars have so far played limited roles. The importance of these initiatives deserves serious scholarly examination of their decision-making processes as well as their effects.

Finally, since the late 1990s a global epistemic community promoting 'competition culture' has begun to take rudimentary shape. Competition lawyers, officials, and scholars now have fora such as the annual Fordham Corporate Law Institute meeting in New York City, where they can meet and discuss competition law from a global and sometimes comparative perspective. They also have publications such as, for example, the *World Competition Law and Economics Review* that are read on a broad transnational basis. In the last few years European scholars and practitioners have founded several new journals with this objective. While their focus tends to be on European and US law, the objective is to become increasingly global in scope. One is *Concurrences*, which is written primarily in French. Another is the *Journal of Competition Law*, which is published in Germany, but includes articles in German, English, and French. A third is the *Journal of Competition Law and Economics*, which is published in the UK. These developments create important incentives and opportunities for comparative competition law scholarship.

2. Lines of Separation: The Pieces and the Whole

While these factors influence comparative competition law scholarship wherever it is written and by whomever it is written, many factors still separate and divide the universe of scholarship in this area. There is not yet a global 'community of comparative competition law scholarship'.

The most prominent lines of division are national and linguistic. Although the beginnings of change are visible in some places, as noted above, those writing about comparative competition law still generally write for audiences that are primarily defined along national and linguistic lines. Although writing in the area is increasingly in English, most of it is still in national languages and directed to national audiences. There has been some regionalization of these audiences, but it has occurred only recently. Moreover, it has been generally limited to Europe, where it has been spurred by the EU developments that became effective in May of 2004 in which primary enforcement responsibilities were decentralized to the member states.

Another dividing line on the map of competition law scholarship is between traditional legal methodology, on the one hand, and economic or 'law and economics' discourse, on the other. Competition law literature is written primarily by lawyers for lawyers, but in recent years the amount of that literature that is written by economists and those using predominantly economic analysis has grown significantly. Some of that literature is accessible to lawyers without special training, but some of it is not (advanced calculus being beyond the competence of most lawyers). This economics-based literature is far more common in the US than elsewhere.

The third factor is more fundamental and more difficult to assess. Ironically, the centrality of US antitrust law to comparative competition law scholars divides their scholarly universe. US antitrust law is the common reference point for competition law scholarship everywhere. All must know about it, and all write in its shadow. This creates two distinct literatures. On the one hand, US writers look out from this experience and usually say 'follow us'. Those outside the US look *at* US antitrust law and relate it to their own situations. The *views from within* and the *views from outside* US antitrust have fundamentally different relationships to the subject-matter.

III. COMPARATIVE COMPETITION LAW SCHOLARSHIP IN THE UNITED STATES

Comparative competition law scholarship in the US reflects the development of US antitrust law, its role in the world, and the power and influence of the US. Pervasive within the US antitrust community is the view that the US has the right answers to basic antitrust questions, specifically, that it has the best methods of analysis and generally the best institutional framework (primarily because it accords a dominant role to courts and private enforcement mechanisms). In this view, others should emulate US antitrust law because it is the best system. We will explore how this view has come to dominate, and we will identify some of its implications.

1. Form and Content

US comparative competition writing is predominantly descriptive scholarship, and there is a vast amount of it. Much of it takes the following form: A practitioner or government official writes a description of an aspect or a component of a foreign competition law that she has encountered and publishes it in one of the many practitioner-oriented or student-run law journals in the US. Two factors make this practice common. One is that there are many US lawyers in large international law firms, and they often encounter issues relating to foreign competition laws. They have professional incentives to 'publicize' that they have had this particular type of experience. The other factor is that publication is relatively easy. There are many law journals of many types in the US, some of which do not have high publication standards, so a prospective author can usually find one somewhere that will publish an article. Such articles may include comments about differences between the encountered foreign law and US law and about the deficiencies of the foreign law in relation to US law, but that is not their main function, and in this context there is little incentive for writers to examine deeper issues of the operation of foreign systems or to engage in careful analytical comparison.

In contrast to the large amount of single-system descriptive scholarship, there is relatively little analytical or normative writing in the area. Material that does fall into this category typically represents what I call 'follow me' scholarship—in which the writer describes a foreign competition law system and then comments at some length about the discrepancies between that system and the US system, often suggesting that the foreign law or practice should more closely approximate the US model.[2]

Several features of the US system tend to be prominent in these comparisons by US writers. Most prominent is the role of economic analysis. Specifically, the common assumption is that economic analysis should be the exclusive basis for competition law and that it should utilize the 'consumer welfare' standard of economic analysis employed in US antitrust. Foreign systems tend to be criticized where they pursue goals other than efficiency or do not rely on the consumer welfare standard for analysis. A second prominent feature is the role of private enforcement. US scholars typically criticize systems that do not have extensive private enforcement. Third, they also tend to see the enforcement of prohibitions of cartel agreements as the most important feature of antitrust and to assign relatively little importance to most other forms of anticompetitive conduct. Finally, US writers in the area tend to disparage the concept of abuse of a dominant position, which is frequently found in competition law systems outside the US, criticizing it for being too vague and potentially too restrictive.

In terms of subject-matter, a high percentage of comparative competition law writing in the US relates to the competition law of the EU. This is the foreign competition law that tends to be enforced most vigorously and is, therefore, the one that is of greatest practical concern for businesses and their advisors. It is also the one that is most likely to be encountered by them. Writers typically find EU law to be deficient to the extent that it differs from US antitrust law.

---

[2] For a thoughtful example referring to Japanese competition law enforcement, see eg Harry First, 'Antitrust Enforcement in Japan', (1995) 64 *Antitrust LJ* 137.

In recent years, it has been criticized, in particular, for not being sufficiently economics-oriented.[3]

2. The Leadership Perspective

The perspective from which most US comparative material is written is best seen as a 'leader's' perspective. As noted above, the assumption is typically that the US antitrust system is superior and that others should follow the US model. This perspective is the result of the unique evolution of the US system and special features of its relations with other competition law systems.

The US system was the first prominent antitrust system, and this long ago accustomed members of the US antitrust community to seeing their system as the 'father' of modern competition law and to having it seen as such by others. This father image has tended to generate and support the impression that others do and should look to the US system for leadership and that US antitrust law cannot be expected to learn from others.

This image was strengthened in the aftermath of World War II. The US promoted antitrust as an export that could help to democratize countries such as Germany and Japan, even imposing a self-styled antitrust system in both countries during the occupation period and requiring that some form of competition law be continued after the occupation was over.[4] These steps have led many to forget that there had been a different model of competition law in Europe in the 1920s and to associate the concept of competition law with US antitrust and with US political hegemony and economic success.

The fall of the Soviet Union and the successes of the US economy in the 1990s brought renewed attention to this area of law around the world, and this attention has tended to emphasize the leadership role of US antitrust. The US has promulgated its version of antitrust in many areas, touting it as an important factor in building economic progress and political stability in countries previously operating on non-market principles. It has been prominent in providing technical assistance to developing countries, and US officials and lawyers have generally been in the forefront of international initiatives in this area. All of this reinforces the image of the US as the most prominent antitrust system—that is, the 'leader' in the field.

Developments within US antitrust are also part of this story. One involves the domestic prominence of antitrust during the 1950s and 1960s. It developed during this period into a central factor in business planning in the US, because the

---

[3] See eg Barry E. Hawk, 'System Failure: Vertical Restraints and EC Competition Law', (1995) 32 *Common Market LR* 973.

[4] See John O. Haley, *Antitrust in Germany and Japan: The First Fifty Years, 1947–1998* (2001).

antitrust laws were interpreted broadly and enforced vigorously. This required business decision-makers and their legal advisors to pay close attention to it, and it led to much writing on the subject. One result was a vast fund of cases and a deep scholarly literature. Another consequence, however, was much resentment among American businesses, who complained about what they considered the extensive interference in their decisional latitude that antitrust represented.

This combination of prominence and resentment led to radical changes in US antitrust law's basic principles and modes of analysis. It also provided US antitrust with a 'message' that has helped to reinforce its leadership role. Dissatisfaction with the expansive view of antitrust that prevailed in the 1960s helped to generate the so-called 'antitrust revolution' that began in the late 1970s. Scholars identified with the 'law-and-economics' (L&E) movement argued that the goals of antitrust should be defined much more narrowly than they traditionally had been, specifically, that they should be determined *solely* by reference to economic theory.[5] They further specified a specific type of economic theory that should serve as the basis of antitrust analysis. It is often referred to as 'Chicago School' analysis. It uses the language and methods of price theory in assessing whether conduct is anticompetitive. These ideas about goals and methods of antitrust quickly won acceptance during the 1980s, riding the political popularity of the 'leave business alone' reforms of President Ronald Reagan.

The rapid victory of this conception of antitrust has imbued members of the US antitrust community with confidence that the current US system represents the 'right answers' to basic antitrust questions. The image of US antitrust history that took shape then and that has been nurtured continually since then is that antitrust law is important, but that it took a 'wrong turn' in the US in the 1950s and 1960s, when it allowed general concerns about fairness and bigness to influence decisions rather than grounding those decisions in sound economic theory. In this image, US antitrust law has learned from its mistakes, and scholars and judges came to realize that law and economics methodology provides a better grounded and more intellectually convincing basis for antitrust. This image of the early mistakes of US antitrust is important for our purposes because it leads US scholars to scorn forms of antitrust that resemble those earlier 'mistakes'. A common refrain is that 'we did that, and we know that it doesn't work'.

The rapid 'victory' of the law and economics conception of antitrust law has also created a kind of post-victory mode of scholarship in which there is often little willingness to consider perspectives other than those of the victors. The 'big battle' over goals and methods has been won, and there is little reason to pay attention to the views of the 'losers'. When this lens is applied internationally, it readily leads to the conclusion that foreign systems that are concerned with issues

---

[5] The classic work is Robert Bork, *The Antitrust Paradox* (1978). See also Richard Posner, *Economic Analysis of Law* (5th edn, 1998).

such as fairness that have been discredited in the US domestic context deserve little respect.

3. Internal Dynamics: Shaping Factors

Several features of the institutional and intellectual context of comparative competition law writing are particularly influential. One is the identity of academic writers. Analytical comparative competition law scholarship in the US is done primarily by scholars of US antitrust law rather than by comparative law specialists—that is, those that are either trained or primarily interested in analysing differences among legal systems. This means that they belong to the US antitrust community and are subject to the pressures and expectations of that community. While this undoubtedly brings deeper knowledge of the US side of the comparison, it may also narrow the scope and depth of comparative analysis.

This situation reflects the lack of interest shown by the comparative law community in competition law issues. Its agenda has traditionally focused on private law issues and, despite occasional appeals among its members for a broadening of the focus, this remains generally true. Perhaps more fundamentally, the general assumption that the US has little or nothing to learn from other systems significantly restricts incentives for comparative work. This will undoubtedly change as globalization forces a reorientation of priorities, but academic communities often react slowly to such external changes.

Given that those writing in comparative competition law come primarily from the antitrust community rather than the comparative law community, they are more likely to reproduce the perspectives of the antitrust community than if they came from the comparative law community. The US antitrust community is dominated by practitioners, with relatively few academics accorded high status within it. As a result, the interests and values of practitioners can be expected to play an important role in comparative scholarship, directly or indirectly. These values and interests vary, but practitioners have incentives to 'sell' the US model, because greater interest in that model from other countries tends to generate greater influence (and profits) for US practitioners. Moreover, a principal feature of the US model is extensive reliance on private enforcement, and this tends to benefit US lawyers by providing them with fee opportunities.

The patterns of influence and power within the US law school community also play a role in shaping comparative antitrust scholarship. A particularly salient factor here is that both comparative law and antitrust law tend to have limited influence in US law schools. This translates into limited support for comparative competition law scholarship. Comparative law scholarship has long been marginal in US law faculties for many reasons. One is the general tendency for US legal academics to assume that the US system has relatively little to gain by looking at other legal systems. Another is the fact that comparative scholarship tends to be relatively expensive compared with domestic scholarship, because it requires that scholars be supported in foreign travel and provided with foreign-language books and periodicals. Contemporary intellectual currents also tend to discourage support for comparative scholarship. For example, much value is attached within the legal academy to the proposition that scholarship should be directed at finding theoretical (and thereby also universal) 'truths', and this creates little space for comparative analysis.

Antitrust law now plays a relatively marginal role in the US law school world, although it was once highly influential. In the first three decades after the end of World War II antitrust scholarship was important because antitrust practice was important, but the law and economics revolution has tended to reduce the scope and severity of antitrust law, and this has correspondingly reduced the value attached to antitrust scholarship. Where antitrust scholarship has limited support, comparative scholarship in the area is likely to receive even less. This effect is enhanced by two assumptions of law and economics: (1) that law and economics is the only appropriate basis for antitrust law and (2) that it produces universally applicable principles. This leaves little room for comparative competition law writing.

This brief review of comparative competition law in the US and of the factors that influence it reveals the perspective from which it is written as well as some of its assumptions and biases. The almost universal assumption within the US antitrust community that US antitrust law and its methods are simply superior to other competition laws narrows the intellectual space within which comparative competition law can operate. It skews and somewhat denatures the comparative enterprise because it does not allow for assessment of the strengths, weaknesses, and consequences of different approaches to competition law. It also significantly distances US writing in the area from most of the writing produced elsewhere.

IV. COMPARATIVE COMPETITION LAW SCHOLARSHIP OUTSIDE THE UNITED STATES

The centrality of US antitrust law puts writers outside the US in a radically different intellectual position from that of their US analogues. It creates different perspectives and objectives, and it subjects writers to different influences and assumptions. 'Should we follow US law?' is a question that frames virtually all writing in the area, whether or not there is specific reference to it. In this section, I look first at traits common to non-US scholarship and then look more closely at such scholarship in specific regions.

1. US Antitrust Law as a Source of Data

It is important to distinguish between two very different uses of US antitrust experience. In one, US competition law is used as a source of data. The long history of US antitrust law makes it a valuable source of antitrust experience. There is an unparalleled depth of cases spanning more than a century of development, and the judicial opinions often contain far more factual material than is available in other systems. In addition, there is a rich body of scholarly writing about antitrust law that includes a wide variety of theoretical perspectives related to varied economic and political circumstances. Moreover, it is available in English, and it is thus far more accessible than it would have been in any other language. On the practical level, the value to non-US writers of knowing about US law and demonstrating publicly one's knowledge is particularly high, in large part because of the size of the US market and the large number of foreign companies operating there who are likely to need advice about US antitrust law. US antitrust law is thus a common reference point for all writing in the area, and this in itself represents a potent source of influence.

The other use is normative. US antitrust is often used as a source of authority for claims in foreign systems about what the law should be. In this use, a proponent of a particular viewpoint or decision in a foreign system seeks to strengthen her argument by showing that what is proposed is the same as or similar to US law or practice in the area. In this sense, US antitrust represents 'authority' that can be used in support of a proposition. Similarity to the US system in and of itself supports the proposition. No further analysis is required. This gives descriptive comparison implied normative force, because all that is necessary to support a normative claim is to establish identity or similarity.

Authority for this use of US antitrust law rests on several factors. One is the 'father' image. The status of US antitrust as the oldest and best-established antitrust system in the world itself tends to confer authority on it. A decision-maker in another country, particularly one with a poorly developed competition law, can often find support for her positions by identifying them as borrowing from the US just because it is the oldest and best-established system. A more sophisticated version of this claim is that the long history of US antitrust does not by itself justify its authority, but that US antitrust has undergone a long process of trial and error learning that has revealed mistakes and produced a better system. US writers are fond of using this latter version of the claim.

US economic successes, particularly since the early 1990s, tend to further justify this use. The soaring US economy of the 1990s led many economic and legal policy-makers to see it as a confirmation of the superiority of US economic policy. Antitrust is part of that economic policy package and derives authority from the success of that package. Ideological factors sometimes enhance this attractiveness and thus augment the authority attached to the package. US antitrust is associated with 'US-style capitalism', which for many means reduced government interference with business, and thus those who support this basic value structure may support US antitrust because it is assumed to be based on these values. This is particularly attractive today, because the current form of US antitrust is significantly less restrictive in many areas than were earlier forms of US law. The claim is not based on careful analysis of the relationship between US antitrust law and particular economic outcomes, but on the attractiveness of the policy package in which antitrust is included and on assumptions about its ideological underpinnings.

US antitrust law also gains authority and attractiveness by virtue of its role as a surrogate for an international standard. In the context of globalization, a competition law decision-maker can often expect support for a proposition that represents 'what others are doing'—that is, an international standard. There is no international standard, however, and US antitrust law is often assumed to be the closest available approximation of such a standard, the point to which all converge.

Note that the low cost of arguments based on authority makes them particularly attractive for use by those with limited resources and those for whom lack of experience or other access constraints create higher costs for engaging in more sophisticated analysis of the issues. This means that such arguments are likely to be most attractive to those who are least likely to be in a position to evaluate them—for example, in developing countries.

Quite apart from the conscious uses of US antitrust law just described, there is also a cognitive dimension to its influence that is seldom noticed. Because of its long-standing position as the central point of reference in the conceptual world of writers in the area, it naturally frames views and imbeds assumptions. This occurs at the cognitive level, often without the writer's conscious awareness of its influence on what is being written. The use of US antitrust law as a standard of reference also simplifies and structures the potentially relevant data, thereby making the decision-maker's task easier.

US economic and political power sometimes also directly supports the influence of US antitrust law on non-US writing. Here the issue is the capacity of public and private interests in the US to influence foreign competition law decisions through the application of pressure, the explicit or implicit offer of resources, or simply through the perception among foreign decision-makers that either of these tools might be employed. These issues are seldom discussed in the comparative competition law literature, but their influence can be extensive. Where these kinds of factors have significant influence on decisions, there are likely to be few incentives for serious scholarship, because scholars have few opportunities even to learn of them, much less to evaluate them in any meaningful way.

One form of power is governmental. The US government actively seeks to influence decisions in foreign systems. Sometimes this is overt and well-publicized, as, for example, during the early 1990s when the US government pressured the government of Japan to increase enforcement of its antitrust laws, thereby hoping to increase the access of US firms to the Japanese market and reduce the balance of payments imbalance between the two countries. More commonly, it takes place in the context of negotiations and technical assistance programmes, where a country can expect to gain US support and/or assistance by conforming its conduct to the wishes of the US.

Private power plays similar, less obvious, but potentially more pervasive roles. Large multinational corporations represent a potentially significant source of income for lawyers and legal consultants in the competition law field. This creates incentives that encourage writers to reach conclusions that tend to be preferred by such firms. In addition, during the last few years, very large international law firms have formed, primarily to provide services to these businesses. For many foreign legal professionals, the potential professional benefits of finding favour with such law firms can be a powerful incentive to write in some ways and not to write in others. This factor can be expected to have its greatest impact on scholarship where law professors are also heavily engaged in private practice, which is common in many parts of the world.

Such factors often shape and sometimes distort writing in the area. Where, for example, competition law decisions are made on the basis of tacit assumptions of US predominance or actual concerns for US political or economic power, the room for serious inquiry into those decisions tends to be limited. Where, for example, statutory texts are enacted in order to send signals to US officials or businesses rather than with the intent of enforcing those provisions, scholars have little reason to take the provisions seriously.

The influences discussed in this section do not affect comparative competition law writers in the US. Here the expectations are reversed. For example, a claim that a US antitrust decision-maker should take a decision in order to conform to the competition law of Japan or France is likely to be met with incredulity, and it would be far more likely to weaken than to strengthen the claim. One role for comparative competition law scholarship is to reveal the extent of these influences, so that each group of writers can more readily recognize the influences that may affect the other.

2. General Characteristics and Influences

We can now identify some general characteristics of this writing and some of the factors that influence those characteristics. These tend to be related to the Civil law context of most of the relevant systems,[6] although in the competition law area writing from common law legal systems (eg Australia) often exhibits patterns similar to those in Civil law countries.

One trait is the sparsity of the literature. With notable exceptions for Japan and a few countries in Europe, there has been relatively little writing in the area, and what has been written is primarily descriptive. Several factors may account for this. Perhaps most important is the general lack of support for comparative competition law within universities. Analytical writing is usually done by scholars, but in most countries competition law itself is relatively new and undeveloped, and thus it is of often limited practical importance and enjoys relatively little serious scholarly attention. This is often compounded by the lack of an intellectual 'home' for competition law, particularly in countries of the Civil law tradition. In these systems there is often a sharp distinction in thought and institutions between the realms of public and of private law, and competition law does not fit easily into either of the two categories. It tends in most places to be seen as part of administrative law. Yet it protects rights that can be and sometimes are understood as private in nature because they protect a private sphere of action against other economic actors, and in some systems they can be enforced in at least some cases in private law courts. Given this situation, there are often few incentives for scholars to engage in this type of scholarship.

A second prominent trait in this writing is its administrative focus. This results from the predominantly administrative character of competition law in most countries outside the US, and it tends to colour not only the issues that are treated, but also the goals and methods of scholarship. It means, for example, that administrative issues such as the range of discretion for administrative decision-making are prominent in the literature. It also tends to limit the amount of legal information available to scholars. In many systems, for example, reported decisions contain little information, and there is little or no judicial review of administrative decisions, so there are comparatively few cases available for analysis. Furthermore, decision-making in the area often involves significant discretion and opacity, with the result that scholars often have little data to investigate. Finally, in some systems competition law decisions can be significantly influenced by political factors, and this also limits incentives for legal scholars to write in the area.

The third general trait is less obvious, but it pervades the literature. It is a general sense of uncertainty about the nature and status of competition law. Should it be viewed as administrative law or private law or some hybrid? What are its benefits and harms? Is our law merely a token that was required by international considerations (such as qualifying for a loan from the World Bank)? If so, why should we enforce it seriously? Is it even law? Uncertainty about the fundamental characteristics of

---

[6] This legal tradition includes legal systems derived from or closely related to the legal culture of continental Europe (eg Latin America and, to a lesser extent, some countries of Asia and Africa).

competition law and its relation to legal, political, and economic systems often lurks in the background of comparative competition law writing.

3. Europe

We now look more closely at particular places on the map of comparative competition law scholarship outside the US. Most of it comes from Europe, where there is a significant amount of analytical comparative writing in this area. Until recently, however, most of the writing was concentrated in a small number of European countries.

(a) The Evolution of Competition Law in Europe

A brief look at the development of competition law in Europe provides the key to understanding the current status of comparative competition law scholarship there.[7] Comparative writing about competition law has deeper roots in Europe than is often assumed, primarily because the history of competition law in Europe is longer and richer than is often assumed. Arguably, this form of scholarship developed even earlier in Europe than it did in the US.

The starting-point for this evolution is the 1890s in Vienna, where a highly educated administrative elite recognized the potential value of a law that could protect the competition process from distortion and drafted legislation that sought that objective. Although the proposal was not enacted, its basic ideas gained the attention of important groups in Germany, where there were unsuccessful efforts in the early 1900s to pass competition legislation. In both contexts serious comparative writing accompanied the legislative efforts.

During the 1920s, the first modern European competition laws were enacted in several countries, the most important of which was Germany. This led to significant interest in the issue in Germany and in a few other countries, and by the end of the decade Europe was developing its own form of competition law, one that differed significantly from US antitrust. It centred on giving administrative agencies the authority to intervene in cases in which companies 'abused' their economic power. This evolution was accompanied by significant comparative literature in the area, again primarily in Germany. Some writers had some knowledge of US law and experience, but it was usually quite limited. Most considered the US model to be ineffective, even counterproductive, and certainly not appropriate for European conditions. The economic depression of the 1930s, fascism, and then World War II swept away the existing legislation.

---

[7] This section is based on the detailed examination in David J. Gerber, *Law and Competition in Twentieth Century Europe: Protecting Prometheus* (1998, paperback edn, 2001).

The end of World War II brought a fundamentally changed situation for competition law and for comparative scholarship in the area. Pre-war experience in Europe was generally discredited by the events of the 1930s and 1940s. Attention now focused on the US and its promotion of competition law as a weapon in the battle for freedom and against the forces of collectivism. Two paths emerged from this situation, and they have only recently been rejoined.

Spurred by the disasters of the first decades of the twentieth century and by the perceived need to reconstruct Germany along lines very different than those that had prevailed in those decades, Germany constructed a competition law system that quickly became the best-developed system in Europe and that has remained so, at least until recently. It was constructed on the basis of (1) ideas and plans generated by a small group of legal scholars and economists that had operated underground during the Nazi period and World war II (the so-called 'ordoliberals') and (2) experience with antitrust law acquired during the Occupation.

European countries other than Germany were slow to develop their own competition law systems. Most introduced some form of administrative control of abusive and anticompetitive practices, but many of these systems were for decades of marginal practical importance. They typically operated primarily as policy instruments with little principled content and minimal legal development. Only gradually have these countries developed systems that are important factors in business and legal operations. Many, but not all, of these systems had begun to have significant independence and significantly increased importance by the 1990s.

One of the key factors in the development of competition law in Europe has been the process of European integration. The Rome Treaty, which created the predecessor of the European Union in 1957, contained provisions for the protection of competition. These were gradually given legal contours and institutional support, and by the 1970s they represented a well-developed competition law that contained elements of both the administrative control model found at the national level in most Member States and a more juridically oriented system similar to the one in Germany.[8] The development of EU-level competition law encouraged awareness of competition law issues among practitioners and businesses, and since the 1980s most national level systems have evolved along lines similar to those of the EU. In 2004, major reforms were introduced that, *inter alia*, give primary enforcement responsibility to the Member States and weave their enforcement systems together with the European Commission in a 'network' of cooperation and mutual obligations. These reforms also required that European Community competition law generally be applied in all cases other than those whose effects are limited to one state. Thus, for the first time, all Member States are required to apply the same substantive law in most cases.

---

[8] For further analysis and comparison of US and EU competition law and experience, see David J. Gerber, 'Competition', in *Oxford Handbook of Legal Studies* (2004), 510 ff.

(b) EU-Level Comparisons

Much of the comparative writing on competition law in Europe relates EU law to US law. In addition to large amounts of descriptive writing, there is also significant analytical and normative writing. Much of it is framed by the issue of the extent to which the EU should adopt elements of the US system. This has created a basic pattern for the writing in which some authors argue for adoption of US elements, usually citing the successes of the US system and its methodological and/or juridical superiority. Other writers resist the move, typically arguing that the conditions in Europe differ from those in the US and that therefore the US system is inappropriate for Europe. This pattern sets a tenor for the genre which constrains the range of arguments and of intellectual inquiry. In particular, it puts those sceptical of US orthodoxy in a defensive posture.

While this basic structure has remained largely unchanged, the relative strength of the two basic arguments has varied over time. Until roughly the mid-1990s, the debates focused primarily on specific doctrinal issues. There were extensive debates, for example, about the propriety of including something like the US 'rule of reason' in EU law. Given the highly developed state of US antitrust law and the relative newness of EU law, European writers acknowledged the value of looking to US experience, particularly regarding the analysis of particular kinds of conduct. There was, however, relatively little direct borrowing of major elements of US antitrust law or of its procedural, methodological, or institutional elements. The argument that US antitrust law was not appropriate for European circumstances was generally successful in these contexts.

Beginning in the late 1990s, however, the balance seemed to shift toward the introduction of more US elements into EU law and to embrace more methodological and institutional issues. The comparative literature has focused on issues such as, for example, the introduction of a leniency programme into EU law. Most important, however, is the current debate over whether to adopt the basic analytical methods of US antitrust law. 'Should the EU change its basic methods to rely more heavily on the type of economic analysis used in US antitrust?' is a question that has been very prominent in the literature. Such issues are impliedly comparative, because the arguments in favour of introducing these elements usually rest on the influence and example of US antitrust law. The Commission has moved in the direction of US antitrust in both of the above examples and in others. The claim that US experience may not be appropriate for Europe seems to have weakened. There has been an increasing tendency to assume that for these purposes the US antitrust system is directly comparable to the EU system, and since the economic vitality of the US in relation to the EU is often attributed to differences in regulatory burdens, this had led to greater willingness to adopt US methods.

(c) National Level Comparative Writing

Comparative competition law writing in Europe also has a national dimension in which European writers analyse the relationship between their national systems and other national systems. Prior to the modernization reforms in 2004, European national competition systems developed and operated independently of each other and of the EU. Even where they did look at other European systems, political and nationalistic considerations often deterred them from acknowledging 'borrowing'. The 2004 reforms have changed this situation dramatically. On the one hand, they have significantly reduced the importance of substantive differences between the systems. On the other hand, however, they now require that competition officials deal with each other frequently and often intensely, making knowledge of other European systems increasingly valuable. In particular, procedural, institutional, and methodological differences take on increased importance.

Germany has produced the most extensive body of comparative competition law scholarship in Europe. It includes not only descriptive material, but also much analytical and normative writing. German scholars have been actively engaged with the issue of comparative competition law since the 1920s, when, for example, the Norwegian competition law experience was regularly reported on and analysed in the leading German competition law journal. The impetus for this scholarship came initially from the practical consideration that Germany adopted an early form of competition law in 1923 and from the participation of large German firms in cartel activities during this period.

The end of World War II spurred renewed interest in comparative competition law, but turned attention to US law, as writers sought to use US experience in developing the new German system that was instituted in 1957.[9] The strong comparative law tradition in German universities and legal circles gave support to this development, as did the commitment of two generations of scholars to develop intellectual and institutional bulwarks against the kinds of totalitarian tendencies that befell Germany in the first half of the twentieth century. German scholars have paid relatively little attention to comparisons involving institutional and methodological comparisons and have focused predominantly on issues of substantive law. In recent years, however, some have begun to pay increasing attention to the role of economics and its role in competition law analysis.

Most other Western European countries have seen some comparative competition law writing, but it has varied widely in amount and in focus, depending on factors such as the practical importance of the domestic competition law, the country's relationship to the EU, and university and intellectual structures and interests. Most of the national level comparisons have related to US law, although smaller states generally have paid less attention to this comparison. Until recently,

---

[9] See eg Wolfgang Fikentscher, *Wettbewerb und Gewerbicher Rechtschutz* (1957).

the only European country that was used to any significant extent for comparative purposes was Germany. The similarities of its legal system to other continental countries, its rich experience, and the deep literature that accompanies it made comparison particularly useful. Given the limited knowledge of German among scholars in many countries, however, its use has been limited. Moreover, the politics of European integration often call for concealment of national influences on EU developments, and this has combined with lingering resentments of the war years and fears of German domination to further limit comparative writing focusing on Germany.

Since the introduction of major reforms in 1998 in the UK, the competition law system of the UK has developed rapidly, and it is now increasingly looked to by other Europeans for comparative purposes. The new UK system has emphasized an increased use of price-theoretic economic analysis, and thus the turn toward such analysis in the European Commission has led to much interest in UK experience. The competition law systems of Italy and the Netherlands have also been used for comparative purposes in recent years. A few examples of comparative writing at the national level will give a sense of its variety and of some of its more important patterns.

In France, for example, comparative competition law was long relatively neglected. There were a few scholars with interest in the area, but it has not generally been considered an important area until recently. French competition law was itself relatively unimportant until recently, and, as a result, courses in French universities have traditionally been rare. French traditions of managing key aspects of the economy from Paris and allowing government to support particular companies and particular industries have tended to minimize interest in competition law. Yet several important French scholars of comparative competition law have emerged in recent years.[10] Other European countries with similar etatistic traditions present similar patterns.

Comparative competition law writing in the UK was relatively limited until the late 1990s, when the above-mentioned reforms began to generate serious comparative analysis and promised to increase significantly the practical importance of competition law issues. In the early 2000s, interest in the topic increased even further, as the rapid growth of transnational law firms and reform of the EU's competition law system seemed to open new opportunities for UK institutions and individuals. Most of the interest has focused on comparisons with the US system.[11]

Comparative writing about competition law was generally limited in Sweden until Sweden began the process of applying for membership in the EU in the early

---

[10] See eg Laurence Idot, 'L'internationalisation du droit de la concurrence', *Cahiers Droit de l'Entreprise—La Semaine Juridique* (2000), 27 ff.

[11] See eg Valentine Korah, 'From Legal Form toward Economic Efficiency—Article 85(1) of the EEC Treaty in Contrast to US Antitrust', (1990) *Antitrust Bulletin* 1009 and Richard Whish, *Competition Law* (5th edn, 2003).

1990s.[12] Its political-business elite had decided in the 1950s that competition law could be useful in sharpening the competitive capacities of some of its industries, so competition law was given a degree of institutional support, but there was relatively little comparative writing about it. When Sweden applied for membership in the EU, however, it had to assess the impact of membership on its own laws and institutions, and thus a few important scholars engaged in serious comparisons with EU law and, to a lesser extent, with other European competition laws (primarily German competition law).[13]

Italy presents a very different picture. Although it was a founding member of the EU and thus was confronted with competition law issues from the inception of the European integration process, Italy chose not to have its own competition law until 1990. One reason for this delay was the claim that it was simply better to let the European Commission worry about competition issues. There was a widely expressed concern that if Italy established a competition law system, it might not work effectively. Others feared that if it did work effectively, it would hamper Italian economic development. When Italy did enact a competition law system, however, it did so with careful comparative preparation, and a comparative literature quickly developed in conjunction with it.[14]

(d) Vertical Comparison: EU and Member States

A third dimension of comparative writing in Europe focuses on the relationship between EU law and national laws. This dimension was of minor importance until the idea of decentralizing competition law enforcement began to gain momentum in the late 1990s, and with the impetus of the 2004 reforms it has developed rapidly. With all Member States now required to apply EU competition law in most cases, officials and lawyers have strong incentives to learn about the similarities and differences between their systems and the EU system. While in the early stages of modernization this interest has often related to substantive law issues, the focus is turning to procedural and methodological comparisons.

4. Asia and the Development Issue

Outside Europe and the US, serious interest in competition law tends to be a recent phenomenon about which there has been little writing. With the rapid growth in the number of competition law systems during the 1990s and their growing importance, however, this situation is changing rapidly. Increasing numbers of

---

[12] There was, however, one major exception. See Ulf Bernitz, *Marknadsraett* (1969).

[13] See eg Nils Wahl, *Konkurrensskada* (2000).

[14] See eg Franco Romani, 'Pensiero economico, pensiero giuridico e concorrenza', in Nicolo Lipari and Ignazio Musu (eds), *La Concorrenza tra economia e diritto* (2000), 47.

scholars and others are now pursuing comparative competition law themes. Writing in these areas shares some of the general traits discussed above with European scholarship, but two factors distinguish it from European writing. One is the economic situation of most countries in this area. The need for rapid economic development tends to be a key theme in both competition policy thinking and in legal writing. The other is the role of European law and experience. Whereas in Europe the comparative focus is on the US, in Asia and elsewhere European law represents an alternative to the US model.

Japan is in many ways an anomaly in this context. In contrast to most of Asia, it has had a highly developed economy for decades. Moreover, its post-war experience is like none of the others in the group. Finally, Japanese scholars have written extensively in the comparative competition law area. Yet it also represents two issues that characterize the perspectives of the Asian group. Its comparative writing often looks to both European and US experience, and rapid development of export potential has been a central theme, at least until quite recently.

Japanese scholars have paid far more attention to comparative competition law than elsewhere in Asia, because competition law itself has played a larger role in Japan than elsewhere in Asia.[15] Although the US-style competition law that was imposed on Japan after World War II went largely unenforced until the 1980s, its importance has grown significantly since then. This has led to the development of a competition law community that includes perhaps 100 or so law professors who focus on competition law as well as a number of practitioners who write in the area. Much of the attention of this group centres on comparative issues. The group has its own professional association and publishes its own academic journal.

Two other Asian systems began to take competition law seriously in the 1980s—the Republics of Korea and China (Taiwan). In both cases, outside pressures (from sources such as the US and the World Bank) appear to have been major factors in this development. Nevertheless, increased enforcement has been accompanied by limited but serious academic interest in comparative competition law writing. One theme in this writing has been the relative value of the US and European models of competition law for the domestic legal system, as groups of scholars have formed around each, often on the basis of where they have studied.

China and India have only recently begun to take competition law seriously, and thus there has so far been little writing in the area. In China, this situation is changing rapidly, because Chinese leaders have been seriously considering the enactment of an anti-monopoly law since the late 1990s, and they have given indications that such a law will be enacted in the near future. This has led a small group of scholars and officials to study foreign competition law experience carefully, with the objective of deciding how to construct and implement a competition

---

[15] See eg Mitsuo Matsushita, *International Trade and Competition Law in Japan* (1993).

law.[16] One factor impeding the growth of this type of scholarship is the general weakness of comparative scholarship in Chinese law faculties. India passed new competition legislation in 2003, but its implementation has been embroiled in controversy, and serious scholarship in the area is still in the early stages of development.

5. Institutional Scholarship: International Organizations

One form of comparative competition law scholarship that has grown in importance recently comes from international organizations. It typically takes the form of reports either from the organization itself or from groups within or related to it. For example, the Organization for Economic Cooperation and Development (OECD) and the United Nations Commission on Trade and Development (UNCTAD) both produce reports on competition law that often have significant comparative components. Although they are often descriptive, they increasingly include serious collaborative scholarship that analyses differences and similarities among systems and provides insights into divergent ways of responding to the problems associated with them. Since its inception in 2001, the ICN (International competition network), a 'virtual' (Internet-based) organization consisting almost exclusively of competition law officials and practitioners, has begun to produce reports that have informational value, but at least so far it has not produced analytical scholarship to any significant extent. The value of this new type of comparative competition law scholarship is likely to continue to increase.

6. Conclusions

Comparative competition law scholarship outside the US thus presents a fundamentally different image than that produced by US-based writers. In contrast to the virtually uncontested confidence of US writers in the superiority of the US system, non-US scholars write in the shadow of perceived deficiencies. They are confronted with the image of US law as an older, better established system that also happens currently to be associated with economic vitality and supported by political and economic power. Their perspectives tend to be coloured and structured by the relationship of their own systems to the US system and to the question of what should be borrowed from US antitrust.

In Europe, comparative competition law writing has changed its focus in recent years, as the economic and political situations have changed. The economic

---

[16] See eg Xiaoje Wang, 'Chinese Anti-Monopoly Law: Issues Surrounding the Drafting of China's Anti-Monopoly Law', (2004) 3 *Washington University Global Studies L Rev* 285.

successes of the US, the increasing integration of Europe, and the 'modernization' of European competition law have made decision-makers and scholars increasingly open to the idea of borrowing from US antitrust. Yet there is also awareness that the needs of European integration, especially in light of the eastward expansion of the EU, may continue to call for competition law to play roles that it does not play in the US. In the context of integration, issues of the use of economic power and of the need for fairness—issues that have often driven European competition law development—sometimes resonate very differently than they do in the US context.

Outside Europe, the international pressures to adopt competition legislation and strengthen competition law systems encounter legal dynamics that differ sharply from those in the US and economic situations that place very different demands on competition law. In most of these countries, the economic development issue was (Japan) or remains (the others) central in analysing the operation of competition law institutions. This creates profound uncertainty about how the concepts and institutions of competition law can be adapted to their needs.

In both situations, the tools of comparative analysis that are currently deployed are often inadequate to the tasks involved. Analytical comparison is central to the entire enterprise of competition law because it can play an important role in revealing the various forces that influence competition law decisions and in identifying options for decision-makers. Its potential is, however, seldom realized.

V. Potential Roles for Comparative Competition Law Scholarship

Economic globalization frames comparative competition law scholarship and will continue to do so for the foreseeable future. It provides and structures opportunities and incentives for scholarship in ways and on levels that have not previously been part of scholarly agendas. As more markets and investments become transnational and global, situations in which the norms and procedures of two or more competition-law systems may apply to the same conduct increase correspondingly. This increases contact surfaces for competition laws and increases the potential for harmful and wasteful conflicts, but it also increases the potential value of cooperation and mutual understanding. Globalization also intensifies contacts between competition-law decision-makers and those who seek to influence them. This raises new points at which an enriched competition law agenda can add both private and public value. It also calls for tools that have been little developed in traditional national legal settings. In this context, decision-makers relate to each other across institutional, cultural, and linguistic boundaries that influence how they perceive the actions of others, how they interpret facts and statements, and how they react to them. So far comparative law scholarship has done little to develop such tools.[17]

1. The Changing Contexts of Comparative Competition Law

Comparative competition law can play roles in three main contexts associated with globalization. One involves private interests. As businesses develop strategies within a context of increasingly numerous competition laws and increasingly powerful competition authorities, the capacity to assess effectively the potential impact of these laws and to influence the potential decision-makers increases in value. Yet information and insights into these factors are costly and difficult to acquire, because the gap between formal statements of the law and actual decisional outcomes is particularly wide in competition law. This means that comparative competition law scholarship that focuses on how legal systems actually operate and on how they interact can be of great value. It can, for example, increase the capacity of business firms to predict legal and regulatory responses to particular forms of conduct. It can also be of central importance in negotiating with regulators and in structuring mutually beneficial transactions that might be subject to the competition laws of one or more states.

A second context relates to national interests. States have many interests in the operation of foreign competition law systems. For example, understanding foreign competition laws and recognizing similarities and differences among systems is valuable for competition law officials engaged in negotiations with their counterparts in other systems regarding how to deal with specific enforcement issues. As the web of laws in this area becomes denser and the interactions of officials become more frequent and intense, the value of knowledge and insights that enable officials to acquire influence among their peers grows, and it typically translates into benefits for the employing state. A further example relates to negotiations with businesses. Most states seek to attract investment from outside their borders, and sound and insightful knowledge of the field of competition law can be of value in attracting such investment and negotiating with firms about investments. Finally, the future development of competition law regimes in many countries remains highly contested, and the future forms of international cooperation in applying competition law norms are still very open. This helps explain why the EU, the US, and others have been competing to influence the development of competition laws in other parts of the world such as Asia and Latin America. The capacity of officials

---

[17] For further discussion, see David J. Gerber, 'Globalization and Legal Knowledge: Implications for Comparative Law', (2001) 75 *Tulane LR* 949 ff.

to influence those decisions will often depend at least in part on the depth of their knowledge of competition law regimes.

Third and from an academic standpoint perhaps most important is the public policy context. In part, the rapid spread of competition laws in recent years is a function of increased recognition of the potential public value of such regimes. Where competition is recognized as the primary mechanism for protecting and promoting economic well-being and producing the political and social benefits that tend to be associated with such wealth creation, laws to protect competition gain salience. There is, therefore, a significant public policy stake in understanding the operations and evolution of various forms of competition law and of developing regimes that effectively deal with the varying economic conditions around the world.

In each of these contexts, comparative competition law scholarship can provide value. It provides a means for better understanding foreign competition laws and their operations, but it also provides the only means of effectively evaluating past experience from other countries and relating it to current needs. As noted, the enactment and implementation of competition laws are subject to often powerful economic and political pressures that can lead to short-term political compromises, hasty and poorly informed decisions, and, ultimately, major mistakes. Knowledge and insights into competition law experience provide an important means of at least partially counterbalancing these forces.

2. Enriching the Comparative Competition Law Agenda

In order to respond effectively to these opportunities, comparative competition law agendas will need to be both broader and deeper. The traditional focus on formal rules, official acts, and published doctrinal statements will not disappear, but the new circumstances call for the addition of other perspectives and methods.

(a) Breadth and Depth

A broader scope of analysis is important for two main reasons. One is obvious; the other perhaps less so. The obvious reason is that many of the important issues will involve countries that have recently enacted significant competition laws for the first time (eg India) or that expect do so in the near future (eg China). In order to be relevant to their decisions, comparative competition law will have to address the specific situations in those countries. The less obvious reason is that the traditional focus on competition law experience in Europe and the US reflects the concerns and interests of politically stable and economically developed countries, and thus it treats a narrower set of issues than those that arise in countries that are less economically developed or that have unstable political and social regimes.

This greater breadth also combines with the forces of globalization to call for greater depth of analysis. Where competition law systems play different political and economic roles than the ones they traditionally have played in the US and Europe, comparative law scholarship needs to address those differences. Analysis of statutory texts and the decisions of courts and regulators is insufficient. It becomes important to understand all factors that influence decisions. The guiding question should be 'what is actually happening in the production of legal decisions?' This means that analysing institutions, procedures, power structures, and the like should become integral to comparative analysis.

(b) Interaction across Difference

Increased interaction among competition law systems and individuals that operate within them calls for fundamentally new thinking about comparative competition law. Comparative law has paid little attention to the issues of interaction among decision-makers. It has understood its task to be the analysis of systems and their components as objects that are related to each other through the analysis itself. The comparatist's analysis is what relates them, but otherwise they are not in contact. The process of comparison is seen as an assessment of objective states or conditions. Individual knowers and decision-makers are assumed to operate within largely closed systems.

As we have seen, however, this conception of comparison is inadequate in the context of globalization, where legal actors interact across differences in systems, and their perceptions of each other's actions shape those interactions. Here the systems interact in the minds, actions, and communications of legal actors. The ways in which they process information, construct and interpret messages, and use language are of paramount importance, and thus it is critical for comparative analysis to examine and illuminate those interactions.

One example suffices to illustrate the problem in the context of competition law. The EU's rejection in 2001 of a merger between two very large US companies (GE and Honeywell) that had been approved in the US is an example that led to conflict, acrimony, and various kinds of harm to transatlantic interactions. Much of the harm was the result of inadequate and erroneous information about differences in systems, failure to recognize differences in the ways in which information was interpreted on opposite sides of the Atlantic, and major misperceptions of the actions and communications of participants in the process.[18] Comparative competition law can provide insights and knowledge that should reduce these kinds of harms.

---

[18] See David J. Gerber, 'The European Commission's GE/Honeywell Decision: US Responses and their Implications', (2003) *Journal of Competition Law* 87.

3. Fashioning the Tools

The tools used in current comparative competition law are inadequate to respond to these needs and opportunities. They focus on formal uses of language—for example, statutes, cases, and administrative pronouncements, but this kind of analysis is often of little or no value for many of the tasks highlighted above.

Two types of deficiencies are prominent. One relates to the lack of interpretive context—the information necessary to identify what affects decisions. In a domestic context, the writer and the audience share extensive background knowledge about that system—that is, about the context in which formal decisions are made. They share knowledge about the institutions, relationships, and basic assumptions of decision-makers. In the comparative context, on the other hand, the author and the audience may share little or no knowledge of this kind. Official language may be largely useless in predicting outcomes, because readers are not in a position to assess the factors that influence decisions. In order to be useful, therefore, comparative law must recreate that context through analysis of patterns of influence on decision-making. The need for tools to recreate this context or acquire insights into it are nowhere greater than in the competition law area, precisely because of the particularly wide gap between official pronouncements and actual decision-making factors. Another is the incapacity of traditional tools to analyse interactions among legal actors and between legal actors and foreign systems. They are simply not designed to penetrate the cognitive dimensions of these interactions.

In fashioning tools to respond to these deficiencies, an interdisciplinary approach will be necessary that contains several elements. One element is provided by law and economics literature. This discipline is particularly important for the competition law area, because one of the main issues in competition law, as we have seen, is the role of economics. More fundamentally, however, this discipline uses economic methodology in legal contexts and provides a means of gaining insight into the interests that are likely to influence decision-making. In analysing interests and incentives, it in effect helps to recreate the context of decision-making that may be otherwise opaque to the foreign observer.[19] A second component is provided by behavioural sciences such as psychology, sociology, and political science. Such approaches have recently become more common in related areas such as public international law, but they continue to be rare in the area of comparative law. They can help illuminate, for example, the issues of communicating across cultural boundaries and structuring knowledge from foreign sources.

While these disciplines provide the material for fashioning comparative competition law tools, they will need to be specifically adapted to the needs we have

---

[19] For a comparative discussion, see Ugo Mattei, *Comparative Law and Economics* (1997).

outlined. Here there is neither theoretical guidance nor significant relevant experience. One way of doing this is to focus on legal decisions in relation to the various
systemic factors that influence them. I refer to this type of analysis as decisional
analysis.[20] Without going into details here, the concept is that systems shape the
decisions of actors in systematic ways that can be analysed and used to provide
insights into the kinds of issues discussed here. I include five basic categories of
influences: texts, interests, institutions, communities, and patterns of thought.
Relating them to legal decisions provides a means of fashioning more effective
comparative tools.

Finally, empirical scholarship should be used to investigate the actual operations
of these and other factors. In particular, correlations between interests and decisional outcomes can be subjected to rigorous empirical analysis. Before empirical
analysis can be employed effectively, however, conceptual and theoretical analysis
will be needed to provide relevant hypotheses of cause and effect. Such developments are likely to have to come from comparative law scholars rather than antitrust scholars who look at foreign legal systems, because the task calls for close
attention and examination of the process of comparison.

VI. Concluding Comments

The thinness, distortions, and general lack of development of comparative competition law are unfortunate. The rapid pace of economic globalization and the
proliferation of competition laws in most parts of the world greatly increase the
potential value of knowledge about competition law and insights into experiences
with it. They call for a body of literature that can serve as a source of perspectives,
analysis, and information. Yet the existing scholarship in the area seldom provides
more than superficial and often distorted presentations of competition law experience. As a result, decision-makers and scholars are often forced to rely on myths,
inaccurate images, and ideological categories in making their decisions and in
analysing and presenting competition law experience.

Nevertheless, this situation also provides opportunities. It means that the field is
not encumbered by established methods, dominant figures, or entrenched ways of
thinking. It is open for development and for new ideas about how to develop,
evaluate, and use knowledge about competition law, particularly in relation to the
phenomenon of economic globalization. Without the weight of a well-established

---

[20] For further discussion, see David J. Gerber, 'System Dynamics: Toward a Language of Comparative
Law', (1998) 46 *AJCL* 719 ff.

tradition, writers can more easily experiment, and they may also be in a better position both to draw on and to contribute to other scholarly traditions and communities.

Efforts to respond to these opportunities face major obstacles. One is the prospect of limited institutional support. Such an agenda has higher costs than many other forms of legal scholarship, while its value is not yet readily perceived. A second obstacle is the lack of expectations regarding this area of scholarship. Because it has not been prominent on the agendas of either competition law or comparative law, scholars have limited incentives to pursue interests in this area. The practical needs of business and public officials will undoubtedly increase expectations and opportunities and thus increase these incentives, but it remains to be seen how quickly academic communities respond to these factors. At least as important, as this chapter has revealed, are contemporary attitudes and perspectives about competition law. For example, those who are convinced that they have little or nothing to learn from other legal systems tend not to be particularly interested in the experience of foreign systems and have few incentives to invest in understanding and learning about such systems.

One factor that is likely to be central in overcoming these obstacles is greater awareness of the potential value of developing more extensive, more relevant, and more effective comparative competition law knowledge. Ironically, of course, increasing this awareness is difficult unless the scholarship in the area demonstrates its value. The onus thus falls on scholars to begin to develop the appropriate tools. Awareness of the challenges of globalization is likely to heighten interest in this approach. For example, for US writers, the need to work with and influence officials from other competition law systems is likely to increase recognition of the need to understand those systems more deeply and recognize the differences between their contexts and those of the US. For non-US writers, US law and experience will undoubtedly remain important to writing and thinking in this area, but it is now critical to examine that experience more carefully and to relate it analytically to the conditions found in other countries. For all, there is a critical need to reconceive competition law and to understand it as an international public good that can, if properly understood and used, bring much benefit. One task of writing in this area is to understand how these benefits can be achieved and this public good can be shared.

The development of transnational and eventually global communities of competition law scholarship could be of great value in achieving these objectives. To the extent that those interested in understanding and relating competition law dynamics and experience create and support such communities, they will generate a process that can, in turn, provide both incentives and support for advancing the kind of agenda sketched here. This has already begun to happen, but only to a very limited extent. International organizations sometimes seek to develop some of this knowledge, but their focus is generally on policy suggestions, and research is often subjected to the political and other agendas of the organization. There are also increasing numbers of transnational conferences in the area, but these are typically dominated by practitioners and government officials who tend to be primarily interested in practical issues and generally have little incentive to pursue the kinds of academic and scholarly projects to which I am referring. What is now needed is a greater focus on deeper understanding of the phenomenon of competition law in its varying forms and contexts.

BIBLIOGRAPHY

Edwards Corwin, *Trade Regulation Overseas: The National Laws* (1966)

Hervé Dumez and Alain Jeunemaitre, *La Concurrence en Europe* (1991)

Tony Freyer, *Regulating Big Business: Antitrust in Britain and America, 1880–1990* (1992)

Mitsuo Matsushita, *International Trade and Competition Law in Japan* (1993)

G. Bruce Doern and Stephen Wilks (eds), *Comparative Competition Policy* (1996)

Giuliano Amato, *Antitrust and the Bounds of Power* (1997)

Hanns Ullrich (ed), *Comparative Competition Law: Approaching an International System of Antitrust Law* (1997)

Spencer Waller, *Antitrust and American Business Abroad* (3rd edn, 1997)

David J. Gerber, *Law and Competition in Twentieth Century Europe: Protecting Prometheus* (1998, paperback edn, 2001)

John Haley, *Antitrust in Germany and Japan: The First Fifty Years, 1947–1998* (2001)

Jürgen Basedow (ed), *Limits and Control of Competition with a View to International Harmonization* (2002)

Josef Drexl, *The Future of Transnational Antitrust—From Comparative Competition Law to Common Competition Law* (2003)

Ky P. Ewing, *Competition Rules for the 21st Century* (2003)

Michael S. Gal, *Competition Policy for Small Market Economies* (2003)

Richard Whish, *Competition Law* (5th edn, 2003)

CHAPTER 38

COMPARATIVE CONSTITUTIONAL LAW

MARK TUSHNET

Harvard

I. Introduction: The Evolution of the Field of Comparative Constitutional Law

THE study of comparative constitutional law began when the study of comparative law did, but the waves of constitution-making during the twentieth century reinvigorated the field. Montesquieu's *Spirit of the Laws*, a predecessor to all contemporary comparative legal scholarship, can readily be taken as an inquiry into comparative constitutional law. Yet, systematic study of comparative constitutional law rests on several related phenomena, which emerged in the generation after Montesquieu. First, the systematic study of comparative constitutional law requires that people believe that they can design institutions by 'reflection and choice' rather than having institutions imposed on them by 'accident and force', as Alexander Hamilton put it in the first *Federalist Paper*. Second, that study probably requires that there be some significant examples of *written* constitutions for scholars to compare. Writing a constitution, of course, is an exercise of reflection and choice. Finally, the constitutions to be studied must have some serious relation to the actual operation of a nation's institutions, going beyond the simple provision of a framework within which government takes place. A constitution that merely creates institutions for making policy offers little to study unless the policies that emerge differ depending on what the institutions are.

For these reasons, the study of comparative constitutional law arose roughly contemporaneously with the adoption of the US Constitution. Not surprisingly, in light of their understanding of the task before them, major figures in that constitution's drafting, John Adams and James Madison, engaged in extensive surveys of constitutional practices in other nations and throughout history, in an effort to discern the features of institutions that would help resolve the political and economic problems that motivated the effort to create a new constitution. Consistent with one of the themes of comparative legal scholarship generally, scattered efforts to borrow constitutional ideas occurred through the nineteenth century. Juan Buatista Alberdi, for example, based his prescriptions for Argentine constitutional design in part on his reflections on the US Constitution.

The study of comparative constitutional law deepened early in the twentieth century, largely as a reaction to observations outside the United States to what the US Supreme Court was doing. In 1921 the French scholar Eduard Lambert published *Le gouvernement des juges et la lutte contre la législation sociale aux États-Unis*, a critical examination of decisions by the US Supreme Court invalidating laws regulating wages and hours. Working in a tradition dating to pre-revolutionary France, Lambert used the US example to demonstrate why empowering judges to set aside legislation was unwise. The German jurisprude Hans Kelsen, relying on the same experience, drew a somewhat different conclusion: Constitutions should include provisions for judicial review, but the ordinary courts should not be given the power to exercise it because of the important policy and political components of constitutional adjudication.[1] The drafters of the Irish Constitution of 1937, emulated a decade later by the drafters of the Indian Constitution, took a third course. Responding to constitutional principles shared by secular socialists and Roman Catholics influenced by their church's social teaching, the Irish Constitution contained constitutional guarantees of social welfare rights, but expressly insulated legislation dealing with such rights from judicial review by including them in a section labelled, 'Directive Principles of Social Policy'.

Neither the creation of constitutions for the nations that had been colonies of European powers, nor sporadic revisions of Western constitutions, provoked substantial scholarship on comparative constitutional law. There were of course studies of how particular problems were treated in different constitutions, and some scholarship on the subject of constitutional borrowing.[2] Prior to the 1950s, the US Supreme Court was the only constitutional court that did enough worth studying, but the emergence of the German Constitutional Court as a creative constitutional interpreter basically doubled the number of constitutional courts whose work product provided fertile ground for scholarship, enabling true comparative studies of constitutional law as actually implemented and interpreted.

The field took off in the 1980s. Canada's effort to patriate its constitution (ie to make constitutional revision in Canada possible without recourse in any way to the British Parliament) and the negotiations that led to both patriation and the adoption of the Canadian Charter of Rights and Freedoms were driven by a deep conceptualization of the role of constitutions in creating and possibly transforming national identity by Pierre Trudeau, a law professor turned politician. The return of democratic constitutionalism to Latin America through the 1980s was relatively little noticed by scholars of constitutional law outside the region, perhaps because it was a return that seemed to need little explanation or to provide interesting new material for scholarship.

---

[1] For a discussion of Kelsen's views on constitutional design, see Klaus von Beyme, 'The Genesis of Constitutional Review in Parliamentary Systems', in Christine Landfried (ed), *Constitutional Review and Legislation* (1988), 21–38.

[2] See eg Louis Henkin and Albert J. Rosenthal (eds), *The Influence of the United States Constitution Abroad* (1990).

That could not be said of the transition to democracy in Central and Eastern Europe from 1989 on, or of the end of apartheid and the establishment of democracy in South Africa in the early 1990s. For all practical purposes, those developments created the field of comparative constitutional law as it exists in the early twenty-first century. Partly out of the urgent need to create democratic institutions and to institute constitutionalism, partly out of enthusiasm over the possibilities of an invigorated democracy in formerly totalitarian nations, and (especially for Europeans) partly out of the importance of ensuring that one's neighbours were governed decently, scholars of constitutional law turned their attention to constitutional developments around the world. Constitution-drafters in Central and Eastern Europe and in South Africa consulted experts from the United States and Western Europe, consultations that were facilitated by the practice in modern constitution-drafting of relying heavily on technical specialists to develop the precise language to be used in new constitutions. More problematic was the possible development of a federated Europe out of the European Community and European Union. Debate over whether a constitution required a pre-existing political community, or whether a liberal constitution could consolidate an existing but unrecognized polity, produced important scholarship.[3] The emergence of the field was signalled in the usual way, by the establishment in 2003 of a scholarly journal dedicated to comparative constitutional law, the *International Journal of Constitutional Law.*

II. COMPARATIVE CONSTITUTIONAL LAW, POLITICS, AND INTERNATIONAL HUMAN RIGHTS

Constitutions lie at the intersection of law and high politics, and distinguishing between the study of comparative constitutional law and the study of comparative politics is sometimes particularly difficult. Recently another distinction has become increasingly difficult to draw: between the study of comparative constitutional law and the study of constitutionalism as such, including internationally recognized human rights.

Consider this problem. Constitution-makers might find themselves facing a choice between instituting a system in which the executive is the head of the

---

[3] The most important early work was Joseph H. H. Weiler, 'Does Europe Need a Constitution? Reflections on Demos, Telos and the German Maastricht Decision', (1995) 1 *European LJ* 219–58.

party controlling the legislature or one in which the executive is elected separately from the legislature, for example. That choice may have important consequences for the system's functioning, by affecting its stability or the vigour with which contested policies can be developed and implemented. Students of comparative constitutional law, though, have relatively little to contribute to the analysis of that choice, compared to what political scientists or political sociologists can contribute.

Yet, limiting the study of comparative constitutional law to distinctively legal topics approached in a distinctively legal way would eliminate from the field the connection between constitutional law as law and constitutional law as high politics. In addition, some topics properly studied in comparative constitutional law can only be understood by drawing on some concepts and conclusions developed in political science. Consider recent scholarship in the latter field on how judicial review becomes a firmly established and socially significant institution. Several authors have argued that it does so when the leaders of a political coalition that has controlled the legislative and executive branches of government for a long period foresee the possibility that they will lose office in the relatively near future. They establish or reinvigorate judicial review as a means by which they can ensure that the policies they advanced in the political branches will remain in force, now constitutionalized and enforced by the courts.[4] This argument describes important features of the institutionalization of judicial review, and at least offers a substantial supplement to more purely legal analyses that root judicial review in constitutional text and ideas about the rule of law.

The connection between constitutional law and high politics gives some issues commonly studied in comparative law a different coloration when the subject is constitutional law. Constitution-makers do borrow provisions they find in other constitutions, and constitutional ideas do migrate. Yet, nationalist concerns may affect the way in which such provisions and ideas are assimilated into national constitutions differently from the way in which such concerns affect the assimilation of ideas in private law, and probably have a more dramatic effect as well. Further, questions of sovereignty may arise when a constitution's designers and, even more, its interpreters look to constitutional experience elsewhere for guidance. The impulse expressed by US Supreme Court justice Antonin Scalia in one prominent opinion, that interpreting a domestic constitution calls for examining domestic sources alone,[5] is widely shared though often resisted. The concern is that

---

[4] See Ran Hirschl, *Towards Juristocracy: The Origins and Consequences of the New Constitutionalism* (2004) (discussing the adoption of judicial review in four nations in the late twentieth century); J. Mark Ramseyer, 'The Puzzling (In)Dependence of Courts: A Comparative Approach', (1994) 23 *Journal of Legal Studies*, 721–47 (discussing Japan); Tom Ginsburg, *Judicial Review in New Democracies: Constitutional Courts in East Asia* (2003); Matthew Stephenson, 'Independent Judicial Review', (2003) 32 *Journal of Legal Studies*, 32 (2003), 59–89 (developing a formal model of the process).

[5] *Stanford v Kentucky* (1989) 492 US 361.

interpreting a domestic constitution in light of experience elsewhere might lead to some degree of surrender of national sovereignty, and exacerbates the compromise of popular sovereignty that exists whenever judicial review does. Yet, despite the inevitable nationalist components of domestic constitutional law, there is reason to believe that at least in some areas constitutional law in many nations has begun to converge on some general analytic approaches if not on particular substantive results (see Section VII below).

III. Constitutionalism and Constitutional Law

A second challenge for the study of comparative constitutional law is to resist the temptation to elide the distinction between constitutional law and constitutionalism. Some states have constitutions but do not have constitutionalism, and the study of comparative constitutional law cannot exclude from its purview such states by defining its interest as one in constitutionalism.[6]

Constitutionalism, a normative concept, tends to be the focus of comparative studies strongly influenced by the strains of universalism that appear in comparative legal study more generally. Constitutionalism is a threshold concept. All legal systems to which the term can be applied must satisfy some minimum requirements, but can vary substantially in the way in which those requirements are fleshed out in institutional detail. Constitutionalism's components include these, and perhaps not much more: First, a commitment to the rule of law, understood to mean a generally observed disposition to exercise public power pursuant to publicly known rules, adherence to which actually provides a substantial motivation for acting or refraining from acting; second, and related, a reasonably independent judiciary; and third, reasonably regular and reasonably free and open elections, with a reasonably widespread franchise.

The study of constitutionalism is basically a philosophical one. It is the branch of the study of classical and modern liberalism concerned with institutional design and fundamental rights. Analysis of the threshold systems must cross to be constitutionalist illuminates the range within which systems might differ from each

---

[6] In this regard, compare the approaches taken in the two leading US course-books on comparative constitutional law. Vicki Jackson and Mark Tushnet, *Comparative Constitutional Law* (2nd edn, 2005), deals with constitutions generally, with a substantial emphasis on government structure, whereas Norman Dorsen, Michel Rosenfeld, Andràs Sàjo, and Suzanne Baer, *Comparative Constitutionalism: Cases and Materials* (2003), focuses on constitutionalism and individual rights issues.

other and yet all be constitutionalist. The later work of Jürgen Habermas exemplifies the study of comparative constitutional law as the study of constitutionalism. At a rather high level of abstraction, Habermas examines the way in which constitutional institutions, particularly a well-designed system of judicial review, can instantiate his dialogic understanding of how human communication fits together with liberalism's philosophical foundations.[7]

The twentieth century saw a transformation in the notion of constitutionalism. Originally, constitutionalism was an idea clearly associated with classical liberalism. Its concern was ensuring that government power not be abused. Structures of government were designed to guard against the adoption of abusive legislation and bills of rights enumerated guarantees that no legislation could permissibly touch. The rise of socialist and social democratic parties in the late nineteenth century, and the response of the Catholic Church to those parties' critique of capitalism and their political programmes, led those who thought about constitutions to expand the scope of constitutional guarantees from classical rights to civil and political participation, and to equality, to incorporate guarantees of social and economic rights. Social and economic rights included rights to shelter, a decent job, and minimally adequate nutrition, for example. Like civil and political rights, these 'second generation' rights could be enjoyed by individuals, although implementing them required affirmative government intervention in the economy, in a way that implementing classical rights seemingly did not. Later the second-generation rights were further supplemented by a third generation of rights to cultural preservation and environmental quality, rights that, it was thought, were inherently available only to groups and communities taken as aggregates.

As some scholars put forth the idea that there could be second- and third-generation constitutional rights, controversy arose over whether such rights were appropriately included in constitutions. One line of criticism was conceptual. Rights, some scholars argued, necessarily entailed the existence of correlative duties located in some identifiable person or body. Yet, against whom was the right to shelter to be asserted? Who had a duty to provide shelter? Supporters of second- and third-generation rights responded that there was no conceptual difficulty in imposing a duty to provide shelter on the government as a whole.[8] The conceptual controversy was resolved in practice by the political necessity that to receive popular support, modern constitutions simply had to include at least second-generation rights.

The conceptual controversy then migrated to the institutional arena. Classical civil and political rights could be enforced by the courts through traditional

---

[7] See especially Jürgen Habermas, *Between Facts and Norms: Contributions to a Discourse Theory of Law and Democracy* (trans William Rehg, 1996).

[8] For a discussion of the conceptual controversies, see Cécile Fabre, *Social Rights Under the Constitution: Government and the Decent Life* (2000).

methods of injunctions, declaratory judgments, and related devices within each nation's remedial system. Critics of social and economic rights pointed out that courts would correctly find it difficult to enforce such rights. Guaranteeing everyone a right to shelter, for example, might impose back-breaking fiscal burdens on governments facing other demands on the national budget. The constitutional formulations of social and economic rights take these concerns into account in various ways, such as the Irish Constitution's 'Directive Principles of Social Policy' (see Section 1 above). The Constitution of South Africa addresses fiscal concerns by directing the government to seek to guarantee the constitution's social and economic rights through 'progressive realisation', and 'within [the government's] available resources'.

Some courts resisted efforts to deny them the ability to enforce second-generation rights, or to direct them to enforce such rights only by applying a loose standard of reasonableness. The Indian Supreme Court, for example, used a judicially enforceable constitutional provision protecting against deprivations of life or liberty as the vehicle for importing into constitutional adjudication rights that were contained in the constitution's enumeration of directive principles that had been modelled on the Irish provisions. The development of weak-form systems of judicial review (see Section VI.3 below) might provide a new mechanism for enforcing second-generation rights in ways that address the fiscal concerns opponents of such rights continue to raise.

The study of constitutionalism necessarily deals only with a subset of all systems with constitutions. In contrast, the study of comparative constitutional law includes the study of the constitutions of totalitarian governments, about which one might ask *why* they have constitutions, and the constitutions of failed or failing nations, about which one might ask whether there is some relation between the constitution and the nation's failure. Why do nations have constitutions without constitutionalism?[9] Some reasons are obvious. Constitutions are a convenient—and, in the modern world, probably a necessary—way of creating or at least identifying the institutions that make law. In constitutionalist systems such institutions would include the elected legislature, but in non-constitutional ones with written constitutions the relevant institution might be the Supreme Leader or the ruling party. In addition, in the modern world having a constitution, or at least having some readily identifiable source of law-making authority of a sort easily embodied in a constitution, may be a prerequisite to recognition as a political actor by the world's other nations. Entities without constitutions might be rebel groups, or terrorists, or military forces with *de facto* control over territory, but they will not be nations entitled to participate in international institutions. Related, having a

---

[9] See H. W. O. Okoth-Ogendo, 'Constitutions without Constitutionalism: Reflections on an African Political Paradox', in Douglas Greenberg, Stanley N. Katz, Melanie Beth Oliviero, and Steven C. Wheatley (eds), *Constitutionalism and Democracy: Transitions in the Contemporary World* (1993).

constitution might signal that a nation aspires to become constitutionalist, or that the nation's leaders understand that for domestic political reasons they must send a signal to their own and other nations that they have such aspirations, however badly realized at the moment.

Political scientists have suggested that some constitutions might interfere with constitutionalism.[10] A stylized version of their argument involves a nation whose constitution creates a presidency elected by the nation as a whole and a legislature elected independently of the president and with proportional representation. Such a nation, political scientists suggest, is quite likely to face problems of policy grid-lock, in which a divided legislature is unable to address pressing national problems in an acceptable way. The president may respond by asserting that, having a national constituency, he and he alone speaks for the nation, and does so by suspending the operation of the legislature—ruling by executive decree rather than by law. As with all arguments from political science, this one identifies tendencies, albeit ones supported by substantial empirical evidence, not necessities. The argument shows, though, why it is important to distinguish between constitutions and constitutionalism.

The study of comparative constitutionalism today intersects with the study of international human rights law. The reason, in part, is that many constitutional systems are subject to the supervision of international institutions that apply international human rights law: the European Court of Human Rights, the United Nations Human Rights Commission, and many more. Often one cannot today understand the way in which human rights norms are articulated in domestic constitutional law without understanding the degree to which domestic decision-makers might be responding to concerns about international supervision. It seems reasonably clear, for example, that the United Kingdom's adoption of the Human Rights Act 1998 was in part a response to the fact that the European Court of Human Rights had held, with some regularity, that practices approved by the British courts violated the European Convention on Human Rights. At present, then, in some aspects the study of comparative constitutional law is continuous with the study of international human rights law.

---

[10] See Juan J. Linz and Arturo Valenzuela (eds), *The Failure of Presidential Democracy* (1994); Carlos Santiago Nino, 'Transition to Democracy, Corporatism and Presidentialism with Special Reference to Latin America', in Greenberg *et al.* (n 9).

IV. Constitutional Foundings
and Transformations

A long-standing tradition in the comparative study of constitutional law deals with the question of how constitutions get off the ground in the first place. The issue is focused when there is a relatively dramatic regime shift—when a fully domestic constitution replaces rule by a colonial power, or when a dictatorship (perhaps under a sham constitution) is overthrown and a new constitution put in place. The prior regime is, by hypothesis, discredited, so that the norms for effectuating constitutional change embedded in *its* constitutional order carry no legitimacy. Frequently, perhaps always, substantial constitutional transformations occur outside the forms prescribed by existing constitutions and are sometimes criticized as illegal for that reason. If not from the existing constitution, where do the forces instituting a new constitution get their legitimacy from?

Classical constitutional theory offers an answer cast in abstract theoretical terms, which are, however, often difficult to match up with social and political reality. That theory distinguishes between the *pouvoir constituant* and the *pouvoir constitueé*. The former, the constituent power or capacity, is always authorized to institute new fundamental arrangements; the latter, the constituted power, is the regime in place at any one time. The theoretical work is done by observing that the constituted power is always subordinate to the constituent power, implying that the norms embedded in any existing constitution, which are the forms the constituted power takes, cannot in principle regulate actions by the constituent power. Specifically, the distinction means that the observation that the constituent power has acted outside the forms of existing legality carries no normative weight.

The real difficulty, though, lies in giving institutional form to this conceptual distinction. Consider, for example, the common practice of convening a constituent assembly to draft and submit new constitutions for approval. There must be some rules for the appointment or election of members to the constituent assembly. The discredited old regime can hardly be the legitimate source of such rules, although sometimes it generates such rules in default of any other mechanism for doing so. Legitimacy comes from general public acceptance of the rules for selecting the constituent assembly, not from laws already in place purporting to say how the existing constitution can be amended or replaced.

Bruce Ackerman's account of constitutional transformations in the United States provides a vivid account of how such legitimacy can arise, although one must not assume that the processes Ackerman identifies for the United States operate universally—an assumption that Ackerman himself sometimes makes.[11] Ackerman distinguishes between what he calls periods of ordinary politics and what he calls constitutional moments. The people pay close attention to 'high politics' during constitutional moments. Politicians mobilize the people themselves over questions of fundamental political organization, rather than working through interest groups to determine public policy.

Ackerman's metaphor of constitutional moments has been quite influential, but it must be employed cautiously. In Ackerman's interpretation of US constitutional history, constitutional moments occur during rather compressed time periods, but there is no general reason to believe that the process of constitutional transformation must be quite as abrupt as the metaphor suggests. Nor is it necessarily true that the people during periods of ordinary politics always neglect questions of fundamental constitutional design, although Ackerman is probably correct in perceiving that the amount of attention people can devote to such questions is always limited. The importance of Ackerman's metaphor lies in its ability to provide an explanation of how the *various* forms by which the constituent power exercises itself gain legitimacy: They do so, on his account, because the mobilizations that occur during constitutional moments provide popular endorsement, and therefore normative value, to whatever institutions emerge to transform the constitutional order.

Those institutions historically have taken a wide variety of forms. Perhaps the most common has been the constituent assembly charged solely with drafting and seeking approval of a new constitution. The advantage of constituent assemblies lies in their focused attention to constitutional design; their disadvantages lie in the possibilities that their members may design constitutions either irresponsibly (because they themselves will have no role in the new constitutional order) or with an eye to promoting their own positions in that order. The most prominent alternative to constituent assemblies for constitution-drafting is the existing legislature. Even in situations where dramatic regime-change is about to occur, the existing legislature may be the only institution that political forces can agree on, perhaps as everyone's second choice, to draft a new constitution. This may be especially true when the political forces supporting the existing regime retain some political or economic power and must be accommodated by the new regime; sometimes the political process leads to modest alterations in the composition of the legislature in place, giving it just enough legitimacy with all parties for it to serve as the constitution-making body. Here the difficulty lies in the fact that the legislature has a dual role. It must continue to govern in the ordinary course even as it creates a new constitution. People chosen because they will be good legislators may be not be good constitution-makers, particularly if Ackerman is correct in seeing a difference between the orientation of ordinary legislators to deal-making and interest

[11] Bruce Ackerman, *We the People: Foundations* (1991); Bruce Ackerman, *We the People: Transformations* (1998).

groups and the orientation of constitution-makers to matters of fundamental principle.

Modern constitution-making faces an imperative of transparency. The US Constitution was drafted in a closed session, and its contents were not revealed to the public until the final document was ready. Such a practice would be unacceptable in most nations today. Transparency at the drafting stage has the important advantage of inducing deliberation and rational argument, but perhaps the equally important disadvantage of discouraging bargaining.[12] Public discussions typically invoke basic principle, thereby educating the observing public about the choices being made as the constitution-drafters create a full constitution. Speaking in public, advocates must take responsibility not only for their arguments but for the provisions they support. Public sessions, though, make it difficult to strike what might be essential compromises that can be defended only as necessary to get the constitution adopted but not as based on fundamental principle.

Transparency occurs at another stage. Historically, constitutions are drafted, submitted to the public, and ratified or rejected. An intermediate stage has recently been introduced into the constitution-making process. In this stage, a constitutional draft is submitted for public comment and revised in light of the public reaction, after which the revised constitution is presented for ratification or rejection. The stage of public comment allows the public to begin to gain a sense of its responsibility for the constitution. Given the difficulties of constitution-drafting, though, often the public comments are merely compiled, and only the ones easiest to integrate into the document are placed in the final constitution. The new or modified provisions may not be the ones about which the public was most concerned, and to that extent the public dissemination of the draft constitution may sometimes come close to being a mere public relations effort.

Still, revising a draft constitution can contribute to its legitimacy. The process of adopting the South African Constitution of 1996 illustrates how. The political dimensions of the transition from apartheid to democracy made it impossible to craft a constitution immediately. No body created under the apartheid regime could have the legitimacy, in the white, coloured, and African communities, to develop a constitution that had a chance of being widely accepted. Complex negotiations led, first, to the adoption of an interim constitution in 1993, enacted by the apartheid regime's legislature. A parliament was elected, and a constitutional court created, under that constitution. The new parliament sat as a constituent assembly to draft a final constitution. The negotiations leading to the adoption of the interim constitution produced two additional important conditions: The negotiators agreed that the final constitution had to comply with thirty-four 'basic principles', and that the new constitutional court would have to

---

[12] Jon Elster, 'Forces and Mechanisms in the Constitution-Making Process', (1995) 45 *Duke LJ* 364–96.

certify that the final constitution did so. The final constitution was adopted by parliament and then submitted for certification. The constitutional court found that the proposed final constitution was generally consistent with the thirty-four principles, but found as well that several proposed provisions needed revision.[13] The most important of these was that the mechanism for insulating basic rights from later amendment had to be strengthened. Parliament modified the final constitution, and the constitutional court then certified that the constitution comported with all of the basic principles. Although the mechanism of external review of proposed constitutional provisions has not yet been widely emulated, the South African process offers valuable insights into the ways in which institutional innovation can help solve some problems associated with constitutional transitions.

The South African example shows one way in which new constitutions can be adopted—by action of an elected parliament. The composition of that parliament is of course particularly important when large-scale transitions are involved. In South Africa the existing parliament was reconstituted before the new constitution was developed and ratified. Elsewhere extra-parliamentary negotiations have led to agreements on new constitutions; formally, the existing parliament adopts the new constitution, but in doing so it is merely ratifying the agreements reached outside its walls. Alternatively, new constitutions can be submitted to the public for ratification in referenda. Voting rules may be set to fit the nation's political requirements, so that, for example, majorities in each of the nation's sections must vote in favour of adopting the constitution. Direct public participation is frequently valuable, but it has its costs. The vote is essentially yes-or-no, with the public unable to reject particular provisions. From the point of view of securing agreement, presenting the new constitution as a package allows bargains struck at the drafting stage to stick, but voting on a package may undermine the ability of the constitution to garner deep public commitment. Public participation in a ratification referendum may be relatively uninformed, as the question presented is abstract and may not convey to the public how the new constitution will actually operate. And, of course, the number of people who vote may not be large enough to give the new constitution the legitimacy its authors hope for.

Problems of legitimacy arise as well when constitutions are imposed, whether in the large or with respect to particular provisions. The post-war constitutions of Germany and Japan drew upon some domestic liberal constitutionalist elements, but both were also substantially imposed by the nations' occupying powers. International demands may place important constraints even on constitutions that are developed through largely domestic processes. After the fall of communism

---

[13] *In re Certification of the Constitution of the Republic of South Africa,* 1996 (4) SA 744 (Constitutional Court, South Africa).

in Central and Eastern Europe, for example, those creating new constitutions believed it politically essential that their nations be seen as part of Europe, which meant acceding somehow to the nominally optional 'Protocol Six' of the European Convention on Human Rights, abolishing the death penalty. Hungary accomplished this through the first decision of its constitutional court rather than in the constitution itself, Poland by legislation, but whatever the mechanism, this basic decision, often at odds with the apparent preferences of each nation's people as revealed in public opinion polls, was at least as much imposed as chosen.

Strikingly, though, the post-war German and Japanese constitutions were among the most successful of the twentieth century. Their successes indicate an important way in which constitutions can gain legitimacy. Attention to the mechanisms of constitution-drafting and ratification, or to constitutional moments, may suggest that legitimacy arises out of the circumstances of a constitution's creation and adoption. The German and Japanese examples suggest that constitutions can become embedded in a nation's political-legal culture by accretion, as the institutions created by the constitution are seen by the public to work reasonably well. Indeed, adequate performance may overcome problems, obvious at the moment of creation, that theorists concerned with constitutional abstractions and concepts might have thought insurmountable.

No constitutions are perfect, and all must therefore contain some means by which they can be changed to address problems with the original document and new circumstances. Constitutional amendments lie along a continuum beginning with minor adjustments in technical provisions, running through more substantial though still relatively confined alterations, to transformations so substantial that scholars can fairly claim that a new constitutional order has replaced the prior one even though much in the prior system seems untouched.

The most important variations in provisions for constitutional amendment affect the relative ease of amendment.[14] At one limit, an amendment procedure might authorize a constitutional amendment by a majority vote in a single legislative session; constitutional amendments under such a system are not much different from ordinary legislation. Layers of difficulty can be added, by requiring a super-majority vote in the legislature to adopt an amendment, by requiring adoption by successive legislatures (perhaps after an intervening election), by requiring approval of amendments by popular referendums or other methods, and the like.

At the other limit lie constitutional provisions that cannot be amended. Placing such provisions in a document that otherwise authorizes amendments poses something of a conceptual puzzle. Consider the provision in the US Constitution purporting to bar amendments that deprive states of their equal representation in the

---

[14] See Sanford Levinson, *Responding to Imperfection: The Theory and Practice of Constitutional Amendment* (1995).

Senate.[15] Could equal representation none the less be eliminated by a two-step process, in which the ban on eliminating equal representation by amendment was itself eliminated by amendment, and then equal representation, no longer protected against amendment, was itself eliminated? As a matter of pure legal form it seems hard to find that process impermissible, and yet it seems inconsistent with the point of asserting that the underlying provision is unamendable.

The highest constitutional courts in Germany and India have asserted that some constitutional provisions are unamendable even though the constitution does not itself expressly identify those provisions. Those courts have said that some constitutional provisions are part of the nation's 'basic' constitutional structure, and cannot be changed even by processes that conform to the letter with the processes laid out in the constitution for amending it. The German Constitutional Court has simply asserted the possibility that some constitutional amendments might be unconstitutional,[16] and the Indian Supreme Court engaged in a substantial analysis of whether amendments affecting the courts altered the nation's basic structures, in what observers describe as a confusing set of opinions that concluded by upholding the amendments.[17] The conceptual puzzles about constitutions' provisions asserting their own amendability disappear in this setting, because the courts as decision-makers external to the document determine which provisions are unamendable. Those puzzles, though, are replaced by another: Because constitutional amendments can have so substantial an effect as to amount to a change from one constitutional order to another, why should not constitutional amendments that transform a nation's 'basic structure' be treated as revolutionary interpositions? They would have the form but not the substance of legality, but none the less could have the legitimacy that comes from revolutionary success.

Amendment procedures are tied as well to questions about constitutional interpretation. The burden of adjusting constitutions to new conditions can be discharged by easy amendment processes. In contrast, the more difficult it is to amend a constitution directly, the more pressure there will be on constitutional courts to interpret existing provisions in ways that address the problems posed by new conditions. This will be particularly true if the difficult-to-amend constitution is an old one, as is the case in the United States, where it can fairly be said that the Supreme Court has recurrently amended the constitution by decisions purporting to interpret it.

---

[15] US Constitution, art V.

[16] BVerfGE 1, 14 (1951) (Federal Constitutional Court of Germany) (The Southwest Case).

[17] See Granville Austin, *Working a Democratic Constitution: The Indian Experience* (1999), 258–77 (describing *Kesavananda Bharati v State of Kerala*, 1973 (4) SCC 225 (Supreme Court of India)).

V. CONSTITUTIONAL STRUCTURES

Constitutions are blueprints for operating a government. Political scientists typically have more insight than lawyers into the way the structures based on those
blueprints actually operate. Federal structures, for example, might promote national
solidarity in divided societies, but they might also exacerbate divisions, depending
on a range of factors, many of which have nothing to do with law. Another example
is provided by the choice among presidential, semi-presidential, and purely parliamentary systems, a choice that seems quite likely to be consequential but that
implicates relatively little law as such.

Perhaps, though, law as such might play some role as courts rely on constitutional law to enforce the bargains, struck at the time of a constitution's adoption,
that are reflected but only imperfectly expressed in the details of constitutional
structure. Parties to a deal about allocating power among a nation's regions, for
example, might retain a continuing interest in reopening the deal whenever they
can, and may seize upon constitutional ambiguities as the mechanism for doing
so. Judicial review might be helpful in enforcing the original deal for enough time
that other structures of bargaining can develop to accommodate changes in the
interests and power of competing regions and the like.

Studies of comparative constitutional law might illuminate some *general* features of some aspects of constitutional structure. The treatment of emergencies in
national constitutions provides an example. Emergencies take a wide range of
forms: natural disasters, terrorist threats, sustained or sporadic domestic disorder,
economic distress, and more. Emergency conditions may induce political leaders to
suspend some aspects of ordinary constitutional legality. They may seek to enact
regulations by executive decree, bypassing the legislature. Or they may limit civil
liberties in ways that might be unjustified outside the emergency context. These
decisions might be wise or unwise, and constitution designers have struggled
to devise methods of reducing the occasions for and the extent and duration of
unwise exercises of emergency powers.

One question designers must face is the extent to which the constitution will
attempt to define what constitutes an emergency. The US Constitution is among
the thinnest in the world, referring only to 'rebellion or invasion'.[18] The French
Constitution of 1958 refers to situations in which the nation's institutions 'are
under serious and immediate threat', which clearly includes domestic disorder.[19]
Other constitutions do not identify emergency circumstances as such, but instead
provide that emergencies can be declared only pursuant to the terms of an organic
law, understood as a statute with a status somewhere between that of the constitution and that of an ordinary law.

---

[18] US Constitution, art I, § 9, cl 2.   [19] Constitution of France, art 16(1).

It is unclear whether constitutions can actually identify, in a helpful way, the occasions on which emergency powers might be necessary. The difficulty lies in the fact that constitution-makers, even drawing upon a wide range of experience throughout the world, cannot fully anticipate what circumstances will impel political leaders to seek to exercise such powers. Defining 'emergencies' broadly allows those leaders to trigger their emergency powers when they feel the need, but fails to constrain their choices. Defining them narrowly may lead to evasions of the constitution's apparent constraints, either through creative interpretation—such as seeing economic turmoil as a threat to the nation's institutions as the French Constitution requires—or through blatant disregard, justified by the constitution's failure. The German political theorist Carl Schmitt, whose work was discredited for a generation by his association with the German fascist regime but was somewhat rehabilitated in the 1980s and 1990s, argued that constitutions could never identify the circumstances for declaring an emergency. For Schmitt, sovereignty resided precisely in the power to declare an exception to ordinary legality, and even written constitutions could not displace the ultimate sovereign power.[20]

A second question for constitution designers is, What is the basic strategy for controlling the exercise of emergency powers once they are invoked? Probably the predominant strategy combines two features: The executive can suspend legality only for a limited period, and can restrict only some, not all, constitutional liberties; and these limitations on the executive are to be enforced by the courts. Whether this strategy is effective is unclear. Executive officials are often able to devise credible legal arguments that their actions fall within the scope of authorized actions during an emergency. And, probably more important, judges have found it difficult to resist executive actions during declared emergencies, either accepting strained arguments that the executive's actions are lawful or implicitly acknowledging that they as judges lack the force or moral credibility to stand against the executive's actions.

Another strategy, reflected in some decisions by the US Supreme Court, might be called a separation-of-powers strategy. Rather than relying on the courts directly to enforce restrictions on executive emergency power, the separation-of-powers strategy relies on politics to constrain the executive. This strategy is easiest to discern in formal separation-of-powers systems, in which a legislature elected independently of the executive can mobilize itself against executive actions.[21] Courts can play a role in the separation-of-powers strategy as well. They can insist that executive actions that seem constitutionally troublesome or excessive be expressly authorized by the legislature. When the courts do so, they are not, at

[20] 'Sovereign is he who decides on the exception.' Carl Schmitt, *Political Theology: Four Chapters on the Theory of Sovereignty* (trans George Schwab, 1986), 5.

[21] A related, though perhaps weaker, version can be seen in parliamentary systems, though. Where the parliament is governed by a coalition, reluctant coalition partners might pressure 'their' prime minister to avoid excessive uses of emergency powers.

least formally, barring the executive from taking action the executive deems necessary. As a result, the courts might not face the difficulties of legitimacy and effectiveness that arise when they seek directly to enforce constitutional restrictions on emergency powers.

The separation-of-powers strategy for controlling emergency power demonstrates the inevitable connection between what constitutional law has to say about government structure and what political science has to say. The extent to which the strategy will be effective will vary, and not entirely with the extent to which a nation's constitutional structure is parliamentary or divides powers between the executive and the legislature. How politics actually operates will matter as well, perhaps more—and legal scholars have relatively little to contribute to understanding that process.

VI. Structures of Judicial Review

Much in the study of comparative constitutional law involves examination of judicial review. There are now two main axes for examining the structures of judicial review. The first is of long-standing, and distinguishes between the specialized and centralized form of judicial review devised by Hans Kelsen for Austria after World War I and emulated in many European nations thereafter, and the generalist and dispersed form of judicial review characteristic of the United States. The second has arisen more recently, and distinguishes between strong-form systems of judicial review, in which the constitutional court's interpretations are final and unrevisable except by means of constitutional amendment or overruling by the court itself, perhaps after a change in membership, and weak-form review, in which the constitutional court's interpretations are subject to revision through a process of relatively short-term dialogue with the nation's political branches.[22]

1. Diffuse, Generalist, Strong-Form Review: The United States

The world's first constitutional court, the United States Supreme Court, exemplifies strong-form review in a generalist and dispersed system. That Court is a generalist one because it is authorized to interpret the national constitution *and*

---

[22] See Stephen Gardbaum, 'The New Commonwealth Model of Constitutionalism', (2001) 49 *AJCL*, 707–60; Mark Tushnet, 'Alternative Forms of Judicial Review', (2003) 101 *Michigan LR* 2781–802.

national statutes, and even to develop 'common law' rules where distinctively national interests are involved and neither the Constitution nor the national legislature provides appropriate rules. Notably, the Supreme Court can interpret national statutes even when no constitutional questions are implicated. In addition, every court in the United States, including the lowest trial-level court in a small town, the lower national courts, and state supreme courts, is authorized, and indeed required, to resolve properly raised constitutional questions. In this sense judicial review in the United States is dispersed. But, in another sense, it is centralized in the Supreme Court, which sits at the top of a pyramid, authorized to hear appeals from all lower courts in which constitutional questions are properly raised.

The dispersal of the power of constitutional review in the United States is connected to the historical circumstances of the creation of judicial review in the United States, to the nation's prevailing conception of adjudication, and to the typical methods by which judges are appointed in the United States. The idea of judicial review was reasonably well-accepted in the early years of the national constitution, but the nation's institutions were at a rudimentary stage. The nation was geographically extended, and the national government lacked the personnel to implement national policy directly throughout the nation. If judicial review was to be effective, it had to be exercised on the local level. Also from early in the nation's history, Americans believed that constitutional law was a special kind of law, to some extent enforced by the people themselves but in any event rather different from the ordinary law of contract and property because of its strong political components.[23] Controlling judicial review by keeping its exercise visible to the people lent force to the dispersed system of judicial review. Finally, judges in the United States hold their offices as a result of processes that incorporate important political elements. Judges in the national judicial system are nominated by the President and confirmed by the upper house of the national legislature; judges in most state judicial systems are elected, or at least must face election within a few years after their appointment. These political components of the appointment process support a dispersed system of judicial review to the extent that every judge is connected to the electorate, directly or indirectly.

The political components of the appointment process also help explain the acceptance in the United States of strong-form judicial review. An important concern about expansive exercises of judicial review has been that judicial review allows judges to displace the choices made by the people's representatives and so is in tension with democratic self-governance. The judges speak in the name of the constitution, and to the extent that they can credibly treat constitutional law as similar to ordinary law they can defuse some of this countermajoritarian concern. But, the high political component of constitutional law means that it can never be merely a specialized area of law alone, and the democratic anxieties

---

[23] Larry Kramer, *The People Themselves: Popular Constitutionalism and Judicial Review* (2004).

about judicial review cannot be entirely eliminated. This is particularly so when the view becomes widely held, as it is in the United States, that the constitutional interpretations proffered by judges unavoidably invoke—explicitly or implicitly—the judges' own values. The fact that US judges have some connection to the political process alleviates some of these concerns.

In the early years of the US Constitution, there was significant support for what has been called 'departmentalism'. Departmentalism took several forms. In one, each department—the judiciary, the legislature, the President—was entitled to interpret and act on its own interpretations of the Constitution, taking into account the rational merits of the interpretations offered by other branches but not compelled to accept them. In another, each department would have the final say on the constitutionality of legislation affecting its own operations. In its strongest version, departmentalism would allow a President to disregard the coercive orders entered by courts in adjudicated cases. Yet, allowing that outcome seems in severe tension with the requirements of the rule of law, and few theorists in the United States ever adhered to such a strong departmentalist view.

Instead, rejecting the seemingly anarchic implications of that form of depart-mentalism, members of the political branches came to accept first the final author-ity of the courts in adjudicated cases and then, gradually, strong-form review itself, in which the judiciary's pronouncements are taken to provide authoritative consti-tutional interpretations, articulating principles that the political branches must follow even in enacting new legislation. Of course the courts' interpretations can be overridden by constitutional amendment, which is however quite difficult in the United States. More important, the composition of the national judiciary in the United States is affected by politically driven decisions through the process of nomination and appointment by the President and upper house of the national legislature. The judiciary's constitutional interpretations can be altered as new judges are placed on the courts.

2. Centralized and Specialized Review: The Kelsenian Constitutional Court

The US Supreme Court's generalist mandate reflects the view that constitutional interpretation is continuous with other forms of legal interpretation, different only in small degree from statutory interpretation because of the role that high politics plays in constitutional interpretation. Hans Kelsen developed an alternative insti-tutional model for judicial review.[24] Kelsen's model began with the insight that constitutional law differed from ordinary law because of its connection to high

---

[24] For a discussion, see von Beyme (n 1).

politics. For Kelsen, judicial review was continuous with the legislative process, not sharply distinguished from it. To avoid the complete displacement of democratic politics by judges on constitutional courts, Kelsen argued that such courts could act only in a negative capacity, invalidating legislation that was inconsistent with constitutional limitations on public power. In addition, Kelsen believed that the political component of constitutional law required that judges on constitutional courts not be mere legal specialists. In the European context in which Kelsen worked, judges were bureaucrats expert in the law alone. Kelsen therefore insisted that judicial review be exercised not by ordinary judges but by a specialized constitutional court, to which appointments would be made with an eye to the fact that constitutional law had a political component. For related reasons, Kelsen's model centralized constitutional review in the specialized constitutional court. And, finally, in most versions of the model access to the constitutional court was limited to a selected list of political actors—some executive officials, representatives of the national legislature, officials of subnational governments—to place a politically controlled screen between the constitutional court and the constitution considered in its entirety.

Many nations have adopted centralized and specialized constitutional courts, even as they have abandoned other components of Kelsen's model. The vision of the constitutional court as a negative legislator only was compatible with the commitments of the classically liberal state, which saw the primary threats to constitutional order in improvident exercises of public power. A constitutional court that was a negative legislator, though, would necessarily stand in the way of some legislation that altered the status quo. Such an institution could not survive the development of the modern social welfare state, one of whose premises was that improvident exercises of private power—that is, some of the consequences of the status quo—were as troubling as some exercises of public power. The idea of the constitutional court as a negative legislator became inconsistent with the ideological commitments of the social welfare state, although it did not follow that such courts necessarily became positive legislators. Further, placing limits on access to constitutional courts was in tension with the ideal that ordinary citizens should be able to participate in the decision-making processes of institutions that exercised substantial public power. Most modern constitutional courts therefore provide some form of procedure for citizens to complain to such courts.

Centralized and specialized constitutional courts face distinctive problems in coordinating their interpretations of the constitution with the actions of the ordinary courts, which in the purist Kelsenian system are prohibited from ruling on constitutional objections. So-called 'battles of the courts', between the constitutional courts and the highest courts charged with implementing non-constitutional law, were particularly common in the post-Communist systems created in the 1990s, though skirmishes have occurred in nearly every system with a specialized constitutional court.

There are a number of devices to secure coordination, none entirely satisfactory. The ordinary courts can be required to refer constitutional objections to the constitutional court whenever they appear. The broad scope of modern constitutions makes a referral mechanism awkward; it would flood the constitutional court with cases while delaying the ultimate resolution of those cases substantially. Constitutional courts can interpret legislation to make it compatible with the judges' interpretation of the constitution, but then they may face resistance from the judges on the ordinary courts charged with the general enforcement of those statutes. Constitutional courts can exercise some control over the ordinary courts by imposing on those courts an obligation to apply the ordinary law in their charge in a manner sensitive to constitutional concerns. The large number of cases in which litigants might claim that the ordinary courts had not been sufficiently sensitive to constitutional norms means that the constitutional court must as a practical matter accord a substantial degree of deference to the ordinary courts. This deference, and related concessions to the ordinary courts when other mechanisms of coordination are used, has led the constitutional courts to win the battle of the courts, though not always on the terms the judges of the constitutional courts set out when the battles began.

3. Weak-Form Judicial Review

The second contrast in institutions of judicial review is between strong-form and weak-form systems. Discussions of constitutional review in the mid-twentieth century laid the groundwork for the development of weak-form systems. Those discussions distinguished between the so-called *erga omnes* effects of constitutional determinations made by the US Supreme Court, and the merely *intra partes* effects said to be characteristic of Kelsenian courts. Judgments have *erga omnes* effects when they 'bind' all legal actors. The precise nature of the binding effect is sometimes unclear, but in a precedent-based system decisions are binding in the sense that they provide a strong basis for predicting that the same judgment will be reached by the constitutional court in any later case presenting the same issue. That prediction gives legal actors strong prudential reasons for conforming their actions to the judgments. In contrast, a judgment has a merely *intra partes* effect when it binds only the parties to the judgment, leaving all other actors free, at least as a matter of law, to disregard the judgment. *Intra partes* effects can be quite significant, of course, in systems where the parties to the judgment include the legislature that enacted a statute found to be unconstitutional.

As a practical matter, the distinction between *erga omnes* and *intra partes* effects might not have been as significant as it was in legal theory. The same predictive evaluations that give judgments a wide effect in a precedent-based system can usually be made in one formally committed to merely *intra partes* effects. What the distinction did, though, was to suggest that some forms of constitutional review might reduce the tension between judicial review and democratic self-governance that many thought characterized the US system, by limiting the scope of judgments of unconstitutionality.

The Canadian Charter of Rights and Freedoms, adopted in 1982, utilized an innovative form of weak-form review.[25] As a result of political compromise, the Charter contains a 'notwithstanding' clause, authorizing legislatures to declare that a statute will be effective notwithstanding its inconsistency with selected Charter guarantees. Canada's Supreme Court interpreted the clause to authorize pre-emptive declarations, issued before a court found the statute unconstitutional, and blanket declarations insulating a large number of statutes from unconstitutionality. It did so in a case closely bound up with the Canadian political controversy over Quebec's status within or independent of Canada. Perhaps as a result, the notwithstanding clause has rarely been invoked in Canada, although some commentators suggest that the mere existence of the provision affects legislative and judicial judgments.[26]

Commentators argue that the notwithstanding clause, along with other features of the Canadian Charter, promote a valuable dialogue between courts and legislatures over the meaning of constitutional terms.[27] At least in theory if not in practice, the dialogue could proceed with the legislature enacting a statute believing it to be constitutional because of a considered judgment the legislature made about constitutional meaning, the courts finding the statute unconstitutional because inconsistent with the judiciary's different judgment about meaning, and the legislature responding either by accepting the court's judgment or by insisting on its own judgment by invoking the notwithstanding clause. Such a dialogic approach to judicial review has the attractive feature that it encourages deliberation about constitutional meaning in the legislature without inevitably displacing the legislature's judgment and without enforcing unconsidered judgments.

Other variants of weak-form review exist. The weakest is the pure interpretive mandate, illustrated by New Zealand's Bill of Rights, which directs the courts to interpret later-enacted legislation to be consistent with the provisions in the Bill of Rights, where such an interpretation is fairly possible without violating ordinary rules invoked in statutory interpretation. The British Human Rights Act 1998 contains an interpretive mandate bolstered by a power in the courts to make a statement that legislation is incompatible with the provisions of the European Convention on Human Rights.

[25] One of its substantive provisions, the limitations provision discussed in Section VII.1 below, can be understood as a version of weak-form review as well.

[26] Lorraine Weinrib, 'Learning to Live with the Override', (1990) 35 *McGill LJ* 541–71.

[27] Peter Hogg and Alison Bushell, 'The Charter Dialogue between Courts and Legislatures (Or Perhaps the Charter of Rights Isn't Such a Bad Thing after All)', (1997) 35 *Osgoode Hall LJ* 75–124.

Stephen Gardbaum calls these institutional innovations the 'New Common-wealth Model' of judicial review,[28] a label that raises questions about whether weak-form systems are institutionally stable. As Gardbaum's label suggests, the innovations emerge from constitutional systems previously committed to strong versions of parliamentary supremacy. Weak-form judicial review might be a polit-ically acceptable first step away from parliamentary supremacy, to be followed, as parliamentary supremacy recedes, by the adoption of stronger-form systems. There is some reason to think that, in both New Zealand and Canada, systems that remain formally weak-form have become in practice rather stronger than initially appeared.

4. Adjudicatory Procedures

How do constitutional courts limit or invite access? Drawing on concepts from the common law, the US Supreme Court in the twentieth century began to articulate so-called 'standing' limitations on who could raise constitutional challenges, and related 'ripeness' and 'mootness' limitations on the timing of such challenges. These limitations were said to derive from the US Constitution's requirement that the national courts consider only 'cases', and were also said to have an irreducible constitutional—that is, legal—component. The US Supreme Court also developed a doctrine precluding it from addressing what it called 'political questions', a relatively narrow category of cases best understood as including only legal contro-versies the resolution of which was left by the Constitution itself to the national legislature or executive.[29]

In various ways, most other constitutional courts have rejected such limitations, at least when they are conceived of as arising from law rather than from discretion-ary choices by the judges about which cases warrant full consideration. Many constitutional courts are generous in allowing persons not directly affected by a statute to challenge its constitutionality, typically on the ground that those directly affected face practical impediments in presenting their challenges. Some will issue advisory opinions on the constitutionality of proposed legislation, usually at the instance of some political actors such as the legislature's leadership. Rather than dismissing challenges to government actions as raising questions not committed to judges, constitutional court judges will give the political actors a wide range of discretion and defer to their decisions within that range while reserving the power to overturn as unconstitutional actions that are truly arbitrary.

Limitations on access to constitutional courts are in tension with the modern

---

[28] Gardbaum (n 22), (2001) 49 *AJCL* 707 ff.
[29] For a discussion, see Joel B. Grossman and T. J. Donahue, 'Political Questions', in Kermit L. Hall (ed), *The Oxford Companion to the Supreme Court of the United States* (2nd edn, 2005) 754–7.

idea, noted earlier, that all citizens should see themselves as active participants in the entire process of governance according to constitutional norms. And, indeed, even in the United States the limitations on access are more theoretical than real. Individuals or groups troubled by some statute or executive action can usually construct a constitutional challenge that surmounts the procedural hurdles the US Supreme Court has erected, although often it will take quite careful lawyering to do so.

VII. Generic Constitutional Law

Constitutions of course vary widely in their specific provisions. Cataloguing the differences between the ways in which constitutional systems provide protection for freedom of expression, guarantee equality, or authorize or restrict affirmative action programmes might identify some themes important for comparative constitutional analysis. For example, the Indian and US experiences with affirmative action show how constitutional language might affect outcomes. In both nations, courts initially took constitutional provisions dealing with equality in general terms to impose substantial limits on affirmative action. The Indian Constitution was then amended to authorize affirmative action expressly, after which the courts upheld affirmative action programmes that arguably fell outside the specific terms of the authorization. In the United States, the courts came to accept some degree of affirmative action, but it may be that the presence of only a general equality provision inhibited the development of a more robust jurisprudence of affirmative action there.

1. The Justifications for Proportionality Analysis in Constitutional Law

Beyond the specifics of a particular constitution, there is the possibility that what one scholar calls 'generic constitutional law' (Law) has begun to emerge.[30] Generic constitutional law deals with the ways in which constitutions protect individual rights, and specifically with the ways in which constitutions identify when and how such rights can be limited.

The 'when' question arises because no rights can sensibly be absolute, subject

---

[30] David S. Law, 'Generic Constitutional Law', (2005) 89 *Minnesota LR*, 652–742.

to no limitation whatsoever. One uncontroversial limitation is that one person's rights must sometimes be limited to avoid violations of another's rights. More troublesome are situations, universally encountered, in which it seems that exercises of individual rights will interfere with important social or public interests. A right of privacy in the home may interfere with the government's ability to identify criminals; exercises of a right of free expression may cause public disorder.

Prior to the emergence of generic constitutional law, constitutional systems used either a balancing or a categorical approach to determining when rights can be limited. The balancing approach asked judges to consider all the interests at play in the circumstances, public interests as well as individual rights, and to determine whether, on balance and taking all the relevant considerations into account, a limitation on the individual rights was justified. This approach had important flaws. It proved easy to proliferate public interests that could outweigh the individual rights and, perhaps more important, judges frequently seemed to give excessive weight to asserted public interests and therefore overrode individual rights more often than seemed appropriate, at least in retrospect. Further, the relatively unstructured nature of balancing seemed at odds with basic requirements of the rule of law, because neither the components of the balancing nor the weights to be given them could readily be specified in advance of a decision dealing with a particular problem.

The categorical approach avoided most of balancing's difficulties, but came with its own costs. Under the categorical approach, courts would identify entire areas of activity that simply were not covered by the relevant constitutional right. Commercial advertising, for example, simply would not count as 'speech' protected by guarantees of free speech. Among the difficulties of categorical approaches were these: Explaining why some activities were protected by constitutional provisions while others that seemed closely related were categorically excluded from protection proved difficult. It mattered a great deal that an activity fell on one or the other side of the line dividing protected from unprotected activities. That meant that identifying the location of the line was extremely important, often seemingly beyond the capacity of language to capture effectively.

Generic constitutional law offers a formula for limiting rights that, its defenders argue, does not require the courts to identify categories of unprotected activities in order to ensure that the proper projects of a constitutional government not be thwarted by overly broad protections of individual rights, and that also provides more structure to legal analysis than balancing does. The Canadian Charter of Rights and Freedoms, which drew upon formulations in the European Convention on Human Rights and the Indian Constitution, provides a lucid version of the formula: Rights are guaranteed, according to the Charter, 'subject only to such reasonable limits prescribed by law as can be demonstrably justified in a free and democratic society'.[31] Each component in this formula provides structure for analysing the permissibility of limitations. 'Prescribed by law' means that an executive official can invoke a limitation only when the official's action is authorized by legislation (or by what should be taken to be a rather narrow category of prerogative powers). The kinds of public interest that can be invoked must be consistent with the requirements of 'a free and democratic society'. Restrictions must be 'demonstrably justified', placing the burden on the government to explain why the limitation on rights is a reasonable one.

The second component of generic constitutional law addresses *how* limitations can be justified, or, put another way, what it takes to demonstrate that a limitation is justified. Many constitutional systems articulate the test for justification as a requirement of proportionality, which David Beatty describes as the 'ultimate rule of law'.[32] The Canadian Supreme Court's formulation provides further structure to the proportionality inquiry.[33] First, the government interest must be an important one. If so, it must be reasonable to think that the restriction actually advances that interest. Beyond that, though, the restriction must limit the right as little as possible in doing so (sometimes referred to as a 'minimal impairment' or 'least restrictive means' requirement). Finally, the test requires a direct evaluation of proportionality, that is, whether the benefits obtained from the restriction, in terms of the amount to which the restriction advances the government's interests, are large enough to outweigh the costs of limiting the affected right.

Proportionality requirements do give some structure to inquiries that seek to balance protected rights and government interests. They do not, though, entirely avoid the concern that balancing approaches allow judges to substitute their evaluation of the importance of government goals for that of the legislature. Consider the 'least restrictive means' requirement. It is well-known that one can always show that the means chosen are the least restrictive ways of accomplishing a complex set of government goals, or, put another way, that any alternative would inevitably do worse in advancing that set of goals than the one chosen; the usual example is that it may be more expensive to administer the proposed alternative, so that the chosen means is indeed the least restrictive method of accomplishing some substantive goal at a specified cost. Finding a restriction disproportionate because there is a less restrictive alternative therefore amounts to substituting the court's judgment about the importance of government policies for the legislature's different judgment.

Whatever the analytic difficulties of the proportionality test, it has become an important component of generic constitutional law. Even courts that refrain from

---

[31] Constitution Act, 1982, enacted as Schedule B to Canada Act 1982, ch 11, Charter of Rights and Freedoms § 1.

[32] David Beatty, *The Ultimate Rule of Law* (2004).

[33] *Regina v Oakes* [1986] 1 SCR 103 (Supreme Court of Canada).

using the language of proportionality and the carefully staged analytic structure developed by the Canadian Supreme Court not infrequently invoke the concepts that go into a proportionality inquiry. Notably, the US Supreme Court, which has not adopted any general test of proportionality, is the origin of the phrase 'least restrictive means'.[34]

2. The Issue of Horizontal Effect

A third component of generic constitutional law is the resolution of the question of a constitution's 'horizontal effect', that is, the extent to which constitutional norms directly and without legislative implementation bind non-governmental actors such as corporations and private employers. The question of horizontal effect arises when, for example, a private employer refuses to hire a person because of the applicant's race or gender. The question was most pressing when constitutions were widely understood in classical liberal terms, as mechanisms for empowering yet limiting government institutions. Giving a constitution horizontal effect expands the scope of normative regulation, from government institutions to the entire society. Such an expansion might seem incompatible with the aspirations of classical liberal constitutions: Designed to *limit* government power, such constitutions would seemingly grant enormous power to the courts charged with enforcing constitutional norms.

The practical consequences of giving a constitution horizontal effect were greatly diminished by the expansion of the legislative authority of the modern social welfare state. Horizontal effect might be important when legislative regulation of the private economy was rare, but as such regulation increased, as for example with the adoption of statutes prohibiting discrimination in employment, the doctrine of horizontal effect came to play a residual role, dealing only with those areas in which statutory regulation had not taken hold. As a result, the practical stakes of having an expansive doctrine of horizontal effect were reduced.

The ideological stakes, that is, the conception of the constitution's purposes, remain important, though, and most constitutional systems have had difficulty directly addressing the question of horizontal effect. The formulation in the Constitution of South Africa exemplifies the difficulties. According to that constitution, a constitutional norm 'binds ... juristic persons if, and to the extent that, it is applicable, taking into account the nature of the right and the nature of any duty imposed by the right'.[35] To the extent that this formulation expresses some enforceable doctrine, it seems to urge on the courts some sort of balancing approach, but precisely what is to be balanced remains unclear.

---

[34] See *Shelton v Tucker* (1960) 364 US 479 (using the phrase 'less restrictive means').
[35] Constitution of the Republic of South Africa, § 8(2).

The difficulty of articulating a clear doctrine of horizontal effect has led many constitutional courts to a solution in which constitutional norms are given indirect effect. First developed by the German Constitutional Court, the doctrine of indirect effect has two components, the first an insistence that constitutional norms do not apply directly to non-government actors, and the second and more important, a rule that the ordinary courts must develop the ordinary law applicable in controversies between non-government actors in a way that fairly takes constitutional norms into account.[36] Libel cases have been a primary vehicle for the development of doctrines of indirect horizontal effect. Constitutional courts direct the ordinary courts to develop the law of libel in a way that is sensitive to the effects of libel doctrine on free expression. Constitutional courts that themselves have the power to develop the ordinary law take the same approach. Rather than saying that constitutional norms apply directly to non-government actors, they hold that the law regulating such actors must be sensitive to constitutional norms. Again, the South African Constitution is exemplary. It states, 'When interpreting any legislation, and when developing the common law or customary law, every court, tribunal or forum must promote the spirit, purport and objects of the Bill of Rights'.[37]

It should be noted that the US Supreme Court is unable to adopt a doctrine of indirect horizontal effect when it confronts the problem, known in the United States as that of 'state action'. The reason arises out of the structure of the US court system: Many state action problems arise in the application of the ordinary law developed in state courts, that is, the courts of the subnational units in the United States. And, as a matter of both constitutional and statutory law, the US Supreme Court has no power to direct state courts to alter the ordinary law except when that law is itself unconstitutional and not merely inadequately sensitive to constitutional norms.

VIII. COMPARATIVE CONSTITUTIONAL LAW AND NATIONAL IDENTITY

In contrast to studies of comparative constitutional law focusing on a universalistic idea of constitutionalism, other studies pursue the Montesquiean theme that each nation's constitution is distinctively suitable to that nation alone. Preambles and

---

[36] BVerfGe 7, 198 (1958) (Federal Constitutional Court of Germany) (The Lüth Case).
[37] Constitution of the Republic of South Africa, § 39(2).

similar components of constitutions are particularly useful sources for discerning the vision of national identity embedded in the constitution. The preamble to the Irish Constitution of 1937, for example, begins with the invocation of 'the Most Holy Trinity' as the 'final end' to whom 'all actions both of men and States must be referred', linking the nation's identity as tightly as possible to its Roman Catholic heritage. It continues by '[g]ratefully remembering [the] heroic and unremitting struggle to regain the rightful independence of our Nation', indicating how the constitution embodies the nation's radical break with its colonial legacy. The preamble to the South African Constitution, in successive phrases, acknowledges the injustices of apartheid and attempts to incorporate all South Africans, black and white, into the nation's new constitutional project: 'We, the people of South Africa, Recognise the injustices of our past; Honour those who suffered for justice and freedom in our land; Respect those who have worked to build and develop our country; and Believe that South Africa belongs to all who live in it, united in our diversity.'

Studies of the way in which specific subjects are dealt with in different constitutional systems can also reveal aspects of national identity. The German Constitutional Court alluded to the nation's experience during the Nazi regime in explaining why the provision in the Basic Law guaranteeing a 'right to life' to 'everyone' required that the legislature make it a criminal offence to obtain an abortion: 'Underlying the Basic Law are principles . . . that may be understood only in light of the historical experience and the spiritual-moral confrontation with the previous system of National Socialism'. Article 9 of the Japanese Constitution of 1946 states that 'the Japanese people forever renounce war as a sovereign right of the nation', and purports to ban the maintenance of 'land, sea, and air forces'. As Japan recovered its place in the international domain, the ban on maintaining armed forces was unsustainable, and the supreme court approved the creation of what were denominated 'self defence forces', eventually becoming one of the largest military forces in the world, sometimes deployed outside the nation's boundaries. By the turn of the twenty-first century, a substantial campaign developed to eliminate Article 9, a campaign that was controversial precisely because constitutional revision would entail a reconceptualization of the nation's identity. An astute analysis of the constitutional (and related) law of privacy and dignity in the United States and Europe locates the origin of differences in the doctrinal treatments of those doctrines in different social and ideological understandings of the way in which equality can best be achieved—in Europe, by making available to everyone the privileges previously available only to the elite, in the United States, by eliminating those privileges and subjecting everyone to the same low level of dignity and privacy previously accorded the less privileged classes.[38]

[38] James Q. Whitman, 'Enforcing Civility and Respect: Three Societies', (2000) 109 *Yale LJ* 1279–398.

An additional feature of comparative constitutional law as made by national courts is the extent to which they advert to constitutional developments elsewhere (and international law that might not be directly effective domestically) in interpreting the nation's constitution. The South African Constitution states that the constitutional court must consider international law, and may consider foreign law.[39] The Canadian Supreme Court alluded to the nation's role in promoting international human rights in explaining why it could no longer allow routine extradition of those subject to the risk of a death sentence.[40] The United States Supreme Court's modest references to non-US law in decisions dealing with the death penalty and gay rights provoked a substantial political controversy,[41] with proponents of such references urging that reasonable decision-makers take guidance and information from whatever sources seem helpful, and opponents charging that such references undermine national sovereignty. Beneath this controversy one can see a dispute about national self-understanding, between those who see the United States as a cosmopolitan nation fully participating in the world's lawmaking processes, and those who emphasize the distinctive place the United States has as an 'exceptional' nation in the world. A similar dispute occurs with respect to the claim that some Asian nations have a distinctive understanding of human rights, justifying their departures from human rights norms widely enforced elsewhere.

The controversy over so-called Asian values illustrates one of the limits of comparative constitutional law. Everyone acknowledges that different nations face different problems, and that an acceptable resolution of a problem in one nation might entail restrictions on liberty that would be unjustified in another nation. The European Court of Human Rights, which enforces a continent-wide set of rights, recognizes this fact in its doctrine giving each nation a 'margin of appreciation' in the application of those rights. Except in federal systems where subnational units are defined not by accidental geographical features but by real cultural or other diversity, the margin-of-appreciation doctrine cannot be an element in domestic constitutional law, and for that reason it is not truly a concern of the study of comparative constitutional law. But the idea that underlies the doctrine— that national differences can explain and justify differences in the interpretation of seemingly similar provisions—surely is.

---

[39] Constitution of the Republic of South Africa, § 39(1).
[40] *United States v Burns* (2001) SCR 283.
[41] See, most recently, *Roper v Simmons* 543 US 551.

IX. Conclusion

Innumerable comparative studies address the ways in which different constitutions and constitutional systems deal with specific topics, such as privacy, free expression, and gender equality. However valuable such studies have been in bringing information about other constitutional systems to the attention of scholars versed in their own systems, their analytic payoff is sometimes questionable. Indeed, enumeration of provisions and summaries of court decisions may sometimes obscure more than they illuminate. Scholarship in comparative constitutional law is perhaps too often insufficiently sensitive to national differences that generate differences in domestic constitutional law. Or, put another way, that scholarship may too often rest on an implicit but insufficiently defended preference for the universalist approach to comparative legal study over the particularist one.

As noted in Section VIII, in some areas national history obviously matters a great deal. More subtly, so do institutional and doctrinal structures. So, for example, the position taken with respect to the constitutionality of regulating hate speech in the United States on the one hand and in Canada and Great Britain on the other might be affected by the much greater centralization of prosecutorial authority in the latter nations, a centralization that limits the possibility of abusive hate speech prosecutions much more substantially than the highly dispersed prosecutorial authority in the United States.

Comparisons across systems must also be sensitive to differences in doctrinal structures. For example, systems fairly described as constitutionalist may tend to impose a reasonably high standard before the government can punish speakers who merely criticize government policy. Yet, the precise doctrinal formulation of that standard might be quite consequential. Constitutional scholars in the United States, for example, know that there is a real difference between the 'clear and present danger' test, well-known around the world, and the less well-known test requiring that the government show that speech critical of government policy uses words of incitement, must be intended to incite, and must be likely to bring about imminent lawless conduct (*Brandenburg v Ohio*, 1969). Scholars of comparative constitutional law might be less sensitive to those doctrinal differences. Still, the twenty-first century might well see a convergence among constitutionalist systems, prodded in part by the emergence of universal norms of international human rights and a gradual decrease in the size of the margin of appreciation for local variation, and in part by exchanges among constitutional court judges.[42]

The growth of scholarship on comparative constitutional law in the late

---

[42] See Anne Marie Slaughter, *A New World Order* (2004). For a recent example, see the conversations transcribed in Robert Badinter and Stephen Breyer, *Judges in Contemporary Democracy: An International Conversation* (2004).

twentieth century deepened the field's analytic foundations. Enumeration and juxtaposition began to be replaced by genuinely comparative studies, informed by insights from political science, sociology, and related fields. Scholars must be cautious about inferring too much about specific constitutions, specific constitutional provisions, and constitutionalism itself from the early years of experience with the constitutions whose adoption in the 1990s provided such energy for the field. Taken together with the knowledge available from longer established constitutional systems, though, this new information seems likely to continue to infuse the field of comparative constitutional law with analytic rigour.

BIBLIOGRAPHY

Carlos Santiago Nino, 'Transition to Democracy, Corporatism and Presidentialism with Special Reference to Latin America', in Douglas Greenberg, Stanley N. Katz, Melanie Beth Oliviero, and Steven C. Wheatley (eds), *Constitutionalism and Democracy: Transitions in the Contemporary World* (1993)

Juan J. Linz and Arturo Valenzuela (eds), *The Failure of Presidential Democracy* (1994)

J. Mark Ramseyer, 'The Puzzling (In)Dependence of Courts: A Comparative Approach', (June 1994) 23 *Journal of Legal Studies* 721–47

Jon Elster, 'Forces and Mechanisms in the Constitution-Making Process', (November 1995) 45 *Duke LJ* 364–96

James Q. Whitman, 'Enforcing Civility and Respect: Three Societies', (April 2000) 109 *Yale LJ* 1279–398

Stephen Gardbaum, 'The New Commonwealth Model of Constitutionalism', (Fall 2001) 49 *AJCL* 707–60

Norman Dorsen, Michel Rosenfeld, András Sàjo, and Suzanne Baer, *Comparative Constitutionalism: Cases and Materials* (2003)

Tom Ginsburg, *Judicial Review in New Democracies: Constitutional Courts in East Asia* (2003)

Matthew Stephenson, 'Independent Judicial Review', (January 2003) 32 *Journal of Legal Studies* 59–89

Mark Tushnet, 'Alternative Forms of Judicial Review', (August 2003) 101 *Michigan LR* 2781–802

David M. Beatty, *The Ultimate Rule of Law* (2004)

Anne-Marie Slaughter, *A New World Order* (2004)

Ran Hirschl, *Towards Juristocracy: The Origins and Consequences of the New Constitutionalism* (2004)

Vicki Jackson and Mark Tushnet, *Comparative Constitutional Law* (2nd edn, 2005)

David S. Law, 'Generic Constitutional Law', (February 2005) 89 *Minnesota LR* 652–742

CHAPTER 39

COMPARATIVE ADMINISTRATIVE LAW

JOHN S. BELL

Cambridge

COMPARATIVE administrative law is a long-standing discipline. The study of other administrative law systems both in order to understand one's own system better and to find models for improvement has been occurring for over 150 years.[1] In the earliest periods, the focus was very much on comparing the institutions of government, central and local,[2] whereas today much more attention is spent on rules and procedures for the exercise of control over the administration and remedies for the deficiencies of administrative action.

Unlike the comparison of private law, it is not possible for administrative lawyers to assume that there is a single, universal function that the law serves in most countries. Administrative law is closely bound up with national institutions and traditions, as well as national constitutional values and ways of operating. Any comparative approach has to take full account of the institutional context in which a particular problem or procedure occurs and to ensure that full account of these nationally specific features is taken before any attempt is made to generalize or compare. For this reason, much work by comparative lawyers involves the study in depth of one other administrative law system, which is then explained in terms familiar to those from the comparatist's own system.[3] The best of this work is explicitly comparative in terms of the questions asked about the other system and the explanations offered for the particular character of the system's development. Comparisons with more than one system are often less successful. If a single author undertakes such an enterprise, then it is often difficult for her or him to have an adequately deep understanding of how the governmental systems of all the different countries work. If there is a collective work, then the explanation of the national systems has to be undertaken in a genuinely comparative way, which is not always easy for national legal experts. This requires a close interaction between the reporters. As a result, there are fewer examples of successful comparative

---

[1] An illustration would be the appreciation expressed by A. V. Dicey of R. von Gneist, 'Englisches Verwaltungsrecht' (1867) in *An Introduction to the Study of the Law of the Constitution* (1st edn, 1886; 10th edn, 1959), 87, 183, and 184. It is interesting to note that the first book on English administrative law was written by a German: Otto Koellreutter, *Verwaltungsrecht und Verwaltungsrechtsprechung im modernen England: Eine rechtsvergleichende Studie* (1912). In many ways, the English distinctive definition of the subject has come out of intense comparison with other jurisdictions.

[2] A good example is Frank Johnson Goodnow, *Comparative Administrative Law* (1902).

[3] Very good examples are the works of Schwartz and Hamson, below n 26.

administrative law spanning many jurisdictions than in private law. More recent attempts to identify and promote deep collaboration of this kind at a European level have been more successful, notably the European Centre of Public Law and the work of Jürgen Schwarze.[4] Both rely on the underpinning of common standards between the jurisdictions studied through the European Convention on Human Rights and European Union law.

I. The Scope of the Subject

1. Definition of 'Administrative Law'

Studies labelled as 'comparative administrative law' are apt to suffer from a confusion about the meaning of 'administrative law'. In the continental European traditions, administrative law (*droit administratif, Verwaltungsrecht*) is concerned with the powers and organization of the executive organs of the state. The common law use of the term 'administrative law' is more synonymous with 'administrative litigation' (*contentieux administrative, Verwaltungsgerichtsbarkeit*), and even in the common law world the topic is often called 'judicial review (of administrative action)'. For the purposes of this study, administrative law establishes both primary rules governing how the administration is authorized to work (its organization, powers, and procedures), as well as the secondary rules governing the remedies (judicial or other) available in cases of a failure to observe the primary rules. To this extent, the broader continental definition is to be preferred.[5]

A second area of difficulty in comparison lies in the scope of administrative law. In one important sense, administrative law includes all the rules and principles that apply to the administration. But this usage would be unnecessarily encyclopaedic. If the distinctive feature of administrative law is the organization and exercise of state power, then our attention should focus on aspects that involve the exercise of state authority or the organization of public services, rather than on everything that a state body might do. There is no particular reason why the ordering of newspapers for the common room of city councillors or liability for an accident caused by the mayor's official car should be governed by rules that are different from those governing similar activities in the lives of ordinary individuals.

---

[4] See the journal *European Public Law* and Jürgen Schwarze (ed), *Administrative Law under European Influence* (1996).

[5] See also Goodnow (n 2), 9–11

Some administrative law rules will be of general application, and some will be confined to specific administrative bodies (eg local authorities) or specific activities (eg public services, education, and so on). There are good comparative studies of the latter, special branches of administrative law, but they are often described simply as 'comparative environmental law', 'comparative tax law', and so on. In this chapter, 'administrative law' will be used to identify a body of general principles that govern the powers and obligations of public authorities.

2. Public Law and Private Law

There is no universally applicable distinction between the distinctive administrative law rules and the rules that are shared between administrative bodies and private individuals and bodies. Legal systems typically distinguish between 'public law' and 'private law' to draw the boundary. This is often a major topic of comparative law enquiry.[6] There are two approaches to the definition of the distinction between public law and private law, and these reveal different aspects of the deep structure of the legal systems. One approach is *ideological* and focuses on the mission and values of public law. The second approach is *institutional* and focuses in particular on the different courts and tribunals through which redress for administrative wrongdoing is provided.

In terms of *ideology*, many continental European legal systems attribute a distinctive mission to public law. Public law is concerned with the common good, not private advantage, a point made by Ulpian in the third century.[7] The state is given special powers and is authorized to act only if it serves the public good. A good example would be the law of expropriation of private property for public utility.[8] Another area would be emergency powers.[9] In both cases, the state is authorized to restrict the rights of individuals without their consent in order to promote the common good. The interesting question for comparison between systems is whether the 'common good' has some generic meaning in such a context, or whether it is simply a framework for decisions to be made about specific national policy. Traditionally, it would have been said that the existence of the common good had to be identified simply as part of the national political process. In more recent times, the emphasis has been on the need for at least some minimum set of requirements that must be satisfied by a claim to the 'common good' in order to satisfy international standards of human rights protection.

The mission to promote the common good may not only authorize the state to

---

[6] eg Centre d'Études et de Recherche sur l'Administration Publique, *Le contrôle juridictionnel de l'Administration* (1991).

[7] D. 1, 1, 1, 2   [8] See Gavin M. Erasmus (ed), *Compensation for Expropriation* (1990).

[9] International Commission of Jurists, *States of Emergency: Their Impact on Human Rights* (1983).

interfere with the rights of private individuals, but may confer on the state special privileges. This occurs, for example in the provision of public services, where a public provider is exempt from many of the restrictions of competition law in order to enable it to provide a service in the general interest.

Although the distinction between actions undertaken for the common good and those undertaken for private advantage is easy to state, it is hard to apply. In some situations, the administration merely offers one mechanism among many to provide social activities, for example port facilities. If these happen to be run collectively, rather than individually, there is often no special social policy that makes the administrative activity different in character from that of the private sector.[10] For example, there are divergent views about the distinctiveness of some public services, such as electricity, gas, or ports.[11] Whereas the French tradition would confer on these activities a special mission in the service of the public good, other traditions, such as in the United Kingdom and the Netherlands, would see nothing specially governmental about such activities.

In terms of *institutions*, there are three issues for debate in this area: the distinctive functions of the administration compared with the private sector, the distinctive organization of the administration, and the distinctive courts that judge complaints against the administration. Studies of comparative public administration focus more on the core of any distinctive functions and institutions of the administration, than do debates in comparative law.[12] All the same, these differences are important in a European context. If one member state is claiming that its services run by public bodies are in the general interest and so should be exempt from competition law, and another member state has similar services provided by the private sector, which is subject to competition law, then the coherence of the internal market is affected. In order to resolve competition law issues of this kind, it is necessary that some comparative administrative law is undertaken. Comparative lawyers are generally more interested in whether systems have distinct courts for dealing with the administration, and upon what criteria the distinction is made between matters appropriate to the administrative courts and those for the ordinary courts. This is discussed in more detail below.

The distinctiveness of administrative law lies as much in its core concepts as in its distinct mission. There are a number of major organizing concepts in public law that differ from those of private law.[13] The core relations of public law are those between the state, the citizen, and the general interest. The relationships

[10] See Spyridon Flogaitis, *Administrative law et droit administrative* (1986), ch II.

[11] See below p. 000.

[12] eg Christopher Pollitt and Geert Bouckaert, *Public Management Reform: A Comparative Analysis* (2000) and a rare example from a comparative lawyer Sabino Cassese, *La nuova constituzione economica* (1995).

[13] John Bell, 'Public Law in Europe: Caught between the National, the Sub-National and the European?', in Mark Van Hoecke (ed) *Epistemology and Methodology of Comparative Law* (2004), ch 13.

between the state and its citizens involve the authority of the state to impose duties and burdens unilaterally, but also its duty to afford protection, respect, and participation to the citizen, and all this in a context of the state determining and implementing the common good. This core idea of public law gives rise to a number of distinctive concepts in administrative law.

3. Administrative Law and Public Administration

National administrative law has to be understood in the context of the character of national public administration, and this is significant for comparative law. In the modern world, the administration is a set of often large organizations. These provide the setting within which the legal norms operate. It is not possible to understand the law from the legal norms without also considering the organizational setting and procedures. As a result, there is a close connection between the discipline of administrative law and that of public administration.[14] Public administration is concerned with the institutional arrangements for the provision of public services and the regulation of governmental activities. Its focus is the organization, management, and effectiveness of those institutional arrangements. It is also concerned with values such as 'good government' and 'best practice'. Administrative law examines these arrangements in terms of values such as legality, fair procedure, and proportionate use of power. All the same, the normative standards governing the public administration are often related to those that are applied in administrative law. Sabino Cassese distinguishes two roles for administrative law. The first describes and systematizes the legal order relating to the public administration. The second engages in critical and constructive evaluation of the public administration from the perspective of standards of legality.[15] It is in this second area that comparative administrative law is particularly valuable. Whereas the literature on public administration involves many empirical studies, the scholarly literature on administrative law is rarely empirical, a point to which we return shortly.[16]

4. With Which Systems is Comparison Useful?

Comparative law studies should be more than the mere collation or confrontation of information about different legal systems. They should be able to provide

---

[14] See eg Yong Zhang, *Comparative Studies on the Judicial Review Systems in East and South-east Asia* (1997), 253. A good illustration would be the extent to which the organization and principles of the public administration form a substantial part of books entitled 'administrative law', eg Georges Vedel and Pierre Delvolvé, *Droit administratif* (12th edn, 1990), part IV; Cassese (n 12), chs 6, 7, and 8.

[15] Sabino Cassese, *Le Basi de diritto amministrativo* (1995), 12.   [16] Below, Section I.1(e).

insights either into the nature of the problems confronting different systems or into the way in which they operate and develop. To that extent, a work that presents different legal systems according to a reasonably similar framework of issues and then leaves the comparison to the reader would be inadequately comparative.[17] A useful comparison may analyse certain issues that are emerging in the different systems, such as the organization of the regulatory state, or it may be that the studies seek to discern the emergence of general principles.[18] On the whole, this is difficult to achieve, if one tries to cover the full range of administrative law, both rules on powers and procedures, as well as remedies.[19] In order to present a deep understanding of administrative law, it is necessary to confine a study to a small number of jurisdictions or to a small range of cognate topics.

(a) Comparison with Ideological Communities

Most comparative studies have been conducted in relation to countries that share a liberal political ideology. That ideology supports the fundamental values such as the rule of law, accountability, and fair procedure. Of course rules of administrative law have existed in other systems, and many of the contemporary rules were developed in times of autocratic government. But the usefulness of comparing the rules of law within different institutional and value systems is limited. If one wishes to have a contextualized understanding of the rules and how they work, then it is necessary to limit research. A number of general comparative studies did try to include the Soviet Prokuratura system within a comparison of the control of the administration. But the results were not particularly enlightening. In order to explain that part of the system effectively, it was necessary to explain much more of the context in which it operated. An even greater problem is met with the study of the Chinese control of the administration.[20] The assumption that 'the control of the administration' was a common phenomenon between systems of fundamentally different political character did not really stand scrutiny. Of course, there are activities to be administered and social benefits to be distributed in all systems, but the values that underpin the relationships between the parties is not the same in systems with a radically different ideology.

---

[17] See René Seerden and Frits Stroink (eds), *Administrative Law of the European Union, its Member States and the United States: A Comparative Analysis* (2002).

[18] Ibid 346. Pieter van Dijk, *Judicial Review of Governmental Action and the Requirement of an Interest to Sue* (1980) offers a clear example of this approach.

[19] This would be a criticism of Seerden and Stroink's work that it tries to cover both sets of topics in seven jurisdictions.

[20] See H. B. Jacobini, *An Introduction to Comparative Administrative Law* (1991), chs VI and VII; Hermann Mosler, *Gerichtsschutz gegen die Executive* (1967); Yong Zhang (n 14) has similar problems.

(b) Comparison within Legal Families

There is a long tradition of comparative research within what might be termed 'legal families' or legal traditions. The grouping of systems according to legal families is different from that of private law. To begin with, there was not the same heritage from Roman law, though there were common concepts and institutions inherited from Canon law. There has not been the export of codes, as in private law, mainly because much of the law has been uncodified until recently. Furthermore, administrative law has developed as part of the organization of the national state, and so has varied from country to country much more than private law.

The common law tradition involving in particular England, Ireland, Canada, Australia, New Zealand, and, for these purposes, Scotland, Malaysia, and South Africa has been an active forum of debate. Because they were administered as part of the British Empire, there was a close connection between the administrations of the different countries and this persisted, even after independence. Particularly where countries are federal, they may have significant differences from Britain in their modern organization. But there is still a significant commonality in traditions and approaches that they can be seen as having a sufficient family resemblance. Initially, there were also strong similarities in the rules developed by the Privy Council for the Commonwealth and the English and Scottish courts, and judges from Britain went out to the Commonwealth and their lawyers were often trained in England. This institutional commonality was reinforced by the principles of judicial review. Decisions from both the Privy Council and the House of Lords were often cited in all countries (especially as they were made typically by many of the same judges). Frequently, academics from the different jurisdictions were also educated in the United Kingdom and taught there for a while. Thus, institutional factors have reinforced the similarities between the systems. Although lying outside the institutional links of the Commonwealth, the United States still shares some features of the common law tradition in terms of judicial institutions and principles and has been hugely influential by reason of its well-developed scholarly writing. In the common law tradition, the American material is not only accessible in terms of language, but also in terms of its broad conceptual structure, even if there are also radical differences.[21] Within such a nexus, the character of the discussion goes well beyond documenting similarities and differences between rules. Rather, the debate seeks to identify solutions to what are perceived as common problems arising not only from a common inherited legal and administrative tradition, but also in the application of common values.[22]

---

[21] For a deep study, see Paul Craig, *Public Law and Democracy in the United Kingdom and the United States of America* (1990) and earlier Bernard Schwartz and Henry William Rawson Wade, *Legal Control of Government* (1972).

[22] A good example is Michael Taggart (ed), *The Province of Administrative Law* (1997), which has contributions from academics in Australia, Canada, New Zealand, the United Kingdom, and the USA.

There have also been similar kinds of debates within countries that have inherited the French tradition of administrative law, both substantive law and procedural matters. Either through colonial administration or by the importing of Napoleonic administration, a number of countries came under this sphere of influence and similarity, and have remained a natural grouping. Within Europe, this would include Portugal, Spain, Italy, Belgium, and Greece, and outside Europe countries as diverse as Lebanon, Chile, and Thailand, as well as former colonies in Africa and Indo-China. Many of these countries, though not all, also share the French tradition of a division between administrative and civil courts, which serves to reinforce differences in legal rules and principles. This similarity of approach is underpinned by frequent exchanges, even though the countries in question now come under different influences. The German tradition is somewhat different in that it does not share many of the institutional features that the French have adopted. Its constitutional and federal traditions, as well as the organization of its bureaucracy under Prussia, have helped to stimulate a distinctive tradition. The distinctive tradition of principles of judicial review has been particularly influential.

(c) Transnational Trends and Comparative Law

Although these historical traditions of legal families continue to have some influence, it has to be recognized that the roles and functions of the administration are subject to a number of transnational trends that extend across the boundaries of these traditions. In the first place, the administration serves conceptions of the public good that are wider than those confined to a single country or tradition. Economic and social goals include the provision of education, medical treatment, social security, transport, and defence, each of which is judged in terms of success by reference to the standards of comparably developed countries, irrespective of their legal tradition. Such comparison is undertaken by organizations such as the OECD and their recommendations influence the development of national administrative policies and institutions.[23] The involvement of many countries in supra-national groupings, such as the European Union, also has an influence on the character of the administration, both in terms of what it is legally permitted to do, and in terms of the influence exercised by the organization on the development of national policies. The incorporation of supra-national legal standards on fundamental rights and administrative behaviour has an influence on the shaping of national standards of judicial review. These may then displace the prestige[24] of other members of an historical legal family and make the point of reference a regional organization or a country seen as advanced, for example, the United States in respect of access to public documents. Thus, the choice of

---

[23] eg OECD, *School Factors Related to Quality and Equity: Results from PISA 2000* (2005).

[24] Rudolfo Sacco, 'Legal Formants: A Dynamic Approach to Comparative Law', (1991) 39 *AJCL* 1.

comparators is by no means limited to traditional ideas of legal families and is fluid.[25]

Useful comparison may therefore focus on one of two aspects of a legal tradition. On the one hand, there is a tradition of public administration and its organization. Some systems have more defined structures for the civil service or public services than others. Some are centralized, others decentralized or federal in terms of organization. When describing the law governing such institutions and activities, it may make most sense to focus on the organizational or institutional tradition. On the other hand, when it comes to the rules and procedures for the control of the administration or remedies for wrongs done, then the tradition of administrative justice may need to be the guide to appropriate comparators. For example, the common law tradition is much more relevant as a grouping in relation to these remedy rules of administrative law than in relation to the rules establishing the powers and procedures of the administration.

Historically, leading administrative law jurists in liberal democracies have been aware of developments outside their traditional circles of reference. Often this has served as a benchmark to assess the quality of national administrative justice and to raise questions about areas that need reform.[26] An important example is the extent to which there are emerging common European standards for administrative law, particularly through the operation of the European Union and the European Convention on Human Rights. Studies in this area will be conducted inductively and deductively. Whereas Schwarze[27] has tried to build up the picture by encouraging the analysis of individual national systems and how far they have changed as a result of European-level norms, Patrick Birkinshaw[28] tries to identify the principles at a supra-national level and see how far they provide a coherent set of standards to be applied nationally. At root there is a question of how far there is a deep commonality between legal systems. Institutions in public law perform tasks in the light of local political agendas and the availability of other local institutions. Education or policing may be national services in one country, but local or regional in others. Religious schools may be part of the public system in one country and part of the private sector in another, often because of the ideology in that country. Beyond the idea of having administrative structures in place to carry out the policies that have been decided by political institutions from time to time, is there a generic function that administrative law performs which is capable of forming the core of administrative law? The difficulty in answering this positively has led many authors to limit themselves to sectoral comparisons, for example, of

[25] Konrad Zweigert and Hein Kötz, *An Introduction to Comparative Law* (trans Tony Weir, 3rd edn, 1998), 69 recognize this.

[26] eg Charles John Hamson, *Executive Discretion and Judicial Control* (1954) and Bernard Schwartz, *French Administrative Law and the Common Law World* (1954).

[27] Jürgen Schwarze (ed), *Administrative Law under European Influence* (1996).

[28] Patrick Birkinshaw, *European Public Law* (2003).

judicial review, administrative liability, local government, education, and so on. It is probably best to suggest that there are not generic social functions that administrative law serves, but rather institutionally situated functions. Accordingly, administrative law comparison is both ideally and typically focused on narrower areas than are covered in national works on administrative law.

(d) Comparative Empirical Research

Empirical research can be defined broadly both positively as the study of the operations and the effects of the law and negatively as work which is not doctrinal or theoretical and which does not rely on secondary sources.[29] Such work is very valuable in understanding the impact of administrative law on the administration and citizens, but it is hard to conduct, even at national level, and is rarely undertaken in a comparative way.

Traditions of such empirical or socio-legal research differ. In relation to judicial review, Halliday suggests that there are three categories of such work:

- studies which propose links between judicial decisions and administrative reaction;
- works reflecting on the impact of judicial review by way of personal professional experience; and
- empirical studies designed to investigate the impact of judicial review on administrative decision-making.[30]

The first kinds of study trace the relationship between the law or judicial decision and the reactions of the administration predominantly from publicly available sources. One can document the changes that the administration has made in its rules or practices as a result of a law or judicial decision. Such studies are relatively straightforward extensions of doctrinal legal approaches. An obvious area for comparative work of this kind is the implementation of common norms, such as EU directives. It is easy to document normative change resulting from the enactment of legislation or the promulgation of rules. It is more difficult to assess the significance of changes without empirical interviews with participants and decision-makers. The research conducted in this way mirrors the work conducted in public administration on the transfer of ideas between administrations in different countries.[31]

The second kind of research involves the reflection of practitioners (often judges) on the way in which administrative law works. Often, there will be colloquia at

---

[29] See John Baldwin and Gwynn Davis, 'Empirical Research in law', in Peter Cane and Mark Tushnet, *The Oxford Handbook of Legal Studies* (2003), 880.

[30] Simon Halliday, 'Researching the Impact of Judicial Review on Routine Administrative Decision-Making', in David Cowan (ed), *Housing, Participation and Exclusion* (1998).

[31] David P. Dolowitz and David Marsh, 'Who Learns What from Whom: A Review of the Policy Transfer Literature', (1996) 44 *Political Studies* 343–57.

which national testimonies are given by practitioners to inform a foreign audience. Such testimonies can provide insights that would not be available by looking at the published sources of the law. The difficulty of such presentations is that sometimes they go little further than repeat what is known doctrinally, or they offer anecdotes that do not have adequate corroboration or assessment of their significance. Professional reflections may well be supported by statistics on case-loads, but it is often not easy to give deeper analysis to ensure that the figures are comparable. The most difficult part of such comparison is to go beyond the simple explanation of the different systems to reach a serious analysis of the different experiences. On the whole, colloquia do not achieve this. Rather, it requires a working group to inter- view the practitioners more systematically and to then hold a workshop in which there is a real confrontation and reflection on positions adopted. An example of the quality of such work and the difficulties encountered can be found in the collection of proceedings of workshops held to celebrate the bicentenary of the *Conseil d'Etat* in France in 1999.[32] The many chapters present the workings of many jurisdictions across the world in comparison with France and this work is valuable. Yet the depth of comparative analysis in the conclusions and overviews is rather limited. For example, Jean Rivero concluded a study on the administration and its citizens by stating that 'we agree on emphasizing the need for a prudent, but effective renewal of protection for the citizen'.[33] This cautious remark came as the culmination of a careful analysis of the different structures for providing redress for citizens' complaints in the various countries studied, which made the production of a more meaningful set of benchmarks difficult to construct.

A third kind of research is rare outside the Anglo-American tradition of legal scholarship. In these jurisdictions, there has been some significant research about the operation of agencies and public bodies that has included a study of the impact of law.[34] As Peter Cane points out, administrative law can be assessed either as an instrumental good, serving values such as efficient government, or as a non-instrumental good, serving constitutional and political values such as the rule of law or respect for human rights.[35] Viewed from an instrumental perspective, it is necessary to examine the impact of legal rules and judicial decisions on the behaviour of the administration. Such research is costly in time and requires special skills that lawyers often do not have. As a result, interdisciplinary research is necessary, but there is only a limited amount. It also requires access to

---

[32] P. Agron *et al.*, *Deuxième centenaire du Conseil d'Etat* (vol II, 2001).

[33] Jean Rivero, 'L'État de Droit', in Charles Debbasch (ed), *Administration et administrés en Europe* (1984).

[34] See eg Genevra Richardson, *Policing Pollution* (1983) and K. Hawkins, *Environment and Enforce- ment* (1984); and generally R. Baldwin and C. McCrudden, *Regulation and Public Law* (1987).

[35] Peter Cane, 'Understanding Judicial Review and its Impact', in Marc Hertogh and Simon Halliday (eds), *Judicial Review and Bureaucratic Impact: International and Interdisciplinary Perspectives* (2004), ch 1.

administrators and their files, which is often not easy to obtain. There are few studies that have been able to conduct this kind of research across jurisdictions. Rather, there has been a confrontation of the empirical research conducted on particular administrations within a specific jurisdiction in the hope of identifying significant similarities and differences. In consequence, Cane concludes that it is necessary for most studies of the administration to accept the importance of non-instrumental values for judicial review as criteria for assessing its acceptability. Within the literature on public administration, there are various attempts to calibrate the effectiveness of the administration, but even these have their difficulties.[36]

II. The Values Served by Administrative Law

1. Constitutional Values and Fundamental Rights

Public law is concerned with the duties and powers of the public administration to serve the common good. *Constitutionally* the public administration is subordinated to the legislative power and must comply with higher norms within the legal order. Doctrinal writers have long made clear the dominance of constitutional principles within administrative law.[37] The fundamental principles governing the administration derive from constitutional law, since this establishes the principal powers and functions of government. Some such principles are nation-specific, such as federalism. Spanish ideas about the functions of autonomous regions are different from the German law on the power of *Länder* or the American law on the powers of states. Principles on the allocation of functions between the government and parliament also differ quite substantially from one system to another. Trends covering a number of jurisdictions can be identified, but they are by no means universal. There are, however, some values common to liberal states that provide more general areas for comparison. Two of these are the rule of law and fundamental rights.

(a) Rule of Law

Although the term 'rule of law' is frequently used to express a fundamental value of

---

[36] Cane (n 35); also eg *OECD Reviews of Regulatory Reform, Regulatory Policies in OECD Countries: From Interventionism to Regulatory Governance* (OECD Publishing, 2002) and <www.oecd.org>.

[37] See Vedel and Delvolvé (n 14), ch 1.

any liberal political system, there are different understandings of this idea among different legal systems. Within the common law tradition, the English-language expression 'rule of law' embraces a number of understandings. In some contexts, it merely refers to conformity to law: an administrative act is authorized by a higher norm. In the view of Dicey, the rule of law emphasized the absence of privileges for the administration and the subordination of the administration to the ordinary law of the land.[38] For him, that entailed the subordination of the administration ultimately to the ordinary courts. In modern times, the idea of compliance with human rights has gained strength and was part of the Delhi declaration of the International Commission of Jurists in 1959. The French conception of l'*état de droit* expresses the idea that all public power is limited by the legal rules which it is bound to respect. It offers the control of power through law. The law is administered, especially by the *Conseil d'Etat* as adviser and judge. But such an expression does not contain substantive content, and it certainly does not entail that the ordinary judges have powers over the administration. In French, the English conception is often translated as 'le règne du droit' in that the law (conceived in the broad sense of legal values) prevails over the administration. The German-language concept of the *Rechtsstaat* has the idea that the administration is given power by the law and is constrained by it.[39] The principle applies to all the administration without immunities. Its concept of the *Gesetzesvorbehalt* (authorization by law) is contrasted with the idea of inherent powers of the administration found in French law and in the English Crown prerogative. The concept is usually understood to include rights of defence against the administration. The German expansion of this into the *sozialer Rechtsstaat* involves a number of substantive rights and social justice. To a great extent, the scope of notions such as 'the rule of law' depends on how far the term is allowed to spread to embrace other constitutional values. The divergence in uses of the terminology and the absence of an exact equivalent in the different languages provides much potential for confusion. All the same, these different terms convey some common liberal messages—that the administration is not free to act as it deems to be right in terms of efficiency or to achieve political goals. The administration has to remain within the constraints set out by law.

(b) Fundamental Rights

Many constitutions, particularly those drafted since 1945, contain enumerations of fundamental rights. These set out further values that the administration must respect and, in some cases, actively promote. A number of types of comparative

---

[38] Dicey (n 1), ch XII. This view he held despite the fact that the Crown then enjoyed immunity from actions in the court.

[39] The concept was coined by von Mohl in 1832: Michael Stolleis, *Geschichte des öffentlichen Rechts in Deutschland* (vol II, 1992), 173.

study have been undertaken to assess the impact of this process. Some simply set in parallel the impact of a specific human rights instrument on national laws. For example, this has been done in relation to the European Convention on Human Rights and Fundamental Freedoms of 1950. Others, however, have tried to compare the extent of the impact and discuss the reasons for the way it has worked in the different legal systems.[40] The concern of such studies is often the outcomes of compliance and an assessment of how far individual legal systems fall short of what the Convention requires. There is less attention to the reasons why national systems absorb such international standards in different ways. The work of Philip Alston,[41] however, has been innovative in examining the processes of introducing fundamental values. The use of bills of rights as legal instruments raises issues of how far the enactment of a legal text has an impact on the way in which the legal system works and what is required to ensure a culture of respect for fundamental values. Although the answers to such questions involve an element of legal sociology, some clues can be found in the extent to which the legal system has adapted to the new culture of rights. Bills of rights are often copied from other constitutions, so there is scope to study legal transplants in this area and to assess how far the embedding of new ideas depends on the legal professions and traditions of the receiving country.[42]

Comparison can be undertaken on how far administrative law reflects certain fundamental values. Many of these values are included in notions of a fair procedure. The influence of fundamental rights is a theme in many general studies of administrative law in Europe.[43] Much of the comparison of fundamental rights occurs in the discussion of influences of international treaties on national law and this applies well outside Europe, though many of the issues are similar.[44]

2. Standards of Good Administration

Operationally, the administration must conform to standards of good administration, including efficiency. Standards of good administration are typically laid down as ideals of administrative practice, rather than legal standards. For example, the moves in the 1990s to treat the user of public services as a form of consumer

---

[40] Compare Conor A. Gearty, *European Civil Liberties and the European Convention on Human Rights: A Comparative Study* (1997) with Andrew Z. Drzemczewski, *European Human Rights Law in Domestic Courts: A Comparative Study* (1983); Robert Blackburn and Jörg Polakiewicz, *Fundamental Rights in Europe* (2001).

[41] Philip Alston (ed), *Promoting Human Rights through Bills of Rights* (1999).

[42] Ibid, especially ch 1.   [43] See Schwarze (n 4).

[44] See Nihal Jayawickrana, *The Judicial Application of Human Rights Law: National, Regional and International Jurisprudence* (2002).

spawned a series of administrative charters, which had no legally binding effect, but which sought to guarantee compensation for failures to meet certain basic standards of public service defined by the administration. In more recent times, the citizen's right to good administration has been enshrined in Art 41 of the Charter of Fundamental Rights and in Art II–41 of the European Constitutional Treaty. A more detailed statement, the Code of Good Administrative Behaviour, was voted by the European Parliament on 6 September 2001. Many such norms do not have legal value, but act as guiding standards that may often form a background to the way in which lawyers and ombudsmen identify how the administration ought to behave, and how legal norms ought to be interpreted. A major area of comparison is administrative procedure (discussed below Section III.3).

III. Comparing the Powers, Organizations, and Procedures of the Administration

1. Powers of the Administration

The concepts of administrative law are not the same in each jurisdiction. In particular, certain terms have particular resonance. A good illustration is the notion of 'public service'.[45] This concept has a particular meaning in French law, where it covers activities provided in the public interest, as this is determined by relevant public authorities. Among the key indicia for an activity to be a public service are its link to a public authority in delivery or authorization, the public interest served, whether it is designed to make a profit or break even, and whether it involves the exercise of powers beyond those normally accorded to private individuals (*les pouvoirs exorbitants*). Once an activity is so classified, then a number of principles apply to its provision, notably the principles of continuity, adaptability, equality, and neutrality. In brief, the state has power to ensure the continuity of the service and to change its specification, but it is required to treat all users equally and to respect the diversity of opinions and beliefs in providing its services. The state is there either as provider or more often as commander of services for the community as a whole, not just for those who can pay for them.

While lawyers in the French tradition readily recognize the concept of 'public

---

[45] See Frank Moderne and Gerard Marcou, *L'idée de service public dans le droit des états de l'union européenne* (2001).

service' with similar legal consequences, those in other traditions do not have a single legal concept that embraces this range of activities. The activities may be very similar to those in France, but they are governed by individual sets of rules governing each particular activity or body. In the common law tradition, 'public service' may be a political concept, but it has no legal definition. In the German and Dutch traditions, there may be special principles that govern the activities of public authorities, but this does not give rise to a general law on public services, including those that are operated by the private sector. This diversity of traditions has made it difficult within the European Union to get agreement on the areas that should be exempted from the normal regime of market competition. Comparative study of these different approaches to the problem shows that there are assumptions and values associated with particular legal concepts and so the conceptual structure of the law makes a difference to how lawyers think.

2. Comparison of Administrative Organizations

The overlap between administrative law and 'administrative science' (*Verwaltungswissenschaft*), often described as 'public administration', is important in most jurisdictions. It is not seriously possible to discuss the norms of administrative law without an appreciation of how the administration works. Furthermore, there are limits to the utility of discussions of general principles of administrative law. The field of administrative law is vast and varied, and the operation of some administrations is substantially different from that of others. As a result, there has been an important strand of comparative research that focuses not on general administrative law, but on particular administrations. Arguments about how the administration should be organized belong to theories of public administration, which the law implements. In particular, modern developments in the nature of the state have focused on the concept of the 'state as regulator', rather than the 'state as provider'.[46] Comparative law looks to see how far these concepts of public administration can illuminate legal structures and powers. Particular attention would be paid to public administration and public finance. For example, practices such as contracting out governmental functions to the private sector or to autonomous agencies have an impact on the character of the state. At the same time, this has a significant impact on the character of public law. Equally, financing public activities through partnerships between public and private finance, which has become common, offers an opportunity for considering the way in which classical

---

[46] See UN Secretariat, *Public Sector Indicators* (*Report for the 15th session of Group of Experts on the United Nations Programme in Public Administration and Finance*) (22 March 2000); Giacinto della Cananea (ed), *European Regulatory Agencies* (2004); Cosmo Graham, *Regulating Utilities: A Constitutional Approach* (2000).

descriptions of administrative law have to be replaced in the face of new forms of administrative structure.

A long-standing area of research has been local administration.[47] Apart from similarity in geographical focus, this topic is actually quite heterogeneous. In the first place, the size of the 'local' unit of government varies enormously. Whereas 'communes' in Latin countries may be very small with limited power, some of the regional governmental bodies in other countries can carry very substantial authority and decide major issues. In the second place, the distribution of powers between central and local government can be very different. For example, in many countries such as France, education is a national public service. In the United Kingdom, it is a local government function. Comparison of local government thus requires a greater precision about the nature of the functions that are being studied. All the same, the issue of how to involve people in the government of their local area is a common theme across countries with different governmental structures.

The scope for public sector enterprises has varied over the past sixty years. In the 1950s until the 1980s, public enterprises were a major governmental vehicle for achieving social goals, and not just a mechanism for delivery. As a result, they were the subject of significant study. Studies led by Wolfgang Friedmann were able to identify purposes that were shared between different countries in their use of such enterprises. Since there was a period trend in favour of this way of functioning, there were important similarities in the way the enterprises operated, as well as significant differences. Both of these were valuable objects of study.[48]

Public employment offers another area in which comparison is valuable, but difficult.[49] A common tradition in continental Europe is that certain state employees have a distinct and protected status. There are special rules for their appointment, career progress, disputes, and dismissal. Public employment law is distinct from private employment, at least for employees performing important state functions. By contrast, common law systems have conceived public employment in essentially private law terms, either as part of the Crown household or as bound by contract. It is only when one considers many administrative practices that the familiar territory of secure employment and distinct procedures and practices are found. These different administrative law structures and concepts may serve to explain the limited amount of comparative law study of public employees, in contrast to the amount of work in public administration. It is easier to note trends and to map the different kinds of provision in the countries studied than to

---

[47] This was a major topic in Goodnow's study of 1893 (n 2), and was a concern of other writers in the period, such as von Gneist (n 1).

[48] Wolfgang Friedmann, *Public and Private Enterprise in Mixed Economies* (1974); Wolfgang Friedmann and Jack Garner, *Government Enterprise* (1970); Michael Moran and Tony Prosser, *Privatization and Regulation in Europe* (1994); Tony Prosser and Cosmo Graham, *Privatizing Public Enterprises: Constitutions, the State and Regulation in Comparative Perspective* (1991).

[49] Tiziano Treu (ed), *Employees' Collective Rights in the Public Sector* (1997).

come up with meaningful common principles.[50] The important areas to be covered include the extent of security of tenure provided to public sector employees, the right to strike and engage in collective bargaining.

3. Comparison of Administrative Procedures

Even if institutions of government are often specific to a particular country, standards for administrative procedure often have more in common. The comparative study of administrative procedures is interesting not just for their content, but also for what this topic illustrates about the sources of administrative law in different jurisdictions. In a number of countries, there are legal codes governing the procedure by which the administration makes decisions, starting in Austria with the General Law on Administrative Procedure of 21 July 1925 and in the United States of America with the Administrative Law Procedure Act 1946. Other examples include the German *Verwaltungsverfahrensgesetz* of 25 May 1976, the Italian law of administrative procedure of 7 August 1990, and the Dutch general law on the administration of 1992. Prior to these statutes, much of the general law was judge-made, though there were specific procedures laid down by statute in relation to specific activities, such as expropriation. In other systems, such as the English common law, that mix of judge-made principles and sector-specific rules remains in force. In addition to these different national sources, there are broadly conceived transnational standards. Some of these transnational standards are not legally binding, but exercise a general influence over the development of the law in particular countries.[51] Other standards are set by international treaties, such as the European Convention on Human Rights. Comparative law is interested not only in comparing the different national standards, but also in how national standards meet international standards.

Such procedural obligations are founded not only on the protection of the subject who is subordinated to the unilateral power of the administration, but also in accountability for its actions to the citizens of the state. Thus the duty to provide reasons not only provides transparency that can enable superiors to exercise control, but also contributes to a better dialogue with citizens. A third reason would be the economy and efficiency of administrative decisions. Simplicity

---

[50] Ibid, Part 1.

[51] See Resolution R (77) 31 of the Council of Ministers of the Council of Europe of 28 September 1977 on the protection of the individual in relations with the state. Rights identified in this Resolution included the access to administrative documents, to legal advice and assistance in preparing a case to the administration, to the reasons for the decision, and to information on rights of appeal. All these involve in some way the right to defend individual interests against the general interest.

and comprehensibility in procedures may avoid excessive cost and improve the comprehensibility of decisions.[52]

Comparison is undertaken at three levels. The first is a discussion of the general principles of administrative procedure. Some experienced commentators suggest that the diversity of the activities and purposes of administrative action is such that any attempt to develop uniform principles to govern the procedure by which the administration acts is bound to fail, either because the duties would be too numerous and burdensome, or because the rules would be so partial and incomplete as to provide inadequate supervision.[53] The procedures appropriate in schools may be inappropriate for dealing with immigration or planning. There may be no particular benefit in having similar procedures for all these organizations. But others consider that there are common standards, grounded in ideas of *fairness* and in the need to simplify procedures for the citizen in his or her dealings with different facets of the administration.[54]

A second level focuses on the procedures of particular administrations or processes. An example would be planning enquiries. Clearly the difficulty here is establishing that the institutional context is sufficiently similar so that the procedures followed can be compared in a useful manner.[55] A third level targets particular procedural duties. Among the issues debated in recent years are the duty of decision-makers to provide reasons for their decisions and the access of the public to information.[56]

IV. COMPARING LEGAL REDRESS

Administrative law organizes a range of forms of redress. There have long been extra-judicial forms of redress that have been very significant. The most important of these has been the Ombudsman movement, which began in Sweden in the early nineteenth century and has grown in the period after the expansion of the welfare state in the 1960s.[57] The law also organizes hierarchical review procedures and,

---

[52] Guido Corso and Francesco Teresi, *Procedimento amministrativo e accesso ai documenti* (1991), 48–50.

[53] See Liusa Torchia (ed), *Il procedimento amministrativi: profili comparati* (1993), 43.

[54] Willem Konijnenbelt, 'The Administrative Procedure in the New Dutch Code of General Administrative Law', in ibid 64.

[55] See the warning of Martin Loughlin, 'The Importance of Elsewhere', [1993] *Public Law* 44 at 57 about the importance of institutional context in deciding whether comparison is useful.

[56] W. J. Ganshof van der Meersch, in Zoltan Peteri and Vanda Lamm (eds), *General Reports to the 10th International Congress of Comparative Law* (1981), 769; Birkinshaw (n 28), ch 6.

[57] See Frank Stacey, *Ombudsmen Compared* (1978).

in more recent times, mediation. Each of these forms an important object of comparative study that lies on the borderline between the disciplines of administrative law and public administration. Much comparative law has concentrated on the institutions of judicial review, the grounds on which it may be awarded, and on the liability of the administration.

1. Comparison of the Procedures and Institutions of Judicial Review

Much of the literature comparing the administrative law in different jurisdictions has concentrated on the issue of how administrative litigation is organized. In part, this has been a result of the interest of administrative judges in discussing how their different systems work. For instance, the volumes published to celebrate the bicentenary of the *Conseil d'Etat* in 1999 include comparisons with many countries in Europe and outside.[58] For the most part, they are concerned with the organization of the administrative courts. It would be conventional to distinguish at least three groups of systems. On the one hand, there are those systems, led by France and Italy, which have distinctive courts, corps of judges, and procedures by which litigation against the administration is brought. Such distinctive courts will certainly have jurisdiction over the legality of administrative acts and may well have competence over administrative liability, administrative contracts, and administrative employment. A second group would include Germany and Spain where there is a distinct branch of the ordinary judiciary which deals with litigation against the administration. The judges engaged in this work are thus specialists. A third group of countries, including England, Scotland, Ireland, and the Netherlands (as well as Scandinavia in the past) have maintained on the one hand a tradition of a common jurisdiction for all matters concerning private and public persons, yet have had a significant number of specialist tribunals that have dealt with specific problem areas, for example, taxation.

This triptych is breaking down in particular in the light of changing European-wide standards. The Scandinavian and Dutch systems were criticized by the European Court of Human Rights in the *Sporrong and Lönnroth* and *Benthem*[59] decisions. In both cases, the system of tribunals was seen to be insufficiently independent. The need for appeal, at least on a point of law, to the courts had been recognized in the British Tribunals and Inquiries Act 1958. The judicialization of the tribunal systems makes them effectively like inferior and specialist courts, often staffed by a combination of lay and lawyer members. In more recent times, the

---

[58] See n 32.

[59] *Benthem v Netherlands* (1985) 8 EHRR 1, Appl No. 1/1984/73/111; *Sporrong and Lönnroth v Sweden* (1982) 5 EHRR 33, Appl No. 7151/75 and 7152/75.

English specialist group of judges dealing with administrative law matters has been relabelled the 'administrative court'. In a different sense, the Americans have developed the concept of the 'administrative judge' offering redress in relation to a particular agency. As far as the extreme separation approach is concerned, this is equally under threat from European standards. In the first place, the standards of a fair judicial procedure in the application of Article 6 of the European Convention do not vary depending on whether a matter is administrative or civil. Second, many of the substantive standards applicable in areas such as public employment, public contracts, and public liability apply in similar ways to the relationships between private parties. Principles of non-discrimination and free movement, notions of competition and competitive tendering, and administrative fault apply to bodies in the public sector, organs of the state, in ways that are not very different from private law. As a result, Italy has moved public employment and public liability within the jurisdiction of the ordinary civil courts. Even the French public law courts borrow procedural devices from the private law courts. There is, of course, the special core issue of the legality of administrative decisions, particularly in the area of the exercise of discretionary power. The rules for this will differ, even from litigation concerning the exercise of powers within a company or private association. Issues of speed, standing, and the extent of scrutiny all argue for a different approach to the relationships between private individuals. But, to the extent that the administration makes use of devices of private law, such as contracts, rather than exercising naked authority in order to achieve its aims, the need for distinctive procedures or judicial institutions becomes less obvious. The distinctiveness of administrative law procedures can best be viewed as essentially pragmatic responses to the special character of some of the issues coming before the courts, rather than being grounded in any deep philosophical distinction between the quality of justice required for administrative law cases and those concerning other matters. The modern question is whether it is necessary to have distinct administrative courts in order to provide adequate redress against the administration.

2. The Grounds of Judicial Review

In many legal systems, there is no code or statute that authorizes the courts to control the legality of administrative action or defines the grounds on which this is done. Accordingly, there is much debate in various countries about the constitutional foundation of judicial review of the administration. For some, it is simply a matter of enforcing the wishes of the legislature. For others, there are more fundamental values that justify a restrictive interpretation of the powers of the administration. The debate on the foundations of judicial review turns around conceptions of the rule of law, discussed above. There is limited comparative discussion of the foundations of judicial review.

Many of the most successful works in comparative law have limited their focus to specific grounds of review in different jurisdictions, though this is often combined with a study of the institutional mechanisms for protecting the citizen.[60] The purpose of such studies has been to understand the differences between national conceptions of administrative justice. A good example is the notion of 'proportionality'. The term has migrated from German administrative law to become a principle recognized in most jurisdictions. Much comparison has been undertaken with the object of clarifying how far there is a real difference between this (often foreign) concept and longer established concepts used in domestic law, such as *erreur manifeste d'appréciation* or *unreasonableness*. The most successful studies of this kind, for example that of Aldo Sandulli, are able to look in depth at the way in which the term is used in the different jurisdictions and the extent to which it represents a difference in the scope of review from traditional terms. In his survey of legal developments in the EU, France, Germany, Italy, and the United Kingdom, Sandulli notes the desire in all countries to prevent the administration exceeding its powers, but there was a divergent degree to which principles of this kind were imposed. National approaches to the control over the administration reflected different views about the scope for the judges to limit the freedom of the administration, especially in the field of discretionary power.[61] Familiarity with regard to the use of this standard in the exercise of EU law competences made many countries more receptive to it. It was difficult to have one standard applied to purely domestic cases and one applied in European cases.[62] All the same, Sandulli notes as do others that the concept of 'proportionality' is used with differing degrees of deference depending on whether a court is controlling a legislative action or the action of the administration.[63] Such work requires considerable attention to the detail of the different systems and how particular issues are handled. In contrast to works in which various experts present the application of such a principle within their own jurisdiction,[64] the kind of study by a single author like Sandulli, or by a collaborative team, can draw comparative conclusions about the nature of legal solutions.

Works examining the development of common European standards of administrative law typically focus on the grounds of review as illustrating the values by which the administration is meant to abide. These values are then used by the European courts as benchmarks to judge the conduct of a transnational

---

[60] See eg Roger Bonnard, *Le contrôle juridictionnel de l'administration. Etude de droit comparé* (1934); Mosler (n 20).

[61] Aldo Sandulli, *La proporzionalità dell'azione amministrativà* (1998), 37–134.   [62] Ibid 132–4.

[63] Ibid 190 and cf Kay Hailbronner, 'The Principle of Proportionality', in Zoltan Peteri and Vanda Lamm (n 56), 831.

[64] eg Evelyn Ellis (ed), *The Principle of Proportionality in the Laws of Europe* (1999); Søren Schønberg, *Legitimate Expectations in Administrative Law* (2001).

administration such as the European Union.[65] In turn, these standards developed by the courts as 'general principles recognized by the member states' are then used to judge the actions of particular member states.[66] There is thus a two-way circulation of ideas.

3. The Liability of the Administration

The liability of the administration provides an example of an area in which the distinctiveness of administrative law will vary from system to system. One focus of analysis would be the values and the basis of liability. Some systems have adopted the view that the liability of the administration should be the same as that for private individuals. Christophe Guettier argues, however, that the specificity of governmental liability is to be found in the balance that has to be struck between protecting the interests of the citizen and preserving the ability of the administration to act in the public interest.[67] Some take the view that specific individuals who suffer disproportionately from actions taken in the public interest should be compensated on a very different basis to those who suffer from the actions of private individuals. At the same time, the risks taken in the public interest may justify a greater caution in terms of the compensation of harms suffered. A public body undertaking a risky activity should not be deterred by the danger that it will have to compensate those who suffer harm as a result. An example would be police actions taken to deal with a sudden threat to public order.

Research in this area has taken various forms. Many have looked at statements of the general principles of liability.[68] This has advantages in bringing out the differences in fundamental values at issue in the field. But most works find it also helpful to focus on specific problem areas to see how far the legal rules make any practical difference to the compensation available to those who suffer from wrongful or excessive administrative action.[69] But it is necessary to go beyond examining merely the results of particular actual or hypothetical cases. Markesinis and his colleagues make this clear through a comparative study of five fact situations in different countries. They set the decision in a legal and socio-economic context to assess its meaning and importance.[70] In addition, attention to individual cases needs to go beyond the reasons given by judges in order to analyse them in terms

[65] Trevor C. Hartley, *The Foundations of European Community Law* (4th edn, 1998), ch 4.

[66] See Schwarze (n 4).   [67] Christophe Guettier, *La responsabilité administrative* (1993), 97.

[68] eg John Bell and Anthony W. Bradley (eds), *Governmental Liability: A Comparative Study* (1991).

[69] This was the structure of the concluding and comparative part of the Max Planck Institute study in 1964 of the topic: Hermann Mosler (ed), *Haftung des Staates für rechtswidriges Verhalten seiner Organe* (1967).

[70] Basil S. Markesinis, J.-B. Auby, Dagmar Coester-Waltjen, and S. F. Deakin, *Tortious Liability of Statutory Bodies: A Comparative and Economic Analysis of Five English Cases* (1999), 107.

of the underpinning ideas. In particular, there is the question of whether the principles setting out the basis of compensation are the same.

Although concepts may vary somewhat from one system to another, it is useful to talk in terms of five general foundations of a right to compensation from a public authority. The first concept is *fault*—a person has a moral responsibility to make good the harm which has been caused by his or her neglect or wrongdoing. Clearly there will be debates about the standards that are expected of a public body, but the key issue is how fault is established. In common law systems, fault involves the breach of a specific duty of care. In other systems, fault simply means a failure by a public authority to conduct itself in a way that can be reasonably expected.[71] Such a standard is close to the failure of the administration to perform its mission, a standard typically used in public administration to criticize 'maladministration'. For some this is too expansive, and they consider that liability will arise only where there has been a breach of an individual right or a materially protected legal position relative to the administration (a kind of 'legitimate interest').[72]

The second concept is that of *risk*. Even without fault, if a body has created a situation of risk of harm for its own purposes (or for the community which it serves), then there is ground for holding it responsible. This idea of sharing benefits and burdens is well acknowledged. In economic terms, a body must internalize the costs of the operation, rather than externalizing them to other people.

Both of these justifications apply equally to public and private persons. But there is a further set of justifications which apply more specifically to public authorities, and which are acknowledged with greater or lesser clarity in the different systems. Roger Errera explains that equality before public burdens justifies French public law liability, both in the areas of fault and risk.[73] This is based on the principle that no one can be expected to contribute an excessive amount for the public good. German lawyers talk about the idea of special sacrifice (*Sonderopfer*) in such circumstances. Now this principle is easy to understand where there is a planned risk created for the public benefit, such as in expropriation.[74] But where there is an unplanned consequence, such as a prisoner on parole committing a bank robbery,[75] the idea of internalizing consequences is less clearly a matter of

---

[71] See Principle 1 of Council of Europe Recommendation R (84) 15 on Public Liability, adopted by the Council 18 September 1984: Reparation should be ensured for damage caused by an act due to a failure of a public authority to conduct itself in a way which can reasonably be expected from it in relation to the injured person.

[72] See Günther Jaenicke, 'Haftung des Staates für rechtswidriges Verhalten seiner Organe', in Mosler (n 69), 867–9.

[73] Roger Errera, 'The Scope and Meaning of No-Fault Liability in French Administrative Law', [1986] *Current Legal Problems* 157.

[74] See Wolfgang Rüfner, 'Basic Elements of German Law on State Liablity', in Bell and Bradley (n 68), ch 11.

[75] CE Sect, 29 April 1987, *Banque populaire de Strasbourg, Actualité Juridique Droit Administratif* 1987, 488.

responsibility. In many ways, the duty to pay compensation in such circumstances is based less on a notion of liability, taking responsibility for one's actions and the harm they cause, and more on *social solidarity*. Such social solidarity offers an alternative basis for requiring the state to pay compensation to those who suffer injury. For example, the French Constitution proclaims the solidarity of all in the face of national calamities. The moral idea is based on the view that, if we find ourselves as part of a community, that situation of mutual dependence generates duties of solidarity. For this reason we offer compensation to those who suffer from the side-effects of a vaccine. Despite the way the issue is presented in some jurisdictions, social solidarity is not a basis of legal liability, but is rather a principle of social justice that could justify a redistribution of resources based on compassion, rather than entitlement.[76] As a result, whilst some countries like France would discuss topics such as vaccine damage under the heading of the *liability* of the administration, other systems would consider it as part of a more general *law on compensation*. The divergence shows a distinction between a view of a moral duty on the state to make reparation only when it has done wrong, and a broader conception of the state as a vehicle for meeting obligations of social solidarity.

V. Influences Shaping Administrative Law

1. Legislators, Professors, and Judges

Administrative law is a relatively modern branch of the law, although it does have roots deep in the medieval period. To a great extent, the courts were responsible for creating many of the remedies for citizens against the administration. In France, Germany, and England, these developed in a piecemeal fashion before the creation of the liberal democratic state. Many of the standards reflected ideas of good administration, rather than the need to keep the state in check. But this latter idea grew later. Judicial initiatives were the predominant vehicle for developing the law. Legislation was rare and tended to be specific. For example, in France there was legislation on liability for public works during the Revolution.

---

[76] See Duncan Fairgrieve, Mads Andenas, and John Bell, *Tort Liability of Public Authorities in Comparative Perspective* (2002), xix–xxii and references therein. Common lawyers have enormous problems in accepting the idea that one has a duty to help those who fall into misfortune: see the discussion of the Bad Samaritan in Joel Feinberg, *Harm to Others* (1984), 163–71.

The development of principles was very much left to textbook writers. Many of the relevant treatises first appeared in the 1880s: Maurer in Germany, Dicey in England, Laferrière in France. Indeed there was quite an interest of the writers in one country for the work of the others. The same has been true in recent times. In England, De Smith (edited now by a senior judge and a professor) provided the academic systematization of the principles of judicial review, whilst Wade provided a more general analysis of administrative law. But it is perhaps symptomatic of the common law that De Smith should have attributed the lack of general principles of administrative law to the lack of a separate system of higher administrative courts.[77]

Studies have been undertaken on the roles of different legal actors in the development of national administrative laws and these do not reflect the same patterns of influence that are seen in national private law. For example, in France, it has been administrative judges as *commissaries du gouvernement*, in acting as the government's legal adviser, or in their course books that have had a major influence on the principles of French administrative law.[78] Their influence has not been simply in making specific decisions, but also on the whole theoretical structure of administrative law. In England, the textbook writers have really shaped the subject and leading judges have drawn their inspiration from them. In this context, it is important to note the role of the Law Commission, a governmental body involving academics and judges, in creating a consensus amongst the legal community and the users of the law before legislation is introduced. Indeed, where legislation has not been introduced, the judges may often draw on its reports for inspiration. The experience of administrative law in Germany, Spain, and Italy has been more similar to that in private law, with principles of administrative law coming from academic literature and the use of academics to prepare legislative measures.

2. Trends in Law and Trends in Public Administration

Much of the study of influences on the development of principles regulating the administration is contained in works on public administration. Much of the legal history of the development of administrative law has focused either on administrative courts or on general administrative law doctrines. This is to take administrative law as a distinct doctrinal legal subject. The attempt to link administrative law

---

[77] Stanley Alexander De Smith, Lord Woolf, and Jeffrey Jowell, *Judicial Review of Administrative Action* (5th edn, 1995), § 1–008; also Henry William Rawson Wade and Christopher Forsyth, *Administrative Law* (9th edn, 2004), 15–19.

[78] J.-J. Bienvenu, 'Les origins et le développement de la doctrine', *Revue Administrative 1997: Le Conseil d'Etat et la Doctrine* 13; Maryse Deguergue, *Jurisprudence et doctrine dans l'élaboration du droit de la responsabilité administrative* (1994), 16–19; generally John Bell, *French Legal Culture* (2001), 182–5.

with the development of the public administration has been a concern of fewer authors. In England, this is an approach associated with the London School of Economics[79] and in France with scholars such as Bourdieu. Because of the specific character of the public administration in each country, it has been rare for scholars involved in this kind of analysis to undertake multi-country studies. As a result, comparative law has to build on the individual national studies as components in a comparative law study.

BIBLIOGRAPHY

Hermann Mosler, *Gerichtsschutz gegen die Exekutive* (1967)
—— *Haftung des Staates für rechtswidriges Verhalten seiner Organe* (1967)
Bernard Schwartz and Henry William Rawson Wade, *Legal Control of Government* (1972)
Wolfgang Friedmann, *Public and Private Enterprise in Mixed Economies* (1974)
Spyridon Flogaitis, *Administrative law et droit administrative* (1986)
Paul Craig, *Public Law and Democracy in the United Kingdom and the United States of America* (1990)
Luisa Torchia, *Il procedimento amministrativi: profili comparati* (1993)
Jürgen Schwarze (ed), *Administrative Law under European Influence* (1996)
Yong Zhang, *Comparative Studies on the Judicial Review Systems in East and South-East Asia* (1997)
Aldo Sandulli, *La proporzionalità dell'azione amministrativà* (1998)
Basil S. Markesinis, J.-B. Auby, Dagmar Coester-Waltjen, and S. F. Deakin, *Tortious Liability of Statutory Bodies: A Comparative and Economic Analysis of Five English Cases* (1999)
Duncan Fairgrieve, Mads Andenas, and John Bell, *Tort Liability of Public Authorities in Comparative Perspective* (2002)
René Seerden and Frits Stroink (eds), *Administrative Law of the European Union, its Member States and the United States: A Comparative Analysis* (2002)
Patrick Birkinshaw, *European Public Law* (2003)
Marc Hertogh and Simon Halliday (eds), *Judicial Review and Bureaucratic Impact: International and Interdisciplinary Perspectives* (2004)

---

[79] Martin Loughlin, *Public Law and Political Theory* (1992).

CHAPTER 40

COMPARATIVE
CRIMINAL LAW

MARKUS DIRK DUBBER

*SUNY-Buffalo**

* Thanks to Jennifer Behrens, Nina Cascio, Carlos Gómez-Jara Díez, Marcelo Ferrante, Tobias Liebau, Lyonette Louis-Jacques, John Mondo, Mathias Reimann, and Leonardo Zaibert for many helpful comments and suggestions, to the Alexander von Humboldt Foundation and Dean Nils Olsen for financial support, and to Bernd Schünemann for exemplary hospitality at the University of Munich.

I. Criminal Law's Parochialism

CRIMINAL law occupies an odd position in the field of comparative jurisprudence. Historically speaking, one can occasionally read that comparative law as a serious academic discipline began as comparative criminal law, either in Germany or in France, or both. And yet, no introduction to comparative criminal law fails to point out that comparative law means, and has meant for quite some time, comparative civil law first and foremost. Textbooks on comparative law feel no need to address, or even acknowledge the existence of, comparative studies in criminal law. The massive *International Encyclopedia of Comparative Law* does not cover criminal law, devoting itself instead to virtually every aspect and variety of 'civil, commercial and economic law'.[1]

It's easy to dismiss academics' complaints about the relative, and undeserved, neglect of their subject—a condition they then set out to rectify—as an all-too familiar scholarly gripe. And yet there is something to the fact that comparative criminal law has attracted little attention, at least as compared to other types of law. The persistent peculiar parochialism of criminal law is deeply bound up with the history of criminal law itself. It is worth exploring not only for its own sake, but also in the hope of framing the challenges the criminal comparatist faces even today.

Of all branches of law, criminal law historically has been the one most closely associated with sovereignty.[2] It's useful to think of criminal law as having emerged from the householder's virtually unlimited discretion to discipline members of his household. The Athenian *oikonomos* or the Roman *paterfamilias* enjoyed the unquestioned power to employ, against insiders and outsiders alike, whatever disciplinary sanctions were necessary to discharge his obligation to look after the welfare of his household (*oikos* or *familia*). The medieval householder wielded the same disciplinary authority, to correct and to punish, over his household—including his wife, offspring, servants, and animals—for the sake of maintaining

---

[1] Adolf Sprudzs, 'The International Encyclopedia of Comparative Law: A Bibliographical Status Report', (1980) *AJCL* 93 ff, 94.

[2] See generally Markus Dirk Dubber, *The Police Power: Patriarchy and the Foundations of American Government* (2005).

the peace (*mund*) of his household.[3] The consolidation and centralization of power, and the eventual creation of a state, consisted of the expansion of this model of household governance from the family to the realm. Criminal law served the function of protecting the 'king's peace'—and still does in English law—by preventing and punishing 'breaches' of that peace, which were considered offences against the (macro) householder, the king, himself. Eventually, in the United States, the concept of the king's peace was replaced by that of the 'public peace', as sovereignty was transferred from the king to 'the people'. In the United States, the intimate connection between criminal law and sovereignty none the less remained in place, even after the fiction of the self-governing and sovereign people had replaced the person, and fiction, of the king as sovereign.

This essentially patriarchal model of criminal law as household discipline was not challenged until the Enlightenment, when the idea of personal autonomy emerged and cast doubt on any account of state power that distinguished radically between governor and governed and denied the latter a say in (their) government altogether. As persons endowed with the capacity to govern themselves, royal subjects were transformed, at least in theory, into citizens, leading eventually to the establishment of democracies as the form of government most consistent with the idea of personal autonomy.

The critique of traditional criminal law formed an important part of the critical project of Enlightenment political theory. Central Enlightenment figures like Voltaire (in France), Kant and P. J. A. Feuerbach (in Germany), Bentham (in England), and—most influentially—Beccaria (in Italy) recognized that the threat and infliction of punitive pain on the newly discovered autonomous citizen posed the most difficult, and the most important, challenge to Enlightenment political theory.[4]

It makes sense, then, that the Enlightenment would trigger a systematic interest in the comparative analysis of criminal law and, in fact, an interest in comparative criminal law first and foremost, before an interest in other forms of comparative analysis. All comparative law bears critical, even subversive, potential by exposing the relativity of apparently ironclad rules.[5] The mere existence of alternative rules suggests that alternatives are possible; and if alternatives are possible, it is only a small step to the suggestion that they might be preferable. If comparative analysis is

---

[3] cf the German offence of *Hausfriedensbruch* (breach of the house peace) even today. StGB § 123.

[4] As a matter of comparative criminal law history, no similar urgency to radically rethink state punishment was felt in the United States. See Markus Dirk Dubber, ' "An Extraordinarily Beautiful Document": Jefferson's Bill for Proportioning Crimes and Punishments and the Challenge of Republican Punishment', in Markus Dirk Dubber and Lindsay Farmer (eds), *Modern Histories of Crime and Punishment* (forthcoming 2007).

[5] See eg Horatia Muir Watt, 'La fonction subversive du droit comparé', (2000) 52 *Revue internationale de droit* 503 ff; George P. Fletcher, 'Comparative Law as a Subversive Discipline', (1998) 46 *AJCL* 683 ff. This critical attitude, however, is not always applied to the study of comparative criminal law itself; closer attention to the history of the subject might prove useful in this regard.

used in conjunction with, or—in Feuerbach's case—as the positive foundation of, natural law arguments, the results of comparative research naturally lead to strong normative claims that the existing arrangements be rendered consistent with the demands of natural justice.

In a pre-Enlightenment system of criminal law, the very idea of comparative law is preposterous. A wise and curious sovereign might wish to consult the experiences of other sovereigns as they exercise quasi-patriarchal power over their households, but accounts of other practices elsewhere would have no critical bite whatsoever— the exercise of disciplinary power over the state household was beyond critique. Criminal law—or rather penal discipline, in so far as, after the Enlightenment, the very concept of law implies the notion of an autonomous legal subject—is the least constrained power of the sovereign since it is the power closest to the very essence of sovereignty. A sovereign who cannot punish as he sees fit is no sovereign.

The significance of Enlightenment critique for the appearance of comparative criminal law as a discipline also helps to account for the fact that comparative criminal law not only began but also has struck considerably deeper roots in continental Europe than in Anglo-American jurisprudence. In the United States in particular, criminal law continues to rest on a quasi-patriarchal foundation. Doctrinally speaking, the criminal law is the most intrusive manifestation of the state's 'police power', which, since Blackstone, has been defined as the power of 'the due regulation and domestic order of the kingdom: whereby the individuals of the state, like members of a well-governed family, are bound to conform their general behaviour to the rules of propriety, good neighbourhood, and good manners'.[6]

In the United States, criminal law to this day is conceived of as protecting the state's sovereignty against 'offences'.[7] The power of the state to reassert its sovereignty against an offence is virtually unlimited within its geographical limits. Territoriality remains the dominant principle of criminal jurisdiction in the United States; any state is free to mete out penal discipline as it sees fit provided it does not interfere with another state's discretion to do likewise within its territory. By contrast, continental criminal law has long recognized active and passive personality, based on the offender's and the victim's citizenship, respectively, as important bases for criminal jurisdiction, along with—more controversially—universal jurisdiction over certain international crimes (eg genocide) regardless of who committed them where against whom.[8] Again unlike in continental criminal law,[9] choice of law

---

[6] William Blackstone, *Commentaries on the Laws of England* (vol 4, 1769), at 162; see generally Dubber, (n 2).

[7] See Markus Dirk Dubber, 'Toward a Constitutional Law of Crime and Punishment', (2005) 55 *Hastings LJ* 509 ff.

[8] See eg StGB §§ 3–7; see Markus D. Dubber and Mark G. Kelman, *American Criminal Law: Cases, Statutes, and Comments* (2005), ch 2.F.

[9] See Albin Eser, 'The Importance of Comparative Legal Research for the Development of Criminal Sciences', in Roger Blanpain (ed), *Law in Motion* (1997), 492 ff, 499 (passive personality jurisdiction).

questions cannot arise in American criminal cases, since no sovereign could assert another's authority; the very act of indirect reassertion would merely reaffirm the other state's lack of authority. Similarly, double jeopardy protections do not apply: a single act that violates two states' criminal norms gives offence to two sovereigns and, in that sense, constitutes not one offence but two, so that the constitutional prohibition of twice putting a defendant in jeopardy of life or limb for 'the same offence' does not come into play.[10] In the pre-Enlightened American view, sovereignty requires nothing less than leaving it to the discretion of each sovereign to decide whether, and how, to respond punitively to offences against its authority.

Even in countries where the Enlightenment's fundamental assault of the traditional quasi-patriarchal regime of state punishment was felt more strongly than in the United States, comparative criminal law emerged only sporadically and without ever achieving anything close to the breadth and depth of work in private law. We now turn to an account of that slow and timid emergence, noting along the way the various functions comparative criminal law was meant to fulfil according to its proponents and practitioners over the past two centuries.

II. Histories and Functions of Comparative Criminal Law

The story of comparative criminal law is one of great promise followed by disappointing practice, even drudgery. Following a theoretically ambitious start at the turn of the nineteenth century, when its aims were laid out with great verve and high hopes, comparative criminal law flattened out quickly. By the second generation, it had been turned over to professional comparatists who lacked the broad vision that animated its creation and were largely content to accumulate foreign law materials, often in the service of some reform project or other.

At the outset of our historical inquiry, it must be noted that the study of comparative criminal law can be oddly ahistorical. Quite often criminal comparatists are content to note the similarities and differences between doctrinal rules in two legal systems, without spending much time on their respective historical roots.[11] This is not only regrettable, but also surprising since comparative law and legal history are so obviously related. History, after all, can be seen as one form of

---

[10] See Dubber (n 7), 509 ff.

[11] There are notable exceptions, of course. See eg George P. Fletcher, *Rethinking Criminal Law* (1978), ch 2.

comparison, across time. As the contemporary criminal comparatist might try to detail—and, if she feels ambitious, perhaps even to explain[12]—the differences in the criminal laws of various states, countries, regions, cities, and so on across space, so the historian would set out to capture, and hopefully to account for, the inter-temporal differences in various legal rules, institutions, or practices. (Of course the practitioner of comparative legal history faces the formidable task of comparing across two dimensions.[13]) It is often said that comparative law highlights the relativity of legal rules; but intertemporal comparison illustrates the relativity of current law no less clearly than does interspatial comparison.

And yet, even exhortations to expand the scope of comparative criminal law beyond abstract legal doctrine emphasize the need to consider criminal law in its 'sociocultural' and 'socioeconomic context', as well as its 'political setting', rarely mention the importance of historical context.[14] Clearly, however, comparative research in criminal law without history makes no more sense than comparative criminal law without sociology, and notably criminology, economics, politics, or culture.

This unfortunate lack of historical curiosity also extends to the discipline of comparative criminal law itself. The historiography of comparative criminal law, if it can be called that, can be found in canned histories in the introductory sections of the very few textbooks on comparative criminal law that exist in any language and occasional contributions to essay collections. It is hoped that future scholarship will move beyond the oddly parochial passing remarks on the history of comparative criminal law we currently have; the following preliminary remarks are offered in this spirit.

1. P. J. A. Feuerbach: A Good Place to Start

As far as they go, comments on the history of comparative criminal law tend to locate its origins in Germany in the early nineteenth century—though some authors, particularly French comparatists, also point to roughly contemporaneous developments in France.[15] More specifically, P. J. A. Feuerbach, the influential

---

[12] See James Q. Whitman, 'The Comparative Study of Criminal Punishment', (2005) 1 *Annual Review of Law & Social Science* 17 ff, 20.

[13] For a recent example in the field of comparative criminal legal history, see James Q. Whitman, *Harsh Justice: Criminal Punishment and the Widening Divide between America and Europe* (2003).

[14] See eg Marc Ancel, 'Some Reflections on the Value and Scope of Studies in Comparative Criminal Law', in Edward M. Wise and Gerhard O. W. Mueller (eds), *Studies in Comparative Criminal Law* (1975), 3 ff, 10.

[15] See eg Marc Ancel, *Introduction comparative aux codes pénaux Européens* (1956), 5 (discussing Joseph-Louis-Elzéar Ortolan, *Cours de législation pénale comparée* (2 vols, 1839–41); also Jean Pradel, *Droit pénal comparé* (2nd edn, 2002), 18–19 (discussing comparative aspects of Pellegrino Rossi's *Traité de droit pénal* (1829)).

German jurist, codifier, author, and judge, is often identified as the father of modern comparative criminal law and, in fact, of modern comparative law in general.[16] Feuerbach's 1800 essay on Islamic criminal law[17] in particular tends to be mentioned as a formative document.[18] This early attempt at legal anthropology—written at a time of frequent anthropologizing and intense interest in the exotic world of Muslim culture—today is remembered not for its forgettable observations about the 'criminal jurisprudence of the Koran', but for programmatic pronouncements such as the following:

Without knowledge of the real and the existing, without comparison of different legislations, without knowledge of their relation to the various conditions of peoples according to time, climate, and constitution, a priori nonsense is inevitable.[19]

Feuerbach's insistence on the comparative method in criminal law thus must be seen as part of his general rejection of traditional natural law, which attempted to deduce substantive principles of right, or justice, from reason alone. Feuerbach instead developed a formal theory of natural law, insisting that universal principles of law be derived from a thorough appreciation of the legal norms of particular societies, which was impossible without the required careful study of each society's 'constitution'. Note that Feuerbach's conception of comparative law incorporates the study of legal history, among other things.

Still, Feuerbach's critique of natural law should not be misunderstood as a rejection of natural law, which at the time was thought to be synonymous with legal theory.[20] Feuerbach did not doubt the possibility of deriving universal principles of law; he simply thought traditional natural law had been going about that derivation in the wrong, purely rationalistic, and insufficiently positivistic, way.

For decades Feuerbach laboured on a large comparative project, which he alternately described as a 'world history of legislation', a 'universal legal history', or simply a 'universal jurisprudence'. To that end, he collected materials not only from Europe, but also from East Asia, Southeast Asia, the Middle East, and the United States.

Feuerbach never managed to complete his grand comparative opus. Still, he better captured the theoretical ambitions of comparative law than anyone since, and placed them within the context of a larger human and scientific endeavour, the discovery of universals:

[16] See eg Walther Hug, 'The History of Comparative Law', (1932) 45 *Harvard LR* 1027 ff, 1054 (Feuerbach 'the first to conceive the science of comparative law').

[17] Paul Johann Anselm Feuerbach, 'Versuch einer Criminaljurisprudenz des Koran', (1804) 2 *Bibliothek für die peinliche Rechtswissenschaft und Gesetzkunde* 163 ff.

[18] On Feuerbach as comparatist, see Gustav Radbruch, *Paul Johann Anselm Feuerbach: Ein Juristenleben* (3rd edn, 1969), 190 ff.

[19] Feuerbach (n 17), 163 ff, 164.

[20] See the subtitle of Hegel's *Philosophy of Right* of 1821: *Natural Law and State Science in Outline* (*Naturrecht und Staatswissenschaft im Grundrisse*).

Why does the legal scholar not yet have a comparative jurisprudence? . . . Just as the comparison of various tongues produces the philosophy of language, or linguistic science proper, so does a comparison of laws and legal customs of the most varied nations, both those most nearly related to us and those farther removed, create universal legal science, i.e., legal science without qualification, which alone can infuse real and vigorous life into the specific legal science of any particular country.[21]

Here Feuerbach makes explicit the connection between comparative jurisprudence and another, far better known, comparative enterprise: comparative linguistics associated with Jacob Grimm and Wilhelm von Humboldt and, more generally, comparative language studies, which also included comparative dictionary projects as well as attempts to work out a 'philosophical universal linguistics'.[22] Humboldt went on to posit that a universal linguistic competence, or 'sense of language' (or grammar), could be distilled from comparative linguistic studies— an idea later revived by Noam Chomsky.[23] Although Feuerbach is credited with introducing the concept of a 'sense of law' (or justice), this juristic competence turned out to be distinctly non-universal. Feuerbach invoked the sense of justice to make a very parochial point: he argued against importing the French jury, which he praised as a theoretical matter, into German criminal procedure on the ground that early nineteenth-century Germans lacked the sense of justice required for the jury to protect, rather than to threaten, individual rights.[24]

If Feuerbach's project sounds very much like Montesquieu's *Spirit of Laws* (1748), not only in the reference to climate, that's no accident. Feuerbach was a great admirer of Montesquieu's; he occasionally referred to his overarching comparative project as his 'German esprit des lois'. Unlike Feuerbach, however, Montesquieu showed virtually no interest in comparative criminal law, or in other matters of criminal law generally—beyond his general but influential call for punishment 'in the spirit of' the crime.[25]

A little later, Cesare Beccaria, whose essay *Of Crimes and Punishments* (1764) kicked off the Enlightenment attack on established penal practices—and notably

---

[21] Paul Johann Anselm Feuerbach, *Anselm Feuerbachs kleine Schriften vermischten Inhalts* (1833), 163.

[22] See Barbara Kaltz, 'Christian Jacob Kraus' Review of "Linguarum totius orbis vocabularia comparativa" (ed. Peter Simon Pallas, St Petersburg, 1786): Introduction, Translation and Notes', (1985) 12 *Historiographia Linguistica* 229 ff.

[23] See generally Markus Dirk Dubber, *The Sense of Justice: Empathy in Law and Punishment* (forthcoming 2006).

[24] See Markus Dirk Dubber, 'The German Jury and the Metaphysical *Volk*: From Romantic Idealism to Nazi Ideology', (1995) 43 *AJCL* 227 ff. The jury, and lay participation generally, has remained one of the key topics in comparative criminal procedure to this day. See eg Thomas Weigend. 'Lay Participation and Consensual Disposition Mechanisms', (2001) 72 *Revue international de droit penal* 595 ff; Markus Dirk Dubber, 'American Plea Bargains, German Lay Judges, and the Crisis of Criminal Procedure', (1997) 49 *Stanford LR* 547 ff.

[25] On Montesquieu's two 'very simple and almost simplistic' comments on comparative criminal law in *Spirit of Laws*, see Jean Pradel, (n 15), 15; see also David Carrithers, 'Montesquieu's Philosophy of Punishment', (1998) 19 *History of Political Thought* 213 ff.

of the use, or at least overuse, of capital punishment—in earnest, likewise took an acomparative approach to the subject of criminal law, or rather of state punishment. 'Follow[ing] the steps' of the 'immortal Montesquieu' who 'has but slightly touched on this subject', Beccaria's famous essay analyses human society in general and critiques laws throughout Europe and throughout history, rather than drawing detailed contrasts and comparisons among individual systems of criminal law. Beccaria here 'pleads the cause of humanity', applying 'philosophical truths' that are 'eternally the same' to state punishment, chief among them of course the universal principle that a good law is one that pursues 'the greatest happiness of the greatest number'.

Bentham took from Beccaria not only his greatest happiness principle, but also his ahistorical and acomparative approach. There is no trace of comparative sensibility in Bentham's systematic, and often tedious, application of Beccaria's principle to every corner of law, including all aspects of penal law, from substance, to procedure, to modes of punishment execution. Bentham was indiscriminately abstract: he attacked Blackstone's common law and the American Revolution's natural law from the same high perch of rigorous utilitarianism. Bentham's inability, or unwillingness, to consider comparative nuance or context was particularly ironic, and ultimately self-defeating, in light of his repeated offers to draft criminal codes for governments throughout the world, including the federal and state governments in the United States, all of which were rejected. Bentham's interest in what he termed 'international law' is not to the contrary; in his view, international law concerned itself not with a community of nations marked by apparently irreconcilable historical, cultural, and economic—yes, even climatic— differences, but with the drafting of a 'universal international code'.

None the less, it would be a mistake to think of Bentham's project as an attempt to export a superior legal system to other less fortunate, or less enlightened, countries, a common occurrence in the history of comparative law, and comparative criminal law in particular. Bentham thought the English common law required radical utilitarian reform just as much as, if not more so than, the legal systems of other countries. His project was universalistic, not chauvinistic, though acomparative all the same.

In an important sense, in fact, the common law—the frequent object of Bentham's withering ridicule—can be viewed as an essentially, and increasingly, comparative project. In Bentham's (and Blackstone's) day, the only comparative dimension of the common law was intertemporal. In Blackstone's *Commentaries on the Laws of England* (1764–9), which Bentham so gleefully criticized, non-English criminal law appears nowhere—nor does Blackstone, it must be said, even follow his common-law predecessors, most importantly Coke, in carefully tracing the development of criminal law doctrine over time. References to foreign law of any kind in Blackstone's discussion of criminal law are limited to vague references to exotic, and essentially non-English and therefore presumptively threatening, customs, such as polygamy. The foreigners themselves occasionally pop up in the form of 'outlandish persons calling themselves Egyptians, or gypsies', association with whom is punished by death or of 'Jews and other infidels and heretics' not entitled to benefit of clergy.

At the same time, it's worth noting that, as a matter of procedure, English law specifically provided for the disposition of foreign criminal (and civil) defendants. From 1190 until 1870, foreigners—notably Jews and foreign merchants—were tried before a mixed jury (*de medietate linguae*). This procedural device, however, hardly turned trials of foreigners into an opportunity for the exploration of comparative criminal law. The mixed jury applied the same substantive common law (or law merchant, as the case may have been) as the unmixed jury deciding the faith of a native Englishman. Still, even if the mixed jury did not introduce choice of law questions into English criminal trials, it at least recognized the existence, and interests, of non-English defendants, who for 'oeconomic' reasons of household governance—as opposed to considerations of their individual rights—were put under the king's protection.[26]

2. Two Modes of Comparative Criminal Law

Common criminal law analysis became more explicitly comparative when it left the English motherland and entered the colonies. Here, two types of inter-action between English and colonial (or Commonwealth) law might be distinguished: (1) the consideration of foreign law by English courts, notably the Privy Council, and (2) the consideration of English law by colonial (or postcolonial) courts. In both cases, courts have turned to comparative analysis, be it between various non-English legal systems or between non-English and English law.

(a) The View from Above

The first—*hierarchical* or *unidirectional*—mode of comparative analysis operates within an imperialist framework that guides English courts' application of English law to resolve disputes and to help develop other, lesser, systems of law. This framework should not be obscured by frequent references to the application and development of a uniform common law within the British Empire or the Commonwealth, which by definition recognizes no distinction between English and 'foreign' law.[27]

In this, imperialist, mode of comparative criminal law, the comparison proceeds from the assumption that the domestic system is superior to the foreign one.

---

[26] On the traditional concept of 'oeconomy' and its connection to 'police', see Dubber (n 2).

[27] See, in this regard, Esin Örücü, *Critical Comparative Law: Considering Paradoxes for Legal Systems in Transition* (1999).

Arguably, imperialist comparative law does not qualify as comparative law in the first place, at least in so far as, in the formulation of Hans-Heinrich Jescheck, 'the basic intellectual approach toward all comparative work consists of the willingness to learn'.[28] Imperialist comparative law seeks, at best, to teach and, at worst, to oppress, but never to learn.

The most obvious instance of imperialist comparative law in the area of criminal law is the exportation of criminal codes to colonies, a common practice among colonial powers in the nineteenth century.[29] The most prominent example is Macaulay's Indian Penal Code (1837). Macaulay looked to Indian customs—which, as is standard colonial practice, were denied the status of laws, thus making comparative law impossible by definition—only in so far as they indicated the need for extraordinary legal measures—as, for instance, to combat Indians' presumed predilection for perjury—or might help render the code more effective by placing its commands within a familiar local context—as evidenced by his innovative use of illustrations of code sections.[30]

There is a contemporary—non-colonial—version of this imperialist approach to comparative criminal law. It also operates from a position of superiority, but without the aid of open political might and, ordinarily, with greater subtlety. The sense of superiority of non-colonial exporter nations in comparative criminal law comes in different forms. German scholars of comparative criminal law, for instance, may be convinced of the superior, and even unmatched, complexity of their domestic law's doctrine of substantive criminal law, which is taken as an indication of the superiority of German substantive criminal law as a matter of scientific progress.[31] Note, for instance, that Jescheck, in the same programmatic essay cited above, remarks that German substantive criminal law has little use for comparative research as a source of alternative approaches because it 'has largely exhausted the field of doctrinal possibilities'.[32] In fact, in his popular criminal law textbook, Jescheck argued for the need to develop a complex doctrinal system of substantive criminal law in part by attributing what he considered the wrong result in a landmark nineteenth-century English criminal case to what he perceived as

[28] Hans-Heinrich Jescheck, *Entwicklung, Aufgaben und Methoden der Strafrechtsvergleichung* (1955), 38.

[29] On the (much neglected) history of German colonial criminal law, see Wolfgang Naucke, 'Deutsches Kolonialstrafrecht 1886–1918', (1988) 7 *Rechtshistorisches Journal* 297 ff.

[30] On the exportation of Macaulay's code to Asia and Africa, and James Fitzjames Stephen's Code of Criminal Law and Procedure (1878–80) to Canada, New Zealand, and Australia, see Sir Rupert Cross, 'The Making of English Criminal Law: (5) Macaulay', (1978) *Crim LR* 519 ff; Sir Rupert Cross, 'The Making of English Criminal Law: (6) Sir James Fitzjames Stephen', (1978) *Crim LR* 652 ff. For an altogether different model of European influence on criminal law reform in a developing but independent nation, see Steven Lowenstein, *Materials on Comparative Criminal Law as Based Upon the Penal Codes of Ethiopia and Switzerland* (1965).

[31] On the scientific ambitions of German criminal law, see Markus Dirk Dubber, 'The Promise of German Criminal Law: A Science of Crime and Punishment', (2005) 6 *German LJ* 1049 ff.

[32] Jescheck (n 28), 28.

English criminal law's lack of doctrinal sophistication.[33] Here comparative criminal law is used not as an opportunity for critical reflection, but as an opportunity for self-affirmation.

Germany has been a major exporter of criminal law doctrine and theory over the past century: the sun never sets on German criminal law theory. Leading textbooks on German criminal law—including Jescheck's—have been translated into several languages, including Spanish, Portuguese, Chinese, Japanese, and Korean. Scores of budding scholars have studied with German criminal law professors, often with generous German foundation support, returning to their home countries to spread German criminal law doctrine.[34] German criminal law theory has been particularly influential in Spain, Latin America, Japan, South Korea, and Taiwan, as well as in several Eastern and Southern European countries (eg Greece, Poland, Turkey).

In criminal procedure, Germany has been less influential, though Turkey adopted the German criminal procedure code as an effort at Westernization, along with the Italian criminal code of 1899. In the area of comparative criminal procedure, the United States is far more likely to suffer from a superiority complex.[35] US criminal procedure, of course, was entirely forgettable both domestically and internationally until the so-called Warren Court Revolution in Criminal Procedure, which turned the subject into a subdiscipline of constitutional law. Claims to the superiority of US criminal procedure law do not invoke scientific progress, but assert a political, even moral, superiority, and perhaps for that reason are advanced most vigorously not by scholars, but by government and foundation representatives who are dispatched to criminal law reform projects throughout the world to do battle with champions of the inquisitorial model.[36]

Scientific or moral chauvinism has been less common in the comparative law of punishment execution and sanctions. There a less ideologically charged exchange of ideas and practices has occurred since the late eighteenth century, when European reformers first took an interest in American penitentiaries; Beaumont and Tocqueville were only the most famous among many foreign visitors and

---

[33] Hans-Heinrich Jescheck and Thomas Weigend, *Lehrbuch des Strafrechts: Allgemeiner Teil* (5th edn, 1996), 195 (discussing the famous cannibalism on the high seas case of *Regina v Dudley and Stephens*, [1884] 14 QBD 273)).

[34] See eg Hans Joachim Hirsch (ed), *Krise des Strafrechts und der Kriminalwissenschaften?* (2001) (proceedings of a conference of foreign criminal law scholars who have received funding from the Alexander von Humboldt Foundation). Between 1953 and 2000, the Humboldt Foundation alone sponsored almost 200 foreign scholars doing research on criminal law in Germany.

[35] Domestically, however, the American criminal process has come under attack from comparatists who claim a European, and notably a German, advantage in criminal procedure. Compare John H. Langbein, 'Land without Plea Bargaining: How the Germans Do It', (1979) 78 *Michigan LR* 204 ff with Dubber, 'American Plea Bargains', (n 24), 547 ff; see also Symposium, 'The European Advantage in Criminal Procedure', (2001) 100 *West Virginia LR* 765 ff.

[36] See Eser, (n 9), 492 ff, 516 ('common-law missionaries' in 'the successor states to the ex-Soviet Union').

inquirers at the time.[37] Today, the two illustrious Frenchmen would have no reason to study American penal institutions, which have long since abandoned the correctional project, unless they were charged with learning about private or maximum security prisons.

It is no accident that, when Jescheck set out to illustrate the successes of comparative criminal law as an engine of domestic criminal law reform in German, every example was drawn from the law of punishment execution and sanctions: (1) 'uniform type of imprisonment' (citing Italian and Austrian practice in support of abandoning the traditional distinction among *Zuchthaus* (penal servitude), *Gefängnis* (imprisonment), and *Haft* (detention) in German criminal law), (2) 'the day-fine system' (drawing on a Scandinavian model that tailors the amount of the daily fine to the economic resources of the defendant and the number of daily fines to the seriousness of her offence), and (3) 'warning combined with suspended fine' (looking to English, French, Italian, and East German law—but apparently not to US law—to develop a new type of alternative sanction).[38]

(b) Muddling Through

A second—*egalitarian* or *multidirectional*—mode of comparative criminal law in the common law world emerged in the United States after the American Revolution. Every federal system composed of independent bodies of state law offers opportunities for comparative analysis of law.[39] American criminal law, for the first hundred years or so of its existence, relied almost exclusively on English precedent. Eventually, however, as each state—and more recently federal law as well—developed its own jurisprudence on a wide range of issues in criminal law, an American court could consider a wide palette of approaches to a given issue before it. Decisions from other states, and to a lesser extent from federal courts, could then be considered alongside English decisions. English law thus became integrated into a comparative analysis, rather than functioning as the model against which lesser colonial efforts must be measured.

This comparative criminal lawmaking was still thought of as a form of common lawmaking, with the various, and increasingly differing, rules fitting together into an increasingly incoherent whole. As time went on, and differences continued to emerge, it became increasingly difficult, however, to maintain the fiction of a

---

[37] Gustave de Beaumont and Alexis de Tocqueville, *Du système pénitentiaire aux États-Unis, et de son application en France; suivi d'un appendice sur les colonies pénales et de notes statistiques* (1833); on the influence of the American penitentiary movement on German criminal law, see Markus Dirk Dubber, 'The Right to be Punished: Autonomy and its Demise in Modern Penal Thought', (1998) 16 *Law & History Review* 113 ff.

[38] Hans-Heinrich Jescheck, 'The Significance of Comparative Law for Criminal Law Reform', (1981) 5 *Hastings International & Comparative Law Review* 1 ff, 20 ff.

[39] cf already Karl Stooß, *Die Schweizerischen Strafgesetzbücher zur Vergleichung zusammengestellt* (1890), *Die Grundsätze des Schweizerischen Strafrechts vergleichend dargestellt* (1892–3).

common law of crimes. The Model Penal Code of the American Law Institute, completed in 1962, attempted to systematize the internally inconsistent body of American criminal law that had accumulated over the years.[40] 'The common law' is ordinarily thought of as the Model Penal Code's raw material, and as its doctrinal alternative in jurisdictions that did not follow the Code. The Code drafters, however, in fact engaged in a comprehensive comparative analysis of the general principles of criminal law in the various American state and federal jurisdictions, drawing on statutes as well as on case law. Based on this systematic exercise in comparative criminal law, the drafters proposed rules that retained certain features of the criminal laws in American jurisdictions while rejecting others, in an effort to render American criminal law as a whole more consistent both internally and in light of what they regarded as the basic functions of a modern system of criminal law (legality, deterrence, treatmentism).

In the wake of the widespread reform and codification of criminal law in jurisdictions throughout the United States—with notable exceptions, such as California and federal criminal law—American criminal law today is essentially a creature of domestic comparative criminal law.[41] There is no American 'common law' of crime; there are only separately codified independent systems of criminal law that are developed in occasional reference to other American systems of criminal law.[42] The myth of a uniform common law of crimes—which is often, in a particularly anachronistic twist, treated as though it included even English criminal law—continues to shape American thinking about, and teaching of, criminal law. It is hoped that the internally comparative dimension of American criminal law will be recognized more fully so that the study of American criminal law, as well as the jurisprudence itself, can become conscious of, and eventually refine, its method. Even without a full-blown comparative investigation, the comparatist's sceptical eye for apparent similarities and apparent differences in doctrinal questions and answers, her sensitivity to procedural, institutional, theoretical, and even historical context, would serve American criminal law well, as its practitioners and theoreticians draw on statutes and court opinions from throughout the land to resolve a given issue.[43]

[40] On the Model Penal Code project, see Markus Dirk Dubber, 'Penal Panopticon: The Idea of a Modern Model Penal Code', (2000) 4 *Buffalo Criminal LR* 53 ff; Markus Dirk Dubber, *Criminal Law: Model Penal Code* (2002).

[41] Consider in this regard the Model Penal Code for Latin America, a self-consciously (transnational) comparative project inspired by the ALI's Model Penal Code and Uniform Commercial Code. Juan Bustos Ramirez and Manuel Valenzuela Bejas, *Le système pénal des pays de L'Amerique Latine* (trans Jacqueline Bernat de Celis, 1983), 7; see also Jescheck (n 38), 1 ff, 18 (Model Penal Code as example of 'regional' comparative criminal law reform project).

[42] On American criminal law as domestic comparative law, see Markus Dirk Dubber, 'Reforming American Penal Law', (1999) 90 *Journal of Criminal Law & Criminology* 49 ff.

[43] For a casebook based on this approach, see Dubber and Kelman (n 8).

3. Domesticating Comparative Criminal Law

The idea of internal comparative criminal law might be further developed to extend beyond the boundaries of criminal law itself. As a matter of theory, as well as of doctrine, the study of criminal law requires a comparative dimension that places its subject within the broader context of law, and, ultimately, of state action generally speaking. The discipline of criminal law rumbles along in almost complete ignorance of other areas of law. American criminal law has yet to develop a satisfactory account of its relation to the law of torts, contracts, or property, or for that matter, to the law of taxation or bankruptcy. As a result, American criminal law has the least to say about the very issues that matter the most in criminal law-making—namely the proper role of criminal law in public policy, and the proper scope and definition of offences within that role.

As a species of law, criminal law must be distinguished from other modes of state governance, most importantly administrative regulation.[44] In addition, criminal law must be differentiated from other legal modes of governance, including both so-called public and private law. This differentiation requires a comparative analysis of the various doctrinal points of contact between criminal law and other areas of law, including—if we use tort law as an example—act, commission through omission, harm, voluntariness, intention, recklessness, negligence, strict liability, causation, mistake, reasonableness, justification, public and private necessity, self-defence, use of force in law enforcement, consent, excuse, insanity, infancy, attempt, as well as—in the special part—protected interests and the host of torts paralleling criminal offences, such as assault, battery, false imprisonment, trespass on land, and trespass to chattels.

The Model Penal Code drafters did not engage in this sort of interdisciplinary domestic comparative law analysis. As a result, some critical features of the Model Code remain troublingly indeterminate. The drafters failed to account for their adoption of differing definitions of similar, if not identical, concepts—for example, rejecting an affirmative definition of the fundamental concept of an act along the lines of the American Law Institute's own Restatement of Torts. What's more, the relationship between criminal law and other areas of law remains unarticulated even where the Model Code makes specific reference to non-criminal law—for example, in justification defences that turn on the general, criminal and civil, 'lawfulness' of the conduct in question.

The drafters of the Model Penal Code were not particularly interested in transnational, as opposed to intranational, comparative criminal law. Eager to devise a piece of model legislation with a chance of adoption in American jurisdictions throughout the land, they instead focused on American law. The only foreign

[44] See Markus Dirk Dubber, 'Policing Possession: The War on Crime and the End of Criminal Law', (2002) 91 *Journal of Criminal Law & Criminology* 829 ff.

criminal law system that received some attention was English law. Even English law, however, appeared not so much in the form of primary materials, that is, cases and to a lesser extent statutes, but through the work of a contemporary commentator, Glanville Williams, who is widely regarded as the father of modern English criminal law scholarship. It is no accident that the publication of Williams's groundbreaking work, *Criminal Law: The General Part*, coincided with the drafting of the Model Code between 1952 and1962. The Code drafters cited German criminal law only very rarely, even though the Code's basic analytic framework bears a certain resemblance to that developed by German criminal law scholars at the beginning of the twentieth century (see Section III.1.(e) below).[45]

It is worth nothing at this point that the Model Penal Code, in its primarily internal comparative approach, resembled Feuerbach's criminal law textbook, *Textbook of the Common Criminal Law in Force in Germany*, which dominated German criminal law teaching during the first half of the nineteenth century. As the textbook's title makes clear, Feuerbach faced a challenge not unlike that encountered by the Model Code drafters. What's more, he viewed his task in similar terms—as revision, reform, and rationalization of an existing, often hopelessly self-contradictory and arbitrary, 'common' criminal law that had evolved over centuries. Like the Model Code drafters, Feuerbach also realized that this formidable critical project presupposed a different, but no less daunting, analytical one: a careful comparative study of the rules of law as they existed at the time. Note that, in Feuerbach's telling, the sources of criminal law included 'the philosophy of criminal law, insofar as it has not been limited in its application through positive statutory provisions'.

Feuerbach was criticized—not without justification—for paying too much attention to the philosophy of criminal law, and too little to positive law, common and otherwise. Recall, however, that under his view, philosophical principles themselves should derive from a careful study of positive law. The Model Penal Code drafters, by contrast, studiously avoided extended discussions of criminal theory, preferring instead to cast their Code as animated by a spirit of 'principled pragmatism'.

4. Foreign Law as Comparative Criminal Law

The more telling contrast, however, pits Feuerbach and the Model Penal Code, on the one hand, against what has come to be regarded as traditional comparative law, on the other. Feuerbach—both in his textbook and his path-breaking Bavarian

---

[45] For rare citations to the German criminal code in the official Commentaries to the Model Code, see eg *Model Penal Code Commentaries* (1985), § 3.02, at 11, § 210.3, at 65. On the similarity between the structure of the Model Code and German criminal law, see Dubber and Kelman (n 8), 182–9.

Criminal Code of 1813, which was based closely on the views laid out in the textbook and other, more theoretical, writings—and the Model Penal Code exemplify the use of internal comparative analysis of legal rules in the service of criminal law reform. Comparative analysis was of integral, and in fact foundational, importance to the law reform projects undertaken by Feuerbach and the Model Penal Code drafters. The materials subjected to comparative analysis were the very subject-matter of the reform effort itself.

Contrast this integral and internal form of comparative analysis with the use of comparative law in other criminal law reform efforts, which self-consciously turn to studies of foreign law to aid domestic projects. The prime example of this style of reform-oriented comparative criminal law is the publication of a sixteen-volume 'comparative depiction of German and foreign criminal law', published under the auspices of the German Justice Ministry between 1905–9 in connection with proposals for reform of the German criminal code.[46] This collection is a treasure trove of information about non-German criminal systems as of the early twentieth century. It is, however, at bottom a work of reportage, a series of essays on how the French do it, how the English do it, and so on. It is fascinating as a study of 'foreign' criminal law, from a German perspective. It tells us a great deal about non-German systems of criminal law and, at least as interesting, about German criminal law thought at a time of great scholarly creativity, when the basic building blocks of German criminal law theory were being assembled.

It is not, however, a work of comparative law. These very building blocks, for instance, were developed without any reference to the extensive study of foreign criminal law.[47] There is also no indication that this enormous project had any influence on the effort to reform the German criminal code, which failed at any rate. The code was not fundamentally revised until the 1960s. At that time, another foreign criminal law study was commissioned by the German Justice Ministry, with far less impressive results, however, which likewise had no noticeable effect on the reform of the code.

The accumulation of materials on, references to, and brief—or not so brief—summaries of foreign criminal law has a long tradition in comparative criminal law. Already Feuerbach's textbook bears its early traces, in the run-on notes of its later editions. These editions were the work of Carl Joseph Anton Mittermaier, who spent his early years collecting and translating foreign criminal codes for Feuerbach. Mittermaier went on to great fame, becoming the internationally best-known German jurisprude of his time.[48] If Feuerbach established the modern discipline of comparative criminal law, Mittermaier was the first professional

---

[46] *Vergleichende Darstellung des deutschen und ausländischen Strafrechts: Vorarbeiten zur deutschen Strafrechtsreform* (16 vols, 1905–9).

[47] Instead, they were largely derived from a phenomenology of crime curiously above all comparative nuance. See generally Dubber (n 31), 1049 ff.

[48] Gerd Kleinheyer and Jan Schröder, *Deutsche Juristen aus fünf Jahrhunderten* (3rd edn, 1989), 182.

criminal law comparatist. Unlike Feuerbach, Mittermaier had no theoretical ambitions for his work in general, or for comparative criminal law in particular. He
spent his long career amassing accounts of foreign criminal law, ultimately with an
eye toward criminal law reform, notably the reform of the German criminal process in light of the English and French systems and the abolition, or at least
limitation, of capital punishment.

Mittermaier's main contribution to Feuerbach's textbook, apart from critiquing
Feuerbach's preoccupation with matters philosophical and adding countless footnotes, consisted of inserting long lists of snapshots of foreign criminal law. In
Mittermaier's hands, then, Feuerbach's textbook came to contain a miniature version of the still more ambitious foreign criminal law project of 1905–9. The reader
could find out quickly—though not necessarily reliably—how the French, the
English, and so on dealt with a particular question, without any attempt, however,
to integrate these descriptions into the textbook's doctrinal analysis of German
criminal law.

One finds the same use of foreign criminal law in Jescheck's textbook on
German criminal law more than a century later. Here, too, discussions of German
criminal law are often followed—in smaller print, indicating their relative
insignificance—by capsules of foreign criminal law. These one-sentence summaries, which generally consist of citations to criminal code sections from one country
after another, are as a rule not incorporated into the discussion of German criminal law, nor are they interconnected across topics, preventing the reader from
gleaning a parallel view of non-German systems of criminal law across the book.
They serve no analytic purpose, though they may help to satisfy the curiosity of
anyone looking for a thumbnail sketch of where some non-German criminal law
systems address a given issue in their criminal code, assuming they have a code. In
the end, they are impressive displays of cosmopolitan erudition.

Not surprisingly, integrating a comparative approach into one's exploration of
issues in criminal law becomes more difficult when the points of comparison are
drawn from a foreign legal system, rather than from another constituent jurisdiction of the same legal system. Making US criminal law relevant to a treatment of
German criminal law is more challenging than bringing California criminal law to
bear on New York criminal law with an eye toward rationalizing American criminal law. Getting foreign criminal law right is just as difficult as any other inquiry
into foreign law. Different systems draw on different sources of criminal law,
ranked in different orders of significance, and functioning in different ways.

The comparatist interested in US criminal law, for instance, would do well to
consult not only the Model Penal Code, but also the relevant jurisdictions' criminal
codes (should they exist), non-criminal codes (if any), unconsolidated criminal
and non-criminal statutes, sentencing guidelines, code commentaries (which may
not exist and, if they do, may differ dramatically in form, content, and ambition),
secondary literature, treatises, and—of course—the jurisprudence of the relevant

courts, in addition to that of the US Supreme Court. One must learn not only how to find the relevant sources, but also how to read them. And once the comparatist has assembled an image of a foreign legal rule, she must be prepared to adjust that image in light of current developments. It is no accident that examples of external comparative criminal law that attempt to engage a foreign system of criminal law, rather than merely citing a necessarily oversimplified nutshell to add foreign flavour to one's doctrinal explorations, are quite rare. One such example from the German literature is Thomas Weigend's nuanced and careful consideration of the Model Penal Code's *mens rea* scheme, as adopted and interpreted in New York criminal law, in the context of a searching exploration of the doctrine of intention in German criminal law.[49]

Retaining for the moment our focus on the comparative analysis on German and US criminal law, it should be noted that neither shows much interest in the other. German criminal law finds it difficult to take US substantive criminal law seriously and, for that reason, sees no particular need to go beyond capsule summaries of US doctrine. At the same time, US criminal law pays just as little attention to German criminal law—or for that matter to the criminal law of any other nation—though not out of a sense of superiority but for simple lack of interest, aside from the obvious language barriers that plague all comparative law work. Interest in German criminal law in the United States, however, has grown over the past fifty years in the wake of the work of Jerome Hall, G. O. W. Mueller, and—most importantly—George Fletcher.

5. Toward a General Theory of Criminal Law

Fletcher's work distinguishes itself not only from other comparative, and non-comparative, criminal law scholarship in the United States, but also from much comparative criminal law scholarship in other countries through its intellectual ambition and instrumental approach to comparative research. Fletcher's mode of comparative scholarship recalls Feuerbach more than it does Mittermaier. In fact, Fletcher even uses a contemporary version of Feuerbach's linguistic analogy; he compares his project to Chomsky's search for a universal grammar.[50] Fletcher pursues an essentially theoretical project, unattached to any particular legal system; aspects of various criminal law systems throughout the world—notably German criminal law and Anglo-American criminal law, and, to a lesser extent, French, Italian, Israeli, and Russian criminal law—are pressed into service in the pursuit of a universal criminal theory. Unlike Weigend, for instance, Fletcher does not turn to

---

[49] Thomas Weigend, 'Zwischen Vorsatz und Fahrlässigkeit', (1981) 93 *Zeitschrift für die gesamte Strafrechtswissenschaft* 657 ff.

[50] George P. Fletcher, *Basic Concepts of Criminal Law* (1998), 5.

comparative analysis to address problems in domestic criminal law; foreign criminal law materials thus aren't integrated into an underlying domestic framework.
There is no domestic law, no foreign law; there is only one criminal law, and
all criminal law is comparative. In Fletcher's work, the point of comparative criminal law is not reform, nor ornamentation; comparative criminal law serves the
establishment of a 'universal jurisprudence', in Feuerbach's term.

Fletcher's work on substantive criminal law theory fits into the comprehensive
programme for a 'general theory of criminal law' encompassing all branches of
criminal law—including substantive criminal law, procedural criminal law, and the
law of punishment execution and sanctions—that was eloquently sketched by
Jescheck in 1955, with obvious Feuerbachian roots:

As there is a general theory of the state and a general theory of macroeconomics, a *general
theory of criminal law* also must be possible, namely one that derives not only from general-
philosophical preconditions, but also proceeds from empirical-comparative foundations.
For as much as the conditions of criminality might differ from country to country, the same
variables are always at issue: human conduct, the violation of legal norms and legal interests, guilt and atonement, protection and rehabilitation, juveniles, adolescents, and adults,
first-time offenders and recidivists, and the great problem of the selection and design of
sanctions.[51]

This ambitious, and exciting, project still awaits serious scholarly attention;
instead, since Mittermaier, comparative criminal law scholars—including Jescheck
himself—have devoted themselves largely to the collection of foreign legal materials. The greatest achievement of comparative criminal law in Germany, France,
Italy, and the United States remains the publication of foreign criminal codes
in translation, with no evident effort to incorporate these primary materials into
the analysis of domestic criminal law or, for that matter, a 'general theory of
criminal law'.

The danger of an abstract approach to comparative criminal law is, of course,
that it neglects the very detail and context—the local nuances—that distinguish
comparative criminal law from pure criminal philosophy—or 'natural law', in the
old terminology. Comparative criminal law thus might be reduced to serve as a
ready-made grab bag of possible solutions to problems that the theoretician did
not, or could not, generate using her powers of thought and imagination. At the
same time, there is always the danger of confusing the established doctrines of
one's domestic criminal law system with the dictates of reason, thus reducing
comparative criminal law to a unilateral campaign of civilization and enlightenment—or, if you prefer, a type of criminal law missionary work. There is also the
less dramatic concern that the resulting theory is beside the point, or entirely self-
referential. Comparative criminal law theorizing that claims independence from
any domestic system of law may, in the end, say a great deal about nothing in

---

[51] Jescheck (n 28), 27 (emphasis in original).

particular as it becomes too disconnected from any single body of law to affect actual doctrine anywhere in the world.

These concerns about theoretical comparative criminal law are at least as old as Feuerbach. Feuerbach cleverly, and unusually, evaded the charge of insufficient attention to positive criminal law by creating his very own positive criminal law—the Bavarian criminal code of 1813. Not every comparatist has that luxury, if only because criminal codes are no longer drafted on royal order.

6. International Criminal Law

Today's theoretical comparatist, however, can point to a body of positive law that simply did not exist in Feuerbach's time, or for that matter, in Jescheck's time: international criminal law. It is only fitting, then, that Fletcher recently has turned his attention to international criminal law, which he contrasts with 'parochial' criminal law.[52] Criminal comparatists are hard at work assembling a 'general part' of international law, which attempts to draw on various legal systems and whatever little precedent there is in the field of international criminal law to create a system of general principles of criminal responsibility, in analogy to the general part of domestic criminal law and of domestic criminal codes.[53]

The notoriously vague and often outright puzzling provisions of the Rome Statute of the International Criminal Court are best read as reflecting negotiated diplomatic compromises rather than some carefully constructed comprehensive view of criminal responsibility. At any rate, they have been taken by criminal comparatists as open invitations to explore how different domestic doctrines of criminal law handle central questions of criminal liability such as intent and other forms of *mens rea*, accomplice and group liability, inchoate criminality (conspiracy, attempt, solicitation), and the availability of defences (eg self-defence, necessity, duress, superior orders, and ignorance of law).

The internationalization—and regionalization[54]—of criminal law is also creating new opportunities for comparative work in procedural criminal law. Left without specific procedural guidelines, international criminal tribunals have been forced to generate procedural rules on the fly, based on general overviews of procedural norms, institutions, and practices in various legal systems across the world prepared by the court's staff. These norms, as well as their application in

---

[52] George P. Fletcher, 'Parochial versus Universal Criminal Law', (2005) 3 *Journal of International Criminal Justice* 20 ff.

[53] See eg Antonio Cassese, *International Criminal Law* (2003); Kai Ambos, *Der Allgemeine Teil des Völkerstrafrechts* (2004); Gerhard Werle, *Principles of International Criminal Law* (2005); see also Philippe Sands (ed), *From Nuremberg to the Hague: The Future of International Criminal Justice* (2003).

[54] See eg the emergence of European criminal law as a subject. Cf Helmut Satzger, *Internationales und Europäisches Strafrecht* (2005).

particular cases, must then be subjected to review under applicable international human rights norms, which in turn cannot be interpreted except in light of the various procedural traditions represented by the tribunal's judges.[55]

III. Selected Topics in Comparative Criminal Law

In this, the final, section we will explore a few issues that have attracted, or might attract, the attention of comparatists in the area of criminal law. Under a familiar analytic scheme, the field of penal law is divided into three aspects. *Substantive criminal law* or criminal law proper concerns itself with the general principles of criminal liability, in its general part, and specific offence definitions, in its special part. *Criminal procedure* deals with the imposition of the general and specific norms of substantive criminal law in particular cases. The law of *punishment execution and sanctions* covers the quantity and quality of sanctions for violation of criminal norms as well as the conditions of their actual infliction on convicted offenders.

The following selection of topics is subjective, and so is the selection of comparative materials. Topics have been drawn from substantive criminal law; no attempt has been made to provide a comprehensive overview of comparative penal law as a whole, or even of comparative substantive criminal law in particular. For simplicity's sake, familiar comparative labels such as 'Anglo-American' and 'continental', 'civil' and 'common' will appear from time to time. Their use does not imply a commitment to the position that any of them capture some distinctive essence; they are used for convenience, and no other purpose. In the end, comparative work always requires careful attention to the law of specific jurisdictions, which may or may not permit generalization to a more abstract—collective or systematic—level of comparison. Comparison that begins with generic contrasts between artificial blocs all too easily descends into the fruitless reaffirmation of unexamined prejudices, particularly if the blocs were assembled for the very purpose of tendentious comparison. This has been a danger particularly in comparative criminal procedure, where 'adversarial' and 'inquisitorial' systems have long, and with increasing futility, locked horns.

Throughout, an effort has been made to highlight issues for comparative

---

[55] See eg the different views of the requirement of 'equality of arms' in the criminal process explored in *Prosecutor v Aleksovski*, Case No. IT-95-14/1-AR73, PP 23–25 (Appeals Chamber, International Criminal Tribunal for the Former Yugoslavia, 16 February 1999).

analysis, rather than to provide a panoramic view of criminal law throughout the world.[56] US law figures prominently in the discussion, reflecting both the author's personal perspective and the increasing significance of US law as a point of reference in comparative analyses of criminal law, particularly for purposes of law reform, where it is often compared and contrasted with German criminal law.

Substantive criminal law, or criminal law proper, traditionally has attracted less comparative interest than its sister disciplines criminal procedure and—at least historically—punishment execution.[57] Even Feuerbach, whose main interest lay in substantive criminal law, showed a programmatic enthusiasm for comparative substantive criminal law, but in fact produced more significant comparative work on criminal procedure (notably on the hotly contested question of lay participation in general, and of the jury in particular).

The relative paucity of comparative work on criminal law is surprising given that theoretical interest in substantive criminal law traditionally has far outpaced theoretical interest in procedural criminal law and, by an even wider margin, in execution law. In fact, within a given criminal subdiscipline, the interest in comparative work appears to be roughly inversely proportional to the interest in theoretical work in that subdiscipline. Unencumbered by theoretical ambitions or broader systematic concerns, criminal procedure and punishment execution have been more likely to scan the world of criminal law for 'better' (generally in the sense of more efficient, if not necessarily more just) processes of case disposition and offender control.

1. General Part

(a) Punishment Theory

Common law and civil law systems generally operate with the same palette of rationales for punishment: retribution, general and specific deterrence, incapacitation, rehabilitation. German criminal law in 1933 adopted a two-track system that distinguishes between punishments and measures; only the latter may rely exclusively on considerations of incapacitation and rehabilitation, while 'true' punishments must reflect the defendant's culpability. This distinction may retain

---

[56] For just such a panoramic view of the law of criminal procedure, see the excellent collection of essays in Craig Bradley, *Criminal Procedure: A Worldwide Study* (1999).

[57] Some of the chestnuts of comparative criminal procedure, touched upon in this essay, include the control, desirability, and inevitability of prosecutorial and police discretion, the roles of judges, prosecutors, and defence attorneys in the criminal process, the place of lay participation in the criminal trial, the control and legitimacy of plea bargaining, and—more recently—the procedural role of victims. Representative general comparative works on all three aspects of penal law appear in the bibliography.

the principled purity of punishments properly speaking, but becomes difficult to maintain once it becomes clear that measures may include indeterminate incarceration for life.[58]

Rehabilitation has fallen into disfavour in the United States, where the dominant rationale for punishment of the War on Crime has been incapacitation, resulting in record incarceration rates and a renaissance of capital punishment. While rehabilitation continues to enjoy greater support in continental systems, a new rationale for punishment has been championed in continental criminal law. 'Positive general prevention' attempts to justify the threat, imposition, and infliction of punishment not in terms of its effect on potential law-breakers but as a means to reinforce the commitment to law among the law-abiding. Positive general prevention is said to avoid both retribution's barbaric pointlessness and deterrence's immoral use of threats to cow citizens into compliance. In the end, however, it is unclear whether it does more than attach a more palatable label to familiar, and familiarly troubled, rationales, not unlike rehabilitation's failed attempt to evade the problem of legitimation altogether by redefining punishment as treatment.[59]

(b) Victims

The victim has undergone a 'rediscovery' in both Anglo-American and continental criminal law in recent decades. In German criminal proceedings, the victim can appear as a parallel prosecutor (*Nebenkläger*), for instance, in sexual assault cases. In cases of petty crime, the victim may even assume the role of private prosecutor (*Privatkläger*), such as in shoplifting prosecutions.[60] In the United States, victims also have been granted various procedural rights, including—most notably—the right to contribute victim impact statements to be considered at sentencing, along with the right to be consulted regarding plea agreements, the right to be accompanied to trial by a 'victim's advocate', and so on.[61]

Upon closer inspection, however, it turns out that the victim's renaissance in US criminal law has very little to do with developments in civil law countries and, for that matter, in other common law countries, including the United Kingdom.[62] In the United States, the rise of the 'victims' rights movement' coincided with the War on Crime and the triumph of incapacitation over other rationales for punishment, and rehabilitation in particular. The pursuit of victims' rights was thought to be inconsistent with the protection of the rights of those suspected of, charged with,

---

[58] See Dubber (n 36), 113 ff, 131.   [59] Ibid.

[60] See William T. Pizzi and Walter Perron, 'Crime Victims in German Courtrooms: A Comparative Perspective on American Problems', (1996) 32 *Stanford Journal of International Law* 37 ff.

[61] See generally Markus Dirk Dubber, 'The Victim in American Penal Law: A Systematic Overview', (1999) 3 *Buffalo Criminal LR* 3 ff.

[62] See generally Symposium, 'Victims and the Criminal Law: American and German Perspectives', (1999) 3 *Buffalo Criminal LR* 1 ff.

and convicted of crime. The fight for victims' rights, in fact, was first and foremost a fight against defendants' rights. So from the very beginning an important component of the victims' rights agenda in the United States included calls for the reform of the law of criminal evidence to require the introduction of all relevant evidence of guilt even where its relevance was outweighed by its potential for confusing or inflaming the jury, the long-term incapacitation of repeat offenders, the reintroduction and expansion of capital punishment, the harshening of prison conditions, and every other item on an ever-growing wish list of tough-on-crime measures.[63]

The rediscovery of the victim elsewhere was considerably less punitive in nature. For instance, one of the central victim-based reforms in German criminal law was the introduction of a provision that permitted the resolution of certain criminal cases through victim-offender mediation, rather than through a traditional criminal trial (StGB § 46 a). By contrast, the mainstream US victims' rights movement showed remarkably little interest in restorative justice programmes or other forms of less punitive responses to crime such as victim compensation laws, which had first appeared in the 1960s.

(c) Jurisdiction

Among the formal prerequisites for the imposition of criminal liability, jurisdiction recommends itself for comparative analysis not only because different legal systems have taken different approaches to the issue but also because they have given it different levels of attention. Anglo American criminal law traditionally has largely ignored the question of criminal jurisdiction (in sharp contrast to the question of civil jurisdiction). Criminal jurisdiction was territorial jurisdiction; it was simply taken for granted that the place of the crime determined jurisdiction. The question attracted no theoretical interest, and doctrinal questions were by and large limited to the issue whether a particular offence was committed in one place or another, or perhaps both, in which case two sovereigns were found to have territorial jurisdiction.

Even today, criminal jurisdiction in Anglo-American law is not covered in criminal law courses and continues to be treated as virtually synonymous with territoriality.[64] This is puzzling since other bases of jurisdiction have begun to enter positive law—largely undetected by the literature—with federal criminal law leading the way in the United States. The non-territorial bases of federal criminal jurisdiction are difficult to detect because the federal criminal law contains no comprehensive provision on jurisdiction. Specific federal statutes, however, have extraterritorial reach, generally on the basis of the passive personality principle,

---

[63] See generally Markus Dirk Dubber, *Victims in the War on Crime: The Use and Abuse of Victims' Rights* (2002).

[64] But see Dubber and Kelman (n 8), ch 2.

which attaches criminal jurisdiction on the basis of the victim's citizenship.[65] Active personality, which turns on the offender's status rather than the victim's, has long since been recognized as not merely one, but the only, basis of military criminal jurisdiction in US law.[66] It also plays an important role in Native American criminal law, which depends crucially on the offender's status (Indian versus non-Indian, Indian tribe member versus Indian non-tribe member)[67] and continues to stump courts accustomed to associating criminal jurisdiction with territoriality.[68]

By contrast, other legal systems recognize the fundamental importance of the question of criminal jurisdiction, conceptualized as part of the more general issue of applicability, which also includes the question of retroactivity, or temporal applicability. Even there, however, the doctrine remains undertheorized as policy considerations, the interpretation of international treaties, and technical questions of extradition have attracted the lion's share of attention in the literature and in the doctrine.[69] Still, the failure to even recognize the need to develop a grounded and comprehensive account of the basis of criminal jurisdiction is symptomatic of a general assumption in Anglo-American criminal law that the power to punish is essentially discretionary and thus beyond the scope of critical inquiry. Once the sovereign has taken offence at the violation of one of its criminal norms, it is free to respond in any way it chooses.

Even the introduction of non-territorial criminal jurisdiction is best seen not as the result of a deep reconsideration of the bases of the state's punitive power, but rather as the reaffirmation of the sovereign's power to reassert its authority even beyond the polity's geographical boundaries. One might argue, for instance, that the active personality principle is more easily justified than, say, territoriality because the offender's citizenship is a better proxy for consent to criminal jurisdiction than the location of the offence. It is no accident that the question of extraterritorial jurisdiction has attracted attention in the United States only when the sovereign itself took offence at the possibility that it, in the person of its official representatives, might be subject to another polity's criminal jurisdiction. The suggestion that a Belgian court might have universal jurisdiction over a former President of the United States and the current Secretary of State (George H. W. Bush and Colin Powell for the bombing of a civilian shelter during the 1991 Gulf War) was rebuffed as a matter of international politics, not on principled grounds of criminal law doctrine. After all, it could hardly be said to violate some as yet undeveloped basic tenets of criminal jurisdiction in US law. US resistance to the international criminal jurisdiction asserted by the international criminal court has followed suit, with the exception that it is has proved

---

[65] See eg 18 USC § 2332 (homicide and serious bodily injury).
[66] See Uniform Code of Military Justice art 2.
[67] Poarch Band of Creek Indians Code § 4–1–2.
[68] See, most recently, *United States v Lara*, 541 US 193 (2004).   [69] StGB § 3, 5, 6, 7.

more difficult to exert political pressure on dozens of signatory nations than on a single country.[70]

(d) Principle of Legality (nulla poena sine lege)

The principle of legality may be widely recognized for its importance. But it means radically different things to different legal systems. In US law, for instance, the legality principle tends to be vaguely associated with two constitutional principles—the prohibition of *ex post facto* and vague criminal laws. The former appears in the federal constitution; the latter has been derived from the general due process guarantee in the federal bill of rights. Both have developed haphazardly and still await integration into a systematic view of criminal law.

For instance, the constitutional *ex post facto* prohibition applies to all laws, including non-criminal ones. Its limitation to criminal laws, which has long been taken for granted, was read into the provision—in dictum, and with very little analysis—by a late eighteenth-century US Supreme Court decision in a civil matter that remains the leading case on retroactivity in American criminal law, and to this day is not merely cited, but extensively quoted, in virtually every judicial, and for that matter scholarly, discussion of retroactivity.[71]

Specificity. Vagueness doctrine has suffered from a similar lack of attention. While it is ordinarily treated as a (Fifth Amendment) due process requirement that presumably would apply to all criminal laws, US courts often struggle to distinguish it from specificity requirements based on (First Amendment) concerns about state interference with protected speech that would apply only to criminal statutes that prohibit speech. Even when the due process foundation of the vagueness prohibition is clear enough, courts often misunderstand it. A 'vagueness' case, for instance, may well strike down a criminal law statute not because it fails to provide potential offenders (or even law enforcement officers) with sufficient notice of what it does and does not criminalize, but because it reaches conduct that lies beyond the state's power to punish, however defined.[72] Moreover, US courts have been decidedly uneven in applying the constitutional prohibition of vagueness. For instance, it appears that courts will uphold patently vague criminal statutes (such as Racketeer Influenced and Corrupt Organizations Act and federal honest services fraud) as long as the legislature specifically designed the statute to be vague— because vague criminal statutes simplify and expedite the state's war on crime.[73]

---

[70] The Belgian parliament revised the universal jurisdiction law in response to US pressure.

[71] *Calder v Bull*, 3 US 386 (1798); cf *Rogers v Tennessee*, 532 US 451 (2001).

[72] *Papachristou v City of Jacksonville*, 405 US 156 (1972) (vagrancy); see Dubber and Kelman (n 8), 143–4.

[73] See eg the federal Racketeer Influenced and Corrupt Organizations Act of 1970, better known as RICO, 18 USC §§ 1961 ff. On RICO's vagueness, see *People v Capaldo*, 151 Misc 2d 114, 572 NYS 2d 989 (1991); see generally Dubber and Kelman (n 8), 740–77.

Vagueness doctrine thus may appear as little more than a guideline for statutory interpretation, as opposed to a constitutional norm. The rule of lenity, which instructs courts to interpret ambiguous criminal statutes in favour of the accused, is often associated with the vagueness prohibition. A court unwilling to strike down a statute on vagueness grounds might interpret it narrowly instead, thus curing it of its vagueness. The rule of lenity is applied even less consistently; courts invoke it in some cases, but ignore it in others. (In fact, modern criminal codes often explicitly abandon lenity as an interpretative guideline in the hope of limiting courts' interpretative discretion to the code's comprehensive conceptual framework.[74]) Like the vagueness prohibition, the rule of lenity is often mistakenly—or at least unnecessarily—invoked, as courts can reach the same result based on an inquiry into legislative intent. Finally, the constitutional foundation of the rule of lenity is at least questionable, despite occasional remarks suggesting a basis in due process.

Legalitätsprinzip. Continental criminal law, by contrast, has developed a more systematic approach to the question of the constraints of legality on criminal law. Driven by the Enlightenment critique of state power in all forms, and in the guise of criminal law in particular, the principle of *nulla poena sine lege* attempted to place principled constraints on official discretion—notably in its judicial and executive manifestations (with legislative constraints lagging behind). In the executive realm, the principle of legality (*Legalitätsprinzip*) was thought to require eliminating official discretion altogether. Prosecutors (who now performed functions traditionally performed by judges, in an attempt to limit judicial discretion) and police were obligated—under threat of criminal punishment—to pursue all reasonably suspected violations of a criminal statute.

Judges in turn were forbidden from interpreting criminal law statutes by analogy, as they had done in the past; criminal statutes were instead to be interpreted strictly and *in dubio pro reo*. In fact, judges who intentionally misinterpreted the statute were themselves subject to criminal liability.[75] As a result, legislatures indirectly were required to draft comprehensive criminal codes rather than passing occasional and broad laws that judges could apply as they saw fit. Legality concerns, however, have remained clearly focused on the judiciary (and the executive), rather than on the legislature. And by all accounts, judges have remained remarkably faithful to the prohibition of interpretation by analogy. Oddly, the one example of a violation of the prohibition which is cited *ad nauseam* is not a judicial decision at all, but a statute: the 1935 amendment to section 2 of the German Criminal Code authorizing punishment of 'an act which the law declares to be punishable *or which deserves punishment according to the fundamental principle of a penal statute and the healthy sentiment of the people*' (emphasis added).

---

[74] See eg Model Penal Code § 1.02(3).   [75] StGB § 339 (*Rechtsbeugung*).

Legislativity. It is one thing for a judge to interpret a criminal statute by analogy. It is quite another for a judge to create the criminal offence in the first place. Under the continental understanding of the legality principle, the former was unacceptable; the latter would have been unthinkable. Yet this is precisely what common law courts, first in England and then in the United States, did for centuries.[76] In the United States, the principle of legality was never invoked to question the court's power to make criminal law. Modern US criminal codes did shift criminal lawmaking power from the judiciary to the legislature, but not on the ground that judicial criminal lawmaking violated constitutional prohibitions of retroactivity, vagueness, or some more fundamental requirement of fair notice. Judicial criminal lawmaking in the United States was not abolished; it slowly faded away, after having survived well into the twentieth century, when US courts finally stopped recognizing new 'common law misdemeanours' that constituted offences against 'the public police and oeconomy'.[77]

Today, executive criminal lawmaking by regulatory agencies and quasi-agencies like sentencing commissions poses a far more significant threat to the principle of legality in US criminal law. The US Supreme Court's recent downgrading of the federal sentencing guidelines from what *de facto*, if not *de jure*, amounted to a comprehensive regulatory code of sentencing law to a discretionary set of guidelines does not reflect a commitment to the principle of legality. That decision instead was motivated by a new-found desire to protect the jury's role in the criminal process.[78]

Prospectivity. Retroactivity is condemned in continental law as it is in US criminal law, though without necessarily having recourse to constitutional rights.[79] Retroactivity in fact was hotly debated in German criminal law long before the appearance of a jurisprudence of constitutional rights in Germany. Karl Binding famously argued that retroactive application of criminal statutes is not necessarily illegitimate because criminal statutes represented only one possible manifestation of a prohibitory norm that might also find recognition in civil statutes or other state action (such as the publication of the norm itself—do not do X). In Binding's view, only the prohibitory norm could not be retroactively applied. As long as the offender had notice of the background norm, the particular, prospective or retrospective, way in which the state chose to respond to its violation was entirely up to the state.

---

[76] See Stanislaw Pomorski, *American Common Law and the Principle Nullum Crimen Sine Lege* (2nd edn, 1975).

[77] See eg *Commonwealth v Keller*, 35 Pa D & C 2d 615 (1964) (creating common law offence of 'indecent disposition of a dead body').

[78] See Dubber and Kelman (n 8), 119–23.

[79] That's not to say that there aren't constitutional prohibitions of retroactivity. See eg GG art 103(2).

Constitutional Law. Outside US law, the problem of vague criminal statutes is not necessarily framed as a constitutional issue. Rather than striking down the statute on vagueness grounds, courts are more likely to interpret it narrowly. Also, continental criminal law tends to be more generous in its interpretation of mistake of law defences based on claims of a good-faith misinterpretation of an unclear statute, as a matter of criminal rather than constitutional law.[80] (US criminal law instead traditionally has taken a very dim view of ignorance of law claims, at least in so far as they are not based on an official misinterpretation of applicable law.)

Only recently have non-US courts begun to explore the connection between the principle of legality (along with other basic principles of criminal law) with the norms of domestic constitutional law and international human rights law. Unlike their counterparts elsewhere, US courts cannot fall back on a well-developed jurisprudence of criminal law; instead they are more likely to draw on a long-standing US constitutional jurisprudence. Viewing an issue in constitutional terms does give courts the power to strike down legislation, thus subjecting the legislature to scrutiny not found elsewhere. By contrast, the finding by a non-US court that a given statute violates this criminal law principle or that does not imply the statute's invalidity. At the same time, however, US courts tend to disregard the criminal nature of an issue. Notably in the special part of criminal law, US courts investigate the state's authority to regulate certain conduct in general, rather than its power to punish that conduct by means of the criminal law.

The legality principle in the United States, then, is considerably narrower than in other countries. Violations of those (few) aspects of the legality principle that are recognized in the United States, however, face a stiffer sanction than mere judicial disapproval: they result in the invalidation of the offending statute. Also note that the (non-constitutional) norms that add up to a broad legality principle in non-US countries are not always as categorical as they might at first appear. The well-known (non-constitutional) principle of compulsory prosecution (*Legalitätsprinzip*) in the German Code of Criminal Procedure, for instance, has for some time been subject to an exception that has begun to threaten the rule—the (non-constitutional) *Opportunitätsprinzip*, or principle of appropriateness. The latter principle releases prosecutors (but, at least in theory, not police officers, who are thought not to deserve the same level of trust) from the former in cases where the public interest does not require prosecution. As one might suspect, the principle of appropriateness played a central role in the spread of plea bargaining in Germany over the past few decades, after—and even while—this practice was universally disavowed and, in fact, derided as a typical example of the pervasive lawlessness of

---

[80] But see Wolfgang Naucke, 'Staatstheorie und Verbotsirrtum', in Bernd Schünemann, Hans Achenbach, Wilfried Bottke, Bernhard Haffke, and Hans-Joachim Rudolphi (eds), *Festschrift für Claus Roxin* (2001), 503 ff.

the US criminal process and the principled superiority of German criminal procedure law.[81]

Codification. A commitment to a broad principle of legality in civil law countries also has not interfered with an approach to codification that leaves considerable room for interpretation and to developments in what is framed as a science of criminal law. The German Criminal Code, for instance, does not define the various mental states required for criminal liability (*Vorsatz, Fahrlässigkeit*). By contrast, the centrepiece of the Model Penal Code project in the United States was a comprehensive and systematic definition of the subjective element of crime, resulting in a taxonomy of mental states including purpose, knowledge, recklessness, and negligence.[82] The German Criminal Code also does not define the basic objective element of criminal liability, conduct. Here too, the Model Penal Code includes a lengthy, if not particularly systematic, provision—which, in the end, evades the thorny question of what constitutes voluntary conduct simply by listing conduct that would not qualify as voluntary.[83] Finally, the German Criminal Code provides no definition of possession, a crucial concept in modern criminal law where possession (of drugs, weapons, instruments of crime, stolen goods, and so on) is increasingly criminalized as a form of early preventive detention that attaches even before the point of preparation—never mind an attempt—to commit an offence.[84] In the case of possession, a definition is particularly important since, without more, criminal liability for possession (a relationship between a person and an object) cannot be squared with the general principle that criminal conduct be limited to conduct. (The Model Penal Code at least attempts a definition, even if it proves unsatisfactory in the end.[85])

German criminal law, of course, has developed a highly sophisticated account of the objective and subjective elements of criminal liability. In fact, one entire school of German criminal law theory, *Finalismus*, which dominated criminal law thought in Germany and German-influenced countries for the better part of the twentieth century, derived an entire system of criminal liability from the ontology of actness, which purportedly implied an essentially human intentionality. Likewise, the discussion of the distinctions among the various types of *Vorsatz* and *Fahrlässigkeit*, or *dolus* and *culpa*, fills volumes. The point here is simply that none of these distinctions is based on the criminal code (except in the loose, and ultimately

---

[81] See Dubber, 'American Plea Bargains', (n 24), 547 ff.

[82] Model Penal Code § 2.02; see Markus D. Dubber, *Criminal Law* (n 40), § 4.2.

[83] Model Penal Code § 2.01; see Dubber, *Criminal Law* (n 40), § 4.1.

[84] On German criminal law, see Cornelius Nestler, 'Rechtsgüterschutz und Strafbarkeit des Besitzes von Schußwaffen und Betäubungsmitteln', in *Vom unmöglichen Zustand des Strafrechts* (1995), 65; Eberhard Struensee, 'Besitzdelikte', in Erich Samson, Friedrich Dencker, and Peter Frisch (eds), *Festschrift für Gerald Grünwald* (1999), 713; Ken Eckstein, *Besitz als Straftat* (2001); on US criminal law, see Dubber (n 44), 829 ff.

[85] Model Penal Code § 2.01(4); see Dubber, *Criminal Law* (n 40), § 4.1(d).

circular, sense that the code reflects a certain conceptual structure, which is itself external to it).

The vast bulk of German criminal law (and therefore of much of criminal law in civil law countries) stems not from codes, nor from courts interpreting these codes, but from the academic literature. Traditionally, the main manufacturers of German criminal law doctrine have been German criminal law professors who regard themselves as engaged in the continuing enterprise of criminal law science, a branch of legal science. (In fact, the definitions of mental states were omitted from the German Criminal Code specifically to allow for continued scientific debate on this issue.[86]) This is not the place to scrutinize the considerable and highly influential achievements of German criminal law science over the past centuries. Suffice it to highlight the tension between the principle of legality and a system of criminal law that relies crucially on the jurisgenerative authority of unelected experts engaged in a highly exclusive and increasingly impenetrable scientific project.[87]

(e) Analysis of Criminal Liability

It is generally assumed that the analysis of criminal liability differs widely in common law and civil law, with one system requiring *actus reus* and *mens rea*, and the other *Tatbestandsmäßigkeit* (*tipicidad, tipicità*), *Rechtswidrigkeit* (*antijuricidad, antigiuridicità*), and *Schuld* (*culpabilidad, colpevolezza*). The significance of these structural matters tends to be exaggerated; none the less, they are worth one's attention if only because supposed structural incompatibility is an unnecessary impediment to comparative analysis.

Modern US criminal law uses an analytic structure that is easily compatible with the German scheme.[88] The Model Penal Code defines a crime as 'conduct that unjustifiably and inexcusably inflicts or threatens substantial harm to individual or public interests'.[89] Criminal liability thus has three basic components: (1) conduct, (2) without justification, and (3) without excuse. To count as a crime, 'conduct' must, however, meet several additional criteria, namely it must: (a) inflict or threaten (b) substantial harm to individual or public interests. If we put the two together, we get the Model Penal Code's complete scheme of criminal liability. A person is criminally liable if he engages in (1) conduct that (a) inflicts or threatens (b) substantial harm to individual or public interests (2) without justification and (3) without excuse.

This scheme is easily mapped onto the traditional common law scheme. It is

---

[86] For a recent suggestion that German criminal law professors be recognized as a 'fourth branch of government', see Bernd Schünemann, 'Strafrechtsdogmatik als Wissenschaft', in Schünemann *et al.* (n 80), 1, 8.

[87] Dubber (n 31), 1049 ff.   [88] See Dubber and Kelman (n 8), ch 3.

[89] Model Penal Code § 1.02; see Dubber, *Criminal Law* (n 40), § 3.

impossible to crystallize a single coherent liability analysis from hundreds of years of Anglo-American common law. Let's assume, for present purposes, that a crime in the common-law sense consists of two 'offence' elements, (1) *actus reus* (the guilty act) and (2) *mens rea* (the guilty mind). *Actus reus* and *mens rea* are necessary, but not sufficient, prerequisites of criminal liability under the common law; criminal liability requires both a criminal 'offence' (consisting of *actus reus* and *mens rea*) and the absence of 'defences'. Particularly in the law of homicide, which has always managed to attract the lion's share of doctrinal attention, courts generally divided these defences into two types, justifications and excuses. Criminal liability thus attached to an offence committed (2) without justification and (3) without excuse. The analytic schemes of the Model Penal Code and the common law therefore are more or less interchangeable depending on how one views the connection between conduct and *mens rea*. The Model Code defines conduct as encompassing both: conduct is 'an action or omission and its accompanying state of mind'. Replacing '*actus reus* and *mens rea*' with 'conduct', the common-law scheme of criminal liability therefore looks like this: (1) conduct, (2) without justification, and (3) without excuse.

The similarity to the German tripartite scheme now is clear. (1) The inquiry into *Tatbestandsmäßigkeit* asks whether the accused's conduct matches the definition of a criminal offence, and is thus criminal in the formal sense. (2) The second level probes the formally criminal conduct's *Rechtswidrigkeit*, or unlawfulness, which is easily reframed as an inquiry into the presence or absence of a justification. (3) Assuming *Tatbestandsmäßigkeit* and *Rechtswidrigkeit*, the third and final prerequisite for criminal liability is *Schuld*, which might be rendered as guilt, responsibility, or perhaps blameworthiness, or—to put it differently once again—the absence of an excuse.

Despite this basic structural compatibility, which should suffice for meaningful comparative analysis, some general differences remains (besides the inevitable distinctions in specific rules). For one, US criminal law attaches far less significance to the definitions of, and distinctions among, the various levels of inquiry. Even the Model Penal Code considered them as no more than occasionally convenient analytic devices. Unlike in other traditions (notably in German criminal law), they are not generally thought to reflect the ontology, or the phenomenology, of criminal liability.[90] Moreover, even modern Anglo-American criminal has retained the basic distinction between offence and defence, classifying justifications and excuses (themselves defensive concepts) as types of defence, rather than as preconditions for the attachment of criminal liability. This distinction, which is largely ignored in continental criminal law, reflects the continued dominance of procedure over substance in Anglo-American criminal law. The distinction, however arbitrary, also carries considerable doctrinal significance as it separates issues that must be proved

---

[90] See generally Dubber (n 31), 1049 ff.

by the state, beyond a reasonable doubt, from those that the defendant may be required to prove.[91]

(f) General Principles of Criminal Liability

Criminal liability requires conduct; mere thoughts or beliefs may not be criminalized. That much is clear, at least as a matter of principle (notwithstanding the criminalization of attempt and conspiracy, for instance). Unlike other systems, US criminal law has constitutionalized the so-called act requirement, though it is unclear whether the constitutional norm limits criminal liability to acts or, more narrowly, to voluntary acts.[92] Also unusually, US criminal law distinguishes between acts (as mere bodily movements) and voluntary acts. The constitutional norm does not reach the widespread criminalization of possession, which is widely recognized as a non-act; it bars the criminalization of the status of being a drug addict, but not the criminalization of drug possession by that same addict.[93]

Generally speaking, US criminal law in particular, and Anglo-American criminal law in general, is thought to be less inclined to criminalize another non-act: omission, or the failure to act by one who is obligated to act. The general German omission statute is regularly held up as a model for more callously individualistic criminal law systems to follow. It's worth noting that this provision originally was added to the German Criminal Code in 1935. It proscribed violations of one's 'duty according to sound popular sentiment', a central concept of National Socialist law, which regarded all serious crime as an act of treason, that is, as the violation of one's loyalty to the *Volk* community or its personal manifestation, the *Führer*.

The connection between the *mens rea* schemes in modern Anglo-American criminal law (which has been heavily influenced by the US Model Penal Code) and in continental (German-influenced) criminal law still awaits detailed exploration. The great comparatist Jimenez de Asúa surely oversimplified matters when he claimed that the Model Penal Code drafters merely rediscovered (and relabelled) the traditional civil law mental states of *dolus* (purpose), *dolus eventualis* (knowledge), conscious *culpa* (recklessness), and unconscious *culpa* (negligence).[94] For one, the Model Code concept of recklessness lacks the subjective element of conditional acceptance that is generally thought to be required for conscious *culpa* (though an argument can be made that the Model Code's concept of recklessness makes room for an element of acceptance by requiring 'conscious disregard' of a risk, rather than mere awareness of it).[95]

---

[91] Dubber and Kelman (n 8), 203–5.   [92] Ibid, ch 4.B.

[93] See *People v Davis*, 33 NY 2d 221 (1973).

[94] Luis Jimenez de Asúa, *Tratado de Derecho Penal* (vol 1, 1964), 669. See generally L. A. Zaibert, 'Philosophical Analysis and the Criminal Law,' (2001) 4 *Buffalo Criminal LR* 100 ff. For a careful comparative reading of the Model Code scheme, see Weigend (n 49), 657 ff.

[95] Dubber, *Criminal Law* (n 40), 73–6.

After traditionally opposing corporate criminal liability, civil law countries have gradually moved closer to the contrary Anglo-American position. Even Germany, which in principle continues to maintain that corporate entities are capable neither of engaging in criminal conduct (see finalism's rich concept of conduct, mentioned above) nor of forming culpable mental states, has quietly recognized corporate 'order offences' (*Ordnungswidrigkeiten*), to be distinguished from corporate 'crimes' (*Straftaten*). These 'order offences' are subject to 'monetary fines' (*Geldbußen*), to be distinguished from 'monetary penalties' (*Geldstrafen*).[96]

In general, the modern US law of complicity—which is related to corporate liability in so far as it involves imputing one (natural) person's conduct to another (juristic) person—today resembles continental law less than it did before the Model Penal Code. The distinctions in traditional Anglo-American criminal law among principals in the first and in the second degree and accessories before, at, and after the fact rivalled the continental taxonomy of *Täter, mittelbarer Täter, Mittäter, Nebentäter,* and *Teilnehmer* in complexity, if not in systematic rigour. The Model Penal Code flattened the law of complicity, retaining only a distinction between principal and accomplice and expanding criminal liability to attempted complicity.[97] While the requirement of purpose was retained for accomplice liability, some US jurisdictions now criminalize non-purposive facilitation as a separate offence.

In the law of defences, some historical differences have been eroding. German criminal law continues to reject a formal proportionality requirement in the law of self-defence. None the less, it has begun to recognize limits on the right to stand one's ground that in the final analysis approximate the long-standing Anglo-American requirement that even those who are in the right must retreat if they can do so in complete safety. In the law of necessity, Anglo-American criminal law continues to have some difficulty with a defence of circumstantial (as opposed to personal) duress, which has long been recognized in German criminal law. At the same time, German criminal law continues to insist that necessity cannot provide a defence in homicide cases because it is improper, or impossible, to measure the value of human life. This position also retains strength in Anglo-American criminal law, despite the countervailing influence of the Model Penal Code which rejected the taboo in favour of a general lesser-evil rule.[98]

The traditional Anglo-American position on insanity, which recognized only a

---

[96] Dubber (n 31), 1049 ff, 1068; see generally Albin Eser, Günter Heine, and Barbara Huber (eds), *Criminal Responsibility of Legal and Collective Entities* (1998).

[97] Markus D. Dubber, 'Criminalizing Complicity: A Comparative Analysis', *Journal of International Criminal Justice* (forthcoming 2007); cf Carl Erik Herlitz, *Parties to a Crime and the Notion of a Complicity Object: A Comparative Study of the Alternatives Provided by the Model Penal Code, Swedish Law and Claus Roxin* (1992).

[98] The taboo may be weakening even in Germany. See eg Michael Pawlik, '§ 14 Abs. 3 des Luftsicherheitsgesetzes: Ein Tabubruch?', (2004) *Juristenzeitung* 1045 ff (legitimacy of statute authorizing the use of arms to intercept aircraft that threaten human lives).

limited defence in case of incapacity to know the difference between right and wrong, has shown remarkable resilience (and, in fact, many US jurisdictions abandoned, or at least significantly limited, the insanity defence in the wake of John Hinckley's 1982 insanity acquittal for his botched assassination attempt of Ronald Reagan[99]). The Model Penal Code position, which was adopted in several US jurisdictions, more closely resembles the continental position in also recognizing insanity based on the volitional incapacity to control one's behaviour.[100] Anglo-American criminal law remains hostile to intoxication as a defence, either precluding it altogether or, more commonly, limiting it to certain offences (eg those requiring intent or knowledge, rather than recklessness).[101] German criminal law places no such limitations on the use of intoxication as a defence, but then criminalizes the intoxication itself (StGB § 323a).[102]

2. Special Part

Any attempt to provide even a preliminary overview of the enormous number and variety of criminal offences that constitute the special parts of various jurisdictions found in various criminal law systems would far exceed the scope of this essay. (Given the continuous expansion of modern criminal law in criminal and non-criminal, consolidated and unconsolidated, statutes and administrative rules and regulations, capturing the breadth of the special part of any single jurisdiction would be difficult enough.) For that reason we will focus on some of the broader characteristics of special parts in common and civil law systems, rather than on specific offences.

The concept of *Rechtsgut* (*bien jurídico, bene giuridico*) plays a central role in the structure of the special part of continental criminal law, as well as in its theory of criminal law in general.[103] A crime is defined as a violation of a *Rechtsgut*, and the special part consists of offences designed to protect various *Rechtsgüter*. There is no similar concept in Anglo-American criminal law, which instead vacillates between ill-defined concepts such as 'individual or public interests' and 'harm or evil'. At the same time, it is worth noting that the all-important question of what qualifies as a *Rechtsgut* remains unsettled. While it is easy enough to define a *Rechtsgut* as any interest that a criminal provision is designed to protect, a

---

[99] See *Clark v Arizona*, 126 S Ct 2709(2006); *Finger v State*, 27 P 3d 66 (Nev 2001).

[100] Compare StGB §§ 20 & 21 with Model Penal Code §§ 4.01 & 4.02; see generally Dubber and Kelman (n 8), ch 7.H.

[101] See generally Dubber and Kelman (n 8), ch 5.G.

[102] cf Brian Foley, 'Same Problem, Same Solution? The Treatment of the Voluntarily Intoxicated Offender in England and Germany', (2001) *Trinity College LR* 119 ff.

[103] See Markus Dirk Dubber, 'Theories of Crime and Punishment in German Criminal Law', (2006) 53 *AJCL* 679 ff.

circular definition of this sort has no critical bite. Even if one could identify a criminal statute that does not protect an interest that could be classified as a *Rechtsgut*, it is unclear what such a finding would imply. Given that the *Rechtsgut* is grounded in preconstitutional criminal law theory rather than in a constitutional guarantee, it is generally understood that an offence without a *Rechtsgut* is not, for that reason alone, unconstitutional or invalid. Even without critical force, however, the *Rechtsgut* may provide a useful analytic device for statutory interpretation that could take the place of a hodgepodge of concepts used by Anglo-American courts for that purpose.

Without a concept of *Rechtsgut*, US courts have turned to constitutional law, rather than criminal law, in cases that raise the question of the permissible scope of the special part. For instance, the US Supreme Court considered whether homosexual sex may be criminalized in keeping with the constitutional right to privacy of consenting adults,[104] whether the private consumption of pornography may be punished in keeping with the right to freedom of thought,[105] whether criminalizing assisted suicide violates a constitutionally recognized right to die,[106] and so on.

Both common law and civil law extend the protection of the relevant interests or rights to acts that fall short of actual interference. Apart from the law of inchoate offences such as attempt, a criminal offence may be consummated by posing a threat or even engaging in conduct that ordinarily poses a threat of harm even if it may not have posed a threat in the particular case. Anglo-American criminal law boasts a wide and ever-expanding variety of implicit and explicit endangerment offences, even if the taxonomy of criminal offences has not been mapped out as systematically as in continental criminal law.[107]

Traditionally, the Anglo-American law of inchoate (incomplete, preparatory, anticipatory) offences has differed rather dramatically from continental criminal law. Notably the offence of conspiracy, which historically could attach not only to any criminal offence but even to non-criminal yet otherwise objectionable ('corrupt, dishonest, fraudulent, or immoral') behaviour, has no direct analogue in continental criminal law, as the Allies noticed as they prepared for the Nuremberg Trials:

During much of the discussion, the Russians and French seemed unable to grasp all the implications of the concept; when they finally did grasp it, they were genuinely shocked. The French viewed it entirely as a barbarous legal mechanism unworthy of modern law, while the Soviets seemed to have shaken their head in wonderment—a reaction, some cynics may believe, prompted by envy. But the main point of the Soviet attack on

---

[104] *Lawrence v Texas*, 539 US 558 (2003) (no); but see *Bowers v Hardwick*, 478 US 186 (1986) (yes).

[105] *Stanley v Georgia*, 394 US 557 (1969) (yes).

[106] *Washington v Glucksberg*, 521 US 702 (1997) (no).

[107] For a recent analytic effort in this regard, see Markus Dirk Dubber, 'The Possession Paradigm: The Special Part and the Police Power Model of the Criminal Process', in R. A. Duff and Stuart Green (eds), *Defining Crimes: Essays on the Criminal Law's Special Part* (2005), 91 ff.

conspiracy was that it was too vague and so unfamiliar to the French and themselves, as well as to the Germans, that it would lead to endless confusion.[108]

The Model Penal Code retained the offence of conspiracy, though limiting it to criminal objectives. It may well be that modern continental criminal law can achieve much of the same result through a broad use of doctrines of complicity and attempt.[109] Still, it should be kept in mind that even the modern US view of conspiracy remains extremely broad: The Model Penal Code expanded conspiracy to cover so-called 'unilateral' conspiracies that require merely the belief that one has entered into an agreement with another and generally punished conspiracies (and all other inchoate offences) as harshly as consummated offences. Federal criminal law, in fact, provides for harsher punishments of conspiracies to commit an offence than for the commission of the offence itself, permits punishment for both the conspiracy to commit an offence and its commission, and generally treats proof of conspiracy as sufficient for liability for complicity in the object offence. The Model Penal Code in turn significantly broadened the scope of attempt liability to include any act that amounts to a substantial step toward the commission of the object offence, provided that act is indicative of the defendant's criminal purpose.[110] Note also that in US law—unlike in German law, for instance— attempt, conspiracy, and solicitation are general inchoate offences that attach to any criminal offence, including misdemeanours.

IV. COMPARATIVE CRIMINAL LAW IN CONTEXT

Comparative criminal law is best seen as one way to gain critical distance from a given system of criminal law by placing it within a larger context. Criminal law history is another. So is other transdisciplinary research, drawing on the tools and insights of the social sciences and humanities. Within comparative criminal law, transnational analysis is only one possible approach among many. Others include intranational comparison among various types of law (torts, contracts, property,

---

[108] Stanislaw Pomorski, 'Conspiracy and Criminal Organizations', in *The Nuremberg Trial and International Law* (1990), 213, 218–19 (quoting Bradley F. Smith, *Reaching Judgment at Nuremberg* (1977), 51).

[109] See generally Dubber n 97.

[110] cf George Fletcher, 'Is Conspiracy Unique to the Common Law?', (1995) 43 *AJCL* 171 ff (reviewing Elisabetta Grande, *Accordo criminoso e conspiracy: Tipicità e stretta legalità nell'analisi comparata* (1993)).

taxation, victim compensation) and regulation within a given jurisdiction and among criminal law systems across domestic jurisdictions.

It is important, in other words, to place comparative criminal law itself within a larger context. Detached from a broader vision of thinking about, teaching, and critiquing law, comparative criminal law all too easily slips into essayistic travel reportage or the collection of criminal exotica, if not the considerably less harmless confirmation of preconceived notions about the superiority—or inferiority—of one's domestic criminal law system. Comparative criminal law has the potential to make an important contribution to criminal law, a subject that is both more parochial *and* more in need of critical analysis than any other form of state action through law. That potential remains as yet unrealized.

BIBLIOGRAPHY

Luis Jiménez de Asúa, *Tratado de derecho penal* (4th edn, 1964)

Juan Bustos Ramírez and Manuel Valenzuela Bejas, *Derecho penal latinoaméricano comparado* (1981)

Mirjan R. Damaška, *The Faces of Justice and State Authority: A Comparative Approach to the Legal Process* (1986)

Markus D. Dubber and James Q. Whitman, *Comparative Perspectives on Criminal Law* (forthcoming 2007)

Markus D. Dubber and Kevin J. Heller (eds), *Handbook of Comparative Criminal Law* (forthcoming 2007)

Albin Eser, George P. Fletcher, and Karin Cornils (eds), *Justification and Excuse: Comparative Perspectives* (1987)

George P. Fletcher, *Basic Concepts of Criminal Law* (1998)

Craig Bradley, *Criminal Procedure: A Worldwide Study* (1999)

Mireille Delmas-Marty and J. R. Spencer (eds), *European Criminal Procedures* (2002)

Jean Pradel, *Droit pénal comparé* (2nd edn, 2002)

Stephen C. Thaman, *Comparative Criminal Procedure: A Casebook Approach* (2002)

James Q. Whitman, *Harsh Justice: Criminal Punishment and the Widening Divide between America and Europe* (2003)

Alberto Cadoppi, *Introduzione allo studio del diritto penale comparato* (2nd edn, 2004)

Liora Lazarus, *Contrasting Prisoners' Rights: A Comparative Examination of Germany and England* (2004)

Richard Vogler, *A World View of Criminal Justice* (2005)

CHAPTER 41

COMPARATIVE CIVIL PROCEDURE

JOACHIM ZEKOLL

New Orleans and Frankfurt

I. INTRODUCTION

PROCEDURAL law, and civil procedure in particular, was long neglected by comparative scholars. Perceived as painstaking, ministerial, and ultimately boring, the subject was dreaded by students and avoided by professors who had higher aspirations. It was considered an unattractive candidate for comparative study because it appeared to be nothing more than a technical framework designed to define, assign, and enforce rights in the domestic courtroom. To the extent one focuses on purely technical matters, such as time limits for filing appeals, it is indeed true that comparative civil procedure does not promise a great deal of insight. Yet, in comparative law, the emphasis on the restatement or juxtaposition of black-letter rules has by and large been overcome in the last couple of decades. Accordingly, scholars have begun to examine comparative procedure's many facets, its purposes and methodology. On the other hand, comparative research in procedural areas is still at a relatively early stage. More importantly, a solid theoretical foundation that would include a theory of comparison and would guide and connect the various research efforts has yet to emerge. As comparative law in general,[1] this nascent sub-discipline generates knowledge without necessarily advancing the cause or formation of a greater comparative enterprise. While comparative procedural thinking has thus not realized its potential, it is increasingly employed in a variety of areas. The inquiries into procedural regimes range from concrete practical concerns, such as improving civil justice at home (by adopting foreign procedural law) or handling issues of international litigation, to pondering broad epistemological questions such as the relationship between forms of procedure and their cultural and political environment.

This essay will first examine the attempts to categorize and label procedural systems (Section II), an impulse that many comparatists cannot, but should, resist. The focus will then shift to procedural harmonization, a term that encompasses a number of topics of increasing importance to proceduralists (Section III). This section forms the centrepiece of the essay because it is here that most opportunities to benefit from comparative scholarship present themselves—and are still being missed. After illustrating the dynamics and results of regional, particularly European, and supra-regional harmonization initiatives, we will look at trends towards harmonization through private rule making and at principles that determine the scope of, and limits to, procedural harmonization. Section IV will address the growing concern about access to justice, specifically cost considerations and claim aggregation techniques, which prompt the somewhat related

---

[1] On the theoretical shortcomings in comparative law generally, see Mathias Reimann, 'The Progress and Failure of Comparative Law in the Twentieth Century', (2002) 50 *AJCL* 671, 685 ff.

questions of whether and to what extent one legal system can borrow procedural rules from another one.

II. Taking Stock—Legal Procedural Families and Other Attempts to Categorize

Historically, comparative law was concerned with the study of substantive law. One of its objectives was to organize legal systems into a number of distinct families, by distinguishing, for example, between Romanic, Germanic, and Anglo-American law.[2] This process of 'mapping' the legal world marks early attempts by comparative scholars to learn enough about various systems to assign them to one family or another. While these typologies may have served as a useful launching pad for subsequent comparative inquiries, the very act of creating categories invites generalizations that run the risk of drawing attention away from the meticulous work needed to uncover and appreciate the make-up of individual legal systems, including their philosophical, political, and cultural roots. Focusing on legal families also does little to improve our understanding of the growing body of transnational law that has arisen from the voluntary transfer of sovereignty to international bodies and treaty regimes, as well as from private law-making activities (eg *lex mercatoria*).

1. Traditional Labels

While the comparative study of procedural laws as defining elements of certain legal families is also unlikely to yield useful insights, a historic examination of the specific structure of a procedural system or, by extension, of the differences between procedural systems that continue to exist, remains a particularly useful tool for understanding the procedural features and preferences of any given regime.[3] Nevertheless, the historical perspective no longer supports the idea that procedural systems can be neatly divided into the traditional legal families of Romanic, Germanic, and Anglo-American procedure.

---

[2] See eg Konrad Zweigert and Hein Kötz, *Introduction to Comparative Law* (3rd edn, 1998), 63 ff.
[3] See eg Benjamin Kaplan, 'Civil Procedure—Reflections on the Comparison of Systems', (1959) 9 *Buffalo LR* 409, 414–21.

Nor can meaningful insights be gained by adhering to another, frequently employed typology, which limits itself to a distinction between adversarial and inquisitorial procedures. The former focuses on the strictly party-driven features of traditional Anglo-American procedure, such as the litigants' control and presentation of evidence, and the passive role of judges. The latter assumes, by contrast, that in Continental European models, and in their non-European offshoots, it is the decision-maker who exerts control throughout the proceedings with only modest powers left to the parties and their representatives. Whatever the historical truth and ramifications of these assumptions, the distinction is moot for purposes of assessing civil justice systems in the Western world today. In reality, Continental civil systems are not 'inquisitorial'; rather, they vest parties with a great deal of autonomy in shaping the proceedings, for example, by determining which evidence will be introduced at trial. And, in many instances, the judge in the so-called 'Anglo-American' procedure is no longer the passive arbiter who merely presides over the case and leaves its development to the parties.

Recently, English law in particular has taken a major step away from the so-called 'adversarial' model. Aimed at reducing the length of judicial proceedings, a comprehensive reform of English civil procedure has severely curtailed the power of parties and strengthened the authority of courts to manage cases. That shift is particularly evident in Part 32.1 of the new Civil Procedure Rules which reads:

(1) The Court may control the evidence by giving directions as to—
    (a) the issues on which it requires evidence;
    (b) the nature of the evidence which it requires to decide those issues; and
    (c) the way in which the evidence is to be placed before the court.
(2) The court may use its power under this rule to exclude evidence that would otherwise be admissible.
(3) The court may limit cross examination.

Together with other changes, such as the limitation of document discovery,[4] this shifting of control places English civil procedure more in line with Continental European, Latin American, and international arbitration models than with US-American law.

Some reallocation of authority between parties and courts has also occurred in the United States, albeit to a lesser extent. Pre-trial conferences, in which the court dictates the course of the proceedings, are now common. Complex multi-party litigations require active management skills and considerable creativity on the part of the court that cannot easily be reconciled with traditional perceptions of 'the adversarial system'. These developments notwithstanding, American procedure, its institutions, and actors remain in many ways unique. No other system allows for such aggressive lawyering and nowhere else does lay participation in the form of

---

[4] See eg Practice Direction supplementing Part 31 of the English Civil Procedure Rules, <http://www.dca.gov.uk/civil/procrules_fin/contents/practice_directions/pd_part31.htm>

the jury trial play such a significant role. The underpinnings and worldwide impact of this procedural regime are the subject of numerous comparative studies and will be recurrent themes in this essay.

Overall, the development of procedural law governing civil litigation has resulted in the emergence of hybrid systems. There is a growing approximation driven by 'a worldwide procedural civilization which has developed independently from national preconditions'.[5] This development will be explored in greater detail below. For present purposes, it suffices to point out that the trend towards harmonization is not due only to procedural reforms through state action and the introduction of procedural rights and guarantees through international treaty obligations;[6] it can also be found in the context of private initiatives (ALI-UNIDROIT) and non-state dispute resolution mechanisms (arbitration), which complement the worldwide production of norms without state input in various fields of substantive law. There are, of course, procedural rules that have proven resistant to harmonization. Institutional settings, that is, the structure of court systems, the role and status of the actors operating these systems, as well as the scope and course of appellate procedures, often reflect long-standing traditions that continue to vary from one system to another.

It would thus go too far to claim that the harmonization of procedural law has led to widespread convergence, that is, to a state in which national idiosyncrasies have largely vanished. It would also be patently unwise to withdraw scholarly attention from the differences that do remain, for example, from the effort to unearth the origins of certain procedural rules. However, today, taxonomies that dwell on legal families, or merely distinguish between adversarial and inquisitorial systems, do not adequately capture the differences and similarities in current procedural law.

2. Damaska's Categories

This scepticism applies as well to more elaborate and ambitious efforts that aim at categorizing legal styles. The best known among them, Mirjan Damaska's *The Faces of Justice and State Authority*,[7] seeks to develop recognizable, and distinguishable,

---

[5] Rolf Stürner, 'Inaugural Speech. Procedural Law and Legal Cultures', in Peter Gilles and Thomas Pfeiffer (eds), *Prozeßrecht und Rechtskulturen—Procedural Law and Legal Cultures* (2003), 18.

[6] For details on the impact of the European Convention for the Protection of Human Rights and Fundamental Freedoms and the American Convention of Human Rights, see Mauro Cappelletti and Briant G. Garth, 'Civil Procedure', ch 1 in *International Encyclopedia of Comparative Law* (vol 16, 1987).

[7] See Mirjan R. Damaska, *The Faces of Justice and State Authority: A Comparative Approach to the Legal Process* (1986).

features of civil and common law procedure by focusing on two themes. One involves the organization of authority in general and the organization of procedural authority in particular; the other addresses the role of procedural law in common and civil law systems. The organization-of-authority element of this scheme distinguishes between a hierarchical (vertical) and a coordinate (horizontal) ordering ideal. Civil law jurisdictions, it is argued, adhere by and large to a hierarchical ordering principle. Among other things, these systems favour career judges who are appointed to distinct echelons within a tightly organized bureaucratic structure, multi-stage trials, the legalistic (and impersonal) application of the law that favours the use of written rather than oral evidence, and decisions that are regularly not accompanied by dissenting opinions but are subject to comprehensive review. By contrast, common law procedure is said to unfold in a coordinate or horizontal structure of judicial authority consisting of lay personnel or elected officials. This system prefers oral evidence, focuses on facts rather than doctrine, and produces decisions which are subject to minimal appellate review. To be sure, these observations produce valuable insights in their own right, but they do not lead to an understanding of the actual functioning of regimes. Hierarchically organized systems, for example, historically have produced very different types of judges, ranging from very active to rather uninvolved.[8]

The second component of Damaska's model relates to the functions of government because 'dominant ideas about the role of government inform views on the purpose of justice, and the latter are relevant to the choice of many procedural arrangements'.[9] The study contrasts two extreme types of government, the reactive state and the activist state. The former is associated with common law proceedings while the latter is linked to the civil law world, including former communist nations. The reactive (common law) state is uninvolved. It merely provides a bare bones framework for a civil society that allows citizens to manage their own affairs. Law in such a setting is not a consequence of state activity, but rather the result of 'agreements, contracts and pacts' (p 75). Conflict resolution manifests itself in a *contest* between private citizens. The reactive state leaves it largely to individuals to pursue their rights, initiate legal disputes, and have them resolved by courts that function as neutral supervisors and disinterested arbiters of fact and (contractarian) law.

By contrast, the activist (civil law) state assumes the role of a social welfare provider. It is the primary forum for political activity and the principal source of norm production (p 80 f). Legal norms thus epitomize state interests and the judicial process serves as means for the *implementation of policies* that promote societal objectives (p 82). While reactive systems strive for 'fair' results in the individual case, the goal in activist systems is to generate the 'right' decision in line with policies embodied in legal norms. Thus, procedural rules in the activist state must be flexible and, if necessary, even dispensable in the pursuit of higher societal

---

[8] Stürner (n 5), 26–7.   [9] Damaska (n 7), 11.

goals through substantive decisions in individual disputes. The activist state accomplishes this by vesting state officials with strong interventionist powers and control over legal proceedings. As opposed to the reactive (common law) state, the prevailing procedural form in the activist (civil law) state is *inquest* rather *contest.*

Neither the organization of authority (hierarchical versus coordinate), nor the purposes of adjudication (reactive versus activist government) in Damaska's model are meant accurately to describe real world settings. They represent ideal types of procedural designs to which existing systems can be compared. The model is thus built on the understanding that every procedural regime exhibits some of the characteristics of each of its four constituent elements. Hierarchically organized (civil law) systems must also solve two-party conflicts and, according to Damaska, these systems will employ adversarial tools to do so. Conversely, legal proceedings in coordinate (common law) systems face disputes that require policy input, and the procedural forms employed to solve such disputes are said to be inquisitorial.[10] This model thus acknowledges the existence of hybrid systems. Coupled with a wealth of illustrations of mixed procedural patterns, it provides more and deeper insights than the traditional undifferentiated classificatory schemes.

Nevertheless, Damaska's model is still rooted in the dubious distinction between common and civil law procedure. It also is suspect in its claim that the organization of authority must entail certain consequences. Further, it rests on the assumption that policy implementation and conflict resolution settings—no matter where they present themselves—reflect more or less distinct categories that can be used as 'markers' for classificatory purposes. Conceptually, it is difficult to think of either category as serving only one purpose or the other.[11] First, policy implementation (inquests) settles real life conflicts not only by way of *inquest* but on the basis of individual *contest* as well. Criminal procedural law in Continental Europe, Damaska's prime example of an inquest-driven, policy implementation process, involves such a contest between the individuals pursuing their rights and the state seeking punishment. That contest involves bargaining, albeit within narrower limits than the open plea bargaining regime that characterizes the American criminal justice system. Continental European criminal justice, therefore, is more than a mere reflection of policy implementation interests. Second, dispute resolution (*contests*) settings provide the venue for the implementation of state policies. This is nowhere more visible than in the United States where generous standing rights encourage individuals to press claims that also serve larger public interest objectives (eg to avoid violations of antitrust laws, improve prison conditions, or overcome racial

---

[10] Damaska (n 7), 12.

[11] For a detailed critique of this part of Damaska's model, see Markovits, 'Playing the Opposite's Game: On Mirjan Damaska's The Face of Justice and State Authority', (1989) 41 *Stanford LR* 1313, 1328 ff.

discrimination).[12] Damaska's own study is rich with illustrations of how litigation purposes and, respectively, procedural forms increasingly overlap and blend.[13]

While it is difficult to agree with Damaska's claim that grouping procedural systems into categories is either possible or useful, at the end of the day, his findings are invaluable and prove the need to pay attention to historical detail and the contemporary political, economic, and cultural conditions that prevail in individual systems. Before exploring the trend towards greater harmonization and functional overlap, which also undermines the effort to compartmentalize procedural systems, a brief account of American procedure and its institutions is necessary to clarify the special status of that system.

3. The Special Status of American Law

American procedural law, specifically as it unfolds in first instance civil and criminal proceedings, represents a category of its own—one that fits into Damaska's coordinate ideal like no other regime. The most important institutional reason for this aspect of American 'exceptionalism'[14] is the presence of the jury and, specifically, its power to decide the outcome at the conclusion of the trial. Lay participation of this magnitude does not exist anywhere else. It fosters a peculiar procedural style that is both informal and formal. It is informal because the presentation of facts, as well as the legal instructions directed at the jury, must be couched in language that is accessible to lay persons. The formal dimension manifests itself in rigid evidentiary rules designed to shield the lay jury from exposure to overly speculative or inflammatory presentation of facts. Oral eloquence, employing clear, simple, and even populist, language, is a key ingredient in the successful court-room performance of a trial lawyer. Constitutionally mandated, and anchored in the American version of egalitarianism, the jury system is fundamentally incompatible with managerial judging. The judge, though vested with the power to instruct the jury on legal matters and to overrule civil verdicts in cases of grave errors, remains largely passive in this setting.[15] The input and initiative available to the parties through their attorneys is correspondingly large.

Although fewer than 3 per cent of all cases ultimately get decided by a jury, this institution shapes American procedural dynamics in other respects as well. Rather than involving various trial stages, which professional judges elsewhere use to

---

[12] Markovits, (1989) 41 *Stanford LR* 1313, 1334.

[13] With respect to public interest litigation in the United States, see Damaska (n 7), 238.

[14] More generally on American *exceptionalism* as such, see Seymour Martin Lipset, *American Exceptionalism: A Double-Edged Sword* (1996).

[15] It is true, however, that American judges have become more managerial, if not activist, in complex litigation. See eg below with respect to their special role in class action, nn 107–8 and accompanying text.

monitor and develop a case over an extended period, the American trial must be a single, uninterrupted event so as to conclude the proceedings before jurors whose service is limited to a single block of time (eg a week), and who cannot be reconvened after that time has expired. The single event concept, in turn, has been one reason for the comprehensive, party-driven, pre-trial proof-taking proceedings (discovery) that can entail massive information exchanges. American discovery rules enable private litigants to obtain access to information held by their opponent or third parties to a much greater extent than any other legal system. American attorneys request, and routinely receive, information that would be unavailable in civil litigation elsewhere. Thus, plaintiffs in the American judicial process can develop a case which is initially supported by little or no evidence and which might not make it to court or even settlement negotiations in other systems. Prejudicial surprises at trial are rare under these circumstances. Settlements, in contrast, occur frequently. One reason to settle arises when discovery has unearthed facts that clearly favour one party. More frequently, however, cost considerations prompt an out-of-court resolution of the dispute. Under the American rule of cost, each party bears its own expenses. The costs to engage in and defend against discovery efforts are so substantial that a settlement is often less costly than winning at trial without the possibility of recouping the expenses associated with trying a case. Abuse in this setting is a real danger and there are defendants who settle for the nuisance value of the suit. Finally, the jury, and its perceived lack of rational decision-making and predictability, plays a role in a decision to accept an early settlement. On the other hand, the negotiations leading to the settlement proceed in the 'shadow of the law', that is, they are influenced by results reached in actually adjudicated cases and by an assessment of what a potential jury trial would yield in this particular dispute.[16] Although a high rate of settlements occurs in other systems as well, this short account should suffice to explain that American civil procedure unfolds within a unique institutional framework and produces dynamics that are not found elsewhere. Thus, while there has been a certain approximation of procedural systems over the last two decades, at least in the West, American procedure remains a case apart.

III. Harmonization

There are a number of procedural principles that are widely shared. For instance, the power of the litigants, rather than the judges, to initiate civil proceedings, to control their scope, and to terminate the litigation by withdrawal, admission, or

---

[16] Joachim Zekoll, 'Liability for Defective Products and Services', (2002) 50 (Supp) *AJCL* 121, 150.

settlement, is a defining principle in all Western legal regimes and has become a basic premise in many former socialist systems as well. Public trials, the independence and impartiality of courts, the procedural equality of the parties, and the right to be heard are likewise commonplace. Yet, the remaining differences are numerous and, in some cases, significant. High on the agenda of many comparative proceduralists today is the effort to examine the harmonization of those procedural elements that are not universally acknowledged principles, but rather domestic idiosyncrasies. This part focuses on the sources, dynamics, and scope of various aspects of procedural harmonization. We begin with observations on comparative law as an instrument of integration, a traditional goal that has fallen out of fashion with post-modern comparatists but that has retained much of its practical relevance.

The success of greater economic integration, worldwide or regionally, depends in part on a harmonized body of *substantive* legal rules that facilitate the free movement of persons, goods, services, and capital. Arguably, furthermore, legal systems compete with one another for the most practical set of rules, that is, norms that provide a transparent foundation for the fair and predictable outcome of disputes, or are capable of avoiding disputes altogether. Whether the resultant rules emanate from 'above', through legislative action, or emerge at a sub-legislative level through 'private law production' (eg soft law, *lex mercatoria*), harmonization of the evolving *substantive* legal framework would hardly be effective without the approximation of the underlying *procedural* regimes. This is so because different procedural and institutional frameworks tend to produce different substantive results. Conversely, similar procedural regimes and institutional conditions promote comparable outcomes. As to the latter, consider the Louisiana Civil Code, which is grounded in French and Spanish civil law. These roots notwithstanding, litigation in Louisiana produces results that are not markedly different from those elsewhere in the United States. Among other things, the reasons lie in the procedural and institutional framework in which litigation occurs. Thus, contingent fee arrangements, jury trials, discovery, and the expectations of all participants in this process generate the same dynamics in the Louisiana justice system as in other states.

The observation that differences in procedural devices and other framework factors can result in divergent substantive litigation outcomes can also be illustrated by reference to the special American conditions. For example, substantive American product liability law, including the concept of strict liability, is similar to the corresponding European black-letter rules. However, the frequency of litigation and settlement, as well as the amounts of damages claimants receive in the United States, are significantly higher than in Europe. While there are a number of reasons for these differences, such as the use of private actions as a substitute for a largely absent social insurance safety net, there are specific procedural and institutional conditions that shape the American litigation experience.

While these factors are substantially more similar in other Western systems, the remaining differences can be significant enough to pose obstacles to greater integration. For example, the effort to create greater regional integration has prompted procedural approximation projects in Latin America. Particularly in the member states of MERCOSUR, the Model Code of Civil Procedure for Iberoamerica has been a catalyst for harmonization. Drafted by the Iberoamerican Institute of Procedural Law in the 1960s, the model law has been adopted almost verbatim by Uruguay as its code of civil procedure and has inspired procedural reforms in Argentina, Bolivia, Brazil, Costa Rica and Peru.[17]

1. Harmonization of Procedural Law in the European Union

In the European Union, both diverging substantive laws and varying levels of procedural protections for market participants, such as their ability to access the judiciary, are perceived as obstacles to market integration. In the following sections we will examine the harmonization of procedural law in Europe, first with a view towards domestic law applicable in intra-state disputes and, second, with respect to rules that govern cross-border litigation in the European Union.

(a) Domestic Law for Intra-state Disputes in Europe

In 1990, the EU Commission brought together a group of procedural law experts from every European Union member state and asked them to render an opinion on the feasibility and content of a future European Code of Civil Procedure. Led by the Belgian Marcel Storme, the group sought to produce a draft EU Code of Civil Procedure, that is, a model code with rules that could be adopted by the member states. It soon became apparent, however, that the group lacked sufficient consensus to produce the envisaged draft. Instead, the experts formulated and commented on fourteen articles which were thought to restate procedural principles generally agreeable to all member states in the European Union.[18] Published in 1994, these principles address, in more or less general terms, court-conducted mediation ('conciliation'), the commencement of proceedings, the subject-matter of litigation, proof-taking rules pertaining to documents and witnesses, the withdrawal of claims, default judgments, costs, provisional remedies, the order for payment, enforcement of judgments and penalty payments. The idea behind these principles—that they could constitute the foundation for a comprehensive future

---

[17] John A. Jolowicz, 'On the Comparison of Procedures', in James A. R. Nafziger and Symeon C. Symeonides (eds), *Law and Justice in a Multistate World, Essays in Honor of Arthur T. von Mehren* (2002), 721, 727.

[18] Marcel Storme (ed), *Rapprochement du Droit Judiciaire de l'Uion Européenne—Approximation of Judiciary Law in the European Union* (1994).

harmonization of domestic procedural law through EU legislation—was widely opposed. Among other things, the critics pointed to the cultural identity that they saw reflected in the existing diversity of domestic rules.[19] The EU Commission, initially supportive of the comprehensive European Code of Civil Procedure project, has apparently abandoned it. Instead, European piecemeal initiatives, aimed primarily at harmonizing various procedural aspects of consumer protection, have prevailed.[20] These measures, like the substantive law initiatives they complement, were not the result of comparative, let alone historical, research but were inspired by the perception that a level playing field for consumer protection law can serve both consumer interests and the free movement of goods and services throughout the Union.

In addition to such legislative initiatives, the case law of the European Court of Justice (ECJ) has established certain uniform procedural obligations in domestic courts for cases addressing the application of EU law. Among other things, this type of 'Europeanization' of domestic procedural law makes it mandatory for domestic courts, in certain circumstances, to raise issues of substantive EU law on their own motion even though domestic procedural law only permits—but does not require—an ex officio court examination of the issue.[21] This procedural obligation is meant to facilitate the widespread implementation of EU law principals, such as the freedom of establishment, through the domestic courts. Whether this and other European impositions on domestic legal procedure will actually lead 'towards European procedural primacy in national systems'[22] is far from certain. In fact, the ECJ itself has repeatedly acknowledged the principle of procedural autonomy of the EU member states. It is true, none the less, that EU member states have lost some of their traditional independence in procedural matters.

As with the harmonization of substantive law, Europeanization of procedural law also occurs irrespective of EU legislative or judicial activities. There have been several domestic law reform initiatives aimed at refining procedural law by adopting features favoured in the procedural law of neighbouring states. The German legislature, for example, explicitly acknowledged such 'borrowing' in the recent revision of the German Code of Civil Procedure. Thus, key components of the reform, including the strengthening of single-judge trials, limited review of facts in appellate proceeding, and greater access to evidence, reflect a conscious adaptation to presumably superior competing models in Europe.[23]

---

[19] See eg Haimo Schack, *Internationales Zivilverfahrensrecht* (3rd edn, 2002), 12.
[20] See eg Directive 98/27/EC of the European Parliament and of the Council of 19 May 1998 on injunctions for the protection of consumers' interests.
[21] See eg *van Schijndel and van Veen v SPF*, joined cases C–430, 431/93 [1995] ECR I–4705.
[22] Ioannis S. Delicostopoulos, 'Towards European Procedural Primacy in National Systems', in *Festschrift für Kostas E Beys* (2003), 229.
[23] *Zivilprozessreformgesetz, Regierungsentwurf Bundestags-Drucksache* 14/4722, p 70.

(b) Unified Rules for Cross-Border Litigation in Europe

Even those who would resist any attempt to reduce the diversity of domestic procedural laws, do not dispute the need for greater uniformity in international litigation settings. In the European Union, questions of international jurisdiction and the recognition of foreign judgments have been governed by uniform law for more than thirty years. Here, too, the driving force behind the unification was the desire to advance market integration in Europe. The EEC Treaty aimed at the creation of a common market and, for that purpose, contained explicit rules for the free movement of persons, goods, services, and capital. Market integration, however, requires more. Among other things, it also depends on the free movement of judgments, that is, the ability of market participants involved in private and commercial disputes to seek redress before the courts of one member state and to swiftly enforce the resultant judgment in another. Although the EEC Treaty did not contain specifically applicable rules facilitating judgment recognition throughout the Community, the drafters recognized that need by calling on member states to enter into negotiations with a view towards that end.[24] In 1968, these negotiations resulted in the so-called 'Brussels Convention',[25] a treaty which not only established the rules for the recognition of judgments in civil and commercial litigation but also set out a limited number of circumstances in which courts may exercise personal jurisdiction over defendants domiciled in contracting states.[26]

The adoption of an exclusive set of jurisdictional rules proved crucial for the success of the Convention. The consensus over when the exercise of personal jurisdiction is appropriate was the result of an exercise in 'normative' comparative law and effectively removed a major obstacle to transnational judgment recognition.[27] Courts which are faced with a request to recognize and enforce a judgment that was rendered under these rules in another member state need not and, for all practical purposes, must not, review the jurisdictional findings of the first tribunal.[28] Because other potential objections to foreign judgments, that is, public policy concerns and service of process flaws, are also narrowly defined, recognition

---

[24] Art 220(4) (now Art 293(4)) calling for negotiations with a view towards the 'simplification of formalities governing the reciprocal recognition and enforcement of judgments of courts or tribunals and of arbitration awards'.

[25] Convention on Jurisdiction and the Enforcement of Judgments in Civil and Commercial Matters, 27 September 1968, 1972 OJ L299/32, as amended by 1990 OJ C 189/1; in force since 1973.

[26] Twenty years later, in 1988, the EC member states and the members of the European Free Trade Association (at the time Austria, Finland, Iceland, Norway, Sweden, and Switzerland) entered into the so-called Lugano Convention, which contains, for the most part, provisions that are identical with those of the Brussels Convention. See Convention on Jurisdiction and the Enforcement of Judgments in Civil and Commercial Matters, 16 September 1988, 1988 OJ L319/9.

[27] It should be noted, though, that prior to the entering into force of the Brussels Convention, there were already a number of bilateral treaties within and outside Europe that facilitated the mutual recognition and enforcement of judgments.

[28] Art 28 of the Brussels Convention; Art 35 of the Brussels Regulation.

and enforcement occur almost as a matter of course. In essence, the Brussels Convention and its successor, Regulation 44/2001, operate much like the Full Faith and Credit Clause in the American Constitution,[29] which likewise guarantees the liberal enforcement of other (American) states' judicial decisions. Unlike under American law, however, courts which exercise jurisdiction under the rules of the Convention do not engage in any due process analysis and are therefore unencumbered by the layer of constitutional inquiry that often results in lengthy and expensive threshold litigation before American courts.

Overall, the jurisdictional rules of the Brussels Convention have produced a high degree of legal certainty as well as outcomes that are considered fair for purposes of intra-community litigation. Yet, there have been cases in which the application of these rules to particular facts was not a simple matter. In these instances, domestic courts, uncertain about the application of a Brussels Convention provision, stayed the proceedings before them and referred the question to the European Court of Justice.[30] The case law generated by that court has significantly improved the even-handed application of these jurisdictional rules by domestic courts in European member states. Indeed, the Court's comprehensive interpretations of structural elements of the Convention, such as the meaning of 'cause of action' or the difference between tort and contract claims, transcend the limited scope of the Convention and inspire a reconsideration of domestic rules in light of this case law. This process in itself may generate a degree of procedural harmonization of domestic rules.

In 2002, the Convention was replaced by Council Regulation 44/2001.[31] This regulation introduced some, but no major, changes. Thus the existing case law produced by the European Court of Justice under the Convention will continue to provide important guidance in many future cross-border disputes. The shift from (Brussels) Convention, to (Brussels) Regulation, that is, to an EU legislative instrument directly applicable in every member state, was made possible through changes introduced by the Treaty of Amsterdam. In force since 1999, these changes widened the legislative competence of the Council of the European Union to adopt measures in the field of judicial cooperation in civil matters with cross-border implications (Art 61 c and Art 65 EC Treaty). According to Article 65 EC Treaty, 'the field of judicial cooperation' includes cross-border service of process, taking of evidence, the recognition and enforcement of judgments, the harmonization of conflict of laws and jurisdictional rules, as well as the harmonization of civil procedural rules in the member states if that is necessary to ensure the proper functioning of civil proceedings.

---

[29] Article IV, § 1 of the US Constitution, as implemented in the Full Faith and Credit Statute, 28 USC § 1738.

[30] Art 234 of the EC Treaty.

[31] Council Regulation 44/2001 on Jurisdiction and the Recognition of Judgments in Civil and Commercial Matters; OJ L12/1 (16 January 2001); not applicable in Denmark.

In addition to Regulation 44/2001, the European Union has made use of this newly acquired legislative competence in many ways. The most recent enactment entering into force is a regulation creating the first uniform European Enforcement Order for uncontested claims.[32] For this type of claim, the regulation obviates the need for any domestic intermediate enforcement proceedings. Judgments, court settlements, and authentic instruments to which the regulation applies are enforceable throughout all member states on the basis of the original enforcement order issued in the member state in which the dispute was originally pending. Although currently the European Enforcement Order is limited to uncontested claims, the plan is to expand the concept to all types of decisions in civil and commercial matters, thus dispensing with the time-consuming enforcement procedures in the forum where the judgment debtor's assets are located.

Other examples illustrating the Europeanization of procedural rules applicable to cross-border disputes include a regulation concerning the service of judicial and extrajudicial documents in civil or commercial matters,[33] a regulation on cooperation between the courts of the member states in the taking of evidence in civil or commercial matters,[34] and a regulation on insolvency proceedings.[35] Additional legislative initiatives, also grounded on Articles 61 and 65 EC Treaty, are in the preparatory stage. For example, there is a proposal for a regulation creating a European order for a rapid payment procedure,[36] which may ultimately apply not only to cross-border disputes but even to purely internal cases as well. In addition, a regulation establishing a European small claims procedure has been proposed.[37] Disputes involving claims of up to €2,000.00 would be subject to a fast-track, uniform European procedure. A proposal for a directive on certain aspects of mediation in civil and commercial matters is also in the pipeline.[38]

More harmonization projects related to both cross-border and domestic disputes are certain to arise. The pressure on domestic systems to stay competitive by individually adapting to modern developments in neighbouring states will not relent, either. Whether, and to what extent, comparative scholarship will play a proactive rather than reactive and descriptive role in this process is another question. So far, the Europeanization of procedural law has occurred primarily in response to practical needs associated with market integration objectives. Comparative scholarship devoted to the phenomena of approximation or harmonization of procedural concepts is still not very highly developed although it is very much needed if legislative and judicial activism without adequate reflection is to be avoided. Scholarly input would be invaluable in many respects: it could test the

---

[32] Regulation (EC) No. 805/2004 of the European Parliament and of the Council of 21 April 2004; OJ L143/15.

[33] Council Regulation (EC) No. 1348/2000 of 29 May 2000; OJ L160/37.

[34] Council Regulation (EC) No. 1206/2001 of 28 May 2001; OJ L174/1.

[35] Council Regulation (EC) No. 1346/2000 of 29 May 2000; OJ L160/1.

[36] COM (2006) 57.   [37] COM (2005) 87 final.   [38] COM (2004) 718.

need for harmonization, evaluate its feasibility, and determine the reach and limits of concrete projects. For that purpose, it could help to identify particular political, economic, or historical conditions that have shaped existing domestic procedural rules. And if the choice is indeed harmonization, rather than continued diversity, implementation studies could and should assess the actual functioning of a body of law that was meant to apply uniformly in systems with different institutional cultures and legal personnel.

For any of these tasks to be performed, however, scholarship would first have to gain access to, and have an impact on, the decision-making process. In recent years, that input was rarely noticeable in the harmonization measures that emanated from the institutions of the European Union. Instead, EU civil servants and bureaucrats representing the member states controlled much of the process. Things 'got done' but not necessarily with a view towards the more fundamental questions inherent in harmonization projects of this magnitude.

2. Supra-regional Harmonization of Procedural Law

Diverging rules pertaining to international jurisdiction, service of process, and obtaining evidence located abroad, as well as differing attitudes towards the recognition and enforcement of foreign judgments, have worldwide implications. These differences increase the costs and risks for litigants and sometimes may even cause tensions between sovereign states. The following sub-sections provide an overview of the strategies formulated to avoid these problems. After an introduction to the most ambitious project in this respect, the failed attempt to draft a worldwide convention on jurisdiction and judgment recognition, the focus will shift to private law-making efforts aimed at mitigating the frictions in international disputes through model rules and arbitration.

(a) The Hague Judgment Project

In many cases of transnational litigation in which the resultant judgment must be enforced abroad, international treaties provide fast and effective relief for the judgment creditor. American judgments, however, do not fare so well in foreign courts. Although the United States signed and ratified the 1958 New York Convention on international arbitral awards which greatly facilitates their enforcement in more than 130 states,[39] the United States is not a member of any bilateral or multilateral treaty on the mutual recognition and enforcement of judgments. Absent any treaty benefits, judgments handed down by American courts often

---

[39] UN Convention on the Recognition and Enforcement of Foreign Arbitral Awards, 10 June 1958, 21 UST 2517, 330 UNTS.

encounter difficulties abroad. Chief among the reasons for the reluctance of courts worldwide to enforce American judgments are higher damage awards, the types of damages (eg punitive or treble), and procedural rules governing American litigation. In contrast, American courts overall have been relatively generous in the enforcement of foreign decisions. In light of this real or perceived imbalance, the US delegation to the Hague Conference proposed in 1992 that the Conference attempt to prepare a convention on jurisdiction and the recognition and enforcement of foreign judgments in civil and commercial matters. Similar to the Brussels Convention, this instrument was intended to regulate the circumstances in which the exercise of international jurisdiction by a court would be appropriate (white list) and the circumstances in which it would not (black list).

It soon became apparent that even though the European model had successfully bridged the gap between Continental and English procedural law, it could not easily be transposed into a worldwide convention. The disagreements centred on certain American rules, such as the exercise of general jurisdiction based on unrelated activities of the defendant in the forum or on the defendant's transitory presence there.[40] In order to accommodate these and other differences, the American delegation proposed a so-called *convention mixte* which divided rules of jurisdiction into three categories. In addition to the white and black lists of jurisdictional bases which mandated and excluded recognition of the resultant judgment, the American proposal introduced a 'grey' zone. This category would be open-ended, permitting member states to assume jurisdiction on grounds not listed in the new Convention as either permitted or prohibited.[41] A judgment on such a grey-zone jurisdictional ground would neither be entitled to nor excluded from recognition in the enforcing forum. The jurisdictional bases in the grey zone would be handled as if there were a treaty: The question of enforceability would depend exclusively on the law of the forum where enforcement is sought. This category reflected, ultimately, the inability to reach agreement on which jurisdictional bases should be permitted and should thus enter the white list.[42] Despite, or perhaps because of, the proposed compromise of a grey zone, and the disagreement over how to compartmentalize various jurisdictional rules, including those pertaining to electronic commerce, the project was never completed as envisaged. Many representatives, particularly the Europeans, insisted on a draft that traced rather closely the successful Brussels Convention model which, from the American perspective, did not exhibit enough flexibility and tolerance for American jurisdictional idiosyncrasies.

---

[40] *Frummer v Hilton Hotels Int'l, Inc* (NY 1967) 227 NE 2d 851; *Burnham v Superior Court of California* (1990) 495 US 604.

[41] Arthur T. von Mehren, 'Recognition and Enforcement of Foreign Judgments: A New Approach for the Hague Conference?', (1994) 57 *Law & Contemporary Problems* 271, 283.

[42] Joachim Zekoll, 'The Role and Status of American Law in the Hague Judgments Convention Project', (1998) 61 *Albany LR* 1283, 1291.

With the failure of the initial plan to create a comprehensive jurisdiction and recognition agreement, the parties shifted their focus. In 2005, they eventually settled on a very narrow facet of the original project: the treatment of choice of court agreements in business transactions.[43] While this rather modest work product cannot be considered a success in light of the original ambitions, the intense dispute and discourse accompanying the original project yielded other benefits. Even though the disagreements proved insurmountable, they triggered a great deal of attention as is evident from the numerous publications on the subject.[44] This extensive exchange in itself constitutes a comparative exercise and sensitizes the participants on all sides of the controversy to the need to identify common ground and recognize its limits.

(b) The American Law Institute's Judgment Recognition Initiative

Several subsequent private law-making projects indicate that this process is, indeed, under way. Assuming that the Hague Judgment Convention would be concluded as planned, the American Law Institute (ALI) commissioned a draft text of a federal statute that would have been submitted as a proposal for legislation transposing the Convention into domestic law. The work on this statute continued even after it became clear that the project at the Hague would fail. The proposed final draft is entitled 'Recognition and Enforcement of Foreign Judgments: Analysis and Proposed Federal Statute'. It embraces some solutions that respond positively to foreign concerns. The underlying principle of the draft legislation—to create a uniform body of federal law replacing the variety of currently governing state practices—is squarely in line with the outcome for which the non-American negotiators at The Hague had bargained. The draft establishes original, albeit concurrent (with state courts), jurisdiction for federal courts in foreign judgment recognition cases and the right of the defendant to remove such cases from state to federal court (§ 8). The preference for a uniform national approach in this area of the law is apparent in other provisions as well. Even the controversial reciprocity requirement (§ 7), which precludes recognition of foreign judgments in American courts if the foreign court will not recognize a comparable American judgment, is premised on a uniform standard designed to prevent forum shopping and uncertainty.

Furthermore, the draft statute precludes, in principle, the recognition of a judgment if personal jurisdiction was based on service of process on a defendant who was only transitorily present in the forum (§ 6 a iv). This stance against 'tag

[43] Convention on Choice of Court Agreements of 30 June 2005, <http://www.hcch.net/index_en.php?act=conventions.text&cid=98>

[44] The Conflict of Laws Section of the American Association of Law Schools even sponsored a Symposium on the topic under the heading: 'Could a Treaty Trump Supreme Court Jurisdictional Doctrine?' The papers were published in (1998) 61 Albany LR 1159 ff.

jurisdiction', though aimed at foreign judgments and subject to an exception in cases of human rights violations in which no other adequate forum is available, reflects an international standard that is contrary to long-established American practice.[45]

In arriving at these and other rules, the authors of the draft statute drew substantially on international scholarship and jurisprudence.[46] In several instances, they adopted foreign positions and thus engaged, at least to some extent, in the kind of 'borrowing' that marks the conclusion of a successful comparative exercise. To be sure, the reporters in charge of drafting the statute still represent only a small, cosmopolitan elite of American legal thinkers. There are many sceptics among ALI members, whether professors or practitioners, and there is opposition within interest groups who adhere to a traditional, more insular outlook. Indeed, there is a good chance that the statute will never be enacted or that conservative courts will interpret the occasionally broad language to support old approaches. That, however, is not the point. History has shown that practitioners, judges, and lawyers alike can mount considerable opposition to change.[47] In fact, anecdotal evidence suggests that the recently reformed rules of English procedure have resulted in less change than expected, largely due to the resistance of practitioners to employ them as intended. But changes do occur if they make (eg commercial) sense and if those who advocate them gain enough momentum.[48] While it is an open question whether that will actually be the case for the ALI Foreign Judgment Statute, this project is evidence that American scholarship increasingly exhibits an interest in foreign or transnational law alternatives. There are also institutional and organizational settings that reflect a new, non-isolationist mindset. For example, the group of reporters and advisors working on the most recent ALI cross-border procedural project includes representatives from several countries.[49] A decade ago this type of drafting exercise would have been essentially an exclusively American enterprise.

(c) The Joint ALI/UNIDROIT Project

Even more remarkable is the first joint project of the ALI and UNIDROIT which resulted in 'The Principles of Transnational Civil Procedure'.[50] For the ALI, which traditionally concerns itself with the approximation of domestic legal rules in the various states, this undertaking marked its first attempt to harmonize a body of law on an international scale. Notably, the law at issue, civil procedure, has been universally considered the most difficult candidate for worldwide harmonization.

---

[45] See *Burnham v Superior Court of California* (1990) 495 US 604.

[46] As is evident from the extensive Reporters' notes accompanying every draft rule.

[47] Lawrence M. Friedman, *A History of American Law* (2nd edn, 1985), 393 ff.

[48] See Friedman (n 47), 396.

[49] *Intellectual Property: Principles Governing Jurisdiction, Choice of Law, and Judgments in Transnational Disputes*; available through <https://www.ali.org/>.

[50] Available through <https://www.ali.org/>.

That these difficulties do exist is manifested in two aspects of the final work product. First, the Principles consist of rather broad statements. What began as an attempt to agree on relatively detailed rules, was subsequently reduced to the formulation of broader principles that could win approval by both sides. Second, the Principles were drafted for purely commercial disputes to be decided by judges or arbitrators, not by juries. No legal regime, whether consisting of rules or principles, could gain worldwide approval if it provided for jury trials and American-style discovery. Conversely, rules (or principles) that excluded these two prototypical procedural features of American personal injury cases and other non-commercial litigation would not be acceptable in the United States.

Despite their limited scope and overall lack of specificity, the Principles suggest that the potential for a common core of procedural law is more substantial than expected. The inclusion of a modest version of *forum non conveniens* as a means of declining jurisdiction is a concession by the European side,[51] as is the acceptance of transient jurisdiction as *ultima ratio* in cases in which 'no other forum is reasonably available'.[52] Other Principles are evidence of American flexibility. One vests party agreements to exclusive jurisdiction with preclusive effects, that is, to oust the jurisdiction of any other court.[53] Another is the inclusion of a *lis pendens* concept that, subject to limited exceptions, requires courts 'to decline jurisdiction or suspend the proceeding, when the dispute is previously pending in another court competent to exercise jurisdiction'.[54] These and other jurisdictional principles mirror in part the draft rules of the Hague Jurisdiction and Judgment Convention project and thus provide a late vindication for the efforts to arrive at compromises which had been unsuccessful in their original context.

There are other pronouncements in the Principles, outside the jurisdictional sphere, that rise above generalities and indicate potential for harmonization where there seemed to have been little of it before. The most important area is that of obtaining evidence, a subject that is particularly conflict-laden when transnational litigation is pending in the United States. Here, the Principles seek to strike a balance between the invasive American discovery practice and the more narrowly circumscribed evidence-gathering procedures that prevail elsewhere. On the one hand, courts and litigants are entitled 'to relevant and non-privileged evidence';[55] on the other, the Principles impose the strictures of fact-pleading to the effect that 'the parties must present in reasonable detail the relevant facts . . . and describe

---

[51] Principle 2.5.   [52] Principle 2.2.1.   [53] Principle 2.4.

[54] Principle 2.6, which goes on to provide an escape clause by stating: '. . . unless it appears that the dispute will not be fairly, effectively and expeditiously resolved in that forum'. To agree that the first chosen forum generally pre-empts jurisdiction of courts chosen later by the opponent is easy for Europeans who embrace a rigid *lis pendens* concept for, among other things, purposes of legal certainty; see Art 27 Brussels Regulation. For the American side, this rule is more difficult to accept because other, or at least additional, factors besides the 'race to the forum' should count in the final determination of whether to exercise or decline jurisdiction.

[55] Principle 16.1.

with sufficient specification the available evidence to be offered in support of their allegations'.[56] Although this specificity requirement is subject to an exception when the party is unable to meet it,[57] transnational evidence taking procedures emanating from American courts under this principle would be freed of much of their potential to cause conflict with other systems. The emphasis is on 'would', because it is far from certain whether, where, and to what extent the non-binding Principles will be adopted. The experience that even binding instruments do not necessarily achieve their intended purpose also cautions against too much optimism. In the field of obtaining evidence abroad, for example, the Hague Evidence Convention was thought to provide a body of binding international law aimed at reducing the tensions between the United States and its trading partners.[58] By and large, however, American courts have applied domestic law instead, holding that the Hague Evidence Convention is merely an optional instrument that does not preclude parties who seek access to evidence located abroad from employing the far-reaching Federal Rules of Civil Procedure.[59] The Principles, on the other hand, are a recent work product, built on decades of experience with judicial conflicts between the United States and its trading partners and thus reflect a much deeper understanding about the forces that drive procedural systems than did the Hague Evidence Convention.[60]

In the end, of course, the limited scope of the Principles, as well as the built-in exceptions and omissions, require few sacrifices by either side and do not really generate approximation where basic similarity did not already exist. It may thus be doubtful whether the Principles, as they stand now, actually present an adoptable body of law, prove inspirational for future legislative processes, or simply represent a kind of restatement of the law of civil procedure.[61] It may even be questionable whether they will influence interpretations of existing rules in court or arbitration proceedings as envisaged by their authors. As far as international arbitration is concerned, it actually appears that the rules generated through such proceedings influenced the formulation of some of the Principles, particularly those dealing with evidence-taking procedures.[62] On the other hand, the Principles may have

---

[56] Principle 11.3.

[57] See ibid: 'When a party shows good cause for inability to provide reasonable details of relevant facts or sufficient specification of evidence, the court should give due regard to the possibility that necessary facts and evidence will develop later in the course of the proceeding'.

[58] Hague Convention on the Taking of Evidence Abroad in Civil and Commercial Matters, 23 UST 2555, 847 UNTS 241 (in force for the United States since 7 October 1972).

[59] *Société Nationale Industrielle Aerospatiale v US District Court* (1987) 107 S Ct 2542.

[60] Particularly unattractive from the American perspective proved Art 23 of the Convention, which enables member states to exclude the discovery of documents, a quintessential element of the American discovery process. All but three states exercised this option.

[61] These appear to be the main goals. See Rolf Stürner, 'The Principles of Transnational Civil Procedure', (2005) 69 *RabelsZ* 201, 209 ff.

[62] See below (n 73).

reverberating effects on the further development of arbitration proceedings. It would not be the first time that a reform effort drawn from an existing set of rules influences those rules in turn.[63] Be that as it may, from a comparative perspective, which is less concerned with instant practical utility, this private law-making effort, undertaken by two of the most influential non-governmental organizations in the field of legal harmonization, offers valuable insights. The rigorous intellectual effort, sustained over many years with input from dozens of individuals, to comprehend foreign procedural settings in their various contexts and to ascertain the extent of rule compatibility, reveals the maximum degree of harmonization that civil procedure can undergo at this point in time.

The reporters in charge of the ALI /UNIDROIT project worked hard to ensure its high visibility. They commissioned the translation of the text of the Principles into ten languages. Abundant resources allowed them to go on a veritable road tour with stops in several continents to solicit more input and to showcase the project as a means of broadening the base of support. This tremendous marketing effort may indeed turn out to be a real asset for future transatlantic and transpacific cooperation in this area, which might eventually manifest itself in the formulation of more concrete rules.

(d) Procedural Harmonization through International Arbitration

A great majority of international commercial disputes are resolved through arbitration. One of its attractions is the neutrality of the forum that most, though certainly not all, parties associate with this type of dispute settlement. Among other things, neutrality refers to a procedural framework that does not represent the procedural 'home turf' of either party. Neutrality in this sense is unavailable in domestic courts for they will always apply the procedural law of the forum. Arbitration proceedings, by contrast, allow for the use of customized rules or the choice of institutional arbitration rules that offer the desired procedural equilibrium and may be tailored to the specific needs and expectations of the parties. The emergence of these 'private' norms is directly related to the high degree of party autonomy that prevails in this area. The freedom of parties (or arbitrators) to shape the procedures is, in turn, often state-sanctioned. That arbitration procedure is primarily a matter for party stipulation is already implicit in the rules of the widely adopted 1958 New York Convention.[64] The UNCITRAL Model Law on International Commercial Arbitration[65] affirms this freedom and provides that the parties are in

---

[63] Friedman (n 47), 397 (with reference to Field's procedural code and the English Judicature Act of 1873).

[64] Art V(1)(d) permits the refusal of the foreign award if '. . . the arbitral procedure was not in accordance with the agreement of the parties . . .', see above (n 39).

[65] UNCITRAL Model Law on International Commercial Arbitration of 1985, <http://www.uncitral.org/uncitral/en/uncitral_texts/arbitration/1985Model_arbitration.html>.

principle 'free to agree on the procedure to be followed by the arbitral tribunal in conducting the proceedings'.[66] Further, in the absence of such an agreement, the tribunal may conduct the arbitration in such a manner as it considers appropriate, and that power includes the determination of admissibility, relevance, materiality, and weight of any evidence.[67]

More than other legislative acts that reform domestic law by borrowing from foreign legal regimes, the widespread adoption of the Model Law was driven by obvious competitive strategies.[68] The German government, for example, advocated its adoption by expressing in no uncertain terms the desire to bring German procedural law in line with modern international standards thus making Germany a more attractive venue for the rendering of valuable arbitration services.[69] As of 2005, the UNCITRAL Model Law has been adopted by more than forty countries. While this regime has been a principal force behind the approximation of arbitral proceedings, additional catalysts had a role in this development. Among them are the UNCITRAL Arbitration Rules of 1976 and institutional arbitration regimes, such as the Rules on Arbitration of the International Chamber of Commerce (ICC) in Paris and Conciliation as well as the Rules of the London Court of International Arbitration. Particularly instrumental in the growing standardization of evidence taking in international commercial arbitration are the IBA Rules,[70] which strike a successful balance among the various legal traditions in this area. Thus, contrary to the view prevailing in some civil law jurisdictions, these rules start from the premise that discovery is an important tool. For example, a party is, in principle, under the obligation to produce documents requested by the other party.[71] Yet, the IBA rules preclude US-style fishing expeditions by imposing rather rigid specificity and relevancy requirements on the requesting party. These include a description of the document, or a description in sufficient detail (including subject-matter) of a narrow and specifically requested category, as well as a description of how the documents requested are relevant to the outcome of the case.[72] Furthermore, the tribunal exerts much more control over the discovery process than do American courts.[73] In light of these and other dispute resolution features dominating international arbitration, the once popular assumption that

---

[66] See ibid, Art 19(1).   [67] Ibid, Art 19(2).

[68] See Christopher R. Drahozal, 'Regulatory Competition and the Locations of International Arbitration Proceedings', (2004) 24 *International Review of Law and Economics* 371 ff.

[69] BT-Drucks 13/5274 of 12 July 1996 *Gesetzentwurf der Bundesregierung Entwurf eines Gesetzes zur Neuregelung des Schiedsverfahrensrechts (Schiedsverfahrens-Neuregelungsgesetz—SchiedsVfG).*

[70] IBA Rules on the Taking of Evidence in International Commercial Arbitration adopted 1 June 1999, <http://www.asser.nl/ica/documents/cms_ica_4_1_IBA_ROE2.pdf>

[71] See ibid, Art 3(4).   [72] Ibid, Art 3(3).

[73] For more details, see Gabrielle Kaufmann-Kohler, 'Globalization of Arbitral Procedure', (2003) 36 *Vanderbilt Journal of Transnational Law* 1313, 1327–8.

international commercial arbitration proceedings are largely Americanized[74] has turned out to be unfounded. In fact, this quasi-system-neutral model of carefully calibrated and controlled access to evidence proved inspirational to the drafters of the Principles of Transnational Civil Procedure,[75] who sought to find a compromise between the American practice and its foreign counterparts.

The main actors in arbitration proceedings, that is, counsel and the tribunal, often adopt the IBA rules or other institutional guidelines in whole or, in some instances, draw on them selectively. As stated above, such reliance introduces neutrality, minimizing the frictions among representatives of different legal traditions. While this generality is historically correct, one might add that these rules probably do meet the expectations of the (Western) professionals involved in this process. After all, the rules were largely drafted by international practitioners for international practitioners who operate in venues like London, Geneva, Stockholm, and New York. Some of these individuals are becoming cosmopolitan representatives of their profession. Although the legal culture in which they were educated is likely to generate some distinct expectations and legal styles, an increasing number of individuals in this group are less committed to a particular domestic legal background than were their predecessors of a few decades ago. Multilingual and often holding degrees from several legal systems,[76] the leading members of this group have become transcultural agents for an emerging transnational legal regime.

This development has lead to pressing, and not yet fully resolved, questions centred on the status and legitimacy of the rules that this new '*homo arbitrator*' generates and applies in arbitral disputes. For example, do these rules represent a *lex mercatoria* that has attained the status of an independent source of law, a 'global law without a state'?[77] To what extent is this private norm production a reflection of an overall shift away from top-down regulation towards self-regulation and privatization; a shift that is noticeable in many areas of state governance structures?[78] What is the role of the international arbitration regime in disputes involving parties from developing nations on one side and opponents from the Western world on the other?[79] While each of these questions lends itself to comparative inquiry by examining, for example, the relationship between globalization and comparative law, any elaboration in this direction would exceed the scope of this chapter. However, there are some readily available answers to the more mundane

---

[74] See eg Nicolas C. Ulmer, 'A Comment on "The 'Americanization' of International Arbitration?" ', (2001) 16 *Mealey's Int'l Arb Rep* 24.

[75] See Stürner (n 61), at 213 n 54.

[76] On the background of arbitrators, see Yves Dezalay and Bryant G. Garth, *Dealing in Virtue: International Commercial Arbitration and the Construction of a Transnational Legal Order* (1996), 18 ff.

[77] For some tentative responses with respect to several fields of substantive law see the contribution in Gunther Teubner (ed), *Global Law without a State* (1997).

[78] For an overview, see Orly Lobel, 'The Renewal Deal: The Fall of Regulation and the Rise of Governance in Contemporary Legal Thought', (2004) 89 *Minnesota LR* 342.

[79] See Dezalay and Garth (n 76), 93–5.

inquiry that forms the heading of this sub-section. It is fair to say that, overall,[80] international arbitral procedure is subject to increasing standardization, that state-sanctioned party autonomy is at the heart of this development, and that the resulting rules, though handled with some flexibility, are considered binding by those who adopt and operate under them.

It could hardly be claimed by extension, however, that state procedural systems show significant signs of corresponding developments. To the extent that the phrase 'state procedural systems' refers to domestic arbitration proceedings, harmonization trends are conceivable, but not likely. Some countries, such as Paraguay, have adopted the UNCITRAL Model Law for both international and domestic arbitration thus opening the door for the introduction of international standards into the domestic realm.[81] But then, the actors in strictly domestic arbitration are, for the most part, representatives of the same legal system. They come to a dispute with similar, domestically coined preconceptions and tend to import familiar domestic litigation patterns into the arbitration process. If there is a general trend among different state procedural systems, it is one towards 'privatizing' justice by having disputes settled outside overburdened court systems so as to avoid a further drain on already scarce state resources. In addition to arbitration, other, non-binding alternative dispute resolution (ADR) mechanisms, such as mediation and conciliation, are gaining in importance world-wide. However relevant this world-wide trend towards self-governance of this variety may be, it does not speak at all to the content of such alternative dispute resolution proceedings. They are driven by the specific needs that prevail in distinct 'dispute cultures'. These may vary widely, particularly with respect to the expectations and strategies brought to the consensus-building process even within identical structures of the negotiation process. However, as the recently approved UNCITRAL Model Law on International Conciliation suggests, alternative dispute resolution techniques in the commercial arena may be subject to greater approximation.[82]

3. Some Principles Regarding the Scope of and Limits to Procedural Harmonization

General state procedural regimes concerned with domestic litigation are not likely to be influenced by rules that emerge from transnational dispute resolution. To be sure, a common core of procedural values has evolved in most procedural systems,

---

[80] There are exceptions. For example, the question is unsettled whether substantive law must be treated like facts to be proven by one or the other party or whether it is for the tribunal to ascertain the content of the applicable norms.

[81] Jan Kleinheisterkamp, *International Commercial Arbitration in Latin America* (2005), 10.

[82] <http://www.uncitral.org/pdf/english/texts/arbitration/ml-conc/ml-conc-e.pdf>.

irrespective of the developments occurring in the world of international dispute resolution. As with arbitration, this common core revolves around personal liberties manifested in procedural party autonomy. Entering into a binding forum selection clause is one example. The principle of party disposition, mentioned above, provides another important illustration: in every mature procedural regime, the parties are entitled to determine the beginning, scope, and even the end of the proceedings if they determine to settle or abandon them. But compared to the institutions of arbitration which cater to corporate interests in the global marketplace, state procedural systems are subject to additional political, constitutional, and ideological restraints. Consider the example of contractual forum selection: many state law systems contain restrictive rules that protect systemically weaker parties, such as consumers or workers, from having to litigate away from home. The underlying policy concerns can be so strong that the rules which embody them may be non-negotiable.[83] If these policy concerns also manifest themselves in substantive law, as they do in legislation to protect consumer interests, the procedural rules serving these interests will be resistant to change until and unless the underlying substantive norm is subject to change as well.

Thus, while state systems are competing individually through rule adaptations that may occur from above or from below, as well as collectively through harmonization projects for the sake of greater regional prosperity, these processes do not necessarily entail the erosion or approximation of the central procedural features of a given system. Furthermore, some procedural rules and institutions are, in and of themselves, considered central principles of a judicial system. On a continuum that reflects vulnerability to change, these rules or institutions sit at one end and might be called core elements of a procedural system (though matters are rarely static and this status may be downgraded over time). Whether by historical accident or conscious design, many of these rules are entrenched in their respective systems, sometimes even constitutionally mandated, and common sense suggests that these core elements will not be sacrificed lightly. At the other end of the spectrum are norms that embody either insignificant or universally acknowledged values, such as certain procedural time limits, that aim at the speedy disposition of a dispute. These rules can be easy targets of harmonization, particularly when market integration strategies so demand.[84]

This still leaves us with the question as to when and why a particular rule can be considered a core element of a procedural system. In looking for an answer, the usual approach today is to examine political traditions, philosophical underpinnings, and cultural roots. Such research is almost always enlightening in some

---

[83] Indeed, in the European Union they became a uniform benchmark applicable to all disputes to which the Brussels Convention or the Brussels Regulation applies.

[84] Konstantinos D. Kerameus, 'Angleichung des Zivilprozeßrechts in Europa', (2002) 66 *RabelsZ* 1, 4–9

respect, but not always entirely successful in identifying the conditions necessary for the evolution of procedural rules and their dynamics. To illustrate this point, let us consider the two core elements of American civil procedure—jury participation and discovery—which have been subject to thorough examination. As we will see immediately below, the political and cultural roots of jury trials are readily identifiable and are undeniably strong, while matters are not so simple with respect to the American variant of discovery.

The institution of lay juries is said to reflect fundamental American cultural and political values, such as egalitarianism and populism.[85] This observation is an old one and shared by many, even non-American, observers. As long ago as 1835, the travelling Frenchman Alexis de Tocqueville saw the jury as a key ingredient of American democracy when he stated that '. . . the jury, which is the most energetic means of making the people reign, is also the most efficacious means of teaching them to reign'.[86] Even if one did not agree with him on this particular point, a quick (and legalistic) reference to the Federal Constitution (sixth and seventh Amendments), and to its counterparts in the various states, demonstrates that trials by jury represent a fundamental value that is here to stay. Of course, the fact that the institution is constitutionally anchored does not necessarily reflect its present status in American contemporary political, cultural, and legal thought. Dozens of books and law review articles published even within a single decade reveal a great deal of controversy over, and pride in, this institution that sets America so far apart from every other legal system in the Western world.

American pre-trial discovery may also be an expression of cultural preferences. Perhaps it reflects a profound American interest in transparency although that virtue is embraced elsewhere as well, without American-style discovery. Perhaps the procedure is rooted in what has been termed 'competitive individualism',[87] although it is not quite clear what that is and why the obligation to disclose evidence would foster individualism. Also, individualism, while widespread, is not necessarily ubiquitous in the American justice system. American judges who certify class actions essentially endow a few with the representation of the many, thus effectively pre-empting the individual pursuit of claims unless opt-out rights are exercised. Nevertheless, even if 'culture' as an explanation is found to be somewhat persuasive, one might add—or content oneself with—the observation expressed earlier,[88] which is that jury trials very much lend themselves to pre-trial discovery of evidence. Recall that jury participation entails the single event concept and that, in turn, calls for comprehensive, pre-trial prove-taking proceedings so as to avoid irremediable surprises for either party at trial.

On the other hand, this finding still does not explain the amazing breadth of

[85] Oscar Chase, 'American "Exceptionalism" and Comparative Procedure', (2002) 50 *AJCL* 277, 289.
[86] Alexis de Tocqueville, *Democracy in America* (orig 1835) (2000), 264.
[87] De Tocqueville (n 86), 295.   [88] Section II.3.

discovery, its intrusiveness, and the relative absence of judicial oversight in this process. What then are the forces at work here? An honest response would admit that we don't really know. Of course, it is as accurate to describe America as 'a society profoundly rooted in law'[89] as it is to conclude that that law is premised on 'Adversarial Legalism'.[90] Also, the legal *Weltbild* of law as a means of change through individual action does have peculiar connotations including the aggressive and far-reaching search for evidence that is dominated by lawyers rather than judges. But what caused this procedural device to become so different from its foreign, including other common law, counterparts? It is often claimed that the reasons lie in 'broader American traditions . . . and interest group pressures'.[91] But these traditions are probably not that old, and interest group pressures aim in more than one direction. American discovery as we know it is a creature of the twentieth century and there is no evidence that this system, with all its idiosyncrasies, was the inevitable consequence of something inherent in older structures or beliefs. As far as the impact of interest groups is concerned, one only has to recall that these include businesses and business lawyers and that in these circles American-style discovery appears to be dispensable, at least for purposes of international arbitration. Further, the relative weight of these factors (as well as others including feeble governmental structures and mistrust towards governmental action) that are frequently cited to describe the dynamics at work in the American judicial system and to explain the forces that resist change is unclear. In short, political traditions and legal culture do not satisfactorily explain why this particular procedural device developed the way it did. Perhaps, this finding confirms a more general observation that, 'it is dubious whether systems of procedure fit particular cultures so snugly . . .'.[92]

In any event, while it is not entirely clear why discovery seems immune to reform through adaptation, borrowing, or harmonization, it is certain that change, if any, will come slowly. Over the past thirty years, discovery rules have been revised at both the federal and state levels, but these revisions were quite limited and seldom inspired by comparative thought. This is all the more surprising because the goal of finding the truth in the course of judicial proceedings is a universal one. Surely, there are conflicting interests at work, raising questions that may lead to different responses in different legal systems. How invasive may this process be? To what extent do we entitle litigants and/or courts to obtain information held by the opponent, or by non-parties? What weight do we attribute to concerns regarding unrestricted access to facts controlled by others such as privacy interests, professional privileges, and commercial and trade secrets? Considering, furthermore, that greater access to evidence entails a greater investment of time, where is the breaking point between finding the truth and wasting resources? And finally, who

---

[89] See Lipset (n 14), 270.
[90] Robert A. Kagan, *Adversarial Legalism: The American Way of Law* (2001).
[91] Kagan (n 90), 15.   [92] Friedman (n 47), 396.

should pay for what is being spent in the course of this process? Because every judicial system must ponder and decide these questions, it would seem only natural to take cognizance of responses developed elsewhere and to examine them with a view towards improving justice at home.

Although this type of comparative thought is not widespread in American legal literature, it is not altogether absent. The most prominent example is contained in John Langbein's 1985 law review article entitled 'The German Advantage in Civil Procedure'.[93] If the title of the article was provocative, its content proved explosive, sending shockwaves through American legal academia and beyond. In essence, the author argued that discovery wastes public and private resources, does not generate truthful fact-finding, and entails lopsided access to justice, limited to those who can afford lawyers. By contrast, the more judge-centred procedure in Germany would help avoid most of these shortcomings. While not all of the immediate reactions were entirely negative,[94] most were critical,[95] perhaps not so much because of the criticism of the American system but because the suggested remedy, to take lessons from a foreign model, did not sit well with a majority of American scholars at that time. While the debate probably did not change the mindset of the participants,[96] many of the immediately published responses to this article have proved quite inspirational for subsequent reflection on American civil procedure, comparative inquiry, and procedural transplants.[97]

IV. ACCESS TO JUSTICE

An important practical reason for comparing procedural regimes is the search for the best tools to improve civil justice at home. For example, every judicial process is geared towards seeking the truth in a given conflict and yet, as we just saw, the

[93] John H. Langbein, (1985) 52 *University of Chicago LR* 823 ff.

[94] Herbert L. Bernstein, 'Whose Advantage After All?: A Comment on the Comparison of Civil Justice Systems', (1988) 21 *University of California at Davis LR* 587 ff.

[95] Samuel R. Gross, 'The American Advantage: The Value of Inefficient Litigation', (1987) 85 *Michigan LR* 734 ff.

[96] Those include Ronald J. Allen, Stefan Köck, Kurt Riechenberg, and D. Toby Rosen, 'The German Advantage in Civil Procedure: A Plea for More Details and Fewer Generalities in Comparative Scholarship', (1988) 82 *Northwestern University LR* 763; John Reitz, 'Why We Probably Cannot Adopt the German Advantage in Civil Procedure', (1990) 75 *Iowa LR* 987; and Ernst Stiefel and James Maxeiner, 'Civil Justice Reform in the United States—Opportunity for Learning from "Civilized" European Procedure instead of Continental Isolation', (1994) 42 *AJCL* 147 ff.

[97] See eg Amalia D. Kessler, 'Our Inquisitorial Tradition: Equity Procedure, Due Process, and the Search for an Alternative to the Adversarial', (2005) 90 *Cornell LR* 1181 ff.

approaches to meeting that goal may differ significantly. There is agreement, too, that the effort to attain truth must be embedded in a rational process that provides access for those with meritorious claims (and defences), avoids delay, utilizes resources proportionately, and protects other legitimate interests of the parties and of society as a whole. There is a growing sense, however, that a number of procedural regimes do not meet these goals. Some even perceive the current state of affairs as 'Civil Justice in Crisis'.[98] That this is not just a catchy title aimed at promoting a book is illustrated in Italy where the proverbial admonishment 'justice delayed is justice denied' has long been a sad reality. The final disposition of civil cases often takes ten years or more.[99]

1. Financing Litigation

Even if one considers legal reform, it is often difficult to achieve the above goals simultaneously because they require choices among competing concerns. Take the example of contingency fee arrangements under which American attorneys are entitled to remuneration only if they obtain a favourable decision for their client. Coupled with the rule that each party pays its own costs regardless of the outcome of the litigation, these '*quota litis*' contracts enable indigent plaintiffs to pursue their claims. In addition to lowering access barriers for many prospective plaintiffs, this system encourages early settlements, which, in principle, is desirable, too.[100] Among other things, it reduces the delay associated with lengthy proceedings and enforcement efforts, and helps minimize the impact on already clogged court dockets. On the other hand, this allocation of litigation costs has serious undesirable side-effects. Litigation without financial risks to plaintiffs encourages the pursuit of unwarranted and frivolous claims, provided, of course, that an attorney is willing to assume the risk; in that case, defendants may be forced into early settlements that do not necessarily reflect the merits of the case. Defendants with valid defences but no prospect of recouping their costs tend to refrain from going to trial because a victorious outcome is often more expensive than settling the case.

Furthermore, the above-described dynamics tend to benefit only plaintiffs whose stakes in a given dispute are high enough to attract an attorney. By contrast, the absence of cost-shifting in American litigation operates as a prohibitive barrier

---

[98] Adrian A. Zuckerman (ed), *Civil Justice in Crisis—Comparative Perspectives of Civil Procedure* (1999).

[99] See Zuckerman (n 98), 23.

[100] See eg Federal Rules of Civil Procedure Rule 16(a)(5), which declares settlement to be one of the objectives of pre-trial conferences.

in cases with small sums in controversy, regardless of the likelihood of success.[101] Prospective litigants have difficulty finding a lawyer willing to enter into a risk-shifting contingency fee contract if his prospective fee is at or below the value of the time he is likely to invest in the case. The alternative, to pay the lawyer an hourly rate not linked to the outcome of the litigation, likewise operates as a bar to those with small claims. Here, too, the cost-benefit relationship between a small amount to be gained through litigation and significant, non-recoverable legal fees prevents many potential plaintiffs from seeking redress through the court system.

Pursuing the same goal of providing reasonable access to courts, a goal that is often constitutionally mandated, a majority of legal systems favour a less entrepreneurial method of financing litigation by allocating costs differently. These systems often prohibit contingency fee arrangements and require the loser to pay all expenses, including those incurred by the prevailing party. In contrast to the American rule, this solution tends to deter prospective plaintiffs, particularly those with limited means and claims whose merits are uncertain. Over-deterrence in some, but not all, of these systems is avoided by the availability of legal expense insurance policies and publicly financed legal aid. Of course, such financial assistance may create the mirror image problem, that is, it may promote litigiousness. But where institutional and financial assistance is poorly developed, as in Italy, for example, litigation is often not an option at all. It is noteworthy that, while the population in Italy doubled from 1894 until 1994, the number of claims fell by roughly one half.[102]

2. Mass Claims

Conflicting interests and dynamics present themselves in other areas of procedure as well. The occurrence of multiple related claims constitutes a challenge to every judicial system. The need to address the problems associated with mass claims has led to comparative inquiries with a view towards the adoption of foreign procedural law. The feasibility of legal 'transplants' has been a focus of comparative research for some time, and this section illustrates that 'borrowing' foreign procedural law is possible, that it actually occurs, but that it occurs with modifications so as to avoid compatibility problems with pre-existing domestic procedural structures and preferences.

---

[101] One study showed that about one-fifth of all claimants seeking legal representation were turned away by attorneys. Cost considerations and small sums in controversy were among the reasons for refusing to represent the claimants. See Deborah R. Hensler, M. Susan Marquis, Allan F. Abrahamse, Sandra H. Berry, Patricia A. Ebener, Elizabeth G. Lewis, E. Allan Lind, Robert J. MacCoun, Willard G. Manning, Jeannette A. Rogowski, and Mary E. Vaiana, *Compensation for Accidental Injuries in the United States, Rand The Institute for Civil Justice* (1991), 133.

[102] Sergio Chiarloni, 'Civil Justice: An Italian Perspective', in Zuckerman (n 98), 267.

Mass claims can arise in several settings. For example, a single incident, such as a catastrophic accident that injures many individuals, or fraudulent corporate conduct such as large-scale misrepresentations on capital markets, causes losses to numerous investors. Every justice system is under pressure to process mass claims and complex litigation efficiently, that is, in a way that guarantees the continued functioning of the justice system. On the other hand, the procedural rights and freedoms of all participants must be guarded. Those rights and freedoms, in turn, reside in two basic, but potentially conflicting, principles: The first is party disposition, that is, the freedom to largely control how, and to some extent when and where, a claim will be asserted for judicial resolution. The second principle is to provide reasonable access to justice which, as we have seen, is often largely unavailable to individuals with small claims. Aggregating claims can be one way of providing affordable access to the legal system. But access to justice does not only impact the individual dimension of this right; the ability to bring mass claims also promotes state interests in regulating conduct through the threat of effective law enforcement.

This mixture of interests and objectives regarding the degree and method of claim aggregation has generated different policy choices in different systems. All procedural regimes originally focused on the resolution of disputes between two individual parties, with the exceptional inclusion or joinder of third parties under certain circumstances. That model remains, of course, at the heart of every procedural system, because most disputes are bilateral.

With the advent of the consumer protection movement and the nowadays widespread perception that mass injuries are the result of some corporate or governmental wrongdoing, the demand arose to accommodate multilateral settings more effectively. Many legislatures have long resisted these pressures, and many still refuse to add procedural instruments to the existing arsenal, while in other systems, group litigation is not unknown, but is often quite restrictive. Several systems limit it, for example, to representative suits aimed at the vindication of group interests in fields such as consumer protection and environmental law.[103] The standing requirements tend to be strict and successful litigants are often limited to obtaining injunctive relief. Based on the understanding that every legal dispute should, in essence, be treated like a bilateral dispute, with res judicata effects only extending to the immediate parties, group litigation mechanisms to pursue monetary claims for individual damages either did not exist at all or were available only in exceptional circumstances. The respective legislatures' failure to change that situation was due not only to inertia, but reflected ideological preferences to preserve the status quo which limited the exposure of corporate defendants.

---

[103] Catherine Kessedjian, 'L'action en Justice des Associations de Consommateurs et d'Autres Organisations Représentatives d'Intérêts Collectifs en Europe', (1997) 33 *Rivista di Diritto Internazionale Privato e Processuale* 281.

The traditionalist view has been changing in a number of jurisdictions over time, however. New methods of procedural aggregation have become available, with the most far-reaching approach embodied in the American class action. This procedural device avoids a multitude of two-party suits by enabling one or more persons (the class representative) to litigate as plaintiffs or as defendants on behalf of themselves and those absent members who share a common interest. Historically, class actions were intended to provide redress for parties with small claims who otherwise could not—or would not want to—afford litigation. Thus, when taxis or gas stations systematically overcharge their customers, for example, American courts will certify a plaintiffs' class. However, contrary to a common preconception, American courts have been reluctant to certify classes in mass tort settings.[104] The reason for this reluctance lies in the legal requirements that the questions of law or fact common to the class members *predominate* over questions affecting only individual members and that the class action be *superior* to alternative methods of adjudicating the controversy.[105] In mass injury cases, such as drug liability disputes, these requirements are difficult to meet.[106] The courts tend to emphasize the interest of the claimants to control the prosecution of their claims individually in this setting.

If a suit is allowed to proceed as a class action, a judicial ruling binds the representatives and absent class members alike, unless the latter exercise their opt-out rights. This presents a striking departure from the traditional model of individual dispute resolution and highlights the increased responsibility assumed by judges in multi-party litigation. Courts that decide to certify a class must act as quasi-fiduciaries for the class whose members have only limited control over the disposition of their claims. Particular scrutiny is necessary when class actions are concluded by settlements, as is the rule. They frequently occur immediately after class certification because both sides have an incentive to avoid full-blown litigation. The defendant faces the risk of a verdict awarding an exorbitant amount of damages. The class representatives—and particularly their lawyers, who often act as entrepreneurs by pooling resources to 'find' cases and move them towards certification—are motivated to settle the case early so as to avoid additional expenses and contingencies and thus secure the return on their investment. That return, in the form of 'reasonable attorney fees'[107] as determined by the court, can be substantial and, in large cases, may amount to millions of dollars. Given these potential

---

[104] Courtland H. Peterson and Joachim Zekoll, 'Mass Torts', (1994) 42 (Supp) *AJCL* 79, 108.

[105] FRCP Rule 23(b)(3). Several state procedural codes are more generous, but the 2005 federal Class Action Fairness Act (CAFA) ensures that class action certification will increasingly be gauged by federal standards. The primary provisions of the Class Action Fairness Act are contained in 28 USC 1332(d).

[106] Predominance is often lacking because questions of causation vary among individual victims and cannot be resolved on a class-wide basis. Furthermore, courts have denied the superiority of the class action device when individual plaintiffs seek high damage awards for personal injuries.

[107] FRCP Rule 23(h).

conflicts of interest, settlements after certification require the approval by the court.[108] Once approved, however, the result confers *res judicata* effects on all class members, including the great majority who are absent. From a broader perspective, then, class actions epitomize the tension that may arise between the objective of efficient case administration and the interests of individual litigants to pursue their claims in the manner they wish.

Outside the United States, legal reform introducing new methods to aggregate claims has been slower and, overall, more cautious. In several systems it is still a work in progress, in others there is no prospect of changing the status quo.[109] Regardless of the content of the reforms that have occurred, the American model has prompted, or at least inspired, the debate over greater group litigation rights everywhere in the world. Resulting reform legislation is a good example of successfully transplanting foreign legal ideas—by processing and customizing them so as not to upset the host system.

A primary concern in these reform efforts is the scope of the *res judicata* effect produced by a court decision in group litigation. One alternative to the American opt-out solution is to adhere to the traditional *res judicata* principle by extending the effects of the judicial decision only to those parties that undertook the affirmative step to become a class member. A recently enacted law in Sweden ('*om Grupprättegang*—LGR') illustrates this opt-in concept by permitting group actions ('*Grupptalan*') while avoiding the sweeping effects of the American opt-out concept of the model. To become a member of the class, the prospective plaintiff must join it within a certain period fixed by the court.[110] As in American law, contingency fee arrangements ('*riskavtal*') are an option in Sweden. Nevertheless, the number of such actions has been significantly lower than in the United States during the first two years since enactment. Several factors will likely prevent future litigation rates from coming close to American levels including the modest remuneration of lawyers in Sweden, the lower damages amounts, and the absence of other American procedural devices, such as juries and discovery.

By contrast, a 1992 reform in Australia appears to have stimulated the initiation of class action suits. This reform applies to suits brought before the Australian federal courts where they are governed by the opt-out concept. Although contingency fee arrangements are more restricted in Australia, there are a number of procedural factors that make class actions even more likely to occur than in the United States. Perhaps most important is the absence of a certification requirement which derails many potential mass torts class actions in the United States. In

---

[108] FRCP Rule 23(e).

[109] An overview of the current status of group proceedings is provided by Mathias Reimann, 'Liability for Defective Products at the Beginning of the 21st Century: Emergence of a Worldwide Standard?', (2003) 51 (Supp) *AJCL* 751, 819–22.

[110] § 14 LGR.

Australian federal courts, the onus is instead on the defendant to convince the court that the proceedings should be deemed inadmissible.[111]

To conclude this survey of jurisdictions that have adopted the class action device with modifications that reflect domestic preferences, Brazil must be mentioned because it adopted yet another rule to regulate the *res judicata* effect of consumer class actions. The pertinent provision, Article 103 of the Brazilian Consumer Code, differentiates among various types of group rights and operates as follows: If the class representatives prevail on the merits, the result will inure to the benefit of all members, absentees included. If the case is lost, the *res judicata* effect bars the relitigation of the case as a class action. However, the adverse decision does not bar absent class members from pursuing their individual damages claims.[112] An even more radical departure from traditional modes of litigation is the rule that a dismissal in certain types of class actions has no *res judicata* effect if it was due to insufficient evidence. Provided the cause of action is not time barred, the same case may thus be relitigated, perhaps years after the initial decision was rendered, if new evidence surfaces subsequent to that decision.[113] The main rationale behind this striking legislative decision to undermine the finality of judgments is to compensate for the lack of effective Brazilian discovery proceedings (as gauged, apparently, by American standards).[114]

To conclude, the foreign adoption of some American class action features, and the exclusion or modification of others, illustrates the viability of partial 'transplants' of legal institutions that meet local needs without compromising local policy objectives. At times, as in the Brazilian example, internal changes (to the effects of *res judicata*) that do not represent a reception of foreign law (discovery) may effectively emulate its effects.

BIBLIOGRAPHY

Benjamin Kaplan, 'Civil Procedure—Reflections on the Comparison of Systems', (1959) 9 *Buff LR* 409

John H. Langbein, 'The German Advantage in Civil Procedure' (1985) 52 *University of Chicago LR* 823

Mirjan R. Damaska, *The Faces of Justice and State Authority: A Comparative Approach to the Legal Process* (1986)

Mauro Cappelletti (ed), Civil Procedure in: *International Encyclopedia of Comparative Law* (vol 16, 1987)

---

[111] S. Stuart Clark and Christina Harris, 'Multi-plaintiff Litigation in Australia: A Comparative Perspective', (2001) 11 *Duke Journal of Comparative & International Law* 289.

[112] For details see Antonio Gidi, 'Class Actions in Brazil—A Model for Civil Law Countries', (2003) 51 *AJCL* 311, 388–99.

[113] See Gidi (n 112), 392.   [114] See Gidi (n 112), 394–95.

Samuel R. Gross, 'The American Advantage: The Value of Inefficient Litigation', (1987) 85 *Michigan LR* 734 ff

Marcel Storme (ed), *Rapprochement du Droit Judiciaire de l'Uion Européenne—Approximation of Judiciary Law in the European Union* (1994)

Yves Dezalay and Bryant G. Garth, *Dealing in Virtue: International Commercial Arbitration and the Construction of a Transnational Legal Order* (1996)

Mirjan R. Damaska, *Evidence Law Adrift* (1997)

Adrian A. Zuckerman (ed), *Civil Justice in Crisis—Comparative Perspectives of Civil Procedure* (1999)

John A. Jolowicz, 'On the Comparison of Procedures', in James A. R. Nafziger and Symeon C. Symeonides (eds), *Law and Justice in a Multistate World, Essays in Honor of Arthur T. von Mehren* (2002), 721 ff.

Konstantinos D. Kerameus, 'Angleichung des Zivilprozeßrechts in Europa', (2002) 66 *RabelsZ* 1

Serge Guinchard *et al.*, *Droit processuel. Droit commun et comparé du procès* (3rd edn, 2005)

CHAPTER 42

··

COMPARATIVE LAW AND PRIVATE INTERNATIONAL LAW

··

MATHIAS REIMANN

*Michigan**

* Thanks to Jacob Dolinger, Diego Fernandez-Arroyo, Alejandro Garro, Barbara Juenger, and especially Symeon Symeonides for the information they provided about comparative conflicts law in various regions of the world. Obviously, the responsibility for the text is entirely mine.

COMPARATIVE law and private international law (conflict of laws)[1] have long had an intimate relationship (Section I). Traditionally, comparative law has interacted with private international law in three basic dimensions which can loosely be termed academic, legislative, and judicial: Comparative law has made private international law the object of scholarly study; it has assisted in the making of private international law rules; and it has provided a method for the application of existing conflicts norms (Section II). Recently, however, the emergence of supra-national legal orders has had a significant impact on the relationship between these disciplines, which are now jointly facing the challenges posed by the coexistence of overlapping legal regimes on multiple levels (Section III). These challenges can only be met through even greater cooperation than in the past (Section IV).

I. An Intimate Relationship

Private international law has a more intimate relationship with comparative law than all the other subject-areas addressed in Part III of this *Handbook*. The main reason is that both disciplines deal with foreign legal systems—comparative law

---

[1] Both terms are often used interchangeably. As has been pointed out repeatedly, both are equally infelicitous. 'Private international law' is misleading for two reasons. First, the respective principles and rules are not 'private law', at least not in the traditional sense of directly regulating private relationships and entitlements; instead, they are secondary law telling decision-makers how to proceed, eg, what law to apply in transboundary cases. Second, such law is not really 'international' in the traditional sense because most of it is simply part of national legislation and case law; it merely deals with international cases. 'Conflict of laws' is also misleading because the subject is not necessarily about resolving such conflicts at all. In several areas (jurisdiction, judgments recognition), there is usually no conflict because the forum's own rules govern without further ado. Even with regard to choice-of-law regimes (determining which jurisdiction's substantive or procedural rules apply), their rules do not necessarily conflict but can often be reconciled or combined.

because it studies them directly, private international law because it needs to solve potential conflicts between domestic and foreign law. Private international law has to deal with foreign law in all its three main branches. This is most obvious with regard to choice of law as its core, that is, the set of principles and rules telling decision-makers in transboundary cases which of the several involved jurisdictions' laws they should apply. But it is also often true for questions of jurisdiction which may require looking at the respective foreign rules. Finally, the recognition of foreign judgments can easily raise questions about the law of the judgment's country of origin.

To be sure, significant differences between the disciplines remain. Most importantly, comparative law is not a body of rules but rather an academic discipline as well as a legal method and thus comparable (and related) to, for example, legal history. Thus its primary purpose is academic, that is, the pursuit of knowledge in and of itself,[2] its enormous practical utility notwithstanding. By contrast, private international law *is* a body of positive rules and thus comparable (and related) to, for example, civil procedure. Its primary goal is practical, that is, the decision of transboundary issues in actual disputes, though it is also of considerable theoretical and academic interest. As we shall see, these differences actually foster the two fields' quasi-symbiotic relationship because their respective orientations complement each other in numerous ways.

How much the two disciplines tend to go hand-in-glove is also visible on the personal and institutional level. Comparative law scholars are often also private international law scholars and vice versa. This is because both fields presuppose an interest in thinking beyond one's own legal system, because both have traditionally shared a focus on private law, and also because both cater to individuals with foreign language capabilities. This combination of jobs, however, is much more common in some countries (like Germany, Switzerland, or the United States) than in others (like France, Italy, or Japan). Institutions often also pair the disciplines together. This is largely because both fields engender similar kinds of work, require a foreign law library, and thrive on relationships with foreign countries. The most famous example of such an institutional combination is the Max Planck Institute for Foreign and International Private Law in Hamburg. Another manifestation is the frequent combination of university chairs for comparative and private international law in some countries. Yet, this close personal and institutional relationship is gradually diminishing as both disciplines grow more specialized and complex so that keeping up in both fields becomes increasingly impossible.

Despite the intimacy of their relationship, comparative law and conflicts law can, in some sense, actually be at loggerheads. At least in the tradition dominant throughout much of the twentieth century, comparative law has displayed a strong

---

[2] See Konrad Zweigert and Hein Kötz, *Einführung in die Rechtsvergleichung* (3rd edn, 1998), 14.

bias in favour of international legal uniformity, mainly as an agenda for legal unification,[3] but also by focusing on the similarity of actual outcomes.[4] Viewed from that perspective, comparative law is, of course, the enemy of private international law: where comparative law overcomes the diversity of law through international unification (or at least tends to find similarity of actual results), conflicts among laws tend to disappear, and so does the need for a discipline to handle them. In short, the success of comparative law as a uniformity agenda deprives private international law of its *raison d'être*[5]—a point to which we shall return in the context of recent developments (Section III). Yet, there is no reason for conflicts lawyers to fear for their existence. Experience has shown that international unification of law is an extremely difficult and rarely successful enterprise; that even where it succeeds, it does not cover all the issues; and even where it covers an issue, it leaves plenty of room for divergent interpretation and results. In a world consisting of different legal systems, comparative law provides a certain centripetal force but, at least on a global level, the centrifugal forces will always remain strong enough to create conflicts and thus to guarantee a place for private international law.

II. Traditional Interactions

As mentioned, comparative law plays three principal roles *vis-à-vis* private international law. First, it is a possible method of studying private international law: it can subject domestic and foreign conflicts law to comparative inquiry (subsection 1). Second, comparative law is a foundation for private international law: it often assists in the process of making conflicts law by informing lawmakers about the existing material and available options (subsection 2). Finally, comparative law is a tool serving the application of private international law: it helps decision-makers to operate conflicts norms in a variety of ways (subsection 3). To be sure, these three roles overlap and interact. Still, they are sufficiently distinct to merit separate analysis.

---

[3] Ibid 24–31.   [4] See eg Zweigert and Kötz's famous '*praesumptio similitudinis*', ibid 39.
[5] See Bénédicte Fauvarque-Cosson, 'Comparative Law and Conflict of Laws: Allies or Enemies? New Perspectives on an Old Couple', (2001) 49 *AJCL* 407, 413–17.

1. Comparative Law as a Method of Study: Comparing Conflicts Regimes

Comparative law has long made private international law one of its favourite topics.[6] With regard to the *specific rules* (the special part), particularly those determining which country's law governs a particular issue, comparative conflicts law is nothing out of the ordinary. These rules are rules like many others and can be compared just like those of contract, tort, or family law. In this regard, comparative conflicts law employs the usual techniques (identifying similarities and differences, and so on) and pursues essentially the usual goals (recognition of alternative solutions, better understanding of one's own system, inspiration for law reform, and so on). Given the particularly close relationship between the two disciplines, comparison of specific conflicts rules may come more naturally than in other fields, but beyond that, it is pretty much business as usual. Yet, with regard to the *general concepts* of private international law (its general part), comparative conflicts law transcends the usual juxtaposition and evaluation of different regimes: 'the worldwide exchange of ideas, which is taking place with regard to the general doctrines of private international law, is more than mere comparative law—to a certain degree, it is the expression of an international legal community'.[7] As a result of the strong academic tradition in conflicts law, and especially of the centuries-long international interaction between conflicts scholars, there is a universally shared stock of basic principles, problems, and solutions which transcend national borders. One who has mastered these basics will feel immediately at home in virtually every conflicts regime in the world. In this regard, comparative conflicts law approaches the ideal of a worldwide jurisprudence.

The study of comparative conflicts law is essentially a scholarly enterprise (although it may serve eminently practical ends[8]). We will begin by looking at its origins and development from the nineteenth through the mid-twentieth century (subsection a), then survey the more contemporary scholarship in various geographic regions (subsection b), and finally outline the major areas of debate (subsection c).

(a) The Development of the Field

The comparative study of conflicts law in the modern sense of looking for similarities and differences between national laws began in the nineteenth century. Of course, the theory and practice of private international law were highly developed

---

[6] Ulrich Drobnig (ed), *The International Encyclopedia of Comparative Law* (1971 ff) allocates an entire volume (III), K. Lipstein (ed), comprising almost 2,000 pages, to private international law.

[7] Jan Kropholler, 'Die vergleichende Methode und das internationale Privatrecht', (1978) 77 *Zeitschrift für vergleichende Rechtswissenschaft* 3 (the translation is mine).

[8] See below Section II.2 and II.3.

even before that time. But as long as the discipline was simply part of the general *ius commune*, that is, of an internationally shared body of legal knowledge, there were no distinct systems to compare. It was only when private international law, like many other areas, began to be enshrined in the codes or statutes of the modern nation state that it lost its essential unity and became divided into various national regimes. This process began in the later eighteenth, and then characterized the whole nineteenth, century.[9] Once positive rules of conflicts law were established on the national level, they could be studied comparatively. Of course, at this point, private international law had lost its truly international character: it had become national law dealing with transboundary cases.

The first full-fledged comparative study of the field[10] was presented by the German-French jurist Jean-Jacques Gaspard Foelix in his *Traité du Droit international privé ou Du conflit de lois de différentes nations en matière de droit privé* in 1843. At around the same time, his German colleague Wilhelm Schaeffner published his *Entwicklung des internationalen Privatrechts*, which was similarly oriented. Yet, at the time, these books were more the exception than the rule. Most other conflicts scholars in the nineteenth century paid scant or no attention to comparative aspects. This is also true for Friedrich Carl von Savigny whose treatise on private international law was clearly the most influential work not only of that period but probably of the whole modern era.[11]

At the beginning of the twentieth century, the famous Paris Congress on Comparative Law (1900) included several presentations on private international law topics. The following decades then brought a fairly steady stream of comparative studies of conflicts law. Some appeared as books[12] while many others were published as articles in various law journals. But none of these studies endeavoured to encompass the whole body of private international law on a worldwide level.

That step was taken by Ernst Rabel around the middle of the twentieth century. Rabel, who had become the director of the prestigious *Kaiser-Wilhelm Institut für ausländisches und internationales Privatrecht* in Berlin[13] in 1926, and who was arguably the most eminent comparative law scholar of his generation, lost all

---

[9] There were some choice-of-law provisions already in the Bavarian codification (*Codex Maximilianeus Bavaricus Civilis*) of 1756 and in the Prussian General Land Law (*Allgemeines Landrecht für die Preußischen Staaten*) of 1794. Yet, the first conflicts provision with a long-lasting impact was the famous Art 3 of the French civil code (*Code civil*) of 1804, which is still in force and, despite its rudimentary character, has formed the basis for French private international law ever since.

[10] Curiously, though, the first modern conflicts works displaying comparative perspectives appeared not in Europe but in the United States, see below.

[11] Friedrich Carl von Savigny, *System des heutigen römischen Rechts* (vol 8, 1849).

[12] See Arthur Nußbaum, *Deutsches internationales Privatrecht. Unter besonderer Berücksichtigung des österreichischen und schweizerischen Rechts* (1932); Arthur K. Kuhn, *Comparative Commentaries on Private International Law or Conflict of Laws* (1937); Henri Batiffol, *Les conflits de lois en matiére de contrats. Etude de Droit international privé comparé* (1938).

[13] The *Institut* was the predecessor of the present *Max Planck Institut für ausländisches und internationales Privatrecht* in Hamburg.

his positions when he was forced to flee Nazi Germany in 1937. Two years later, he emigrated to the United States where he found a new academic home at the University of Michigan Law School in Ann Arbor. Here, marooned in the American Midwest, Rabel wrote his *magnum opus*, *The Conflict of Laws: A Comparative Study* (1945–58). Deeply international by professional experience and conviction, Rabel pursued the goal of initiating 'a radical turn of choice-of-law rules from provincial to world-wide thinking'.[14] In four volumes comprising almost 2,500 pages (not counting various introductions and indices), his study presents a comparative review of the conflicts rules (including many procedural norms) applicable in roughly a hundred jurisdictions throughout the world. It is organized not by country but rather by subject-matter and presents not only the black-letter rules but also analyses the material from a functional and practical perspective. In both its sweep and its unfailing control of massive amounts of material, it is truly a work of monumental proportions. It could only be written by a multilingual scholar of enormous erudition and over a period of many years. *The Conflict of Laws* is a classic of legal scholarship and continues to be considered the definitive comparative study on private international law even today. It is one of those law books, like Blackstone's *Commentaries on the Laws of England* (1765–69) 200, or Savigny's *System des heutigen römischen Rechts* (1840–9) 100 years before, whose contents become inevitably dated but whose accomplishment remains timeless.

While no other comparative study of conflicts law has rivalled Rabel's work (no author has even tried), the fifty-plus years that have passed since its completion have none the less yielded a fairly impressive crop in that field. To a considerable extent, this is due to the influence of Rabel's call for a sustained comparative perspective in conflicts law and to the example he had set.

Since the 1950s, a major source of comparative private international scholarship has been the series of lectures given annually at the Hague Academy of International Law (especially the General Courses on Private International Law) by the most prominent private international law scholars in the world. The lectures are published by the Hague Academy in *Recueil des cours* and, subsequently, often in book form as well. Together they constitute a sizeable library on comparative conflicts law, which by now consists of several dozen volumes.

(b) A Regional Survey

A complete survey of the comparative conflicts scholarship in the various countries of the world is neither possible nor necessary here. It is interesting to look at a few geographic regions, however, because it shows both that there is a substantial body of work out there and that there are considerable regional (or country-specific) differences in the development of comparative conflicts law.

---

[14] Ernst Rabel, *The Conflict of Laws: A Comparative Study* (vol I, 1945), 98.

In many parts of continental Europe, comparative conflicts scholarship has become fairly common as well as quite highly developed in the last half-century. French private international law has often suffered from a reputation of nationalism but this reputation is no longer justified, if it ever was. In recent decades, the studies of Henri Batiffol, Paul Lagarde, Pierre Lalive, and Marc Ancel have often gone beyond national boundaries. Today, a younger generation of scholars keeps producing comparative conflicts work, and the *Revue critique de droit international privé* regularly publishes articles and reviews in that genre. In Germany, comparative perspectives are virtually *de rigueur* in conflicts scholarship. The leading treatise by Gerhard Kegel is replete with foreign and comparative references[15] and the current generation of scholars has continued and solidified that tradition. The Max Planck Institute for Foreign and International Private Law in Hamburg is probably the world's major centre of comparative conflicts law, and the *Rabels Zeitschrift,* edited by its directors, is a leading journal in that area. Similarly live traditions of comparative conflicts scholarship have long existed in many of the smaller European countries, especially in Switzerland, but also in Austria, Belgium, and the Netherlands. If we turn south, however, the picture becomes more uneven. In some Mediterranean countries, comparative conflicts scholarship has a solid and live tradition, as in Italy and Greece, while that is less true in others, such as Spain. In Central and Eastern Europe, comparative conflicts scholarship is experiencing a gradual revival after long hibernation during the communist period.

On the other side of the channel, the comparative element in private international law has, on the whole, been weaker than on the continent. Still, there is considerable comparative conflicts law in England as well. In part, the work has been done by the previous generation (R. H. Graveson *et al*) which included some prominent German immigrants (especially Kurt Lipstein and Otto Kahn-Freund); in considerable part, it also comes from academics active today. Notably, the United Kingdom is the birthplace of the recent *Journal of Private International Law.* According to the prospectus, this periodical it is not only 'the first English language journal devoted exclusively to private international law', it also pursues explicitly comparative goals, that is, 'the sharing of information and ideas from legal systems around the world'.

US-American conflicts scholarship has often been criticized for its parochialism but the picture in the United States is neither so simple nor so bleak. Certainly, the nineteenth-century beginnings were anything but parochial. In fact, the earliest conflicts works including serious comparative elements were published not in Europe but in the United States. In 1828, Samuel Livermore presented his *Dissertations on the Questions which Arise from the Contrariety of Positive Laws of Different States and Nations.* Six years later, Harvard law professor

---

[15] Gerhard Kegel and Klaus Schurig, *Internationales Privatrecht* (8th edn, 2000).

and United States Supreme Court Justice Joseph Story published a much fuller treatment in his *Commentaries on the Conflict of Laws* (1834), in which he drew heavily on foreign learning. And in 1872, Francis Wharton's *Treatise on the Conflict of Laws* bore the subtitle *A Comparative Study of Anglo-American, Roman, German, and French Jurisprudence*. At the beginning of the twentieth century, even Joseph Beale, much maligned by later generations for the narrow-mindedness of his vested rights approach, was more widely read in foreign conflicts law than all but a handful of American conflicts scholars today.[16] It has really only been the 1920s, and especially with the advent of legal realism, that American conflicts scholarship has taken a decidedly parochial turn.[17] This trend worsened during the so-called 'choice-of-law revolution' of the 1950s through the 1980s.[18] Its leaders (especially Brainerd Currie) showed no interest in foreign approaches, and the intense theoretical discussions of these decades hardly ever looked beyond American borders. It is not surprising therefore, that, despite early efforts to bring in comparative perspectives,[19] the *Second Restatement of Conflicts* (1971) shows scant influence of foreign ideas (with the exception of some English approaches). It was at this point that mainstream American conflicts scholars and theories were indeed, as Gerhard Kegel famously put it, 'stewing in their own juices'.[20] Still, even in those decades, there were always a few American conflicts scholars with a soundly comparative outlook. Not accidentally, most of them were European immigrants (Albert Ehrenzweig, Friedrich Juenger, Kurt Nadelmann, and Arthur Nussbaum[21]) but the group included some indigenously American scholars as well (especially Arthur von Mehren and Hessel Yntema). But particularly in the last two decades, American conflicts scholarship has overcome most of its erstwhile parochialism.[22] Today, comparative scholarship is both

---

[16] See Joseph Beale, *A Treatise on the Conflict of Laws* (1916); Beale's 66-page bibliography lists works from all over the world in half a dozen languages.

[17] In 1945, Hessel Yntema justly lamented that 'inadequate attention has been given in this country to the relations between the doctrines of conflicts of law as here evolved and those of foreign countries other than England', Hessel Yntema, 'Foreword', in Rabel (n 14), vol I, xci.

[18] For an authoritative review, see Symeon Symeonides, *The American Choice-of-Law Revolution in the Courts: Today and Tomorrow* (2003).

[19] In fact, Ernst Rabel's comparative study of conflicts law was originally planned as a contribution to a Second Restatement of Conflicts. It was based on an initiative, and largely financed by, the ALI for that purpose. Soon, however, Rabel's work took on a life of its own; see William Draper Lewis, 'Foreword', in Rabel (n 14), vol I, ix–x.

[20] ('Kochen im eigenen Saft'), Gerhard Kegel, 'Wandel auf dünnem Eis', in Friedrich Juenger (ed), *Zum Wandel des internationalen Privatrechts* (1974), 35, at 41.

[21] See eg Albert Ehrenzweig and Erik Jayme, *Private International Law, A Comparative Treatise on American International Conflicts Law Including the Law of Admiralty* (3 vols, 1967); Friedrich Juenger, *Choice of Law and Multistate Justice* (1993); Kurt Nadelmann, *Conflict of Laws, International and Interstate* (1972); Arthur Nußbaum (ed), *American-Swiss Private International Law* (1951, 2nd edn, 1958); Arthur Nußbaum (ed), *Bilateral Studies in Private International Law* (vols 2–13, 1953–65).

[22] See eg 'Symposium, International Issues in Common Law Choice of Law: American Conflicts Teaching Exits the Middle Ages', (1995) 28 *Vanderbilt Journal of Transnational Law* 361.

frequent and part of the mainstream, thanks especially to the work of Symeon Symeonides (another immigrant)[23] but also thanks to a sizeable group of others who pay regular attention to the comparative and international dimensions of their discipline. As a result, the heyday of American parochialism in conflicts law is definitely over.[24]

In fact, at least as far as the *transatlantic* dimension is concerned, conflicts scholars in the United States today pay *more* attention to comparative perspectives than their European colleagues. This is the result of almost diametrically opposed developments on both sides of the Atlantic over the last two decades. In the 1960s through the 1980s, mainstream American conflicts scholarship was preoccupied with the profound changes occurring on its domestic choice-of-law scene. When the dust of the choice-of-law revolution settled (and the theoretical debates became tiresome) in the 1980s, American conflicts law discovered the challenges of economic globalization. It began to look outward again, especially to Western Europe with its new crop of conflicts legislation, so that today, European conflicts law is frequently discussed, or at least referenced, in the American literature. The European development began from the opposite end. Private international law scholars in the 1970s and early 1980s frequently looked across the Atlantic because they were intrigued by the American choice-of-law revolution and intensely debated its merits and dangers as a potential model for European reform.[25] Over time, however, continental conflicts theory lost interest in American developments for three reasons: what American ideas appeared useful had by and large been absorbed;[26] in many European countries, new conflicts legislation was enacted, and after the legislature had spoken further theoretical debate seemed rather pointless; and, perhaps most importantly, beginning in the late 1980s, European conflicts scholars focused their attention on the new and urgent problems created by the acceleration of European integration. Especially because of these new challenges at

[23] See eg Symeon Symeonides, *Private International Law at the Turn of the Twenty-First Century, Progress or Regress?* (1999); see also Mathias Reimann, *Conflict of Laws in Western Europe, A Guide through the Jungle* (1995).

[24] For a more detailed and nuanced assessment, see Mathias Reimann, 'Parochialism in American Conflicts Law', (2001) 49 *AJCL* 369. Of course, this is not to deny that more can, and should, be done; see Friedrich Juenger, 'The Need for a Comparative Approach to Choice-of-Law Problems', (1999) 73 *Tulane LR* 1309 ff.

[25] See especially Christian Joerges, *Zum Funktionswandel des internationalen Privatrechts* (1971); Friedrich Juenger, *Zum Wandel des internationalen Privatrechts* (1974); Gerhard Kegel, 'Paternal Home and Dream Home: Traditional Conflict of Laws and the American Reformers', (1979) 27 *AJCL* 615; 'Symposium "The Influence of Modern American Conflicts Theories on European Law" ', (1982) 30 *AJCL* 1.

[26] A prime example is the principle that in tort cases, the law of the parties' common domicile (if any) may trump the law of the place of the wrong. This principle was first openly announced by the New York Court of Appeals in 1963 (*Babcock v Jackson*, 191 NE 2d 279, NY 1963) and has since become widely accepted in Europe and beyond, see Mathias Reimann, 'Codifying Torts Conflicts: The 1999 German Legislation in Comparative Perspective', (2000) 60 *Louisiana LR* 1297.

home, European private international law began to turn inward, and today, continental scholars rarely look beyond the boundaries of the European Union any more.[27] In that sense, European conflicts scholarship is more parochial today than its American counterpart. The Europeans would be well-advised to heed Ulrich Drobnig's recent admonition: 'In our preoccupation with Europe, let us not forget the world'.[28]

In Latin America, the comparative approach to conflicts law has a long tradition.[29] This tradition goes back to the nineteenth century (eg Pimenta Bueno in Brazil), gathered strength in the earlier decades of the twentieth century, especially with the work of A. Sanchez de Bustamante (Cuba). It was continued, *inter alia*, by Quintin Alfonsin (Uruguay) and Jacob Dolinger (Brazil), and it is very much alive today in the work of a younger generation. Here, we also find significant regional studies of the private international law of the Andean countries[30] and of the MERCOSUR members.[31]

In several Asian countries (Japan, Korea, the People's Republic of China, and Taiwan), conflicts scholars have also frequently looked at foreign developments, with Europe and the United States receiving the lion's share of attention. With regard to Europe, this reflects the original reception of continental (especially French and German) conflicts doctrine in many parts of Asia in the nineteenth and twentieth centuries. With respect to the United States, it is a result of the global impact of American law in general as well as of the fascination with the bold innovations generated during the American choice-of-law revolution in particular.

(c) Fundamental Issues

Much comparative conflicts law deals with the myriad specific rules governing a huge variety of particular issues. These issues range from the more traditional question of exactly which law applies in transboundary cases in matters of contract, tort, and family law to more recent questions of intellectual property rights, electronic commerce, and the Internet generally. But they also include discussions of diverse international jurisdiction principles and rules, especially in the American-European context. Finally, comparative conflicts law addresses problems of various judgments recognition regimes, most recently with regard to the failed

[27] Notable exceptions are Jan Kropholler and Jan von Hein, 'From Approach to Rule-Orientation in American Tort Conflicts?', in James Nafziger and Symeon Symeonides (eds), *Law and Justice in a Multistate World* (2002), 317; Frank Vischer, 'New Tendencies in European Conflict of Laws and the Influence of U.S. Doctrine—A Short Survey', ibid 459.

[28] Ulrich Drobnig, 'Die Geburt der modernen Rechtsvergleichung. Zum 50. Todestag von Ernst Rabel', (2005) *Zeitschrift für europäisches Privatrecht* 821, at 831.

[29] For an overview, see Werner Goldschmidt, 'Droit international privé latino-americain', (1973) 100 *Journal de Droit International (Clunet)* 65.

[30] Mario A. Gomez de la Torre, *Sistemas de Derecho Internacional Privado en los Paises del Area Andina (Separata No. 1 de la Revista Anuario Ecuatoriano de Derecho Internacional)* (vol IV, 1976–80).

[31] Diego Fernandez-Arroyo, *Derecho internacional privado de los Estados del MERCOSUR* (2003).

project of a comprehensive Hague Convention on that topic. The comparative conflicts law literature in these and other special areas is so vast that no one can seriously claim to have a complete overview.

Beyond all these specifics, however, lie about half-a-dozen pervasive issues which go to the very heart of choice-of-law theory and practice. While these issues have a long pedigree, they have come to the fore with renewed vigour in the last three decades. They have been put into sharp relief by the clash between two fundamentally different choice-of-law models as the traditional (originally European) model with its essentially multilateralist and territorial rules was challenged, and in part overcome, by the (American) choice-of-law revolution with its preference for more unilateralist and policy-oriented approaches. Since the older tradition is often identified with European conservatism while the newer model resulted from American iconoclasm, the discussion of fundamental choice-of-law issues is often imbedded in a comparison between the respective regimes on both sides of the Atlantic.[32] In other words, the theoretical debate about the most fundamental choice-of-law issues and the actual comparison between the European tradition and the American revolution have often been just different sides of the same coin.[33]

While there are several plausible ways to define and organize these major issues,[34] it may be helpful (albeit somewhat artificial) to put them into two groups. The first group comprises three questions pertaining to the fundamental orientation and goals of the choice-of-law system in general. The second group contains three questions about the character of choice-of-law norms in particular. As the reader will soon notice, these issues overlap in multiple ways.

With regard to the basic orientation and goals of private international law in general, the most fundamental question (logically antecedent to all others) is whether the law applicable in transboundary cases should be selected by choice-of-law rules at all ('selectivism') or whether such cases should rather be governed by a particular set of substantive rules specifically made for such cases ('substantivism'). More recently, the substantivist agenda was espoused by one of the most prominent comparative conflicts scholars, Friedrich Juenger. Juenger engaged in a thorough comparative analysis of the major choice-of-law regimes and found all of them badly wanting, arguing that the choice of one set of laws (over another) is never a truly satisfactory solution to the specific problems of transboundary cases.[35]

[32] See the contributions to the 'Symposium', (1982) 30 *AJCL* 1.

[33] This is not to deny, of course, that much of the debate continues to take place outside that comparative context.

[34] For a somewhat different, though equally plausible, definition and organization, see Symeon Symeonides, 'American Choice of Law at the Dawn of the 21st Century', (2001) 37 *Willamette LR* 1. Despite the differences between his line-up and mine, I draw heavily on Symeonides's analysis throughout this subsection.

[35] Friedrich Juenger, *Choice of Law and Multistate Justice* (orig 1993, special edn 2005; with comments by ten international conflicts scholars).

Despite Juenger's efforts, however, the majority of private international law regimes remain rather firmly committed to choice-of-law rules, albeit perhaps only as a lesser evil.[36]

If choice-of-law norms determine the applicable law, we are immediately faced with a second fundamental issue concerning goals: should such norms aim at 'conflicts justice' or try to do 'material justice'?[37] Is the objective of the choice-of-law process (merely) to decide *which set of domestic rules* has the better claim to application (regardless of their content)? Or should choice-of-law norms directly aim at doing justice *between the parties*? In the former case, choice-of-law is a self-contained enterprise; in the latter, it is merely a way of reaching the desired final result. This is not the place to discuss the deep jurisprudential and philosophical issues underlying this dichotomy. Suffice it to say that the more traditional approach to choice of law, which continues to prevail (though with many modifications) in Europe and most other parts of the world, has been leaning towards the goal of 'conflicts justice' while the more modern approaches, especially in the United States, have put greater emphasis on 'material justice'.

This issue is intimately connected to the third basic problem of orientation, that is, whether choice of law should be 'jurisdiction selecting' or 'law selecting'. Should conflicts norms select just the *state or country* from which the applicable law will then be taken, no matter what that law says? Or should private international law choose *a law* in full view of its substance? The traditional model has mainly been jurisdiction selecting and has permitted a look at the substance of the involved laws only by way of (public policy) exception. The more modern models pushed by the American conflicts revolution provide for a choice in consideration of the content of the laws involved. This is most obvious with regard to the 'better law' approach but also implicit in interest analysis which requires that the policies underlying the respective rules be consulted. While law-selecting notions of better law and interest analysis have recently had some influence outside the United States as well, in most of the world, they have affected the prevailing essentially jurisdiction-selection approach merely at the margin.

When it comes to the more specific issues pertaining to the character of conflicts norms, the threshold question is whether these norms should be 'multilateral' or 'unilateral'. Under a 'multilateralist' paradigm, the applicable law must be determined according to predefined norms which rely on neutral criteria; employing such norms, the judge must make the decision from a perspective external to his or her own state, treating all respective laws as equal candidates

---

[36] See Mathias Reimann, 'Remarks by an Embarrassed but Unrepentent Multilateralist', ibid (special edn), lxv.

[37] See Kegel and Schurig, above (n 15), 114 ('*materiellprivatrechtliche Gerechtigkeit*' versus '*internationalprivatrechtliche Gerechtigkeit*').

(at least in theory). Under a 'unilateralist' approach, the basic choice-of-law idea is that a law will be applied if it has a proper claim to application (eg according to its underlying policy); such a norm asks the judge to make the decision from an internal point of view, and since he or she will usually consider the applicability of forum law first, this approach tends to be inherently biased in favour of the *lex fori*. Since the work of Friedrich Carl von Savigny in the middle of the nineteenth century,[38] conflicts law has strongly trended towards multilateralism, but during the American choice-of-law revolution, unilateralism experienced a strong come-back. Today, most choice-of-law regimes contain doses of both. Still, it is fair to say that European conflicts law remains more strongly committed to multilateralism while several US-American variants have made (neo-)unilateralism their major paradigm.

The second problem regarding the character of choice-of-law norms is whether they should consist of 'rules' or 'approaches'.[39] A rule provides for an unequivocal result, as in Art 3 s 1 of the Dutch conflicts statute on tort: 'Obligations arising from tort are governed by the law of the state on whose territory the act was committed'.[40] In contrast, an approach does not preordain a definite outcome but only provides decision-making guidelines for the judge, an example being § 145(1) of the Second Restatement of Conflicts (1): 'The rights and liabilities of the parties with respect to an issue in tort are determined by the local law of the state which, with respect to that issue, has the most significant relationship to the occurrence and the parties under the principles stated in § 6'.[41] The traditional conflicts model is heavily rule-oriented while many modern choice-of-law regimes tend to prefer 'approaches'. With regard to contracts, there is actually evidence of a worldwide convergence towards somewhat indeterminate norms.[42] Today, many European conflicts regimes are quite open-ended as well.[43] Still, by and large conflicts lawyers in the civil law orbit are more comfortable with rules while their common law colleagues find approaches more easily acceptable.

Finally, and closely related to the issue of 'rules' versus 'approaches', there is the question of what criteria conflicts norms should employ. Should they rely on hard-and-fast reference points such as the geographic location of events or the domicile or nationality of the parties? Or should they rather utilize other, more malleable criteria, such as policy analysis, or even value judgments, such as the choice of the

---

[38] The foundation of modern multilateralism was laid in Friedrich Carl von Savigny, *System heutigen römischen Rechts* (vol 8, 1849).

[39] See Willis Reese, 'Choice of Law: Rules or Approach', (1972) 57 *Cornell LR* 315.

[40] *Wet conflictenrecht onrechtmatige daad*, of 11 April 2001.

[41] § 145(2) then lists four criteria to be taken into account.

[42] The principle that a contract is governed by the law with which it has the 'closest connection' or 'most significant relationship' is becoming more and more widely accepted, see Mathias Reimann, 'Savigny's Triumph? Choice of Law in Contracts Cases at the Close of the Twentieth Century', (1999) 39 *Virginia Journal of International Law* 571.

[43] See Kropholler and von Hein (n 27).

'better law'?[44] Again, on the whole, civilian conflicts lawyers have by and large opted for more unequivocal factors[45] while their common law brethren have been more accepting of softer criteria.

Ultimately, the desirable character of choice-of-law norms depends on how one weighs certainty and predictability of outcomes against flexibility and justice in the individual case. The more a system is committed to the former values, the more it will rely on hard-and-fast rules employing neutral and unambiguous criteria. The more a system pursues the latter objectives, the more it will prefer broader approaches relying on malleable (perhaps multi-factor) tests. While there are, arguably, overall tendencies of convergence towards a middle ground, the world's choice-of-law regimes continue to present a fairly broad spectrum of varying answers to all of these questions. Thus, they continue to provide fertile ground for comparative studies.

2. Comparative Law as a Foundation: Assisting the Making of Conflicts Law

For the last century or so, the drafting of written conflicts rules has usually been based on the study of already existing models. In this context, comparative conflicts law serves the lawmaker. This is true particularly regarding the efforts at an international unification of conflicts law but it is also the case, albeit perhaps more inconsistently, with respect to national legislation.

(a) The International Unification of Conflicts Law[46]

Efforts at the international unification of conflicts law go back for more than a hundred years. Their most important manifestation are the conferences on private international law regularly held at The Hague since 1893. After World War II, the Hague Conference on Private International Law became a firmly established institution with its own permanent bureau and staff. Beginning as a European club with thirteen members, it has developed into a worldwide organization with

---

[44] *Conklin v Horner*, 157 NW 2d 579, 586 (Wisc 1968). Another example is the choice of the law of the state whose 'interest would be more impaired if its policy were subordinated to the policy of another state', *Bernhard v Harrah's Club*, 546 P 2d 719 (Cal 1976).

[45] There are, however, notable exceptions, such as the German rule that damage claims based on foreign law cannot 'go significantly further than is necessary for an adequate compensation of the injured party', Art 40 s 3 ss 1, EGBGB.

[46] A related, but different, matter is the international unification of substantive law, for example, of the law of commercial contracts in general and of sales law in particular; see below, n 88.

delegates from currently sixty-five countries.[47] Given both its composition and its mission, it goes without saying that the Hague Conference is the veritable embodiment of comparative conflicts law. The Conference has so far generated thirty-nine Hague Conventions on a large variety of issues, ranging from choice of law to jurisdiction and from civil procedure to judgments recognition.[48] In terms of ratification by states, some of these conventions have been more successful than others but even where countries did not outright adopt a particular convention, they often followed it as a model.

Beyond the Hague Conference, various other organizations draft and publish international conventions dealing with conflicts issues. Some of them aim at worldwide unification, such as the United Nations Commission on International Trade Law (UNCITRAL). Other projects have a regional character, such as the series of private international law conferences held in Latin America (with the participation of the United States) since the late nineteenth century. They produced, *inter alia*, the *Bustamante Code*, a uniform codification of conflicts law adopted by a sizeable group of Latin American countries in the Convention on Private International Law in 1928 in Havana.[49] Today, the Interamerican Specialized Conference on Private International Law continues to promote the integration of conflicts law in that region.[50] In the post-World War II era, regional unification of conflicts law also became a major European agenda under the auspices of the Council of Europe and of the European Community. Needless to say, their projects are based on comparative studies as well. Take, for example, the (European Community) Convention on the Law Applicable to Contractual Obligations of 1980 (Rome Convention) which now provides uniform choice-of-law rules in contracts cases throughout the European Union. Its drafting team not only consulted the laws of the various EC member states but also considered a variety of international conventions both in force and at the drafting stage.[51]

As a result of these comparative law-based efforts, conflicts law has undergone

---

[47] Kurt Lipstein, 'One Hundred Years of Hague Conferences on Private International Law', (1993) 42 *ICLQ* 553; 'Symposium: The Hague Conference on Private International Law', (1994) 57 *Law and Contemporary Problems* 1.

[48] Hague Conference on Private International Law, Collection of Conventions 1893–2003 (2004). The latest product is the Hague Convention on Choice of Forum Agreements (2005).

[49] League of Nations Treaty Series LXXXVI No. 1950 (1929). The Code entered into force in 1935; about a dozen Latin American countries are members. For an overview in English, see Ernest Lorenzen, 'The Pan-American Code of Private International Law', (1930) 4 *Tulane LR* 499.

[50] In 1994, it adopted an Inter-American Convention on the Law Applicable to International Contracts (Mexico City Convention), see Friedrich Juenger, 'The Inter-American Convention on the Law Applicable to International Contracts: Some Highlights and Comparisons', (1994) 42 *AJCL* 381; on the developments since then, see Diego Fernandez-Arroyo and Jan Kleinheisterkamp, 'The VIth Inter-American Specialized Conference on Private International Law (CIDIP VI): A New Step Towards Interamerican Legal Integration', (2002) 4 *Yearbook of Private International Law* 237.

[51] Mario Guiliano and Paul Lagarde, *Report on the Convention on the Law Applicable to Contractual Obligations, Official Journal C 282* (31 October 1980), 0001–0050.

more unification on a regional or even worldwide level than most other areas
of law. Of course, substantial differences remain. But the trend towards convergence is strong and persistent, particularly among the members of the Hague
Conference and within the European Union.[52] The more a country resists this
trend, as is often the case with the United States, the more it tends to become an
outlier.

(b) Modern Conflicts Legislation

In the last thirty years, and especially since the 1990s, there has been an almost
worldwide wave of national conflicts legislation. The trend originated in continental Europe and then spread to many other parts of the globe, including some
common law jurisdictions. By now, dozens of states have updated or reformed
their private international law by enacting new conflicts statutes, and the trend
appears to continue unabated.[53] Some of these reforms were driven by the adoption of international conventions, others resulted from purely domestic initiatives.
Yet, on the whole, it is fair to see this wave of conflicts legislation as a response
to the globalization of the economy and the increased mobility of people. These
phenomena have led to a surge in transboundary transactions and disputes,
creating an urgent need for modern, functional, conflicts rules.

The nature and scope of the various statutes differs considerably. In most cases,
such legislation either updates or supersedes older (usually more fragmentary)
statutes (as in Germany, Japan, and Liechtenstein), in a few others, it codifies
choice-of-law rules for the first time (as in Belgium,[54] the United Kingdom, or
Oregon). Some statutes encompass private international law as a whole, that is,
including jurisdiction, judgments recognition, and perhaps other topics (as in Italy,
Switzerland, or Slovenia); others focus just on choice of law (as in Austria, the
Netherlands, or Quebec). Some are integrated into larger (civil or procedural)
codes (as in Bulgaria, Louisiana, or Russia); many are free-standing acts (as in
Poland, Turkey, or Venezuela).[55]

While it is hard to gauge, exactly, how much comparative work went into the
preparation of each and every new conflicts statute, in most cases, drafting experts
or teams looked at the conflicts rules of other countries as well as at the pertinent
international conventions. This is especially true where the principal draftsperson
was an academic. Take, for example, the making of the Swiss Federal Act on Private

---

[52] On the Europeanization of international private law, see below, Section III.1.

[53] A major exception is France. This is somewhat ironic since, in general, the French legal tradition
is, in a sense, the very symbol of codification.

[54] It is true that Belgium had had some conflicts provisions in its civil code but these provisions
were so rudimentary that they did not constitute anything like a codification of private international
law.

[55] For a collection of European conflicts legislation in the original languages with a German
translation, see Wolfgang Riering (ed), *IPR-Gesetze in Europa* (1997).

International Law of 1987[56] which was largely the work of a professor of private international law at the University of Basle, Frank Vischer. Vischer, who commands a broad and deep knowledge of comparative conflicts law,[57] drew not only on the national regimes of many countries in Europe and beyond, he also considered several international conventions (some still at the draft stage) as well as the writings of conflicts scholars especially in Europe and the United States.[58] Another vivid example is the Louisiana codification of choice-of-law rules of 1992. Its principal draftsman, Symeon Symeonides, then a professor of private international law at Louisiana State University, is perhaps the world's leading expert on comparative conflicts law today. Working on the Louisiana rules, he looked way beyond American cases to the conflicts law of, *inter alia*, Austria, (the former) East and West Germany, Hungary, Poland, Portugal, Spain, Switzerland, and the (draft) project for Puerto Rico as well as the pertinent international (Hague) conventions.[59]

Since even national conflicts legislation thus normally builds on comparative foundations, the individual statutes tend to be but variations on a common set of themes. It remains true that some continue to rely on nationality as the crucial connection between a person and a state while others look to domicile or habitual residence; that some happily embrace the doctrine of *renvoi* while others by and large reject it; and that some display more rigid reliance on territorial factors while others take a more flexible stance. Yet, despite these and other differences, the particular statutes all tackle universal problems by drawing on a globally shared fund of possible solutions.

3. Comparative Law as a Tool: Operating Conflicts Norms

As a tool in the hands of a private international lawyer, comparative law serves a primarily practical goal: it assists in the operation of existing conflicts norms and thus helps to resolve actual transboundary issues. Here, it addresses itself mainly to the judge. In this context, it performs several distinct functions.

---

[56] *Bundesgesetz über das internationale Privatrecht vom 18. Dezember 1987*; for an English translation see Jean-Claude Cornu, Stéphane Hankins, and Symeon Symeonides, 'Swiss Federal Statute on Private International Law of December 18, 1987', (1989) 37 *AJCL* 187.

[57] See Frank Vischer, 'General Course on Private International Law', (1992-I) 232 *Recueil des cours* 21.

[58] Frank Vischer, 'Drafting National Legislation on Conflict of Laws: The Swiss Experience', (1977) 41 *Law and Contemporary Problems* 131; Frank Vischer, 'Das Problem der Kodifikation des schweizerischen internationalen Privatrechts', (1971) *Zeitschrift für Schweizerisches Recht* 1.

[59] Symeon Symeonides, 'Problems and Dilemmas in Codifying Choice of Law for Torts: The Louisiana Experience in Comparative Perspective', (1990) 38 *AJCL* 421.

(a) Information about Foreign Law

On the most basic level, comparative law simply provides the information about foreign law that private international law requires. Of course, as has often been pointed out, simple information about foreign law is not comparative law in the proper sense of the term—since nothing is being compared, it is merely a matter of knowledge of foreign law (in German: *Auslandsrechtskunde*). Still, providing foreign law information does belong to the discipline of comparative law for two reasons. First, supplying such information is much of what comparative lawyers actually do in their scholarship and practical work, simply because they are typically experts in more than one legal system. Second, while it is true that, in principle, any foreign lawyer could provide information about his or her home country, often only a comparatist can make that information intelligible to someone from another country. That typically requires acts of (linguistic, conceptual, cultural, etc) translation which can only be performed by someone who is at home in both systems. Thus, when attorneys or judges handling a transboundary case under private international law need information about foreign law, they like to turn to someone who understands both the domestic and the foreign regimes governing the respective subject-matter, that is, to a comparatist.

The need for information about foreign law arises in many contexts. It is most obvious when a private international law rule calls for the application of foreign law in a transboundary case. For example, the most basic choice-of-law principle in tort cases is that torts are subject to the law of the place where the wrong occurred (*lex loci delicti*).[60] Thus if a court in the People's Republic of China finds that a tort was committed in Korea, it may have to apply Korean law[61] and in order to do so, it must find out what that law says. A comparative lawyer (specializing in Korean law) can provide that information and make it intelligible to the Chinese lawyer or judge. In this scenario, private international law and comparative law work hand-in-hand: the former decides what law applies and the latter tells us what that law says.[62]

---

[60] This rule quickly loses its simplicity, of course, if, for example, the act constituting the tort occurs in one jurisdiction while the damage ensues in another. In addition, in many, if not most, jurisdictions today, this rule is subject to various qualifications and exceptions, most prominently the principle that the law of the common domicile (or habitual residence) of the parties (if any) may displace the law of the place of the wrong; see Mathias Reimann, 'Codifying Torts Conflicts: The 1999 German Legislation in Comparative Perspective', (2000) 60 *Louisiana LR* 1297 ff.

[61] See Art 146 of the Common Principles of Private Law; for an English translation and an explanation, see Tung-Pi Chen, 'Private International Law of the People's Republic of China: An Overview', (1987) 35 *AJCL* 445, at 468.

[62] There can also be a need to learn about foreign private international law rules. This is most obviously the case where domestic conflicts provisions refer to these rules. Choice-of-law norms often provide that if foreign conflicts provisions refer the case back to forum law, such a reference back shall be accepted so that forum law applies. This doctrine of *renvoi* is fairly common in many legal systems, see eg Art 4 § 1 of the Polish private international law statute (*Prawo prywatne miedzynarodowe*) of 1965.

Yet, even the application of private international law norms themselves may require knowledge of foreign law (ie regardless of whether or not foreign law is ultimately found applicable). In that case, comparative law is a tool for the operation of the private international law machine. This is frequently the case in all three major areas of private international law. A choice-of-law example is a dispute in which an Italian court has to judge the formal validity of a testament made by a Finnish citizen resident in Sweden while vacationing in Morocco. According to Art 48 of the Italian private international law statute, a testament is valid if it complies with the form of the state either where it was made or of which the testator was a national or in which he resided.[63] Thus the Italian court will have to check the laws of Finland, Sweden, and Morocco. A jurisdictional illustration derives from the English principle of *forum conveniens*: an English court with proper jurisdiction under domestic law may still decline to hear the case, say against a South African defendant, if there is a more convenient forum elsewhere. This, of course, requires that a court in another country have proper jurisdiction.[64] The English judge must therefore assure himself of jurisdiction under foreign, for example, South African, law. Finally, a Swiss court asked to recognize a foreign judgment can do so only 'if the judgment is no longer subject to ordinary recourse or if it is a final judgment'.[65] Whether these conditions are fulfilled depends, of course, entirely on foreign law.

While private international law is thus often highly dependent on the information services of comparative law, these services are not fundamentally different from those rendered by comparative law in many other international contexts. When a Greek lawyer advises his client about Canadian immigration rules, applies for an Australian business licence, or evaluates the effect of a Lebanese arrest warrant, he or she also has to obtain the requisite information about Canadian, Australian, and Lebanese law respectively and will often turn to the expertise of a comparative law specialist for that purpose. Yet, handling transboundary cases often requires more than simple information: it frequently calls for a proper comparison of domestic and foreign law.

(b) Specific Comparative Analysis

As a service provider to private international law, comparative law really comes into its own where it delivers a specific comparative analysis of the domestic and foreign law involved in an international case. Here, the relationship between the two fields is most intimate because both cooperate very closely in resolving specific issues.

Often, private international law norms clearly require a comparative analysis of

---

[63] Legge 31 maggio 1995, No. 218.

[64] *Spiliada Maritime Corp v Consulex Ltd* [1986] 3 All ER 843; see Lawrence Collins (ed), *Dicey and Morris on the Conflict of Laws* (vol I, 13th edn, 2000), 385 ff.

[65] See Cornu *et al*, (1989) 37 *AJCL* 193 ff, at 201.

domestic and foreign (substantive or procedural) laws. This is most frequent in the choice-of-law context. Some choice-of-law rules are explicit in that regard. An example is Art 22 of the Austrian Federal Statute of 15 June 1978 on International Private Law.[66] It provides that the prerequisites for the legitimation of illegitimate children through the parents' subsequent marriage depend on the law governing the personal status of the parents; if, however, the parents are subject to different personal status laws, the court must apply the law which is more favourable to the legitimation of the child. Obviously, the judge must compare the status laws involved in order to decide which is more favourable. Another, similar, example is the 'better law' approach embraced by several US-American states in tort disputes.[67] It requires, at least *inter alia*, that among the potentially applicable laws, the court pick the 'better' one. Here, the rule calls for a comparative evaluation of the laws' respective merits, whatever the criteria may be.[68]

In the jurisdictional context, such comparative exercises are much rarer, simply because the competence of courts is usually judged (only) by the *lex fori*. Still, comparison may be required here as well, though the requirement is usually more implicit than explicit. For instance, before a United States federal court with proper jurisdiction can dismiss a case under the doctrine of *forum non conveniens*, it must assure itself that the alternative (foreign) country provides a fair system of justice and that the plaintiff has at minimum a fighting chance. This almost inevitably leads to a comparison between the respective procedural regimes, as well as between the generally available remedies, in the United States court versus the foreign forum.[69]

Decisions about the recognition of foreign judgments can also require comparative analysis. Probably the most obvious trigger is the virtually ubiquitous rule that a foreign judgment cannot be recognized if it violates the recognition state's public policy (*ordre public*). Whether that is the case can be properly determined only by comparing the foreign judgment with its hypothetical domestic counterpart. Take, for example, the German Supreme Court's decision whether a judgment rendered by a California court violated German public policy because it granted not only very substantial compensatory but also punitive damages. The court engaged in a lengthy and thorough comparative discussion which remained admirably conscious of the overall context of the case. This resulted in the recognition of the

---

[66] *Bundesgesetz vom 15. Juni 1978 über das internationale Privatrecht.*

[67] They include Arkansas, New Hampshire, Rhode Island, and Wisconsin; whether Minnesota still belongs in this group is questionable; see the overview in Eugene F. Scoles, Peter Hay, Patrick Borchers, and Symeon Symeonides, *Conflict of Laws* (4th edn, 2004), 85 ff. The approach is based on Robert Leflar, 'Choice-Influencing Considerations in Conflicts Law', (1966) *New York University LR* 41, 267 ff.

[68] A well-known example is *Conklin v Horner*, 157 NW 2d 579 (Wisc 1968).

[69] A vivid example is *In Re Union Carbide Corp*, 809 F 2d 195 (1987). Note, however, that the United States Supreme Court has held that the foreign remedies do not have to be equivalent to the domestic ones so that an elaborate comparison between the substantive laws of the countries involved is not required, *Piper Aircraft Company v Reyno*, 454 US 235 (1981).

compensatory damage award but in the rejection of the punitive damages because the former were sufficiently comparable to German remedies while the latter were incompatible with basic tenets of the German legal system.[70]

In all of these contexts and instances, the need for a comparative analysis is fairly obvious, generally accepted in theory, and widely fulfilled in practice. Beyond this area of easy agreement, however, lies a much more complicated and contested question.

(c) The Construction of Routine Conflicts Norms

Simply put, the question is this: must courts engage in comparative analysis even when applying private international law norms which do *not* expressly require, or at least more or less openly invite, such an approach? In other words, should the comparative method pervade (at least most of) private international law in action?

The most prominent manifestation of that question is the problem of 'qualification'.[71] The problem appears under various names: 'qualification' in French and German ('Qualifikation'), 'classification' in British English, 'characterization' in American English, and so on, and we will use these terms interchangeably here. Even though we can address it here only on a very simple level, it is not free from difficulty. Still, it is worth discussing because it illustrates how intricately interrelated private international law and comparative law are.

The matter is best grasped by way of an example, and the time-honoured question how to treat statutes of limitation provides a good one. Assume that a plaintiff from Mexico City sues a defendant from Detroit, Michigan. The suit is brought in Mexico City but is based on an accident in Detroit. Before the Mexican court, the Michigan defendant invokes the statute of limitations because the accident occurred two and a half years ago. Under Mexican law, the basic limitation period for torts is two years, in Michigan it is three. Is the action time-barred? That, of course, depends on which statute of limitations applies. As mentioned, the basic choice-of-law rule for torts is that the law of the place of the wrong (*lex loci delicti*) governs; this would be Michigan law with its three-year limitation period so that the action could proceed. But is the statute of limitations really a matter of 'tort', that is, part of substantive law (because it determines for how long one has a right)? Or is it rather a matter of procedure (because it determines how long one can sue)? If the latter, the general choice-of-law rule is a very different one: matters of procedure are subject to the law of the forum (*lex fori*); that would be Mexican law

---

[70] BGH judgment of 4 June 1992, *Entscheidungen des Bundesgerichtshofs in Zivilsachen* 118, 312 ff. For an analysis see Joachim Zekoll, 'The Enforceability of American Money Judgments Abroad: A Landmark Decision by the German Federal Court of Justice', (1992) 30 *Columbia Journal of International Law* 30, 64 ff.

[71] The question can arise in other contexts as well; for an overview, see Jan Kropholler, 'Die vergleichende Methode und das internationale Privatrecht', (1978) 77 *Zeitschrift für vergleichende Rechtswissenschaft* 8 ff.

with its two-year limitation period so that the case would have to be dismissed. In other words, the outcome depends on whether the Mexican judge 'qualifies' the statute of limitations as 'substantive' or 'procedural'.

We can see here that 'qualification' is essentially a matter of interpreting conflicts rules: what exactly do 'tort' or 'procedure' mean in the respective norms? Note that similar issues will arise all the time. Especially in choice of law, most core provisions operate with concepts requiring such interpretation. When they point to a certain law for issues of a 'person', 'marriage', 'child support, 'contract', 'delict', and so on, they always require a decision as to what exactly is covered by these terms. To make matters worse, similar issues will also arise with regard to jurisdiction[72] and judgments recognition.[73] In short, the problem of 'qualification' is pervasive in private international law.

Since the issue was first discovered towards the end of the nineteenth century, scholars (and sometimes courts) have spilled enormous amounts of ink over the question how best to approach it. There are essentially three options. First, a court can simply classify the respective phenomenon according to the *lex fori*, that is, its own conceptions. In our example, the Mexican judge would then classify statutes of limitations in conflicts cases just as in purely domestic cases under Mexican law. The problem is, of course, that that may not really do justice to the international nature of the case, not to mention that it might lead to undesirable differences in outcome in different fora. Second, a court can qualify according to the law governing the substance of the case (*lex causae*). The Mexican court would thus adopt the characterization of statutes of limitations in Michigan; yet, that can lead to circular reasoning: after all whether Michigan law counts depends on which conflicts rules apply (tort or procedure) and that, in turn, depends on the qualification issue itself. Third, a court can refuse to be bound by either the *lex fori* or the *lex causae* and instead construe the conflicts norm in light of both its own *and* the potentially applicable foreign law(s), that is, through a comparative analysis.

The latter, comparative, approach was propagated in a famous essay published in 1931 by Ernst Rabel.[74] Rabel's main argument was that in order to fulfil its function as a link (or switch) between several legal orders, a conflicts law norm cannot be

---

[72] For example, Romanian courts will exercise (personal) jurisdiction over defendants in contract disputes if (at least part of) the contractual obligation must be fulfilled in Romania, see Art 149 of the Romanian Statute No. 105 on the Regulation of Legal Relationships in Private International Law (*Legea nr. 105 din 22 septemrie 1992 cu privire le reglementarea reporturilor de drept international privat*). Is the pre-contractual duty to negotiate in good faith, as recognized under German law (see § 311 s 2 BGB), a contractual obligation?

[73] For instance, Art 34 of the Turkish Law No. 2675 on International Private and Procedural Law (*Milletlerarasi Özel Hukuk ve Usul Hukuku Hakkinda Kanun*) provides for the recognition of foreign private law judgments. Is a US-American judgment for punitive damages a matter of private law as envisaged by this provision?

[74] Ernst Rabel, 'Das Problem der Qualifikation', (1931) 5 *RabelsZ* 241 ff. For an English account of his views, see Ernst Rabel, *The Conflict of Laws: A Comparative Study* (vol I, 1945), 49 ff. Rabel was Austrian by birth but held most of his appointments in German universities and research institutions.

understood solely in light of one or the other. Certainly, it cannot be interpreted exclusively from the perspective of forum law. Instead, private international law 'must . . . make use of comparative law'.[75] Although it is somewhat of an over-simplification, it is fair to say that according to Rabel, the comparative method must therefore pervade private international law.

The fight between the advocates of the *lex fori*, the *lex causae*, and the comparative methods raged for decades.[76] In particular, Rabel's comparative approach was hotly debated by scholars in many legal systems. Now that the dust has settled, one can see that, by and large, Rabel has lost the battle but won the war.

Rabel has lost the battle because his claim that a comparative analysis must be the basic approach to the 'qualification' problem did not prevail. Quite aside from its own theoretical problems, his postulate is simply too demanding in practice, at least for national courts. After all, it would require almost every judge deciding a private international law dispute to become a full-fledged comparative lawyer. This is not only unrealistic in terms of the routinely available time and resources, it is also fraught with error in understanding foreign, indeed often completely alien, law. Comparative analysis is not something that a non-specialist can easily do on the side—and well. Thus today, most scholars as well as most courts support the much more user-friendly basic rule that qualification is essentially governed by the *lex fori*.[77]

Still, Rabel won the war because it soon became understood that even under this basic rule, comparative analysis is virtually inevitable.[78] It is not hard to see why. A court applying a conflicts norm cannot avoid deciding whether the foreign phenomenon at issue falls under that norm, and that cannot be done without some (perhaps barely conscious) comparative considerations.[79] Imagine a judge in Montreal who must determine which law governs the rights between a Saudi Arabian couple before him. At the very outset, he will have to decide whether the Saudi Arabian union between the man and the woman is a 'marriage' in the sense of his domestic conflicts norms (Arts 3088–9 of the Quebec Civil Code). In order to do so, however, he must perform at least a casual comparison between the Saudi Arabian and the Quebecois notions of 'marriage'. The need for a comparative analysis is even more obvious in cases in which a foreign phenomenon is

---

[75] Ibid 287.

[76] For an overview, see Dicey and Morris (n 64), at 33 ff; from a German point of view, see Kegel and Schurig (n 15), 276 ff (providing an extensive bibliography). The French perspective is summarized by Henri Batiffol and Paul Lagarde, *Droit international privé* (8th edn, 1993), 474–90.

[77] For an overview of the approaches in France, Germany, and Great Britain, see Veronique Allarousse, 'A Comparative Approach to the Conflict of Characterization in Private International Law', (1991) *Case Western Reserve International LR* 23, 479 ff. In some instances, this is legislatively mandated, see eg § 3 of the Hungarian Law on Private International law (1979. *évi 12, törvényereju rendelet a nemzetközi maganjogrol*). See also § 7(3) of the Restatement (Second) Conflict of Laws (1971).

[78] See A. N. Makarov, *Internationales Privatrecht und Rechtsvergleichung* (1949), 26 ff.

[79] Kropholler (n 7).

completely unknown in the forum. A famous example is the Anglo-American trust, which has no direct equivalent in most civil law countries. Qualification purely according to the *lex fori* is simply not possible since the trust does not comfortably fit any of the Roman-law-based notions of property prevailing in continental Europe. Only a comparison between the trust and its closest equivalents in the forum state can help. Another, even more striking, example, is the Islamic *mahr*—a gift the husband is obligated to make to the wife on the occasion of marriage. Such an institution does not exist in most Western legal systems. Should a judge in, say, Germany, consider it a matter of marital property law (subject to the law of the spouses' common nationality, if any, Art 14, 15 EGBGB), of spousal support (subject to the law of the creditor's habitual residence, Art 17 EGBGB) or, perhaps, simply as a gift (subject, as essentially a contract, probably to the law of the donor's habitual residence, Art 28 EGBGB)? The judge can only make that decision by comparing the *mahr* to its closest German equivalent(s).

As a result, in many legal systems today, scholars and courts refine and supplement the interpretation of conflicts norms according to the *lex fori* by looking at the purpose and function of both the private international law norm to be applied and the substantive laws involved.[80] The qualification of a trust may thus vary with its concrete purpose, for example whether it was to benefit a charitable institution or to leave money to the donor's surviving children. Such an approach, however, is basically a variation on the functional method in comparative law which asks what problem the respective rules were meant to solve. This approach was famously propagated by Rabel himself and has prevailed in comparative law for the last two generations.[81] Thus it is widely acknowledged today, especially in Europe, that private international law is highly dependent on the comparative method even with regard to the routine interpretation and application of standard conflicts norms.

(d) The Interpretation of International Conventions

In our time, an increasing number of private international law norms originate not in a particular domestic order but rather stem from international conventions adopted by a growing number of states.[82] This is especially true among the member countries of the Hague Conference on Private International Law. The construction of norms in, or those based on, such conventions poses particular challenges and is especially dependent on a comparative approach.

This is mainly because the very purpose of such conventions is the (worldwide

---

[80] For England, see Dicey and Morris (n 64), 36 ff; for France, Battifol and Lagarde (n 76), 474 ff; for Germany, Bernd von Hoffmann and Karsten Thorn, *Internationales Privatrecht* (8th edn, 2005), 231 ff.

[81] See Ralf Michaels, 'The Functional Method of Comparative Law', Chapter 10 of the present *Handbook*.

[82] Normally, such conventions themselves are the product of comparative studies, see above, Section II.2(a).

or regional) unification of private international law rules. Obviously, courts would defeat that purpose if they were to interpret convention rules in different ways, for example, by looking only to their respective forum laws for purposes of qualification. It is therefore widely recognized that conventions must be interpreted on their own terms ('autonomously') and that guidance must be sought by looking to the other signatory states' substantive laws and practices.[83]

The most impressive manifestation of this approach is the rich case-law of the European Court of Justice pertaining to the so-called Brussels Convention.[84] Here, one can see private international law and comparative law go hand-in-glove in the routine practice of an international tribunal. Today, such a comparative approach is also embraced by many national courts, especially in Europe. The track record of American courts is decidedly mixed in that regard. In two major decisions interpreting private international law conventions, the United States Supreme Court duly looked at the negotiation history of the respective conventions and at the foreign law background but made no visible effort to consider whether foreign courts had faced the same, or similar, issues and how they had decided them.[85] Lower courts, however, have occasionally considered foreign decisions and strived to construe international conventions from an international, rather than a domestic, point of view.[86]

III. The Emergence and Impact of Supra-national Legal Orders

For many decades, the traditional interactions between comparative law and conflicts law have, on the whole, been both stable and harmonious. Since the late twentieth century, however, there has been trouble in paradise as the two

---

[83] Thus, Art 18 of the 1980 Convention on the Law Applicable to Contractual Obligations (Rome Convention) among the members of the EU, 1980 OJ L266, provides: 'In the interpretation and application of the preceding uniform rules, regard shall be had to their international character and to the desirability of achieving uniformity in their interpretation and application'.

[84] Convention on Jurisdiction and the Enforcement of Judgments in Civil and Commercial Matters, 1989 OJ L285/1. As we will see below, the Convention is now superseded by the Council Regulation No. 44/2001 on Jurisdiction and the Enforcement of Judgments in Civil and Commercial Matters, 2001 OJ L12/1.

[85] See *Société Industrielle Aerospatiale v United States District Court*, 482 US 522 (1987) (construing the Hague Evidence Convention); *Volkswagenwerk AG v Schlunk*, 486 US 694 (1988) (construing the Hague Service Convention).

[86] For references, see Reimann (n 24), 378–9.

disciplines—and thus their relationship—have been affected by the emergence of supra- or international legal orders.[87] The most visible manifestation of this phenomenon is the Europeanization of private international law (subsection 1). A more diffuse, and as of yet more uncertain, development is the growing influence of fundamental rights (subsection 2). These, and similar, developments are beginning to change the interaction between private international law and comparative law.[88]

1. The Europeanization of Private International Law

(a) From Cooperation to Command

'Europeanization' can signify (at least) two very different things. First, it can mean an academic and educational agenda aiming at the gradual harmonization of law among the countries of Europe (with legislation perhaps following suit); this process works by and large from the bottom up.[89] Second, Europeanization can mean that national law is being prescribed, or even displaced, by European Union law; this essentially works from the top down. With regard to private international law, we have recently witnessed a transition from the first to the second kind of Europeanization.

Private international law has long been in the process of Europeanization in the first sense. Conflicts scholarship has drawn on all-European ideas for decades (if not centuries), and conflicts scholars have seen themselves as members of a community of colleagues at home in all of Europe (if not the world). If anything is new here, it is the explicit academic search for a body of common principles for all of European conflicts law.[90] At least for the time being, this kind of Europeanization

---

[87] This Section draws on, but also goes beyond, three articles with overlapping coverage: Bénédicte Fauvarque-Cosson, 'Droit comparé et droit international privé: la confrontation de deux logiques à travers l'exemple des droits fondamentaux', (2000) *Revue international de droit comparé* 797; Bénédicte Fauvarque-Cosson, 'Comparative Law and Conflict of Laws: Allies or Enemies? New Perspectives on an Old Couple', (2001) 49 *AJCL* 407 (especially 417–26); and Mathias Reimann, 'Beyond National Systems: A Comparative Law for the International Age', (2001) 75 *Tulane LR* 1103.

[88] A similar development is the emergence of an internationally uniform law of contracts—on a global level, see the 1980 UN Convention on the International Sale of Goods (CISG) and, in unofficial form, the Unidroit Principles of International Commercial Contracts (3rd edn, 2005). On the European level, see Ole Lando and Hugh Beale (eds), *Principles of European Contract Law*, Parts I and II (1999), and Ole Lando, Eric Clive, André Prüm, and Reinhard Zimmermann (eds), *Principles of European Contract Law*, Part III (2003). On these developments, see Chapter 29 of the present *Handbook*.

[89] This meaning prevails in the private law discussion where Europeanization signifies mainly the emergence of an all-European approach to scholarship and teaching with the long-term goal of an all-European body of law. On this aspect, see Chapter 16 of the present *Handbook*.

[90] See Thomas Kadner Graziano, *Gemeineuropäisches internationales Privatrecht* (2002).

does not seriously change the traditional interplay between the two disciplines; instead, it rather confirms it in the form of comparative conflicts law.

Europeanization in the second sense, however, is a more recent, as well as more dramatic, phenomenon.[91] Beginning in the 1980s, more and more conflicts law has been taken over by the European Community with the result that national law has been displaced.[92] At first, this happened in a piecemeal fashion. The EC Council began to promulgate directives on private law, many of which contained conflicts rules in their respective, highly specific, contexts. Since these rules were apparently enacted without regard to, if not in sheer ignorance of, the pertinent national provisions, they often caused confusion and consternation among conflicts experts and courts. Still, up to that point, EC conflicts law was no more than an occasional interference with national regimes. Around the turn of the last century, however, EC institutions began to enact comprehensive conflicts legislation, making law for whole, core, areas of the field.[93] The most dramatic takeover to date occurred in the area of jurisdiction and judgments recognition when the Brussels Convention, a treaty concluded among the member states in 1968, was superseded by an EC Council regulation, a legislative act with direct effect in the member states, in 2002.[94] These kinds of takeovers are now on the horizon for choice of law as well: after they had adopted the so-called Rome Convention governing choice of law in contracts cases in 1980, the EC member states had begun to work towards a complementary agreement on non-contractual obligations ('Rome II'). In the meantime, however, the EU institutions have taken control of the project and published a draft regulation on that very topic.[95] Thus, if Europe arrives at uniform choice of law rules for torts as well, it will not happen through a treaty but by

[91] This process has been chronicled by Erik Jayme and Christian Kohler in a series of detailed and critical articles since the late 1980s, published in the *Praxis des internationalen Privat- und Verfahrensrechts* (*IPRax*), see ibid 9, 337 (1989); 10, 353 (1990); 11, 361 (1991); 12, 346 (1992); 13, 357 (1993); 14, 405 (1994); 15, 343 (1995); 16, 377 (1996); 17, 385 (1997); 18, 417 (1998); 19, 412 (1999); 20, 454 (2000); 21, 501 (2001); 22, 461 (2002); 23, 485 (2003); 24, 481 (2004); 25, 481 (2005). See also Barbara Dauner-Lieb (ed), *Systemwechsel im europäischen Kollisionsrecht* (2002).

[92] The Treaty of Amsterdam (1999) amended the original EC Treaty and gave the European Community broad competence to legislate in the area of conflicts law, see Treaty Establishing the European Community (as amended by the Treaty of Nice 2003), Arts 61 and 65; for an analysis, see Jürgen Basedow, 'The Communitarization of the Conflict of Laws under the Treaty of Amsterdam', (2000) 37 *Common Market LR* 687.

[93] Under the supremacy doctrine established by the ECJ in *Costa v ENEL*, Case 6/64, [1964] ECR I–585, European Community law trumps the national laws of the member states.

[94] Council Regulation (EC) No. 44/2001 of 22 December 2000 on Jurisdiction and the Recognition and Enforcement of Judgments in Civil and Commercial Matters, OJ L012, 0001–0023 (16 January 2001). Other Council Regulations overtook various international conventions (which had not yet entered into force) regarding international insolvency proceedings, jurisdiction and judgments recognition in family law matters, and transboundary service of process; see Council Regulations 1346/2000, 1347/2000, and 1348/2000 (all of 29 May 2000).

[95] Proposal of the European Parliament and the Council on the Law Applicable to Non-Contractual Obligations ('Rome II'), 22 July 2003, COM (2003) 427 final.

legislation from above. It is probably just a matter of time before we see even the original Rome Convention on contract conflicts displaced by EC legislation as well.

Even though the takeover by the EC institutions has, so far, not entailed massive substantive changes, the overall effect of these developments is of enormous importance: private international law is decreasingly left to the individual member states as co-equal sovereigns, that is, less and less a matter of national legislation or voluntary international cooperation through convention-making. Instead, conflicts law is increasingly turned over to central institutions wielding superior legislative authority, that is, made by command from above.

(b) The Changing Role of Comparative Law

The impact of this process on the relationship between conflicts law and comparative law is complex and ambiguous. While comparative law tends to lose conflicts law as an object of study, it continues to matter for the making of European private international law and, once such law is in place, becomes more important than ever as an interpretive tool for operating the respective provisions.

On the one hand, the Europeanization of private international law tends to deprive comparative law of a time-honoured subject. The reason is quite simple: to the extent that conflicts law is made at the European level, it becomes an internationally uniform regime superseding the various national systems. Yet, without a variety of such national systems, there is nothing to compare, at least not within Europe. To be sure, scholars can then compare the European regime with other parts of the world, but once the former is cast in stone by legislation, the incentives to do so are much diminished.

On the other hand, comparative law should remain important as a foundation, that is, for the very making of European private international law. This, of course, presupposes that the European institutions do not simply act by fiat but take account of the member states' conflicts laws. At least with regard to the more ambitious projects, such as the 'Rome II' regulation, there are some indications that comparative law will continue to matter.[96] Still, one wonders whether with regard to comparative preparatory work, bureaucrats in Brussels have the same motivation (not to mention expertise) as the scholars and other experts representing their countries in international convention making, such as in the Hague.

Finally, while one may suspect that help from comparative law is no longer needed once the uniform regime is in place, the discipline continues to be important even then, namely as a tool for operating the European rules. Such rules make sense only if they are applied in a manner that ensures, or at least promotes, uniformity of outcomes. Consequently, judges interpreting European conflicts rules must free themselves from their national predilections and consider what

---

[96] See Guiliano and Lagarde (n 51), at 4–6.

their colleagues elsewhere have done or are likely do to, in similar cases. The necessary comparative approach is not entirely new because it has been considered indispensable with regard to international conventions for some time.[97] But such an approach becomes even more essential with regard to European conflicts law because its very point is to reach maximum uniformity throughout the whole European Community.

2. The Emergence of Fundamental Rights

(a) The Impact of Universal Rights Norms

It has been widely accepted (in the United States for much longer than in Europe[98]) that even conflicts law must not violate fundamental rights. But as long as those rights stemmed only from the various domestic constitutions, this remained a purely domestic affair. As such, it did not seriously affect the international variety of conflicts law. In the last two-and-a-half decades, however, international rights have entered the picture. This is visible in several contexts. In Europe, such rights have mainly been invoked to *limit* what states can do in private international law. The European Court of Justice, for example, has repeatedly invoked the European Union Treaty, especially the four freedoms (movement of goods, people, services, and capital) and the non-discrimination principle, for that purpose.[99] At least on one occasion, the Court has also relied on the European Convention on Human Rights.[100] In a similar vein, French courts have rejected the application of foreign law and refused the recognition of foreign judgments because of violations of the same

---

[97] See above, Section II.3(d).

[98] The United States Supreme Court has subjected personal jurisdiction to the limits of the due process clause of the fourteenth amendment since *Pennoyer v Neff*, 95 US 714 (1877) and began checking choice-of-law decisions under the same provision in *New York Life Insurance Co v Dodge*, 246 US 357 (1918). For later developments, see Scoles *et al*, above (n 67), at 149–77, 288–320. In Europe, the idea first came to the fore in the German Constitutional Court's famous 'Spanierentscheidung' of 4 May 1971, *Entscheidungen des Bundesverfassungsgerichts* 31, 78. Italy followed suit in 1987, *Corte costituzionale* 5 marzo 1987, n 71, *Foro italiano* 1987, I, 2316; *Corte costituzionale* 10 dicembre 1987, n 477, *Foro italiano* 1987, I, 1456.

[99] For example, the traditional rule, long prevailing in many continental European countries, that corporations are subject to the law of the place of their seat cannot be invoked to deny a business incorporated in one member state the right to establish itself (and to be recognized, etc) in another; see *Centros v Erhvervs-og Selskabsstryrelsen*, Case C–212/97, [1999] ECR-I, 1459. The impact of this case, and of several subsequent decisions of the ECJ, on the 'seat theory' of private international law continues to be debated. See also Luca Radicati di Brozolo, 'L'influence sur les conflits des lois des principes de droit communitaire en matière de liberté de circulation', (1993) 82 *Revue critique de droit international privé* 401.

[100] The scope of the public policy exception to the duty to recognize other member states' civil judgments must be construed with due regard to the European Convention on Human Rights, *Krombach v Bamberski*, Case C–7/98, [2000] ECR I–1935.

Convention.[101] On the other side of the Atlantic, international human rights have mainly been used to *expand* what courts can do in transboundary private disputes. The primary example here is the case-law under the Alien Tort Claims Act.[102] That statute provides for federal jurisdiction 'of any civil action by an alien for a tort only, committed in violation of the law of nations or a treaty of the United States'.[103] Since 1980, this act has spawned a wave of claims seeking compensation for human rights violations through civil litigation. The alleged wrongs were almost invariably committed outside the United States. Since neither the Alien Tort Claims Act itself nor the invoked human rights norms as such provide a cause of action, these cases raise the classic conflicts question which substantive law applies.

(b) The Coordination of Multiple Legal Orders

Again, the impact of these developments on private international law, comparative law, and their interaction is not uniform.

From one point of view, the impact of fundamental rights threatens to make conflicts law, as well as its need for comparative law, (partially) obsolete. Where international fundamental rights norms dictate the outcome of transboundary issues, they pre-empt, so to speak, the field, forcing all countries and courts respecting those norms to reach the same result. If, for example, a binding norm of international human rights law dictates that forced labour is a form of slavery and thus strictly prohibited,[104] a state is not allowed to consider such a practice legal, regardless of what its internal law says (and perhaps even regardless of what its law said at some earlier time, as in the case of Germany during World War II). The universality of the higher norm entails uniformity, and uniformity is the death of conflicts law. And if conflicts law is dead, comparative law can neither study it nor be of any use to it.

Viewed from another angle, however, both conflicts law and comparative law become perhaps more important than ever where human (or other fundamental) rights begin to affect transboundary issues. The reason is that such rights can in fact complicate, rather than eliminate, the potential conflicts among competing legal regimes. This is because international human (and other) rights add a layer of norms on top of the coexisting national regimes. This, in turn, creates the need

---

[101] See Fauvarque-Cosson, Comparative Law and Conflict of Laws (n 87), 422–3.

[102] The seminal case is *Filartiga v Pena-Irala*, 630 F 2d 876 (2d Cir 1980); recently, the United Supreme Court has limited the scope of the Alien Tort Claims Act in *Sosa v Alvarez-Machain*, 124 S Ct 2739 (2004). In the meantime, other countries have had their share of similar problems, such as Germany facing compensation claims by foreigners for being forced into labour during World War II, see eg Decision of the German Constitutional Court of 13 May 1996; *Entscheidungen des Bundesverfassungsgerichts* 94, 315.

[103] 28 United States Code § 1350.   [104] See eg *Doe v Unocal Corp*, 395 F 3d 932 (2002).

to regulate the interplay between several levels of law. As a result, conflicts questions become, in a sense, multidimensional: they must deal both with the relationship between the international and the domestic level norms and with the variety of the laws of the involved nation states. Take, for example, a typical case brought under the Alien Tort Claims Act[105] for violation of human rights in a foreign country. Is such a case governed by the norms of international law allegedly violated (although these norms contain no explicit private cause of action?), by the law of place of the wrong (although it may not provide adequate remedies precisely because individual rights are not respected there?), by the *lex fori* (although neither the parties nor the events are really connected with the forum state?), or by a combination of all of the above?[106] Does, perhaps, the law of the place of the wrong provide the basic cause of action, international law the standard of wrongfulness, and forum law the remedies?

This essay is not the place to pursue these questions, especially since they are far from being resolved.[107] Asking them, however, suggests that answering them requires not only new conflicts rules going beyond traditional private international law but also a comparative understanding of all the legal regimes involved— national as well as supra- or international. Note that the emergence of a multi-layered legal universe is of course not limited to the rise of fundamental rights. To the extent that other international regimes mature into legal orders directly affecting the law of their member states, we will face the same, or similar, complexities. This is already beginning to happen with regard to international trade regimes, such as NAFTA. In all these contexts, we will be able fully to understand and effectively to resolve the respective conflicts only on the basis of a comparative analysis that tells us to what extent the various legal orders involved are similar or different, compatible or incompatible, fulfilling the same or diverse functions. In sum, comparative law must help conflicts law to perform the 'task of coordination' among multiple legal regimes operating on different levels.[108]

---

[105] Above (n 103).

[106] In *Doe v Unocal Corp* (n 104), the United States Court of Appeals for the Ninth Circuit discussed the choice of law question under the Alien Tort Claims Act and decided to apply international law, rather than the law of the place of the alleged wrong (Myanmar), to crucial aspects of the case.

[107] For a discussion, see Axel Halfmeier, 'Menschenrechte und Internationales Privatrecht im Kontext der Globalisierung', (2004) 68 *RabelsZ* 653 at 671–80.

[108] The concept is borrowed from Richard Buxbaum, 'Die Rechtsvergleichung zwischen nationalem Staat und internationaler Wirtschaft', (1996) 60 *RabelsZ* 201.

IV. Concluding Remarks

Three decades ago, Arthur von Mehren, one of the leading experts in both fields, concluded that 'no system of private international law can escape involvement with the discipline of comparative law'.[109] Fortunately, conflicts lawyers and comparatists have often worked closely together for well over a century. In the relatively simple world consisting only of co-equal (nation) states with their domestic legal systems, this cooperation took place in the resolution of conflicts on the horizontal level, so to speak. To be sure, since nation states and their legal systems will continue to coexist for the foreseeable future, the work on that level also needs to continue. But the challenge common to both disciplines today is also to handle the problems resulting from the emergence of multiple and overlapping legal orders on various levels in the world. The disciplines will thus have to cooperate in resolving conflicts arising in the vertical dimension as well.

Meeting this challenge will require increasing amounts of teamwork not only between private international lawyers and comparative lawyers but with other specialists as well. As mentioned, handling the multiplicity of legal orders today entails an understanding of various inter- or even supra-national regimes and their interplay with national systems. At minimum, these regimes include several branches of public international law, European Union law, and international trade, not to mention various forms of regional integration in Latin America, Asia, and perhaps even Africa. To make matters worse, all these areas are undergoing constant growth and rapid change. As a result, individual conflicts or comparative law scholars can no longer hope to master the resulting complexities single-handedly—even if they were of the calibre of Ernst Rabel.

Bibliography

A. N. Makarov, *Internationales Privatrecht und Rechtsvergleichung* (1949)

Ernst Rabel, *The Conflict of Laws: A Comparative Study* (4 vols, 1945–58)

Albert Ehrenzweig and Erik Jayme, *Private International Law* (3 vols, 1967–77)

Henri Batiffol, 'Les rapports du droit comparé au droit international privé', (1970) *Revue international de droit comparé* 661

Kurt Lipstein (ed), *Private International Law* (vol III), in Ulrich Drobnig (ed), *International Encyclopedia of Comparative Law* (1971 ff)

---

[109] Arthur von Mehren, 'The Contribution of Comparative Law to the Theory and Practice of Private International Law', (1977–8) 26 *AJCL* 32, 33. See also Arthur von Mehren, 'Choice-of-Law and the Comparative-Law Problem', (1975) 23 *AJCL* 751.

Werner Goldschmidt, 'Droit international privé latino-americain', (1973) 100 *Journal de Droit International* (*Clunet*) 65

Arthur T. von Mehren, 'The Contribution of Comparative Law to the Theory and Practice of Private International Law', (1977–8) 26 *AJCL* 32

Jan Kropholler, 'Die vergleichende Methode und das internationale Privatrecht', (1978) 77 *Zeitschrift für vergleichende Rechtswissenschaft* 3

Friedrich Juenger, *Choice of Law and Multistate Justice* (1993, special edn, 2005)

Mathias Reimann, *Conflict of Laws in Western Europe: A Guide through the Jungle* (1995)

Petar Šarčević and Paul Volken (eds), *Yearbook of Private International Law* (1999 ff)

Symeon Symeonides, *Private International Law at the End of the Twentieth Century: Progress or Regress* (1999)

Bénédicte Fauvarque-Cosson, 'Droit comparé et droit international privé: la confrontation de deux logiques à travers l'exemple des droit fondamentaux', (2000) *Revue international de droit comparé* 797.

Patrick Borchers and Joachim Zekoll (eds), *International Conflict of Laws for the Third Millennium* (2001)

Friedrich Juenger, *Selected Essays on the Conflict of Laws* (2001)

Thomas Kadner Graziano, *Gemeineuropäisches Internationales Privatrecht* (2002)

Arthur T. von Mehren, *Theory and Practice of Adjudicatory Authority in Private International Law: A Comparative Study of the Doctrine, Policies, and Practices of Common- and Civil-Law Systems* (2003)

INDEX

....